RECORDS OF CIVILIZATION

SOURCES AND STUDIES

EDITED UNDER THE AUSPICES OF THE
DEPARTMENT OF HISTORY, COLUMBIA UNIVERSITY

RECORDS OF CIVILIZATION

SOURCES AND STUDIES

NUMBERS LIV - LVI

INTRODUCTION TO ORIENTAL CIVILIZATIONS

INTRODUCTION TO ORIENTAL CIVILIZATIONS

Wm. Theodore de Bary, EDITOR

Sources of
Indian Tradition

COMPILED BY

Wm. Theodore de Bary
Stephen Hay
Royal Weiler
Andrew Yarrow

COLUMBIA
UNIVERSITY
PRESS
NEW YORK 1958

The addition to the "Records of Civilization: Sources and Studies" of a group of translations of Oriental historical materials, of which this volume is one, was made possible by funds granted by Carnegie Corporation of New York. That Corporation is not, however, the author, owner, publisher, or proprietor of this publication, and is not to be understood as approving by virtue of its grant any of the statements made or views expressed therein.

SPECIAL CONTRIBUTORS

A. L. BASHAM

R. N. DANDEKAR

PETER HARDY

I. H. QURESHI

V. RAGHAVAN

J. B. HARRISON

PREFACE

This book, part of a three-volume series dealing with the civilizations of Japan and China, as well as India and Pakistan, contains source readings that tell us what the peoples of India have thought about the world they lived in and the problems they faced living together. It is meant to provide the general reader with an understanding of the intellectual and spiritual traditions which remain alive in India and Pakistan today. Thus, much attention is given to religious and philosophical developments in earlier times which still form part of the Indian heritage and have experienced a considerable revival in the nineteenth and twentieth centuries. On the other hand, attention is also given to political, economic, and social thought, which other surveys, concentrating on classical Indian philosophy, have generally omitted.

Although our aim has been to combine variety with balance in the selection and presentation of materials, a few words are perhaps necessary concerning special points of emphasis. A glance at the contents will show that religion has furnished the general categories under which traditional Indian civilization is treated. This implies no judgment that religion was always the dominant factor in Indian life, but only that in the body of literature which provides us our texts, religious identities and continuities are more clearly distinguishable than are those based upon historical chronology or dynastic associations. Next, in this volume somewhat more attention is given to Theravāda Buddhism than to Mahāyāna because the latter is given fuller treatment in the volumes in this series dealing with China and Japan. In the case of Hinduism the reader will find that relatively greater emphasis is placed upon the social and devotional aspects of the religion, which have affected great numbers of Hindus, than upon the philosophical speculations which have generally commanded the first attention of educated Indians and Westerners and have already been widely reproduced in translation. In Parts One to Four, dealing with traditional Indian and Muslim civilization, most of the translations are new and many of them are of texts previously untranslated into any Western language. In the chapters on modern India and Pakistan, on the other hand, a majority of the readings are from English originals or existing translations.

Because of the unfamiliarity and complexity of many subjects not previously presented in translation, we have found it necessary to include more historical and explanatory material than is usual in a set of source readings. Nevertheless, the reader who seeks a fuller knowledge of historical and institutional background will do well to supplement this text by referring to a general survey of Indian history and culture.

Given the limitations of an introductory text, we could not hope to deal with every thinker or movement of importance, but have had to select those examples which seem best to illustrate the major patterns of Indian thought in so far as they have been expressed and preserved in writing. In the modern period the necessity for such selectivity is most apparent. Here particular prominence has been given to persons actively engaged in leading organized religious and political movements.

Compilation of this volume was originally undertaken by Dr. Andrew Yarrow in connection with the general education program in Columbia College. In their present form these readings have been substantially revised by the general editor with the assistance of Dr. Royal Weiler of Columbia, and supplemented by Dr. Stephen N. Hay of the University of Chicago. It goes without saying that this volume could not have been compiled without the cooperation of our principal contributors: R. N. Dandekar of the Bhandarkar Oriental Research Institute, Poona; V. Raghavan of the University of Madras; A. L. Basham, Peter Hardy, and J. B. Harrison of the School of Oriental and African Studies, University of London; and I. H. Qureshi of the Center for Pakistan Studies, Columbia University. Their contribution is all the more appreciated because of the patience and forbearance they have shown in regard to adjustments which the general editor has had to make in order to achieve uniformity and balance in the volume as a whole. For this reason, it should be emphasized, the editor must bear primary responsibility for the selection and presentation of the materials contained here.

More material than could be included was originally prepared not only by our principal contributors but by other collaborators as well. These include Dr. Mohammad Habib and Mr. K. A. Nizami of the Muslim University, Aligarh; and Drs. Aloo Dastur, A. R. Desai, Usha Mehta, and P. R. Brahmananda of the School of Economics and Sociology, University of Bombay. To the director of the latter institution, Dr. C. N. Vakil, an especial debt of gratitude is owed for his help in the early stages of this long project. To Professor Habib an additional debt is acknowledged by Dr. Hardy for the privilege of consulting his manuscript translations from the historian Barni. The compilers also wish to thank Mr. Arthur Michaels and Professor Holden Furber of the University of Pennsylvania for their assistance and advice in regard to the influence of British thought in India.

The final version of these readings owes much to the critical examination and comment of scholarly colleagues. Dr. Basham wishes to record his appreciation to Dr. A. K. Warder for his reading of the draft on Jainism and Buddhism. Dr. Hay is similarly indebted to Sir Percival Spear, Professor Richard Park, and Mr. Marshall Windmiller of the University of California at Berkeley; to Professor Amiya Chakravarty of the School of Theology, Boston University; and to Dr. R. C. Majumdar, Dr. J. A. B. Van Buitenen and Mr. Sudhindranath Datta at the University of Chicago, for reading and criticizing the chapters on modern India. Dr. S. M. Ikram of the Center for Pakistan Studies, Columbia University, is also to be thanked for reading the chapters on Muslim India and Pakistan. In the editing of Parts One and Three, Visudh Busyakul of the University of Pennsylvania gave Dr. Weiler invaluable advice and assistance, as did Marjorie A. Weiler. Saul Guggenheim performed the exacting task of preparing the chapter decorations for Chapters I–XX. The remainder were drawn by Eloise Hay, who was also one of our most discerning and helpful critics. Lastly mention must be made of the indefatigable and competent service of Miss Eileen J. Boecklen in preparing the manuscript for publication, and of our good fortune in having Joan McQuary and Eugenia Porter guide it through the Press.

This series of readings has been produced in connection with the Columbia College General Education Program in Oriental Studies, which has been encouraged and supported by the Carnegie Corporation of New

York. For whatever value it may have to the general reader or college student seeking a liberal education that embraces both East and West, a great debt is owed to Dean Emeritus Harry J. Carman, Dr. Taraknath Das, and Dean Lawrence H. Chamberlain of Columbia College, who contributed much to the initiation and furtherance of this program.

WM. THEODORE DE BARY

EXPLANATORY NOTE

The sources of translations given at the beginning of each selection are rendered as concisely as possible. Full bibliographical data can be obtained from the list of sources at the end of the book. In the reference at the head of each selection, unless otherwise indicated, the author of the book is the writer whose name precedes the selection. Where excerpts have been taken from existing translations, they have sometimes been adapted or edited in the interests of uniformity with the book as a whole.

Indic words appearing in italics as technical terms or titles of works are rendered in accordance with the standard system of transliteration as found in Louis Renou's *Grammaire Sanskrite* (Paris, 1930), pp. xi–xiii, with the exception that here ś is regularly used for ç. To facilitate pronunciation, other Sanskrit terms and proper names appearing in roman letters are rendered according to the usage of Webster's New International Dictionary, 2d edition, Unabridged, except that here the macron is used to indicate long vowels and the Sanskrit symbols for ś (ç) and ṣ are uniformly transcribed as sh. Similarly, the standard Sanskrit transcription of c is given as ch. In connection with Theravāda Buddhism, the form of technical terms is that of Pali rather than Sanskrit; the latter, however, is retained in connection with Jainism. Thus, in Buddhism Pali *dhamma* for Sanskrit *dharma,* but in Jainism Sanskrit *poṣadha* for Prakrit *posaha.* Deviations from these principles may occur in passages directly quoted from Indian writers of the seventeenth through twentieth centuries. A word list giving standard Indic equivalents for roman transcriptions will be found at the end of this volume.

In the pronunciation of Indic words, the accent is usually on the next to final syllable if long; otherwise on the nearest long syllable before it. The long syllable is indicated by the macron (e.g., ā, ī, ū) or a diphthong (e, o, ai, au), or a vowel followed by more than one consonant (except h).

Guide to Pronunciation

a	as *u* in but
ā	as *a* in father
i	as *i* in pin
ī	as *i* in machine
u	as *u* in pull
ū	as *u* in rule
ri (ṛ), a vowel	as *er* in river
e	as *ay* in say
ai	as *ai* in aisle
o	as *o* in go
au	as *ow* in how
ch (c)	as in church
sh (ś, ṣ)	as *sh* in shape
g	as *g* in get
kh	as *kh* in lakehouse
gh	as *gh* in doghouse
th	as *th* in anthill
dh	as *dh* in roundhouse
bh	as *bh* in clubhouse
ph	as *ph* in uphill
ṃ or ṅ	as *ng* in sing

Guide to the Pronunciation of Persian and Indo-Persian Words

Short Vowels

a	Intermediate between the vowels in the English words *bed* and *bad*
i	As the vowel sound in the English *fen*
u	As in the English word *put*

Long Vowels

ā	as *a* in father
ī	as *i* in police
ū	as *u* in prude

Diphthongs

ai	as *ey* in they
au	as *ou* in out

In Indo-Persian the majhūl vowel sound ō rhymes with *toe;* the short vowel a is closer to the *u* in *sun;* and the diphthong au tends more to the majhūl sound, as the *o* in *hose* or *toe.*

' represents the Arabic and Persian letter *'ayn.* In Arabic *'ayn* is a strong guttural preceding a vowel. In Persian, however, *'ayn* at the beginning of a word is not pronounced separately from the vowel which goes with it; in the middle of a word, it has a sound—*sa‘d* (or *sa‘d*) like the bleating of a sheep; at the end of a word, in Persian, it is either silent or, more usually given a slight pronunciation between short "a" and "e" on a rising intonation.

' represents the *hamza* or glottal stop in Arabic words. It is a jerked hiatus; the Cockney pronunciation of "butter," "better," or "bottle" gives the sound in the middle of Arabic words; at the beginning of Arabic words it is indistinguishable from the vowel that goes with it; at the end it is like the Persian pronunciation of *‘ayn* at the end of words.

In Persian words, ' also represents *hamza* when used to indicate a hiatus between two long vowels, as in the English pronunciation (very distinct) of "India Office," i.e., "India" (pause) "Office." (Example: Badā’ūnī.)

R.W. AND P.H.

CONTENTS

PART ONE
BRAHMANISM

Prehistoric Period

B.C. c.2700–1700 Indus Valley civilization and height of Harappa Culture.
     c.1500–1200 Aryan invasions of the Indian subcontinent; composition of the earliest hymns of the *Rig Veda*.

Vedic Period

     c.1200–900 Composition of the *Rig Veda*.
     c.900 The great war depicted in the *Mahābhārata* epic.
     c.900–500 Period of later Vedas, Brāhmanas, and early Upanishads.
     c.800 Aryans reach eastern Bihar and Bengal.
     c.600 End of Brāhmana period.

INTRODUCTION

Brahmanism, while not necessarily representing the most ancient religion of the Indian subcontinent, is that system of belief and ritual practice to which Indians have, historically, looked back as the source of their religious traditions. Whether in later Hinduism, which tenaciously holds to much of the Brahmanical tradition, or in Buddhism, which rejects much of it, there is presupposed this highly conscious and articulate cult, the central feature of a way of life made known through the ages by the earliest body of formal literature, the Veda.

As seen today, the earliest religious thought in India is known or deduced from archaeological evidence, such as seals, figurines, tablets, and other artifacts, belonging to a pre-Aryan civilization which existed in the valley of the Indus River during the latter part of the third millennium B.C. The only conclusions which may be drawn with any certainty, however, from materials associated with the culture uncovered at the site of Harappa, are a preoccupation with fertility symbols (e.g., terra-cotta figurines of pregnant females, stone phallic symbols, and the like) and the worship of a divinity similar to the god Shiva, the ascetic par excellence of historic Hinduism, who is frequently associated with a bull and is also often represented by a phallic symbol. Besides representations of fertility symbols, which imply the existence of a Mother or Earth Goddess cult, and the divinity reminiscent of Shiva, the Indus civilization also seemed to attach religious significance to certain animals, such as the tiger, buffalo, crocodile, elephant, and even multiheaded monsters and hybrid creatures, as well as trees and auspicious symbols, such as the swastika. Some seals point to religious motifs found in Mesopotamia, such as the Gilgamesh legend, the ibex, trefoil designs, and others, and suggest a possible origin of religious ideas even earlier than the datable artifacts of the Indus Valley civilization. Though it is difficult to establish a definite continuity in the development of religious ideas in India dating from the Indus civilization to modern times, it is, however, possible to distinguish a clearly non-Aryan—which may or may not be pre-Aryan—source for many of the concepts which characterize that religion which is known as "Hinduism" in India today.

A second, and perhaps somewhat more significant, source of Indian religious ideas was introduced by the Aryans who invaded India from the northwest about 1500 B.C., or earlier, and who may themselves have been responsible for the destruction of the Indus civilization. These Aryan invaders brought with them religious concepts consisting mainly of a pantheon of naturalistic or functional gods, a ritualistic cult involving the sacrificial use of fire and an exhilarating drink called *soma,* as well as the rudiments of a social order. To a certain extent their religion derived from primitive Indo-European times; that is to say, some of the gods mentioned in the scriptures of these people are found to have mythological counterparts in other Indo-European traditions, particularly those of Iran, Greece, and Rome, and thus indicate a common origin of such gods in antiquity. In addition to such specifically Indo-European concepts, the religion of the Aryans involved other ideas which may have developed in the course of their eastward migrations or may have resulted from the assimilation of indigenous religious notions encountered in the Indian subcontinent itself. From a sociological standpoint, the religion introduced by the Aryan invaders was limited to persons of Aryan birth, though some non-Aryan beliefs seem to have been accepted in a modified form or at least tolerated by the priesthood of the conquering Aryans.

The religion thus developed by the Aryans from the time of their invasion of India until roughly 500 B.C. was embodied in a collection of hymns, ritual texts, and philosophical treatises, called the *Veda.* From Aryan times down to the present, Hindus have regarded the Veda as a body of eternal and revealed scripture. Its final authority is accepted to some extent by all Hindus as embodying the essential truths of Hinduism. The earliest portion of the Veda consists of four metrical hymnals, known as *Samhitās,* being the *Rig Veda, Yajur Veda, Sāma Veda,* and *Atharva Veda.* The earliest of these texts is that of the *Rig Veda,* and it is this collection of hymns (*ṛc*) which constitutes the earliest source of knowledge concerning the Aryan religion. The most recent of these canonical collections is the *Atharva Veda,* which is somewhat more representative of the popular religion of Vedic times than are the other Vedas, which are more sacerdotal in character. The metrical hymns and chants of these texts gave

rise to elaborate ritualistic prose interpretations called *Brāhmanas* and *Āranyakas* ("forest books"). Toward the end of the Vedic period, the earlier emphasis on ritual was translated symbolically. Thus, Vedic ideas of sacrifice and mythology were reinterpreted in terms of the macrocosm and microcosm. Cosmological inquiries of some of the later hymns of the *Rig Veda* were extended and an investigation of the human soul was undertaken. The speculations and interpretations along these lines were formulated by various philosophical schools in treatises collectively called *Upanishads*. Thus, the whole of Vedic literature consists of four Vedas or Samhitās, several expository ritual texts attached to each of these Vedas called Brāhmanas, and speculative treatises, or Upanishads, concerned chiefly with a mystical interpretation of the Vedic ritual and its relation to man and the universe.

Although the relationship between the various deities of the *Rig Veda* is not always clear, and different deities—often personifications of natural forces—may each in turn be regarded as the supreme god, nevertheless Indra (often referred to as *eka deva* "One God") stands out as pre-eminent and the core myth of the *Rig Veda* recounts his deeds. In terms of this central myth, creation proceeded when Indra, the champion of the celestial gods, slew a serpent demon, Vritra, who enclosed the waters and the sun requisite for human life. When Indra split open the belly of this demon the essentials of creation—moisture, heat, light—were released and cosmic order (rita) was established under the administration of the god Varuna. Gods and men then had specific functions (*vrata*) to perform in accordance with this cosmic order. After death those individuals who had fulfilled their obligations under the cosmic order went to a heavenly realm presided over by Yama, the first mortal. Two mythical dogs guarded the righteous on the path to this region, but the sinful were fettered and, unprotected, fell prey to various demons.

Cult practices developed an elaborate ritual based on a fire sacrifice, personified as the god Agni, and included various oblations of clarified butter and the production of the soma juice, deified as the god Soma, from an unidentified plant known also from Iranian sources. This ritual naturally necessitated a highly specialized priesthood. Just as the crackling of the sacrificial fire was viewed as the voice of Agni, the priest par excellence, so, too, great significance was attached to the chanting of hymns and invocations by the human priesthood. Later the sacrifice itself

was viewed cosmologically and the correct performance of the sacrifice possessed a magical potency which could coerce even the gods. This magical power inherent in the sacrificial prayers thus developed into spells, called *bráhman*. He who recited them was a "pray-er" (*brahmán*), or one related to prayer (*bráhmana*). From this concept developed the brāhman, or priestly, caste.

The spiritualization of prayer (brahman) and its relation to the gods and the universe through ritual sacrifice constitute the central conception of this early phase of Indian religious thought. When the Upanishads coupled this notion with an investigation of the individual self (ātman)—an idea closely allied to the earlier personification and deification of "Wind" or "Air" (*Vāyu*) and referring to human "breath"—the brahman came to be viewed as a universal principle. Thus, an essential feature of Vedic ritual, the "prayer" itself, was given cosmological and cosmogonic implications and became the principal subject of later Indian philosophical inquiry. It is on the basis of these ritualistic Vedic concepts that the earliest definable religious thought of India is identified as Brahmanism.

CHAPTER I

THE COSMIC ORDER IN
THE VEDIC HYMNS

Long before they entered into India the Vedic Aryans must have started producing prayers and songs (mantras) relating to their religion. The character of this religion was determined by the kind of life they had been living. At that early stage of their cultural history, the Vedic Aryans lived close to nature—as a part of it, rather than apart from it. It was, therefore, the vastness and brilliance of nature, its blessings and maledictions, and, above all, the inexorable and subtly operating law which regulated all its manifestations, that dominated their religious ideology. The earliest hymns of the Vedic Aryans, accordingly, pertained to this cosmic religion, to which they gave expression through such mythological concepts as those of the divine parents, Heaven and Earth, the cosmic law (rita), and the sustainer of that law, Varuna. Side by side with this cosmic religion, the Vedic Aryans had also developed a kind of fire worship. The cosmic religion of the Vedic Aryans tended toward anthropomorphism, but it was not idolatrous. Fire was, therefore, regarded as the liaison between gods and men.

Sun worship, which also figures prominently in the Veda, is, in a sense, just an aspect of fire worship; but it has greatly influenced many mythological concepts in the Veda with the result that divinities like Vishnu, who had originally little to do with the solar phenomenon, came to be regarded as sun-gods at some stage in the evolution of their character.

In the course of time there occurred a change in the conditions of life of the Vedic Aryans and consequently in their religious ideology. They set out toward India on campaigns of conquest and colonization, fought on their way a series of battles with several antagonistic tribes, whom they collectively called *Dāsas,* and finally emerged as victorious colonizers of that part of India which was known as the land of seven rivers, the present Punjab. In this epoch-making warlike enterprise the Vedic Aryans were apparently led by their heroic leader, Indra, whom they soon made into a god. Gradually history came to be transformed into mythology. In this process several elements were derived from an ancient primitive myth of the Hero and the Dragon. And later the Vedic Aryan war-god came to be invested with a cosmic character. This hero-religion eventually dominated the hymns produced by the Vedic poets, priests, and warriors.

Perhaps with a view to counteracting the growing influence of a mythology glorifying military prowess, the Vedic poets and priests deified the magical potency of their prayers and priestcraft in the forms of Brahmanaspati (Lord of Prayer), who is in some respects modeled after Indra, and Vāch, the goddess of Speech or Holy Word. He embodies prayer (*brahman*) itself, as well as ritual activity in general. Moreover, in the person of Brahmanaspati ritual and cosmological aspects are blended. He is often associated with Agni, the sacrifice personified, on the one hand, and Indra, the later cosmogonic principal (*tad ekam*), on the other. Thus the hymns dedicated to this god represent the emergence of prayer (*brahman*) as an extremely significant concept in early Vedic thought. It is not at all surprising then that the importance of ritual in Vedic religion should give rise to the central conception of later Vedic philosophical speculation regarding the true nature of the cosmological concept *brahman* and its relation to the human self.

Like many other primitive communities, the Vedic Aryans believed that the creation of the universe and the procreation of the human race were the result of a primeval sacrifice, namely of the self-immolation of a cosmic being. This cosmic being is represented in the Veda as the male, Purusha. Apart from this concept of the primeval cosmic sacrifice as the starting point of creation, there are represented in the Veda other significant currents of cosmogonic thought. According to one of them the source of all powers and existences, divine as well as earthly, was conceived as the "golden germ" (*hiraṇyagarbha*)—a form assumed by an unnamed Ur-god. This "golden germ" is the precursor of the universal egg (*brahmāṇḍa*) of the later cosmogony. Another cosmogonic theory is far more profound. It seeks to controvert the view that the world has evolved out of "nonbeing" (asat). At the same time this theory asserts that the source of this world cannot be, strictly speaking, characterized as "being" (sat). In the beginning there was neither "nonbeing" nor "being," nevertheless That One (*tad ekam*) breathed, though breathless, through its own inherent power. Besides it nothing existed. This idea may suggest the mythological creation of the world by Indra, the One God (*eka deva*), who destroyed the cosmic demon Vritra. Finally, in the *Atharva Veda* both "being" and "nonbeing" have *brahman* as their source.

Side by side with the ritual, eschatology, mythology, and cosmogony of the upper classes among the Vedic Aryans there had also existed a religion of the non-Aryan subject peoples. This religion comprised a variety of charms, imprecations, and exorcistic practices which were primarily intended "to appease, to bless, and to curse." The motif recurring throughout this religion was, of course, magic.

Agni

The discovery of fire constitutes a significant landmark in the history of human civilization and it is not unnatural that fire should have been held in great awe from early times. The Aryans, however, developed the worship of Agni or Fire to an extraordinary degree.

The god Agni is the personification and deification especially of the sacrificial fire. He is the priest of the gods and the god of the priests. In the *Rig Veda* he is second only to Indra in prominence. He has three forms: terrestrial as fire, atmospheric as lightning, and celestial as the sun. Thus, his function as the sacrificial fire of the priests serves as a kind of liaison between man and the heavenly gods—specifically he carries the oblations which the brāhman priests pour into the fire to the gods. The correct propitiation of Agni in the Vedic ritual was thus of considerable importance to Aryan man.

[From *Rig Veda*, 1.1]

I extol Agni, the household priest, the divine minister of the sacrifice, the chief priest, the bestower of blessings.

May that Agni, who is to be extoled by ancient and modern seers, conduct the gods here.

Through Agni may one gain day by day wealth and welfare which is glorious and replete with heroic sons.

O Agni, the sacrifice and ritual which you encompass on every side, that indeed goes to the gods.

May Agni, the chief priest, who possesses the insight of a sage, who is truthful, widely renowned, and divine, come here with the gods.

O Agni, O Angiras ["messenger"], whatever prosperity you bring to the pious is indeed in accordance with your true function.

O Agni, illuminator of darkness, day by day we approach you with holy thought bringing homage to you,

Presiding at ritual functions, the brightly shining custodian of the cosmic order (rita), thriving in your own realm.

O Agni, be easy of access to us as a father to his son. Join us for our wellbeing.

Heaven and Earth

As the divine parents, Heaven and Earth are symbolic of the vastness, brightness, and bounty of nature. The myth of their conjugal union dates from primitive Indo-European times and probably represents the earliest Vedic conception of creation based on an indissoluble connection of the two worlds, celestial and terrestrial.

Note the constant emphasis in these prayers on the hope of obtaining material rewards.

[From *Rig Veda*, 6.70]

Rich in ghee [i.e., clarified butter considered as fertilizing rain], exceedingly glorious among beings, wide, broad, honey-dispensing, with beautiful forms, Heaven and Earth are, in accordance with Varuna's cosmic law (dharma), held asunder, both ageless and rich in seed.

Nonexhausting, many-streamed, full of milk, and of pure ordinance, the two dispense ghee for the pious one. You two, O Heaven and Earth, ruling over this creation, pour down for us the seed [rain] which is wholesome to mankind.

The mortal, who, for the sake of a straightforward course of life, has offered sacrifice unto you, O Heaven and Earth, O Sacrificial Bowls, he succeeds; he is reborn through his progeny in accordance with the cosmic law. Your poured semen becomes beings of manifold forms, each fulfilling his own function.

With ghee are covered Heaven and Earth, glorious in ghee, mingled with ghee, growing in ghee. Wide and broad, these two have precedence at the time of the selection of officiating priests. The wise ones invoke these two with a view to asking them for blessings.

May Heaven and Earth, honey-dropping, honey-dispensing, with honeyed courses, shower down honey for us, bringing unto the gods sacrifice and wealth, and for us great glory, reward, and heroic strength.

May Heaven and Earth swell our nourishment, the two who are father and mother, all-knowing, doing wondrous work. Communicative and wholesome unto all, may Heaven and Earth bring unto us gain, reward, and riches.

Varuna

Varuna is the administrator of the cosmic law (rita, dharma), which regulates all activities in this world, big and small. It is he, for instance, who has spread out the earth and set the sun in motion, and who pours out the rain but sees to it that the one ocean is not filled to overflowing by many rivers. He is, therefore, rightly called the world-sovereign. Naturally enough, this upholder of cosmic order is also regarded as the lord of human morality. It is the function of Varuna to ensure that there occurs no transgression of the law, cosmic or human.

[From *Rig Veda*, 5.85]

Unto the sovereign lord sing a sublime and solemn prayer (*brahman*), one dear unto glorious Varuna, who has spread out the earth, as the butcher does the hide, by way of a carpet for the sun.

Varuna has extended the air above the trees; he has put strength in horses, milk in cows, will-power in hearts, fire in waters, the sun in the heaven, and soma upon the mountain.

Varuna poured out the leather-bag, opening downward, upon the heaven and the earth and the mid-region. Thereby does the lord of the whole creation moisten thoroughly the expanse of earth, as rain does the corn.

He moistens the broad earth and the heaven. When Varuna would have it milked [i.e., would shower rain] then, indeed, do the mountains clothe themselves with clouds and the heroes, showing off their might, loosen those clothes [i.e., disperse the clouds].

This great magic-work (māyā) of renowned spiritual Varuna will I proclaim loudly; of Varuna, who, standing in the mid-region, has measured the earth with the sun as with a measuring rod.

No one, indeed, dare impugn this great magic-work of the wisest god, namely, that the many glistening streams, pouring forth, do not fill up one ocean with water.

If we, O Varuna, have offended against a friend, befriended through Aryaman or through Mitra [i.e., gods of hospitality and friendship], or if we have offended against an all-time comrade or a brother or an inmate —whether belonging to us, O Varuna, or a stranger—do you remove that offense from us.

If we have deceived, like gamblers in a game of dice, and whether we really know it or not, all that do you unbind from us, like loosened fetters, O god. Thus may we be dear unto you, O Varuna.

Dawn

In hymns such as this we find most movingly expressed the profound awe and sensitivity to the beauties of nature which underlie much of Vedic mythology. Here, however, there is less of the tendency to personify and deify natural forces which is so prominent a feature of Vedic religious thought, than a majestic description of the actual dawn itself in metaphorical language, giving us an insight into the cosmic harmony of man and nature. While later Indian philosophies often viewed nature and the visible world as in some sense evil or unreal, this loving appreciation of nature is characteristic not only of the more optimistic, life-affirming attitude of the Vedas but also of an important strain in Indian literature from the early epics and plays of Kālidāsa down to the modern works of Rabindranath Tagore.

We have chosen the excellent metrical translation of Professor Macdonell which suggests the stately rhythm and cumulative power of the original.

[From A. A. Macdonell, *Hymns from the Rigveda*, p. 38]

This light has come, of all the lights the fairest:
The brilliant brightness has been born effulgent.
Urged onward for god Savitar's uprising,
Night now has yielded up her place to morning.

Bringing a radiant calf she comes resplendent:
To her the Black One has given up her mansions.
Akin, immortal, following each other,
Morning and Night fare on, exchanging colors.

The sisters' pathway is the same, unending:
Taught by the gods alternately they tread it.
Fair-shaped, of form diverse, yet single-minded,
Morning and Night clash not, nor do they tarry.

Bright leader of glad sounds she shines effulgent:
Widely she has unclosed for us her portals.
Pervading all the world she shows us riches:
Dawn has awakened every living creature.

Men lying on the ground she wakes to action:
Some rise to seek enjoyment of great riches,
Some, seeing little, to behold the distant:
Dawn has awakened every living creature.

One for dominion, and for fame another;
Another is aroused for winning greatness;
Another seeks the goal of varied nurture:
Dawn has awakened every living creature.

Daughter of Heaven, she has appeared before us,
A maiden shining in resplendent raiment.
Thou sovereign lady of all earthly treasure,
Auspicious Dawn, shine here today upon us. . . .

Indra

Indra is the most prominent divinity in the *Rig Veda*. He is an atmospheric god often identified with thunder and wielding a weapon, called *vajra* ("thunderbolt"). As such he destroys the demons of drought and darkness and heralds the approach of the rain so vital to life in India. In the Veda, the most significant myth which recounts his deeds centers about his slaying of the demon Vritra, who encloses the waters (i.e., the rains) and the sun, and who is the very embodiment of cosmic chaos. Historically considered, this myth may represent the conquest of India by the Aryans inspired by a warrior-champion, Indra. From a mythological standpoint, the destruction of Vritra and the subsequent release of the essentials of life—water, heat, light—may be allegorically regarded as an early cosmogonic theory.

[From *Rig Veda*, 1.32]

Indra's heroic deeds, indeed, will I proclaim, the first ones which the wielder of the vajra accomplished. He killed the dragon, released the waters, and split open the sides of the mountains.

He killed the dragon lying spread out on the mountain; for him Tvashtar fashioned the roaring vajra. Like bellowing cows, the waters, gliding, have gone down straightway to the ocean.

Showing off his virile power he chose soma;[1] from the three *kadrukas*[2] he drank of the extracted soma. The bounteous god took up the missile, the vajra; he killed the first-born among the dragons.

When you, O Indra, killed the first-born among the dragons and further overpowered the wily tricks (māyā) of the tricksters, bringing forth, at that very moment, the sun, the heaven, and the dawn—since then, indeed, have you not come across another enemy.

Indra killed Vritra, the greater enemy, the shoulderless one, with his mighty and fatal weapon, the vajra. Like branches of a tree lopped off with an axe, the dragon lies prostrate upon the earth.

For, like an incapable fighter, in an intoxicated state, he [Vritra] had challenged the great hero [Indra], the mighty overwhelmer, the drinker of soma to the dregs. He did not surmount the onslaught of his fatal weapon. Indra's enemy, broken-nosed,[3] was completely crushed.

Footless and handless he gave battle to Indra. He [Indra] struck him with the vajra upon the back. The castrated bull, seeking to become a compeer of the virile bull, Vritra lay shattered in many places.

Over him, who lay in that manner like a shattered bull[4] flowed the waters for the sake of man.[5] At the feet of the very waters, which Vritra had [once] enclosed with his might, the dragon [now] lay [prostrate].

Vritra's mother had her vital energy ebbing out; Indra had hurled his fatal weapon at her. The mother lay above, the son below; Dānu[6] lay down like a cow with her calf.

In the midst of the water-streams, which never stood still nor had any resting place, the body lay. The waters flow in all directions over Vritra's secret place; Indra's enemy lay sunk in long darkness.

With the Dāsa as their lord[7] and with the dragon as their warder, the waters remained imprisoned, like cows held by the Pani.[8] Having killed

[1] Presumably the juice of soma was originally used for ritualistic purposes only. In view of the peculiar strength-giving, entrancing properties of the drink, however, the war-lord Indra later used it to inspirit himself for his heroic deeds.

[2] *Kadrukas* are traditionally explained as the three days in a six-day soma-sacrifice. Perhaps the word originally meant the three wooden bowls from which soma was drunk.

[3] Or, the breaker of chariots.   [4] Or, reed.

[5] Manu. The exact meaning is unclear.   [6] Vritra's mother.

[7] Literally "having the demon as their lord" (*dāsapatnīs*). After Indra's victory over the demon, the waters became *arya-patnīs* (*Rig Veda*, 10.43.8), that is, "having the Aryans as their lord." Apart from its mythological significance, this fact may have an historical basis in the conflict of the Aryan invaders with indigenous tribal people.

[8] That is, the leader of the Panis, a gypsy-like, nomadic, trading people, who stole the cows belonging to the Aryans.

Vritra, [Indra] threw open the cleft of waters which had been closed.

You became the hair of a horse's tail, O Indra, when he [Vritra] struck at your sharp-pointed vajra—the one god (*eka deva*) though you were. You won the cows, O brave one, you won soma; you released the seven rivers, so that they should flow.

Neither did lightning nor thunder, nor mist nor hailstorm, which he [Vritra] had spread out, prove efficacious when Indra and the dragon fought. And the bounteous god remained victorious for all time to come.

Whom did you see, O Indra, as the avenger of the dragon, that fear entered into your heart, after you had killed the dragon, and frightened, you crossed nine and ninety rivers and the aerial regions like the falcon? [9]

Indra, who wields the vajra in his hand, is the lord of what moves and what remains rested, of what is peaceful and what is horned.[10] He alone rules over the tribes as their king; he encloses them as does a rim the spokes.

The Primeval Sacrifice

The origin of the universe from a primeval sacrifice, in which a cosmic being offers himself as an oblation, is not unknown in primitive mythological traditions. However, the sacrifice of the male Purusha here is not so much the primordial sacrifice of a world-giant or the type *Ur-mensch* found in Norse or Germanic mythology, as it is a cosmogonic idea based on ritual sacrifice itself as the origin of the universe. Thus, the nature of the Purusha is a secondary blend of characteristics derived from the Vedic deities Agni, the sacrifice personified and the typical male principle; Sūrya, the sun; and Vishnu, another solar deity who embraces earth, atmosphere, and sky. Emphasized here is the universality of Purusha and his function as the cosmic sacrifice. In this way the ritual sacrifice performed on earth by a priestly class eventually was translated into terms of cosmological significance by a process identifying microcosmic, with macrocosmic, elements.

This hymn makes the earliest reference to the four social orders, later known as castes. The passage is important in that it emphasizes the magico-ritualistic origin of castes. The brāhmans formed the highest social order, the literate intelligentsia which gave India its priests, thinkers, law-givers, judges, and ministers of state. The rājanyas, later called kshatriyas or rulers, were the

[9] Does this refer to some temporary setback which Indra suffered in his battles with the Dāsas?

[10] And, therefore, aggressive.

second social order, the Indian counterpart of feudal nobility: from this class were recruited kings, vassals, and warriors. The vaishyas formed the class of landowners, merchants, and moneylenders, while the shūdras, originally those peoples conquered by the Aryans, were workers, artisans, or serfs.

[From *Rig Veda*, 10.90]

Thousand-headed Purusha, thousand-eyed, thousand-footed—he, having pervaded the earth on all sides, still extends ten fingers beyond it.

Purusha alone is all this—whatever has been and whatever is going to be. Further, he is the lord of immortality and also of what grows on account of food.

Such is his greatness; greater, indeed, than this is Purusha. All creatures constitute but one quarter of him, his three quarters are the immortal in the heaven.

With his three quarters did Purusha rise up; one quarter of him again remains here. With it did he variously spread out on all sides over what eats and what eats not.

From him was Virāj [11] born, from Virāj the evolved Purusha. He, being born, projected himself behind the earth as also before it.

When the gods performed the sacrifice with Purusha as the oblation, then the spring was its clarified butter, the summer the sacrificial fuel, and the autumn the oblation.

The sacrificial victim, namely, Purusha, born at the very beginning, they sprinkled with sacred water upon the sacrificial grass. With him as oblation the gods performed the sacrifice, and also the Sādhyas [a class of semidivine beings] and the rishis [ancient seers].

From that wholly offered sacrificial oblation were born the verses [*ṛc*] and the sacred chants; from it were born the meters (*chandas*); the sacrificial formula was born from it.[12]

From it horses were born and also those animals who have double rows [i.e., upper and lower] of teeth; cows were born from it, from it were born goats and sheep.

When they divided Purusha, in how many different portions did they arrange him? What became of his mouth, what of his two arms? What were his two thighs and his two feet called?

[11] The precise meaning of Virāj is uncertain. Here it seems to represent a kind of cosmic source—perhaps the waters themselves—from which creation proceeds.

[12] The verses (*ṛc*), the sacred chants (*sāma*), and the sacrificial formula (*yajus*) may refer to the three Vedas.

His mouth became the brāhman; his two arms were made into the rājanya; his two thighs the vaishyas; from his two feet the shūdra was born.

The moon was born from the mind, from the eye the sun was born; from the mouth Indra and Agni, from the breath (prāna) the wind (vāyu) was born.

From the navel was the atmosphere created, from the head the heaven issued forth; from the two feet was born the earth and the quarters (the cardinal directions) from the ear. Thus did they fashion the worlds.

Seven were the enclosing sticks in this sacrifice, thrice seven were the fire-sticks made, when the gods, performing the sacrifice, bound down Purusha, the sacrificial victim.

With this sacrificial oblation did the gods offer the sacrifice. These were the first norms (dharma) of sacrifice.[13] These greatnesses reached to the sky wherein live the ancient Sādhyas and gods.

The Origin of the World

In the early Indra creation myth, the demon Vritra had to be slain before creation could proceed. Indra as the personal demiurge brought order out of chaos (asat); that is to say, he brought about the existent (sat) from the nonexistent (asat). In later Vedic cosmogonic speculation, the personal creator, Indra as the One God (*eka deva*) is conceived of as an impersonal creative impulse called That One (*tad ekam*). When the question arises (vs. 1) as to "what enclosed all," the answer is no longer Vritra according to the old myth, but rather that creation proceeds from a principle motivated by desire outside, or over and beyond, "being" and "non-being." In terms of this new cosmological interpretation of creation, only the sages were able to fathom in their hearts the relation of "being" and "nonbeing." The hymn ends on a note of skepticism, which anticipates the questioning mood of the Upanishads—"he who is the highest overseer in heaven, he certainly knows, on the other hand, perhaps he does not."

[From *Rig Veda*, 10.129]

Neither not-being nor being was there at that time; there was no air-filled space nor was there the sky which is beyond it. What enveloped all? And where? Under whose protection? What was the unfathomable deep water?

---

[13] The later sacrifices are modeled after the primeval cosmic sacrifice and are believed to be actually furthering the purpose of that sacrifice by ensuring the proper organization and functioning of the world and human society.

Neither was death there, nor even immortality at that time; there was no distinguishing mark of day and night. That One breathed without wind in its own special manner. Other than It, indeed, and beyond, there did not exist anything whatsoever.

In the beginning there was darkness concealed in darkness; all this was an indistinguishable flood of water. That, which, possessing life-force, was enclosed by the vacuum, the One, was born through the power of heat from its austerity.

Upon It rose up, in the beginning, desire, which was the mind's first seed. Having sought in their hearts, the wise ones discovered, through deliberation, the bond of being and nonbeing.

Right across was their [i.e., the wise ones'] dividing line extended. Did the below exist then, was there the above? There were the seed-planters, there were the great forces of expansion. Below there was self-impulse, above active imparting.

Who knows it for certain; who can proclaim it here; namely, out of what it was born and wherefrom this creation issued? The gods appeared only later—after the creation of the world. Who knows, then, out of what it has evolved?

Wherefrom this creation has issued, whether he has made it or whether he has not—he who is the superintendent of this world in the highest heaven—he alone knows, or, perhaps, even he does not know.

The Brahmachārī

The term *brahmachārī* means "going to, or according to, *bráhman* (the holy word)." Since the prayer or sacred word (*brahman*) came to be identified with the Vedic hymns or invocations themselves, a brahmachārī was regarded as a student of the Veda as well as a disciple of Brahman. In later Hinduism this remnant of early Brahmanism was preserved as the first prescribed stage (āshrama) of Aryan life, characterized by studentship under a competent teacher (guru) or authority on the Vedic texts, and adherence to a vow of celibacy. This stage itself is called *brahmacharya*. In this particular hymn, from the *Atharva Veda*, the brahmachārī is glorified in a cosmological sense as the sun "clothed in heat" and "with a long beard" (that is, with many rays), who is the primeval principle of the universe. The heat of the sun and the fervor generated through austerities are both called *tapas*, often seen as a factor in creation. Thus when Mahatma Gandhi later glorified *brahmacharya*, it was as a creative force sublimated by sexual continence.

[From *Atharva Veda*, 11.5.1–8, 17–26]

The Brahmachārī travels animating the two hemispheres; the gods become like-minded in him. He sustains earth and heaven; he fills his teacher with fervor.

The fathers, the god-folk, and all the gods collectively follow the Brahmachārī; the six thousand three hundred and thirty-three Gandharvas went after him. He fills all the gods with fervor.

When the teacher accepts the Brahmachārī as a disciple, he treats him as an embryo within his own body. He carries him for three nights in his belly; when he is born, the gods assemble to see him. . . .

Born prior to Brahman, clothing himself in heat, the Brahmachārī arose with his fervor. From him were born Brahmahood, the highest Brahman, and all the gods together with immortality.

The Brahmachārī goes forth, kindled by sacred fire-sticks, clothing himself with black-antelope skin, consecrated, long-bearded. Within one single day does he go from the eastern to the northern ocean; having gathered together the worlds, he fashions them repeatedly.

The Brahmachārī, begetting Brahman, the waters, the world, Prajāpati [Lord of Creatures], the most exalted one, creative force, having become an embryo in the womb of immortality, indeed, having become Indra, has shattered the demons.

The preceptor fashioned both these hemispheres, the wide and the deep, namely, earth and heaven. These two the Brahmachārī protects with his fervor; in him the gods become like-minded. . . .

Through Brahmacharya, through fervor, a king protects his kingdom. A teacher through Brahmacharya seeks a Brahmachārī for his student.

Through Brahmacharya a maiden finds a young husband. Through Bramacharya a steer or horse strives to obtain food.

Through Brahmacharya, through fervor, the gods dispelled death. Through Brahmacharya Indra brought heaven to the gods.

Plants, past and future, trees, the year and its seasons were all born from the Brahmachārī.

Animals of the earth and those of heaven, wild and domestic, wingless and winged, were all born from the Brahmachārī. . . .

The Brahmachārī fashioned these things on the back of the waters. He stood in the sea performing austerities. When he has performed ritual ablution, he shines extensively over the earth, brown and ruddy.

A Charm Against Jaundice

The contents of the *Atharva Veda* relate mainly to what may be considered indigenous traditions of popular religion. This religion consists of charms and imprecations accompanied by certain exorcistic practices, for the proper knowledge of which one has to depend entirely on an ancillary text of the Veda, like the *Kauśika Sūtra*. It is needless to add that the principal basis of these practices is symbolic magic.

   [From *Atharva Veda*, 1.22]

Unto the sun let them both go up—your heartburn and your yellowness; with the color of the red bull do we envelop you.

   With red colors do we envelop you for the sake of long life; so that this person may be free from harm and may become non-yellow.

   Those cows [1] that have Rohiṇī [the Red One] as presiding divinity, as also cows which are red—their every form and every power—with them do we envelop you.

   Into the parrots do we put your yellowness and into the yellow-green *ropaṇākā*-birds. Similarly into the turmeric [or yellow wagtail?] do we deposit your yellowness.

Exorcism of Serpents

The tradition designates this charm specifically to keep serpents away from the premises.

   [From *Atharva Veda*, 6.56]

Let not the serpent, O gods, slay us with our children and with our men. The closed jaw shall not snap open, the open one shall not close. Homage to the divine folk [i.e., the serpents, by way of exorcistic euphemism].

   Homage be to the black serpent, homage to the one with stripes across its body, homage to the brown constrictor [?], homage to the divine folk.

   I smite your teeth with tooth, I smite your two jaws with jaw; I smite your tongue with tongue; I smite your mouth, O Serpent, with mouth. [2]

---

[1] Or herbs.
[2] Presumably the exorcist strikes the tooth, jaw, etc. of the symbolic figure of a serpent with the tooth, jaw, etc. of, perhaps, a dead serpent.

CHAPTER II

THE RITUAL ORDER IN
THE BRĀHMANAS

To each of the four Samhitās or collections of hymns are attached certain expository liturgical texts called *Brāhmanas*. These somewhat bulky prose treatises give, in tedious detail, explanations of the Vedic ritual and its performance. Thus their principal concern is with the nature and use of the holy word, utterance, prayer, invocation, or divine power in the sacrifice, that is, *brahman*. The Sanskrit term *brāhmaṇa* means "relating to Brahman" or simply "brahmanic." Since the Veda contains both terms *bráhman* "prayer" and *brahmán* "pray-er," the Brāhmanas can be considered as either referring to the knowledge of *bráhman* or as belonging to the priesthood (*brāhmaṇa*), though the former interpretation seems more likely.

The Brāhmanas are significant for several reasons. First of all, they represent the oldest known specimens of Indo-European prose narrative, though earlier prose formulae are found in some of the hymn collections. Secondly, they constitute a fountainhead of information dealing with sacrifice, ritual, and priesthood. Thirdly, much of this ritualistic material is inspirited and illustrated by numerous myths and legends of all types. Even though the personalities of the gods of the *Rig Veda* tend to lose their virility and become submerged in a maze of ritual formulae, still this mythological and legendary lore provides numerous themes for poets and other writers of later times. Thus the Vedic tradition is kept very much alive even in the minds of that vast majority of Indians belonging to social classes considered beneath the priesthood.

The Brāhmana texts deal mainly with the theory and practice of sacrifice. The institution of sacrifice, elaborated by the brahmanic priests, is an amazingly intricate and complex affair. There are three principal categories of sacrifice—the cooked-food sacrifice, to be offered on the domestic fire, the oblation sacrifice, and the *soma*-sacrifice, the last two to be offered on the sacred *śrauta* (Vedic) fires. It is chiefly with the last two categories that the Brāhmana texts concern themselves. Broadly speaking, the contents of a Brāhmana text may be classified under two main heads—the precepts and the explanation. The precepts are detailed injunctions relating to the place and time, priests and sacred fires, deities and ritualistic formula, oblations and sacrificial utensils, priests' fees and expiatory rites, and several sacerdotal details in respect of a particular sacrifice. The explanation, as it were, seeks to "rationalize" these injunctions—the method of such rationalization often being, paradoxical as it may seem, not logical but magical. One of the commonest ways of emphasizing the appropriateness of any particular ritualistic detail was by taking recourse to etymology. For instance, water (*āpaḥ*) was used in connection with the preparation of a fire-place because "by means of water (*āpaḥ*), indeed, is all this world obtained [*āpta* from a different root, *āp*]; having thus obtained all this, as it were, by means of water, he sets up the sacred fire." Obviously most of such etymological exercises will not stand the test of modern scientific philology. Another way of justifying and, to a certain extent, glorifying a sacerdotal detail was by presenting it as a significant item in some myth, which latter often took the form of a contest for superiority between the gods and the demons. Then, too, there was the usual tendency to establish a kind of mystic bond between an item of the sacrificial procedure and some aspect of cosmic phenomena.

The Collection of Materials for the Sacred Fires

All *śrauta* (Vedic, as opposed to domestic) sacrifices presuppose the formal setting up of the sacred fires, usually three in number. The following extract deals with the collection of the specific materials to be used in connection with the preparation of a fire-place. An attempt is made to make the translation as literal as possible in order to bring out the peculiarities of the style developed in the Brāhmanas.

    [From *Śatapatha Brāhmaṇa*, 2.1.1. 1–14]

Since, indeed, he collects (*sam + bhṛ*) them from this place and from that—that is why the materials used in connection with the preparation of the fire-place are called "collection" (*sambhāra*). In whatever place the essence of Agni (Fire) is inherent, from that very place he collects the materials. Collecting in this way, he thereby here makes him [Agni] thrive partly with glory, as it were, partly with cattle, as it were, partly with a mate, as it were.[1] Then the officiating priest draws with the wooden sword three lines on the spot selected for the fire-place. Whatever part of this earth is trodden upon or is defiled by being spit upon, that part of hers, indeed, he thereby symbolically digs up and removes away, and thus he sets up the sacred fires upon the earth which is now rendered worthy of being sacrificed upon: that is, indeed, why he draws lines upon the spot selected for the fire-place. Then he sprinkles the lines with water. This, indeed, constitutes the collecting of water [as a material for the preparation of the fire-place], namely, that he sprinkles the lines with water. That he collects water as a material in this connection is due to the fact that water is food; for, water is, indeed, food: hence, when water comes to this world, there is produced plentiful food in this world. By sprinkling water he makes him [Agni] thrive with plentiful food itself. Moreover, water is, indeed, female and Agni is male. By sprinkling water he makes him thrive with a procreating mate. By means of water (*āpah*), indeed, is all this world obtained [*āpta*]; having thus obtained all this, as it were, by means of water, he sets up the sacred fire. That is why he collects water. . . . [The officiating priest then collects a piece of gold, representing the divine *semen virile;* saline soil, representing cattle and the flavors of heaven and earth; earth dug out by a wild rat, representing the flavor of this earth, affluence; and gravel, representing firmness of the earth, as proved by an *ad hoc* mythological story. He thus makes fire thrive with the magic potency derived from these materials.]

These five materials (*sambhāra*), indeed, does he collect (*sam + bhṛ*); for, five-fold is the sacrifice, five-fold is the sacrificial victim, five are the seasons of the year. As for the statement that there are five seasons in a year, they say: "Six, surely, are the seasons in a year [according to the Indian system]. There is thus a kind of deficiency in the foregoing prescription." But, verily, this very deficiency (*nyūna*) is rendered a procreative mate. For, it is from the *nyūna* [that is, the lower part of the body— a pun on the two meanings of the word *nyūna*] that progeny is procreated. Further, this fact, namely, that there are only five materials instead of six actually ensures for the sacrificer some scope for progress toward prosperity in future. That is why there are only five materials collected in connection with the preparation of the fire-place, even though there are

---

[1] The essence of Agni which is scattered in various places is, as it were, collected together and is again symbolically bestowed upon him so as to make him full and complete.

six seasons in a year. And if they still persist in arguing that there are, surely, six seasons in a year, we may retort by saying that Agni himself is the sixth among those materials and that, therefore, this whole procedure, surely, becomes nondeficient.

The Fetching of Sacrificial Grass

The *Śrauta Sūtras* are the most exhaustive and comprehensive manuals of Vedic sacrifice. They are the outcome of vigorous efforts made to systematize and consolidate the brahmanic ritual. It will be seen from the following passage how ritualist teachers added—perhaps purposefully—to the already existing complexities of the sacrificial procedure by expressing a variety of opinions even about a minor detail, such as the thickness of the bunch of sacrificial grass for the new-moon and full-moon sacrifices.

The text of the *Baudhāyana Śrauta Sūtra* and its supplements, *Dvaidha* and *Karmānta,* has been here rearranged so as to make it yield a connected account about this particular item in the sacrificial procedure. Baudhāyana was the preceptor of an eminent school of ritualists belonging to the Taittirīya branch of the *Black Yajur Veda.* Shālīki was another ritualist-preceptor, whose views were presumably treated with great respect.

[From *Baudhāyana Śrauta Sūtra,* 1.2; 20.2; 24.24–25]

With the formula, *devānām pariṣūtam asi* [1] [the officiating priest] should trace [by means of the sickle] a line round as small a cluster of *darbha*-grass as he considers to be sufficient for being used as strewing grass. As for the tracing round: Baudhāyana, indeed, says that [the officiating priest] should recite the formula three times and repeat the action of tracing a line round the *darbha* cluster also three times. He should act similarly at the time of tracing a hole for the sacrificial post, similarly at the time of tracing the foot-print [of the cow] with which soma is to be purchased, similarly at the digging of the hole for the branch of the *udumbara* tree, and similarly at the preparation of the [four] resonant pits. Shālīki on the other hand says that he should recite the formula only once, but should repeat the action of tracing round a line three times.

Then he should brush [the blades in the *darbha* cluster from the bottom] to the top [by means of the sickle] with the formula, *varṣavṛddham asi.* He should seize it by means of the sickle with the formula, *devabarhir mā.* . . . He should cut off [as much grass as can be cut off in one

[1] In most cases, the Sūtra texts give only the initial words of a formula to indicate the whole formula.

stroke with the formula] *ācchettā te mā riṣam.* He should touch the stumps of grass remaining after the cutting with the formula, *devabarhiḥ śatavalśaṃ vi roha.* As for cutting off of the grass: The view expressed above is that of Baudhāyana. Shālīki on the other hand says that this formula should, indeed, be regarded as bestowing an indirect blessing. There should, therefore, be only indirect touching [of the stumps] by means of the formula. With the formula, *sahasravalśā vi vayaṃ ruhema,* he should touch himself [that is, he should touch his own heart]. He should cut off the *darbha* cluster entirely. Having tied up the *darbha* blades into a bunch to serve as strewing grass, he should place it aside with the formula, *pṛthivyāḥ sampṛcaḥ pāhi.*

For being used as strewing grass there should be tied up a bunch of *darbha* blades having a circumference equal to the one produced by joining the tips of nails [of the thumb and forefinger]—such is the view of some teachers. A bunch should be tied up of as many *darbha* blades as could be cut off in one stroke—such is the view of some teachers. . . . It should be tied up so as to be as thick as the handle of the sacrificial spoon—such is the view of some teachers. It should be tied up so as to be as thick as the thigh-bone—such is the view of some teachers. It should be tied up so as to be as thick as the thumb-joint—such is the view of some teachers. It should be tied up without being measured—such is the view of some teachers.

CHAPTER III

THE ULTIMATE REALITY IN THE UPANISHADS

Toward the end of the Brāhmana period, that is, c.600 B.C., another class of religious texts appeared called *Āranyakas* ("forest books"). The exact implication of this term is uncertain, but it seems probable that these works were recited by hermits living in the forests. The retirement to the forest prior to attaining religious salvation is usually considered the third prescribed stage (āshrama) in the life of the orthodox Hindu even as studentship (brahmacharya) represented the first. The Āranyakas contain transitional material between the mythology and ritual of the Samhitās and Brāhmanas on the one hand and the philosophical speculations of the Upanishads on the other. The ritual is given a symbolic meaning, and knowledge of this becomes more important than the actual performance of the ritual itself. This principle then becomes the starting point of Upanishadic speculation.

Like the Brāhmanas, each Upanishad is attached to one of the four Vedic Samhitās. The Upanishads represent both the final stage in the development of Vedic religious thought and the last phase of Brahmanism. They are thus the end of the Veda (*vedānta*). Later philosophical schools of classical Hinduism which base their tenets on the authority of the Upanishads are therefore called *Vedānta*.

The Upanishads cannot be regarded as presenting a consistent, homogeneous, or unified philosophical system, though there are certain doctrines held in common. Divergences of method, opinion, and conclusion are everywhere apparent even within a single Upanishad. It is for this reason that the Upanishads are considered speculative treatises. Another significant feature of the Upanishads, particularly the older ones, is that practically every basic idea expounded has its antecedent in earlier Vedic texts. What distinguishes the Upanishads is not so much their originality as their probing for new interpretations of the earlier Vedic concepts to obtain a more coherent view of the universe and man. Here the link between man and the cosmos is, as we have said, no longer the ritual act, but a knowledge of the forces symbolically represented in the ritual. These allegorical and symbolic interpretations are characteristic of the Upanishads. They are developed by Upanishadic thinkers in two ways: 1) by setting up various levels of comprehension suited to different individual intellectual capacities, and 2) by identifying partially or by degrees two seemingly dissimilar elements and arriving at a type of equation which, though at first sight irrational, will on further analysis or introspection reveal a unity. This pursuit of a unifying principle suggests that the duality apparent in the world is to some extent or in some sense unreal. The macrocosm is viewed universally as an extension of Vedic mythological and ritualistic concepts, specifically *brahman*. As a parallel to this, the microcosmic nature of the human self or soul (ātman) is explained. From this results the most significant equation of the Upanishads: *brahman* = *ātman*. It is the transcendent knowledge of this essential identity that is the chief concern of Upanishadic sages.

The Sacrificial Horse

The most elaborate and stupendous sacrifice described in the Brāhmanas is the horse-sacrifice (*aśvamedha*). It is an ancient rite which a king might undertake to increase his realm. In the following selection from perhaps the oldest of the Upanishads, the *Bṛhad Āraṇyaka* (Great Forest Text), the horse-sacrifice is given cosmological significance by equating various parts of the sacrificial horse with corresponding elements of the cosmos. To Upanishadic thinkers the real meaning of the horse-sacrifice was gained through a realization of the identity of the parts of this sacrifice and the universe. This type of mystical or transcendent knowledge is based on equations stressed by the word "verily" (*vai*) and is characteristic of the early Upanishads in particular. It should be noted that dawn, the sun, the wind, etc., besides being elements of the cosmos, were also deified naturalistic forces in Vedic mythology and still retain their identity as such in the following passage.

[From *Bṛhad Āraṇyaka Upaniṣad*, 1.1.1]

Dawn verily is the head of the sacrificial horse. The sun is his eye; the wind, his breath; the universal sacrificial fire (*agni-vaiśvānara*), his open mouth; the year is the body (ātman) of the sacrificial horse. The sky is his back; the atmosphere, his belly; the earth, his underbelly [?]; the directions, his flanks; the intermediate directions, his ribs; the seasons, his limbs; the months and half-months, his joints; days and nights, his feet; the stars, his bones; the clouds, his flesh. Sand is the food in his stomach; rivers, his entrails; mountains, his liver and lungs; plants and trees, his hair; the rising sun, his forepart; the setting sun, his hindpart. When he yawns, then it lightnings; when he shakes himself, then it thunders; when he urinates, then it rains. Speech (*vāc*) is actually his neighing (*vāc*).

Sacrifices—Unsteady Boats on the Ocean of Life

Some later Upanishads represent a reaction to the glorification of the sacrifice in which the brahmanic ritualists indulged. The teacher of the *Muṇḍaka Upaniṣad* quoted below seems to concede a place for sacrifice in man's life— by way of religious discipline; but he concludes that sacrifice is ineffectual as a means to the knowledge of the highest reality and to spiritual emancipation. On the other hand, as is suggested by the passage cited above, some earlier Upanishadic teachers substituted a kind of "spiritual" or "inner" sacrifice for the "material" or "external" sacrifice.

[From *Muṇḍaka Upaniṣad,* 1.2. 1, 2, 7–13]

This is that truth. The sacrificial rites which the sages saw in the hymns are manifoldly spread forth in the three [Vedas]. Do you perform them constantly, O lovers of truth. This is your path to the world of good deeds.

When the flame flickers after the oblation fire has been kindled, then, between the offerings of the two portions of clarified butter one should proffer his principal oblations—an offering made with faith. . . .

Unsteady, indeed, are these boats in the form of sacrifices, eighteen in number, in which is prescribed only the inferior work. The fools who delight in this sacrificial ritual as the highest spiritual good go again and again through the cycle of old age and death.[1]

Abiding in the midst of ignorance, wise only according to their own estimate, thinking themselves to be learned, but really hard-struck, these fools go round in a circle like blind men led by one who is himself blind.

Abiding manifoldly in ignorance they, all the same, like immature children think to themselves: "We have accomplished our aim." Since

---

[1] That is, they are reborn again and again in the phenomenal world. The doctrine of transmigration or reincarnation was probably unknown to the brāhman ritualists, but in the Upanishads man's salvation from this cycle of rebirths became a matter of great concern. It is suggested that the Vedic sacrifices could bring only a temporary respite in the abode of a god, not permanent release from the cycle.

the performers of sacrificial ritual do not realize the truth because of passion, therefore, they, the wretched ones, sink down from heaven when the merit which qualified them for the higher world becomes exhausted.

Regarding sacrifice and merit as most important, the deluded ones do not know of any other higher spiritual good. Having enjoyed themselves only for a time on top of the heaven won by good deeds [sacrifice, etc.] they re-enter this world or a still lower one.

Those who practice penance (tapas) and faith in the forest, the tranquil ones, the knowers of truth, living the life of wandering mendicancy— they depart, freed from passion, through the door of the sun, to where dwells, verily, that immortal Purusha, the imperishable Soul (ātman).

Having scrutinized the worlds won by sacrificial rites, a Brāhman should arrive at nothing but disgust. The world that was not made is not won by what is done [i.e., by sacrifice]. For the sake of that knowledge he should go with sacrificial fuel in hand as a student, in all humility to a preceptor (guru) who is well-versed in the [Vedic] scriptures and also firm in the realization of Brahman.

Unto him who has approached him in proper form, whose mind is tranquil, who has attained peace, does the knowing teacher teach, in its very truth, that knowledge about Brahman by means of which one knows the imperishable Purusha, the only Reality.

The Five Sheaths

In this passage an attempt is made to analyze man on five levels—proceeding from the grosser forms to the subtler, and therefore more real, forms. The "real" man transcends the physical, vital, mental, and intellectual aspects and has to be identified with the innermost, beatific aspect. It is, in the end, suggested that the real self of man is identical with Brahman, the ultimate principle, the absolute, which is his *raison d'être*.
[From *Taittirīya Upaniṣad, 2.1–6 passim*]

From this Self (ātman), verily, space arose; from space, wind; from wind, fire; from fire, water; from water, the earth; from the earth, herbs; from herbs, food; from food, man (purusha). This man here, verily, consists of the essence of food. Of him possessing the physical body made up of food, this, indeed, is the head; this, the right side; this, the left side; this, the body (ātman); this, the lower part, the foundation. . . . From food, verily, are produced whatsoever creatures dwell on the earth. More-

over, by food alone do they live. And then also into it do they pass at the
end. . . . Verily, different from and within this body which consists of
the essence of food is the body which consists of breath. The former body
is filled with the latter. The latter body also is of the shape of man. According to the former one's being of the shape of man this latter body is
of the shape of man. Of him possessing the body consisting of breath,
the out-breath is head; the diffused breath, the right side; the in-breath,
the left side; space, the body; the earth, the lower part, the foundation.
. . . Verily, different from and within this body which consists of vital
breaths is the body which consists of mind. The former body is filled
with the latter. The latter body is also of the shape of man. . . . Verily,
different from and within this body which consists of mind is the body
which consists of intellectuality [or consciousness]. The former body is
filled with the latter. That one also is of the shape of man. . . . Verily,
different from and within this body which consists of intellectuality [or
consciousness] is the body which consists of bliss.[1] The former body is
filled with the latter. The latter body also is of the shape of man. . . .
As to that, there is also this verse: "Nonexistent (asat), verily, does one
become if he knows (believes) that Brahman is nonexistent.[2] If one
knows that Brahman exists, such a one people thereby know as existent."

The Real Self

In this famous parable, the real, essential Self is successively identified with
the bodily self, the dream self, and the self in deep sleep, and it is suggested
that all these three teachings are quite inadequate, for in none of the three
conditions, namely, of wakefulness, of dream, and of deep sleep, can the nature
of Self be said to conform to the description given in the very first sentence
of this passage. The real Self is neither body nor mind nor a complete negation
of consciousness. The Self is certainly conscious, but of nothing else but itself.
It is pure self-consciousness as such and it is in this condition that it is identical
with the highest reality.

[From *Chāndogya Upaniṣad,* 8.7–12 *passim*]

"The Self (ātman) who is free from evil, free from old age, free from
death, free from grief, free from hunger, free from thirst, whose desire

[1] Each succeeding body is within the preceding one and is, therefore, subtler and more
real than it. The body of bliss is the most internal body. Bliss, accordingly, is the true nature
of man.

[2] Man has, indeed, no existence as apart from Brahman. For a man to say that Brahman
is non-existent is a contradiction in terms.

is the Real [*satya,* or truth], whose intention is the Real—he should be sought after, he should be desired to be comprehended. He obtains all worlds and all desires, who, having found out that Self, knows him." Thus, indeed, did the god Prajāpati speak. Verily, the gods and the demons both heard this. They said among themselves: "Aha! Let us seek after that Self—the Self, having sought after whom one obtains all worlds and all desires." Then Indra from among the gods went forth unto Prajāpati, and Virochana from among the demons. Indeed, without communicating with each other, those two came into the presence of Prajāpati with sacrificial fuel in hand [i.e., as students willing to serve their preceptor]. For thirty-two years the two lived under Prajāpati the disciplined life of a student of sacred knowledge (brahmacharya). Then Prajāpati asked them: "Desiring what have you lived the disciplined life of a student of sacred knowledge under me?" They said: " 'The Self, who is free from evil, free from old age, free from death, free from grief, free from hunger, free from thirst, whose desire is the Real, whose intention is the Real—he should be sought after, he should be desired to be comprehended. He obtains all worlds and all desires, who, having found out that Self, knows him.' These, people declare to be the venerable master's words. Desiring him [the Self] have we lived the student's life under you." Prajāpati said to them: "That Purusha who is seen in the eye—he is the Self (ātman)," said he. "That is the immortal, the fearless; that is Brahman." "But this one, Sir, who is perceived in water and in a mirror—who is he?" Prajāpati replied: "The same one, indeed, is perceived in all these." "Having looked at yourself in a pan of water, whatever you do not comprehend of the Self, tell that to me," said Prajāpati. They looked at themselves in the pan of water. Prajāpati asked them: "What do you see?" They replied: "We see here, Sir, our own selves in entirety, the very reproduction of our forms, as it were, correct to the hairs and the nails." Then Prajāpati said to them: "Having become well ornamented, well dressed, and refined, look at yourselves in a pan of water." Having become well ornamented, well dressed, and refined, they looked at themselves in a pan of water. Thereupon Prajāpati asked them: "What do you see?" They replied: "Just as we ourselves here are, Sir, well ornamented, well dressed, and refined. . . ." "That is the Self," said he. "That is the immortal, the fearless; that is Brahman." Then they went away with a tranquil heart. Having looked at them, Prajāpati said to himself:

"They are going away without having realized, without having found
out the Self. Whosoever will accept this doctrine as final, be they gods or
demons, they shall perish." Then Virochana, verily, with a tranquil heart,
went to the demons and declared to them that doctrine, namely: One's
self [one's bodily self] [1] alone is to be made happy here; one's self is to be
served. Making oneself alone happy here, serving oneself, does one obtain both worlds, this world and the yonder. Therefore, here, even now,
they say of one who is not a giver, who has no faith, who does not offer
sacrifices, that he is, indeed, a demon; for this is the doctrine of the
demons. They adorn the body of the deceased with perfumes, flowers,
etc., which they have begged, with dress and with ornaments, for they
think they will thereby win the yonder world.

But then Indra, even before reaching the gods, saw this danger: "Just
as, indeed, the bodily self becomes well ornamented when this body is
well ornamented, well dressed when this body is well dressed, and refined when this body is refined, even so that one becomes blind when this
body is blind, lame when this body is lame, and maimed when this body
is maimed. The bodily Self, verily, perishes immediately after the perishing of this body. I see no good in this." With sacrificial fuel in hand, he
again came back to Prajāpati. [Indra states his objection to Prajāpati, who
admits its truth and asks him to live as a student under him for another
thirty-two years.] Indra lived a student's life under Prajāpati for another
thirty-two years. Then, Prajāpati said to him: "He who moves about happy
in a dream—he is the Self," said he. "That is the immortal, the fearless;
that is Brahman." Thereupon, with a tranquil heart, Indra went away.

But then, even before reaching the gods, he saw this danger: "Now,
even though this body is blind, the Self in the dream-condition does not
become blind; even though this body is lame, he does not become lame;
indeed, he does not suffer any defect through the defect of this body. He
is not slain with the slaying of this body. He does not become lame with
the lameness of this body. Nevertheless, they, as it were, kill him; they,
as it were, unclothe him. He, as it were, becomes the experiencer of what
is not agreeable; he, as it were, even weeps. I see no good in this." [Again
Indra returns to Prajāpati with his objection. The latter admits its truth
but asks Indra to be his student for another thirty-two years.] Then
Prajāpati said to him: "Now, when one is sound asleep, composed, serene,

---

[1] Ātman can refer to one's bodily self as well as the Supreme Self.

and knows no dream—that is the Self," said he. "That is the immortal, the fearless; that is Brahman." Thereupon, with a tranquil heart, Indra went away.

But then, even before reaching the gods, he saw this danger: "Assuredly, this Self in the deep sleep condition does not, indeed, now know himself in the form: 'I am he'; nor indeed does he know these things here. He, as it were, becomes one who has gone to annihilation. I see no good in this." [Indra once more returns to Prajāpati, who promises to tell him the final truth after another five years of studentship.] Indra lived a student's life under Prajāpati for another five years. The total number of these years thus came to one hundred and one; thus it is that people say that, verily, for one hundred and one years Maghavan [Indra, the Rewarder] lived under Prajāpati the disciplined life of a student of sacred knowledge. Then Prajāpati said to him: "O Maghavan, mortal, indeed, is this body; it is taken over by death. But it is the basis of that deathless, bodiless Self. Verily, the Self, when embodied, is taken over by pleasure and pain. Verily, there is no freedom from pleasure and pain for one who is associated with the body. The wind is bodiless; cloud, lightning, thunder—these are bodiless. Now as these, having risen up from yonder space and having reached the highest light, appear each with its own form, even so this serene Self, having risen up from this body and having reached the highest light, appears with its own form. That Self is the Supreme Person (*uttama puruṣa*).

The Essential Reality Underlying the World

Looking "outwards," the Upanishadic thinker comes to the realization that this world is merely a bundle of fleeting names and forms, that there is only one permanent reality underlying this manifold phenomenal world, and that, in the ultimate analysis, that reality (elsewhere called Brahman, but here sat, i.e., being, essence) is identical with the essential reality in human personality, namely, the Self (ātman).

[From *Chāndogya Upaniṣad*, 6.1–3, 12–14, *passim*]

There, verily, was Shvetaketu, the son of Uddālaka Āruni. To him his father said: "O Shvetaketu, live the disciplined life of a student of sacred knowledge (brahmacharya). No one, indeed, my dear, belonging to our family, is unlearned in the Veda and remains a brāhman only by family connections as it were." He, then, having approached a teacher at the age of twelve and having studied all the Vedas, returned at the age of twenty-four, conceited, thinking himself to be learned, stiff. To him his father said: "O Shvetaketu, since, my dear, you are now conceited, think yourself to be learned, and have become stiff, did you also ask for that instruction whereby what has been unheard becomes heard, what has been unthought of becomes thought of, what has been uncomprehended becomes comprehended?" "How, indeed, Sir, is that instruction?" asked Shvetaketu. "Just as, my dear, through the comprehension of one lump of clay all that is made of clay would become comprehended—for the modification is occasioned only on account of a convention of speech,[2] it is only a name; while clay as such alone is the reality. Just as, my dear, through the comprehension of one ingot of iron all that is made of iron would become comprehended—for the modification is occasioned only on account of a convention of speech, it is only a name; while iron as such alone is the reality. . . . So, my dear, is that instruction." "Now, verily, those venerable teachers did not know this; for, if they had known it, why would they not have told me?" said Shvetaketu. "However, may the venerable sir tell it to me." "So be it, my dear," said he.

"In the beginning, my dear, this world was just being (sat), one only, without a second. Some people, no doubt, say: 'In the beginning, verily, this world was just nonbeing (asat), one only, without a second; from that nonbeing, being was produced.'[3] But how, indeed, my dear, could it be so?" said he. "How could being be produced from nonbeing? On the contrary, my dear, in the beginning this world was being alone,[4] one only, without a second. Being thought to itself: 'May I be many; may I procreate.' It produced fire. That fire thought to itself: 'May I be many, may I procreate.' It produced water. Therefore, whenever a person grieves or perspires, then it is from fire [heat] alone that water is produced. That water thought to itself: 'May I be many; may I procreate.' It produced food. Therefore, whenever it rains, then there is abundant food; it is from water alone that food for eating is produced.

[2] The various objects made of clay, such as plate and pitcher, are *essentially* nothing but clay. But for the sake of convenience different names are, by convention, assigned to the different shapes or modifications which that clay is made to assume. Within the world of the objects made of clay, clay alone is essential, while the different names and forms of those objects are only incidental. This is the doctrine of extreme nominalism.

[3] As in *Rig Veda,* 10.72.   [4] Compare *Rig Veda,* 10.129, above.

. . . That divinity [5] (Being) thought to itself: 'Well, having entered into these three divinities [fire, water, and food] by means of this living Self, let me develop names and forms.[6] Let me make each one of them tripartite.' That divinity, accordingly, having entered into those three divinities by means of this living Self, developed names and forms. . . . It made each one of them tripartite. . . ."

"Bring hither a fig from there." "Here it is, sir." "Break it." "It is broken, sir." "What do you see there?" "These extremely fine seeds, sir." "Of these, please break one." "It is broken, sir." "What do you see there?" "Nothing at all, sir." Then he said to Shvetaketu: "Verily, my dear, that subtle essence which you do not perceive—from that very essence, indeed, my dear, does this great fig tree thus arise. Believe me, my dear, that which is the subtle essence—this whole world has that essence for its Self; that is the Real [*satya,* truth]; that is the Self; that [subtle essence] art thou, Shvetaketu." [7] "Still further may the venerable sir instruct me." "So be it, my dear," said he.

"Having put this salt in the water, come to me in the morning." He did so. Then the father said to him: "That salt which you put in the water last evening—please bring it hither." Even having looked for it, he did not find it, for it was completely dissolved. "Please take a sip of water from this end," said the father. "How is it?" "Salt." "Take a sip from the middle," said he. "How is it?" "Salt." "Take a sip from that end," said he. "How is it?" "Salt." "Throw it away and come to me." Shvetaketu did so thinking to himself: "That salt, though unperceived, still persists in the water." Then Āruni said to him: "Verily, my dear, you do not perceive Being in this world; but it is, indeed, here only: That which is the subtle essence—this whole world has that essence for its Self. That is

[5] Being, which has been referred to in an impersonal manner so far, is now spoken of as a personalized divinity with a view to indicating that pure, essential "Being," as such, is in no way connected with the process of creation—this latter being only the result of nominalism.

[6] Being penetrates into fire, water, and food as their life-force and thereby invests them with the capacity further to function in the process of creation, thus helping the evolution of the phenomenal world which is in reality but a bundle of names and forms.

[7] In this statement, which is repeated a number of times in this chapter of the *Chāndogya Upaniṣad,* the following important points have been made: sat or Being, which is the cause of this gross world, is itself subtle and imperceptible. It is Being which constitutes the true Self (ātman) or life-force of this world. In other words, without Being the world cannot exist. The only absolute reality, therefore, is Being. This Being is identical with the Self (ātman), which is the essential reality in human personality. There is, thus, one single essential reality underlying man and the world.

the Real. That is the Self. That art thou, Shvetaketu." "Still further may the venerable sir instruct me." "So be it, my dear," said he.

"Just as, my dear, having led away a person from Gandhāra [8] with his eyes bandaged, one might then abandon him in a place where there are no human beings; and as that person would there drift about toward the east or the north or the south: 'I have been led away here with my eyes bandaged, I have been abandoned here with my eyes bandaged'; then as, having released his bandage, one might tell him: 'In that direction lies Gandhāra; go in that direction.' Thereupon he, becoming wise and sensible, would, by asking his way from village to village, certainly reach Gandhāra. Even so does one who has a teacher here know: 'I shall remain here [in this phenomenal world] only as long as I shall not be released from the bonds of nescience. Then I shall reach my home.' "

[8] The western limit of Indian civilization.

PART TWO
JAINISM AND BUDDHISM

B.C.   817   Traditional date of the birth of the Jain savior Pārshva-
nātha.

c.563–483 [or, 558–478]   Siddhārtha Gautama, the Buddha.

c.542–490   Bimbisāra, king of Magadha.

c.490–458   Ajātashatru, king of Magadha.

c.480   First Buddhist Council at Rājagriha.

c.468 [or, 487, 477]   Death of Vardhamāna Mahāvīra.

327–325   Invasion by Alexander of Macedon.

Maurya Period

c.322–298 [or, 317–293]   Chandragupta

c.300   Megasthenes, Greek ambassador of Seleucus Nicator
visits court of Chandragupta.

c.298–273   Bindusāra.

c.273–237 [or, 269–232; 268–233]   Ashoka.

c.247–207   King Devanampiya Tissa of Ceylon converted to Buddhism by Thera Mahinda.

c.200–200 A.D.   Period of greatest Buddhist and Jain influence in India.

c.190   Greek Kingdoms in North-West India.

c.185 [or, 183]   End of dynasty.

Age of Invasions

c.185–173 [or, 183–171]   Shunga Dynasty.

c.185–149   Pushyamitra Shunga.

c.170–165   Yueh-chi (Iranians) invade India.

c.150   Milinda (Gk. Menander), greatest of Indo-Greek kings.

c.90   Shakas invade North-West India.

A.D.   c.early 1st century Kushānas invade India.

c.79 [or, 82]   Division of Jains into Shvetāmbara and Digambara sects.

c.78–101   Kanishka.

c.100–200   Rise of Mahāyāna Buddhism. Ashvaghosha's *Buddhacarita*. Prominence of Mādhyamika School of Nāgārjuna
(until 5th century).

c.200–400   Kundakunda, Jain teacher of Digambara sect.

c.400–500   Mahāyāna philosophers Asanga and Vasubandhu. Founding of great Buddhist monastery at Nālandā.

c.454	Writing of Jain oral tradition at Council at Valabhī in Saurashtra.
c.500–1000	Prominence of Mahāyāna Buddhist School of Yogāchāra or Vijñānavāda.
c.600–700	Appearance of Tantricism in organized Buddhism.
c.700–800	Buddhism spreads to Nepal and Tibet.
c.770–810	Buddhist King Dharmapāla rules in Bihar and Bengal.
c.900–1000	Sahajayāna or Sahajīya Tantric School marks last phase of Buddhism in India.
c.1192	Muslim defeat of Hindus under Prithivi Rāj. Buddhism disappears as an organized religious force in India.

INTRODUCTION

THE BACKGROUND OF JAINISM
AND BUDDHISM

Between the seventh and the fifth centuries B.C. the intellectual life of India was in ferment. It has been pointed out many times that this period was a turning point in the intellectual and spiritual development of the whole world, for it saw the earlier philosophers of Greece, the great Hebrew prophets, Confucius in China, and probably Zarathustra in Persia. In India this crucial period in the world's history was marked on the one hand by the teaching of the Upanishadic sages, who admitted the inspiration of the Vedas and the relative value of Vedic sacrifices, and on the other hand by the appearance of teachers who were less orthodox than they, and who rejected the Vedas entirely. It was at this time that Jainism and Buddhism arose, the most successful of a large number of heterodox systems, each based on a distinctive set of doctrines and each laying down distinctive rules of conduct for winning salvation.

The social background of this great development of heterodoxy cannot be traced as clearly as we would wish from the traditions of Jainism and Buddhism, which have to some extent been worked over by editors of later centuries. But it would appear that heterodoxy flourished most strongly in what is now the state of Bihar and the eastern part of Uttar Pradesh. Here the arrival of Aryan civilization and brahmanical religion seems to have been comparatively recent at the time. The people were probably little affected by the Aryan class system, and the influence of the brāhman was by no means complete. Quite as much attention was devoted to local chthonic gods such as yakshas and nāgas, worshiped at sacred mounds and groves (chaityas), as to the deities of the Aryan pantheon. Cities had arisen, where a class of well-to-do merchants lived in comparative opulence, while the free peasants who made up the majority of the population enjoyed, as far as can be gathered, a somewhat higher standard of living than they do today, when pressure of population and exhaustion of the soil have so gravely impoverished them.

The old tribal structure was disintegrating, and a number of small regional kingdoms had appeared, together with political units of a somewhat different type, which preserved more of the tribal structure, and are generally referred to as "republics" for want of a better word. Most of these republics were of little importance politically, and were dependent on the largest of the kingdoms, Kosala, which controlled most of the eastern part of modern Uttar Pradesh; one such was that of the Shākyas, in the Himalayan foothills, which might well have been forgotten entirely were it not for the fact that the founder of Buddhism was the son of one of its chiefs. The most important of these republics was that generally referred to as the Vajjian Confederacy, of which the largest element was the tribe of the Licchavis; this controlled much of Bihar north of the Ganges, and was apparently governed by a chief who derived his power from a large assembly of tribesmen, and ruled with the aid of a smaller council of lesser chiefs. Much of Bihar south of the Ganges formed the kingdom of Magadha. King Bimbisāra, who ruled Magadha during most of the time in which the Buddha taught, seems to have had more initiative in political organization than his rivals, and managed his little state with more efficiency and closer centralized control than any other chief or king of his time. His son, Ajātasattu, who began to reign some seven years before the Buddha's death, embarked upon a policy of expansion. Magadha soon absorbed the Vajjis and Kosala, and her growth continued until, about two hundred years later, the great emperor Ashoka annexed Kalinga, and Pātaliputra (modern Patna) became the capital of the whole Indian subcontinent except the southern tip.

The development of organized states and the advance of material culture were accompanied by the rapid spread of new religious ideas which were soon to become fundamental to all Indian thought. It is remarkable that in the Vedas and the earlier Brāhmana literature the doctrine of transmigration [1] is nowhere clearly mentioned, and there is no good reason to believe that the Aryans of Vedic times accepted it. It first ap-

---

[1] We use this term, which is the most usual one, with reference to the general Indian doctrine of reincarnation and rebirth; but it must be remembered that it is misleading when applied to Buddhism, which maintains that no entity of any kind migrates from one body to another (see p. 97).

KAMBOJA

GANDHĀRA

Taxila

Indus

KASHMIR HIMALAYA

PUNJAB

Jhelum

Chenab

Ravi

Sutlej

Mt. Kailasa

MTS.

Harappa

Indraprastha

Brahmaputra

Mohenjodaro

RĀJPUTĀNA

Brindavan
Mathura

Kanauj

NEPAL

Savatthi

Kapilavastu
Lumbini
Kusinara
Vaishali
Mithilā

Champa

KĀMARŪPA

Chanhu-Daro

Ajmir

Ayodhyā

Ganges

RAJASTHĀN

Prayaga

Sarnath

Kāshi

Patali-
putra
Nalanda

Jumna

MĀLWĀ
AVANTI

Bharhut

Khajuraho

Bodhgaya

Gaya

Rajagaya

BIHAR
MAGADHA

Ujjain

Sauchi

Narbadā

GUJARAT

VINDHYA MTS.

MAHĀKOSALA

Mahānadi

BENGAL

MOUTHS OF THE INDUS

SURĀSHTRA

Valabhi

Girnar

Surat

Tapti

MOUTHS OF THE GANGES

MAHĀRĀSHTRA

KALINGA

Konarak
Puri

Arabian
Sea

Poona

Godavari

ANDHRA

Bay of
Bengal

Krishna

Talikota

Vengi
Amaravati

Bādāmi

DECCAN

Vijayanagar

Tungabhadra

KĀRNĀTAKA

CHOLA PALLAVA

Kānchipuram

Māmallapuram

Mysore

Kāveri

KERALA

Shrirangam

Tanjore

Madura

PĀNDYA

India

BEFORE 1200

Anurādhāpura
Polonnāruva

Kandy

LANKA-SIMHALA

0   100   200   300   400   500

Scale in Miles

pears, in a rather primitive form, in the early Upanishads as a rare and new doctrine, to be imparted as a great mystery by master-hermits to their more promising pupils. In the next stratum of India's religious literature, the Jain and Buddhist scriptures, the doctrine of transmigration is taken for granted, and has evidently become almost universal. With this belief in transmigration came a passionate desire for escape, for union with something which lay beyond the dreary cycle of birth and death and rebirth, for timeless being, in place of transitory and therefore unsatisfactory existence. The rapid spread of belief in transmigration throughout the whole of northern India is hard to account for; it may be that the humbler strata of society had believed in some form of transmigration from time immemorial, but only now did it begin to affect the upper classes. It is equally difficult to explain the growth of a sense of dissatisfaction with the world and of a desire to escape from it. Several reasons have been suggested to account for this great wave of pessimism, occurring as it did in an expanding society, and in a culture which was rapidly developing both intellectually and materially. It has been suggested that the change in outlook was due to the break-up of old tribes and their replacement by kingdoms wherein ethnic ties and the sense of security which they gave were lost or weakened, thus leading to a deep-seated psychological unease affecting all sections of the people. Another suggested cause of the change in outlook is the revolt of the most intelligent people of the times against the sterile sacrificial cults of the brāhmans. No explanation is wholly satisfactory, and we must admit our virtual ignorance of the factors which led to this great change in the direction of religious thought which was to have such an effect on the life of India and the world.

Both the sages of the Upanishads and the heresiarchs of the unorthodox schools taught the way of knowledge, as opposed to the way of works. Their primary aim was to achieve salvation from the round of birth and death, and to lead others to achieve it. Most of them maintained that salvation could only be obtained after a long course of physical and mental discipline, often culminating in extreme asceticism, but this was chiefly of value as leading to the full realization of the fundamental truths of the universe, after which the seeker for salvation was emancipated from the cycle of transmigration and reached a state of timeless bliss in which his limited phenomenal personality disintegrated or was absorbed in pure being. The basic truths of the various schools differed widely.

In many passages of the Buddhist scriptures we read of six unorthodox teachers (often rather inaccurately referred to as "heretics"), each of whom was the leader of an important body of ascetics and lay followers. In one passage (*Digha Nikāya* 1.47 ff.) short paragraphs are quoted which purport to give the basic tenets of their systems. A glance at these will give some impression of the bewildering variety of doctrines which were canvassed by the ascetic groups of the time.

The first of the teachers mentioned, Pūrana Kassapa, was an antinomian, who believed that virtuous conduct had no effect on a man's karma:

He who performs an act or causes an act to be performed, . . . he who destroys life, the thief, the housebreaker, the plunderer, . . . the adulterer and the liar . . . commit no sin. Even if with a razor-sharp discus a man were to reduce all the life on earth to a single heap of flesh he would commit no sin, neither would sin approach him. . . . From liberality, self-control, abstinence, and honesty is derived neither merit nor the approach of merit.

The second "heretic," Makkhali Gosāla, was the leader of the sect of Ājīvikas, which survived for some two thousand years after the death of its founder. He agreed with Pūrana that good deeds did not affect transmigration, which proceeded according to a rigid pattern, controlled by an all powerful cosmic principle which he called *Niyati,* Fate.

There is no deed performed either by oneself or by others [which can affect one's future births], no human action, no strength, no courage, no human endurance or human prowess [which can affect one's destiny in this life]. All beings, all that have breath, all that are born, all that have life, are without power, strength, or virtue, but are developed by destiny, chance, and nature. . . . There is no question of bringing unripe karma [2] to fruition, nor of exhausting karma already ripened, by virtuous conduct, by vows, by penance, or by chastity. That cannot be done. Samsāra [3] is measured as with a bushel,

[2] It is perhaps unnecessary to mention that karma is the effect of any action upon the agent, whether in this life or in a future one. Most Indian sects believed that karma operated as a sort of automatic moral sanction, ensuring that the evil-doer suffered and the righteous prospered; but Pūrana, Makkhali, and Pakudha appear to have disagreed with this view, while Ajita the materialist evidently denied the existence of karma altogether. The Jains, as we shall see, still look on karma as a sort of substance adhering to the soul, and it would appear that the "heretics" did likewise, although later Hinduism and Buddhism take a less materialistic view of it.

[3] The cycle of transmigration, the round of birth, death, and rebirth.

with its joy and sorrow and its appointed end. It can neither be lessened nor increased, nor is there any excess or deficiency of it. Just as a ball of thread will, when thrown, unwind to its full length, so fool and wise alike will take their course, and make an end of sorrow.

The third heterodox teacher, Ajita Kesakambala, was a materialist. The passage in which his views are given is one of the earliest expressions of complete unbelief in immaterial categories in the history of the world's thought:

There is no [merit in] almsgiving, sacrifice, or offering, no result or ripening of good or evil deeds. There is no passing from this world to the next. . . . There is no after-life. . . . Man is formed of the four elements; when he dies earth returns to the aggregate of earth, water to water, fire to fire, and air to air, while the senses vanish into space. Four men with the bier take up the corpse; they gossip [about the dead man] as far as the burning ground, where his bones turn the color of a dove's wing, and his sacrifices end in ashes. They are fools who preach almsgiving, and those who maintain the existence of immaterial categories speak vain and lying nonsense. When the body dies both fool and wise alike are cut off and perish. They do not survive after death.

Pakudha Kacchāyana, the fourth of the six, was an atomist, a predecessor of the Hindu Vaisheshika school, putting forward his theories probably a century or more before Democritus in Greece developed a similar doctrine of eternal atoms:

The seven elementary categories are neither made nor ordered, neither caused nor constructed; they are barren, as firm as mountains, as stable as pillars. They neither move nor develop; they do not injure one another, and one has no effect on the joy or the sorrow . . . of another. What are the seven? The bodies of earth, water, fire, air, joy and sorrow, with life as the seventh. . . . No man slays or causes to slay, hears or causes to hear, knows or causes to know. Even if a man cleave another's head with a sharp sword, he does not take life, for the sword-cut passes between the seven elements.[4]

The fifth teacher, Nigantha Nātaputta,[5] was no other than Vardhamāna Mahāvīra, the leader of the sect of Jains, which survives to this day, and the teachings of which will be considered presently. The sixth and last, Sanjaya Belatthiputta, was, as far as can be gathered from the passage attributed to him, a sceptic, who denied the possibility of certain knowledge altogether:

[4] These doctrines were apparently taken up by the Ājīvikas, who in later times maintained a theory of seven elements, which was evidently derived from that of Pakudha.

[5] Pāli, *Nigaṇṭha Nātaputta;* Skt. *Nirgrantha Jñātṛputra.*

If you asked me "Is there another world?", and if I believed that there was, I should tell you so. But that is not what I say. I do not say that it is so; I do not say that it is otherwise; I do not say that it is not so; nor do I say that it is not not so.

It must be emphasized that the salvation promised by these teachers, and by others like them, was not dependent on the mere acceptance of the doctrine on the word of the teacher, or on belief in it on a cool logical basis. To achieve release from transmigration it was necessary that the fundamental doctrine should be realized in the inmost being of the individual, and such a realization could only be achieved by the mystical and ascetic practices generally known in the West as yoga. Each group, even that of the materialists who followed Ajita, had its special system of meditation and mental or spiritual exercises, each its organized body of followers, usually ascetics, pledged to strive together for emancipation. Lay devotees and patrons were generally thought to be on the lowest rungs of the spiritual ladder, and there was little or no chance of full salvation outside the disciplined order.

CHAPTER IV

THE BASIC DOCTRINES
OF JAINISM

Originating at the same time and in the same region of India as Buddhism, Jainism has experienced its moments of triumph, periods when mighty kings supported it and the finest craftsmen in India worked on the embellishment of its temples. But it has never spread, like Buddhism, beyond the land of its origin to become one of the world's great religions; on the other hand it has not disappeared from India as Buddhism has, but has survived to the present day, a small but significant element in the religious life of the subcontinent.

THE ORIGIN AND DEVELOPMENT OF JAINISM

The figure to whom Jains look back as their great teacher, Vardhamāna Mahāvīra ("The Great Hero"), was a contemporary of the Buddha, often mentioned in the Buddhist scriptures under the name Nigantha Nātaputta, "the naked ascetic of the clan of the Jnātrikas." Mahāvīra is believed by the Jains to have been the twenty-fourth and last Tīrthankara ("Fordmaker") of the present period of cosmic decline. Pārshva, the twenty-third Tīrthankara, is said to have lived only two hundred and fifty years before Mahāvīra, and it would seem that in fact the latter teacher based his new community on existing groups of asectics, some of whom looked back to the earlier preacher Pārshva. The legends told by the Jains about Mahāvīra are in many ways less attractive than those told by Buddhists about Buddha, and most of them are equally doubtful from the point of view of the historian, but the main outline of his life-story is probably true. Mahāvīra is said to have been the son of Siddhārtha, a chief of the warrior clan of the Jnātrikas, and his wife Trishalā, sister of Chetaka, chief of the larger kindred tribe of the Licchavis; both tribes

dwelled around the important city of Vaishāli, in what is now North
Bihar. Thus, like the Buddha, Mahāvīra was a scion of the tribal "re-
publican" peoples of India. He is said to have left his home at the age of
thirty in order to seek salvation and to have wandered for twelve years
far and wide in the Ganges valley, until, at the age of forty-two, he
found full enlightenment, and became a "completed soul" (kevalin) and
a "conqueror" (jina). From a derivative form of the second title the
Jains take their name. Mahāvīra taught his doctrines for some thirty
years, founding a disciplined order of naked monks and gaining the
support of many layfolk. He died at the age of seventy-two at Pāvā, a
village not far from Patna, which is still visited by thousands of Jains
annually and is one of their most sacred places of pilgrimage. Most authorities believe that the date of his death was 468 B.C., although the Jains
themselves place it some sixty years earlier.

Probably for a century or so after Mahāvīra's death the Jains were comparatively unimportant, because both the Jain and the Buddhist scriptures,
though not wholly ignoring the existence of the other sect, look on the
sect of the Ājīvikas as the chief rival of their respective faiths. Jainism,
like Buddhism, began to flourish in the days of the Mauryas. A very
strong Jain tradition maintains that the first Maurya emperor, Chandragupta (c. 317–293 B.C.), was a patron of Jainism and ultimately became a
Jain monk. It is to this period that the great schism in Jainism is attributed by tradition. Between the death of Mahāvīra and this time, the
order had been led by a series of pontiffs called *Gaṇadharas* ("Supporters
of the Communities"). Bhadrabāhu, the eleventh *Gaṇadhara,* foresaw that
a great famine would soon occur in northern India, and so, with a great
following of naked monks, among whom was the ex-emperor Chandragupta, he departed for the Deccan, leaving behind many monks who refused to follow him, under the leadership of another teacher, Sthūlabhadra. When the famine was over Bhadrabāhu and many of the exiles returned to find that those who had remained in the north had adopted
many dubious practices as a result of the distress and confusion of the
famine, the most censurable of which was the wearing of white robes.

This, however, was not the only misfortune resulting from the famine.
Bhadrabāhu was the only person who knew perfectly the unwritten
sacred texts of Jainism. In order to conserve them Sthūlabhadra called
a council of monks at Pāṭaliputra, but Bhadrabāhu was not present—

horrified at the corruption of the Order he had departed for Nepal, to end his days in solitary fasting and penance. So the original canon of Jainism was reconstructed as well as possible from the defective memory of Sthūlabhadra and other leading monks in the form of the eleven *Limbs (Aṅga)*. Thus, according to tradition, Jainism was divided into two great sections, though in fact the division may have existed in germ in the days of Mahāvīra himself and did not become final until about two centuries later. On the one hand were the *Digambaras,* the "Space-clad," who insisted on the total nudity of their monks and who did not admit the full authenticity of the eleven *Limbs,* and on the other the Shvetāmbaras, or "White-clad," whose monks wore white robes and who accepted the *Limbs.* Today the Digambaras are to be found chiefly in the Deccan, especially in Mysore, while the Shvetāmbaras, who are much in the majority, dwell chiefly in Gujarat and Rajasthan. Though the teachers of the one group would in the past often write and speak very acrimoniously about the practices of the other, there has never been any fundamental difference in doctrine. There was no development in Jainism at all comparable to that which produced Mahāyāna Buddhism from Theravāda. All Jains, whatever their sect, maintain the same fundamental teachings, which have probably been little altered since the time of Bhadrabāhu. Though there have been superficial compromises with Hinduism, Jainism remains what it was over two thousand years ago.

There is no doubt that Jain monks did much to spread northern culture in the Deccan and the Tamil land, and in the early medieval period, until the eleventh century, many important south Indian kings gave Jainism their support. But the great wave of devotional theism which arose in South India almost overwhelmed it, and it never again became a major force in the religious life of the peninsula. In the west, too, after a period of triumph in the twelfth century, when King Kumārapāla of Gujarat became an earnest Jain, the religion declined. But its layfolk, unlike those of Buddhism, were bound to their faith by carefully regulated observances and the pastoral care of the monks. Solidly knit communities of well-to-do merchants forming their own castes, the Jains resisted both the violent attacks of the Muslims and the constant peaceful pressure of the brāhmans; where Buddhism perished Jainism survived.

Indeed in recent centuries Jainism has shown signs of vitality and

growth. At Surat, in the early eighteenth century, a further significant
schism occurred in the Shvetāmbara sect, under the leadership of a Jain
monk named Vīrajī who, basing his views on those of earlier less successful reformers, taught that true Jainism should not admit iconolatry or
temple worship. This schism, which undoubtedly owes some of its inspiration to Islam, is comparable on a much smaller scale to the Protestant
Reformation in Christianity; it has resulted in the emergence of a new
sect of Jainism which has given up the complex ritual dear to the Indian
heart, and holds its religious meetings in the austere and unconsecrated
sthānakas ("buildings") from which the sect has acquired its usual name
—*Sthānakavāsī*.

In some respects the debt of Indian culture to Jainism is as great as
it is to Buddhism. Of all the religious groups of India Jainism has always been the most fervent supporter of the doctrine of nonviolence
(ahimsā), and undoubtedly the influence of Jainism in the spread of
that doctrine throughout India has been considerable. But even if Jainism
had never existed, it is probable that the idea of ahimsā would still have
been almost as widespread in India as it actually is. It is in other and
unexpected ways that Jainism has so greatly affected Indian life. Despite
their very stern asceticism Jain monks have always found time for study,
and, more than the Buddhists, they have devoted much attention to secular learning. The Jain monk is allowed and indeed encouraged to com-
pose and tell stories if these have a moral purpose, and thus much
medieval literature in Sanskrit, Prākrit, and the early vernaculars is the
work of Jain monks, who also helped to establish and develop the literature of certain vernacular languages, notably Canarese and Gujarātī.
Mallinātha, the author of the standard commentary on the works of India's greatest poet, Kālidāsa, was a Jain. Jain monks also contributed
much to the indigenous sciences of mathematics, astronomy, and
linguistics, and their libraries preserved from destruction many important ancient texts, often of non-Jain origin. In modern times also Jainism
has had some significant influence, for Mahātmā Gāndhi was born in a
part of India where Jainism is widespread, and he has himself admitted
the great impression made on him by the saintly Jain ascetics whom he
met in his youth. Many factors contributed to mold the mind of the young
lawyer who was to become one of the greatest men of the twentieth century, and of these Jainism was not the least important.

JAIN DOCTRINES AND PRACTICES

The basic teaching of Jainism may be expressed in a single sentence: The phenomenal individual consists of a soul closely enmeshed in matter, and his salvation is to be found by freeing the soul from matter, so that it may regain its pristine purity and enjoy omniscient self-sufficient bliss for all eternity. In essence the Jain teaching closely resembles that of the early Sānkhya school of Hindu philosophy, and it is possible that both Jainism and Sānkhya share a common source in primitive hylozoistic ideas which were widespread in the Ganges valley before the time of Mahāvīra.

The Jain view of life is essentially materialistic, using that word in its strict sense. Jainism, in fact, looks back to a stage in the evolution of Indian thought when it was almost impossible to conceive of any entity except on the analogy of solid matter. For the Jain the soul, called *jīva* ("life") in contrast to the Vedāntic *ātman* ("self"), is finite, and of definite though variable dimensions. The primitive roots of Jainism are also shown in its attribution of souls to objects not generally thought of as living. Buddhism does not allow that plants have life in the sense of gods, human beings, or animals. Jainism, on the other hand, finds souls not only in plants, but in the very elements themselves. Among the many classifications of Jainism is one which divides all living things into five categories, according to the number of senses they possess. The highest group, possessing five senses, includes men, gods, the higher animals, and beings in hell. Of these men, gods, and infernal beings together with certain animals (notably monkeys, cattle, horses, elephants, parrots, pigeons, and snakes) possess intelligence. The second class contains creatures thought to have four senses only—touch, taste, smell, and sight; this class includes most larger insects such as flies, wasps, and butterflies. The class of three-sensed beings, which are thought to be devoid of sight and hearing, contains small insects such as ants, fleas, and bugs, as well as moths, which are believed to be blind because of their unfortunate habit of flying into lighted lamps. Two-sensed creatures, with only the sense of taste and touch, include worms, leeches, shellfish, and various animalculae. It is in the final class of one-sensed beings, which have only the sense of touch, that the Jain classification shows its most original feature.

This great class is in turn divided into five sub-classes: vegetable bodies, which may be simple, as a tree, containing only one soul, or complex, as a turnip, which contains countless souls; earth-bodies, which include earth itself and all things derived from the earth, such as stones, clay, minerals, and jewels; water-bodies, found in all forms of water—in rivers, ponds, seas, and rain; fire-bodies, in all lights and flames, including lightning; and wind-bodies, in all sorts of gases and winds.

Thus the whole world is alive. In every stone on the highway a soul is locked, so tightly enchained by matter that it cannot escape the careless foot that kicks it or cry out in pain, but capable of suffering nevertheless. When a match is struck a fire-being, with a soul which may one day be reborn in a human body, is born, only to die a few moments afterwards. In every drop of rain, in every breath of wind, in every lump of clay, is a living soul.

Like the monad of Leibnitz the jīva of Jainism in its pure state is omniscient, and mirrors the whole universe; but the soul's natural brightness and wisdom is clouded over by layers of matter, and every thought, word, or action is believed to affect the material integument of the soul. Karma, the cause of the soul's bondage, is thought of in Jainism as a sort of subtle matter, flowing in chiefly through the organs of sense. Acts of selfishness and cruelty result in the influx of much very heavy and inauspicious karma, which results in unhappy rebirths; good deeds, on the other hand, have no such serious effects; while suffering willingly undertaken dissipates karma already accumulated. The soul can never gain liberation until it has rid itself of its whole accumulation of karma, and therefore Jain ascetics subject themselves to rigorous courses of penance and fasting in order to set their souls free of the karma already acquired, while all their actions are most carefully regulated to prevent the further influx of karma in serious quantities. Actions carried out with full consciousness which do no harm to other living things and are not undertaken for unworthy motives or for physical satisfaction attract only very slight karma, which is dispelled almost immediately; on the other hand the unintentional killing of an ant through carelessness may have very serious consequences for the soul. Though a deliberate act of cruelty is more culpable than an accidental one, even the latter must be paid for dearly. If the soul at last escapes from all the layers of its material envelope, being lighter than ordinary matter, it rises to the top of the universe, where it remains forever in omniscient inactive bliss.

Injury to one of the higher forms in the scale of being involves more serious consequences to the soul than injury to a lower form; but even the maltreatment of earth and water may be dangerous for the soul's welfare. For the layman it is impossible not to harm or destroy lives of the one-sensed type, but even wanton and unnecessary injury to these is reprehensible. The Jain monk vows that as far as possible he will not destroy even the bodies of earth, water, fire, or wind. In order to remain alive he must of course eat and drink, but he will not damage living plants in order to do so, preferring to leave this to the lay supporters who supply him with food. The monk will not eat potatoes or other root vegetables, since these contain large colonies of plant-lives; he strains his drinking water, in order to do as little harm as possible to the souls within it; he wears a face-cloth, rather like a surgeon's mask, to ensure that he does no serious injury to the wind-lives in the air he breathes; he will not run or stamp his feet, lest he harm the souls in earth and stones, or destroy small insects; he refrains from all quick and jerky movements for fear of injuring the souls in the air. His whole life must be circumspect and thoroughly regulated. Buddhism demands similar circumspection on the part of its monks, though not taken to such extreme lengths, but with the Buddhist the purpose of this is to develop the monk's spiritual powers. With the Jain its purpose is simply to avoid injury to the lower forms of life and thereby to prevent the influx of karma in dangerous quantities.

The number of lives or souls in the universe is infinite. The consequences of this proposition were worked out by the Jains with ruthless logic. Most souls have no hope of full salvation—they will go on transmigrating indefinitely. This is inevitable, for the number of souls is infinite, and however many pass to the state of ultimate bliss an infinite number will still remain bound in the toils of matter, for infinity remains infinity, however much is subtracted from it.

Thus the process of transmigration continues eternally, and the universe passes through an infinite number of phases of progress and decline. Unlike the similar cyclic doctrines of Hinduism and Buddhism, in the Jain system there is no sharp break at the end of the cycle, but rather an imperceptible process of systole and diastole. Each cosmic cycle is divided into two halves, the ascending (*utsarpiṇī*), and the descending (*avasarpiṇī*). We are now in the phase of descent, which is divided into six periods. In the first, the "very happy" (*suṣama-suṣamā*), men were of enormous stature and longevity, and had no cares; they were spontaneously virtuous, so had no need of morals or religion. In the second period, the "happy" (*suṣamā*), there was some diminution of their stature, longevity, and bliss. The third period, called "happy-wretched" (*suṣama-duḥṣamā*), witnessed the appearance of sorrow and evil in mild forms. At first mankind, conscious of the decline in their fortunes, looked to patriarchs (*kulakara*) for guidance and advice, until the last patriarch, Rishabhadeva, knowing the fate which was in store for the world, established the institutions of government and civilization. He then took to a life of asceticism, making his son Bharata the first Universal Emperor (*Cakravartin*). Rishabhadeva was the first of the twenty-four Tīrthankaras ("Fordmakers" through life) of Jainism, and, according to Jain tradition, was the true founder of Jainism in this age, for religion was now necessary in order to restrain the growing evil propensities of men. Moreover with the cosmic decline men's memories had become so bad that they needed to commit their thoughts to writing; so Brahmī, the daughter of Rishabhadeva, invented the numerous alphabets of India. The fourth period, "wretched-happy" (*duḥṣama-suṣamā*), was one of further decline, and saw the birth of the other twenty-three Tīrthankaras, the last of whom was Mahāvīra. The fifth period, the "wretched" (*duḥṣamā*), began some three years after Mahāvīra's death, and is at present current. Its duration is 21,000 years, during which Jainism will gradually disappear, and the stature, virtue, and longevity of men will gradually diminish. The sixth and last period, the "very wretched" (*duḥṣama-duḥṣamā*), will also last for 21,000 years, and at its end the nadir of decline will be reached. People will live for only twenty years, and will be only a cubit tall. Civilization will be forgotten, and men will live in caves, ignorant of even the use of fire. Morality will be nonexistent, and theft, incest, adultery, and murder will be looked upon as normal. At the end of this age there will be fierce storms which will destroy many of the remaining pygmy inhabitants of the earth; but some will survive, and from now on the state of the world will imperceptibly grow better, for the age of ascent will have commenced. The six periods will be repeated in reverse order until the peak of human happiness and virtue is reached once more, and the cycle begins again.

In a universe which continually repeats itself in this way there seems little scope for human effort, but though on a large scale the processes of nature are strictly determined by natural law and neither men nor gods can influence them, the individual is free to work out his own salvation. The Jains vigorously rejected the fatalism of the Ājīvikas. It was to a life of earnest striving for perfection that Mahāvīra called his followers, whether laymen or monks.

Jainism differs from Buddhism in that its layfolk are expected to submit themselves to a more rigid discipline and are given more definite and regular pastoral care by the Jain clergy. The layman should in theory spend full- and new-moon days in fasting and penance at a Jain monastery. Few modern Jains keep this sabbath, called *poṣadha,* in so rigorous a form, except at the end of the Jain ecclesiastical year, usually in July, when there takes place a sort of Jain Lent, called *paryuṣaṇā,* which lasts for eight days with the Shvetāmbaras and for fifteen with the Digambaras. The year ends with a general penance in which all good Jains, monk and layman alike, are expected to confess their sins, pay their debts, and ask forgiveness of their neighbors for any offenses, whether intentional or unintentional. This ceremony of general confession and pardon, extending beyond the Jain church to embrace members of other religions and even animals, is perhaps the finest ethical feature of Jainism.

Despite their insistence on kindliness and nonviolence, Jain ethical writings often have a rather chilly character, their altruism motivated by a higher selfishness. The Jain scriptures contain nothing comparable for instance to the *Mettā Sutta* of the Buddhists (see Chapter VI), and the intense sympathy and compassion of the Bodhisattva of Mahāyāna Buddhism is quite foreign to the ideals of Jainism; for an advanced ascetic such sentiments are further bonds to be broken, mere evidence of human weakness, destroying the impassivity acquired after many years of hardship and penance. The chief reason for doing good is the furtherance of one's own spiritual ends. Violence is chiefly to be avoided not so much because it harms other beings as because it harms the individual who commits it. Charity is good because it helps the soul to break free from the bonds of matter. To implicate one's own feelings with those of others is dangerous to the welfare of the soul. The virtuous layman is encouraged to do good works and to help his fellows not for love of others but for love of his own soul; the monk turns the other cheek when attacked for the same reason.

We must not overemphasize this feature of Jainism. Moralists of all religions and none have often appealed to enlightened self-interest as the chief spur to virtuous conduct; moreover many passages in the Jain scriptures do encourage a more positive and truly altruistic morality. But their attitude is often one of cold detachment which, to the unbeliever, is rather unattractive.

In everyday life the Jains have been much influenced by the Hindus. They often perform all the domestic rites of Hinduism, employing brāhmans for the purpose. They worship many of the Hindu gods, who are believed to bestow temporal blessings, and they have their own versions of the most famous Hindu legends. Nevertheless Hinduism has made little impression on the heart of Jainism, which remains much as it was over two thousand years ago—a primitive science, purporting to give an explanation of the whole universe and to show man his way through it to its topmost point, where the conquerors and completed souls dwell forever in omniscient bliss. There have been no great changes in Jainism over the centuries, and it remains what it always has been—an atheistic ascetic system of moral and spiritual discipline encouraging honesty and kindliness in personal relations, and a rigid and perhaps sometimes exaggerated nonviolence.

JAIN LITERATURE

The Jain canon, as preserved by the Shvetāmbara sect, consists of forty-five texts of moderate size, chiefly composed in the Ardha-māgadhī dialect of Prākrit, in both prose and verse. These consist of eleven *Limbs* (*Aṅga*), twelve *Secondary Limbs* (*Upāṅga*), ten *Miscellaneous Texts* (*Prakīrṇaka*), six *Separate Texts* (*Chedasūtra*), four *Basic Texts* (*Mūlasūtra*), and two separate texts which do not fall into any of the foregoing categories, the *Blessing* (*Nandīsūtra*), and the *Door of Enquiry* (*Anuyogadvāra*). The Jains themselves, as we have seen, do not claim that these texts are the authentic productions of the founder of Jainism, but maintain that the eleven *Limbs* were codified some two hundred years after Mahāvīra's death, while the whole canon did not receive its definitive form until the fifth century A.D., when it was finally established at a council held at Valabhī in Saurashtra. In fact the canon contains matter of very varying date; it has received far less study than the canon of Pāli Buddhism, and much further work must be done on it before it can be arranged in chronological order. It appears, however, that the *Secondary, Miscellaneous,* and *Basic Texts* contain some material which is quite as old as much of the contents of the eleven *Limbs,* while much of the latter is probably no earlier than the beginning of the Christian era. However, the canon also contains matter with a very archaic flavor, which may be more or less correctly transmitted from the days of the founder himself. The language, allusions, and general atmosphere of the Jain canon show, however, that it is broadly speaking later than that of Theravāda Buddhism.

The canon contains passages of grace and beauty, especially in its verse portions, but its style is generally dry; lengthy stereotyped passages of description are repeated over and over again throughout the series of texts, and the passion for tabulation and classification, which can be detected in much Indian religious literature, is perhaps given freer rein here than in the scriptures of any other sect. From the literary point of view the Jain canon is inferior to that of the Buddhists.

There is, however, much noncanonical Jain literature in various Prākrits, Apabhramsha, Sanskrit, several vernaculars of India, and in English, and some of the medieval narrative literature is of considerable literary merit. *Legends* (*Purāṇas*) were composed on the Hindu model, together with lengthy tales of the lives of the Tīrthankaras and other worthies of Jainism. Gnomic poetry is very plentiful. Commentarial literature was produced in very large quantities in Sanskrit, as well as manuals of doctrine, and refutations of the views of other systems. Moreover Jain scholars wrote treatises on politics, mathematics, and even poetics, giving their works a Jain slant. The total of medieval Jain literature is enormous, and is often more interesting and attractive than the canonical works.

The brief anthology which follows includes passages from both the canon and later Jain literature. Some liberty has been taken in places with the originals, and here and there passages have been drastically abridged in order to make them more easily understandable to the Western reader. According to the conventional usage works in Prākrit are generally referred to by their Sanskrit titles.

Of Human Bondage

The opening verses of *The Book of Sermons* (*Sūtrakṛtāṅga*)[1] epitomize the teaching of Jainism. The text from which they are taken, a series of separate passages of various origin in prose and verse, is one of the oldest sections of the canon. The insistence on nonviolence and the disparagement of human emotions are among the leading themes of Jainism from its origin to the present day.

[From *Sūtrakṛtāṅga*, 1.1.1.1–5]

One should know what binds the soul, and, knowing, break free from bondage.

What bondage did the Hero[2] declare, and what knowledge did he teach to remove it?

He who grasps at even a little, whether living or lifeless, or consents to another doing so, will never be freed from sorrow.

If a man kills living things, or slays by the hand of another, or consents to another slaying, his sin goes on increasing.

The man who cares for his kin and companions is a fool who suffers much, for their numbers are ever increasing.

All his wealth and relations cannot save him from sorrow.

Only if he knows the nature of life, will he get rid of karma.

The Man in the Well

This famous parable is to be found in more than one source, and is known to the Hindus. The version given below in an abridged form is taken from *The Story of Samarāditya*, a lengthy tale in mixed prose and verse[3] written in Prākrit by Haribhadra, who lived in the seventh century. The story tells of the adventures of its hero in nine rebirths, and is intended to show the effects of karma, but its author was a master of words, and his moral purpose is often lost in descriptive writing of a charming floridity. In the grim little story which follows, told by a Jain monk to a prince in order to persuade him of the evils of the world, he remembers his main purpose. The parable needs little comment, for Haribhadra has interpreted it himself.

[From *Samarādityakathā*, 2.55–80]

A certain man, much oppressed by the woes of poverty,
Left his own home, and set out for another country.

[1] Prākrit, *Sūyagaḍaṅga*. The correct interpretation of the Prākrit term is very doubtful. Our title is based on the conventional Sanskrit equivalent.
[2] That is, "The Great Hero," Mahāvīra.   [3] A genre known as *campū*.

He passed through the land, with its villages, cities, and harbors,
And after a few days he lost his way.

And he came to a forest, thick with trees . . . and full of wild beasts. There, while he was stumbling over the rugged paths, . . . a prey to thirst and hunger, he saw a mad elephant, fiercely trumpeting, charging him with upraised trunk. At the same time there appeared before him a most evil demoness, holding a sharp sword, dreadful in face and form, and laughing with loud and shrill laughter. Seeing them he trembled in all his limbs with deathly fear, and looked in all directions. There, to the east of him, he saw a great banyan tree. . . .

And he ran quickly, and reached the mighty tree.
But his spirits fell, for it was so high that even the birds could not fly over
  it,
And he could not climb its high unscalable trunk. . . .
All his limbs trembled with terrible fear,
Until, looking round, he saw nearby an old well covered with grass.
Afraid of death, craving to live if only a moment longer,
He flung himself into the well at the foot of the banyan tree.
A clump of reeds grew from its deep wall, and to this he clung,
While below him he saw terrible snakes, enraged at the sound of his
  falling;
And at the very bottom, known from the hiss of its breath, was a black
  and mighty python
With mouth agape, its body thick as the trunk of a heavenly elephant,
  with terrible red eyes.
He thought, "My life will only last as long as these reeds hold fast,"
And he raised his head; and there, on the clump of reeds, he saw two
  large mice,
One white, one black, their sharp teeth ever gnawing at the roots of the
  reed-clump.
Then up came the wild elephant, and, enraged the more at not catching
  him,
Charged time and again at the trunk of the banyan tree.
At the shock of his charge a honeycomb on a large branch
Which hung over the old well, shook loose and fell.

The man's whole body was stung by a swarm of angry bees,
But, just by chance, a drop of honey fell on his head,
Rolled down his brow, and somehow reached his lips,
And gave him a moment's sweetness. He longed for other drops,
And he thought nothing of the python, the snakes, the elephant, the mice,
   the well, or the bees,
In his excited craving for yet more drops of honey.
This parable is powerful to clear the minds of those on the way to free-
   dom.
Now hear its sure interpretation.
The man is the soul, his wandering in the forest the four types of exist-
   ence.[4]
The wild elephant is death, the demoness old age.
The banyan tree is salvation, where there is no fear of death, the elephant,
But which no sensual man can climb.
The well is human life, the snakes are passions,
Which so overcome a man that he does not know what he should do.
The tuft of reed is man's allotted span, during which the soul exists em-
   bodied;
The mice which steadily gnaw it are the dark and bright fortnights.[5]
The stinging bees are manifold diseases,
Which torment a man until he has not a moment's joy.
The awful python is hell, seizing the man bemused by sensual pleasure,
Fallen in which the soul suffers pains by the thousand.
The drops of honey are trivial pleasures, terrible at the last.
How can a wise man want them, in the midst of such peril and hardship?

Kinsfolk Are No Comfort in Old Age

If in this brief anthology we quote several passages which lay stress on the
miseries of ordinary life, we do but preserve the proportion of such passages
in the Jain scriptures themselves. The following extract is taken from *The
Book of Good Conduct,* the first *Limb* of the canon, which contains some of
the most ancient passages of Jain literature.
   [From *Ācārāṅga Sūtra,* 1.2.1]

[4] Divine, human, animal, and infernal.
[5] Until the introduction of Western methods of recording time the week was not used in
India except in astronomy. In its place was the *pakṣa,* the "wing" of the lunar month, the
bright *pakṣa* covering the period from new moon to full and the dark from full moon to
new.

He who desires the qualities of things is deluded and falls into the grip of great pain. For he thinks, "I have mother, father, sister, wife, sons and daughters, daughters-in-law, friends, kin near and remote, and acquaintances. I own various properties, I make profits. I need food and clothes." On account of these things people are deluded, they worry day and night, they work in season and out of season, they crave for fortune and wealth, they injure and do violence, and they turn their minds again and again to evil deeds. Thus the life of many men is shortened.

For when ear and eye and smell and taste and touch grow weak, a man knows that his life is failing, and after a while his senses sink into dotage. The kinsfolk with whom he lives first grumble at him, and then he grumbles at them. . . . An old man is fit for neither laughter, nor playing, nor pleasure, nor show. So a man should take to the life of piety, seize the present, be firm, and not let himself be deluded an hour longer, for youth and age and life itself all pass away. . . .

Understanding the nature of all kinds of pain and pleasure, before he sees his life decline, a wise man should know the right moment [for taking up a life of religion]. . . . Before his senses weaken he should pursue his own true welfare.

All Creation Groans Together in Torment

The following passage is taken from the *Book of Later Instructions,* one of the *Basic Texts,* and of later date than the *Limbs* of the canon, from which we have quoted. The eloquent verses translated below are part of a long speech delivered by a prince named Mrigaputra, in order to persuade his parents to allow him to take up a life of religion. Much of this passage consists of a very gory description of the pains of purgatory, which we omit. The reader should remember what we have said about the hylozoism of the Jains—the iron on the blacksmith's anvil is also in pain.

[From *Uttarādhyayana Sūtra*, 19.61–67, 71, 74]

From clubs and knives, stakes and maces, breaking my limbs,
An infinite number of times I have suffered without hope.
By keen-edged razors, by knives and shears,
Many times I have been drawn and quartered, torn apart and skinned.
Helpless in snares and traps, a deer,
I have been caught and bound and fastened, and often I have been killed.
A helpless fish, I have been caught with hooks and nets;

An infinite number of times I have been killed and scraped, split and
    gutted.
A bird, I have been caught by hawks or trapped in nets,
Or held fast by birdlime, and I have been killed an infinite number of
    times.
A tree, with axes and adzes by the carpenters
An infinite number of times I have been felled, stripped of my bark, cut
    up, and sawn into planks.
As iron, with hammer and tongs by blacksmiths
An infinite number of times I have been struck and beaten, split and
    filed. . . .
Ever afraid, trembling, in pain and suffering,
I have felt the utmost sorrow and agony. . . .
In every kind of existence I have suffered
Pains which have scarcely known reprieve for a moment.

Creatures Great and Small

The following verses from the *Book of Sermons* exemplify the cardinal
Jain doctrine that life pervades the whole world and that the lives of even the
humblest living things should be respected. The first verse lists the various
categories of life; the first two lines giving the five sub-classes of one-sensed
beings, and the second two a fourfold subdivision of beings with two or more
senses.
    [From *Sūtrakṛtāṅga*, 1.1–9]

Earth and water, fire and wind,
    Grass, trees, and plants, and all creatures that move,
Born of the egg, born of the womb,
    Born of dung, born of liquids [6]—

These are the classes of living beings.
    Know that they all seek happiness.
In hurting them men hurt themselves,
    And will be born again among them. . . .

Some men leave mother and father for the life of a monk,
    But still make use of fire;

---

[6] Creatures born of dung are lice, bugs, and similar insects; those born of liquids are
minute water insects, etc.

But He [7] has said, "their principles are base
    Who hurt for their own pleasure."

The man who lights a fire kills living things,
    While he who puts it out kills the fire;
Thus a wise man who understands the Law
    Should never light a fire.

There are lives in earth and lives in water,
    Hopping insects leap into the fire,
And worms dwell in rotten wood.
    All are burned when a fire is lighted.

Even plants are beings, capable of growth,
    Their bodies need food, they are individuals.
The reckless cut them for their own pleasure
    And slay many living things in doing so.

He who carelessly destroys plants, whether sprouted or full grown,
    Provides a rod for his own back.
He has said, "Their principles are ignoble
    Who harm plants for their own pleasure."

The Eternal Law

For the Jains the term *dharma* has two meanings. In one sense the term is used
to imply a sort of secondary space, without which movement would be impossible. In most contexts, however, *dharma* for the Jain is the universal rule
of nonviolence, the eternal Law. The following passage on this theme is from
the *Book of Good Conduct.*
    [From *Ācārāṅga Sūtra,* 1.4.1]

Thus say all the perfect souls and blessed ones, whether past, present,
or to come—thus they speak, thus they declare, thus they proclaim: All
things breathing, all things existing, all things living, all beings whatever,
should not be slain or treated with violence, or insulted, or tortured, or
driven away.

    This is the pure unchanging eternal law, which the wise ones who

[7] Mahāvīra.

know the world have proclaimed, among the earnest and the not-earnest, among the loyal and the not-loyal, among those who have given up punishing others and those who have not done so, among those who are weak and those who are not, among those who delight in worldly ties and those who do not. This is the truth. So it is. Thus it is declared in this religion.

When he adopts this Law a man should never conceal or reject it. When he understands the Law he should grow indifferent to what he sees, and not act for worldly motives. . . .

What is here declared has been seen, heard, approved, and understood. Those who give way and indulge in pleasure will be born again and again. The heedless are outside [the hope of salvation]. But if you are mindful, day and night steadfastly striving, always with ready vision, in the end you will conquer.

Respect for Life

Though "enlightened self-interest" is very frequently stated in the Jain scriptures to be the most important reason for leading the good life, numerous passages show that even the unimpassioned Jain monks who composed the canon were not entirely devoid of human feeling. The following extract, a much abridged version of the first chapter of the first *Limb* of the Jain canon, the *Book of Good Conduct,* exemplifies this point.
    [From *Ācārāṅga Sūtra,* 1.1]

Earth is afflicted and wretched, it is hard to teach, it has no discrimination. Unenlightened men, who suffer from the effects of past deeds, cause great pain in a world full of pain already, for in earth souls are individually embodied. If, thinking to gain praise, honor, or respect, . . . or to achieve a good rebirth, . . . or to win salvation, or to escape pain, a man sins against earth or causes or permits others to do so, . . . he will not gain joy or wisdom. . . . Injury to the earth is like striking, cutting, maiming, or killing a blind man. . . . Knowing this a man should not sin against earth or cause or permit others to do so. He who understands the nature of sin against earth is called a true sage who understands karma. . . .

And there are many souls embodied in water. Truly water . . . is alive. . . . He who injures the lives in water does not understand the nature of sin or renounce it. . . . Knowing this, a man should not sin

against water, or cause or permit others to do so. He who understands
the nature of sin against water is called a true sage who understands
karma. . . .

By wicked or careless acts one may destroy fire-beings and, moreover,
harm other beings by means of fire. . . . For there are creatures living
in earth, grass, leaves, wood, cowdung, or dustheaps, and jumping creatures which . . . fall into a fire if they come near it. If touched by fire,
they shrivel up, . . . lose their senses, and die. . . . He who understands
the nature of sin in respect of fire is called a true sage who understands
karma.

And just as it is the nature of a man to be born and grow old, so is
it the nature of a plant to be born and grow old. . . . One is endowed
with reason, and so is the other; [8] one is sick, if injured, and so is the
other; one grows larger, and so does the other; one changes with time,
and so does the other. . . . He who understands the nature of sin
against plants is called a true sage who understands karma. . . .

All beings with two, three, four, or five senses, . . . in fact all creation,
know individually pleasure and displeasure, pain, terror, and sorrow. All
are full of fears which come from all directions. And yet there exist people
who would cause greater pain to them. . . . Some kill animals for sacrifice, some for their skin, flesh, blood, . . . feathers, teeth, or tusks; . . .
some kill them intentionally and some unintentionally; some kill because
they have been previously injured by them, . . . and some because they
expect to be injured. He who harms animals has not understood or renounced deeds of sin. . . . He who understands the nature of sin against
animals is called a true sage who understands karma. . . .

A man who is averse from harming even the wind knows the sorrow of
all things living. . . . He who knows what is bad for himself knows what
is bad for others, and he who knows what is bad for others knows what is
bad for himself. This reciprocity should always be borne in mind. Those
whose minds are at peace and who are free from passions do not desire
to live [at the expense of others]. . . . He who understands the nature of
sin against wind is called a true sage who understands karma.

In short he who understands the nature of sin in respect of all the six
types of living beings is called a true sage who understands karma.

[8] The commentary justifies this statement. Plants manifest a degree of reason in knowing
the right season in which to bear flowers and fruit, and in growing upwards and not
downwards.

The Hero of Penance and Self-Control

To gain salvation a man must be absolutely sinless, and to achieve such complete purity he must become a Jain monk. His goodness must be such that he will not even accidentally tread on the insect which crosses his path. In order to avoid such acts of violence Jain monks often carry feather dusters, with which they sweep the ground on which they sit or walk. The following passage, exemplifying these teachings, is taken from the canonical *Book of Sermons.*
  [From *Sūtrakṛtāṅga,* 1.2.1.10–14]

Oh man, refrain from evil, for life must come to an end.
Only men foolish and uncontrolled are plunged in the habit of pleasure.

Live in striving and self-control, for hard to cross are paths full of insects.
Follow the rule that the Heroes [9] have surely proclaimed.

Heroes detached and strenuous, subduing anger and fear,
Will never kill living beings, but cease from sin and are happy.

"Not I alone am the sufferer—all things in the universe suffer!"
Thus should man think and be patient, not giving way to his passions.

As old plaster flakes from a wall, a monk should make thin his body by
    fasting,
And he should injure nothing. This is the Law taught by the Sage.[10]

Cheerfully Endure All Things

The ideal which the Jain monk, and indeed as far as may be the Jain layman, strives for is complete imperturbability. But behind this he should feel a calm, patient cheerfulness in the knowledge that, whatever his hardships, he is wearing away his karma and preparing for the bliss of full salvation.
  [From *Uttarādhyayana Sūtra,* 2.24–37]

If another insult him, a monk should not lose his temper,
For that is mere childishness—a monk should never be angry.
If he hears words harsh and cruel, vulgar and painful,
He should silently disregard them, and not take them to heart.
Even if beaten he should not be angry, or even think sinfully,
But should know that patience is best, and follow the Law.
If someone should strike a monk, restrained and subdued,
He should think, "[It might be worse—] I haven't lost my life!" . . .

---

[9] The twenty-four Tīrthankaras.   [10] Mahāvīra.

If on his daily begging round he receives no alms he should not be grieved,
But think, "I have nothing today, but I may get something tomor-
row!" . . .
When a restrained ascetic, though inured to hardship,
Lies naked on the rough grass, his body will be irritated,
And in full sunlight the pain will be immeasurable,
But still, though hurt by the grass, he should not wear clothes.
When his limbs are running with sweat, and grimed with dust and dirt
In the heat of summer, the wise monk will not lament his lost comfort.
He must bear it all to wear out his karma, and follow the noble, the su-
preme Law.
Until his body breaks up, he should bear the filth upon it.[11]

Wise Men and Fools

The following passage from the *Book of Good Conduct* repeats a theme very
common in Jain literature, the contrast between the life of the world and the
life of religion.
[From *Ācārāṅga Sūtra*, 1.2, 3]

Who will boast of family or glory, who will desire anything, when he
thinks that he has often been born noble, often lowly, and that his soul,
[his true self] is neither humble nor high-born, and wants nothing?

Thus a wise man is neither pleased nor annoyed. . . . A man should
be circumspect and remember that through carelessness he experiences
many unpleasantnesses and is born in many wombs, becoming blind,
deaf, dumb, one-eyed, hunchbacked, or of dark or patchy [12] complexion.
Unenlightened, he is afflicted, and is forever rolled on the wheel of birth
and death.

To those who make fields and houses their own, life is dear; they want
clothes dyed and colored, jewels, earrings, gold, and women, and they
delight in them. The fool, whose only desire is for the fullness of life,
thinks that penance, self-control, and restraint are pointless, and thus he
comes to grief. . . .

There is nothing that time will not overtake. All beings love themselves,

[11] Normally a Jain monk should not wash, for by doing so he is liable to injure both
water-lives and the vermin on his body.
[12] *Śabala*, probably a reference to the skin disease leucoderma, very widespread in India,
which produces white blotches on the skin.

seek pleasure, and turn from pain; they shun destruction, love life, and desire to live. To all things life is dear. They crave for riches and gather them together, . . . using the labor of servants both two-footed and four-footed; and whatever a man's share may be, whether small or great, he wants to enjoy it. At one time he has a great treasure, . . . while at another his heirs divide it, or workless men steal it, or kings loot it, or it is spoiled or vanishes, or is burned up with his house. The fool in order to get riches does cruel deeds which in the end are only of benefit to others, and stupidly comes to grief on account of the pain which he causes.

This the Sage (Mahāvīra) has declared—such men cannot and do not cross the flood; they cannot, they do not reach the other shore; they cannot, they do not get to the other side.

Though he hears the doctrine such a man never stands in the right place,
But he who adopts it stands in the right place indeed.
There is no need to tell a man who sees for himself,
But the wretched fool, delighting in pleasure, has no end to his miseries,
    but spins in a whirlpool of pain.

Two Ways of Life

For all the severity of the discipline of the Jain ascetic, the Jain scriptures contain numerous passages which mention the quiet inner happiness of the homeless life. The great sense of relief, of freedom, which comes with the abandonment of family ties, is often described in Hindu, Buddhist, and Jain texts. Moreover the life of asceticism is not looked on as weakly giving way before the sorrows of the world, but as a great spiritual struggle to be entered upon with courage and resolution like that of the soldier. These ideas are well expressed in the following passage, taken from the Book of Later Instructions, wherein we read of a semi-legendary king of Mithilā (North Bihar), who became an ascetic, and evidently did not regret it.

[From Uttarādhyayana Sūtra, 9]

With the fair ladies of his harem King Nami enjoyed pleasures like those
    of heaven,
And then he saw the light and gave up pleasure. . . .
In Mithilā, when the royal sage Nami left the world
And took to the life of a monk, there was a great uproar.
To the royal sage came the god Indra, disguised as a brāhman,
And spoke these words:

"There is fire and storm, your palace is burning!
Good sir, why don't you take care of your harem?"
Nami replied:
"Happy we dwell, happy we live, who call nothing whatever our own.
Though Mithilā burn, nothing of mine is burned!
When a monk has left his children and wives, and has given up worldly
    actions,
Nothing is pleasant to him, nothing unpleasant.
There is much that is good for the sage, the houseless monk
Set free from all ties, who knows himself to be alone."
Indra said:
"Build a wall, with gates and turrets,
And a moat and siege-engines; then you will be a true warrior."
Nami replied:
"With faith as his city, hardship and self-control the bolt of the gate,
Patience its strong wall, impregnable in three ways.[13]
With effort as his bow, circumspection in walking its string,
And endurance as its tip, with truth he should bend his bow,
And pierce with the arrow of penance the mail of his enemy, karma.
Thus the sage will conquer in battle, and be free [from samsāra]!"
Indra said:
"By punishing thieves and burglars, pickpockets and robbers,
Keep the city in safety; then you will be a true warrior."
Nami replied:
"Often men punish unjustly,
And the guiltless are put in prison, the guilty set free."
Indra said:
"Bring under your yoke, O lord of men, those kings
Who do not bow before you; then you will be a true warrior."
Nami replied:
"Though a man conquer a thousand thousand brave foes in battle,
If he conquers only himself, this is his greatest conquest.
Battle with yourself! Of what use is fighting others?
He who conquers himself by himself will win happiness." . . .

Throwing off his disguise, and taking his real shape,
Indra bowed before him and praised him with sweet words:

[13] By means of the three "defenses"—self-control in thought, word, and deed.

"Well done! You have conquered anger!
Well done! You have vanquished pride!
Well done! You have banished delusion!
Well done! You have put down craving!
Hurrah for your firmness!
Hurrah for your gentleness!
Hurrah for your perfect forbearance!
Hurrah for your perfect freedom! . . ."
Thus act the enlightened, the learned, the discerning.
They turn their backs on pleasure, like Nami the royal sage.

The Refuge of All Creatures

Here and there in the Jain scriptures the virtue of compassion (*dayā*) is
praised, though for the monk it should never be allowed to lead to emotional
involvement with other beings. In the following passage, however, the monk
is declared to have other duties than merely working out his own salvation; in
practice Jain monks have always been ready to help others with preaching,
consolation, and spiritual advice.
    [From *Ācārāṅga Sūtra,* 1.6, 5]

In whatever house, village, city, or region he may be, if a monk is attacked
by men of violence, or suffers any other hardship, he should bear it all
like a hero. The saint, with true vision, conceives compassion for all the
world, in east and west and south and north, and so, knowing the Sacred
Lore, he will preach and spread and proclaim it, among those who strive
and those who do not, in fact among all those who are willing to hear
him. Without neglecting the virtues of tranquillity, indifference, patience,
zeal for salvation, purity, uprightness, gentleness, and freedom from care,
with due consideration he should declare the Law of the Monks to all that
draw breath, all that exist, all that have life, all beings whatever. . . . He
should do no injury to himself or anyone else. . . . The great sage becomes a refuge for injured creatures, like an island which the waters cannot overwhelm.

The Final Penance

Though strongly opposed by the Buddhists, religious suicide is known to both
Hindu and Jain ascetics, and Mahāvīra himself is said to have voluntarily

starved himself to death by the protracted fast known as *itvara* or *sallekhanā*. A Jain monk who wishes to end his life in this way, and thereby rid his soul of a great deal of karma and perhaps even obtain full salvation, must prepare for the final penance by a course of graduated fasting lasting for as long as twelve years. If, however, he is sick and unable to maintain the course of rigid self-discipline to which he is vowed, he may starve himself to death without the preliminary preparation. The following passage from the *Book of Good Conduct,* though it refers to the rite as a "terrible penance," looks on it as the triumphant end to a life of spiritual struggle, and finds it no cause for tears.

[From *Ācārāṅga Sūtra,* 1.7, 6]

If a monk feels sick, and is unable duly to mortify the flesh, he should regularly diminish his food. Mindful of his body, immovable as a beam, the monk should strive to waste his body away. He should enter a village or town . . . and beg for straw. Then he should take it and go to an out-of-the-way place. He should carefully inspect and sweep the ground, so that there are no eggs, living beings, sprouts, dew, water, ants, mildew, drops of water, mud, or cobwebs left on it. Thereupon he carries out the final fast. . . . Speaking the truth, the saint who has crossed the stream of transmigration, doing away with all hesitation, knowing all things but himself unknown, leaves his frail body. Overcoming manifold hardships and troubles, with trust in his religion he performs this terrible penance. Thus in due time he puts an end to his existence. This is done by those who have no delusions. This is good; this is joyful and proper; this leads to salvation; this should be followed.

Moral Verses

Among the great classics of Tamil is *The Four Hundred Quatrains (Nālaḍi-nānnūrru),* better known simply as *The Quatrains,* a collection of fine verses on morality, perhaps of the fifth or sixth century A.D. They are known and loved by all Tamils, whether Hindu, Jain, Muslim, or Christian, since they contain much which all religions would approve, and little to which any would object; but they are by tradition the work of a large company of Jain monks who in a time of famine were sheltered and fed by a Tamil king, and, when they departed from his court, left each a quatrain as a blessing for his benevolence. The traditional ascription is borne out by the contents of the collection. Unlike the kindred collection of Tamil gnomic verse, the *Couplets (Kuṛal),* which is theistic in outlook, the *Quatrains* contain no references to the gods, and their earnest and rather pessimistic attitude to life is very similar to that of literature of known Jain origin. They differ, however, from much other Jain literature in their warmth and real humanity—for the authors of the *Quatrains* right conduct was not merely the avoidance of doing evil and the performance of cold acts of charity, but was rooted in fellowship, sympathy, and love. The verses below are a small representative sample of the whole.

[From *Nāladiyār*]

There is no passing the fixed day [of death]. No one
   On earth has escaped death, and fled, and gone free.
You who hoard up wealth, give it away! Tomorrow
   The funeral drum will beat. [6]

My mother gave me birth, left me, and went
   To seek her mother, who had gone on the same quest.
And so goes on the search of each man for his mother.
   This is the way of the world. [15]

Men come uninvited, join the family as kinsmen,
   And silently depart. As silently the bird
Flies far from the tree where its old nest remains,
   Men leave their empty bodies to their kin. [30]

The skulls of dead men, with deep caves for eyes,
   Horrid to see, grinning, address the living—
"Take heed, and keep to the path of virtue.
   That is the blessing that makes the body worth having." [49]

When men rise up in enmity and wish to fight,
   It is not cowardice, say the wise, to refuse the challenge.
Even when your enemies do the utmost evil,
   It is right to do no evil in return. [67]

If you send a little calf into a herd of cows
   It will find its mother with unfailing skill.
So past deeds search out the man who did them,
   And who must surely reap their fruit. [107]

Cows are of many different forms and colors;
   Their milk is always white.

The path of virtue, like milk, is one;
  The sects that teach it are manifold. [118]

Those who snare and keep encaged the partridge or the quail,
  Which dwell in the wilds where beetles hum around the flowers,
Shall [in a later life] till black and hungry soil,
  Their legs in fetters, as slaves to alien lords. [122]

Learning is a treasure that needs no safeguard;
  Nowhere can fire destroy it or proud kings take it.
Learning's the best legacy a man can leave his children.
  Other things are not true wealth. [134]

In the city of the gods, in the after-life,
  We shall learn if there is any greater joy
Than that when wise men, with minds as keen as steel,
  Meet together in smiling fellowship. [137]

You may bite the sugar-cane, break its joints,
  Crush out its juice, and still it is sweet.
Well-born men, though others abuse or hurt them
  Never lose their self-respect in words of anger. [156]

The greatness of the great is humility.
  The gain of the gainer is self-control.
Only those rich men are truly wealthy
  Who relieve the need of their neighbors. [170]

People speak of high birth and low—
  Mere words, with no real meaning!
Not property or ancient glory makes a man noble,
  But self-denial, wisdom and energy. [195]

This is the duty of a true man—
  To shelter all, as a tree from the fierce sun,
And to labor that many may enjoy what he earns,
  As the fruit of a fertile tree. [202]

Better hatred than the friendship of fools.
  Better death than chronic illness.
Better to be killed than soul-destroying contempt.
  Better abuse than praise undeserved. [219]

If I do not stretch out my hand and risk my life
  For a friend in need,
May I reap the reward of one who seduces the wife of a friend,
  While the wide world mocks me in scorn. [238]

Best is a life passed in penance,
  Middling, that spent with those one loves,
Worst, the life of one never satisfied,
  Cringing to rich men who care nothing for him. [365]

As a scroll read by one who well understands it,
  As wealth to the man of generous spirit,
As a sharp sword in the warrior's hand,
  Is the beauty of a faithful wife. [386]

CHAPTER V

JAIN PHILOSOPHY AND
POLITICAL THOUGHT

Two of the most interesting and individual features of Jainism are the kindred doctrines of "Viewpoints" (*nayavāda*) and "Maybe" (*syādvāda*), which are often called together "the Doctrine of Manysidedness" (*anekāntavāda*). These ideas certainly existed in embryo at the time of Mahāvīra and the Buddha, as is evident from the passages in the Buddhist scriptures attributed to the teacher Sanjaya which appear to be based on a garbled version of some such "manysided" doctrine; but there is no good evidence that they were propounded by Mahāvīra, and they may have been introduced into Jainism some time after his death.

Western thought, from the days of the Greeks onward, has been largely governed by the logical rule known as the law of the excluded middle—"either *a* or not-*a*." Socrates must be a mortal or not-mortal—there is no other possibility. In India, on the other hand, this law of thought has never been so strongly emphasized as in Europe, and the Jains allow not two possibilities of predication, but seven. These are known as "the Sevenfold Division" (*saptabhaṅgī*) or "the Doctrine of Maybe" (*syādvāda*):

1. We may truthfully affirm a given proposition (*syādasti*). Thus when in winter I come home after a walk in the open air, I may say that my room is warm.

2. But from another point of view it is possible to negate the same proposition (*syānnāsti*). Thus someone who has been sitting in the same room for some time may say with equal truth that it is not warm.

3. Hence it is possible to predicate the truth of a proposition and its negation at one and the same time (*syādastināsti*). The room is both warm and not-warm.

4. But the true character of the room, which we have seen is from different points of view warm, not-warm, and warm-and-not-warm, may

be said to be indescribable (*syādavaktavya*). Its true character, *sub specie aeternitatis,* eludes us.

The first four of the seven divisions are fairly clear and intelligible. The last three divisions, on the other hand, are a pendantic refinement of the theory, and some early Jain schools did not accept them:

5. A characteristic may be predicated about an entity which is otherwise recognized to be indescribable (*syādastyavaktavya*).

6. It may not possess that characteristic and be otherwise indescribable (*syānnāstyavaktavya*).

7. It may both have and not have the same characteristic, and be otherwise indescribable (*syādastināstyavaktavya*).

Closely related to the doctrine of "Maybe" is that of "Viewpoints," which shows the seven ways of approaching an object of knowledge or study:

1. We may consider an object of thought, say a certain man, concretely (*naigama-naya*), as at the same time an individual and a member of the human species.

2. Or we may consider him purely as a representative of mankind, not taking note of his individual character, but thinking only of the characteristics which he has in common with other men (*saṃgraha-naya*).

3. On the other hand we may think of him primarily as, for instance, our old friend John Smith, with all his personal traits and idiosyncrasies, hardly considering him in relation to the human species at all (*vyavahāra-naya*).

4. We may think of him as at the present moment, taking no note of his past or future, as a mere phenomenon in a limited area of space and time (*rjusūtra-naya*).[1]

As with the Sevenfold Division, the last three viewpoints seem somewhat pedantic, and are connected rather with the words used to define objects and concepts than with the objects and concepts themselves:

5. We may think of him from the point of view of his specific name "man," considering its synonyms and its implications (*śabda-naya*). This is supposed to prevent misuse of words and terms.

6. We may think of him from the point of view of the conventional meaning of the word only, without considering its etymological implications (*samabhirūḍha-naya*).

---

[1] One of the chief Jain criticisms of the Buddhists was that they tended to view the world exclusively from the viewpoint of *rjusūtra*, virtually ignoring the others.

7. Or finally we may consider an object with respect to the etymology of its name (*evambhūta-naya*). This viewpoint cannot be well illustrated with the word "man." A favorite Jain illustration is the consideration of the god Shakra (better known as Indra) as a manifestation of pure power, because his name is derived from the root *śak,* "to be able."

Though the Jain doctrine of manysidedness, in its finished form, shows pedantic refinements which are perhaps the work of an unfruitful scholasticism, it is, in its fundamentals, a remarkable achievement of Indian thought. Implicit in the epistemological relativity of *anekāntavāda* is a recognition that the world is more complex than it seems, that reality is more subtle than we are inclined to believe. Our knowledge is less certain than we think. A given proposition, though generally accepted as true, may only be relatively so, and the absolute and whole truth can only be seen by the perfected soul, the siddha, who surveys the whole universe in a single act of timeless knowledge. There is a famous Indian parable, occurring in many sources, which tells of a king who, in a fit of practical joking, assembled a number of blind men and told them each to touch an elephant and tell him what they felt. The man who touched the trunk declared that it was a snake, he who touched the tail, a rope, he who touched the leg, a tree-trunk, and so on. The story concludes with violent altercations, each blind man maintaining that he knew the whole truth. So man, incapable of seeing things whole and from all aspects at once, must be satisfied with partial truths. All too often he maintains that he knows the whole truth, and his one-sided approach results in anger, bigotry, and strife. The Jain, trained in the doctrine of manysidedness, realizes that all ordinary propositions are relative to the aspect from which they are made, and tries to know the objects of his attention as thoroughly as possible by considering them from all points of view. Jain philosophers have often been just as forthright in their criticism of other systems as the teachers of rival Indian schools of thought, but Jainism has a record of tolerance and friendliness toward other sects which is at least in part due to the doctrine of the manysidedness of truth.

Of Space and Time

Jain theories of space, time, and matter are of considerable subtlety, and suggest the non-Euclidean conceptions of modern relativity physics. There are in Jainism three types of space: *ākāśa,* sometimes translated "ether," but which we translate as "space," the function of which is to contain other substances, and a secondary and a tertiary space, which permit movement and rest respectively. These latter are strangely called *dharma* and *adharma* ("non-dharma"). This *dharma* must not be confused with the term as used in its religious and ethical sense, which we translate as "the Law" or "Righteousness." In our translation below *dharma* and *adharma* in the special sense of Jain physics are left untranslated. As will be seen, space is made up of an infinite number of points and of time, which, as in relativity physics, almost takes on the character of a fourth dimension, and consists of an infinite number of atomic instants. Substances are composed of atoms. There seems to have been some uncertainty as to whether or not a single atom had dimension. Kundakunda, the author whom we quote, apparently believed that the material atom was infinitesimal.

The *Essence of the Doctrine* is the work of a teacher of the Digambara sect, Kundakunda, who is believed to have lived in the third or fourth century A.D. It is a concise versified outline of the main doctrines of Jainism, written in Shauraseni Prakrit. It was commented on at considerable length in Sanskrit by Amritachandra, of the tenth century, and our notes are largely based on his work. The passage we quote outlines the nature of the six substances of Jain physics—souls, matter, space, *dharma, adharma,* and time—which constitute the whole universe. One of our chief reasons for including this passage is to show the great subtlety of which early Indian thought was capable. Our notes do not half exhaust the matter discussed by the commentator, and they might be prolonged indefinitely. It is largely on account of their extremely recondite nature that we have included so little from the purely philosophical texts of Jainism and Buddhism.

[From *Pravacanasāra*, 2.41–49, 53]

The quality of space is to give room, of *dharma* to cause motion, of *adharma* to cause rest.[1]

The quality of time is to roll on, of the self,[2] awareness.

You should know, in short, that all these qualities are formless.

---

[1] The existence of *dharma* as a secondary space is proved to the Jain's satisfaction from the fact of motion; this must be caused by something; it cannot be due to time or the atoms, since they have no spatial extension, and that which is spaceless cannot give rise to movement in space; it cannot be due to the soul, since souls do not fill the whole universe, but motion is possible everywhere; it cannot be due to space, for space extends even beyond the universe, and if space was the basis of motion the bounds of the universe would fluctuate, which they do not; therefore motion must be caused by some other substance which does not extend beyond the universe, but pervades the whole of it; this is what is called *dharma*. The existence of *adharma* is proved by similar arguments.

[2] Here Kundakunda employs the Prakrit term *appa* (Skt. *ātman*) in the sense of *jīva*, the usual Jain term for soul.

Souls, aggregates of matter, *dharma, adharma,* and space
Contain innumerable dimensional points,[3] but time has no dimensional
    points [i.e., no dimensions].

Space is both in the universe and in that which is beyond it. *Dharma* and
    adharma extend throughout the universe only;
Likewise time, because it depends on the other two substances, these other
    substances being souls and matter.[4]

As the dimensional points of space, so are the dimensional points of other
    substances [except time].
The atom has no dimensional point, but hence is explained the develop-
    ment of dimensional points.[5]

But a moment has no dimensional point. It occurs when a substance with
    a single dimensional point
Crosses a dimensional point of space.

[3] *Pradeśa,* elsewhere translated "infinitesimal spatial units," or "spatial minima." The *pradeśa,* though it roughly corresponds to the point in Euclidean geometry, is not quite the same concept. The Euclidean point has no dimensions; the *pradeśa* has dimensions but they are infinitesimally small. It is a sort of atom of space, perhaps comparable to the point in the Gaussian system of geometry used by Einstein. The paradoxical "dimensional point" is perhaps as good a translation of this difficult term as any other.

[4] Time does not exist beyond the confines of the universe, because it can only function in relation with souls and matter, which do not exist except in the universe. Note that the universe (*loka*) is unique, and poised in absolutely empty space (*aloka,* "non-universe"). Unlike the Buddhists, the Jains do not admit the existence of a plurality of universe.

[5] The obvious interpretation of this is that the ultimate atom has no dimension, but that upon the juxtaposition of nondimensional atoms in different relationships dimensionally measurable substances are produced. The commentator, however, notices that three verses later Kundakunda defines the dimensional point as the space occupied by an atom. As the dimensional point possesses dimension, albeit in an infinitesimally minute measure, we are faced with a crux. The best Amritachandra can do to solve it is as follows: "Though, as has been said, matter, considered as a substance, is without dimensional points, on account of its having one dimensional point only, yet it has the characteristic of being the originator of dimensional points, through its innate nature, which has the power of developing qualities of viscousness and roughness (implying attraction and repulsion) of such character as to be the cause of the production of two or more dimensional points." It seems that "dimensional point" is here used in two senses, the distinction between which is not thoroughly recognized by the writer. Matter in the form of the atom is quite without dimension; the dimensional point, however, in which the atom is contained, is infinitesimally small, but not wholly without dimension, not an absolute Euclidean point; the nondimensional atoms of matter, in their infinitesimally small areas of space, create a specious sense of extension or dimension in material substances by their mutual attractions and repulsions.

A moment is equal to the time taken for an atom to move [from one
    dimensional point to another].
What lies before and after that moment is time. The moment originates
    and perishes.[6]

The space occupied by an atom is called a dimensional point.
It can find room for all atoms.[7]

One, two, many, innumerable or infinite
Are the dimensional points contained by substances, as are the moments of
    their duration.[8] . . .

The world is full of objects with spatial extension, complete and eternal.
That which knows it is the soul,[9] bound to the four vital forces.[10]

There Is No Creator

Jainism, though not denying the existence of superhuman beings, is fundamentally atheistic. Moreover, it never compromised with theism, or devised
a pantheon of substitute gods, as did Mahāyāna Buddhism. From the earliest
times to the present day Jains have strenuously rejected the doctrine that
the universe is created or guided by a divine will or a divine mind—for
them natural law is a sufficient explanation. Their literature contains many
criticisms of the theist's position.
    The following example of Jain dialectic is taken from the *Great Legend*

[6] The commentator points out that time as substance has no beginning or end, but as
modified by its relations with other substances it originates and is subject to annihilation.
    [7] Thus all the atoms in the universe can be contained in a single dimensional point. This
is only logically possible if the atoms are infinitely small or completely without dimension.
    [8] On this verse Amritachandra makes a remarkable comment: "The complex of dimensional
points is horizontal, while that of which the function is characterized by moments is
vertical." This clearly implies the concept of time as a sort of fourth dimension.
    [9] The belief in soul-substance is said to be one of the most primitive features of Jainism,
but the verses quoted will show how far Jain thought on the subject transcended primitive
concepts. The soul is certainly a substance, but it is not material substance, any more than
are space and time. Its chief function is knowledge, of which the other five substances are
the objects.
    [10] *Prāṇa:* this term literally means "breath." In the later Vedic literature it often has the
sense of "the breath of life," hence "spirit" or "soul." In Hindu literature the word is
used for one of the five "winds" of the body, residing in the heart and responsible for
respiration. The Jains, however, used the word in a completely different sense; with them
there were four prāṇas, which were particularly potent forms of karma, binding the soul
within the body, and conditioning its powers of sensation, strength, longevity, and respiratory
capacity respectively.

(*Mahāpurāṇa*), a lengthy poem in excellent Sanskrit, composed by the Digambara teacher Jinasena in the ninth century. This work is modeled on the Hindu Purāṇas and consists mainly of cosmology and legends of the patriarchs, Tīrthankaras, and other great men of former days. Like the Hindu Purāṇas again, it contains numerous philosophical and polemic excursi of which the following passage is one.

[From *Mahāpurāṇa*, 4.16–31, 38–40]

Some foolish men declare that Creator made the world.
The doctrine that the world was created is ill-advised, and should be rejected.

If God created the world, where was he before creation?
If you say he was transcendent then, and needed no support, where is he now?

No single being had the skill to make this world—
For how can an immaterial god create that which is material? [1]

How could God have made the world without any raw material?
If you say he made this first, and then the world, you are faced with an endless regression.[2]

If you declare that this raw material arose naturally you fall into another fallacy,
For the whole universe might thus have been its own creator, and have arisen equally naturally.

If God created the world by an act of his own will, without any raw material,
Then it is just his will and nothing else—and who will believe this silly stuff? [3]
If he is ever perfect and complete, how could the will to create have arisen in him?

[1] A very common line of argument among the Jains. One type of substance cannot produce another with completely different characteristics.

[2] He had previously to make the raw-material of the raw-material, and so on. The endless regression is a type of fallacy as well known in Hindu logic as in Western.

[3] The appeal to practical experience, with which Jains, like Samuel Johnson at a later date, made short work of idealist philosophers!

If, on the other hand, he is not perfect, he could no more create the universe than a potter could.

If he is formless, actionless, and all-embracing, how could he have created the world?
Such a soul, devoid of all modality, would have no desire to create anything.

If he is perfect, he does not strive for the three aims of man,[4]
So what advantage would he gain by creating the universe?

If you say that he created to no purpose, because it was his nature to do so, then God is pointless.
If he created in some kind of sport,[5] it was the sport of a foolish child, leading to trouble.

If he created because of the karma of embodied beings [acquired in a previous creation]
He is not the Almighty Lord, but subordinate to something else. . . .

If out of love for living things and need of them he made the world,
Why did he not make creation wholly blissful, free from misfortune?

If he were transcendent he would not create, for he would be free;
Nor if involved in transmigration, for then he would not be almighty.

Thus the doctrine that the world was created by God
Makes no sense at all.

And God commits great sin in slaying the children whom he himself created.
If you say that he slays only to destroy evil beings, why did he create such beings in the first place? . . . .

Good men should combat the believer in divine creation, maddened by an evil doctrine.

___

[4] Righteousness (dharma), profit (artha), and pleasure (kāma), a traditional Indian classification.
[5] An attack on the Vedāntic doctrine of creation.

Know that the world is uncreated, as time itself is, without beginning and
    end,
And is based on the principles,[6] life and the rest.

Uncreated and indestructible, it endures under the compulsion of its own
    nature,
Divided into three sections—hell, earth, and heaven.

The Plurality of Souls

Jain theorists never tired of attacking the idealist monism of Vedāntic Hinduism and Mahāyāna Buddhism, usually basing their arguments on appeals to
experience and sturdy common sense. For the Jain the material universe is
an ineluctible datum, not to be explained away by specious arguments how-
cvcr subtle. The existence of innumerable living beings in the universe is an
obvious fact of experience. The fact of their being alive can be explained by the
hypothesis that they possess a certain substance, life (jīva). But as their bodies
are separate, so their lives are separate. And the life, for the Jain, is the soul.
    This criticism of Vedānta is taken from the *Debates with the Disciples* of
Jinabhadra, a Jain writer who probably lived in the early seventh century. The
text purports to contain a series of discussions between Mahāvīra and the
eleven ascetics who were later to become his chief disciples; in it each of these
puts forward a proposition, and, after some discussion, is convinced of its fal-
laciousness and becomes a follower of Mahāvīra. The work is part of a longer
one, a lengthy appendix (*niryukti*) to the canonical *Book of Obligatory Practices* (*Avaśyaka Sūtra*), and is composed in Prākrit verse.
    [From *Gaṇadharavāda*, 1.32–39]

You should know that the chief characteristic of the soul is awareness,
    And that its existence can be proved by all valid means of proof.
Souls may be classified as transmigrant and liberated,
    Or as embodied in immobile and mobile beings.

If the soul were only one,
    Like space pervading all bodies,

---

[6] *Tattva*, more accurately "facts." These, according to Jain classification, are seven—souls
(*jīva*, lit. "life"); the other five substances (see p. 76) which are classified as non-soul
(*ajīva*); the influx of karmic matter into the soul (*āsrava*); the bondage of the soul, arising
from this (*bandha*); the stopping of the influx of karma (*saṃvara*); the destruction and
expulsion of karmic matter previously absorbed (*nirjarā*); and final emancipation from
bondage to karma (*mokṣa*).

Then it would be of one and the same character in all bodies.
   But the soul is not like this.
There are many souls, just as there are many pots and other things
   In the world—this is evident from the difference of their characteristics.

If the soul were only one
   There would be no joy or sorrow, no bondage or freedom.[1]
The awareness, which is the hallmark of the soul,
   Differs in degree from body to body.
Awareness may be intense or dull—
   Hence the number of souls is infinite.[2]

If we assume the monist hypothesis, since the soul is all-pervading,
   There can be no liberation or bondage, [for the soul is uniform] like
      space.
Moreover thus the soul is neither agent nor enjoyer, nor does it think,
   Nor is it subject to transmigration—again just like space.

Again assuming monism, there can be no soul enjoying final bliss,
   For there are many maladies in the world, and thus the world-soul can
      only be partly happy;
Moreover, as many phenomenal souls are in bondage
   The world-soul cannot be released from transmigration, but only partly
      so.[3]

The soul exists only within the body,[4] just as space in a jar,
   Since its attributes are only to be detected therein,

[1] These words are, of course, intended in their special sense of bondage to and freedom from karma and matter.

[2] The logic of the argument is not clear. The twelfth-century commentator Maladhārī Hemachandra (not to be confused with the great Hemachandra) gives an interpretation which may be paraphrased as follows: The awareness of the different souls may vary in degree from the all-embracing knowledge of the perfected being (siddha) to the almost complete senselessness of the stone. Between the one and the other there are an infinite number of gradations. Therefore the number of souls is infinite. The logic is still evidently unsatisfactory.

[3] Maladhārī Hemachandra expands this by comparing the fortunate Brahman of Vedānta to a man whose whole body is diseased with the exception of one finger, or to one whose whole body is fettered, with the same exception. The Jains, perhaps justly accused of pessimism, would have no truck with the unrealistic optimists who declared that all evil and sin were in some sense illusory.

[4] This does not involve materialism of the Western positivist type. The Jains, in common with most other Indian sects, believe that the soul is wrapped in a series of inner sheaths of subtle matter, which form an invisible body surrounding it. The statement of the text is

And since they are not to be found elsewhere,
  As a pot is different from a piece of cloth.

Therefore action and enjoyment,
  Bondage and release, joy and sorrow,
And likewise transmigration itself,
  Are only possible on the hypothesis that souls are many and finite.

A Modern Jain Apologist

In the last hundred years the Jains of India, one of the wealthiest and best-educated communities of the subcontinent, have maintained their solidarity and have tried to adapt their doctrines to modern needs and conditions. A good deal of money and labor has been spent on propaganda, not only to prevent younger members of the community from succumbing to the temptations of twentieth-century materialism, but also to obtain sympathizers, and even converts, from other communities. Among the most active Jain propagandists was the late Mr. Champat Rai Jain, an able barrister with a good command of English, Hindi, and Urdu, and a wide knowledge of his own and other religions, who devoted many years with self-sacrificing wholeheartedness to writing and speaking in favor of Jainism. In keeping with the earlier teachers of his faith, who interpreted the Hindu scriptures figuratively in a Jain sense, Mr. Jain, who had read widely in Christian and Muslim theology, succeeded in proving to the satisfaction of himself and many of his co-religionists that both the Bible and the Qur'an taught the eternal truths of Jainism, that the only God of any significance was the eternal soul of man, who should liberate himself from matter and karma as quickly as possible by ahiṃsā and ascesis. We cannot, however, give an extract from Mr. Jain's brilliant if unscientific interpretations of the stories of the Old Testament and the teachings of the New. Perhaps his most interesting achievement was in his use of modern concepts taken from psychology and science in the service of his religion. The passage below, based largely on the arguments of earlier Jain philosophers, but well expressed in twentieth-century terms, aims at showing that the soul, which for the Jain includes consciousness and indeed has conscious awareness as its chief characteristic, is a simple substance, and therefore in its uncompounded state is eternal.
  [From C. R. Jain, *Essays and Addresses,* pp. 89–92]

Knowledge is an affection or feeling—the sense of awareness of an object or thing. Outside me are things, not knowledge; inside me is knowledge, not things.

---

not quite correct, for the siddhas, the perfected beings completely emancipated from karma who dwell in eternal omniscient bliss at the summit of the universe, are souls in a state of complete nakedness, according to orthodox Jain teaching.

The current of vibrations (sensory stimulus) that comes from the external object is not loaded with knowledge. It is only matter in motion or motion of matter (that is, matter or energy in one form or another). Only in contact with a conscious substance does it occasion knowledge (perception); otherwise only a material or mechanical phenomenon will ensue.

The mere formation of the outline of an object on the retinae or elsewhere will not account for perception. No image is formed through the senses other than sight. Visual perception itself only gives us an inverted image, which is the reverse of how things are perceived. There is, again, a great difference between the microscopic retinal image and the mental percept, which may represent half the world. The main difficulty remains yet to be stated. How is the retinal image itself perceived? Is it its outline that is *felt?* And by whom? Does perception merely consist in a feeling of contact with the image formed in the eye, or further back, say in the perceptive centers of the brain? If so it will only give us a number of simultaneous touch-feelings—a coextensive series of sensations of touch along the outlines or over the area filled by the image. But how shall we account for the brightness and color that play such an important part in visual perception? The external stimulus, it would thus seem, merely calls out what is already there *inside;* it is not itself transformed into perception—color, smell, sounds, etc.

Again, perception will be impossible for a composite substance. A composite substance lacks in individualization. Different parts of a composite substance, e.g., a mirror, will reflect different limbs or parts only of an object; the object in its entirety will not be, cannot be, reflected in any of the parts of the reflecting surface. It will, therefore, be impossible for any part of a composite perceiver to perceive the whole of an object. A compound, of course, does not cease to be a compound merely because it is given a simple name.

Consciousness perceives the whole as well as the parts of an object simultaneously. It must therefore be a simple (uncompounded) thing, unlike the mirror, which is devoid of individuality. . . .

Knowledge radically differs from the object in the world outside. The rose on the bush in the garden took a long time in putting in its appearance; a small cutting was first stuck in the soil; it germinated after a time; then appeared leaves and shoots; then a tiny little bud slowly formed on one of the branches; and after a time it bloomed into a rose.

Nothing like this tedious process occurs in consciousness at the moment of perception. The knowing faculty there and then produces from its mysterious nursery an exact *facsimile* of the external rose, and that without trouble. It would as easily produce two, three, four, or a basketful of roses, or any and all other flowers, whole gardens. . . . Its producing capacity is really wonderful—it is infinite!

Are these epistemological facsimiles of outside objects manufactured in any way in the background of consciousness? But knowledge is not atomistic, nor made of parts. Suppose you try to break up an idea, e.g., the percept of a house, into bits and parts. The physical structure can be demolished. . . . But with what instruments shall we demolish the mental counterpart of the material edifice? . . .

What does it all signify then? Is it meant that loose ready-made ideas are stocked in an immense "stores" somewhere in the mind?

No; for our consciousness is unitary and not composite. Loose ideas will be like external objects and will have to be perceived as external objects are perceived. With loose ideas the mind will itself become idealess, and devoid of knowledge. But knowledge consists, really, only in the states of the perceiving consciousness, which are inseparable from it.

The unity of knowledge may be further illustrated by another example. A man enters the field of my vision, and is perceived as one. A little later another man joins him. In my consciousness also the first man is joined by the second. Now in the world outside the two men are separate; the first remained where he was; the second merely came and sat down beside him. But in the mind the two constitute but one percept. While the second man was approaching the first one, the mind was continually furnishing new and ready-made mental pictures corresponding to the scene and the movements going on in the world outside. When the two men came together finally there was no blending or pasting together of two different percepts in the mind. . . . The secret is only this, that with each act of perception a new mental image is evoked and appears in the limelight.[1] . . . Thus a new percept is presented every moment by our consciousness, and it is a noncomposite, partless, and unbreakable presentation.

Furthermore I can have an idea of an object that may be rough, smooth,

[1] Outside the limelight of consciousness knowledge is not destroyed, but exists in the "sub-conscious" condition, owing to the inimical influence of the matter which is in association with the soul. [Author's footnote.]

hot, cold, light, heavy, hard, or soft; but the idea itself, that is my knowledge of the object, is neither cold, nor hot, nor smooth, nor rough, nor hard, nor soft. In the like manner color is to be found in the objects outside in the world; but none in the mind. This will also hold good of taste, smell, and sound.

Knowledge then: 1) consists in the states of a noncomposite and partless . . . substance; 2) is natural to, that is inherent (unmanufactured) in, the perceiving faculty; 3) is infinite; and 4) is devoid of material qualities, color, taste and the like.

Now a thing that is not made up of parts is eternal, being unbreakable, indestructible and indissoluble. The faculty of knowledge, the partless substance whose function is conscious perception, is, then, immortal. As such it is, and may properly be, termed soul.

The Ideal King I

The Jain attitude to rulership and government varied considerably. The state is a necessary feature of society in the period of decline in which we now find ourselves. It maintains the social order and is conducive to the good life, leading to liberation. In this respect Jain thought differs very little from that of Hinduism. In fact Jain writers set much the same ideals before rulers as do those of Hinduism, and their thought on the subject has few original features. A sample of typical Jain advice to kings is given later. Exceptional ideas, however, are to be found in the writings of Hemachandra, who appears to have had real influence on politics, which may still be indirectly felt in India to the present day. This teacher, the greatest doctor of Jainism, was born in or about 1089 in Gujarat. Entering the Jain order as a boy, he rapidly acquired a great reputation for learning, and was much patronized by the powerful king of the Chaulukya dynasty, Jayasimha (1094–1143), despite the fact that the latter was an orthodox Hindu. Jayasimha died childless, and was succeeded by Kumārapāla (1143–72) a distant relation who seized the throne by force. Under Hemachandra's influence Kumārapāla became a Jain, and, if we are to believe later Jain sources, enforced ahimsā so rigorously that two merchants were mulcted of all their wealth for the crime of killing fleas. There is no doubt that Kumārapāla did attempt to enforce ahimsā quite stringently, under the guidance of his Jain mentor, who composed several works in his honor. Hemachandra died a little before his pupil at the age of eighty-four, by fasting to death; Kumārapāla is said to have died in the same manner. His successor, Ajayapāla, introduced something of an orthodox reaction, and is referred to by the Jains as a violent persecutor of their faith.

Hemachandra was evidently a man of great versatility; among his works are philosophical treatises, grammars of Sanskrit and Prākrit, lexica of both languages, a treatise on poetics, and much narrative poetry which, if judged according to the canons of the time, is often very beautiful and brilliantly clever. The longest of his poems is *The Deeds of the Sixty-three Eminent Men* (*Triṣaṣṭiśalākāpuruṣacarita*), an enormous work telling the stories of the twenty-four Tīrthankaras and of other eminent figures in Jain mythology, including the patriarchs and various legendary world emperors. The last section of this forms an independent whole, *The Deeds of Mahāvīra,* and records the life story of the historical founder of Jainism. In its course Mahāvīra is said to have prophesied in his omniscience the rise to power of Hemachandra's patron Kumārapāla, and to have forecast the reforms he would inaugurate. It will be seen that Hemachandra's ideal king is a rigorous puritan, and that he has a rather pathetic faith that man could be made good by legislation.

[From *Mahāvīracarita,* 12.59–77]

The vows, especially those concerning . . . food,
He will keep regularly, and he will be generally celibate.
The king will not only avoid prostitutes
But will encourage his queens to remain chaste. . . .

He will not take the wealth of men who die sonless [1]—
This is the fruit of insight, for men without insight are never satisfied.

Hunting, which even the Pāndus [2] and other pious kings did not give up,
He will abjure, and all men will do likewise at his command.

When he forbids all injury there will be no more hunting or other cruel
    sports.
Even an untouchable will not kill a bug or a louse.

When he puts down all sin the wild deer of the forest
Will ever chew the cud unharmed, like cows in a stall. . . .

Even creatures who eat meat by nature, at his command,
Will forget the very name of meat, as an evil dream. [3]

---

[1] According to earlier Hindu law books, if a man died sonless and without male relatives the king was entitled to appropriate his property, though he was responsible for the maintenance of the widow and the dowering of the dead man's daughters. In accordance with the precept of the *Yājñavalkya Smṛti* Kumārapāla allowed the widow to inherit in such cases.

[2] The heroes of the *Mahābhārata.*

[3] It was a commonplace of Indian thought that the king had jurisdiction not only over the human beings of his kingdom, but also over the animals. His virtue or lack of it, moreover, was supposed directly to affect the course of nature.

Drink, which even pious [Jain] laymen had not given up,
He, perfect of soul, will forbid everywhere. . . .
Drunkards, whose fortunes were ruined by calamitous drink
Will once more prosper, when they have given it up at his command.

Gambling, which even princes such as Nala [4] could not abandon,
He will utterly put an end to, like the name of his worst enemy.[5]

Under his glorious rule, throughout the earth
There will be no more pigeon races or cock fights.

Continually bestowing his wealth on all men, he will redeem the debts of
    the whole world,
And will establish his own era upon earth.[6]

The Ideal King II

Other Jain writers set somewhat less puritanical ideals before their kings, and
their concept of good conduct in matters of government differed little from that
of the Hindus. This is exemplified in the *Nectar of Aphorisms on Polity* of
Somadeva, a Digambara teacher of the tenth century. This is a collection of
gnomic sentences on politics and good conduct, written in Sanskrit prose. We
quote some of those concerning the ideal king.
     [From *Nītivākyāmṛta, 17.180–84*]

A true lord is he who is righteous, pure in lineage, conduct and associates,
    brave, and considerate in his behavior.
He is a true king who is self-controlled whether in anger or pleasure, and
    who increases his own excellence.
All subjects are dependent on the king. Those without a lord cannot ful-
    fill their desires.
Though they be rich, subjects without a king cannot thrive. How can
    human effort be of any avail in cultivating a tree without roots?
If the king does not speak the truth all his merits are worthless. If he
    deceives, his courtiers leave him, and he does not live long.

    [4] A famous king of the *Mahābhārata* legend, who was ruined by gambling.
    [5] This line shows, as is quite clear from other sources, that Hemachandra's idea of
ahimsā did not include the renunciation of war.
    [6] Several great kings of Hindu India established new eras, but that of Kumārapāla did
not survive his death.

He is dear to the people who gives of his treasure.

He is a great giver whose mind is not set on frustrating the hopes of suppliants.

Of what use is the barren cow, which gives no milk? Of what use is the king's grace, if he does not fulfill the hopes of suppliants?

For an ungrateful king there is no help in trouble. His frugal court is like a hole full of snakes, which no one will enter.

If the king does not recognize merit the cultured will not come to his court.

The king who thinks only of filling his belly is abandoned even by his queen.

Laziness is the door through which all misfortunes enter. . . .

A king's order is a wall which none can climb. He should not tolerate even a son who disobeys his commands. . . .

He should never speak hurtfully, untrustworthily, untruthfully, or unnecessarily.

He should never be improper in dress or manners.

When the king is deceitful, who will not be deceitful? When the king is unrighteous who will not be unrighteous? . . .

He should personally look into the affairs of his people. . . .

He should not make offering to the spirits of the night. . . .

Bribery is the door through which come all manner of sins. Those who live by bribery cut off their mother's breasts. . . .

The king is the maker of the times. When the king rightly protects his subjects all the quarters are wishing-cows,[1] Indra rains in due season, and all living things are at peace.

Practical Advice on War and Peace

Though charity and forgiveness are, of course, looked on as cardinal virtues, the highest virtue, for the Jain, is nonviolence, the importance of which is repeated over and over again in Jain literature, with many variations. It is noteworthy that, despite its nonviolence, Jainism never strongly opposed militarism; several great Jain kings were conquerors, and the ideal Jain king, Kumārapāla, who is said to have enforced vegetarianism throughout his realm, is nowhere said to have given up warfare. No Jain monarch had the enlightened sentiments of Ashoka in this respect, and nowhere in the whole body of Jaina literature is a plea for peace between states to be found such as that in the

[1] Legendary divine cows, which granted all the wishes of those who milked them.

Buddhist *Excellent Golden Light Sūtra.* Yet, in normal personal relations, ahimsā is repeatedly stated to be the greatest virtue.

With very few exceptions, Indian thinkers looked on warfare as legitimate. There were, however, two schools of thought on the subject. One, typified by the *Mahābhārata* and the *Lawbook of Manu (Manusmṛti)*, looked on war as good in its own right, a very exciting, if very grim sport, and sometimes even as a religious duty. There was no question of justified and unjustified warfare here; wars of aggression, if waged fairly and with humanity toward the wounded, prisoners, and noncombatants, were just as legitimate as wars of self-defense. The other school of thought, most clearly expressed in the famous treatise on polity (*Arthaśāstra*) ascribed to Kautilya, looked on war as a "continuation of policy by other means," a legitimate last resort in achieving the aims of statecraft, but not to be embarked on lightly, since it was expensive, troublesome, and uncertain in its outcome.

Jainism supported the second point of view; the Jain writer on polity, Somadeva, who on practical grounds advises war only as a last resort, like the Hindu political theorists, looks on it as a normal activity of the king.

[From *Nītivākyāmṛta,* 344–56 *cento*]

The force of arms cannot do what peace does. If you can gain your desired end with sugar, why use poison? . . .

What sensible man would abandon his bale [of merchandise] for fear of having to pay toll on it? [2]

For when the water is drained from the lake the crocodile grows as thin as a snake.[3]

A lion when he leaves the forest is no more than a jackal.

And a snake whose fangs are drawn is a mere rope.

In union is strength. Even a mad elephant will trip on a twisted clump of grass. And the elephants of the quarters [4] are held by ropes of twisted fibers.

But what is the use of other means when the enemy can only be put down by force? Such expedients are like a libation of ghee poured on the fire [which makes it burn more fiercely].

The Miseries and Dangers of Politics

The passages which we have quoted from the work of Hemachandra and Somadeva typify two Jain attitudes to political life. The first saw it as a

---

[2] Implying that it is better for a king to pay tribute to a more powerful enemy, rather than to fight to the last and lose his kingdom altogether, and probably his life also.

[3] Thus even if the enemy conquers, and seems immensely powerful, he may yet lose much of his power by one means or another, and it will then be possible to resist him.

[4] Mythical divine elephants presiding over the cardinal points.

means of enforcing morality as Jainism understood it upon those who would not accept the restraints of religion willingly; the second, as a necessary feature of everyday life, which was perfectly legitimate provided it was conducted justly. A third attitude is that shown by Somaprabha, an author of the late twelfth century, in the passage which we quote. The work from which it is taken is a didactic poem, the *Arousing of Kumārapāla,* which purports to tell of the conversion of King Kumārapāla by Hemachandra, and of his reforms. The work is written in mixed Sanskrit, Prākrit, and Apabhramsha; our quotation is taken from a section composed in Apabhramsha.

Though both his main characters were keen politicians, Somaprabha, in the course of one of the stories told by the monk to the king, declares that political activity is inevitably sinful, and advises Jains to have nothing to do with it.

[From *Kumārapālapratibodha,* Apabhramsha sections, 2.51–60 (Alsdorf, 105)]

The achievement of the three aims [1]
  Is the essence of man's life,
But advancement in office
  Is a hindrance thereto.

For when it pleases the king's mind
  A minister must harm others, and that is the source of sin.
How then can perfect righteousness arise in him,
  Through which he may gain eternal bliss?

And the fortune which an officer extorts by force from others,
  Like a leech sucking blood,
His master may take from him,
  For he [the king] extorts from everyone.

Subservient to another, full of fears and cares,
  Responsible for manifold affairs of state,
How can officials know the joys of love,
  In which great happiness reveals itself? . . .

After tossing on the ocean of being, of which birth and death are waves,
  You have come to man's estate.
Avoid the things of sense and pluck the fruit of human birth.[2]
  Why give up ten million for the sake of a mere penny? . . .

[1] Righteousness, profit, and pleasure.
[2] Only human beings are capable of achieving complete salvation. The gods cannot gain it unless they are reborn as men, for in heaven there is not enough sorrow and pain to work off the residual evil karma.

If you spend only five days in the service of a king
  You bring sin upon yourself,
And you must go, O soul, to the dark gulf of hell,
  With its inevitable, intolerable, innumerable woes.

So give up the king's service; though it seems sweet as honey,
  It brings scorn and disillusion, it is basically wretched.
Work, O soul, for righteousness, and put aside your lethargy,
  Lest in hell you find not a few unpleasantnesses.

The soul that in youth does not strive after righteousness
  And does not avoid all reprehensible actions,
Will wring its hands in the hour of death,
  And be left like an archer with a broken bowstring.

CHAPTER VI

THERAVĀDA BUDDHISM

As we have already seen, the centuries which saw the rise of Buddhism and Jainism in India were marked by continuing social change and profound intellectual ferment. What has been said above about the conditions in which the heterodox systems developed in the sixth and fifth centuries must be borne in mind in the study of Buddhism.

The founder of Buddhism was the son of a chief of the hill-tribe of the Shākyas, who gave up family life to become an ascetic when he was some twenty-nine years old, and, after some years, emerged as the leader of a band of followers who pursued the "Middle Way" between extreme asceticism and worldly life. The legends which were told about him in later times are mostly unreliable, though they may contain a grain of historical truth here and there. Moreover many of the sermons and other pronouncements attributed to the Buddha [1] are not his, but the work of teachers in later times, and there is considerable doubt as to the exact nature of his original message. However, the historicity of the Buddha is certain, and we may believe as a minimum that he was originally a member of the Shākya tribe, that he gained enlightenment under a sacred pīpal tree at Gayā, in the modern Bihar, that he spent many years in teaching and organizing his band of followers, and that he died at about the age of eighty in Kusinārā, a small town in the hills. The Sinhalese Buddhists have preserved a tradition that he died in 544 B.C., but most modern authorities believe that this date is some sixty years too early.

The band of yellow-robed *bhikkhus* [2] which the Buddha left behind him to continue his work probably remained for some two hundred years one small group among the many heterodox sects of India, perhaps fewer in numbers and less influential than the rival sects of Jains and Ājīvikas.

---

[1] "The Enlightened" or "Awakened," a religious title with which we may compare the Christian "Christ" (i.e., "Anointed") and "Savior." The Buddha's real name was Siddhārtha Gautama (Pāli, Siddhattha Gotama).

[2] Literally, "beggars." This is the Pāli form, used by the Theravāda Buddhists. The Sanskrit form is *bhikṣu*. Here the word is generally translated "monk."

Though by Western standards its rule was rigid, involving continuous movement from place to place for eight months of the year and the consumption of only one meal a day, which was to be obtained by begging, it was light in comparison with the discipline of most other orders, the members of which were often compelled to take vows of total nudity, were not permitted to wash, and had to undergo painful penances. It is evident that between the death of the Buddha and the advent of Ashoka, the first great Buddhist emperor, over two hundred years later, there was considerable development of doctrine. Some sort of canon of sacred texts appeared, though it was probably not at this time written down, and the Buddhists acquired numerous lay followers. For the latter, and for the less spiritually advanced monks, the sect adapted popular cults to Buddhist purposes—notably the cult of stūpas, or funeral mounds, and that of the sacred pīpal tree. We have seen that these had probably been worshiped in the Ganges valley from time immemorial, and with such cults both Hinduism and Buddhism had to come to terms. Buddhist monks began to overlook the rule that they should travel from place to place except in the rainy season and took to settling permanently in monasteries, which were erected on land given by kings and other wealthy patrons, and were equipped with pīpal trees and stūpas, theoretically commemorating the Buddha's enlightenment and death respectively.

Quite early in the history of Buddhism sectarian differences appeared. The tradition tells of two great councils of the Buddhist order, the first soon after the Buddha's death, the second a hundred years later. At the latter a schism occurred, and the sect of *Mahāsaṅghikas* ("members of the Great Order") is said to have broken away, ostensibly on account of differences on points of monastic discipline, but probably on doctrinal grounds also. The main body, which claimed to maintain the true tradition transmitted from the days of the founder, took to calling their system *Theravāda*[3] ("The Teaching of the Elders"). By little over a century after this schism the whole of India except the southern tip had been unified politically by Magadha, after a long and steady process of expansion, which culminated in the rise of the first great Indian imperial dynasty, that of the Mauryas. The third and greatest of the Mauryas, Ashoka, became a Buddhist. According to his own testimony he was so moved by

---

[3] In Sanskrit *Sthaviravāda*, but the Pāli form is generally used, as Pāli was the official language of the sect.

remorse at the carnage caused by an aggressive war which he had waged that he experienced a complete change of heart and embraced Buddhism. His inscriptions, the earliest intelligible written records to have survived in India, testify to his earnestness and benevolence.

Buddhism seems to have received a great impetus from Ashoka's patronage. He erected many stūpas, endowed new monasteries, and enlarged existing Buddhist establishments. In his reign the message of Budhism was first carried over the whole of India by a number of missionaries, sent out, according to tradition, after a third council which met at Pātaliputra (the modern Patna) in order to purify the doctrine of heresy. It was in Ashoka's reign that Ceylon first became a Buddhist country, after the preaching of the apostle Mahinda, said to have been Ashoka's son, who had become a monk. From that day onwards Ceylon has remained a stronghold of the Buddhism of the Theravāda school; Mahāyāna and other Buddhist sects, though they have at times been influential, have never seriously shaken the hold of the form of Buddhism which Ceylon looks on as particularly its own.

It is probable that, by the end of the third century B.C., the doctrines of Theravāda Buddhism were in essentials much as they are now. The monks taught a dynamic phenomenalism, maintaining that everything in the universe, including the gods and the souls of living beings, was in a constant state of flux. Resistance to the cosmic flux of phenomena, and craving for permanence where permanence could not be found, led to inevitable sorrow. Salvation was to be obtained by the progressive abandonment of the sense of individuality, until it was lost completely in the indescribable state known as Nirvāna (Pāli, *Nibbāna,* "blowing out"). The Buddha himself had reached this state, and no longer existed as an individual; nevertheless he was still rather inconsistently revered by his followers, and the less-learned Buddhist layfolk tended to look on him as a sort of high god.

The fundamental truths on which Buddhism is founded are not metaphysical or theological, but rather psychological. Basic is the doctrine of the "Four Noble Truths": 1) that all life is inevitably sorrowful; 2) that sorrow is due to craving; 3) that it can only be stopped by the stopping of craving; and 4) that this can only be done by a course of carefully disciplined and moral conduct, culminating in the life of concentration and meditation led by the Buddhist monk. These four truths, which are the common property of all schools of Buddhist thought, are part of the true Doctrine (Pāli, *dhamma;* Skt. *dharma*), which reflects the fundamental moral law of the universe.[4]

All things are composite. Buddhism would dispute the Hegelian theory that units may organize themselves into greater units which are more than the sum of their parts. As a corollary of the fact that all things are composite they are transient, for the composition of all aggregates is liable to change with time. Moreover, being essentially transient, they have no eternal Self or soul, no abiding individuality. And, as we have seen, they are inevitably liable to sorrow. This threefold characterization of the nature of the world and all that it contains—sorrowful, transient, and soulless—is frequently repeated in Buddhist literature, and without fully grasping its truth no being has any chance of salvation. For until he thoroughly understands the three characteristics of the world a man will inevitably crave for permanence in one form or another, and as this cannot, by the nature of things, be obtained, he will suffer, and probably make others suffer also.

All things in the universe may also be classified into five components, or are composed of a mixture of them: form and matter (*rūpa*), sensations (*vedanā*), perceptions (*saññā*), psychic dispositions or constructions (*saṃkhārā*), and consciousness or conscious thought (*viññāna*). The first consists of the objects of sense and various other elements of less importance. Sensations are the actual feelings arising as a result of the exercise of the six senses (mind being the sixth) upon sense-objects, and perceptions are the cognitions of such sensations. The psychic constructions include all the various psychological emotions, propensities, faculties, and conditions of the individual, while the fifth component, conscious thought, arises from the interplay of the other psychic constituents. The individual is made up of a combination of the five components, which are never the same from one moment to the next, and therefore his whole being is in a state of constant flux.

The process by which life continues and one thing leads to another is

---

[4] The word *dharma* is employed in Buddhism a little differently from its use in Hinduism, and is strictly untranslatable in English. One leading authority has translated it as "the Norm"; in our extracts it is translated "the Doctrine," "Righteousness," or "The Law of Righteousness" according to context. The term *dharma* in Buddhism has also other connotations. Phenomena in general are dharmas, as are the qualities and characteristics of phenomena. Thus the Buddha's last words might be translated: "Growing old is the dharma of all composite things."

explained by the Chain of Causation (*Paṭicca-samuppāda,* lit. Dependent Origination). The root cause of the process of birth and death and rebirth is ignorance, the fundamental illusion that individuality and permanence exist, when in fact they do not. Hence there arise in the organism various psychic phenomena, including desire, followed by an attempt to appropriate things to itself—this is typified especially by sexual craving and sexual intercourse, which are the actual causes of the next links in the chain, which concludes with age and death, only to be repeated again and again indefinitely. Rebirth takes place, therefore, according to laws of karma which do not essentially differ from those of Hinduism, though they are explained rather differently.

As we have seen, no permanent entity transmigrates from body to body, and all things, including the individual, are in a state of constant flux. But each act, word, or thought leaves its traces on the collection of the five constituents which make up the phenomenal individual, and their character alters correspondingly. This process goes on throughout life, and, when the material and immaterial parts of the being are separated in death, the immaterial constituents, which make up what in other systems would be called the soul, carry over the consequential effects of the deeds of the past life, and obtain another body accordingly. Thus there is no permanent soul, but nevertheless room is found for the doctrine of transmigration. Though Buddhism rejects the existence of the soul, this makes little difference in practice, and the more popular literature of Buddhism, such as the *Birth Stories* (*Jātaka*), takes for granted the existence of a quasi-soul at least, which endures indefinitely. One sect of Buddhism, the *Sammitīya,* which admittedly made no great impression on the religious life of India, actually went so far as to admit the existence of an indescribable substratum of personality (*pudgala*), which was carried over from life to life until ultimately it was dissipated in Nirvāna, thus fundamentally agreeing with the pneumatology of most other Indian religions.

The process of rebirth can only be stopped by achieving Nirvāna, first by adopting right views about the nature of existence, then by a carefully controlled system of moral conduct, and finally by concentration and meditation. The state of Nirvāna cannot be described, but it can be hinted at or suggested metaphorically. The word literally means "blowing out," as of a lamp. In Nirvāna all idea of an individual personality or ego ceases to exist and there is nothing to be reborn—as far as the individual is concerned Nirvāna is annihilation. But it was certainly not generally thought of by the early Buddhists in such negative terms. It was rather conceived of as a transcendent state, beyond the possibility of full comprehension by the ordinary being enmeshed in the illusion of selfhood, but not fundamentally different from the state of supreme bliss as described in other non-theistic Indian systems.

These are the doctrines of the Theravāda school, and, with few variations, they would be assented to by all other schools of Buddhism. But the Mahāyāna [5] and quasi-Mahāyāna sects developed other doctrines, in favor of which they often gave comparatively little attention to these fundamental teachings.

Of the Lesser Vehicle only one sect survives, the Theravāda, now prevalent in Ceylon, Burma, Thailand, Cambodia, and Laos. There were several others in earlier times, some of which had distinctive metaphysical and psychological systems which approached more closely to those of the Greater Vehicle than did that of the Theravāda. The most important of these sects was perhaps that of the Sarvāstivādins, which stressed the absence of any real entity passing through time in transmigration, but on the other hand maintained the ultimate reality of the chain of events which made up the phenomenal being or object. A sub-sect of the Sarvāstivādins, the Sautrāntikas, emphasized the atomic nature of the component elements of the chain—every instant a composite object disappeared, to be replaced by a new one which came into being as a result of the last. This view of the universe, which appears in the systems of other Buddhist sects in a less emphatic form, is akin to the quantum theory of modern physics.

Another very interesting sect of the Lesser Vehicle was the Mahāsanghika, said to have been the first to break away from the main body of Buddhism. Subdivided into numerous schools, its chief characteristic was the doctrine that the things of the phenomenal world were not wholly real; thus it paved the way for the idealist world-view of Mahāyāna philosophy. Buddhas, on the other hand, according to the fully developed

[5] With the rise of the Mahāyāna form of Buddhism, Buddhist sects became divided into two major groups. The newer sects referred to their doctrine as the "Mahāyāna," the Greater Vehicle (to salvation), and to their rivals' as the "Hīnayāna," the Lesser Vehicle. We have generally preferred to call the latter group Theravāda from the name of its major sect.

doctrine of the Mahāsanghikas, had full reality, as heavenly beings in a state of perpetual mystic trance, and earthly Buddhas such as the historical Gautama were mere docetic manifestations of the Buddhas in their true state. It is possible that gnostic doctrines from the Middle East influenced this form of Buddhism, which came very close to Mahāyānism, differing only in the doctrine of bodhisattvas.

Buddhism also taught an advanced and altruistic system of morality, which was a corollary to its metaphysics, since one of the first steps on the road to Nirvāna was to do good to others, and thereby weaken the illusion of egoity which was the main cause of human sorrow. Buddhism set itself strongly against animal sacrifice and encouraged vegetarianism, though it did not definitely impose it. It tended towards peace, even if Ashoka's successors did not heed his injunctions to avoid aggression. Its attitude to the system of class and caste is not always definite; while passages in the Buddhist scriptures can be found which attack all claims to superiority by right of birth, the four great classes seem to have been recognized as an almost inevitable aspect of Indian society; but the Buddhist classification of these classes varies significantly from that of the Hindus, for in Buddhist sources the warrior is usually mentioned before the brāhman.

The total literature of Buddhism is so large that it is quite impossible for a single individual to master it in his lifetime. Each of the numerous sects of Buddhism had its version of the sacred scriptures written either in a semi-vernacular Prākritic language or in a form of Sanskrit with peculiar syntax and vocabulary, generally known as "Buddhist Sanskrit." Besides these there was a great body of commentarial literature, and much philosophical and devotional writing of all kinds. Much of the literature of the sects other than the Theravāda has been lost, or only survives in Chinese or Tibetan translations, but the complete canon of Theravāda Buddhism has been fully preserved in Ceylon. It is therefore of fundamental importance in any study of Buddhism. It is written in Pāli, a language related to Sanskrit, and based on an ancient vernacular, probably spoken in the western part of India.

The canon is generally known as *Tripiṭaka* (the *Three Baskets*) after the three sections into which it is divided, namely *Conduct* (*Vinaya*), *Discourses* (*Sutta*), and *Supplementary Doctrines* (*Abhidhamma*). The first *Piṭaka* contains the rules of conduct of the Buddhist order of monks and nuns, usually in connection with narratives which purport to tell the circumstances in which the Buddha laid down each rule. The second *Piṭaka* is the most important; it contains discourses, mostly attributed to the Buddha, divided into five sections: the *Long Group* (*Dīgha Nikāya*) containing long discourses; the *Medium Group* (*Majjhima Nikāya*) with discourses of shorter length; the *Connected Group* (*Saṃyutta Nikāya*), a collection of shorter pronouncements on connected topics; the *Progressive Group* (*Aṅguttara Nikāya*), short passages arranged in eleven sections according to the number of topics dealt with in each—thus the three types of sin, in act, word and thought, occur in section three, and so on; and finally the *Minor Group* (*Khuddaka Nikāya*), a number of works of varying type, including the beautiful and very ancient Buddhist poems of the *Way of Righteousness* (*Dhammapada*) and a collection of verses which are filled out by a lengthy prose commentary to form the *Birth Stories* (*Jātaka*) relating the previous births of the Buddha.

The third *Piṭaka, the Supplementary Doctrines,* is a collection of seven works on Buddhist psychology and metaphysics, which are little more than a systematization of ideas contained in the *Discourses,* and are definitely later than the main body of the canon.

There is considerable disagreement about the date of the canon. Some earlier students of Buddhism believed that the *Conduct* and *Discourse Baskets* existed in much the same form as they do now within a hundred years of the Buddha's death. Later authorities are inclined to believe that the growth of the canon was considerably slower. On the other hand many of the discourses may look back to the Buddha himself, though all have been more or less worked over, and none can be specified with certainty as being his own words. The orthodox tradition itself admits that the *Basket of Supplementary Doctrines* (*Abhidhamma Piṭaka*) is later than the other two, and was not completed until the time of Ashoka. Sinhalese tradition records that the canon was not committed to writing until the reign of King Vaṭṭagāmani (89–77 B.C.), and it may not have finished growing until about this time. Thus it is possible that it is the product of as many as four centuries.

There are numerous other works in Pāli which are not generally considered canonical. Perhaps the most important of these works are the standard commentaries on the books of the canon, most of which, it is said, were compiled in Ceylon by the great doctor Buddhaghosa, of the fifth century A.D., from earlier commentaries. As well as passages of explanatory character, the commentaries contain much ancient Buddhist tradition not to be found elsewhere, and the elucidation of the *Jātaka* verses, in plain and vigorous prose, contains some of the finest narrative literature of the ancient world. Buddhaghosa is also the reputed author of a valuable compendium of Buddhist doctrine, *The Way of Purification* (*Visuddhimagga*). Another very important Pāli work of early date is *The Questions of King Menander* (*Milindapañha*), from which several passages are translated here. The inscriptions of Emperor Ashoka (c. 273–232 B.C.) must also be included in any survey, since they are inspired by Buddhism and are at least in part intended to inculcate the morality of Buddhism.

BASIC DOCTRINES OF THERAVĀDA BUDDHISM

The Four Noble Truths

According to Buddhist tradition this was the first sermon preached by the Buddha. After gaining enlightenment under the Tree of Wisdom at Gayā he proceeded to Vārānasī [1], where, in a park outside the city, he found five ascetics who had formerly been his associates, and who had left him in disgust when he gave up self-mortification and self-starvation as useless in his quest for supreme wisdom. In the presence of these five the Buddha "set in motion the Wheel [2] of the Law" by preaching this sermon, which outlines the Four Noble Truths, the Noble Eightfold Path, and the Middle Way, three of the most important concepts of Buddhism.

[From *Saṃyutta Nikāya*, 5.421 ff.[3]]

Thus I have heard. Once the Lord was at Vārānasī, at the deer park called Isipatana. There he addressed the five monks:

There are two ends not to be served by a wanderer. What are these two? The pursuit of desires and of the pleasure which springs from de-

---

[1] The ancient name of Banaras, now officially revived by the Indian government.

[2] The chariot wheel in ancient India symbolized empire and hence this phrase may be paraphrased as: "embarked on his expedition of conquest on behalf of the Kingdom of Righteousness."

[3] In all quotations from the Pāli scriptures, except where specified, reference is made to the Pāli Text Society's edition of the text.

sire, which is base, common, leading to rebirth, ignoble, and unprofitable; and the pursuit of pain and hardship, which is grievous, ignoble, and unprofitable. The Middle Way of the Tathāgata [4] avoids both these ends. It is enlightened, it brings clear vision, it makes for wisdom, and leads to peace, insight, enlightenment, and Nirvāna. What is the Middle Way? . . . It is the Noble Eightfold Path—Right Views, Right Resolve, Right Speech, Right Conduct, Right Livelihood, Right Effort, Right Mindfulness,[5] and Right Concentration. This is the Middle Way. . . .

And this is the Noble Truth of Sorrow. Birth is sorrow, age is sorrow, disease is sorrow, death is sorrow; contact with the unpleasant is sorrow, separation from the pleasant is sorrow, every wish unfulfilled is sorrow—in short all the five components of individuality [6] are sorrow.

And this is the Noble Truth of the Arising of Sorrow. It arises from craving, which leads to rebirth, which brings delight and passion, and seeks pleasure now here, now there—the craving for sensual pleasure, the craving for continued life, the craving for power.

And this is the Noble Truth of the Stopping of Sorrow. It is the complete stopping of that craving, so that no passion remains, leaving it, being emancipated from it, being released from it, giving no place to it.

And this is the Noble Truth of the Way which Leads to the Stopping of Sorrow. It is the Noble Eightfold Path—Right Views, Right Resolve, Right Speech, Right Conduct, Right Livelihood, Right Effort, Right Mindfulness, and Right Concentration.

The Nature of Consciousness and the Chain of Causation

The following *Discourse,* though it purports to be a single utterance of the Buddha, is evidently a conflation of separate passages, bearing on the character of consciousness. It contains a short statement of the contingent nature of consciousness or conscious thought, an appeal for an objective and clear realization that everything whatever is dependent on causes outside itself, an enumeration of the elements of the Chain of Causation, given first in reverse order, an exhortation to the monks not to bother unduly about the question of the survival of the personality and to realize the facts of the Doctrine for themselves, not taking them from the lips of the Teacher, and finally an impressive passage

[4] "He who has thus attained," one of the titles of the Buddha.

[5] *Sati,* lit. "memory." At all times the monk should as far as possible be fully conscious of his actions, words, and thoughts, and be aware that the agent is not an enduring individual, but a composite and transitory collection of material and psychic factors.

[6] Forms, sensations, perceptions, psychic dispositions, and consciousness.

comparing the life of the ordinary man with that of the Buddha, which we have not space to give here.

[From *Majjhima Nikāya*, 1.256 ff.]

Once a certain monk named Sāti, the son of a fisherman,[1] conceived the pernicious heresy that, as he understood the Lord's teaching, consciousness continued throughout transmigration. When they heard this several monks went and reasoned with him . . . but he would not give in, but held firm to his heresy. . . . So they went to the Lord and put the matter to him, and he sent a monk to fetch Sāti. When Sāti had come the Lord asked him if it was true that he held this heresy . . . and Sāti replied that he did hold it.

"What, then," asked the Lord, "is the nature of consciousness?"

"Sir, it is that which speaks and feels, and experiences the consequences of good and evil deeds."

"Whom do you tell, you foolish fellow, that I have taught such a doctrine? Haven't I said, with many similes, that consciousness is not independent, but comes about through the Chain of Causation, and can never arise without a cause? You misunderstand and misrepresent me, and so you undermine your own position and produce much demerit. You bring upon yourself lasting harm and sorrow!" . . .

Then the Lord addressed the assembled monks:

"Whatever form of consciousness arises from a condition is known by the name of that condition; thus if it arises from the eye and from forms it is known as visual consciousness . . . and so with the senses of hearing, smell, taste, touch, and mind, and their objects. It's just like a fire, which you call by the name of the fuel—a wood fire, a fire of sticks, a grass fire, a cowdung fire, a fire of husks, a rubbish fire, and so on."[2]

"Do you agree, monks, that any given organism is a living being?" "Yes, sir."

"Do you agree that it is produced by food?" "Yes, sir."

"And that when the food is cut off the living being is cut off and dies?" "Yes, sir."

---

[1] In theory the origins of a monk, once he had become a full member of the Order, were irrelevant, but the authors of the Pāli scriptures often mention the fact that a given monk was of humble birth. It would seem that they were not altogether free from class-consciousness.

[2] The implication is that just as fire is caused by fuel and varies according to the fuel used, so consciousness is caused by the senses and their objects, and varies accordingly.

"And that doubt on any of these points will lead to perplexity?" "Yes, sir."

"And that Right Recognition is knowledge of the true facts as they really are?" "Yes, sir."

"Now if you cling to this pure and unvitiated view, if you cherish it, treasure it, and make it your own, will you be able to develop a state of consciousness with which you can cross the stream of transmigration as on a raft, which you use but do not keep?" "No, sir."

"But only if you maintain this pure view, but don't cling to it or cherish it . . . only if you use it but are ready to give it up?" [3] "Yes, sir."

"There are four bases which support all organisms and beings, whether now existing or yet to be. They are: first, food coarse or fine, which builds up the body; second, contact; third, cogitation; and fourth, consciousness. All four derive and originate from craving. Craving arises from sensation, sensation from contact, [4] contact from the six senses, the six senses from physical form, physical form from consciousness, consciousness from the psychic constructions, and the psychic constructions from ignorance. . . . To repeat: Ignorance is the cause of the psychic constructions, hence is caused consciousness, hence physical form, hence the six senses, hence contact, hence sensations, hence craving, hence attachment, hence becoming, hence birth, hence old age and death with all the distraction of grief and lamentation, sorrow and despair. This is the arising of the whole body of ill. . . . So we are agreed that by the complete cessation of ignorance the whole body of ill ceases.

"Now would you, knowing and seeing this, go back to your past, wondering whether you existed or didn't exist long ago, or how you existed, or what you were, or from what life you passed to another?" "No, sir."

"Or would you look forward to the future with the same thoughts?" "No, sir."

"Or would you, knowing and seeing this, trouble yourselves at the

---

[3] Buddhism is a practical system, with one aim only, to free living beings from suffering. This passage apparently implies that even the most fundamental doctrines of Buddhism are only means to that end, and must not be maintained dogmatically for their own sake. It suggests also that there may be higher truths, which can only be realized as Nirvāna is approached.

[4] Here we are told that craving arises from contact, through sensation, while in the previous sentence contact arises from craving. There is no real paradox, because the chain is circular, and any one link is the cause of any other.

present time about whether or not you really exist, what and how you are, whence your being came, and whither it will go?" "No, sir."

"Or would you, possessing this knowledge, say, 'We declare it because we revere our teacher'?" "No, sir."

"Or would you say, 'We don't declare it as from ourselves—we were told it by a teacher or ascetic'?" "No, sir."

"Or would you look for another teacher?" "No, sir."

"Or would you support the rituals, shows, or festivals of other ascetics or brāhmans?" "No, sir."

"Do you only declare what you have known and seen?" "Yes, sir."

"Well done, brethren! I have taught you the doctrine which is immediately beneficial, eternal, open to all, leading them onwards, to be mastered for himself by every intelligent man."

False Doctrines About the Soul

The early Buddhists never ceased to impress upon their hearers the fact that the phenomenal personality was in a constant state of flux, and that there was no eternal soul in the individual in anything like the Hindu sense. On the other hand the perfected being had reached Nirvāna, and nothing could be meaningfully predicated about him. The following passage, attributed to the Buddha himself, criticizes the soul theories of other sects.
[From *Dīgha Nikāya*, 2.64 ff.]

It is possible to make four propositions concerning the nature of the soul— "My soul has form and is minute," "My soul has form and is boundless," "My soul is without form and is minute," and "My soul is without form and boundless." Such propositions may refer to this life or the next. . . .

There are as many ways of not making propositions concerning the soul, and those with insight do not make them.

Again the soul may be thought of as sentient or insentient, or as neither one nor the other but having sentience as a property. If someone affirms that his soul is sentient you should ask, "Sentience is of three kinds, happy, sorrowful, and neutral. Which of these is your soul?" For when you feel one sensation you don't feel the others. Moreover these sensations are impermanent, dependent on conditions, resulting from a cause or causes, perishable, transitory, vanishing, ceasing. If one experiences a happy sensation and thinks "This is my soul," when the happy sensation ceases he will think "My soul has departed." One who thinks thus looks on his soul as something impermanent in this life, a blend of happiness and sorrow with a beginning and end, and so this proposition is not acceptable.

If someone affirms that the soul is not sentient, you should ask, "If you have no sensation, can you say that you exist?" He cannot, and so this proposition is not acceptable.

And if someone affirms that the soul has sentience as a property you should ask, "If all sensations of every kind were to cease absolutely there would be no feelings whatever. Could you then say 'I exist'?" He could not, and so this proposition is not acceptable.

When a monk does not look on the soul as coming under any of these three categories . . . he refrains from such views and clings to nothing in the world; and not clinging he does not tremble, and not trembling he attains Nirvāna. He knows that rebirth is at an end, that his goal is reached, that he has accomplished what he set out to do, and that after this present world there is no other for him. It would be absurd to say of such a monk, with his heart set free, that he believes that the perfected being survives after death—or indeed that he does not survive, or that he does and yet does not, or that he neither does nor does not. Because the monk is free his state transcends all expression, predication, communication, and knowledge.

The Simile of the Chariot

This passage from the *Questions of King Menander* is among the best known arguments in favor of the composite nature of the individual. The Greek king Milinda, or Menander, ruled in northwestern India about the middle of the second century B.C. According to the text he was converted to Buddhism by Nāgasena, and the wheel which appears on some of his numerous coins would suggest that he was in fact influenced by the Indian religion. The style of the *Questions* is in some measure reminiscent of the Upanishads, but some authorities have thought to find traces of the influence of Plato and have suggested that the author or authors knew Greek. Though in its present form the work may be some centuries later, its kernel may go back to before the Christian era.

[From *Milindapañha* (Trenckner ed.) pp. 25 f.]

Then King Menander went up to the Venerable Nāgasena, greeted him respectfully, and sat down. Nāgasena replied to the greeting, and the

King was pleased at heart. Then King Menander asked: "How is your reverence known, and what is your name?"

"I'm known as Nāgasena, your Majesty, that's what my fellow monks call me. But though my parents may have given me such a name . . . it's only a generally understood term, a practical designation. There is no question of a permanent individual implied in the use of the word."

"Listen, you five hundred Greeks and eighty thousand monks!" said King Menander. "This Nāgasena has just declared that there's no permanent individuality implied in his name!" Then, turning to Nāgasena, "If, Reverend Nāgasena, there is no permanent individuality, who gives you monks your robes and food, lodging and medicines? And who makes use of them? Who lives a life of righteousness, meditates, and reaches Nirvāna? Who destroys living beings, steals, fornicates, tells lies, or drinks spirits? . . . If what you say is true there's neither merit nor demerit, and no fruit or result of good or evil deeds. If someone were to kill you there would be no question of murder. And there would be no masters or teachers in the [Buddhist] Order and no ordinations. If your fellow monks call you Nāgasena, what then is Nāgasena? Would you say that your hair is Nāgasena?" "No, your Majesty."

"Or your nails, teeth, skin, or other parts of your body, or the outward form, or sensation, or perception, or the psychic constructions, or consciousness? [1] Are any of these Nāgasena?" "No, your Majesty."

"Then are all these taken together Nāgasena?" "No, your Majesty."

"Or anything other than they?" "No, your Majesty."

"Then for all my asking I find no Nāgasena. Nāgasena is a mere sound! Surely what your Reverence has said is false!"

Then the Venerable Nāgasena addressed the King.

"Your Majesty, how did you come here—on foot, or in a vehicle?"

"In a chariot."

"Then tell me what is the chariot? Is the pole the chariot?" "No, your Reverence."

"Or the axle, wheels, frame, reins, yoke, spokes, or goad?" "None of these things is the chariot."

"Then all these separate parts taken together are the chariot?" "No, your Reverence."

"Then is the chariot something other than the separate parts?" "No, your Reverence."

[1] The five components of individuality (see p. 96).

"Then for all my asking, your Majesty, I can find no chariot. The chariot is a mere sound. What then is the chariot? Surely what your Majesty has said is false! There is no chariot! . . ."

When he had spoken the five hundred Greeks cried "Well done!" and said to the King, "Now, your Majesty, get out of that dilemma if you can!"

"What I said was not false," replied the King. "It's on account of all these various components, the pole, axle, wheels, and so on, that the vehicle is called a chariot. It's just a generally understood term, a practical designation."

"Well said, your Majesty! You know what the word 'chariot' means! And it's just the same with me. It's on account of the various components of my being that I'm known by the generally understood term, the practical designation Nāgasena."

Change and Identity

After convincing Menander of the composite nature of the personality by the simile of the chariot, Nāgasena shows him by another simile how it is continually changing with the passage of time, but possesses a specious unity through the continuity of the body.

[From *Milindapañha* (Trenckner ed.), p. 40]

"Reverend Nāgasena," said the King, "when a man is born does he remain the same [being] or become another?"

"He neither remains the same nor becomes another."

"Give me an example!"

"What do you think, your Majesty? You were once a baby lying on your back, tender and small and weak. Was that baby you, who are now grown up?"

"No, your Reverence, the baby was one being and I am another."

"If that's the case, your Majesty, you had no mother or father, and no teachers in learning, manners, or wisdom. . . . Is the boy who goes to school one [being] and the young man who has finished his education another? Does one person commit a crime and another suffer mutilation for it?"

"Of course not, your Reverence! But what do you say on the question?"

"I am the being I was when I was a baby," said the Elder . . . "for through the continuity of the body all stages of life are included in a pragmatic unity."

"Give me an illustration."

"Suppose a man were to light a lamp, would it burn all through the night?" "Yes, it might."

"Now is the flame which burns in the middle watch the same as that which burned in the first?" "No, your Reverence."

"Or is that which burns in the last watch the same as that which burned in the middle?" "No, your Reverence."

"So is there one lamp in the first watch, another in the middle, and yet another in the last?"

"No. The same lamp gives light all through the night."

"Similarly, your Majesty, the continuity of phenomena is kept up. One person comes into existence, another passes away, and the sequence runs continuously without self-conscious existence, neither the same nor yet another."

"Well said, Reverend Nāgasena!"

The Process of Rebirth

In this little passage Nāgasena presses the analogy of the lamp further, and shows Menander how rebirth is possible without any soul, substratum of personality, or other hypothetical entity which passes from the one body to the other.

[From *Milindapañha* (Trenckner ed.), p. 71]

"Reverend Nāgasena," said the King, "is it true that nothing transmigrates, and yet there is rebirth?"

"Yes, your Majesty."

"How can this be? . . . Give me an illustration."

"Suppose, your Majesty, a man lights one lamp from another—does the one lamp transmigrate to the other?"

"No, your Reverence."

"So there is rebirth without anything transmigrating!"

Karma

Buddhism accepted the prevailing doctrine of karma, though it had an original explanation of the process whereby karma operated. In this passage from the

Questions of King Menander karma is adduced as the reason for the manifest inequalities of human fate and fortune. Had Nāgasena been disputing with an Indian king instead of with a Greek one the question would not have been asked, for the answer would have been taken for granted.

[From *Milindapañha* (Trenckner ed.), p. 65]

"Venerable Nāgasena," asked the King, "why are men not all alike, but some short-lived and some long, some sickly and some healthy, some ugly and some handsome, some weak and some strong, some poor and some rich, some base and some noble, some stupid and some clever?"

"Why, your Majesty," replied the Elder, "are not all plants alike, but some astringent, some salty, some pungent, some sour, and some sweet?"

"I suppose, your Reverence, because they come from different seeds."

"And so it is with men! They are not alike because of different karmas. As the Lord said . . . 'Beings each have their own karma. They are . . . born through karma, they become members of tribes and families through karma, each is ruled by karma, it is karma that divides them into high and low.' "

"Very good, your Reverence!"

Right Mindfulness

The following passage is of interest as showing the means which the monk should take in order thoroughly to realize the transience and otherness of all things, and thus draw near to Nirvāna. The *bhāvanās,* or states of mind, are practiced by Buddhist monks to this day, and are part of "Right Mindfulness," the seventh stage of the Noble Eightfold Path. The translation is considerably abridged.

[From *Majjhima Nikāya,* 1.420 ff.]

The Lord was staying at Sāvatthī at the monastery of Anāthapindaka in the Grove of Jeta. One morning he dressed, took his robe and bowl, and went into Sāvatthī for alms, with the Reverend Rāhula [1] following close behind him. As they walked the Lord, . . . without looking round, spoke to him thus:

"All material forms, past, present, or future, within or without, gross or subtle, base or fine, far or near, all should be viewed with full understanding—with the thought 'This is not mine, this is not I, this is not my soul.' " [2]

---

[1] The Buddha's son, who, after his father's enlightenment, became a monk.
[2] Or "self" (*atta*).

"Only material forms, Lord?"

"No, not only material forms, Rāhula, but also sensation, perception, the psychic constructions, and consciousness." [3]

"Who would go to the village to collect alms today, when he has been exhorted by the Lord himself?" said Rāhula. And he turned back and sat cross-legged, with body erect, collected in thought.

Then the Venerable Sāriputta,[4] seeing him thus, said to him: "Develop concentration on inhalation and exhalation, for when this is developed and increased it is very productive and helpful."

Towards evening Rāhula rose and went to the Lord, and asked him how he could develop concentration on inhalation and exhalation. And the Lord said:

"Rāhula, whatever is hard and solid in an individual, such as hair, nails, teeth, skin, flesh, and so on, is called the personal element of earth. The personal element of water is composed of bile, phlegm, pus, blood, sweat, and so on. The personal element of fire is that which warms and consumes or burns up, and produces metabolism of food and drink in digestion. The personal element of air is the wind in the body which moves upwards or downwards, the winds in the abdomen and stomach, winds which move from member to member, and the inhalation and exhalation of the breath. And finally the personal element of space comprises the orifices of ears and nose, the door of the mouth, and the channels whereby food and drink enter, remain in, and pass out of the body.[5] These five personal elements, together with the five external elements, make up the total of the five universal elements. They should all be regarded objectively, with right understanding, thinking 'This is not mine, this is not me, this is not my soul.' With this understanding attitude a man turns from the five elements and his mind takes no delight in them.

"Develop a state of mind like the earth, Rāhula. For on the earth men throw clean and unclean things, dung and urine, spittle, pus and blood, and the earth is not troubled or repelled or disgusted. And as you grow like the earth no contacts with pleasant or unpleasant will lay hold of your mind or stick to it.

"Similarly you should develop a state of mind like water, for men

---

[3] The five components of individuality.   [4] One of the Buddha's chief disciples.
[5] This interesting passage will give the reader some notion of ancient Indian ideas of anatomy and physics, as it would have been assented to by most schools of thought. In

throw all manner of clean and unclean things into water and it is not troubled or repelled or disgusted. And similarly with fire, which burns all things, clean and unclean, and with air, which blows upon them all, and with space, which is nowhere established.

"Develop the state of mind of friendliness, Rāhula, for, as you do so, ill-will will grow less; and of compassion, for thus vexation will grow less; and of joy, for thus aversion will grow less; and of equanimity,[6] for thus repugnance will grow less.

"Develop the state of mind of consciousness of the corruption of the body, for thus passion will grow less; and of the consciousness of the fleeting nature of all things, for thus the pride of selfhood will grow less.

"Develop the state of mind of ordering the breath, . . . in which the monk goes to the forest, or to the root of a tree or to an empty house, and sits cross-legged with body erect, collected in thought. Fully mindful he inhales and exhales. When he inhales or exhales a long breath he knows precisely that he is doing so, and similarly when inhaling or exhaling a short breath. While inhaling or exhaling he trains himself to be conscious of the whole of his body, . . . to be fully conscious of the components of his mind, . . . to realize the impermanence of all things, . . . or to dwell on passionlessness . . . or renunciation. Thus the state of ordered breathing, when developed and increased, is very productive and helpful. And when the mind is thus developed a man breathes his last breath in full consciousness, and not unconsciously."[7]

The Last Instructions of the Buddha

The following passage occurs in the *Discourse of the Great Passing-away* (*Mahāparinibbāna Sutta*) which describes the last days and death of the Buddha. The Master, an old and ailing man, is on the way to the hills where he was born, and where soon he is to die. These are among his last recorded instructions to his disciples. Unfortunately we cannot be sure of their authenticity; the fine phrases concerning "the closed fist of the teacher" are particularly suspect, for they are just the sort of interpolation which an earnest Theravāda monk would be likely to make, in order to discredit

---

many passages Buddhist texts admit only four elements, rejecting space, which is looked on as an element in orthodox Hindu theory.

[6] Friendliness, compassion, joy, and equanimity are the four cardinal virtues of Buddhism.

[7] The state of mind in the last moments before death was considered extremely important in its effect on the next birth. Some of the Chinese and Japanese Buddhist sects perform rites at the deathbed similar to the Roman Catholic extreme unction.

the doctrines of schismatics of a Mahāyānist type, who claimed to possess the esoteric teachings of the Master. But, whether authentically the Buddha's words or not, the following passage perhaps gives the quintessence of Theravāda Buddhism, with its call for self-reliant striving against all that seems base and evil.

[From *Dīgha Nikāya*, 2.99 f., 155–56]

Soon after this the Lord began to recover, and when he was quite free from sickness he came out of his lodging and sat in its shadow on a seat spread out for him. The Venerable Ānanda went up to him, paid his respects, sat down to one side, and spoke to the Lord thus:

"I have seen the Lord in health, and I have seen the Lord in sickness; and when I saw that the Lord was sick my body became as weak as a creeper, my sight dimmed, and all my faculties weakened. But yet I was a little comforted by the thought that the Lord would not pass away until he had left his instructions concerning the Order."

"What, Ānanda! Does the Order expect that of me? I have taught the truth without making any distinction between exoteric and esoteric doctrines; for . . . with the Tathāgata there is no such thing as the closed fist of the teacher who keeps some things back. If anyone thinks 'It is I who will lead the Order,' or 'The Order depends on me,' he is the one who should lay down instructions concerning the Order. But the Tathāgata has no such thought, so why should he leave instructions? I am old now, Ānanda, and full of years; my journey nears its end, and I have reached my sum of days, for I am nearly eighty years old. Just as a worn out cart can only be kept going if it is tied up with thongs, so the body of the Tathāgata can only be kept going by bandaging it. Only when the Tathāgata no longer attends to any outward object, when all separate sensation stops and he is deep in inner concentration, is his body at ease.

"So, Ānanda, you must be your own lamps, be your own refuges. Take refuge in nothing outside yourselves. Hold firm to the truth as a lamp and a refuge, and do not look for refuge to anything besides yourselves. A monk becomes his own lamp and refuge by continually looking on his body, feelings, perceptions, moods, and ideas in such a manner that he conquers the cravings and depressions of ordinary men and is always strenuous, self-possessed, and collected in mind. Whoever among my monks does this, either now or when I am dead, if he is anxious to learn, will reach the summit." [p. 99 f.]

"All composite things must pass away. Strive onward vigilantly." [pp. 155–56]

The Buddha in Nirvāna

This brief passage from the *Questions of King Menander* illustrates the Theravāda conception of Nirvāna. It is not total annihilation, but at the same time it involves the complete disintegration of the phenomenal personality—a paradox which cannot be explained in words.

[From *Milindpañha* (Trenckner, ed.), p. 73]

"Reverend Nāgasena," said the King, "does the Buddha still exist?"

"Yes, your Majesty, he does."

"Then is it possible to point out the Buddha as being here or there?"

"The Lord has passed completely away in Nirvāna, so that nothing is left which could lead to the formation of another being. And so he cannot be pointed out as being here or there."

"Give me an illustration."

"What would your Majesty say—if a great fire were blazing, would it be possible to point to a flame which had gone out and say that it was here or there?"

"No, your Reverence, the flame is extinguished, it can't be detected."

"In just the same way, your Majesty, the Lord has passed away in Nirvāna. . . . He can only be pointed out in the body of his doctrine, for it was he who taught it."

"Very good, Reverend Nāgasena!"

The City of Righteousness

This fine passage, from the latter part of the *Questions of King Menander,* is probably the work of a hand different from that which composed the dialogues which we have already quoted. In it the Buddha almost takes on the character of a savior god, who, like Amitābha in the developed Mahāyāna mythology, built a heaven for his followers. Nirvāna is not described in negative terms, but in very positive ones, and the metaphor of the busy, populous, and prosperous city hardly suggests the rarified Nirvāna of the previous passage, but a heaven in which personality is by no means lost. It suggests in fact to the Western reader the New Jerusalem of the Book of Revelation. Clearly this passage is the work of a writer whose attitude approached closely to that of

Mahāyāna, but it must be remembered that Theravāda Buddhists look on the text from which it is taken as semi-canonical.

[From *Milindapañha* (Trenckner ed.), pp. 330 ff.]

The builder of a city . . . first chooses a pleasant and suitable site; he makes it smooth, and then sets to work to build his city fair and well proportioned, divided into quarters, with ramparts round about it. . . . And when the city is built, and stands complete and perfect, he goes away to another land. And in time the city becomes rich and prosperous, peaceful and happy, free from plague and calamity, and filled with people of all classes and professions and of all lands . . . even with Scythians, Greeks, and Chinese. . . . All these folk coming to live in the new city and finding it so well planned, faultless, perfect, and beautiful exclaim: "Skilled indeed must be the builder who built this city!"

So the Lord . . . in his infinite goodness . . . when he had achieved the highest powers of Buddhahood and had conquered Māra [1] and his hosts, tearing the net of false doctrine, casting aside ignorance, and producing wisdom, . . . built the City of Righteousness.

The Lord's City of Righteousness has virtue for its ramparts, fear of sin for its moat, knowledge for its gates, zeal for its turrets, faith for its pillars, concentration for its watchman, wisdom for its palaces. The *Basket of Discourses* is its marketplace, the *Supplementary Doctrines* its roads, the *Conduct* its court of justice, and earnest self-control is its main street. . . .

The Lord laid down the following subjects for meditation: the ideas of impermanence, of the nonexistence of an enduring self, of the impurity and of the wretchedness of life, of ridding oneself of evil tendencies, of passionlessness, of stopping the influx of evil tendencies, of dissatisfaction with all things in the world, of the impermanence of all conditioned things, of mindful control of breath, of the corpse in disintegration, of the execution of criminals with all its horrors; the ideas of friendliness, of compassion, of joy, of equanimity, [2] the thought of death, and mindfulness of the body. . . . Whoever wishes to be free from age and death takes one of these as a subject for meditation, and thus he is set free from passion, hatred, and dullness, [3] from pride and from false views; he crosses

---

[1] The spirit of the world and the flesh, the Buddhist Satan.
[2] The four cardinal virtues of Buddhism.
[3] The three "influxes" (*āsava*), the cardinal sins of Buddhism.

the ocean of rebirth, dams the torrent of his cravings, is washed clean of the threefold stain [of passion, hatred, and dullness], and destroys all evil within him. So he enters the glorious city of Nirvāna, stainless and undefiled, pure and white, unaging, deathless, secure and calm and happy, and his mind is emancipated as a perfected being.

THE ETHICS OF THERAVĀDA BUDDHISM

In the sphere of personal relations Buddhism inculcated a morality gentler and more humanitarian than the stern early Hindu ethic, based chiefly on duty rather than fellowship. The four cardinal virtues of Buddhism—friendliness, compassion, joy, and equanimity—are extolled in many passages of the scriptures. The *Birth Stories* teach friendly relations between man and man and between man and animal, and encourage the warm virtues of family love, brotherhood, and honesty (not to speak of shrewdness) in one's dealings with others. Though the surviving Buddhist religious literature is chiefly intended for the monastic community Buddhism certainly had, and still has, a message going far beyond the monastery to the millions of ordinary believers who have no hope of Nirvāna until after many lives, but who may yet rise in the scale of being by faith in the teaching of the Buddha, by service to the Buddhist Order, and by fair dealing with their fellows.

In this connection we would draw attention to the most important passage on lay morality in the Pāli scriptures—the *Discourse of Admonition to Singāla (Singālovāda Sutta)*. It is a solid bourgeois morality that this text encourages. Like many older writings of Protestant Christianity it stresses the virtue of thrift—expensive ceremonies and domestic rituals are wasteful as well as useless; fairs and festivals lead men to squander precious time and wealth; from the layman's point of view drink and gambling are evil chiefly for the same reasons; to increase the family estates is a meritorious act. But there is more in the *Discourse* than this. In modern terms the ideal it sets forth is of a society in which each individual respects the other's personality, an intricate network of warm and happy human relationships, where parents and children, teachers and pupils, husbands and wives, masters and servants, and friends and friends look on one another as ends in themselves, and dwell together in mutual respect and affection, each helping the other upward in the scale of being through a cosmos which, though theoretically a vale of tears, yet contains pleasant places and gives many opportunities for real if transient happiness in fellowship with friends and kin. And the inevitable sorrow of all who are born only to grow old and pass away, the lonely anguish of the individual being who finds himself at odds with an unfriendly universe, can only be lessened, at least for the ordinary layman, by brotherhood.

The Morals of the Monk

The following extract is part of a long panegyric of the Buddha, leading up to a description of his perfect wisdom. The moral virtues attributed to him in the earlier part of the passage, which is quoted here, are those after which every monk should strive; and, allowing for their different circumstances, the monk's example should be followed as far as possible by the layman.

[From *Dīgha Nikāya,* 1.4 ff.]

The monk Gautama has given up injury to life, he has lost all inclination to it; he has laid aside the cudgel and the sword, and he lives modestly, full of mercy, desiring in compassion the welfare of all things living.

He has given up taking what is not given, he has lost all inclination to it. He accepts what is given to him and waits for it to be given; and he lives in honesty and purity of heart. . . .

He has given up unchastity, he has lost all inclination to it. He is celibate and aloof, and has lost all desire for sexual intercourse, which is vulgar. . . .

He has given up false speech, he has lost all inclination to it. He speaks the truth, he keeps faith, he is faithful and trustworthy, he does not break his word to the world. . . .

He has given up slander, he has lost all inclination to it. When he hears something in one place he will not repeat it in another in order to cause strife, . . . but he unites those who are divided by strife, and encourages those who are friends. His pleasure is in peace, he loves peace and delights in it, and when he speaks he speaks words which make for peace. . . .

He has given up harsh speech, he has lost all inclination to it. He speaks only words that are blameless, pleasing to the ear, touching the heart, cultured, pleasing the people, loved by the people. . . .

He has given up frivolous talk, he has lost all inclination to it. He speaks at the right time, in accordance with the facts, with words full of meaning. His speech is memorable, timely, well illustrated, measured, and to the point.[1]

He does no harm to seeds or plants. He takes only one meal a day, not eating at night, or at the wrong time.[2] He will not watch shows, or attend fairs with song, dance, and music. He will not wear ornaments, or adorn himself with garlands, scents, or cosmetics. He will not use a high or large bed. He will not accept gold or silver, raw grain or raw meat. He will not accept women or girls, bondmen or bondwomen, sheep or goats, fowls or pigs, elephants or cattle, horses or mares, fields or houses. He will not act as go-between or messenger. He will not buy or sell, or falsify with scales, weights, or measures. He is never crooked, will never bribe, or cheat, or defraud. He will not injure, kill, or put in bonds, or steal, or do acts of violence.

Care of the Body

The Buddhist Order was very solicitous for the bodily health of its members, and the Buddha is reported to have said, on one occasion: "He who would care for me should care for the sick." [1] Buddhist monasteries often served as dispensaries, and it has been suggested that one of the reasons for the spread of Buddhism in Southeast Asia and elsewhere was the medical lore of the Buddhist monks, which, though of course primitive by modern standards, was superior to anything known to the local inhabitants, and thus added to the reputation of the new religion.

The *Questions of King Menander* explains the apparent anomaly that a system which stressed so strongly the evils of the things of the flesh should also value physical wellbeing so highly.

[From *Milindapañha* (Trenckner ed.), pp. 73-74]

The King said: "Reverend Nāgasena, is the body dear to you wanderers?"

"No, your Majesty."

"Then why do you feed it and care for it so well?"

"Have you ever gone to battle, and been wounded by an arrow?"

---

[1] The layman in Buddhism is expected to follow the example of Gautama in all the points of morality above, except, of course, that in place of complete celibacy legitimate sexual relations are allowed. Many of the points that follow would be regarded as subjects of supererogation for the layman, though he might adhere to some of them for specified periods. It should be remembered, incidentally, that the vows of the Buddhist monk are not taken in perpetuity, and a Buddhist layman will often take the monk's vows for a short period.

[2] That is, after midday.   [1] *Vinaya Piṭaka* 1. 302 (*Mahāvagga* 8. 26).

"Yes, your Reverence, I have."

"And in such a case isn't the wound smeared with ointment, anointed with oil, and bound with a bandage?"

"Yes, that's what is done."

"And is the wound dear to you, your Majesty, that you care for it so well?"

"Certainly not! All those things are done to make the flesh grow together again."

"So, you see, wanderers do not hold the body dear, your Majesty! Without clinging to it they bear the body in continence, for the Lord declared that the body was like a wound. . . .

'Covered with clammy skin, with nine openings, a great wound,
The body oozes from every pore, unclean and stinking.' "

"Well spoken, Reverend Nāgasena!"

"Lay Not Up for Yourselves Treasures upon Earth. . . ."

In theory "right views" about the nature of the world are the first step along the Eightfold Path. But the Buddhist literature meant chiefly for laymen tends to emphasize right actions rather than right views. Whatever the beliefs of a man may be, his good deeds and self-discipline are an unfailing source of merit, and lead to a happier rebirth, which may give him the opportunity for further spiritual progress. We quote the following little passage partly because it recalls a famous verse of the Sermon on the Mount. Notice that the treasure "cannot be given to others." This is the doctrine of the Theravāda sect. The Mahāyāna teaches that the merit accruing from good deeds can be transferred by a voluntary act of will, and men are encouraged, by the example of the compassionate bodhisattvas (See Chapter VII), to make such transfers of merit.

[From *Khuddaka Pāṭha*, 8]

A man buries a treasure in a deep pit, thinking: "It will be useful in time of need, or if the king is displeased with me, or if I am robbed or fall into debt, or if food is scarce, or bad luck befalls me."

But all this treasure may not profit the owner at all, for he may forget where he has hidden it, or goblins may steal it, or his enemies or even his kinsmen may take it when he is careless.

But by charity, goodness, restraint, and self-control man and woman alike can store up a well-hidden treasure—a treasure which cannot be given to others and which robbers cannot steal. A wise man should do good—that is the treasure which will not leave him.

The Virtue of Friendliness

The following poem is evidently a conflation from two sources, for in the middle of the third verse its whole tone changes, and in place of a rather pedestrian enumeration of the Buddhist virtues we have an impassioned rhapsody on the theme of friendliness (*mettā*), the first of the four cardinal virtues. "Mindfulness of friendliness" is among the daily exercises of the monk, and can also be practiced by the layman; he detaches himself in imagination from his own body, and, as though looking down on himself, pervades himself with friendliness directed towards himself, for it is impossible to feel true friendliness or love for others unless, in the best sense of the term, one feels it for oneself; then he proceeds in imagination to send waves of friendliness in every direction, to reach every being in every corner of the world. After pervading the world with love he may repeat the process with the three other cardinal virtues—compassion, joy, and equanimity. These forms of the practice of "right mindfulness" are known as *Brahma-vihāras,* freely translated "sublime moods." They are still practiced by Buddhists throughout the world, and it is believed, especially among the Mahāyānist sects, that the waves of friendliness constantly poured out by many thousands of meditating monks have a very positive effect on the welfare of the world.

[From *Sutta Nipāta,* p. 143 ff.]

This a man should do who knows what is good for him,
Who understands the meaning of the Place of Peace [i.e., Nirvāna]—
He should be able, upright, truly straight,
Kindly of speech, mild, and without conceit.

He should be well content, soon satisfied,
Having few wants and simple tastes,
With composed senses, discreet,
Not arrogant or grasping. . . .

In his deeds there should be no meanness
For which the wise might blame him.

May all be happy and safe!
May all beings gain inner joy—

All living beings whatever
Without exception, weak or strong,
Whether long or high
Middling or small, subtle or gross,
Seen or unseen,
Dwelling afar or near,
Born or yet unborn—
May all beings gain inner joy.

May no being deceive another,
Nor in any way scorn another,
Nor, in anger or ill-will,
Desire another's sorrow.

As a mother cares for her son,
Her only son, all her days,
So towards all things living
A man's mind should be all-embracing.
Friendliness for the whole world,
All-embracing, he should raise in his mind,
Above, below, and across,
Unhindered, free from hate and ill-will.

Standing, walking or sitting,
Or lying down, till he falls asleep,
He should remain firm in this mindfulness,
For this is the sublime mood.
Avoiding all false views,
Virtuous, filled with insight,
Let him conquer the lust of the passions,
And he shall never again be born of the womb.

Hatred and Love

The idea of "turning the other cheek" in one's personal relations is frequently to be found in Buddhist literature. Nevertheless there are few condemnations of warfare, as distinct from acts of violence on the part of individuals, and the Theravāda scriptures contain no passages on this latter topic as forthright as

Ashoka's Thirteenth Rock-Edict (quoted later). The following verses from the *Way of Righteousness* exemplify these points.

[From *Dhammapada*, 3–5, 201]

"He insulted me, he struck me,
　　He defeated me, he robbed me!"
Those who harbor such thoughts
　　Are never appeased in their hatred. . . .
But those who do not harbor them
　　Are quickly appeased.

Never in this world is hate
　　Appeased by hatred;
It is only appeased by love—
　　This is an eternal law (*sanantana-dhamma*).[1]

Victory breeds hatred
　　For the defeated lie down in sorrow.
Above victory or defeat
　　The calm man dwells in peace.

Buddhism and Everyday Life

The *Admonition to Siṅgāla* is the longest single passage in the Pali scriptures devoted to lay morality. Though put in the mouth of the Buddha, it is probably not authentically his; parts of it, however, may be based on a few transmitted recollections of his teaching. Like many other *Discourses* it seems to emanate from more than one source, for the earlier part, enumerating the many sins and faults to which the layman is liable, and describing the true friend, is divided by a series of verses from the later and finer passage, defining the duties of the layman in his sixfold relationship with his fellows.

The reader should notice the solid, frugal, mercantile virtues which are inculcated, especially in the first part. This sermon is evidently not directed chiefly at the very poor or the very rich, but at the prosperous middle class. Also noteworthy are the paragraphs on the duties of husbands and wives and masters and servants in the second part of the sermon—if read in terms of rights rather than of duties they seem to imply the wife's right to full control of household affairs and to an adequate dress allowance, and the employee's right to fair wages and conditions, regular holidays, and free medical attention.

[From *Dīgha Nikāya*, 3.180 ff.]

[1] Skt. *Sanātana dharma*, a conventional term designating "Hinduism," redefined here in terms of Buddhist ethics.

Once when the Lord was staying in the Bamboo Grove at Rajagaha, Singāla, a householder's son, got up early, went out from Rājagaha, and, with his clothes and hair still wet from his morning ablutions, joined his hands in reverence and worshiped the several quarters of earth and sky— east, south, west, north, above, and below. Now early that same morning the Lord dressed himself, and with bowl and robe went into Rājagaha to beg his food. He saw Singala worshiping the quarters, and asked him why he did so.

"When my father lay dying," Singāla replied, "he told me to worship the quarters thus. I honor my father's words, and respect and revere them, and so I always get up early and worship the quarters in this way."

"But to worship the six quarters thus is not in accordance with noble conduct."

"How then, Sir, should they be worshiped in accordance with noble conduct? Will the Lord be so good as to tell me?"

"Listen then," said the Lord, "and I'll tell you. Mark well what I say!"

"I will, Sir," Singāla replied. And the Lord spoke as follows:

"If the noble lay-disciple has given up the four vices of action, if he does no evil deed from any of the four motives, if he doesn't follow the six ways of squandering his wealth, if he avoids all these fourteen evils— then he embraces the six quarters, he is ready for the conquest of both worlds, he is fortunate both in this world and the next, and when his body breaks up on his death he is reborn to bliss in heaven.

"What are the four vices of action that he gives up? They are injury to life, taking what is not given, base conduct in sexual matters, and false speech. . . .

"What are the four motives of evil deeds which he avoids? Evil deeds are committed from partiality, enmity, stupidity, and fear.

"And what are the six ways of squandering wealth? They are addiction to drink, the cause of carelessness; roaming the streets at improper times; frequenting fairs; gambling; keeping bad company; and idleness.

"There are six dangers in addiction to drink: actual loss of wealth; increased liability to quarrels; liability to illness; loss of reputation; indecent exposure; and weakened intelligence.

"There are six dangers in roaming the streets at improper times: the man who does so is unprotected and unguarded; so are his wife and children; and likewise his property; he incurs suspicion of having committed crime;

he is the subject of false rumors; in fact he goes out to meet all kinds of trouble.

"There are six dangers in frequenting fairs: the man who does so becomes an insatiable addict of dancing; singing; music; story-telling; jugglers; or acrobats.

"There are six dangers in gambling: the winner incurs hatred; the loser regrets his lost money; there is obvious loss of wealth; a gambler's word is not respected in the law courts; he is scorned by his friends and counselors; and he is not cultivated by people who want to marry their daughters, for the rogue who's always dicing isn't fit to keep a wife.

"There are six dangers in keeping bad company: a man who does so has as his friends and companions rogues; libertines; drunkards; confidence men; swindlers; and toughs.

"And there are six dangers in idleness; A man says, 'it's too cold' and doesn't work; or he says, 'it's too hot'; or 'it's too early'; or 'it's too late'; or 'I'm too hungry'; or 'I'm too full.' And so all the while he won't do what he ought to do, and he earns no new wealth, but fritters away what he has already earned.

"There are four types who should be looked on as enemies in the guise of friends: a grasping man; a smooth-spoken man; a man who only says what you want to hear; and a man who helps you waste your money.

"The grasping man is an enemy on four grounds: he is grasping; when he gives a little he expects a lot in return; what duty he performs he does out of fear; and he only serves his own interests.

"The smooth-spoken man is an enemy on four grounds: he speaks you fair about the past; he speaks you fair about the future; he tries to win you over by empty promises; but when there's something to be done he shows his shortcomings.[1]

"The man who only says what you want to hear is an enemy on four grounds: he consents to an evil deed; he doesn't consent to a good one; he praises you to your face; but he runs you down behind your back.

"The wastrel is an enemy on four grounds: he is your companion when you drink; when you roam the streets at improper times; when you go to fairs; and when you gamble.

---

[1] The commentator Buddhaghosa gives a quaint example of the conduct of such a false friend—you send a message asking him to lend you his cart, and he replies that the axle is broken.

"But there are four types who should be looked on as friends true of heart: a man who seeks to help you; a man who is the same in weal and woe; a man who gives good advice; and a man who is sympathetic. . . .

> The friend who is a helper,
>   The friend in weal and woe,
> The friend who gives good counsel,
>   The friend who sympathizes—
> These the wise man should know
>   As his four true friends,
> And should devote himself to them
>   As a mother to the child of her body.

> The wise and moral man
>   Shines like a fire on a hilltop,
> Making money like the bee,
>   Who does not hurt the flower.
> Such a man makes his pile
>   As an anthill, gradually.
> The man grown wealthy thus
>   Can help his family
> And firmly bind his friends
>   To himself. He should divide
> His money in four parts;
>   On one part he should live,
> With two expand his trade,
>   And the fourth he should save
> Against a rainy day.[2]

"And how does the noble lay-disciple embrace the six quarters? He should recognize these as the six quarters: mother and father as the east;

---

[2] These verses are undoubtedly popular gnomic poetry, adapted with little or no altera-
tion to Buddhist purposes. They effectively give the lie to the picture, still popular in some
circles, of ancient India as a land of "plain living and high thinking." The last three verses
are evidently the product of a society quite as acquisitive as that of present-day Europe or
America. The commentator Buddhaghosa found them difficult, for the ideal layman is
here said to plow half his income back into his trade, but to devote nothing to religious
or charitable causes. The phenomenal rate of reinvestment advocated suggests a rapidly
expanding economy.

teachers as the south; wife and children as the west; friends and coun-selors as the north; slaves and servants as below; and ascetics and brāh-mans as above.

"A son should serve his mother and father as the eastern quarter in five ways: having been maintained by them in his childhood he should main-tain them in their old age; he should perform the duties which formerly devolved on them; he should maintain the honor and the traditions of his family and lineage; he should make himself worthy of his heritage; and he should make offerings to the spirits of the departed. And thus served by their son as the eastern quarter his mother and father should care for him in five ways: they should restrain him from evil; encourage him to do good; have him taught a profession; arrange for his marriage to a suitable wife; and transfer his inheritance to him in due time. Thus he embraces the eastern quarter and makes it safe and propitious.

"A pupil should serve his teacher as the southern quarter in five ways: by rising [to greet him when he enters]; by waiting upon him; by willing-ness to learn; by attentive service; and by diligently learning his trade. And thus served by his pupil as the southern quarter a teacher should care for him in five ways: he should train him in good conduct; teach him in such a way that he remembers what he has been taught; thoroughly in-struct him in the lore of every art [of his trade]; speak well of him to his friends and counselors; and protect him in every quarter. Thus he embraces the southern quarter and makes it safe and propitious.

"A husband should serve his wife as the western quarter in five ways: by honoring her; by respecting her; by remaining faithful to her; by giv-ing her charge of the home; and by duly giving her adornments. And thus served by her husband as the western quarter a wife should care for him in five ways: she should be efficient in her household tasks; she should manage her servants well; she should be chaste; she should take care of the goods which he brings home; and she should be skillful and untiring in all her duties. Thus he embraces the western quarter and makes it safe and propitious.

"A gentleman should serve his friends and counselors as the northern quarter in five ways: by generosity; by courtesy; by helping them; by treating them as he would treat himself; and by keeping his word to them. And thus served by a gentleman as the northern quarter his friends and counselors should care for him in five ways: they should protect him when he is careless; they should guard his property on such occasions; they should be a refuge for him in trouble; in misfortune they should not leave him; and they should respect other members of his family. Thus he embraces the western quarter and makes it safe and propitious.

"A master should serve his slaves and servants as the lower quarter in five ways: he should assign them work in proportion to their strength; he should give them due food and wages; he should care for them in sickness; he should share especially tasty luxuries with them; and he should give them holidays at due intervals. Thus served by their master as the lower quarter they should care for him in five ways: they should get up before him; they should go to bed after him; they should be content with what he gives them; they should do their work well; and they should spread abroad his praise and good name. Thus he embraces the lower quarter and makes it safe and propitious.

"In five ways a gentleman should serve ascetics and brāhmans as the upper quarter: by affectionate acts; by affectionate words; by affectionate thoughts; by not closing his doors to them; and by duly supplying them with food. Thus served by a gentleman as the upper quarter they should care for him in six ways: they should restrain him from evil; they should encourage him to do good; they should feel for him with a friendly mind; they should teach him what he has not heard before; they should encourage him to follow what he has already learned; and they should show him the way to heaven. Thus he embraces the upper quarter and makes it safe and propitious."

SOCIETY AND THE STATE IN THERAVĀDA BUDDHISM

Few pages in the massive literature of Buddhism lay down definite instructions on social or political life, and the amount of speculation by Buddhist authors on the problems of state and society is not large. Indeed Buddhism has sometimes been stigmatized as not a true religion at all, but a mere system of self-discipline for monks, with no significant message for the ordinary man except that he should if possible leave the world and take the yellow robe. In fact Buddhists have always realized that not every layman was morally or intellectually capable of becoming a monk, and the scriptures, as we have seen above, do contain here and there instructions especially intended for layfolk, together with occasional passages with a social or political message. Nevertheless it may be that one of the reasons for the disappearance of Buddhism in the land of its birth was that it left the laymen too dependent on the ministrations of the brāhmans, and, instead of giving a lead in political and social matters, was too often willing to compromise with the existing ways of everyday life.

Though in practice Buddhism seems to have accepted the existence of a society with sharp class divisions and to have made no frontal attack on it, there are many passages in Buddhist literature in which the four classes of Hindu society are declared to be fundamentally equal, and in which men are said to be worthy of respect not through birth, but only through spiritual or moral merit. Though we cannot show that Buddhism had any definite effect on the Indian system of class and caste, its teachings obviously tended against the extremer manifestations of social inequality. In those lands where Buddhism was implanted upon societies little influenced by Hindu ideas the caste system in its Indian form is not to be found.

In politics Buddhism definitely discouraged the pretensions of kings to divine or semidivine status. While Hindu teachers often declared that kings were partial incarnations of the gods and encouraged an attitude of passive obedience to them, the Buddhist scriptures categorically state that the first king was merely the chosen leader of the people, appointed by them to restrain crime and protect property, and that his right to levy taxation depended not on birth or succession but on the efficient fulfillment of his duty. The *Birth Stories,* among the most influential of the Buddhist scriptures, contain several tales of wicked kings overthrown as a result of popular rebellion. Thus Buddhism had a rational attitude to the state. The constitution of the Buddhist order, in which each monastery was virtually a law unto itself, deciding major issues after free discussion among the assembled monks, tended toward democracy, and it has been suggested that it was based on the practices of the tribal republics of the Buddha's day. Though Buddhism never formulated a distinctive system of political ethics it generally tended to mitigate the autocracy of the Indian king.

On the question of war Buddhism said little, though a few passages in the Buddhist scriptures oppose it. Like the historical Ashoka, the ideal emperor of Buddhism gains his victories by moral suasion. This did not prevent many Buddhist kings of India and Ceylon from becoming great conquerors and pursuing their political aims with much the same ruthlessness as their Hindu neighbors. Two of pre-Muslim India's greatest conquerors, Harsha of Kanauj (606–647) and Dharmapāla of Bihār and Bengal (c.770–810), were Buddhists. In fact Buddhism had little direct effect on the political order, except in the case of Ashoka, and its leaders seem often to have been rather submissive to the temporal power. An Erastian relationship between church and state is indicated in the inscriptions of Ashoka, and in Buddhist Ceylon the same relationship usually existed.

Early travelers have left a number of valuable accounts of conditions in ancient India. Two of these, that of the Greek Megasthenes (c.300 B.C.) and that of the Chinese pilgrim Fa-hsien (A.D. c.400), are of special interest for our purposes, for the first was written before Buddhism had become an important factor in Indian life, and the second when it had already passed its most flourishing period and had entered on a state of slow decline. Megasthenes found a very severe judicial system, with many crimes punished by execution or mutilation. The existence of such a harsh system of punishment is confirmed by the famous Hindu text on polity, the *Arthaśāstra,* the kernel of which dates from about the same time. Under Chandragupta Maurya, the grandfather of Ashoka, the state was highly organized and all branches of human activity were hemmed in by many troublesome regulations enforced by a large corps of government officials. Fa-hsien, on the other hand, found a land where the death penalty was not imposed, and mutilation was inflicted only for very serious crime; and he was especially impressed by the fact that human freedom was respected and people were able to move freely from one part of the land to the other without passports or other forms of interference from the government. In Megasthenes' day all classes freely ate meat, while in the time of Fa-hsien only the outcastes did so.[1] It seems certain that Buddhism had something to do with the great change in the direction of mildness and nonviolence which had taken place in the seven hundred years between the two travelers. Certainly Buddhism was not the only factor in the change, for sentiments in favor of tolerance, mildness,

---

[1] If we are to believe the pilgrim, who may have exaggerated somewhat.

and nonviolence are to be found also in Hindu and Jain writings, but it is very probable that Buddhism was the greatest single factor, for it was the most active and vigorous religion in the period in question.

Though Ashoka was practically forgotten by India his message calling for good relations between rulers and ruled was not, and echoes of it may be heard in many non-Buddhist sources of later date. On the other hand his fond hope that aggressive wars would cease forever as a result of his propaganda was unfulfilled, and the successors of Ashoka seem to have been if anything more militant than his predecessors. It would seem that Buddhism had little effect in encouraging peace within the borders of India.

How the World Evolved

Buddhism, like all Indian religious systems, believed that the world goes through periods of evolution and decline. While it did not reject the existence of the gods, it denied that they had any significant effect upon the cosmic process. Brahmā, at the time of the Buddha a much more important figure than he became in later Hinduism, imagines that he is the creator, when in fact the world came into being through the operation of natural laws. In Brahmā's case the primal ignorance, which affects gods and men alike, has led to the wish fathering the thought. The following passage is attributed to the Buddha himself.
[From *Dīgha Nikāya*, 3.28 ff.]

There are some monks and brāhmans who declare as a doctrine received from their teachers that the beginning of all things was the work of the god Brahmā. I have gone and asked them whether it was true that they maintained such a doctrine, and they have replied that it was; but when I have asked them to explain just how the beginning of things was the work of the god Brahmā they have not been able to answer, and have returned the question to me. Then I have explained it to them thus:

There comes a time, my friends, sooner or later, . . . when the world is dissolved and beings are mostly reborn in the World of Radiance.[1] There they dwell, made of the stuff of mind, feeding on joy, shining in their own light, flying through middle space, firm in their bliss for a long, long time.

Now there comes a time when this world begins to evolve, and then

[1] *Ābhassara,* the third Buddhist heaven, above the World of Brahmā.

the World of Brahmā appears, but it is empty. And some being, whether because his allotted span is past or because his merit is exhausted, quits his body in the World of Radiance and is born in the empty World of Brahmā, where he dwells for a long, long time. Now because he has been so long alone he begins to feel dissatisfaction and longing, and wishes that other beings might come and live with him. And indeed soon other beings quit their bodies in the World of Radiance and come to keep him company in the World of Brahmā.

Then the being who was first born there thinks: "I am Brahmā, the mighty Brahmā, the Conqueror, the Unconquered, the All-seeing, the Lord, the Maker, the Creator, the Supreme Chief, the Disposer, the Controller, the Father of all that is or is to be. I have created all these beings, for I merely wished that they might be and they have come here!" And the other beings . . . think the same, because he was born first and they later. And the being who was born first lived longer and was more handsome and powerful than the others.

And it might well be that some being would quit his body there and be reborn in this world. He might then give up his home for the homeless life [of an ascetic]; and in his ardor, striving, intentness, earnestness, and keenness of thought, he might attain such a stage of meditation that with collected mind he might recall his former birth, but not what went before. Thus he might think: "We were created by Brahmā, eternal, firm, everlasting, and unchanging, who will remain so for ever and ever, while we who were created by the Lord Brahmā . . . are transient, unstable, shortlived, and destined to pass away."

That is how your traditional doctrine comes about that the beginning of things was the work of the god Brahmā.

The Origin of Society and the State

This most important and interesting legend should be read as a sequel to the former passage, since it describes a further stage in the process of cosmic evolution. It tells of the gradual progress of humanity, on account of its own greed, from the blissful golden age when there was no need of food or clothing to a fully evolved society with a king and class system. It should be noted especially that neither the state nor the class system has any ultimate sanction other than human expediency. The first king holds office by virtue of a contract with his subjects, and this is probably one of the world's oldest versions of the contractual theory of the state. The passage concludes by emphasizing the fundamental equality of all the four classes. Again the words are attributed to the Buddha.

[From *Dīgha Nikāya,* 3.80 ff.]

Sooner or later, after a long, long time . . . there comes a time when this world passes away. Then most living beings pass to the World of Radiance, and there they dwell, made of the stuff of mind, feeding on joy, shining in their own light, flying through middle space, firm in their bliss for a long, long time. Sooner or later there comes a time when this world begins to evolve once more. Then those being who pass away from the World of Radiance are usually born here on earth; but they are still made of the stuff of mind . . . and are firm in their bliss for a long, long time.

At that time the world is wholly covered in water, dark with a blinding darkness. No moon or sun, no constellations are to be seen, nor the forms of stars; there are no nights or days, no phases of the moon or months, no seasons or years. And there are no men or women then, for the beings living on earth are simply reckoned as beings. And for those beings, after a long, long time, a sweet earth is spread out on the waters, just as the skin forms on the surface of hot milk as it cools. And it had [2] color, fragrance and flavor, for it was the color of fine ghee or butter, and sweet as the choicest honey.

Then a certain being, greedy from a former birth, said, "What can this be?" and tasted the sweet earth with his finger. He was delighted with the flavor, and craving overcame him. Then others followed his example, and tasted the earth, . . . until they were all feasting on it, breaking off pieces with their hands. And as they did so their radiance faded; and as it faded the moon and sun appeared, with the constellations and the forms of stars, nights and days, phases of the moon and months, seasons and years. . . .

Beings continued thus, feeding on the sweet earth, for a long, long time. And the more they ate the more solid their bodies became, some beautiful and some ugly. And the beautiful scorned the ugly, boasting of their greater beauty. And as they became vain and conceited because of their beauty the sweet earth disappeared. . . .

Then growths appeared on the soil, coming up like mushrooms, with

---

[2] The change of tense occurs in the original.

color, scent and flavor like those of the sweet earth. The beings began to eat those growths, and so they continued for a long, long time . . . until the growths too disappeared.

Then creeping plants arose, growing like rattans; and the beings lived on them until the creepers too disappeared. . . .

Then, when the creepers had vanished, rice appeared, already ripe in the untilled soil, without dust or husk, fragrant and clean-grained. If they gathered it in the evening and took it away for supper it would grow and be ripe again by the next morning. If they gathered it in the morning for breakfast it would grow and be ripe again by the evening. It grew without a pause. And those beings continued to live on the rice . . . for a long, long time, and their bodies became more and more solid, and their differences in beauty, even more pronounced. In women female characteristics appeared, and in men male. The women looked at the men too intently, and the men at the women, and so passion arose, and a raging fire entered their bodies. In consequence they took to coupling together. When people saw them doing so some threw dust at them, others ashes, others cowdung, and shouted, "Perish, you foul one! Perish, you foul one!! How could one person treat another like that?" And even now people in certain districts, when a bride is led away after a wedding, throw dust or ashes or cowdung, and repeat the custom of long ago, but do not understand its significance.

What was considered immoral in those days is now considered moral. For in those days the people who took to coupling together were not allowed to enter a village or town for a month afterward or even for two. So, as they incurred so much blame for their immorality, they took to building huts in order to conceal it.

Then someone of a lazy disposition thought to himself, "Why do I go to the trouble of fetching rice night and morning? I'll fetch enough for supper and breakfast in one journey!" Then another man saw him and said, "Come on, my friend, let's go and fetch our rice!" "I've got enough," the first man replied, "I've fetched enough in one journey for both supper and breakfast." So the second man followed the first man's example, and fetched enough rice for two days at once. [Thus gradually people took to storing enough rice for as much as eight days at a time]. . . . And from the time that people took to feeding on stored rice the grain became covered with dust, and husks enveloped it; the reaped stems did not grow again, and there were pauses in its growth, when the stubble stood in clumps.

Then the people gathered together and lamented, saying: "Evil customs have appeared among men. Once we were made of the stuff of mind . . . and were firm in our bliss for a long, long time. . . . But now, through our evil and immoral ways, we have degenerated until our grain has become covered with dust . . . and the stubble stands in clumps. So let us divide the rice fields, and set up boundary marks."

Then someone of a greedy disposition, while watching his own plot, appropriated another plot that had not been given to him, and made use of it. The people seized him and said: "You've done an evil deed in taking and using a plot which was not given to you. Don't let it happen again!" "Very well," he replied. But he did the same thing again and yet a third time. Once more the people seized him and admonished him in the same terms, but this time some of them struck him with their hands, some with clods, and some with sticks. From such beginnings arose theft, censure, false speech, and punishment.

Then the people gathered together and lamented, saying: "Evil ways are rife among the people—theft, censure, false speech, and punishment have appeared among us. Let us choose one man from among us, to dispense wrath, censure, and banishment when they are right and proper, and give him a share of our rice in return. So they chose the most handsome, . . . attractive, and capable among them and invited him to dispense anger, censure, and banishment. He consented and did so, and they gave him a share of their rice.

Mahāsammata means approved (*sammata*) by the whole people (*mahājana*), and hence Mahāsammata was the first name to be given to a ruler. He was lord of the fields (*khettānam*) and hence *khattiya* [Skt. *kṣatriya*] was his second name. He pleases (*rañjeti*) others by his righteousness—hence his third name, *rājā*.[3] This was the origin of the class of kshatriyas, according to the tale of long ago.[4] They originated from those same folk and no others, people like themselves, in no way different; and their origin was quite natural and not otherwise.

Then it happened that some men thought, "Evil ways are rife among

[3] It is hardly necessary to say that these etymologies of *khattiya* and *rājā* are false, as are those which follow. They are significant nevertheless.

[4] It is noteworthy that in the Pāli scriptures the kshatriya is regularly mentioned before the brāhman.

the people. . . . Now let us put away such evil and unwholesome ways."
The word *brāhman* implies that they put away (*bāhenti*) such evil and
unwholesome ways, and so brāhman became their earliest name. They
built themselves huts of leaves in the woodland, and there they sat and
meditated. They had no more use for charcoal or the smoke of cooking,
or for the pestle and mortar, but they went out to villages, towns, or cities,
seeking their food, in the evening their supper, in the morning their
breakfast. When they had enough to eat they came back and meditated in
their huts, and so they were given the second name of mystics (*jhāyaka*)
because they meditated (*jhāyanti*).

Now some of them grew tired of meditating in their huts, and so they
went away, settled on the outskirts of villages and towns, and made
books.[5] When they saw this the people said, "These good folk can't meditate!", and so they were called teachers (*ajjhāyaka*),[6] and this became their
third name. In those days these teachers were looked on as the lowest of
brāhmans, but now they are thought the best. This was the origin of the
class of brāhmans. . . . They originated quite naturally and not otherwise.

There were other people who married and took to all kinds of crafts
and trades; and because they took to all kinds (*vissa*) of crafts and trades
they were called *vessa* [Skt. *vaiśya*]. This was the origin of the class of
vaishyas. . . . They originated quite naturally and not otherwise.

Those who remained were hunters. Those who live by hunting (*ludda*)
have a mean (*khudda*) trade, and thus they were called *sudda* (Skt.
śūdra). This was the origin of the class of shūdras. . . . They originated
quite naturally and not otherwise.

Then there came a time when a kshatriya, scorning his own way of life,
went out from his home and took up the homeless life, thinking to become
an ascetic—[and then a brāhman, a vaishya, and a shūdra did the same].
From these four classes arose the class of ascetics. . . . And they too
originated quite naturally and not otherwise.

A kshatriya who has led a bad life, whether in deed, word, or thought,
and who has had wrong views about the world, because of his outlook and
his deeds will be reborn after parting with his body in the waste and woe-

---

[5] According to the commentary, the three Vedas.

[6] An untranslatable play on words. *A-jhāyaka* means a non-meditator, and *ajjhāyaka* a
reciter or teacher of the Vedas.

ful pit of purgatory. And a brāhman, a vaishya, and a shūdra will fare likewise. If on the other hand they lead good lives in thought, word, and deed, and have right views about the world, they will be reborn in the happy world of heaven. If their lives and their views are mixed they will be reborn in a state where they feel both happiness and sorrow. But if they are self-restrained in body, speech and mind . . . they may find Nirvāna, even in this present life.

For whoever from among the members of these four classes becomes a monk and later a perfected being, with all his stains destroyed, has done what he had to do; he has laid down his burden, gained salvation, destroyed the bonds of becoming; he is free in his perfect wisdom. And he is declared to be to the chief of them all, by the law of Righteousness and not otherwise; for the Law is the best thing men can have, both in this life and the next.

The Ideal of Government, and the Decay and Growth of Civilization

The following *Discourse*, again attributed to the Buddha, attempts, like the preceding one, to account for the origin of crime and evil, but it gives a different answer. According to a former passage crime began in the state of nature, and kingship was introduced to suppress it. Here government precedes crime. The golden age has its governments and indeed its conquests, but they are not conquests by the sword. It seems more than likely that this account of the Universal Emperor's peaceful victories over his neighbors is in some way linked with Ashoka's "Conquest by Righteousness," and we are inclined to believe that the present passage is post-Ashokan. Note that sin and crime, and the consequent lowering of the standards of civilization and of human conditions generally, are said to be due to the shortcomings of the ruler, and especially to his failure to continue the policy of his predecessors in caring for the poor. Hence crime appears, morality declines, and with it the standards of life deteriorate, until, after a brief period of complete anarchy, human love and fellowship again prevail, and gradually restore the golden age. Interesting is the reference to Metteya (Sanskrit, *Maitreya*), the future Buddha. This indicates that the *Discourse* is a comparatively late one. Our version is considerably abridged.

[From *Dīgha Nikāya,* 3.58 ff.]

In the past . . . there was a king called Dalhanemi. He was a Universal Emperor . . . a king of Righteousness, a conqueror of the four quarters, a protector of his people, a possessor of the Seven Jewels—the Wheel, the Elephant, and Horse, the Gem, the Woman, the Householder, and the General.[7] He had over a thousand sons, all heroes brave of body, crushers of enemy armies.[8] He conquered the earth from ocean to ocean and ruled it not by the rod or by the sword, but by the Law of Righteousness.

Now after many thousands of years King Dalhanemi ordered one of his men thus: "When you see that the Divine Wheel has sunk or slipped from its place, come and tell me." . . . And after many thousand years more the man saw that the Divine Wheel had sunk . . . and went and told the King. So King Dalhanemi sent for his eldest son, and said: "Dear boy, the Divine Wheel has sunk, and I've been told that when the Wheel of a Universal Emperor sinks he has not long to live. I have had my fill of human pleasure—now the time has come for me to look for divine joys. Come, dear boy, you must take charge of the earth. . . ." So King Dalhanemi duly established his eldest son on the throne, shaved his hair and beard, put on yellow robes, and left his home for the state of homelessness. And when the royal sage had left his home seven days the Divine Wheel completely vanished.

Then a certain man went to the King, the anointed warrior, and told him that it had vanished. He was beside himself with sorrow. So he went to the royal sage his father and told him about it. "Don't grieve that the Divine Wheel has disappeared," he said. "The Divine Wheel isn't an heirloom, my dear boy! You must follow the noble way of the Universal Emperors. If you do this and keep the fast of the full moon on the upper terrace of your palace the Divine Wheel will be seen again, complete with its thousand spokes, its tire, its nave, and all its other parts."

"But what, your Majesty, is the noble way of the Universal Emperors?"

"It is this, dear boy, that you should rely on the Law of Righteousness, honor, revere, respect, and worship it. You should be yourself the banner

[7] A Universal Emperor (Pāli, *Cakkavatti;* Skt. *Cakravartin*) is a figure of cosmic significance, and corresponds on the material plane to a Buddha on the spiritual. Thus, according to the legend of the Buddha, it was prophesied at the birth of Siddhārtha Gautama that he would either become a Buddha or a Universal Emperor. Universal Emperors invariably have the Seven Jewels, which are perfect specimens of their kinds, and are the magical insignia of their owners. The Woman is of course the chief queen. In most lists the Crown Prince takes the place of the Householder.

[8] The Universal Emperor is not thoroughly adapted to the ethics of Buddhism, and though he conquers by force of character even the Buddhist author cannot disconnect him wholly from the usual militancy of the Indian king.

of Righteousness, the emblem of Righteousness, with Righteousness as your master. According to Righteousness you should guard, protect, and watch over your own family and people, your armed forces, your warriors, your officers, priests and householders, townsmen and country folk, ascetics and brāhmans, beasts and birds. There should be no evil-doing throughout your domains, and whoever is poor in your land should be given wealth. . . . Avoid evil and follow good. That is the noble way of the Universal Emperors."

"Very good, your Majesty," the King replied, and he followed the way of the Universal Emperors, until one day the Divine Wheel revealed itself . . . complete and whole. And he thought: "A king to whom the Divine Wheel reveals itself thus becomes a Universal Emperor—so may I now become such a Universal Emperor." He uncovered one shoulder, took a pitcher of water in his left hand, and sprinkled the Divine Wheel with his right, saying: "Roll on, precious Wheel! Go forth and conquer, lordly and precious Wheel!"

Then the precious Wheel rolled on toward the east, and the King followed it with his fourfold army. Wherever the Wheel stopped the Universal Emperor encamped with his army, and all the kings of the east came to him and said, "Come, your Majesty! Welcome, your Majesty! All this is yours, Your Majesty! Command, us, your Majesty!" And the Universal Emperor said, "Do not take life; do not take what is not yours; do not act basely in sexual matters; do not tell falsehoods; do not drink spirits.[9] Now enjoy your kingdoms as you have done in the past." And all the kings of the east submitted to him.

Then the Divine Wheel plunged into the eastern ocean, and rose again and rolled towards the south. And so the Wheel conquered the south, west, and north, until it had covered the whole earth from sea to sea. Then it returned to the capital, and stood at the door of the Universal Emperor's private apartments, facing the council hall, as though fixed to the place, adorning the inner palace.

With the passage of many thousands of years other kings did as this one had done, and became Universal Emperors—and it all happened as it had done before. But one day a Universal Emperor left his palace to become an ascetic, and his son, who succeeded him, heard that the Divine Wheel had vanished, but, though grieved at its disappearance, did not go

[9] These are the five precepts which all Buddhist laymen must do their best to follow.

to his father, the royal sage, to ask about the noble way of the Universal Emperors. He ruled the land according to his own ideas, and the people were not governed as they had been in the past; so they did not prosper as they had done under former kings who had followed the noble way of the Universal Emperors.

Then the ministers and counsellors, the officers of the treasury, the captains of the guard, the ushers, and the magicians, came to the King in a body and said: "The people do not prosper, your Majesty, because you govern them according to your own ideas. Now, we maintain the noble way of the Universal Emperors. Ask us about it and we will tell you." The King asked them about it and they explained it to him. When he had heard them he provided for the care and protection of the land, but he did not give wealth to the poor, and so poverty became widespread. Soon a certain man took what had not been given to him, and this was called stealing. They caught him and accused him before the King.

"Is it true that you have taken what was not given to you?" asked the King.

"It is, your Majesty," replied the man.

"But why did you do it?"

"Because I'd nothing to live on, your Majesty."

Then the King gave him wealth, saying, "With this keep yourself alive, care for your father and mother, children and wife, follow a trade, and give alms to ascetics and brāhmans, to help yourself along the way to heaven."

"I will, your Majesty," he replied.

And another man stole and was accused before the King, and the King rewarded him in just the same way. People heard of this and thought that they would do the same in order to receive wealth from the King. But when a third man was brought before the King and accused of theft the King thought: "If I give wealth to everyone who takes another man's property theft will increase. I'll put a stop to this! I'll sentence him to execution and have him beheaded!"

So he ordered his men to tie the culprit's arms tightly behind him with a strong rope, to shave his head with a razor, to lead him from street to street and from square to square to the strident sound of the drum, and to take him out of the southern gate of the city, and there to cut off his head. And they did as the King commanded.

But when people heard that thieves were to be put to death they thought: "We'll have sharp swords made, and when we steal we'll cut off the heads of those we rob." And they did so, and looted in village and town and city, besides committing highway robbery.

Thus, where formerly wealth had been given to the poor, poverty became widespread. Hence came theft, hence the sword, hence murder . . . and hence the span of life was shortened and men lost their comeliness, until where the fathers had lived for eighty thousand years the sons lived for only forty thousand.

Then it happened that a certain man stole and was accused, and when the King asked him whether it was true that he had stolen he replied, "No." Thus lying became widespread, and where the fathers had lived for forty thousand years the sons lived for only twenty thousand.

And again, when a certain man took what was not given him, another man came to the King and said: "So and so has taken what was not given him, he has committed . . . theft." Thus he spoke evil of the thief. So speaking evil of others became widespread, until where the fathers had lived for twenty thousand years the sons lived for only ten thousand.

Now some people were handsome and some ugly. And the ugly were jealous of the handsome, and took to committing adultery with other men's wives. So base conduct in sexual matters became widespread, and men's life-span and comeliness diminished until where the fathers had lived for ten thousand years the sons lived for only five thousand.

Next abusive speech and foolish gossip increased, and so where the fathers had lived for five thousand years the sons lived some for two thousand five hundred and some for two thousand years. Then cupidity and ill-will increased, and the life-span became only one thousand years. With the growth of false doctrines it fell to five hundred, and then incest, inordinate greed, and unnatural lust spread, and hence the span of life dropped to two hundred and fifty or two hundred years. Finally three further sins—disrespect for father and mother, disrespect for ascetics and brāhmans, and refusal to heed the head of the family—reduced man's life to one hundred years.

A time will come when the descendants of these people will live for only ten years, and when girls will reach puberty at the age of five. Then there will not be even the taste of ghee, butter, sesamum oil, sugar, or salt, and the finest food of the men of that time will be mere millet, where now it is rice and curry. Among those men . . . good deeds will entirely disappear, and evil deeds will flourish exceedingly—there will not even be a word for good, much less anyone who does good deeds. Those who do not honor mother and father, ascetic and brāhman, and those who do not heed the head of the family will be respected and praised, just as today those who do these things are respected and praised.

Among those people there will be no distinction of mother or aunt or aunt-by-marriage or teacher's wife—society will be just as promiscuous as goats and sheep, fowls and pigs, dogs and jackals. There will be bitter enmity one with another, bitter ill-will, bitter animosity, bitter thoughts of murder, and parents will feel toward their children, children toward their parents, brothers toward their brothers . . . as a hunter feels toward a deer.

Then there will be a transitional period of the Seven Days of the Sword, during which men will look upon one another as wild beasts, and with sharp swords in their hands will take one another's lives. . . . But a few will think: "We don't want anyone to kill us and we don't want to kill anyone. Let us hide in grassland, in jungle, in hollow trees, in river-marshes, or in the rough places of the mountains, and live on the roots and fruits of the forest."

And thus they will survive. And after the Seven Days of the Sword are passed they will come out and embrace one another, and with one accord comfort one another, saying, "How good it is, my friend, to see you still alive!" Then they will say: "We have lost so many of our kins-folk because we took to evil ways—now we must do good! But what good deed can we do? We must stop taking life—that is a good custom to adopt and maintain!"

They will do this, and increase in both age and comeliness. And their virtues will increase until once more they live to the age of eighty thousand years and girls reach puberty at the age of five hundred. . . . India will be rich and prosperous, with villages and towns and cities so close together that a cock could fly from one to the next. India will be as crowded then as purgatory is now, as full of people as a thicket is of canes or reeds. Vārānasī . . . will be a rich and prosperous capital, full of people, crowded, and flourishing, and there will be born Sankha, a Universal Emperor, who will . . . like Dalhanemi . . . conquer the earth from ocean to ocean and rule it . . . by the Law of Righteousness.

And among those people will be born the Lord Metteya, the perfected being, the fully enlightened, endowed with wisdom and virtue, the blessed, the knower of all the worlds, the supreme guide of willing men, the teacher of gods and men, a Lord Buddha, even as I am now. Like me, with his own insight, he will know the world and see it clearly, with its spirits, with Māra, with Brahmā, with its ascetics and brāhmans, with its gods and men. He will teach the Law of Righteousness in spirit and in letter, lovely in its beginning, lovely in its middle, lovely in its end, and he will live the pure life of celibacy in all its completeness, just as I do now. But he will have thousands of monks as his followers, where I have only hundreds.

Conditions of the Welfare of Societies

The following passage occurs in the *Discourse of the Great Passing-away*, which describes the last days and death of the Buddha. Though the words are put into his own mouth, it is quite likely that the passage is based on a series of popular aphorisms current among the Vajjian tribesmen themselves. It is followed by a longer passage in which the Buddha is purported to have adapted the list of the seven conditions of the welfare of republics to the circumstances of the Buddhist Order. According to a tradition preserved by the commentator Buddhaghosa, King Ajātasattu's wily minister Vassakāra, hearing the Buddha's words, set to work by "fifth column" methods to sow dissension among the leaders of the Vajjis, with the result that Magadha was able to annex their lands within a few years.

Notice especially the third condition. No early Indian sect took kindly to innovation, and according to orthodox Hindu thought the purpose of government was not to legislate, but only to administer the eternal law (*Sanātana-dharma*). Though the Buddhists had a somewhat different conception of dharma they shared the conservatism of the Hindus in this respect. Nevertheless new legislation was enacted from time to time, as will be seen later in the edicts of Ashoka.

[From *Dīgha Nikāya*, 2.72 ff.]

Once the Lord was staying at Rājagaha on the hill called Vulture's Peak . . . and the Venerable Ānanda was standing behind him and fanning him. And the Lord said: "Have you heard, Ānanda, that the Vajjis call frequent public assemblies of the tribe?" "Yes, Lord," he replied.

"As long as they do so," said the Lord, "they may be expected not to decline, but to flourish."

"As long as they meet in concord, conclude their meetings in concord, and carry out their policies in concord; . . . as long as they make no laws not already promulgated, and set aside nothing enacted in the past, acting in accordance with the ancient institutions of the Vajjis established in olden days; . . . as long as they respect, esteem, reverence, and support the elders of the Vajjis, and look on it as a duty to heed their words; . . . as long as no women or girls of their tribes are held by force or abducted; . . . as long as they respect, esteem, reverence, and support the shrines of the Vajjis, whether in town or country, and do not neglect the proper offerings and rites laid down and practiced in the past; [10] . . . as long as they give due protection, deference, and support to the perfected beings among them so that such perfected beings may come to the land from afar and live comfortably among them, so long may they be expected not to decline, but to flourish.

Birth Is No Criterion of Worth

Though in practice it would seem that Indian Buddhists maintained the system of class and caste, the theoretical attitude of Buddhism was equalitarian. We have seen that the division of the four classes was believed to be a functional one, with no divine sanction. The Buddhist view is summed up in the verse of the *Discourse Section* (*Sutta Nipāta*, verse 136):

> No brāhman is such by birth.
> No outcaste is such by birth.
> An outcaste is such by his deeds.
> A brāhman is such by his deeds.

In the following passage the Buddha puts forward numerous arguments in favor of this view, though many other passages show that lay Buddhists were encouraged to treat worthy brāhmans with respect.
[From *Majjhima Nikāya*, 2.147 ff.]

Once when the Lord was staying at Sāvatthī there were five hundred brāhmans from various countries in the city . . . and they thought: "This ascetic Gautama preaches that all four classes are pure. Who can refute him?"

At that time there was a young brāhman named Assalāyana in the city, . . . a youth of sixteen, thoroughly versed in the Vedas . . . and in all brāhmanic learning. "He can do it!", thought the brāhmans, and so they

---

[10] Note the respect paid to popular religion, which Buddhism adapted in the cults of the sacred tree and the stūpa, and later in that of the image.

asked him to try; but he answered, "The ascetic Gautama teaches a doctrine of his own,[1] and such teachers are hard to refute. I can't do it!" They asked him a second time . . . and again he refused; and they asked him a third time, pointing out that he ought not to admit defeat without giving battle. This time he agreed, and so, surrounded by a crowd of brāhmans, he went to the Lord, and, after greeting him, sat down and said:

"Brāhmans maintain that only they are the highest class, and the others are below them. They are white, the others black; only they are pure, and not the others. Only they are the true sons of Brahmā, born from his mouth,[2] born of Brahmā, creations of Brahmā, heirs of Brahmā. Now what does the worthy Gautama say to that?"

"Do the brāhmans really maintain this, Assalāyana, when they're born of women just like anyone else, of brāhman women who have their periods and conceive, give birth and nurse their children, just like any other women?"

"For all you say, this is what they think. . . ."

"Have you ever heard that in the lands of the Greeks and Kambojas and other peoples on the borders there are only two classes, masters and slaves, and a master can become a slave and vice versa?"

"Yes, I've heard so."

"And what strength or support does that fact give to the brāhmans' claim?"

"Nevertheless, that is what they think."

"Again if a man is a murderer, a thief, or an adulterer, or commits other grave sins, when his body breaks up on death does he pass on to purgatory if he's a kshatriya, vaishya, or shūdra, but not if he's a brāhman?"

"No, Gautama. In such a case the same fate is in store for all men, whatever their class."

"And if he avoids grave sin, will he go to heaven if he's a brāhman, but not if he's a man of the lower classes?"

---

[1] *Dhammavādi:* Our translation is on the basis of Buddhaghosa's commentary as generally interpreted. Dr. A. K. Warder suggests that the term may here mean "a teacher maintaining that the world is governed by natural law."

[2] According to the *Puruṣa Sūkta* (*Rig Veda,* 10.90) brāhmans are born from the head of the primeval man, while the other three classes are born from his arms, trunk, and feet, respectively.

"No, Gautama. In such a case the same reward awaits all men, whatever their class."

"And is a brāhman capable of developing a mind of love without hate or ill-will, but not a man of the other classes?"

"No, Gautama. All four classes are capable of doing so."

"Can only a brāhman go down to a river and wash away dust and dirt, and not men of the other classes?"

"No, Gautama, all four classes can."

"Now suppose a king were to gather together a hundred men of different classes and to order the brāhmans and kshatriyas to take kindling wood of sāl, pine, lotus or sandal, and light fires, while the low class folk did the same with common wood. What do you think would happen? Would the fires of the high-born men blaze up brightly . . . and those of the humble fail?"

"No, Gautama. It would be alike with high and lowly. . . . Every fire would blaze with the same bright flame." . . .

"Suppose there are two young brāhman brothers, one a scholar and the other uneducated. Which of them would be served first at memorial feasts, festivals, and sacrifices, or when entertained as guests?"

"The scholar, of course; for what great benefit would accrue from entertaining the uneducated one?"

"But suppose the scholar is ill-behaved and wicked, while the uneducated one is well-behaved and virtuous?"

"Then the uneducated one would be served first, for what great benefit would accrue from entertaining an ill-behaved and wicked man?"

"First, Assalāyana, you based your claim on birth, then you gave up birth for learning, and finally you have come round to my way of thinking, that all four classes are equally pure!"

At this Assalāyana sat silent . . . his shoulders hunched, his eyes cast down, thoughtful in mind, and with no answer at hand.

Ashoka: The Buddhist Emperor

The great emperor Ashoka (c.268–233 B.C.), third of the line of the Mauryas, became a Buddhist and attempted to govern India according to the precepts of Buddhism as he understood them. His new policy was promulgated in a series of edicts, which are still to be found, engraved on rocks and pillars in many parts of India. Written in a form of Prākrit, or ancient vernacular, with several local variations, they can claim little literary merit, for their style is crabbed and often ambiguous. In one of these edicts he describes his conversion, and its effects:

[From the Thirteenth Rock Edict]
When the king, Beloved of the Gods and of Gracious Mien, had been consecrated eight years Kalinga [1] was conquered, 150,000 people were deported, 100,000 were killed, and many times that number died. But after the conquest of Kalinga, the Beloved of the Gods began to follow Righteousness (Dharma), to love Righteousness, and to give instruction in Righteousness. Now the Beloved of the Gods regrets the conquest of Kalinga, for when an independent country is conquered people are killed, they die, or are deported, and that the Beloved of the Gods finds very painful and grievous. And this he finds even more grievous—that all the inhabitants—brāhmans, ascetics, and other sectarians, and householders who are obedient to superiors, parents, and elders, who treat friends, acquaintances, companions, relatives, slaves, and servants with respect, and are firm in their faith—all suffer violence, murder, and separation from their loved ones. Even those who are fortunate enough not to have lost those near and dear to them are afflicted at the misfortunes of friends, acquaintances, companions, and relatives. The participation of all men in common suffering is grievous to the Beloved of the Gods. Moreover there is no land, except that of the Greeks, where groups of brāhmans and ascetics are not found, or where men are not members of one sect or another. So now, even if the number of those killed and captured in the conquest of Kalinga had been a hundred or a thousand times less, it would be grievous to the Beloved of the Gods. The Beloved of the Gods will forgive as far as he can, and he even conciliates the forest tribes of his dominions; but he warns them that there is power even in the remorse of the Beloved of the Gods, and he tells them to reform, lest they be killed.[2]

For all beings the Beloved of the Gods desires security, self-control, calm of mind, and gentleness. The Beloved of the Gods considers that

[1] The coastal region comprising the modern Orissa and the northern part of Āndhra State.

[2] Note that Ashoka has by no means completely abandoned the use of force. This passage probably refers to the wild uncivilized tribesmen of the hills and jungles, who still occasionally cause trouble in Assam and some other parts of India, and in ancient days were a much greater problem.

the greatest victory is the victory of Righteousness; and this he has won here (in India) and even five hundred leagues beyond his frontiers in the realm of the Greek king Antiochus, and beyond Antiochus among the four kings Ptolemy, Antigonus, Magas, and Alexander.[3] Even where the envoys of the Beloved of the Gods have not been sent men hear of the way in which he follows and teaches Righteousness, and they too follow it and will follow it. Thus he achieves a universal conquest, and conquest always gives a feeling of pleasure; yet it is but a slight pleasure, for the Beloved of the Gods only looks on that which concerns the next life as of great importance.

I have had this inscription of Righteousness engraved that all my sons and grandsons may not seek to gain new victories, that in whatever victories they may gain they may prefer forgiveness and light punishment, that they may consider the only [valid] victory the victory of Righteousness, which is of value both in this world and the next, and that all their pleasure may be in Righteousness. . . .

Ashoka's Buddhism, as his title shows, did not lessen his belief in the gods. Here he expresses his faith in Buddhism, and declares that the gods have appeared on earth as a result of his reforms: [4]

[From a minor Rock Edict (Maski Version)]
Thus speaks Ashoka, the Beloved of the Gods. For two and a half years I have been an open follower of the Buddha, though at first I did not make much progress. But for more than a year now I have drawn closer to the [Buddhist] Order, and have made much progress. In India the gods who formerly did not mix with men now do so. This is the result of effort, and may be obtained not only by the great, but even by the small, through effort—thus they may even easily win heaven.

Father and mother should be obeyed, teachers should be obeyed; pity . . . should be felt for all creatures. These virtues of Righteousness should be practiced. . . . This is an ancient rule, conducive to long life.

[3] Antiochus II Theos of Syria, Ptolemy II Philadelphus of Egypt, Antigonus Gonatas of Macedonia, Magas of Cyrene, and Alexander of Epirus. Classical sources tell us nothing about Ashoka's "victories of Righteousness" over these kings. Probably he sent envoys to them, urging them to accept his new policy and his moral leadership. Evidently he never gave up his imperial ambitions, but attempted to further them in a benevolent spirit and without recourse to arms.

[4] Some authorities have put different interpretations on the relevant phrases, but in our opinion there can be little doubt about their meaning.

[From the Ninth Rock Edict]
It is good to give, but there is no gift, no service, like the gift of Righteousness. So friends, relatives, and companions should preach it on all occasions. This is duty; this is right; by this heaven may be gained—and what is more important than to gain heaven?

The emphasis on morality is if anything intensified in the series of the seven Pillar Edicts, issued some thirteen years after the Rock Edicts, when the king had been consecrated twenty-six years:

[From the First Pillar Edict]
This world and the other are hard to gain without great love of Righteousness, great self-examination, great obedience, great circumspection, great effort. Through my instruction respect and love of Righteousness daily increase and will increase. . . . For this is my rule—to govern by Righteousness, to administer by Righteousness, to please my subjects by Righteousness, and to protect them by Righteousness.

Ashoka's solicitude extended to the animal life of his empire, which in ancient India was generally thought to be subject to the king, just as was human life. He banned animal sacrifices at least in his capital, introduced virtual vegetarianism in the royal household, and limited the slaughter of certain animals; his policy in this respect is made clear in his very first Rock Edict:

[From the First Rock Edict]
Here [5] no animal is to be killed for sacrifice, and no festivals are to be held, for the king finds much evil in festivals,[6] except for certain festivals which he considers good.

Formerly in the Beloved of the God's kitchen several hundred thousand animals were killed daily for food; but now at the time of writing only three are killed—two peacocks and a deer, though the deer not regularly. Even these three animals will not be killed in future.

[From the Second Pillar Edict]
I have in many ways given the gift of clear vision. On men and animals, birds and fish I have conferred many boons, even to saving their lives; and I have done many other good deeds.

[5] There is some reason to believe that the adverb implies the royal capital of Pāṭaliputra.
[6] Samāja, generally interpreted as a fair or festival, but perhaps a society or club. A tone of rather pompous puritanism is sometimes evident in the edicts, and suggests a less congenial side of Ashoka's character.

In accordance with the precepts of Buddhism Ashoka, for all his apparent other-worldliness, did not neglect the material welfare of his subjects, and was specially interested in giving them medical aid:

[From the Second Rock Edict]
Everywhere in the empire of the Beloved of the Gods, and even beyond his frontiers in the lands of the Cholas, Pāndyas, Satyaputras, Keralaputras,[7] and as far as Ceylon, and in the kingdoms of Antiochus the Greek king and the kings who are his neighbors, the Beloved of the Gods has provided medicines for man and beast. Wherever medicinal plants have not been found they have been sent there and planted. Roots and fruits have also been sent where they did not grow, and have been planted. Wells have been dug along the roads for the use of man and beast.

Ashoka felt a moral responsibility not only for his own subjects, but for all men, and he realized that they could not lead moral lives, and gain merit in order to find a place in heaven, unless they were happy and materially well cared for:

[From the Sixth Rock Edict]
I am not satisfied simply with hard work or carrying out the affairs of state, for I consider my work to be the welfare of the whole world, of which hard work and the carrying out of affairs are merely the basis. There is no better deed than to work for the welfare of the whole world, and all my efforts are made that I may clear my debt to all beings. I make them happy here and now that they may attain heaven in the life to come. . . . But it is difficult without great effort.

He speaks in peremptory tones to the officers of state who are slow in putting the new policy into effect:

[From the First Separate Kalinga Edict]
By order of the Beloved of the Gods. Addressed to the officers in charge of Tosali.[8] . . . Let us win the affection of all men. All men are my children, and as I wish all welfare and happiness in this world and the next for my own children, so do I wish it for all men. But you do not realize what this entails—here and there an officer may understand in part, but not entirely.

[7] Tamil kingdoms, in the southern tip of the Peninsula.
[8] The chief town of Kalinga, the region conquered by Ashoka in his last war of aggression.

Often a man is imprisoned and tortured unjustly, and then he is liberated for no [apparent] reason. Many other people suffer also [as a result of this injustice]. Therefore it is desirable that you should practice impartiality, but it cannot be attained if you are inclined to habits of jealousy, irritability, harshness, hastiness, obstinacy, laziness, or lassitude. I desire you not to have these habits. The basis of all this is the constant advoidance of irritability and hastiness in your business. . . .

This inscription has been engraved in order that the officials of the city should always see to it that no one is ever imprisoned or tortured without good cause. To ensure this I shall send out every five years on a tour of inspection officers who are not fierce or harsh. . . . The prince at Ujjain shall do the same not more than every three years, and likewise at Taxila.

Later, in his Pillar Edicts, Ashoka seems more satisfied that his officers are carrying out the new policy:

[From the Fourth Pillar Edict]
My governors are placed in charge of hundreds of thousands of people. Under my authority they have power to judge and to punish, that they calmly and fearlessly carry out their duties, and that they may bring welfare and happiness to the people of the provinces and be of help to them. They will know what brings joy and what brings sorrow, and, conformably to Righteousness, they will instruct the people of the provinces that they may be happy in this world and the next. . . . And as when one entrusts a child to a skilled nurse one is confident that . . . she will care for it well, so have I appointed my governors for the welfare and happiness of the people. That they may fearlessly carry out their duties I have given them power to judge and to inflict punishment on their own initiative. I wish that there should be uniformity of justice and punishment.

In numerous passages Ashoka stresses the hard work which the new policy demands of him. He has given up many of the pleasures of the traditional Indian king in order to further it, including, of course, hunting:

[From the Eighth Rock Edict]
In the past kings went out on pleasure trips and indulged in hunting and similar amusements. But the Beloved of the Gods . . . ten years after

his consecration set out on the journey to Enlightenment.[9] Now when he goes on tour . . . he interviews and gives gifts to brāhmans and ascetics; he interviews and gives money to the aged; he interviews the people of the provinces, and instructs and questions them on Righteousness; and the pleasure which the Beloved of the Gods derives therefrom is as good as a second revenue.

As we have seen, Ashoka, though a Buddhist, respects brāhmans and the members of all sects, and he calls on his subjects to follow his example:

[From the Twelfth Rock Edict]
The Beloved of the Gods . . . honors members of all sects, whether ascetics or householders, by gifts and various honors. But he does not consider gifts and honors as important as the furtherance of the essential message of all sects. This essential message varies from sect to sect, but it has one common basis, that one should so control one's tongue as not to honor one's own sect or disparage another's on the wrong occasions; for on certain occasions one should do so only mildly, and indeed on other occasions one should honor other men's sects. By doing this one strengthens one's own sect and helps the others, while by doing otherwise one harms one's own sect and does a disservice to the others. Whoever honors his own sect and disparages another man's, whether from blind loyalty or with the intention of showing his own sect in a favorable light, does his own sect the greatest possible harm. Concord is best, with each hearing and respecting the other's teachings. It is the wish of the Beloved of the Gods that members of all sects should be learned and should teach virtue. . . . Many officials are busied in this matter . . . and the result is the progress of my own sect and the illumination of Righteousness.

Though he was by no means a rationalist, it appears that Ashoka thought little of the many rituals and ceremonies of Indian domestic life:

[From the Ninth Rock Edict]
People perform various ceremonies, at the marriage of sons and daughters, at the birth of children, when going on a journey . . . or on other occasions. . . . On such occasions women especially perform many cere-

[9] This phrase probably merely implies that Ashoka made a pilgrimage to the Bodhi Tree at Gayā.

monies which are various, futile, and useless. Even when they have to be done [to conform to custom and keep up appearances] such ceremonies are of little use. But the ceremonies of Righteousness are of great profit —these are the good treatment of slaves and servants, respect for elders, self-mastery in one's relations with living beings, gifts to brāhmans and ascetics, and so on.[10] But for their success everyone—fathers, mothers, brothers, masters, friends, acquaintances, and neighbors—must agree— "These are good! These are the ceremonies that we should perform for success in our undertakings . . . and when we have succeeded we will perform them again!" Other ceremonies are of doubtful utility—one may achieve one's end through them or one may not. Moreover they are only of value in this world, while the value of the ceremonies of Righteousness is eternal, for even if one does not achieve one's end in this world one stores up boundless merit in the other, while if one achieves one's end in this world the gain is double.

We conclude this selection of the edicts of Ashoka with his last important inscription, in which the emperor, eighteen years after his conversion, reviews his reign:

[From the Seventh Pillar Edict]
In the past kings sought to make the people progress in Righteousness, but they did not progress. . . . And I asked myself how I might uplift them through progress in Righteousness. . . . Thus I decided to have them instructed in Righteousness, and to issue ordinances of Righteousness, so that by hearing them the people might conform, advance in the progress of Righteousness, and themselves make great progress. . . . For that purpose many officials are employed among the people to instruct them in Righteousness and to explain it to them. . . .

Moreover I have had banyan trees planted on the roads to give shade to man and beast; I have planted mango groves, and I have had ponds dug and shelters erected along the roads at every eight kos.[11] Everywhere I have had wells dug for the benefit of man and beast. But this benefit is but small, for in many ways the kings of olden time have worked for the welfare of the world; but what I have done has been done that men may conform to Righteousness.

[10] With this compare the *Admonition to Singāla* (p. 122 ff.).
[11] There is some uncertainty about the interpretation of this phrase. If that given above is correct, it implies intervals of about sixteen miles, or a day's journey.

All the good deeds that I have done have been accepted and followed by the people. And so obedience to mother and father, obedience to teachers, respect for the aged, kindliness to brāhmans and ascetics, to the poor and weak, and to slaves and servants, have increased and will continue to increase. . . . And this progress of Righteousness among men has taken place in two manners, by enforcing conformity to Righteousness, and by exhortation. I have enforced the law against killing certain animals and many others, but the greatest progress of Righteousness among men comes from exhortation in favor of noninjury to life and abstention from killing living beings.[12]

I have done this that it may endure . . . as long as the moon and sun, and that my sons and my great-grandsons may support it; for by supporting it they will gain both this world and the next.

[12] For all his humanitarianism, Ashoka did not abolish the death penalty, as was done by some later Indian kings.

CHAPTER VII

MAHĀYĀNA BUDDHISM: "THE GREATER VEHICLE"

From about the first or second century A.D. onwards, a new and very different kind of Buddhism arose in India. The new school, which claimed to offer salvation for all, styled itself *Mahāyāna*, the Greater Vehicle (to salvation), as opposed to the older Buddhism, which it contempuously referred to as *Hīnayāna,* or the Lesser Vehicle. The Mahāyāna scriptures also claimed to represent the final doctrines of the Buddha, revealed only to his most spiritually advanced followers, while the earlier doctrines were merely preliminary ones. Though Mahāyāna Buddhism, with its pantheon of heavenly buddhas and bodhisattvas and its idealistic metaphysics, was strikingly different in many respects from the Theravāda, it can be viewed as the development into finished systems of tendencies which had existed long before—a development favored and accelerated by the great historic changes taking place in northwestern India at that time. For over two hundred years, from the beginning of the second century B.C. onwards, this region was the prey of a succession of invaders—Bactrian Greeks, Scythians, Parthians, and a Central Asian people generally known to historians of India as Kushānas. As a result of these invasions Iranian and Western influences were felt much more strongly than before, and new peoples, with backgrounds very different from those of the folk among whom the religion arose, began to take interest in Buddhism.

A tendency to revere the Buddha as a god had probably existed in his own lifetime. In Indian religion, divinity is not something completely transcendent, or far exalted above all mortal things, as it is for the Jew, Christian, or Muslim, neither is it something concentrated in a single unique, omnipotent, and omniscient personality. In Indian religions godhead manifests itself in so many forms as to be almost if not quite ubiquitous, and every great sage or religious teacher is looked on as a special manifestation of divinity, in some sense a god in human form. How much more divine was the Buddha, to whom even the great god Brahmā himself did reverence, and who, in meditation, could far transcend the comparatively tawdry and transient heavens where the great gods dwelt, enter the world of formlessness, and pass thence to the ineffable Nirvāna itself? From the Buddhist point of view even the highest of the gods was liable to error, for Brahmā imagined himself to be the creator when in fact the world came into existence as a result of natural causes. The Buddha, on the other hand, was omniscient.

Yet, according to theory, the Buddha had passed completely away from the universe, had ceased in any sense to be a person, and no longer affected the world in any way. But the formula of the "Three Jewels"— "I take refuge in the Buddha, I take refuge in the Doctrine, I take refuge in the Order"—became the Buddhist profession of faith very early, and was used by monk and layman alike. Taken literally the first clause was virtually meaningless, for it was impossible to take refuge in a being who had ceased to exist as such. Nevertheless the Buddha was worshiped from very early times, and he is said to have himself declared that all who had faith in him and devotion to him would obtain rebirth in heaven. In some of the earliest Buddhist sculpture, such as that of the stūpa of Bharhut (second or first century b.c.), crowds of worshipers are depicted as ecstatically prostrating themselves before the emblems of the Buddha—the wheel, the footprints, the empty throne, or the trident-shaped symbol representing the Three Jewels. At this time it was evidently not thought proper to portray the Buddha or to represent him by an icon; but in the first century a.d., whether from the influence of Greco-Roman ideas and art forms or from that of indigenous popular cults, the Buddha was represented and worshiped as an image.

A further development which encouraged the tendency to theism was the growth of interest in the *bodhisattva*. This term, literally meaning "Being of Wisdom," was first used in the sense of a previous incarnation of the Buddha. For many lives before his final birth as Siddhārtha Gautama the Bodhisattva did mighty deeds of compassion and self-sacrifice, as he gradually perfected himself in wisdom and virtue. Stories of the Bodhisattva, known as *Birth Stories* (*Jātaka*) and often adapted from popular legends and fables, were very popular with lay Buddhists, and numerous illustrations of them occur in early Buddhist art.

It is probable that even in the lifetime of the Buddha it was thought that he was only the last of a series of earlier Buddhas. Later, perhaps through Zoroastrian influence, it came to be believed that other Buddhas were yet to come, and interest developed in *Maitreya*, the future Buddha, whose coming was said to have been prophesied by the historical Buddha, and who, in years to come, would purify the world with his teaching. But if Maitreya was yet to come the chain of being which would ultimately lead to his birth (or, in the terminology of other sects, his soul) must be already in existence. Somewhere in the universe the being later to become Maitreya Buddha was already active for good. And if this one, how many more? Logically the world must be full of bodhisattvas, all striving for the welfare of other beings.

The next step in the development of the new form of Buddhism was the changing of the goal at which the believer aimed. According to Buddhist teaching there are three types of perfected beings—*Buddhas,* who perceived the truth for themselves and taught it to others, *Pratyeka-buddhas,* "Private Buddhas," who perceived it, but kept it to themselves and did not teach it, and *Arhants*,[1] "Worthies," who learned it from others, but fully realized it for themselves. According to earlier schools the earnest believer should aspire to become an Arhant, a perfected being for whom there was no rebirth, who already enjoyed Nirvāna, and who would finally enter that state after death, all vestiges of his personality dissolved. The road to Nirvāna was a hard one, and could only be covered in many lives of virtue and self-sacrifice; but nevertheless the goal began to be looked on as selfish. Surely a bodhisattva, after achieving such exalted compassion and altruism, and after reaching such a degree of perfection that he could render inestimable help to other striving beings, would not pass as quickly as possible to Nirvāna, where he could be of no further use, but would deliberately choose to remain in the world, using his spiritual power to help others, until all had found salvation. Passages of Mahāyāna scriptures describing the self-sacrifice of the bodhisattva for the welfare of all things living are among the most passionately altruistic in the world's religious literature.

The replacement of the ideal of the Arhant by that of the bodhisattva is the basic distinction between the old sects and the new, which came to

---

[1] Pāli, *arahant,* usually translated "perfect being" in our extracts.

be known as *Mahāyāna*. Faith in the bodhisattvas and the help they afforded was thought to carry many beings along the road to bliss, while the older schools, which did not accept the bodhisattva ideal, could save only a few patient and strenuous souls.

The next stage in the evolution of the theology of the new Buddhism was the doctrine of the "Three Bodies" (*Trikāya*). If the true ideal was that of the bodhisattva, why did not Siddhārtha Gautama remain one, instead of becoming a Buddha and selfishly passing to Nirvāna? This paradox was answered by a theory of docetic type, which again probably had its origin in popular ideas prevalent among lay Buddhists at a very early period. Gautama was not in fact an ordinary man, but the manifestation of a great spiritual being. The Buddha had three bodies—the Body of Essence (*Dharmakāya*), the Body of Bliss (*Sambhogakāya*) and the Body of Magic Transformation (*Nirmāṇakāya*). It was the latter only which lived on earth as Siddhārtha Gautama, an emanation of the Body of Bliss, which dwelled forever in the heavens as a sort of supreme god. But the Body of Bliss was in turn the emanation of the Body of Essence, the ultimate Buddha, who pervaded and underlay the whole universe. Subtle philosophies and metaphysical systems were developed parallel with these theological ideas, and the Body of Essence was identified with Nirvāna. It was in fact the World Soul, the *Brahman* of the Upanishads, in a new form. In the fully developed Mahāyānist cosmology there were many Bodies of Bliss, all of them emanations of the single Body of Essence, but the heavenly Buddha chiefly concerned with our world was *Amitābha* ("Immeasurable Radiance"), who dwelt in *Sukhāvatī,* "the Happy Land," the heaven of the West. With him was associated the earthly Gautama Buddha, and a very potent and compassionate Bodhisattva, Avalokiteshvara ("the Lord Who Looks Down").

The older Buddhism and the newer flourished side by side in India during the early centuries of the Christian era, and we read of Buddhist monasteries in which some of the monks were Mahāyānist and some Hīnayānist. But in general the Buddhists of northwestern India were either Mahāyānists or members of Hīnayāna sects much affected by Mahāyānist ideas. The austerer forms of Hīnayāna seem to have been strongest in parts of western and southern India, and in Ceylon. It was from northwestern India, under the rule of the great Kushāna empire (first to third centuries A.D.) that Buddhism spread throughout central Asia to China; since it emanated from the northwest, it was chiefly of the Mahāyāna or near-Mahāyāna type.

We have already outlined the typical Mahāyāna teaching about the heavenly Buddhas and bodhisattvas, which is a matter of theology rather than of metaphysics. But Mahāyāna also produced philosophical theories which were argued with great ability, and which were influential on the thought of Hinduism, as well as on that of the Far East. The two chief schools of Mahāyāna philosophy were the *Mādhyamika* (Doctrine of the Middle Position) and the *Vijñānavāda* (Doctrine of Consciousness) or *Yogācāra* (The Way of Yoga). The former school, the founder of which was Nāgārjuna (first to second centuries A.D.), taught that the phenomenal world had only a qualified reality, thus opposing the doctrine of the Sarvāstivādins. A monk with defective eyesight may imagine that he sees flies in his begging bowl, and they have full reality for the percipient. Though the flies are not real the illusion of flies is. The Mādhyamika philosophers tried to prove that all our experience of the phenomenal world is like that of the short-sighted monk, that all beings labor under the constant illusion of perceiving things where in fact there is only emptiness. This Emptiness or Void (*Śūnyatā*) is all that truly exists, and hence the Mādhyamikas were sometimes also called *Śūnyavādins* ("exponents of the doctrine of emptiness"). But the phenomenal world is true pragmatically, and therefore has qualified reality for practical purposes. Yet the whole chain of existence is only real in this qualified sense, for it is composed of a series of transitory events, and these, being impermanent, cannot have reality in themselves. Emptiness, on the other hand, never changes. It is absolute truth and absolute being—in fact it is the same as Nirvāna and the Body of Essence of the Buddha.

Nāgārjuna's system, however, went farther than this. Nothing in the phenomenal world has full being, and all is ultimately unreal. Therefore every rational theory about the world is a theory about something unreal evolved by an unreal thinker with unreal thoughts. Thus, by the same process of reasoning, even the arguments of the Mādhyamika school in favor of the ultimate reality of Emptiness are unreal, and this argument against the Mādhyamika position is itself unreal, and so on in an infinite regress. Every logical argument can be reduced to absurdity by a process such as this. The ontological nihilism of Mādhyamika dialectic led to the development of a special sub-school devoted to logic, the *Prāsaṅgika* [2] which produced works of great subtlety.

The effect of Mādhyamika nihilism was not what might be expected. Sceptical philosophies in the West, such as that of existentialism, are generally strongly flavored with pessimism. The Mādhyamikas, however, were not pessimists. If the phenomenal world was ultimately unreal, Emptiness was real, for, though every logical proof of its existence was vitiated by the flaw of unreality, it could be experienced in meditation with a directness and certainty which the phenomenal world did not possess. The ultimate Emptiness was here and now, everywhere and all-embracing, and there was in fact no difference between the great Void and the phenomenal world. Thus all beings were already participants of the Emptiness which was Nirvāna, they were already Buddha if only they would realize it. This aspect of Mādhyamika philosophy was specially congenial to Chinese Buddhists, nurtured in the doctrine of the *Tao,* and it had much influence in the development of the special forms of Chinese and Japanese Buddhism, which often show a frank acceptance of the beauty of the world, and especially of the beauty of nature, as a vision of Nirvāna here and now.

The Vijnānavāda school was one of pure idealism, and may be compared to the systems of Berkeley and Hume. The whole universe exists only in the mind of the perceiver. The fact of illusion, as in the case of the flies in the short-sighted monk's bowl, or the experience of dreams, was adduced as evidence to show that all normal human experience was of the same type. It is possible for the monk in meditation to raise before his eyes visions of every kind which have quite as much vividness and semblance of truth as have ordinary perceptions; yet he knows that they have no objective reality. Perception therefore is no proof of the independent existence of any entity, and all perceptions may be explained as projections of the percipient mind. Vijnānavāda, like some Western idealist systems, found its chief logical difficulty in explaining the continuity and apparent regularity of the majority of our sense impressions, and in accounting for the fact that the impressions of most people who are looking at the same time in the same direction seem to cohere in a remarkably consistent manner. Bishop Berkeley, to escape this dilemma,

---

[2] So called from its preoccupation with *prasaṅga* the term used in Sanskrit logic for the *reductio ad absurdum.*

postulated a transcendent mind in which all phenomena were thoughts. The Vijnānavādins explained the regularity and coherence of sense impressions as due to an underlying store of perceptions (*ālayavijñāna*) evolving from the accumulation of traces of earlier sense-impressions. These are active, and produce impressions similar to themselves, according to a regular pattern, as seeds produce plants. Each being possesses one of these stores of perception, and beings which are generically alike will produce similar perceptions from their stores at the same time. By this strange conception, which bristles with logical difficulties and is one of the most difficult of all Indian philosophy, the Vijnānavādins managed to avoid the logical conclusion of idealism in solipsism. Moreover they admitted the existence of at least one entity independent of human thought—a pure and integral being without characteristics, about which nothing could truly be predicated because it was without predicates. This was called "Suchness" (*Tathatā*) and corresponded to the Emptiness or Void of the Mādhyamikas, and to the Brahman of Vedānta. Though the terminology is different the metaphysics of Mahāyāna Buddhism has much in common with the doctrines of some of the Upanishads and of Shankara. The latter probably learned much from Buddhism, and indeed was called by his opponents a crypto-Buddhist.

For the Vijnānavāda school salvation was to be obtained by exhausting the store of consciousness until it became pure being itself, and identical with the Suchness which was the only truly existent entity in the universe. The chief means of doing this, for those who had already reached a certain stage of spiritual development, was yogic praxis. Adepts of this school were taught to conjure up visions, so that, by realizing that visions and pragmatically real perceptions had the same vividness and subjective reality, they might become completely convinced of the total subjectivity of all phenomena. Thus the meditating monk would imagine himself a mighty god, leading an army of lesser gods against Māra, the spirit of the world and the flesh. The chief philosophers of the school were Asanga (fourth century A.D.) and Vasubandhu,[3] of about the same period. According to tradition Dinnāga, the greatest of the Buddhist logicians, was a disciple of Vasubandhu.

The canons of the Mahāyāna sects contain much material which also

[3] There may have been two Vasubandhus, one the approximate contemporary of Asanga and the other about a century later.

occurs in Pāli, often expanded or adapted, but the interest of the
Mahāyānists was largely directed to other scriptures, of which no counterparts exist in the Pāli canon, and which, it was claimed, were also the
pronouncements of the Buddha. These are the *Vaipulya Sūtras,* or "Expanded Discourses," of greater length than those in the Pāli *Basket of
Discourses (Sutta Piṭaka),* and written in Buddhist Sanskrit; in them the
Buddha is supposed to have taught the doctrine of the heavenly Buddhas
and bodhisattvas. Of these Mahāyāna sūtras pride of place must be taken
by *The Lotus of the Good Law (Saddharmapuṇḍarīka),* which pro-
pounds all the major doctrines of Mahāyāna Buddhism in a fairly simple
and good literary style with parables and poetic illustrations. In translation it is the most popular Buddhist scripture in China and Japan, the
Japanese Buddhists of the Nichiren sect making it their sole canonical
text. An important group of Mahāyāna texts is the *Discourses on the
Perfection of Wisdom (Prajñāpāramitā Sūtras),* of which several exist,
generally known by the number of verses[4] they contain, ranging from
700 to 100,000. The primary purpose of these is to explain and glorify the
ten perfections *(pāramitā)* of the Bodhisattva, and especially the perfection of wisdom (prajnā), but they contain much of importance on other
aspects of Buddhism. Other Mahāyāna sūtras are too numerous to mention.

The Bodhisattva

The essential difference between Mahāyāna and Theravāda Buddhism is in the
doctrine of the bodhisattva, who, in Mahāyāna, becomes a divine savior, and
whose example the believer is urged to follow. It must be remembered that all
good Buddhists, from the Mahāyāna point of view, are bodhisattvas in the
making, and the many descriptions of bodhisattvas in Mahāyāna texts provide
ideals for the guidance of monk and layman alike. One of the chief qualities
of the bodhisattva is his immense compassion for the world of mortals.

[From *Aṣṭasāhasrikā Prajñāpāramitā,* 22.402–3]

The bodhisattva is endowed with wisdom of a kind whereby he looks on
all beings as though victims going to the slaughter. And immense compassion grips him. His divine eye sees . . . innumerable beings, and he is
filled with great distress at what he sees, for many bear the burden of past

---

[4] Or more correctly the number of verses of 32 syllables each which they would contain if they had been versified. They are actually in prose.

deeds which will be punished in purgatory, others will have unfortunate rebirths which will divide them from the Buddha and his teachings, others must soon be slain, others are caught in the net of false doctrine, others cannot find the path (of salvation), while others have gained a favorable rebirth only to lose it again.

So he pours out his love and compassion upon all those beings, and attends to them, thinking, "I shall become the savior of all beings, and set them free from their sufferings."

The Mahāyāna Ideal Is Higher Than That of the Theravāda

Mahāyāna teachers claimed that the ideal of the Theravādins—complete loss of personality as perfected beings in Nirvāna—was fundamentally selfish and trivial. The truly perfected being should devote all his powers to saving suffering mortals. The following passage elucidates this point. It purports to be a dialogue between the Buddha and one of his chief disciples, Shāriputra (Pāli *Sāriputta*).

[From *Pañcaviṃśatisāhasrikā Prajñāpāramitā,* pp. 40–41]

"What do you think, Shāriputra? Do any of the disciples [1] and Private Buddhas [2] ever think, 'After we have gained full enlightenment we will bring innumerable beings . . . to complete Nirvāna'?"

"Certainly not, Lord!"

"But," said the Lord, "the bodhisattva (has this resolve). . . . A firefly . . . doesn't imagine that its glow will light up all India or shine all over it, and so the disciples and Private Buddhas don't think that they should lead all beings to Nirvāna . . . after they have gained full enlightenment. But the disc of the sun, when it has risen, lights up all India and shines all over it. Similarly the bodhisattva, . . . when he has gained full enlightenment, brings countless beings to Nirvāna.

The Suffering Savior

In many passages of the Mahāyāna scriptures is to be found what purports to be the solemn resolve made by a bodhisattva at the beginning of his career. The following fine passage will appear particularly striking to Western readers, for in it the bodhisattva not only resolves to pity and help all mortal beings,

---

[1] *Śrāvaka,* literally "hearer," a term often applied by Mahāyāna writers especially to adherents of Theravāda.

[2] *Pratyeka-buddha,* one who has achieved full enlightenment through his own insight, but does not communicate his saving knowledge to others.

but also to share their intensest sufferings. Christians and Jews cannot fail to note resemblances to the concept of the suffering Savior in Christianity and to the "Servant Passages" of Isaiah (53:3–12). It is by no means impossible that there was some Christian influence on Mahāyāna Buddhism, for Christian missionaries were active in Persia very early, and it became a center from which Nestorian Christianity was diffused throughout Asia. From the middle of the third century A.D. Persian influence in Afghanistan and Northwestern India, which had always been felt, was intensified with the rise of the Sāsānian Empire; and it was in these regions that Mahāyāna Buddhism developed and flourished. Thus Christian influence cannot be ruled out. But it is equally possible that the similarities between the concepts of the suffering savior in Buddhism and Christianity are due to the fact that compassionate minds everywhere tend to think alike.

The work from which the following passage is taken, Shāntideva's *Compendium of Doctrine,* dates from the seventh century. It is extremely valuable because it consists of lengthy quotations from earlier Buddhist literature with brief comments by the compiler, and many of the passages quoted are from works which no longer survive in their original form. The following passages are quoted from two such works, the *Instructions of Akṣayamati (Akṣayamati Nirdeśa)* and the *Sūtra of Vajradhvaja (Vajradhvaja Sūtra).*

[From *Śikṣāsamuccaya,* pp. 278–83]

The bodhisattva is lonely, with no . . . companion, and he puts on the armor of supreme wisdom. He acts himself, and leaves nothing to others, working with a will steeled with courage and strength. He is strong in his own strength . . . and he resolves thus:

"Whatever all beings should obtain, I will help them to obtain. . . . The virtue of generosity is not my helper—I am the helper of generosity. Nor do the virtues of morality, patience, courage, meditation and wisdom help me—it is I who help them.[3] The perfections of the bodhisattva do not support me—it is I who support them. . . . I alone, standing in this round and adamantine world, must subdue Māra, with all his hosts and chariots, and develop supreme enlightenment with the wisdom of instantaneous insight!" . . .

[3] These six, generosity (*dāna*), moral conduct (*śīla*), patience (*kṣānti*), courage or energy (*vīrya*), meditation (dhyāna) and wisdom (prajñā) are the *Pāramitās,* or virtues of the bodhisattva, which he has developed to perfection. Many sources add four further perfections—"skill in knowing the right means" to take to lead individual beings to salvation according to their several characters and circumstances (*upāyakauśalya*), determination (*praṇidhāna*), strength (*bala*), and knowledge (jñāna). Much attention was concentrated on these perfections, especially on the Perfection of Wisdom (*Prajñāpāramitā*), which was personified as a goddess, and after which numerous Buddhist texts were named.

Just as the rising sun, the child of the gods, is not stopped . . . by all the dust rising from the four continents of the earth . . . or by wreaths of smoke . . . or by rugged mountains, so the bodhisattva, the Great Being, . . . is not deterred from bringing to fruition the root of good, whether by the malice of others, . . . or by their sin or heresy, or by their agitation of mind. . . . He will not lay down his arms of enlightenment because of the corrupt generations of men, nor does he waver in his resolution to save the world because of their wretched quarrels. . . . He does not lose heart on account of their faults. . . .

"All creatures are in pain," he resolves, "all suffer from bad and hindering karma . . . so that they cannot see the Buddhas or hear the Law of Righteousness or know the Order. . . . All that mass of pain and evil karma I take in my own body. . . . I take upon myself the burden of sorrow; I resolve to do so; I endure it all. I do not turn back or run away, I do not tremble . . . I am not afraid . . . nor do I despair. Assuredly I must bear the burdens of all beings . . . for I have resolved to save them all. I must set them all free, I must save the whole world from the forest of birth, old age, disease, and rebirth, from misfortune and sin, from the round of birth and death, from the toils of heresy. . . . For all beings are caught in the net of craving, encompassed by ignorance, held by the desire for existence; they are doomed to destruction, shut in a cage of pain . . . ; they are ignorant, untrustworthy, full of doubts, always at loggerheads one with another, always prone to see evil; they cannot find a refuge in the ocean of existence; they are all on the edge of the gulf of destruction.

"I work to establish the kingdom of perfect wisdom for all beings. I care not at all for my own deliverance. I must save all beings from the torrent of rebirth with the raft of my omniscient mind. I must pull them back from the great precipice. I must free them from all misfortune, ferry them over the stream of rebirth.

"For I have taken upon myself, by my own will, the whole of the pain of all things living. Thus I dare try every abode of pain, in . . . every part of the universe, for I must not defraud the world of the root of good. I resolve to dwell in each state of misfortune through countless ages . . . for the salvation of all beings . . . for it is better that I alone suffer than that all beings sink to the worlds of misfortune. There I shall give myself into bondage, to redeem all the world from the forest of purgatory, from rebirth as beasts, from the realm of death. I shall bear all grief and pain in my own body, for the good of all things living. I venture to stand surety for all beings, speaking the truth, trustworthy, not breaking my word. I shall not forsake them. . . . I must so bring to fruition the root of goodness that all beings find the utmost joy, unheard of joy, the joy of omniscience. I must be their charioteer, I must be their leader, I must be their torchbearer, I must be their guide to safety. . . . I must not wait for the help of another, nor must I lose my resolution and leave my tasks to another. I must not turn back in my efforts to save all beings nor cease to use my merit for the destruction of all pain. And I must not be satisfied with small successes."

The Lost Son

One of the reasons for including this passage is its remarkable resemblance to the famous parable of St. Luke's Gospel (15:11–32). As the *Lotus of the Good Law,* from which the Buddhist story is taken, was probably in existence well before Christian ideas could have found their way to India via Persia, it is unlikely that this parable owes anything to the Christian one. Similarly it is unlikely that the Christian parable is indebted to the Buddhist. Probably we have here a case of religious minds of two widely separated cultures thinking along similar lines, as a result of similar, though not identical, religious experience. For this reason the resemblances and differences of the two stories are most instructive.[4]

The Prodigal of the Christian story squanders his patrimony in riotous living. The son in the Buddhist story is a wretched creature who can only wander about begging. His fault is not so much in squandering his property as in failing to acquire wealth (i.e., spiritual merit). The Prodigal returns to his father by his own free choice, after repenting his evil ways. In the Buddhist story it is only by chance that the son meets his father again; moreover the son does not recognize the father, though the father recognizes his son—thus the heavenly Buddha knows his children and works for their salvation, though they do not recognize him in his true character, and, if they get a glimpse of him, are afraid and try to avoid him—they feel much more at ease among their own earthbound kind, in "the poor quarter of the town," where their divine father sends his messengers (perhaps representing the Bodhisattvas) to find

---

[4] The text itself purports to give an interpretation of the parable in which the son toiling as a menial in his father's house is compared to the Hīnayāna monk, who is unaware of the true glory of the enlightenment to which he is heir. There is little doubt, however, that the story here turned to purposes of sectarian propaganda was originally meant to have a wider significance, and we believe our interpretation to be that demanded by the spirit of the parable.

them, bringing them home by force if need be. Here there is no question of a positive act of repentance, as in the Christian parable.

Unlike the Prodigal's father in the Christian story, who kills the fatted calf for his long-lost son, the father in the Buddhist story makes his son undergo a very long period of humble probation before raising him to the position which he merits by his birth. The heavenly Buddha cannot raise beings immediately from the filth and poverty of the earthly gutter to the full glory of his own heavenly palace, for they are so earthbound that, if brought to it at once, they would suffer agonies of fear, embarrassment, and confusion, and might well insist on returning to the gutter again. So they must undergo many years of preparation for their high estate, toiling daily among the material dross of this world, earnestly and loyally striving to make the world a tidier place. Like the father in the story, the heavenly Buddha will cover his glory with earthly dust and appear to his children as a historical Buddha to encourage and instruct them. Thus the Buddha shows the perfection of "skill in means," that is to say, in knowing the best means to take to lead each individual to the light according to the circumstances in which he is placed.

Gradually the son grows more and more familiar with the father, and loses his former fear of him, but still he does not know that he is his father's child. So men, even though pious and virtuous, and earnestly carrying out the Buddha's will, do not know that they are already in Heaven; their lives are still to some extent earthbound, and though the Buddha offers them all his wealth of bliss long habit keeps them from enjoying it.

Only when the father is near death does he reveal himself to his son. This seems at first to weaken the analogy, for heavenly Buddhas do not die. But in fact the conclusion of the parable is quite appropriate, for when man has fulfilled his tasks and carried out his stewardship, that is to say when he has reached the highest stage of self-development, he finds that the heavenly Buddha has ceased to exist for him, that nothing is truly real but the great Emptiness which is peace and Nirvāna.

[From *Saddharmapuṇḍarīka*, 4.101 ff.]

A man parted from his father and went to another city; and he dwelt there many years. . . . The father grew rich and the son poor. While the son wandered in all directions [begging] in order to get food and clothes, the father moved to another land, where he lived in great luxury, . . . wealthy from business, money-lending, and trade. In course of time the son, wandering in search of his living through town and country, came to the city in which his father dwelled. Now the poor man's father . . . forever thought of the son whom he had lost . . . years ago, but he told no one of this, though he grieved inwardly, and thought: "I am old, and well advanced in years, and though I have great possessions I have no son.

Alas that time should do its work upon me, and that all this wealth should perish unused! . . . It would be bliss indeed if my son might enjoy all my wealth!"

Then the poor man, in search of food and clothing, came to the rich man's home. And the rich man was sitting in great pomp at the gate of his house, surrounded by a large throng of attendants, . . . on a splendid throne, with a footstool inlaid with gold and silver, under a wide awning decked with pearls and flowers and adorned with hanging garlands of jewels; and he transacted business to the value of millions of gold pieces, all the while fanned by a fly-whisk. . . . When he saw him the poor man was terrified . . . and the hair of his body stood on end, for he thought that he had happened on a king or on some high officer of state, and had no business there. "I must go," he thought, "to the poor quarter of the town, where I'll get food and clothing without trouble. If I stop here they'll seize me and set me to do forced labor, or some other disaster will befall me!" So he quickly ran away. . . .

But the rich man . . . recognized his son as soon as he saw him; and he was full of joy . . . and thought: "This is wonderful! I have found him who shall enjoy my riches. He of whom I thought constantly has come back, now that I am old and full of years!" Then, longing for his son, he sent swift messengers, telling them to go and fetch him quickly. They ran at full speed and overtook him; the poor man trembled with fear, the hair of his body stood on end . . . and he uttered a cry of distress and exclaimed, "I've done you no wrong!" But they dragged him along by force . . . until . . . fearful that he would be killed or beaten, he fainted and fell on the ground. His father in dismay said to the men, "Don't drag him along in that way!" and, without saying more, he sprinkled his face with cold water—for though he knew that the poor man was his son, he realized that his estate was very humble, while his own was very high.

So the householder told no one that the poor man was his son. He ordered one of his servants to tell the poor man that he was free to go where he chose. . . . And the poor man was amazed [that he was allowed to go free], and he went off to the poor quarter of the town in search of food and clothing. Now in order to attract him back the rich man made use of the virtue of "skill in means." He called two men of low caste and of no great dignity and told them: "Go to that poor man . . . and hire him in your own names to do work in my house at double the normal daily wage; and if he asks what work he has to do tell him that he has to help clear away the refuse-dump." So these two men and the poor man cleared the refuse every day . . . in the house of the rich man, and lived in a straw hut nearby. . . . And the rich man saw through a window his son clearing refuse, and was again filled with compassion. So he came down, took off his wreath and jewels and rich clothes, put on dirty garments, covered his body with dust, and, taking a basket in his hand, went up to his son. And he greeted him at a distance and said, "Take this basket and clear away the dust at once!" By this means he managed to speak to his son. [And as time went on he spoke more often to him, and thus he gradually encouraged him. First he urged him to] remain in his service and not take another job, offering him double wages, together with any small extras that he might require, such as the price of a cooking-pot . . . or food and clothes. Then he offered him his own cloak, if he should want it. . . . And at last he said: "You must be cheerful, my good fellow, and think of me as a father . . . for I'm older than you and you've done me good service in clearing away my refuse. As long as you've worked for me you've shown no roguery or guile. . . . I've not noticed one of the vices in you that I've noticed in my other servants! From now on you are like my own son to me!"

Thenceforward the householder called the poor man "son," and the latter felt towards the householder as a son feels towards his father. So the householder, full of longing and love for his son, employed him in clearing away refuse for twenty years. By the end of that time the poor man felt quite at home in the house, and came and went as he chose, though he still lived in the straw hut.

Then the householder fell ill, and felt that the hour of his death was near. So he said to the poor man: "Come, my dear man! I have great riches, . . . and am very sick. I need someone upon whom I can bestow my wealth as a deposit, and you must accept it. From now on you are just as much its owner as I am, but you must not squander it." And the poor man accepted the rich man's wealth, . . . but personally he cared nothing for it, and asked for no share of it, not even the price of a measure of flour. He still lived in the straw hut, and thought of himself as just as poor as before.

Thus the householder proved that his son was frugal, mature, and mentally developed, and that though he knew that he was now wealthy he still remembered his past poverty, and was still . . . humble and meek. . . . So he sent for the poor man again, presented him before a gathering of his relatives, and, in the presence of the king, his officers, and the people of town and country, he said: "Listen, gentlemen! This is my son, whom I begot. . . . To him I leave all my family revenues, and my private wealth he shall have as his own."

Against Self-Mortification

Buddhists of both "vehicles" strongly deprecated the exaggerated ascetic practices of other sects, as they did taboos connected with food and ritual purity. Suffering, for the Buddhist, has no intrinsic value or purificatory effect, unless it is undertaken voluntarily for the sake of others, in the manner of the bodhisattva, who elects to dwell in all the purgatories in order to relieve the beings in torment there. The man who mortifies the flesh in order to gain rebirth in heaven is completely selfish and misguided, and his last state will be worse than his first.

The following verses are from the *Deeds of the Buddha,* a metrical life of the Buddha by Ashvaghosha (first to second centuries A.D.), which is among the masterpieces of Sanskrit poetry and one of the earliest known poems in the courtly style. Though it is written in Sanskrit it contains no specifically Mahāyāna features; but it is included among Mahāyāna literature, since it was preserved by the Mahāyānist sects. The verses are spoken by the future Buddha during his period of spiritual apprenticeship, when he realizes that self-mortification is useless and wrong.

[From *Buddhacarita,* 7.20 ff.]

Penance in its various forms is essentially sorrowful;
    And, at best, the reward of penance is heaven.
Yet all the worlds are liable to change,
    So the efforts of the hermitages are of little use.

Those who forsake the kin they love and their pleasures
    To perform penance and win a place in heaven
Must leave it in the end
    And go to greater bondage.

The man who pains his body and calls it penance
    In the hope of continuing to satisfy desire

Does not perceive the evils of rebirth,
And through much sorrow goes to further sorrow.

All living beings are afraid of death
And yet they all strive to be born again;
As they act thus death is inevitable,
And they are plunged in that which they most fear.

Some suffer hardship for mere worldly gain;
Others will take to penance in hope of heaven.
All beings fail in their hopeful search for bliss,
And fall, poor wretches, into dire calamity.

Not that the effort is to be blamed which leaves
The base and seeks the higher aim,
But wise men should labor with an equal zeal
To reach the goal where further toil is needless.

If it is Right to mortify the flesh
The body's ease is contrary to Right;
Thus if, by doing Right, joy is obtained hereafter
Righteousness must flower in Unrighteousness.

The body is commanded by the mind,
Through mind it acts, through mind it ceases to act.
All that is needed is to subdue the mind,
For the body is a log of wood without it.

If merit comes from purity of food [5]
Then even the deer gain merit,
And those who do not win the reward of righteousness
But by an unlucky fate have lost their wealth. . . .

And those who try to purify their deeds
By ablutions at a place which they hold sacred—

---

[5] From the context it appears that this verse is specially directed at the Jains, whose monks were given to very severe fasting, sometimes even to death.

These merely give their hearts some satisfaction,
For water will not purify men's sin.

Joy in All Things

Joy is one of the cardinal virtues of Buddhism, and the bodhisattva, who is
the example which all Mahāyāna Buddhists are expected to follow as far as
their powers allow, has so trained his mind that even in the most painful and
unhappy situations it is still full of calm inner joy. The following passage is
from the *Compendium of Doctrine;* the first paragraph is the work of the
author, Shāntideva, while the second is quoted from a lost sūtra, the *Meeting
of Father and Son (Pitṛputrasamāgama).*
[From *Śikṣāsamuccaya,* 181 f.]

Indeed nothing is difficult after practice. Simple folk, such as porters,
fishermen and plowmen, for instance, are not overcome by depression, for
their minds are marked by the scars of the many pains with which they
earn their humble livings, and which they have learned to bear. How
much the more should one be cheerful in a task of which the purpose is
to reach the incomparable state where all the joys of all beings, all the
joys of the bodhisattvas are to be found. . . . Consciousness of sorrow
and joy comes by habit; so, if whenever sorrow arises we make a habit
of associating with it a feeling of joy, consciousness of joy will indeed
arise. The fruit of this is a contemplative spirit full of joy in all things. . . .

So the bodhisattva . . . is happy even when subjected to the tortures of
hell. . . . When he is being beaten with canes or whips, when he is
thrown into prison, he still feels happy.[6] . . . For . . . this was the resolve of the Great Being, the bodhisattva: "May those who feed me win
the joy of tranquillity and peace, with those who protect me, honor me,
respect me, and revere me. And those who revile me, afflict me, beat me,
cut me in pieces with their swords, or take my life—may they all obtain
the joy of complete enlightenment, may they be awakened to perfect and
sublime enlightenment." With such thoughts and actions and resolves he
cultivates . . . and develops the consciousness of joy in his relations with
all beings, and so he acquires a contemplative spirit filled with joy in all
things . . . and becomes imperturbable—not to be shaken by all the
deeds of Māra.

[6] Here a long list of the most gruesome tortures is omitted.

The Good Deeds of the Bodhisattva

We have seen that the bodhisattva has ten "Perfections." A further list of good qualities is sometimes attributed to him. Notice that the emphasis is on the positive virtues of altruism, benevolence, and compassion.

[From *Tathāgataguhya Sūtra, Śikṣāsamuccaya*, p. 274]

There are ten ways by which a bodhisattva gains . . . strength: . . . .
He will give up his body and his life . . . but he will not give up the Law
  of Righteousness.
He bows humbly to all beings, and does not increase in pride.
He has compassion on the weak and does not dislike them.
He gives the best food to those who are hungry.
He protects those who are afraid.
He strives for the healing of those who are sick.
He delights the poor with his riches.
He repairs the shrines of the Buddha with plaster.
He speaks to all beings pleasingly.
He shares his riches with those afflicted by poverty.
He bears the burdens of those who are tired and weary.

The Evils of Meat-Eating

According to the scriptures of the Theravāda school the Buddha allowed his followers to eat flesh if they were not responsible for killing the animal providing the meat, and if it was not specially killed to feed them. To this day most Buddhists in Ceylon and other lands where Theravāda prevails eat meat and fish, which are supplied by Muslim or Christian butchers or fishermen. Like the great Ashoka, however, many Buddhists have felt that meat-eating of any kind is out of harmony with the spirit of the Law of Righteousness, and have been vegetarians. The following passage criticizes the Theravāda teaching on meat-eating, and enjoins strict vegetarianism. The words are attributed to the Buddha.

[From *Laṅkāvatāra Sūtra*, pp. 245 ff.]

Here in this long journey of birth-and-death there is no living being who . . . has not at some time been your mother or father, brother or sister, son or daughter. . . . So how can the bodhisattva, who wishes to treat all beings as though they were himself, . . . eat the flesh of any living being. . . . Therefore, wherever living beings evolve, men should feel toward them as to their own kin, and, looking on all beings as their only child, should refrain from eating meat. . . .

The bodhisattva, . . . desirous of cultivating the virtue of love, should not eat meat, lest he cause terror to living beings. Dogs, when they see, even at a distance, an outcaste . . . who likes eating meat, are terrified with fear, and think, "They are the dealers of death, they will kill us!" Even the animalculae in earth and air and water, who have a very keen sense of smell, will detect at a distance the odor of the demons in meat-eaters, and will run away as fast as they can from the death which threatens them. . . .

Moreover the meat-eater sleeps in sorrow and wakes in sorrow. All his dreams are nightmares, and they make his hair stand on end. . . . Things other than human sap his vitality. Often he is struck with terror, and trembles without cause. . . . He knows no measure in his eating, and there is no flavor, digestibility, or nourishment in his food. His bowels are filled with worms and other creatures, which are the cause of leprosy; and he ceases to think of resisting diseases. . . .

It is not true . . . that meat is right and proper for the disciple when the animal was not killed by himself or by his orders, and when it was not killed specially for him. . . . Pressed by a desire for the taste of meat people may string together their sophistries in defense of meat-eating . . . and declare that the Lord permitted meat as legitimate food, that it occurs in the list of permitted foods, and that he himself ate it. But . . . it is nowhere allowed in the sūtras as a . . . legitimate food. . . . All meat-eating in any form or manner and in any circumstances is prohibited, unconditionally and once and for all.

The Gift of Food

From the Buddhist point of view, as Ashoka said, there is no greater gift than the gift of the Law of Righteousness; but Buddhism never disparaged the value or merit of practical acts of kindness and charity. The Buddhists, as we have seen, set much store on physical wellbeing. The passage which follows will show that poverty and hunger, unless voluntarily undertaken for a worthy cause, were looked on as unmitigated evils, liable to lead to sin and hence to an unhappy rebirth.

This passage is from the Tamil classic *Maṇimēgalai,* perhaps of the sixth century A.D., which is wholly Buddhist in inspiration, and concludes with an exposition of Mahāyāna logic and the doctrine of the Chain of Causation. The poem tells of Manimēgalai, a beautiful girl who, after many adventures, realized the uselessness and sorrow of the world and became a Buddhist nun. Here, led by a demi-goddess, she finds a magic bowl, which gives an inexhaustible supply of food.

[From *Maṇimēgalai*, 11.55–122]

The bowl rose in the water and . . . moved toward her hand. She was glad beyond measure, and sang a hymn in praise of the Buddha:
"Hail the feet of the hero, the victor over Māra!
Hail the feet of him who destroyed the path of evil!
Hail the feet of the Great One, setting men on the road of Righteousness!
Hail the feet of the All Wise One, who gives others the eye of wisdom!
Hail the feet of him whose ears are deaf to evil!
Hail the feet of him whose tongue never uttered untruth!
Hail the feet of him who went down to purgatory to put an end to suffering. . . .
My tongue cannot praise you duly—All I can do is to bend my body at your feet!"

While she was praying thus Tīvatilagai told her of the pains of hunger and of the virtue of those who help living beings to satisfy it. "Hunger," she said to Manimēgalai, "ruins good birth, and destroys all nobility; it destroys the love of learned men for their learning, even though they previously thought it the most valuable thing in life; hunger takes away all sense of shame, and ruins the beauty of the features; and it even forces men to stand with their wives at the doors of others. This is the nature of hunger, the source of evil craving, and those who relieve it the tongue cannot praise too highly! Food given to those who can afford it is charity wasted,[7] but food given to relieve the hunger of those who cannot satisfy it otherwise is charity indeed, and those who give it will prosper in this world, for those who give food give life. So go on and give food to allay the hunger of those who are hungry."

"In a past life," said Manimēgalai, "my husband died . . . and I mounted the pyre with him. As I burned I remembered that I had once given food to a Buddhist monk named Sādusakkāra; and I believe it is because of this virtuous thought at the moment of death that this bowl of

[7] This may be a criticism of the Hindu virtue of *dāna*, which is usually translated "charity," but includes feasts given to brāhmans who may be much richer than the donor.

plenty has come into my hands. Just as a mother's breast begins to give milk at the mere sight of her hungry baby, so may this bowl in my hand always give food . . . at the sight of those who suffer hunger and wander even in pouring rain or scorching sun in search of food to relieve it."

The Three Bodies of the Buddha

The following passage expounds the doctrine of the Three Bodies (*Trikāya*). It is taken from Asanga's *Ornament of Mahāyāna Sūtras,* a versified compendium of Mahāyāna doctrine, with a prose commentary. The latter is quoted where it throws light on the difficult and elliptical verses.

[From *Mahāyānasūtrālaṅkāra,* 9.60–66]

The Body of Essence, the Body of Bliss,[8] the Created Body—these are the bodies of the Buddhas.
The first is the basis of the two others.
The Body of Bliss varies in all the planes of the Universe, according to region,
In name, in form, and in experience of phenomena.
But the Body of Essence, uniform and subtle, is inherent in the Body of Bliss,
And through the one the other controls its experience, when it manifests itself at will.

Commentary: The Body of Essence is uniform for all the Buddhas, Because there is no real difference between them. . . .

The Created Body displays with skill birth, enlightenment, and Nirvāna,
For it possesses much magic power to lead men to enlightenment.
The Body of the Buddhas is wholly comprised in these three bodies. . . .
In basis, tendency, and act they are uniform.
They are stable by nature, by persistence, and by connection.

Commentary: The Three Bodies are one and the same for all the Buddhas for three reasons: *basis,* for the basis of phenomena[9] is indivisible; *tendency,* because there is no tendency particular to one Buddha and not

---

[8] *Sambhoga,* more literally "enjoyment"; in some contexts it implies little more than "experience."

[9] *Dharmadhātu,* the Absolute.

to another; and *act,* because their actions are common to all. And the Three Bodies have a threefold stability: by *nature,* for the Body of Essence is essentially stable; by *persistence,* for the Body of Bliss experiences phenomena unceasingly; and by *connection,* for the Created Body, once it has passed away, shows its metamorphoses again and again.

Emptiness

The doctrine of *Śūnyatā,* "Emptiness" or "the Void," is aptly expressed in these fine verses from the *Multitude of Graceful Actions,* a life of the Buddha in mixed verse and prose, replete with marvels and miracles of all kinds, which formed the basis of Sir Edwin Arnold's famous poem, *The Light of Asia.*

[From *Lalitavistara,* 13.175–77]

All things conditioned are instable, impermanent,
    Fragile in essence, as an unbaked pot,
Like something borrowed, or a city founded on sand,
    They last a short while only.

They are inevitably destroyed,
    Like plaster washed off in the rains,
Like the sandy bank of a river—
    They are conditioned, and their true nature is frail.

They are like the flame of a lamp,
    Which rises suddenly and as soon goes out.
They have no power of endurance, like the wind
    Or like foam, unsubstantial, essentially feeble.

They have no inner power, being essentially empty,
    Like the stem of a plantain, if one thinks clearly,
Like conjuring tricks deluding the mind,
    Or a fist closed on nothing to tease a child. . . .

From wisps of grass the rope is spun
    By dint of exertion.
By turns of the wheel the buckets are raised from the well,
    Yet each turn of itself is futile.

So the turning of all the components of becoming
    Arises from the interaction of one with another.
In the unit the turning cannot be traced
    Either at the beginning or end.

Where the seed is, there is the young plant,
    But the seed has not the nature of the plant,
Nor is it something other than the plant, nor is it the plant—
    So is the nature of the Law of Righteousness, neither transient nor
      eternal.

All things conditioned are conditioned by ignorance,
    And on final analysis they do not exist,
For they and the conditioning ignorance alike are Emptiness
    In their essential nature, without power of action. . . .

The mystic knows the beginning and end
    Of consciousness, its production and passing away—
He knows that it came from nowhere and returns to nowhere,
    And is empty [of reality], like a conjuring trick.

Through the concomitance of three factors—
    Firesticks, fuel, and the work of the hand—
Fire is kindled. It serves its purpose
    And quickly goes out again.

A wise man may seek here, there, and everywhere
    Whence it has come, and whither it has gone,
Through every region in all directions,
    But he cannot find it in its essential nature. . . .

Thus all things in this world of contingence
    Are dependent on causes and conditions.
The mystic knows what is true reality,
    And sees all conditioned things as empty and powerless.

Faith in Emptiness

The following passage needs little comment. Belief in *Śūnyavāda,* the doctrine of Emptiness, encourages a stoical and noble equanimity.

[From *Dharmasaṅgīti Sūtra, Śikṣāsamuccaya,* p. 264]

He who maintains the doctrine of Emptiness is not allured by the things of the world, because they have no basis. He is not excited by gain or dejected by loss. Fame does not dazzle him and infamy does not shame him. Scorn does not repel him, praise does not attract him. Pleasure does not please him, pain does not trouble him. He who is not allured by the things of the world knows Emptiness, and one who maintains the doctrine of Emptiness has neither likes nor dislikes. What he likes he knows to be only Emptiness and sees it as such.

Karma and Rebirth

In an illusory world, rebirth is also illusory. The things a man craves for have no more reality than a dream, but he craves nevertheless, and hence his illusory ego is reborn in a new but equally illusory body. Notice the importance of the last conscious thought before death, which plays a very decisive part in the nature of the rebirth. The chief speaker in the following dialogue is said to be the Buddha.

[From *Pitṛputrasamāgama, Śikṣāsamuccaya,* pp. 251–52]

"The senses are as though illusions and their objects as dreams. For instance a sleeping man might dream that he had made love to a beautiful country girl, and he might remember her when he awoke. What do you think— . . . does the beautiful girl he dreamed of really exist?"

"No, Lord."

"And would the man be wise to remember the girl of his dreams, or to believe that he had really made love to her?"

"No, Lord, because she doesn't really exist at all, so how could he have made love to her—though of course he might think he did under the influence of weakness or fatigue."

"In just the same way a foolish and ignorant man of the world sees pleasant forms and believes in their existence. Hence he is pleased, and so he feels passion and acts accordingly. . . . But from the very beginning his actions are feeble, impeded, wasted, and changed in their course by circumstances. . . . And when he ends his days, as the time of death approaches, his vitality is obstructed with the exhaustion of his allotted span of years, the karma that fell to his lot dwindles, and hence his previous actions form the object of the last thought of his mind as it disappears. Then, just as the man on first waking from sleep thinks of the country girl about whom he dreamed, the first thought on rebirth arises from two causes—the last thought of the previous life as its governing principle, and the actions of the previous life as its basis. Thus a man is reborn in the purgatories, or as an animal, a spirit, a demon, a human being, or a god. . . . The stopping of the last thought is known as decease, the appearance of the first thought as rebirth. Nothing passes from life to life, but decease and rebirth take place nevertheless. . . . But the last thought, the actions (karma), and the first thought, when they arise come from nowhere and when they cease go nowhere, for all are essentially defective, of themselves empty. . . . In the whole process no one acts and no one experiences the results of action, except by verbal convention.

Suchness

The Vijnānavādin school called their conception of the Absolute *Tathatā* or "Suchness," in which all phenomenal appearances are lost in the one ultimate being.

The following passage is taken from a text which was translated into Chinese in the seventh century from a recension more interesting than the extant Sanskrit form. The whole passage considers the "Suchness" of the five components of being in turn. Here we give only the passage relating to the first of these.[10]

[From *Mahāprajñāpāramitā*, ch. 29, 1]

What is meant by . . . knowing in accordance with truth the marks of form? It means that a bodhisattva . . . knows that form is nothing but holes and cracks and is indeed a mass of bubbles, with a nature that has no hardness or solidity. . . .

What is meant by . . . knowing in accordance with truth the origin and extinction of form? It means that a bodhisattva . . . knows . . . that when form originates it comes from nowhere and when it is extin-

---

[10] Translated by Dr. Arthur Waley from the Chinese version of Hsüan Tsang. Reprinted by permission of Messrs. Bruno Cassirer, Oxford, from *Buddhist Texts through the Ages,* ed. by Edward Conze, Oxford, 1954, p. 154 f.

guished it goes nowhere, but that though it neither comes nor goes yet its origination and extinction do jointly exist. . . .

What is meant by knowing . . . in accordance with truth about the Suchness of form? It means that a bodhisattva . . . knows . . . that Suchness of form is not subject to origination or extinction, that it neither comes nor goes, is neither foul nor clean, neither increases nor diminishes, is constant in its own nature, is never empty, false or changeful, and is therefore called Suchness.

All Depends on the Mind

The following passage expresses the idealism of Mahāyāna thought.
[From *Ratnamegha Sūtra, Śikṣāsamuccaya*, p. 121–22]

All phenomena originate in the mind, and when the mind is fully known all phenomena are fully known. For by the mind the world is led . . . and through the mind karma is piled up, whether good or evil. The mind swings like a firebrand,[11] the mind rears up like a wave, the mind burns like a forest fire, like a great flood the mind bears all things away. The bodhisattva, thoroughly examining the nature of things, dwells in ever-present mindfulness of the activity of the mind, and so he does not fall into the mind's power, but the mind comes under his control. And with the mind under his control all phenomena are under his control.

Nirvāna Is Here and Now

The two following passages, the first Mādhyamika, and the second Vijñā-navādin in tendency, illustrate the Mahāyāna doctrine that Nirvāna, the highest state, Pure Being, the Absolute, the Buddha's Body of Essence, is present at all times and everywhere, and needs only to be recognized. Thus the older pessimism of Buddhism is replaced by what is almost optimism. With this change of outlook comes an impatience with the learned philosophers and moralists who repeat their long and dreary sermons on the woes of samsāra, the round of birth-and-death. Though this attitude may have contributed to the antinomian tendencies of tantric Buddhism, it will probably stir an answering chord in many Western minds. Most people are like the man in the parable of the Lost Son, who year after year cleared away the refuse of his father's house without knowing that he was the son and heir.

[11] An allusion to a famous simile. The world is like a firebrand which, when swung round in the hand, resembles a solid wheel of flame.

[From *Śikṣāsamuccaya*, p. 257]

That which the Lord revealed in his perfect enlightenment was not form or sensation or perception or psychic constructions or thought; for none of these five components come into being, neither does supreme wisdom come into being . . . and how can that which does not come into being know that which also does not come into being? Since nothing can be grasped, what is the Buddha, what is wisdom, what is the bodhisattva, what is revelation? All the components are by nature empty—just convention, just names, agreed tokens, coverings. . . .

Thus all things are the perfection of being, infinite perfection, unobscured perfection, unconditioned perfection. All things are enlightenment, for they must be recognized as without essential nature—even the five greatest sins [12] are enlightenment, for enlightenment has no essential nature and neither have the five greatest sins. Thus those who seek for Nirvāna are to be laughed at, for the man in the midst of birth-and-death is also seeking Nirvāna.

[From *Laṅkāvatāra Sūtra*, pp. 61–62]

Those who are afraid of the sorrow which arises from . . . the round of birth-and-death seek for Nirvāna; they do not realize that between birth-and-death and Nirvāna there is really no difference at all. They see Nirvāna as the absence of all . . . becoming, and the cessation of all contact of sense-organ and sense-object, and they will not understand that it is really only the inner realization of the store of impressions.[13] . . . . Hence they teach the three Vehicles,[14] but not the doctrine that nothing truly exists but the mind, in which are no images. Therefore . . . they do not know the extent of what has been perceived by the minds of past, present, and future Buddhas, and continue in the conviction that the world extends beyond the range of the mind's eye. . . . And so they keep on rolling . . . on the wheel of birth-and-death.

Praise of Dharma

Dharma, the cosmic Law of Righteousness proclaimed by the Buddha, was revered quite as highly by the Mahāyānists as by the Theravādins. The ulti-

[12] Murdering one's mother, murdering one's father, murdering a perfected being (*arhant*), trying to destroy the Buddhist Order, and maliciously injuring a Buddha.

[13] *Ālayavijñāna* (see p. 160).

[14] The two "Lesser Vehicles" (to salvation) of the older Buddhism—namely, those of the disciples and of Private Buddhas—and the vehicle of the bodhisattva.

mate body of the Buddha, which was roughly equivalent to the World-Soul of
the Hindus, was called the Dharma-body, and the basic element of the universe
was also often known as *Dharma-dhātu,* "the Raw-material of the Law," especially by the Vijñānavāda.[15] The following passage, perhaps originally intended
for liturgical purposes, exemplifies the mystical attitude toward Dharma, which
was widespread in later Buddhism. Here Dharma seems to have much in common with the *Tao* of Lao Tzu. Notice that it is prior to the heavenly Buddhas
themselves.

[From *Dharmasaṅgīti Sūtra, Śikṣāsamuccaya,* pp. 322–23]

The blessed Buddhas, of virtues endless and limitless, are born of the Law
of Righteousness; they dwell in the Law, are fashioned by the Law; they
have the Law as their master, the Law as their light, the Law as their
field of action, the Law as their refuge. They are produced by the Law
. . . and all the joys in this world and the next are born of the Law and
produced by the Law. . . .
The Law is equal, equal for all beings. For low or middle or high the Law
cares nothing.
  So must I make my thought like the Law.
The Law has no regard for the pleasant. Impartial is the Law.
  So must I make my thought like the Law.
The Law is not dependent upon time. Timeless is the Law. . . .
  So must I make my thought like the Law.
The Law is not in the lofty without being in the low. Neither up nor
down will the Law bend.
  So must I make my thought like the Law.
The Law is not in that which is whole without being in that which is
broken. Devoid of all superiority or inferiority is the Law.
  So must I make my thought like the Law.
The Law is not in the noble without being in the humble. No care for
fields of activity has the Law.
  So must I make my thought like the Law.
The Law is not in the day without being in the night. . . . Ever firm is
the Law.
  So must I make my thought like the Law.
The Law does not lose the occasion of conversion. There is never delay
with the Law.

[15] Or, as many philosophers of this school would have interpreted it, "the Raw-material
of Phenomena," since *dharma* in Buddhism had also a special philosophical connotation.

So must I make my thought like the Law.
The Law has neither shortage nor abundance. Immeasurable, innumerable is the Law. Like space it never lessens or grows.
So must I make my thought like the Law.
The Law is not guarded by beings. Beings are protected by the Law.
So must I make my thought like the Law.
The Law does not seek refuge. The refuge of all the world is the Law.
So must I make my thought like the Law.
The Law has none who can resist it. Irresistible is the Law.
So must I make my thought like the Law.
The Law has no preferences. Without preference is the Law.
So must I make my thought like the Law.
The Law has no fear of the terrors of birth-and-death, nor is it lured by Nirvāna. Ever without misgiving is the Law.
So must I make my thought like the Law.

Perfect Wisdom Personified

Prajñāpāramitā, the Perfection of Wisdom, is praised in many passages of Mahāyāna literature. As with the early Jews, the divine Wisdom was personified,[16] but the process went much further with the Buddhists than with the Jews, for in India *Prajñāpāramitā* became a goddess worshiped in the form of an icon. She was especially cultivated in the Vajrayāna, but by no means neglected in Mahāyānist sects.

[From *Aṣṭasāhasrikā Prajñāpāramitā,* 7.170–71]

Perfect Wisdom spreads her radiance, . . . and is worthy of worship. Spotless, the whole world cannot stain her. . . . In her we may find refuge; her works are most excellent; she brings us to safety under the sheltering wings of enlightenment. She brings light to the blind, that all fears and calamities may be dispelled, . . . and she scatters the gloom and darkness of delusion. She leads those who have gone astray to the right path. She is omniscience; without beginning or end is Perfect Wisdom, who has Emptiness as her characteristic mark; she is the mother of the Bodhisattvas. . . . She cannot be struck down, the protector of the unprotected, . . . the Perfect Wisdom of the Buddhas, she turns the Wheel of the Law.

[16] Compare especially Proverbs 8 and 9:1–6.

The Blessings of Peace [17]

The following passage is one of the few in the literature of early India which call upon the many kings of the land to forget their quarrels and live together in peace. It seems to contain an implicit criticism of the Hindu ideals of kingship, which encouraged kings to aim at territorial aggrandizement, and to attack their neighbors without good reason, in order to gain homage and tribute.

In the sixth section of the *Sūtra of the Excellent Golden Light,* the four great Kings Vaishravana, Dhritarāshtra, Virūdhaka, and Virūpāksha, who are the gods guarding the four quarters of the earth and correspond to the *Lokapālas* or world-protectors of Hindu mythology, approach the Buddha and declare that they will give their special protection to those earthly kings who patronize monks who recite the sūtra, and encourage its propagation in their domains. The Buddha replies with the words which follow. The sūtra probably belongs to the third or fourth century A.D., before the full expansion of the Gupta empire, when warfare was widespread. The reference to the title *devaputra,* "Son of the Gods," in the passage quoted after the following suggests that it emanated from northwestern India, where *devaputra* was a royal title of the Kushāna kings.

[From *Suvarṇaprabhāsottama Sūtra,* 6, pp. 73–75]

Protect all those royal families, cities, lands, and provinces, save them, cherish them, guard them, ward off invasion from them, give them peace and prosperity. Keep them free from all fear, calamity, and evil portent. Turn back the troops of their enemies and create in all the earthly kings of India a desire to avoid fighting, attacking, quarreling, or disputing with their neighbors. . . . When the eighty-four thousand kings of the eighty-four thousand cities of India are contented with their own territories and with their own kingly state and their own hoards of treasure they will not attack one another or raise mutual strife. They will gain their thrones by the due accumulation of the merit of former deeds; they will be satisfied with their own kingly state, and will not destroy one another, nor show their mettle by laying waste whole provinces. When all the eighty-four thousand kings of the eighty-four thousand capital cities of India think of their mutual welfare and feel mutual affection and joy, . . . contented in their own domains, . . . India will be prosperous, well-fed, pleasant, and populous. The earth will be fertile, and the months and

---

[17] We are indebted to Dr. Edward Conze for drawing our notice to this and the following passage, which have not hitherto received from historians the attention they deserve.

seasons and years will all occur at the proper time.[18] Planets and stars, moon and sun, will duly bring on the days and nights. Rain will fall upon earth at the proper time. And all living beings in India will be rich with all manner of riches and corn, very prosperous but not greedy.

The Divine Right (and Duty) of Kings

As we have seen, the early Buddhists evolved the story of the first king Mahāsammata, which implies a doctrine of social contract. In Hinduism, however, ideas of a different kind developed, and from early in the Christian era it was widely proclaimed in Hindu religious literature that the king was "a great god in human form," made of eternal particles of the chief gods of the Hindu pantheon. It became usual to address the king as Deva or "god," and the older ideas of Buddhism on kingship were, at least in Mahāyāna circles, modified in consequence.

The Sūtra of the Excellent Golden Light, as well as the striking call for peace previously quoted, contains one of the few passages in the Mahāyāna scriptures in which problems of government are discussed. It is not admitted that the king is a god in his own right, but he holds his high estate by the authority of the gods, and therefore is entitled to be addressed as Deva, and as "Son of the Gods." This doctrine of divine appointment may be compared with that widely proclaimed in England during the Stuart period, and it is also closely akin to the Chinese doctrine of the "mandate of Heaven." Like the Son of Heaven in imperial China, the Indian "Son of the Gods" held his title on condition of fulfilling his function properly, and might incur the anger of his divine parents. The verses quoted implicitly admit the moral right of revolt against a wicked or negligent king, for in conspiring against him his subjects are serving the heavenly purpose, and plotting the overthrow of one who no longer enjoys the divine blessing on which his right to govern depends. This too is a doctrine well known in China.

This poem on government, in Buddhist Sanskrit, purports to be a speech of the high god Brahmā, delivered to the four Great Kings, whom we have met in the previous extract.

[From Suvarṇaprabhāsottama Sūtra, 12 (cento)]

How does a king, who is born of men, come to be called divine?
Why is a king called the Son of the Gods?

---

[18] Note that, as we have seen elsewhere, the welfare of the whole land, and even the regularity of the calendar and of heavenly phenomena generally, were believed to be dependent on the morality of men, and more especially on the morality of ruling kings. This idea, which is also found in Hinduism, was well known in China, where it developed independently.

If a king is born in this world of mortals,
How can it be that a god rules over men?

I will tell you of the origin of kings, who are born in the world of mortals,
And for what reason kings exist, and rule over every province.
By the authority of the great gods a king enters his mother's womb.
First he is ordained by the gods—only then does he find an embryo.

What though he is born or dies in the world of mortals—
Arising from the gods he is called the Son of the Gods.

The thirty-three great gods assign the fortune of the king.
The ruler of men is created as son of all the gods,
To put a stop to unrighteousness, to prevent evil deeds,
To establish all beings in well-doing, and to show them the way to heaven.
Whether man, or god, or fairy, or demon,
Or outcaste, he is a true king who prevents evil deeds.
Such a king is mother and father to those who do good.
He was appointed by the gods to show the results of karma. . . .

But when a king disregards the evil done in his kingdom,
And does not inflict just punishment on the criminal,
From his neglect of evil, unrighteousness grows apace,
And fraud and strife increase in the land.

The thirty-three great gods grow angry in their palaces
When the king disregards the evil done in his kingdom.

Then the land is afflicted with fierce and terrible crime,
And it perishes and falls into the power of the enemy.
Then property, families, and hoarded wealth all vanish,
And with varied deeds of deceit men ruin one another.

Whatever his reasons, if a king does not do his duty
He ruins his kingdom, as a great elephant a bed of lotuses.

Harsh winds blow, and rain falls out of season,
Planets and stars are unpropitious, as are the moon and sun,

Corn, flowers, and fruit and seed do not ripen properly,
And there is famine, when the king is negligent. . . .

Then all the kings of the gods say one to another,
"This king is unrighteous, he has taken the side of unrighteousness!"
Such a king will not for long anger the gods;
From the wrath of the gods his kingdom will perish. . . .

He will be bereft of all that he values, whether by brother or son,
He will be parted from his beloved wife, his daughter will die.
Fire will fall from heaven, and mock-suns also.
Fear of the enemy and hunger will grow apace.
His beloved counselor will die, and his favorite elephant;
His favorite horses will die one by one, and his camels. . . .

There will be strife and violence and fraud in all the provinces;
Calamity will afflict the land, and terrible plague.

The brāhmans will then be unrighteous,
The ministers and the judges unrighteous.

The unrighteous will be revered,
And the righteous man will be chastised. . . .
Where the wicked are honored and the good are scorned
There will be famine, thunderbolts, and death . . .
All living beings will be ugly, having little vigor, very weak;
They will eat much, but they will not be filled.
They will have no strength, and no virility—
All beings in the land will be lacking in vigor. . . .

Many ills such as these befall the land
Whose king is partial [in justice] and disregards evil deeds. . . .

But he who distinguishes good deeds from evil,
Who shows the results of karma—he is called a king.
Ordained by the host of gods, the gods delight in him.
For the sake of himself or others, to preserve the righteousness of his land,

And to put down the rogues and criminals in his domains,
Such a king would give up [if need be] his life and his kingdom. . . .

Therefore a king should abandon his own precious life,
But not the jewel of Righteousness, whereby the world is gladdened.

Magical Utterances

It would be wrong to depict Mahāyāna Buddhism as simply a system of idealist philosophy, with a pantheon of benevolent and compassionate deities and an exalted and altruistic ethical system. It contained many elements from a lower stratum of belief, as will be made clear from the following extract from the *Laṅkāvatāra Sūtra,* one of the most important sacred texts of Mahāyāna Buddhism, from which we have already given two quotations.

Belief in the magical efficacy of certain syllables, phrases, and verses is as old as the *Rig Veda*. The Pāli scriptures, however, pay little attention to this aspect of popular religion, and it would seem that the early Buddhists who were responsible for the compilation of these texts took a comparatively rationalistic view of the world. The criticism of vain and useless rituals contained in the Pāli texts and in Ashoka's edicts was probably intended to cover the vain repetition of mantras or magical utterances. But from early in the Christian era onwards, such things became more and more closely associated with Buddhism, especially with the Mahāyāna sects. Hinduism and Buddhism alike developed schools which taught that the constant repetition of mantras was a sure means of salvation. The following passage is not strictly tantric, for it does not attribute to the mantras it quotes any efficiency other than in the dispelling of evil spirits; but the importance given to the mantras, and the fact that they are attributed to the Buddha himself, show that Mahāyāna Buddhism was, by the fourth or fifth century A.D., permeated with the ideas which were to lead to fully developed tantricism.

[From *Laṅkāvatāra Sūtra,* pp. 260–61]

Then the Lord addressed the Great Being, the Bodhisattva Mahāmati thus:

Mahāmati, hold to these magic syllables of the *Laṅkāvatāra,* recited . . . by all the Buddhas, past, present, and future. Now I will repeat them, that those who proclaim the Law of Righteousness may keep them in mind:

Tuṭṭe tuṭṭe vuṭṭe vuṭṭe paṭṭe paṭṭe kaṭṭe kaṭṭe amale amale vimale vimale nime nime hime hime vame vame kale kale kale kale aṭṭe maṭṭe vaṭṭe tuṭṭe jñeṭṭe spuṭṭe kaṭṭe kaṭṭe laṭṭe paṭṭe dime dime cale cale pace pace

*bandhe bandhe añce mañce dutāre dutāre patāre patāre arkke arkke sarkke
sarkke cakre cakre dime dime hime hime ṭu ṭu ṭu ṭu ḍu ḍu ḍu ḍu ru ru ru
ru phu phu phu phu svāhā.* . . .

If men and women of good birth hold, retain, recite, and realize these
magical syllables, nothing harmful shall come upon them—whether a
god, a goddess, a serpent-spirit, a fairy, or a demon.[19] . . . If anyone
should be in the grip of misfortune, let him recite these one hundred and
eight times, and the evil spirits, weeping and wailing, will go off in another direction.

[19] The names of many other supernatural beings follow.

CHAPTER VIII

THE VEHICLE OF THE THUNDERBOLT AND THE DECLINE OF BUDDHISM IN INDIA

The early centuries after Christ were very prosperous ones for Buddhism. In the Northwest it seems to have been the major religion, for hardly any specifically Hindu remains of this period are to be found there. Elsewhere the influence of Buddhism can be measured by the numerous remains of stūpas and monasteries to be found in many parts of India, which are among the finest and most beautiful relics of ancient Indian civilization. From India Buddhism spread not only to Central Asia and China but also to many parts of Southeast Asia. It is certain that it had some effect on the religious thought of the Middle East, and Buddhist influence has been traced in Neo-Platonism, Gnosticism, and Manichaeism. Many authorities believe that early Christianity was influenced, directly or indirectly, by Buddhist ideas. In the Eastern churches the story of Buddha's abandonment of his home for a life of asceticism, "the Great Going-forth," has been adapted as a Christian legend, the name of its protagonist, St. Josaphat, being evidently a corruption of the word *bodhisattva*.

But never in any part of India did Buddhism wholly supplant the other cults and systems. Theistic Hinduism continued to develop even during the period when Buddhism was strongest, as did the six orthodox philosophical systems. Layfolk, though they might support Buddhist monks and worship at Buddhist shrines, would usually patronize brāhmans also, and call on their services for the domestic rites such as birth ceremonies, initiations, marriages, and funerals, which played and still play so big a part in Indian life. Outside the monastic order those who looked on themselves as exclusively Buddhist were at all times probably comparatively few, and Ashoka, when he called on his subjects to respect the members of all sects and patronized Buddhists and Ājīvikas and probably other sects also, merely followed the practice of most religiously minded Indians down to the present day. It must be remembered that Indian religion is not exclusive. The most fanatical sectarian would probably agree that all the other sects had some qualified truth and validity. Hence Buddhism was never wholly cut off from the main stream of Indian religion.

The fourth century A.D. saw the rise of a second great empire, which at its zenith controlled the whole of northern India from Saurashtra to Bengal. This was the empire of the Guptas, whose greatest emperors were Hindus and gave their chief patronage to Vaishnavism.[1] From this period Buddhism began to lose ground in India. Its decline was at first almost imperceptible. The Chinese traveler Fa-hsien, who was in India at the very beginning of the fifth century, testified to the numerous well-populated Buddhist monasteries in all parts of the land. He noted, however, that Buddhists and Hindus joined in the same religious processions, as though Buddhism was looked on as a branch of Hinduism, rather than as an independent religion. In the seventh century the later Chinese travelers such as Hsüan Tsang and I Tsing reported a considerable decline in Buddhism. Numerous monasteries, even in the sacred Buddhist sites, were deserted and in ruins, and many monks were said to be corrupt, and given to superstitious and un-Buddhist practices. Some access of strength no doubt resulted from the support of Harsha (606–647), one of the last Hindu emperors to control the major part of northern India, who is said by Hsüan Tsang to have ended his life as a devotee of Buddhism. The chief stronghold of Buddhism from this time onward was Bihar and Bengal. In Bihar the great Buddhist monastery of Nālandā, probably founded in the fifth century A.D., was one of the chief centers of learning in the whole of India, to which students came from as far afield as China and Java. In eastern India Buddhism continued to flourish until the twelfth century, with the support of the Pāla dynasty, which ruled Bihar and Bengal, and the kings of which, though by no means exclusive in their religious allegiance, gave their chief support to Buddhism. It was from this region that Buddhism was carried in the eighth century to Nepal and Tibet, to be revived and strengthened by later missions in the eleventh century.

The Buddhism which prevailed in India at this time was of a type very

[1] The cult of Vishnu.

different from that known to the pious emperor Ashoka. The Hīnayāna schools had almost disappeared in eastern India, and allegiance was divided between the Mahāyāna and a new branch of Buddhism, often referred to as a separate vehicle, "the Vehicle of the Thunderbolt" (*Vajra-yāna*). From the middle of the fifth century onwards, with the decline of the Gupta empire, Indians began to take more and more interest in the cults of feminine divinities and in the practice of magico-religious rites, which were believed to lead to salvation or to superhuman power, and which often contained licentious or repulsive features. There is no reason to believe that such practices were new—they can be traced in one form or another right back to the Vedas. But until this time they are little in evidence either in literature or in art, and we must assume that they had not much support among the educated, but were practiced chiefly by the lower social orders. As with many other features of Hinduism, they gradually influenced the upper classes, until in the Middle Ages groups of initiates, both Hindu and Buddhist, were to be found all over India, who practiced strange secret ceremonies in order to gain the magic power which, it was believed, would lead to salvation.

Earlier Buddhism had never been so rationalistic as to reject the supernatural. Thus it was taken for granted that the monk who was highly advanced in his spiritual training was capable of supranormal cognition and of marvelous feats such as levitation. The Buddha himself is said to have made a mango tree grow from a stone in a single night and to have multiplied himself a thousandfold; but these miracles were only performed on a single occasion to show the superiority of Buddhism over other sects, and the Master gave explicit instructions to his followers that they were not to make use of their magical powers, the exercise of which might lead them astray from the straight path to Nirvāna. There were, however, at all times hermit monks, living apart from the monasteries in solitude or semi-solitude, and it was probably among such monks that the practice of magic grew.

The new magical Buddhism, like the magical Hinduism which arose at about the same time, is often known as *Tantricism,* from the *Tantras,* or scriptures of the sects, describing the spells, formulas, and rites which the systems advocated. Probably Tantricism did not appear in organized Buddhism until the seventh century, when Hsüan Tsang reported that certain monastic communities were given to magical practices. Tantric Buddhism was of two main branches, known as Right and Left Hand, as in Tantric Hinduism. The Right Hand, though it became very influential in China and Japan, has left little surviving literature in Sanskrit; it was distinguished by devotion to masculine divinities. The Left Hand sects, to which the name *Vajrayāna* ("Vehicle of the Thunderbolt") was chiefly applied, postulated feminine counterparts or wives to the Buddhas, bodhisattvas, and other divinities of the mythology of later Buddhism, and devoted their chief attention to these *Tārās,* or "Savioresses." As in Hinduism they were thought of as the personified active aspects of the deities in question. The lore of this form of Buddhism was not generally given to the ordinary believer, but was imparted only to the initiate, who need not be a monk, but might be a layman. Adepts who had learned the secrets of Vajrayāna at the feet of a spiritual preceptor (guru) would meet together, usually at night, in small groups to perform their secret ceremonies.

Among the chief features of the ritual of Vajrayāna was the repetition of mystical syllables and phrases (mantra), such as the famous *Oṃ maṇi padme hūṃ.*[2] Yoga postures and meditation were practiced. But the Tantric groups also followed more questionable methods of gaining salvation. It was believed that once the adept had reached a certain degree of spiritual attainment the normal rules of moral behavior were no longer valid for him, and that their deliberate breach, if committed in an odor of sanctity, would actually help him on the upward path. Thus drunkenness, meat-eating, and sexual promiscuity were often indulged in, as well as such repulsive psychopathic practices as eating ordure, and sometimes even ritual murder. Such antinomianism was perhaps the logical corollary of one of the doctrines which Tantric Buddhism took over from the Yogācāra school of Mahāyāna, that all things in the universe were on ultimate analysis the illusory products of mind.

We must not believe that the whole of Tantric Buddhism is included in the practice of unpleasant secret rites. Many Tantric circles practiced such rites only symbolically, and their teachers often produced works of

---

[2] "Ah! The jewel is indeed in the lotus!" Though there are other interpretations this seems the most probable significance of the mysterious and elliptical phrase, which is specially connected with the Bodhisattva Avalokiteshvara, and is still believed in Tibet to have immense potency. Its significance may be sexual, implying that the Bodhisattva has united with his Tārā.

considerable philosophical subtlety, while the ethical tone of some passages in the Tantricist Saraha's *Treasury of Couplets* (*Dohākośa*), one of the last Buddhist works produced in India is of the highest.

The Vajrayāna developed its own system of philosophy by adapting the doctrines of the Vijnānavādins and Mādhyamikas to its own world view. It admitted the emptiness of all things, but maintained that, once the emptiness was fully recognized, the phenomenal world was not to be disparaged, for it was fundamentally identical with the universal Emptiness itself. Thus the adept was encouraged to utilize the phenomenal world for his psychic progress to supreme wisdom. The world was a Means (*upāya,* a masculine noun in Sanskrit), and full consciousness of the Emptiness of all things was the Supreme Wisdom (prajnā, a feminine noun), often personified both in Mahāyāna and Vajrayāna circles as a goddess. Final bliss was to be obtained by the union of the phenomenal Means with the noumenal Wisdom, and the most vivid symbol of such union was sexual intercourse. Thus a philosophical basis was found for the erotic practices of Tantric Buddhism. The Vajrayāna position was rather like that of certain deviationist Christian sects, the morals of which were completely antinomian, because their members were the Elect, and thus above the law.

The end of Buddhism in India is still not completely elucidated. Buddhist monasteries survived in many parts of the land until the time of the Muslim invasions at the very end of the twelfth century. Though there had been some loss of ground to Hinduism, it is clear that the great monasteries of Bihar and Bengal were inhabited down to this time. Fine illustrated manuscripts of Mahāyāna and Tantric scriptures were produced in Eastern India, some of which found their way to Nepal, where they have survived to this day. Inscriptions and archaeological evidence show that there were still fairly prosperous Buddhist monasteries at the sacred sites of Sarnath, near Vārānasī, where the Buddha preached his first sermon, and Shrāvastī, in northern Uttar Pradesh, where he spent much of his actual life. In the Deccan and the Dravidian South there are few evidences of Buddhism after the tenth century, though here and there it survived. It would seem that the life of the monasteries became gradually more and more estranged from that of the people, and that the activities of the monks, grown wealthy from long standing endowments, became increasingly confined to small circles of initiates. This, however, is not the whole story, for Buddhists were among the earliest writers of Bengali, and this would indicate an attempt to make contact with a popular audience. Thus the end of Buddhism was not wholly due to the divorce of Buddhism and everyday life, or to corruption and decay, as some have suggested.

By the time of the Guptas we find the Buddha worshiped in his shrines as a Hindu god, with all the ritual of pūjā,[3] and Buddhist monks and Hindu priests joined in the same processions. The Pāla kings, who claimed to be "supreme worshipers of the Buddha," were also proud of the fact that they maintained all the rules of Hindu dharma,[4] and many of their ministers were orthodox brāhmans. We can perhaps imagine the attitude of the layman to Buddhism from this analogy. For ordinary folk living near a Buddhist monastery, Buddha would be one god among many; they might pay him special homage and worship because their ancestors had done so and because his temple was nearby, but they would not look upon his worship as in any way excluding them from the Hindu fold. Medieval Hinduism knew many sects, each specially devoted to one or other of the gods, who was looked upon as supreme, the lesser gods being mere emanations or secondary forms of the great one. From the point of view of the layman this would be the position of Buddhism—a sect of Hinduism with its own special order of devotees, the monks, pledged to the service of their god. It cannot be too strongly emphasized that Hinduism has always tended to assimilate rather than to exclude.

At this time anti-Buddhist activity was not completely unknown. There are traditions, most of them preserved only in Buddhist sources and therefore suspect of exaggeration, of occasional fierce persecution by anti-Buddhist kings, chiefly Shaivites,[5] some of whom are said even to have gone as far as to place a price on the head of every Buddhist monk. Allowing for all exaggerations, it is clear that some kings were strongly anti-Buddhist and took active steps to discourage Buddhism. More serious opposition came from certain medieval Hindu philosophers and their disciples. Teachers such as Kumārila and Shankara are said to have traveled far and wide throughout India preaching their own doctrines and attacking those of their rivals, and Buddhism seems to have been singled

[3] Worship of an idol with offerings of lights, flowers, food, etc.
[4] The Sacred Law.   [5] Worshipers of Shiva.

out for special attention by those reformers. Anti-Buddhist propaganda of one kind or another may have had a significant influence in the decline of Buddhism.

By the time of the Muslim invasion (1192 A.D.) Buddhism was rapidly merging in the body of Hinduism. The process is exemplified in the doctrine of the incarnations of Vishnu, which does not appear in its final form until just before the Muslim invasion. Here the Buddha figures as an incarnation of the Supreme God, who took human form in order either to put a stop to the sacrifice of living animals, or, according to some formulations, to destroy the wicked by leading them to deny the Vedas and so accomplish their own perdition. Thus the Buddha was placed, in theory at least, on the same exalted level as the great popular divinities Krishna and Rāma, and his devotees might worship him as a full member of the orthodox pantheon. There is no reason to believe that the cult of Buddha as a Hindu god was ever widespread, but certainly in the great temple of Gayā, the scene of the Master's enlightenment, he was adored by simple Hindu pilgrims with all the rites of Hinduism as a Hindu god until very recent times, when the ancient temple was transferred back to Buddhist hands. Other traces of Buddhism survive in parts of eastern India. Thus it is said that the peasants of Bengal and Orissa still worship a divinity called Dharma, who seems to be a faint folk recollection of the ancient religion of the land.

When the Turkish horsemen occupied Bihar and Bengal, slew or expelled the "shaven-headed brāhmans," as they called the Buddhist monks, and destroyed their monasteries and libraries, Buddhism was dead in India. The *purohitas* (chaplains) of Hinduism, who performed the domestic rites for the layfolk, and the Hindu ascetics who wandered from place to place, were in need of no organization and could survive the disruption of the Muslim invasion and the aggressive propaganda of the alien faith. Buddhism, dependent on the monasteries for its survival and without the same lay support as Hinduism received, was destroyed by the invader. It is noteworthy that Islam had its greatest success in those parts of India where Buddhism had been strongest, in the Northwest, and in Bengal. Only in the Himālayan regions, especially Nepal, did Buddhism survive, kept alive largely by contact with Tibet. Though in many parts of Asia it has flourished, and indeed spread and developed in the last seven hundred years, in the land of its birth it has died. Only in the last few decades have intelligent Indians begun once more to take an interest in the religion founded by India's greatest son. Thanks largely to the work of the Mahābodhi Society the sacred sites of Buddhism are once more cared for, and Buddhist monasteries again exist in many parts of India. Though the number of professing Buddhists in India and Pakistan is still very small, there is no doubt that the doctrines of Buddhism are beginning to influence more and more Indians, and Buddhism may well become a force to be reckoned with in the India of the future.

To the Pure All Things Are Pure

The doctrine that the round of birth-and-death was really the same as Nirvāna, the cult of feminine divinities, and the growing interest in magic, especially magical utterances, led to the appearance of Vajrayāna, or Tantric Buddhism. The rather dangerous view that all things are legitimate to those who fully know the truth is already to be found in specifically Mahāyāna texts. In the texts of Vajrayāna it is developed further, for it is declared that, at a certain stage of self-development, to give way to the passions, especially the sexual passions, is a positive help along the upward path. This passage is taken from a Tantric poem, *Disquisition on the Purification of the Intellect,* composed by Āryadeva [1] toward the end of the seventh century.

[From *Cittaviśuddhiprakaraṇa,* pp. 24-38]

> They who do not see the truth
>   Think of birth-and-death as distinct from Nirvāna,
> But they who do see the truth
>   Think of neither. . . .
>
> This discrimination is the demon
>   Who produces the ocean of transmigration.
> Freed from it the great ones are released
>   From the bonds of becoming.
>
> Plain folk are afflicted
>   With the poison of doubt. . . .
> He who is all compassion . . .
>   Should uproot it completely.

[1] Not the same as an earlier Āryadeva, disciple of Nāgārjuna and author of the *Four-hundred Stanzas* (*Catuḥśataka*).

As a clear crystal assumes
  The color of another object,
So the jewel of the mind is colored
  With the hue of what it imagines.

The jewel of the mind is naturally devoid
  Of the color of these ideas,
Originally pure, unoriginated,
  Impersonal, and immaculate.

So, with all one's might, one should do
  Whatever fools condemn,
And, since one's mind is pure,
  Dwell in union with one's divinity.[2]

The mystics, pure of mind,
  Dally with lovely girls,
Infatuated with the poisonous flame of passion,
  That they may be set free from desire.

By his meditations the sage is his own Garuda,[3]
  Who draws out the venom [of snakebite] and drinks it.
He makes his deity innocuous,
  And is not affected by the poison. . . .

When he has developed a mind of wisdom
  And has set his heart on enlightenment
There is nothing he may not do
  To uproot the world [from his mind].

He is not Buddha, he is not set free,
  If he does not see the world
As originally pure, unoriginated,
  Impersonal, and immaculate.

[2] That is, the woman with whom the Tantricist practices his rites.
[3] A mythical, divine bird, the enemy and slayer of snakes.

The mystic duly dwells
  On the manifold merits of his divinity,
He delights in thoughts of passion,
  And by the enjoyment of passion is set free.

What must we do? Where are to be found
  The manifold potencies of being?
A man who is poisoned may be cured
  By another poison, the antidote.

Water in the ear is removed by more water,
  A thorn [in the skin] by another thorn.
So wise men rid themselves of passion
  By yet more passion.

As a washerman uses dirt
  To wash clean a garment,
So, with impurity,
  The wise man makes himself pure.

Everything Is Buddha

The last phase of Buddhism in India was the school of Tantricism sometimes known as *Sahajayāna* or *Sahajiya,* "the Vehicle of the Innate," which stressed the doctrine that Ultimate Being was ever present in all things living, a view not strange to Buddhism, and very well known in Hinduism. The Sahajayāna teachers, like other Tantricists, strongly supported the view that sexual activity and other forms of worldly pleasure were positive helps to salvation for those who made use of them in the proper spirit, but their teaching was distinguished by its emphasis on simplicity—it was possible for the ordinary layman, living a normal life in every respect, to achieve salvation, simply by recognizing the Buddha within himself and all things.

The teachers of this school began to write in the vernaculars, and a number of their poems and series of verses, composed either in Apabhramsha [1] or Old Bengali, survive from among the many which must now be lost. All these works date from the tenth to the twelfth centuries. Unlike Sanskrit poetry their verses are rhymed and they employ meters which are still widely used in

[1] The early medieval vernaculars, which had moved much further from Sanskrit than had Pāli or the Prākrits, and were much closer to the modern languages of India.

the vernaculars. For these reasons they give an impression very different from that of earlier Buddhist poetry. In their simplicity of style, and in the simplicity of their doctrines, they seem to look forward rather than back—towards the simple mystical verse of Kabīr, who also taught that the Ultimate Being was to be found in one's own home, as one went about one's daily work. Like Kabīr's verses again they sometimes have a strong ethical content; for all their emphasis on the value of sex as a means of salvation, the Sahajayāna teachers, like all Buddhists, taught the virtues of compassion, kindliness, and helpfulness.

The following verses are taken from the *Treasury of Couplets* ascribed to Saraha, and written in Apabhramsha in the eleventh or twelfth century.

[From Saraha, *Dohākośa,* v. 102-end; as translated by D. S. Snellgrove in Conze, *Buddhist Texts,* pp. 238–39]

As is Nirvāna so is Samsāra.[2]
  Do not think there is any distinction.
Yet it possesses no single nature,
  For I know it as quite pure.

Do not sit at home, do not go to the forest,
  But recognize mind wherever you are.
When one abides in complete and perfect enlightenment,
  Where is Samsāra and where is Nirvāna?

Oh know this truth,
  That neither at home nor in the forest does enlightenment dwell.
Be free from prevarication
  In the self-nature of immaculate thought!

"This is my self and this is another."
  Be free of this bond which encompasses you about,
And your own self is thereby released.

Do not err in this matter of self and other.
  Everything is Buddha without exception.
Here is that immaculate and final stage,
  Where thought is pure in its true nature.

___

[2] Transmigration, i.e., this world.

The fair tree of thought that knows no duality,
   Spreads through the triple world.
It bears the flower and fruit of compassion,
   And its name is service of others.

The fair tree of the Void abounds with flowers,
   Acts of compassion of many kinds,
And fruit for others appearing spontaneously,
   For this joy has no actual thought of another.

So the fair tree of the Void also lacks compassion,
   Without shoots or flowers or foliage,
And whoever imagines them there, falls down,
   For branches there are none.[3]

The two trees spring from one seed,
   And for that reason there is but one fruit.
He who thinks of them thus indistinguishable,
   Is released from Nirvāna and Samsāra.

If a man in need approaches and goes away hopes unfulfilled,
   It is better he should abandon that house
Than take the bowl that has been thrown from the door.

Not to be helpful to others,
   Not to give to those in need,
This is the fruit of Samsāra.
   Better than this is to renounce the idea of a self.

He who clings to the Void
   And neglects Compassion,
Does not reach the highest stage.

[3] All things are ultimately one in the eternal and infinite Emptiness which is the body of the Buddha; therefore there is no real distinction between self and others, and on analysis the "fair tree" is nonexistent. But, as we shall see in the following verse, on a still higher plane of thought it shares the reality of the Ultimate Being, and therefore, to the man who sees the world with complete clarity, acts of mercy and kindness are still valid.

But he who practices only Compassion,
    Does not gain release from toils of existence.
He, however, who is strong in practice of both,
    Remains neither in Samsāra nor in Nirvāna.

PART THREE
HINDUISM

B.C.	c.500–500 A.D.	Period of Hindu lawbooks, epics, and development of the six orthodox systems of philosophy.
	c.300	Earliest core of Kautilya's *Artha Śāstra*.
	c.100–100 A.D.	*Composition of Bhagavad Gītā.*
A.D.	c.100–200	Early law code of Yājnavalkya.
	c.200–400	Bharata's *Treatise on Dramaturgy*.

Gupta Period

c.300–500   Īshvarakrishna's *Sāṅkhya Kārikās*. Christian community of the Nestorian (Syrian) sect in existence at Cochin in South India.

c.300–888   Pallava rulers of Kāñchī in South India.

c.319 [or 318, 320]–335   Chandragupta I.

c.335–376   Samudragupta.

c.376–415   Chandragupta II.

c.400–500   Vātsyāyana's Aphorisms on Love.

c.405   Fa-hsien, Chinese pilgrim arrives in Magadha.

c.454   First Hūna invasion.

c.495   Second Hūna invasion.

c.540   End of Gupta dynasty.

c.550–753 [or, 757]   Kingdom of Western Chālukyas in Deccan.

606–647   Rule of King Harsha of Kanauj in North India.

c.629–645   Chinese pilgrim Hsüan-tsang visits India.

c.630–970   Eastern Chālukyas in Deccan.

Medieval India

c.700–800   Tamil saint Māṇikkavāchakar in Mathurai. Dandin, Sanskrit author and rhetorician.

c.760–1142   Pālas of Bihar and Bengal.

c.788–820   Traditional dates of Shankara.

c.800–900   *Bhāgavata Purāṇa. Policy of Shukra*. Jinasena's *Great Legend* (*Mahāpurāṇa*). Sundaramūrti, Shaiva *Nāyanār* of South India. Vāmana and Ānandavardhana, Hindu rhetoricians and aesthetic philosophers.

c.907–1310 [or, c.850–1267]   Chola Empire at Tanjore.

c.973–1189	Second Chālukya dynasty in Western and Central Deccan.
c.1000–1100	Abhinavagupta. Yāmuna Āchārya's (Tamil' Ālavandār) *Āgamaprāmāṇya*. Saraha's *Dohākośa*. Rise of Hindu Tantricism.
c.1018–1055	King Bhoja of Mālwā.
c.1100–1200	Mammata's *Kāvyaprakāśa*. Basavarāja founds Vīrashaiva movement in South India.
c.1137	Death of Rāmānuja.
c.1197–1276 [or, 1199–1278]	Madhva Āchārya.
c.1200–1300	Shārngadeva's treatise on music, *Sangītaratnākara*. Lokāchārya's *Triad of Categories*.
1216–1327	Pāndyas of Mathura.
c.1275–1296	Jnāneshvara's *Jñāneśvarī*.
c.1300–1400	Lallā, poetess of Kashmir.
1336–1565	Vijayanagara, last great Hindu kingdom in India.
c.1420 [or, 1550]	Mīrā Bāī, Rājput poetess.
1440–1518	Kabīr.
c.1449–1568	Shankaradeva, Vaishnava saint of Assam.
c.1475 [or, 1479]–1531	Vallabha, Vedānta philosopher.
c.1480–1564	Purandaradāsa, poet-saint of Karnataka.
c.1485–1533	Chaitanya of Bengal.
c.1500–1600	Sūrdās, blind poet of Agra. Vādirāja's *Kṛṣṇastuti* and *Haryaṣṭaka*.
c.1532–1623	Tulasī Dās.
c.1542	St. Francis Xavier arrives in India.
c.1609–1649 [or, 1598–1649]	Tukārāma, Mahārāshtra poet-saint.
c.1700–1800	Baladeva, Vaishnava mystic in Bengal.
c.1718–1775	Rāmaprasād in Bengal.
c.1767 [or, 1759]–1847	Tyāgarāja, saint-musician of South India.

INTRODUCTION

Buddhism and Jainism, which appear from archaeological evidence to have achieved considerable influence in India from c.200 B.C. to A.D. c.200, were gradually displaced by what came to be known as Hinduism, so-called because at the time of the Muslim conquest (A.D. c.1200) it was already the religion of the vast majority of Indians (Persian *Hindū,* "Indian"). Even today, despite the long period of Muslim rule (thirteenth to eighteenth centuries), with its numerous conversions to Islam, and the century or two (depending on the area) of British rule, Hindus account for three-fourths of the inhabitants of the subcontinent; the Buddhists have disappeared except in outlying areas (e.g., Tibet, Ceylon, Southeast Asia, etc.); and the Jains form a minority of little but commercial significance.

Hinduism is divided into innumerable sects and has no well-defined, large-scale ecclesiastic organization. Its two most general characteristics are the caste system and agreement about the sacredness of its most ancient scriptures, the Veda, which though considered essentially eternal, were revealed to the sages, the rishis. The caste system is itself supposed to rest on the authority of the Veda and in a sense the whole society forms an ecclesiastical organization, with its own canon law, the Sacred Law (dharma), also based on the Veda. The apex of the pyramidal caste system is the brāhman class, who because they are the authoritative interpreters and transmitters of the Veda, and sole ministrants of the religious sacraments, are likewise considered sacred. The hierarchy of caste is based upon how close a caste comes in its way of life to the pattern set by the brāhmans, who are themselves ranged into a hierarchy of castes on the basis of scriptural learning, adherence to the Sacred Law, and birth (that is, on the recognition won by their particular caste over a long period of time).

Hindus generally believe that the soul is eternal but is bound by the law of karma ("action") to the world of matter, which it can only escape after spiritual progress through an endless series of births. Different schools and sects have different views about metaphysics and the nature and method of release (moksha) from transmigration. The *Song of the Lord* (*Bhagavad Gītā*) sets forth three basic paths: those of knowledge, selfless action, and devotion to God. They are regarded as complementary rather than mutually exclusive. As understood today, the path of knowledge implies an awareness that reality is one and spiritual, the Brahman, with which each apparently individual soul is identical, and which is sat, chit, ānanda—pure being, intelligence, and bliss. All distinctions, including the entire phenomenal world, have only a relative reality but are ultimately false and the result of the creative illusion (māyā) of the Brahman. The path of devotion implies belief in a supreme personal god as the ultimate reality, the creator, preserver, and destroyer of the universe; salvation, viewed as various degrees of nearness to, and communion with, God, is dependent on God's grace in response to the devotee's intense and unswerving devotion and service. The major division in Hinduism is between the devotees of Vishnu and those of Shiva.

Neither the path of knowledge nor that of devotion need be, or ordinarily is, strictly monistic or monotheistic in practice. After all, man's desires, needs, and sufferings are many, and corresponding to these there are hosts of minor gods as well as various incarnations, manifestations, and aspects of the major gods. All these are generally united mythologically to one or the other major god. Thus Krishna and Rāma are the most important incarnations of Vishnu; Shiva's spouse is the Mother Goddess, known as Devī, Kālī, etc. As the Hindu generally does not follow any rigid dogma, there is a great deal of interpenetration between the various views of the divine, with the result that in India there are polytheistic monists, dualistic monotheists, etc. The various views are ordered by the monists, who follow the philosophy of the Upanishads as interpreted by Shankara (ninth century A.D.) into descending levels of apprehension of one and the same truth. The monistic view, whether pure monism or not, is often referred to as Higher Hinduism, the other views as Popular or Sectarian Hinduism. Included in the latter are more humble beliefs among the lowest strata of the population, such as the worship of various animals, trees, diseases, and even stones.

Devotion to the devotee's chosen deity (*iṣṭa-devatā*) may be purely spiritual, but it is usually manifested by pūjā, the ritual of worship and service of an idol of the deity (bathing the idol, offerings of food and water, flowers, lights, music and dancing). Just as sacrifice (yajna) was characteristic of early Brahmanism, renunciation (sannyāsa) of the Upanishads (and Theravāda Buddhism and Jainism), pūjā is character-istic of Hinduism (and Mahāyāna Buddhism). The idol or idols must be housed and cared for, and this requires temples and priests. Temples grew more and more elaborate with time, as did the ritual of worship. In fact, temples came to play a most important religious, cultural and artistic, and even economic role in medieval India.

The orthodox Hindu believes that the ultimate truth in matters of re-ligion is to be found in the Veda, which is called *Shruti,* revelation. Later scriptures represent interpretations or codifications of that truth and are therefore called *Smriti* (human) tradition. The sectarian may also believe that his god revealed a more explicit doctrine in some still more recent scripture (āgama or tantra). Thus the Hindu sees religious development in Hinduism as the emphasis of now this, now that aspect of the Veda, or as a gradually deeper and more complete perception of the truth which was there in the Veda all the time. Thus the six orthodox systems of phi-losophy all claim Vedic authority, a claim which later Hindus have ac-cepted in the belief that all were complementary visions (darshanas) of the one Truth. Even the Hindu's major gods, Vishnu or Shiva, had been worshiped in Vedic times too (though both were quite minor figures in the early Veda), so that later theistic movements were seen as a con-tinuation and expansion of an earlier faith.

We have seen how the ideal of cosmic ethical interdependence of the earliest (the hymnal) portion of the Veda, the Samhitā, gave way to the principle of ritualistic—sacrificial and magical—cosmic interdependence in the Brāhmana period, and the latter, in turn, to the conclusion that ultimate reality was one, the Brahman, identical with man's Self, Ātman, as revealed in the concluding portion of the Veda, namely, the Upanishads. The doctrine of the Upanishads was really only the expression within the Vedic or Brahmanical tradition of a great quietistic movement char-acterized by a deep disillusionment with life, probably closely associated with the elaboration of the doctrines of karma and rebirth. The same movement was the basis of the heterodox faiths of Buddhism and Jainism. Thus if the earlier periods of the Brahmanical tradition had emphasized the positive values of life, symbolized by the ritual designed to help achieve those values, namely, the sacrifice (yajna), the last period was pessimistic and its ideal was renunciation (sannyāsa) of worldly life for the life of a religious mendicant.

The new outlook affected first and most profoundly those groups of brāhmans who had been given to theosophical speculations since late Rig-Vedic times, many of whom already lived in forest hermitages. But the ritualists, who formed the great majority of brāhmans, were also affected to some extent and adopted, in the Sacred Law, renunciation as the ultimate religious ideal of man, though to be followed only after a man had fulfilled all his social obligations during most of his adult life. (The elaboration of the Sacred Law is contemporary with the Upanishads in its beginnings but continued on for several centuries after Christ.)

Side by side with these developments in hieratic and intellectual circles, there are indications cropping up even in early texts of more popular religious movements centering around the worship of various supreme gods. This may well be a popular expression of the same search for cosmic unity in an Absolute which we found at the intellectual level in the Veda: e.g., the Brahmā (Sanskrit *Brahman,* a masculine noun) of the *Mahābhārata,* an early supreme creator god, is a personalized form of the Upanishadic Brahman (neuter in Sanskrit). These theistic movements must have grown in importance over a long period before they took on the trappings of philosophical thought, e.g., in a late Upanishad glorifying Shiva, the *Śvetāśvatara,* and from this time we can follow the development of theism through its own vast literature. The somewhat later and much more famous *Song of the Lord* (*Bhagavad Gītā*), dedicated to Krishna further advocates action according to dharma, ordained duty, and thus the Sacred Law comes to form a part of the new dispensation. Thus fortified by philosophy and the Brahmanical Sacred Law, Hinduism, as the new theistic movements are called, spread rapidly and to a great extent absorbed the rival faiths of Buddhism and Jainism.

Intellectually, the Upanishadic doctrine of an eternal, immutable essence of all things was easier to reconcile with theism than the Buddhist doctrine of universal impermanence. Socially, the Sacred Law, evolved chiefly on the basis of the older Brahmanism, became the property of Hinduism and was applied and propagated by both kings and brāhmans. Politically, the monistic, monotheistic, and socially hierarchical tendencies of Hinduism accorded better with the growing power and divinization of kings. Finally, by slight adjustments of the mythology the Hindu gods could be given an antiquity far beyond human traditions, as well as the scriptural authority of the Veda. Thus Krishna became an avatār (incarnation) of the Vedic Vishnu, Shiva another name for the Vedic Rudra, and the other gods of the new pantheon were somehow brought into derivative relationship to these two. The mantle of Vedic authority also covered the Sacred Law, the orthodox systems of philosophy, and, in fact, the whole of Hinduism. Hinduism is thus both a new religion and, in certain respects, a continuation of the older Brahmanism.

In contrast to the earlier Brahmanism which was restricted in principle to those of Aryan birth, and in contrast also to Theravāda Buddhism and Jainism, which offered the prospect of immediate salvation only to the monk, the new theistic movements offered an easy path to salvation for all, the path of devotion to God, without the need for forsaking life in society. The new ideal was also egalitarian as regards the hope of salvation—were not all devotees, from whatever class, equally dear to God? Hinduism thus offered a strong religious bond, transcending class or caste distinctions, to a society threatened with disintegration by the foreign invasions and rule of the second century B.C. to A.D. c.300 and later.

The periods in which these developments were brought to their fullest expression in Hindu culture were the dynasties of the Guptas in the North (fourth and fifth centuries A.D.) and the Pallavas (c. fourth to ninth centuries A.D.) and Cholas (c. ninth to c. twelfth centuries) in the South. The Gupta Age is the classical period of Hindu culture, which was to be imitated but not surpassed by later ages. It was brought to an end in the North c.500 by repeated invasions of the Huns which must have greatly impoverished northern India and which ushered in what we refer to as the Indian medieval period, distinguished from the earlier, classical age not by any break in cultural continuity but rather by lesser creativity and the spread of popular religious movements centered on devotionalism and magic. Politically there was a gradual disintegration and centralized empires gave way to looser, more feudalistic types of political organization, which were no match for the Turkish Muslim raiders and invaders from Ghazni and Ghur in present Afghanistan (c.1000–1200).

While the Dravidian South, which had never been Brahmanical, had early been converted to Buddhism or Jainism, in the North from the Shunga (second to first centuries B.C.) to the Gupta period Hinduism had made much headway against the heterodox religions. From the North, probably due in part to the prestige of the Guptas, the movement spread to the South, and the Pallava rulers were converted to Hinduism. It was with their help and that of their successors, the Cholas, that southern India became the stronghold of the Hindu tradition after the Muslim invasions in the north.

From the foregoing it will be clear that Hinduism was much more than an aggregation of devotional cults and philosophical schools—it was a way of life. To understand this way of life in its fullness and variety, we must first see how the major fields of human endeavor were ordered, according to the traditional Hindu conception, in relation to the ultimate ends of man.

CHAPTER IX

THE FOUR ENDS OF MAN

One of the main concepts which underlies the Hindu attitude to life and daily conduct is that of the four ends of man (purushārtha). The first of these is characterized by considerations of righteousness, duty, and virtue. This is called *dharma*. There are other activities, however, through which a man seeks to gain something for himself or pursue his own pleasure. When the object of this activity is some material gain, it is called *artha;* when it is love or pleasure, it is *kāma*. Finally, there is the renunciation of all these activities in order to devote oneself to religious or spiritual activities with the aim of liberating oneself from the worldly life; this is *mokṣa*. These four are referred to as "the tetrad" (*caturvarga*).

In early texts it is more usual to find the aspirations of man stated as three: dharma, material gain, and love or pleasure. Dharma then refers to the religio-ethical ideal, which we may translate as "virtue." The basic meaning of dharma, a word derived from the root *dhṛ,* "to sustain," is the moral law, which sustains the world, human society, and the individual. Dharma thus replaced the Vedic word rita, the principle of cosmic ethical interdependence. Though dharma generally refers to religiously ordained duty, in other passages it may just mean morality, right conduct, or the rules of conduct (mores, customs, codes, or laws) of a group. When Upanishadic mysticism and quietism came to be included in the religio-ethical ideal, dharma was classified into two aspects, the one relating to activity (*pravṛtti*) and the other to retirement from life (*nivṛtti*). Then *nivṛtti* itself later became a separate end of man under the name moksha, spiritual liberation. When moksha, now representing the higher religious ideal, is opposed to dharma, the latter no longer refers to the whole of religion but continues to include all ritual activities and ethical duties and ideals, such as right, righteousness, virtue, justice, propriety, morality, beneficence, and nonviolence. Dharma is in fact a key word of Hindu culture, and Hinduism itself is sometimes designated as Sanātana Dharma, the Eternal Dharma.

The great epic, the *Mahābhārata,* carries dharma as its burden, for it states at the end as the essence of its teachings: "With uplifted arms I cry, none heeds; from dharma [religious duty], material gain and pleasure flow; [1] then, why is not dharma pursued? Neither for the sake of pleasure, nor out of fear or avarice, no, not even for the sake of one's life should one give up dharma; dharma stands alone for all time; pleasure and pain are transitory." While this great epic makes its hero, Yudhishthira, the very son of the God of Dharma (*Dharma-putra*) and one who had no enemy (*Ajātaśatru*), the other epic, the *Rāmāyaṇa,* makes its hero, Rāma, dharma itself in flesh and blood.

The pursuits of material gain and pleasure are both necessary for life— for no one can live without either acquiring some goods or enjoying things to some extent—but they should be controlled by considerations of dharma. While material gain and pleasure refer to actuality, dharma refers to an ideal principle or rule or norm to which man should conform in his activities in the world, with reference to himself or in relation to his fellow-beings. Dharma is therefore assigned first place, because it is the regulating factor, except for which the pursuit of material gain and pleasure would lead man to ruin or into conflict with his fellow-beings. The Upanishads call upon man not to covet another's wealth (*Īśāvāsya,* 1.1). Even kings, whose role in life is so closely bound up with material activities and considerations, are asked to observe and enforce dharma; [2] they are considered merely regents and executors of dharma. A king who follows the injunctions of dharma is called a royal sage (*rāja-ṛṣi*); his victories, the victories of dharma (as the poet Kālidāsa says); and his rule, the rule of dharma. The *Lawbook of Yājnavalkya* (*Yājñavalkya Smṛti*) states that where there is a conflict between principle and policy, righteousness and material advantage, dharma and artha, the former should prevail. Similarly control by dharma is insisted upon for love or pleasure (kāma) also. In a well-known passage, the *Bhagavad Gītā* (7.11) makes the Lord identify Himself with such desire (kāma) as is consistent with dharma. The Hindu ideal does not preach abstinence from pleasure for all or at all stages; it rather preaches, universally, the

---

[1] Fulfilling one's religious duties, which included both ritual and ethical duties, was thought to lead to material rewards and pleasures both in this life and in heaven.

[2] Ordained duty, especially justice, the first and main religious duty of a king, and social duties (i.e., the class system).

ideal of chastened love, or pleasure regulated by considerations of both morality and material wellbeing.

The pursuit of moksha or liberation is placed last, as according to the Hindu scheme of values, it ought to be the final and supreme aspiration of man. The desire for liberation from the endless cycle of transmigration to which the spirit is subjected is so ingrained in the Hindu that however much he may wander about in life, he does not fail in his later years to pursue this yearning of the soul. Even in these days of Western education many who have led a modern life find a change coming over them and heed the nostalgic call of the Hindu spirit. Examples of this change are not wanting even among politicians; be they Moderates, Congressmen, or Praja-Socialists, they hear that inner voice to which the national poet Kālidāsa gave expression as he laid down his pen: "And as for me, may Shiva, the almighty, end this cycle of rebirth."

From the Science of Dharma

Each of the first three ends of man was the subject-matter of a separate science: dharma, religion, of the *Dharma Śāstra,* the science of dharma, which we translate freely as the Sacred Law; artha, material gain, of the *Artha Śāstra,* the science of material gain; and kāma, love or pleasure, of the *Kāma Śāstra,* the science of love. Moksha, spiritual liberation, is not separately mentioned in the readings given below, but is included under dharma.

[From *Manu Smṛti,* 2.224]
Some say that dharma [virtue] and material gain are good, others that pleasure and material gain are good, and still others that dharma alone or pleasure alone is good, but the correct position is that the three should co-exist without harming each other.

[From *Yājñavalkya Smṛti,* 2.2.21]
The science of dharma is of greater authority than the science of material gain.

From the Science of Material Gain: The Conduct of
the Ideal King
   [From *Kauṭilīya, Artha Śāstra,* 1.7]

Therefore by abandoning the six internal enemies,[1] one should gain the
control of his senses; he should gain knowledge by associating himself
with elders, use his intelligence department as his eye, acquire and conserve things by exertion, establish righteous rule by commands and
directives, and discipline among the people by the extension of education, endear himself to the people by gifts, and provide livelihood to
them with what is beneficial to each.

Having brought his senses under discipline he must avoid betaking to
others' women, appropriating others' wealth, and injuring others; he
must avoid also long sleep, fickleness, falsehood, gaudy dress, associations
which would bring him to grief, and activities that are unrighteous and
unprofitable.

He should enjoy pleasure without detriment to virtue or material gain;
he ought not to deprive himself of pleasure. Or he should take to pursuits virtuous, profitable, and pleasant in such a manner that they are
mutually helpful. Of these, virtue, material gain and pleasure, if one is
pursued by him to the exclusion of the others, it affects him adversely as
well as others.

From the Science of Love
   [From Vātsyāyana, *Kāma Sūtra,* 1.1.1; 1.2.1, 14, 49]

Obeisance to virtue, material gain, and pleasure. [1.1.1]

Man, who could normally live up to a hundred years, must apportion
his time and take to virtue, material gain, and pleasure in such a way that
these are mutually integrated and do not harm each other. As a boy he
must attend to accomplishments like learning; in youth he should enjoy
himself; in later life he should pursue the ideals of virtue and spiritual
liberation. [1.2.1]

When there are all three, virtue, material gain, and pleasure, their
mutual superiority is in the order of their precedence. [1.2.14]

Thus taking to material gain, pleasure, and virtue, man attains here as

---
[1] Lust, anger, avarice, delusion, pride, and envy.

well as in the hereafter happiness which is unimpaired and complete.
[1.2.49]

From the Rāmāyaṇa

The *Rāmāyaṇa*, one of the two national epics of India, is ascribed to Sage
Valmīki.
    [From *Rāmāyaṇa*, 2.21.57–58; 3.9.30]

My dear one! In this world, virtue, material gain, and pleasure are all
to be found in the fruit accruing from the pursuit of virtue; I am sure
they will all be found there even as in the case of a chaste wife who is also
beloved and blessed with offspring. If there is a case in which the three
are not found together, one should do only that in which there is virtue, for one who is intent solely on material gain is to be hated and to
be engrossed completely in pleasure is also not praiseworthy. [2.21.57–58]
    From dharma issue profit and pleasure; one attains everything by
dharma, it is dharma which is the essence and strength of the world.
[3.9.30]

From Kālidāsa

Kālidāsa (c. 400 A.D.), the foremost Indian poet, has enunciated the fundamental concepts of Hindu thought and culture in his poems and plays.
    [From *Raghuvaṃśa*, 1.25; 17.57]

In that wise King Dilīpa, who punished only to maintain order and married only for the sake of progeny, even material gain and love [1] were
based on virtue [i.e., religious duty]. [1.25]
    King Atithi did not put a strain on virtue by his pursuit of material
gain and pleasure, nor did he allow these two to suffer by his pursuit of
virtue; he did not betake to pleasure at the cost of material gain nor vice
versa; he was devoted to the three in a harmonious manner. [17.57]

---

[1] The basic meaning of kāma is clearly required in this context. The meaning is that
the king performed the sexual act not for its own sake but for the sake of the male
progeny required to "pay the debt to the Fathers" by continuing the rites to his ancestors.
Likewise material possession, in the form of kingly rule, was for the sake of maintaining
law and order.

CHAPTER X

DHARMA, THE FIRST END OF MAN

The older Brahmanism of the Samhitās and Brāhmanas, when faced with the popularity of the non-Brahmanic religions and the appeal among intellectuals of Upanishadic mysticism, began to consolidate, reorganize, and revitalize the Brahmanic way of life and thought. In this process a synthesis was achieved between the older Brahmanical ideal of action—of life viewed as a ritual—and the newer, quietistic ideal of withdrawal and renunciation developed in the Upanishadic period. This revivalist movement within Brahmanism touched all spheres of human life—religious, academic, domestic, and social. Indeed, it was then for the first time that conscious efforts were made to evolve a definite pattern of Brahmanical society. The movement found expression in the texts of the Sacred Law (*Smṛti* or *Dharma Śāstra*) as well as in the Epics, the *Mahābhārata* and *Rāmāyana,* and in literature generally, even that dedicated to such profane subjects as material gain or love.

For vast numbers of Hindus throughout the ages there has been no more inspiring symbol of dharma than the hero of the epic *Rāmāyana,* a text which gives expression to the two main tendencies of the new revivalist movement—social and devotional. Rāma, eldest son and rightful heir to Dasharatha, King of Ayodhyā, is deprived of the throne by his stepmother's sudden demand that Dasharatha, in fulfillment of a boon granted long before, crown her own son king and banish Rāma. So that his father may keep his pledge to his wife, Rāma voluntarily withdraws to live in the wilderness for fourteen years with his faithful wife Sītā. In the forest the sages who have been leading a life of penance and austerity seek help from the great warrior Rāma against demons who are harassing them. This brings Rāma into conflict with the demons, whose king abducts Sītā and keeps her captive in his stronghold, hoping to win her love. After many struggles Rāma and his allies, the monkeys, overcome Rāvana and rescue

Sītā. Thereupon Rāma is restored to his throne in Ayodhyā and sets an example as king of the most righteous and benevolent rule.

Rāma's noble example of devotion to duty, to his father, and to his people, as well as Sītā's long-suffering fidelity to Rāma, have been looked to as religious and ethical ideals down through the ages. Rāma is seen as the embodiment of dharma, and his triumph over wicked Rāvana as the overcoming of vice (*adharma*) in order that virtue and the moral law might prevail in personal and public life. Rāma, the embodiment of dharma, is also adored as the incarnation of the Supreme Lord who has come into the world to restore the moral order. In this form he became the object of a great devotional movement which swept the country in the first centuries A.D. Generation after generation, poets have celebrated Rāma in poems and plays, in both Sanskrit and vernacular; temples have been built to him, where sculpture, song, and drama told of his glory and enthroned him in the hearts of the masses. Eventually the *Rāmāyaṇa* spread to the whole world of Southeast Asia where one can still see Rāmāyana sculptures and Rāmāyana plays. Even today, the epic, in its original Sanskrit or its vernacular versions, is read and expounded to large gatherings of devout listeners and in the national struggle for freedom which Mahātmā Gandhi waged, he held forth the establishment of *Rāma-rājya,* a reign of truth and nonviolence, as the ideal.

The Sacred Law and the epics are viewed by the Hindus as only slightly less sacred than the Vedas and together form the body of semi-canonical scriptures called *Smriti* "(human) Tradition"—as opposed to the Vedas, which are *Shruti* "(divine) Revelation." Smriti is supposed to be based on Shruti, as indeed it largely is, and its authority is therefore only derivative. It is best represented in the Lawbooks, namely, the earlier *Aphorisms on the Domestic Ritual (Gṛhya Sūtras)* and *Aphorisms on Dharma (Dharma Sūtras),* in prose, and the later expanded versified codes, called *Dharma Śāstras* or *Smṛtis,* and related texts. The most famous of these latter codes are the *Lawbook of Manu (Manu Smṛti,* Shunga period, second to first centuries B.C.) and that of Yājnavalkya (*Yājñavalkya Smṛti,* early Gupta period, c. fourth century A.D.).

In time the major period of Smriti (the Lawbooks and epics) covers roughly a thousand years (c.500 B.C. to A.D. c.500). Smriti gave India an integrated philosophy of life and social organization which stood the test, on the one hand, of foreign invasions and rule over several centuries (second century B.C. to A.D. c.300), and on the other, of the heterodox religions, furnishing a pattern for the integration and absorption of both. The same period of foreign invasions and rule saw the rapid spread of theistic devotional cults, which after early opposition came to accept the authority of the Sacred Law and the Vedic scriptures, and in return gained the support of orthodox Brahmanism. The alliance soon grew into the single, dynamic movement—though divided into several schools and sects—known as Hinduism. In contrast to Brahmanism, Hinduism was a mass movement, which brought together into a single culture and polity, presided over by the Sacred Law of the brāhmans, various peoples, classes, and religious traditions. This fusion of diverse forces produced one of the world's great classical periods, that of Hindu culture in the Gupta Age (fourth and fifth centuries A.D.).

The central concept which was elaborated and emphasized by Smriti was that of dharma. The word has been used in most of the Brahmanic texts from the *Rig Veda* downwards, and in different contexts, as we have seen, it has denoted different ideas, such as, Vedic ritual, ethical conduct, caste rules, and civil and criminal law. The Sacred Law is the codification of dharma. Actually, the concept of dharma is all-comprehensive and may be, broadly speaking, said to comprise precepts which aim at securing the material and spiritual sustenance and growth of the individual and society. Another significant characteristic of dharma which deserves to be specially noted is that it was regarded as not being static. The content of dharma often changed in the changing contexts of time, place, and social environment.

In spite of the comprehensive character of dharma, in its most common connotation it was limited to two principal ideals, namely the organization of social life through well-defined and well-regulated classes (varnas) and the organization of an individual's life within those classes into definite stages (āshramas). Thus, in popular parlance, dharma almost came to mean just varna-āshrama-dharma, that is the dharmas (ordained duties) of the four classes and the four stages of life.

The system of the four classes has come to be regarded as the most essential feature of Brahmanic society. Even later Hinduism, which differs from Brahmanism in many significant respects, has scrupulously preserved this peculiar social organization. Though the word *varna-vyavasthā* is generally translated as caste system, it should be remembered that, strictly speaking, varna does not denote caste as we understand it today. Caste system is *jāti-vyavasthā,* which, no doubt, represents a ramification of the original system of classes. From the early Brāhmanic texts we can derive but little historical information regarding the origin and development of classes and castes. The aim of those texts was avowedly to glorify and defend the social organization governed by the concepts of classes and castes. They either speak of the divine origin of those social phenomena or give some mythical accounts in respect to them. A complex social phenomenon such as the caste system must be the result of the interaction of a variety of factors. The word *varṇa* (color, complexion) itself would indicate that one of these basic factors was racial distinction. In the *Rig Veda* we actually come across references to the *ārya varṇa* (the "Aryan color," i.e., the Vedic Aryans) and the *dāsa varṇa* ("the Dāsa color," the name collectively given to all racial groups other than the Vedic Aryans). In territories where the Aryans were dominant, the color-line dividing the three upper Aryan social orders from the fourth, that of the despised shūdras, was very strict. Draconian penalties were prescribed for the shūdra who struck or insulted an Aryan, or even presumed to sit on the same seat with him. This social cleavage was given religious sanction and was thus preserved to this day in the distinction between caste Hindus and shūdras. The shūdras were denied all access to the Veda, the Vedic sacrifices, and the Aryan sacraments, especially the investiture with the sacred thread symbolic of the Aryan child's admittance to membership in his class.

Another important factor was magico-ritualistic in character. The four main classes were distinguished from one another on account of the specific roles which they played in connection with the communal sacrifice. These were determined by certain definite concepts of taboo, pollution, and purification. Corresponding to their roles in the ritual these classes were assigned distinct colors, which fact also seems to have confirmed the use of the word *varṇa* with reference to them. This magico-ritualistic origin of the four classes is indirectly indicated by their mention in the Purusha Sūkta (*Rig Veda,* 10.90), as the limbs of the cosmic sacrificial Purusha. Then there was the impact on the social organization of the Vedic Aryans of the pattern of social life already evolved by the indigenous Indian communities, which must have also been responsible for the consolidation of this social phenomenon. In the initial stages,

these classes were more or less fluid and elastic. But in course of
time they hardened into a definite social system characterized by a large
number of endogamous and commensal castes, sub-castes, and mixed
castes. Elaborate discussions occur in texts of the Sacred Law regarding
their respective duties, and social and legal privileges and disabilities.

Within these classes and castes, an individual's life was organized into
four distinct stages, called āshramas, in such a manner that the individual
should be enabled to realize, through a properly graded scheme, the four
ends of life. These four stages of life are those of the student, the householder, the hermit or recluse, and the ascetic. It will be seen that the
system of the four stages of life seeks to resolve the conflict between two
ideals, namely, consolidation and progress of society on the one hand and
the spiritual emancipation of the individual on the other. In connection
with the scheme of the four stages the texts of the Sacred Law have
stated clearly and at some length the Brahmanic ideals regarding such
topics as education, position of woman, and family life. Attempts have
also been made to render the broad scheme of the four stages more
viable and effective by prescribing various sacraments (samskāras), which
are, as it were, the lampposts on the road leading to the full-fledged
growth of man's personality. These sacraments cover man's whole life,
beginning from the prenatal and ending with the post-mortem condition.

It will thus be seen that the Brahmanists had developed a most comprehensive system of social thought. This system continues to constitute—
though in a more or less modified form—the basis of Hindu society even
to this day.

What Is Dharma?

It is difficult to find any one single passage wherein the comprehensive character of dharma is adequately brought out. Some typical passages are, therefore,
given below with the idea that they might cumulatively indicate some characteristic features of this highly significant concept in Brahmanism and Hinduism.

[From *Taittirīya Āraṇyaka,* 10.79]
Dharma is the foundation of the whole universe. In this world people go
unto a person who is best versed in dharma for guidance. By means of

dharma one drives away evil. Upon dharma everything is founded. Therefore, dharma is called the highest good.

[From *Mahābhārata*, 12.110.10–11]
For the sake of the promotion of strength and efficacy among beings the
declaration of dharma is made. Whatever is attended with nonviolence
(ahimsā),[1] that is dharma. Such is the fixed opinion.

Dharma [from a root *dhṛ*, "to sustain"] is so called on account of its
capacity for the sustenance of the world. On account of dharma, people
are sustained separately in their respective stations.[2]

[From *Vaiśeṣika Sūtra*, 1.1.2]
That from which result material gain and spiritual good is dharma.

[From *Manu Smṛti*, 8.15]
Dharma, when violated, verily, destroys; dharma, when preserved, preserves: therefore, dharma should not be violated, lest the violated dharma
destroy us.

The Sources and Extent of Dharma

A discussion about the more tangible nature and extent of dharma, as it is
generally understood, is given in the following passages.

[From *Yājñavalkya Smṛti*, 1.1.1–3, 6–9]

Having paid homage to Yājnavalkya, the lord of yogins, the sages said:
Please expound to us fully the dharmas of the four classes, the four stages
of life, and others.

The lord of yogins, living in Mithilā [capital of Videha], having meditated for a moment, said to the sages: The laws of that country in which
the black antelope roams freely,[3] do you understand carefully.

The four Vedas, together with the Purāṇas,[4] logic, the science of Vedic
interpretation, the Sacred Law [Dharma Shāstra], and the [six] limbs of

[1] In thought, word, and deed: violence of any kind disturbs the proper functioning of
the individual and society, and, therefore, represents the negation of dharma.

[2] Confusion regarding the respective duties and functions (and privileges and disabilities)
of different classes unbalances society. One of the king's chief duties is to prevent such
confusion.

[3] That is, the open grazing lands of the north Indian plain. According to Manu (2.23),
such a country alone is fit for sacrifice, that is, for Aryan habitation.

[4] Semihistorical and religious legends.

the Veda,[5] constitute the fourteen seats of sciences and of dharma. . . .

In a certain country, at a certain time, through certain means, when a thing is given over to a deserving person with faith—then, in that case, all these items, among others, indicate the concept of dharma.[6]

The Vedic scriptures [Shruti], the Sacred Law [Smriti], the practices of the good, whatever is agreeable to one's own self, and the desire which has arisen out of wholesome resolve—all these are traditionally known to be the sources of dharma.

Over and above such acts as sacrifice, traditional practices, self-control, nonviolence, charity, and study of the Veda, this, verily, is the highest dharma, namely, the realization of the Self by means of yoga.

Four persons versed in the Vedas and dharma, or a group of those who are adept only in the three Vedas, constitute a court. Whatever that court declares would be dharma; or that, which even one person who is the best among the knowers of the lore of the Self declares, would be dharma.

This passage, which is of the nature of a table of contents, indicates the scope and extent of the Sacred Law, as it was traditionally understood.

[From *Manu Smṛti*, 1.111–18]

The creation of the universe, the procedure in respect of the sacraments, the practices relating to the vow of studentship [the respectful behavior toward teachers, etc.], the highest rule regarding the ceremonial bath [to be taken at the termination of studentship],

The taking of a bride, the definitions of various kinds of marriages, the regulations concerning the great sacrifices, the eternal rule of the obsequies,

The definition of the modes of gaining subsistence, the vows of a graduate in Vedic studies [i.e., of a brāhman householder], the rules regarding what may be eaten and what may not be eaten, the purification of men and the purification of things,

The laws concerning women, the rules relating to a hermit's life, spiritual emancipation, renunciation of worldly life, the whole set of the duties of a king, the deciding of law-suits,

The rules regarding the examination of witnesses, the law governing the relation between husband and wife, the law of inheritance and parti-

---

[5] They are: science of correct pronunciation and accentuation, aphorisms concerning Vedic ritual, etc., grammar, Vedic etymology, Vedic metrics, and astronomy.

[6] The various constituents of the activity of giving away, which is, indeed, the main basis of all dharma, at least in the final age of a cycle, form, according to the commentator, the causative attributes of dharma.

tion of ancestral property, the law concerning gambling, the removal of men who prove to be thorns of society,

The behavior of vaishyas and shūdras, the origin of mixed castes, the law for all four classes in times of distress, similarly the expiatory rites,

The threefold course of transmigration resulting from a person's karma, the spiritual good, the examination of merits and demerits of actions,

The laws of specific countries, the laws of specific castes, the eternal laws of individual families, the laws of heretics and [tribal] communities —all these topics Manu has expounded in this treatise.

Dharma Is Not Static

The following passage brings out a very significant characteristic of dharma, namely, that the concept and content of dharma change in accordance with the changing circumstances. Ancient tradition speaks of four ages (yugas)—Krita, Tretā, Dvāpara, and Kali—their duration, respectively, 1,728,000; 1,296,000; 864,000; and 432,000 human years. It is believed that each of these four succeeding ages is characterized by an increasing physical and spiritual deterioration. No one uniform set of dharmas can, therefore, be made applicable to all the four ages. It is further believed that when one cycle of four ages is completed, there occurs the end of the universe, which is followed by a new creation and a new cycle.

[From *Manu Smṛti*, 1.81–86]

Four-footed and complete is dharma in the Krita age—it is, verily, identical with Truth. Through behavior contrary to dharma, no gain of any kind accrues to men.

In the other three ages, by reason of some kind of gain [accruing to men even through behavior contrary to dharma], dharma is deprived successively of one foot [i.e., one-fourth]. On account of the prevalence of theft, falsehood, and deceitfulness, dharma disappears successively quarter by quarter.

In the Krita age men are free from disease, accomplish all their aims, and live four hundred years; but in the ages beginning with the Tretā, their span of life decreases successively by one quarter.

The span of life of mortals mentioned in the Veda, the desired results of sacrificial rites, and the special spiritual powers of the embodied souls (that is, of mortals)—these result as fruits of men's actions in this world in accordance with the character of a particular age.

One set of dharmas is prescribed for men in the Krita age, other sets of dharmas in the Tretā and the Dvāpara ages and still another set of dharmas in the Kali age, in accordance with the increasing deterioration characterizing each successive age.

Austerities [tapas] constitute the highest dharma in the Krita age; in the Tretā, sacred knowledge is declared to be the highest dharma; in the Dvāpara they speak of the performance of sacrifice as the highest dharma; giving alone is the highest dharma in the Kali age.[7]

Varna-Dharma or Organization of the Four Classes

As far as the Brahmanic-Hindu way of life was concerned, the essence of all dharma consisted in the proper functioning of the organization of the four classes or of its later complex development, namely, the caste system. Each class had its own set of duties and obligations (sva-dharma) definitely prescribed and, for the sake of the solidarity and progress of society as a whole, each class or social unit was expected to act up to the following teaching of the Bhagavad Gītā (3.35): "Far more conducive to the ultimate good is one's own code of conduct (sva-dharma), even though deficient in quality, than an alien code of conduct, far easier to be practiced though it may be."

The four classes of those born from the mouth and limbs of Purusha—the brāhman (priest), kshatriya (noble), vaishya (the bourgeois), the shūdra (serf) —formed a well-knit, almost self-sufficient society.[8]

Below this society, yet economically tied to it, were a number of "excluded" castes, whose contact, shadow, or even sight polluted. They performed impure work such as scavenging, disposing of the dead, leather-work, etc., and had to live outside Aryan communities. They were made to bear distinctive marks and to strike a piece of wood to warn people of their approach. The concept of excluded castes is continued today in the untouchable castes, some of which may go back to ancient times, others probably being added from time to time from primitive tribes coming to live near more settled communities.

Large parts of India were not conquered by the Aryans but were held by various indigenous peoples, some tribes or classes of whom were observed to have a status and occupations similar to those of the corresponding twice-born

[7] Disparity (particularly in respect of material possessions), which is, indeed, the root cause of all evil and ill-will among men in the present Kali age, can be removed only by "giving away." It is interesting to view in this light such movements in modern India as Bhū-dāna (giving away of land), Sampatti-dāna (giving away of wealth), Śrama-dāna (making physical labor available to society), etc.

[8] The brāhmans, kshatriyas, and vaishyas are called dvija or twice-born, because they are entitled as Aryans to the sacrament of initiation to the study of the Veda, which is regarded as their second or spiritual birth. The study or even overhearing of the Vedic scriptures by the non-Aryan shūdras was forbidden under the most drastic penalties.

classes. These were called *Vrātyas* and were thought to be twice-born castes degraded by neglect of the Vedic rites. Though assimilated in principle to shūdras, they were eligible to admission into the caste system as brāhmans, kshatriyas, or vaishyas by having a special sacrifice performed by brāhman priests. This device may have been largely responsible for the integration among the twice-born both of the non-Aryan upper classes found in India by the Aryans and of later invaders such as the Huns. All other foreigners were despised "barbarians" (*Mlecchas*).

[From *Manu Smṛti*, 1.87–98, 102, 107, 108]

For the sake of the preservation of this entire creation, [Purusha], the exceedingly resplendent one, assigned separate duties to the classes which had sprung from his mouth, arms, thighs, and feet.[9]

Teaching, studying, performing sacrificial rites, so too making others perform sacrificial rites, and giving away and receiving gifts—these he assigned to the brāhmans.

Protection of the people, giving away of wealth, performance of sacrificial rites, study, and nonattachment to sensual pleasures—these are, in short, the duties of a kshatriya.

Tending of cattle, giving away of wealth, performance of sacrificial rites, study, trade and commerce, usury, and agriculture—these are the occupations of a vaishya.

The Lord has prescribed only one occupation [karma] for a shūdra, namely, service without malice of even these other three classes.

Man is stated to be purer above the navel than below it; hence his mouth has been declared to be the purest part by the Self-existent One.

On account of his origin from the best limb of the Cosmic Person, on account of his seniority, and on account of the preservation by him of the Veda [brahman]—the brāhman is in respect of dharma the lord of this entire creation.[10]

For the Self-Existent One, having performed penance, produced the

[9] Cf. *Rig Veda*, 10.90. The divine origin of the four classes is indicated here. It is, therefore, almost sacrilegious for a lower order to assume the duties of a higher one.

[10] Even from the point of view of civil law the brāhman enjoyed certain special privileges. In connection with the treasure-trove, for instance, the *Manu Smṛti* lays down (8.37) that if a brāhman finds it he may keep the whole of it "for he is master of everything," while persons belonging to other classes cannot do so. The punishments prescribed for a brāhman offender are more lenient than those prescribed for the same offense by persons belonging to other classes. For perjury, persons of the three lower classes shall be fined and banished, but a brāhman shall only be banished. Similarly, a brāhman is not liable to corporal punishment (*Manu Smṛti* 8.123–24).

brāhman first of all, from his own mouth, for the sake of the conveying of the offerings intended for the gods and those intended for the manes and for the sake of the preservation of this entire universe.

What created being can be superior to him through whose mouth the gods always consume the oblations intended for them and the manes those intended for them?

Of created beings, those which are animate are the best; of the animate, those who subsist by means of their intellect; of the intelligent, men are the best; and of men, the brāhmans are traditionally declared to be the best;

Of the brāhmans, the learned ones are the best; of the learned, those whose intellect is fixed upon ritual activity; of those whose intellect is fixed upon ritual activity, those who carry out ritual activity; of those who carry out ritual activity, those who realize the Brahman.

The very birth of a brāhman is the eternal incarnation of dharma. For he is born for the sake of dharma and tends toward becoming one with the Brahman. . . .

For the sake of the discussion of the brāhman's duties and of those of the other classes according to their precedence, wise Manu, the son of the Self-existent One, produced this treatise. . . .

In this treatise there are expounded in entirety dharma, the merits and demerits of [human] actions, and the eternal code of conduct of the four classes.

The code of conduct—prescribed by scriptures and ordained by sacred tradition [the Sacred Law]—constitutes the highest dharma; hence a twice-born person, conscious of his own Self [seeking spiritual salvation], should be always scrupulous in respect of it.

The Origin of Mixed Castes

This is a conventional description of the origin and nature of the various castes and mixed castes. It can by no means be regarded as reflecting the complex system of more than three thousand real castes, subcastes, mixed castes, and exterior (untouchable) castes, which prevails in India at present. Only one factor is considered in relation to the complex variety of the caste system, namely, mixed marriages; no reference is made to such other factors as occupations, specific religious functions, enforcement of deliberate economic and administrative policies, etc.

[From *Yājñavalkya Smṛti*, 1.90–96]

By husbands belonging to a particular class upon wives belonging to the same class—the husbands and wives having been united in unblemished marriages—are begotten sons who belong to the same caste as that of the father and the mother [11] and who are capable of continuing the line.

The son [12] begotten by a brāhman upon a kshatriya woman is called *Mūrdhāvasikta;* upon a vaishya woman, *Ambastha;* upon a shūdra woman, *Nisāda* or even *Pārasava.*[13]

The sons begotten upon vaishya and shūdra women by a kshatriya are known by tradition respectively as *Māhisya* and *Ugra*. The son begotten by a vaishya upon a shūdra woman is known as *Karana*. This rule is laid down only in respect of married persons.

The son [14] begotten upon a brāhman woman by a kshatriya is called *Sūta;* by a vaishya, *Vaidehaka;* by a shūdra, *Cāndāla,* who is excluded from all considerations of dharma.

A kshatriya woman procreates from a vaishya a son called *Māgadha;* and from a shūdra, *Ksattr*. A vaishya woman procreates from a shūdra a son called *Āyogava.*

By a Māhishya is begotten upon a Karana woman a son called *Rathakāra.*[15] As bad and good are to be regarded respectively the sons born of hypogamous [pratiloma] and hypergamous [anuloma] marriages.

The progressive advance in the social status [16] [of the various mixed

[11] There is a threefold division of Hindu marriage: 1) that in which the husband and the wife belong to the same class; 2) hypergamy, in which the husband belongs to a higher class than the wife; 3) hypogamy, in which the wife belongs to a higher class than the husband. The offspring of hypogamous unions was especially despised, in direct proportion to the disparity between the ranks of the parents: the Chāndāla, said to be the offspring of a shūdra by a brāhman woman, is the lowest untouchable.

[12] This and the next stanza refer to the mixed castes resulting from hypergamous marriages. The sons of hypergamous unions between Aryan parents were also Aryan, though of mixed caste.

[13] Two very low castes.

[14] This and the next stanza refer to the mixed castes resulting from hypogamous unions.

[15] The *Sūta* (charioteer, bard), *Ksattr* (doorkeeper), *Māhisya* (attendant on cattle), *Rathakāra* (chariot-maker) must have originally had occupational significance. The Nishādas were an aboriginal tribe in origin and lived by fishing and hunting. *Ambastha* (healer, doctor), *Vaidehaka,* and *Māgadha* (trader) are clearly regional names, implying that these castes came from Ambashtha, Videha, or Magadha. It may be seen how the castes named in this treatise had the most varied origins and were somehow integrated into a hierarchical system based on the theory of hypergamy. We must admire, however, the Brāhman author's ingenuity in choosing appropriate occupational castes for the offspring of different hybrid unions.

[16] This stanza is important in that it speaks of the possibility of a mixed caste being

castes] should be known as resulting in the seventh or even in the fifth union.[17] In cases of inversion of duties one is reduced to the status equal [to that of the caste whose way of life he adopts also at the end of the same period]. The higher and lower [status of sons born of unions between real castes and mixed castes] is to be determined on the same principle as before [the principle of hypergamy].

Initiation to Studentship

A brāhman, kshatriya, or vaishya boy is formally taken to a preceptor to be initiated to the disciplined life of a student of sacred knowledge. This initiation (upanayana) constitutes his second or spiritual birth—his birth from his parents being only a physical birth. Persons belonging to the first three classes are therefore called *dvijas* or twice-born. With the initiation commences the first stage of life (āshrama), namely, Vedic studentship or brahmacharya. The different initiation ages for the various classes suggest that their courses of study were different. The brāhman boy's was without doubt intellectually the hardest and he was probably the only one expected to master a whole Veda. The kshatriya's education was also in the hands of a brāhman preceptor, but much emphasis must have been given to training in military arts and government. As we can see from the selection given below from a work dating several centuries before Christ, a long period of education was compulsory in principle for all Aryans, who thus learned a common language (Sanskrit) and acquired a common culture. The superior linguistic, cultural, and social cohesion of the Aryans vis-à-vis the various non-Aryan tribes and peoples insured Aryan domination—political, social, and cultural—over the greater part of India even more than their military victories.

[From *Āśvalāyana Gṛhya Sūtra*, 1.19.1–13; 20.1–7; 21.5–7; 22.1–5]

In the eighth year one should initiate a brāhman; or in the eighth year from the conception in the embryo; in the eleventh year, a kshatriya; in the twelfth, a vaishya. Until the sixteenth year the proper time for initiation has not passed for a brāhman; until the twenty-second year, for a

---

elevated to the status of the next higher real caste. It also makes the significant point that a change in occupation (in normal circumstances) often implies a change in caste. In other words, birth is not the only factor which determines caste, for a Brāhman family which lives by the profession of a shūdra continuously through seven generations becomes shūdra. It is interesting that there is no mention of a person following the profession of a social order higher than his.

[17] For instance a brāhman begets upon a shūdra wife of Nishāda daughter. Another brāhman marries this Nishāda daughter and begets a daughter. Upon the daughter born in this way in the sixth generation a brāhman husband would beget a son who is himself a brāhman and not a member of any mixed caste.

kshatriya; until the twenty-fourth year, for a vaishya. After that they become banished from Sāvitrī.[18] One should not initiate them, nor teach them, nor officiate at their sacrifices; people should not have any dealings with them.

One should initiate a boy who has put on ornaments, the hair on whose head is properly taken care of, who is clothed in a new garment that has not yet been washed, or in an antelope skin if he is a brāhman, in the skin of a spotted deer if he is a kshatriya, in a goat's skin if he is a vaishya. If they put on garments, they should put on colored ones: a brāhman, a reddish-yellow one; a kshatriya, a light red one; a vaishya, a yellow one. As for their girdles: that of a brāhman should be made of *muñja* grass; that of a kshatriya, a bow-string; that of a vaishya, woolen. As for their staffs: that of a brāhman should be of *palāśa* wood; that of a kshatriya, of *uḍumbara* wood; that of a vaishya, of *bilva* wood; or all sorts of staffs are to be used by students belonging to all classes.

Having offered an oblation while the student touches him on the arm [implying participation in the offering], the teacher should station himself to the north of the sacred fire facing toward the east. To the east of the sacred fire facing toward the west should the student station himself. The teacher should then fill with water the two cavities of the hands of himself and of his student and with the formula *tat savitur vṛṇīmahe* . . . should make the water flow down upon the full cavity of the student's hands by means of the full cavity of his own hands. Having thus poured out the water upon the student's hands, he should with his own hand take the student's hand together with the thumb with the words: "By the impulse of the god Savitar [the Impeller, i.e., the sun god], with the arms of the two Ashvins [heavenly physicians], with Pūshan's hand [god of prosperity] I take thee by thy hand, O so-and-so!" The teacher should take the student's hand a second time with the words: "Savitar has taken your hand, O so-and-so." The teacher should take the student's hand a third time with the words: "Agni [Fire, the god of sacrificial rites] is thy teacher, O so-and-so!" The teacher should make the student look at the sun and should then say: "God Savitar, this is thy student of sacred knowledge [brahmachārī]; protect him; may he not die." . . .

Having seized the student's hands with the student's garment and his

---

[18] From initiation and hence from class and Aryan society, Sāvitrī being the Vedic verse used at initiations.

own hands, the teacher should recite the Sāvitrī verse firstly fourth by fourth, then verse-half by verse-half, and finally the whole of it. He should make the student recite the Sāvitrī after himself as far as he is able to do so. On the region of the student's heart the teacher should place his hand with the fingers stretched upwards and say: "Into my vow I put thy heart; after my mind may thy mind follow; with single-aimed vow do thou rejoice in my speech; may God Brihaspati [heavenly priest of the gods] join thee to me."

Having tied the girdle round the student and given him the staff, the teacher should instruct him in the disciplined life of a student of sacred knowledge (brahmacharya) with the words: "A student of sacred knowledge thou art; sip water [a purification rite]; do the ritual act (karma); do not sleep in the daytime; remaining under the direction of the teacher study the Veda." For twelve years lasts the studentship for the Veda; or until the student has properly learned it. The student should beg food in the evening and in the morning. He should put fuel on the sacred fires in the evening and in the morning.[19]

Marriage and Householder's Duties

The second stage of life, that of the householder, is often characterized as the basis and support of the other three. It is, indeed, the only stage which affords full scope for the realization of the first three ends of man, namely, pleasure (kāma), material gain (artha), and virtue (dharma).

[From *Āśvalāyana Gṛhya Sūtra*, 1.5.1–3; 6.1–8]
One should first examine the family [of the intended bride or bridegroom], those on the mother's side and on the father's side, as has been said above.[20] One should give his daughter in marriage to a young man endowed with intelligence. One should marry a girl who possesses the characteristics of intelligence, beauty, and good character, and who is free from disease. . . .

The father[21] may give away his daughter after decking her with orna-

---

[19] The student lived with the teacher at his residence and helped him in connection with, among other things, his religious observances. He begged food daily for himself and his teacher. Society bore the responsibility for the maintenance of teachers and students.

[20] That is, through ten generations, as has been prescribed in Āshvalāyana's *Aphorisms on the Vedic Ritual* (*Ā. Śrauta Sūtra*, 9.3.20).

[21] This passage describes the eight forms of marriage. The three main factors involved in these different forms are money, love, and physical force. Traditionally, the first four forms

ments and having first offered a libation of water: This is the *Brāhma* form of marriage. A son born to her after such a marriage purifies twelve descendants and twelve ancestors on both her husband's and her own sides. The father may give her away after decking her with ornaments to an officiating priest while a Vedic sacrifice is being performed: that is the *Daiva* [22] form of marriage. A son born of such a marriage purifies ten descendants and ten ancestors on both sides. "Practice dharma together," —a marriage performed with this imposition on the bride and the bridegroom is the *Prajāpatya* form of marriage. A son born of such marriage purifies eight descendants and eight ancestors on both sides. A person may marry a girl after having first given a cow and a bull to her father: that is the *Ārṣa* [23] form of marriage. A son born of such marriage purifies seven descendants and seven ancestors on both sides. A person may marry a girl after having made a mutual agreement with her. That is the *Gāndharva* [24] form of marriage. A person may marry a girl after having satisfied her father with money: that is the *Āsura* ["demonic"] form of marriage. A person may carry off a girl while her people are sleeping or are careless about her: that is the *Paiśāca* ["devilish"] form of marriage. Having killed her people and broken their heads, a person may carry off a girl, while she is weeping, from her relatives who are also weeping: that is the *Rākṣasa* ["fiendish"] form of marriage.

[From *Yājñavalkya Smṛti,* 1.97–105, 115–16]
A householder should perform every day a Smriti rite [i.e., a domestic rite prescribed by the Sacred Law, Smriti] on the nuptial fire or on the fire brought in at the time of the partition of ancestral property. He should perform a Vedic rite on the sacred fires.

Having attended to the bodily calls, having performed the purificatory rites, and after having first washed the teeth, a twice-born [Aryan] man should offer the morning prayer.

Having offered oblations to the sacred fires, becoming spiritually composed, he should murmur the sacred verses addressed to the sun god. He should also learn the meaning of the Veda and various sciences.

of marriage are accepted as proper, while the remaining four are condemned. This becomes clear not only from the names given to the various forms but also from the conventional mention in respect of the first four forms of marriage of the purifying capacity of sons born of those marriages.
[22] Lit. "pertaining to the [Vedic] gods."   [23] Lit. "pertaining to the [Vedic] sages."
[24] Lit. "pertaining to the heavenly musicians."

He should then go to his lord for securing the means of maintenance and progress. Thereafter having bathed he should worship the gods and also offer libations of water to the manes.

He should study according to his capacity the three Vedas, the *Atharva Veda,* the Purānas, together with the Itihāsas [legendary histories], as also the lore relating to the knowledge of the Self, with a view to accomplishing successfully the sacrifice of muttering prayers [*japa-yajña*].

Offering of the food oblation [bali], offering with the utterance *svadhā,* performance of Vedic sacrifices, study of the sacred texts, and honoring of guests—these constitute the five great daily sacrifices [25] dedicated respectively to the spirits, the manes, the gods, the Brahman, and men.

He should offer the food oblation to the spirits [by throwing it in the air] out of the remnant of the food offered to the gods. He should also cast food on the ground for dogs, untouchables, and crows.

Food, as also water, should be offered by the householder to the manes and men day after day. He should continuously carry on his study. He should never cook for himself only.

Children, married daughters living in the father's house, old relatives, pregnant women, sick persons, and girls, as also guests and servants— only after having fed these should the householder and his wife eat the food that has remained. . . .

Having risen before dawn the householder should ponder over what is good for the Self. He should not, as far as possible, neglect his duties in respect of the three ends of man, namely, virtue, material gain, and pleasure, at their proper times.

Learning, religious performances, age, family relations, and wealth— on account of these and in the order mentioned are men honored in society. By means of these, if possessed in profusion, even a shūdra deserves respect in old age.

The Position of Women

Contradictory views have been expressed concerning the social status of a Hindu woman. On the one hand it is enjoined that she should be shown the

[25] This is an expansion of the older and basic concept of Brahmanical thought, that of the three debts, to the ancestors or manes, to the gods, and to the rishis or sages. The debt to the manes was discharged by marrying and continuing the race and thus the ceremonies originally intended to feed the ancestors. The debt to the gods was discharged by sacrifices and worship and that to the sages through the study and preservation of the scriptures.

utmost respect, while, on the other, she is said to deserve no freedom. This contradiction is more apparent than real, for the emphasis in the latter case is not so much on the denial of any freedom to a woman as on the duty of her near ones to protect her at all costs.

[From *Manu Smṛti*, 3.55–57; 9.3–7, 11, 26]

Women must be honored and adorned by their fathers, brothers, husbands, and brothers-in-law who desire great good fortune.

Where women, verily, are honored, there the gods rejoice; where, however, they are not honored, there all sacred rites prove fruitless.

Where the female relations live in grief—that family soon perishes completely; where, however, they do not suffer from any grievance—that family always prospers. . . .

Her father protects her in childhood, her husband protects her in youth, her sons protect her in old age—a woman does not deserve independence.

The father who does not give away his daughter in marriage at the proper time is censurable; censurable is the husband who does not approach his wife in due season; and after the husband is dead, the son, verily, is censurable, who does not protect his mother.

Even against the slightest provocations should women be particularly guarded; for unguarded they would bring grief to both the families.

Regarding this as the highest dharma of all four classes, husbands, though weak, must strive to protect their wives.

His own offspring, character, family, self, and dharma does one protect when he protects his wife scrupulously. . . .

The husband should engage his wife in the collection and expenditure of his wealth, in cleanliness, in dharma,[26] in cooking food for the family, and in looking after the necessities of the household. . . .

Women destined to bear children, enjoying great good fortune, deserving of worship, the resplendent lights of homes on the one hand and divinities of good luck who reside in the houses on the other—between these there is no difference whatsoever.

The Hermit and the Ascetic

In the third stage of life man is expected to retire from active family and social life and seek seclusion. But he should be available for advice and guidance to the family and society whenever they need them. In the last stage, namely, that

[26] Ordained duty, especially here religious rites.

of the life of an ascetic (sannyāsin), man completely renounces this worldly life and devotes himself exclusively to spiritual self-realization.

[From *Manu Smṛti,* 6.1–3, 8, 25, 33, 42, 87–89]

Having thus lived a householder's life according to the prescribed rules, a twice-born householder should, making a firm resolve and keeping his sense-organs in subjection, live in a forest as recommended in the Sacred Law.

When a householder sees his skin wrinkled and his hair gray and when he sees the son of his son, then he should resort to the forest.

Having given up food produced in villages [by cultivation] and abandoning all his belongings, he should depart into the forest, either committing his wife to the care of his sons or departing together with her. . . .

He should be constantly engaged in study and should be self-controlled, friendly toward all, spiritually composed, ever a liberal giver and never a receiver, and compassionate toward all beings. . . .

Having consigned the sacred fires into himself [27] in accordance with the prescribed rules, he should live without a fire, without a house, a silent sage subsisting on roots and fruit. . . .

Having thus passed the third part of his life in the forest, he should renounce all attachments to worldly objects and become an ascetic during the fourth part of his life. . . .

He should always wander alone, without any companion, in order to achieve spiritual perfection—clearly seeing that such attainment is possible only in the case of the solitary man, who neither forsakes nor is forsaken. . . .

The student, the householder, the hermit, and the ascetic—these constitute the four separate stages of life, originating from and depending upon the householder's life.

All these stages of life, adopted successively and in accordance with the Shāstras, lead the brāhman [28] following the prescribed rules to the highest state.

Of all these, verily, according to the precepts of the Veda and the Smriti

[27] The three sacred fires are the symbol of a householder's life. During the latter part of his life as a forest hermit the Hindu gives up his sacred fires; these are not to be destroyed but are symbolically consigned into his own self.

[28] And also persons belonging to the next two social orders.

the householder is said to be the most excellent, for he supports the other three.

The Sacraments

The sacraments (samskāras) help to render the scheme of the four stages of an individual's life more tangible and definite. They represent, as it were, the various landmarks in man's progress through the course of life, which aim at building up a full-fledged physical and spiritual personality. The following passage represents the earliest enumeration of the sacraments. Note the author's subordination of external ritual to moral qualities at the end of the passage.

[From *Gautama Dharma Sūtra,* 8.14–26]

1) The ceremony relating to the conception of the embryo; 2) the ceremony relating to the desired birth of a male child; 3) the parting of the pregnant wife's hair by the husband [to ward off evil spirits]; 4) the ceremony relating to the birth of the child; 5) the naming of the child; 6) the first feeding; 7) the tonsure of the child's head; 8) the initiation; 9–12) the four vows taken in connection with the study of the Veda; 13) the ceremonial bath [graduation]; 14) the union with a mate who would practice dharma together with him [i.e., marriage]; 15–19) the daily performance of the five sacrifices to gods, manes, men, spirits, and the Brahman; 20–26) and the performance of the following sacrifices, that is, of the seven cooked-food sacrifices . . . ; 27–33) the seven kinds of oblation sacrifices . . . ; 34–40) the seven kinds of soma sacrifices . . . these are the forty sacraments.

Now follow the eight good qualities of the soul, namely, compassion to all beings, forbearance, absence of jealousy, purity, tranquillity, goodness, absence of meanness, and absence of covetousness. He who is sanctified by these forty sacraments but is not endowed with the eight good qualities of the soul does not become united with the Brahman, nor does he even reach the abode of the Brahman. On the other hand, he who is, verily, sanctified by a few only of the sacraments but is endowed with the eight good qualities of the soul becomes united with the Brahman, he dwells in the abode of the Brahman.

CHAPTER XI

ARTHA, *THE SECOND END OF MAN*

As we have seen, the ancient Indian concept of dharma as religiously ordained duty touched all aspects of man's relation with the society. One such aspect was political in character and often manifested itself in the form of the relation between the subject and the state. In view of the fact that the state in ancient India was mostly monarchical, this aspect of dharma was known as the *Rāja-dharma,* the dharma (duty) of kings. Naturally enough, the *Rāja-dharma,* which, by and large, corresponded with political science, formed but one of the many topics dealt with in the larger scheme of Dharma Shāstra. The latter was normally divided into three main sections, namely, rules of conduct (*ācāra*), civil and criminal law (*vyavahāra*), and expiation and punishment (*prāyascitta*). The *Rāja-dharma* was included in the section embodying the rules of conduct. In the course of time, however, polity came to be considered important enough to be recognized as an independent branch of knowledge, under the name of *Artha Shāstra,* the science of profit or material gain. As against Dharma Shāstra, Artha Shāstra may be said to have given quite a new orientation to political theory and practice. This new orientation reflected, at least to a certain extent, the increasing intensity of the struggle for power in ancient India and the growing complexity of the methods used to gain and keep control over the land and its peoples. Indeed, it is possible to find some indications of this new political ideology in the *Mahābhārata* itself. In order to overpower the Kaurava warriors like Bhīshma, Drona, and Karna, the Pāndavas often employed, under the active direction of Lord Krishna himself, ruses and stratagems which were not in strict accordance with the traditional rules of righteous war (*dharma-yuddha*). The ultimate victory of the Pāndavas over the Kauravas symbolizes, in a sense, the predominance of the new Artha Shāstra ideal over the older epic ideal of chivalry. As for the essential difference between the sacred law and the science of material gain, it may be stated in broad and rather oversimplified terms as follows: While Dharma Shāstra insisted on the righteousness of both the means and the ends, Artha Shāstra concerned itself primarily with the attainment of the ends irrespective of the nature of the means employed for that purpose. It is not unlikely that one of the reasons why Artha Shāstra is traditionally believed to be a science ancillary to the *Atharva Veda* is the similarity of their attitude toward the means and the ends. The Artha Shāstra ideology completely dominated the polity of ancient India. Attempts were made, however, from time to time to reassert the superiority of Dharma Shāstra over Artha Shāstra by prescribing that, in case of conflict between the two, Dharma Shāstra should prevail.

It is probable that besides the mostly theoretical *Dharma Sūtras* (Aphorisms on Dharma) which do not seem to have been specifically related to any particular set of social and political conditions, there had existed some kind of Artha Shāstra literature—presumably in the form of sūtras or aphorisms and more realistic in outlook—which served as a practical guide for the pursuit and exercise of power. That literature is now unfortunately not available—except perhaps in fragments—and is mainly known through references to it in later works. In 1905, however, a remarkable monument belonging to the second phase of the evolution of that literature—the phase of thorough amplification of the older aphorisms—first came to public attention. This is the well-known *Treatise on Material Gain (Artha Śāstra)* [1] attributed to Kautilya, the minister of Chandragupta Maurya, who was a contemporary of Alexander the Great. Though the kernel of the work may perhaps look back to the fourth century B.C., in its present form it is possibly as late as the fourth century A.D. This work is of exceptional interest and value, for it has almost revolutionized the traditional view regarding certain aspects of ancient Indian history and culture.

The *Treatise on Material Gain* of Kautilya reflects, in a striking manner, the social and political forces which were at work in India during the fourth century B.C. Alexander's incursions into India (326–325 B.C.) had helped to emphasize the need for establishing a central political and military power. The *Treatise on Material Gain* has, accordingly, laid down policies aimed at welding together, into a more or less unified pattern and under the control—direct or indirect—of a single authority, the multi-

[1] *Śāstra* means treatise, collectively "a discipline *or* science."

plicity of smaller states that had crowded the stage of Indian history at
that time. Interstate relations thus constitute one of the main topics in
Kautilya's *Treatise*. Kautilya defines Artha Shāstra as the science which
treats of the means of acquiring and maintaining the earth, and indeed
deals with practical government administration more fully than with
theorizing about the fundamental principles of political science. In social
matters, Kautilya has transcended the exclusiveness of ancient Brahmanism and has at the same time successfully counteracted the renunciatory
tendencies of the Upanishads and early Buddhism. The exaltation of royal
power in the legislative sphere and the elaboration of a complex bureaucracy in the executive sphere were certainly new to Indian polity. It is not
unlikely that in these matters Kautilya has derived inspiration from foreign—more particularly, Hellenistic—sources.

To the intense political and military activity of the early Maurya period,
which is reflected in the teachings of the science of material gain, there
was a reaction in the reign of Ashoka (c.273–232 B.C.), the grandson of
Chandragupta and the third Maurya emperor, who turned away from the
Machiavellian ways of Artha Shāstra to the ways of righteousness or
dharma, and in particular to the teachings of the Buddha. Under Ashoka's
patronage Buddhism received great impetus and, consequently, threw
out a strong challenge to the ancient Brahmanic traditions. The last
Maurya monarch's commander-in-chief, Pushyamitra Shunga, who overthrew his master and thereby established his own dynasty in Magadha,
was, on the other hand, a strong adherent of Brahmanism. Therefore,
when he came to power he made a bold bid to resuscitate the Brahmanic
way of life and thought. He performed the traditional horse sacrifice,
helped the promotion of the Sanskrit language and literature, and tried
to reestablish the Brahmanic ideals in the social sphere. It is out of this
last activity that the *Lawbook of Manu* (*Manu Smṛti*) has presumably
evolved, but in whatever little the author has said about polity one finds
hardly anything original. The epic *Mahābhārata,* which is, in its final literary form, more or less contemporaneous with the *Lawbook of Manu,*
is definitely richer in political speculations. The entire *Rāja-dharma*
("dharma of kings") section of the *Śāntiparvan* ("the Book of Peace," the
twelfth book), for instance, constitutes a veritable compendium of political
theories, rules of diplomacy, and details of administration. But the main
achievement of the *Mahābhārata* consists in the synthesis of the older the-

ories which it has attempted rather than in the enunciation of any new ones. And perhaps more significant than such theoretical discussions are the indications of political thought and practice which can be gleaned from the events actually described in the epic. At any rate, the total polity of Hindu India throughout its history from the Shunga period (second to first centuries B.C.) onward may be said to have been the result of a blending together of the political ideology of Kautilya's *Treatise on Material Gain* (in its present or an earlier form) and the social ideology of the *Lawbook of Manu.*

Among later works in Sanskrit dealing with the subject of political science may be mentioned the *Lawbook of Yājnavalkya,* the *Essence of Policy of the School of Kāmandakī (Kāmandakīya Nīti Sāra),* and the *Policy of Shukra (Śukra Nīti).* What the Lawbook of Manu was in relation to the Shunga period, the *Lawbook of Yājnavalkya* may be said to have been in relation to the Gupta period (fourth to fifth centuries A.D.). Though the latter, like its predecessor, makes no original contribution to ancient Indian polity, it reflects, to a large extent, the social changes which had been brought about by the beginning of the Gupta epoch. The Gupta lawgivers brought all persons, irrespective of caste, property, and position in society, under the purview of the king's supreme law. No person was regarded as being above the law. For instance, the *Lawbook of Yājnavalkya* denied to the brāhmans several legal concessions which they had previously enjoyed. It also did away with the many legal inequities from which the shūdra suffered. The law relating to women was also considerably revised and brought in line with their changed social status. The Gupta rulers were by no means bent on social revolution; indeed they retain much that has the sanction of orthodox tradition. Nevertheless, it is significant that whereas in earlier lawbooks there is no distinction between secular and religious law, in the *Lawbook of Yājñavalkya* these two aspects of law are clearly separated and *vyavahāra* or law proper is discussed far more systematically. It further lays greater stress on private law than on criminal law.

The *Essence of Policy* . . . which also is traditionally ascribed to the Gupta period (A.D. c.400), is but a metrical conspectus of Kautilya's *Treatise on Material Gain.* Its author shows no originality whatsoever nor are any traces to be found in it of any practical experience of governmental administration on his part. The *Essence of Policy* indicates on the one hand the unique sway which Kautilya's work held over ancient Indian polity, and on the other, the general decline of political thought in the succeeding periods. The same may be said of the *Kural*, a comprehensive work in Tamil by Tiruvalluvar, which deals with the three ends of man. This work probably dates from A.D. 450–500 and, like most of the Tamil literature produced in that period, shows unmistakable influence of earlier Sanskrit works. Even a casual perusal of the section on polity in the *Kural* would make it quite evident that Tiruvalluvar was closely acquainted with Kautilya's *Treatise* and has derived his inspiration and material from that work. Contrary to our expectations, therefore, the *Kural* does not contain any political thought which can be characterized as peculiar to South India. The last phase of the history of ancient Indian polity is represented by the *Policy of Shukra*, which is usually ascribed to about A.D. 800. This work also is in the nature of a conspectus of earlier works on polity, but it is remarkable for its detailed treatment of the administrative machinery, foreign relations, and military policy.

Dharma As the Supreme Authority

The normal form of the state in ancient India was monarchy. Temporal sovereignty, however, was usually considered to be based on religious authority. Thus, the dharma, the religious and moral law, elaborated and preserved by the brāhmans, was thought to be the source of kshatra, the sovereign power of the king, and therefore superior to it. The coronation ceremony, it is true, represented the application of this spiritual power in the temporal realm, and in that respect the custodians of spiritual power on earth were regarded as subordinate to the temporal authority vested in the king. Nevertheless, the king's chaplain (purohita), who was considered the embodiment of brahman, spiritual power, served as the king's mentor in temporal as well as spiritual matters. In this capacity he and other brāhman advisers attempted to guide and restrain the king's exercise of power, reminding him that it was not absolute. In so far as they actually succeeded in inspiring respect for dharma in the ruler, the brāhmans were thereby able to serve as a kind of check on the monarchy.

Social prosperity and the harmonious functioning of society were believed to depend upon a society composed of the four social orders, namely, brāhman, kshatriya, vaishya, and shūdra, representing respectively spiritual authority, temporal power, wealth, and labor. The society could not flourish in the absence of any of its four constituents. The regulation and prosperity of such an ordered society was not so much the function of the king as it was of dharma or law. Thus, in the *Rig Veda* each person in the ordered universe (sat) had a particular function (*vrata*) to perform. The regulation of this ordered universe was established by cosmic law or order, rita or dharma. Hence, the performance of duty in accordance with this law brought about a state of harmony with the ordered universe (sat) and was regarded as *satya* (truth). In this way, cosmic law was identified with truth and was regarded as the ultimate authority to which even the king was obliged to yield. This supremacy of dharma is the basic concept of ancient Indian social and political thought.

[From *Bṛhad Āraṇyaka Upaniṣad*, 1.4.11–14]

Verily, in the beginning this [world] was brahman, being only one. That brahman, being one, did not prosper. It therefore brought forth an excellent form, kshatra, such as those among the gods who are embodiments of kshatra, namely Indra, Varuna. . . . Therefore, there is nothing higher than kshatra. Therefore, the brāhman sits below the kshatriya at the coronation [*rājasūya*] sacrifice. Thereby, indeed, brahman confers honor on kshatra. The source of kshatra, however, is this very brahman. Therefore, even though the king attains supremacy, finally he has to resort to brahman, which is, indeed, his own source. So a king who injures a brāhman attacks his own source. He becomes more sinful as does one who injures his superiors.

Still he did not prosper. He created the community [*viś*, i.e., the vaishyas], such as those classes of gods, who are designated by groups, namely, the Vasus, the Rudras, the Ādityas. . . .

Still he did not prosper. He created the menial class [*śūdra-varṇa*], such as Pūshan among the gods. Verily, this earth is Pūshan for it nourishes all this, whatever there is.[1]

Still he did not prosper. That brahman brought forth an excellent form, dharma [law]. This dharma is the sovereign power ruling over kshatra itself. Therefore, there is nothing higher than dharma. Thereby, even the weak can overcome the strong with the help of dharma as with the help of a king. Verily, that which is dharma is truth [*satya*]. Therefore, they say of a man who speaks dharma, that he speaks the truth, for, verily, these two are one and the same.

The Origin of Kingship

In Vedic literature there are various speculations, mostly embodied in mythical legends, about such topics as the origin and nature of kingship, the functions

---

[1] Pūshan is a Vedic deity represented as a pastoral divinity and pathmaker *par excellence*. The principal functions indicate his service to gods and men. Similarly, the shūdras are the servants of the three higher classes. There is here, too, a pun on Pūshan and the earth which nourishes (*puṣyati*) the world.

of the king, and types of sovereignty. Though the most frequent theory expounded is that of the divine origin of kingship, in the Vedic literature itself references to any divinity attaching to the person of an historical king are rare. Occasionally in the *Rig Veda* or *Atharva Veda* a king is referred to as half-god or even a god above mortals. In ancient India, however, the king is not regarded as an incarnation on earth of any one particular deity, though he is often represented as the embodiment of a number of divinities. The idea of the personality of a king having been formed of essential particles derived from different gods was developed, perhaps for the first time, in the *Lawbook of Manu* (e.g. *Manu Smṛti,* 7.4–8).

In some older texts there are also suggestions that the king was selected or chosen, usually on account of some pressing need or special urgency, such as war, and was expected to fulfill certain obligations to the people. Public opinion expressed itself through popular assemblies or councils (*sabhā, samiti*) and something akin to a social contract between the king and his subjects was understood to exist. However this may be, it should be remembered that the normal form of state in ancient India was monarchy, usually with some form of religious sanction, and that the normal form of monarchy was hereditary.

One theory of the divine origin of kingship is found in the *Mahābhārata,* where, for instance, Brahmā or Prajāpati, the lord of creatures, is said to have rescued the human race from a state of nature by laying down a code of conduct for all people and by creating the institution of kingship. In the following passage three distinct stages in the evolution of kingship are indicated, namely, the golden age of stateless society under the regulation of dharma, in which individuals were conscious of their duties toward themselves and their fellow men, and external agencies, like state or government, were unnecessary; the period of decadence characterized by the prevalence of a state of nature; and finally the period which saw the divine establishment of law and the first king, Virajas, as administrator of law.

[From *Mahābhārata,* 12.59.5, 13–30, 93–94]

Yudhishthira said: "This word 'king' (*rājā*) is so very current in this world, O Bhārata; how has it originated? Tell me that, O grandfather."

Bhīshma said: "Certainly, O best among men, do you listen to everything in its entirety—how kingship originated first during the golden age (krita-yuga). Neither kingship nor king was there in the beginning, neither scepter (*daṇḍa*) nor the bearer of a scepter. All people protected one another, by means of righteous conduct (dharma). Thus, while protecting one another by means of righteous conduct, O Bhārata, men eventually fell into a state of spiritual lassitude. Then delusion overcame them. Men were thus overpowered by infatuation, O leader of men, on account of the delusion of understanding; their sense of righteous conduct was lost.

When understanding was lost, all men, O best of the Bhāratas, overpowered by infatuation, became victims of greed. Then they sought to acquire what should not be acquired. Thereby, indeed, O lord, another vice, namely desire, overcame them. Attachment then attacked them, who had become victims of desire. Attached to objects of sense, they did not discriminate between right and wrong action, O Yudhishthira. They did not avoid, O king of kings, pursuing what was not worth pursuing, nor, similarly, did they discriminate between what should be said and what should not be said, between the edible and inedible, and between right and wrong. When this world of men had been submerged in dissipation, all spiritual knowledge [brahman] perished; and when spiritual knowledge perished, O king, righteous conduct also perished.

"When spiritual knowledge and righteous conduct perished, the gods were overcome with fear, and fearfully sought refuge with Brahmā, the creator. Going to the great lord, the ancestor of the worlds, all the gods, afflicted with sorrow, misery, and fear, with folded hands said: 'O Lord, the eternal spiritual knowledge, which had existed in the world of men has perished because of greed, infatuation, and the like, therefore we have become fearful. Through the loss of spiritual knowledge, righteous conduct also has perished, O God. Therefore, O Lord of the three worlds, mortals have reached a state of indifference. Verily, we showered rain on earth, but mortals showered rain [i.e., oblations] up to heaven. As a result of the cessation of ritual activity on their part, we faced a serious peril. O grandfather, decide what is most beneficial to us under these circumstances.'

"Then, the self-born lord said to all those gods: 'I will consider what is most beneficial; let your fear depart, O leaders of the gods.'

"Thereupon he composed a work consisting of a hundred thousand chapters out of his own mind, wherein righteous conduct (dharma), as well as material gain (artha) and enjoyment of sensual pleasures (kāma) were described. This group, known as the threefold classification of human objectives, was expounded by the self-born lord; so, too, a fourth objective, spiritual emancipation (moksha), which aims at a different goal, and which constitutes a separate group by itself.

"Then the gods approached Vishnu, the lord of creatures, and said: 'Indicate to us that one person among mortals who alone is worthy of the highest eminence.' Then the blessed lord god Nārāyana reflected, and brought forth an illustrious mind-born son, called Virajas [who became the first king]."

The Science of Polity

The important place of political and economic thought, in relation to the other major fields of human inquiry and speculation, is set forth in the passages which follow.

[From *Kauṭilīya Artha Śāstra*, 1.2, 3, 4, 7]
Philosophy, the Veda, the science of economics, and the science of polity—these are the sciences. . . .

Sānkhya, Yoga, and materialism—these constitute philosophy. Distinguishing, with proper reasoning, between good and evil in the Vedic religion, between profit and nonprofit in the science of economics, and between right policy and wrong policy in the science of polity, and determining the comparative validity and invalidity of these sciences [under specific circumstances], philosophy becomes helpful to the people, keeps the mind steady in woe and weal, and produces adroitness of understanding, speech, and action. . . .

The *Sāma Veda,* the *Rig Veda,* and the *Yajur Veda* constitute the trilogy of the *Vedas.* These, the *Atharva Veda,* and the *Itihāsa Veda* (the Veda of history and legends) make up the Vedas. Phonetics, ritual, grammar, etymology, metrics, and astronomy—these are the limbs [ancillary sciences] of the Veda. The way of life taught in the trilogy of the Vedas [and other Vedic works] is helpful on account of its having laid down the duties of the four classes and the four stages of life. . . .

Agriculture, cattle-breeding, trade, and commerce constitute the main topics dealt with in the science of economics; it is helpful on account of its making available grains, cattle, gold, raw material, and free labor. Through the knowledge of economics, a king brings under his control his own party and the enemy's party with the help of treasury and army.

The scepter [1] (*daṇḍa*) is the means of the acquisition and the preservation of philosophy, the Veda, and economics. The science treating with the effective bearing of the scepter is the science of polity (*Daṇḍa Nīti*). It conduces to the acquisition of what is not acquired, the preservation of what has been acquired, the growth of what has been preserved, and the

[1] That is, government as opposed to anarchy.

distribution among worthy people of what has grown. It is on it [the science of polity] that the proper functioning of society [lit., the world] depends. . . .

"Of the three ends of human life, material gain is, verily, the most important." So says Kautilya. "On material gain depends the realization of dharma and pleasure." [2]

[From *Śukra Nīti,* 1.4–19]

Other sciences treat of one or another field of human activity, while the science of policy (Nīti Shāstra) [3] is helpful in all respects and conduces to the stability of human society.

As the science of policy is the source of dharma, material gain, and pleasure, and as it is traditionally said to lead to spiritual emancipation, a king should always study it diligently.

Through the knowledge of the science of policy, kings and others become conquerors of their foes and conciliators of their own people. Kings who are skillful in working out the right policy always prevail.

Can the knowledge of words and their meanings not be acquired without the study of grammar, and of material categories without the study of logic, and the science of reasoning and of ritual practices and procedures without the study of the *Pūrva Mīmāṃsā?* [4] Can the limitations and destructibility of bodily existence not be realized without the study of the Vedānta texts? [5]

Further, these sciences treat only of their own special subjects. They are, accordingly, studied only by such persons as follow their respective teachings. Their study implies mere adroitness of intellect. Of what avail are they to people interested and engaged in everyday affairs? On the other hand, the stability of any human affairs is not possible without the science of policy, in the same way as the functioning of the physical bodies of men is not possible without food.

The science of policy conduces to the fulfillment of all desires and is, therefore, respected by all people. It is quite indispensable even to a king, for he is the lord of all people.

Just as diseases are bound to make their appearance in the case of per-

---

[2] Consequently the Artha Shāstra, the science of material gain (i.e., polity), is the most important science.

[3] Lit., science of wise conduct (*nīti*), another name for the science of material gain or polity (Artha Shāstra).

[4] The philosophy of ritual.   [5] The Upanishads.

sons who eat unwholesome foods, so do enemies make their appearance—
some immediately and some in course of time—in respect of kings who
are devoid of the knowledge of the science of policy; but it never happens
that they do not make their appearance at all.

The primary duty of a king consists of the protection of his subjects and
the constant keeping under control of evil elements. These two cannot
possibly be accomplished without the science of policy.

Absence of the knowledge of the science of policy is, verily, the weakest point of a king—it is ever dangerous. It is said to be a great help to
the growth of the enemy and to the diminution of one's own power.

Whoever abandons the science of policy and behaves independently
[that is, without any consideration for the teachings of the science] suffers from misery. Service of such an independent [i.e., self-willed, capri-
cious] master is like licking the sharp edge of the sword.

A king who follows the science of policy is easily propitiated,[6] while
one who does not follow it cannot be easily propitiated. Where both—
right policy and might—exist, there prevails all-round glory.

In order that the entire kingdom should, of its own accord, become
productive of good, right policy should be employed and maintained by
a king. This should, indeed, be done by a king also for his own good.

A kingdom divided within itself, the army disintegrated, the civil
service headed by ministers disorganized—these are always the result of
the ineptitude of a king who is devoid of the knowledge of the science of
policy.

Duties of a King

Ancient Indian polity does not treat specifically of the rights and the privileges
of the subject but leaves them to be inferred from the duties and the responsibilities of the king, with which it deals at some length. The following passage,
which deals with the duties of a king, prescribes that the king regulate his
activities according to a definite timetable. A king was expected to keep himself in touch with every department of administration. Special emphasis was
put on the inadvisability of his isolation from his subjects.

[From Kauṭilīya Artha Śāstra, 1.19]

Only if a king is himself energetically active, do his officers follow him
energetically. If he is sluggish, they too remain sluggish. And, besides,

[6] Or: has his own desires easily fulfilled.

they eat up his works.[1] He is thereby easily overpowered by his enemies. Therefore, he should ever dedicate himself energetically to activity.

He should divide the day as well as the night into eight parts. . . . During the first one-eighth part of the day, he should listen to reports pertaining to the organization of law and order and to income and expenditure. During the second, he should attend to the affairs of the urban and the rural population. During the third, he should take his bath and meal and devote himself to study. During the fourth, he should receive gold and the departmental heads. During the fifth, he should hold consultations with the council of ministers through correspondence and also keep himself informed of the secret reports brought by spies. During the sixth, he should devote himself freely to amusement or listen to the counsel of the ministers. During the seventh, he should inspect the military formations of elephants, cavalry, chariots, and infantry. During the eighth, he, together with the commander-in-chief of the army, should make plans for campaigns of conquest. When the day has come to an end he should offer the evening prayers.

During the first one-eighth part of the night, he should meet the officers of the secret service. During the second, he should take his bath and meals and also devote himself to study. During the third, at the sounding of the trumpets, he should enter the bed chamber and should sleep through the fourth and fifth. Waking up at the sounding of the trumpets, he should, during the sixth part, ponder over the teachings of the sciences and his urgent duties for the day. During the seventh, he should hold consultations and send out the officers of the secret service for their operations. During the eighth, accompanied by sacrificial priests, preceptors, and the chaplain, he should receive benedictions; he should also have interviews with the physician, the kitchen-superintendent, and the astrologer. Thereafter, he should circumambulate by the right[2] a cow with a calf and an ox and then proceed to the reception hall. Or he should divide the day and the night into parts in accordance with his own capacities and thereby attend to his duties.

When he has gone to the reception hall, he should not allow such persons, as have come for business, to remain sticking to the doors of the hall [i.e., waiting in vain]. For, a king, with whom it is difficult for the people to have an audience, is made to confuse between right action and wrong

[1] That is, spoil or bring to naught his works.   [2] As a mark of respect or reverence.

action by his close entourage. Thereby he suffers from the disaffection of his own subjects or falls prey to the enemy. Therefore he should attend to the affairs relating to gods,[3] hermitages, heretics, learned brāhmans, cattle, and holy places as also those of minors, the aged, the sick, those in difficulty, the helpless, and women—in the order of their enumeration or in accordance with the importance or the urgency of the affairs.

A king should attend to all urgent business, he should not put it off. For what has been thus put off becomes either difficult or altogether impossible to accomplish.

Seated in the fire-chamber and accompanied by the chaplain and the preceptor he should look into the business of the knowers of the Veda and the ascetics—having first got up from his seat and having respectfully greeted them.

Only in the company of the adepts in the three Vedas, and not by himself, should he decide the affairs of the ascetics as also of the experts in magical practices—lest these become enraged.

The vow of the king is energetic activity, his sacrifice is constituted of the discharge of his own administrative duties; his sacrifical fee [to the officiating priests] is his impartiality of attitude toward all; his sacrificial consecration is his anointment as king.

In the happiness of the subjects lies the happiness of the king; in their welfare, his own welfare. The welfare of the king does not lie in the fulfillment of what is dear to him; whatever is dear to the subjects constitutes his welfare.

Therefore, ever energetic, a king should act up to the precepts of the science of material gain. Energetic activity is the source of material gain; its opposite, of downfall.

In the absence of energetic activity, the loss of what has already been obtained and of what still remains to be obtained is certain. The fruit of one's works is achieved through energetic activity—one obtains abundance of material prosperity.

The Seven Limbs of the State

Though monarchy was the normal form of state in ancient India, the sovereign power was never concentrated in the person or the office of the monarch alone.

[3] This refers to endowments, etc. in the name of the gods. Note the relatively high importance of the "heretics," mostly Buddhists and Jains, coming right after Hindu temples and brāhman hermitages.

The state or sovereignty was regarded as an organic whole made up of seven constituents, which are called the "limbs" of the body politic—the monarch being just one of those constituents. The state can function effectively only if these constituents remain properly integrated with one another. Modern political theorists mention territory, population, and central government as together constituting the state. It is interesting to note the additional constituents mentioned by Kautilya, who is first among ancient Indian writers to advance the theory of the seven constituents of the state.

[From *Kauṭilīya Artha Śāstra*, 6.1]

The king, the ministers, the country, the forts, the treasury, the army, and the allies are the constituents of the state.

Of these, the perfection of the king is this: Born of a high family; non-fatalistic; endowed with strong character; looking up to [experienced] old men [for guidance]; religious, truthful in speech; not inconsistent [in his behavior]; grateful; having liberal aims; full of abundant energy; not procrastinating; controller of his feudatories; of determined intellect; having an assembly of ministers of no mean quality; intent on discipline—these are the qualities by means of which people are attracted toward him. Inquiry; study; perception; retention; analytical knowledge; critical acumen; keenness for the realization of reality—these are the qualities of the intellect. Valor; impetuosity; agility; and dexterity—these are the qualities of energy. Of profound knowledge; endowed with strong memory, cogitative faculty, and physical strength; exalted; easily controlling himself; adept in arts; rid of difficulties;[4] capable bearer of the scepter; openly responding both to acts of help and harm; full of shame [to do anything evil]; capable of dealing adequately with visitations of nature and the constituents of state; seeing far and wide; utilizing for his work the opportunities afforded by the proper place, time, and personal vigor; skilled in discriminating between conditions which require conclusion of a treaty and manifestation of valor, letting off the enemies and curbing them, and waiting under the pretext of some mutual understanding and taking advantage of the enemies' weak points; laughing joyfully, but guardedly and without loss of dignity; looking straight and with uncrooked brow; free from passion, anger, greed, obstinacy, fickleness, heat, and calumny; capable of self-management; speaking with people smilingly but with dignity; observing customs as taught by elderly people—these are the qualities of the personality.

[4] Or: not addicted to vices.

The perfection of the ministers has been described earlier.[5]

Firm in the midland and at the boundaries; capable of affording sub-sistence to its own people and, in case of difficulties, also to outsiders; easy to defend; affording easy livelihood to the people; full of hatred for the enemy; capable of controlling [by its strategic position] the dominions of the feudatories; devoid of muddy, rocky, salty, uneven, and thorny tracts, and of forests infested with treacherous animals and wild animals; pleasing; rich in arable land, mines, and timber and elephant forests; wholesome to cows; wholesome to men; with well-preserved pastures; rich in cattle; not depending entirely on rain; possessing waterways and overland roads; having markets full of valuable, manifold, and abundant ware; capable of bearing the burden of army and taxation; having indus-trious agriculturists, stupid masters,[6] and a population largely consisting of the lower classes [i.e., the economically productive classes, vaishyas and shūdras]; inhabited by devoted and respectable men—this is the perfection of the country.

The perfection of the forts has been described earlier.[7]

Lawfully inherited from his ancestors or earned by the king himself; mainly consisting of gold and silver; full of manifold and big precious stones and bars of gold; and such as would endure a calamity even of a long duration and also a state of things which brought in no income—this is the perfection of the treasury.

Coming down from father and grandfather; constant in its loyalties; obedient; having the sons and wives of soldiers contented and well pro-vided for; not becoming disintegrated in military campaigns in foreign lands; everywhere unassailable; capable of bearing pain; experienced in many battles; expert in the science of all the weapons of war; regarding the rise and the downfall of the king as equivalent to their own and conse-quently not double-dealing with him; mainly consisting of kshatriyas [nobles]—this is the perfection of the army.

Coming down from father and grandfather; constant in their loyalties;

---

[5] *Kauṭilīya Artha Śāstra* 1.9. It is mentioned there that a minister should be, among other things, native, born of high family, influential, trained in arts, endowed with foresight, bold, eloquent, possessed of enthusiasm, dignity, endurance, etc.

[6] According to the *Essence of Policy* . . . (4.54), the leading personalities in the country should be stupid. The commentator explains: Where the leaders of the community are foolish, the king can rule according to his own sweet will and without any obstruction.

[7] *Kauṭilīya Artha Śāstra* 2.3. On all the boundaries of the kingdom there should be de-fensive fortifications. Mention is made of water-forts, mountain-forts, desert-forts, and forest-forts. Details regarding their construction are also given.

obedient; not double-dealing; capable of preparing for war on a large scale and quickly—this is the perfection of the allies.

Not born of a royal family; greedy; having an assembly of ministers who are mean; with his subjects antagonistic toward him; inclined toward injustice; non-diligent; overcome by calamities; devoid of enthusiasm; fatalistic; indiscreet in his actions; helpless; supportless; impotent; and ever doing harm to others—this is the perfection of the enemy. For such an enemy is easy to uproot.

Excepting the enemy these seven constituents, characterized by the development of their respective qualities and serving as limbs of sovereignty, are said to be intended for promoting the perfection of the sovereignty.

A king endowed with a significant personality makes the imperfect constituents perfect. A king without personality, on the other hand, destroys the constituents even though they are well developed and effectively attached to one another.

Therefore, even the ruler of the four ends of the earth, the constituents of whose sovereignty are spoiled and who is not endowed with a significant personality, is either destroyed by the constituents themselves or is overpowered by his enemies.

On the other hand, a ruler who is endowed with a significant personality, is blessed with perfect constituents of sovereignty, and is a knower of statecraft, though possessing a small dominion, verily, conquers the entire earth—he does not suffer a setback.

The Circle of States and Interstate Policy

The theory of the circle of states and that of the sixfold interstate policy, as formulated by the political theorists of ancient India, may appear rather doctrinaire, but they clearly involve certain principles which must have been derived from practical political experience. The normal state of affairs is seen as a balance of power among the various states, but the ruler is impressed with the need for always remaining on his guard, for tactfully watching the situation, and, whenever an opportunity offers itself, for acting as a hammer unto others lest he himself be turned into an anvil.

[From *Kauṭilīya Artha Śāstra*, 6.2; 7.1]

Repose and activity constitute the source of acquisition and maintenance of wealth. Effort toward the acquisition of the fruits of works undertaken is activity. Effort toward the continuance of the enjoyment of the fruits of works is repose. The source of repose and activity is the sixfold policy. Its possible results are deterioration, stagnation, and progress. Its human aspect is constituted of right policy and wrong policy; its divine aspect of good luck and bad luck. For the divine working and the human working together keep the world going. That which is brought about by unseen forces is the divine. Thereby, the acquisition of the desired fruit denotes good luck; that of the undesired, bad luck. That which is brought about by the visible forces is the human. Thereby, the accomplishment of acquisition and maintenance denotes right policy; nonaccomplishment, wrong policy. The human aspect can be thought about [and taken care of]; the divine cannot be thought about [and taken care of].

The king who is endowed with personality and the material constituents of sovereignty and on whom all right policy rests is called the conqueror.[8] That which encircles him on all sides and prevails in the territory immediately adjacent to his is the constituent of the circle of states known as the enemy. Similarly, that which prevails in the territory which is separated from the conqueror's territory by one [namely, by the enemy's territory] is the constituent known as friend. A neighboring prince having the fullest measure of antagonism is an enemy. When he is in difficulty, he should be attacked; when he is without support or has weak support, he should be exterminated. In contrary circumstances [that is, when he is strong or has strong support], he should be harassed or weakened. These are the peculiar attitudes to be taken toward an enemy.

From the enemy onward and in front of the conqueror are the friend, the enemy's friend, the friend's friend, and the enemy's friend's friend, ruling over the consecutively adjacent territories. In the rear of the conqueror there are the rear-seizer,[9] the challenger,[10] the ally of the rear-seizer, and the ally of the challenger [ruling over the consecutively adjacent territories].

The prince ruling over the territory immediately adjacent to that of the conqueror is the conqueror's "natural" enemy. One who is born in the same family as the conqueror is his "born" enemy. One who is himself

[8] The conqueror is the king with reference to whom all the teachings of Kautilya's *Treatise* are taught. He may, indeed, be said to be the hero of this treatise. It is he who is the center of the circle of states and who is expected to employ the sixfold interstate policy. A king, according to Kautilya, must always aim at victories over others.

[9] An inimical prince who attacks the rear of the conqueror.

[10] *Ākranda,* lit. one who shouts, is a prince who "challenges" the rear-seizer on behalf of the conqueror or who warns the conqueror of the rear attack.

antagonistic to the conqueror or creates antagonism toward him among others is his "factitious" enemy. The prince ruling over the territory immediately beyond the one adjacent to that of the conqueror is his "natural" friend. One who is related to the conqueror through the father or the mother is his "born" friend. One with whom the conqueror has sought refuge for the sake of wealth or life is his "factitious" friend.

The prince who rules over the territory adjacent to those of the enemy and of the conqueror and who is capable of favoring both of them, whether they are united or not, or of keeping them under restraint when they are not united, is the middle king.

The prince who rules over a territory lying beyond those of the enemy, the conqueror, and the middle king, who is stronger than the other kings constituting the circles of states, and who is capable of favoring the enemy, the conqueror, and the middle king, whether they are united or not, or of keeping them under restraint when they are not united, is the neutral king.

These twelve [11] are the primary kings constituting the circles of states.

The conqueror, his friend, and friend's friend are the three primary constituents of his own circle of states. They are, each of them, possessed of the five constituents of sovereignty, namely, minister, country, fort, treasury, and army. Each circle of states, accordingly, consists of eighteen constituents.[12] Hereby are explained also the circles of states belonging to the enemy, the middle king, and the neutral king.

Thus there are in all four circles of states.[13] There are twelve primary kings; [14] and sixty constituents of sovereignty; [15] in all, there are seventy-two constituents.[16] [6.2]

The circle of states is the source of the sixfold policy. The teacher says: "Peace, war, marking time, attack, seeking refuge, and duplicity are the

[11] Namely: conqueror, enemy, friend, enemy's friend, friend's friend, enemy's friend's friend, rear-seizer, challenger, rear-seizer's ally, challenger's ally, the middle king, and the neutral king.

[12] That is, six constituents of sovereignty for each state, omitting the seventh, the ally, which is already implicit in the scheme.

[13] Namely, those of the conqueror, the enemy, the middle king, and the neutral king.

[14] Namely, the same four main kings and their respective friends and friends' friends. The rear-seizer, the challenger, and their respective allies do not seem to have been included in this number.

[15] Each of the twelve kings has five constituents of sovereignty (besides himself), omitting the ally as above.

[16] The above sixty plus the twelve kings.

six forms of interstate policy." "There are only two forms of policy," says
Vātavyādhi, "for the sixfold policy is actually accomplished through peace
and war." Kautilya says: "The forms of policy are, verily, six in number,
for conditions are different in different cases."

Of these six forms: binding through pledges means peace; offensive
operation means war; apparent indifference means marking time;
strengthening one's position means attack; giving oneself to another [as
a subordinate ally or vassal] means seeking refuge; keeping oneself engaged simultaneously in peace and war with the same state means duplicity. These are the six forms of policy.

When one king [the would-be conqueror] is weaker than the other
[i.e., his immediate neighbor, the enemy], he should make peace with
him. When he is stronger than the other, he should make war with him.
When he thinks: "The other is not capable of putting me down nor am
I capable of putting him down," he should mark time. When he possesses
an excess of the necessary means, he should attack. When he is devoid of
strength,[17] he should seek refuge with another. When his end can be
achieved only through the help of an ally, he should practice duplicity.
So is the sixfold policy laid down. [7.1]

State Administration

This statement about the qualifications and functions of the principal ministers
of the king clearly indicates a very complex and highly specialized governmental
organization. It is also typical of the ancient Indian writings on polity, which
concerned themselves more with the concrete administrative details than with
abstract political theorizing.

[From *Śukra Nīti*, 2.69, 70, 77–108]

The chaplain, the deputy, the premier, the commandant, the counsellor,
the judge, the scholar, the economic adviser, the minister, and the ambassador—these are the king's ten primary officers. . . .

Well-versed in ritual formulas and practices, learned in the three Vedas,
diligent about religious duties, conqueror of his sense-organs, subduer of
anger, devoid of greed and infatuation, possessed of the knowledge of the

---

[17] Strength, as Kautilya has said elsewhere, is of three kinds: strength of wise counsel
(which is made up of knowledge and wisdom), strength of sovereignty (which is made up
of treasury and army), and strength of personal enterprise (which is made up of the will
to martial glory).

six limbs of the Veda and of the science of archery together with its
various branches, one fearing whose anger even the king becomes devoted to righteous conduct and right policy, skilled in polity and the science of weapons, missiles, and military tactics—such should the chaplain
be; such a chaplain is, verily, also the preceptor—capable of cursing and
blessing alike. Those with reference to whom the king thinks: "Without
the proper advice of these primary officers, my kingdom may be lost and
there may be a general setback"—they should be regarded as good ministers. Is the growth of the kingdom possible without such ministers
whom the king does not fear? Just as women are to be adorned with
ornaments, dresses, etc., so too should these ministers be adorned and
propitiated. What is the use of those ministers, whose counsels conduce
neither to any aggrandizement of kingdom, population, army, treasury,
and good kingship, nor to destruction of the enemy?

He who can discriminate between what is to be done and what is not
to be done is traditionally known to be qualified for the office of the
deputy. The premier is the supervisor of all things, and the commandant
is well versed in military science and technique. The counsellor is skilled
in polity and the scholar is the master of the essential tenets of righteous
conduct. The judge possesses the knowledge of popular customs and
principles of law. One who possesses an insight into the proper time and
place for any action is called the minister, while one who knows the income and expenditure of the state is known as the economic adviser.
One who can delve into the innermost thoughts and the secret actions,
who has good memory, who has an insight into the proper time and
place for any action, who is a master of the sixfold policy, who is an
effective speaker, and who is fearless—such a one should be made the
ambassador.

The deputy should always advise the king about a thing which, though
unwholesome, has to be done, about the time when a thing is fit to be
done instantly, and about a thing which, though wholesome, should
not be done. He should make him act, or himself act, or should neither
act nor advise.[1] The premier should, indeed, find out whether a thing is
effective or ineffective, and watch over all the working in connection with
the state functions entrusted to all officers. The commandant should be in
charge of elephants, as also of horses, chariots, and foot-soldiers, so of

[1] When he feels that such action or advice is not necessary.

strong camels and, verily, of oxen; of those who are studied in military musical instruments, code-languages, ensigns, and battle-arrays, of vanguards and rearguards; of bearers of royal emblems, weapons, and missiles; of menial servants; and of servants of middle and high grades. He should find out the efficacy of missiles, missile-throwers, and cavalry; he should also find out how many among the troops are capable of action, how many are old, and how many new; he should further find out how many among the troops are incapable of action, how many are equipped with arms, ammunition, and gunpowder, and how much is the quantity of war material. Having carefully thought over all this the commandant should properly report to the king as to what is to be done. The counsellor should consider as to how, when, and in respect of whom the policies of conciliation, bribery, dissension, and punishment are to be employed and as to what their result would be—whether great, moderate, or small. He should then decide on some action and report it to the king. The judge should always advise the king after examining, while seated in the court with his assessors, the plaints brought forth by men, by means of witness, written documents, rights accruing from possession, artifices, and ordeals —first finding out as to which of these means is effective in which suits —and after getting the decisions agreed upon by the majority confirmed through the application of logic, direct observation, inference, and analogy as also of popular customs. The scholar should study the rules of conduct which are current, which have become archaic, and which are observed by the people, which are prescribed in scriptures, which are not applicable at a particular time, and which are opposed to scriptures and popular customs, and recommend to the king such rules as would be conducive to happiness in this life and hereafter. The economic adviser should report to the king on the following items: the quantity of commodities like grass, etc., stored during a particular year; the quantity spent; and the quantity in movables and immovables which has been left as balance. The minister should investigate and report to the king on how many cities, villages, and forests there are, how much land is under cultivation, who received rent from it and how much, how much remains after paying off the rent, how much land is uncultivated, how much revenue is realized in a particular year by way of taxes and fines, how much revenue accrues from uncultivated land and how much from forests, how much is realized from mines and how much from treasure-troves, how much is added to the state treasury as not belonging to any-body, as lost [and found], as recovered from thieves, and as stored up.

The characteristics and functions of the ten ministers are thus briefly mentioned. The king should judge their competence by looking into their written reports and oral instructions. He should appoint them to each post by rotation. He should never make these officers more power-ful than himself; he should invest these ten primary officers with equal authority.

moves, how much is added to the state treasury as not below, and to anybody as just [and found], as recovered from thieves, and the characteristics and dimensions of the ten offices previously mentioned. The king should judge from these records their written reports and oral instructions. He should appoint to each post . . . . the honest and capable officers; moreover, careful that himself, he should invest these honest officers with equal authority.

CHAPTER XII

KĀMA, THE THIRD END OF MAN

The place of kāma or the pursuit of love and pleasure in the balanced Hindu scheme of life derives from the importance attached to the life of the married householder (*grhastha*). In more than one authoritative text, the householder's life is considered to be the greatest of the four stages of life. Hinduism does not hold up monasticism or eremitism as a common ideal for all; it considers, rather, that the strains and trials of household management, family life, and social obligations are a useful discipline contributing to the preparation of man for the final life of retirement and spiritual endeavor. The place assigned to pleasure provides also for its regulated enjoyment, rather than its suppression, and thus for the development of a well-rounded personality. Constantly reminding the householder of his duties (i.e., dharma) as also of the higher nature of the Ultimate Reality which was the final goal to be attained, the Hindu code of conduct saw to it that the normal man did not degenerate into an epicure or profligate. Love chastened by suffering was held up even by poets and dramatists as capable of effecting a lasting spiritual union, and some of the best poetry in Sanskrit reflects this spirit and attitude toward love. The longing of hearts in love was taken as the most effective image to depict the yearning of the devotee to God or the seeking by the individual soul of the Supreme Soul, a symbolism which is at the base of a greater part of the erotic art of India. Hindu aesthetes explained the philosophy of beauty in terms of the enjoyment or perception of a state of sublime composure or blissful serenity which was a reflection, intimation, image, or glimpse of the enduring bliss of the spirit in its true realization through knowledge.

As in the case of the science of material gain (i.e., of polity), the science of love or pleasure (Kāma Shāstra) also was studied systematically and in exhaustive detail, the object being to comprehend all types of persons and situations, normal and otherwise. The separate disciplines and techniques elaborated upon, however, as well as the special cases and situations dealt with, should be considered in relation to the general view of life from which these branches of knowledge were evolved, and which continued to regulate and guide them. The history of the growth of these separate disciplines is set forth at the outset in texts like the *Aphorisms on Love* (*Kāma Sūtra*) of Vātsyāyana, where it is said that it was the gods and sages that promulgated these sciences of material gain and pleasure, along with the sacred law, and that at the beginning it was all one comprehensive code of conduct. As time went by, each section was separately elaborated by later sages and teachers, in conformity with the comprehensive scheme of values represented by duty (dharma), material gain, pleasure, and spiritual emancipation.

The cultured person and in particular the courtesan of Sanskrit literature (the Indian equivalent of the Japanese geisha) was expected to be educated in sixty-four *kalās* (arts and sciences), a term often equated with *śilpa* "art" or *vidyā* "science." Though this number may vary in older Jain and Buddhist texts, a standard list of sixty-four is given by Vātsyāyana in the *Kāma Sūtra* and a slightly different one in the *Policy of Shukra*. These arts include dancing, singing, acting, flower-arranging, gambling, legerdemain, distillation of spiritous liquors, sewing and embroidery work, first-aid, metallurgy, cooking, chemistry, posture, dueling, gymnastics, horology, dyeing, architecture and engineering, minerology, calligraphy, swimming, leatherwork, archery, driving horses and elephants, composition and solution of riddles and other puzzles, nursing and rearing of children, and the like.

The Man of Taste and Culture

In contrast to the characterization of the Hindu outlook as pessimistic and other-worldly, is the following description, taken from Vātsyāyana's *Aphorisms on Love* (c. A.D. 400), of the man-about-town who enjoys the good things of life, has a cultured taste, and moves in the most refined social and artistic circles.

The word for civilization in Sanskrit is, like its Western counterpart, associated with the town and city (nagara). The *nāgaraka* in Sanskrit means the civilized or cultured urban individual.

[From Vātsyāyana, *Kāma Sūtra*, 1.4]

After acquisition of learning, a person should with the help of the material resources obtained by him through gifts from others, personal gain, commerce or service,[1] marry and set up a home, and then follow the ways of the man of taste and culture (*nāgaraka*).

He may make his abode, in accordance with the calling chosen by him, in a city, in a commercial center, or a town; any of these that he chooses should be inhabited by good people.

There he should make for himself a house, with water nearby, having a garden, provided with separate apartments for different activities, and having two retiring rooms.

In the retiring room in the forepart of the house, there shall be a fine couch, with two pillows, pliant at the center, having a pure white sheet; there shall be by its side another couch of lesser height [for lying down]; at the head, there shall be a wicker-seat [for doing his prayers] and a platform for the sandal paste left over after the night's use, a garland, a box for wax and scents, peelings of pomegranate fruit [a mouth deodorant] and betel leaves; a spittoon on the ground; a lute hanging on a bracket on the wall, a painting-board and box of colors, some books and garlands of *kurantaka* flowers; not far away on the floor, different kinds of seats; a dice-board; outside the room, cages for the birds kept for playing with; and at a remote end [outside], things for private use.

In the garden a swing, well covered and under the shade of a tree, as also an earthen platform strewn with the falling flowers of the garden. Such is to be the layout of his residence.

He must get up early in the morning, answer the calls of nature, wash his teeth, smear his body with just a little [2] fragrant paste, inhale fragrant smoke, wear some flower, just give the lips a rub with wax and red juice, look at his face in the mirror, chew betel leaves along with some mouth deodorants, and then attend to his work.

Every day he must bathe; every second day, have a massage; every third day, apply *phenaka* [3] to the legs; every fourth day have a partial shave and clipping of the nails; every fifth [?] or tenth day a more complete

---

[1] These four means of acquiring wealth—acceptance as gift, personal gain, commerce, and service—apply respectively to the four classes, brāhman, kshatriya, vaishya, and shūdra. This suggests that the refined accomplishments, cultural preoccupations, and pursuit of art and pleasure were not restricted to any single segment of society.

[2] The commentary hastens to state that too much of these do not speak well of the person's refinement.

[3] To ward off stiffness of the legs.

shave; he must frequently wipe off the perspiration in the armpit; have his food in the forenoon and afternoon.[4]

After eating [in the forenoon] comes playing with parrots and myna birds and making them talk; and indulging in cock and ram fights and in other artistic activities; also attending to the work he has with his friends and companions. Then a little nap. In the forenoon still, he dresses and goes out for social calls and for enjoyment of the company of others. In the evening he enjoys music and dance. At the end of it, in his own apartments, decorated and fragrant with smoke, he awaits, along with his companions, his beloved who has given him an engagement, or else sends her a message and himself goes out to meet her. . . . Such is the daily routine.

He should arrange excursions in parties for attending festivals, salons for enjoying literature and art, drinking parties, excursions to parks, and group games. Once a fortnight or month, on the day sacred to particular deities, the actors and dancers attached to the temple of Sarasvatī [the Goddess of learning] gather and present shows [for the cultured citizens of the place]; or visiting actors and musicians from other places present their programs in the Sarasvatī temple.

AESTHETIC SPECULATIONS

Beauty has been a subject of Indian comment and speculation since the earliest times. The Rig Vedic poet reveled in the beauties of both nature and man; he attached the highest value to beauty of expression in the art of poetry, and had, besides several general terms, the specific names Lakshmī and Shrī for beauty. In the supplementary hymns of the *Rig Veda* he had already devoted a poem to the concept of a deity presiding over beauty and prosperity. In the Brāhmanas we come upon the word *śilpa*, the common term for art in the sense of a perfect or refined form or replica, and the whole world is described as a brilliant piece of divine art or handiwork. The Upanishads, which conceive of the ultimate reality as the one imperishable substratum of the form of existence, knowledge, and bliss, speak of it also as the fullness of perfection and the fountainhead of all enjoyment, *rasa* (*Taittirīya*, 2.7); from it proceed literature and other

[4] But in the forenoon and evening, according to the medical authority Chārāyana.

forms of artistic expression (*Bṛhad Āraṇyaka,* 2.4.10); and to it, as in praise
of the Supreme Being, all song is sung (*Chāndogya* 1.7.6). The epics, the
Rāmāyaṇa and the *Mahābhārata,* along with the Purāṇas, set forth the
conception of a personal God, who is the embodiment of all beauty, and
the object of man's devotion, service, and rapturous exaltation. Whatever
is beautiful here in this world is so because of the spark of this divine beauty
in it, says the *Bhagavad Gītā* (10.41).   ·

Musicians later developed their philosophy along lines indicated by
the Vedas and Upanishads, according to which music and spiritual endeavor were closely linked. All songs were to be composed and sung in
praise of God; less lofty themes were not considered acceptable. Furthermore, the very act of singing was likened to the yogic discipline involving
the control of breath and concentration. Indian music is, unlike the
harmonic system of the modern West, a melodic or modal system in
which the highest form of art is the continued singing of pure melody
(rāga) unaided by any words. This pure melodic elaboration helps both
the singer and listener to become absorbed in the depths of his own being
or transported to a plane where all mundane memory ceases to intrude
or disturb the blissfulness, restfulness, or poise which the spirit achieves.
The high spiritual value set upon music is not only attested in the texts
and the songs, but is also demonstrated by the fact that all the great
musicians of India have been revered as saints.

The art of sculpture, iconography, and painting, as exemplified in the
temples and rockcut caves, had a similar spiritual inspiration, content, and
purpose.

It is in the fields of drama and poetry that a theory of art was systematically developed. Though the popular roots of the drama are shown in
some of its social forms, the highest type of drama was conceived to be
the heroic play in which the acts of gods, incarnations of the Supreme
Divinity, or the sublime royal heroes of the epics were "imitated" or "represented"; similarly the highest form of the poetic art was also the epic
or the grand poem which was a continuation of the *Rāmāyaṇa* and the
Mahābhārata, following them in theme and treatment, though at less
length. The holding forth before the people of elevated character and action was, nevertheless, a secondary purpose; critics agreed that the didactic aspect of a play or poem should always be subordinated to the primary
aim of artistic enjoyment.

But if enjoyment of poetry and drama is the primary end, what then is the essence of this enjoyment? If poetry and drama depict a variety of characters and actions, with a consequent mixture of pleasant and unpleasant feelings, how is it all rendered equally or uniformly relishable? What is there in art that distinguishes it from the world and nature? If the poem, play, or picture presents a different reality, what is the nature of this reality? To questions such as these Indian critics have addressed themselves.

For them the essential thing in poetry or drama is not story and character as such, but the emotion which they embody and which the poet tries to communicate. The emotional interest of a work centers around certain primary sentiments felt by all human beings, around which other secondary emotions hover. Thus love, heroism, pathos, and a few others are seen as ultimate sentiments which constitute their own explanation; not so the subsidiary or transitory feelings such as doubt or despondency, anxiety, longing, or jealousy—all of which require further and multiple explanations as to their causes. Now these major enduring sentiments (*sthāyī-bhāvas*) are embedded as impressions in every heart, and the portrayal of situations in poems and plays touches the corresponding emotional instincts in the cultivated reader or spectator. Though any human being possesses a similar emotional endowment, only the cultivated person can respond fully to artistic presentations. In others the response may be hindered either by a lack of culture or by momentary preoccupations arising from irrelevant and distracting circumstances. In overcoming or eliminating the latter, the artistic atmosphere of the theater, the music, the poetic diction are all helpful. One who is thus responsive is called "a person of attuned heart" (*sa-hṛdaya*), one who identifies himself with the representation. Because the rapport is achieved through an emotional response and appreciation, such a person is also called a *rasika,* one who has aesthetic taste (rasa, lit. "flavor," "relish"). These words *rasa* and *rasika* are as much key words of Indian culture as *dharma* or *brahman,* and suggest how in Indian culture there is an imperceptible shading-off from the spiritual to the aesthetic, and vice versa.

How can the designated emotions, circumscribed by person, time, and place, be shared by spectators or readers? In life, one's emotions produce in onlookers quite varied reactions; what happens to them, then, in art? Bharata said in his *Treatise on Dramaturgy* (*Nāṭya Śāstra,* c. second century B.C. to second century A.D.), and this was further elucidated by the tenth-century critic Bhatta Nāyaka,[1] that in the emotions of the world a process of universalization occurs, thanks to their artistic expression, in music, acting, etc., and it is in their universal aspect, as love or heroism as such, and not as the love and the heroism of such and such characters, that a spectator finds them appealing to his own corresponding instincts. Along with this universalization, there is also a process of abstraction which detaches a painful situation from its painful setting. When the worldly emotion ceases to have its former personal reference, its painfulness, loathsomeness, etc., are all transcended. Thus, all the emotions presented in art are transferred to a supramundane plane, and the so-called enjoyment comes to represent a unique category of experience unlike anything that is known to result from ordinary worldly pleasures. This universalization and sublimation also disassociates the emotion from its particularized form, e.g., love, etc., so that it is relished simply as aesthetic emotion (rasa).

This aesthetic emotion is therefore of the nature of a serenity (viśrānti) of the heart or spirit, a condition in which the restlessness attendant upon mundane activity [2] is stilled by the play of artistic presentation. It is in this respect that aesthetic bliss is considered akin to the Supreme Beatitude. This is not, of course, the same as the Supreme Beatitude, from which, when once attained, there is no falling away. The realization of aesthetic bliss is a condition brought about and brought to an end by the presentation and withdrawal of the artistic stimulus. Yet it offers a momentary glimpse of the Supreme Bliss, and continuous efforts to partake of it are a means of preparing the soul for its supreme self-realization.

Now the artistic stimulus which brought forth this end is neither real nor unreal; it is indescribable; the cognition of this is again unique, being none of the known types of actual perception, inference, memory, etc. It is best described by analogy to the nature of the world as seen in idealistic metaphysics such as that of Kashmir Shaivism or Shankara's Advaita (monism). Like Shaivism and Advaita, Sānkhya also contributed its

---

[1] His work is called the *Mirror of the Heart* (*Hṛdayadarpaṇa*).

[2] The critic Abhinavagupta adopts here the Sānkhya psychology of the three qualities or dispositions of the mind: the sublime, "purity"; the restless, "passion"; and the stupid, "darkness" (see below under Sānkhya). Sorrow is the outcome of the restless disposition of "passion," but thanks to the artistic presentation, the sublime disposition of "purity" dominates over it and sublimates the tragic situation.

ideas to the theory set forth above; it is from the Sānkhya system that Abhinavagupta (A.D. c.1000),[3] the foremost exponent of this point of view, seeks assistance when explaining the phenomenon of our enjoyment of tragic plays and the sentiment of pathos.

This notable theory of aesthetic bliss is first adumbrated in both its broad outlines and technical details in Bharata's comprehensive *Treatise on Dramaturgy,* which is the earliest extant work in the field. Later, critics asserted that the emotional theory applied primarily to drama, where the actual impersonation of characters by different actors, and actual acting, made emotional communication direct, while in poetry this communication was indirect, since everything had to be put into words. Therefore, according to these early rhetoricians, Bhāmaha, Dandin, Vāmana [4] (seventh, eighth, and ninth centuries) who dealt with poetry primarily, emotion or rasa was subordinated to expression, which was embellished by various elements such as style, figure, and elegance. Subsequently the school of neo-critics headed by Ānandavardhana [5] (ninth century) unified criticism by treating the problems of poetry and drama as fundamentally identical, and restoring the supreme place to emotion.

Ānandavardhana's thesis was elucidated and developed further by the Kashmirian Shaiva philosopher Abhinavagupta, but even after the work of this writer, some younger critics like Kuntaka,[6] almost contemporary with Abhinavagupta, reargued the case for poetic art being one preeminently of expression, to which everything else was subordinated. Bhatta Nāyaka, whose contribution to the problem of aesthetic emotion in the theory of universalization has already been noted, and who wrote a little before Abhinavagupta, also upheld the expressionistic view of poetry. He clearly distinguished poetry from scriptural injunction on the one hand, and story or news on the other. In scripture, the words or the letter of the text was the chief thing; in story or narrative, the ideas alone mattered; but in poetry the *way,* the *manner* in which one used words or put his ideas, was what mattered.

Even those who took their stand on rasa or emotion as the essence of

---

[3] Author of a commentary on Bharata's *Treatise on Dramaturgy* and another on the *Light on Suggestion* (*Dhvanyāloka*) of Ānandavardhana.

[4] The works of these writers are called, respectively: the *Ornaments of Poetry* (*Kāvyālankara*), the *Mirror of Poetry* (*Kāvyādarśa*), and *Aphorisms on the Ornaments of Poetry* (*Kāvyālankāra Sūtra*), with commentary by the same author.

[5] His classic is called the *Light on Suggestion.*

[6] Author of the *Life of Striking Expression* (*Vakroktijīvita*).

poetry had to take into consideration the unique character of poetic expression; they were required to explain how this communication of emotion took place. While ideas actually can be conveyed by words, emotions cannot be evoked by mere mention of them. Poetry must represent the attendant emotional factors, the human participants, the background of nature, and the actions resulting from those feelings which come in the train of a major sentiment. It is through these that the sentiments of love, etc., are aroused in a responsive reader or spectator. Now this realm of emotion is something which lies beyond the reach of either the primary sense or its secondary metaphorical shifts; it is only through *suggestion* that emotion can be communicated. Therefore the leading neo-critic, Ānandavardhana, expounded the doctrine of suggestion (*dhvani, vyañjanā*) or revelation (*prakāśa*) as the chief means by which art achieves its highest communication. This *dhvani,* which has to do with the overtones of words, could render even the communication of ideas and figurative turns more charming by the power of suggestion than by straightforward statement. One paramount reason adduced by Ānandavardhana in support of his claim that suggestion is the sole means of communication was the emotional response produced by music through the inarticulated sounds of pure melody, where there obviously could be no question of verbal communication, primary or secondary. And this was as true of sight as of sound. The look in a lady's eye might have a profound emotional significance, unexplainable except in terms of suggestion.

There were, however, a few critics who still refused to acknowledge the need to ascribe to words such an intangible quality as suggestion when known processes of verbal import or cognition existed, such as the speaker's intention, presumption, and inference. King Bhoja [7] (eleventh century), who tried to take a rather dispassionate view of the Kashmirian contributions from his distant Malwa, found it more reasonable to take an eclectic approach, which would not reject the idea of suggestion, but would make it part of the poet's intention. He tried also to reconcile the ancients and the neo-critics in regard to the respective importance of expression and emotion. The most noteworthy contribution of Bhoja lies in his theory of aesthetic emotion, which, however, few after him understood properly. Bhoja tackled the problem of poetry and the world

[7] His two works in this field are the *Necklace of Sarasvatī* (*Sarasvatīkaṇṭhābharaṇa* [Sarasvatī is the Goddess of learning]) and the *Illumination of Love* (*Śṛṅgāraprakāśa*).

together and tried to find some common basis for explaining culture itself. Aesthetic emotion, according to him, is a refinement of the human ego (ahamkāra) or the development of one's self-consciousness (*abhimāna*) which takes one's personality to that peak of perfection at which one reflects upon one's Self and feels the joy of its fulfillment. Such was the interpretation given to the word *śṛṅgāra* which ordinarily means love, but which to Bhoja meant the Self's Love for Itself, and of which the love for various persons and things in the world is only an empirical manifestation. This inner Self, not so much at rest with itself as aglow with its own essential energy of love, is the one aesthetic emotion which is fed and nourished by the other feelings arising out of it and surrounding it, like the flames of a fire. The poetic emotions, such as love, heroism, etc., only enkindle this inner fire of the Self; and in the measure of their contribution to the burnishment of this inner Self—this sublimated ego—the poetry, art, or cultural activity of the world may be considered fruitful.

Among the lesser critics, there was about the same time (eleventh century) in Kashmir, the pupil of Abhinavagupta, Kshemendra,[8] who worked out the idea of proportion and propriety, *jīvita,* as the very life of poetic beauty. Lastly, we might mention Jagannātha Pandita,[9] who flourished in the seventeenth century. Following in the main school of thought handed down by Abhinavagupta, he defined poetry as words which convey an idea of beauty, and beauty as the delectation of a unique category of supramundane joy.

DRAMATURGY

Bharata's Treatise on Dramaturgy

[From *Nātya Śāstra,* 1.14–15, 17, 104–8, 113–14; 6.10, 15–21, 31, 32; 27.49–53, 55, 56, 59–62; 36.72, 74–76]

[God Brahmā said:] I will create the lore of drama which promotes dharma [virtue], material gain, and fame, which will show for posterity all activities, which is enriched with the ideas of all branches of knowledge and presents all the arts; I shall create it, along with the story required for its theme, with its teachings and the summary of its topics.

---

[8] Author of the tract *Examination of Propriety* (*Aucityavicāracarcā*).
[9] Author of the *Ocean of Aesthetic Emotion* (*Rasagaṅgādhara*).

. . . Brahmā extracted the text from the *Rig Veda,* songs from the
Sāma Veda, actions from the *Yajur Veda,* and the emotions from the
Atharva Veda. [1.14–17]

[Brahmā said:] The drama is a representation of the nature or feelings of the whole universe. In some place it depicts dharma, play somewhere else, material gain at another place, quietude in yet another, fun
at one place, fight at another place, love at one place, and killing at
another. The drama that I have devised is a representation of the activities of the world; the virtuous ones have here virtue, and the amor-
ous ones, love; the undisciplined ones are tamed here, and the disciplined ones exhibit their discipline; it emboldens the weak, energizes
the heroic, enlightens the ignorant, and imparts erudition to the scholars;
it depicts the gaiety of lords, teaches fortitude to those tormented by
misery, shows gains to the materially minded, and firmness to the agitated; thus it is endowed with variegated feelings and embodies varied
states. [1.104–8]

There is no knowledge, craft, learning, art, practical skill, or action
which is not found in drama. [1.113–14]

Emotions, their subsidiary moods, actions, technique, style, mode, production and success, song and instrumentation, and theater—these form
the resume of the topics of dramaturgy. [6.10]

The great Brahmā mentioned eight emotions: love, humor, pathos, violence, heroism, fear, loathsomeness, and wonder.[1] The enduring moods
from which these aesthetic emotions develop are love, laughter, sorrow,
anger, effort, fear, loathing, and surprise. The transitory feelings are
thirty-three, despondency, langor, apprehension, envy, elation [etc.].
[6.15–21]

We shall speak first of the emotions [rasas]. Nothing goes on in a
drama without emotion. This emotion is manifested by the interaction of
cause, effect, and accessory moods. What is the illustration? Just as a
dish or culinary taste is brought about by the mingling of various
viands, even so is an emotional state engendered by the coming together
of various feelings or emotional conditions; just as by molasses and other
food-materials, the six culinary tastes are made, even so the eight perma-

---

[1] Some recensions of the text read a ninth emotion, quietude; later, from the eighth century onwards, the ninth was not only accepted, but also considered the greatest of all the
emotions.

nent emotional moods are brought to a state of relishability by the interaction of manifold emotional conditions. The Sages asked: What is the meaning of the word *rasa* [emotion; lit. flavor, relish]? The reply given is: rasa is so called because it is relished. How is rasa relished? The reply is: Just as healthy men, eating food dressed with manifold accessories, enjoy the different tastes [the sweet, the sour, etc.], and derive exhilaration, etc., even so, the spectators with attuned minds relish the permanent emotional states [love, heroism, etc.], which are presented and nourished with manifold feelings and their actions through limbs, speech, and involuntary physical manifestations. [6.31, 32]

I shall now set forth the characteristics of spectators. They should be men of character and pedigree; endowed with composure, conduct, and learning; intent on good name and virtue; unbiased; of proper age; well versed in drama and its constituent elements; vigilant, pure, and impartial; experts in instruments and make-up; conversant with dialects; adepts in arts and crafts; knowledgeable in the dexterous art of gesticulation and in the intricacies of the major and minor emotional states; proficient in lexicon, prosody, and different branches of learning—such men are to be made spectators for witnessing a drama. He who is satisfied when the feeling of satisfaction is portrayed, himself becomes sorrow-stricken when sorrow is shown, and attains the state of helplessness when helplessness is enacted—he is the proper spectator in a drama. [27.49-53, 55]

It is not expected that all these qualities will be present in a single spectator. . . . Those in youth will be pleased with the love portrayed, the connoisseurs with the technical elements, those devoted to mundane things with the material activities presented, and the dispassionate ones with the efforts toward spiritual liberation depicted; of varied character are those figuring in a play and the play rests on such variety of character. The valorous ones will delight in themes of loathsomeness, violence, fights, and battles, and the elders will always revel in tales of virtue and mythological themes. The young, the common folk, the women would always like burlesque and striking make-up. Thus he who is, by virtue of the response of the corresponding feeling or situation, able to enter into a particular theme is considered a fit spectator for that kind of theme, being endowed with those qualities needed for being a proper spectator. [27.56, 59-62]

The science and production of drama helps the intellectual growth of people; it has in it the activity of the whole universe, and presents the knowledge contained in all its branches. . . .

He who listens to this branch of knowledge promulgated by God Brahmā, he who produces a drama, and he who attentively witnesses it —such a person attains to that meritorious state which those versed in the Vedas, the performers of sacrifices, and the donors of gifts attain. Among the duties of the king, provision for the enactment of plays is said to be highly useful; to present to the people a play is a gift esteemed highly among various kinds of gifts. [36.72, 74–76]

POETICS

Mammata's Illumination of Poetry

A standard textbook of neo-criticism written c. A.D. 1100.
[From Mammata, *Kāvyaprakāśa*, Chapters 1, 4]

The muse of the poet is all glorious, bringing into being as it does a creation beautified by the nine sentiments [lit. flavors], free from the limitations imposed by nature, uniformly blissful, and not dependent on anything else. . . .

Poetry is for fame, material gain, worldly knowledge, removal of adversity, immediate realization of supreme bliss, and for instruction administered sweetly in the manner of one's beloved wife. . . .

The bliss that arises immediately on the delectation of the emotions depicted in the poem and which makes one oblivious of every other cognition forms the highest of all the fruits of poetry.

Scriptural texts like the Veda command like masters and in them the very letter of the text is the chief thing. The stories of the mythological books and epics have their main emphasis on just conveying the meaning, and they instruct like friends. Poetry, on the other hand, is different from these two kinds of writings. Poetry is the activity of the poet who is gifted in depicting things on a supramundane plane; his writing is consequently such that in it word and meaning are together subservient and the emphasis is on the unique poetic activity which aims at evocation of emotional response; [1] therefore poetry like a beloved spouse, makes

[1] This explanation of the difference between poetic expression and other writing was given by the critic Bhatta Nāyaka. According to him, poetry is an emphasis on the *manner* of saying a thing.

one absorbed in one emotion, wins over both the poet and the reader alike with its message that one should be virtuous like Rāma and not vicious like Rāvana.[2] Hence, one should put forth effort in the direction of poetic composition.

This poetry is word and sense devoid of flaws, and from it occassionally the figures [of speech and sound] may be absent; that is, word and sense in poetry always have the figures, but if in some place, the figure is not clearly recognizable, the fact of the expression being poetry is not affected. . . .

This poetry, the wise say, is the highest and is called "poetry of suggestion" if its suggested element excels the expressed one. . . . The poetry is middling and called "poetry in which the suggested is subordinated to the expressed" if the suggested is not dominant over the expressed. . . . That category of poetry is inferior in which there is no suggested element and there is only some strikingness of sound or sense. Strikingness includes stylistic qualities and figures. [Ch. 1]

Among the suggested elements are those in which the sequence of the process is not noticeable and another in which it is noticeable.[3] As, however, the causes, effects, and accessory feelings of an emotion are not themselves the aesthetic emotion [rasa], but are the conditions which bring that aesthetic emotion into being, there does exist a sequence in the process of their suggestion also; but this sequence is not perceivable. The emotion, its basic and accessory feelings, their semblance, the gradual fall, rise, and admixture of these, which are all imperceivably suggested, form the very "soul" of poetic expression; as such they are to be distinguished from the state in which they are subordinated to the charm of expression and function as embellishments thereof. . . .

Sage Bharata has said: "Emotion is manifested by the interplay of the causes, effects, and the accessory moods." This is expounded thus:

The causes of emotions are (a) the human substratum, and (b) the exciting conditions of environment, etc.; e.g., in love the woman is the human substratum and the garden, etc., form the exciting conditions. The permanent emotional state called love is engendered by this twofold cause. The effects or ensuants which render the emotion cognizable comprise, for instance in love, the sidelong glances, the disporting of the

[2] The hero and villain respectively of the epic *Rāmāyaṇa*.
[3] The former is the case of the emotions, rasas.

arms, etc. The attendant accessory moods which nourish the permanent emotional state, in the case of love, are despondency, langor, etc. The emotion [so nourished] is primarily in the character presented, e.g., Rāma; it is also seen in the actor by virtue of our contemplating Rāma's character in him. Such is the nature of emotion as Bhatta Lollata and other ancient writers expounded it. . . .

Bhatta Nāyaka said: This aesthetic relish [rasa] is not apprehended as existing either independently or in oneself; also, it is neither originated nor revealed; but in poetry and drama, there is, beyond the primary significance of the expression, a function [called "that which makes for imaginative enjoyment"], which universalizes the particular causes, ensuants, and accessories [belonging to a given context]; by this universalizing power the permanent emotional mood [like love] is called forth; there is then a state of repose of the consciousness, a blissfulness, engendered by the upsurge of the sublime mental quality; in that state the emotional mood is relished.

The blessed teacher Abhinavagupta observed: In the world one makes out the permanent mood [like love] from causes like woman; in poetry and drama, the same give up their [prosaic] character of causes, etc., and by reason of their artistic evocative nature come to be called by non-worldly designations vibhāvas,[4] etc. They are not apprehended as one's own, the enemy's or the middle man's, nor as not being one's own, the enemy's, or the middle man's; they are apprehended in their universal aspect, there being no mental resolve either to take or to discard a particular relation to oneself as friend, foe, or neutral. The permanent emotional state such as love is embedded as impression in the hearts of spectators and is manifested by these causes [vibhāvas], etc., and apprehended in their universalized aspect. Through the strength of the same universalization, this permanent emotional state, though appearing only in a particular cognizer, is yet apprehended as if by a cognizer who has awakened into an unbounded state, because, for the time being, his limited cognizership drops and he becomes rid of the touch of any other object of cognition. In this unlimited state, on account of the universalization enabling one to be in unison with all hearts, the permanent emotional mood, though, like one's Self, not really different, is yet brought within the range of apprehension. This apprehension or realization is essentially of the form

---

[4] "Cause," in dramaturgy.

of a relish and strictly confined to the duration of the evoking artistic conditions, causes, etc.; its relish is unitary like that of a composite drink in which the ingredients do not taste separately; this unique relish is such that it seems to quiver in front of one, it seems to throw everything else into oblivion, it seems to make one experience the ineffable beatitude of the Supreme Being; it produces a supramundane delectation; such is the nature of the experience of aesthetic emotion, love and the like. . . . The means of its cognition are not indeterminate, because the knowledge of causes, etc., is essential to it; nor is it determinate, for it is relished as a supramundane bliss, certified by one's own Self-experience. Being of neither form or of both forms, it shows only, as already stated, its non-worldly character, and no contradiction whatsoever. [Ch. 4]

The Ocean of Aesthetic Emotion [1]
[From Jagannātha, Rasagaṅgādhara, Chapter 1]

THE DEFINITION OF POETRY

Words which convey an *idea* endowed with *beauty* constitute *poetry*. *Beauty* is that whose contemplation gives rise to a *non-worldly delight*. . . . The means of realizing this is repeated contemplation, an activity of imagination, directed toward the thing characterized by that non-worldly delectation. "A son has been born to you," and "I shall give you money" —these are also sentences whose meaning produces delight but that delight is not non-worldly; therefore there can be no question of poetry in those sentences. Thus poetry is words conveying an idea whose imaginative contemplation is productive of a supramundane delectation. [Ch. 1]

MUSIC

From a Brāhmana
[From Taittirīya Brāhmaṇa, 3.9.14]

Two brāhman lutists are singing to the lute; this thing, the lute, is verily the embodiment of beauty and prosperity; and these musicians of the lute do verily endow him [the patron] with prosperity.

[1] The term rendered here as "ocean" probably refers to Shiva as the Bearer of the Ganges (gaṅgādhara) and as the embodiment of emotion (rasa).

From an Upanishad
[From *Chāndogya Upaniṣad* 1.7.6]

These that sing to the lute indeed sing of Him [the Supreme Brahman] only; hence it is that they attain riches.

From a Lawbook (*c. fourth century* A.D.)
[From *Yājñavalkya Smṛti*, 3.4.112–15]

One attains the Supreme Being by practicing continuously the chanting of the *sāmans* [the sacred Vedic mantras set to music] in the prescribed manner and with mental concentration. The singing of the songs *Aparānta, Ullopya,* [etc.] . . . the songs composed by Daksha and Brahman, constitutes indeed liberation. One who knows the correct playing of the lute, has mastered the subtle semitones, and understands the rhythms, attains the path of liberation without any strain.

From the Purānas (*early medieval*)

[From *Viṣṇu Purāṇa*, 1.22.84]
Whatever poetic utterances there are, and the songs in all their entirety, are aspects of Lord Vishnu in his sonant form.

[From *Skanda Purāṇa, Sūta Saṃhitā*, 4.2.3.114–16]
The knowledge of music becomes an effective means of attaining oneness with Lord Shiva; for by the knowledge of music, one attains to a state of absorption and it is by attaining such a state that oneness with Shiva could be obtained. . . . One ought not to indulge, out of delusion, in worldly songs. . . .

From a Tantra (*medieval*)
[From *Vijñānabhairava Tantra*]

To the yogin whose spirit attains a unified state in the uniform bliss engendered by the delectation of objects like music, there occurs an absorption and anchoring of the mind in that bliss. Where there is a continuous and long flow of sounds from stringed instruments, one becomes freed of other objects of cognition and becomes merged in that ultimate and verily of the form of that Supreme Ether [the Brahman].

From a Standard Music Treatise (thirteenth century A.D.)

[From Shārngadeva, *Saṅgītaratnākara*, 1.3.1–2]

We adore that Supreme Being of the form of sound [Nāda-Brahman] which is the one bliss without a second, and the light of consciousness in all beings that has manifested itself in the form of the universe. By the adoration of sound [*nāda*] are also adored Gods Brahmā [the Creator], Vishnu [the Preserver], and *Maheśvara* [Shiva, the Destroyer], for they are the embodiments of sound.

From the Songs of Tyāgarāja

Tyāgarāja (1767–1847) was the famous saint-musician of South India. The songs are translated from the Telugu.

SAṄGĪTAJÑĀNAMU [1] (MELODY: *Sālagabhairavi*)

O Mind! The knowledge of the science and art of music bestows on a person the bliss of oneness with the Supreme Being.

Music such as is accompanied by the blissful oceanlike stories of the Lord which are the essence of love and all the other sentiments blesses a person with oneness with the Lord.

Music such as that cultivated by the discerning Tyāgarāja bestows on a person affection [for fellow beings], devotion [to God], attachment to good men, the Lord's Grace, austere life, mental concentration, fame, and wealth.

RĀGASUDHĀRASA (MELODY: *Āndolikā*)

O Mind! drink and revel in the ambrosia of melody; it gives one the fruit of sacrifices and contemplation, renunciation as well as enjoyment; Tyāgarāja knows that they who are proficient in sound, the mystic syllable *Oṃ,* and the music notes [2]—which are all of the form of the Lord Himself—are liberated souls. [3]

---

[1] Indian songs are usually identified, as here, by their beginning words.

[2] From abstract sound, the mystic syllable *Oṃ* appears and from it the seven notes of music. *Oṃ* is uttered at the beginning, and sometimes also at the end, of a Vedic recitation, prayer, or chant. In the Upanishads (especially the *Chāndogya*) *Oṃ* came to be regarded as the essence of the Vedas, indeed of the whole world.

[3] That is *jīvanmuktas,* those who are released from bondage while yet in an embodied state.

CHAPTER XIII

MOKSHA, THE FOURTH END OF MAN

The fourth and final aim of man, moksha, is the culmination of the other three, but especially of the religious ideal originally associated with dharma. In the earliest phase of Indian thought the observance of the cosmic and moral law (rita) and the performance of dharma in the form of sacrifice were believed in as means of propitiating the gods and gaining heavenly enjoyment in the afterlife. From this idea—that an act of dharma achieved some merit or benefit which might be enjoyed on death —developed the karma theory and its corollary, the doctrine of rebirth. At this point, however, the thought that one thus passed from life to life and that there was no end to this series led to deeper reflection. An act being finite cannot produce a result different from it or more lasting; a thing that does not last is imperfect and cannot be the ultimate truth; what has been conditioned by acts, namely, this life, is therefore perishable and hence not capable of producing real happiness. To one perplexed with this problem, Death itself, as in the *Katha Upaniṣad,* revealed the secret. As one passed from birth to birth and death to death, what was it that endured and continued as the substratum of conditioned experience, of the happy and unhappy results of acts? What was it in man that formed the basis of all this transmigratory drama? If there was something which endured such changes, it might yield the secret of restfulness, infinite peace, and lasting happiness. To attain it, one would naturally have to turn away from the so-called limited good or happiness and the equally circumscribed means to it. To one intent on the supreme good or everlasting bliss, even the pleasures of life were no different from its miseries, as both lead to an endless cycle of experience and have to be transcended. As anything done within the sphere of cause and effect was caught up in the same chain, action was no remedy; knowledge of the truth alone could help one to rise above the transmigratory cycle or the world of cause and effect.

This line of thought serves as the common background for later systems which expounded the goal or the reality or the path in different ways. All were agreed that experience in this life was on the whole to be considered miserable and that deliverance (moksha) from it or its cessation was to be sought. The Upanishads considered that knowledge of the truth would lead to realization of the Self as such, beyond the conditioned existence in which it was involved; and that behind this world of cause and effect, underlying the phenomenon of things that come into being, change, decay, and disappear, there was one permanent reality: existence (sat), changeless and consequently sorrowless, and of which knowledge was not a quality but its very form. The Upanishads, for the most part, held this monistic view of one transcendent absolute, but sometimes they spoke also of the truth as a transcendent personality. While the former view led to a monism such as Shankara's, the latter view led to theistic schools, which considered one supreme god as the creator, sustainer, and destroyer of the universe, and which developed the doctrine of devotion, love, and surrender. To them release from the world (moksha or mukti) brought absorption into or essential identity with the Lord.

Like the first mentioned pantheistic Upanishadic or Vedāntic school, there were others which also took their stand on knowledge as the means of attaining the everlasting good. They likewise turned away from sacrifices and similar ritual to inquire into the nature of reality. Sage Kanāda, the founder of the Vaisheshika system, examined creation and the universe whose creation he attributed to atoms as the material cause; God was for him an efficient cause and also a teacher and helper; knowledge of all physical, mental, and spiritual categories—which comprised matter, mind, spirit or soul, both human and divine—and their respective qualities and differences contributed to the attainment of the everlasting good, *niḥśreyasa*.

Sage Gotama, the founder of the Nyāya school, asserted that the misery experienced by man was due to birth (which involved death), the latter to activity, activity to desire and dislike, and these to erroneous knowledge —a causal chain akin to that which the Buddha preached. The followers of this school were theists, pluralists, and realists, and for them release or moksha was a state in which the soul of man was absolutely rid of all experience of sorrow (inclusive of so-called "pleasure") and was like unto a stone.

The Sānkhya of Sage Kapila, whose doctrines are found echoed in the Upanishads, considered release from the misery of all life here and in the heavens as attainable by the knowledge of the truth concerning Self or soul, on the one hand, and the material universe on the other. The truth about these two is that all experiences are due solely to the latter and not to the ever-pure soul. It is only imagined that they belong to the soul because of its proximity to matter and its erroneous identification with matter as agent and enjoyer. The Yoga of Sage Patanjali set forth the process of psychological discipline by which one could attain this release (moksha) or isolation (*kaivalya*) of the soul from involvement with matter and its doings.

Now all these five schools of Hindu philosophy aimed at release from the misery (*duḥkha*) of mundane experience and transmigration (samsāra), and all emphasized knowledge of one kind or another. Among these, the school which primarily based itself on the Upanishads, the Vedānta, took different forms, monistic and pantheistic or theistic. The Mīmāmsā alone, as a school, still stood for the performance of ordained duties (dharma) and sacrificial and meritorious acts (karma). Action, of course, could not be eliminated so long as a man lived; the most philosophy could do was to take the sting out of action. The monistic philosophers, recognizing the disciplinary value of acts and duties, as indeed of ethics, accordingly assigned them a place under *sādhanas* or preparatory disciplines. Acts could function in this way as ancillary to knowledge providing they were not done with the expectation of personal gain, or from the theistic view, as an expression of devotion, provided they were dedicated to the Lord. Either way, the doer abandoned not the act, but the desire for its fruit. Thus when action was adjusted to Vedānta and qualified by knowledge or devotion, it too became a means of liberation.

This reconciliation of action with knowledge and devotion, which also removed the contradiction between dharma and moksha, was the great contribution of the *Bhagavad Gītā*. In modern times, when increased activity has become a dominant feature of Indian life, it is to this text with its philosophy of selfless and dedicated action that the whole Indian nation has turned for inspiration.

THE BHAGAVAD GĪTĀ

The *Song of the Lord* (*Bhagavad Gītā*), which is by far the best known religio-philosophical text in Sanskrit, may be considered the most typical expression of Hinduism as a whole and an authoritative manual of the Krishnaite religion (i.e., the popular cult of Krishna) in particular.

Even in very early times there had existed, side by side with the hieratic Vedic religion, several popular, tribal religions. The gods and goddesses of these tribal people differed from the divinities of the official Vedic pantheon, and the religious practices associated with them also differed fundamentally from the religious practices of the Vedic Aryans. Nevertheless, these indigenous religions eventually found a place under the broad mantle of the Vedic religion. While Brahmanism remained in the ascendancy, their sphere of influence was restricted to the tribes among which they had originated. But the gradual decline of Brahmanism, in the face of competition from Buddhism and Jainism, afforded these popular religions an opportunity to assert themselves; and indeed, the Brahmanists themselves seem to have encouraged this development to some extent as a means of meeting the challenge of the more heterodox movements. At the same time, among the indigenous religions, with their variety of gods and religious practices, a common allegiance to the authority of the Veda provided a thin, but nonetheless significant, thread of unity. This is the genesis of Hinduism, which brought together under its banner large masses of people, and, at the same time, kept the Vedic tradition alive.

One significant constituent of this all-embracing Hinduism was Krishnaism, which seems to have originated and spread among the tribes of Western and Central India, like the Vrishnis, the Sātvatas, the Ābhīras, and the Yādavas. Its principal teacher was Krishna, who was associated with the above-mentioned tribes as either their temporal or their spiritual leader, and was in course of time, transformed into a tribal god. That this tribal god and the religious movement inspired by him were originally not countenanced by the Vedic religion is suggested by the episode at the Govardhana mountain (*Harivaṃśa,* 72–73), which describes the antagonism to and subsequent subjugation by Krishna of the chief Vedic god Indra. This is clearly symbolic of the growing predominance of the popular religion over the hieratic Brahmanic religion. But the religion of Krishna typifies the paradoxical characteristic of Hinduism mentioned above, namely, that it was a fundamental departure from Brahmanism which nonetheless remained within the bounds of loyalty to the Veda.

The *Gītā*[1] forms part of the great epic of India, the *Great Poem* (or *War*) *of the Descendants of Bharata* (*Mahābhārata*), which has gathered a veritable encyclopedia around the epic story of the rivalry between the Kauravas, led by Duryodhana, and their cousins the Pāndavas, led by Yudhishthira. Both houses were descended from Kuru and ultimately from the famous Vedic tribe of the Bharatas which gave India her name *Bhārat*. The struggle culminated in the great war won by the Pāndavas and their allies with the help of Krishna. Chiefly due to its numerous and elevated passages on the subjects of wisdom, duty, and liberation from mundane existence, the epic, which probably underwent its last major revision c. fourth century A.D. in the Gupta period, became sacred to later Hindus as part of the Smriti scriptures.

When in the course of the growth of the *Mahābhārata,* the bardic historical poem relating to the Kuru-Bharatas was being transformed into an early form of the epic, two principal processes had been in operation, namely, the bardic enlargement of the original ballad-cycle relating to the Kuru-Bharatas, and the Krishnaite redaction of the bardic material. The *Gītā* must indeed have served as the cornerstone of this Krishnaite superstructure. Though the *Gītā* mainly epitomizes the teachings of Krishna, after it had been included in the epic it also was subjected, like the rest of the epic, to the final process of Brahmanic revision.

The religion of Krishna differed from the Upanishads, as well as from Buddhism and Jainism, first and foremost in its teaching about the goal of human life. The Upanishads generally put forth the view that, since this phenomenal world and human existence are in some sense unreal, man should renounce this worldly life and aim at realizing the essential identity of his soul with the Universal Self, which is the one and only absolute reality. The Upanishadic attitude toward life and society is fundamentally individualistic. The *Gītā,* on the other hand, teaches that man has a duty to promote *lokasaṅgraha* or the stability, solidarity, and progress of society. Society can function properly only on the principle of the

[1] The abbreviated title of the *Bhagavad Gītā.*

ethical interdependence of its various constituents. As an essential constituent of society, therefore, man must have an active awareness of his social obligations. The *sva-dharma* (lit. one's own dharma, set of duties) or the specific social obligations of different types of men are, according to the *Gītā*, best embodied in the doctrine of the four classes. The *Gītā*, however, emphasizes the metaphysical significance of that scheme, according to which all classes are equal and essential, while it insists mainly on man's active recognition of *sva-dharma* or his own specific social obligations.

The second fundamental point on which the *Gītā* differs from Upanishadic thought follows logically from the first. The Upanishadic ideal of spiritual emancipation through knowledge involves the acceptance of the unreal character of the phenomenal world. Through his actions, consciously or unconsciously, man becomes involved in the tentacles of this fictitious world and is thus removed farther and farther from his goal. A complete abnegation of action, therefore, came to be regarded almost as a *sine qua non* of a true seeker's spiritual quest. The ideal of social integrity (*lokasaṅgraha*) through *sva-dharma* enjoined by the *Gītā*, on the other hand, implies an active way of life. The *Gītā*, indeed, most often speaks in terms of yoga (application to work or self-discipline) rather than of moksha (release or liberation). The teacher of the *Gītā* has discussed, at great length, the why and the how of the yoga of action (karma-yoga). The activism inculcated by the *Gītā* is, however, not of the common variety. It is tinged—perhaps under the influence of Upanishadic and Buddhist thought—with an element of renunciation. It argues that action, as such, is not detrimental to one's attainment of his spiritual goal. It is only one's attachment to the fruits of action that keeps one eternally involved in the cycle of birth and death. The *Gītā*, therefore, teaches the art of "acting and yet not acting," i.e., acting without becoming personally involved in the action.

Whereas Vedic ritual practices were exclusive in character, Krishna sponsors a way of spiritual life in which all can participate. It is the yoga of devotion (bhakti yoga). In contrast to ritual sacrifice the *Gītā* offers a concept of sacrifice embracing all actions done in fulfillment of one's *sva-dharma* and without attachment to their fruits. This way of devotion presupposes the recognition of a personal god—in the present context, of course, Krishna himself—who is regarded as being responsible for the creation, preservation, and destruction of the universe. The devotee serves that God like a loyal servant, always craving some kind of personal communion with Him. The criterion of true worship, according to the doctrine of devotion, is not the richness or profuseness of the materials used for worship nor the number and variety of religious observances involved in it. It is rather the earnestness, the faith, and the sense of complete surrender to the Divine on the part of the devotee (bhakta). Such a devotee—whatever his age, sex, learning, and social status—compels God to become his friend, guide, and philosopher. The way of devotion is thus more simple, more direct, and more effective than any other religious practice. To this teaching of devotion, however, Krishna makes one significant addition. He insists that a true practitioner of the yoga of action (karmayogin) also become a true devotee, for, by following his own duty (*sva-dharma*), the karmayogin is doing the will of God and participating in the divine project.

Krishnaism cannot boast of any independent philosophical system of its own. The great virtue of the *Gītā* is that, instead of dilating upon the points of difference among the various systems of thought and practice, it emphasizes the points of agreement among them and thereby brings about a philosophical and religious synthesis. We have already suggested that the *Gītā* underwent a kind of Brahmanic reorientation. One of the more significant results of this reorientation, as far as the personality of Krishna is concerned, was that this tribal god, who was essentially non-Vedic in origin and whose character had already become syncretic, came to be regarded as an avatār (incarnation) of the Vedic god Vishnu, and as identical with the Upanishadic Brahman.

Due no doubt to this synthetic character, study of the *Bhagavad Gītā* has given rise to a variety of problems pertaining both to its form and its content. It is, for instance, asked whether the text of the *Gītā*, as we have it today, actually represents its "original" text. Then there is the question concerning the relation between the *Gītā* and the *Mahābhārata*. Can the elaborate teaching embodied in the *Gītā* have been imparted by Krishna to Arjuna just when the great battle of Kurukshetra was on the point of commencing? Further, can the various teachings of Krishna be said to have been presented in the present text of the *Gītā* in a logical sequence? Would a rearrangement of the text not yield better results in this respect? Coming to the teachings of the *Gītā*, some scholars aver that its main metaphysical foundations have been derived from the Sānkhya system, the Vedāntic (monistic) tendencies being superimposed on them only in a superficial manner, while other scholars are of the opinion that it is just the other way around. Arguments are again adduced in support of the two opposing views that the *Gītā* in its original form was a philosophical treatise only later adopted by Krishnaism, and, on the other hand, that basically it embodied the kshatriya code of conduct as sponsored by Krishna, the philosophical speculations having found their way in it only incidentally. There is also the problem concerning the norm of ethical conduct. The views expressed on the subject by the *Gītā* itself do not appear to be quite consistent. At some places (5.14; 18.59) it is said that it is man's inherent nature (*svabhāva* or prakriti) which determines his actions, while elsewhere (11.33; 18.61) man is described as functioning only as an instrument of the Divine Will. It is further suggested (2.35) that one should act in such a manner that he is not thereby subjected to public disgrace. The teacher of the *Gītā* also points (16.24) to scripture as the authority for determining what should be done and what should not be done, and concludes by saying (18.63) that, reflecting fully on the doctrine declared by him, one should act as one chooses. These are only some typical problems of the many which are often discussed in connection with the work. The *Gītā* need not be approached as if it were a systematic treatise, in which the principal subject is treated with scientific or logical rigor. Being included in the popular epic, the *Gītā* also inherited epic characteristics of style and presentation. Nevertheless, this original compendium of Krishnaite religion, philosophy, and ethics has been presented in the epic on a very dramatic background and in such a manner that there should be no ambiguity so far as its principal teachings are concerned.

You Have To Fight

When the armies of the Kauravas and the Pāndavas were arrayed on the battlefield of Kurukshetra, waiting for the signal to commence the fight, the Pāndava hero, Arjuna, seeing that relatives and friends were ranged against each other, was suddenly overcome by deep spiritual despondency. It would be sinful, he felt, to kill his own kindred for the sake of kingdom. Therefore, not as a coward, but as a morally conscientious and sensitive person, he lay down his bow and declared to his friend and charioteer, Krishna, that he would not fight. Krishna then attempted to convince Arjuna that he would be committing a sin if he failed to perform his own duty (*sva-dharma*) as a warrior. As for his concern over taking the lives of others, this arose from a delusion which Krishna proceeds to dispel in the following passage:

[From *Bhagavad Gītā*, 2.11–37]

The Blessed Lord said:

You grieve for those who should not be mourned, and yet you speak words of wisdom! The learned do not grieve for the dead or for the living.

Never, indeed, was there a time when I was not, nor when you were not, nor these lords of men. Never, too, will there be a time, hereafter, when we shall not be.

As in this body, there are for the embodied one [i.e., the soul] childhood, youth, and old age, even so there is the taking on of another body. The wise sage is not perplexed thereby.

Contacts of the sense-organs, O son of Kuntī, give rise to cold and heat, and pleasure and pain. They come and go, and are not permanent. Bear with them, O Bhārata.

That man, whom these [sense-contacts] do not trouble, O chief of men, to whom pleasure and pain are alike, who is wise—he becomes eligible for immortality.

For the nonexistent (asat) there is no coming into existence; nor is there passing into nonexistence for the existent (sat). The ultimate nature of these two is perceived by the seers of truth.[1]

Know that to be indestructible by which all this is pervaded. Of this imperishable one, no one can bring about destruction.

These bodies of the eternal embodied one, who is indestructible and incomprehensible, are said to have an end. Therefore fight, O Bhārata.

He who regards him [i.e., the soul] as a slayer, and he who regards him as slain—both of them do not know the truth; for this one neither slays nor is slain.

He is not born, nor does he die at any time; nor, having once come to be will he again come not to be. He is unborn, eternal, permanent, and primeval; he is not slain when the body is slain.

Whoever knows him to be indestructible and eternal, unborn and immutable—how and whom can such a man, O son of Prithā, cause to be slain or slay?

[1] Cf. *Rig Veda*, 10.129.

Just as a man, having cast off old garments, puts on other, new ones, even
so does the embodied one, having cast off old bodies, take on other, new
ones.

Weapons do not cleave him, fire does not burn him; nor does water
drench him, nor the wind dry him up.

He is uncleavable, he is unburnable, he is undrenchable, as also undryable.
He is eternal, all-pervading, stable, immovable, existing from time immemorial.

He is said to be unmanifest, unthinkable, and unchangeable. Therefore,
knowing him as such, you should not grieve [for him].

And even if you regard him as being perpetually born and as perpetually
dying, even then, O long-armed one, you should not grieve for him.

For, to one who is born death is certain and certain is birth to one who
has died. Therefore in connection with a thing that is inevitable you
should not grieve.

Unmanifest in their beginnings are beings, manifest in the middle stage,
O Bhārata, and unmanifest, again, in their ends. For what then should
there be any lamentation?

Someone perceives him as a marvel; similarly, another speaks of him as a
marvel; another, again, hears of him as a marvel; and, even after hearing of him, no one knows him.

The embodied one within the body of everyone, O Bhārata, is ever un-
slayable. Therefore, you should not grieve for any being.

Further, having regard to your own dharma [duty] you should not falter.
For a kshatriya there does not exist another greater good than war
enjoined by dharma.

Blessed are the kshatriyas, O son of Prithā, who get such a war, which
being, as it were, the open gate to heaven, comes to them of its own
accord.

But if you do not fight this battle which is enjoined by dharma, then you
will have given up your own dharma as well as glory, and you will incur
sin.

Moreover, all beings will recount your eternal infamy. And for one who
has been honored, infamy is worse than death.

The great car warriors will think of you as one who has refrained from
battle through fear; having been once greatly respected by them, you
will then be reduced to pettiness.

Those who are not favorably inclined toward you will speak many unutterable words, slandering your might. What, indeed, can be more painful than that?

Either, being slain, you will attain heaven; or being victorious, you will enjoy [i.e., rule] the earth. Therefore arise, O son of Kuntī, intent on battle.

Why Karma-Yoga?

In the preceding passage, Krishna has addressed himself specifically to the case of Arjuna. Now he initiates a more or less general discussion of the theory and practice of the yoga of action, arguing against the view that renunciation entails only physical renunciation of all activity, or that such a renunciation, by itself, is conducive to the attainment of one's spiritual goal.

[From *Bhagavad Gītā*, 3.4–24]

Not by nonperformance of actions does a man attain freedom from action; nor by mere renunciation of actions does he attain his spiritual goal.

For no one, indeed, can remain, for even a single moment, unengaged in activity, since everyone, being powerless, is made to act by the dispositions (gunas) of matter (prakriti).[2]

Whoever having restrained his organs of action still continues to brood over the objects of senses—he, the deluded one, is called a hypocrite.

But he who, having controlled the sense-organs by means of the mind, O Arjuna, follows without attachment the path of action by means of the organs of action—he excels.

Do you do your allotted work, for action is superior to nonaction. Even the normal functioning of your body cannot be accomplished through actionlessness.

Except for the action done for sacrifice,[3] all men are under the bondage of action. Therefore, O son of Kuntī, do you undertake action for that purpose, becoming free from all attachment.

Having, in ancient times, created men along with sacrifice,[4] Prajāpati

[2] Cf. note 19.

[3] That is, action done in the spirit of sacrifice does not entangle the doer in its consequences.

[4] In this and the following six stanzas Krishna develops another argument in favor of the yoga of action, namely, that every man has to recognize his role in the scheme of cosmic ethics and has actively to promote its functioning. If he fails to do so, the cosmos will be turned into chaos. This is the basic theory of early Brahmanism.

said: "By means of this [sacrifice] do you bring forth. May this prove
to be the yielder of milk in the form of your desired ends.

"Do you foster the gods by means of this and let those gods foster you;
[thus] fostering each other, both of you will attain to the supreme good.

"For the gods, fostered by sacrifice, will grant you the enjoyments which
you desire. Whoever enjoys the enjoyments granted by them without
giving to them in return—he is, verily, a thief."

The good people who eat what is left after the sacrifice [5] are released from
all sins. On the other hand, those sinful ones who cook only for themselves—they, verily, eat their own sin.

From food creatures come into being; from rain ensues the production of
food; from sacrifice results rain; sacrifice has its origin from action
(karma).[6]

Know action to originate from the Brahman and the Brahman to originate from the Imperishable. Therefore, the Brahman, which permeates
all, is ever established in sacrifice.

Whoever, in this world, does not help in the rotating of the wheel thus
set in motion—he is of sinful life, he indulges in mere pleasures of sense,
and he, O son of Prithā, lives in vain.

But the man whose delight is in the Self alone, who is content with the
Self, who is satisfied only within the Self—for him there exists nothing
that needs to be done.

He, verily, has in this world no purpose to be served by action done nor
any purpose whatsoever to be served by action abnegated. Similarly, he
does not depend on any beings for having his purpose served.

Therefore, without attachment, always do the work that has to be done,
for a man doing his work without attachment attains to the highest goal.

For, verily, by means of work have Janaka and others attained perfection.
You should also do your work with a view to the solidarity of society
[lokasangraha].

Whatever a great man does, the very same the common man does. Whatever norm of conduct he sets up, that the people follow.

There is not for me, O son of Prithā, in the three worlds, anything that

[5] That is, those whose first and foremost concern is the promotion of cosmic order which
sacrifice sustains, and not any selfish interest.

[6] Action is, indeed, the basic force which sets and keeps in motion the cosmic wheel:
action—sacrifice—rain—food—creatures—action.

has to be done nor anything unobtained to be obtained; and yet I continue to be engaged in action.

For if ever I did not remain engaged in action unwearied, O son of Pṛthā,
men would in every way follow in my track.

These worlds would fall into ruin if I did not do my work. I would then
be the creator of chaos and would destroy these people.

The Technique of Karma-Yoga

The *Gītā* essentially embodies a code of conduct. After having theoretically
established that, in order to fulfill one's social obligations, one has inevitably
to do one's appointed work, the *Gītā* now lays down the practical course by
following which one can, even while engaging oneself in work, remain unin-
volved in its consequences. The *Gītā* thereby meets the most common objection
to the way of work. It is, indeed, this practical aspect of the yoga of action
(karma-yoga) which has been dilated upon in the major part of the poem.

[From *Bhagavad Gītā*, 3.25–35; 4.13–20; 2.39–50]

The Blessed Lord said:

Just as the unwise act being attached to their action, even so should the
wise act, O Bhārata, but without attachment, and only with a view to
promoting the solidarity of society.

One should not create any conflict in the minds of the ignorant who are
attached to action. On the contrary the wise man, himself acting in accordance with the technique of the yoga of action, should induce them
willingly to undertake all [prescribed] actions.

Actions of every kind are actually done by the dispositions of matter
[prakriti]; [7] and, still, a person whose mind is deluded by the ego
thinks: "I am the doer [of those actions]."

But he, O Mighty-armed One, who knows the truth of the distinctness of
the soul from the dispositions of matter and from the actions [resulting
therefrom], does not become attached [to the results of actions], realizing that the dispositions operate upon the dispositions.

Those who are deluded by the dispositions of matter become attached to
the disposition and the actions [resulting from them]. One who knows
the whole truth should not make such dullards, who do not know the
whole truth, falter [by himself renouncing all action].

[7] Cf. note 23.

MOKSHA: THE FOURTH END

Renouncing into Me all actions, with your mind fixed on the Self, and
becoming free from desire and all sense of "my-ness," do you fight, freed
from your spiritual fever.

Those men, who, full of faith and without malice, always follow this
My teaching—they are, verily, freed from the bondage of actions.

Those, on the other hand, who, treating My teaching with superciliousness, do not follow it—know them, who are utterly confounded in
wisdom and are senseless, to be completely lost.

Even the man of knowledge acts in accordance with his own innate nature. Beings have to follow the dictates of their innate nature. What can
repression avail?

The attraction and aversion of a sense-organ in respect of the objects of
that sense-organ are inherently determined. One should not come under
their sway for they are his waylayers.

Better is one's own dharma [class duties] which one may be able to fulfill
but imperfectly, than the dharma of others which is more easily accomplished. Better is death in the fulfillment of one's own dharma. To adopt
the dharma of others is perilous. . . .

The fourfold class system was created by Me in accordance with the varying dispositions and the actions [resulting therefrom]. Though I am its
creator, know Me, who am immutable, to be a non-doer.[8]

Actions do not cling to Me, for I have no yearning for their fruit. He who
knows Me thus [and himself acts in that spirit] is not bound by actions.

So knowing was action done even by men of old who sought liberation.
Therefore do the same action [i.e., your class duties] which was done
by the ancients in ancient times.

What is action? What is inaction?—as to this even the wise sages are

---

[8] In this stanza, three propositions have been set forth: 1) The scheme of the four classes,
which ensures the promotion of social solidarity (*lokasaṅgraha*) in the most efficient manner, is created by God. Therefore all men, surrendering themselves to the Divine will,
should fulfill their respective duties (*sva-dharma*) in accordance with that scheme. 2) That
scheme is designed by God in accordance with the varying propensities and capacities of
different sets of people. It is not arbitrary. 3) God created the four-class system as a part
of His *sva-dharma*. He had to act in the fulfillment of that *sva-dharma*, but He acted
in a perfectly disinterested and unattached manner. Therefore, even in spite of action, He
remained free from bondage to action. In other words, though He was a "doer," as far as the
consequences of His action were concerned, He was a "non-doer." He has thus demonstrated the efficacy of the technique of karma-yoga. It would appear that, out of these three
propositions, in the present context, it is the last one which Krishna wants particularly to
emphasize.

confounded. I will expound action to you, knowing which you will be liberated from evil.

One has to realize what is action; similarly, one has to realize what is wrong action; and one has also to realize what is inaction. Inscrutable, indeed, is the way of action.

He who sees inaction in action and action in inaction, he is discerning among men, expert in the technique of karma-yoga, the doer of the entire action [enjoined by his dharma].

He whose undertakings are all devoid of motivating desires and purposes and whose actions are consumed by the fire of knowledge—him the wise call a man of learning.

Renouncing all attachment to the fruits of actions, ever content, independent[9]—such a person even if engaged in action, does not do anything whatever.[10]

This concept has been set forth for you according to Sānkhya.[11] Listen now to this one according to Yoga, being endowed with which mental attitude, O son of Prithā, you will cast away the bondage of actions.[12]

Herein there is no loss of any effort, nor does there exist any impediment. Even a little practice of this dharma saves one from great fear.

In this [technique], one's mind is fixed on action alone [not its fruits]; it is single-aimed, O Joy [i.e., scion] of the Kurus, while the thoughts of those whose minds are not fixed on action alone are many-branched and endless.

This flowery speech, which the undiscerning proclaim, who are fondly attached to the Vedic [ritualistic] doctrine and who, O son of Prithā, assert that there is nothing else, whose minds are full of desires and who are intent on heaven—a speech which yields nothing but birth after birth as the fruit of action and which lays down various specialized rites for the attainment of enjoyment and supremacy—by that speech of the ritualists the minds of those who are attached to enjoyment and supremacy are carried away, and their minds, which should be fixed exclusively on action, are not established in concentration.

The Vedas have the operation of the three constituent properties of matter

[9] That is, not depending on any attachment or aversion to action.
[10] As far as the bondage of action is concerned.
[11] Cf. earlier selection, "You Have To Fight."
[12] Sānkhya and Yoga here represent respectively the theoretical approach and the practical approach to Arjuna's problem.

[i.e., the phenomenal world] as their subject-matter; transcend, O Arjuna, the operation of the three constituent properties. Become free from dualities,[13] ever abiding in pure essence (*sattva*), indifferent to acquisition and preservation, possessed of the Self.

As much purpose there is in a pond in a place which is flooded with water everywhere, so much purpose there is in all the Vedas for a brāhman who possesses true knowledge.

Action alone is your concern, never at all its fruits. Let not the fruits of action be your motive, nor let yourself be attached to inaction.

Steadfast in Yoga, engage yourself in actions, Dhananjaya, abandoning attachment and becoming even-minded in success and failure. Such even-mindedness is called *yoga*.

Far inferior is mere action to action done according to the technique of karma-yoga, O Dhananjaya. Seek refuge in the [right] mental attitude. Wretched are those who are motivated by the fruits of action. One who acts according to the technique of karma-yoga casts off, in this world, the consequences of both his good acts and his bad acts. Therefore take to this yoga. Yoga is skill in actions.

The Doctrine of Devotion

The *Bhagavad Gītā,* like most of the texts relating to popular Hinduism, recommends devotion (bhakti) as the most efficacious form of religion. Devotion, as described in the *Gītā,* presupposes the recognition of a personal God, who is omnipresent, omniscient, and omnipotent, and who confers His grace on the devotee—however lowly he may be—when he surrenders himself unreservedly to Him.

[From *Bhagavad Gītā,* 9.4-14]

GOD AND THE CREATION

The Blessed Lord said:

By Me is all this world pervaded through My non-manifest form. All beings abide in Me, but I do not abide in them.[14]

And yet the beings do not abide in Me; behold My supreme yoga, Sustainer of beings, but not abiding in beings, is My Self, the bringer into being of all beings.

[13] The pairs of opposites, such as pleasure and pain, attachment and aversion, etc.
[14] The distinction between the incarnate God and the transcendental Godhead is emphasized in this and the next stanza.

Just as the mighty air, always moving everywhere, abides in the sky, even
so do all beings abide in Me.[15] Understand this well!

All beings, O son of Kuntī, pass into My material nature [prakriti, primal
matter] at the close of the world cycle; and at the beginning of the next
world cycle I again bring them forth.

Having recourse to My own material nature, I bring forth, again and
again, this entire multitude of beings, which is helpless under the control of matter.

These acts do not, however, bind Me, O Dhananjaya, for I remain as if
unconcerned, unattached to these acts.

With Me as the overseer does primal matter give birth to this world—
movable and immovable; and by reason of this, O son of Kuntī, does
the world keep revolving in its course.

The deluded despise Me, the great lord of beings, who have assumed a
human body, not realizing My higher existence.

They of vain hopes, of vain actions, of vain knowledge, and devoid of
wisdom partake of the deluding nature of fiends and demons.

The great-souled ones, on the other hand, O son of Prithā, partaking of
the divine nature, worship Me with undistracted mind, knowing Me
as the immutable source of all beings.

Ever glorifying Me, always striving in My service, and steadfast in vows,
bowing down to me with devotion, they worship Me with constant
application.

Divine Manifestations

Though God is universally immanent, His presence is to be realized through
his most striking manifestations, that is to say, through whatever is endowed,
in a special way, with glory, majesty, and vigor.

[From *Bhagavad Gītā*, 10.20–24, 40–42; 11.3–4, 8, 14–17, 21, 26–27, 31–34;
9.22–34; 18.66–69]

I am, O Gudākesha [i.e., Arjuna], the Self abiding in the hearts of all
beings; I am the beginning, the middle, and also the end of beings.

Of the Ādityas I am Vishnu; of the luminaries, the radiant sun; I am
Marīchi of the Maruts; of the stars I am the moon.

---

[15] The beings abide in God in the same sense and to the same extent as air abides in the
infinite, universal space. That is to say, they do not in any way affect the immutable character of God.

Of the Vedas I am the *Sāma Veda;* of the gods I am Indra; of the sense-organs I am the mind; of living beings I am the sentience.

Of the Rudras I am Shankara [Shiva]; Kubera I am of the Yakshas and Rakshasas; of the Vasus I am Agni; Meru I am of peaked mountains.

Of the officiating priests, know me, O son of Prithā, to be the chief—Brihaspati; of the army commanders I am Skanda; of water reservoirs I am the ocean. . . .

There is no end to My divine manifestations, O Tormentor of the Foe. Here, however, has been proclaimed by Me the extent of My divine glory only through a few illustrations.

Whichever entity is endowed with glory and with majesty, and is, verily, full of vigor—each such entity do you know to have originated from a fraction of My splendor.

Or rather, what need is there, O Arjuna, for this detailed knowledge on your part? This entire world do I support and abide in with only a single fraction of Myself.

GOD'S OMNIFORM

Arjuna said:

As You have declared Your Self to be, O Supreme Lord, even so it is. I desire to see Your supreme form, O Supreme Person.

If You think that it can be seen by me, O Lord, then reveal to me Your immutable Self, O master of yoga. . . .

The Blessed Lord said:

But you cannot see Me just with this your own human eye. Here I give you the divine eye. Behold My supreme yoga. . . .

Then he, Dhananjaya, overcome with amazement, his hair standing on end, bowed down his head and, with folded hands, said to the God.

Arjuna said:

I see all the gods in Your body, O God, as also the various hosts of beings, the Lord Brahmā enthroned on a lotus-seat and all the seers and divine serpents.

I see You possessing numberless arms, bellies, mouths, and eyes, infinite in form on all sides. Neither Your end, nor Your middle, nor yet Your beginning do I see, O Lord of the universe, O omniformed.

Wearing the crown and bearing the mace and the discus, a mass of splendor radiating on all sides, I see you—hard to gaze at—all around me, possessing the radiance of a blazing fire and sun, incomprehensible. . . .

These hosts of gods here enter into You and some, in fright, extol You
   with folded hands. And bands of the great seers and the perfected ones,
   crying "Hail," praise You with manifold hymns of praise. . . .

And here all these sons of Dhritarashtra [i.e., the Kauravas] together
   with the hosts of kings, and also Bhīshma, Drona, and Karna, along
   with the chief warriors on our side too, are rushing forward and entering into Your fearful mouths which have formidable tusks. Some,
   caught between the teeth, are seen with their heads pulverized. . . .

Tell me who You are—You of formidable form. Salutation unto You, O
   Foremost among the gods, confer Your grace on me. I desire to know
   you fully, the primal one, for I do not comprehend Your working.

The Blessed Lord said:

Time am I, bringing about the destruction of the world, grown mature,
   now engaged in drawing in the worlds within Myself.[16] Even without
   you will they all cease to be—these warriors who are arrayed in the
   opposing armies.

Therefore arise and win glory; conquering the foes enjoy a prosperous
   kingdom. By Me, verily, are they even already slain; become a mere
   instrument, O Savyasāchin, and slay Drona, Bhīshma, Jayadratha,
   Karna, and likewise other warriors, who have been already slain
   by Me. Feel not distressed. Fight, you shall conquer your enemies in
   battle.

GOD AND THE DEVOTEE

Those persons who, meditating on Me without any thought of another
   god, worship Me—to them, who constantly apply themselves [to that
   worship], I bring attainment [of what they do not have] and preservation [of what they have attained].

Even the devotees of other divinities, who worship them, being endowed
   with faith—they, too, O son of Kuntī, [actually] worship Me alone,
   though not according to the prescribed rites.

For I am the enjoyer, as also the lord of all sacrifices. But those people do
   not comprehend Me in My true nature and hence they fall.

Worshipers of the gods go to the gods; worshipers of the manes go to

[16] This passage may suggest that Time (*kāla*) is the ultimate principle underlying the
world, but it has not been further developed metaphysically. More probably, however, the
rerference to Time means simply Death. Cf. *Gītā* 10.30, 33, 34 *passim*.

the manes; those who sacrifice to the spirits go to the spirits; and those who worship Me, come to Me.

A leaf, a flower, a fruit, or water, whoever offers to Me with devotion— —that same, proffered in devotion by one whose soul is pure, I accept.

Whatever you do, whatever you eat, whatever you offer in sacrifice, whatever you give away, whatever penance you practice—that, O son of Kuntī, do you dedicate to Me.

Thus will you be freed from the good or evil fruits which constitute the bondage of actions. With your mind firmly set on the way of renunciation [of fruits], you will, becoming free, come to Me.[17]

Even-minded am I to all beings; none is hateful nor dear to Me. Those, however, who worship Me with devotion, they abide in Me, and I also in them.

Even if a person of extremely vile conduct worships Me being devoted to none else, he is to be reckoned as righteous, for he has engaged himself in action in the right spirit.

Quickly does he become of righteous soul and obtain eternal peace. O son of Kuntī, know for certain that My devotee perishes not.

For those, O son of Pṛthā, who take refuge in Me, even though they be lowly born, women, vaishyas, as also shūdras—even they attain to the highest goal.

How much more, then, pious brāhmans, as also devout royal sages? Having come to this impermanent, blissless world, worship Me.

On Me fix your mind; become My devotee, My worshiper; render homage unto Me. Thus having attached yourself to Me, with Me as your goal, you shall come to Me. . . .

Abandoning all [other] religious practices (dharma), betake yourself unto Me alone as shelter. I shall deliver you from all sins whatsoever; be not grieved.

Never is this to be spoken by you to one who does not lead a life of austerity, who is not a devotee, and who is not anxious to hear, or to one who treats Me with superciliousness.

He, on the other hand, who proclaims this supreme secret among My devotees, showing the highest devotion to Me, shall without doubt come straight unto Me.

---

[17] In this and the preceding stanza, the *Gītā* coordinates its two principal teachings, namely, devotion (bhakti) and the yoga of action.

There is none among men who does dearer service to Me than he; nor shall there be another dearer to Me than he in the world.

Philosophical Synthesis

The *Bhagavad Gītā* does not endorse any one system of philosophy among those current in its time, but rather aims at achieving a synthesis of the most prominent among them, the Sānkhya yoga, and the Vedānta. Though one cannot speak of any consistent metaphysical viewpoint underlying the *Gītā's* teaching, the author tends toward a kind of theistic Sānkhya which embraces the spirit-matter dualism of the Sānkhya, the ultimate monism of the Vedānta, and the all-powerful God of devotional religion, realized through the disciplined activity and meditation of the yoga.

[From *Bhagavad Gītā*, 13.19–23; 14.3–8; 15.16–19; 5.4, 5]

Primal matter [prakriti] and spirit [purusha]—know them both to be beginningless.[18] The modifications and the constituent properties [19]— know them as originated from primal matter.

Primal matter is said to be the cause in respect to the creatorship of the cause and effect [relation in the phenomenal world]. The spirit is said to be the cause in respect of being the experiencer of pleasure and pain.

For the spirit abiding in primal matter experiences the constituent properties born of primal matter. Its attachment to the constituent properties is the cause of its births in good or evil wombs.

And the Supreme Spirit in this body is called the Witness, the Permitter, the Supporter, the Experiencer, the Great Lord, as also the Supreme Self.[20]

He who thus knows the spirit and primal matter together with the con-

[18] According to Sānkhya, there are two ultimately and independently existing principles, primal matter (prakriti) and spirit (purusha). The spirit is sentient (cetana) but incapable of modification while primal matter is nonsentient but capable of modification. In the unmodified form of primal matter, its three constituent properties (gunas), namely, purity (sattva), passion (rajas), and darkness (tamas) are in a state of equipoise. This state of equipoise is disturbed as the result of the "seeing" of primal matter by the spirit. Primal matter then begins to be modified, according to a fixed plan, into the manifold phenomenal world. The various aspects of the phenomenal world, accordingly, are made up of the three constituent properties combined in different proportions.

[19] That is, the different combinations of the three constituent properties which constitute the phenomenal world.

[20] The concept of the Supreme Spirit over and above matter and the individual spirit or soul is unknown to the original Sānkhya. It reflects the monistic Vedānta concept of the highest Brahman (cf. "the Supreme Self," *paramātman,* in this stanza) and thus facilitates a kind of synthesis between Vedānta monism and Sānkhya dualism. For another, the Supreme Spirit is identified with the all-god (Krishna; cf. "the great lord," *maheśvara*) of devotional religion.

stituent properties [21]—even though he engages himself in action in any way, he is not born again. . . .

My womb is the Great Brahman; [22] in it I deposit the seed. Therefrom occurs the origination of all beings, O Bhārata.

Whatever forms are produced in all wombs, O son of Kuntī—of them the Great Brahman is the primal womb and I am the father implanting the seed.

Purity, passion, and darkness—these constituent properties born of primal matter bind down the immutable embodied one [i.e., the soul] within the body, O mighty-armed.[23]

Of these, purity, on account of its taintlessness, produces light and health. Through attachment to happiness and through attachment to knowledge it binds one down, O sinless one.

Know passion to be of the nature of emotion, the source of longing and attachment. It binds down the embodied one, O son of Kuntī, through attachment to action.

But know darkness to be born of ignorance and as causing infatuation to all embodied ones, It binds one down, O Bhārata, through negligence, indolence, and sleep. . . .

There are two spirits in this world, the mutable and the immutable; the

[21] That is, one who knows the true nature of spirit and matter and preserves the true nature of the spirit, namely, of being essentially isolated from matter, by not allowing it to become attached to the various modifications of primal matter.

[22] This expression is made up of two technical terms, one of which—the Great One (Mahat)—is borrowed from Sānkhya while the other—the Brahman—is taken from the Vedānta. According to Sānkhya, the first evolute of primordial matter is "the Great One," which is the source of all further evolution; while in Vedānta the Brahman is the ultimate essence and cause of the world. This entity (the Great Brahman), which clearly refers here to primordial matter, is presided over by Krishna, who infuses it with life (his "seed")—an attempt at a synthesis between theism and both schools of philosophy.

[23] Matter includes not only the external world and the body, but also what we would call the mind. The latter is regarded as active, like all of matter, but unconscious, consciousness being the fundamental characteristic of the spirit. The spirit is deluded by the ego faculty of the mind into identifying itself with the body-mind complex. All of matter is made up of the three dispositions (gunas). The word guṇa literally means "strand," as the strands of a rope, but it also came to mean "quality." Though the gunas had both cosmic and psychological significance, the latter use predominates in the Gītā. The translation "disposition" is more suggestive of this connotation. The three dispositions manifest themselves in the highest or directing faculty of the mind, i.e., the intellect (buddhi), as three fundamental tendencies or drives, which are present in all of us in various proportions. Even when "purity," the drive toward knowledge and liberation, predominates, it binds the soul to the world of matter and therefore to karma and rebirth; but once the intellect reaches the saving knowledge, the drive for knowledge and liberation, and a fortiori the other dispositions, now without purpose, wither away, leaving the soul, freed from specious connections to the phenomenal world, to enjoy its own immutable bliss.

mutable [i.e., matter] comprises all beings; what remains unchanged is called the immutable [the spirit or soul].

But other than these two is the Highest Spirit (*uttama-puruṣa*), called the Supreme Self, who, the Eternal Lord (*īśvara*), permeating the three worlds, sustains them.[24]

Since I surpass the mutable and am higher even than the immutable, therefore, I am celebrated as the Highest Spirit (*puruṣa-uttama*) among people and in scripture [lit. in the Veda].

Whoever, undeluded, thus knows me to be the Highest Spirit, he is the knower of all and worships me with his whole being, O Bhārata. . . .

Fools, not the wise, declare that Sānkhya and Yoga are different; a person who resorts to one of these correctly, obtains the fruit of both.

The position obtained by followers of Sānkhya is also obtained by the followers of Yoga. He who sees that Sānkhya and Yoga are one, he truly sees.

The Ideal Man

The *Gītā* mentions in different contexts the characteristics of the man who can be regarded as perfect according to Krishnaism. He is referred to variously as of steadfast wisdom, yogin, devotee, etc. In the characterization of the Ideal Man the principal teachings of the *Gītā* are also reflected.

[From *Bhagavad Gītā*, 2.55–59; 6.16–23; 12.13–19]

When one renounces all the desires which have arisen in the mind, O son of Pṛithā, and when he himself is content within his own Self, then is he called a man of steadfast wisdom.

He whose mind is unperturbed in the midst of sorrows and who entertains no desires amid pleasures; he from whom passion, fear, and anger have fled away—he is called a sage of steadfast intellect.

He who feels no attachment toward anything; who, having encountered the various good or evil things, neither rejoices nor loathes—his wisdom is steadfast.

When one draws in, on every side, the sense-organs from the objects of sense as a tortoise draws in its limbs from every side—then his wisdom becomes steadfast.

The objects of sense turn away from the embodied one [the soul] who

[24] Cf. note 20.

ceases to feed on them, but the taste for them still persists. Even this taste, in his case, turns away after the Supreme is seen. . . .

Yoga, indeed, is not for one who eats in excess nor for one who altogether abstains from food. It is, O Arjuna, not for one who is accustomed to excessive sleep nor, indeed, for one who always keeps awake.[25]

For one who is disciplined in eating and recreation, who engages himself in actions in a disciplined manner,[26] who properly regulates his sleep and wakefulness—for him yoga proves to be the destroyer of sorrow.

When one's properly controlled mind becomes steadfast within the Self alone and when one becomes free from all desires, then he is said to have accomplished yoga.

"Just as a lamp in a windless place flickers not"—this is the simile traditionally used in respect of a yogin whose mind is properly controlled and who practices the yoga of the Self.

Wherein the mind, restrained by the practice of yoga, is at rest; and wherein he, seeing the Self through the Self, finds contentment within his own Self;

wherein he finds that supreme bliss, which is perceived by the intellect alone and which is beyond the ken of the sense-organs; wherein, being steadfast, he does not swerve from reality;

having obtained which, he does not consider any other gain to be greater than it; and being steadfast in which, he is not shaken by even a heavy sorrow;

that state, one should know as the one called yoga—the disconnection from union with sorrow. This yoga should be practiced with resoluteness and with undepressed mind. . . .

He who does not entertain hatred toward any being, who is friendly and ever compassionate, free from all sense of "my-ness," free from egoism, even-tempered in pain and pleasure, forbearing;

he who is ever content, the yogin, possessing self-control, of unshakable resolve; who has dedicated to Me his mind and intellect—he, My devotee, is dear to Me.

---

[25] The *Gītā* prescribes a way of life which can be practiced by the common man. It was generally believed that yoga presupposed some austere physical and mental discipline. This kind of yoga was obviously beyond the reach of the common man. The *Gītā*, therefore, here teaches a different kind of yoga or self-discipline, the most essential feature of which is temperateness.

[26] A reference to the yoga (discipline) of action.

He from whom the world shrinks not and who does not shrink from the
world; and who is free from elation, impetuosity, fear, and perturbation
—he too is dear to Me.

He who has no expectation; who is pure, dexterous, unconcerned, and un-
troubled; who renounces all acts [27]—he, My devotee, is dear to Me.

He who neither exults nor hates, neither grieves nor yearns; who renounces good and evil; who is full of devotion—he is dear to Me.

He who behaves alike to foe and friend; who, likewise is even-poised in
honor or dishonor; who is even-tempered in cold and heat, happiness
and sorrow; who is free from attachment;

who regards praise and censure with equanimity; who is silent, content
with anything whatever; who has no fixed abode,[28] who is steadfast
in mind, who is full of devotion—that man is dear to Me.

HINDU PHILOSOPHY

The Upanishadic doctrine concerning the identity of the individual self
(ātman) with the Absolute Brahman, which represented the culmination
of philosophic thought in the Vedas, also served as the point of departure
for Hindu philosophical speculation in later times. The term Vedānta,
as we have seen, means "end of the Veda" (that is, the Upanishads), and
came to be applied to those later texts which, accepting the scriptural
authority of the Upanishads, attempted to formulate more systematically
its teaching concerning the nature of Brahman. The *Brahma* or *Vedānta
Sūtras,* from which readings are given below, are ascribed to Vyāsa or
Bādarāyana. Other thinkers who expounded the doctrines of the Vedānta
and are referred to by Vyāsa in the course of these discussions include
such names as Jaimini, Āshmarathya, Audulomi, and Kāshakritsna.

Closely related to the Vedānta was another school devoted to the hymns
and formulae found in the Samhitā portion of the Veda, with which different deities were to be propitiated and merit thereby accumulated for
the attaining of heavenly enjoyment. These meritorious acts enjoined by
the former part of the Veda constitute dharma, and the nature of this

---

[27] Namely, acts springing from selfish desires and emotions; or: the fruits of such acts.

[28] A fixed abode is the symbol of one's attachment to the experiences of this phenomenal
world.

dharma as taught by the Veda in its ritualistic portion (*Karma Kāṇḍa*) is expounded in a system of thought called *Mīmāṃsā* ("inquiry") by the sage Jaimini. It is also referred to as *Pūrva* (earlier) *Mīmāṃsā;* while the *Vedānta* is, in this respect, referred to as *Uttara* (later) *Mīmāṃsā*. According to the earlier interpreters of the Vedic teachings, these two schools were taken together and it was considered proper to study first the Pūrva Mīmāmsā and then the Uttara Mīmāmsā. But Shankara Āchārya (Shankara the Teacher, A.D. c.850) the greatest exponent of Advaita,[1] showed that the philosophy of the Brahman and its pursuit have nothing to do with acts; acts can, according to him, serve only as a disciplinary accessory, aiding mental purification.

Apart from this, the Pūrva Mīmāmsā gave a whole system of exegetical principles employed in the interpretation of the Vedic texts, which are of use in the sphere of civil and religious law also.

Also closely related to the *Vedānta* is the system of thought called *Sānkhya,* which figures so importantly in the *Gītā*. *Sānkhya* means reasoning. Traces of the development of Sānkhya thought are met with in the Samhitā and Upanishads, and in Buddhism. The sage who supposedly first propounded this school was Kapila, a name already met in one of the more important later Upanishads. According to Kapila, there are two entities, spirit and matter, purusha and prakriti; the phenomenal world that we see, the beings and their activities, are all the manifold manifestations of matter. Matter is nonsentient and is constituted of three dispositions called *guṇa*[2]—purity (*sattva*), passion (*rajas*), and darkness (*tamas*). *Sattva* is light, revealing, and happy; *rajas* is active, passionate, restless, and sorrowful; *tamas* is heavy, stupid, and obscuring. When these three constituents are in a state of equilibrium, matter is static; but when the equilibrium is disturbed and one or the other constituent gains the upper hand, matter starts evolving into cosmic intellect, egoity, the subtle elements, and so on. The cause of this disturbance of equilibrium is the proximity of the spirit. The spirit alone is intelligent, and its intelligence is reflected in the evolutes of matter, namely, intellect, ego, mind, and senses (intellect and ego have both a cosmic and an individual function). The spirit, whose association with matter is responsible for evolution, experience, and misery, being by nature a mere spectator not actually involved in the doings of matter, real knowledge consists of the realiza-

[1] Lit. "non-duality," the monistic school of Vedānta.   [2] Lit. "strands."

tion of the distinctness of the spirit from matter and recognition of all mundane activities as due to the interplay of the material dispositions. By such isolation, one frees oneself from material bondage and the consequent sufferings. The *Vedānta Sūtras* refute the Sānkhya in many places by pointing out that insentient matter cannot explain creation and that a sentient Supreme Being alone can be the source of this universe.

Closely related to the Sānkhya is the school of Yoga, the aphorisms of which are ascribed to Sage Patanjali. The Yoga is presupposed by the Upanishads and Buddhism. This school accepts the philosophical doctrines of the Sānkhya, with one important difference in that it accepts a God (Īshvara) as the Supreme Omniscient ever-existing Teacher. For the rest, the Yoga sets forth a system for controlling the mind and body through physical and ethical disciplines, and for helping that one-pointed concentration by which the aspirant could see the spirit established in its intelligence and isolated completely from the modifications and contaminations of matter. The Yoga is thus of practical value.

Two other systems of thought also arose which used logic to a large extent, the Vaisheshika and Nyāya, both realistic and pluralistic in their tenets. The Vaisheshika developed a view of the physical universe through its atomic theory according to which objects were constituted of atoms (*aṇu*), the ultimately analyzable units, and as each was distinct by virtue of its own ultimate particular quality called *viśeṣa,* the school came to be known as *Vaiśeṣika*. The philosophy of the Vaisheshika is acceptable to the Nyāya, which specialized in the methodology of thought and reasoning. The Nyāya accepted God only as an efficient cause, the architect of the universe, and used the teleological argument to prove His existence. The followers of both these schools were theists and worshiped Shiva as the Supreme God.

The above were the six schools of philosophy developed by the orthodox, as against the heterodox thinkers. All of these orthodox schools accepted the Vedas as authoritative. Opposed to them were the purely materialist thinkers called *Cārvākas* or *Lokāyatas* for whom there was no Self or entity beyond the material body and its needs, as also the schools of Buddhism and Jainism which repudiated Vedic authority.

One of the chief characteristics of the Indian systems of thought is that they postulate at the very outset the criteria or sources of valid knowledge (*pramāṇas*) which each of them proposes to use and rely upon. Of the sources of valid knowledge, it is only the materialistic school which accepts direct sense perception (*pratyakṣa*) as the sole source of knowledge. The rest accept a number of sources of knowledge, two, three, four, and so on. The chief of these sources of knowledge are the direct perception already mentioned, inference (*anumāna*), analogy (*upamāna*), and verbal testimony (*śabda*), the last of which includes the words of a reliable person and the scriptural utterances. Just as each school sets forth the sources of knowledge acceptable to it, it enumerates also the categories of knowable objects (*prameyas*) accepted by it.

Among these schools, use is made to a varying degree of logic and inference on the one hand and scriptural authority on the other. The two Mīmāṃsās assign the primary place to scripture, and according to the Vedānta, reasoning occupies only the secondary place, being resorted to only to interpret and reinforce revelation. Mere inference is like groping in the dark, says the grammarian and poet Bhartrihari. In the logical school of Nyāya also, where even God is proved on logical grounds, the authority of the Veda as the word of God is accepted. To the Indian thinker, philosophy is no mere intellectual game but a darshana or vision of Truth revealed by a seer and an experience realized and relived by the aspirant. Consequently, each school sets forth its own conception of the goal aimed at by the inquiry. All are agreed that the goal of the philosophical quest is liberation from the misery of going from birth to death and death to birth, and the attainment of everlasting Bliss. In some cases, the everlasting bliss is simply release (mukti or moksha) from the transmigratory cycle (samsāra) or the suffering caused by the material enslavement of the spirit; the Sānkhya-Yoga schools envisage their liberation thus; in Nyāya also, it is of the same type, though here, as in Yoga, God's grace is sought as a help. In the theistic schools, of which an example is given below, the *summum bonum* is conceived in terms of different relationships to a personal God. In monistic Advaita, the final state which the aspirant strives for is the realization of the unity of his Self with Brahman.

As Indian philosophy aims at experiencing the Truth, all the schools include disciplines (*sādhanas*), practical means for the attainment of the spiritual goal. The Yoga, mentioned already, is the chief *sādhana* accepted by the orthodox as well as heterodox schools. Devotion to God, fulfillment of obligatory and ordained duties, ethical behavior—all these are likewise part of the means employed. As all the schools have such a practical side, all of them emphasize the need and importance of a spiritual preceptor or teacher—a guru.

In their inquiry into the nature of reality, the schools adopt different theories of causation, and in epistemology, they have similarly different theories of truth and error. There are three main theories of causation—origination (*ārambha*), transformation (*pariṇāma*), and apparent transfiguration (*vivarta*). The logical Nyāya school holds the first view, the effects being, according to them, created from out of several causes; here the effect was previously nonexistent in any one cause (*asatkārya-vāda*). The Sānkhya school adopts the second view where the effect exists already in the cause and is merely brought out in a different form (*sat-kārya-vāda*). On the third theory, which the idealistic school of Advaita adopts, the effect is only an apparent manifestation on the basis of the cause which is thereby transfigured. In accordance with the first view, illustrated by the example of the potter making a pot out of clay, God creates the universe as an agent. In the second case, which resembles milk curdling into a different form, the entire phenomenal world represents but manifold evolutions of the same matter. The third view is exemplified by a rope mistaken for a snake, or water seen in a mirage; in the same manner, the entire phenomenal universe is but an appearance projected by the basic reality called the *brahman*. It will be seen that from the first theory to the second and from the second to the third, there is a progressive reduction of difference and increase in identity between cause and effect.

In the same manner, when there arises a wrong cognition, different schools explain the nature of error in different ways. This consideration is essential to understanding the conception of the universe and experience in the different schools. Consider the example of a piece of nacre shining as silver to an onlooker who rushes to take it, but is disappointed on closer examination. Here, according to the Nyāya, what is one thing shines as something else; this is *anyathā-khyāti* or misapprehension. According to one sub-school of Pūrva Mīmāmsā, erroneous cognition is a case of nonapprehension of something (*akhyāti*); that is, one sees nacre, not as nacre, but as just "this object in front"; the strong memory of silver experienced by him previously forces itself now to the fore and without being able to distinguish between actual cognition and a recollection, he rushes to the knowledge that it is silver. Among the Vedāntic schools, that of Rāmānuja thinks that in all such experiences, there is nothing invalid; and in reality, certain silver-elements inhere in nacre as a consequence of which such a cognition arises. This is an eclectic view of *akhyāti-cum-satkhyāti*. In Shankara's theory of the appearance of one thing on the substratum of another and the superimposition of something unreal on a basic reality, the case of seeing silver in nacre, with which the whole phenomenal world and experience are compared, is simply an apparent reality whose nature cannot be determined one way or the other as either real or unreal. It has a *relative* reality for the duration of the erroneous perception, when one rushes to pick it up as silver, but is *ultimately* unreal, being sublated on the rise of the correct perception of its being only nacre.

Of these schools of philosophy, each played its notable part for a time and became superseded later, leaving only some distinctive subsidiary aspect of it as its contribution. The Sānkhya was once the most widely and influentially expounded school, against which even Buddhism had to contend. The very name Sānkhya became synonymous with knowledge. Moreover, despite some earlier tendencies toward atheism, after the addition of a God in a more substantial manner than in Yoga, the Sānkhya became absorbed by the Purānas. At the same time, the rise of Vedānta made it superfluous, its doctrine of primordial matter being paralleled by the Vedāntic nescience (*avidyā*) or illusion (māyā) and its conception of unaffected spirit or purusha by the Vedāntic ātman or Brahman (the only difference being that in Sānkhya, spirit (purusha) was not one but many). In its concept of the three dispositions (gunas), the Sānkhya bequeathed a vital idea which was useful in all schools of thought and fields of activity for evaluating things and grading them as good, middling, and bad. The cognate system of Yoga, however, was likewise adopted by all schools and today has spread even beyond the confines of India. The word *yoga* has come to mean spiritual or religious path in general.

For a long time the logical school of Nyāya performed a great service in defending, against the attacks of Buddhistic atheists and nihilists, the doctrines of the existence of God, the reality of the world, the continuity of experience, and the substantiality of wholes as distinct from parts. Later, when Vedānta took over the task of criticizing Buddhist metaphysics, the Nyāya with its realism and pluralism, directed its criticism against Advaitic idealism and monism. As a school of philosophy the Nyāya was unable to maintain a separate existence, but its methodology in logical analysis—in definition, inference, sentence, word and meaning, etc.—came to be utilized by all schools of philosophy in their own dialectic. The Mīmāmsā,[3] for its part, had served to restore the authority of the Veda when it was assailed by the Buddhists; and Kumārila, one of its outstanding exponents in the seventh century, was responsible for defending and strengthening Hindu teachings against Buddhism. With the rise of Vedānta and the progressive decline of the belief in sacrificial rites and the path of acts, Mīmāmsā became more and more a theoretical scholastic discipline, its writers being, in conviction, Vedāntins of one school or another.

It is the remaining school, the Vedānta, that became, from the time of Shankara, the prevailing philosophy of India. The readings which follow are representative of the monistic or nondualistic (*Advaita*) school of Vedānta as expounded by Shankara in his commentary on the *Vedānta Sūtras*. Later interpretations of the *Vedānta Sūtras* were those of the Rāmānuja school of qualified nondualism (*Viśiṣṭādvaita*) and of Madhva Āchārya (Madhva the Teacher, 1199–1278) which inculcated a more theistic and pluralistic (*Dvaita*) interpretation of Vedānta.

The exact nature of the relation between the Supreme Being and the individual soul is the central problem in these systems. Already in the *Vedānta Sūtras* (1.4.20–22), the sages, Āshmarathya, Audulomi and Kāshakritsna, are seen to have held different views on this question. The first held that the individual souls, even as sparks issuing forth from a fire, were neither different from the Brahman nor non-different from It. The second held that the individual souls are different from the Supreme, but with the dropping of their embodied limitation, they become one with the Supreme. According to the third, it is the Supreme Soul that exists also as the individual soul. The early interpreters of the *Vedānta Sūtras* before Shankara mostly adopted the first view of difference-*cum*-identity (*bheda-abheda*), holding the evolutionary theory of the origin of things from the Brahman, and in the period immediately following Shankara also, this view was maintained by writers like Bhāskara (A.D. c.850) and Yādavaprakāsha (A.D. c.1100). Shankara, as also his grand-preceptor Gaudapāda, followed the third view, of Kāshakritsna, and expounded

[3] The Pūrva Mīmāmsā.

the identity of the two, of the individual soul as a state of the Supreme.

In Rāmānuja's (d. A.D. 1137) interpretation, the sentient and the non-sentient universe constitute the body of the Supreme Being, which is thus a personality endowed with attributes and is identified with the God Vishnu. While the sentient and nonsentient (i.e., souls and matter) are thus characteristic of the one Brahman and cannot exist independently of Him, there is nonetheless an inherent distinction between them. It is in this sense that Rāmānuja's nondualism is "qualified." Rāmānuja's understanding of the *Vedānta Sūtras* differs from Shankara's nondualism in that Brahman is for Rāmānuja not intelligence itself, as Shankara maintains, but is a Supreme Being whose chief attribute is intelligence. This latter conception of the Supreme Being as the cause of the universe and as possessing various attributes gives the Rāmānuja school of Ve-dānta a theistic character. It has tended to stress devotion (bhakti) rather than knowledge as the chief means of salvation. In fact, however, this devotion to Vishnu—the theistic Brahman—is seen to derive from knowl-edge, and to represent only a more direct path to salvation. Unbelief rather than ignorance is regarded as the fundamental obstacle to this goal.

Madhva was a realist and pluralist to whom the world was real, the souls were many and different, the Supreme God was Vishnu and the individual souls, His servants. Besides Shankara, Rāmānuja, and Madhva, there were other South Indian exponents of the *Vedānta Sūtras* who explained this relationship between the Supreme and the individ-ual self in slightly different terms and who established in North India sects which are still widely followed there. Nimbārka, for instance, adopted the old standpoint of difference-*cum*-identity; and Vallabha Āchārya (A.D. c.1500) adopted Shankara's view with greater stress on the personal God and His grace. In Bengal Vaishnavism, founded by Chaitanya (b. A.D. 1485), Baladeva (eighteenth century) interpreted the relation between God and the individual soul as an inscrutable difference-*cum*-identity. All these schools were markedly theistic and practiced fer-vent devotion to God in the form of Krishna, the Lover Supreme.

ISHVARAKRISHNA
The Sāṅkhya Kārikās

This exposition of the Sānkhya is taken from the best-known compendium of
that school dating perhaps from the fourth century A.D. The original is in
pithy verse (kārikās) and to give an easy flow to the English version, the text
is rendered in some places in an expanded manner.

[From Īshvarakrishna, *Sāṅkhyā Kārikās,* 1–33, 38–42, 44–45, 55–69]

Owing to man being assailed by the three kinds of misery,[1] there arises
the desire in him to know the means for the removal of such misery.
Such an inquiry into the cause of the removal of misery is not rendered
useless because there are known and ready remedies, for such remedies
are neither invariably nor completely effective. Like those worldly remedies are those that one knows from the scriptures [namely, the performance of Vedic sacrifices to attain the joyous status of heaven]; for
that scriptural remedy is impure as sacrifices involve injury [to animals],
and its fruits are both perishable[2] and liable to be excelled by other kinds
of pleasure.[3] Therefore a remedy which is the opposite of these [the
seen one of the world and the heard one of the scriptures] is more beneficial; and that remedy is to be had by knowledge, the discrimination of
the manifest material creation, its unmanifest cause [the object], and the
presiding sentient spirit [the subject].

Primordial Matter is not an effect [modification]; the intellect, etc.,
seven in number, are both cause and effect; there are sixteen categories
which are only effects; the spirit is neither cause nor effect.[4]

The categories of knowledge are known from means of correct knowledge and in Sānkhya, three sources of valid knowledge are accepted:
perception, inference, and valid testimony; all other means of correct

---

[1] Mental and physical; that caused by fellow beings, animals and nature; and that caused
by atmospheric conditions, spirits and heavenly beings.

[2] The heavenly status is strictly governed by the duration of the fruit of sacrifices and at
its lapse, the performer of the sacrifice enjoying heavenly status reverts to earthly existence.
A limited act, such as it is, cannot produce a result which is everlasting, a state from which
there is no lapse.

[3] Such a fruit admits of degrees, one doing a bigger sacrifice gaining a higher heaven
or a bliss of longer duration; varying degrees are part and parcel of artificial acts operating
under the laws of specific cause-and-effect relationships.

[4] These are the twenty-five categories of Sānkhya.

knowledge are included in these three. Perception is the determination of objects by their contact with the respective senses perceiving them. Inference is of three kinds, and it results from the knowledge of a characteristic feature and of an object invariably accompanied by that feature.[5] Valid testimony is what one hears from a reliable authority. Perception provides knowledge of sensible objects. Of things beyond the senses, knowledge is had through inference based on analogy;[6] and those that are completely beyond the senses and cannot be established even through that process of inference are ascertained through valid testimony. A thing may not be perceived because of too great distance, of too much proximity, injury to the senses, inattention of mind, smallness or subtlety, an intervening object, suppression by another, or merging in a similar thing.

Primordial matter is not perceived because it is too subtle, not because it does not exist; for it is known from its products [the phenomenal world]. And those products are intellect, etc.; products born of primordial matter are, in their characteristics, partly like it and partly unlike it.[7]

The effect already exists in the cause for the following reasons: what is nonexistent cannot be produced; for producing a thing, a specific material cause is resorted to; everything is not produced by everything; a specific material cause capable of producing a specific product alone produces that effect; there is such a thing as a particular cause for a particular effect.

The evolved [i.e., the product] has the following characteristics: it has been caused, it is noneternal, nonpervasive, attended by movement, manifold, resting on another, an attribute of its source in which it finally merges, endowed with parts, and depending on another for its existence. The nonevolved [i.e., the cause, primordial matter] is the opposite of all this. But the evolved and the unevolved [primordial matter] have these common properties: they are composed of three dispositions [gunas];

[5] Such a characteristic feature is, for instance, smoke which accompanies fire invariably. Thus, from the appearance of smoke on a mountain, the existence of fire on the mountain is inferred. The stock example of a five-membered inference is: 1) *thesis to be proved:* the mountain is on fire; 2) *ground:* because it has smoke; 3) *illustration:* everything that has smoke, e.g., a kitchen, has fire; 4) *application:* the mountain is such a thing; 5) *conclusion:* therefore the mountain is on fire.

[6] For example, when we infer, from the different positions of the sun that it moves, on the analogy of a person seen at different places owing to his movement.

[7] That is, an effect takes a new form but at the same time carries the features of the cause; there is a difference-*cum*-identity between cause and effect.

they are nondiscriminating and nonsentient; they are object; they are common; and their nature is to evolve. The spirit is opposed in its qualities both to one and to the other.

The three dispositions: they are of the form of pleasure, pain, and dejection; their purposes are illumination, activation, and checking; they function by prevailing over one another, resorting to one another, engendering one another, and acting in cooperation with one another.[8] They are purity [sattva], passion [rajas], and darkness [tamas]. Purity is light, revealing and desirable; passion is stimulating and active; darkness is dense and obscuring; their harmonious functioning is directed by unity of purpose, as in the case of a lamp [in which the ingredients, fire, oil, and wick, conjointly function for the one purpose of producing light].[9]

The properties like absence of discriminatory knowledge can be proved to exist in the evolved by reason of the latter being composed of the three dispositions and by the absence of this threefold composition of its opposite, namely the spirit. The existence of an unevolved primary cause is proved by the fact that the effect has the same properties as the cause.

The unevolved exists as the primordial cause because the diverse evolutes are all attended by limitations, because common features subsist through all of them [arguing inheritance from a common cause], because the evolved has come into being as the result of the potentiality of a cause, because the distinction of cause and effect apply to the entire world without exception.

The unevolved acts [evolves] through its three dispositions [purity, etc.] and through them conjointly, changing like water according to the difference pertaining to each of those dispositions.

As all aggregates imply one different from themselves whom they subserve, as that for whom they are intended should differ from their own nature, namely, being composed of three dispositions, etc., as such objects should have one as their presiding authority, as objects imply an

---

[8] All nature is composed of these three dispositions. They are not to be understood as attributes of nature, but they are the three modes in which nature itself is constituted. They are nature. All modifications of nature are but the products of the different kinds of proportions of the interplay or intermingling of these three modes.

[9] Opposed in nature and individually possessed of mutually destructive properties, these cooperate for the sake of a common object; even so the three modes of nature, whose common object is to allow the spirit to attain through experience discriminative knowledge and ultimate emancipation.

enjoyer, and as there is seen through evolution a striving for liberation, there exists the spirit. The plurality of spirits is proven because of the specified nature of birth, death, and faculties in respect of each person, because of the absence of simultaneous activity on the part of all, and because of the diversity of the nature of the three dispositions in different beings. By the same reason of differences from the unevolved [primordial matter] which is composed of the three dispositions, the spirit is proved to be only a spectator, distinct and unaffected, endowed with cognition but free of agency.

Hence, as a result of union with the spirit, the evolved though non-sentient, yet appears to be sentient; and on its part, the spirit, too, though the dispositions of matter alone act, appears to act but is really indifferent. It is for the sake of enlightenment of the spirit and the eventual withdrawal from primordial matter [i.e., liberation of the spirit from matter] that the two come together, even as the lame and the blind [10] come together for mutual benefit; creation proceeds from this union.

From primordial matter proceeds intellect; from it ego; from that the group of sixteen [the five subtle elements governing sound, touch, form, taste, and smell, the five senses of knowledge, the five of action, and the mind which is the internal sense presiding over the other ten senses]; from the five [subtle elements] among those sixteen, the five gross elements [ether, air, fire, water, and earth].

The intellect is of the form of determination; its sublime [purity-dominated] forms are virtue, knowledge, dispassion, and mastery; the opposites of these [darkness-dominated vice, ignorance, passion, and powerlessness] represent its forms in delusion.

Ego is of the form of identification; from it proceed twofold creation, the group of eleven [senses] and the five subtle elements. From that state of ego called *vaikṛta* [i.e., dominated by purity] proceed the eleven purity-dominated evolutes [the faculties]; from the state called *bhūtādi* [dominated by darkness, lit. the origin of gross natural elements], the five subtle elements, which are dominated by darkness; and from the state called *taijasa* [dominated by passion] both of these [the faculties as well as the subtle elements] proceed. [11]

---

[10] The blind can carry the lame and the lame can direct the blind; sentient spirit is lame as it is devoid of activity and active matter is blind as it is devoid of cognition.

[11] The sublime purity-dominated state is inactive, even so the degraded darkness-dominated state; to make each of these active and productive of their respective evolutes, namely,

The senses of knowledge are eye, ear, nose, tongue, and skin; those of action are voice, hands, feet, and the organs of excretion and generation. The mind is of both forms [of knowledge and action]: it is of the form of reflection and it is called a sense because of its similarity to the senses. The variety of organs is due to the modifications of the constituents, and so is the variety of objects comprehended by the senses. The function of the five organs of knowledge in respect of form, etc. [their respective objects] is of the form of indeterminate perception; of the five organs of action, speech, taking, moving, discharge, and enjoyment form the function. What has been set forth above forms the characteristic and distinctive function of each of these three [the senses of knowledge, those of action, and of the mind]; the five vital breaths [12] constitute their conjoint function.

In respect of a perceptible object the functioning of the four [intellect, ego, mind, and one of the senses] is known to be sometimes simultaneous, sometimes gradual.[13] In respect of the unseen the operation of the three [internal instruments of knowledge: intellect, ego, and mind] is based on a prior sense perception. The external and internal instruments of knowledge function in their respective capacity in coordination; the motive of their activity is only to subserve the purpose of the spirit; [besides this] there is naught else that promulgates the activity of the instruments. These instruments [intellect, etc.] are of thirteen kinds: [five organs of knowledge; five of action; and intellect, ego, and mind]; they gather, hold together, and reveal [their objects]; their results are tenfold [the five sense-perceptions and five activities], gathered, assimilated, and revealed. The inner organ is threefold [intellect, ego, and mind]; the external organs are ten [the five of knowledge and the five of action] and they form the object of the former triad; the external ones are confined to the present time, the internal organs comprehend all the three phases of time [present, past, and future]. . . .

The subtle elements are not of any specific character; from these five, the five gross elements of matter proceed and these gross elements have specified characters, peaceful, violent, and dormant [according to the relative preponderance of any of the three gunas]. These three specified

the eleven faculties and the five subtle elements, the association of passion, the principle of activity, is needed; hence the middle state (taijasa) is for the benefit of both states.

[12] The five vital breaths are those that sustain life, discharge excreta, etc.

[13] Gradual in cases of doubt at the first instance and resolution after reflection.

forms have again a threefold manifestation [in living beings]; the subtle body,[14] the gross body born of parents, together with the gross elements; the subtle ones endure [through transmigration], the gross ones are perishable. The former called the *liṅga*[15] is of unknown antiquity, not subject to any obstruction, is enduring, and comprises intellect, ego, mind, and the five subtle elements; it is not yet capable of experience [being without a gross body], but overlaid with the impressions of acts, it migrates from birth to birth. Just as there cannot be a picture without a substratum or a shadow without objects like the post, even so, the instruments of experience cannot exist without the subtle body [composed of the subtle elements]. According to the exigencies of the causes—virtue, vice, etc.—and the resultant higher or lower births, the subtle body (*liṅga*) prompted by the purpose of the spirit (viz. its liberation) makes its appearance like an actor in different guises, thanks to the capacity of the primary cause (prariti) to manifest diverse forms. . . .

By virtue one progresses toward higher forms of embodied existence; by vice, one goes down toward lower forms; by knowledge liberation is gained and by its opposite bondage; by nonattachment to mundane objects, one reaches the state of merging in primordial matter;[16] from desire impelled by passion further transmigration results; unimpeded movement is gained through the attainment of mastery and from its opposite, the opposite of free movement. . . .

In this transmigratory journey, the sentient spirit experiences the misery due to old age and death till such time as the subtle body also falls away; hence, in the very nature of existence, everything is misery.

Thus this activity caused by primordial matter starting with intellect and ending with gross elements is for the release of each individual spirit; it is really for the spirit, though it appears to be for itself. Just as insentient milk flows out for the purpose of the growth of the calf, even so is the activity of primordial matter intended for the release of the spirit. Just as

[14] This is the form in which one is said to transmigrate from one kind of birth to another.

[15] The subtle body is called *liṅga* because it is eventually "merged" (*līyate*) back into primordial matter.

[16] This is an intermediate state from which one proceeds to final release or to further transmigration. There are three kinds of bondage due to three kinds of mistaken notion: considering the performance of various acts of merit as being enough; identifying the spirit with one of the intruments of knowledge; and mistaking primordial matter to be the spirit. Those engaged in acts continue to be involved in bodies produced by the effects; the other two produce a state of merger in primordial matter.

to rid oneself of a longing, one indulges in activities in the world, even so does primordial matter act for freeing the spirit [from its own experience]. Just as a danseuse displays her art to the public and retires, even so does primordial matter unfold itself before the spirit and then retire. She [matter], the helpful lady, endowed with all the dispositions, selflessly carries out, by manifold means, the purpose of the spirit which, in reality, plays no helpful part in this activity, not being made of the three dispositions.[17] Methinks, there is nothing more tender than primordial matter, that poor thing which, once it has come within the sight of the spirit, never again appears before him.

Therefore, surely, no spirit is bound, none is released, none transmigrates; primordial matter, taking different forms, transmigrates, binds herself and releases herself. By her own seven forms [virtue and vice, ignorance, detachment and attachment, mastery and the lack of it], matter binds herself; and for the purpose of the spirit, she herself, with one of her forms, namely knowledge, causes release.

"I am not like this," "This is not mine," "This is not myself"—by repeated cognizance of this truth, pure knowledge, free from all error and of the form of the discrimination of the spirit from matter, arises. Whereby the spirit, remaining unaffected like a spectator, merely looks on at primordial matter, who has, on the cessation of her purpose,[18] ceased to evolve and has turned away from her sevenfold modification.[19] The one [spirit] is indifferent, because he has seen through matter; the other [primordial matter] has ceased to be active, because she has been seen through; even though their union continues for a time, there is no evolution. When virtue, etc., have ceased to be operative as cause, as a result of the rise of perfect knowledge, the spirit continues to be in an embodied state as a result of the impressions [caused by previous karma], even as a potter's wheel.[20] When the body falls [dies], and primordial

[17] The verse is couched in a poetic vein with *double entendre* depicting the activity of primordial matter (prakriti, a feminine noun) as that of a helpful housewife and the part of the spirit (purusha, a masculine noun) as that of the idle, sit-at-home husband.

[18] The experience of the spirit and his eventual release.

[19] The eighth, knowledge, being really not her form, but a reflection of the spirit and being the cause and itself the form of that discrimination which constitutes release; the other seven, virtue, vice, etc., which constitute bondage, good and bad, are mentioned as the forms from which matter now desists.

[20] Even though the pot has been produced and the potter has ceased to rotate the wheel, the wheel yet continues its revolutions owing to the prior momentum; similarly, when perfect knowledge has been produced, no more fresh evolution of matter or its modification

matter having fulfilled her role has retired, the spirit attains release which is both certain and complete.

This secret doctrine intended for the release of the spirit was declared by the Supreme Sage [Kapila]; here are analyzed the existence, origin, and merger of beings.

SHANKARA
Commentary on the Vedānta Sūtras

If Vedānta is the dominant philosophy of India today, the credit is due almost entirely to the genius of Shankara. Shankara's expressed aim was to promote the Truth revealed in the Upanishads, which he regarded as the highest message of the Veda. He wrote commentaries to several Upanishads and to the *Gītā*, besides the present one on the *Vedānta Sūtras*, and he tried to show that all these works expressed one and the same system, i.e., the system of pure monism (Advaita).

The basic principles of Shankara's philosophy derive from this concept of absolute nonduality. All plurality is seen as unreal and as superimposed upon the absolute unqualified Brahman which is one without a second. The false notions of plurality and causality arise from delusion or māyā which though without beginning may be eliminated through knowledge. Similarly, the individual soul, which appears different from other souls and also from Brahman is in fact nothing but the one unitary Brahman. Since ignorance lies at the root of the seeming duality, knowledge alone is regarded as the means to liberation. Religious actions have only a secondary function in that they may direct the mind to knowledge, but in themselves can never bring about liberation. Devotion, too, plays a role, though subordinate. For while Brahman is absolute existence, intelligence, and bliss, it may be regarded as possessing auspicious attributes characteristic of a personalized god (*īśvara*). Contemplation of this more limited conception of Brahman purifies the mind and prepares it for the higher knowledge of the unqualified Brahman. Much of Shankara's dialectic is based on this dual standard of absolute and relative—or higher and lower—knowledge. That knowledge which leads to liberation is not mere reasoning, but involves the introspective realization of the absolute unity of the individual soul and Brahman.

The *Aphorisms on the Brahman* or *on the Upaniṣads* (*Brahma* or *Vedānta*

---

take place, but those modifications that had already begun must run their course and they do so as long as that body lasts; on the fall of that body, the spirit is completely released. This applies to the Vedāntic theory of knowledge and release also. The state in which one is enlightened and yet embodied, the Vedānta calls *Jīvanmukti*.

Sūtras) of Bādarāyana is an ancient codification into a single unified system of the thought of the Upanishads, whose kernel may go back several centuries before Christ. In Shankara's time it was already considered an authoritative interpretation of the Upanishads. The manner in which Shankara expounds his philosophy, in the form of a commentary on this text, is highly illustrative of his general method, which is based on the rational interpretation of revealed truth. In the introduction to his commentary, Shankara demonstrates the essential duality between the subject (Self or soul) and the object (matter). The portion extracted here forms Shankara's commentary (bhāshya) on the first four aphorisms (sūtras) which are generally taken as a concise introduction to and epitome of his extensive commentary on the whole of the *Vedānta Sūtras*.

[From Shankara, *Brahmasūtra Bhaṣya*, 1.1.1–4]

INTRODUCTION ON "SUPERIMPOSITION"

When it is well understood that "object" and "subject," comprehended as "you" and "I" and opposed in nature like darkness and light, cannot be of each other's nature, much less could the properties of the two be of each other's nature; therefore when one superimposes on the "subject" comprehended as "I" and consisting of intelligence, the "object" comprehended as "You" and its properties, and superimposes the "subject" which is the reverse thereof and its properties on the "object," this superimposition, it stands to reason to believe, is a thing to be denied.

Still, superimposing the nature and attributes of one thing on those of another and without discriminating from each other the two totally distinct things, namely, the "object" and the "subject," there is this natural usage in the world, *"I am this"* and *"This is mine,"* which is due to a sublative notion and represents a confusion of the true and the false.

One may ask, what is this thing called "superimposition"? We say, it is the "appearance" in something of some other thing previously experienced and consists of a recollection.[1] Some call it the superimposition of the attributes of one thing on another; some say that where a thing is superimposed on another, it is the illusion due to the nonperception of their difference; still others hold that where there is a superimposition, it is the fancying in a thing of a property contrary to its nature. In any case, it does not cease to have the character of one thing appearing to

---

[1] For example, you have met John in London; when you come upon X in New York and accost him as John, you have really met someone in whom you recollect the likeness of John whom you have previously seen; the flash of John's likeness in X is later sublated when you come closer and say, "I am sorry . . ."; here John-ness is superimposed on X.

possess another's property. And so is our experience in the world: nacre shines like silver, and one moon, as if it had a second.

But how does the superimposition of "object" and its properties on the inner Self, which is not the "object," come about? On a thing before oneself one superimposes another thing, but you say, the inner Self, which falls outside the scope of what is comprehended as "you," is never an "object." The reply is: This inner Self is not a nonobject at all times, for it is the object of the notion "I" and there is the knowledge of the inner Self by immediate intuition.[2] There is no such rule that a superimposition has to be made only in an object that exists in front of one; for even in an imperceivable thing like the ether, boys superimpose a surface, dirt, etc. Thus it is not contradictory to speak of superimposition on the inner Self of things which are non-Self.

The superimposition so characterized, the learned consider to be nescience, and the determination of the real nature of a thing by discriminating that which is superimposed on it, they say is knowledge. When this is so, that on which a thing is superimposed is not affected in the slightest degree by either the defect or the merit of the superimposed thing. And it is due to this superimposition over one thing of another in respect of the Self and the non-Self—which is termed nescience—that all worldly transactions, of the means of knowledge and the objects thereof, take place, and [under the same circumstance] again, do all the scriptures, with their injunctions, prohibitions, and means of liberation operate.

But how do you say that sources of valid knowledge like perception and the scriptures fall within the purview of that which is conditioned by nescience? I shall reply: One devoid of the sense of "I" and "Mine" in the body, senses, etc., cannot be a cognizer and cannot resort to a means of cognition; for without resorting to the senses, there can be no activity of perception, etc.; and without a basis [the body] the activity of the senses is not possible; and none ever acts without a body on which the sense of the Self has not been superimposed. Nor could the Self, the unattached, be a cognizer, when none of these [body, senses, etc.] exist; and without a cognizer, the means of cognition do not operate. Hence it is under what

[2] As a conditioned Self it is presented as object in cognitions of "I" and as the unconditioned Self, it is known by immediate intuitive knowledge; in the latter case, as the Self itself consists of knowledge and does not depend on anything outside for its knowledge, it is by courtesy that a subject-object relation is stated.

is conditioned by nescience that all means of knowledge, perception, etc., as also the scriptures, come. . . .

In respect of activities relating to scriptural teachings, although an intelligent person does not become eligible to enter upon them unless he knows the Self as having a relation to the other world, still that truth called Self, which is to be known from the Upanishads, which transcends the physical needs like hunger and the distinctions like brāhman, kshatriya, etc., and which is not subject to transmigration, is not to be included in the eligibility [for scriptural activities], because that Self is of no use and is opposed to this kind of eligibility.[3] Operating as it does before the rise of the knowledge of that kind of Self, the scripture does come under things conditioned by nescience. Thus scriptural injunctions like "A brāhman shall perform the sacrifice" operate, consequent on the superimposition on the Self of particularities like class, stage, age, and condition.

We said that superimposition is the seeing of a thing in something which is not that; thus, when son, wife, etc., are all right or not, one considers one's own Self as all right or not, one superimposes external attributes on the Self; even so does one superimpose on the Self the attributes of the *body* when one considers that "I am corpulent, I am lean, I am fair, I stand, I go, I jump"; similarly attributes of the *senses* when one says, "I am dumb, one-eyed, impotent, deaf, blind"; and in the same manner the properties of the *internal organs,* e.g., desire, volition, cogitation, and resolution. Even so, man superimposes the [conditioned] Self presented in the cognition of "I" on the inner Self which is the witness of all the activities of the internal organ; and that inner Self, the very opposite and the witness of all, on the inner organ.

Thus without beginning or end, existing in the very nature of things, this superimposition which is of the form of a knowledge that is subject to sublation and is responsible for the agency and experience of man, is something which the whole world knows. It is for casting away this superimposition which is the cause of [all] evil and for gaining the knowledge of the oneness of the Self that all the Upanishads are begun. And how this is the purport of all the Upanishads, we shall show in this system of thought called the investigation into the Self that presides over the body [Śārīraka Mīmāṃsā].

[3] That real Self which neither acts nor enjoys is beyond the realm of a desire for such result as may accrue from a meritorious act or an activity intended for attaining such a desire.

Of this system of thought [also] called the *Vedānta Mīmāṃsā* [the enquiry into the purport of the Vedānta, i.e., the Upanishads], which it is my desire to explain, this is the first aphorism:

THEN THEREFORE THE DESIRE TO KNOW THE BRAHMAN

In the commentary to this aphorism Shankara defends his position against the related system called Pūrva Mīmāṃsā ("First Inquiry") in which the nature of ordained duty (dharma) and ordained action or ritual (karma) are investigated. Shankara devotes much of his attention to the refutation of other systems of thought, both orthodox and heterodox. In the passages quoted he tries to refute the claims of the Pūrva Mīmāmsakas that theirs was the only valid interpretation of the Vedas. Both schools of Mīmāmsakas ("scriptural exegetes") grew in response to the challenge of other systems of thought, chiefly Buddhism. Since the Veda was infallible it *a fortiori* had to be consistent, and to produce such a consistent system based on the Vedic scriptures was the aim of both schools. According to the Pūrva Mīmāṃsā the sole purpose of scripture was to set forth ordained duty, which was otherwise unknowable; this was done in scriptural passages stating injunctions or prohibitions. Since no Vedic passage could be lacking in purpose, all other passages were viewed as *arthavāda,* helpful explanations, praises, or condemnation in connection with some injunction or prohibition. Shankara criticizes the Pūrva Mīmāṃsā for holding that the meaning of the Veda consists only of prescriptions for action, whereas the Upanishads deal not with action but with knowledge (of the Brahman).

When it is accepted that the "then" [in the aphorism] has the meaning of "after" [something], just as the inquiry into dharma [duty] presupposes invariably the study of the Vedas which has just gone before that inquiry, so also, in the case of this inquiry into the Brahman, we must state what it is that has necessarily preceded it. That it is after the study of the Vedas is something common to both the inquiries, i.e., that into dharma and that into the Brahman, but is there not a difference here that the inquiry into the Brahman follows the knowledge of dharma? No; it is possible that one may have a desire to know the Brahman if one had read the Upanishads, even though one had not inquired into what dharma is. In scriptural texts like the one on the sundering of the heart [in sacrificing an animal], there is a fixed sequence of things, sequence being intended there [by the word "then"]; sequence that way is not meant here; for between the inquiry into dharma and the Brahman, there is no authority to show that one is complementary to the other or that a person qualified in the former [dharma] becomes eligible for the latter [Brahman].

Further between the two there is difference in respect of fruit as well as the object of the inquiry; the knowledge of dharma has the fruit of prosperity and it is dependent on observance of the respective duties; on the other hand, the knowledge of the Brahman has the fruit of everlasting bliss and is not dependent on any other activity. Also dharma which is desired to be known is a thing yet to come into being, as it is dependent on the person doing it; but the Brahman desired to be known here is a thing which exists already, because it is eternal and not dependent on the activity of a person. There is also difference between the two in regard to the operation of their respective sacred injunction: The sacred injunction[4] which defines dharma enlightens a person even as it engages him in the activity intended by it; on the other hand, the text relating to the Brahman[5] only enlightens a person; as knowledge is the direct result of the text, the person is not enjoined to an activity of knowing; just as an object is known when there is the contact of the sense organ and the object, even so is it here.

Therefore something must be set forth [as the preceding consideration] in close succession to which the inquiry into the Brahman is taught. I shall set it forth; the sense of discrimination as to things permanent and evanescent, nonattachment to objects of enjoyment here or in the hereafter, the accumulation of accessories like quietude and self-control,[6] and a desire to be liberated. When these are present, whether before an inquiry into dharma or after it, it is possible for one to inquire into the Brahman and know it, not when they are absent. Therefore, by the word "then," it is taught that this desire to know the Brahman follows immediately after the full acquisition of the spiritual accessories set forth above. . . .

Now that Brahman may be well known or unknown; if it is well known, there is no need to desire to know it; if on the other hand, it is unknown, it could never be desired to be known. The answer to this objection is as follows: The Brahman exists, eternal, pure, enlightened, free by nature, omniscient, and attended by all power. When the word "Brahman" is explained etymologically, it being eternal, pure and so on, are all understood, for these are in conformity with the meaning of the root *bṛh* [from which Brahman is derived]. The Brahman's existence is

---

[4] For example, "He who desires heaven shall perform the sacrifice" and so on.
[5] For example, "The Brahman is to be known" and so on.
[6] Others are retirement from activities, forbearance, mental concentration, and faith.

well known, because it is the Self of all; everyone realizes the existence of the Self, for none says, "I am not"; if the existence of the Self is not well known, the whole world of beings would have the notion "*I* do not exist." And the Self is the Brahman.

It may be contended that if the Brahman is well known in the world as the Self, it has already been known, and again it becomes something which need not be inquired into. It is not like that, for [while its existence in general is accepted], there are differences of opinion about its particular nature. Ordinary people and the materialists are of the view that the Self is just the body qualified by intelligence; others think that it is the intelligent sense-organs themselves that are the Self; still others, that it is the mind; some hold it as just the fleeting consciousness of the moment; some others as the void; [7] certain others say that there is some entity, which is different from the body, etc., and which transmigrates, does and enjoys; [8] some consider him as the enjoyer and not as the doer; [9] some that there is, as different from the above entity, the Lord who is omniscient and omnipotent.[10] According to still others, it is the inner Self of the enjoyer.[11] Thus, resorting to reasonings and texts and the semblances thereof, there are many who hold divergent views. Hence one who accepts some view without examining it might be prevented from attaining the ultimate good, and might also come to grief. Therefore, by way of setting forth the inquiry into the Brahman, here is begun the discussion of the meaning of the texts of the Upanishads, aided by such ratiocination as is in conformity to Scripture and having for its fruit the Supreme Beatitude.

It has been said that the Brahman is to be inquired into; on the question as to the characteristics of that Brahman, the blessed author of the aphorisms says:

WHENCE IS THE ORIGIN . . . OF THIS

. . . Of this universe made distinct through names and forms, having many agents and enjoyers, serving as the ground of the fruits of activities attended by specific places, times, and causes, and whose nature and design cannot be conceived even in one's mind—that omniscient, omnipotent cause wherefrom the origin, maintenance, and destruction of such a uni-

---

[7] The Buddhists.   [8] The Nyāya school.   [9] The Sānkhya school.
[10] This is according to the Yoga school where, besides the individual souls, there is a God.
[11] According to the Vedāntins, to whom the present text and its expounder belong.

verse proceed is the Brahman; such is the full meaning that is to be understood. . . .

It is not possible to discard the Lord, characterized as above, and suppose anything else, primordial matter devoid of intelligence,[12] atoms,[13] nonexistence, or a person subject to the transmigratory cycle as the cause of the origin, etc., of the universe characterized above.[14] Nor can it proceed from the very nature of things, for we require here [for production of a thing] a specific place, time, and cause.

This itself is taken by those philosophers who speak of the Lord as the cause of the universe, as an inference capable of demonstrating the existence, etc., of a Lord, different from the transmigrating individuals. And here, too, in the present aphorism, "whence, etc.," [15] is it not the same idea that is propounded? It is not so, for the aphorisms string together the flowers of the statements in the Vedānta [Upanishads]; [16] it is the Upanishadic statements that are cited in the form of aphorisms and examined. It is by the examination of the meaning of the scriptural texts and determining it exactly that Brahman-realization is achieved, not by inference and other sources of knowledge. The Vedāntic texts which speak of the cause of the origin, etc., of the world being there, inference, which would strengthen the understanding of their meaning and would be in conformity with the Vedāntic text, is not precluded from being one of the sources of knowledge; for ratiocination is accepted by scripture itself as an aid. Thus the Scripture says: "That Self is to be listened and thought over" [17] and shows in the text "Just as an intelligent man who has been well informed would reach the Gandhāra country," even so here, he who has a teacher knows" [18] that the Scripture takes the aid of human intellect. As

---

[12] This is the Sānkh'ya theory, refuted more fully later.

[13] This is the view of the Vaisheshika school, refuted more fully later.

[14] From aphorism four onward, these opposing views are tackled and refuted.

[15] Texts, aphorisms, verses, etc., were usually identified by citing the beginning word or words.

[16] What is meant by Shankara is that the second aphorism is not to be taken as supplying the inference to prove God, or as implying that inference is the main source of our knowledge of God; that may be so for logicians (followers of the Nyāya school), but certainly not for students of Vedānta for whom the scriptural statement about God forms the primary source of knowledge. The aphorisms are primarily a collection of statements from the scripture; when saying this Shankara presses into service also the meaning "thread," which the word sūtra has.

[17] Brhad Āraṇyaka Upaniṣad, 2.4.5.

[18] Chāndogya Upaniṣad, 6.14.2. In this text the usefulness of a personal teacher for pointing the way on the spiritual path is mentioned, and the illustration is given of an intelligent

far as the inquiry into the Brahman is concerned, scripture, etc., are not
the sole source of knowledge as in the case of the inquiry into dharma;
scripture, etc., and direct experience, etc., according to the occasion, are
sources of knowledge; for the knowledge of the Brahman has for its object something which already exists and completes itself in its direct experience. In a thing which is to be *done,* there is no need for experience, and
scripture, etc., may alone be the source of knowledge, for the thing to be
done depends, for its very coming into being, on the person [who proposes
to do it]. An act, whether mundane or ordained by scripture, may be done,
may not be done at all, or may be done in a different manner; likewise,
with reference to the scripture-ordained acts, the texts say: "One takes the
ṣoḍaśin cup in the *Atirātra* ritual" and also [elsewhere]: "One does not
take the *ṣoḍaśin* cup in the *Atirātra*"; also: "One offers oblations after
sunrise" and [elsewhere] "One offers oblations before sunrise." Injunctions and prohibitions too have meaning in this sphere, as also optional
rules and exceptions. But a thing as such does not admit of alternative
propositions like "It is thus" and "It is not thus," "It is" and "It is not";
alternative suppositions depend on the human mind, but knowledge of the
truth of a thing is not dependent on the human mind; on what then does
that depend? It is solely dependent on the thing itself. In respect of a
pillar the knowledge of its true nature cannot take the form, "This is
either the pillar or a man or something else"; "This is a man or something
else" is suppositious knowledge; "This is really a pillar" is correct knowledge, because the question depends on the nature of the thing. In this
manner, the validity of knowledge in respect of objects which are already
in existence depends on the things themselves.

Thus the knowledge of the Brahman too is dependent on the thing,
because the knowledge refers to a thing already in existence. The objection may be raised that, in so far as the Brahman is an object already in
existence, it can be surely comprehended by other means of knowledge
and the discussion on the Vedāntic texts becomes futile; this objection cannot hold because the Brahman is not within the provenance of the senses,
the invariable relation between it and its effect is not apprehensible in its
case; by nature, senses have for their object things of the world, not the
Brahman. It is only when the Brahman can be the object of sense-per-

---

man who wants to reach the Gandhāra country, but not knowing the way, asks men and
with the help of their information and direction, reaches his destination.

ception that one can apprehend that there is an effect which is related to the Brahman [its cause]; when the effect alone is apprehended [by the senses], it is not possible to decide if it is related to the Brahman or to something else; therefore the present aphorism mentioning origin, etc., is not for setting forth a theistic syllogism. But then what is it for? It is to draw attention to a Vedāntic text. What is the Vedāntic text that is intended to be indicated in this aphorism? It is the text [19] which begins with the words "Bhrigu, son of Varuna, approached his father Varuna with the request, 'O Blessed one, teach me the Brahman,'" and states: "That from which all these beings are born, that by which those born subsist and that into which those dying enter, that do you try to know; that is the Brahman." Of this Brahman [so characterized] the text which clinches its nature is the following: "From bliss it is that these beings are born; by bliss are those born sustained and into bliss do those dead enter." [20] Other texts of this kind, which speak of its being by nature eternal, pure, enlightened, and free, and of its being omniscient, and of the form of the Self and the cause, are also to be cited.

By showing the Brahman as the cause of the universe it has been suggested that the Brahman is omniscient; now to reinforce that omniscience the author of the aphorisms says:

AS IT IS THE SOURCE OF THE SCRIPTURE

Of the extensive scripture [Shāstra] comprising the *Rig Veda,* etc., reinforced and elaborated by many branches of learning, illumining everything even as a lamp, and like unto one omniscient, the source [lit. womb] is the Brahman. Of a scripture of this type, of the nature of the *Rig Veda* and the like, endowed with the quality of omniscience, the origin cannot be from anything other than the omniscient one. Whatever teaching has, for purposes of elaborate exposition, come forth from an eminent personage, as the science of grammar from Pānini, etc., though it is comprehensive of that branch of knowledge, it is well understood in the world that its exponent [e.g., Pānini] possesses knowledge far more than what is in his work; it therefore goes without saying that unsurpassed omniscience and omnipotence is to be found in that Supreme Being from whom, as the source, issued forth, as if in sport and without any effort, like the breathing of a person, this scripture in diverse recensions,

---

[19] *Taittiriya Upaniṣad,* 3.1.   [20] *Ibid.,* 3.6.

called *Rig Veda,* etc., which is the repository of all knowledge and is responsible for the distinctions into gods, animals, humans, classes, stages of life, etc.; this is borne out by scriptural texts like: "This that is called *Rig Veda* [and so on] is the breathings out of this Great Being." [21]

Or the scripture consisting of *Rig Veda,* etc., is the source, i.e., the authoritative means of knowing this Brahman in its real form; what is meant is that it is from the authoritative source of scripture that the Brahman, the cause of the origin, etc. of the universe is known.[22] The scriptural text concerned was cited under the previous aphorism: "That from which these things have their birth, etc." Wherefore then the present aphorism, when the Brahman being knowable from the scriptural source has already been shown by the previous aphorism which cites scriptural texts of this class? The reply is: In the previous aphorism the scripture has not been expressly stated and one might doubt that by that aphorism, "whence, etc.," a syllogistic proof of the Brahman has been set forth; to remove such a doubt, this aphorism came in, saying, "As it has the scripture as its source."

But how is it said [a Pūrva Mīmāmsaka might contend] that the Brahman is known from scripture? It has been shown by the statement: "As the scripture has action as its purpose such texts as do not have that purport are useless," [23] that the scripture refers to ritual action; therefore the Upanishads are useless as they do not have action as their purport; or as revealing the agent, the deity, etc., they are subservient to the texts which enjoin ritual action; or they are for enjoining some other activity like meditation. It is not possible that the Veda sets forth the nature of a thing already well established,[24] for a thing well established becomes the object of direct perception and other sources of knowledge; and even if such a thing is set forth, there is no human objective served by it, as there is nothing there to be avoided or desired. For this very reason, texts like "He wept," lest they should become meaningless, have been said to have meaning as recommendatory eulogies,[25] according to the statement "By

[21] *Bṛhad Āraṇyaka Upaniṣad,* 2.4.10.

[22] This is an additional interpretation of the same aphorism which reinforces what Shankara said last under the previous aphorism that the scripture is the primary source of knowledge about the Brahman, and inference or reasoning is only secondary.

[23] This is from the aphorisms of the Pūrva Mīmāmsā.

[24] The purpose of a Vedic text is to reveal what has not been known through well-known sources of knowledge.

[25] This is from a Vedic text of the class called *arthavāda,* which extols an injunction or

reason of syntactic unity with the injunctive texts, they might be for praising the injunctions." [26] Of the Vedic texts called mantras, e.g., "Thee for
nourishment," [27] the intimate association with the ritual has been shown,
as they speak of an act and its accessories; no Vedic text is seen anywhere
nor can it be justified without some relation to the enjoining of an act.
Such enjoining of an act is not possible in respect of the nature of a thing
which is well established, for injunction has for its object an action.
Therefore, by reason of revealing the nature of the agent, the deity, etc.,
required for the ritual, the Upanishads are complementary to the texts
enjoining ritual acts. If, however, this standpoint is not accepted, out of
the fear that the Upanishads represent a different context altogether, still,
the Upanishads may be held to have their purport in an activity like the
meditation set forth in their own texts. Therefore the Brahman is not to
be known from the scriptural source. In the face of that objection it is
said:

THAT, HOWEVER, IS SO BECAUSE OF TEXTUAL HARMONY

The word "however" is for warding off the *prima facie* view. That
Brahman, omniscient, omnipotent, and cause of the birth, existence, and
dissolution of the universe *is* known from the scripture as represented by
the Upanishads. How? "Because of textual harmony." In all the Upanishads the texts are in agreement in propounding, as their main purport,
this idea. For example, "Dear one! this thing Existence alone was at the
beginning"; [28] "The one without a second"; [29] "The Self, this one only,
existed at first"; [30] "This Brahman, devoid of anything before or after,
inside or outside"; [31] "This Self, the Brahman, the all-experiencing
one"; [32] "At first there was only this Brahman, the immortal one." [33]
When it is decisively known that the purport of the words in these texts
is the nature of the Brahman, and when unity is seen, to imagine a different purport is improper, as thereby one will have to give up what is
expressly stated and imagine something not stated. Nor could it be concluded that their purport is to set forth the nature of the agent, deity, etc.;

condemns its opposite by various means, etymological significance, a legendary illustration,
and so on. The Brāhmana part of the Veda has such texts. The present example "He wept"
is from the explanation of the name Rudra.

[26] This is another aphorism from the Pūrva Mīmāmsā.

[27] Used in a particular act in one of the sacrifices.   [28] *Chāndogya Upaniṣad*, 6.2.1.

[29] *Ibid.*   [30] *Aitareya Upaniṣad*, 1.1.1.   [31] *Bṛhad Āraṇyaka Upaniṣad*, 2.5.19.

[32] *Ibid.*   [33] *Muṇḍaka Upaniṣad*, 2.2.11.

for there are texts like "Then whom should It see and with what?," [34] which refute action, agent, and fruit.

Because the Brahman is a thing already well established, it cannot be held to be the object of perception by senses, etc.; for the truth that the Brahman is the Self, as set forth in the text "That thou art," [35] cannot be known without the scripture. As regards the objection that since there is nothing here to be avoided or desired, there is no use in teaching it, it is no drawback; it is from the realization that the Self is the Brahman, devoid of things to be avoided or desired, that all miseries are ended and the aspiration of man is achieved. If the mention of deity, etc., means the meditations expressed in the texts themselves, there is really no contradiction; thereby, the Brahman cannot become complementary to a text enjoining a meditation; for, because the Brahman is one and devoid of things to be avoided or desired, it stands to reason that It overcomes the notion of all duality of action, agent, etc. Once thrown out by the knowledge of oneness in the Brahman, the dualistic notion cannot have that resurgence whereby one could hold that the Brahman is subservient to the meditative injunction. Although, in other parts of the scripture, texts may not be authoritative without some relation to the injunction enjoining actions, yet it is not possible to repudiate the authoritativeness of that part of the scripture concerning the knowledge of the Self, for this knowledge is seen to lead to its fruit [36] [Self-realization]. The authoritativeness of scripture is not to be deduced by inference [37] for which there is a need to look for an analogical instance experienced elsewhere. Therefore it is established that the Brahman is authoritatively known from scripture.

THE WAY OF DEVOTION

The characteristic feature of medieval Hinduism is the great upsurge and spread of devotional movements. However intense was activity in the domain of metaphysics, the worship of a personal God, in one form or another, became the dominant trend and influenced even the schools of

[34] *Bṛhad Āraṇyaka Upaniṣad*, 2.4.13.   [35] *Chāndogya Upaniṣad*, 6.8.7.
[36] This is in reply to the objection of futility.
[37] That is, a syllogism based on the argument of fruitfulness as applicable to injunctive texts which prescribe action. The Nyāya school employs the analogy of the medical science in a syllogism to prove the authoritativeness of scripture.

philosophy in the direction of theism. Unquestionably the most important literary sources of this movement were the two epics, the *Rāmāyaṇa* and the *Mahābhārata,* which enshrined in the hearts of the people a divine personality adored as the fountainhead of all beauty and goodness and as the repository of infinite excellences. Following the epics, the Purānas, which dealt with the missions that the Lord fulfilled in the world by taking upon Himself many incarnations, had a wide appeal among the masses. Like the epic, the Purāna, by presenting to us the origin and cosmography of the world, the process of time, the rise and fall of kingdoms, and the conflicts of good and evil forces, reminds us that mundane possessions are ephemeral, that the Almighty alone is worth aspiring for. The Purānas, in fact, became the bibles of popular Hinduism. They expatiated on the glories and exploits of different forms of divinity, set forth in extenso the types of worship, and described the sacred shrines in different holy places to which pilgrimages were made by the devout. These Purānas were recounted to large popular audiences, who also thronged to temples which kings had dedicated to the various gods and where the same stories could be seen depicted in attractive sculpture and painting. When music, dance, and drama were added to the regular daily service of these deities, the temples not only proved great centers of attraction for the people, but also came to play a role second only to the kings as patrons of all the arts. As practices accessory to devotion, the observance of vows and austerities (*vratas*) and pilgrimages to holy waters (*tīrthas*) for baths were also approved and encouraged in the Purānas. The development of dispassion and detachment (*vairāgya*), sacrifice of possessions (*tyāga*), abstinence and moderation, and the cultivation of tranquillity and retirement were likewise recommended.

The eighteen main Purānas, the eighteen minor Purānas, and the many Samhitās and other Purāna-like compilations all dealt with the subjects set forth above. Among them, the *Purāna of the Lord* (*Bhāgavata Purāna,* c. eighth or ninth century A.D.) gained, by its extraordinary popularity, a place rivaled only by that of the epic *Rāmāyaṇa.* This Purāna deals with the incarnations that the Lord repeatedly takes to restore the balance of values in the world, by putting down evil and reviving virtue. The book is noteworthy for its own unique way of dealing with the story of the Lord in His incarnation as Krishna and the ecstatic type of devotion exemplified by the cowherd lasses (*gopīs*) for the Lord. There is the Supreme

Being, the Brahman, of which the Personal God is a form assumed freely for blessing the universe. That one omniscient, omnipotent God, transcendent as well as immanent, takes for the further benefit of humanity manifold forms and incarnations through His mystic potency (māyā). In these forms, He engages Himself in action in the world without being contaminated by the stain of action and its fruit, which would otherwise produce bondage and transmigration. In this role the Lord—living in the world and yet out of it, acting at His own instance, selflessly and regardless of fruit—is the exemplar of the path of true and noble action, karma-yoga, and to all who want to serve the world (lokasaṅgraha), He, the Yogin and expert doer (karma-kuśala) is the model. Emulating Him, walking in His footsteps, taking refuge under Him, abandoning the sense of oneself as the agent, having faith in His grace and compassion rather than in one's own capacity, confessing one's shortcomings and praying to Him, adoring Him, repeating His name, wearing emblems to identify oneself as belonging to Him, singing or writing of Him, worshiping Him in an image at one's home or in a temple, communing with fellow worshipers, seeing His immanence in all beings and therefore venerating all humanity—all these are ways of practicing devotion to Him and thereby realizing Him.

Each of these fundamental ideas of the cult of devotion tended to be developed into a systematic doctrine and school of its own. Thus "surrendering oneself to God" was the theme of schools which advocated one kind of surrender or another. So, too, with the doctrine of the Lord's grace. Among the Shrīvaishnavas [1] of the South, there are two well-known doctrines, one of which insists that the Lord's grace must be met with an effort on one's own part as well, while the other contends that man need do no more than place himself meekly and completely in the hands of God, who will protect the supplicant. The reciting of the Lord's name, like surrender to Him, became of great importance; throughout the nation men and women ceased to adopt fanciful proper names and everyone was named after a god or goddess, so that whatever name was uttered, one might indirectly be calling upon God. One counted God's name on a rosary or sang a hymn containing a string of the Lord's names and epithets. A body of ideas and writings grew up on the efficacy of reciting God's name and on how to do it.

[1] *Śrīvaiṣṇavas*, devotees of Vishnu with the Goddess Shrī (*Śrī*) as Mediator.

Each school of devotion had its own sacred formula or mantra, embodying the most significant of the names of the deity. For example, the celebrated five-syllabled mantra of the worshipers of Shiva runs: *Oṃ Namaḥ Śivāya,* meaning "*Oṃ,* Obeisance to Shiva." Similarly the eight-syllabled mantra of the worshipers of Vishnu-Nārāyana is: *Oṃ Namo Nārāyaṇāya,* "*Oṃ,* Obeisance to Nārāyana." The initiation into this mantra and its recitation was had at the hands of one's spiritual teacher (guru), who in all schools was esteemed as next or equal to God.

These various ways in which God was worshiped came to be codified into the school of devotion, the Bhakti Mīmāmsā (Inquiry into Bhakti), which apart from the major theistic systems of philosophy, had its own sūtras (aphoristic texts), expositions, and subsidiary literature. There are two sets of aphorisms on devotion (*Bhakti Sūtras*) ascribed to Sage Shāndilya and Nārada, which define what devotion is, emphasize its importance and superiority, and classify its forms. To illustrate the nature of man's approach to God and the degree or intensity of his devotion, various analogies were made with the relationship between friends, servant and master, son and father, etc. The most ecstatic form of devotion was considered to be that which resembled the yearning of separated lovers for each other, just as the cowherd lasses yearned for Krishna.

The three deities upon which the principal devotional movements centered were Vishnu, Shiva, and Shakti or Devī the Goddess. Each of these was worshiped under various aspects, the two most popular incarnations of Vishnu being Rāma and Krishna. The concept of the Mother Goddess Shakti carried with it a host of minor goddesses and female deities, worshiped according to esoteric practices set forth in texts called *Tantras.* Among the more prominent subsidiary sects were the worship of the Sun; Ganesha, the elephant-headed god; and Kumāra-Kārttikeya, the war-god. Even such powers as the planets (*graha*) were propitiated. Among minor devotional movements there were also some which centered around celebrated teachers and saints.

Among theistic schools of philosophy there were monistic and dualistic schools of Shaivism, chiefly in Kashmir and South India. The Nyāya system was, on its religious side, affiliated with different sects of Shaivites. The Vedānta offered a variety of interpretations of the relation between the Supreme Soul and the individual soul as developed by Bhāskara,[2]

---

[2] He came immediately after Shankara and held an identity-*cum*-difference in respect of the relation between the Supreme Soul and the individual soul.

Rāmānuja (d. 1137), Shrīkantha, Madhva (1199–1278), Vallabha (1479–1531), Nimbārka, and the followers of Chaitanya (b. 1485). The followers of Rāmānuja looked upon the souls as constituting the body (*śeṣa*) of the Lord (*Śeṣin*) who was the Supreme Soul. Madhva conceived of God and man as totally distinct and as Master and servant. The conception of deliverance (mukti, moksha) or salvation also differed. In most of these religious schools, emancipation was to be enjoyed in a sublime and unique world or heaven, in which case the substance of deliverance was defined as gaining a place in the Lord's world (*sālokya*) and precious proximity to Him (*sāmīpya*). According to two other views, devotees who had achieved the realization of God attained the same form as their God (*sārūpya*) or became in some way absorbed in Him (*sāyujya*).

Even the monistic philosophy of Shankara and his followers had a place for devotion to the personal God, whose grace was considered necessary to that spiritual awakening or knowledge of the Self which led to emancipation. Some of the most appealing devotional hymns are attributed to Shankara and his followers. Tradition also informs us of the reorganization of temple worship at many centers by Shankara. The distinctive feature of Shankara's teaching concerning devotion is that the various forms and names are seen as representing but one principle of divinity, whereas in the other schools one particular form and name, Shiva or Vishnu, alone is the God to be worshiped. A devotee of Shankara's school may find that a particular form of divinity appeals to him most, but he will be quite catholic in his veneration or worship of other deities; in the latter case, however, the approach is definitely sectarian.

There was thus no school of thought which failed to attach a very high value to devotion. Advocates of devotion insisted that without it all austerities, rituals, virtues, learning, or any other aspect of spiritual endeavor would be meaningless and ineffective. It was devotion that gave one real status, not birth. Among devotees there was no caste, no distinction of high or low, except that those who lacked devotion were considered the lowliest. Such a view naturally gave God's grace, called forth by true and intense devotion, an overriding power over the fate that beset one as a result of one's own actions.

The literature and school of thought styled *Āgama* and *Tantra* may best be appreciated when taken together with the literature and school of devotion. The word *Āgama*, originally applied to the Veda, means strictly a tradition of knowledge or practice handed down from teachers to pupils;

later *Āgama* came to mean a school of texts and practices of devotion to different deities, which was outside the strict scope of the Vedic teachings. A large body of texts, which their adherents believed as much revealed scriptures as the Veda, grew up under Āgama, relating to the worship of different deities, chiefly Shiva, Vishnu, and Devī or Shakti. All schools of Shaivism and Vaishnavism freely draw upon the authority of the Āgamas to reinforce their interpretation of Vedānta. The Āgama expatiates on the philosophical position, the greatness of the particular divinity upheld, and the modes and specifications of the worship of that deity. Accordingly they comprise the sections jnāna, yoga, kriyā, and charyā (philosophy, the esoteric teachings, the worship of images in temples, and religious conduct and practices).

The Tantras are of a like nature, but revel more in esoteric teachings. Apart from the teaching of mystic formulas, mantras, which are common to the Āgamas and other theistic schools, they have developed a complex mystic symbolism of letters, and employ, along with images, mystic diagrams or charts called *yantras* or *cakras*.

THE TEACHERS
NĀRADA

Aphorisms on Devotion
[From *Bhakti Sūtras*, 1–22, 25–70, 72–84]

Now then, we shall expound devotion. Devotion consists of supreme love for God. It also consists of immortality.[1] On obtaining that, man has achieved everything, he becomes immortal, he is completely satisfied. Having got it, he desires nothing else, he grieves not, he hates nothing, he delights not in anything else, he strives for nothing; having realized which, man becomes as if intoxicated, and benumbed; he delights in his own intrinsic bliss.

Devotion is not like ordinary passion, as it is the suppression of all other preoccupations. This suppression of preoccupations is the giving up of the activities of the world as well as those [namely, the rituals] ordained by the Vedas.

Devotion is complete and exclusive absorption in God and indifference

---

[1] Or, is supremely delectable like ambrosia. This is the double meaning of *amṛta*.

to things opposed to Him. Completeness or exclusiveness of devotion to Him means the abandoning of anything else or anybody else as one's prop and support. And indifference to things opposed to Him means the doing and observance of only those things in the world or the Vedas which are conducive to devotion towards Him.

One may observe the scriptural ordinances after one's faith in God has been firmly established, for otherwise the devotee may be deemed to have fallen off from the standard of ordained conduct. Similarly, worldly activities, like taking food, should be kept up by the devotee only to the extent needed for keeping his body.

I shall set forth the characteristics of devotion according to different views: Sage Vyāsa says that devotion is the continuous desire one has to perform the worship, etc., of God. Sage Garga opines that such a desire to listen to the stories, etc., of God is devotion. Sage Shāndilya holds that all such desires [for worship, listening to the Lord's story, etc.] should be without detriment to one's delight in the Self. But Nārada [i.e., the present author] describes devotion as dedication of all acts to God and the intense anguish when one slips from his absorption in God: there have been examples of such devotion, as in the case of the cowherd lasses of the Brindāvan.[2] . . .

Devotion is superior to action, knowledge, or yogic contemplation; for devotion is itself its fruit, and God loves the meek and dislikes those who are proud [of their attainments].

Some say that knowledge alone is the means of acquiring devotion to God, but others opine that knowledge and devotion are interdependent. According to Nārada [the writer], devotional love is itself its end. We can see this in cases like one's knowledge of a palace or a feast; certainly by one's knowledge of a palace one does not gain the satisfaction that he is a king or by one's knowledge of a feast one's hunger is not appeased. Therefore those desiring salvation should take to devotion alone.

Now, the means of acquiring devotion are set forth by teachers: 1) renunciation of sense pleasures and mundane associations; 2) ceaseless adoration of the Lord; 3) even when one is with others, engaging oneself in the listening to and the singing of the glory of the Lord; 4) chiefly the grace of the great souls or a particle of divine grace itself.

[2] The cowherd village on the banks of the Yamunā where Lord Krishna spent his childhood.

The association of the great souls [mahātman] is hard to acquire, hard to be had completely, but is always fruitful. For gaining even that association, one requires God's blessing; for between God and His men there is no difference. So try to acquire the company of the holy souls; strive for that.

And, by all means, shun evil company; for that is responsible for passion, wrath, delusion, loss of the thought of the Lord, the loss of knowledge, in fact all kinds of loss; these evil traits swell up like an ocean by reason of bad company.

Who crosses over the illusion of phenomenal existence? He who gives up evil association, who waits upon the high-souled ones, who becomes freed of the ego; he who resorts to a secluded spot, uproots worldly bondage, transcends the three dispositions and stops worrying himself about acquiring something or safeguarding something acquired; he who abandons the fruit of actions, renounces all action, and thereby transcends the pairs of joy and sorrow, gain and loss, and so on; he who lays aside even scriptures and cultivates solely uninterrupted love for God. He saves himself and becomes also the savior of the world.

Devotion is something indescribable; it is like the taste that a dumb man enjoys. But it is occasionally revealed when there is somebody deserving of it. It is absolute, not vitiated by desire for anything, multiplying every minute of its existence, and is uninterrupted; it is a highly sublime form of experience. One who has it looks at it only, listens to it alone, and thinks of nothing else.

Devotion may also be qualified in these ways, by reason of the three dispositions, as of purity, of passion, and of darkness, or by reason of the condition of the devotee, namely, one in distress, one who is curious to know, and one who has an object in view. Of these three varieties, the preceding ones are superior to the succeeding ones.

Compared to other paths, devotion is easiest. It stands in need of no external proof and it is its own proof; for it is of the very form of tranquillity and supreme bliss.

The devotee should have no anxiety if the world slips away from him; for has he not surrendered himself, the world, and the scriptures to the Lord? However, even when one is established in devotion, one should not voluntarily give up normal activities, but he should certainly give up the fruits of his actions and learn how to give them up.

The devotee should not listen to accounts of women's beauty, riches, and what unbelievers say; should cast away pride and vanity. Offering up all his activities to God, he should show his desire or anger or pride only in activities on His behalf.

Transcending the tripartite distinction of love, lover, and object of love, one should develop that love which consists of continuous service and is like the yearning of a beloved for her lover. Those who are exclusive lovers are the chief devotees; with choked voices and streaming eyes, they commune among themselves; they are the souls who sanctify our homes and the world; they make holy spots holy, sanctify acts, and render scriptures sacred. For they are full of God. . . .

Among such devotees there is no distinction of birth, learning, appearance, pedigree, wealth, or profession; for they belong to God.

A devotee should not get involved in discussion about God; for reasoning cuts in anyway and there is no finality about it. Texts which speak of devotion should be honored and the acts taught therein followed. Anxious to gain a time free from the preoccupation of pleasure or pain, desire or gain, one should not waste even a split second. One should observe nonviolence, truth, purity, compassion, faith, and other virtues.

Ever and with all heart, devotees should, without any other thought, worship only the Lord. When He is sung of, He hastens to present Himself and bestow on devotees His experience. Devotion to God is true for all times and is superior to everything else; it is superior.

Devotion, which is really one, yet takes eleven forms: attachment to the greatness of the Lord's qualities, to His form; being engrossed in His worship, and His thought; attachment to Him as a servant, as a friend, as a child or as toward a child, and as a beloved; surrendering oneself unto Him; seeing Him everywhere; and inability to bear the separation from Him.

So do they declare in one voice, without fear of what people say, the teachers of the path of devotion, Kumāra, Vyāsa, Shuka, Shāndilya, Garga, Vishnu, Kaundinya, Shesha, Uddhava, Āruni, Bali, Hanumān, Vibhīshana, and others. He who has faith in this wholesome teaching that Nārada has given gains devotion and gains that most beloved object [God]; indeed he gains that Dearest Thing.

KAPILA
The Purāna of the Lord

The *Purāṇa of the Lord,* dedicated to the different incarnations of the Lord including that of Krishna, has probably served to inspire and unify the devotional movements more than any other single text. Here, in one of the earlier books, Sage Kapila teaches the path of devotion to his mother Devahūti. Sage Kapila is identified as one of the manifestations of the Lord and as the promulgator of the Sānkhya philosophy. The account of the Sānkhya in Purānic literature is always theistic and the *Purāṇa of the Lord* completely integrates it with the path of devotion. The treatment of the doctrine also is remarkable for the way in which the same Purāna criticizes the aberrations and empty forms and rites which may unfortunately parade as devotion instead of being the true realization of the presence of the Lord everywhere.

[From *Bhāgavata Purāṇa,* 3.29.7–34; 6.1.11–18; 6.2.14; 7.5.24; 11.3.18–32; 11.27.7–51]

THE PATH OF DEVOTION (Bhakti-yoga)

[The Lord, Sage Kapila, tells His mother Devahūti:]

Blessed lady! The path of devotion is conceived in various ways according to different approaches; for by reason of nature, qualities, and approach, the minds of men differ.

That devotee, who, in a harmful manner, with vanity and intolerance, goes about ostentatiously, making distinctions between one being and another, and practices devotion, is of the lowest type, impelled by ignorance.[1]

Contemplating material enjoyment, fame, or riches, he who, still making distinctions, worships Me in images, etc., is of the middling type, impelled by desire.[2]

He who adores Me with a view to put an end to all actions [good or bad] or offering up all his actions to Me, the Supreme Being, or worships Me because I must be worshipped,[3] he is of the superior type, though he has yet the sense of difference. . . .

The characteristic of pure devotion to the Supreme Being is that it has no motive and is incessant. . . .

That devotion is described as absolute by which one transcends the

[1] The manifestation of the disposition of "darkness."
[2] The manifestation of "passion."   [3] The manifestation of "purity."

three dispositions [purity, passion, and darkness] and renders himself fit to become one with Me. . . .

I am always present in all beings as their soul and yet, ignoring Me, mortal man conducts the mockery of image-worship. He who ignores Me resident in all beings as the Soul and Master, and, in his ignorance, takes to images, verily pours oblations on ash [i.e., worships in vain]. The mind of that man who hates Me abiding in another's body, who, in his pride, sees invidious distinctions and is inimically disposed to all beings, never attains tranquillity. Blessed lady! when the worshiper is one who insults living beings, I am not satisfied with his worship in My image, however elaborate the rites and manifold the materials of his worship. Doing one's appointed duty, one should adore Me, the Master, in images and the like, only so long as one is not able to realize in one's own heart Me who am established in every being. That man of invidious perception who draws the line between himself and another, him Death pursues with his dangerous fear.

Therefore, with charity and honor and with friendship toward all and a nondifferentiating outlook, one should worship Me, the Soul of all beings, as enshrined in all beings. . . .

Honoring them, one should mentally bow to all the beings, realizing that the Lord the Master has entered them with an aspect of His own being. [3.29.7–34]

DEVOTION TO GOD THE GREATEST EXPIATION

The removal of sinful acts by expiatory rites which are also acts is not final; [4] expiatory acts are for the unintelligent; knowledge is expiation. When one keeps eating only wholesome food, diseases do not assail him; therefore one who observes the disciplines gradually qualifies himself for the supreme welfare. . . . But some, dependent solely on God, cast away all sin completely, even as the sun sweeps away the fog, solely through devotion to God. If one is averse to the Lord, no amount of expiation will purify him. [6.1.11–18]

[4] An act also carries with it the possibility of lapses; if expiation for a lapse is sought by another act, that expiatory act is liable to further lapses and so on ad infinitum; therefore an expiation of another order or plane alone can be final and that is taught here as devotion to the Lord and the recital of His name with devotion.

THE LORD'S NAME

The Teachers consider the utterance of the Lord's name as destructive of sin completely, even when the utterance is due to the name being associated with something else, or is done jocularly, or as a result of involuntary sound, or in derision.[5] [6.2.14]

NINE KINDS OF DEVOTION

Listening to the Lord's glory, singing of Him, thinking of Him, serving His feet, performing His worship, saluting Him, serving Him, friendship with Him, declaring oneself as His [surrendering oneself to Him][6] —if man could offer unto the Lord devotion of these *nine* kinds, that indeed I would consider as the greatest lesson one has learned. [7.5.24]

THE DOINGS OF THE DEVOTEE[7]

One should therefore resort to a teacher, desiring to know what constitutes the supreme welfare. . . . Taking the teacher as the deity, one should learn from him the practices characteristic of the Lord's devotees. . . . First detachment from all undesirable associations, then association with the good souls, compassion, friendliness, and due humility toward all beings, purity, penance, forbearance, silence, study of sacred writings, straightforwardness, continence, nonviolence, equanimity, seeing one's own Self and the Lord everywhere, seeking solitude, freedom from home, wearing clean recluse robes, satisfying oneself with whatever comes to one, faith in the scriptures of devotion and refraining from censure of those of other schools, subjugation of mind, speech, and action, truthful-

---

[5] This is the doctrine generally subscribed to on the popular level; but at the higher levels it is insisted that the true recital of God's name is that in which the devotee understands the full significance of the Lord's glory and realizes the omnipresence of the Lord.

[6] Complete surrender to the Lord, called *prapatti* or *śaraṇāgati* is the cardinal doctrine of the theology of South Indian Shrīvaishnavism; accordingly this school considers *Bhagavad Gītā*, 18.66, in which the Lord tells Arjuna: "Giving up all duties, take refuge under Me alone; I shall deliver you from all sins," as the final teaching (*carama-śloka*); and the chief sacred formula of the school, which has two parts, runs: 1) I seek as refuge the feet of Nārāyaṇa, Lord of the Goddess of Fortune; 2) Obeisance to Nārāyaṇa, Lord of the Goddess of Fortune (*Śrīman-nārāyaṇa-caraṇau śaraṇam prapadye; Śrīmate nārāyaṇāya namaḥ*). The Goddess from whom the Lord cannot be separated acts as the mediator between the devotee and the Lord.

[7] The following selections are taken from the eleventh book of the *Purāṇa of the Lord;* the second and the third selections form the part of the teachings of Lord Krishna to His best friend, devotee and kinsman, Uddhava. The range of the topics in the selections given here corresponds to that of the contents of Vaishnava Āgamas and Tantras.

ness, quietude, restraint, listening to accounts of the Lord's advents, exploits, and qualities, singing of the Lord, contemplation of the Lord of wonderful exploits, engaging in acts only for His sake, dedicating unto the Lord everything—the rites one does, gifts, penance, sacred recital, righteous conduct and whatever is dear to one like one's wife, son, house, and one's own life—cultivating friendship with those who consider the Lord as their soul and master, service to the Lord and to the world and especially to the great and good souls, sharing in the company of fellow devotees the sanctifying glory of the Lord, sharing with them one's delight, satisfaction and virtues of restraint, remembering oneself and reminding fellow-worshipers of the Lord who sweeps away all sin; bearing a body thrilled with devotion and ecstatic experience of the Lord, now in tears with some thought of the Lord, now laughing, now rejoicing, now speaking out, now dancing, now singing, now imitating the Lord's acts, and now becoming quiet with the blissful experience of the Supreme—such are the Lord's devotees, who behave like persons not of this world. [11.3.18–32]

THE METHOD OF WORSHIPING GOD IN HIS SYMBOL

[The Lord says;] My worship is of three kinds, Vedic, Tantric, and mixed. . . . In an image, on ground, in fire, in the sun, in the waters, in one's own heart, or in a brāhman, one should with suitable materials, with love, and without deception, worship Me, the Master.

First at dawn, one should have his bath, after washing his teeth, etc. . . . then do the worship of the *sandhyā* [8] and other duties ordained by the Veda; and with the rites and mantras prescribed in the Veda, one should conduct My worship, taking the resolve [9] properly; it is indeed My worship that sanctifies the observance of other duties. [10]

God's images are of eight kinds: of stone, wood, metal, plaster, painting,

[8] The *sandhyās* are the three junctions of the day, sunrise, noon, and sunset, when a twice-born is to worship *Gāyatrī*, the deity presiding over solar energy and the stimulator of intellect.

[9] This is what is called *saṅkalpa* or the utterance of the resolution of the mind that I, so and so, will perform such and such a rite or religious act for such and such a deity or other object of propitiation for such and such a purpose or according to such and such a scriptural injunction.

[10] After the first establishment of the complete theistic conviction, Vedic rites acquired a theistic orientation; the performance of *sandhyā*, of *śrāddha* in honor of manes, feasting of brāhmans, everything was for the propitiation of, and as dedication to, the Supreme Lord; and to this effect a statement was expressly made at the beginning or end of the act.

sand, *mind,* and precious gem. The image in which My spirit dwells is of two kinds, the fixed and the moving; in worship with a fixed image, there is to be no periodic calling forth of the divine presence in it and the bringing to an end of such divine presence; with a moving image, these may be done; and in a symbolic image on the ground such invocation and calling off of the divine presence have to be done. . . .

Without any deceit, the devotee should conduct My worship with well-known materials that are available and with love in his heart.

When I am worshiped in an icon, bathing Me and decorating Me are welcome; when I am worshiped on ground, the method of worship is to invoke there with the appropriate mantras the divine presence of the respective deities; when worshiped in fire, worship takes the form of the oblations with ghee. When I am to be worshiped in the sun, adoration by prostration, offering of water with mantras, muttering of prayer, etc., are best; when worshiped in the waters, the offering of water with mantras is to be done; for even some water offered to Me with love by a devotee pleases Me most; even elaborate offerings, sandal, incense, flowers, light, food, etc., made by one who is devoid of devotion, do not satisfy Me.

WORSHIP IN AN IMAGE

Having purified oneself and having gathered the materials of worship, the devotee should sit on his seat of sacred *darbha* grass, facing east or north and conduct the worship with the image in front of him. He should then utter the incantations with appropriate gestures [mudrās] which render his different limbs and hands duly charged with spiritual power; he should then invoke with mantras and proper gestures My presence in the image.

He should keep in front a vessel of sanctified water and with that water sprinkle thrice the image, the materials of worship, himself, and the vessels.

Then the devotee should, in his own body purified by the control of breath and the awakening of fire [slumbering at the basic plexus, *mūlādhāra*], contemplate in the lotus of his heart My subtle form, the form which the men of realization meditate upon as abiding on the fringes of *Oṃ*.[11] When the devotee's whole being has become pervaded

---

[11] *Oṃ* or *praṇava* is the greatest of all the mystic spells (mantras) of Hinduism; it is composed of five parts, A, U, M, the stop (*bindu*), and the resonance (*nāda*); beyond the

by My form, which is the inner Soul of all beings, the devotee shall, having become completely immersed in Myself, make My presence overflow into the image, etc., established in front of him, and then, with all the paraphernalia, conduct My worship.

He must first offer Me seat; My seat is made of nine elements, virtue, knowledge, dispassion, and mastery as the four feet and the opposites of these as the enclosed plank on which I sit; the other parts of My seat are the three sheets spread over the sitting plank, these three representing the three dispositions [purity, etc.] of which My own mystic potency [māyā] is composed; there are also to be established on the seat My nine powers [shakti]; [12] and at the center of the seat an eight-petalled lotus, shining with its pericarp and filaments; and having prepared My seat thus, the devotee should, by the Vedic and Tantric methods and for the attainment of the two fruits of welfare here and in the hereafter, make to Me the different offerings of worship. . . .

When offering Me the bath with fragrant water, the Vedic mantras beginning with *Suvarṇagharma*,[13] the *Puruṣa Sūkta*,[14] and the *Sāma Veda* chants like *Rājana* [15] should be recited.

With clothes, sacred thread, jewels, garlands, and fragrant paste, My devotee should decorate My form suitably and with love. With faith, My worshiper should then offer Me water to wash, sandal, flower, unbroken rice,[16] incense, light, and food of different kinds; also attentions like anointing, massage, showing of mirror, etc., and entertainments like song and dance; these special attentions and entertainments may be done on festive days and even daily.

EMOTIONAL ADORATION

One should engage himself in singing of Me, praising Me, dancing with My themes, imitating My exploits and acts, narrating My stories or listening to them.

---

realm of the fifth dwells the Lord. No worship in a material image is good without such mental contemplation of the Lord.

[12] All these details which give the inner significance to the gross rituals and materials of worship are briefly referred to in the text and explained fully in the commentary. The nine powers or shaktis of the Lord are purity, exaltation, knowledge, action, mystic union, inclination, truth, mastery, and grace.

[13] *Taittirīya Āraṇyaka*, 3.11.   [14] *Rig Veda*, 10.90.

[15] Beginning with the words, *"Indram naro."* These give an indication of how the Vedic hymns were adapted to the later devotional development.

[16] Unbroken rice grain is scattered on a person or image as an auspicious act during festivities, marriage, worship, blessing, etc.

With manifold hymns of praise of Me, taken from the *Purāṇas* or from the local languages (Prakrits),[17] the devotee should praise and pray to Me that I bless him and prostrate himself completely before Me. With his head and hands at My feet, he should pray, "My lord, from the clutches of death [i.e., the cycle of birth and death], save me who have taken refuge under You." . . .

Whenever and wherever one feels like worshiping Me in images, etc., one should do so; I am, however, present in oneself and in all beings; for I am the Soul of everything.

Thus worshiping me with Vedic and Tantric methods, one attains through Me the desired welfare here and in the hereafter.

PUBLIC WORSHIP

Having consecrated an image of Me one should build a firm temple for Me, and beautiful flower gardens around for conducting daily worship and festivals. For the maintenance of My worship, etc., in special seasons as well as every day, one should bestow fields, bazaars, townships, and villages,[18] and thereby attain to My own lordship. [11.27.7–51]

LOKĀCHĀRYA
The Triad of Categories

The *Triad of Categories* (*Tattvatraya*) of Lokāchārya (thirteenth century) belongs to the literature of South Indian Shrīvaishnavism or Vishishtādvaita (i.e. the nondualism of the qualified Supreme), founded by Rāmānuja. Shrīvaishnavism is the most typical theistic system of thought, whose ideology inspired new devotional movements all over north India. The text followed here is a Sanskrit version of the original work written in a mixed Sanskrit-Tamil style, frequently employed by the South Indian Shrīvaishnava teachers.
    [From Lokāchārya, *Tattvatraya*, pp. 85 f., 121 f.]

THE LORD .

The Lord is exclusively endowed with a nature that is opposed to all evil, unlimited, and of the form of knowledge-bliss; is adorned with

---

[17] Cf. the section entitled, "Songs of the Saints," below. This illustrates the integration of the learned and the popular trends and traditions.

[18] The bulk of the inscriptions and grants unearthed and published by the Indian Archaeological Department relate to the foundation of these temples and the endowments made to them for divine service.

auspicious qualities, knowledge, power, etc.; He is the author of the creation, maintenance, and annihilation of the entire universe; is resorted to by the four kinds of persons [specified in the text of the *Gītā*]: namely, one in difficulty, one making a scholarly inquiry, one desirous of material gain, and one desirous of wisdom; is the bestower of the four kinds of fruits consisting of virtue, material gain, pleasure, and spiritual liberation; is possessed of a unique personality and is the consort of the three goddesses called Lakshmī, Bhūmī, and Nīlā. . . .

"His auspicious qualities, knowledge, power, etc."—these are eternal, unbounded, numberless, natural, unvitiated; there is nothing to compare them with nor to excel them; of these the objects of His qualities like affection [such as accessibility, softness, etc.] are His devotees; everybody forms the object of His qualities of knowledge, power, etc. which are at the basis of His other qualities; of the Lord's knowledge, the object is those in ignorance; of power, the weak; of forgiveness, those who have sinned; of compassion, those in misery; of affection, those who have shortcomings; of superior conduct, the inferior ones; of straightforwardness, the crooked ones; of friendliness, those who are of bad heart; of softness, those who are afraid of separation from Him; of accessibility, those who yearn to see Him. And so on.

Thus, because He is endowed with all auspicious qualities, the Lord, when He sees the sufferings of others exclaims, "Alas!" and shows His compassion; thinks always, without an exception, of their good; without either pure selfishness or a selfishness mingled with altruism, He exists exclusively for others' sake even as moonlight, southern breeze, sandal, and cool water; sees not in those who resort to Him their inferiority to Himself in respect of birth, knowledge and conduct; becomes Himself the savior when people find themselves as well as others as of no avail; performs impossible miracles like the bringing back of Sage Sāndīpini's son [drowned in the sea] [2] and the like; fulfills their desires; even creates for them [for His devotees] previously nonexistent positions like that of the Pole-star; [3] extends to them also Himself and all that is His, on the principle that what is one's own is enjoyed by oneself; [4] on the fulfillment of His devotees' purposes, He feels as if He Himself had accom-

---

[2] This is a story from the Purānas; the text adds one more instance also which is left out in the translation.

[3] This the Lord created and gave to the little boy-devotee, Dhruva.

[4] That is, as the beings are part of the Lord's own body, what is His is theirs also.

plished a purpose of His own; without a thought of even a single good He has done, He thinks only of the particle of a good act that the devotee might do; He Himself becomes the object of such constant delectation to the devotee that one is made to forget immemorially ingrained tastes; like a father seeing with his eyes the mistakes of his wife and sons, He goes on without minding at heart the mistakes of His devotees; even when the goddess Lakshmī [his consort] points out flaws in a devotee, He opposes Her and firmly stands by the devotee and protects him; like a lover courting even the untidy things of his beloved, He indeed accepts even the flaws of His devotees as something pleasing to Him; He is absolutely straight toward them in thought, word, and action; when they are separated, He troubles Himself so that their misery might end; places Himself freely at their service, even rendering Himself so easy as to be bound and beaten by them; and just as the mother cow, in her affection for her just-delivered calf, scares with its horns and hoofs even those who come to give feed to the calf, so the Lord wards off even Mother Lakshmī and the eternally enlightened teachers and Himself goes on displaying His own affection toward His devotees. . . .

His "personality" is, in form and qualities, something which He has taken according to His own desire; it is eternal and uniform; it is supramundane; just as a jewel cup will show transparently the gold placed in it, even so, it does not, unlike the human body which shrouds the inner Self, hide the divine nature which is of the form of knowledge, but reveals it; it is of the form of limitless effulgence; it is a reservoir of a multitude of auspicious qualities, gracefulness and the like; it is to be contemplated by yogins, so enrapturing the entire universe that one develops distaste for every other kind of mundane enjoyment; it is enjoyed by the ever-liberated souls; like a pool of lotuses blooming forth as the rays of the rising Sun strike them, it removes every kind of heat in one; it is the root of endless incarnations; it is the protector of all and resort of all; it shines adorned with arms and ornaments.

THE LORD'S FORM

The Lord's form is five-fold: the transcendent one [*para*], the manifestations [*vyūha*], the incarnations [*vibhava*], the immanent spirit [*antaryāmin*], and the images [*arcā*].

By "transcendent" is meant that it is beyond time and is in the further heaven of unbounded bliss where the eternally free souls revel in His presence. By "manifestation" is meant His taking the forms *Saṅkarṣaṇa, Pradyumna,* and *Aniruddha* for purposes of creation, maintenance, and destruction, for protecting the souls in transmigration and to bless the devotees. In the transcendent form, all the six qualities, knowledge, strength, lordship, heroism, power, and effulgence, are full; in each of the three manifestations, two of the six qualities become manifest. . . .

The "incarnations" are manifold, but chiefly of two distinct kinds, the main and subsidiary. . . . Of the incarnations, the cause is His desire; the purpose, the protection of the good, the destruction of the bad and the restoration of righteousness. "Immanence" is to enter into and control; it is also the remaining of the Lord with all sentient selves during all their states like their sojourns through heaven and hell, even as a companion who is unable to leave them; it is also the residence of the Lord in the lotus of one's heart, so that one might meditate upon Him in an auspicious form and He too, like one's kith and kin, safeguard one. The incarnation in "images" is the abiding of the Lord in temples and homes in materials of men's choice [metal, stone, etc.]; it is different from the several manifestations, Rāma, Krishna, etc., as these images are not circumscribed by the place, time, and associates connected originally with those manifestations; and all their activities are under the control of their priests whose shortcomings the Lord overlooks. Inducing the religious attitude [which any amount of mere spiritual reading does not produce], attracting the auspicious feelings of the devotee's heart, being the resort of the whole world, enjoyability—all these qualities are found to the maximum in the incarnation in images. Reversing the relationship of subordinate and Master and appearing to be innocent of knowledge, power and worship because of the overpowering influence of His unbounded compassion, He bestows on His devotee whatever the latter expects.

HYMNS IN SANSKRIT

The vast hymnal literature in Sanskrit not only gives expression to a wide range of devotional ideas and varied phases of the devotional life, but also embodies tenets of the followers of the path of devotion, the Lord's forms, incarnations, qualities, compassion, and efficacy of devotion, the potency of the Lord's name, surrender and dedication to the Lord, etc.

Devotion Alone Essential

[From Kulashekhara, *Mukundamālā*]

The Lord Nārāyana [Vishnu] is all-glorious in the absence of devotion to whose lotus feet the recital of the Vedas becomes a cry in the wilderness, the daily austerities only a means to reduce one's corpulence, all public benefactions but oblations on ash, and baths in holy waters like the bath of the elephant.[1]

[From *Bhāgavata Purāṇa,* 7.9.10]

Even a low-caste man is superior to a brāhman who is endowed with the twelve excellences but who is averse to the lotus feet of the Lord; if the former has dedicated his mind, speech, desire, and objects, and his life itself to the Lord, he sanctifies his whole race, not so the latter who is stuck up in his own enormous pride.

[From *Brahma Purāṇa,* ch. 49]

What is the use of pedigree, conduct, learning, nay even the life of those who have no devotion toward the Lord, the creator of the Universe?

[From *Bhāgavata Purāṇa,* 6.11.25]

O Lord who are the most proper object of desire! Leaving You, I desire not heaven or the status of the creator, lordship over this or the nether world, not even miraculous yogic attainments or release from rebirth!

[From Chaitanya, *Śikṣāṣṭaka* [2]]

Wealth, men, women, poesy—none of these, O Lord of the universe, do I desire; in every birth of mine, may there be unmotivated devotion to You, the Lord.

The Lord's Incarnations

[From *Bhāgavata Purāṇa,* 11.4.33]

May that Supreme Lord who, devoid of name, form, or end, yet took, for blessing those who adored His feet, names and forms through incarnations and exploits, be gracious unto me.

[1] An elephant's bath is proverbial as a futile act, for the elephant, as soon as it gets out of water, takes and throws the dirt of the street all over its body.

[2] Chaitanya (b. 1485), the founder of the Bengal school of fervent devotion to Krishna, did not write extensively. The *Octad of Instruction* (*Śikṣāṣṭaka*) extracted here is one of his two Sanskrit hymns.

The Lord's Name

[From *Vāmana Purāṇa,* ch. 83.96–99]
The sin that has accrued to me through the desire for others' women and possessions and treachery to others, through reviling others to their great agony and traducing the great ones, the sin committed by me in childhood, boyhood, youth, and old age, and in another birth—may all that sin disappear as a result of the recital of the Lord's [Vishnu's] names, Nārāyana, Govinda, Hari, and Krishna, even as a cup of salt in water.

[From Shrīdhara Venkatesha,[3] *Hymn of Sixty Verses on the Lord's Name* (*Ākhyāṣaṣṭi*)]
O Name of the Lord! Let there be the Vedas by hundreds, and by hundreds the piles of Purānas and Āgamas; are these capable of giving the thought of the Lord without You? On the other hand, You who remove all weariness completely without any effort, can bestow that thought of the Lord without the aid of any of those.

The Lord's Compassion

[From Nīlakantha Dīkshita,[4] *Ānandasāgarastava*]
If you have the compassion towards me that I should be saved, save me; why weigh my good and bad acts? You who are powerful enough to make and unmake the universe, to abide by the laws of one's karma![5] Who will be taken in by this deception?

[From *Ādyādimahālakṣmīhṛdaya Sūtra*]
If I had not been created, there would be no question, O Lord, of Your being compassionate; if diseases had not been created, the discovery of medicine would be futile.

[3] A saint of c.1700 who lived in Tanjore District, South India, and was one of those responsible for the spread of the cult of reciting the Lord's name and the singing of congregational prayers and praises (*bhajans*).

[4] Poet and devotee of the Mother Goddess at Mathurai, South India, seventeenth century.

[5] There is always the conflict between the sphere of the Lord's mercy and the law of karma; according to the karma doctrine, one has to undergo the suffering consequent on the acts done by him, for what has been done will have its effect. But is the Lord to abide by the course of karma, which is after all subject to His sway, or will He bring His compassion into operation to save a devotee? It depends on the intensity of one's devotion to bring forth this grace of the Lord.

Serving the Lord

[From *Narasiṃha Purāṇa,* ch. 11]

That [alone] is a tongue which praises the Lord, that [alone] is a mind which is given up to You, O Lord! those alone are praiseworthy arms which do Your worship.

[From Shankara, *Subrahmaṇyabhujaṅga,* 26]

The Lord's form before the eyes, His glory in the ears, His sanctifying story always in my mouth, His work on my hand, and His service on my body—may all the aspects of my being be absorbed in God *Subrahmaṇya!* [6]

[From Shankara, *Saundaryalaharī,* 27]

Whatever I speak is the muttering of Your prayer; all art is the symbol of Your worship; all my movement is going round You in veneration; eating, etc., is offering oblations to You; if I lie down it is prostration to You; all my enjoyments are in a spirit of dedication to You; O Goddess! whatever I do may it be a synonym of Your worship.

[From Shankara, *Kāśīpañcaka,* 5]

The body is Banaras; knowledge is the expansive Ganges, the mother of the three worlds, flowing here; this devotion, this faith is the Gayā; [7] the meditation on the feet of one's spiritual teacher is Prayāga; [8] Lord *Viśveśvara* [9] is the inner Self, the witness of the minds of all and transcending the three states [of wakefulness, dream, and sleep]; if everything abides in my own body, what other shrine is there besides that?

[Verse uttered at the end of every ritual and religious act.]

Whatever I do with my body, word, mind, senses, intellect, soul, or by the course of nature, all that I dedicate to the Supreme Lord Nārāyana.

[From Utpaladeva of Kashmir, [10] *Śivastotrāvali*]

Enjoying within myself the delectation of devotion and closing my

---

[6] Kumāra or Kārttikeya, son of Shiva.

[7] The famous sacred spot in Bihar; associated also with the Buddha.

[8] Allahabad, place of pilgrimage at the confluence of the Ganges and Yamuna Rivers with the celestial river Sarasvati.

[9] The name of Shiva in the temple at Banaras.

[10] The school of Kashmir Shaivism is a theistic-*cum*-monistic school which incorporated the Tantric ideologies and methods of worship. One of its chief exponents is Utpaladeva (c. 900–950). The present extracts are from his beautiful hymns expressing his mystic love of Shiva.

eyes in that bliss, may I remain saying, "Obeisance to Myself, the Lord Shiva" and adoring even blades of grass!

This in brief is the definition of happiness and misery as far as I am concerned; listen to it, O Lord! Union with you is all happiness, the separation from my Lord is all misery.

To me, filled with your devotion, let there be adversity; may I not have even a succession of happy events, if they are to turn me away from your devotion.

In that seeking of Lord Shiva, all miseries become happiness, poison becomes nectar, and this life itself becomes liberation.

Laying All Burdens on the Lord and Surrendering to His Grace

[From *Pañcarātra, "Jitam te"* hymn] [11]
What is beneficial to me, that You Yourself order for me, O Lord! I am Yours, O God of gods! I have no capacity to do Your worship or praise; I am solely looking forward to Your compassion; [12] bless me please.

[From Shankara, *Śivabhujaṅga,* 16]
I am poor, wretched, broken, stricken with anguish and sorrow, exhausted, and rent into pieces; O Lord, You are the inner soul of all beings and You do not know my distress! O Lord, protect me.

[From Vedānta Deshika,[13] *Aṣṭabhujāṣṭaka*]
O Lord of the Goddess of prosperity! [14] You, by Yourself, must protect me who am solely dependent on You; if You take the initiative [to save], wherefore my exertions? And if You do not take the initiative, of what use even then are my efforts?

[From Vādirāja,[15] *Kṛṣṇastuti*]
I know not my good, I know not what is not to my good; I am powerless

[11] There are two traditions of Vishnu worship, the *Vaikhānasa* and the *Pañcarātra,* the former older, but the latter more widespread.

[12] This attitude accords with the "southern" or more popular school of South Indian Shrīvaishnavism which says that all that man can do is, without pretending to put forth any effort of his own, realize his own meekness and keep himself ready and fit to receive the Lord's grace. The other school, called the "northern," holds that God helps those who help themselves.

[13] A brilliant, versatile, and prolific writer of the Vishishtādvaita (qualified nondualism) school (1268–1369), he wrote in Sanskrit and Tamil.

[14] The mediator between God and the devotee, according to Shrīvaishnava theology.

[15] Vādirāja (sixteenth century) is a teacher of the dualistic and pluralistic school of theism started by Madhva in South India. In the interpretation of the Vedānta according to this school, God is only the efficient cause, not the material cause also as the schools of Shankara and Rāmānuja hold.

either to do or to refrain from doing; just as a puppet dances, even so, I exist purely at the direction of Lord Hari.

[From Vādirāja, *Haryaṣṭaka*]

O Lord Hari! Does an animal fallen into the well know how to lift itself by its own effort? Throwing about its feet and bellowing frequently, it can only excite pity, O Lord!

[From Yāmuna, *Stotraratna*] [16]

I am not one firmly established in the observance of duties; I have not known what the Self is; nor have I any devotion to Your lotus feet; destitute of everything, with no other way open, O you protector of refugees! I have taken refuge at Your feet.

There is not one despised act in the world which I have not done a thousand times; O Lord! at this hour when my sin is bearing its consequences, I am crying before you, without any other way.

O Lord! Whatever I have, whatever I am—all that is only Yours; rather, knowing full well that all this, of course, belongs to You, what shall I offer You?

[From Rāmānuja,[17] *Śaraṇāgatigadya*]

Giving up all other ordained observances, abandoning all my desires inclusive of salvation, O Lord! I took refuge under Your feet that measured the whole universe.

You alone are my mother, my father, my kinsman, my teacher, my learning, my wealth; O God of gods! You are my everything.

THE SONGS OF THE SAINTS OF MEDIEVAL HINDUISM

Just as Buddhism had gone about consolidating itself in the frontier regions and countries neighboring India—Ceylon in the south, Burma in the east, Tibet and Central Asia in the north and northwest—even so within

---

[16] Yāmuna Āchārya (Tamil name, Ālavandār, eleventh century), South India; one of the founders of Shrīvaishnavism in the South. Noteworthy among his three Sanskrit treatises is the *Authoritativeness of the Āgamas* (*Āgama-prāmāṇya*) which tries to establish the authority of the Āgama texts alongside of the Vedas.

[17] This great Shrīvaishnava teacher of South India and founder of the Vishishtādvaita (qualified non-dualism) school died in 1137. According to his interpretation of the Vedānta, the Lord is the efficient and material cause of the universe, but He is different from the sentient and nonsentient creation; souls are many, not one, and they are not identical with Him, but constitute His body and are dependent on Him.

India, it had gained a stronghold in areas where Brahmanical traditions were weakest. Thus the missionaries of Buddhism and Jainism established themselves in South India. Later, the leaders of the Brahmanical way found that the masses in these areas could be won over only by going to them and speaking to them in their own language. Accordingly, the truths of the Upanishads, the conclusions of the philosophical systems, the basic beliefs and practices of Hinduism—all these were brought to the people in their own language, often in a homely style, enlivened with poetry, wit, and satire, through songs by men of spiritual realization, the saints. Thus arose all over the country popular religious poetry and song.

In each region a school or succession of teachers appeared who went about making the whole countryside resound with their songs. These saints from different parts of the country subscribed to different schools of philosophy, but there was a common approach and method in their work among the people. Most of them were followers of the path of devotion (bhakti) to a personal God, and therefore their lives were marked either by continued pilgrimages to famous temples and sacred places, (which helped also their work of propagation), or by intense worship at a particular place or of a specific form of God (*iṣṭa-devatā*) to which they were most attached.

A circumstance which contributed greatly to their popularity and the success of their movement among the masses is that these saints did not come only from the highest-born and best-educated classes of society, but from every stratum of society down to the untouchables. Thus emphasis was laid on character and sincerity, not on high birth or learning.

This popular religious movement began in South India in the Tamil-speaking area where saints arose from the time of the Pallava rulers of Kāñchī (c. fourth to ninth centuries A.D.). In reclaiming the kings and the people for Hinduism, they went about singing their psalms to deities enshrined at different temples. From the Tamil country this movement of saint-singers of philosophical and religious songs in regional languages spread to the Kannada-speaking area, whence the spark was ignited in Maharashtra; then the Hindi-speaking areas took it up and the whole of North India was aflame with this resurgent and fervent faith. This popular presentation of the teaching of the Upanishads, the philosophical schools, and the Purānic lore, coincided with the linguistic phenomenon of the growth of the neo-Indo-Aryan languages of the North and the flowering forth of the literatures in the Dravidian family of languages in the South.

These songs comprised not merely stray philosophical, religious, ethical, and didactic pieces, but often musical versions of whole texts from the Sanskrit epics and Purānas. Now, under the inspiration of Vālmīki and his *Rāmāyana* in the original Sanskrit, the *Rāmāyana* came to be retold or sung in the local language, e.g. that of Kamban in Tamil and of Tulasīdās in Hindi. In recent times, there has been no greater votary of Rāma than Mahātmā Gāndhi, who imbibed this fervor for Rāma and his kingdom from the *Rāmāyana* of Tulasīdās, as well as from the soul-stirring songs written in Gujarati and Hindi. Yet not only the *Rāmāyana,* but the Upanishads, the *Gītā,* and the Purānas also had their effect. Indeed the literary renaissance of the neo–Indo-Aryan and Dravidian languages came about through the impregnation of the ideas and themes of classical Sanskrit literature, original production in which now was weakened as a result of the upsurge of creative effort in the vernacular. At the same time, popular songs, which became a dual heritage of the religiously devout and the musically minded, served as forerunners also of a musical renaissance. In them a new form of musical composition took shape, and a repertoire was provided not only for concerts but also for congregational worship or service in temples. It is these songs that one might have heard in Gāndhi's prayer meetings; it is these, too, that one hears again and again on the All-India Radio. In various localities where people met, sang, and went into devotional ecstasies, halls were erected called *bhajan maths* or *nām ghars.* From the dim past when sages (rishis) in the forest hermitages (āshramas) put forth their Upanishads, to these apostles of popular spiritual culture, the saint-musicians and their *bhajan* halls, which still continue in force all over the country even in modern cities like New Delhi, Bombay, Calcutta, and Madras—the basic unity and rich flow of this spiritual heritage is clearly seen.

The readings which follow are selections from the psalms and songs of these saint-musicians of India, representing not only the geographical and linguistic regions of India, but also the chronological movement from the seventh century to the beginnings of the nineteenth.[1]

---

[1] Where there are no specific printed sources given for the texts of the songs which follow, they are to be understood as taken from popular printed collections of such songs available in each of the languages.

TAMIL-NĀD [2]

The Tamil saints appeared in the great days of the Pallavas when art and literature blossomed forth and Hindu culture spread from the South across the seas into the East Indies. The saints sang of Shiva and Vishnu in the temples which were then coming into prominence; the hymns on Shiva are called *Devāram* and those on Vishnu, *Divya Prabandham,* both names underlining their sacred character. Revered by the Tamils as the *Tamil Veda,* they embody the teachings of the Upanishads, and are sung to different melodic modes. The inscriptions in temples provide for endowments to maintain their recitals as part of the temple-service. The saints who adored Shiva are called *Nāyanārs,* and those who sang of Vishnu, *Ālvārs;* the contributions of these two groups of saints form the bedrock of Tamil culture and still form the most appealing part of Tamil literature. The period from the seventh century to the ninth century covers the ages of the more important ones among these; others followed and kept the tradition in full vogue throughout the subsequent centuries.

TIRUNĀVUKKARASHU

Tirunāvukkarashu (Vāgīsha, seventh century A.D.), "Master of Speech" or Appar, was reconverted to Shaivism from Jainism by his sister Tilakavatī, and in turn reconverted the Pallava King, Mahendra Varman.

We are not subject to any; we are not afraid of death; we will not suffer in hell; we live in no illusion; we feel elated; we know no ills; we bend to none; it is all one happiness for us; there is no sorrow, for we have become servants, once for all, of the independent Lord, and have become one at the beautiful flower-strewn feet of that Lord.

JNĀNASAMBANDHA

Jnānasambandha (seventh century) vanquished the Jains at Mathurai [3] and reconverted the Pāndyan king to Shaivism.

---

[2] *Nāḍ, nāḍu* in Tamil means country.

[3] Mathurai, the second largest city of the Tamil country, the ancient Pāndyan capital and fabled seat of Tamil learning.

The Lord's Names

The Lord's names are medicines; they are sacred mantras; they are the way to salvation in the other world, they are all the other good things, too; through them all acute miseries are destroyed; meditate only upon those names of the Lord.

The Lord Is Everything

Thou art flaw, Thou art merit, O Lord of Kūḍal Ālavāi![4] Thou art kith and kin, Thou art Master. Thou art the light that shines without a break. Thou art the inner meaning of all the sacred texts learned. Material gain, emotional gratification [kāma], all these that man seeks art Thyself. What can I utter in praise before Thee?

MĀNIKKAVĀCHAKAR

Māṇikkavāchakar ("the Ruby-worded Saint," eighth century), a minister of the Pāṇḍyan court at Mathurai fought Buddhism and revived Shaivism. His songs are surcharged with much feeling. The collection of his devotional poems is called compendiously the *Sacred Utterances*.
    [From *Tiruccataḳam, 90*]

I am false, my heart is false, my love is false; but I, this sinner, can win Thee if I weep before Thee, O Lord, Thou who art sweet like honey, nectar, and the juice of sugar-cane! Please bless me so that I might reach Thee.

From his poem on union with the Lord, called the *Puṇarcci-p-pattu,* which is typical of devotional ecstasy and the symbolism of "divine nuptials."

Melting in the mind, now standing, now sitting, now lying and now getting up, now laughing and now weeping, now bowing and now praising, now dancing in all sorts of ways, gaining the vision of the Form [of the Lord] shining like the rosy sky, with my hairs standing on end— when will I stand united with, and entered into, that exquisite Gem of mine [the Lord]!

SUNDARAMŪRTI

Sundaramūrti (ninth century) was the most humanistic of the Shaiva Nāyanārs.

_____
[4] Meaning Mathurai.

[O Lord!] Without any other attachment, I cherished within my mind only Thine holy feet; I have been born with Thy grace and I have attained the state whereby I will have no rebirth. O Benevolent Lord at Kodumudi,[5] worshiped and lauded by the learned! Even if I forget you, let my tongue go on muttering your mantra *Nomah Śivāya*.[6]

POIHAI, BHŪTAM, AND PEY

Poihai of Kānchīpuram, Bhūtam of Mahābalipuram, and Pey of Mylapore, Madras, were the first three Ālvārs. On a rainy night, at Tirukkōvilūr, all three were taking shelter together in a small room which was all dark; the Lord also pressed into that small space, and to find out who the newcomer was, each of the three saints lit a lamp. What the lamp was that each lit is told by them in their verses.

Poihai: With earth as the lamp, with the swelling sea as the ghee, with the burning sun as the flame, I have seen the Lord. . . .

Bhūtam: With love as the lamp, ardent yearning as the ghee, and the mind melting in joy as the wick, I lit the light of knowledge. . . .

Pey: Lighting in my heart the bright lamp of knowledge, I sought and captured Him; softly the Lord of Miracles too entered my heart and stayed there without leaving it. . . .

NAMMĀLVĀR

Nammālvār was the most important and prolific of the Ālvār psalmists.

The Lord as Lover

This is a mood of devotion in which the devotee places himself in the position of the beloved and yearns for the Lord as the Lover. The mood is found already in the Vedic hymns; it is quite common in devotional literature and the outpourings of the mystics; in music, there is a whole body of songs, chiefly in dance, which adore the Lord in this manner.

[From *Tiruvāymoei*, 2.4.1]

---

[5] A Shiva shrine in Tamil country.
[6] This is typical of the devotee's complete preoccupation with the Lord and the cult of adoring the Lord by the incessant recital of His name. *"Namah Śivāya"* means "Obeisance to Shiva" and forms the great "five-syllabled" mantra of Shiva; it is extracted from the Veda and is held so sacred by Shaivites that they take the expression *Namah-Śivāya* as a personal name.

Tossing about restlessly, with a mind that has melted, singing again and again and shedding tears, calling upon You as Narasimha [7] and seeking You everywhere, this beautiful maid [8] is languishing.

The God with Form and Beyond Form
[From *Tiruvāymoei*, 2.5.10]

He is not a male, He is not a female, He is not a neuter; He is not to be seen; He neither is nor is not; when He is sought, He will take the form in which He is sought, and again He will not come in such a form. It is indeed difficult to describe the nature of the Lord.

PERIYĀLVĀR OR VISHNUCHITTA
[From *Tiruvāymoei*, 5.2.6]

O ye ills tormenting me for long! listen, I tell you now, this body of mine has become the holy shrine of the great Lord, the Cowherd Krishna; know that, o ye ills that oppress me! I tell you one more word, you have no longer any hold here; know that and go away! This is not the old town, it has now been taken over as a protected place.

TIRUMANGAIMANNAR

Tirumangaimannar, an Ālvār and chief of a division of the Cola country, was opposed to Buddhism, of which there was a famous center in his neighborhood, at Nāgapattina on the seacoast of Tanjore.

The Lord's Name Nārāyaṇa

Nārāyaṇa is the most venerated of all the names of Vishnu as the Supreme God; the sacred formula (mantra) in which the devotees of Vishnu are initiated and which they go on repeating is *"Namo Nārāyaṇāya"*—"Obeisance to Lord Nārāyana."

The following is a widely recited verse and puts concisely all that the Lord's name and faith in it mean to the Hindu devotee.
[From *Periatirumoei*, 1.1.9]

The name *Nārāyaṇa* will bless one with high birth and affluence; it will obliterate all the sufferings of the devotees; it will endow one with the

---

[7] *Narasiṃha*, foremost man; means also that incarnation of Vishnu in which the Lord appeared as half-man, half-lion.

[8] That is, the heart of the devotee.

heavenly state and the service of the Lord; it will bring success and all good things; it will perform for one more beneficial acts than one's own mother; that word I have found, the name *Nārāyana*.

KARNATAKA

In this region, corresponding roughly to the state of Mysore, Kannada, a Dravidian language, is spoken.

BASAVARĀJA

Basavarāja (twelfth century), a high state official, founded the Vīrashaiva movement, a sect of worshipers of Shiva. His sententious sayings are for the most part addressed to his deity *Kūḍala Saṅgameshvara* (a form of Shiva).

The lamb brought to the slaughterhouse eats the leaf garland with which it is decorated. . . . The frog caught in the mouth of the snake desires to swallow the fly flying near its mouth. So is our life. The man condemned to die drinks milk and ghee. . . .

He who knows only the *Gītā* is not wise; nor is he who knows only the sacred books. He only is wise who trusts in God.

When they see a serpent carved in stone, they pour milk on it; if a real serpent comes, they say, "Kill, kill." To the servant of God, who could eat if served, they say, "Go away, go away"; but to the image of God which cannot eat, they offer dishes of food.

To speak truth is to be in heaven, to speak untruth is to continue in the world of mortals. Cleanliness is heaven, uncleanliness is hell.

Sweet words are equal to all prayers. Sweet words are equal to all penances. Good behavior is what pleases God. . . . Kindness is the root of all righteousness.

Those who have riches build temples for Thee; what shall I build? I am poor. My legs are the pillars; this body of mine is the temple.

PURANDARADĀSA

Purandaradāsa (1480–1564), the foremost and the most prolific of the Hari-dāsas ("Servants of Vishnu"),[9] a sect of saint-composers in Karnataka, is

[9] The Haridāsas were drawn from all classes, Kanakadāsa, one of them, being a shepherd.

deemed to have laid the foundations of the modern phase of the South Indian
music system known as Karnatak music. His songs are remarkable for their
literary merit, devotional fervor, and moral and philosophical teachings.

(Song: *Stomach-austerity* (*Udaravairāgya*); Melody: [10] *Nādanāmakriyā*)

This austerity is really for the sake of the stomach, this austerity devoid of
devotion to the Lord—this rising in early dawn, and telling people, with
a shivering frame, of having bathed in the river,[11] all the time having a
mind filled with jealousy and anger; this display of a large number of
images, like a shop of bronzeware and conducting worship with bright
lights, to impose on others. . . .

All acts done without the abandonment of the sense of "I," without
communion with the holy souls, without belief that everything goes on
only at the instance of the Lord, and without the vision in silence of the
Lord, are merely austerities practiced for livelihood.

MAHĀRĀSHTRA

JÑĀNADEVA OR JÑĀNESHVARA

Jñanadeva (1275–1296) was the foremost Mahārāshtrian saint and founder of
the Marathi language and literature. His most famous work is a Marathi metrical paraphrase of the *Bhagavad Gītā* called the *Jñāneśvarī*.

[From *Jñāneśvarī*, 17.1794–1802]

Let the Lord of the Universe be pleased with this sacred literary activity
of mine, and being pleased, let Him bestow on me this grace: May the
wicked leave their crookedness and cultivate increasing love for the good.
Let universal friendship reign among all beings. Let the darkness of evil
disappear. Let the sun of true religion rise in the world. Let all beings
obtain their desire. . . . May all beings be endowed with all happiness
and offer ceaseless devotion to the Primeval Being. . . .

TUKĀRĀM

Tukārām (1598–1649) was the most popular shūdra saint of Mahārāshtra.

[10] Indian music belongs to the melodic or modal system, not to the harmonic system.
Numberless melodic modes (rāga), based on a progression of notes, have been evolved,
each with its distinct aesthetic ethos.
[11] A purification rite.

I saw my death with my own eyes. Incomparably glorious was the occasion. The whole universe was filled with joy. I became everything and enjoyed everything. I had hitherto clung to only one place, being pent up in egoism [in this body]. By my deliverance from it, I am enjoying a harvest of bliss. Death and birth are now no more. I am free from the littleness of "me" and "mine." God has given me a place to live and I am proclaiming Him to the [whole] world.

GUJARAT

MĪRĀBĀĪ

Mīrābāī (b. 1550) was an unfortunate Rājput princess who, widowed in mundane life, became, in spiritual life, the bride of the Lord whom she adored in the form of Krishna. Her songs, rhapsodies of Krishna-love, have always been popular, even today.

My only consort is Giridhar Gopāl,[12] none else—none else indeed in the whole world which I have seen through and through. I have forsaken my brothers, friends, and relations, one and all, and sitting among saintly souls, have lost regard for worldly fame or honor. My heart swells at the sight of godly persons and shrinks at the sight of the worldly. I have indeed reared the creeper of Godly Love with the water of my tears. Churning the curds, I have extracted the essence, ghee, and have thrown away the whey. The king sent me a cup of poison, even that I have drunk with pleasure! The news is now public, everyone now knows that Mīrā is deeply attached by love to God; it does not matter now; what was fated has happened!

KASHMIR

LALLĀ

Lallā (fourteenth century) was a Shaivite mystic. Her verses (Lallāvākyāni) are even today immensely popular in Kashmir.

---

[12] Names of Krishna, the former referring to his exploit in lifting a mountain, the latter to his role as cowherd.

I, Lallā, went out far in search of Shiva, the omnipresent Lord; after wandering, I, Lallā, found Him at last within my own self, abiding in His own home.

Temple and image, the two that you have fashioned, are no better than stone; the Lord is immeasurable and consists of intelligence; what is needed to realize Him is unified concentration of breath and mind.

Let them blame me or praise me or adore me with flowers; I become neither joyous nor depressed, resting in myself and drunk in the nectar of the knowledge of the pure Lord.

With the help of the gardeners called Mind and Love, plucking the flower called Steady Contemplation, offering the water of the flood of the Self's own bliss, worship the Lord with the sacred formula of silence!

BANARAS (HINDI)

KABĪR

Kabīr (1440–1518), a low caste weaver in Banares, was in many respects the pioneer of Hindi devotional verse, using the vernacular to popularize religious themes drawn from both Hindu and Muslim traditions. Though his fundamental concepts are chiefly Hindu, Muslim influence is reflected in his holding to a strict theism, opposition to all forms of idolatry and rejection of caste. God for Kabīr is usually called Rām (Skt. Rāma), and is frequently regarded as the divine Guru or Teacher. The mystical conceptions and the phraseology itself of Kabīr's verses reflect strong Sūfī influences juxtaposed to traditional Hindu doctrines. His poetry is often ungrammatical and borrows freely from both Sanskrit and Persian vocabularies, yet it is direct and forceful. Numerous couplets and didactic sayings are attributed to Kabīr and constitute much of the folk-wisdom of the average Hindu. During his lifetime Kabīr organized a religious order of monks and nuns, who furnished teachers and leaders of the community and otherwise propagated his teachings. The selections which follow were translated by the modern poet Rabīndranāth Tagore, for whom Kabīr stood as one of the most appealing and inspiring symbols of India's religious heritage.

[From Tagore, Songs of Kabīr, pp. 45–46, 55–57, 108–9, 112]

O servant, where dost thou seek Me?
Lo! I am beside thee.
I am neither in temple nor in mosque: I am neither in Kaaba nor in Kailash:[13]

---

[13] Abode of Shiva.

Neither am I in rites and ceremonies, nor in Yoga and renunciation.
If thou art a true seeker, thou shalt at once see Me: thou shalt meet Me in
   a moment of time.
Kabīr says, "O Sādhu! God is the breath of all breath."   [p. 45]

It is needless to ask of a saint the caste to which he belongs;
For the priest, the warrior, the tradesman, and all the thirty-six castes,
   alike are seeking for God.
It is but folly to ask what the caste of a saint may be;
The barber has sought God, the washerwoman, and the carpenter—
Even Raidās was a seeker after God.
The Rishi Swapacha was a tanner by caste.
Hindus and Moslems alike have achieved that End, where remains no
   mark of distinction.   [pp. 45–46]

Tell Me, O Swan, your ancient tale.
From what land do you come, O Swan? to what shore will you fly?
Where would you take your rest, O Swan, and what do you seek?
Even this morning, O Swan, awake, arise, follow me!
There is a land where no doubt nor sorrow have rule: where the terror
   of Death is no more.
There the woods of spring are a-bloom, and the fragrant scent "He is I"
   is borne on the wind:
There the bee of the heart is deeply immersed, and desires no other
   joy.   [pp. 55–56]

O Lord Increate, who will serve Thee?
Every votary offers his worship to the God of his own creation: each day
   he receives service—
None seek Him, the Perfect: Brahma, the Indivisible Lord.
They believe in ten Avatārs; but no Avatār can be the Infinite Spirit, for
   he suffers the results of his deeds:
The Supreme One must be other than this.
The Yogī, the Sannyāsī, the Ascetics, are disputing one with another:
Kabīr says, "O brother! he who has seen the radiance of love, he is
   saved."   [pp. 50–57]

O brother! when I was forgetful, my true Guru showed me the Way.
Then I left off all rites and ceremonies, I bathed no more in the holy
   water:

Then I learned that it was I alone who was mad, and the whole world
   beside me was sane; and I had disturbed these wise people.
From that time forth I knew no more how to roll in the dust in obeisance:
I do not ring the temple bell:
I do not set the idol on its throne:
I do not worship the image with flowers.
It is not the austerities that mortify the flesh which are pleasing to the
   Lord,
When you leave off your clothes and kill your senses, you do not please
   the Lord:
The man who is kind and who practises righteousness, who remains
   passive amidst the affairs of the world, who considers all creatures on
   earth as his own self,
He attains the Immortal Being, the true God is ever with him.
Kabīr says: "He attains the true Name whose words are pure, and who is
   free from pride and conceit."   [pp. 108–9]

If God be within the mosque, then to whom does this world belong?
If Rām be within the image which you find upon your pilgrimage, then
   who is there to know what happens without?
Hari is in the East: Allāh is in the West. Look within your heart, for
   there you will find both Karīm and Rām;
All the men and women of the world are His living forms.
Kabīr is the child of Allāh and of Rām: He is my Guru, He is my Pīr.[14]
                                     [p. 112]

SŪRDĀS

Sūrdās (sixteenth century) was the blind poet-singer of Agra.
I have danced my full now, O Gopāl! With passion and fury as my pet-
ticoat,[15] with lust for physical pleasure as my necklace, with delusion
jingling as my anklets, with words of abuse as poetry, with mind full of
false ideas as the big drum, with my movement in the company of the
unholy as the steppings, with avarice as the earthen pitcher making sound
inside, beating time in various ways, I have danced enough. I have worn
illusion as my girdle, I have put on material craving as the mark on my

---

[14] Sūfī saint or teacher.   [15] The imagery employed is that of the danseuse.

forehead; I have demonstrated endless movements of my wants, without regard to time or place; O do remove all this nonsense of mine, O Son of Nanda! [16]

TULASĪDĀS

Tulasīdās (1532–1623) was the author of the great bible of the Hindi-speaking peoples, the Hindi *Rāmāyaṇa* called *Sacred Lake of the Deeds of Rāma*.

Where the Lord Dwells
[From *Rāmacaritamānasa*, 2.*Caupāī* 130]

O Rāma! Thou dwellest in the hearts of those who have no lust, anger, infatuation, pride, delusion, avarice, excitement, affection or hatred, hypocrisy, vanity, deceitfulness; those who are dear to all, benevolent to all, equable in joy and sorrow, praise and blame, who speak the truthful and the pleasant and are endowed with discrimination, who, while awake or asleep, have taken shelter under Thee and indeed have no other resort but Thyself; in their minds, O Rāma, dost Thou dwell. Those who consider other men's women as mothers and others' wealth as more poisonous than poison, those who rejoice to see others flourish and are acutely pained to see them afflicted, those to whom Thou art dearer than life, in their minds is Thy blessed abode.
[From *Vinayapattrikā*, No. 116]

O Mādhava! Such is your mystic power of illusion [māyā]; however much one may strive, one does not overcome it unless and until You bless with Your grace. . . . Knowledge, devotion, manifold spiritual means— all these are of course true; none of these is false; but Tulasī says in full confidence that the grace of the Lord alone can dispel that illusion.
[From *Vinayapattrikā*, No. 120]

Many are the means of crossing over the ocean of transmigration which the pure words of the Vedas speak of. But Tulasī says: "Real happiness of heart cannot be attained without giving up the ideas of 'I' and 'mine.'

---

[16] Nanda is the cowherd foster of Krishna.

ASSAM AND BENGAL

SHANKARADEVA

The spread of the Vaishnava devotional movement in Assam was primarily
due to this saint. Shankaradeva (1449–1568) composed devotional narrative
poems, dramas, and songs for prayers and congregational singing; founded
nām ghars, halls for congregational prayer, and *sattras,* monastic establishments
where devotional music, dance, and drama were maintained. He was a fore-
runner of Chaitanya of Bengal. The selection quoted below is a *kīrtanaghoṣa,*
a song with refrain to be taken up by the congregation.

Save me O Rāma! O formless and faultless Hari! have compassion on
Thy devotee and fulfill this his heart's desire. I bow to Thee, O Mādhava.[17] Thou art the giver of Law to the Law-maker.[18] Thou art the
Way, the Mind; Thou art the Author of the World. Thou art the Over-
soul and the sole Lord of the world, and nothing else exists besides Thee.

Thou art the cause and effect [of the world of being], the universe of
the static and the moving, even as an ear ornament is inseparable from
the gold of which it is made. Thou art the animals and the birds, the gods
and the demons, the trees and the shrubs. Only the ignorant taketh Thee
as different [from the Universe].

Being under the spell of Thy māyā, none knows that Thou art the Soul.
Thou art at the heart of all beings. Blind to this truth, they go to seek
Thee outside. Thou art the sole Truth; all else is illusory. The wise know
this and meditate on Thee within their hearts.

I crave not for happiness, nor am I in need of salvation. Let there be
naught but devotion at Thy feet. Let my mouth recite Thy name, let my
ears listen to Thy tale; let Thy lotus feet shine in my heart. Let not the
company of Thy devotees ever forsake me; this is the kindness I beg at
Thy feet.

RĀMAPRASĀD

Rāmaprasād (1718–1775) was from Bengal.

O my mind! I tell you, worship Kālī [19] in whatever fashion you desire,
repeating day and night the mantra given to you by the teacher.[20]

---

[17] Rāma, Hari, and Mādhava are names of Vishnu in his different forms.
[18] Brahmā, one of the Hindu trinity, the Creator.   [19] The Divine Mother.
[20] All schools of thought, devotion, and esoteric practice attach the greatest importance to

When you lie down, think you are doing obeisance to Her; in sleep meditate on the Mother; when you eat, think you are offering oblations to the Mother; whatever you hear with your ear is all the mantras of the Mother; each one of the fifty letters of the alphabet represent Her alone; Rāmaprasād declares in joy that the Mother pervades everything; when you move about in the city, consider that you are circumambulating the Mother.

An Anonymous Bhajan Song
[*Saṃsāra māyā chādiye Kṛṣṇa nāma bhaja mana*]

O Mind! Giving up attachment to the world, adore the name of Krishna. Repeat the name of Krishna and you will discover an invaluable treasure. Craving for worldly objects and all the deception caused by māyā will vanish. If you thirst for beauty, your thirst will be satisfied in an instant, for you will see with your eyes that unblemished gem, the Unbounded Supreme Being; your vision of beauty will be merged in that All-Beautiful in which all nature around is immersed. If the lotus feet of that Lord but touch you, your heart will be filled with wonderful riches.

ANDHRA (TELUGU)

TYĀGARĀJA

Tyāgarāja (1767–1847), the greatest South Indian composer, was a member of a Telugu family living in Tamil country. The major part of the songs heard in South Indian concerts are his compositions. He adored God in the form of Rāma, the incarnation of Vishnu and the hero of Vālmīki's Sanskrit epic. He believed in the full efficacy of repeating the Lord's name. His songs are noteworthy not only for his devotional fervor and ethical and spiritual preachings, but also for proclaiming the role of music an easier spiritual path than even yogic practices. On the other hand, the cultivation of mere music without devotion to the Lord would not lead one to the proper goal.
  (Song: *Svara-rāga-sudhārasa*)

O Mind! devotion associated with the ambrosia of the notes and melodies of music is verily paradise and salvation. . . .

---

the guru or teacher who is to be venerated as the embodiment of divinity and from whom initiation should be taken.

To know and realize the nature of "sound" originating from the basic plexus [*mūlādhāra*] [21] is itself bliss and salvation. Likewise the knowledge of the various resonant centers of the body from which emanate the seven glorious notes of music.

Through philosophical knowledge one attains salvation only gradually after several births; but he who has knowledge of melodies along with natural devotion to God becomes a liberated soul here and now.

[21] According to esoteric physiology, there are in the body of man six centers, from the basic pelvic region to the head; the physico-spiritual energy, as well as sound, pass from the lowest where they are present in their subtlest form, to the higher ones where they become more and more manifest.

PART FOUR
ISLAM IN MEDIEVAL INDIA

1582   Promulgation of Dīn-i-Ilāhī, Akbar's "Divine Faith."
1600   Charter of incorporation granted to the East India Company.
1605–1627   Reign of Jahāngīr.
1627–1658   Reign of Shah Jahān.
1651   Foundation of East India Company's factory at Hugli.
1667–1668   War of Succession between Dārā Shikōh and Aurangzīb.
1707   Birth of Shah Walī-Ullāh. Death of Aurangzīb.
1739   Sack of Delhi by Nādir Shah.
1757   Battle of Plassey.

INTRODUCTION

After the Ghōrid Turkish conquest at the end of the twelfth century A.D. India was, ideologically, the home of a plural society. It is disputable whether the Ghōrids and their successors revolutionized the forms of either the political or the economic life of the country; it can be argued convincingly that they only substituted one set of rulers for another without fundamentally changing the traditional functions of government or the traditional relations of rulers and ruled—that in administration, while introducing a new structure at the center, Delhi, they were conservative at the periphery, in the village; and that in economic life they merely introduced a new group of revenue receivers without changing the ways in which the people of India earned a living. What is indisputable is that, under the protection of their military power, they introduced into the heart of India a new, and in the event, unassimilable interpretation of the meaning and end of life—the Muslim.

With the memory of the partition of India along the religious frontier between Muslim and non-Muslim still fresh, it is difficult to contemplate the place of Muslim civilization in India in calm historical perspective. In the atmosphere generated by the events of 1947, it is easy either to regard Pakistan as a necessary good—as being somehow "in the womb of time" as soon as Muslim political control over Hindustan had been established in the twelfth century—and therefore to magnify the differences between Muslim and non-Muslim cultures in India; or to regard her as an unnecessary evil made possible only by the political maneuvering of modern times—and therefore to minimize the differences between these cultures.

The standpoint taken here is that the treatment of Muslims by Hindus as merely another caste; the interpenetration of Hindu customary law among Muslims in the villages; the creation of a Hindu-Muslim ruling class by the Mughal emperors with a system of rank in the imperial service and common interest in polo, elephant fighting, and common modes of dress; the development of a lingua franca, Urdu, combining Hindi grammar with a largely Arabic and Persian vocabulary; the study of Hindu thought by Muslims like al-Birūnī or Abū'l Fazl; the composition of histories in Persian by Hindus; the syncretist religions of Kabīr and Guru Nānak—all of these notwithstanding—neither educated Muslims nor educated Hindus accepted cultural coexistence as a natural prelude to cultural assimilation. Thus long before British rule and long before modern political notions of Muslim nationhood, the consensus of the Muslim community in India had rejected the eclecticism of Akbar and Dārā Shikōh for the purified Islamic teachings of Shaikh Ahmad of Sirhind and Shah Walī-Ullāh. Cultural apartheid was the dominant ideal in medieval Muslim India, in default of cultural victory.

We are not called upon here to analyze the political consequences of this fact in the modern history of India, still less to suggest what those consequences ought to have been. We may better understand, however, why Islam as an "ideology" remained unassimilated in medieval India, while yet enjoying peaceful coexistence for long periods with non-Muslim, principally Hindu, culture, if we examine briefly its religious and historical background.

CHAPTER XIV

THE FOUNDATIONS OF MEDIEVAL ISLAM

Islam in India, as elsewhere, was a civilization founded upon religion, that is, upon "the recognition on the part of man of some higher unseen power as having control of his destiny, and as being entitled to obedience, reverence, and worship" (in the words of the Oxford Dictionary). The reason for man's existence on earth, the purpose of his daily life, was submission (*islām*) to and worship of the One God, the Omnipotent. Human society was without value save that with which Allāh had endowed it as man's proving ground for eternal salvation. The life on earth was significant—but only because Allāh had given it significance. The world was not an illusion, it was for man a dread reality, portending everlasting bliss or everlasting damnation. Man's existence on earth was not an evil to be avoided but an opportunity for service to God.

Thus the values of this world are for Muslims not of its own creation. Man does not exist merely to serve his own satisfactions according to his own manner of conceiving them. The end of man is not therefore his own perfection, his own self-realization on earth. His beliefs, his way of life, are ordained for him by Allāh who is his sovereign. A Muslim is always on active service for his Lord. No Muslim of whose thinking we have any record in medieval India forgets that he inhabits a world governed by Allāh; as a good subject he never forgets to write in the name of Allāh, nor, however distant from religion his subject may appear in our eyes, to begin with praises to his Lord. He knows that the proper study of mankind is not man but God.

ISLAM AS REVEALED IN THE
QUR'ĀN AND THE SUNNA

As the means of that study Allāh has provided, in so far as He has deemed it fitting, a revealed Book, the Qur'ān, sent down in Arabic through the Angel Gabriel to His messenger the Prophet Muhammad over a period of more than twenty years from about A.D. 610, the original being in heaven as a "well-guarded tablet" (Qur'ān 85.22). But even the Prophet did not receive the whole of this tablet. The records of Muhammad's inspired utterances, found not merely in the memories of men, but according to later tradition written on shoulder blades, palm leaves, and stones, were collected after his death and under the third caliph, 'Uthmān (644–655), formed into an "authorized version" of one hundred and fourteen suras or chapters. Whatever paths Muslim thought might take in the centuries after the recension of the Qur'ān, Muslims found in the Qur'ān the very word of God, authority for those paths. The Qur'ān has remained for all ages the inspiration of the religious life of Islam.

But because the Qur'ān was the Word of God and the Prophet Muhammad the last of the prophets, at his death Divine Guidance for the community of believers came to an end. Where were the faithful to find authoritative directions amid all the vicissitudes of life? As the Arabs conquered vast territories and strange populations with highly developed religions of their own, so the need for guidance increased. The Qur'ān was indeed the final authority, but without interpretation its meaning might elude the believer. It was perhaps natural that, with so many men alive with personal memories of the words and actions of Muhammad, Muslims should seek for a model of what they should believe and do in the discourse and in the deeds of him whom God had chosen to be the bearer of His Message. By the time of the Muslim conquest of North India the principal source of Muslim belief and practice, other than the Qur'ān, had become the Sunna, or usage of the Prophet as reported in the Hadīth, the corpus of canonical tradition about Muhammad. The impression made by the personality of the Prophet upon his contemporaries and the respect paid by the Arabs to the customs (Sunna) of their forefathers provided the impetus to turn tradition into the second source of authority.

The earliest collections of Hadīth were made probably in early Um-

mayad times by the pious for their own edification and by lawyers and
judges who had to administer the Arab conquests. At that time they did
not have an overriding authority, second only to that of the Qur'ān. But
there was a strong feeling among the faithful that, after the Qur'ān, belief
should rest upon the authority of the Prophet and of his Companions and
followers, so that any individual or sect wishing to justify its interpretation
of Islam naturally appealed to a Hadīth. Hence it was not long before men
began to manufacture traditions and put them into circulation. Hadīth
became a report of what the Prophet, his Companions and followers
would have said or done if they had been obliged to do so. The pious did
not at first feel any great uneasiness at these forgeries. They doubtless
thought that since their content was good and true, the Prophet would
certainly have acted or spoken thus. The Hadīth became a microcosm
of the religious history of the Muslim community during its formative
years.

The elevation of the Prophet's Sunna as embodied in the Hadīth to
a position of authority equal to that of the Qur'ān, and the reexamination
of the actual practice of the Muslim community in the light of a thorough reconsideration of the original religious meaning of the Prophet's
mission was, in the realm of jurisprudence, the work of al-Shāfi'ī (767–
820). Unlike his predecessors who were prepared to accept the "living
tradition" of the community as a basis of law, irrespective of whether
that tradition could be attributed to the Prophet himself, al-Shāfi'ī persuaded his fellow Muslims to accept that only traditions from the Prophet
himself should have the force of law and that the model of behavior of
the Muslim community should be the model behavior of Muhammad.
Undoubtedly this at first increased the tendency to invent Apostolic
tradition, but in the longer run it had the effect of subjecting the actual
practice of the community to scrutiny in the light of the religious insights of al-Shāfi'ī's day, and of systematizing the Law and the methods
of discovering the Law. The raising of Apostolic tradition to a religious
status almost equal to that of the Qur'ān was in effect a reconversion of
the Muslim community to Islam at the end of the second and the beginning of the third century Hijra.

This sanctification of Hadīth and the Sunna in the province of jurisprudence hastened the appearance of collections of Hadīth which satisfied
the new principles of criticism. The narrators of Hadīth were required

to cite their authorities going back to the original narrator—usually a Companion of the Prophet, and then the biographies of the narrators were compiled in order to ascertain whether the narrators of the Hadīth were *prima facie* in a position to transmit the Hadīth; whether, for example, one had died before the next had been born, or whether they had ever met.

In the third century after Hijra appeared the first critical collections of Hadīth, the *Genuine Collections (Sahīh)* compiled by al-Bukhārī (d. 870), principally for legal purposes, and Muslim (d. 889), principally for theological purposes. These have a canonical authority in Islam second only to that of the Qur'ān. Thus, three centuries before the Turkish conquest of North India "standard" compendia of Muslim tradition had been collected, which, with the Qur'ān, provided the authoritative sources of Muslim belief.

For the orthodox (Sunni) Muslim these authoritative sources of belief and practice were not the spiritual monopoly of a divinely appointed priesthood. Anyone in the community could devote himself to the study and development of the religious sciences which came to be based upon the study of the Qur'ān and the Sunna of the Prophet as embodied in the canonical collections of Hadīth. The Caliph or head of the Muslim community had no spiritual powers; each believer was equal in his right to study how God must be obeyed (although as will be seen in the section on the Sharī'a he must be bound by the consensus of the community before him). This was not so for unorthodox Islam.

UNORTHODOX ISLAM

The most important schism in Muslim civilization is that caused by the Shī'a—the party of 'Alī.

After the death of Muhammad, a section of the faithful insisted that 'Alī, cousin and son-in-law of the Prophet, was the rightful heir to the headship of the Muslim community. The majority did not agree, and when 'Alī became caliph, the Umayyads resisted him by force of arms. 'Alī lost Syria and Egypt, and in 661 when he was murdered, Mu'awīya, an Umayyad, was proclaimed caliph in Jerusalem. 'Alī's son, Hasan, sold his rights to Mu'āwiya and died a few years later, the Shī'a asserting that he had been poisoned by Mu'āwiya. His younger brother, Husain, who had lived quietly at Medina during Mu'āwiya's reign, rebelled against Yazīd, Mu'āwiya's son. At Karbala Husain's band of two hundred was surrounded by superior forces and, as it refused to surrender, was annihilated. The tenth of Muharram, the day of Husain's death, is the culmination of ten days' lamentations among the Shī'a. 'Alī's party appeared to be finished, but it became a focus for all the discontents of the time. Although Arab in origin, the Shī'a gained support among the clients (*mawālī*), the non-Arabs who had accepted Islam and yet were not exempt from taxes and social disabilities imposed on non-Muslims.

Defeat in politics spurred elaboration of specific Shī'a doctrines. First, the "martyr's" death of Husain led to the introduction of a passion motive; the tragedy of the death of Husain paves the way to Paradise for the Shī'a. Second, the Shī'a developed the doctrine of the *Imām,* an infallible being partaking of the divine attributes sent by God to guide the faithful in every age. Some Shī'a regard the Imām as an incarnation of the Godhead itself, but they are not typical. The Imām is sinless (unlike Muhammad) and infallible, possessing a secret knowledge—the Divine Light—handed down from God to Muhammad and thence to 'Alī and his descendants. He is the final interpreter of the word of God in the Qur'ān. He is appointed by and responsible to God, not by and to the community of the faithful. His powers are much nearer those of a pope than are those of the Sunni caliphs.

The Shī'a split into many sects, the largest was that of the "Twelvers" who recognized twelve Imāms in the line from Fātima and 'Alī, ending with Muhammad al-Mahdī who disappeared from the world in 880 and is believed to be preserved against the day of his second coming to restore justice and righteousness. For the Twelvers the Imām remains mortal, but a divine light is inherent in him.

One of the most important sects of the Shī'a is that of the "Seveners" (or Ismā'īlī), so-called because they recognized as Imām the son of Ismā'īl ibn Ja'far, the sixth Imām, and not his brother Mūsā al-Kāzim. Closely connected with the Ismā'īlī were the Qarmatians who believed that Muhammad ibn Ismā'īl was the last Imām who would reappear on the last day.

In Ismā'īlī beliefs the number seven had magic importance. In their gnostic Neo-Platonic philosophy, there were seven emanations of the world intellect—God, the universal mind, the universal soul, primeval matter, space, time, and the world of earth and man. They forged a chain of manifestations of the world intellect beginning with Adam and passing through Muhammad to the Imāms. Muhammad was not, as in orthodoxy, the seal of the Prophets. They taught that the laws of the Sharī'a were not intended for those with esoteric knowledge and its prohibitions were but mere allegories. The Qur'ān itself had an inner meaning, known only to initiates.

The Ismā'īlī and the Qarmatians appealed primarily to the poor and lowly, to peasants and artisans. The Qarmatians practiced community of property, and according to their enemies, of wives also. They organized workers and artisans into guilds. They considered it legitimate to shed the blood of the orthodox. In 899 they founded an independent state at al-Ahsa on the western shores of the Persian Gulf and launched raids on neighboring Syria and Iraq. In 930 they captured Mecca and carried off the Black Stone. The Qarmatians passed on their doctrines to the Fātimids of Egypt and to the Assassins of Alamut and Syria, who terrorized the Muslim world by raids and assassinations from their mountain fortresses until stamped out by the Mongol Hūlāgū in 1256.

The Ismā'īlī and the Qarmatians owed their strength to the social discontent of later 'Abbāsid times. The disparity between rich and poor, and the decline in prosperity of the empire at the end of the ninth century, made many humble people enemies of Sunni Islam. The latter appeared to condone the social ills of the time. On the eve of the Muslim conquest of India it was customary to stigmatize enemies as Qarmatians or Bātinīs, so great was the abhorrence they aroused among those who supported the existing order.

It must be emphasized, however, that the majority of the Shī'a viewed the Ismā'īlī and the Qarmatians with an alarm equal to that of the Sunnis or orthodox Muslims, for they compromised the unity of God and disregarded the finality of Muhammad's prophethood. The majority of the Shī'a, the Twelvers, accept the Five Pillars of Islam (ritual purification, prayer, alms, fasting, and pilgrimage) and though they do not accept the principle of consensus, their law is based on the Sunna of the Prophet. Their principles occasionally diverge from those of the four Sunni schools —e.g., temporary marriage is allowed; marriage with a Christian or Jewish woman is not. Dogmatically the authority of the Imām tends to overshadow that of the Qur'ān and the Sunna.

Although the Shī'a were influential at the Mughal court in the sixteenth and seventeenth centuries and enjoyed adherents among the rulers of the Deccan Muslim kingdoms which appeared in the fourteenth and fifteenth centuries, their contribution to medieval Muslim thought in India has not been considered sufficiently distinctive in its social and political overtones to be included in the readings. Furthermore, although the Ismā'īlī and the Qarmatians infiltrated into India, they were suppressed by Muslim governments under Sunni influence and have not, so far as has been ascertained, left to posterity any direct evidence of their thought in India.

THE HISTORICAL BACKGROUND

Islam came to South Asia first as a religion, and then as a political force. The peripheral Arab conquest of Sind (beginning A.D. 711) was preceded by Muslim settlements on the western seaboard as were the Ghaznavid invasions (beginning A.D. 1000) preceded by small colonies of Muslims in the southern Punjab.

The timing and nature of Muslim conquests in North India was of decisive significance in defining the character of Muslim thought in India. The early Arab invasions of Sind under Muhammad ibn Qāsim occurred less than a hundred years after the death of the Prophet Muhammad. Islam, in 711, was still a religion composed of a few basic assertions about the oneness of God, the mission of the Prophet, the terrors of the Last Judgment, the need to perform the five daily ritual prayers, to go on the pilgrimage (*hajj*) to Mecca and to give alms (*zakāt*) to the poor. The Arabs were still sitting as pupils at the feet of the peoples they had subdued, learning the arts of civilization. The study of Arab grammar, it is true, had begun under al-Du'alī, al-Khalīl, and the Persian Sībawaih. Traditionists [1] such as al-Hasan al-Basrī, Ibn Zuhrī, and Ibn Sharāhīl al-Sha'bī were putting into circulation the religiously authoritative reports of the sayings and doings of the Prophet or his Companions. Thinkers like Wāsil ibn 'Atā were raising theological issues of divine and human ordination, while sects like the Khārijī and the Shī'a were quarreling over the government of the faithful. Even so, Islam was still forging those

---

[1] That is, specialists in the compilation and interpretation of the "authentic" traditions handed down from the Prophet.

intellectual weapons—the science of tradition, theology, jurisprudence, and history—which would enable it to meet argument with something more than conviction. Islam was still receptive to the impress of those civilizations of Byzantium and Persia which the Arabs had conquered. Within wide limits, Muslims were free to seek after and do God's will in their own ways. There was no established orthodoxy; there was no authority seeking to enforce one.

The century following the Arab conquest of Sind was therefore one in which Hindu culture could encounter the Arabs in the hope of giving more than it was forced to receive. For example, the scientific study of astronomy in Islam commenced under the influence of an Indian work, the *Siddhanta,* which had been brought to Baghdad about 771 and translated. The Hindu numerical system entered the Muslim world about the same time. Later, in the ninth century, India contributed the decimal system to Arab mathematics.

The background to the Ghōrid Turkish conquest of India which commenced in 1175 and blossomed into the Sultanate of Delhi under Iltutmish (1211–1236) was vastly different. The Ghōrid invasions were begun to finance the imperial ambitions of a small mountain principality in Afghanistan, were continued as a profitable outdoor occupation for Turkish adventurers, and ended in providing a home for Muslim refugees from the Mongol catastrophe of the third decade of the thirteenth century.

By the second half of the ninth century, the 'Abbāsid Caliphate had surrendered effective authority first to Persian and then to Turkish military adventurers, who recruited their chief military support from converted, purchased, and immigrant Turkish nomads from the steppes and mountains beyond the Oxus and the Jaxartes. The political headquarters of the Eastern world moved to Nishapur, Samarqand, Bukhara, and Ghaznin. The 'Abbāsid Caliph at Baghdad survived only to legitimize with robes of honor and mandates of appointment whoever had the power to compel him to do so.

Now it was unlikely that the Ghōrids and the motley host of hardy horsemen who followed them—Afghans, Turks, rough mountaineers, newly converted nomads—would themselves be the bearers of a Muslim culture remarkable for depth, variety, or subtlety. They came to Hindustan as raiders, to remain as rulers. They came as soldiers of fortune; they found fortune and stayed to organize it. It would not, therefore, have been surprising if Muslim thought in India had been stillborn of such parents. But although the Ghōrid Turks and Afghans themselves were rude and uncouth, they became nevertheless the guardians of a proud and rich emigré civilization.

For in 1220, the Mongol deluge burst upon the Muslim world; Bukhara, Samarqand, Gurganj, Balkh, Marv, and Ghaznin were in turn destroyed. Many scholars of the eastern Muslim world were killed and libraries burned. In 1258, Hūlāgū, a grandson of Chingis Khān, sacked Baghdad and slew the 'Abbāsid Caliph, Al-Musta'sim. Although by the end of the century the grandson of Hūlāgū, Ghazan Khān, had become a devout Muslim and Hūlāgū's successors (called the Īl-Khāns) had surrounded themselves with Muslim savants such as al-Juwainī and Rashīd ud-dīn, Islam was in eclipse for over half a century in Transoxania, Persia, and Iraq. But apart from a campaign on the left bank of the Indus by Chingis Khān, and forays against Lahore and Multan, India escaped Mongol visitation. The former servants of the Ghōrid sultans were left quietly, and (incidentally) by no military merit of their own, to establish a sultanate at Delhi.

From the work of the contemporary Indo-Muslim historian, Minhāj us-Sirāj Jūzjānī, himself an immigrant, and of the later historian Ziā ud-dīn Barnī, it is evident that the sultanate of Delhi offered a refuge for scholarly fugitives from the Mongols. In the thirteenth century India became a cultural colony of the Muslim world at a time when the center of that world was in enemy hands. It is not surprising, therefore, that the strong conservative trends in Islam at the beginning of the thirteenth century were, in India, strengthened. To re-establish ties with the old, rather than to embrace the new, was a reasonable desire in men who had barely escaped with their lives and who now found themselves precariously situated in an armed camp in North India, open to attack from the Mongols in the northwest and from Hindus all around them.

These immigrant Muslim scholars were now the bearers of a civilization as well as of a faith. Under the early 'Abbāsids, Muslims had not only assimilated the traditions of pre-Islamic Persia and the heritage of classical Greece, but also, in response to their religious needs, had transmuted those contributions into a unique cultural whole greater than any of its individual parts.

In religion the science of Hadīth provided Muslims with a means of formulating and defending true belief and pious practice. Muslim jurisprudence (*fiqh*) had appeared as an imposing corpus of legal princi-ples regulating the personal, commercial, property, and sexual relations of Muslim to Muslim and of Muslim to non-Muslim. The four orthodox schools of jurisprudence, the Hanafite founded by Abū Hanīfa (d. 767), the Mālikite founded by Mālik ıbn Anas (c.715–795), the Shāfi'ite founded by Muhammad ibn Idrīs al-Shāfi'ī (767–820), and the Hanbalite founded by Ahmad ibn Hanbal (d. 855), represent one of the greatest achievements of Islam and one which gave Muslim civilization in India great corporate strength. Migrant or immigrant Muslims from outside India were often appointed *qāḍīs* (religious judges) by the sultans in India, thus promoting Islamic knowledge there.

In theology (*kalām,* or the science of the unity of God) and philosophy, Islam had either come to terms with (or had imposed terms upon) Greek philosophy and now at the end of the twelfth century, in the theology of al-Ash'arī (873–935) and in the philosophy of al-Ghazālī (d. 1111), could rest awhile in an intellectual caravansary sufficiently fortified against assault. The challenge of the Mu'tazilites, who had attempted to interpret Islam in terms of Greek metaphysics—making God and the Qur'ān con-form to human ideas of justice and reason in effect—had been met by al-Ash'arī of Baghdad and al-Māturīdī of Samarqand (d. 944), who had turned the weapons of Greek dialectic to the defeat of the Mu'tazilites in the assertion of God's unlimited sovereignty and the defense of the Qur'ān and the Hadīth.

By the end of the twelfth century, mysticism too had been domesticated in the Islamic world. Potentially a disruptive force emphasizing a direct personal relationship between the individual and his God and tending to ignore, if not to denigrate, the rules of conduct and the credal formula-tions of the orthodox, Sufism (Muslim mysticism) had been made re-spectable by al-Ghazālī. Seeking not academic knowledge but immediate experience of God, he managed to buttress the structure of theological ideas with vivid personal religious experience. It was important for Islam in India that Sufism had found accommodation in orthodox Islam by the time of the Muslim conquest—for not only did the community thereby present a united front against the infidel, but also Sufi modes of thought and worship made an appeal to Hindus so strong that many were con-verted to Islam. It was only after three centuries, in Mughal times, that orthodox lawyers and theologians grew fearful lest the Sufis should stray outside the Muslim fold, and, by going too far to meet kindred Hindu spirits, prepare the internal subversion of Islam in India.

Muslim historiography (*tārīkh*) had also developed as a distinctive cultural form by the time the Ghōrid Turks invaded India. Pre-Islamic Arab oral traditions, tribal genealogy, the traditions of the old Persian *Khudāy-Nāma,* the religious demand for authentic biographies of the Prophet and the early caliphs, the Persian taste for edifying anecdotes and the Turkish rulers' desire for fame, had all contributed to the rise of historical writing eminently fitted to remind Muslims in India of their great heritage. The Ghōrid invasion followed the victory of Persian as the literary language of the eastern Muslim world and, with that victory, the revival of Persian modes of thought in politics and poetry, ethics, and belles-lettres. This was encouraged by the Turkish sultans and their principal officers who found Persian easier to learn than Arabic. Persian poetry and prose with its content of epic royal deeds, its fables and moral anecdotes, its education in polite manners and in the arts of politic government, gave the society of Turkish soldiers of fortune its title deeds to civilization.

Thus the Muslim conquest of India occurred at a period when Islamic civilization had crystallized in a form which, on looking back, one can see it was to retain until the nineteenth and twentieth centuries. The scope for change in response to the challenges of the Indian environment was less than it had been at the time of the Arab invasion of Sind—indeed the Arabs had already made the major Muslim concession to India, the admission *de facto* of the Hindus to the status of *zimmīs* (tolerated and protected unbelievers).

It is remarkable that once Islam was ensconced in India, no important effort was made forcibly to evict it. For this, the political and social character of the Muslim conquest was largely responsible. The Ghōrids, and in the sixteenth century the Mughals, invaded India with organized professional armies; they did not invade India as a folk in search of a home, or as nomads in search of pasture. Neither Turk nor Mughal deprived the Hindu cultivator of his holding or settled in closed colonies on the lands of the dispossessed. Both substituted one group of revenue receivers and military chiefs for another, changing the men at the top of the social pyramid without dislodging the pyramid itself.

The Turks and the Mughals sought paramountcy rather than empire in India, suzerainty rather than government, superintendence rather than control. Neither the Delhi sultanate nor the Mughal empire interfered greatly with the daily life or the religious generality of their subjects. Except for acts in the heat of battle, violence did not normally characterize the relations of Muslim and Hindu. For the most part the mass of Hindus remained indifferent to their new rulers, rather than bitterly antagonistic toward them and their foreign faith.

THE COMING OF ISLAM TO INDIA

Despite the Muslim conquest of the Hindus, even at the height of the Delhi sultanate and the Mughal empire the Muslims remained a minority. Hindu chiefs enjoyed local power under Muslim suzerainty and Hindu clerks staffed all but the directing and executive posts in the administration. In the last resort, it is true, military and political power over the greater part of Hindustan rested with Muslims, yet, as with all political power, its continued exercise depended on the tacit observance of certain conditions, none the less real for being unspecified and unspoken. For the Muslims in India these were first, refraining from trespassing beyond the traditional frontiers of political activity in India, i.e., revenue collection and troop raising, to interfere actively in the beliefs and customs and laws of subject communities; and second, to preserve the cultural and religious identity of the ruling group so that it would instinctively cohere to defend its privileged political position against non-Muslims. It is this second condition with which the present section is concerned.

Before the Ghōrid conquests in India, al-Ghazālī, as will be seen, had largely stilled the theological warfare of the schools and obliged the mystics first to go on the pilgrimage to Mecca. In depriving Greek philosophy of its hold over the educated and by confining scholastic theology to a role strictly defensive of tradition, he had turned Muslims again toward the study of the Qur'ān and the Sunna as the "quickening word" for personal and social religious life. Islam entered India at a time when its learned men ('ulamā), mainly traditionists and canon lawyers rather than theologians, were engaged in just that practical elaboration of the daily witness of a Muslim to his beliefs which favors the solidarity of the community.

Politics, too, enhanced the influence of the ulamā. The Turks who conquered North India at the end of the twelfth century A.D. were military adventurers glad of support from the religious classes. The Ghōrid sultans recognized the legal sovereignty of the Caliph of Baghdad but in practice acted as caliphs in their own dominions, appointing religious judges (*qādīs*) and canon jurists (muftīs) to the principal towns and enforcing their decisions. The *qādīs,* muftīs, and the ulamā who taught in mosque schools and colleges, advocated obedience to the sultan and the powers that be. Although the sultans might disregard the Sharī'a when their own political position and personal habits were in question, the prestige and authority of the state stood behind the ulamā in their education of the Muslim population at large. If the state did not actively impose an orthodoxy itself, it permitted others to do so. It appears that the sultans of Delhi generally appointed orthodox Sunni ulamā of the Hanafite school of jurisprudence to office and to teaching posts.

There were occasions too when the government actively suppressed unorthodoxy. Extreme Shī'a sects—the Ismā'īlī and Qarmatians—had first appeared in Hindustan in upper Sind and established a principality with a capital at Multan. Mahmūd of Ghaznin had defeated and dispersed them in 1005 and from 1009 to 1010, but they continued underground activity in India thereafter. In the reigns of Iltutmish, Raziya, 'Alā ud-dīn Khaljī, and Fīrūz Shāh Tughluq in the thirteenth and fourteenth centuries, their adherents were slaughtered and imprisoned by the government. The Ismā'īlī and Qarmatian denial of the legitimacy of the sultanate, their egalitarian urges and their secret guild organizations caused the Delhi government as much alarm as their rejection of the orthodox caliphate, schools of law, and theology scandalized the Sunni ulamā. The relations between the Delhi sultanate and the ulamā were generally, therefore, close and harmonious, with important consequences for the outward unity and the stability of the Muslim community.

The chief ideological threat to the religious integrity of Islam in India was more subtle and insidious than that offered by the Shī'a and the Qarmatians, because it came from within the orthodox fold, from those whose lives of devotion and gentleness were often compelling arguments for their teachings—namely the mystics. The real religious tension in Indian Islam was between the Sunni ulamā and the Sufis. It was a tension between twin heirs of al-Ghazālī's heritage. The twelfth century A.D. saw the organization of the great mystic orders (*silsila*) outside India and

even before the Ghōrid conquest was complete in 1195, Khwāja Muʿīn
ud-dīn Chishtī of Sistan had settled in Ajmir introducing the Chishtī
order to India. Within the next two centuries the great Sufi orders had
spread their network of "retreats" over most of North India. These
retreats were a powerful force both within and beyond the Indian
Muslim community. The Sufis appealed to all classes of Muslims, particularly those less educated in the traditional sciences. Moreover, they
exhibited a way of life and thought attractive to Hindus in its devotion,
piety, asceticism, tolerance, and, during the sultanate period at least,
in its independence of the ruling power. They were the true missionaries
of Islam as a faith in India.

Nevertheless, the Sufis were under constant critical surveillance by the
ulama lest they surrender Islam in the name of Islam. The fears and
suspicions of the orthodox were strongest after the Mughal conquest,
when Akbar and later Dārā Shikōh seemed to be encouraging or at
least tolerating un-Islamic ideas and practices. The orthodox feared in
Sufism its pantheistic predilections, its toleration of saint worship, and its
tacit encouragement of the neglect of the study and practice of the Sharīʿa.
They feared too the substitution of "retreat" for mosque as the center of
the life and worship of the community. Such tendencies did not need
or imply Hindu influence—they existed in Islam before the conquest of
India—but unless resisted they could have meant cultural absorption for
Islam in India. As it was, the ulamā in their educational work among
"New Muslims" needed to run fast to stand still. (Thus, for example,
within living memory Muslims in Kashmir have worshiped at Buddhist
shrines, Muslim cultivators in western India have offered vows to
Hindu gods at harvest time, and Muslim women in the eastern Punjab
have sacrificed to Sitāla, the goddess of smallpox). The orthodox ulamā
did not want unnecessary hostages held out to "Hindu superstition."

But at the ideological level, the tension between the ulamā and the
mystics must not be exaggerated into a parting of the bond between
them. They were not enemies but rivals; partners in the mutual enjoyment of al-Ghazālī's legacy, no bitter litigants quarreling over its division. Both were traveling toward God, one by the orthodox path (Sharīʿa)
and the other by the mystic Way (tarīqa), from a common starting point.
The mystics remained Muslim mystics and the orthodox who combated
their more dangerous ideas were often mystics themselves (e.g., Shaikh

Ahmad of Sirhind). And even if it sometimes appeared, as in Akbar's and Dārā Shikōh's day, that orthodoxy and mysticism had reached the limits of mutual tolerance, the instinct of the Muslim community for unison, if not unity, in the face of unbelievers asserted itself in the person of Shah Walī-Ullāh (1702-1762) to prevent open schism and heresy hunting.

The readings that follow illustrate the different articulations of one fundamentally religious and "otherworldly" system of thought and system of law. First, we present the exposition of Islam in India by the 'ulamā, which took two main forms. One was the repetition of the mandates of the Sharī'a and of the principles of Muslim jurisprudence as set down in textbooks which were accepted as authoritative by the consensus of the Muslim community. The other was the exposition and defense of Muslim beliefs and outward observances, for the benefit of converts on the one hand and to the discredit of the mystics' extravagances on the other. The latter motive, however, did not become prominent until the fifteenth and sixteenth centuries.

Of these two forms of exposition, legal and theological, it was the former which, as we have seen, increasingly engaged the attention of the ulamā at the time of Islam's introduction to India, and which probably contributed most to the establishment of the Muslim community there. Nevertheless, implicit in this whole structure were certain basic Muslim teachings about the nature of God and Divine worship. Muslim thought in India cannot be understood without a brief appreciation of the features, methods and course of Muslim theology.

FUNDAMENTALS OF MUSLIM FAITH

The Prophet himself was no theologian and the Qur'ān was no theological treatise. Thus the followers of the Prophet were left to reduce the conceptions of the Qur'ān to a system. They were forced to do so partly by political quarrels in which opponents characterized each other as heretics and infidels, and partly by the impact of other creeds or systems of thought, notably Christianity and Greek philosophy, which challenged the convictions of pious Muslims and provoked them to defend their faith by argument.

The Qur'anic concept of Allāh is stated most simply in the formula, "There is no God save Allāh." He is the One, the Living, the Exalted, the Comprehensive, the Powerful, the Self-Sufficing, the Absolute Originator, the Eternal, the Mighty, the Dominant, the Haughty, the Great, the Laudable, the Glorious, the Generous, the Strong, the Firm, the Knower, the Subtle, the Aware, the Wise, the Hearer, the Seer. He is also the Creator, the Shaper, the Giver of Life, and the Giver of Death, the Assembler of All at the Last, the Strengthener, the Guardian, the King, the Governor, the Lord of Kingship, the Prevailer, and the Tyrant. He is the Exalter, the Abaser, the Honorer, and the Advancer. In relation to mankind Allāh is the Compassionate Compassionator, the Forgiver, the Pardoner, the Clement, the Kind, and the Loving. He is the Giver, the Provider, and the Answerer of Prayer. God's power is infinite; so is His knowledge. Although transcendent and without a peer, He is nearer to man than his jugular vein. Although not bound by human ideas of justice, He hates injustice and oppression. Man's relation to Allāh is one of utter submission and dependence. The Qur'ān deals in antinomies, as if to emphasize the temerity of human efforts to comprehend the nature and purposes of Allāh. Thus in the one text God is kind, loving, and patient; in another, He says: "I created not the jinn and mankind save that they should worship me." Again, "Whom Allāh guideth aright, he allows himself to be guided aright; whom He leads astray, they are the losers," in confrontation with "The truth is from your Lord. Let him then who will, believe; and let him be, who will be, an unbeliever," illustrates that the Qur'ān is on the issue of divine or human ordination a mine of texts for later theologians, rather than a text itself. The precise relation of Allāh to His Creation, of His Word to Himself, of His Attributes to His Essence, of Divine Command and human responsibility became questions to trouble succeeding generations of Muslims. With the aid of quotations from the Qur'ān it was possible to assert, with equal force, either the absolute transcendence over, or the complete immanence of Allāh in, His Creation. The first doctrine in general was developed by scholastic theologians, the second by some extreme Sufis.

Immediately after the death of Muhammad, however, the Muslim community in Mecca and Medina subscribed to an expression of faith in the one God, His Prophet, His Book, His Angels, and the Last Day, and to fulfill the duties of pilgrimage to Mecca, alms-giving, and fasting. But disputes among the followers of the Prophet together with the Arab conquest of Syria, Persia, and Egypt wrought a change. When 'Alī submitted his claim to the caliphate to arbitration after the battle of Siffin (657), some of his adherents came out against him claiming his action was unlawful. They (the Khārijites) went on to assert that they alone were true Muslims and that any other so-called Muslims must be killed on sight. This raised the question of what made a Muslim. The propaganda on behalf of the descendants of 'Alī also forced clearer and more elaborate definitions of Islam. Some said the Angel Gabriel had made a mistake and brought to Muhammad the revelation intended for 'Alī; others argued that there were two Gods; one the Imām (leader, ruler) in heaven, the other the Imām ('Alī or his descendants) on earth. The Murji'is arose who would postpone all such questions to the Last Day.

The contact between Christians and Muslims in Syria led to an efflorescence of new concepts about God, his relation to man and to the Qur'ān. Most Muslims believed at first that God was the absolute governor of the world. Christian ideas tended to emphasize human responsibility and under their influence some Muslims, the Qadarīs, affirmed the freedom of man's will. Christian doctrines of the *Logos* probably provoked the Muslim doctrine that the Qur'ān was eternal and uncreated. It was the word of God; God without a Word was unthinkable, therefore the Qur'ān was coeval with God, i.e., eternal and uncreated. His other attributes, being His, were equally eternal and uncreated. These ideas, with parallels in Christian concepts of the Trinity, could destroy his Oneness and Unity, the fundamental dogma of Islam. Another danger was Greek philosophy with its exaltation of human reason and its notions of substance and attributes. Using reason, Muslim thinkers treated the problem of the nature of Allāh in such a way as to make Him devoid of positive attributes. For example, in the Qur'ān, Allāh was the knower; therefore, He must have the quality, "knowledge." But of what was His knowledge, of something within Himself or without? If the first, there was a duality in Himself; if the latter, then His knowledge depended on something outside Himself and was not absolute, therefore He Himself, the possessor of this quality, was not absolute.

In this potentially dangerous situation, three main schools of theological thought appeared in Islam. The first, the "people of tradition," followed theological proofs which they had heard were derived from the Qur'ān, the Sunna of the Prophet, and the consensus of the Muslim community. For them reason must not be employed either to criticize or to develop doctrine; statements of belief must be accepted literally, "without enquiring how." If, for example, in the Qur'ān, it is stated that God is settled on His throne (Qur'ān 20.5), that statement must be believed as it stands without asking how He sits, or whether He sits like a man.

The second school of thought was rational in method, and its chief members were the Mu'tazilites, whose intention was to formulate Islam in philosophical terms acceptable to educated non-Arabs. They founded Muslim scholasticism. Frankly using reason to arrive at their theological position, they nevertheless reasoned from the text of the Qur'ān. Thus it is wrong to describe them as rationalists in an eighteenth-century sense.

The Mu'tazilites were concerned to vindicate Allāh's unity, His justice, and His spirituality. They denied that Allāh could be said to have any essential or eternal qualities. He could be described as Lord, Possessor, the Merciful, and so forth, but not in the sense that lordship, ownership, and mercy were attributes added to the Divine Being; rather they were attributes identical with His essence. The Mu'tazilite doctrine of the Qur'ān was also intended to preserve the unity of Allāh. If the Qur'ān was eternal and uncreated it must be another God, they argued, for it was not God, yet was other than God. Therefore it was created. The Mu'tazilites also upheld the essential justice of Allāh, conceiving Him, under the influence of Greek ideas, as Infinite Justice. All that God does is aimed at what is best for His creation. He does not desire evil and does not ordain it. All man's actions, both good and evil, result from man's free will. Man will be rewarded for his good deeds and punished for his bad. Then, the Mu'tazilites denied all anthropomorphic notions of God, explaining away those texts in the Qur'ān which speak of God's hands, eyes, face, and throne, and of His being upheld in Paradise by believers. They held that since He was infinite, He could not be in one place for that would entail His being finite. God was spirit. Their opponents said that the Mu'tazilites reduced Allāh to a vague unity of negatives. This contrasted with the vivid, personal Allāh of the Qur'ān and was completely unsatisfying to the vast majority of simple believers. The mildness of the Mu'tazilites in rejecting doctrines of absolute predestination contrasted with the hardness of their doctrines of punishment in hell for the choice of evil-doing. Moreover, when their doctrines were made the of-

ficial orthodoxy under the Caliph al-Ma'mūn (813–833), they treated
their opponents with great intolerance and even brutality.

The third school of thought was that which eventually, by the end of
the twelfth century, became the orthodox, i.e., the Ash'arite, so-called
after its founder, al-Ash'arī (873–935). In it the use of reason in Muslim
theology was accepted, only now in defense, not in defiance, of the simple
formulations of the Qur'ān. Applying the methods of Greek dialectic, the
Ash'arites defeated the Mu'tazilites on their own ground. Briefly, their
theology was as follows. God is eternal, without beginning and without
end and without a likeness. He knows by knowledge, lives by life, wills
by will, sees by sight, and speaks by His word. These attributes are eternal, inhere in His essence, are not He and not other than He, yet they do
not detract from the unity of His essence. The Qur'ān is the speech of
Allāh written in books, preserved in memories, recited by tongues, revealed to Muhammad. The speech of God is increate but the speech of
Moses or other Prophets which God quotes in the Qur'ān is created. Man's
pronouncing, writing, or reciting the Qur'ān is created, whereas the
Qur'ān itself is uncreated.

Allāh created creatures free from unbelief and from belief. Then he
gave them commandments and some disbelieved. Their denial was caused
by Allāh's abandoning them. Allāh did not compel any of His creatures to be infidels or faithful. Fault and unbelief are acts of men. All
the acts of man are truly his own acquisition, but Allāh creates them
and they are caused by His will and His knowledge, His decision and
His decree. As for anthropomorphism, God has face, hands, and soul;
these belong to His qualities but it is not legitimate to inquire how.

In so far as any theology was written in medieval Muslim India—
and only commentaries appear to be extant—it was largely Ash'arite in
tone and content.

This is an appropriate place to add something briefly on philosophy in
Islam, although there appears to have been no philosophical speculation
in medieval Indian Islam. (Indeed, as will be evident from the extracts
from Barnī there was sometimes active hostility to philosophy among
Indian Muslims.) Translation of some of the works of Plato and Aristotle
into Arabic stimulated speculation. Under the influence of Neo-Platonism
and Aristotle and against the literal word of the Qur'ān, philosophers
like Ibn Sīnā taught that the world was eternal, that God knew only

universals (cf. the Platonic forms) and not particulars, and that there was no resurrection of the body. They asserted that it is impossible for the accustomed order of things, i.e., natural law, to be violated.

Hence philosophy was anathema to the orthodox and philosophers were often persecuted. Al-Ghazālī expressed the distaste of the orthodox in his *Incoherence of Philosophers* (*Tahāfut al-Falāsifa*), in which he showed that reason could be used to destroy reason and that the philosophers could not prove the ideas which Islam condemned. This book provoked the retort which marked the climax of philosophy in the Muslim world, *The Incoherence of Incoherence* (*Tahāfut al-Tahāfut*) by Ibn Rushd (Averroes), in which he disputes al-Ghazālī's arguments seriatim.

Interesting, from a modern standpoint, is Ibn Rushd's doctrine of nature. For Ibn Rushd the world is eternal, for everything comes into being out of something else. Becoming is the realization of potentiality, there is a causal connection between phenomena, and it is possible to formulate universal concepts which will express that nature of things, e.g. that fire burns wood because that is its nature. It is impossible here to develop Ibn Rushd's points in detail, but his practical defeat by al-Ghazālī may be important in explaining the failure of natural science in Islam to progress beyond a certain point. For the orthodox, fire burns wood because God creates inflammability in the wood when it comes into contact with the fire. Nature is not an order, it is a succession of individual Divine decrees. Space is a series of untouching atoms and time a succession of untouching moments. All change and action in the world is produced by God deciding to maintain or destroy these atoms. For example, God creates in man's mind the will to write; at the same moment He gives him the power to write and brings about the apparent motion of the hand, of the pen, and the appearance of the writing on the paper. No one of these is the cause of the other. God has brought about, by creation and annihilation of atoms, the requisite combinations to produce these appearances. Hence there is no idea of natural law. The universe is sustained by perpetual Divine intervention—in a sense, by a perpetual miracle.

THE LEGACY OF AL-GHAZĀLĪ

It was al-Ghazālī, however, who truncated philosophizing in Islam and who won an ascendancy in the Muslim world which ranks him as perhaps the greatest single force in Islam after the Prophet himself. Al-Ghazālī (1059–1111) had been brought up in an atmosphere of Sufi mysticism, but turned, before the age of twenty, to the study of theology and jurisprudence. Joining the service of the Seljuq wazir Nizām ul-Mulk, he was appointed to the Nizāmiya Madrasa [1] in Baghdad and was soon recognized as the greatest contemporary authority on theology and law. But he found no spiritual satisfaction in either. Reason merely destroyed reason; it proved nothing. Al-Ghazālī lost his faith and in his despair he could no longer teach. Finally he turned to Sufism and in mystical communion with God found peace and certainty. He abandoned his agnosticism in terror of the Divine Wrath and returned to belief in prophecy and the last judgment. After two years in Syria (1095–1097) in complete seclusion, followed by nine years in retreat, during which he wrote his great work, the *Revival of Religious Sciences* (*Ihyā' 'Ulūm al-Dīn*), in 1106 he returned under pressure from the Seljuq sultan to teaching at Nishapur. But he did not stay long in public life, returning to Tus where before his death in 1111 he had charge of a madrasa (mosque school) and a Sufi hospice.

Al-Ghazālī's *Revival of the Religious Sciences* is "a comprehensive statement of dogmatic moral ascetic and illuminative theology." He deposed jurisprudence and theology from the position they had held within Islam, teaching that the intellect should only be used to destroy trust in itself. Philosophy could not reach to the ultimate reality. Al-Ghazālī did not, however, reject dialectic; rather was he prepared, like al-Ash'arī, to use it in defense of traditional dogmas. For him the ultimate source of all knowledge was revelation from God, which reason may elucidate but cannot challenge. Hence he devoted himself to the study of tradition. After al-Ghazālī, the chief function of scholastic theology was defensive—to support and explain the doctrines of the Qur'ān and the Sunna—hence in India particularly the absence of any original theological works and the concentration on Qur'anic commentary and the study of the hadīth.

Al-Ghazālī recalled Muslims to obedience and devotion to God in their daily lives. A *faqīh*, or canon lawyer, second only to the founders of the four orthodox schools of jurisprudence and a moralist without peer in Islam, he presents in his *Revival of the Religious Sciences* the whole duty of man towards God and his fellows with the thoroughness of the ortho-

[1] A famous Muslim school in the Middle Ages.

dox schools of jurisprudence, and with the devotion of the mystic for whom the practice of duty is the cleansing of the spectacles through which the disciple catches a glimpse of God. Al-Ghazālī restored holiness to the Holy Law and law to holiness.

The creed which al-Ghazālī set forth in his *Revival of the Religious Sciences* was fundamentally that accepted by the Sunni ulamā in India and established as orthodox teaching. It is not possible to present that creed fully here, or to discuss its implications against the background of theological controversy which had raged up to his time. Nevertheless, the following represent perhaps the most essential doctrines as they were presented to the mass of the faithful and the newly converted in India:

1. God is One, without partners.

2. He is utterly transcendent, possessing no form and escaping all definition.

3. He is the Almighty Creator.

4. He knows and ordains everything that is.

5. God is all-powerful and in whatever he ordains, he cannot be unjust (that is, human concepts of justice and injustice cannot be applied to him).

6. The Qur'ān is eternal.

7. Obedience to God is binding upon man because He so decreed it through his prophets.

8. Belief in the Prophet's Divine mission is obligatory upon all.

9. Belief in the Day of Judgment is obligatory as revealed by the Prophet.

10. Belief in the excellence of the Prophet's Companions and the first four Caliphs is required by authentic tradition.

MUSLIM ORTHODOXY IN INDIA

It does not seem that any theological originality was shown by Indian Muslims in the medieval period; they sought merely to provide education in the principles of Islam. Dialectic, the study of the Qur'ān and of the Sunna, and the reiteration of the ways of witnessing outwardly to Islam, were three of the chief ways in which the ulamā in India performed this, their most important and most engrossing task. Commentaries upon commentaries upon commentaries were the typical re-

ligious literature of the time other than the mystical. The readings given
are not intended to illustrate the entire range of even a single work of
this class—an impossible task within the present compass—but rather
to suggest the flavor of the whole. For each work quoted a number of
others of its kind exists.

Piety: The Key to Paradise

This work on the goodly Muslim life was compiled not long after 1356 from
various commentaries on the Qur'ān as well as from al-Ghazālī's *Revival of
the Religious Sciences*. The author, Muhammad Mujīr Wajīb Ad:b (dates unknown) was a disciple of the Sufi shaikh Nāsir ud-dīn Chirāgh of Delhi. The
absence of tension between Sunni orthodoxy and Sufism in the fourteenth century is shown by the fact that the author quotes from the *Fawā'id ul-Fuwād*
and the *Khair ul-Majālis*—records of the conversations of Sufi saints.

The *Key to Paradise* treats of the merit of repeating the formula, "There is
no god but God," reading the Qur'ān, legal prayer, ablutions, fasting, alms-
giving, honesty, slander, good manners, and supererogatory prayers. In reading
the apparently simple teachings of *The Key to Paradise,* we should keep in
mind the type of audience—Indian-born Muslims, perhaps not long converted
—to which they are addressed.

[From Adīb, *Miftāh al-Jinān,* folios 4b, 9b–10, 13b, 14b, 20b–21a]

ON PRAISING GOD

It is related that the Prophet said that whoever says every day at daybreak in the name of God the Merciful and the Compassionate, "There is
no god but God and Muhammad is His Prophet," him God Most High
will honor with seven favors. First, He will open his spirit to Islam; second, He will soften the bitterness of death; third, He will illuminate
his grave; fourth, He will show Munkar and Nakīr [1] his best aspects;
fifth, He will give the list of his deeds with His right hand; sixth, He will
tilt the balance of his account in his favor; and seventh, He will pass
him over the eternal bridge which spans the fire of hell into Paradise like
a flash of lightning. [folio 4b]

ON REMEMBERING GOD

It is reported that a man came to the Prophet and said, "O Prophet of
God, the obligations of Islam are many. Advise me a little of what I

[1] The angels Munkar and Nakīr examined the dead and, if necessary, punished them in
their tombs.

should do, in the letter and in the spirit." The Prophet said, "Keep your lips moist by repeating God's name." [folios 9b–10]

ON THE EXCELLENCE OF READING THE QUR'ĀN

In the illuminating commentary [of Fakhr ud-dīn al-Rāzī?] it is set down that the servant of God should make the Qur'ān his guide and his protection. On the Day of Judgment the Qur'ān will precede him and lead him toward Paradise. Whoever does not diligently stay close to the Qur'ān but lags behind, the angel will come forth and striking him on his side will carry him off to hell. . . .

It is reported in tradition that one's rank in Paradise depends upon the extent of one's recitation of the Qur'ān. They say that everyone who knows how to read a small amount of the Qur'ān will enjoy a high position in Paradise and they say that the more one knows how to read it, the higher one's status in Paradise. Utbā ibn 'Amr says that he heard the Prophet say, "Whoever reads the Qur'ān in secret is the same kind of person who gives alms in secret, and whoever reads the Qur'ān openly is like him who gives alms openly." The Prophet said that on the night of his ascent to heaven he was shown the sins of his people. He did not see any greater sin than that of him who did not know and did not read the Qur'ān. [folio 13b]

ON THE EXCELLENCE OF SAYING, "IN THE NAME OF GOD
THE MERCIFUL, THE COMPASSIONATE"

It is reported in the Salāt-i-Mas'ūdī that Khwāja Imām Muhammad Taiyyar reported that on the morning of the Day of Resurrection, the people awaiting judgment will be deserving punishment. The angels will be hauling them up for punishment. They will say to young and old: "Come forth, you who were our followers in the world." Again they will say to the old weak ones: "You are the weak. It may be that God will have mercy on your weakness." Then they will go to the very edge of hell. When they say: "In the name of the merciful and compassionate God," the five-hundred-year-long fire of hell will avoid them. The Lord of Hell will address the fire: "Why do you not take them?" The fire will reply: "How can I take those who repeat the name of the Creator and remember Him as the Merciful and Compassionate?" God's voice will reach them, saying: "They are My servants and the fire is also My servant. He who honors My name, his name too I have held in higher esteem." On the blessings of saying: "In the name of the merciful and compassionate God," God said: "I have freed everyone in the name of God, the Merciful and the Compassionate." Therein are nineteen letters and the flames of hell are nineteen also. Every believer who repeats that rubric, to him God will give refuge from the nineteen flames of hell. [folio 14b]

ON THE MERIT OF SAYING ONE'S PRAYERS

The Prophet was sitting down with his Companions around him with Abū Bakr Siddīq [Caliph after Muhammad's death] sitting at his right hand. A young man came in; the Prophet gave instructions that he should sit nearer to him than Abū Bakr. The Companions began to think this young man was a man of the highest distinction. After the young man had left they questioned the Prophet about it; Muhammad looked toward Abū Bakr and said: "O, chief of the Companions, do not be uneasy that I bade that young man to sit higher up than you." Abū Bakr said: "O Prophet of God, what was there to say? I obeyed your command quite willingly." The Prophet said, "O, Abū Bakr, be in known unto you that this young man has sent me a harvest of such quantity as no one else has done." Abū Bakr said, "But, O Prophet of God, this young man's only occupation is that of being your disciple." The Prophet said, "He is busy with his own affairs, but every day he says his prayers once during the day and once at night. I give him a high place in our assembly because he says his prayers." [folios 20b–21a]

Theology: The Perfection of Faith

The next readings exemplify the use of reason and tradition in medieval Indian Islam to justify orthodox doctrines of God's transcendence and of His power over creation. They are taken from an exposition of Sunni doctrine called *The Perfection of Faith* by 'Abd ul-Haqq al-Dihlawī al-Bukhārī, who was born in Delhi in 1551 and died there in 1642. He was one of the most famous Sunni writers in Mughal India, winning the favor of the Emperor Jahāngīr. After performing the pilgrimage to Mecca about 1587 and studying in the Hijāz, he returned to teach for half a century in Delhi.

'Abd ul-Haqq was a prolific writer, composing biographies of the Prophet, of Indian Muslim saints, commentaries on the traditions of the Prophet, as well as a short history of India. His main contribution to Islam in India was the popularization of the study of Hadīth at a time when Sunni Islam was under the cloud raised by Akbar and the extreme mystical doctrines of Ibn 'Arabī.

The *Perfection of Faith* shows the dialectic used in orthodox theology in support of doctrines whose ultimate basis is divine revelation.

[From 'Abd ul-Haqq al-Dihlawī, *Takmīl ul-Īmān*, folios 2a–3b, 13–15]

THE ATTRIBUTES OF GOD

In truth, the creation and the proper ordering of the world will not come right except with one creator and one governor. . . . The Nourisher of the World is alive, is wise and powerful, and a free agent. Whatever He does is by His own intent and choice and not under compulsion and necessity. Without these attributes such a strange and wonderful world quite certainly would not appear or be conceivable. Such a world is not possible from a dead, ignorant, powerless, or unfree agent. These attributes [of life, wisdom, power and freedom] appear in created things. If they are not in God, from whence do they appear? He is a speaker of speech, a hearer of hearing, and a seer of seeing, because to be dumb, deaf, and blind is to be deficient and deficiencies are not proper to God. The Holy Qur'ān is eloquent as to that. It is impossible to comprehend the reality of these attributes, indeed of the totality of divine attributes by analogy and reason. But God has created a likeness of those in the essence of humankind, which he has interpenetrated in some way or other with His own attributes. But in truth, the attributes of man do not survive as God's attributes survive. "God's eternal attributes remain."

The attributes of God are eternal and are of equal duration with His essence.

Whatever He possesses—perfection and reality—is constant in eternity; because the location of accidents was created it does not become eternal. Except in a body there is neither limitation, cause, nor time; the creator of the world is not body and substance. That is to say, He is not a body and an attribute, that is to say, with the bodily qualities which the body has, like blackness and whiteness. He is not formed so that He has bodily shape and He is not compounded so that He is joined together repeatedly. He is not numbered so that it is possible to count Him. He is not limited so that He has a limit and He is not in a direction, that is to say, He is not above or below, before or after, left or right. He is not in a place and not in a moment, because all these are attributes of the world and the Nourisher of the World is not subject to worldly attributes and His purposes are not subject to time. Time does not include or circumscribe Him. His existence is not dependent upon time. For in that condition when there was not time, there was He. Now also there is time and He exists. Therefore, He is not in time. [folios 2b–3b]

THE TRANSCENDENCE OF GOD

Whatever exists, except God's essence and attributes, is created, that is to say, it comes into existence from nonexistence and is not eternal. As proof, the tradition of the Prophet, "There was God and there was nothing besides Him." As proof too, the world changes and is a place of many vicissitudes. Whatever is of this description is not eternal, and whatever is eternal does not change. We know that there is one real mode of existence—that of God's essence and attributes and there is no way for change in that mode. . . . And Almighty God is capable of extinguishing the world. After existence it passes away. As the Word of God says: "Everything perishes except the mode [Him]." Thus the angels, paradise, hell, and such like things to whose lastingness a tradition has testified, also are perishable. . . . Although God can annihilate in the twinkling of an eye, those who do not die will know that God is the creator of the world who has brought it into existence from nonexistence because, since the world is not eternal, the meaning of creation is that it was not and then it was. Whatever was of that order must have had a creator to bring it from nonexistence into existence because if it was created from itself it must always have been. Since it did not always exist, it was not created by itself but by another. The Nourisher of the World must be eternal. If He were not eternal He would be created. He would be of the world, not the self-existent Nourisher of the World. That is to say that the world's existence is by reason of its own essence and not by reason of something other than itself. But the world needs something other than itself and whatever needs something other than itself is not fit for lordship. The meaning of God's own words is future, that is, He Himself is coming into existence Himself. Certainly it must be that the end of the chain of existences is in one essence which is from itself. Otherwise it will continue in the same way endlessly and this is not reasonable. [folios 2a–2b]

FREE WILL

The next reading attempts to resolve the ethical problem posed by the doctrine of divine omnipotence. It should be noted that 'Abd ul-Haqq al-Dihlawī ap-

peals to the Sharī'a for final illumination. This is typical of his approach to theological issues and evidence of the strong hold of the Holy Law upon the
religious imagination of Muslims.

First it is necessary to understand the meaning of compulsion and
choice so that the essence of this problem may become clear. Man's
actions are of two kinds. One, when he conceives something, and, if that
thing is desired by and is agreeable to his nature, a great desire and passion for it wells up from within him, and he follows that passion and
moves after it. Or if the thing is contrary and repugnant to him, dislike
and abhorrence for it wells up within him and he shuns it. His relation
to the action and to stopping the action before the appearance of the
desire and the loathing were on a par. It was possible that he might act
or not act, whether at the stage of conception when the power to act was
near, or before conceiving the idea when he was farther from acting. This
motion of man is called an optional motion and the action which results
from that motion is called an optional action. The other kind of action
is when there is no conception, arousing of desire and wish, but motion
occurs and then desire, like the trembling of a leaf. This motion is called
compulsory and obligatory. If the meaning of desire and intention (as
distinct from choice) is as stated, it may be objected: "Who says that
man is not discerning and is not perspicacious? The creation of man occurred by choice, and such is the composition of his nature. Who says
that all human motions and actions are compulsory? To say this is to
deny virtue. No intelligent person will agree to this."

But there are difficulties in this conclusion. For, if, after comprehension
and conversance with the eternal knowledge, intentions, decree, and
ordination of God, it is conceived that it is not (really) man who
brings actions into existence, that conclusion will be reached because it
is realized that if God knew from all eternity that a particular action must
be performed by a particular individual, that action must therefore be
so performed, whether without that individual's choice, as in compulsory motion, or with his choice. If the action was optional (in form),
the individual did not (really) have choice either in his decision or in his
action. Furthermore, although the individual may have had choice in
his action, yet he did not have any choice in its first beginnings.

For example, when an eye opens and does not see, there is no image
before it. If after seeing and observing visible objects, they are desired,

a rousing of passion and desire is compulsory and the existence of motion toward them is also obligatory. Thereafter, although this action occurs through the human being's choice, yet in fact this choice is obligatory and compulsory upon him. Obligation and necessity are contrary to the reality of choice. Man has choice but he has not choice in his choice; or to put it another way, he has choice in appearance, but in fact he is acting under compulsion. . . . Imām Ja'far Sādiq, who is a master of the people of the Sufi way and a chief of the people of Truth, says that there is no compulsion or freedom. But he lays down that the truth is to be found between compulsion and freedom. The Jabarites are those who say that fundamentally man has no choice and his motions are like those of inanimate nature. The Qadariya are those who say that man has choice and that man is independent in his transactions. His actions are his own creations. Imām Ja'far says that both these two schools of thought are false and go to extremes. The true school of thought is to be found between them but reason is at a loss and confounded in the comprehension of this middle way; in truth this confusion is found among people of a disputatious and contending sort who wish to found articles of faith upon reason, and who will not acknowledge anything as true and believe in it unless it pleases their reason and falls within their understanding. But for believers, the short proof of this is what is put forward in the Holy Law and the Qur'ān, in which it is written on this problem that God has both power and will and, notwithstanding that, He charges obedience and disobedience to His servants. And He says, God never commits injustice but men have inflicted injustice upon themselves. "God was not one to wrong them but they did wrong themselves."

In this verse He establishes two things. He has imputed creation to Himself and action to men. Therefore we must of necessity believe that both are true and must be believed—that creation is from God and action from man. Although we do not reach to the end of this problem and as the proof of the Holy Law and what is commanded and forbidden is itself a consequence of choice, then it is necessary to believe that. The problem of divine power and ordination and the problem of man's choice become known to us by the traditions of the right path [Sharī'a]. Since both are known from the Sharī'a, what is the controversy and the disputing about? One must believe in both. In this matter faith in the middle way is necessary. In truth, deep thought into this problem is among the indications of

idleness and ignorance because no action and no truth is affected by controversy about it. One has to act. The real truth of the matter is that which
is with God. [folios 13–15]

Propaganda: The Indian Proof

The *Indian Proof,* written during the reign of Jahāngīr by one Ibn 'Umar Mihrābī, avowedly aims at combating "creeping Hinduism" among Muslims living
in villages far from the strongholds of Muslim culture, the towns and fortresses
of the Ganges-Jumna River area. It is written in the form of a dialogue between
a *sharāk* or species of talking bird who asks questions on cosmology and religion and a parrot who gives the Muslim answers. The dialogue is preceded
by a mythical account of its origin. A young and accomplished Muslim falls in
love with the daughter of a Mahratta raja and gives her the two talking birds
whom he has made word perfect in theological discussion. The raja's daughter
becomes a Muslim through listening to the two birds and has their conversation recorded in letters of gold. The golden text passes into the treasury of the
Rai (prince) of Gujrat, Rai Karan, who has it interpreted to him by a young
brahman secretly converted to Islam. On hearing the dialogue Rai Karan also
becomes a Muslim. It is possible that the mythological form of the work is a
response to the Hindu environment.

The *Indian Proof* shows clearly that the orthodox and the mystics in India
were of the same faith, collaborators if not partners in the work of Muslim
education. The parrot frequently quotes a Sufi work, the *Way of Eternity*
(*Marsād ul-Abad*), written about 1223 by Najm ud-dīn Dāyah of Qaisariyah.
Moreover, in the reading given below on the creation of the world, the *Indian
Proof* expresses the doctrine of the Light of Muhammad, or the existence prior
to creation of the soul of Muhammad in the form of light, from which God
makes all things emanate when He decides that the universe shall be. This
doctrine idealizing Muhammad is found among Sunnis, Shī'as, and mystics
after the ninth century A.D. and does not necessarily impair the orthodox assertion of God's unity and transcendence. Its presence in the *Indian Proof,*
however, underlines the unwisdom of forcing a cleavage between ulamā and
mystics upon medieval Indian Islam.

[From Ibn 'Umar Mihrābī, *Hujjat ul-Hind,* folios 11b–13a]

The *sharāk* said: Please be kind enough to explain the manner of the coming into being of all creation and of everything which exists—mankind,
the angels, jinns, devils, animals like wild beasts, birds, vegetation like
trees and plants, the soul and the lower self of man and animals, the earth,
mountains, seas, dry land and water, fire, wind, the skies, the world and
the constellations, the signs of the zodiac, the mansions and the empyrean,

the throne of God, the tablet, the pen, heaven, hell, the dwelling place in time and space of all these. Through your generous instruction it should become clear and known to everyone without doubt or obscurity what is the reality of each, in a way which explains its creation and reassures the heart and mind. And also, when you explain, do it so that all doubts disappear, reality is distinguishable from error and truth from falsehood.

The parrot answered: Know that the *Way of Eternity* (*Marsād ul-Abad*) gives an explanation of the beginning of created existences in this world and in heaven which has become the mode of existent things. If God wills, this explanation will be repeated. Now listen with your mind and from your heart to this other explanation. There is a difference between human souls and the pure soul of Muhammad the Prophet. As the prophets have said, he was the first thing God created. They called him a light and a spirit and he himself was the existence of existences, the fruit and the tree of created beings. As the tradition said, "But for you the heavens would not have been created"; for this, and no other, was the way in which creation began, like as a tree from whose seed spring the chief fruits of the tree. Then God Most High, when He wished to create created beings, first brought forth the light of Muhammad's soul from the ray of the light of His Unity as is reported in the Prophetic traditions. "I am from God and the believers are from me." In some traditions it is reported that God looked with a loving eye upon that light of Muhammad. Modesty overcame Him and the tears dropped from Him. From those drops He created the souls of the prophets. From those lights He created the souls of the saints, from their souls, the souls of believers, and from the souls of the believers He created the souls of the disobedient. From the souls of the disobedient He created the souls of hypocrites and infidels. From human souls He created the souls of the angels and from the rays of the souls of the angels He created the souls of jinns, and from their souls, devils. He created the different souls of animals according to their different kinds of ranks and states, all their descriptions of beings and souls—vegetation and minerals and compounds and elements He also brought forth.

To explain the remainder of creation; from the pearl [tear drop] which had remained, God created a jewel and looked upon that jewel with a majestic glance. With that awesome glance God melted that jewel and it became half water and half fire. Then He caused warm smoke to rise from the fire and the water and to be suspended in the air. From that came the seven heavens and from the sparks which were in the air with the smoke came forth the twinkling constellations. When He had brought forth the sun and the moon, the stars, the signs of the zodiac and the mansions of the moon from the leaping tongues of flame, He threw the wind and the water into confusion; foam appeared upon the surface and forth came the seven surfaces of the earth. Waves rose up and mountains emerged therefrom. From the remainder of the water God created the seas. He created the world in six days.

THE SHARĪʿA OR HOLY LAW OF ISLAM

Medieval Muslim society in word and deed aspired to discern and obey the pleasure of God. God was the only real object of knowledge; the understanding, however partial, of His purposes and the effort to fulfill them on earth, however feeble, was the whole duty of man. Man was thus created for worship and subjecthood, not for dominion over the world. In every thought, word, and action man was accountable to God on the Day of Judgment. Hence Muslim social ideals were not humanist ideals —the balanced and harmonious development of the human faculties or the creation of a man-conceived utopia on earth, for example. A New World for Muslims could only mean one in which they had discovered God's Will and were obeying it more fully than before.

Society was thought of, moreover, as a situation which human beings were forced to accept, rather than a relationship which might be transformed into a willing partnership for mutual companionship and welfare. It was an arithmetical total of human atoms each in geographical contiguity with the other, but significant only in relation to God.

The Muslim's individual relationship to God, however, was not stressed at the expense of social order. Belief in God and His Prophet implied acceptance of the Holy Law revealed through the Qurʾān and the Sunna of Muhammad. This Holy Law governed both doctrine and practice. It defined not merely right belief about God's Unity, His Power, and His Knowledge, but also those external acts of devotion—personal, e.g., prayer or pilgrimage, or social, e.g., almsgiving, avoidance of usury, maintenance of certain discriminations against the unbeliever—compliance with which attested one's membership in God's community before the eyes of the world. Muslim society was an organized society, though not, ideally, a humanly organized society. Its ethic was revealed to it by God, and its public life was to be informed by that revelation. Human institutions as the Muslims encountered them in their career of conquest fell into two types: they either did, or did not, conform to the will of God. If they did not, they had to be either transformed or destroyed. They could not be ignored. Nothing in life was irrelevant to the good life. Muslims were never at leisure in the sight of God. The Sharī'a or the Holy Law set the perfect standard for earthly society; it was the practical embodiment of the unity and the distinctive ideology of Islam.

As has been explained above, the Qur'ān and the Sunna of the Prophet were, after his death the two chief sources of guidance to the believer and hence of the Sharī'a. By the time of the Muslim conquest of North India, however, individuals were not permitted to investigate those sources for themselves. To later generations the knowledge of the Sharī'a is authoritatively communicated through the systems of jurisprudence worked out by the four orthodox schools of law. Jurisprudence is the science of deducing the mandates of the Sharī'a from its bases in the Qur'ān and Sunna, and in addition to the laws regulating ritual and religious observance, it embraces family law, the law of inheritance, property and contract, criminal law, constitutional law, and the conduct of war. From the Muslim viewpoint the ultimate obligation to obey regulations in any section of the Sharī'a is a religious one. They are all equally commands of Allāh. Moreover, according to the jurists, every human action falls into and may be evaluated in one or another of these five categories: commanded, recommended, legally indifferent, reprobated, or forbidden by God Himself.

According to orthodox theory, unambiguous commands or prohibitions in the Qur'ān or in the authenticated Sunna excluded the use of human reason and determination, except in so far as the resources of philology or lexicography were necessary to establish the literal sense of the text. However, when points of law or conduct not covered by a clear statement in the Qur'ān or the Sunna arose, recourse was had to argument from analogy (qiyās) or even to opinion (ra'y). Opinion, however, was rejected by the stricter sort, as introducing a fallible human element in a divine decision. It was in an academic fashion that the theologians and lawyers of the second and third centuries after Hijra developed the all-embracing regulations of the Sharī'a and created a body of jurisprudence unique in that it was the work of theorists rather than of practical men. In this they were encouraged by the 'Abbāsids, the self-proclaimed godly rulers who were determined, so they said, to abandon the ungodly ways of their Umayyad predecessors.

The whole structure was given rigidity and strength by the acceptance, in the second century Hijra, of what became the fourth basis of jurisprudence, the consensus (*ijmā'*) of the Muslim community. This was the real guarantee of the authenticity of the text of the Qur'ān, of the text of the Sunna, and of the acceptability of analogy; it was the real curb on heresy and innovation. Consensus became indeed a third channel of revelation. What the Muslim community was prepared to accept became Divine Law. When the community had attained a consensus, it was regarded as irrevocable; the formation and circulation of new doctrines and practices was in theory impossible, and, in practice, dangerous. Consensus fixed the limit between orthodoxy and heresy; to question an interpretation of Islam so arrived at was tantamount to heresy. However, consensus is not promulgated by any formal body and its existence is perceived only on looking back and seeing that agreement has tacitly been reached and then consciously accepting that tacit agreement. The spiritual mantle of Muhammad fell not upon a church and a priesthood but upon the whole community.

The chief prescriptions of the Sharī'a, founded on the four bases of the Qur'ān, Hadīth, analogy, and consensus as the "knowledge of the rights and duties whereby man may fitly conduct his life in this world and prepare himself for the future life," had been formulated by A.D. 1200. Muslims backed into their future facing the past. God's will for mankind had been revealed for men through His Prophet six hundred years ago, and since men had now worked out their understanding of that will, any impulse for change in the new environment of India would meet with tough resistance.

The good days were the good old days. The history of the world after the death of the Prophet, therefore, was a history of decadence and of retrogression, not of betterment and progresss. Change was *ipso facto* for the worse, and, therefore, to be avoided. If change did occur nevertheless, it would be disguised wherever possible as a return to the purer

Islam of seventh-century Arabia or, if not, it might be sanctified by consensus. It was certain, however, that it would not be sought or welcomed.

Through the Sharī'a Muslim society displayed and displays a deep sense of solidarity and a remarkable resilence under attack. Acceptance of the Sharī'a code of practical obligations distinguishes friend from foe. The Sharī'a itself lessens the risk of apostasy and indifference through ignorance of the practical demands made by religion upon the individual. By impressing upon Muslims that every action and social activity should be an act of worship and of humility before God, the Sharī'a nurtures the interior spiritual life while tilting the balance against the vagaries of individual religious intuition or individual speculation about the nature of God. Yet as al-Ghazālī's achievement suggests, there is room for wide variation of belief and practice within the ambit of the Holy Law. The principle of the consensus of the community has in practice permitted the tacit and peaceful acceptance of change. Muslims have usually been reluctant to extrude anyone from their society who subscribes at least to the simple basic testimony (shahādat, namely, "There is no god but God. Muhammad is the Prophet of God.") There has always been a hope of further education in the true Faith This wide tolerance was to prove a major asset in the survival and the expansion of the Muslim community in India.

The Bases of Jurisprudence

A clear exposition of the bases of Muslim jurisprudence is given in the *Encyclopedia of the Sciences* by Fakhr ud-dīn al-Rāzī (1149–1209), a theologian and canon lawyer who lived for a time (c. 1185) in Ghaznīn and the Punjab under the patronage of the Ghōrid sultans, Ghiyath ud-dīn and Muhammad ibn Sām, who started the conquest of North India.

[From al-Razi, *Jāmi' ul-'Ulūm*, pp. 8–9]

The first basis is the knowledge of the evidences of the mandates of the Holy Law. These are four—God's book, the Sunna [custom and sayings] of the Prophet of God, the consensus of the community, and analogy. The explanation of the Qur'ān and the Sunna of the Prophet has been adduced. It is evident that when the Prophethood of Muhammad became acknowledged and the truth of what he said established, whatever he indicated by his practice and gave witness to as truth is right and true. Further the consensus of the community is established by the fact that God Most High said, "He who resists the Prophet after the right way has been made clear to him, we will cause him to suffer the fate he has earned. We shall cause him to burn in Hell. What an evil fate!" Since in the light of this verse it is forbidden and unlawful to follow other than the way of the believers, it follows that it is right and true to follow the way of the believers. Likewise, the Prophet said, "My community will not agree upon an error." [If a mistake had been possible in the consensus of the community, it would have been a deviation from the right path], for then the falseness of this tradition would necessarily follow and this is untrue. But what analogy proves is that the events and vicissitudes of life are infinite and the evidences are finite. To affirm the infinite by means of the finite is absurd; therefore it is evident that there is no avoiding analogy and the employment of one's own opinion [ijtihād].[1] Therefore it is evident that all the four sources are right and true. . . .

There are ten conditions of legal interpretation. The first is knowledge of God's Holy Book because it is a foundation of the knowledge of the mandates of the Sharī'a. But it is not a necessary condition that there should be knowledge of the whole Book but only of those verses which are relevant to the mandates of the Holy Law—to wit, to the number of five hundred verses, and no more. It is necessary that these verses should be in the mujtahid's memory in such a way that when need of them arises it is possible to attain his object in the knowledge of one of the mandates of the Holy Law. The second condition is knowledge of the traditions of the Prophet. In the same way as in the knowledge of the word of God, where there was no need to know all, but only to remember some points, so it is with the traditions of the Prophet. Thirdly, it is a condition of legal interpretation that one should know the abrogating and the abrogated portions of the Qur'ān and of the Sunna, so that no error should occur in legal interpretation. Fourth, one should discriminate between the reason why a tradition is valid or invalid and discern the true from the false. Fifth, the interpreter of the law should be aware of the problems which have been resolved among the umma[2] because if he is

---

[1] A Muslim legist's interpretation of the Sharī'a, an undertaking requiring deep scholarship and considerable ingenuity on the part of the interpreter (mujtahid), particularly if, as often, he wished to find justification in the Qur'ān and Sunna for some later custom.
[2] The Muslim community.

not aware of them he may deliver a formal legal opinion which is against the consensus of the community and this is not permissible. Sixth, knowledge of the manner of arranging Sharī'a evidence in a way which will bring forth a conclusion and distinguish truth from error in that conclusion. The interpreter of the law should know what are the occasions of error and how many there are, so that he may avoid them. The seventh is awareness of the fundamentals of the faith—knowledge of creation, of the unity of God, and of His freedom from sin and vice. The interpreter of the law should know that the Creator is eternal, knowing, and powerful. The eighth and ninth are that he should know lexicography and grammar to such an extent that by their means he can know the intentions of God and of the Prophet in the Qur'ān and the Traditions. The tenth condition is knowledge of the sciences of the bases of jurisprudence and comprehension of what is commanded and what is prohibited, the universal and the particular, the general and the special, abrogation of Qur'anic verses and the circumstances thereof, Qur'anic commentaries, and preferences and rulings and analogy.

Guidance in the Holy Law

The standard work expounding the principles of jurisprudence according to the predominant school of law in medieval Muslim India, the Hanafī, is the *Guidance* by Maulana Burhān ud-dīn Marghīnānī (d. 1197) of Transoxania. It is a digest or abstract of earlier Hanafī works and was itself the subject of several later commentaries in India. The *Guidance* commences with the compulsory religious duties ('*ibādat*) of ritual purification, prayer, alms, fasting, and pilgrimage. This exposition of religious duty precedes that of the principles of Muslim law relating among other things to marriage, adultery, fosterage, divorce, manumission of slaves, vows, punishments, larceny, holy war and the treatment of infidels, foundlings, treasure trove, loans, gifts, rules of evidence, prohibited liquors, offenses against the person, and wills. The readings given below from the *Guidance* are intended to show only the essentially religious grammar and idiom of Muslim law.

THE ALMS TAX

[From *Hidāya*, 1.1.1.2]

Alms-giving is an ordinance of God, incumbent upon every person who is free, sane, adult, and a Muslim, provided he be possessed, in full property, of such estate or effects as are termed in the language of the law a minimum, and that he has been in possession of the same for the space of one complete year. . . . The reason of this obligation is found in the word of God, who has ordained it in the Qur'ān, saying, "Bestow alms." The same injunction occurs in the traditions, and it is moreover universally admitted. The reason for freedom being a requisite condition is that this is essential to the complete possession of property. The reason why sanity of intellect and maturity of age are requisite conditions shall be hereafter demonstrated. The reason why the Muslim faith is made a condition is that the rendering of alms is an act of piety, and such cannot proceed from an infidel.

OF THE DISBURSEMENT OF ALMS, AND OF THE PERSONS TO WHOSE USE IT IS TO BE APPLIED

[From *Hidāya*, 1.1.7.53–54]

The objects of the disbursement of alms are of eight different descriptions: first, the needy; secondly, the destitute; thirdly, the collector of alms; . . . fourthly, slaves [upon whom alms are bestowed in order to enable them, by fulfilling their contract (i.e., by procuring their purchase price) to procure their freedom]; fifthly, debtors not possessed of property amounting to a legal minimum; sixthly, in the service of God; seventhly, travelers; and eighthly, the winning over of hearts. And those eight descriptions are the original objects of the expenditure of alms, being particularly specified as such in the Qur'ān; and there are, therefore, no other proper or legal objects of its application. With respect to the last, however, the law has ceased to operate, since the time of the Prophet, because he used to bestow alms upon them as a bribe or gratuity to prevent them from molesting the Muslims, and also to secure their occasional assistance; but when God gave strength to the faith, and to its followers, and rendered the Muslims independent of such assistance, the occasion of bestowing this gratuity upon them no longer remained; and all the doctors unite in this opinion. . . .

POLYGAMY

The Qur'anic influence on Muslim jurisprudence is illustrated in the following.

[From *Hidāya*, 1.2.1.88]

It is lawful for a freeman to marry four wives, whether free or slaves; but it is not lawful for him to marry more than four, because God has commanded in the Qur'ān, saying: "Ye may marry whatsoever women are agreeable to you, two, three, or four," and the numbers being thus expressly mentioned, any beyond what is there specified would be unlawful. Shāfi'ī alleges a man cannot lawfully marry more than one woman of the description of slaves, from his tenet as above recited, that "the marriage of freemen with slaves is allowable only from necessity"; the text already quoted is, however, in proof against him, since the term "women" applies equally to free women and to slaves.

TESTIMONY

The law relating to the inadmissibility of the testimony of nonbelievers and others is significant as it measures a man's "credit-worthiness" by his adherence to Muslim faith and rules of conduct.

[From *Hidāya*, 2.21.1.670–71; 2.21.2.690–91]

In all rights, whether of property or otherwise, the probity of the witness, and the use of the word *shahādat* [evidence] is requisite; even in the case of the evidence of women with respect to birth, and the like; and this is approved; because *shahādat* is testimony, since it possesses the property of being binding; whence it is that it is restricted to the place of jurisdiction; and also, that the witness is required to be free; and a Muslim. If, therefore, a witness should say: "I know," or "I know with certainty," without making use of the word *shahādat,* in that case his evidence cannot be admitted. With respect to the probity of the witness, it is indispensable, because of what is said in the Qur'ān: "Take the evidence of two just men." [2.21.1.670–71]

. . . .

The testimony of *zimmīs* [protected unbelievers] with respect to each other is admissible, notwithstanding they be of different religions. Mālik and Shāfi'ī have said that their evidence is absolutely inadmissible, because, as infidels are unjust, it is requisite to be slow in believing anything they may advance, God having said [in the Qur'ān]: "When an unjust person tells you anything, be slow in believing him"; whence it is that the evidence of an infidel is not admitted concerning a Muslim; and consequently, that an infidel stands [in this particular] in the same predicament with an apostate. The arguments of our doctors upon this point are twofold. First, it is related of the Prophet, that he permitted and held lawful the testimony of some Christians concerning others of their sect. Secondly, an infidel having power over himself, and his minor children, is on that account qualified to be a witness with regard to his own sect; and the depravity which proceeds from his faith is not destructive of this qualification, because he is supposed to abstain from everything prohibited in his own religion, and falsehood is prohibited in every religion. It is otherwise with respect to an apostate, as he possesses no power, either over his own person, or over that of another; and it is also otherwise with respect to a *zimmī* in relation to a Muslim, because a *zimmī* has no power over the person of a Muslim. Besides, a *zimmī* may be suspected of inventing falsehoods against a Muslim from the hatred he bears to him on account of the superiority of the Muslims over him. [2.21.2.690–91]

CHAPTER XV

THE MYSTICS

The majority of Muslims neither knew nor understood the theological formulations of their faith. For them life was bounded by the Sharī'a and by the round of mosque, pilgrimage, fasting, alms-giving, and ritual prayer. But many outside the comparatively small circle of scholars found this unsatisfying, particularly if, as often but not always, they were non-Arab converts with different religious traditions. They craved for a more emotional, indeed emotive religion, one in which God appeared as a loving, succoring Friend rather than as an abstract definition of undifferentiated unity incomprehensible in His Essence, inscrutable and arbitrary in His decrees. Moreover, as Islam grew to world power, the pious were scandalized at the compromises of political life and at the readiness of lawyers and theologians to accept service under "ungodly" rulers. Many withdrew into an ascetic seclusion, seeking to avoid the Divine Wrath on the Day of Judgment.

Many Muslims, therefore, found their thirst for God and for piety quenched in mysticism rather than in theology. The religious history of Islam after the twelfth century, particularly in those lands of the Eastern Caliphate which later came under the political dominance of the Turks and the Mongols, was largely that of the Sufi mystic movements and of the struggle of the ulamā to keep those movements within the Muslim fold. Although Islamic mysticism may have been stimulated by Christian, Gnostic, or Hindu mysticism, it already had a firm basis in the inspiration of the Qur'ān and in the early experience of the Prophet. His earlier revelations betray an intense consciousness of God as a living, everpresent reality. "We are nearer to him [man] than his jugular vein" (Qur'ān 50.15), and "Whenever ye turn there is the faith of God. Adore, and draw thou nigh" (96.19), or "He loveth them and they love Him" (5.59). It was this text which was particularly used by later Sufis to justify their attempts to lose themselves in the Divine Love.

Sufism was at the confluence of two streams of thought in Islam—the ascetic and the devotional. But by the second century after Hijra, the second had gained the upper hand. In many, the mystical element of love and adoration overcame the fear of the Day of Judgment. This victory is summed up in the sentence from al-Hasan al-Basrī (643–728): "I have not served God from fear of hell for I should be a wretched hireling if I served Him from fear; nor from love of heaven for I should be a bad servant if I served for what is given; I have served Him only for love of Him and desire for Him," or by the saying of the woman saint, Rabi'a al-Adawīya (d. 801): "Love of God hath so absorbed me that neither love nor hate of any other thing remain in my heart."

Before the second-century Hijra (A.D. 722–822) had ended, the Sufis had already worked out methods of attaining gnosis (ma'rifat) or mystic knowledge of God along a path (tarīqa) to ecstatic union with God or with one of His attributes, either by the indwelling of God in the man, or by the man's ascent to God. The true mystic was he who had cast off self and lost himself in God. The language of the Muslim Sufis during or after the moment of supreme mystical experience was often borrowed from that of inebriation or sexual love. A famous mystic, al-Hallāj, eventually, in 922, executed for heresy in Baghdad, "was so carried away by his ecstatic experience that he did not feel the dual nature of man, that is to say, his existence here as a single creature, and his rapture in mystical communion with the Divine. He taught that man was God incarnate and he looked to Jesus rather than to Muhammad as the supreme example of glorified humanity. God is love, and in His love, He created man after his own image so that man might find that image within himself and attain to union with the Divine Nature." Al-Hallāj expressed the intensity of the feeling of complete harmony with God in the following terms. "I am He whom I love and He whom I love is I. We are two spirits dwelling in one body. If thou seest me, thou seest Him, and if thou seest Him, thou seest us both."

The spiritual life which rises to this climax of insight was usually described as a journey passing through a number of stages. A typical mystic "road map" showed the following as milestones along the journey: repentance, abstinence, renunciation, poverty, patience, trust in God, satisfaction. Only when the Sufi has passed all these stages is he raised to the higher plane of consciousness (gnosis) and realizes that knowledge, knower, and known are one. Repentance is described as the awakening of the soul from the slumber of sin and heedlessness; abstinence and renunciation mean not merely the relinquishing of material pleasures but also the abandonment of all desire—even of the desire to abandon everything itself. Poverty meant the stripping away of every wish which could distract men's thoughts from God. Patience meant both patience in misfortune and patience to refrain from those things which God has forbidden to mankind. Trust in God betokened confidence in His grace toward the sinful pilgrim and satisfaction means for the pilgrim, eager acceptance of Divine decree. All these stages or stations (*maqāmāt*) were arrived at through the efforts of the pilgrim. The later part of the journey toward God was only made possible by the gift of God Himself. Indeed the light of intuitive certainty by which the heart sees God was a beam of God's Own Light cast therein by Himself. The two supreme states (*hāl*) were annihilation and subsistence. Annihilation (fanā) means a transformation of the soul through the utter extinction of all passion and desires, the contemplation of the Divine attributes, and the cessation of all conscious thought. Most Sufis were insistent that the individual human personality was not annihilated in this state. Some said that in this state the Sufi becomes like a drop of water in the ocean. Upon this follows subsistence (*baqā*) or abiding in God. This can mean either, or all, of three things— union with one of the activities symbolized by the names of God, union with one of the attributes of God, or union with the Divine Essence. When the Sufi has attained annihilation and subsistence, the veils of the flesh, of the will, and of the world have been torn aside, Truth is beheld and man is united to God. The wisest mystics, e.g., al-Ghazālī, recognized that this supreme experience could not be expressed in words; others ignored the limitation of language and scandalized the orthodox while often failing to communicate their own experience.

It is perhaps not surprising that Sufis should soon have come under suspicion from the orthodox theologians. Although early Sufis of the ascetic sort lived retired meditative lives, their claim to judge men and themselves by an inner light and to enjoy a direct personal relation to God could not but antagonize the ulamā, the doctors of a Sharī'a which claimed to regulate only outward conduct and who had no sure means of detecting hypocrisy. Although some early mystics were scrupulous in the observance of the Sharīʿa, others were not recognizably within the Muslim fold at all. A friend of the philosopher Ibn Sīna, Abū Saʿīd ibn Abīʾl Khair, a Persian mystic, wrote:

> Not until every mosque beneath the sun,
> Is ruined will our holy work be done,
> And never will true Muslim appear,
> Till faith and infidelity are one.

There was always the danger that, in the intensity of his personal religious experience, the Sufi would deny the value of the mandates of the Sharīʿa. "The mystics learned from God, the ulamā from books." As al-Ghazālī was to ask: "In what do discussions on divorce and on buying and selling prepare the believer for the beyond?" Al-Wāsitī (d. 932) said: "Ritual acts are only impurities."

These dangerous antinomian tendencies were matched by dangerous pantheistic tendencies. It was difficult for orthodox scholars to stomach some of the expressions used by mystics in the moment of supreme insight and experience. Abū Yazīd al-Bistāmī (d. 875) cried: "Praise be to Me!"; al-Hallāj (d. 922): "I am the Truth. Is it Thou or is it I?"; Ibn Sahl Tustarī (d. 896): "I am the Proof of God, in face of the saints of my time"; Ibn Abīʾl Khair: "Beneath my robe there is only God"; Ibn Sabʿīn (d. 1269): "There is nothing but God." The famous Sufi teacher Muhyiʾ ud-dīn ibn al-ʿArabī was a thorough monist. The one reality is God; the universe is His expression of Himself. The universe does not proceed from God by emanations but by manifestations; He makes himself known to Himself in everything. The mystic does not become one with God; he becomes conscious of his oneness with God. Clearly, in such a doctrine, Islam and other faiths are put on an equality. Everything (including infidels and infidelity) is for the best in the best of all possible worlds. The execution of al-Hallāj in 922 in Baghdad was a measure of the antagonism aroused among the lawyers and the dialecticians by such ideas as the above. Moreover under the ʿAbbāsid Caliphs, Sufism was not popular with political authority. In the course of the third century after Hijra Sufism became popular among the artisan and minor trading classes of the cities of Iraq and Persia, uneducated in the traditional religious disciplines and sometimes the victims of the ʿAbbāsid tax machine. Although Sufism was never a revolutionary movement politically, its call for a personal spiritual revival threw into sharp relief the worldliness of the ruling powers.

That orthodoxy was reconciled to mysticism within Islam was largely the achievement of the great theologian and mystic al-Ghazālī, who probably forestalled a schism in Islam. He was an Erasmus who was enough of a Luther to make a Luther unnecessary. In India, the measure of his success may be gauged by the absence of tension between the ulama and the mystics during the sultanate period. In Mughal times, however, partly because some of the Mughal rulers appeared positively to encourage unorthodoxy, antagonism broke out again.

Al-Ghazālī made the personal, emotional relation of the individual to God the core of popular Islam. Man's perfection and happiness consist in trying to imitate the qualities of God, in trying to do His Will. This Will he may discover from theology—but few are equipped to follow that severe discipline. Rather is he likely to discover the real attributes and purposes of God by mystical experience. In winning over Islam to this view, al-Ghazālī won for Sufism an abiding home in Muslim orthodoxy. In doing so, however, he pared away some of the more extreme forms of mystic expression. He refused to try to express what he himself had experienced. "To divulge the secrets of Lordship is unbelief." Al-Ghazālī held Sufism back from pantheism; at the moment of supreme illumination there is still a distinction between God and the mystic.

Al-Ghazālī's monumental exposition of Islam was accepted by consensus within a century of his death. The consequences for the Muslim world were second only perhaps to the deaths of Hasan and Husain at Karbala in 680. Many of the peoples in western Asia, particularly in the lands dominated by the Turks, were finally won over to orthodox Islam. Sufism henceforth became the most vital spiritual force in Islam with its exponents courted by princes as much as by the ordinary man. However, the victory of al-Ghazālī's synthesis altered the whole course of Muslim civilization. It opened the floodgates (and nowhere more so than in India later) to forms of religious belief and practice from which Muhammad himself would have recoiled. Principally these innovations meant the worship of saints in the teeth of the Qur'ān, tradition, and orthodox theology. Many Sufis cared little whether their practices and their teachings were in harmony with received Islamic doctrine. "Know that the principle and foundation of Sufism and knowledge of God rests on saintship," wrote al-Hujwīrī.

The victory of al-Ghazālī was followed by the invasion of Neo-Platonic and gnostic ideas into Sufism. The extreme expression of these ideas is found in Ibn 'Arabī, the Spaniard (1165–1240), in the doctrine of the Light of Muhammad. He taught that things emanate from divine prescience as ideas, and that the idea of Muhammad is the creative and rational principle of the universe. He is the Perfect Man in whom the Divine Light shines, the visible aspect of God. The aim of the Sufi should be to unite with, and in, the Perfect Man who unifies all phenomena into the manifestation of the real. The Perfect Man is "a copy of God." He is a cosmic power on which the universe depends for existence. Later, popular Islam was to attach this idea to the persons of famous mystics. At the head of the community stood prophets, and below them, saints who were the elect of the mystics. The saints formed an invisible hierarchy on which the order of the world depended. It was not surprising therefore that popular sentiment attributed miracles to the Sufi shaikhs or that after death their tombs became places of pilgrimage.

These ideas, and those of an earlier stage of Sufi belief and practice, became institutionalized in the century after al-Ghazālī's death in the great Sufi orders. Already al-Ghazālī had stated that the Sufi disciple must have recourse to a spiritual director for guidance. The novice was received into the fraternity by a ceremony of initiation. The head of the fraternity (shaikh or pīr, lit. elder) claimed the spiritual succession from the founder of the order and through him from the Prophet or 'Alī. The shaikh and his followers lived in a community endowed by supporters (who often included sultans) giving themselves up to spiritual exercises, meditation, and the attainment of mystical experience. In the twelfth century the Muslim world was covered by such retreats as a result of initiates going out from the parent retreat and founding satellite retreats linked to the parent by ties of reverence and common rituals. Membership in the orders was often very broad; it was of two kinds—a class of initiates (murīd) engaged in continual meditation or devotional exercises, and a larger number of "lay members" meeting to partake in "remembrance of God," but otherwise following their normal occupations. The total number of Sufi orders is (and was in the twelfth century) very great. The Muslim conquest of North India was contemporary with the introduction of some of these orders into India. There they were to dominate Muslim thought and social life, reaching out at times toward Hinduism.

SUFISM IN INDIA DURING THE SULTANATE PERIOD (c.1200–1500)

Muslim mysticism in India, like Muslim scholastic theology in India, entered the country in a well-developed form and did not greatly change its ideas (as opposed to its practices) in its new environment. The increasing influence of Ibn 'Arabī's pantheistic doctrines in Mughal times was due to a fresh immigration of Sufi orders new to India, rather than to changes in existing Indo-Muslim mystical schools of thought.

Between the end of the twelfth century and the end of the fifteenth, three great Sufi orders had migrated from Iraq and Persia into northern India, the Chishtī, the Suhrawardī, and the Firdausī. The first was the largest and most popular. Its "sphere of operations" was the area of the present Uttar Pradesh, where its great saints Nizām ud-dīn Auliyā (1238–1325) and Nasīr ud-dīn Muhammad Chirāgh of Delhi (d. 1356) lived and taught. Among its adherents were numbered some of the greatest luminaries of Indo-Muslim culture in the sultanate period—including Amīr Khusrau, the poet, and Ziā ud-dīn Barnī, the historian. The tombs of the mystic-saints of the order are still honored by both Hindus and Muslims. The Suhrawardī order was primarily confined to Sind. The Firdausī order could not establish itself in the Delhi area in face of the Chishtī order, and moved eastward to Bihar.

All these mystic orders were indebted for the theoretical expression of their ideas to a small number of "mystic textbooks" written in the eleventh and twelfth centuries, notably the *Discovery of the Beloved* (*Kashf ul-Mahjūb*) by Shaikh 'Alī Hujwīrī, written partly at Lahore, the capital of the Punjab when annexed by Mahmūd of Ghaznin. In India no such systematic theoretical treatises were written, but to popularize Sufi teaching, disciples of great Sufi teachers recorded the sayings and discourses of their masters or wrote their biographies. Notable among the former is *The Morals of the Heart* (*Fawā'id ul-Fuwād*) by the poet Amīr Hasan Sijzī, a record of the conversations of Shaikh Nizām ud-dīn Auliyā in his retreat at Ghiyāspūr between A.D. 1307 and 1322. Another "Indian Sufi teachers' handbook" is the collection of letters (*Maktūbāt*) of Shaikh Sharaf ud-dīn Yahyā of Manīr, a mystic of the Firdausī order who flourished in Bihar toward the end of the fourteenth or the beginning of the fifteenth century. The letters were addressed to a disciple.

The readings will illustrate the following themes: the Sufi emphasis on the love for God as the principle of human existence on earth and their consequent unworldly attitude; the urge toward union with Him; the stages of the mystic path toward that union; the avoidance of pantheism and monism and the acceptance of the Shari'a by the mystics of the sultanate period; and the role of the saints.

The Love of God
[From Shaikh 'Alī Hujwīrī, *Kashf ul-Mahjūb*, pp. 307–8]

Man's love toward God is a quality which manifests itself in the heart of the pious believer, in the form of veneration and magnification, so that he seeks to satisfy his Beloved and becomes impatient and restless in his desire for vision of Him, and cannot rest with anyone except Him, and grows familiar with the remembrance of Him, and abjures the remembrance of everything besides. Repose becomes unlawful to him and rest flees from him. He is cut off from all habits and associations, and renounces sensual passion and turns toward the court of love and submits to the law of love and knows God by His attributes of perfection. It is impossible that man's love of God should be similar in kind to the love of His creatures toward one another, for the former is desire to comprehend and attain the beloved object, while the latter is a property of bodies. The lovers of God are those who devote themselves to death in nearness to Him, not those who seek His nature because the seeker stands by himself, but he who devotes himself to death stands by his Beloved; and the truest lovers are they who would fain die thus, and are overpowered, because a phenomenal being has no means of approaching the Eternal save through the omnipotence of the Eternal. He who knows what is real love feels no more difficulties, and all his doubts depart.

Contemplation
[From Shaikh 'Alī Hujwīrī, *Kashf ul-Mahjūb*, pp. 329–31]

The Apostle said: "Make your bellies hungry and your livers thirsty and leave the world alone, that perchance you may see God with your hearts";

and he also said: "Worship God as though thou sawest Him, for if thou dost not see Him, yet He sees thee." God said to David: "Dost thou know what is knowledge of Me? It is the life of the heart in contemplation of Me." By "contemplation" the Sufis mean spiritual vision of God in public and private, without asking how or in what manner. . . .

There are really two kinds of contemplation. The former is the result of perfect faith, the latter of rapturous love, for in the rapture of love a man attains to such a degree that his whole being is absorbed in the thought of his Beloved and he sees nothing else. Muhammad b. Wasi' says: "I never saw anything without seeing God therein," i.e., through perfect faith. This vision is from God to His creatures. Shiblī says: "I never saw anything except God," i.e., in the rapture of love and the fervor of contemplation. One sees the act with his bodily eye and, as he looks, beholds the Agent from all things else, so that he sees only the Agent. The one method is demonstrative, the other is ecstatic. In the former case, a manifest proof is derived from the evidences of God; and in the latter case, the seer is enraptured and transported by desire; evidences and verities are a veil to him, because he who knows a thing does not reverence aught besides, and he who loves a thing does not regard aught besides, but renounces contention with God and interference with Him in His decrees and His acts. God hath said of the Apostle at the time of his Ascension: "His eyes did not swerve or transgress" (Qur'ān 53.17), on account of the intensity of his longing for God. When the lover turns his eye away from created things, he will inevitably see the Creator with his heart. God hath said: "Tell the believers to close their eyes" (Qur'ān 24.30), i.e., to close their bodily eyes to lusts and their spiritual eyes to created things. He who is most sincere in self-mortification is most firmly grounded in contemplation for inward contemplation is connected with outward mortification. Sahl b. 'Abdallāh of Tustar says: "If anyone shuts his eye to God for a single moment, he will never be rightly guided all his life long," because to regard other than God is to be handed over to other than God, and one who is left at the mercy of other than God is lost. Therefore the life of contemplatives is the time during which they enjoy contemplation: time spent in seeing ocularly they do not reckon as life, for that to them is really death. Thus, when Abū Yazīd was asked how old he was, he replied: "Four years." They said: "How can that be?" He answered: "I have been veiled [from God] by this world for seventy years, but I have seen Him during the last four years: the period in which one is veiled does not belong to one's life."

Seeking the Path
[From Shaikh Sharaf ud-dīn Maneri, *Maktūbāt-i-Sadi,* pp. 37–38]

The aspiration of the Seeker should be such that, if offered this world with its pleasures, the next with its heaven, and the Universe with its sufferings, he should leave the world and its pleasures for the profane, the next world and its heaven for the faithful, and choose the sufferings for himself. He turns from the lawful in order to avoid heaven, in the same way that common people turn from the unlawful to avoid hell. He seeks the Master and His Vision in the same way that worldly men seek ease and wealth. The latter seek increase in all their works; he seeks the One alone in all. If given anything, he gives it away; if not given, he is content.

The marks of the Seeker are as follows. He is happy if he does not get the desired object, so that he may be liberated from all bonds; he opposes the desire-nature so much that he would not gratify its craving, even if it cried therefor for seventy years; he is so harmonized with God that ease and uneasiness, a boon and a curse, admission and rejection, are the same to him; he is too resigned to beg for anything either from God or from the world; his asceticism keeps him as fully satisfied with his little all—a garment or a blanket—as others might be with the whole world. . . . He vigilantly melts his desire-nature in the furnace of asceticism and does not think of anything save the True One. He sees Him on the right and on the left, sitting and standing. Such a Seeker is called the Divine Seer. He attaches no importance to the sovereignty of earth or of heaven. His body becomes emaciated by devotional aspirations, while his heart is cheered with Divine Blessedness. Thoughts of wife and children, of this world and the next, do not occupy his heart. Though his body be on earth, his soul is with God. Though here, he has already been there, reached the Goal, and seen the Beloved with his inner eye.

This stage can be reached only under the protection of a perfect teacher, the Path safely trodden under his supervision only. . . . It is indispensable for a disciple to put off his desires and protests, and place himself before the teacher as a dead body before the washer of the dead, so that He may deal with him as He likes.

Renunciation
[From Shaikh Sharaf ud-dīn Maneri, *Maktūbāt-i-Sadi*, pp. 49–51, 78]

The first duty incumbent upon a Seeker is the practice of *Tajrīd* and *Tafrīd*. The one is to quit present possessions; the other, to cease to care for the morrow. The second duty is seclusion, outer and inner. Outer seclusion consists in flying from the world and turning thy face to the wall in order that thou mayest give up thy life on the Divine threshold; inner seclusion consists in cleansing the heart of all thoughts connected with the non-God, whether the non-God be earth or heaven. [p. 78]

. . .

Intellect is a bondage; faith, the liberator. The disciple should be stripped naked of everything in the universe in order to gaze at the beauty of faith. But thou lovest thy personality, and canst not afford to put off the hat of self-esteem and exchange reputation for disgrace. . . .

All attachments have dropped from the masters. Their garment is pure of all material stain. Their hands are too short to seize anything tainted with impermanence. Light has shone in their hearts enabling them to see God. Absorbed in His vision are they, so that they look not to their individualities, exist not for their individualities, have forgotten their individualities in the ecstasy of His existence, and have become completely His. They speak, yet do not speak; hear, yet do not hear; move, yet do not move; sit, yet do not sit. There is no individual being in their being, no speech in their speech, no hearing in their hearing. Speakers, they are dumb; hearers, they are deaf. They care little for material conditions, and think of the True One alone. Worldly men are not aware of their whereabouts. Physically with men, they are internally with God. They are a boon to the universe—not to themselves, for they are not themselves. . . .

The knowledge that accentuates personality is verily a hindrance. The knowledge that leads to God is alone true knowledge. The learned are confined in the prison of the senses, since they but gather their knowledge through sensuous objects. He that is bound by sense-limitations is barred from supersensuous knowledge. Real knowledge wells up from the Fountain of Life, and the student thereof need not resort to senses and gropings. The iron of human nature must be put into the melting-pot of discipline, hammered on the anvil of asceticism, and then handed over to the polishing agency of the Divine Love, so that the latter may cleanse it of all material impurities. It then becomes a mirror capable of reflecting the spiritual world, and may fitly be used by the King for the beholding of His Own Image. [pp. 49–51]

THE QUEST FOR GOD THE BELOVED AND FOR KNOWLEDGE OF GOD

The quest for knowledge of God is usually described in terms of a journey or a road (tarīqa); the geography and the stages of the journey are given differently by different mystics but the mode of impulsion is the same. The Sufi must kill desire for the world, trust in God, submit to His will, and await patiently the inflowing of His Divine Grace before being able to proceed to final illumination—annihilation of the self and subsistence in God.

Repentance
[Adapted from Shaikh 'Alī Hujwīrī Kashf ul-Mahjūb, p. 294]

You must know that repentance is the first station of pilgrims on the way to the Truth, just as purification is the first step of those who desire to serve God. Hence God hath said: "O believers, repent unto God with a sincere repentence" (Qur'ān 66.8). And the Apostle said: "There is nothing that God loves more than a youth who repents"; and he also said: "He who repents of sin is even as one who has no sin"; then he added: "When God loves a man, sin shall not hurt him," i.e., he will not become an infidel on account of sin, and his faith will not be impaired. Etymologically tawbat [repentance] means "return," and repentance really involves the turning back from what God has forbidden through fear of what He has commanded. The Apostle said: "Penitance is the act of returning." This saying comprises three things which are involved in repentance, namely, 1) remorse for disobedience, 2) immediate abandonment of sin, and 3) determination not to sin again.

The Steps of a Disciple
[From Shaikh Sharaf ud-dīn Maneri, Maktūbāt-i-Sadi, pp. 60–61, 67–69]

The first step is holy law (Sharī'a). When the disciple has fully paid the demand of religion, and aspires to go beyond, the Path appears before him. It is the way to the heart. When he has fully observed the conditions of the Path, and aspires to soar higher, the veils of the heart are rent, and Truth shines therein. It is the way to the soul, and the goal of the seeker.

Broadly speaking, there are four stages: *Nāsūt, Malakūt, Jabarūt,* and *Lāhūt,* each leading to the next. *Nāsūt* is the animal nature, and functions through the five senses—e.g., eating, contacting, seeing, hearing, and the like. When the disciple controls the senses to the limit of bare necessity, and transcends the animal nature by purification and asceticism, he reaches *Malakūt,* the region of the angels. The duties of this stage are prayers to God. When he is not proud of these, he transcends this stage and reaches *Jabarūt,* the region of the soul. No one knows the soul but with the divine help; and truth, which is its mansion, baffles description and allusion. The duties of this stage are love, earnestness, joy, seeking, ecstasy, and insensibility. When the pilgrim transcends these by forgetting self altogether, he reaches *Lāhūt,* the unconditioned state. Here words fail.

Religion is for the desire-nature; the Path, for the heart; truth for the soul. Religion leads the desire-nature from *Nāsūt* to *Malakūt,* and transmutes it into heart. The Path leads the heart from *Malakūt* to *Jabarūt,* and transmutes it into soul. Truth leads the soul from *Jabarūt* to the divine sanctuary. The real work is to transmute the desire-nature into heart, the heart into soul, and to unify the three into one. "The lover, the Beloved and love are essentially *one.*" This is absolute monotheism. . . .

"The motive of the faithful is superior to their acts." Acts by themselves are of no value: the importance lies in the heart.

It is said that the traveler on the divine Path has three states: 1) action, 2) knowledge, 3) love. These three states are not experienced unless God wills it so. But one should work and wait. He will do verily what He has willed. He looks neither to the destruction nor to the salvation of anyone.

One who wishes to arrive at the truth must serve a teacher. No one can transcend the bondage and darkness of desires unless he, with the help of the Divine Grace, comes under the protection of a perfect and experienced teacher. As the teacher knows, he will teach the disciple according to his capacity, and will prescribe remedies suited to his ailments, so that "There is no God except Allāh" be firmly established in his nature, and the ingress of the evil spirits be cut off from his heart. All the world seeks to tread the divine Path. But each knows according to his inner purity, each seeks and aspires according to his knowledge, and each treads the Path according to his seeking and aspiration. [pp. 67–69]

· · · ·

Khwāja Bāyazīd was asked: "What is the way of God?" He replied: "When thou hast vanished on the Way, then hast thou come to God." Mark this: If one attached to the Way cannot see God, how can one attached to self see God? [pp. 60–61]

The Final Stage
[From Shaikh Sharaf ud-dīn Maneri, *Maktūbāt-i-Sadi*, pp. 2–4]

The fourth stage consists in the pouring forth of the Divine Light so profusely that it absorbs all individual existences in the eyes of the pilgrim. As in the case of the absorption of particles floating in the atmosphere in the light of the sun, the particles become invisible—they do not cease to exist, nor do they become the sun, but they are inevitably lost to sight in the overpowering glare of the sun—so, here, a creature does not become God, nor does it cease to exist. Ceasing to exist is one thing, invisibility is another. . . . When thou lookest through a mirror, thou dost not see the mirror, for thou mergest into the reflection of thy face, and yet thou canst not say that the mirror has ceased to exist, or that it has become that reflection, or that the reflection has become the mirror. Such is the vision of the Divine Energy in all beings without distinction. This state is called by the Sufis absorption in monotheism. Many have lost their balance here: no one can pass through this forest without the help of the Divine Grace and the guidance of a teacher, perfect, open-eyed, experienced in the elevations and depressions of the Path and inured to its blessings and sufferings. . . . Some pilgrims attain to this lofty state only for an hour a week, some for an hour a day, some for two hours a day, some remain absorbed for the greater portion of their time. . . .

THE PRESERVATION OF GOD'S TRANSCENDENCE AT THE SUPREME STAGE OF MYSTIC EXPERIENCE

The avoidance of pantheistic doctrines by most Sufis of the Chishtī, Suhrawardī, and Firdausī orders is a significant feature of the religious history of Islam in India. The urge toward pantheism was very powerful. The Sufi might describe the moment of supreme insight in terms of complete annihilation of the self in God's being or he might develop the Muslim doctrine that God has no partners into the proposition that only God exists. Either way, the transcendence of God over the world disappears. The following readings illustrate how this heresy was avoided.

Subsistence and Annihilation
[From Shaikh ʿAlī Hujwīrī, *Kashf ul-Mahjūb*, pp. 242–45, 246, 278–80]

You must know that annihilation (*fanā*) and subsistence (*baqā*) have one meaning in science and another meaning in mysticism, and that formalists are more puzzled by these words than by any other technical terms of the Sufis. Subsistence in its scientific and etymological acceptation is of three kinds: 1) a subsistence that begins and ends in annihilation, e.g., this world, which had a beginning and will have an end, and is now subsistent; 2) a subsistence that came into being and will never be annihilated, namely, Paradise and hell and the next world and its inhabitants; 3) a subsistence that always was and always will be, namely, the subsistence of God and His eternal attributes. Accordingly, knowledge of annihilation lies in your knowing that this world is perishable, and knowledge of subsistence lies in your knowledge that the next world is everlasting.

But the subsistence and annihilation of a state (*hāl*) denotes, for example, that when ignorance is annihilated knowledge is necessarily subsistent, and that when sin is annihilated piety is subsistent, and that when a man acquires knowledge of his piety his forgetfulness is annihilated by remembrance of God, i.e., when anyone gains knowledge of God and becomes subsistent in knowledge of Him he is annihilated from [entirely loses] ignorance of Him, and when he is annihilated from forgetfulness he becomes subsistent in remembrance of Him, and this involves the discarding of blameworthy attributes and the substitution of praiseworthy attributes. A different signification, however, is attached to the terms in question by the elect among the Sufis. They do not refer these expressions to knowledge or to state but apply them solely to the degree of perfection attained by the saints who have become free from the pains of mortification and have escaped from the prison of stations and the vicissitude of states, and whose search has ended in discovery, so that they have seen all things visible, and have heard all things audible, and have discovered all the secrets of the heart; and who, recognizing the imperfection of their own discovery, have turned away from all things and have purposely become annihilated in the object of desire, and in the very essence of desire have lost all desires of their own, for when a man becomes annihilated from his attributes he attains to perfect subsistence, he is neither near nor far, neither stranger nor intimate, neither sober nor intoxicated, neither separated nor united; he has no name, or sign, or brand, or mark.

In short, real annihilation from anything involves consciousness of its imperfection and absence of desire for it, not merely that a man should say, when he likes a thing: "I am subsistent therein," or when he dislikes it, that he should say: "I am annihilated therefrom"; for these qualities are characteristic of one who is still seeking. In annihilation there is no love or hate, and in subsistence there is no consciousness of union or separation. Some wrongly imagine that annihilation signifies loss of essence and destruction of personality, and that subsistence indicates the subsistence of God in man; both these notions are absurd. In India I had a dispute on this subject with a man who claimed to be versed in Qur'anic exegesis and theology. When I examined his pretensions I found that he knew nothing of annihilation and subsistence, and that he could not distinguish the eternal from the phenomenal. Many ignorant Sufis consider that total annilihation is possible, but this is a manifest error, for annihilation of the different parts of a material substance can never take place. I ask these ignorant and mistaken men: "What do you mean by this kind of annihilation?" If they answer: "Annihilation of substance," that is impossible; and if they answer; "Annihilation of attributes," that is only possible in so far as one attribute may be annihilated through the subsistence of another attribute, both attributes belonging to man; but it is absurd to suppose that anyone can subsist through the attributes of another individual. The Nestorians of Rūm [the Byzantine empire] and the Christians hold that Mary annihilated by self-mortification all the attributes of humanity and that the Divine subsistence became attached to her, so that she was made subsistent through the subsistence of God, and that Jesus was the result thereof, and that He was not originally composed of the stuff of humanity, because His subsistence is produced by realization of the subsistence of God; and that, in consequence of this, He and His Mother and God are all subsistent through one subsistence, which is eternal and an attribute of God. All this agrees with the doctrine of the anthropomorphistic sects of the Hashwiyya, who maintain that the Divine essence is a locus of phenomena and that the eternal may have phenomenal attributes. I ask all who proclaim such tenets: "What difference is there between the view that the eternal is the locus of the phenomenal and the view that the phenomenal is the locus of the eternal, or between the assertion that the eternal has phenomenal attributes and the assertion that the phenomenal has eternal attributes?" Such doctrines involve materialism and destroy the proof of the phenomenal nature of the universe, and compel us to say that both the Creator and His creation are eternal or that both are phenomenal, or that what is created may be commingled with what is uncreated, and that what is uncreated may descend into what is created. If, as they cannot help admitting, the creation is phenomenal, then their Creator also must be phenomenal, because the locus of a thing is like its substance; if the locus is phenomenal, it follows that the contents of the locus are phenomenal too. In fine, when one thing is linked and united and commingled with another, both things are in principle as one.

Accordingly, our subsistence and annihilation are attributes of ourselves, and resemble each other in respect of their being our attributes. Annihilation is the annihilation of one attribute through the subsistence of another attribute. One may speak, however, of an annihilation that is independent of subsistence, and also of a subsistence that is independent of annihilation: in that case annihilation means annihilation of all remembrance of other, and subsistence means subsistence of the remembrance of God. Whoever is annihilated from his own will subsists in the Will of God, because thy will is perishable and the Will of God is everlasting: when thou standest by thine own will thou standest by annihilation, but when thou art absolutely controlled by the Will of God thou standest by subsistence. Similarly, the power of fire transmutes to its own quality anything that falls into it, and surely the power of God's Will is greater than that of fire; but fire affects only the quality of iron without changing its substance, for iron can never become fire. [pp. 242–45]

Now I, 'Alī b. 'Uthmān al-Jullābī, declare that all these sayings are near to each other in meaning, although they differ in expression; and their real gist is this, that annihilation comes to a man through vision of the majesty of God and through the revelation of Divine omnipotence to his heart, so that in the overwhelming sense of His Majesty this world and the next world are obliterated from his mind, and "states" and "station" appear contemptible in the sight of his aspiring thought, and what is shown to him of miraculous grace vanishes into nothing: he becomes dead to reason and passion alike, dead even to annihilation itself; and in that annihilation of annihilation his tongue proclaims God, and his mind and body are humble and abased, as in the beginning when Adam's posterity were drawn forth from his loins without admixture of evil and took the pledge of servantship to God (Qur'ān 7.171). [p. 246]

•   •   •   •

Unification is of three kinds: 1) God's unification of God, i.e., His knowledge of His unity; 2) God's unification of His creatures, i.e., His decree that a man shall pronounce Him to be one, and the creation of unification in his heart; 3) men's unification of God, i.e., their knowledge of the unity of God. Therefore, when a man knows God he can declare His unity and pronounce that He is one, incapable of union and separation, not admitting duality; that His unity is not a number so as to be made two by the predication of another number; that He is not finite so as to have six directions; that He has no space, and that He is not in space, so as to require the predication of space; that He is not an accident, so as to need a substance, nor a substance, which cannot exist without another like itself, nor a natural constitution (tab'i), in which motion and rest originate, nor a spirit so as to need a frame, nor a body so as to be composed of limbs; and that He does not become immanent (hāl) in things, for then He must be homogeneous with them; and that He is not joined to anything, for then that thing must be a part of Him; and that He is free from all imperfections and exalted above all defects; and that He has no like, so that He and His creature should make two; and that He has no child whose begetting would necessarily cause Him to be a stock (asl); and that His essence and attributes are unchangeable; and that He is endowed with those attributes of perfection which believers and Unitarians affirm, and which He has described Himself as possessing; and that He is exempt from those attributes which heretics arbitrarily impute to Him; and that He is living, knowing, forgiving, merciful, willing, powerful, hearing, seeing, speaking, and subsistent; and that His knowledge is not a state (hāl) in Him, nor His power solidly planted (salābat) in Him, nor His speech divided in Him; and that He together with His attributes exists from eternity; and that objects of cognition are not outside of His knowledge, and that entities are entirely dependent on His Will; and that He does that which He has willed, and wills that which He has known, and no creature has cognizance thereof; and that His decree is an absolute fact, and that His friends have no resource except resignation; and that He is the sole predestinator of good and evil, and the only being that is worthy of hope or fear; and that He creates all benefit and injury; and that He alone gives judgment, and His judgment is all wisdom; and that no one has any possibility of attaining unto Him; and that the inhabitants of Paradise shall behold Him; and that assimilation (*tashnīh*) is inadmissible; and that such terms as "confronting" and "seeing face to face" (*muqābalat u muwājahat*) cannot be applied to His being; and that His saints may enjoy the contemplation (*mushāhadat*) of Him in this world.

Those who do not acknowledge Him to be such are guilty of impiety. [pp. 278–80]

True Contemplation Is Ineffable
[From Shaikh 'Alī Hujwīrī, *Kashf ul-Mahjūb*, pp. 332–33]

Some Sufis have fallen into the mistake of supposing that spiritual vision and contemplation represent such an idea of God as is formed in the mind by the imagination either from memory or reflection. This is utter anthropomorphism and manifest error. God is not finite that the imagination should be able to define Him or that the intellect should comprehend His nature. Whatever can be imagined is homogeneous with the intellect, but God is not homogeneous with any genus, although in relation to the Eternal all phenomenal objects—subtle and gross alike—are homogeneous with each other notwithstanding their mutual contrariety. Therefore contemplation in this world resembles vision of God in the next world, and since the Companions of the Apostle are unanimously agreed that vision is possible hereafter, contemplation is possible here. Those who tell of contemplation either in this or the other world only say that it is possible, not that they have enjoyed or now enjoy it, because contemplation is an attribute of the heart and cannot be expressed by the tongue except metaphorically. Hence silence ranks higher than speech, for silence is a sign of contemplation, whereas speech is a sign of ocular testimony. Accordingly the Apostle, when he attained proximity to God, said: "I cannot tell Thy praise," because he was in contemplation, and contemplation in the degree of love is perfect unity and any outward expression in unity is otherness. Then he said: "Thou hast praised Thyself," i.e., Thy words are mine, and

Thy praise is mine, and I do not deem my tongue capable of expressing
what I feel. As the poet says:

> I desired my beloved, but when I saw him
> I was dumbfounded and possessed neither tongue nor eye.

[From Shaikh Sharaf ud-dīn Maneri, *Maktūbāt-i-sadi,* p. 4]

Beyond the four is the stage of complete absorption, i.e., losing the very
consciousness of being absorbed and of seeking after God—for such a consciousness still implies separation. Here, the soul merges itself and the
universe into the Divine Light, and loses the consciousness of merging
as well. "Merge into Him, this is monotheism: lose the sense of merging,
this is unity." Here there are neither formulae nor ceremonies, neither
being nor nonbeing, neither description nor allusion, neither heaven nor
earth. It is this stage alone that unveils the mystery: "All are nonexistent
save Him"; "All things are perishable save His Face"; "I am the True
and the Holy One." Absolute unity without duality is realized here. "Do
not be deluded; but know: everyone who merges in God is not God."

SUFI ACCEPTANCE OF ORTHODOX FORMALIST ISLAM

The Sufi orders whose adherents migrated to India before the end of the
fifteenth century accepted the Islam of the Sharī'a as an essential pre-
condition of true religion. They joined with the ulamā in teaching the
simple observances of the faith to new Muslims, often in country areas
outside the influence of the mosque or mosque school. The ulamā and
Sufis were at peace in the house which al-Ghazālī had built—in different
rooms perhaps but under the same roof.

Orthodox Practice and Spiritual Experience Both Necessary
[From Shaikh 'Alī Hujwīrī, *Kashf ul-Mahjūb,* pp. 13–15, 16]

The object of human knowledge should be to know God and His Commandments. Knowledge of "time" and of all outward and inward circumstances of which the due effect depends on "time" is incumbent upon
everyone. This is of two sorts: primary and secondary. The external division of the primary class consists in making the Muslim's profession of
faith; the internal division consists in the attainment of true cognition.
The external division of the secondary class consists in the practice of devotion; the internal division consists in rendering one's intention sincere.

The outward and inward aspects cannot be divorced. The exoteric aspect of truth without the esoteric is hypocrisy, and the esoteric without the exoteric is heresy. So, with regard to the Law, mere formality is defective, while mere spirituality is vain.

The knowledge of the truth has three pillars: 1) Knowledge of the essence and unity of God; 2) Knowledge of the attributes of God; 3) Knowledge of the actions and wisdom of God.

The knowledge of the law also has three pillars: 1) The Qur'ān; 2) The Sunna; 3) The consensus of the Muslim community.

Knowledge of the divine essence involves recognition, on the part of one who is reasonable and has reached puberty, that God exists externally by His essence, that He is infinite and not bounded by space, that His essence is not the cause of evil, that none of His creatures is like unto Him, that He has neither wife nor child, and that He is the Creator and Sustainer of all that your imagination and intellect can conceive.

Knowledge of the divine attributes requires you to know that God has attributes existing in Himself, which are not He nor a part of Him, but exist in Him and subsist by Him, e.g., knowledge, power, life, will, hearing, sight, speech, etc.

Knowledge of the divine actions is your knowledge that God is the creator of mankind and of all their actions, that He brought the nonexistent universe into being, that He predestines good and evil and creates all that is beneficial and injurious.

Knowledge of the law involves your knowing that God has sent us Apostles with miracles of an extraordinary nature; that our Apostle, Muhammad (on whom be peace!), is a true messenger, who performed many miracles, and that whatever he has told us concerning the unseen and the visible is entirely true. [pp. 13–15]

Muhammad b. Fazl al-Balkhī says: "Knowledge is of three kinds—from God, with God, and of God." Knowledge of God is the science of gnosis whereby He is known to all His prophets and saints. It cannot be acquired by ordinary means, but is the result of divine guidance and information. Knowledge from God is the science of the Sacred Law, which He has commanded and made obligatory upon us. Knowledge with God is the science of the "stations" and the "Path" and the degrees of the saints. Gnosis is unsound without acceptance of the law, and the law is not practiced rightly unless the "stations" are manifested. [p. 16]

The Superiority of the Prophets Over the Saints
[From Shaikh 'Alī Hujwīrī, *Kashf ul-Mahjūb,* pp. 235–37]

You must know that, by universal consent of the Sufi shaikhs, the saints
are at all times and in all circumstances subordinate to the prophets, whose
missions they confirm. The prophets are superior to the saints, because
the end of saintship is only the beginning of prophecy. Every prophet is
a saint, but some saints are not prophets. The prophets are constantly exempt from the attributes of humanity, while the saints are so only temporarily; the fleeting state of the saint is the permanent station of the
prophet; and that which to the saints is a station is to the prophets a veil.
This view is held unanimously by the Sunni divines and the Sufi mystics,
but it is opposed by a sect of the Hashwiyya—the Anthropomorphists of
Khurasan—who discourse in a self-contradictory manner concerning the
principles of unification, and who, although they do not know the fundamental doctrine of Sufism, call themselves saints. Saints they are indeed,
but saints of the Devil. They maintain that the saints are superior to the
prophets, and it is a sufficient proof of their error that they declare an
ignoramus to be more excellent than Muhammad, the Chosen of God. The
same vicious opinion is held by another sect of anthropomorphists, who
pretend to be Sufis, and admit the doctrines of the incarnation of God and
His descent [into the human body] by transmigration, and the division of
His essence. I will treat fully of these matters when I give my promised
account of the two reprobated sects [of Sufis]. The sects to which I am
referring claim to be Muslims, but they agree with the Brahmans in denying special privileges to the prophets; and whoever believes in this doctrine becomes an infidel. Moreover, the prophets are propagandists and
Imāms, and the saints are their followers, and it is absurd to suppose that
the follower of an Imām is superior to the Imām himself. In short, the
lives, experiences, and spiritual powers of all the saints together appear as
nothing compared with one act of a true prophet, because the saints are
seekers and pilgrims, whereas the prophets have arrived and have found
and have returned with the command to preach and to convert the people.
If anyone of the above-mentioned heretics should urge that an ambassador
sent by a king is usually inferior to the person to whom he is sent, as,
e.g., Gabriel is inferior to the apostles, and that this is against my argument, I reply that an ambassador sent to a single person should be inferior

to him, but when an ambassador is sent to a large number of persons or to a people, he is superior to them, as the apostles are superior to the nations. Therefore one moment of the prophets is better than the whole life of the saints, because when the saints reach their goal they tell of contemplation and obtain release from the veil of humanity, although they are essentially men. On the other hand, contemplation is the first step of the apostle; and since the apostle's starting place is the saint's goal, they cannot be judged by the same standard.

The Morals of the Heart

The *Morals of the Heart* (*Fawā'id ul-Fuwād*), the "table-talk" of Shaikh Nizām ud-din Auliyā, is typical of the instruction in simple piety to which all Muslims could willingly assent.

[From Amīr Hasan Sijzī, *Fawā'id ul-Fuwād*]

ON REMEMBERING GOD

Then he [Shaikh Nizām ud-dīn] said: Once upon a time there was a great man who was called Mīra Kirāmī. A dervish wished to visit him. This dervish had the miraculous power whereby whatever he saw in a dream was correct, except for that dream which he had when the desire to see Mīra Kirāmī seized hold of him. He set out to the place where Mīra Kirāmī lived but along the way he halted for the night and fell asleep. In his dreams he heard that Mīra Kirāmī had died. When daybreak came he awoke and cried: "Alas! I have come so far to see him and he is dead. What shall I do? I will go on to the place where he was and lament at his burial place." When he reached the locality where Mīra Kirāmī lived, he began to ask everyone where Mīra Kirāmī's burial place was. They replied: "He is alive, why do you ask for his grave?" The dervish was astonished that his dream was untrue. Finally he went to see Mīra Kirāmī and greeted him. Mīra Kirāmī returned his greeting and said: "Your dream was correct as to its meaning; I am usually engaged in constant recollection of God. But on the night of your dream I was occupied otherwise; therefore the cry went forth to the world that Mīra Kirāmī had died." [conversation of the 19th Jamādī ul-Awwal, 708 after Hijra]

ON TRUST IN GOD

Talk turned to trust in God. Nizām ud-dīn said that trust has three degrees. The first is when a man obtains a pleader for his lawsuits and this pleader is both a learned person and a friend. Then the client believes: "I have a pleader who is both wise in presenting a suit and who is also my friend." In this instance there is both trust and a making of requests. The client says to his lawyer: "Answer this suit thus and bring this or that matter to such and such a conclusion." The first stage of trust is when there is both confidence in another and the giving of instructions to another.

The second degree of trust is that of a suckling whose mother is giving milk. Here there is confidence without question. The infant does not say: "Feed me at such and such times." It cries but does not demand its feed [in so many words]. It does not say, "Feed me." It does not say, "Give me milk." It has confidence in its heart in its mother's compassion.

But the third degree of trust is that of a corpse in the hands of a corpse washer. It does not make requests or change or make any motion or stay quiescent [of its own volition]. As the corpse washer decides, so he turns the corpse about—and so it goes. This is the third and highest degree of trust. [conversation of the 10th Rabīʿ ul-Ākhir, 710 after Hijra]

ON OBEDIENCE TO GOD

On Sunday, third Muharram 708 after Hijra, after paying respect to the shaikh, talk turned to obedience to God. Obedience to God is of two kinds, "intransitive" and "transitive." "Intransitive" obedience is that obedience whose benefits affect only the one person—for example, prayer, fasting, pilgrimage, and praising God. "Transitive" obedience is that whose benefits and comfort reaches another. Whatever kindness in companionship and compassion is shown toward others, they call "transitive" obedience. The rewards of this obedience are very great. There must be sincerity in "intransitive" obedience for it to be acceptable to God. But with "transitive" obedience, whatever one does is rewarded and acceptable to God. [conversation of the 3rd Muharram, 708 after Hijra]

ON GOING TO FRIDAY PRAYERS

A story was told that nonattendance at Friday prayers was being interpreted away [as not obligatory for a Muslim]. Shaikh Nizām ud-din said there is no such interpretation. Unless someone is a captive, on a journey, or ill, he who can go to Friday prayers and does not go has a very stubborn heart. Then he said, if a man does not go to one Friday congregational prayer, one black spot appears on his heart; if he misses two weeks' congregational prayer, then two black spots appear; and if he does not go three times in succession, his whole heart becomes black— which God forbid! [conversation of the 6th Zu'l Hijja, 719 after Hijra]

ON THE PLACE OF THE SUFI IN DAILY LIFE

Shaikh Nizām ud-dīn Auliyā said this on the real position to be adopted about abandoning the world. Abandoning the world is not stripping one-self naked, or sitting wearing only a langūta. Abandoning the world means wearing clothes and eating but not retaining what comes one's way, not acquiring anything or savoring anything, and not being attached to [worldly] things. [conversation of the 5th Shawwāl, 707 after Hijra]

CHAPTER XVI

RELIGIOUS TENSION UNDER THE MUGHALS

The religious unity of Islam in India suffered its greatest stresses during the century from A.D. c.1550 to 1650, the period of the establishment of Mughal rule and of its apogee. Many forces, some political and more religious, were conspiring to weaken the hold over Indian Muslims of Sunni orthodoxy and of "moderate" mysticism.

The Mughals were by ancestry, taste, and conviction seekers and eclectics in religion, characteristics which their political necessities and ambitions tended to confirm. The family of Chingis Khān are reported to have joined in Nestorian, Christian, Muslim, and Buddhist religious observances. Tīmūr showed greater respect to Sufi shaikhs than to the Sunni ulamā. Bābur and his son Humāyūn had been constrained to accept Shī-'ism outwardly while negotiating for the support of the Persian Shī'ite Safavids. Moreover, during the sixteenth and seventeenth centuries, Shī-'ism in India enjoyed political patronage. In the Deccan, Yūsuf 'Ādil Shāh of Bijapur (1489–1510) pronounced himself a Shī'a as did Burhān ud-dīn of Ahmadnagar and Qūlī Qutb Shāh of Golkonda. In North India, Bairam Khān, the guardian and minister of the young Akbar, was a Shī'a with a large Persian Shī'a following who settled down in India.

Furthermore, significant religious developments within the penumbra dividing Muslim from Hindu had softened religious acerbities in India. If from within Islam the mystic had appeared to reach out toward Hinduism, from within Hinduism, Kabīr (b. 1398), Nānak (b. 1469), and Chaitanya (b. 1485), with their condemnation of caste, Hindu rituals, and idolatry appeared to be reaching out toward Islam.

Important changes also occurred in the character of Muslim mysticism in India. New orders were introduced from Persia—the Shattārī, whose shaikh Muhammad Ghawth was Humāyūn's spiritual preceptor; the Qādirī, whose shaikh Mir Muhammad was tutor to the Mughal prince

Dārā Shikōh; and the Naqshbandī order, whose greatest luminary was Shaikh Ahmad of Sirhind. Members of the first two orders in particular were deeply influenced by the frankly pantheistic doctrines of the Spanish Muslim mystic Ibn 'Arabī (1164–1240); they observed few of the restraints in expression characteristic of the earlier Chishtī and Suhrawardī orders. What is more, their adherents were often intimately acquainted with Hindu mysticism.

None of these challenges to Sunni orthodoxy was exactly new; what was new was the political climate in India in which they had to be met. Under the Mughals, until Aurangzīb's time, the Sunni ulamā could not be confident of the exclusive support and patronage of the ruling power. Akbar came to an understanding with the Hindu Rajputs, who served to underpin his empire, and with policy reinforcing his own personal religious inclinations, set his face against Muslim militancy. The orthodox were scandalized not so much by the presence of un-Islamic ideas and practices in the Indian Muslim community as by the absence of political support in resisting them.

But resist they did, and, in the end successfully, though not without the help of a Sunni Mughal emperor, Aurangzīb (1658–1707). Readings have already been given from the works of a great traditionist of the Mughal period, 'Abd ul-Haqq al-Dihlawī. However, the greatest figure in the reaction against Akbar's and the mystics' religious syncretism was Shaikh Ahmad of Sirhind (1564–1624) who, arguing from within mystic experience itself against the pantheism of Ibn 'Arabī, recalled Muslims to a fresh realization of the religious value of traditional observance.

AKBAR'S RELIGIOUS OUTLOOK

Akbar, apparently by deliberate, mature choice, could neither read nor write; it is possible, therefore, only dimly to perceive his religious attitudes through the testimony of witnesses violently prejudiced either in his favor, as was Abū'l Fazl, his friend and confidant; or against him, as was the historian 'Abd ul-Qādir Badā'ūnī, his secret orthodox Sunni opponent, or partly through the testimony of the Jesuit fathers and of a Parsi student of religion, Muhsin-i-Fānī, who wrote half a century after Akbar's death.

As a boy in Kabul, Akbar had been open to Shī'a teachings and to the mysticism of the Persian poets. Although at the outset of his reign, however, his religious officials—the *sadr* ("minister for religious endowments") and the *qāḍīs* (religious judges)—were Sunni, Akbar himself visited Sufi retreats at Ajmir and Sikri. He seems to have been offended by the persecution of the Shī'a by his Sunni *sadr* and chief muftī (canon jurist) which grew violent about 1570. Meanwhile, in 1562, he had married a Hindu Rajput princess, Bihārī Mal of Amber, and had admitted Rajput princes, e.g., Rājā Mān Singh and Todar Mal, to high political and administrative office. After 1574 he was influenced by Abū'l Fazl and his brother Faizī, sons of Shaikh Mubārak Nāgōrī, and all students of Hinduism, indeed of "comparative religion." From this time, they led the discussions in the Hall of Worship which Akbar had built at Fathpur Sikri. These discussions, over which Akbar presided, were attended by Sunni ulamā, Sufi shaikhs, Hindu pundits, Parsees, Zoroastrians, Jains, and Catholic priests from Portuguese Goa. The mere fact of such discussions—in which apparently the Sunni ulamā did not shine—is the measure of the bias against orthodoxy at court. Akbar's personal religious searchings were followed by the Declaration (*Mahzar*) of 1579 that Akbar was accepted by the ulamā as the arbiter in religious disputes, by the enunciation of the "Divine Faith" (*Dīn-i-Ilāhī*), Akbar's own eclectic faith of 1582, and by a series of conciliatory gestures toward the Hindus. The Divine Faith, however, was accepted by only a small number of courtiers and was not enforced throughout the empire by political and administrative pressure.

Akbar ordered the translation of the *Atharva Veda,* the *Rāmāyaṇa,* and the *Mahābhārata.* According to Badā'ūnī he prohibited the killing of cows, refrained from eating meat on certain days and celebrated non-Islamic festivals. However, Akbar emphatically did not wish to destroy Islam in India, as Badā'ūnī implies. His quest for religious truth was that of an eclectic, not of a fanatic. Looking back, the consensus of the community appears to have pronounced against his activities, but this does not mean that they necessarily flouted the concensus at the time.

The following readings will illustrate Akbar's religious quest and the Divine Faith. The Declaration will be given in the next chapter on Muslim political thought.

The Discussion in the Hall of Worship

Readers must recall that the author of these passages is hostile to Akbar.
[Badā'ūnī, *Muntakhab ut-Tawārīkh*, II, 200–201, 255–61 *passim*, 324]

In the year nine hundred and eighty-three the buildings of the 'Ibādat-khāna were completed. The cause was this. For many years previously the emperor had gained in succession remarkable and decisive victories. The empire had grown in extent from day to day; everything turned out well, and no opponent was left in the whole world. His Majesty had thus leisure to come into nearer contact with ascetics and the disciples of his reverence [the late] Mu'īn, and passed much of his time in discussing the Word of God and the word of the Prophet. Questions of Sufism, scientific discussions, inquiries into philosophy and law, were the order of the day. [II, 200–201]

. . . .

And later that day the emperor came to Fathpūr. There he used to spend much time in the Hall of Worship in the company of learned men and shaikhs and especially on Friday nights, when he would sit up there the whole night continually occupied in discussing questions of religion, whether fundamental or collateral. The learned men used to draw the sword of the tongue on the battlefield of mutual contradiction and opposition, and the antagonism of the sects reached such a pitch that they would call one another fools and heretics. The controversies used to pass beyond the differences of Sunni, and Shī'a, of Hanafī and Shāfi'ī, of lawyer and divine, and they would attack the very bases of belief. And Makhdūm-ul-Mulk wrote a treatise to the effect that Shaikh 'Abd-al-Nabī had unjustly killed Khizr Khān Sarwānī, who had been suspected of blaspheming the Prophet [peace be upon him!], and Mīr Habsh, who had been suspected of being a Shī'a, and saying that it was not right to repeat the prayers after him, because he was undutiful toward his father, and was himself afflicted with hemorrhoids. Shaikh 'Abd-al-Nabī replied to him that he was a fool and a heretic. Then the mullās [Muslim theologians] became divided into two parties, and one party took one side and one the other, and became very Jews and Egyptians for hatred of each other. And persons of novel and whimsical opinions, in accordance with their pernicious ideas and vain doubts, coming out of ambush, decked the false in the garb of the true, and wrong in the dress of right, and cast the emperor, who was possessed of an excellent disposition, and was an earnest searcher after truth, but very ignorant and a mere tyro, and used to the company of infidels and base persons, into perplexity, till doubt was heaped upon doubt, and he lost all definite aim, and the straight wall of the clear law and of firm religion was broken down, so that after five or six years not a trace of Islam was left in him: and everything was turned topsy-turvy. . . .

And Samanas [Hindu or Buddhist ascetics] and Brahmans (who as far as the matter of private interviews is concerned gained the advantage over every one in attaining the honor of interviews with His Majesty, and in associating with him, and were in every way superior in reputation to all learned and trained men for their treatises on morals, and on physical and religious sciences, and in religious ecstasies, and stages of spiritual progress and human perfections) brought forward proofs, based on reason and traditional testimony, for the truth of their own, and the fallacy of our religion, and inculcated their doctrine with such firmness and assurance, that they affirmed mere imaginations as though they were self-evident facts, the truth of which the doubts of the sceptic could no more shake "Than the mountains crumble, and the heavens be cleft!" And the Resurrection, and Judgment, and other details and traditions, of which the Prophet was the repository, he laid all aside. And he made his courtiers continually listen to those revilings and attacks against our pure and easy, bright and holy faith. . . .

Some time before this a Brahman, named Puruk'hotam, who had written a commentary on the Book, *Increase of Wisdom* (*Khirad-afzā*), had had private interviews with him, and he had asked him to invent particular Sanskrit names for all things in existence. And at one time a Brahman, named Debi, who was one of the interpreters of the *Mahābhārata,* was pulled up the wall of the castle sitting on a bedstead till he arrived near a balcony, which the emperor had made his bed-chamber. Whilst thus suspended he instructed His Majesty in the secrets and legends of Hinduism, in the manner of worshiping idols, the fire, the sun and stars, and of revering the chief gods of these unbelievers, such as Brahma, Mahadev [Shiva], Bishn [Vishnu], Kishn [Krishna], Ram, and Mahama (whose existence as sons of the human race is a supposition, but whose nonexistence is a certainty, though in their idle belief they look on some of them as gods, and some as angels). His Majesty, on hearing further how much the people of the country prized their institutions, began to look upon them with affection. . . .

Sometimes again it was Shaikh Tāj ud-dīn whom he sent for. This shaikh was son of Shaikh Zakarīya of Ajodhan. . . . He had been a pupil of Rashīd Shaikh Zamān of Panipat, author of a commentary on the *Paths* (*Lawā'ih*), and of other excellent works, was most excellent in Sufism, and in the knowledge of theology second only to Shaikh Ibn 'Arabī and had written a comprehensive commentary on the *Joy of the Souls* (*Nuzhat ul-Arwāh*). Like the preceding he was drawn up the wall of the castle in a blanket, and His Majesty listened the whole night to his Sufic obscenities and follies. The shaikh, since he did not in any great degree feel himself bound by the injunctions of the law, introduced arguments concerning the unity of existence, such as idle Sufis discuss, and which eventually lead to license and open heresy. . . .

Learned monks also from Europe, who are called *Padre,* and have an infallible head, called *Papa,* who is able to change religious ordinances as he may deem advisable for the moment, and to whose authority kings must submit, brought the Gospel, and advanced proofs for the Trinity. His Majesty firmly believed in the truth of the Christian religion, and wishing to spread the doctrines of Jesus, ordered Prince Murād to take a few lessons in Christianity under good auspices, and charged Abū'l Fazl to translate the Gospel. . . .

Fire worshipers also came from Nousarī in Gujarat, proclaimed the religion of Zardusht [Zarathustra] as the true one, and declared reverence to fire to be superior to every other kind of worship. They also attracted the emperor's regard, and taught him the peculiar terms, the ordinances, the rites and ceremonies of the Kaianians [a pre-Muslim Persian dynasty]. At last he ordered that the sacred fire should be made over to the charge of Abū'l Fazl, and that after the manner of the kings of Persia, in whose temples blazed perpetual fires, he should take care it was never extinguished night or day, for that it is one of the signs of God, and one light from His lights. . . .

His Majesty also called some of the yogis, and gave them at night private interviews, inquiring into abstract truths; their articles of faith; their occupation; the influence of pensiveness; their several practices and usages; the power of being absent from the body; or into alchemy, physiognomy, and the power of omnipresence of the soul. [II, 255–261 *passim*, 324]

Note in the next readings the condemnation of prophethood by a philosopher at Akbar's court, which is said to have gone uncensured.

[From Muhsin-i-Fānī, *Dabistān-i-Mazāhib*, III, 78–81]
But the greatest injury comprehended in a prophetic mission is the obligation to submit to one like ourselves of the human species, who is subject to the incidental distempers and imperfections of mankind; and who nevertheless controls others with severity, in eating, drinking, and in all their other possessions, and drives them about like brutes, in every direction which he pleases; who declares every follower's wife he desires legal for himself and forbidden to the husband; who takes to himself nine wives, whilst he allows no more than four to his followers, and even of these wives he takes whichever he pleases for himself; and who grants impunity for shedding blood to whomsoever he chooses. On account of what excellency, on account of what science, is it necessary to follow that man's command; and what proof is there by his simple word? His word, because it is only a word, has no claim of superiority over the words of others. Nor is it possible to know which of the sayings be correctly his own, on account of the multiplicity of contradictions in the professions of faith. If he be a prophet on the strength of miracles, then the deference to it is very dependent; because a miracle is not firmly established, and rests only upon tradition or a demon's romances. . . .

But if it be said that every intellect has not the power of comprehending the sublime precepts, but that the bounty of the Almighty God created degrees of reason and a particular order of spirits, so that he blessed a few of the number with superior sagacity; and that the merciful light of lights, by diffusion and guidance, exalted the prophets even above these intellects —If it be so, then a prophet is of little service to men; for he gives instruction which they do not understand, or which their reason does not approve. Then the prophet will propagate his doctrine by the sword; he says to the inferiors: "My words are above your understanding, and your study will not comprehend them." To the intelligent he says: "My faith is above the mode of reason." Thus, his religion suits neither the ignorant nor the wise.

The Divine Faith

The Divine Faith was Sufi in conception, with ceremonial expressions borrowed from Zoroastrianism. It was strictly monotheistic and incorporated Shī'ite ideas of the role of the mujtahid or interpreter of the faith. In brief, it appears to owe more to Islam than to Hinduism. Unfortunately the beliefs and practices of the Divine Faith are nowhere comprehensively stated. They have to be pieced together from Abū'l Fazl's *Institutes of Akbar* (*Ā'īn-i-Akbarī*), Badā'-ūnī's *Selected Histories* (*Muntakhab ut-Tawārīkh*) and Muhsin-i-Fānī's *School of Religions* (*Dabistān-i-Mazāhib*).

THE DIVINE FAITH'S MONOTHEISM
[From Muhsin-i-Fānī, *Dabistān-i-Mazāhib*, III, 74–75]

Know for certain that the perfect prophet and learned apostle, the possessor of fame, Akbar, that is, the lord of wisdom, directs us to acknowledge that the self-existent being is the wisest teacher, and ordains the creatures with absolute power, so that the intelligent among them may be able to understand his precepts; and as reason renders it evident that the world has a Creator, all-mighty and all-wise, who has diffused upon the field of events among the servants, subject to vicissitudes, numerous and various benefits which are worthy of praise and thanksgiving; therefore, according to the lights of our reason, let us investigate the mysteries of his creation, and, according to our knowledge, pour out the praises of his benefits.

THE DIVINE FAITH'S SUFI PIETY
[From Muhsin-i-Fānī, *Dabistān-i-Mazāhib*, III, 82–84]

In the sequel it became evident to wise men that emancipation is to be obtained only by the knowledge of truth conformably with the precepts of the perfect prophet, the perfect lord of fame, Akbar, "the Wise"; the practices enjoined by him are: renouncing and abandoning the world; refraining from lust, sensuality, entertainment, slaughter of what possesses life; and from appropriating to one's self the riches of other men; abstaining from women, deceit, false accusation, oppression, intimidation, foolishness, and giving [to others] opprobrious titles. The endeavors for the recompense of the other world, and the forms of the true religion may be comprised in ten virtues, namely, 1) liberality and beneficence; 2) forbearance from bad actions and repulsion of anger with mildness; 3) abstinence from worldly desires; 4) care of freedom from the bonds of the worldly existence and violence, as well as accumulating previous stores for the future real and perpetual world; 5) piety, wisdom, and devotion, with frequent meditations on the consequences of actions; 6) strength of dexterous prudence in the desire of sublime actions; 7) soft voice, gentle words, and pleasing speeches for everybody; 8) good society with brothers, so that their will may have the precedence to our own; 9) a perfect alienation from the creatures, and a perfect attachment to the supreme Being; 10) purification of the soul by the yearning after God the all-just, and the union with the merciful Lord, in such a manner that, as long as the soul dwells in the body, it may think itself one with him and long to join him, until the hour of separation from the body arrives.

THE INFLUENCE OF ZOROASTRIANISM
[From Badā'ūnī, *Muntakhab ut-Tawārīkh*, II, 322]

A second order was given that the sun should be worshiped four times a day, in the morning and evening, and at noon and midnight. His Majesty had also one thousand and one Sanskrit names for the sun collected, and read them daily at noon, devoutly turning toward the sun; he then used to get hold of both ears, and turning himself quickly round about, used to strike the lower ends of his ears with his fists. He also adopted several other practices connected with sun-worship.

DĀRĀ SHIKŌH AND PANTHEISM

Akbar's mantle as a religious seeker fell not on his son Jahāngīr or his grandson Shāh Jahān, but on his great-grandson Dārā Shikōh (1615–1659). Dārā Shikōh addressed himself, with perhaps more enthusiasm than insight, to the study of Hindu philosophy and mystical practices. This was the more congenial because he himself was a follower of the Qādirī order of Sufis in the persons of Miān Mīrzā (d. 1635) and Mullā Shāh Badakhshānī (d. 1661).

Dārā Shikōh is important from the present standpoint because he symbolizes the major danger threatening the religious integrity of Islam in India, a mingling of the two seas of Muslim mystical pantheism and Hindu pantheism to batter down the defenses of orthodoxy. He symbolized but did not intend that threat; he himself would have rejected a charge of heresy or unbelief. The widespread Sufi acceptance of Ibn 'Arabī's mystical philosophy and their interest in Hindu mysticism should be condemned as infidelity if Dārā Shikōh is to be condemned for infidelity. However, the subsequent consensus of the Muslim community was that Dārā Shikōh's activities were dangerous to it and there is a strong presumption that Aurangzīb's political instincts were finely tuned to strong waves of Muslim sentiment when, after the war of succession, for his own ambitious purposes he had Dārā Shikōh condemned as a heretic and executed.

The readings which follow are intended to illustrate first the pantheistic tendency in Dārā Shikōh's thought—tendency, not fulfillment, for he appears to stop short of asserting the complete absorption of the mystic in God's essence—and second his efforts to find common ground between Hindu and Muslim.

The Mystic Path
[From Dārā Shikōh, *Risāla-yi-Haqq-Numā*, pp. 24, 26]

Here is the secret of unity (tawhīd), O friend, understand it;
Nowhere exists anything but God.
All that you see or know other than Him,
Verily is separate in name, but in essence one with God.

. . . .

Like an ocean is the essence of the Supreme Self,
Like forms in water are all souls and objects;
The ocean heaving and stirring within,
Transforms itself into drops, waves and bubbles. [p. 24]

So long as it does not realize its separation from the ocean,
The drop remains a drop:
So long he does not know himself to be the Creator,
The created remains a created.

. . . .

O you, in quest of God, you seek Him everywhere,
You verily are the God, not apart from Him!
Already in the midst of the boundless ocean,
Your quest resembles the search of a drop for the ocean! [p. 26]

[From Dārā Shikōh, *Hasanat ul-'Ārifīn*, p. 16]

Dost thou wish to enter the circle of men of illumination?
Then cease talking and be in the "state";

By professing the unity of God, thou canst not become a monotheist,
As the tongue cannot taste sugar by only uttering its name.

[From JRASB, Vol. V, No. 1, p. 168]
Paradise is there where no mullā exists—
Where the noise of his discussions and debate is not heard.

May the world become free from the noise of mullā,
And none should pay any heed to his decrees!

In the city where a mullā resides,
No wise man ever stays.

The Upanishads: God's Most Perfect Revelation

The following is taken from Dārā Shikōh's translation of fifty-two Upanishads, completed in 1657. He uses the third person in referring to himself.
[From Hasrat, *Dārā Shikōh,* pp. 260–68]

Praised be the Being, that one among whose eternal secrets is the dot in the [letter] ب of the bismallāh in all the heavenly books, and glorified be the mother of books. In the holy Qur'ān is the token of His glorious name; and the angels and the heavenly books and the prophets and the saints are all comprehended in this name. And be the blessings of the Almighty upon the best of His creatures, Muhammad, and upon all his children and upon his companions universally!

To proceed; whereas this unsolicitous faqīr [a religious mendicant], Muhammad Dārā Shikōh in the year 1050 after Hijra [A.D. 1640] went to Kashmir, the resemblance of paradise, and by the grace of God and the favor of the Infinite, he there obtained the auspicious opportunity of meeting the most perfect of the perfects, the flower of the gnostics, the tutor of the tutors, the sage of the sages, the guide of the guides, the unitarian accomplished in the Truth, Mullā Shāh, on whom be the peace of God.

And whereas, he was impressed with a longing to behold the gnostics of every sect, and to hear the lofty expressions of monotheism, and had cast his eyes upon many books of mysticism and had written a number of treatises thereon, and as the thirst of investigation for unity, which is a boundless ocean, became every moment increased, subtle doubts came into his mind for which he had no possibility of solution, except by the word of the Lord and the direction of the Infinite. And whereas the holy Qur'ān is mostly allegorical, and at the present day, persons thoroughly conversant with the subtleties thereof are very rare, he became desirous of bringing in view all the heavenly books, for the very words of God themselves are their own commentary; and what might be in one book compendious, in another might be found diffusive, and from the detail of one, the conciseness of the other might become comprehensible. He had, therefore, cast his eyes on the Book of Moses, the Gospels, the Psalms, and other scriptures, but the explanation of monotheism in them also was compendious and enigmatical, and from the slovenly translations which selfish persons had made, their purport was not intelligible.

Thereafter he considered, as to why the discussion about monotheism is so conspicuous in India, and why the Indian theologians and mystics of the ancient school do not disavow the Unity of God nor do they find any fault with the unitarians, but their belief is perfect in this respect; on the other hand, the ignoramuses of the present age—the highwaymen in the path of God—who have established themselves for erudites and who, falling into the traces of polemics and molestation, and apostatizing through disavowal of the true proficients in God and monotheism, display resistance against all the words of unitarianism, which are most evident from the glorious Qur'ān and the authentic traditions of indubitable prophecy.

And after verifications of these circumstances, it appeared that among this most ancient people, of all their heavenly books, which are the *Rig Veda,* the *Yajur Veda,* the *Sama Veda,* and the *Atharva Veda,* together with a number of ordinances, descended upon the prophets of those times, the most ancient of whom was Brahman or Adam, on whom be the peace of God, this purport is manifest from these books. And it can also be ascertained from the holy Qur'ān, that there is no nation without a prophet and without a revealed scripture, for it hath been said: "Nor do We chastise until We raise an apostle" (Qur'ān 17.15). And in another verse: "And there is not a people but a warner has gone among them" (Qur'ān 35.24). And at another place: "Certainly We sent Our apostles with clear arguments, and sent down with them the Book and the measure" (Qur'ān 57.25).

And the *summum bonum* of these four books, which contain all the secrets of the Path and the contemplative exercises of pure monotheism, are called the *Upanekhats* [*Upanishads*], and the people of that time have written commentaries with complete and diffusive interpretations thereon; and being still understood as the best part of their religious worship, they

are always studied. And whereas this unsolicitous seeker after the Truth
had in view the principle of the fundamental unity of the personality and
not Arabic, Syriac, Hebrew, and Sanskrit languages, he wanted to make
without any worldly motive, in a clear style, an exact and literal translation of the *Upanekhat* into Persian. For it is a treasure of monotheism and
there are few thoroughly conversant with it even among the Indians.
Thereby he also wanted to solve the mystery which underlies their efforts
to conceal it from the Muslims.

And as at this period the city of Banares, which is the center of the
sciences of this community, was in certain relations with this seeker of the
Truth, he assembled together the pandits [Hindu scholars] and the sann-
yasis [Hindu ascetics or monks], who were the most learned of their
time and proficient in the *Upanekhat* . . . in the year 1067 after Hijra;
and thus every difficulty and every sublime topic which he had
desired or thought and had looked for and not found, he obtained
from these essences of the most ancient books, and without doubt or suspicion, these books are first of all heavenly books in point of time, and
the source and the fountainhead of the ocean of unity, in conformity with
the holy Qur'ān.

Happy is he, who having abandoned the prejudices of vile selfishness,
sincerely and with the grace of God, renouncing all partiality, shall study
and comprehend this translation entitled *The Great Secret (Sirr-i-Akbar)*,
knowing it to be a translation of the words of God. He shall become
imperishable, fearless, unsolicitous, and eternally liberated.

THE REACTION AGAINST PANTHEISTIC MYSTICISM

The leader of the religious opposition to pantheistic mysticism and to
neglect of the Sharī'a was Shaikh Ahmad Sirhindī al-Mujaddid-i-Alf-i-
Thānī (the Renewer of Islam at the Beginning of the Second Muslim Millennium). Born at Sirhind in the East Punjab in 1564, he frequented the
society of Abū'l Fazl and his brother Faizī at Agra. In 1599 he was initiated into the Naqshbandī order of mystics. He incurred the displeasure
of Jahāngīr for his unbending opposition to the Shī'a who were powerful
at court, but was restored to favor before his death in 1624.

Shaikh Ahmad Sirhindī's great achievement was paradoxically to win Indian Islam away from Sufi extremism by means of mysticism itself. Perhaps his success was due to deep personal understanding of the meaning and value of what he rejected. To explain briefly: the mystical school of Ibn 'Arabī holds that Being is one; is Allāh, and that everything is His manifestation or emanation. God is neither transcendent nor immanent. He is All. Creation is only God's yearning to know Himself by expressing Himself. At the end of the mystic path (fanā) the mystic knows himself to be Himself. God's essence and His attributes (e.g., individual Sufi seekers) are One.

Shaikh Ahmad of Sirhind replied that Ibn 'Arabī and his school were merely talking of the mystic stage of annihilation (fanā) and that this is not the final stage of reality. At the stage of annihilation the mystic is *ipso facto* absorbed in the being of God and utterly oblivious to anything other than God. Ibn 'Arabī is confusing the subjective with the objective. In fact, says Shaikh Ahmad, Ibn 'Arabī must still be aware of the world in order to identify it with God, otherwise he would have talked only of God. Shaikh Ahmad argues that beyond annihilation is a state which, he says, Ibn 'Arabī did not reach, in which the mystic experiences the truth that God is beyond comprehension through intuition. Hence man must revert to revelation and to the religious sciences based on revelation, in other words to the Sharī'a of the ulamā. Shaikh Ahmad insists that the only relation between God and the world is that of Creator and created and all talk of union or identity is heresy born of subjective mystic misconceptions.

These views Shaikh Ahmad propagated in his *Letters* (*Maktūbāt*), written to his disciples and others. About five hundred and thirty in all, they form a great classic of Indo-Muslim religious literature.

Mystic Union With God Is Only Subjective
[From Shaikh Ahmad Sirhindi, *Maktubat*, folios 52–53b]

The divine unity which Sufis encounter on their way is of two kinds, "unity of experience" (*tauhīd-i-shuhūdī*) and "unity of existence" (*tauhīd-i-wujūdī*). "Unity of experience" is seeing only one thing, that is to say, the traveler on the mystic path witnesses only oneness. "Unity of existence" is considering that only one thing exists and conceiving all else as nonexistent, believing that nonexistence is a mere reverse and antithesis [logically] of that one existence. "Unity of existence" is of the order of positive knowledge and "unity of experience" is of the order of absolutely certain knowledge. "Unity of experience" is among the necessary stages of the mystic path because annihilation of the self is not established without this oneness and without that real insight is not possible.

The overwhelming power of the vision of the unity of God is such that it is impossible to see what is beyond the state of annihilation of the self (fanā). Contrary to that is the "unity of existence"; . . . There is nothing in the heart which shall cause the denial of knowledge of what is beyond at the time of attaining knowledge of the unity of God. For example, when someone obtains a certain knowledge of the existence of the sun, the attainment of that knowledge does not cause him to think that the stars do not also exist at the same time. But at the time when he saw the sun he will certainly not see the stars, what he has witnessed will only be the sun. At the time when he does not see the stars, he knows that the stars are not nonexistent; indeed he knows they exist, but are hidden and overcome by the brilliance of the sun. This person is in a position to contradict those who deny the existence of the stars for he knows it was only that the knowledge of their existence had not yet been attained by him. Then the doctrine of unity of existence, which is the denial of everything except the Self of the Divine, is at war with both reason and the Sharī'a in contradistinction to unity of experience in which in its visualizing of unity no opposition to them occurs. For example, at the time of sunrise to deny the existence of the stars is to deny fact. At the same time when the stars are not seen, there is no opposition; rather their invisibility is due to the superiority of the light of the sun; if one's vision becomes so powerful as not to be affected by the light of the sun, the stars will be seen separately from the sun. This power of vision is possible in the "station" of absolute truth.

Thus the statements of some shaikhs who are apparently opposed to the True Way, and lead some men toward the doctrine of unity of existence as, for example, Abū Mansūr al-Hallāj in his statement, "I am God," and Abū Yazīd Bistāmī, "Praise be to Me!" and such like. It is proper that people must be led toward "unity of experience" and that opposition to that doctrine be repelled. Whenever what is other than God Most High was hidden to them, they uttered those phrases in the grip of ecstasy and they did not affirm anything but God. The meaning of "I am the Truth" is that He is the Truth, not "I" [al-Hallāj]; since he does not see himself he [al-Hallāj] does not establish that it is he who sees himself and he calls what he sees God. This is unbelief. Here no one may speak because not to affirm a thing is not [necessarily] to deny its existence and this is exactly what "unity of existence" does. For I say that to affirm nothing is not to deny anything. Indeed at this stage on the mystic path there is utter amazement [at the Glory of God] and all commands become ineffective.

And in "Praise be to Me!" the holiness of God is meant, not the holiness of the mystic, because God has become completely raised beyond the mystic's sight. . . . Some mystics do not give vent to such expressions in the state of real certainty, which is a state of amazement. When they pass beyond this stage and arrive at absolute certainty, they avoid such expressions altogether and do not transgress proper bounds.

In these times, many of those who claim to live as Sufis have propagated "unity of existence" and do not know anything beyond that; they have remained behind in real knowledge and have reduced the statements of the shaikhs to meanings of their own imagining and have held them up as guides for their own generation making current their own wicked secrets by means of these conceptions. If there are expressions in the statements of some of these shaikhs which lead to unity of existence, they must be attacked. . . .

The Sharī'a Is the True Religious Way
[From Shaikh Ahmad Sirhindī, Maktūbāt, folios 46a–b]

The Prophet says that there are three parts to the Sharī'a, knowledge, action, and sincere belief. Until these three parts are verified the Sharī'a is not verified. When the Sharī'a is verified God's satisfaction is obtained and this is superior to all else, "May God Most High be satisfied with all of them!" Therefore the Sharī'a is a guarantee of all these blessings and there is no purpose in seeking anything beyond the Sharī'a. The Way and the Truth, which for the Sufis have become distinct, both are servants of the Sharī'a. On the perfection of the third part of the Sharī'a which is sincere belief—the aim in acquiring the first two parts of the Sharī'a is the perfection of the Sharī'a and not anything else. The states and stations and gnosis which happen to the Sufi along his way are not among the purposes of the Sharī'a. The imaginings, the ideas, and the dark thoughts of the novice of the Way, having passed beyond all these must reach the stage of acquiescence in God, the end of the stages of the pilgrims of the mystic path and the object of the greatest desire. Unfortunately, the aim of passing beyond the stages of the Way to the reality beyond is not just to obtain that sincere belief which is the real cause of acquiescence in God. . . . Short-sighted people count the attainment of the various states and stages of the mystic path among their aims and consider the appearance of God and His manifestations among the things to be most desired. In the end, they remain imprisoned in their thoughts and in their imaginings and deprive themselves of the perfections of the Sharī'a.

Revelation and Inspiration Reconciled
[From Shaikh Ahmad Sirhindī, *Maktūbāt*, folios 50–51b]

The Prophet of God is the beloved of God; everything which is good and desired is for the sake of the beloved of God. As God has said in the holy Qur'ān, "No doubt your conduct and character is the best," and, "You are without doubt among the prophets and on the right path," and, "This is the only right path that you follow, and you do not follow the wrong path." His people have called him the straight road and what is outside his way of life is forbidden. As the Prophet has said, "Thanks should be given that the Prophet has shown a right path for the people." He also said that inner belief perfects outward observance and that there is not a hair-breadth of contradiction between the two. For example, not to tell lies is Sharī'a and to condemn lying thoughts in the heart is the Way (tarīqa) and inner reality (*haqīqat*). If this condemnation is possible but with hesitation and great effort, it is the Way and if it comes about without great hesitation it is inner reality. Then in truth, interior belief, which is both the Way and the Truth, is shown forth; this is the Sharī'a. When the travelers who follow the way of reproach encounter anything which is openly at war with the Sharī'a and adopt it, they fall victim to intoxication and are overcome by the mystic state (*hāl*). If they pass beyond that stage and return to sobriety, opposition to the Sharī'a is completely removed and destroyed.

For example, a group of the intoxicated limit their imagination to themselves and consider the Person of God to be encompassed by the world. This view is opposed to the opinion of the orthodox ulamā. They assert the way of (traditional) knowledge. Whenever, despite the fact that the Person of God is unlimited by any categorical mandates, and despite the fact that to inject something into the Person of God is to oppose the clear statement that He is ineffable and inscrutable, the Sufis assert that His Person is limitrophe with the world, then indeed they dwell in confusion, folly, and mere ignorance. What has God to do with the injection of human ideas and limitations into His Person? The Sufis must give the excuse that their intention is to understand the first manifestation of God and that when they see that manifestation they do not know it for what it is, and they interpret it as God Himself. . . .

The Person of God Most High is most nearly understood by the orthodox ulamā when they say that He is ineffable and incomparable and that whatever is beyond Him is something additional to that manifestation. If that manifestation of Him is proved it will be known that it is beyond the bounds of His essence and it will not be said that the limits of that manifestation are the limits of God's essence. Thus the viewpoint of the ulamā is more lofty than the viewpoint of the Sufis. The Person of God according to the Sufis is in fact implied in the essence of God according to the orthodox ulamā. Nearness and association with the Person of God and the agreement of interior knowledge with the sciences of the Sharī'a is perfect and complete. . . .

The station of truth is higher than the station of saintship; higher than that still is the station of prophethood and the knowledge which came by inspiration and by revelation to the holy Prophet. Between knowledge by revelation and knowledge by inspiration there is only a difference of process. . . . Revelation is clear cut and inspiration, opinion. For revelation is through the medium of angels and angels are innocent; there is no imputation of error to them.

Although inspiration has a high religious status and is of the heart, and the heart is of the Divine Order, nevertheless, it is connected with the reason and the lower self and however much one is on guard against the lower self, it never rises beyond its own qualities. The ability to err finds a home in it. But one must know that the survival of the qualities of the lower self and its contentment is a benefit and an advantage. If the lower self is completely forbidden from manifesting its qualities, the way of moral and spiritual development is obstructed. The soul would attain the rank of an angel and it would be imprisoned. Its progress is by means of opposition between it and the lower self. If no opposition remains how shall development occur?

Against Rulers Misled by Wicked Ulamā
[From Shaikh Ahmad Sirhindī, *Maktūbāt*, folios 58b–59b]

The sultan in relation to the world is like the soul in relation to the body. If the soul is healthy, the body is healthy, and if the soul is sick, the body is sick. The integrity of the ruler means the integrity of the world; his corruption, the corruption of the world. It is known what has befallen the people of Islam. Notwithstanding the presence of Islam in a foreign land, the infirmity of the Muslim community in previous generations did not go beyond the point where the Muslims followed their religion and the unbelievers followed theirs. As the Qur'ān says, "For you, your way, for me, my way." . . .

In the previous generation, in the very sight of men, unbelievers turned to the way of domination, the rites of unbelief prevailed in the abode of Islam, and Muslims were too weak to show forth the mandates of the faith. If they did, they were killed. Crying aloud their troubles to Muhammad, the beloved of God, those who believed in him lived in ignominy and disgrace; those who denied him enjoyed the prestige and respect due to Muslims, and with their feather brains condoled with Islam. The disobedient and those who denied Muhammad used to rub the salt of derision and scorn into the wounds of the faithful. The sun of guidance was hidden behind the veil of error and the light of truth was shut out and obscured behind the curtain of absurdity.

Today, when the good tidings of the downfall of what was prohibiting Islam [i.e., the death of Akbar] and the accession of the king of Islam [i.e., Jahāngīr] is reaching every corner, the community of the faithful have made it their duty to be the helpers and assistants of the ruler and to take as their guide the spreading of the Holy Law and the strengthening of the community. This assistance and support is becoming effective both by word and deed. In the very early days of Islam the most successful pens were those which clarified problems of Holy Law and which propagated theological opinions in accordance with the Qur'ān, the Sunna, and the consensus of the community, so that such errors and innovations as did appear did not lead people astray and end in their corruption. This role is

peculiar to the orthodox ulamā who should always look to the invisible
world.

Worldly ulamā whose worldly aspirations are their religion—indeed
their conversation is a fatal poison and their corruption is contagious. . . .
In the generation before this, every calamity which appeared arose from
the evil desires of these people. They misled rulers. The seventy-two sects
who went on the road of error were lost because the ruler enforced his
errors on others and the majority of the so-called ignorant Sufis of this
time upheld the decisions of the wicked ulamā—their corruption was also
contagious. Obviously, if someone, notwithstanding assistance of every
kind, commits an error, and a schism occurs in Islam, that error should
be reprehended. But these hateful people of little capital always wish to
enroll themselves among the helpers of Islam and to beg importunately.
. . . These disobedient people worm their way into the confidence of the
generous and consider themselves to be like heroes. . . . It is hoped that in
these times, if God wills, the worthy will be honored with royal company.

SHAH WALĪ-ULLĀH

The instinct of Indian Islam for tolerance and flexibility as a condition
of its survival is symbolized in the life and thought of Shah Walī-Ullāh
of Delhi (1703–1762), who wrote during the decline of the Mughal empire
and before Indian Islam felt the impact of Western thought. He translated
the Qur'ān into Persian, wrote Qur'anic commentaries, was a student of
tradition, scholastic theology, and jurisprudence, and practiced Sufism.
His significance as a religious thinker is still being estimated but his writings indicate that Indian Islam had survived the intellectual and religious
trials of the sixteenth and seventeenth centuries without loss of vitality
and catholicity. Shah Walī-Ullāh helped to insure that at least among
Muslims there was no bitter religious strife to complement the political
strife in India after Aurangzīb's death. Shah Walī-Ullāh, in the readings
which follow, is to be observed teaching the old lessons of devotion to
the Sunna of the Prophet and the need for breadth and tolerance in
interpreting the mandates of the Sharī'a.

The Imitation of Muhammad
[From *The Muslim World*, Vol. XLV, No. 4 (tr. by Rahbar), pp. 326–27]

Know that the key of happiness is following the Sunna and imitating God's apostle in all his goings out and comings in, in his movements and times of quiescence, even in the manner of his eating, his deportment, his sleep, and his speech. I do not say that concerning his manners in matters of religious observances alone, because there is no reason to neglect the traditions which have come down concerning them; nay, that has to do with all the matters of use and wont, for in that way unrestricted following arises. God said, "Say, If you love God, follow me and God will love you" (Qur'ān 3.29). And He said, "What the apostle has brought you receive, and what he has forbidden you refrain from" (Qur'ān 59.7). So you must sit while putting on trousers and stand while putting on a turban; you must begin with the right foot when putting on your sandals, and eat with your right hand; when cutting your nails you must begin with the forefinger of the right hand and finish with its thumb; in the foot you must begin with the little toe of the right foot and finish with the little toe of the left. It is the same in all your movements and times of quiescence. Muhammad b. Aslām used not to eat a melon because the manner in which God's apostle ate it had not been transmitted to him. A certain man was unmindful and began to put on the left shoe first, so he made atonement for that with a *kurr* [a measure] of wheat. Now it is not fitting to be lax in such matters and say that this is one of the things which pertain to use and wont, so that there is no point in following the Prophet regarding it, because that will lock against you an important gate of happiness.

Legal Interpretation

Ijtihād or legal interpretation is the process whereby the student of the Sharī'a arrives at determinations of the Holy Law in circumstances not already covered by previous decisions. Legal interpretation is the sole means of adapting the Sharī'a to changing social circumstances while yet preserving the ideal of orthodoxy, i.e., of following in the footsteps of the Prophet in obedience to a God-revealed law. The problem of legal interpretation has come to the fore in every period of crisis for the Indo-Muslim community, whether in the newly founded state of Pakistan or in Shah Walī-Ullāh's eighteenth century, when Muslim power was rapidly disintegrating. Shah Walī-Ullāh advises interpreters of the law to avoid arbitrariness and destructive controversy, and rather to apply the Golden Mean.

[From *The Muslim World*, Vol. XLV, No. 4, pp. 347–54 *passim*; 357–58]

The true nature of legal interpretation (*ijtihād*), as understood from the discourse of scholars, is exhaustive endeavor in understanding the derivative principles of the Holy Canon Law by means of detailed arguments, their genera being based on four departments: 1) The Holy Book [the Qur'ān]; 2) The example and precept of the Prophet [the Sunna]; 3) The consensus of opinion of the Muslim community; 4) The application of analogy.

Let it be understood from this that legal interpretation is wider than [i.e., not confined to] the exhaustive endeavor to perceive the principle worked out by earlier scholars, no matter whether such an endeavor leads to disagreement or agreement with these earlier scholars. It is not limited by the consideration whether this endeavor is made with or without aid received from some of the earlier scholars in their notification of the aspects of questions involved in a given issue and their notification over the sources of the principles through detailed arguments. . . .

[Al-Baghawī said] "An interpreter of the Law is one who combines in himself five types of knowledge: 1) the knowledge of the Book of God the Glorious; 2) the knowledge of the example and precept of the Prophet (peace be on him and his descendants); 3) the knowledge of the speeches of the scholars of yore recording their consensus of opinion and their difference of opinion; 4) the knowledge of the Arabic language; and 5) the knowledge of analogy, which is the method of eliciting the principle from the Qur'ān or the Hadīth when the principle is not found unequivocally in the statutes of the Qur'ān, the Hadīth, and the consensus of opinion.

"It is incumbent that of the knowledge of the Holy Book he should possess the knowledge of the abrogating and the abrogated passages, the summary expressions and the full expressions, the general ordinances and the particular ones, the sound verses and the ambiguous verses, the disapprovals, prohibitions, permissions and approvals, and obligations.

"And of the Hadīth he must recognize the perfectly sound Hadīth, the weak ones, the ones supported by complete chains of narrators going back to the Prophet, the ones in which the chains of narrators omit the names of the Companions who transmitted the Hadīth. And he must know the application of the Hadīth upon the Qur'ān and of the Qur'ān upon the Hadīth, so that if he finds a Hadīth, the outward meanings of which do not conform to the meanings of the Book, he should get guided rightly to bring out its bearing, for the Hadīth is an exposition of the Book, and does not contradict it. Of the Hadīth it is obligatory upon him to know only those which relate to the principles of the Holy Law, and not the rest which contain stories, accounts of events, and admonitions.

"And likewise, it is incumbent that he should possess the lexical knowledge necessary to understand the passages in the Qur'ān and the Hadīth. But it is not required that he should encompass the entire vocabulary of Arabic. He should so polish up his linguistic knowledge that he may be in a position to understand the real import of Arabic phrases to an extent which may guide him to the intended meanings in different contexts and circumstances. This requirement is there because the Holy Canon Law is addressed in Arabic. He who does not know Arabic will not recognize the meaning intended by the Law-giver [i.e., the Prophet], nor will he understand what the companions and the successors of the companions said of principles, nor will he understand the most important judgments given by the jurisconsults of the community. He should know Arabic well so that his judgment does not stand opposed to theirs, in which case his judgment will involve violation of the consensus. And when he knows the major portion of each of these departments of knowledge, he is an interpreter of the Law, and the exhaustive knowledge of all these is not a condition. And if he is ignorant of one of these five departments then his path is to follow [i.e., not to indulge in legal interpretation], even if he is profoundly learned in the school of one of the bygone Imāms [the founders of one of the four schools of Muslim law]. It is not allowable for such a man to be invested with the status of a judge, or to be a candidate for a position in which he might give judgments. And if these sciences are combined in him, and he shuns evil passions and innovations, clothes himself with robes of piety, and abstains from major sins, not persisting in minor sins, then it is allowable that he may take up the responsibility of the office of a judge and may exercise his personal discretion in the Holy Law using legal interpretation and may pronounce his judgment. And he who does not combine in himself these conditions must, in matters that might concern him, follow him who does combine them." [The quotation from al-Baghawī ends here.] . . .

Scholars have differed in the matter of ratification of interpreters of the law, pronouncing differently on the derivative issues where no conclusive judgment is to be found. Is each of these interpreters of the law correct or is only one of them correct? . . . . [The author reviews the opinions of various authorities, and finally quotes al-Baidāwī.]

Al-Baidawī said in *The Stages* (*Al-Minhāj*): "The most preferable view is that which comes soundly from al-Shāfi'i: 'In every occurrence there is a fixed verdict upon which there is an indication.' Whichever interpreter of the law finds out that indication, hits the target, and whichever fails to find it out, misses the target, although he is not sinful on that account, for legal interpretation, which is the sum total of the search of arguments, is preceded by arguments; and the indication upon the error made comes after the verdict. If two different legal interpretations were to be regarded true, this would be a concurrence of two contradictions. And the interpreter of the law, missing the target of truth is not sinful either because the Prophet (peace be on him!) said: 'Whoso hits the target, shall have two rewards, and whoso misses it, shall have only one reward.'

"It is said that if the verdict is fixed, then he whose position is contrary to it does not judge according to what Allāh had revealed, and so is a transgressor, for Allāh the Exalted says: 'Whoso judges not in accordance with what Allāh has revealed, they are the transgressors.' We say answering this objection that he [i.e., the error-maker] pronounced judgments in accordance with what he thought was right, even though his judgment mistook the meaning of what God has revealed." . . .

And in reality the opinion attributed to the four Imams [the opinion that only one legal interpreter out of many, pronouncing on the same issue, is correct] is drawn out from some of their statements and there is no final unequivocal ruling (*nass*) given by them on this matter.

And in fact the community of Islam has not differed from the position that you can ratify legal interpreters pronouncing judgment in a matter wherein the community is given choice by an unequivocal holy text or by consensus (ijmā'), e.g., the Seven Variant Readings of the Qur'ān, the formulae of invocations, and the number of prostrations in Witr Prayers, which may be seven, nine, or eleven. And likewise the ulamā [i.e., scholars] should not differ [from the position that both the legal interpreters could be ratified] in matters wherein choice is given by some indication [if not by an unequivocal text or by consensus].

And the truth is that there are four types of difference: 1) That in which the truth is decisively determined, and it is necessary in such a case that its opposite be contradicted for it is false; 2) That in which the truth is determined by the dominant opinion. The opposite of it is false by dominant opinion; 3) That in which definite choice has been given to adopt any of the two alternative sides of difference; and 4) That in which the above choice is given by the dominant opinion.

And the detailed explanation of the above is that if the issue at hand is such that the verdict of the verdict giver is violated by both the alternative ways of settling it, i.e., if there is found an unequivocal, sound, and well-known Hadīth of the Prophet, and both legal interpretations stand opposed to it, then both will be false. But yes. The legal interpreter in such a matter will sometimes be excused upon grounds of his ignorance of the unequivocal Hadīth of the Prophet (peace be upon him) until that Hadīth reaches him, and the argument gets established. And if the legal interpretation is exercised in the ascertainment of an event which happened but the state whereof becomes dubious, like in the question whether Mr. A is dead or alive, unquestionably the truth in such a case will be one of the two alternatives. But the interpreter making a mistake in such a case will sometimes be excused in his legal interpretation. . . . The important cases of difference are of many types:

1. One interpreter of the law receives a Hadīth and the other one does not. Now in this case the right interpreter is already known.

2. Every interpreter engaged in the same issue has some conflicting Hadīth and he exercises legal interpretation in bringing about congruence between some of them and preference of some over others, and his legal interpretation leads to a certain judgment of his own and so difference of this nature appears.

3. They may differ in the explanation of the words used and their logical definitions, or regarding the supply of what might be considered omitted in speech [and left to be understood], or in eliciting the *manat* [i.e., the common factor which justifies the application of a primary principle from the Qur'ān or the Hadīth to a derivative situation, or in application of general to particulars, etc.].

4. They may differ in primary principles leading to difference in derivative principles.

In all these cases each of any two interpreters of the law will be right provided the sources from which they get support are easily acceptable to intellects. . . .

Now whoever recognizes the true nature of this problem will realize: 1) that in the majority of cases of legal interpretation the truth lies somewhere between the two extremes of difference; 2) that in the matter of religion there is breadth and not narrowness; 3) that being unreasonably stubborn and determined to deny what the opponent says is ridiculous; 4) that the construing of definitions if it aims at bringing concepts closer to the understanding of every literate person, assists knowledge. But if these definitions are far-fetched and try to discriminate between involved matters by means of innovated premises, it will soon lead to an unworthy and innovated system of Sharī'a; 5) the true opinion is that pronounced by Izz al-Dīn 'Abd al-Salām who says: "He attains the goal who stands firm on what is agreed upon by scholars and abstains from what they have unanimously disallowed, and regards allowable that which is unanimously thus regarded by scholars, and does that which is unanimously approved by scholars, and keeps away from that which they have unanimously regarded as hateful."

Shah Walī-Ullāh and Mysticism

In his attitude toward mysticism, Shah Walī-Ullāh was conciliatory. For him, Ibn 'Arabī's doctrine of the unity of existence and Shaikh Ahmad of Sirhind's doctrine of the unity of experience, *i.e.,* the apparent but illusory unity of existence are both true statements about the same thing. In a letter to one Afandī Ismā'īl he writes:

[Adapted from *Visva-Bharati Annals,* IV 35–36 (tr. by Asiri), 1951]

Unity of existence and unity of experience are two relative terms used at two different places in an argument about God. Unity of existence here implies scrutiny of the encompassing truth which has filled the universe by unfolding itself with various commands on which is based knowledge about good and evil. Both revelation and reason support it. One should know that created things are one in one respect and different in another. This can only be perceived by the saints who are really perfect. The stage of unity of experience is higher than unity of existence. . . . Now some Sufis saw the contingent and created as connected with the eternal; also they perceived the modes of God's existence combined with His essence.

This can be explained by the example of wax forms of man, horse and ass, which have wax in common, but different shapes. This is the belief of the real pantheists. But the others maintain that the Universe is a reflection of the names and attributes of the necessary being [God] reflected in their opposite, nonexistence. These attributes and names are reflected in the mirror of nonexistence which is powerless.

In the same manner one can imagine the appearance of each name and attribute of God in the mirror of non-being. The former is unity of existence, and the latter unity of experience. To me both are based on true revelations. Unity of experience of Shaikh Ahmad does not contradict but confirms Ibn 'Arabī's unity of existence. In short, if real facts are taken into account and studied without their garb of simile and metaphor, both doctrines will appear almost the same.

CHAPTER XVII

THE MUSLIM RULER
IN INDIA

For Muslims, God is the all-mighty and ever active sovereign of His Universe who has made His Will and Pleasure for mankind known in His Holy Law (Sharī'a). The government of His community on earth is therefore one of the innumerable and, strictly speaking, indeterminate expressions of this total Divine sovereignty, and "political theory" is merely one specification or aspect of the Holy Law.

The problems to which Muslim thought on temporal government stands as the succession of answers have not been, for example, those of the origin and nature of political power or of the relation of "church" and "state," but of how the pious Muslim might recognize that the government of the community is in the right hands and be assured that it is being exercised for the right purposes. After early attempts to define the conditions of the appointment of legitimate authority over the community however, the majority of the ulamā—the students of Islamic revelation—preferred to concentrate on persuading the *de facto* ruler to do his duty toward Islam no matter how he had gained his position, thereby enabling pious Muslims to obey the "powers that be" with a good conscience. In this they were doubtless impelled by the desire to avoid a political chaos in which the practice of the good Muslim life might become impossible, and by a human reluctance to believe that, in accepting a particular ruler, they had sinned against God.

As long as the Prophet lived, Muslims did not have to "theorize politically." Muhammad was the divinely appointed Messenger of God, communicating to mankind what God had wished them to know. Muhammad united in himself, legislative, executive, and judicial functions. But with him died the Revelation of Divine Command and the exercise of Divine government organically united in one person. However, the period of the *ridda* wars (632–634) against seceding Arab tribes determined

that rebellion was the same as apostasy and that ideally, at least, the community was neither a political nor a religious one, but both.

After the Prophet's death, Muslims could not agree upon one interpretation of God's will for the government of the community. Some, the party
of 'Alī, the Prophet's cousin and son-in-law, thought he should have been
accepted as head of the community at the Prophet's death, in place of those
who were actually accepted successively, namely, Abū Bakr, 'Umar, and
'Uthmān. Faced with opposition, the supporters of the actual succession of
caliphs idealized their rule, and what later generations believed was
their practice, was held to embody true Islamic government on earth.
This, the Sunni doctors of the Holy Law stated, involved the necessity
of a Khalīfa as the divinely ordained ruler of the community, symboliz-
ing the supremacy of the Holy Law. He was selected by the community
(or by the senior members of it) to enforce the Holy Law, but not to
define it himself. The Khalīfa, the Sunnis held, was a magistrate, not
a pope; the guardian, not the chief of the ulamā.

The pious charged the Ummayads (661–750) with introducing a
worldly hereditary monarchy. The 'Abbāsid caliphs (750–1258) advertised
their religiousness and patronized the ulamā, but hardly fulfilled the
ideal of the early caliphate—they were not elected and their authority was
certainly not exercised solely to enforce the Holy Law.

Moreover from the middle of the ninth century, the 'Abbāsid caliphs
were proposed and deposed by their Turkish guards, while between 945
and 1055, they were the puppets of the Buyid princes, Shī'a's who only
recognized the 'Abbāsid caliph as nominal head of the community for
political reasons.

Confronted with this chasm between the ideal and the actual, and unwilling to convict the community of living in sin by reason of its acquiescence, Sunni jurists attempted to sanctify, or at least to condone, the
actual course of history by appeal to texts from the Qur'ān and the Sunna,
and to ijmā'—in this context, passive acceptance of the political *fait accom-
pli*. Faced with the "amirate by seizure"—the forceful imposition of his
rule by a military chief over a part of the Muslim world—a jurist like
al-Māwardī (d. 1058) argued in his *al-Ahkām us-Sultāniyya* that such a
ruler was to be accepted as legitimate providing that he paid deference to
the nominal headship of the caliph and entered into a kind of "concordat"
whereby the caliph invested him with authority in return for an undertaking to rule according to Holy Law and defend Muslim territory.

As for India, the Ghōrid conquerors, the sultans of Delhi, and, *a fortiori,* the Mughals were clearly not agents of the caliph. Although Iltutmish in 1229 received investiture as the lieutenant of the then 'Abbāsid caliph, the Mongol Hūlāgū's slaying of the 'Abbāsid Caliph al-Musta'sim in 1258 denied his successors even that title to legitimacy. Indo-Muslim theory met the situation by stressing the divine ordination of the function of temporal government, the duty of obedience, and the desirability of the sultanate in India acting as caliph *de facto* for its own dominions— that is by ascribing to it those functions, including the defense and maintenance of true religion and the Holy Law, of dispensing justice and of appointing the god-fearing to office, which Sunni jurists had earlier ascribed to the caliphate. The test of the Muslim ruler was not how he came to be where he was, but what he did when he arrived there.

In essence, the bulk of Indo-Muslim writing on government embodies a conception of partnership between the doctors of the holy law and the sultan in the higher interests of the faith—a partnership between pious professors and pious policemen. In the sixteenth century, members of Akbar's circle, under the influence of Shī'ī doctrines and ideas mediated from Greek philosophy, were inclined to allow the "just Imām" discretion to decide points of Holy Law where there was disagreement among the doctors and no clear guidance was offered by the Sharī'a. Still, it is doubtful whether in this they were going beyond the ambit of the administrative discretion (*siyāsa*) already allowed the ruler by some jurists and writers so that he might act in the best interest, though not according to the formal terms, of the Holy Law. Abū'l Fazl, however, appears to associate some of the sanctity which had always attached to the office of the just Imām with the person of the just ruler. The orthodox, for their part, reacted strongly against this, fearing that the supremacy of the Holy Law over a Muslim's realm (and the authority of the ulamā as its interpreters) was about to be abandoned even in principle, as it had long since been ignored for the most part in practice. Certainly Abū-l Fazl's ideas threatened to wipe out the distinction made in later Sunni thought between the religious and the ruling institution.

The readings in this section illustrate the political thinking of writers who accept the sultanate as a necessary fact and who wish to consecrate it to Islamic purposes. They have been taken from the following works of the sultanate period—The *Genealogies* (*Shajara-yi-Ansāb*) written about 1206 by Fakhr ud-dīn Mubārak Shāh, a learned man at the court of Qutb

ud-dīn Aibak; Ziā ud-dīn Barnī's *Rulings on Temporal Government*
(*Fatāwa-yi-Jahāndārī*); and *The Treasuries of Kings* (*Zakhīrat ul-Mulūk*), written in the second half of the fourteenth century by one said
to be largely responsible for the conversion of Kashmir to Islam, Shaikh
Hamadānī. Along with these are presented under each topic pertinent
selections from writing of the Mughal period, including Muhammad
Bāqir Khān's *Advice on Government* (*Mau'iza-yi-Jahāngīrī*); the *Ethics
of Government* (*Akhlāq-i-Jahāngīrī*), written in 1620–1622 by Nūr ud-
dīn Muhammad Khagānī; Abū Tālib al-Husaini's *Institutes of Tīmūr*
(c. 1637); and Abū'l Fazl's *Ā'in-i-Akbarī*.

The Final End of Human Society Is the Worship of God

Ziā ud-dīn Barnī was the most important writer on politics during the era of
the Delhi sultanate (c.1210–1556). Born about 1285, he belonged to the Muslim aristocracy, with his father, paternal uncle, and grandfather all holding important administrative positions under the sultan of Delhi. He himself held
no government post but was a *nadīm* or boon companion of Sultan Muhammad
ibn Tughluq (1325–1351) for over seventeen years. At the death of Muhammad
ibn Tughluq he fell out of favor and was banished from court, suffering imprisonment for a few months. It was during this period of poverty and exile
from court that he wrote his works on government and religion, hoping thereby
both to prepare himself for the hereafter and also to win back the favor of
Sultan Fīrūz Shāh Tughluq. In the latter hope he was disappointed, dying
in poverty not long after 1357.

Barnī wrote to set forth for the sultans of Delhi their duty toward Islam. His
two most important works, the *Rulings on Temporal Government* (*Fatāwa-yi-
Jahāndārī*) and *Fīrūz Shāh's History* (*Tārīkh-i-Fīrūz Shāhī*) form the reverse
and obverse of the same doctrinal coin. Barnī was a Sunni Muslim, hostile to
the Shī'a and to the influence of Greek philosophy, while convinced of the
virtues of Sufi mysticism. In the *Fatāwa-yi-Jahāndārī* he sets forth his conception of the duties of the sultan toward orthodox Sunni Islam, a conception
which, it should be emphasized, is not original in the wider context of Islamic
political or legal thought. In the *Tārīkh-i-Fīrūz Shāhī*, he interprets the history
of the Delhi sultans from Balban (1266–87) to Fīrūz Shāh Tughluq (1351–88)
in such a manner as to convey that sultans who followed his precepts prospered,
and those who sinned against them, met Nemesis.

[From Barnī, *Fatāwa-yi-Jahāndārī*, folios 44b, 143, 199a–199b]

The king of all kings and rulers is God. God maintains the world by His
wrath and His grace and the indications of His grace and His wrath are
manifest in His mercy and His bounty toward the good and the wicked.

He has created Paradise for the good and the obedient and has promised it for them. He has created hell for the wicked and the disobedient and has frightened the stubborn and the infidels with it. He has created Rizwān [the porter at the gate of Paradise] out of his mercy and Malāk [the guardian of hell] out of his wrath. So, earthly "rulers" must [metaphorically speaking] follow the practices of the Real Ruler and treat the inhabitants of their kingdoms in accordance with the contrasting qualities which are essential for temporal government. [folio 199a–b]

. . . .

God is the real king and earthly "kings" are the playthings of His decree and Divine Power. In His government, God forgives some sinners and does not accept the repentance of others and treats them sternly. Some He will punish in the next world and does not punish in this world; others he punishes in this world and will not punish in the next. Some He keeps safe and some He keeps under the umbrella of His protection, compassion, and favor. Some He raises to the pinnacle of esteem, greatness, glory, and good fortune. Others He rolls in the dust of dishonor and disgrace. Upon some He bestows wealth and prosperity, others He causes to live in a middling state, others He keeps in poverty, indigence, and wretchedness. Some He brings to life and some He causes to die. Toward people of every sort, condition and kind He exercises His Lordship by different treatment, in accordance with His Ripe Judgment. He maintains the order of the world and keeps it coherent. He is the real King and to him alone is Kingship proper. [folio 143]

. . . .

Mankind was created for submission to God. As God Most High has said, "We have not created men or jinns except that they may worship Us." [folio 44b]

Prophets and Kings

All power is ultimately God's but is exercised over human society through prophets, the learned, and kings. The substitution of sultans for caliphs is an adjustment of Muslim thinking to the historical situation in the Muslim world after the destruction of the 'Abbāsid caliphate. God ordains the sultanate as a necessary corrective for human weakness and as a necessary means of salvation.

[From Barnī, *Fatāwa-yi-Jahāndārī*, folios 247b–248a]
Religion and temporal government are twins; that is, the head of religion

and the head of government are twin brothers. As the world will not come right or stay right through kingship alone there must be both prophets and kings in the world so that mankind's business in both the worlds may be carried through in accordance with God's wishes. If there be a king and no prophet, then the affairs of this world may come aright, but no one created of God will be saved in the next. If there is a prophet but no king, then without the power and majesty of kingship, the world will seek the right in vain and religious commands will not prevail and affairs will fall into confusion and disorder. Almighty God has adorned prophets and kings with inborn virtues and praiseworthy qualities. These two high attributes—prophethood and kingship—do not mix well with base morals and vile qualities. Almighty God (may His name be glorified) has only created prophets that they may bestow the gift of humble submission to God out of their own nature. He has created them innocent of major and minor sin so that everyone in the world may draw nigh to Him who lacks nothing and become His nearest and dearest. They hear the word of God and bring it to men; they show men the way to those laws which are pleasing to God. They show them the right path and keep them away from the wrong path. Everyone of those so pleased to hearken unto those words and follow their authority draws nearer to God and is worthy of the bounty of Paradise. But he who counts their words as nothing, rejects their prophethood and the commands from God which out of their God-fearing characters the prophets give, is deserving of Hell and remains estranged from God.

[From Shaikh Hamadānī, *Zakhīrat ul-Mulūk,* folio 75a]
Know ye that among the great ones of the learned, those possessed of intelligence and wisdom, it is established and proved that, at the very first moment of creation, by reason of the different qualities and admixture of ability which are bestowed by the bounty of God like a lustrous and bejeweled costume, the souls and natures of men have fallen out differently. Hence, the inclinations, motives and purposes of men have become different and the difference is manifested in all their words, deeds, and fundamental articles of faith.

The qualities of beastliness and of base morals—tyranny and injustice, hatred, and rancor, and avarice are implanted in the dispositions of men. Then, in the perfection of His great Wisdom, God has decreed that there be a just and competent ruler of mankind so that, by the power of judicial

process, the affairs of the progeny of Adam and the rules for managing
the affairs of mankind may be kept and preserved on the right path;
also a ruler has been ordained by God so that he may endeavor, as far as
possible, to put into operation the mandates of the Sharī'a and to be on
guard to preserve the prescriptions and rules of Islam among people of all
classes and, with the prohibitions of punishment and the curb of command, to prevent tyranny over and oppression of the weak by the strong.
Thus the physical world may be assured of stability, the bounds of the
Sharī'a not invaded by the disorder of oppression and innovation, and the
characteristics of brute beasts and camels may not be manifested among
people of all classes.

[From Muhammad Bāqir Khān, *Mau'iza-yi-Jahāngīrī,* folios 5–7]
Moreover, in order to order and arrange the affairs of the world and the
concerns of mankind there must be rules whereby, each living with the
other, no one may suffer injustice and oppression. Therefore God has
raised up from among mankind itself prophets and messengers, each one
of whom is a pearl in the sea of purity and a lodestar in the constellations
possessing the qualities of attachment to the world and of separation from
it, of care for the world and of detachment from it. Thus, having obtained
holiness through separation and detachment from the world, they may,
by their connection and their strong ties with it, guide the rebellious and
those wallowing in black error and eager to be deceived, to the abode of
true guidance and the fountain of divine protection. And they keep those
laws which are called the Sharī'a so that everyone may be put on the
straight road of its mandates and, enjoying security through the majesty
and wrath of God, attain to eternal bliss and felicity. Everyone who strays
from the straight path shall be afflicted by the lash of divine displeasure
and be placed in the next world in "durance vile." . . .

After the time of Muhammad who is the seal and the last of the
prophets, in order that the principles of religion may be established and
properly ordered, the actions of God's servants directed aright and their
welfare secured, and the boon of peace and tranquillity obtained by the
existence of one governor and ruler who should be worthy of imitation
and possessed of exalted power, and whose praiseworthy person should
be adorned with the jewel of justice and equity; in order too, that through
the full exercise of the power or by the nonexercise of the power of a
warrior's wrath, the shadow of man's base and animal passions may be

shunned and avoided in order that all this may be achieved and the
people not forget their sincere friends [the prophets], not follow after
their own desires, not let their lusts overwhelm them, not indulge in
wanton pastimes and arrogant contention for superiority, one against
another—and if the different generations of God's creatures are to live
quietly on a bed of peace and tranquillity, then there is no escaping,
indeed it is necessary and unavoidable, that there shall exist that chosen
being of creation whom they call a king.

He, the king, being created with the morals of a doctor of holy law and
basing his conduct of affairs upon the mandates of the Holy Law shall
therefore make his authority distinguished for some of the qualities which
can be the embroidery of the garments of the sultanate. Furthermore,
directing all his high aspirations toward understanding what wise men
say and opening the secrets of the ulamā, he shall make their advice,
counsel and decisions his model, so that both the head of his kingdom
shall be adorned with the crown of success and the garment of the kingdom be ornamented by respect for religion. Both the kingdom and the
subjects of every prudent king who is distinguished for these worthy
qualities and who is adorned with the jewel of these laudable dispositions,
shall become prosperous, happy, contented, obedient, and loyal, and with
the garden of his authority containing such trees and seeds, year by year
for numberless generations, his reputation for goodness shall remain inscribed on the pages of time.

Obedience to the Sultan Is Commanded by God
[From Fakhr-i-Mudir, *Shajara*, pp. 12–13]

And the Prophet, Peace be upon him! saith: "Whoever obeys me, verily
and truly will have obeyed God and whoever obeys the Imām [leader],
that is to say, the sultan, will have obeyed me, and whoever rebels against
me will have rebelled against God, and whoever rebels against the sultan,
verily and truly he will have rebelled against me." The Prophet also said:
"Obey your kings and governors though they be Abyssinian slaves."

Kingship Is Incompatible with Religious Ideals

Some thinkers, on the other hand, hold that the sultanate is un-Islamic; that it
is an unholy heir of Persian traditions of monarchy. Ziā ud-dīn Barnī, for ex-

ample, insists that monarchy is essentially antithetical to religion and that rulers must consecrate themselves to God's service if they are to have any hope of escaping God's wrath. Only the four Rightly-Guided Caliphs were true Muslim rulers.

[From Barnī, *Fatāwa-yi-Jahāndārī,* folios 87b–100a, 224a–b *passim*]
The governance of men is not feasible and has not been feasible without the ways of rulers and the majesty and pomp of governors. And that one generation when the Rightly-Guided Caliphs exercised the authority of the successors of the Prophet with a life of abstinence and poverty, and the world became subject to them, was only possible because the time of the Prophet Muhammad was so near and the effects of his miracles were still being felt. From Adam's day until the extinction of the world their generation has been and will always be considered the wonder of time and the rarity of the ages. The behavior of these caliphs in all things followed the Sunna of the Prophet. But if succeeding caliphs and kings wished to follow their example they would not be able to maintain their caliphate or royal authority for a single day. Moreover, those four [the Rightly-Guided Caliphs] who did not adopt the habits and customs of sultans for fear of opposing the practice of the Prophet, with all the power of the Prophet's practices, lost their lives. 'Umar, 'Uthmān, and 'Alī were martyred by fearless fanatics. No other Muslim caliph or ruler has found the opportunity— or will ever find it—to rule and to proclaim the practice of the Prophet, by embracing their way of life and livelihood; for the world is full of those who have the character of devils, the habits of carnivorous beasts, of wild animals, and beasts of prey; without the terror and dominion of powerful and successful sultans, command and control over them is never achieved. . . .

The helpers and supporters of the orthodox caliphs were the noble Companions of the Prophet who eagerly sacrificed their lives and property, wives, sons, and belongings in the way of Truth. Because they had been associates, friends, and companions of the Chosen One of the Lord Most High and had witnessed Divine Revelation, they were such lovers of God and the Prophet that the whole world was not worth a farthing in their sight. . . . Because they had such helpers and companions, the path of poverty and self-denial was practicable in the government of the Rightly-Guided Caliphs. . . .

But now . . . real belief in God and certainty and firmness in the true faith remain conspicuous in only a small number of individuals. The outward appearance of Islam has assumed many guises; the world has returned to the ways of mere mimics [i.e., men only follow Islam as a matter of custom] and of seekers after this world. Just as before the advent of the Prophet, the aspirations and desires of mankind were centered on this world, so the same is appearing again. Never will the power and authority of the caliphate be asserted and become well constituted without the terror and majesty and pomp of temporal rulership which are the ways by which rulers secure submission of the unruly, reduce the forward and the rebellious to impotence. Rule, dominion, and conquest are not possible with a life of poverty. Without the majesty and pomp of the sultanate, man will swallow man, the obedient will become disobedient, the prestige of authority will melt away, and obedience to command will completely disappear. No one will fear the governors and *muqta's* whom the Commander of the Faithful has appointed, and they will become without respect or authority; every day revolt and tumult will break out and tyranny and oppression will appear. . . .

After them [the first four caliphs] the caliphs and kings of Islam were faced by two opposed alternatives, both necessary for religion and the realm. If they followed the traditions of the Prophet and his mode of life, government and kingship would be impracticable for them; claiming to be kings and yet living the life of a mendicant they would not remain alive; authority, which is the essence of government, would not be enforced among the people at all.

If they follow the practices of the Khusraus [the Persian emperors] and adopt their mode of sitting and rising, eating and dressing, and their general manner of life—the destruction of the headstrong, the subduing of the forward, and the taking of any steps necessary for the enforcement of authority among the people, it is necessary to transgress the Sunna of the Prophet, the sum and essence of true religion. In the persons and in the environment of kings no traditions are admissible because prophet-hood is the perfection of religiousness, and kingship that of earthly bliss; these two perfections are opposed and contradictory to each other and their combination is not within the bounds of possibility.

For servitude to God is the necessary condition of religion, and the necessary conditions of this servitude are submission, supplication, poverty, self-abasement, abjectness, need, and humility. On the other hand,

the requisites of kingship, which is the perfection of worldly good fortune, are haughtiness, pride, aloofness from others, luxurious and soft living, lack of civility, grandeur, and might. The qualities enumerated here
are among the attributes of God. And since kingship is the deputyship and
the vice-regency of God, kingship is not compatible with the characteristics of servitude.

Consequently, it became necessary for the rulers of Islam to adopt the
customs of the kings of Persia to ensure the greatness of the True Word,
the supremacy of the Muslim religion, the superiority of Truth, the root-
ing out of the enemies of the Faith, the carrying on of the affairs of
religion, and the maintenance of their own authority. . . . Nevertheless,
the religion of Islam totally prohibits the iniquities committed by the
Persian kings.

But just as the eating of carrion, though prohibited, is yet permitted
in time of dire need, similarly the customs and traditions of the sultans
of 'Ajam [1]—the crown and the throne, aloofness from others, pride, rules
about sitting down and getting up in the king's court, high palaces, court
ceremonials, asking people to prostrate themselves before the king, collecting treasures, misappropriating properties, wearing gold garments and
jewels and silk cloth and making other people wear them, putting people
to death on grounds of policy, keeping large harems, spending recklessly
without any right and seizing countries without any claims of inheritance,
and whatever else is a necessity of his aloof status, his pride and haughtiness without which a king is not deemed or called a king—should, from
the viewpoint of truth and the correct faith, be considered like the eating
of carrion in time of dire need. It is the duty of religious kings to fear and
regret the commission of such actions as a danger to religion, to ask for
divine forgiveness during the night with weeping and lamentations, to be
certain themselves that all the customs and traditions of kingship are opposed to the traditions of the Prophet and in that they and their followers
and their servants are involved.

Piety consists in following the practices of the Prophet. During the
period of his mission as Prophet, the Prophet never ate meat by cutting
it with a knife. The Companions asked: "O Prophet of God, is it forbidden to cut meat with a knife and to eat it?" "It is not forbidden," he replied, "but it is one of the practices of the sultans of 'Ajam and I who

[1] 'Ajam, lit. "dumb," refers to the non-Arabs, especially to the inhabitants of Persia.

have been sent to overthrow their customs and practices completely, and forbid them absolutely in my faith, have not eaten in the way that they have eaten."

So, O sons of Mahmūd, know and know well that kingship is not feasible without adopting the customs and practices of kings of 'Ajam. It is known to all the ulamā that the customs and practices of the sultans of 'Ajam are opposed to the Sunna of the Prophet and to his way of life and livelihood. [folios 87b–89b, 99b–100a]

. . . .

It has been said that in former times in 'Ajam, Rūm,[2] Yaman, India, Syria, and Egypt kingship was confined to the royal dynasty of every country and the desire of usurpation did not enter the hearts of the members of any other class of people. Thus, if in 'Ajam the ruler did not belong to the dynasty of the Khusraus, the people did not obey him. Similarly, in Rūm, if the ruler did not belong to the family of the Qaisars, the Romans did not bow their heads to him. Whenever such a principle had become customary among the people for generations and ages, usurpation was not tried. . . . Further, among the ancients, kingship was hereditary, and if a king died, one of his sons, in accordance with his nomination, ascended the throne. He kept the old officers at their posts and did not injure any leader, tribal chief, or noble family. This way and custom was very admirable.

After the rule of these monarchs in whose dynasties kingship had been enduring came to an end, kingship was established in many countries by usurpation and force and no attention was paid to the origin and descent of kings. Anyone who could obtain power, prestige, and a following by any means whatsoever, established himself over a territory, overthrew its previous ruler, took possession of the royal authority and caused himself to be called "king." . . .

Among the Muslims this untoward event came about through the Umayyad sultans who have been called Yazīdīs and Marwānids. During the generation of the Companions of the Prophet the government of the Muslim countries belonged by right to the Rightly-Guided Caliphs through the consensus of the community and appointment by their predecessors. The caliphate passed down to the Commander of the Faithful,

[2] The Eastern Roman or Byzantine Empire.

Hasan, son of 'Alī, both of whom were of the Hāshim clan. Not until Mu'āwiya, Yazīd, and the Marwānids had overthrown the Hāshim clan, their helpers, supporters, friends, and well-wishers, and blackened their own faces in this world and the next, was their eighty years of rule possible. Not until Abū Muslim Marūzī had sought vengeance for the family of the Prophet from the Umayyad sultans and disinterred Mu'āwiya, Yazīd, and the Marwānids from their graves and burnt them and extirpated their helpers, supporters, sympathizers, and sincere friends, did the caliphate of the 'Abbāsids in Baghdad become possible. . . .

Now reflect with a clear mind on how this bad practice and wicked custom has become habitual among the kings of Islam. First, without any rightful claim, external or domestic, they seize a territory; then out of religious or worldly expediency they obtain permission from the caliph of Baghdad for their usurpation. In addition to this, for the preservation of their own lives, which are certainly worthy of ultimate destruction and death, they overthrow and reduce to poverty and distress, by every means that comes to hands, many tribes, families, and illustrious families of the preceding regime. Some they spare, others they kill; some they imprison, others they exile; and some they deprive of their properties. Owing to the weakness of their faith, they do not care for Islam or the rights of Muslims, and they never consider the answer they will have to give on the Day of Judgment. To this sort of "overthrowing" they give the name of "political expediency." [folios 224a–224b *passim*]

[From Shaikh Hamadānī, *Zakhīrat ul-Mulūk*, folios 76a–b]
There were two offices united in Adam's illustrious person—the office of prophet and the office of sultan and ruler. In the office of prophet there is no place for the domination of lust and self-will. Undoubtedly the reality of this office was never manifested except in the pure bodies and open vessels of the prophets (may God bless them all and give them peace). But the conduct of the office of sultan and ruler are as if susceptible to the assaults of passionate and lustful behavior. There is a great measure of the two reprehensible qualities of lust and self-will attaching to the dangerous office of sultan. For that reason, in most ages and seasons it appears as an offensive manifestation and as a vessel of contamination, with its holders drawn from among tyrants, felons, oppressors, and the rich. From the time of Adam there has only been a limited number of

people among the great Prophets—Joseph, Moses, David, Solomon, and Muhammad (Peace be upon him)—and after the prophets, the Rightly-Guided Caliphs—Abū Bakr, 'Umar, 'Uthmān, and 'Alī (may God be satisfied with all of them)—in whose noble persons the good qualities of rulership have been manifested. They attended to the performance of the duties of their office in the way they should and made their own good qualities an argument against the oppressor and the unjust, the unheeding and the contumacious.

A few stories from the annals of the sultanate and governorship of prophets, a few traditions of the government and caliphate of the God-fearing and Rightly-Guided Caliphs have been set down for remembrance in this chapter for the admonition of those evil tyrants and wicked oppressors who have made the office of sultan and ruler over the people of Islam a source of pride and arrogance, and authority and governorship over the Muslim community a base thing of lust and self-will, and who consider wickedness and injustice the normal practice of kingship and corrupt and filthy behavior the normal practice of the great.

The War Between Good and Evil

The world has been created a battlefield between good and evil in which evil cannot be annihilated but only temporarily kept in check. The integral relation between "political theory" and theology should be noted.

[From Barnī, Fatāwa-yi-Jahāndārī, folios 117b–118a]

The meaning of "truth being established at the center" is not that falsehood totally vanishes while truth alone remains in this world. For Almighty God has said: "We have created two spirits"—that is, God has created things in pairs and has brought into existence one thing in opposition to another. Opposite to truth he has created falsehood, for example. Opposite to moral soundness he has created corruption. In the disorder of good, he created evil. Opposite obedience to God there is rebellion against him and opposed to obedience there is disobedience. Similarly, day and night, light and darkness, sky and earth, belief and unbelief, the unity of God and polytheism have been created in pairs and as contraries of each other.

The object of the above preamble is this. "Truth being established at the center" does not mean that falsehood is totally overthrown. For if all the prophets and kings of Islam gather together and try to remove and eliminate falsehood (which includes infidelity, sin, disobedience, and wickedness) from this world so that only truth (which includes Islam, moral soundness, obedience, and virtue) may prevail, they most certainly will not be able to succeed. It is not within the realm of possibility that there should be only goodness on this earth and no evil, only morality and no corruption, only Islam and theism and no infidelity and polytheism. For truth becomes luminous through the existence of falsehood, good through the existence of evil, Islam through the existence of infidelity, and theism through the existence of polytheism. In this way it becomes clear that this is truth and this is falsehood, that this is good and this is evil, that this is Islam and this is polytheism. . . .

Man's Opposing Qualities and Their "Political" Implications

Men have been created with contrasting qualities of good and evil dispositions; so with rulers—only rulers must control and employ their different dispositions so as to ensure the superiority of true religion and the maintenance of peace and order.

[From Barnī, *Fatāwa-yi-Jahāndārī,* folios 193a–195a *passim*]

God Most High has formed man with contrasting qualities. In every creature whom He has created as a human being and taken out of the animal circle, the contradictory qualities of contraction of the heart [against the entry of divine revelation] and its expansion [to receive divine revelation], wrath and grace, generosity and meanness, humility and pride are to be observed. But he in whom contrasting qualities are to be seen to perfection yet whose human nature is very much present is one of the wonders of the world. . . .

All the subjects of the ruler at the time of having dealings with him, or of his exercising temporal authority over them, are dependent upon him, and he is lord and judge over all. Consequently, wrath and grace, power and compassion, severity and sympathy, pride and humility, harshness and softness, anger and forbearance, mercy and hardness of heart, which are opposing qualities, should adorn the king in the most perfect manner and should be employed at proper times and on appropriate occasions. With these perfect dispositions, a king can deal with thousands of men who are different in their qualities and dispositions, temperaments and natures. If all is wrathfulness in the ruler and no kindness, what will become of the submissive, the weak, and the yielding? How will they endure violent usage or conquest? And if there is mildness and no wrathfulness, how will the ruler restrain the rebellious, the contumacious, the refractory and the disobedient from rebellion, contumacy, and disobedience and make them instead obedient, submissive, resourceless, and impotent? The same underlying truth as holds good for the attributes of men and beasts holds good also for the contrasting attributes of the ruler.

It is one of the wonders of the world when the contrasting qualities of the king are perfect and when he shows them forth in all their splendor at the appropriate and fitting occasions, and when he does not show wrath at the time for mildness or mildness at the time for wrath. One so endowed is complete with a portion of Godlike attributes. A person whose contrasting qualities are innate and display themselves to perfection and which are employed on occasions of good and evil, probity and dishonesty, obedience and disobedience, is worthy of and has a claim to kingship—which is the deputyship and vice-regency of God. . . . Such are the kings who have the position of Axes of the World on earth and who find a place in the shadow of the Divine Throne. Recounting their praises and their great deeds becomes a means of salvation and not of perdition.

The Duties and Responsibilities of the True King

The extent to which Muslim thinkers in India transfer the obligations of the caliph to the sultan will be observed in these readings.

The first excerpt indicates the proper relationship between those learned in the Holy Law and political authority. Sultans should be police chiefs to enforce the Shari'a, not legislators.

[From Fakhr-i-Mudir, *Shajara,* pp. 9–14]
It is evident to mankind that after the prophets and the messengers (on whom be peace!) comes the rank and station of the true friends of God, the martyrs and the learned. The learned are also the true friends of God and enjoy superiority over the martyrs; as the Prophet says: "The learned are the heirs of the prophets." He also says: "When the Day of Judgment cometh, they will weigh the ink of the scholar and the blood of the martyr and the ink of the scholar will prevail over the blood of the martyr."

The world is maintained through legal opinions of the learned and by their piety; the world is kept prosperous through the blessings of their knowledge, their adherence to religion, and their fear of God. The mandates of the Sharī'a and the ordinances of divine worship are entrusted to their station. Prohibitions and sins are concealed and hidden through their superintendance and the commands to do what is right are known to them. The religion of God Most High is firm through their persons and the fixing of the limits of punishment and of royal justice is dependent upon their faith in God. The Prophet says: "One wise doctor of jurisprudence is more troublesome to the Devil than a thousand worshipers."

The Prophet also, in giving the reason for the standing and excellence of the learned says: "The best amīrs [rulers] and kings are those who visit men learned in the Sharī'a, and the worst learned men are those who wait on amīrs and kings." This tradition is recorded so that amīrs and kings may seek out learned men and hear wisdom from them, and so that they may take their advice and do what they say, leaving alone what they prohibit. Thus they may be the best of amīrs and kings. It is forbidden for learned men to wait on amīrs and sultans lest they become the worst of learned men. And this is a merciful prohibition against going to visit kings, although it may be necessary, lest someone should despise them and condemn them, for God Most High has made learned men dear to him [pp. 9–11]

. . . .

Some of the mandates of the Sharī'a are dependent upon the person and the orders of kings—as the Friday *Khutba* [sermon], and the two festivals of the breaking of the fast of Ramazān and of sacrifices at Mecca, the fixing of the limits of the land tax and alms, the making of war; the giving of judgment between litigants; the hearing of lawsuits; in addition, the protection of the country from foreign armies, the organization of armies, the provision of rations for the soldiery, the awarding of capital punishment in the interests of the subjects, the doing of justice among the people and the avenging of the oppressed. [pp. 13–14]

[From Barnī, *Fatāwa-yi-Jahāndārī*, folios 7a–9a]
The essence of protection and promotion of the Faith by the ruler is the enforcement in his kingdom of the commands to do what is lawful and the prohibition of what is unlawful, and the making current of the mandates of the Holy Law among the seventy-two creeds. [folio 8a]

. . . .

The greatness of a king who protects religion is beyond description, for it is through his protection and promotion of the faith that Muslims give themselves to obedience to God and the performance of their religious duties in peace of mind, that the mandates of the Holy Law of the Prophet may become operative over different realms, that the pure faith may predominate over others, and that the honor and lives of both Muslims and the protected people are protected and secured and the banners of Islam may reach unto the highest heavens. [folio 7a]

. . . .

The religious scholars of the past have written clearly and in detail concerning the tests of the firm and sincere faith of kings. One of these tests is that they appoint harsh-tempered censors of morals and honest judicial officers in their capitals, cities, and towns, and strengthen their authority in every way, so that these officers can make manifest the splendor of "ordering the good and prohibiting the evil" among the Muslims, and may embitter the lives of all open, persistent, and public sinners through their severe punishments. . . . By the purity of their surveillance of the above sinful acts, they may check wine-sellers, flute-players, and dice-players. If prohibitions, stern orders, and insults cannot restrain them, if in spite of their claim to be Muslims, they do not openly give up their shameless acts of disobedience, and if respect for the Faith and fear of the ruler's orders is unable to dissuade them, then the rich among them should be punished with deprivation of property and the poor with imprisonment and fines. Wine-sellers should be sent out of the towns to live in distant corners; if they happen to be Muslims, they should be treated heartlessly, and it should be so arranged that no Muslim acts as a wine-seller. All male prostitutes should be prevented with severe blows from adorning themselves like women, wailing like women, and indulging in their other sins; they should also be treated with harshness and severity so that they may leave the capital, go to the countryside, and obtain their livelihood there by agriculture and other lawful occupations. . . . These people who have made filthy sin and disobedience their profession, and whose open parade of their behavior in the capital of Islam brings disgrace on the banners of Islam, should be prohibited in all cities and be ordered to leave them and conceal themselves in hovels and out-of-the-way places in the countryside. The construction and public use of pleasure houses should not be permitted; if they have been constructed already, they should be pulled down, "brick by brick." In short, the public practice of anything prohibited by the Law should not be allowed. But if in secret and privately habitual sinners indulge in their practices, severe investigations about their activities should not usually be made. If anything prohibited by the Holy Law is seen by the censors of morals, judicial officers, and the general public, it should be totally suppressed. But what is secret and hidden should not be so revealed and published.

The innovations which are injurious to the traditions should be overthrown as far as possible; at no places where they are seen should innovations, under any pretext, be allowed to become established.

The Muslim should be insistently asked, city quarter by city quarter, street by street, and house by house, to observe the five basic Muslim duties, i.e., reciting the Muslim profession of faith, the five obligatory prayers, the giving of alms, fasting during the month of Ramazan, and the pilgrimage to Mecca. It should be the duty of the censors to warn people who are slack about their obligatory prayers by various means; people who ignore their prayers altogether should be compelled by severe measures to pray. The rich should be asked to give alms (*zakāt*) to the poor and no excuse from them should be heard. And as to those reckless people, who either eat openly or practice their disgusting acts of disobedience in public during the fasting month [Ramazān] regardless of the respect due to the Faith and with no fear of the king, they should be arrested and brought before the ruler, so that as a general warning he may in his discretion and with his firm judgment punish them with long imprisonment, exile to distant places, death, or the shedding of blood. [folios 8a–9a]

In the next reading Barnī is advocating what he suggests was the actual practice of Sultan Mahmūd of Ghaznīn as the ideal for succeeding rulers in the Islamic world—that is, the suppression of the *falāsīfa* (philosophers).

[From Barnī, *Fatāwa-yi-Jahāndārī,* folios 10b, 121a]
No other "sciences" were allowed to be publicly taught in the kingdom of Sultan Mahmūd except Qur'anic commentary, the traditions of the Prophet, and law divested of all false interpretation—in short, apart from the "sciences" which were based on the affirmation, "God has said," and "The Prophet has said," all other "sciences" were banned.

When Sultan Maḥmūd conquered Khwārazm, he heard that Muʻtazilite doctrines were current there and that many men of learning were Muʻtazilites. He ordered these Muʻtazilite scholars to be exiled from Khwārazm; if anyone after the promulgation of this order followed the Muʻtazilite creed or even took its name, he was to be sent bound to Ghaznin. By the God who has succored Sultan Maḥmūd in every difficulty, if Ibn Sīnā, who is the reviver of the philosophy of Greece and the leader of philosophers in Muslim countries, had fallen into the hands of Sultan Maḥmūd, he would have ordered Ibn Sīnā to be cut to pieces and his flesh given to kites. [folio 10b]

Further, if kings like and approve that philosophers and all other people of false doctrine who are opponents of the true religion and enemies of the Prophet should teach their books openly; that these people should give to the sciences of the Greeks, which are the enemies of the traditional commands of the early and later prophets, the name of rational knowledge and to the sciences of the Sharīʻa they give the name of traditional knowledge; that they should proclaim the world to be eternal and consider God not to have a cognition of details; that they should be disbelievers in the Day of Judgment, in the rising up of men from their graves, in the account-taking [on Judgment Day], and in Heaven and Hell (though belief in these things is the basis of the Faith and has been asserted in three hundred and sixty revealed books of the prophets); that they should both speak and write their rationalistic books in denial of these things—now if such people are allowed to live with honor and dignity in the capital of the king, to propagate their doctrines and to affirm their preference for the rationalistic over the traditional—how is the true Faith to prevail over the false creeds, or the banners of Islam raised, or "Truth established at the Center," or the honor of "ordering the good or prohibiting the unlawful," appear? [folio 121a]

[From Abū Ṭālib Husainī, *Tūzuk-i-Tīmūrī*, pp. 338, 340, 342]
It is your duty to act in obedience to the commands of God and of the Prophet of God and to give help to his posterity. Those rulers who feed on the bounty of God, and yet rebel against Him and against His Prophet, you must expel from God's kingdom. Act with justice in the land of your Creator; for it is said that the kingdom of the unbelievers may remain, but that of the unjust, never.

You must root out from God's kingdom all pollution and abomination; for evil practices have that effect on the world which bad food has upon the body.

Do not ascribe the continuance of the tyrant in the world to his own merits; the cause of the long duration of the oppressive and the wicked is this, that they may realize their power for evil in action and then be overtaken by the wrath and fury of Almighty God.

It shall happen that the omnipotence of the Creator shall chastise the cruel, the wicked, and the impious, by chains and imprisonment, by famine and hunger and plague, and by sudden death, all at one time.

And it shall sometimes happen that the just, the devout and the virtuous, and the innocent shall be overtaken and be caught in the disasters which afflict the evil-doers. For the fire which occurs in the reed bed burns both the moist green reeds and the dry reeds.

The general attitude of benevolence toward his Muslim subjects which was expected of the godly Muslim ruler is expressed in the following reading from Shaikh Hamadānī's *Treasuries of Kings*.

[From Shaikh Hamadānī *Zakhīrat ul-Mulūk*, folios 88a–93b]
Subjects are of two kinds, believers and unbelievers, and the mandates for and duties toward them are different according to whether they are believers or unbelievers.

There are twenty duties toward their Muslim subjects which are laid upon governors and kings and which they are obliged to perform.

The first is to show respect toward all Muslims; not to behave haughtily toward any Muslim, in full realization that God considers any haughty tyrant his enemy. . . . Second, not to listen to vulgar tittle-tattle one about another for that only leads in the end to strife and regret; in particular to consider vicious the words of scoundrels, intriguers, the jealous and the greedy, because covetousness will cause harm to a people through greed for a morsel, and envy will destroy all talents. . . . The third duty is that when a ruler becomes angry with a Muslim for some fault or weakness, he should as far as possible not delay forgiveness beyond three days, unless his anger has been caused by some action harmful to religion, wherefore it is permissible for him to shun him for the rest of his life. However, in a worldly matter forgiveness is more fitting. The Prophet [on whom be peace] has said: "Whoever forgives the sin of a brother

ISLAM IN MEDIEVAL INDIA

Muslim will have his sins forgiven by God on the Day of Judgment." . . .

The fourth duty upon rulers is to make the bounty of justice and righteousness general over all the people and in spreading the fruits of benevolence not to discriminate between the worthy and the unworthy; for the king is the shadow of God's justice and as the mercy of God embraces both infidel and believer alike, so the justice of the ruler should embrace both the good and the wicked. . . .

The fifth duty is not, in the arrogance of power, to pry into the private households of Muslims and not to enter the houses and storehouses of subjects without permission, because when the Prophet, in all his glory as a ruler and prophet, approached the door of a Muslim's house, he asked three times for permission to enter; if permission was not given, he went away and was not vexed. . . .

The sixth duty is, in speaking and dealing with all kinds of people, to treat each man according to his own proper rank and degree, neither looking for gentle speech from the mean and the ruffianly, nor elegance from the ignorant, and not demanding the manners of polite society from mountain and desert folk. Show courtesy to each according to his station and excuse every man according to his rank and do not disdain to meet anyone face to face. . . . The seventh duty upon rulers is to hold old men in great respect at meetings and discussion and especially to look upon the godly and the young with a kindly eye. As the Prophet said: "He who does not treat the old men of my people with respect and who is not merciful toward the young of the Muslim community is not one of us." . . .

The eighth obligation upon a ruler is that when he makes a promise in conversation with any Muslim, he keep it and allow nothing contrary to it. As the Prophet said: "Religion is the making of a promise [by the believer]." The Prophet said: "There are three indications of a hypocrite— when he speaks he lies, when he makes a promise he does precisely the opposite, and when he is trusted he acts treacherously." . . .

The ninth duty is not to speak severely when giving judgment and to show an open face to men of all classes and to show benevolence to those in distress. As the Prophet said: "In Paradise there are mansions whose interiors appear from outside to be of wondrous precious stones." They asked: "O Prophet of God, and whose are these mansions?" and he said: "They belong to those who speak pleasantly to the servants of God, to those who feed the hungry, and to those who say their prayers at night when the rest of mankind are asleep."

The tenth duty is to show fairness in the exercise of the royal office and jurisdiction. As the ruler asks fair dealing from his people, so they ask fair dealing from him. Moreover, he should deal with the affairs of Muslims in the same way that he would conclude the bargain with them if they were dealing with him. The Prophet said: "He who wishes to escape hell-fire and enter into the blessings of Paradise should do toward men as he would have them do toward him."

The eleventh duty is to consider the establishment of peace and concord a first duty, so that no delay is permitted in deciding an issue between Muslims and there is no delay in the decision between two opposing sides which might end in the matter becoming a cause of hatred, enmity, and eventual violence. The Prophet said: "I will inform you of a deed better than fasting, almsgiving, and prayer." They said: "Yes, yes, O Prophet of God?" He said: "It is peacemaking between Muslims."

The twelfth duty is not to attempt to investigate Muslims' sins and not to distress unfortunate subjects for their errors; the ruler should wink at his people's faults as far as possible and keep their mistakes hidden. The Prophet said: "Whoever conceals the sins and faults of Muslims will have his sins concealed by God on earth and on the Day of Judgment."

The thirteenth duty is not to arraign the people for acts of disobedience when they follow their own desires; to prevent suspicion and avoid arousing suspicion; if from time to time the ruler succumbs to sin, he should keep the fact concealed because the generality follow their ruler and judge in virtue and in vice, and if they see their ruler on the high road of virtue, they will follow the same path and the reward for that will be credited to his account. If the subjects observe corruption in their ruler they will also stray into iniquity, debauchery, and vice, and the sin of that will be debited to his account. The Prophet said: "Whoever follows good practices will reap the reward for that, and the reward of whoever follows him in those good practices will also be put to his account; whoever follows evil practices will receive the punishment for that, and the punishment of him who acts wickedly as a consequence will also be put down to him who was responsible originally for those evil practices."

The fourteenth duty upon the ruler is, that when a decision on the requirements of a Muslim is held up for words of intercession, to see that he puts in the requisite word of intercession and allows no negligence in carrying the decision out. One of the special features of the work of a judge is that many important matters may be brought to a successful conclusion by one word from him. The ruler should seize the opportunity to obtain the blessings of this reward. The Prophet said: "There is no more excellent act of almsgiving than speech." They asked him: "How so?" He replied: "It is intercession which preserves lives, brings benefit to another, and prevents harm to another."

The fifteenth duty is to keep the position of those who are poor and weak preponderant over that of those who are rich and powerful. Most of the time the ruler should sit with the poor and the people of God and once a day he should brighten the mirror of his heart with the advice and counsel of the pious because the personal superintendence of the business of government and the mixing with all and sundry darkens the heart, as does also association with the worldly and the rich. When these two darknesses embitter the heart, one must fear danger to religion; this is a cause for eternal bondage and everlasting mortification. . . . The Prophet said: "You are sitting with the dead." "O Prophet of God, who are the dead?" "The rich," he replied. . . .

The sixteenth duty is not to neglect the position of the poor and humble and not to allow any omission of almsgiving to the weak and those in distress. The ruler should consider diligent inquiry into the position of orphans an obligation upon himself and should consider the account to be rendered on the Day of Judgment; on that day possessions and a kingdom are no help and all the rightful claimants will demand their dues from the ruler. Today, when he is able, he should strive to redeem his time. Abū Harīra said that the Prophet said: "On the Day of Judgment God will summon his servant. God the Avenger will address him by name. 'O servant of Mine, on earth I asked you for bread and apparel and you did not give me any.' His servant will ask: 'O God, how is that?' and God will say: 'So-and-so was hungry in your company and so and so was naked and you did not look after them and treat them kindly. As you deprived them by your power and might of the means of subsistence so we now deprive you.' "

The seventeenth obligation on rulers is to keep, by punishment, the highways used by Muslims free from the fear of highwaymen and thieves, by exemplary and public punishment to make an example, as a warning to others, of him who causes injury to Muslims on the highroads by molestation and extortion. At every place in the country where there is a dangerous spot infested by robbers, erect buildings there if it is at all possible and, if not, station watchmen there. . . .

The eighteenth duty upon the ruler is, as far as possible, and where there is need, to exert himself in the good work of building bridges and resting places for travelers; not to permit any negligence in this respect. . . . The nineteenth duty is to build a mosque in any place where Muslims congregate and to appoint an Imām and a muezzin and to furnish the means of livelihood for them, so that, in freedom from anxiety they can perform prayer assiduously at the proper times without offering the excuse that seeking the means of carrying out that commandment prevents them in fact from doing so. . . .

The twentieth duty is not to abandon the command of God to do what is lawful and His injunction against doing what is unlawful, and not to deny people of all classes religious exhortation. Also, to command the subjects to perform their religious duties, to prevent them from disobedience to God and by means of punishment restrain them from sin.

One of the most important duties imposed by Muslim writers on the sultanate was the subjection of unbelievers. This was a duty of peculiar importance in India with its large Hindu population.

In practice both the sultans of Delhi and the Mughal emperors extended toleration to their Hindu subjects. It is doubtful whether they levied *jizya* or a poll tax as such upon non-Muslims. There is no evidence that a separate branch of the revenue department existed for this purpose, and those historians who allege that some sultans did levy *jizya* can be shown to be extolling a sultan in stock Islamic idiom. There is no doubt that for orthodox writers, it was a merit to abase the infidel and levy *jizya*. The view of the Muslim legists of the Hanafī school was that payment of *jizya* implying political submission entitled a non-Muslim to toleration, subject to certain discriminations—detailed in the reading later from Shaikh Hamadānī's *Treasuries of Kings*. Strictly, only a "people of a [revealed] book," i.e., Jews, Christians, and Sabaeans (which has been interpreted to cover Zoroastrians), may be accepted as *zimmīs* or "people of the covenant or obligation." Thus, Hindus should be excluded from toleration. Ziā ud-dīn Barnī was dismayed that the sultan of Delhi did tolerate them, as he implies in the first passage below. Barnī's ideals are expressed in the second and third readings. To support his contention he quotes an (uncanonical?) tradition to the effect that unbelievers have only the choice of Islam or the sword.

[From Barnī, *Fatāwa-yi-Jahāndārī*, folios 12a, 119a–20b]

If the desire for the overthrow of infidels and the abasing of idolators and polytheists does not fill the hearts of the Muslim kings; if, on the other hand, out of the thought that infidels and polytheists are payers of tribute and protected persons, they make the infidels eminent, distinguished, honored, and favored; if they bestow drums, banners, ornaments, cloaks of brocade, and caparisoned horses upon them; if they appoint them to governorships, high posts, and offices; and if in their capital [Delhi?] where the raising of the banners of Islam raises those banners in all Muslim cities, they allow idol-worshipers to build houses like palaces, to wear clothes of brocade, and to ride Arab horses caparisoned with gold and silver ornaments, to be equipped with a hundred thousand sources of strength, to live amid delights and comforts, to take Muslims into their service and to make them run before their horses, with poor Muslims begging of them and at their doors in the capital of Islam, through which the palace of Islam raises itself, so that Muslims call them kings, princes, warriors, bankers, clerks, and pandits [Brahman scholars]—how then may the banners of Islam be raised? [folios 120–120b]

· · · ·

If the kings of Islam, with all their majesty and power, take for granted infidelity and infidels, polytheism and polytheists throughout their dominions in return for the land revenue (*kharāj*) and *jizya,* how will the tradition, "If I fight people until they say, 'There is no god but God,' and if they say, 'There is no god but God,' they are immune from me and their persons and property exist only by virtue of Islam," be observed? And how will infidelity and infidels, polytheism and polytheists be overthrown—the purpose of the mission of 124,000 prophets and the domination of sultans of Islam since Islam appeared? If the kings of Islam do not strive with all their might for this overthrow, if they do not devote all their courage and energies to this end for the satisfaction of God and of the prophet, for the assistance of the Faith and the exalting of the True Word; if they become content with extracting the *jizya* and the land tax from the Hindus who worship idols and cow-dung, taking for granted the Hindu way of life with all its stipulations of infidelity, how shall infidelity be brought to an end, now that Muhammad's Prophethood has come to an end—and it was by the prayers of the prophets that infidelity was being ended? How will "Truth be established at the Center" and how will the

Word of God obtain the opportunity for supremacy? How will the True Faith prevail over other religions, if the kings of Islam, with the power and prestige of Islam which has appeared in the world, with three hundred years of hereditary faith in Islam, permit the banners of infidelity to be openly displayed in their capital and in the cities of the Muslims, idols to be openly worshiped and the conditions of infidelity to be observed as far as possible, the mandates of their false creed to operate without fear? How will the True Faith prevail if rulers allow the infidels to keep their temples, adorn their idols, and to make merry during their festivals with beating of drums and *dhols* [a kind of drum], singing and dancing? [folios 119a–b]

. . . .

If Mahmūd . . . had gone to India once more, he would have brought under his sword all the Brahmans of Hind who, in that vast land, are the cause of the continuance of the laws of infidelity and of the strength of idolators, he would have cut off the heads of two hundred or three hundred thousand Hindu chiefs. He would not have returned his "Hindu-slaughtering" sword to its scabbard until the whole of Hind had accepted Islam. For Mahmūd was a Shāfi'ite, and according to Imām Shāfi'i the decree for Hindus is "either death or Islam"—that is to say, they should either be put to death or embrace Islam. It is not lawful to accept *jizya* from Hindus as they have neither a prophet nor a revealed book. [folio 12a]

Shaikh Hamadānī was, however, prepared to admit idol worshipers to the status of *zimmīs,* as the first of his conditions below implies.

[From Shaikh Hamadānī, *Zakhirat ul-Mulūk,* folios 94a–95a]
There is another mandate relating to those subjects who are unbelievers and protected people (*zimmīs*). For their governance, the observance of those conditions which the Caliph 'Umar laid down in his agreement for establishing the status of the fire worshipers and the People of the Book [Jews and Christians] and which gave them safety is obligatory on rulers and governors. Rulers should impose these conditions on the *zimmīs* of their dominions and make their lives and their property dependent on their fulfillment. The twenty conditions are as follows:

1. In a country under the authority of a Muslim ruler, they are to build no new homes for images or idol temples.
2. They are not to rebuild any old buildings which have been destroyed.
3. Muslim travelers are not to be prevented from staying in idol temples.
4. No Muslim who stays in their houses will commit a sin if he is a guest for three days, if he should have occasion for the delay.
5. Infidels may not act as spies or give aid and comfort to them.
6. If any of their people show any inclinations toward Islam, they are not to be prevented from doing so.
7. Muslims are to be respected.
8. If zimmīs are gathered together in a meeting and Muslims appear, they are to be allowed at the meeting.
9. They are not to dress like Muslims.
10. They are not to give each other Muslim names.
11. They are not to ride on horses with saddle and bridle.
12. They are not to possess swords and arrows.
13. They are not to wear signet rings and seals on their fingers.
14. They are not to sell and drink intoxicating liquor openly.
15. They must not abandon the clothing which they have had as a sign of their state of ignorance so that they may be distinguished from Muslims.
16. They are not to propagate the customs and usages of polytheists among Muslims.
17. They are not to build their homes in the neighborhood of those of Muslims.
18. They are not to bring their dead near the graveyards of Muslims.
19. They are not to mourn their dead with loud voices.
20. They are not to buy Muslim slaves.

At the end of the treaty it is written that if zimmīs infringe any of these conditions, they shall not enjoy security and it shall be lawful for Muslims to take their lives and possessions as though they were the lives and possessions of unbelievers in a state of war with the faithful.

A passage from a Mughal writer on the same theme.

[From Abū Tālib Husainī, Tūzuk-i-Tīmūrī, p. 330]
If tyranny and oppression and iniquity exists in any kingdom, it is the duty of sultans, out of a regard for justice, to resolve on the removal and

extirpation of the tyranny and oppression and to conduct a rapid excursion against it. For God Most High will take that kingdom from the oppressor and entrust it to the just ruler. . . . And in every country where the Sharī'a is feeble, where they do not respect those whom God Most High has made great and distress His chosen servants, it is the duty of a conquering sultan, who intends to make current the religion and the law of Muhammad, to invade that country, for the Prophet will strengthen him in that undertaking. Thus I seized the capital of Hindustan from Sultan Mahmūd, the grandson of Fīrūz Shāh, from Mallū Khān, and from Sarang, reestablishing the True Faith and the Sharī'a and destroying the idol temples of that country.

Justice Is Indispensable to Temporal Rulership

Muslim writers in Persia who, after the practical breakdown of the Sunni jurists' theory of the caliphate, discussed the duties of the sultanate (e.g. Nizām ul-Mulk, author of the *Siyāsat-Nāma,* al-Ghazālī in his *Nasīhat ul-Mulūk* and Wassāf in his *Akhlāq us-Sultānat*) were prepared to choose justice in preference to legality, if they could not have both. Although a sultan was often obliged, out of political expediency, to contravene, or to go beyond the ideal prescriptions of the Sharī'a, they argued that he could still serve God if he dispensed justice and equity, thus preventing social disorder provoked by oppression. Indo-Muslim thought was (as usual) very similar.

[From Fakhr-i-Mudir, *Shajara,* p. 13]
And the Prophet also says, "The sultan is the shadow of God. The shadow consists of care and tranquillity because justice and security are found there, and in the shelter and protection of kings there is a resting place for the oppressed and a refuge from the oppressors."

[From Barnī *Fatāwa-yi-Jahāndārī,* folios 43b–44b]
From the time of Adam to our own days the people of all communities throughout history are united in the opinion that justice is a requisite of religion and that religion is a requisite of justice. For it is not possible for men to live without having dealings with each other; and in these mutual dealings a man may be strong or weak, good or bad, Muslim or non-Muslim, wise or foolish, learned or ignorant, townsman or villager, resident or traveler, deceptive or straightforward, ruler or subject, an adult or a minor. Now justice is the balance in which the actions of people, right or wrong, are weighed. The distinction between one's des-

serts and the opposite is clarified by justice. Justice exposes cruelty, oppression, usurpation, and plunder. Consequently, there can be no stability in the affairs of men without justice. No religion which is founded on divine commandments can do without justice. Both ancient and succeeding authorities have said: "Religion and justice are twins." For justice breaks the strong arm of the tyrannical, the oppressive, and the mighty—of misappropriators, plunderers, rebels, the froward, the "people of license," and disbelievers in the Day of Judgment and accounts—to protect the money, property, women, and children of the weak, the obedient, the helpless, the orphans, the submissive, and the friendless. Justice prevents tyranny and oppression through the mandates of religion. If there is no justice or equity on the earth, there will be complete community of women and property; the distinction between one man's property and another's will vanish; no time or place will be free from disorder, and no man will be able to drink his cup of water in his corner in peace or to stretch his legs and sleep on his bed in security for a single night; and, finally, the world will cease to be prosperous owing to immense tumults and disorders. Nevertheless if all the wise men of the earth tried to govern a village, or even a household, through mere policy or precepts of wisdom without judges endowed with power, they would not succeed. The origin of peace and stability is justice and equity which prevails among the people [only] through strong command.

The real justification for the authority of kings and of their power and dignity is the manifestation of justice, so that through their royal power and dignity they may remove all recourse to oppression and cruelty in the dealings of the servants of God, the seventy-two creeds may attain to contentment of heart, and everyone may devote himself to his craft, profession, trade and work, and the world may become populous and prosperous. If there is no justice, there will be no trade and no one will be able to obtain any fruit from his work. Finally, if the affairs of men are not "organized at the center," there will be no permanency in the works of Muslim faith or the commandments, and recompense and punishment will not bear their fruits.

[From Muhammad Bāqir Khān, *Mau'iza-yi-Jahāngīrī*, folios 10a–11a]
Kings must consider their sitting on a throne to be for the sake of dispensing justice and not for the sake of living a life of enjoyment, and

should consider justice and equity the cause of the continuance of their rule, of the persistence of their fame, and of obtaining reward in the next world. . . .

If there is no control by government and administration, great enterprises would not stay in [good] order and if there was no correction and punishment, man's affairs would be ruined. Administration is the ornament of the king and of the state, and it is expedient for both religion and government. Without the kings' rules of administration the mandates of the Shari'a would not be put into effect, nor would the foundations of the sultanate be firm. If the sword of administrative punishment is not drawn from the scabbard of retribution, the foundations of sedition and the basis of oppression will not be subverted and undermined. If the vile dross of injustice is not destroyed by the flame of royal power, the young plant of security will not be nurtured in the garden of hope. When the seditious see that the flame of such punishment is sharp, they will slink away. If they observe little to be alarmed at in the work of administration, there will be rebellion on every side and all kinds of disturbances will ensue.

Moreover, kings must show the mercy which God does toward the good and the peaceable and the wrath of God toward the wicked and the evildoers. They must tip the point of their authority with the honey of kindness and sweeten the bitterness of their harshness with the sugar of kindness. There must be a conjunction of justice and punishment, so that the meadow of the hopes of the good may be kept verdant by the moisture of kindness and the bases of the existence of the wicked may be uprooted by the gale of punishment.

Rulership Is a Sacred Trust

Indo-Muslim writers emphasize the responsibility of rulers before God for the welfare of His creatures. Power is a sacred trust, for which rulers will answer on the Day of Judgment.

[From Nūr ud-dīn Muhammad Khaqānī, *Akhlāq-i-Jahāngīrī*, folio 279b] It is said that when the father of 'Umar ibn 'Abd al-'Azīz lay dying, his son asked him when he would see him again. 'Abd al-'Azīz replied that it would be in the next world. His son said he hoped it would be sooner than that. 'Abd al-'Azīz then said: "You may see me in a dream during the first, second, or third nights [after my death]." Twelve years passed without his son seeing him in a dream. At last he did so. Replying to his son's question why he had not seen him as promised, 'Abd al-'Azīz said: "O son I have been very occupied; near Baghdad there was a broken bridge with no one appointed to keep it in repair. Once when a flock of sheep were passing over it, the forefeet of one of them went through a hole in the bridge. I have been answering [to God] for that until this very moment.

[From Shaikh Hamadānī, *Zakhīrat ul-Mulūk,* folios 72b–73a]
Sulaimān Fāris (may God be satisfied with him) reported that the Prophet of God (on whom be peace) said that every governor who has anything to do with the affairs of Muslims in the exercise of his authority will on the Day of Judgment be brought forward with both hands tied around his neck. Nobody and nothing will release his hands except justice. . . . If he has been a benefactor of mankind, his benevolence frees him; if he has been a wicked man, an oppressor, and a sinner and a rebel against God . . . he falls into the pit; it must be seventy years before he reaches the bottom of that pit.

[From Nūr ud-dīn Muhammad Khaqānī, *Akhlāq-i-Jahāngīrī,* folios 264a– 269]
It is reported from Abū Sa'īd that the Prophet said that every sultan and ruler who does not show compassion toward his subjects will be forbidden to enter Paradise and enjoy its delights. And 'Abdullāh 'Umar al-Khattāb reported that the Prophet said that God will, on the day of need, when the ruler is surrounded by enemies, close the door of His mercy in the face of that ruler who, placed in a position of authority over Muslims, shuts the door of his house against the weak and the needy. And Abū Mūsā Ash'arī said that the Prophet said that the basest fellow in creation is he who as a ruler puts himself in pledge for Muslims and does not discharge that pledge, while the most noble is he who dispenses justice and equity among Muslims. [folios 264a, b]

· · · ·

It is related that in the time of Sultan Abū Sayyid Khudābanda, his amīrs [nobles] were treating his subjects harshly and forcibly confiscating their goods. One day the sultan said to his amīrs: "Until now I have had regard for my subjects, but after today I shall cease doing so. If it is expedient, then we must plunder everybody and not allow them anything from our treasuries; but on the condition, furthermore, that you do not ask for any salary or stipend from me; if henceforth any one of you makes this sort of request to me, I shall punish him." The amīrs said: "How can we do without salaries or stipends, what kind of service can we then perform?" Abū Sayyid replied: "The successful conduct of all our affairs depends on the efforts made by the subjects in building, agriculture, in crafts, and in commerce. When we plunder them, from whom can we expect to receive anything? You should consider that if the mass of the people have their livestock and its products taken away, and their grain eaten, they must of necessity abandon cultivation and engage in it no more; thus there will be no revenue and what will you do?" When the amirs heard these words, they began to treat the people kindly. [folios 268b–269]

The Selection of Officials

If he is to escape divine punishment, the sultan must employ and consult god-fearing aides and officials of true Muslim belief and avoid employing low and impious persons. The aim of the royal officials, as of the sultan himself, must be the furtherance of true religion.

[From Barnī, *Fatāwa-yi-Jahāndārī*, folios 59a, b, 205b–10a]
How can the ruler . . . act according to the Sharī'a in his government without good helpers, praiseworthy supporters, pious friends, and trusty well-wishers who are adorned with lineage, descent, and praiseworthy morals? How can he discharge the duties of such a high and delicate office with the help of the worthless and the shameless, with the assistance and concurrence of the godless and the idle? [folio 205b]

. . . .

In the choice of helpers and companions, religious kings have laid down a few things as obligatory. First, the person selected should be one on whom the search for true religion predominates over the quest for worldly good, even though it be only by a needle's point, for if all his efforts are devoted to religion he will not become one of the helpers and companions of the king and will not dabble in the world's business. . . . From a man whose loyalty and well-wishing toward them springs out of love of the world and desire for place and who is a captive and slave of this world, no deed, which is in the ultimate praiseworthy and commendable, can be expected. . . . A man who is not fit to be trusted in affairs of religion, is not fit to be trusted in affairs of state. [folio 210a]

. . . .

My advice to you, my dear son, is do justice to the qualities of the people of God and make clear the balance and scales for measuring the virtue of the people. Create a rank for every excellence and accordingly confer honor, position, dignity, and grandeur upon every description of people. In the bestowal of robes and gifts, employment in office, the right of sitting and rising, of speaking and listening in your presence, deal with your servants in a manner in keeping with their capacity as wazirs, wise men, learned in the Holy Law, and ascetics. Do not blindly undertake with the servants of God some project affecting your kingdom in an incongruous way and do not start any project which the wise men of your kingdom will attribute to your lack of reason or to self-will. Let it be known to you, my son, that God has made the ruler greater than all human creation, and, with all that greatness, has entrusted the world to him. Thus it is necessary that the great should receive the gift of greatness from the ruler and that he be the cause of their position in the world and their dignity. He should be the means of the prestige which appears among men. Royal actions are indeed very important. The consequences of royal actions quickly appear among the people and remain a long time. It is a long time before a person honored by him becomes base, or a person made contemptible by him becomes excellent. But the honor in which those who forsake the world and retire to an ascetic way of life are held among the generality is due to their renunciation of the world (which is the beloved of mankind) and their withdrawal from human society. The king has no part in conferring this honor and has no hand in its attainment. Thus, my son, it is incumbent upon you not to lower the offices and dignities of your state by conferring them upon the foolish, the ignorant, the sinful, the low-born, and those in the grip of vice. The royal dynasty itself is disgraced and becomes infamous through baseness and infamy among the officers of state. [folios 59a–59b]

[From Muhammad Bāqir Khān, *Mauʿiza-yi-Jahāngīrī*, folios 27b–28b]
The ruler is he who, having nurtured those who are distinguished among their equals for the perfection of their sagacity, probity, ability, chastity,

sincerity, devotion to religion, piety, faithfulness, and loyalty, acquired prestige from the fact of each one being employed in the capacity for which he is fitted. He gives them appointments one by one as occasion arises in accordance with their judgment, courage, intelligence, and capacity. He does not give one person two employments lest an intended task is not completed; one person, one task; one task, one person. The ruler himself should look into the circumstances and the nature of the employments entrusted to his officers and trusted servants so that when they are performed he should know which among his agents cherish his subjects and are upright in religion, and which are treacherous and seditious knaves. So, he who ministers to the people's welfare and sincerely performs the duty assigned to him may be favored by the ruler and enjoy security in his office. He who does not sympathize with the subjects, who neglects the essentials of his duty, does not let slip an opportunity for treachery, and makes baseness his upper and his nether garments—his name is to be struck from the roll of office.

In the following reading, Barnī states that among usurpers are those who do not employ subordinates in those ranks for which God has fitted them; usurpers, thinking of the preservation of their own power and not of God's glory, employ those whom they believe meet for their own worldly purposes, irrespective of merit. The basis of Barnī's moral and religious distinctions, which should be mirrored in social distinctions, is more fully illustrated in the chapter on the Muslim social ideal.

[From Barnī, *Fatāwa-yi-Jahāndārī,* folios 56a, b]
But one who collects a large number of people on his side, caring for no dessert or merit in them except their loyalty to himself, he is to be called "conqueror" and not "king." He rules the country through the power of his followers; he strikes, takes, seizes, and bestows, and thus every day he is able to show more favors to his supporters. He increases their power and dignity, thinking that the permanence of his kingdom is due to them, and he strives for their prosperity without paying any regard to their defects and their merits. The eyes of such a man are turned away from God Almighty; he is all the time exclusively busy with his helpers and supporters till matters come to such a pass that he turns all low, mean, base, defective, and worthless men, who are of bad and low origin, into the pillars of his state, provided he sees in them great loyalty toward himself combined with substantial power and dignity. No doubt thousands

and thousands of such usurpers have risen on this earth from every stock that can be imagined; they have ruled for a while with the support of a body of partisans and have left the world having made themselves and their followers fit for Hell. Thus neither their names nor any traces of them have remained in the conversations or the hearts of the people. But all rulers, whose eyes have been wholly fixed on God Almighty, have made clear scales and measures of merit, real worth, piety, nobility, free-birth, wisdom, skill, and morality, who have discharged their obligations to every merit through the resources of their government and to the full extent of their power, and who in that discharge have looked at everyone with that one vision—their memory will remain till the Day of Judgment among the people of God and this fact will have been a sufficient proof of their salvation and of their status in the next world.

The Importance of Consultation
[From Barnī, *Fatāwa-yi-Jahāndārī*, folios 17a, 23a–24a]

You should know that the supreme object of that part of a man's soul which commands to evil, higher than which it is impossible to conceive, is self-will and self-indulgence. This is specially the case with kings, whose souls owing to their great power become equal in strength to a thousand elephants in heat. If the king subdues this power and madness of his soul, refrains from being self-willed, and decides the affairs of his kingdom in consultation with his counsellors, will not the kindness of God shine on his forehead and all his undertakings end in success and virtue? [folio 17a]

. . . .

Great kings have observed many conditions and have been very cautious in the matter of consultation; consequently, the opinion of their counsellors has seldom erred. The first condition of consultation is the frank expression of the opinion of the counsellors—that is, the very condition of holding a council is that all counsellors should be able to say whatever comes to their minds without fear, to give reasons and arguments for their opinions about the execution of state enterprises, and to consult frankly with each other. Ultimately, when all their minds are in agreement and no objection remains, they should apply themselves to the accomplishment of their purpose. This, in the terminology of consultation, is known as "agreement of opinion." If there is no unanimous agreement about the matter among the counsellors, no reliance can be placed upon any course of action. Secondly, the counsellors ought to be [properly] appointed; they should be nearly equal to each other in their experience, in their loyalty, and in their status before the king. If one counsellor is perfect in intelligence and the other defective, one high in status and the other "on the way down," there will be a danger of incongruity in the decision. Thirdly, all counsellors should be admitted to the secrets of the realm and none of them should be unworthy of being taken into confidence. If a counsellor is not cognizant of the secrets of the realm, he will not be able to arrive at a correct decision, just as a physician cannot prescribe effective remedies unless he knows the real symptoms and diseases of a patient. Fourthly, the counsellors, besides being chosen by the ruler and being near to him, ought to have perfect security of life and position so that they may not for any reason resort to flattery in the council chamber. They should be able to express their real opinion, with lips unsealed, and they should be convinced that this will lead to increased recognition of their loyalty. They should not be afraid of the ill-temper of the ruler, for so long as the fear of the king tortures their breasts, sincere advice will not come from their hearts to their tongues. Fifthly, the king should keep his opinions a secret from his counsellors. He should, first, acquaint himself with the opinion of his counsellors, hear the views they have to express and wait for the decision they arrive at. If the ruler expresses his opinion in the council at the very beginning, the counsellors will find it necessary, willingly or unwillingly, to praise his decision and to suppress their own views. No one will have the courage to oppose the decision of the king or to give reasons against it. This fact has been proved by experience. [folios 23a–24a]

Organizing the Government

Rulers must appoint pious, efficient, and trustworthy army commanders, wazirs or finance officers, judges, and intelligence officers. The task of the latter particularly is to report on the welfare of the people and to bring oppressive acts by officials to the ruler's notice.

[From Muhammad Bāqir Khān, *Mau'iza-yi-Jahāngīrī,* folios 26b–27b]
You should know that "pillars of the state," ministers, and other servants, are essential for sultans and kings. It is an unquestioned need of rulers

to have capable counsellors and trusty officers who have the privilege of intimacy with the king's secrets, and have ability and authority for important undertakings. It is said that a realm has four legs. If one is missing the foundations of important transactions will not be firm. The first leg of the kingdom is the existence of great amīrs, who are the people of the sword and guard the frontiers of the kingdom and prevent the wickedness of enemies from affecting the king and the people. They are the pillars of the dynasty and the foundation of the sultanate. Second are the capable finance officers and religious revenue officers who are the ornament of the kingdoms, the cause of the stable foundations of the sultanate, and the regulators of the affairs of the realm. The undertakings of the ruler of the kingdom do not reach a successful conclusion without the people of the pen, and indeed in some ways, the people of the pen aspire to superiority over the people of the sword, arguing first that the sword is only used for enemies and not for friends, whereas the pen is used both to benefit friends and to ward off enemies, something which the sword cannot do. The second argument is that the people of the sword in secret betray ambitions to be kings themselves. This is something which never happens with the people of the pen. Thirdly, the people of the sword empty the treasury, and the people of the pen fill it, and occasions of income are better than occasions of expenditure. In any event, failure will never overtake nor calamity stalk the kingdom of him who places in charge of his affairs a wise, sensible wazir, with excellent moral qualities, without greed and with high aspirations. For, if the opposite occurs and an unholy wazir with a lewd nature meddles with the business of the realm, however much the ruler may be humane and beneficient himself, the benefits of his own justice and compassion will be prevented from reaching his subjects and fear of him will not cause reports of oppressors to be made to him—just as it is impossible for a thirsty man to touch the pure sweet water which is to be seen on the skin of a crocodile, however thirsty he may be. The third leg of the realm is the judge who, on behalf of the sultan, inquires into the state of the people, obtains justice for the weak from the strong, and abases and subdues the seditious and the forward. The fourth leg is the trusty intelligence officers who report continually the actions of the royal officials and the condition of the subjects. They bring to the royal notice any signs of harshness and negligence. For when information about the country and realm is hidden from the ruler, he is careless of friend or foe, good or evil, and everyone does as he likes. When the ruler is without information, the foundations of his sultanate become shaky from all the rebellions which spring up in all parts of the country.

[From Barnī, *Fatāwa-yi-Jahāndārī,* folios 82a–84a *passim*]

In the appointment of intelligence officers, auditors, and spies, religious rulers have had good intentions and objects. First, when it becomes clear to the officers, judges, governors, and revenue collectors both far and near, that their good and bad actions will be brought to light, they do not demand bribes or accept presents or show favor or partiality. They do not depart from the path of righteousness or take to sinfulness and wrong-doing, and they are always fearful and trembling concerning their own private affairs. Owing to this caution on their part they may be safe from their real superior [God] and from their figurative superior [the sultan].

Secondly, when the people are convinced that the good and bad deeds of all classes are being reported to the king and that officeholders have been appointed for this particular purpose, they will behave like good subjects; they will neither conspire nor rebel nor attempt to overpower each other nor oppress the weak. Thirdly, if revenue collectors and accountants know that their actions will be brought to the notice of the king, they will refrain from stealing and misappropriating and thus remain secure from the ruler and escape dishonor and disgrace. Lastly, it will be an advantage even to the king's sons, brothers, and high officers if they are aware that the king will be informed of all their actions, for they will not then, presuming on their close relationship with the king, step beyond the bounds of justice in their dealings with their own people and strangers, or their slaves and servants. . . .

The intelligence officer should be truthful in speech, truthful in writing, reliable, well-born, worthy of confidence, sober and careful where he lives, and not much given to social and convivial intercourse so that his object, which is obtaining correct information for the king's business, may be attained. But if the intelligence officer is a thief, a man without rectitude, low-born, mean, a frequenter of every place and a caller at every door, corrupt, greedy, covetous, and reckless, then what should be the predicate of the ruler's intentions, his designs and his search for the welfare of his subjects, will become the opposite. For the dishonest and low-born intelligence officer, who is a master of intrigue and "wire-pulling," spins many lies that look like truth, and through his testifying to false information, affairs are thrown into disorder. Where benefits should be rendered, injuries are inflicted; men worthy of punishment are favored while men deserving of favor are punished.

The Army

Following the Persian pre-and post-Muslim tradition Muslim writers on government in India always stress the importance of the maintenance of a large and efficient army. It is doubtful whether this stress is specifically related to the military problems facing the Muslim rulers in India.

[From Barnī, *Fatāwa-yi-Jahāndārī*, folios 64a–b]
O sons of Mahmūd, you and every one whom God raises to be a ruler and a refuge of religion, ought to know that without a large, powerful, and magnificent army, maintained in good order, it has not been possible to exercise government and maintain rule, or plan conquest, to direct administration, to awe the hearts of the people by conquests, to bring the world under rule and government, to overcome the rebellious and the refractory, to bring the stubborn and the disobedient under control, to suppress the contentions of rivals and the opposition of equals and the enmity of the powerful, to overthrow those who injure the religion and realm of Muhammad, to extirpate those who molest the Sharī'a of Muhammad and to make manifest the glory of the true faith over false doctrines and to enforce the mandates of the Sharī'a over the seventy-two creeds, to seize by force countries, regions, provinces, and territories from the irreligious, to obtain booty for the warriors of the faith and those entitled to it among the Muslims, to close all breaches open to the enemies of the kingdom and those troublesome to the dynasty and, in short, to seek relief from the heavy responsibility of rulership.

[From Muhammad Bāqir Khān, *Mau'iza-yi-Jahāngīrī*, folios 35a–b]
Similarly since the world is a place of unforeseen vicissitudes and no one knows what time will have in store, or from what direction rebellion will appear, rulers must consider the raising of a large army their principal concern and must always keep it equipped and ready for war and, having appointed and confirmed amīrs, aides, and pillars of the kingdom, confer

upon each, according to merit, his command (*mansab*) and a *jāgīr*,[1] so that he may maintain his appropriate contingent. From year to year rulers should take care that their armies and amīrs are ready for muster, that all their weapons, equipment, and warlike apparatus is ready and prepared; if sultans and amīrs become so engrossed in collecting money that they do not recruit an army, in an emergency they will be at a loss; there will be no benefit to be derived from their chests of gold and however much "they may bite the finger of regret with the teeth of blame," it will not profit them.

The Perfect Rule

The religious consequences which Muslim writers hoped and believed would flow from sultans taking upon themselves the responsibilities and duties previously borne by the caliphs are perhaps best expressed in the reading below from Barnī's *Rulings on Temporal Government*.

[From Barnī, *Fatāwa-yi-Jahāndārī*, folios 122a–122b; 231b–232a]

Whenever the ruler, with truly pious intent, high aspirations, and all solicitude, strives with the help of his supporters and followers, and with all the might and power of his office in the conviction that the glory of Muhammad's religion is the most important task of his own faith and dynasty [then the following consequences follow]: obedience to the command to do what is lawful and the prohibition of what is unlawful manifests itself in his capital and in the provinces; the banners of Islam are always exalted; virtue and merit grow and good works and obedience to God arise, and arise with the beat of drums; sin and iniquity, wickedness and wrongdoing, sink low and remain concealed and in hiding; justice and beneficence become diffused while oppression and tyranny are doomed and cast out; the sciences of tradition become agreeable to men's minds, and they avoid concealed innovations and the knowledge and the literature of concealed innovations; the religious and the protectors of religion attain to dignity and high positions while members of false sects, men of evil faith and heretics, enemies of true religion, become base and contemptible, powerless, and of no account. Those mandates of true religion are enforced and those forbidden by the Holy Law (Sharī'a)

---

[1] Lands (or land revenues) assigned in return for service to the ruler, originally only for the lifetime of the grantee but often becoming hereditary.

sink low and become as if they had never been; love of God and of the Prophets is strengthened in the Muslim community and love of the world (which is a temptation in the path of truth and a longing and an evil in men's hearts) lessens, and desire for the next world increases and desire for this world becomes wearisome and vexatious. The virtues of the people prevail over their vices; truth and the truthful obtain glory and honor, lying and liars, dishonor. Descendants of Muhammad [Saiyyids], doctors of Sharī'a, mystics, ascetics, devotees, recluses appear great, honored, distinguished, and illustrious in the sight and in the minds of men, while the ignorant, the corrupt, the irreligious, the negligent [in performing their prayers], and the shameless appear contemptible, powerless, and unworthy in men's sight. In Holy War sincere zeal is manifested, and the desire for martyrdom graces the warriors and strivers for the faith. Truth and honesty become such; perfidy and dishonesty are reduced to a sorry plight; the good and the just take up occupations in religion and government; the tyrannical and the wicked are left to roam at large "unwept, unhonored, and unsung," or by a change in their dispositions, to behave justly and well; the rich and propertied discharge their obligations to God, and give alms, and perform charitable good works; the poor and the needy are not left in want and are freed from hunger and nakedness. [folios 122a, b]

However, if rulers do not fulfill their religious duty and act as tyrants, no "constitutional" remedy is provided. Tyranny is a visitation from God.

If God Most High views the people of a country and clime with eyes of wrath, and wishes them to remain in toil, trouble, suffering, distress, and disorder, he appoints over them a ruler who is a slave to innate depravity, so that they may be at a loss to know what to do through his evil character and filthy habits, and be utterly confounded through his vicious qualities. [folios 231b–232a]

Abū'l Fazl's Theory of Rulership

The next reading is taken from the preface to the famous *Institutes of Akbar* and "imperial gazeteer" of Akbar's empire. Abū'l Fazl 'Allāmī, friend and companion of the Mughal emperor Akbar, was born in 1551 at Agra. His father, Shaikh Mubārak, was a prominent scholar and mystic, and Abū'l Fazl, though given an orthodox education, stood at the confluence of the many religious currents of his age. He was presented at court by his brother, the poet Faizī, in 1574, and soon gained the emperor's favor by his wit, learning, and moral earnestness. He joined in influencing Akbar against Sunni orthodoxy and in obtaining the assent of Muslim doctors of law to a declaration giving Akbar the deciding voice on religious questions in narrowly defined circumstances. Abū'l Fazl attracted the enmity of Prince Salīm (Jahāngīr) for his influence over Akbar and was murdered at the former's instance in 1602.

Abū'l Fazl's thinking on government was influenced by Shī'ī teachings and by ideas mediated from classical Greece by Muslim philosophers (falāsifa). The Shī'a believed that from the creation of Adam a divine light had passed into the substance of a chosen one in each generation and that this Imam possessed esoteric knowledge of God and enjoyed immunity from sin. By Mughal times, this conception of an immaculate and infallible guide for mankind had been transferred to the person of the temporal ruler (pādshāh). Furthermore, the Platonic idea of "philosopher kings" had been received into the Muslim world and transmitted with Islamic overtones by such writers, for example, as al-Fārābī (d. 950), Ibn Rushd (d. 1198), and al Rāzī (d. 1209), reaching Indian Mughal circles through Jalāl ud-dīn Dawwānī's Akhlāq-i-Jalālī (Jalālī's Ethics), written in Persia about 1470. In his writing, Abū'l Fazl treated Akbar as an incarnation of these conceptions. Akbar himself, of a deeply religious and inquiring mind, was not loath to exercise that initiative in religious questions which Abu'l Fazl was willing to allow him in theory.

[From Abū'l Fazl, Ā'īn-i-Akbarī, pp. ii–iv]

No dignity is higher in the eyes of God than royalty, and those who are wise drink from its auspicious fountain. A sufficient proof of this, for those who require one, is the fact that royalty is a remedy for the spirit of rebellion, and the reason why subjects obey. Even the meaning of the word Pādshāh [emperor] shows this; for pād signifies stability and possession. If royalty did not exist, the storm of strife would never subside, nor selfish ambition disappear. Mankind, being under the burden of lawlessness and lust, would sink into the pit of destruction; this world, this great market place, would lose its prosperity, and the whole world become a barren waste. But by the light of imperial justice, some follow with cheerfulness the road of obedience, while others abstain from violence through fear of punishment; and out of necessity make choice of the path of rectitude. Shāh is also a name given to one who surpasses his fellows, as you may see from words like shāh-suwār [royal horseman], shāh-rāh [royal road]; it is also a term applied to a bridegroom—the world, as the bride, betroths herself to the king, and becomes his worshiper.

Silly and shortsighted men cannot distinguish a true king from a selfish ruler. Nor is this remarkable, as both have in common a large treasury, a numerous army, clever servants, obedient subjects, an abundance of wise men, a multitude of skillful workmen, and a superfluity of means of enjoyment. But men of deeper insight remark a difference. In the case of the former, these things just now enumerated are lasting, but in that of the latter, of short duration. The former does not attach himself to these things, as his object is to remove oppression and provide for everything which is good. Security, health, chastity, justice, polite manners, faithfulness, truth, and increase of sincerity, and so forth, are the result. The latter is kept in bonds by the external forms of royal power, by vanity, the slavishness of men, and the desire of enjoyment; hence everywhere there is insecurity, unsettledness, strife, oppression, faithlessness, robbery.

Royalty is a light emanating from God, and a ray from the sun, the illuminator of the universe, the argument of the book of perfection, the receptacle of all virtues. Modern language calls this light the divine light, and the tongue of antiquity called it the sublime halo. It is communicated by God to kings without the intermediate assistance of anyone, and men, in the presence of it, bend the forehead of praise toward the ground of submission.

Again, many excellent qualities flow from the possession of this light:

1. A paternal love toward the subjects. Thousands find rest in the love of the king, and sectarian differences do not raise the dust of strife. In his wisdom, the king will understand the spirit of the age, and shape his plans accordingly.

2. A large heart. The sight of anything disagreeable does not unsettle him, nor is want of discrimination for him a source of disappointment. His courage steps in. His divine firmness gives him the power of requittal, nor does the high position of an offender interfere with it. The wishes of great and small are attended to, and their claims meet with no delay at his hands.

3. A daily increasing trust in God. When he performs an action, he considers God as the real doer of it [and himself as the medium] so that a conflict of motives can produce no disturbance.

4. Prayer and devotion. The success of his plans will not lead him to neglect, nor will adversity cause him to forget God and madly trust in man. He puts the reins of desire into the hands of reason; in the wide field of his desires he does not permit himself to be trodden down by restless-

ness; nor will he waste his precious time in seeking after that which is improper. He makes wrath, the tyrant, pay homage to wisdom, so that blind rage may not get the upper hand, and inconsiderateness overstep the proper limits. He sits on the eminence of propriety, so that those who have gone astray have a way left to return, without exposing their bad deeds to the public gaze. When he sits in judgment, the petitioner seems to be the judge, and he himself, on account of his mildness, the suitor for justice. He does not permit petitioners to be delayed on the path of hope; he endeavors to promote the happiness of the creatures in obedience to the will of the Creator, and never seeks to please the people in contradiction to reason. He is forever searching after those who speak the truth and is not displeased with words that seem bitter, but are in reality sweet. He considers the nature of the words and the rank of the speaker. He is not content with committing violence, but he must see that no injustice is done within his realm.

The Declaration of Akbar's Status as a Mujtahid

The next reading is the Declaration (*mahzar*) by certain of the ulamā at Akbar's court allowing limited powers of religious interpretation to the Mughal emperor. It should be emphasized that these powers were allowed only when there was no clear prescription already in the Holy Law and only where there was disagreement among the ulamā. It is quite wrong to conceive Akbar as being granted "papal" powers by those who subscribed to the *mahzar*.

[From 'Abd ul-Qādir Badā'ūnī, *Muntakhab ut-Tawārīkh*, II, 271–72]

The intention in laying this foundation and accepting this statement is that, since Hindustan has become a center of security and peace and a land of justice and beneficence through the blessings of the ruler's justice and policy, groups of people of all classes, especially learned scholars and men accomplished in minute study, have migrated to Hindustan and have chosen this country for their home, having left the lands of "'Arab and 'Ajam." All the distinguished scholars who embrace the study of the roots and derivations of the Sharī'a and the sciences based on reason and tradition, and who are characterized by religious faith, piety, and honesty, have very carefully and deeply considered the abstruse meanings of the Qur'anic verse: "Obey God and obey the Prophet and those who have authority among you," and the sound traditions: "Surely the man who is dearest to God on the Day of Judgment is the just Imām [leader, king]. Whoever obeys the amīr [commander], obeys you and whoever rebels against him rebels against you." Also other proofs established by reason and report. The learned have given a decision that the status of a just king is greater before God than the status of an interpreter of the Law (mujtahid) and that the Sultan of Islam, the asylum of the people, the Commander of the Faithful, the shadow of God over mankind, Abū'l Fath Jalāl ud-dīn Muhammad Akbar Pādshāh Ghāzī (whose kingdom God perpetuate!) is a most just, most wise king and one most informed of God.

Accordingly if a religious problem arises regarding which there are differences among the interpreters of the Law, and if His Majesty with his penetrating understanding and clear wisdom chooses one side with a view to facilitating the livelihood of mankind and the good order of the world's affairs and gives the decision to that side, that shall be agreed upon and it shall be necessary and obligatory for everyone of all sorts and conditions to follow it. Furthermore, if, in accordance with his own just opinion, he should promulgate a decision which is not opposed to the [clear] text of the Qur'ān and the Traditions and would be for the convenience of mankind, it is necessary and obligatory for everyone to act upon it and opposition to it shall be a cause of hardship in the next world and of detriment in both religious and worldly affairs.

This sincere written statement, for the sake of God and the promulgation of the duties of Islam, is signed as a declaration of the scholars of religion and of the holy lawyers. (Done in the month of Rajab 987 after Hijra [August–September, 1579])

CHAPTER XVIII

THE IDEAL SOCIAL ORDER

Writing in medieval India on the ideal Muslim social order, as on other aspects of the Islamic revelation, was confined to those educated in Muslim religious sciences. Therefore its approach is academic and doctrinaire. This is no crisis-literature; it does not offer practical answers to contemporary social problems, but rather repeats ideas which entered Hindustan from the ouside Muslim world. Any correspondence between the ideal categories of Muslim "social" thought and the actualities of the Indian scene is attributable more to the general similarity of the economic order and class structure of Asian society in the pre-industrial age, whether in Hindustan, Persia, or Iraq, than to actual observation of society in India.

The ideal Muslim social order is essentially a religious order. Society is not a venue for individual self-realization, a contrivance for the satisfaction of human wants; the only kind of human happiness which it should make possible is the happiness which comes from obedience to God. Since obedience to God meant obedience to a revealed Holy Law, the Shari'a, Muslim social ideals envisage a conservative order in which repetition and submission are reckoned more worthy than innovation and enterprise. The good society was the old society—that which existed during the lifetime of the Prophet. The modern American hopes and intends change to be for the better; the medieval Muslim believed it to be for the worse.

As has been seen, for the Muslim, earthly society should be so ordered as to make possible the godly life and the welfare of the students of the godly life, the ulamā and the mystics. Harmony is the keyword; man should be in harmony with God, nature, and his fellows. If he is not in harmony with his fellows, his attention will be diverted from God, for then he will be intent upon self-preservation. But harmony depends upon being in his proper place and a man's proper place is that for which his nature fits him. The ultimate whole within which each individual finds his place is not economic, although economic activity is essential to the welfare of that whole. The ultimate whole is Islamic—the Muslim community defending itself successfully against attack from outside, devoting itself to the practice of the True Faith, and providing itself with a livelihood sufficient both to bear the cost of its own defense and to keep its members alive and active in the service of God.

In India (following pre-Muslim Iranian tradition) society is seen as four main classes—men of the pen, men of the sword, men of business, and men of the soil. The first are guardians of religion and learning, the second are the guardians of those guardians, and the third and fourth are the sustainers of the first two classes. Attempts by any member of any class to change from his class can only, it is believed, result in chaos and disorder. Muslim social ideas are essentially hierarchical and organic. But how was each to be sure of his proper class and function? Indo-Muslim thinkers, adapting Greek and Persian ideas, answered that God had decided the problem at the creation. Social harmony between classes of men endowed with different aptitudes is willed by God.

The ideal social classification advocated by Indo-Muslim theorists of the ulamā class did correspond in large measure to the social stratification, viewed from a Muslim point of observation, in that area of Hindustan under Muslim rule—except that the people of the sword took precedence in practice over the people of the pen and often ignored them. But it was nevertheless very much the theory of a pen-man's utopia which ignored actual social differences in Muslim India—the distinction between Turk and non-Turk in the first century of Muslim rule, between immigrant Muslim and Indian-born Muslim, between hereditary Muslim and converted Muslim, Delhi Muslim and Bengali Muslim, between descendants of Afghan tribes and non-Afghans, between those with light skins and those with dark, between slaves and free men. However, in its picture of a static society in which men performed those duties for which heredity and inherited education had designated them—of soldiers who would not conceive of becoming agriculturists or traders, and of traders who would not think of becoming ulamā or soldiers—the idea was not very far from the actual: a society of small cultivators and traders supporting, with its labor and taxes, a military and learned aristocracy.

The institution of slavery was important in politics, administration, and in household economy in medieval India under Muslim rule; it does not figure as an important theme in Indo-Muslim writing on the ideal social order. Turkish rulers like Qutb ud-dīn Aibak (1206–1210), Iltutmish (1211–1236), and Balban (1266–1287), began their careers as slaves, and slaves from within the sultans' households were often appointed to high administrative and military offices, but no organized system of slave training, promotion and rule, similar to the Janissary system under the Ottoman Turks, existed in medieval India.[1]

Similarly, the status of women in Muslim law and thought did not change with the conquest of Hindustan by Muslims, although, in practice, Hindu customary law was influential among certain groups of Muslim converts from Hinduism.[2]

For statements on the social and political discrimination which, ideally, should be enforced against non-Muslims, reference should be made to Chapter XVII.

The Four-Class Division of Society

The first reading has been taken from a Persian work on ethics written outside India in the second half of the fifteenth century. The work is *Jalālī's Ethics* (*Akhlāq-i-Jalālī*), by Muhammad ibn Asad Jalāl ud-dīn al-Dawwānī (1427–1501). It was popular in Mughal India.

[From Thompson, *Practical Philosophy of the Muhammadan People*, pp. 388–90]

In order to preserve this political equipoise, there is a correspondence to be maintained between the various classes. Like as the equipoise of bodily temperament is effected by intermixture and correspondence of four elements, the equipoise of the political temperament is to be sought for in the correspondence of four classes.

1. *Men of the pen,* such as lawyers, divines, judges, bookmen, statisticians, geometricians, astronomers, physicians, poets. In these and their exertions in the use of their delightful pens, the subsistence of the faith and of the world itself is vested and bound up. They occupy the place in politics that water does among the elements. Indeed, to persons of ready understanding, the similarity of knowledge and water is as clear as water itself, and as evident as the sun that makes it so.

[1] For an extensive discussion of the status of slaves under Muslim law, see the article, " 'Abd" in the *Encyclopaedia of Islam* (new edition, 1954). No changes in legal doctrine on slavery appear to have occurred in medieval Muslim India; readings from lawbooks used in India have not been given.

[2] See the article, " 'Āda" in the *Encyclopaedia of Islam* (1954).

2. *Men of the sword,* such as soldiers, fighting zealots, guards of forts and passes, etc.; without whose exercise of the impetuous and vindictive sword, no arrangement of the age's interests could be effected; without the havoc of whose tempest-like energies, the materials of corruption, in the shape of rebellious and disaffected persons, could never be dissolved and dissipated. These then occupy the place of fire, their resemblance to it is too plain to require demonstration; no rational person need call in the aid of fire to discover it.

3. *Men of business,* such as merchants, capitalists, artisans, and crafts-men, by whom the means of emolument and all other interests are adjusted; and through whom the remotest extremes enjoy the advantage and safeguard of each other's most peculiar commodities. The resemblance of these to air—the auxiliary of growth and increase in vegetables—the reviver of spirit in animal life—the medium by the undulation and movement of which all sorts of rare and precious things traverse the hearing to arrive at the headquarters of human nature—is exceedingly manifest.

4. *Husbandmen,* such as seedsmen, bailiffs, and agriculturists—the superintendents of vegetation and preparers of provender; without whose exertions the continuance of the human kind must be cut short. These are, in fact, the only producers of what had no previous existence; the other classes adding nothing whatever to subsisting products, but only transferring what subsists already from person to person, from place to place, and from form to form. How close these come to the soil and surface of the earth—the point to which all the heavenly circles refer—the scope to which all the luminaries of the purer world direct their rays—the stage on which wonders are displayed—the limit to which mysteries are confined—must be universally apparent.

In like manner then as in the composite organizations the passing of any element beyond its proper measure occasions the loss of equipoise, and is followed by dissolution and ruin, in political coalition, no less, the prevalence of any one class over the other three overturns the adjustment and dissolves the junction. Next attention is to be directed to the condition of the individuals composing them, and the place of every one determined according to his right.

The four-class classification is found in India in Abū'l Fazl, by whom the learned are relegated to the third position.

[From Abū'l Fazl, *Ā'īn-i-Akbarī*, iv–v]
The people of the world may be divided into four classes:

1. *Warriors,* who in the political body have the nature of fire. Their flames, directed by understanding, consume the straw and rubbish of rebellion and strife, but kindle also the lamp of rest in this world of disturbances.

2. *Artificers and merchants,* who hold the place of air. From their labors and travels, God's gifts become universal, and the breeze of contentment nourishes the rose-tree of life.

3. *The learned,* such as the philosopher, the physician, the arithmetician, the geometrician, the astronomer, who resemble water. From their pen and their wisdom, a river rises in the drought of the world, and the garden of the creation receives from their irrigating powers, a peculiar freshness.

4. *Husbandmen and laborers,* who may be compared to earth. By their exertions, the staple of life is brought to perfection, and strength and happiness flow from their work.

It is therefore obligatory for a king to put each of these in its proper place, and by uniting personal ability with due respect for others, to cause the world to flourish.

Social Precedence

The essentially religious color of the medieval Muslim ideal social order is brought out in the following passage, which purports to be an order by the Caliph Ma'mūn establishing social precedence. The passage is from the *Rulings on Temporal Governments,* by Ziā ud-dīn Barnī.
[From Barnī, *Fatāwa-yi-Jahāndārī,* folios 128a–129b *passim*]

It is commanded that the inhabitants of the capital, Baghdad, and the entire population of the Muslim world should hold in the greatest honor and respect all men of the Hāshimite family who are related to the Prophet by ties of blood, especially the 'Abbāsids to whose line the caliphate of the Muslim community has been confirmed, and, in particular the saiyids whose descent from and relationship to the Prophet is certain. In all circumstances they should strive to reverence and honor them and not allow them to be insulted and humiliated. They should consider the

rendering of honor and respect to them to be among their religious duties
and a way of doing homage to the Prophet himself. People should consider the causing of any harm or injury to them as equal to infidelity and
unbelief.

In accordance with God's commands, a share of the fifth of the spoils
of war which accrues to the public treasury, after having been converted
to cash, should be delivered to them at their homes for their maintenance.
They are to have precedence in seating over all my [the Caliph Ma'mūn's]
helpers, supporters, courtiers, and high officers and dignitaries of the
realm. In other assemblies and meetings, religious scholars, shaikhs, wazirs,
maliks [princes], and the well-known and distinguished people of Baghdad are to sit below them. All classes of the Baghdad population are to
pay them due regard and to deem the salvation of Muslims of all classes
attainable through paying the relations of the Prophet honor and respect.

As regards the Sunni religious scholars and the Sufis of Baghdad, it
is commanded that they should be respected in the capital; to do them
honor is to be considered a part of piety. It should be thought that the
mandates of the True Faith are adorned by their words and deeds and
the elevation of the banners of Islam is a result of honor paid to them.

[And Ma'mūn ordered that] in accordance with the instructions of the
Chief Qādī and with the records kept by the Shaikh ul-Islām, they should
cause religious scholars and Sufis to be given what would be sufficient
and salutary for them, and enable them to live in the best of circumstances and to avoid that neediness which makes both knowledge and
the learned contemptible.

For the warriors and champions of the Faith, he commanded sufficient
salaries, allowances, and assistance to be given them in cash from the
public treasury of the Muslims, in accordance with the instructions of the
muster master at Baghdad and the ranks and grades named and fixed by
the muster master's department. Respect and honor are to be paid to
holy warriors both in the caliph's palace and in all Baghdad, for they are
the protectors of the territory of Islam and of its inhabitants. They fight
in the way of God and overthrow the enemies of God and of His Prophet.

Divine Origin of the "Division of Labor"

Ideally a man's status in the godly society is related to his innate virtues or vices
for which God as Creator is responsible. A man's occupation denotes his moral

degree in God's sight. The superior social rank of the learned and the literary, implied in the first reading, should be noted.

[From Barnī, *Fatāwa-yi-Jahāndārī*, folios 216b–217b]

All men in creation are equal and in outward form and appearance are also equal. Every distinction of goodness and wickedness which has appeared among mankind has so appeared as a result of their qualities and of their commission of acts. Virtue and vice have been shared out from all eternity and were made the associate of their spirits. The manifestation of human deeds and acts is a created thing. Whenever God obliges good actions and wicked actions, and good and evil, He gives warning of it so that those good and bad deeds, that good and that evil, may be openly manifested, and when, in the very first generation of Adam, the sons of Adam appeared and multiplied, and the world began to be populated, and in their social intercourse the need for everything befell mankind, the Eternal Craftsman imparted to mens' minds the crafts essential to their social intercourse. So in one he implanted writing and penmanship, to another horsemanship, to one the craft of weaving, to another farriery, and to yet another carpentry. All these crafts, honorable and base, from penmanship and horsemanship to cupping and tanning, were implanted in their minds and breasts by virtue of those virtues and vices which, in the very depths of their natures, have become the companions of their spirits. To the hearts of the possessors of the virtues, by reason of their innate virtue, have fallen the noble crafts, and in those under the dominion of vice, by reason of their innate vice, have been implanted the ignoble occupations. Those thus inspired have chosen those very crafts which have been grafted upon their minds and have practiced them, and from them have come those crafts and skills and occupations with which they were inspired; for them the bringing of those crafts into existence was made feasible.

These crafts, noble and ignoble, have become the hidden companions of the sons of the first sons of Adam. In accordance with their quickness of intelligence and perspicacity, their descendants have added to the crafts of their ancestors some fine and desirable features, so that every art, craft, and profession, of whose products mankind has need, has reached perfection.

As virtues were implanted in those who have chosen the nobler occupations, from them alone come forth goodness, kindness, generosity, valor, good deeds, good works, truthfulness, keeping of promises, avoidance of slander, loyalty, purity of vision, justice, equity, recognition of one's duty, gratitude for favors received, and fear of God. These people are said to be noble, freeborn, virtuous, religious, of high lineage, and of pure birth. They alone are worthy of offices and posts in the realm and under the government of the ruler who, in his high position as the supreme governor, is singled out as the leader and the chief of mankind. Thus the government of the ruler and his activities are given strength and put in an orderly condition.

But whenever vices have been inserted into the minds of those who chose the baser arts and the mean occupations, only immodesty, falsehood, miserliness, perfidy, sins, wrongs, lies, evil-speaking, ingratitude, stupidity, injustice, oppression, blindness to one's duty, cant, impudence, bloodthirstiness, rascality, conceit and godlessness appear. They are called lowborn, bazaar people, base, mean, worthless, "plebeian," shameless, and of impure birth. Every act which is mingled with meanness and founded on ignominy comes very well from them. The promotion of the low and the lowborn brings no advantage in this world, for it is impudent to act against the wisdom of creation.

Rulers to Preserve the Social Order Willed by God
[From Barnī, *Fatāwa-yi-Jahāndārī*, folios 58a–58b, 130a]

It is a [religious] duty and necessary for kings whose principal aims are the protection of religion and stability in affairs of government to follow the practices of God Most High in their bestowal of place. Whomsoever God has chosen and honored with excellence, greatness, and ability, in proportion to his merit so should he be singled out and honored by kings. . . . He whom God has created with vile qualities and made contemptible in his sin, rascality, and ignorance, who as a sport of the Devil has been brought into existence as a slave of this world and a helpless victim of his lower self, should be treated and lived with according to the way he was created, so that the wisdom of the creation of the Creator may illumine the hearts of all. But if the ruler, out of a natural inclination or base desire, self-will, or lack of wisdom honors such a scoundrel, then the ruler holds God in contempt and treats Him with scorn. For the ruler has honored, in opposition to the wisdom of creation, one whom God has dishonored and treats him as one distinguished and honorable, making him happy out of the bounty of his power and greatness. Such a ruler is not worthy of the caliphate and deputyship of God. To use the name of king for him becomes a crime for he has made the incomparable bounty of God into an instrument of sin. Opposition to the wisdom of creation hurts him in this world and finally he will be punished in the next world.

. . . . .

Teachers of every kind are to be strictly enjoined not to thrust precious stones down the throats of dogs or to put collars of gold round the necks of pigs and bears—that is, to the mean, the ignoble, the worthless; to shopkeepers and the lowborn they are to teach nothing more than the mandates about prayer, fasting, alms-giving, and the pilgrimage to Mecca, along with some chapters of the Qur'ān and some doctrines of the Faith, without which their religion cannot be correct and valid prayers are not possible. They are to be instructed in nothing more lest it bring honor to their mean souls. They are not to be taught reading and writing, for plenty of disorders arise owing to the skill of the lowborn in knowledge. The disorders into which all the affairs of religion and government are thrown is due to the acts and words of the lowborn, whom they have made skillful. For by means of their skill they become governors, revenue-collectors, accountants, officers, and rulers. If the teachers are disobedient and it is discovered at the time of investigation that they have imparted knowledge or taught letters or writing to the lowborn, inevitably punishment for their disobedience will be meted out to them. [folio 130a]

The next two readings from the Mughal period express a similar point of view to Barnī's. The first work, Muhammad Bāqir Khān's *Admonitions on Government,* was written in 1612–13; the second, though entitled *Institutes of Timūr,* was written about 1637 by Abū Tālib al-Husainī.

[From Muhammad Bāqir Khān, *Mau'iza-yi-Jahāngīrī,* folios 29–31 *passim*]

Rulers should not permit unworthy people with evil natures to be put on an equality with people with a pure lineage and wisdom and they should consider the maintenance of rank among the fundamental customs and usages of rulership. For, if the differences between classes disappear and the lowest class boast of living on an equality with the "median" class, and the "median" boast of living on an equality with

the upper, rulers will lose prestige and complete undermining of the
bases of the kingdom will appear. For this reason rulers of former days
used not to allow base people of rascally origin and who had been
taught writing to understand problems of fulfilling promises and rules
of order because, when this habit is perpetuated and they emerge from
their professions to take their place among the servants of the government, verily, injury will spread and the life of all classes become disordered. . . . Consider worthy of education him who has an intrinsically
fine nature and avoid educating rascals with an intrinsically bad nature,
for every stone does not become a jewel nor all blood fragrant musk.
In him who has a vile person, a base nature, and an inner nastiness, there
will not be seen either sincerity, capacity for government, or regard for
religion—and when the quality of sincerity and of piety, which is the
root of intellect, has been removed, every fault which it is possible to
have can be expected from him.

[From Abū Tālib al-Husainī, *Tūzuk-i-Tīmūrī*, pp. 158–60]
Fourthly, by advice and institute, I regulated the affairs of my household
and by advice and institute I firmly established my authority so that the
amirs [nobles] and ministers, soldiers and subjects, could not transgress
the just bounds of their ranks and degrees, and each one was the keeper
of his own station. [p. 160]

. . . .

Be it known to Abū Mansūr Tīmūr (on whom be the blessing of Almighty God!) that the organization of the business of this world is pat-
terned on the organization of the business of the next, in which there
are public functionaries and officials, deputies and chamberlains, each in
his own station performing his own work. They do not overstep their
bounds and they await the commands of God. Therefore you must
take precautions that your wazirs, soldiers, officials, servants, and officials, each being within the confines of their own stations, await your
commands. Keep every class and group within their proper limits so
that your dominion may be properly established and ordered. But if you
do not keep everything and everybody in their proper place, then chaos
and sedition will make their way into your state. Therefore you should
watch that everything and everybody remain in their rank and degree.
[p. 158]

CHAPTER XIX

THE IMPORTANCE OF THE
STUDY OF HISTORY

Medieval Indo-Muslims, no less than medieval Arab or Persian Muslims, were historically minded people. The Muslim conquest of Hindustan ushered in a succession of historical works, chiefly written in Persian, without precedent (except for the Kashmir Chronicle, 1148–49) and certainly without parallel in Hindu India. Such well-known works as Ziā ud-dīn Barnī's *Tārīkh-i-Fīrūz Shāhī* (c.1357), Abū'l Fazl's *Akbar-Nāma* (1590s), and 'Abd ul-Qādir Badā'ūnī's *Muntakhab ut-Tawārīkh* (c.1596) are but the most imposing peaks of a Himalayan range of histories.

Islam as a religion had intensified and redirected the pre-Muslim Arab interest in the past, which had found expression in the oral battle-day traditions (*ayyām*) and tribal genealogies (*ansāb*). The Qur'ān was the confirmation of a progressive revelation in history of God's will for man (6.92; 35.31), recalling mankind to an awareness of a Truth previously communicated by an historical succession of prophets (4.163), but neglected. Man should study the history of the world before Muhammad for the good of his soul. Furthermore, the Qur'ān emphasizes man's accountability to God for his deeds—that is to say, for his history—on the Day of Judgment (17.13, 14). Hence the facts about what men do are instinct with a truly awful significance.

Then too, the study of the life of the Prophet, his actions, and his sayings, and those of his Companions, was essentially an historical study. For most Muslims this had added significance inasmuch as they viewed the good life as one modeled upon the life of the Prophet and upon those of his Companions. Again, the dogma of the infallibility of consensus, and for Sunnis, the belief that the religious role of Muhammad had descended upon the community as a whole, invested a record of the past with a new seriousness. Such a record was essential for true servant-hood of God and a reasonable hope of salvation.

Before the Muslim conquests in India, interest in history in the Muslim world had also been excited by such nonreligious considerations as pride in the story of Muslim conquests and in the part played therein by family and tribe, and by the emergence of independent military rulers who encouraged the production of histories retailing their power, piety, and patronage of learning. Such rulers were as interested in enjoying stories and traditions from pre-Muslim Iran and Turkestan as in knowing the biography of the Prophet and the story of the infant Muslim community after his death. Tabarī's (d. 923) monumental *History of Prophets and Kings (Tārīkh ul-Rusūl wa'l Mulūk)* stood at the confluence of both the Islamic and the non-Islamic streams in Muslim historiography.

Indo-Muslim historiography (as indeed that elsewhere in the Muslim world), reflected, and sometimes consciously propagated, the religio-politico-social ideas illustrated in the previous chapters. Written chiefly by courtiers, royal confidants, and officials, the purpose of Indo-Muslim histories was utilitarian in the sense that they aimed some to teach true religion by historical example, some to preserve a record of great deeds for the edification of succeeding generations of Muslims, some to glorify the history of Islam in Hindustan, some to praise a particular ruler or a line of rulers, and some to do all these. Many such histories were written either at the behest of the ruler or in hope of his patronage.

Medieval Muslim historiography in India, as in medieval Muslim Persia, implicitly accepted therefore (where it did not seek actively to underpin) notions of a religious and social order founded upon a tacit partnership between the ulamā and their patron and protector, the godly ruler, in the furtherance of the good life. Furthermore, by concentrating upon the deeds of the ruling power, Indo-Muslim historians helped to confirm autocracy as the typical Indo-Muslim political institution. Such tendencies will be illustrated from the preface to Abū'l Fazl's *Akbar-Nāma,* where he indeed destroys even the theory of a balance between separate religious and ruling institutions.

Almost all Indo-Muslim historians assume that only the history of Muslims is deserving of attention. Many, particularly after the establishment of Mughal rule, give a conspectus of the political history of Muslims in Hindustan from the time of the Ghōrid conquest, or sometimes perhaps, of the raids of Mahmūd of Ghaznin. The stimulation among the literate and the powerful of an Indo-Muslim awareness of themselves as a separate community, divided from the Hindus by history as well as by ideology, must be accounted an important by-product of Indo-Muslim historical writing.

Relevance and space do not permit the discussion and illustration of Indo-Muslim historical technique. The aim of the readings is merely to illustrate three themes related to those of earlier chapters. It is not suggested that they are even an index to the scope of Indo-Muslim historical writing.[1]

The Study of History As an Integral Support of the Orthodox Muslim Conception of World Order

[From Barnī, *Tārikh-i-Fīrūz Shāhī*, pp. 9–17]

After the science of Qur'anic commentary, of tradition, of jurisprudence, and the mystic path of the Sufi shaikhs, I have not observed such advantages from any branch of learning as I have from history. History is the knowledge of the annals and traditions of prophets, caliphs, sultans, and of the great men of religion and of government. Pursuit of the study of history is particular to the great ones of religion and of government who are famous for the excellence of their qualities or who have become famous among mankind for their great deeds. Low fellows, rascals, unfit and unworthy persons, inferior people, and those with base aspirations, people of unknown stock and mean natures, of no lineage and low lineage, loiterers and bazaar loafers—all these have no connection with history. It is not their trade and skill. A knowledge of history does not advantage such people and profits them in no circumstance. For history is the annals of the good qualities of greatness and the story of the virtues, excellences, and the fine deeds of great men of religion and government, and not a record of the vices of rascals, low fellows, people of inferior birth and bazaar stock, who love base qualities by reason of their rascally nature and who have no desire for history. Rather it is harmful to base and mean fellows for them to read and know history, not an advantage at all. What higher honor for history is it possible to conceive than that mean and low people have no desire or inclination for this rare form of knowledge, that it is of no profit to them in their low dealings and filthy

[1] For this see C. A. Storey, "Persian Literature," Section II, 2, *History of India* (London, 1939).

morals, and that history is the only science of learning in any quarter from which they desire no benefit whatever?

But those who have been born of excellent lineage and good stock, in whose seed the honor of greatness and of great birth has been inscribed— they cannot escape knowing history and employing it. They cannot live without using history. Among great people, those born great, those of high lineage and those born of high lineage, the historian is dearer than life and they wish to follow the footsteps of historians whose writings are a means whereby the great people of religion and of government find eternal life.

Leaders of religion and of government have spoken at length on the value of history. The first value is that the heavenly books which are the word of God are filled with reports of most of the deeds of prophets—the best of created beings—and of the annals of sultans—the rulers of men— their violence and oppression. History is the form of knowledge which provides a stock of warnings to be heeded by those with eyes to see. Second, the science of Hadīth—all the words and deeds of the Prophet and the most precious form of knowledge after Qur'anic commentary, the discovery and confirmation of narrators, and of events recorded in tradition, the warlike activities of the Holy Prophet, the establishment of a chronology, the abrogation of traditions—all these are connected with history and it is on this account that the science of history is entirely bound up with the science of tradition. The great Imāms of tradition have said that history and tradition are twins and if the traditionist is not an historian he will not be informed of the activities of the Holy Prophet, and of the Companions who are the original reporters of Hadīth. Without history, the true circumstances of the real Companions and the followers of the Companions as distinct from spurious companions and followers will become evident. Whenever the traditionist is not an historian, their activities will not be authenticated and the traditionist will not be able to give a true account of tradition or explain it correctly. Furthermore, the circumstances and events which occurred in the time of the Prophet and his companions and their explanation and analysis—which is a cause of encouragement and confidence for the hearts of all generations of the Muslim community—these too became known through history.

The third boon to be derived from history is that it is a means of increasing the intelligence and understanding and also a means of correct decision and planning [a course of action]. From the study of the expe-

rience of others a person becomes experienced himself and through knowing, by a knowledge of history, what has previously happened, a firm
resolve emerges. Aristotle and Buzurjmihr [wazir to the Sassanian ruler
Noshirwan] have stated that a knowledge of history strengthens and
confirms right judgment in that the knowledge of previous circumstances
is a testimony to the justice and soundness of subsequent opinion.

The fourth advantage to be gained from history is that through its
knowledge, and through awareness of events both recent and remote in
time, the hearts of sultans, maliks, wazirs, and other great men remain
firm and if some terrible calamity from heaven happens to rulers, they
do not lose their serenity and the remedy for healing the ills of the kingdom becomes clear to them from the remedies applied by their predecessors. In their hearts they may avoid schemes and projects which they
would otherwise have planned and they observe signs of untoward happenings before they occur. This advantage is one of the greatest possible.

The fifth advantage from history is that the knowledge of the annals
of the prophets and their vicissitudes, and the way in which they accepted
whatever came to them, patiently and with resignation, may become a
cause of patience and resignation for those who know history. The eventual finding by the prophets of salvation from calamity becomes a means
of hope for those who know history. Since it became evident from history
that calamities of all kinds have rained upon prophets (who are the best
of men), the hearts of Muslims will not despair when unforeseen calamity
descends upon them.

The sixth advantage from a knowledge of history is that the natural
qualities of the elect, of the just, and of the benevolent, their salvation
and their high status, find a seat in the heart and the evil deeds of the
contumacious, the tyrannical, and the oppressive, their ultimate destruction and the plague affecting them become evident to the sultans, wazirs,
and rulers of Islam. The rewards of virtue and the results of evil deeds
are proved in the affairs of worldly government, and fortunate caliphs,
sultans, and rulers incline toward virtue and excellence, and kings of Islam do not fall into the clutches of tyranny and oppression, avoid haughty
behavior in exercising their dominion, and do not abandon what their
character as servants of God requires. The benefits of the right dealing
of caliphs and sultans, wazirs and rulers, spread among all the people
and stretch near and far.

The seventh benefit from history is that it is inseparable from truth.

Great men of religion and government in all ages have said that the foundation of the science of history has been placed on truth. Thus Abraham made this request from God and offered this prayer: "May I have a good report among later generations." In rebuking those who write lies, God has said: "They corrupt the Word from its proper meaning." God has made lying and slandering perilous matters.

The composition of history is special to great men and the sons of great men who are connected with the administration of justice, freedom, truth, and right, because history is the narration of good and evil, justice and injustice, merit and unmerit, praiseworthy qualities and offensive qualities, acts of obedience and acts of disobedience, virtues and vices, in times gone by so that succeeding readers may take warning from them and comprehend the advantages and the dangers of worldly government and the benevolence and the wickedness of empire and follow that benevolence and avoid that wickedness. And if, which God forfend! a liar and rogue uses falsehoods, and, with his low and filthy nature grafts a story of unfitting actions upon the lives of previous great men, incorporates it in his writing and gives currency to lying and slander with many colored accounts, makes lies seem like truth, and writes them down, and does not, out of criminality, fear either this world or the next, and does not fear having to answer on the Day of Judgment so that the good are called and described as wicked for hidden crimes of which they speak—all this is terrible and worse. To speak and write of the wicked as if they were good, that is the worst form of evil conduct.

Since the annals of history are without [written] warrant and proclaim the dealings of sultans and great men, therefore, it is necessary that the historian be one of the kind worthy of respect and known and famous for his truth and just dealing, so that students may have firm confidence in what he writes without written authority and so that he may obtain credit among the honorable. For there is no assurance for the honorable unless in the writing of one worthy of respect and unless there is not the slightest doubt as to his true faith and piety. . . .

It must be known that whatever people worthy of respect have written in their histories has been relied upon by others, and whatever the self-willed people of unknown stock have written, the wise have not trusted. History written by rascals has grown old in booksellers' shops and has been returned to the papermakers for repulping.

As the historian must be among the notables and the respected, so the soundness of his religion and sect is a condition of his writing history. Otherwise, what happens is as in the case of some people of wrong religion and of evil faith from hereditary prejudice and hereditary hatred—such as the Shi'a and the Khārijites who have woven lying tales about the Companions of the Prophet. Previous writers of wrong faith and evil religion have mixed truth and error in their histories. They have set down well-known and rejected traditions in their works. Whenever the religion, sect, and evil belief of an historian is not evident to readers and they reckon the writers of history among their predecessors, they think that perhaps they are writing the truth. Whoever does not recognize the deceits of people of false religion—that the way of such people is to keep their erroneous beliefs and filthy faith hidden among the Sunnis and mix the lies and tissue of inventions which have found a place among their horrid doctrines with the kinship of well-known true traditions; that they set them down in their own rejected writings so that the student who has not had warning of previous circumstances may come to know of their false beliefs and their crooked ways and understand the religion of lying historians—trouble will indeed come upon his own true faith by studying those writers who have mingled with error, and he will consider correct what irreligious authors have composed.

One great benefit from the understanding of history is that through it the Sunnis of time gone by become known from the unorthodox, those of true from those of untrue belief, and faithful supporters of Islam from unfaithful. Trustworthy accounts of events are distinguished from rejected doctrines and the Imāms of the Sunna and the community turn with renewed strength to the orthodox faith.

One of the indispensable conditions of history writing, and one which is absolutely obligatory in the interests of piety, is that when the historian writes of the excellences, the good deeds, the justice and equity of the ruler or of a great man, he must also not conceal his vices and evil deeds and not employ the ways of conviviality in writing history. If he considers it expedient he should speak openly, but if not, he should speak by insinuations, in hints, and in covert and learned allusions. If out of fear and terror he cannot write about the crimes of contemporaries he is excused, but he must write the truth about the past. If the historian has received blows from the ruler, wazir, or great men of his time, or has received much favor and patronage, he should write in such a way that it is impossible to perceive that he has received kindness or ill treatment, patronage or payment from the great, lest as a consequence he should write against truth of excellences and of vices that were not, and of deeds and events that did not happen. But the attention of the truthful, pious, and sincere historian should be directed toward writing the truth. He should be in fear of answering on the Day of Judgment. . . .

In sum, history is a rare and useful form of knowledge and its writing is a very great obligation. Its advantages spread far and wide, both as regards spreading the knowledge of deeds and praiseworthy qualities and perpetuating them on the scrolls of time and as regards the many boons it confers upon readers when they study it. The historian has many duties and responsibilities toward those of whose annals and deeds he writes and spreads on the pages of time. If they are alive, the publication of their deeds becomes a means whereby they are loved, spoken well of, and wished well. Friendship for them becomes engraved on the hearts both of those who know them and of strangers. If they are dead, the recollection of their deeds ensures them a second life, and they become greatly deserving of God's mercy. The historian also has duties toward the readers and hearers of history because by means of his writing they may obtain considerable rewards.

[From Badā'ūnī, *Muntakhab ut-Tawārīkh,* II (tr. by Lowe), 272]
I have made bold to chronicle these events, a course very far removed from that of prudence and circumspection. But God (He is glorious and honored!) is my witness, and sufficient is God as a witness, that my inducement to write this has been nothing but sorrow for the faith, and heartburning for the deceased religion of Islam. . . .

[From Badā'ūnī, *Muntakhab ut-Tawārīkh,* III (tr. by Haig), 529, 530 *passim*]
I shall now explain what it was that originally led me to collect these fragments. Since a complete revolution, both in legislation and in manners, greater than any of which there is any record for the past thousand years, has taken place in these days, and every writer who has had the ability to record events and to write two connected sentences has, for the sake of flattering the people of this age, or for fear of them, or by reason of his ignorance of matters of faith, or of his distance from court, or for his own selfish ends, concealed the truth, and, having bartered his faith

for worldly profit, and right guidance for error, has adorned falsehood with the semblance of truth, and distorted and embellished infidelity and pernicious trash until they have appeared to be laudable . . . it is incumbent on me, who am acquainted with some, at least, of the affairs narrated, and have even been intimately connected with these transactions, to place on record what I have seen and what I have heard, for my evidence regarding these things is that of an eyewitness who is certain of what he relates, and does not spring from mere supposition and guesswork ("and when can that which is heard resemble that which is seen?") in order that, on the one hand, my record may be an expiation of the writings, past and present, which I have been compelled and directed to undertake, and, on the other, right may be proved to be on the side of the Muslims and mercy may be shown to me.

Historical Literature in the Service of Autocracy

Indo-Muslim historiography tended to focus on the deeds of the ruler, who was sometimes glorified in the extreme, as is shown by this excerpt from Nizām ud-dīn Ahmad's *Tabaqāt-i-Akbarī*, written in 1592–93.

[From Nizām ud-dīn Ahmad, *Tabaqāt-i-Akbarī*, I (tr. by De), iii–v *passim*]

But, after that, this insignificant particle—Nizām ud-dīn Ahmad, the son of Muhammad Muqīm the Harāwī, who is a humble dependent and a faithful adherent of the sublime Court of the Great Emperor, the Sultan of the Sultans of the world, the beneficent shadow of God, the viceregent of the Omnipotent, the strengthener of the pillars of world-conquest, the founder of the rules for governing the world, the ruler of the world and of all who inhabit it, the lord of all time and of all that exists in it, the embodiment of Divine secrets, the personification of spiritual essences, the most potent conqueror and the most successful ruler, the lion in the wilderness of political and religious warfare Abū'l Fath Jalāl ud-dīn Muhammad Akbar Pādshāh Ghāzī; may God perpetuate his dominion and empire, and fill the table of his justice and benefaction!—represents that from his childhood, according to the instructions of his worthy father, he occupied himself with the study of historical works, which brightens the intellect of the studious, and inspires the intelligent with awe. . . . Now that all the provinces and divisions of Hindustan have been conquered by the world-opening sword of His Majesty, the viceregent of God, and the many have been unified into the one, and even many of the countries

outside of India, which had never been acquired by any of the former
great sultans have become part and parcel of his dominions, and it is
hoped, that the seven climes would become the abode of peace and quiet
under the shadow of His Majesty's auspicious standard, it came to the
dull understanding of the author, that he should, with the pen of truth
and candor, write a comprehensive history which should present in a clear
style, in its different sections, an account of the Empire of Hindustan from
the time of Sabuktigīn which began with the year 367 after Hijra when
Islam first appeared in the country of Hindustan, to the year 1001 after
Hijra, corresponding with the thirty-seventh year of the Divine era, which
was inaugurated at the epoch-making accession of His Majesty, the viceregent of God; and should embellish the glorious army, which is as it
were an introduction to the sublime chronicle of renown. . . .

The next reading, from Abū'l Fazl's *Akbar-Nāma,* betrays his efforts to have
Akbar regarded as heir both to the prophets and to caliphs and kings.
      [From Abū'l Fazl, *Akbar-Nāma,* I (tr. by Beveridge), 16–17]

So long as the spiritual supremacy over the recluse, which is called Holiness, and the sway over laymen, which is called Sovereignty, were distinct,
there was strife and confusion among the children of Noah [mankind].
Now that in virtue of his exaltation, foresight, comprehensive wisdom,
universal benevolence, pervading discernment, and perfect knowledge
of God, these two great offices (mansab) which are the guiding thread
of the spiritual and temporal worlds, have been conferred on the opener
of the hoards of wisdom and claviger of Divine treasuries, a small portion
at least—if his holy nature grant the necessary faculty—may be brought
from the ambush of concealment to the asylum of publicity. Knowest thou
at all who is this world-girdling luminary and radiant spirit? Or whose
august advent has bestowed this grace? 'Tis he who by virtue of his enlightenment and truth is the world-protecting sovereign of our age, to wit,
that Lord (Shāhanshāh) of the hosts of sciences—theater of God's power
—station of infinite bounties—unique of the eternal temple—confidant of
the dais of unity—jewel of the imperial mine—bezel of God's signet-ring
—glory of the Gurgān family—lamp of the tribe of Tīmūr—lord of incomparable mystery—heir of Humāyūn's throne—origin of the canons
of world-government—author of universal conquest—shining forehead
of the morning of guidance—focus of the sun of holiness—[etc., etc.] . . .
Akbar.

PART FIVE

SIKHISM

CHAPTER XX

THE RELIGION AND SOCIAL
ORGANIZATION OF THE SIKHS

Sikhism is the religion of some six and a quarter million Indians. The homeland of the Sikhs is the Sutlej valley, the region around Amritsar, Jullundur, and Ludhiana, in the Punjab. Smaller numbers of Sikhs, in service or commerce, are to be found in many other parts of India, especially since the exodus from West Pakistan at the time of partition. The Sikhs are not racially distinct from other Punjabis, from whose main stocks they are drawn.

Sikhism began as one of the many religious movements called forth in northern India by the confrontation of Hinduism and Islam. What has survived of the teaching of its founder, Nānak, is not so vigorous as that of his predecessor Kabīr, nor so original as that of the later Dādu, both of whom founded small sects which survive to this day. But Sikhism revealed a power of growth, religious and political, not possessed by the Kabīr- or Dādū-panthīs, so that whereas they are today minor sects, the Sikh community is still politically important. Sikhism has a double interest then, as an example, first, of syncretist religious thought in Nānak's teaching, and second, of the clothing of a spiritual idea in corporate institutions.

The Punjab, when Nānak was born (A.D. 1469), had been for four centuries under Muslim rule and influence. More particularly, from the thirteenth century onward the Sufi orders had been active, first the Chishti and Suhrawadi, and then the Qadiri and Naqshbandi orders. The teaching and shrines of the Sufi saints alike were venerated—by Hindus as well as by Muslims. The Punjab was also influenced profoundly by the Bhakti movement, that outburst of devotional religion which swept across India, a vigorous Hindu reaction to the shock of persecution and the monotheistic teaching of the Muslim invaders.

Between the two movements, Sufi and Bhakti, for both of which doctrine was unimportant and the personal, emotional relation of the individual to God vital, there was much in common. The three successive exponents in northern India of this new religious approach were a Muslim, Kabīr (1440–1518), a Hindu, Nānak (1469–1538), and a Muslim, Dādu (1544–1603). All three used a common Bhakti vocabulary to preach a message which, under different emphasis, remained at root the same. Indeed the Sikh and Dādūpanthī scriptures incorporate much of Kabīr's teaching and verse. Both Hindus and Muslims were attracted by their preaching, and the popular accounts of Kabīr and Nānak picture Muslims and Hindus claiming the bodies of the dead teachers as theirs to bury and to cherish.

So far did the *rapprochement* go that the orthodox on either side took alarm. At the very moment when, under Aurangzib, orthodox Muslims were acting to restrain the Sufis, orthodox Hindus were denouncing the Sikh gurus for betraying Hinduism. As Dādu cried: "Fierce and terrible have they become, when they saw I was of neither faction."[1]

NĀNAK AND HIS TEACHING

The founder of Sikhism, Nānak, was a Hindu and a kshatriya. His native village, largely Hindu, had a Muslim zamīndār (landholder), however, and it is said that a Muslim neighbor provided for Nānak's further education after he had finished the schooling given by the village pandit.[2] Nānak married a Hindu girl, who bore him two sons, and possibly a daughter also. Through his brother-in-law's influence he secured a job as storekeeper in the service of Daulat Khān Lodi, the great Afghan governor of the province.

Nānak's early life thus illustrates the interdependence of Muslims and Hindus in the Punjab. The accounts of his life also speak of his early interest in the teachings of wandering ascetics; Muhsin-i-Fānī[3] suggests that Nānak, a Hindu, finally decided to adopt the wandering religious life at the prompting of a Muslim darwish. Leaving the service of Daulat Khān Lodi in early middle age, he abandoned his wife and family, and, accompanied by a Muslim musician, Mardāna, began a period of wandering which traditionally took him all over India, to Ceylon, and even to

[1] W. G. Orr, *A Sixteenth-century Indian Mystic,* p. 63.
[2] Ghulām Husayn Khān Tabātabā'i, *Siyar-ul-Mutaak-khirin,* I, 110.
[3] Muhsin-i-Fānī, *Dabistān-i-Mazāhib,* II, 247–48.

Mecca and Medina. At intervals he revisited the Punjab where he spent the last ten or fifteen years of his life at Kartarpur, a newly founded "Sikh" village. There he lived with his family as a householder,[4] preaching in the villages and teaching the disciples gathered round him, until his death in 1538.

Nānak was not a systematic theologian, and his thought, drawn from many sources, is not always coherent. But his personal working faith proclaims insistently the majesty and unity of God, the comparative insignificance of prophets or avatārs, the fleeting vanity of worldly life, and the need to approach God in fear and love. God creates, God disposes, but God is gracious. All can approach Him, therefore, in a spirit of service and devotion, without which all formal ritual is worthless.

God, and the worship of God, rather than man's salvation, is at the center of Nānak's preaching. His Being is beyond men's capacity to know, relate, or understand, shrouded in mystery, "The Unseen, Infinite, Inaccessible, Inapprehensible God."[5] But if there is something here of the Hindu attitude (or the Mu'tazilite), defining God by negatives until God becomes a mere philosophical abstraction, normally Nānak stresses the reality of God, whose power and glory are displayed in His creation. "There is but one God whose name is true, the Creator."[6] Here the influence of Islam is evident and strong. And it is seen again in the vision of God sustaining and disposing by His will. This transcendence and omnipotence are carried indeed to the logical conclusion of orthodox Islam, to predestination and a fatalistic acceptance of God's decree.

But the background of Nānak's thought is Hindu—the metaphors and basic concepts of Hinduism come naturally to him. So, though in his writings as a whole, the vision of God the Creator is dominant, there are also passages about the immanence of God—"He Himself is the Relisher; He Himself is the relish; He Himself is the Enjoyer"[7]—which strike a quite different note. In the same way he accepts the Hindu doctrines of māyā and rebirth, though forcing them into a form which is scarcely reconcilable with Hindu philosophy. Thus the almost autonomous system of karma to which that philosophy consigns men is in Nānak made subject to the will of God. The round of transmigration becomes a punishment, a hell, to which God may condemn men, but from which, whatever

[4] Bhāi Gurdās, War, I, 38.　　[5] M. A. Macauliffe, The Sikh Religion, I, 330.
[6] Ibid., I, 195.　　[7] Ibid., I, 265.

his burden of evil action, God in His grace may save man. "Even if he be drowning in sin, God will still take care of him." [8]

What then is the relationship of men and God? It has already been suggested that for the Muslim "the reason for man's existence on earth, the purpose of his daily life, was submission to and worship of the One God, the Omnipotent." Nānak, when he is thinking of God as omnipotent, likewise urges absolute and joyful submission. He stresses man's weakness, his own consciousness of failure or sin, and his consequent wholeome fear of the Lord.

But he also thinks of God as a loving God—a bestower of unmerited grace:

As a herdsman guardeth and keepeth watch over his cattle,
So God day and night cherisheth and guardeth man and keepeth him in happiness.
O Thou compassionate to the poor, I seek Thy protection; look on me with favor.[9]

In this mood Nānak throws himself upon God's mercy, calling upon Him also to pity all suffering humans.

But Nānak does not conceive of man as merely passive. Man may be misled by māyā—but here māyā is not that pure illusion of Vedantic monism which keeps man from the realization that God alone exists, but something much nearer the Puritans' view of a snare and a delusion. If man chooses the world, the flesh, and the devil, he is to some degree responsible; Nānak contritely recognizes that he has sinned, if only by omission, "I have done no good act." [10] He outlines how responsible men should act in this world so as to "abide pure amid the impurities of the world." [11]

There is no constant belief, however, in human free will, and even where man chooses the good life, he is still utterly dependent upon God's grace. He cannot earn, still less compel the gift of salvation. "God cannot be overcome by other ceremonial acts." [12] Nevertheless, worship and devotion are given as the means of approaching God. He is in fact bounteous, the great giver, but even if He were not, wholehearted devotion would be man's only way.

---

[8] Macauliffe, *The Sikh Religion*, I, p. 107.   [9] *Ibid.*, p. 301.
[10] *Ibid.*, p. 178.   [11] *Ibid.*, p. 60.   [12] *Ibid.*, I, 308.

Man can avoid entanglement in māyā by surrender and devotion to God.

> By obeying Him wisdom and understanding enter the mind.
> By hearing the Name [God revealed] sorrow and sin are no more.[13]

But God does not reveal Himself directly, nor can man learn to love the Creator unaided. A mediator is needed between the transcendent Lord and man. That mediator is the guru.

With Nānak, who had no human guru of his own, the word is used less of human guides than for God Himself, for the Holy Spirit. But his teaching accorded well with the ancient Hindu doctrine of the teacher being all in all for the pupil, with the emphasis on the relationship of pīr and murīd among Sufis, even perhaps with the Shī'a doctrine of the Imām. The doctrine of the guru was one destined to grow in importance in Sikhism.

Finally, what of the negative, the puritan, aspect of Nānak's teaching? There is an attack upon whatever sunders man from the One True Name —pride in book learning, pride in fasts and penances, pride in ritual purity or the five prayers daily made. There is an attack upon whatever is set up as a substitute for God, whether it be prophet or avatār. There is an attack upon whatever distracts—wealth, leisure, even family ties. And there is the most relentless attack upon idol worship.

Kabīr had been a trenchant iconoclast: "The beads are of wood, the gods of stone, the Jumnā of water. Rāma and Krishna are dead. The four Vedas are fictitious stories." [14] Nānak's monotheism is not quite so unqualified. Sometimes he echoes Kabīr, pointing out the inconsistencies in the four Vedas,[15] the false lesson taught in the *Rāmāyaṇa* and *Mahābhārata*.[16] He several times makes the point contained in the lines

> At God's gate there dwelt thousands of Muhammads, thousands of Brahmas,
>   of Vishnus, and of Shivs
> There is one Lord over all spiritual lords, the Creator, whose name is true.[17]

But the Prophet, or the Hindu Gods, though created, have a reality, and honest worship of them has some value. It is hard to be a good Muslim or Hindu, hard to give alms, fast, or say one's prayers meaningfully, but to be or do so is good. Caste, which he treats as irrelevant, is seen as a source

---

[13] *Ibid.*, I, 201.   [14] G. H. Westcott, *Kabir and the Kabir Panth*, p. 58.
[15] Macauliffe, *The Sikh Religion*, I, 236.   [16] *Ibid.*, I, 269.   [17] *Ibid.*, I, 40–41.

of spiritual pride. In all of these what Nānak deplores is the confusion of outward form for inner purpose. "Thou shalt not go to heaven by lip service, it is by the practice of truth thou shalt be delivered." [18]

NĀNAK

The teachings of Nānak, which have come down in the *Ādi Granth,* are in the form of hymns and of sayings, often short and pithy, which are made more memorable by being in vigorous verse. His verses, like those of all the gurus, are often repetitious, for they represent his preaching to many different audiences, and to unlettered villagers at that.

Sikhs hold that the essence of Nānak's teaching is found in the Japji, or morning prayer. From it, the opening invocation, three of the thirty-eight verses, and the conclusion are given below. Here we find Nānak's conception of God, the transcendent Creator, the Disposer of all things; and also his view of man, predestined, sinful, brought to judgment.

[From M. A. Macauliffe, *The Sikh Religion,* I, 195–98, 204, 217]

There is but one God, whose name is true, the Creator, devoid of fear and enmity, immortal, unborn, self-existent; God the great and bountiful. Repeat His Name.

The True One was in the beginning, the True One was in the primal age, The True One is now also, O Nānak; the True One also shall be. By His order bodies are produced; His order cannot be described. By His order souls are infused into them; by His order greatness is obtained. By His order men are high or low; by His order they obtain preordained pain or pleasure. By His order some obtain their reward; by His order others must ever wander in transmigration. All are subject to His order; none is exempt from it. He who understandeth God's order, O Nānak, is never guilty of egoism.

[pp. 195–96]

. . . .

True is the Lord, true is His name; it is uttered with endless love. People pray and beg, "Give us, give us"; the Giver giveth His gifts;

[18] Macauliffe, *The Sikh Religion,* I, 39.

Then what can we offer Him whereby His court may be seen?

What words shall we utter with our lips, on hearing which He may love us?

At the ambrosial hour of morning meditate on the true Name and God's greatness.

The Kind One will give us a robe of honor, and by His favor we shall reach the gate of salvation.

Nānak, we shall thus know that God is altogether true.   [pp. 197-98]

. . . .

Numberless are the fools appallingly blind;

Numberless are the thieves and devourers of others' property;

Numberless are those who establish their sovereignty by force;

Numberless the cut-throats and murderers;

Numberless the liars who roam about lying;

Numberless the filthy who enjoy filthy gain;

Numberless the slandered who carry loads of calumny on their heads;

Nānak thus describeth the degraded.

So lowly am I, I cannot even once be a sacrifice unto Thee.

Whatever pleaseth Thee is good.

O Formless One, Thou art ever secure.   [p. 204]

. . . .

Merits and demerits shall be read out in the presence of the Judge.

According to men's acts, some shall be near, and others distant from God.

They who have pondered on the Name and departed after the completion of their toil,

Shall have their countenances made bright, O Nānak; how many shall be emancipated in company with them!   [p. 217]

The Guru and the Ungodly
[From Macauliffe, *The Sikh Religion*, I, 228, 272-83, 326-31]

As a fish out of water, so is the infidel—dying of thirst.

If thy breath be drawn in vain, O Man, thou shalt die without God.

O Man, repeat God's name and praises;

But how shalt thou obtain this pleasure without the guru? It is the guru who uniteth man with God.

Meeting the society of holy men is as a pilgrimage for the holy.
[pp. 330–31]

. . . .

Man is led astray by the reading of words; ritualists are very proud.
What availeth it to bathe at a place of pilgrimage, if the filth of pride be
    in the heart?
Who but the guru can explain that the King and Emperor dwelleth in
    the heart?
All men err; it is only the great Creator who erreth not.
He who admonisheth his heart under the guru's instruction shall love the
    Lord.
Nānak, he whom the incomparable Word hath caused to meet God, shall
    not forget the True One.   [pp. 272–73]

. . . .

The Hindus have forgotten God, and are going the wrong way.
They worship according to the instruction of Nārad.
They are blind and dumb, the blindest of the blind.
The ignorant fools take stones and worship them.
O Hindus, how shall the stone which itself sinketh carry you across?
[p. 326]

. . . .

What power hath caste? It is the reality that is tested.
Poison may be held in the hand, but man dieth if he eat it.
The sovereignty of the True One is known in every age.
He who obeyeth God's order shall become a noble in His court. [p. 283]

They who have meditated on God as the truest of the true, have done real
    worship and are contented;
They have refrained from evil, done good deeds, and practiced honesty;
They have lived on a little corn and water, and burst the entanglements of
    the world.
Thou art the great Bestower; ever Thou givest gifts which increase a
    quarterfold.
They who have magnified the great God have found Him. [p. 228]

THE DEVELOPMENT OF SIKHISM AS A DISTINCT RELIGION

Tolerance, a belief that there are many roads to God, is a feature of Hinduism. The Bhakti and Sufi movements both subordinated doctrine to the establishment of a direct communion with God. Akbar attempted an eclectic approach; Dārā Shikōh argued that nothing separated Muslim and Hindu but terminological differences. Kabīr or Dādu called God indifferently Allāh, Rāma, Karīm. For his part Nānak probably sought neither to fuse Islam and Hinduism, nor to found a new religion of his own. He did allow that the Muslim or Hindu who lived up to the best in his creed achieved something—but of incomparably less value than the worship of the True Name. God was within—the externals of Islam or Hinduism could not lead man to Him. On the other hand, as far as the records go, he did little or nothing to organize those whose spirit he had quickened, to prescribe for them a distinctive way of life, or a distinctive form or ritual of worship.

Yet Nānak's personal influence did not die away; Sikhism emerged as a distinct religion. Nānak's personal rejection of the ascetic life, and of his son Sri Chand because he had formed a quietist sect, may have been one factor, along with his stress on living the good life in this world, which contributed to a distinctive Sikh way of life. His unusual decision to appoint a successor, whom he regarded as the guru for his followers, certainly was another, for it made possible the emergence of the Sikhs as a separate body.

The guruships of Nānak's first four successors—Angad (1539–1552), Amar Dās (1552–1574), Rām Dās (1574–1581), and Arjun (1581–1606)— passed in peaceful development. Akbar admired their saintly lives and there was no quarrel with Islam or the State. But each added something to the separate identity of Sikhism.

Angad elaborated a distinctive script, Gurmukhi, based on that of the Punjab moneylenders, in which to write down Nānak's life and teaching. He also made the institution of the *langar,* or free kitchen, more important. Under Amar Dās the self-conscious organization of Sikhism went further. It may have been in his day that "the active and domestic Sikhs" were set apart from the ascetic Udasis who followed Sri Chand.[1] By thus barring the ascetic, Sikhism acquired a distinctive social character. Amar Dās, by even greater stress upon the *langar,* possibly weakened caste feeling among those who shared the common meal. He certainly provided a common purpose for the Sikhs who contributed to support of the *langar,* as he did when the great step-well (*bawali*) was built at Goindwal, the first Sikh place of pilgrimage. His appointment of three days in the year on which Sikhs should foregather, his provision of specifically Sikh funeral and marriage ceremonies, his discouragement of sati and indulgence in wine all served further to separate the Sikhs from their fellow Punjabis, Hindu or Muslim. Moreover there were so many recruits, from both communities, as to require the setting up of some twenty-two *manjas* or circles, each under a pious Sikh, where the Sikhs assembled for worship and whence missionaries were sent out. (This congregational worship is perhaps another Islamic contribution.)

Rām Dās completed the most famous shrine of Sikhism, the *amritsar,* tank of nectar, from which the town takes its name, and began the Golden Temple in its midst. He took the significant step of sending out agents (*masands*) to collect funds for this. His successor, Guru Arjun, was still more active in organizing the circles (*manjas*) and the collection of the tithe levied on the faithful through his agents. Amritsar in his day became a center for all Sikhs. His greatest contribution, however, was the compilation of the *Ādi Granth* (first book), the official collection of the hymns and sayings of Nānak and his successors, together with a very large selection from Kabīr and other Bhaktas and Sufis whose message was consonant with that of Nānak. Sikhism now had its Book, which was to receive the reverence among Sikhs given by Muslims to the Qur'ān. By Arjun's day Sikhism had a distinctive language, scripture, ritual, communal life, and center. He himself emphasized this fact:

> I have broken with the Hindu and the Muslim,
> I will not worship with the Hindu, nor like the Muslim go to Mecca.
> I shall serve Him and no other.[2]

This claim, however, conceals the fact that Sikhism was turning more strongly against Islam than Hinduism. Angad and Amar Dās had been

---

[1] Sir J. Malcolm, *Sketch of the Sikhs,* p. 27. (Nānak, Angad, and Amar Dās were all married, family men.)
[2] Cf. Macauliffe, *The Sikh Religion,* III, 422.

zealous Hindus before their conversion, and the writings of Amar Dās, Rām Dās, and Arjun are very Hindu in tone. There were some Muslim but many more Hindu converts. Moreover since the Sikhs were now emerging as an organized community under gurus with great temporal power, there was more likelihood of friction and conflict developing between them and their Muslim rulers. In 1606 Arjun was involved in the unsuccessful rebellion of Prince Khusrau against his father, the Emperor Jahāngīr. Punished with a fine, Arjun refused to pay and was executed. Though Jahāngīr, once secure on his throne, was almost as tolerant in religious matters as his father, Akbar, nevertheless in the eyes of the Sikhs Arjun became a martyr and the Muslims their enemies.

Hargobind (1606–1645) succeeded Arjun at the age of eleven, and obeying his last injunction, assembled a military force about him. There were several clashes with Mughal troops during his guruship, notably in 1628, 1631, and 1634, and conflicts also with the rājas of the Himālayan foothills. The guru had become a military as well as spiritual leader. Later the ninth guru, Tegh Bahādur (1664–1675)—who had served with the Mughals in Assam—was called to Aurangzib's court and offered the choice of conversion to Islam or death. He chose martyrdom.

It was his son, Gobind Singh (1675–1708), who completed the final transformation of the Sikhs into a militant community.[3] His father, he said, had died "to protect the frontal marks and the sacred threads of the Hindus."[4] Now he would uproot tyranny from the land. Gobind Singh's life is a record of continuous warfare, largely unsuccessful against the Mughals, more successful against the hill rājas. But if he failed as a soldier, he succeeded as a Sikh. In 1699 he inaugurated the khālsa, the sworn brotherhood of fighting Sikhs. At baptism into the khālsa, Sikhs were given five signs marking them off from Hindu or Muslim—notably the uncut hair and beard—and received the name of Singh. Their joint drinking from one bowl of baptismal nectar cut at caste within Sikhism. Association with Hindu or Muslim was declared sinful. Paradise was promised to those who died in the Sikh cause.

In the fighting with the Mughals Gobind Singh lost all his sons. He provided in two ways for the succession to the guruship, first, by making

[3] Not all the Sikhs had approved of this conflict with the Mughal authority, either in Hargobind's day or in Gobind Singh's.
[4] Macauliffe, The Sikh Religion, IV, 392.

his obeisance and offering to the *Granth Sahib* (he had added a considerable body of his own writings to the *Ādi Granth*), with the instruction, "Obey the *Granth Sāhib*. It is the visible body of the guru"; [5] and second, by making the khālsa likewise an embodiment of the guru: "Wherever there are five Sikhs assembled who abide by the guru's teaching know that I am in the midst of them. Henceforth the guru shall be the khalsa and the khālsa the guru." [6]

In the institutions of Gobind Singh may be seen the coming together of three distinctive strands in Sikhism, the idea of the guru, of the *Granth Sāhib,* and of the Brotherhood of the Sikhs. Nānak had said, "Through the guru, man obtaineth real life," [7] and the same stress is laid upon the guruship's importance by the succeeding gurus. This was no more than Kabīr had done, however. What gave the guruship such importance was the practice of the guru choosing his successor, to whom he made an offering and obeisance. That choice was made, in the case of Angad and Amar Dās, from among the disciples, on the grounds that these two excelled all others in the completeness of their surrender to the guru's will. Rām Dās, the fourth guru, was the son-in-law of Amar Dās, but even so it was stressed that he excelled in submission and humility. Here was emphasized for all Sikhs, the merit of absolute obedience to the guru. There was also developed the theory that the gurus were in fact one spirit, passing from one body to another. Since from Rām Dās the guruship passed by hereditary succession, it was easy for the Sikh to think of the guru as somehow divine. The gurus, notably Gobind Singh, denounced any such idea as sacriligious, but it persisted. Indeed when boys of five or nine (Har Kishan and Gobind Singh) were recognized as spiritual leaders, it is clear that the idea of incarnation had superseded that of the human teacher.

Something of the same process is seen in the Sikh attitude to the *Granth Sāhib*. To the concept of a book were added the overtones associated with Nānak's mystical use of the words *The Name,* or *The Word,* until the book itself became sacred and an object of worship.

The third basic concept was that of the Sikh brotherhood (compare this with the brotherhood of Islam). The union of Sikhs in cooperative efforts —sometimes opposed by Muslims or Hindus—gave a practical sense of

---

[5] Macauliffe, *The Sikh Religion,* V, 244.   [6] *Ibid.,* V, 243–44.
[7] *Ibid.,* I, 149.

corporate life. To this was added a sense of being elect. Rām Dās cursed those who left the community, and promised the faithful sure salvation. "God himself is the protector of the True Guru, and will save all who follow him." [8] The true Sikh was not merely saved himself, he could save others.[9] The fellowship of these saints was likewise given a peculiar sanctity, until Gobind Singh could equate any five of the khālsa gathered together with the guru himself. These ideas, and the practical organization achieved under the gurus, served to preserve Sikhism and the Sikh community in the very difficult years after the death of the last of the gurus.

ANGAD

The Succession to the Guruship

Little from Angad has survived, but these lines from the Coronation Ode by the minstrel Balwand reflect the growing *mystique* of guruship and the importance of obedience as the prime qualification for it. Here "Lahina" refers to Angad (1539–1552).

[From Macauliffe, *The Sikh Religion*, II, 25, 26]

Guru Nānak proclaimed the accession of Lahina as the reward of service.
He had the same light, the same ways; the king merely changed his own body. [p. 25]
The divine umbrella waved over him; he obtained possession of the throne in the place of Guru Nānak. . . .
Lahina obeyed what the guru had ordered him, and earned the reward of his acts. [p. 26]

AMAR DĀS

The third guru, Amar Dās (1552–1574), was a powerful preacher, who to Nānak's teaching added even greater stress upon the guru—the *human* guru— together with a sharper disdain of Brāhmans and those who reject Sikhism.

[From Macauliffe, *The Sikh Religion*, II, 166–67, 221, 238]

They who turn their faces from the true guru, shall find no house or home.

[8] Macauliffe, *The Sikh Religion*, II, 301.
[9] "He had saved himself and his family, and he shall save twenty one generations, yea the whole world." *Ibid.*, II, 292.

They shall wander from door to door like divorced women of bad character and evil reputation.

Nānak,[1] they who are pardoned through the guru's instruction shall be
blended with God.   [p. 221]

Let none be proud of his caste.
He who knoweth God is a Brāhman.
O stupid fool, be not proud of thy caste;
From such pride many sins result.
Everybody saith there are four castes,
But they all proceed from God's seed.
The world is all made out of one clay,
But the Potter fashioned it into vessels of many sorts.
The body is formed from the union of five elements;
Let anyone consider if he hath less or more in his composition.
Saith Nānak, the soul is fettered by its acts.
Without meeting the true guru salvation is not obtained.   [p. 238]

If the perverse be admonished, will they ever heed the admonition?

If the perverse meet the good, these will not associate with them; they
are doomed to transmigration.

There are two ways—one the love of God, the other of mammon; the way
man treadeth dependeth on God's will.

The believer chasteneth his heart and applieth to it the touchstone of the
Word.

It is with his heart he quarreleth, with his heart he struggleth, he is engaged with his heart.

Whoever loveth the true Word shall receive what his heart desireth.

He shall ever eat the ambrosia of the Name, and act according to the
guru's instruction.

They who quarrel with others, instead of quarreling with their own hearts,
waste their lives.

The perverse are ruined by obstinacy and by the practice of falsehood and
deception.

---

[1] As may be judged from the preceding examples, it was a poetic convention for the
poet's name to appear in the last lines. Use of the name Nānak by later gurus reflects the
belief that his spirit spoke through them.

He who by the guru's instruction subdueth his heart, shall fix his affection on God.

Nānak, the believer practiceth truth; the perverse suffer transmigration, [pp. 166–67]

RĀM DĀS

Rām Dās (1574–1581), the fourth guru, gave further form to Sikh religion by his teaching and direction of the Sikh community.
[From Macauliffe, *The Sikh Religion,* II, 264]

Let him who calleth himself a Sikh of the true guru, rise early and meditate on God;

Let him exert himself in the early morning, bathe in the tank of nectar,

Repeat God's name under the guru's instruction, and all his sins and transgressions shall be erased.

Let him at sunrise sing the guru's hymns, and whether sitting or standing meditate on God's name.

The disciple who at every breath meditateth on God, will please the guru's heart.

The guru communicateth instruction to that disciple of his to whom my lord is merciful.

The slave Nānak prayeth for the dust of the feet of that guru's disciple who himself repeateth God's name and causeth others to do so.

ARJUN

Guru Arjun (1581–1606) wrote a great deal and, unlike the second, third, and fourth gurus, addressed Hindus and Muslims alike.
[From Macauliffe, *The Sikh Religion,* III, 13, 28–29, 64, 311, 422]

I practice not fasting, nor observe the [month of] Ramazan:

I serve Him who will preserve me at the last hour.

The one Lord of the earth is my God,

Who judgeth both Hindus and Muslims.

I go not on a pilgrimage to Mecca, nor worship at Hindu places of pilgrimage.

I serve the one God and no other.

I neither worship as the Hindus, nor pray as the Muslims.

I take the Formless God into my heart, and there make obeisance unto
  Him.
I am neither a Hindu nor a Muslim.
The soul and the body belong to God whether He be called Allāh or Rām.
Kabīr hath delivered this lecture.
When I meet a true guru or pīr, I recognize my own Master.   [p. 422]

Without the society of the saints, man, ever wavering, suffereth great
  misery:
By love of the one Supreme God the profit of God's essence is earned.
                                                                    [p. 311]

. . . .

To the Word and the Name are now added as instruments of salvation bathing
in the Amritsar tank, and the *Ādi Granth* compiled by the guru.

By bathing in the tank of Rām Dās
All the sins that man commiteth shall be done away,
And he shall become pure by his ablutions.
The perfect Guru hath given us this boon.
When we meditate on the Guru's instructions,
God bestoweth all comfort and happiness,
And causeth the whole cargo to cross over safely.
In the association of the saints uncleanness departeth,
And the supreme Being abideth with us.
Nānak by meditating on the Name
Hath found God the primal Being.   [p. 13]

. . . .

Three things have been put into the vessel [the *Ādi Granth*]—truth, pa-
  tience, and meditation.
The ambrosial name of God, the support of all, hath also been put therein.
He who eateth and enjoyeth it shall be saved.
This provision should never be abandoned; ever clasp it to your hearts.
By embracing God's feet we cross the ocean of darkness; Nānak, every-
  thing is an extension of God.   [p. 64]

. . . . .

O my soul, grasp the shelter of the Supreme and Omnipotent God.

Repeat the name of God who supporteth the regions of the earth and the
universe.

O saint of God, abandon thine intellectual pride, understand the will of
God, and thou shalt be happy.

Accept the act of God as good: in weal and woe meditate on Him.

The Creator saveth in a moment millions of fallen ones, and in this there
is no delay.

The Lord is the destroyer of the pain and sorrow of the poor; He reward-
eth whom He pleaseth;

He is mother and father, cherisher of life and soul, and a sea of comfort
for all.

There is no deficiency in the Creator's gifts; He is omnipresent, and a
mine of jewels.

The beggar beggeth Thy name, O Lord; Thou abidest in every heart.

The slave Nānak hath entered the sanctuary of Him from whom nobody
departeth empty.   [pp. 28–29]

GOBIND SINGH

The tenth guru, Gobind Singh (1675–1708), was founder of the khālsa, the
sworn brotherhood of fighting Sikhs. His hymns sound a warlike note.
[From Macauliffe, *The Sikh Religion*, V, 117, 261–62, 286]

May we have the protection of the immortal Being!
May we have the protection of All-steel!
May we have the protection of All-death!
May we have the protection of All-steel!   [pp. 261–62]

. . . .

Thou art the Subduer of countries, the Destroyer of the armies of the
wicked, in the battle-field Thou greatly adornest the brave.

Thine arm is infrangible, Thy brightness refulgent, Thy radiance and
splendor dazzle like the sun.

Thou bestowest happiness on the good, Thou terrifiest the evil, Thou scat-
terest sinners, I seek Thy protection.

Hail! hail to the Creator of the world, the Savior of creation, my Cherisher, hail to Thee, O Sword!   [p. 286]

Finally, as an example of how far Sikhism had traveled since Guru Nānak's day, here is part of Guru Gobind's instructions on the means of salvation.

Have dealings with every one, but consider yourselves distinct. Your faith and daily duties are distinct from theirs. Bathe every morning before repast. If your bodies endure not cold water then heat it. Ever abstain from tobacco. Remember the one immortal God. Repeat the Rahirās in the evening and the Sohila at bedtime. Receive the baptism and teaching of the guru, and act according to the *Granth Sāhib*. Cling to the boat in which thou hast embarked. Wander not in search of another religion. Repeat the guru's hymns day and night. Marry only into the house of a Sikh. Preserve thy wife and thy children from evil company. Covet not money offered for religious purposes. Habitually attend a Sikh temple and eat a little sacred food therefrom.   [p. 117]

LATER DEVELOPMENTS IN SIKHISM

It is evident that in Gobind Singh's day there were many among the Sikhs who clung to Hindu ways, despite the elaboration of a distinctive pattern for Sikh life by the gurus. The years of Mughal proscription, from the days of Aurangzib's attack upon both Hindus and Sikhs, threw the Sikhs into the arms of the Hindus, to whose civil usages and customs they largely adhered. At the death of Ranjīt, founder of the Sikh kingdom in the Punjab, the Hindu rite of satī was observed. Veneration of the cow, never taught by the gurus, led to rigid prevention of cow slaughter. Malcolm stresses the tremendous strength of caste within Sikhism, ruling absolutely over marriage, but also affecting commensality.

This continued drift away from the teaching of the gurus called forth a series of reform movements. First was that of Dyāl Dās (1783–1855), the *Nirankāris* (the formless), who attacked the worship of idols—even images of the gurus. He also attacked the adoption of Hindu marriage ceremonies and pilgrimage. His son Bhāi Dārā did win back the Sikhs to ceremonial conforming to the scriptures. There was also an antimilitarist element in the movement. The *Nāmdhari* movement of Sāīn Sāhib (d. 1862) attacked the introduction of caste distinctions and taboos, satī, and idol worship. Later in the nineteenth century, when Hindu and Christian missionaries were active, the *Singh Sabhā* (or Association) was formed.

Its influence was marked in fostering Sikh education, with particular emphasis on the teaching of Gurmukhi and the Scriptures. Missionaries were appointed and the Khālsa Tract Society formed to distribute religious literature.

One unexpected aid to the reformers was provided by the attitude of the British military authorities. Impressed by Sikh fighting capacity and grateful for Sikh aid during the Mutiny, they freely recruited Sikhs into the Indian army. The army insisted, however, on recruiting khālsa Sikhs; an order of the commander-in-chief read, "Every countenance and encouragement is to be given to their comparative freedom from the bigoted prejudices of caste, every means adopted to preserve intact the distinctive characteristics of their race, their peculiar conventions and social customs."

In the twentieth century the most powerful reformist movement was the Akāli, whose greatest achievement was the Sikh Gurdwāras Bill, passed in 1925, which restored to the Sikh community control of the gurdwāras (temples), which had in many cases fallen into the hands of mahants (priests) who were far more Hindu than Sikh but who exercised a hereditary control. With the intensification of the Indian struggle for independence, the Akāli movement took up increasingly the political cause of the community, the latest aspect of which is the demand for a separate Sikh state in East Punjab.[1]

[1] For a full account of the reform movements, see Khushwant Singh, *The Sikhs* (London, 1953).

India and Pakistan

Scale in Miles

1897	Swami Vivekānanda (1862–1902) receives triumphant welcome on return to India; founds Rāmakrishna Mission.
1901	Death of Justice M. G. Rānade (born 1842).
1905	Partition of Bengal arouses nationalist agitation, in which Surendranāth Banerjea (1848–1926), Bāl Gangādhar Tilak (1856–1920), Rabīndranāth Tagore (1861–1941), Brahmabāndhab Upādhyāy (1861–1907) and Aurobindo Ghose (1872–1950) take prominent part.
1906	Muslim League founded.
1907	Indian National Congress split by quarrel between Moderates and Extremists.
1909	Morley-Minto Reforms grant Muslim demand for separate electorates.
1911	Partition of Bengal annulled. Transfer of the Indian capital from Calcutta to Delhi announced.
1913	Rabīndranāth Tagore awarded Nobel Prize for his *Gītāñjali*.
1915	Death of G. K. Gokhale (born 1866).
1916	Moderate, Extremist and Muslim League leaders agree on demand for a national legislative assembly to be elected on a communal basis.
1919	Montagu-Chelmsford Reforms provide for legislative assembly to begin in 1921. Amritsar massacre.
1920	Death of Tilak. Gāndhi starts first nation-wide civil disobedience movement (suspended in 1922 after outbreaks of violence).
1920–1924	Khilāfat Movement, led by Muhammad Ālī (1879–1930).
1930	Muhammad Iqbāl (1873–1938) proposes separate state for India's Muslims.
1930–1934	Second nation-wide civil disobedience movement.
1935	Government of India Act grants provincial self-government.
1940	Muslim League, under President Jinnāh, demands creation of Pakistan.
1941	Subhās Chandra Bose (1897–1945) escapes to join the Axis powers.
1942	Congress rejects Cripps' offer, demands British quit India.
1945–1947	Amid communal rioting and threats of mutiny, the British Labor government prepares to grant India complete self-government.
1947	India, under Prime Minister Jawaharlāl Nehru (1889–), and Pakistan, under Prime Minister Liāquat Ālī Khān (1895–1951) become independent dominions.
1948	Gāndhi assassinated in New Delhi. Death of Muhammad Ālī Jinnāh (born 1876).
1950	India becomes a republic within the Commonwealth.
1951–1952	Congress Party wins national elections. First Five-Year Plan begins.
1956	Pakistan adopts Islamic Constitution.

CHAPTER XXI

THE OPENING OF INDIA
TO THE WEST

The spreading of European power and civilization over the entire surface
of the globe in recent centuries can be viewed as a continuing series of
intrusions into the cultures of the non-European world. Nowhere in Asia
have the effects of this penetration been more profoundly felt than in
India. Because she was the first to receive the impact of European expansion, and the only major civilization on the continent to fall directly
under foreign rule, the influence of the West on her life and thought has
been deep and lasting.

The first Europeans to reach India by sea were the Portuguese. Their
intrepid captain, Vasco da Gama, landed on the Malabar coast in 1498.
Seventy-five years later we find them received at the Mughal court by the
solicitous Emperor Akbar. In the words of Akbar's biographer: "They
produced many of the rarities of their country, and the appreciative Khe-
dive [the Emperor] received each one with special favor and made inquiries about the wonders of Portugal and the manners and customs of
Europe. It seemed as if he did this from a desire of knowledge, for his
sacred heart is a depot of spiritual and physical sciences. But his boding
soul wished that these inquiries might be the means of civilizing (*istīnās*,
i.e. familiarity or sociability) this savage [unsocial] race." [1] Akbar later
summoned Jesuit missionaries from Goa to expound the principles of
their religion, in which he was much interested, but he laughingly preferred his three hundred wives to the Christian ideal of monogamy.

When the French and British East India Companies first established
their tiny trading settlements along the eastern and western coasts of India
in the seventeenth century, the great empire of the Mughals still held
sway. A century later it had collapsed, and various Muslim and Hindu
chieftains were fighting among themselves for possession of its remnants.

[1] Abū'l Fazl, *Akbar-Nāma* (tr. by H. Beveridge), III, 37.

In protecting their commercial interests the sea-borne Europeans were drawn into the struggle. When in the early nineteenth century the British finally emerged victorious over both the local contenders and their French rivals, they found themselves masters of a population speaking fourteen different major languages, with two-ninths of them following Islam and most of the rest belonging to various Hindu castes and sub-castes, and with small minorities professing Sikhism, Jainism, Buddhism, Zoroastrianism, Nestorian Christianity and Judaism. Onto this cultural crazy-quilt the new rulers of India imposed a pattern of their own—not a religious but a secular one. Law and order, efficient government and free trade, were the new gods, and all Indians hoping for worldly success bowed down to them and worshiped them.

While some Indians opposed and the majority ignored the coming of the new order, others actively abetted the opening of their country to the West. Four representative men, each of whom played a notable part in the history of this period and left to posterity written records of his thinking, are considered in this chapter—one a Hindu merchant of the 1740s and 50s, the second a Muslim aristocrat of the early 1800s, the third a Christian of mixed European and Indian ancestry, and the fourth a brāhman scholar-reformer and founder of a new religious movement. The last two were active in Calcutta in the 1820s—just at the time the British were overcoming their earlier reluctance to interfere with established cultural patterns, and shortly before they took the decisive step of introducing English education.

Although these four men came from quite different religious and regional backgrounds, the question of what to do about the Westerner and his culture was in the forefront of their minds. All showed an inclination toward some aspects of the new culture and (except for the Christian) an aversion toward other aspects, but even in their likes and dislikes they differed noticeably. The attitudes which each reveals in his writings therefore give us unique insights into the complexity of Indian society in this crucial period, and furnish us with valuable clues to the later evolution of Indian thought as it responded to the incessant challenge of the West.

ĀNANDA RANGA PILLAI: HINDU AGENT FOR THE FRENCH

India in the eighteenth century was a land rife with internal dissensions and devoid of any central political power. Muslim governors and Hindu chieftains vied with each other for the remnants of the Mughal empire, while most of the population pursued their traditional occupations in relative indifference to the religious or regional origins of their rulers. Under these circumstances, the scattered seacoast settlements of the European trading companies attracted little attention, except from the Indian merchants who found it profitable to act as intermediaries between the foreign traders and the people of the hinterland.

The Hindu merchant Ānanda Ranga Pillai (1709–1761) rose to a position of great trust and influence as chief agent for the French colony of Pondichéry. Thanks to the diary which he kept faithfully for twenty-five years, we have an almost Pepysian record of the life of the tiny settlement and of its leading Indian citizen. Although most of the diary is a rather tedious chronicle of business transactions and political intrigue, we can find in it occasional glimpses of the attitude of an important Hindu toward his French masters and toward his own society.

One striking feature of *The Private Diary of Ananda Ranga Pillai* is the total absence in its author of national consciousness or sense of political loyalty to fellow Indians, as opposed to Europeans. Trade was his family's hereditary occupation and he therefore entered naturally into a symbiotic relation with the merchants from across the sea. He ardently supported the empire-building ambitions of his sponsor, François Dupleix, and identified the latter's fortunes with his own, regarding Dupleix not as a foreigner but simply as an individual with whom he enjoyed a mutually profitable connection. At the same time Ānanda Ranga remained a staunch and orthodox Hindu, never violating in the slightest the rules of his religion. In this respect he is representative of many generations of Indians from his day down to our own whose interest in things Western remained at the level of externals, and for whom European culture and thought seemed of little importance in comparison with the time-tested value of their traditional beliefs.

ĀNANDA RANGA PILLAI
On the Greatness of Dupleix

It is clear from his diary that Ānanda Ranga Pillai admired the brilliant French adventurer and preferred his rule to that of the Marāthā or Muslim potentates then contending for power in South India.

[From *The Private Diary of Ananda Ranga Pillai,* I, 299–301]

The English have captured the ships bound for Pondichéry, and have received a reinforcement of men-of-war from England and other places. This accounts for their activity; nevertheless they are much troubled owing to their leader, the governor, being a worthless fellow, and a man devoid of wisdom. Although Pondichéry receives no ships, her government lacks funds, the enemy has seized her vessels, she is feeble and wanting in strength, and her inhabitants are in misery; although she has all these disadvantages, no sooner is mention made of her than the nawabs [governors], and other magnates in the interior, become alarmed. When her name is uttered, her enemies tremble, and dare not stir. All this is owing to the ability, readiness, and luck of the present governor, M. Dupleix. His method of doing things is not known to any one, because none else is possessed of the quick mind with which he is gifted. In patience he has no equal. He has peculiar skill in carrying out his plans and designs; in the management of affairs, and in governing; in fitting his advice to times and persons; in maintaining at all times an even countenance; in doing things through proper agents; in addressing them in appropriate terms; and in assuming a bearing at once dignified and courteous towards all. . . .

Owing to these qualities, he has acquired such a reputation as to make all people say that he is the master, and that others are useless individuals. Because God has favored him with unswerving resolution, and because he is governing Pondichéry on an occasion when she is threatened with danger, her inhabitants are confident and fearless, and are even able to defy the people of towns opposed to them. This is due solely to the skill and administrative ability of the governor. If he did not occupy this position, and if the danger had occurred in the times of his predecessors, the inhabitants of this city would be a hundred times more disturbed and terrified than the followers of the invader: such is the general opinion regarding M. Dupleix. Besides this, if his courage, character, bearing, greatness of mind, and skill in the battlefield, were put to the test, he could be compared only with the Emperor Aurangzib, and Louis XIV; and not with any other monarch. But how am I to paint all his high and praiseworthy characteristics? I have described him only so far as my simple mind allows me. People of better capacity could do this more completely than I.

An Astrological Misfortune

Ānanda Ranga was a firm believer in astrology. It struck him as a calamity, explainable only by reference to the stars, that his brother should be so unusually devoid of worldly ambition.

[From *The Private Diary of Ananda Ranga Pillai,* III, 9–10]

Although my brother is thirty-four or thirty-five years old, he has no desire to acquire wealth, and no ambition to figure conspicuously in the service of the Company. He is, further, too retiring to hold any intercourse with Europeans. Far from accusing him, however, I can only worry myself with the thought that God has created him thus, and blame my own ill-luck. The young men of these days become, from their fifth year, thoroughly filled with aspirations. The great desire for employment, coupled, as it is, with a strong craving to acquire wealth, that is evinced by them is quite extraordinary, and is beyond one's comprehension and powers of expression. The very opposite to this, my brother—who is hard on thirty-five—although naturally possessed of the gifts of high culture, excellent parts, guarded temper, winning manners, handsome presence, and fortunate birth, is not blessed with the courage and spirit of enterprise which are indispensable to raising oneself to distinction. It is this defect that induces him to cast aside all aspirations to greatness, and to prefer to remain at home in obscurity. This warp in his mind I attribute to the weak and fruitless star which, according to my horoscope, will cast its shadow over me for some months to come. I cannot but impute to this circumstance his desire to resign his post in that city of Kubera [The God of Wealth], which has recently come under our rule, and to return emptyhanded. This bears out the predictions of astrologers that my career, up to my thirty-eighth year, will not be marked by success. I entertain no doubt as to the truth of their statements, and shall, therefore, not lay any blame at his door.

An Improper Feast

When his arch-rival, a convert to Christianity, gave a public feast for Hindus
and Christians alike, Ānanda Ranga's sense of propriety was offended. The
firm maintenance of Hindu custom his attitude exemplifies was to be a major
stumbling-block to social reformers of the succeeding centuries.

[From *The Private Diary of Ananda Ranga Pillai*, I, 293–95]

This day, there was an event worthy of record. In the village of Reddi-
palaiyam, to the east of Ozhukarai, a church has been constructed by
Kanakarāya Mudali, and he has placed some images therein. In honor
of this, he invited, without distinction, all the Brāhmans, Vellāzhas,
Kōmuttis, Chettis, goldsmiths, weavers, oil-mongers, and people of other
castes; and all Europeans and Christians, and entertained them with a
feast at Ozhukarai. Choultries [hostels] and gardens were allotted for the
preparation of food by Brāhman cooks, and meals for Vellāzhas were
cooked in the house of Agambadaiyans. All the arrangements were made in
strict conformity with the religious scruples of each caste, and the people
who attended received every attention. Meals for Europeans were prepared at Pondichéry, and brought over to Ozhukarai. Tables were procured for them to dine at, and every comfort was provided for them. The
Governor M. Dupleix, and his consort, in company with all the members
of Council, repaired thither, and partook of the banquet. He remained
until five in the evening, and then returned to Mortāndi Chāvadi. All the
people of Pondichéry who went to Ozhukarai enjoyed themselves, and
proceeded homewards in the evening. Neither in the arrangements which
Kanakarāya Mudali made, nor in the supplies which he procured, was
there anything wanting. Nevertheless, despite the heavy cost of the entertainment, and the elaborate nature of the preparations, there was
something which detracted from the splendor, grace, and excellence of
the hospitalities. Persons of every persuasion should abide by the rules
prescribed for them: their conduct so regulated would look consistent.
Although of a different persuasion, he followed the practice of a Hindu;
assembled people of that religion; and gave them a treat which afforded
room for dispraise and derision, and every man gave vent to his criticisms
as he saw fit. If he wished to conform to the rules of his church, and the
commands of his scriptures, he should have entertained only the Euro-

peans, native Christians, pariahs,[1] and such others; whose associations brought them in touch with his religion. Even this would be considered derogatory to one of his position and reputation. However magnificent may be the style of any social act in which one indulges, if it be at variance with the established practice of the community concerned, it cannot redound to one's credit. If a man who has forsaken his religion, and joined another, reverts to the manners and customs of his former belief, he must inevitably draw upon himself contempt.

The Doctrine of Predestination

Commenting on Dupleix's ignominious departure from Pondichéry in 1754, Ānanda Ranga revealed his belief that all a man's thoughts and actions are preordained.

[From *The Private Diary of Ananda Ranga Pillai*, IX, 54]

This great man has been arrested and put with his property on board ship. Such is the fate of the man who seeks his own will without the fear of God; but he who acts with circumspection, and refrains from molesting the upright, escapes falling into sin. But a man's thoughts depend upon the times and seasons. Who then can be blamed? Such is the world. He who is destined to happiness will be wise; and he who is destined to misery will be foolish. Do not the Vedas say so? What was to be has come to pass.

The Collapse of the Old Order

Toward the end of French domination over South India, an inexperienced governor appointed a man of low caste to the position formerly held by Ānanda Ranga. Reflecting on the changes which the French had introduced into hierarchical Hindu society, the diarist commented bitterly.

[From *The Private Diary of Ananda Ranga Pillai*, XI, 318]

In times of decay, order disappears, giving place to disorder, and justice to injustice. Men no longer observe their caste rules, but transgress their bounds, so that the castes are confused and force governs. One man takes another man's wife and his property. Everyone kills or robs another. In short, there is anarchy. Who among the low is lower than a pariah beggar? And what worse can be imagined than for such a one to rule?

[1] A low caste of Hindus in South India.

Unless justice returns, the country will be ruined. This is what men say, and I have written it briefly.

ABŪ TĀLEB: MUSLIM TRAVELER TO THE WEST

Although Europeans had been visiting India since the days of Marco Polo, few Indians had the curiosity or the wherewithal to acquaint themselves at first hand with Europe and its culture. Hindus considered overseas travel to be defiling, and automatically outcast those who ventured abroad. Muslims, on the other hand, were not only free from such restrictions but had the example of Muhammad—a great traveler—and the duty of a pilgrimage to Mecca to encourage them in venturing overseas. It is, therefore, not surprising that one of the first educated Indians to travel to Europe should be a Muslim.

Mirza Abū Tāleb Khān was born in Lucknow in 1752 of Persian and Turkish descent. His mature life was spent in the service of the governors of Bengal and of Oudh, but a jealous prime minister retired him and cut off his pension. Abū Tāleb then sought employment with the British, whom he had assisted in putting down a rebellious Hindu prince. He moved his family to Calcutta and seems to have learned English fairly well, but his hopes of securing a good position were disappointed. He grew very despondent, and when a Scottish friend suggested they travel to England together at his expense, he reflected, ". . . that, as the journey was long and replete with danger, some accident might cause my death, by which I should be delivered from the anxieties of the world, and the ingratitude of mankind. I therefore accepted his friendly offer, and resolved to undertake the journey."

Despite his pessimistic frame of mind, Abū Tāleb seems by his own account to have greatly enjoyed his three years in Europe. No sooner had he arrived in London than he was presented to the king and queen, dubbed "the Persian prince," and lionized by the English aristocracy. He had ample opportunity to observe his hosts, and when writing his recollections did not hesitate to enumerate their national vices as well as their virtues.

The Travels of Mirza Abū Tāleb Khān, written in Persian on his re-

turn to Calcutta, gives us a unique insight into the reactions of an aristocratic Indian Muslim to English life. For the most part a careful account
of the curiosities and customs he observed, the book is remarkably barren of reflections on the cultural and religious foundations of Western
civilization, leaving the impression that as a Muslim he regarded them as
unworthy of serious attention. On the other hand, the lighter side of London life greatly appealed to him, as it has to other Indians since his day.
Abū Tāleb's comments on English characteristics, though superficial, are
important as indicative of the major differences in outlook between the
Indo-Persian culture created by the Mughals and the Indo-British culture
which superseded it.

ABŪ TĀLEB

Muslim Indifference to Learning About the West

Abū Tāleb realized that his interest in Europe was exceptional and correctly
predicted in the introduction to his book that his fellow-Muslims would continue to ignore Western learning out of "zeal for their religion."
[From *The Travels of Mirza Abū Tāleb Khān,* I, 1–6]

Glory be to God, the Lord of all worlds, who has conferred innumerable
blessings on mankind, and accomplished all the laudable desires of his
creatures. Praise be also to the Chosen of Mankind [Muhammad], the
traveler over the whole expanse of the heavens, and benedictions without
end on his descendants and companions.

The wanderer over the face of the earth, Abū Tāleb, the son of
Mohammed of Ispahan, begs leave to inform the curious in biography,
that, owing to several adverse circumstances, finding it inconvenient to
remain at home, he was compelled to undertake many tedious journeys,
during which he associated with men of all nations and beheld various
wonders, both by sea and by land.

It therefore occurred to him, that if he were to write all the circumstances of his journey through Europe, to describe the curiosities and
wonders which he saw, and to give some account of the manner and
customs of the various nations he visited, all of which are little known
to Asiatics, it would afford a gratifying banquet to his countrymen.

He was also of opinion, that many of the customs, inventions, sciences, and ordinances of Europe, the good effects of which are apparent

in those countries, might with great advantage be imitated by Mohammedans.

Impressed with these ideas, he, on his first setting out on his travels, commenced a journal, in which he daily inserted every event, and committed to writing such reflections as occurred to him at the moment: and on his return to Calcutta, in the year of the Hejira 1218 (A.D. 1803), having revised and abridged his notes, he arranged them in the present form.

[Here Abū Tāleb changes from the third to the first person, and laments:] I have named this work . . . "The Travels of Tāleb in the Regions of Europe"; but when I reflect on the want of energy and the indolent dispositions of my countrymen, and the many erroneous customs which exist in all Mohammedan countries and among all ranks of Mussulmans, I am fearful that my exertions will be thrown away. The great and the rich, intoxicated with pride and luxury, and puffed up with the vanity of their possessions, consider universal science as comprehended in the circle of their own scanty acquirements and limited knowledge; while the poor and common people, from the want of leisure, and overpowered by the difficulty of procuring a livelihood, have not time to attend to their personal concerns, much less to form desires for the acquirement of information on new discoveries and inventions; although such a passion has been implanted by nature in every human breast, as an honor and an ornament to the species. I therefore despair of their reaping any fruit from my labors, being convinced that they will consider this book of no greater value than the volumes of tales and romances which they peruse merely to pass away their time, or are attracted thereto by the easiness of the style. It may consequently be concluded, that as they will find no pleasure in reading a work which contains a number of foreign names, treats on uncommon subjects, and alludes to other matters which cannot be understood at the first glance, but require a little time for consideration, they will, under pretense of zeal for their religion, entirely abstain and refrain from perusing it.

Ode to London

Shortly after his arrival in London, Abū Tāleb composed a poem in praise of that city and its beauties. The following is a literal translation from the Persian.

[From *The Travels of Mirza Abū Tāleb Khān*, I, 218–20]

Henceforward we will devote our lives to London, and its heart-alluring
   Damsels:
Our hearts are satiated with viewing fields, gardens, rivers, and palaces.

We have no longing for the Toba, Sudreh, or other trees of Paradise:
We are content to rest under the shade of these terrestrial Cypresses.

If the Shaikh of Mecca is displeased at our conversion, who cares?
May the Temple which has conferred such blessings on us, and its Priests,
   flourish!

Fill the goblet with wine! If by this I am prevented from returning
To my old religion, I care not; nay, I am the better pleased.

If the prime of my life has been spent in the service of an Indian Cupid,
It matters not: I am now rewarded by the smiles of the British Fair.

Adorable creatures! whose flowing tresses, whether of flaxen or of jetty
   hue,
Or auburn gay, delight my soul, and ravish all my senses!

Whose ruby lips would animate the torpid clay, or marble statue!
Had I a renewal of life, I would, with rapture, devote it to your service!

These wounds of Cupid, on your heart, Tāleba, are not accidental:
They were engendered by Nature, like the streaks on the leaf of a tulip.

The Evil of Western Materialism

Abū Tāleb's catalogue of the vices of the English is one of the most interesting
parts of his book. In criticizing their irreligion, worldliness and love of luxury,
he anticipated the argument widely used by Indian nationalists a century later,
i.e., that Westerners were incurably materialistic and therefore unfit to rule a
religious country like India. In fairness to the English, he later added a shorter
list of their virtues.

   [From *The Travels of Mirza Abū Tāleb Khān*, II, 128–31]

The first and greatest defect I observed in the English is their want of
faith in religion, and their great inclination to philosophy [atheism]. The
effects of these principles, or rather want of principle, is very conspicuous
in the lower orders of people, who are totally devoid of honesty. They
are, indeed, cautious how they transgress against the laws, from fear of

punishment; but whenever an opportunity offers of purloining any thing without the risk of detection, they never pass it by. They are also ever on the watch to appropriate to themselves the property of the rich, who, on this account, are obliged constantly to keep their doors shut, and never to permit an unknown person to enter them. At present, owing to the vigilance of the magistrates, the severity of the laws, and the honor of the superior classes of people, no very bad consequences are to be apprehended; but if ever such nefarious practices should become prevalent and should creep in among the higher classes, inevitable ruin must ensue.

The second defect most conspicuous in the English character is pride, or insolence. Puffed up with their power and good fortune for the last fifty years, they are not apprehensive of adversity, and take no pains to avert it. Thus, when the people of London, some time ago, assembled in mobs on account of the great increase of taxes and high price of provisions, and were nearly in a state of insurrection—although the magistrates, by their vigilance in watching them, and by causing parties of soldiers to patrole the streets day and night, to disperse all persons whom they saw assembling together, succeeded in quieting the disturbance—yet no pains were afterwards taken to eradicate the evil. Some of the men in power said it had been merely a plan of the artificers to obtain higher wages (an attempt frequently made by the English tradesmen); others were of opinion that no remedy could be applied; therefore no further notice was taken of the affair. All this, I say, betrays a blind confidence, which, instead of meeting the danger and endeavoring to prevent it, waits till the misfortune arrives, and then attempts to remedy it. Such was the case with the late king of France, who took no step to oppose the Revolution till it was too late. This self-confidence is to be found, more or less, in every Englishman; it however differs much from the pride of the Indians and Persians.

Their third defect is a passion for acquiring money and their attachment to worldly affairs. Although these bad qualities are not so reprehensible in them as in countries more subject to the vicissitudes of fortune, (because, in England, property is so well protected by the laws that every person reaps the fruits of his industry, and, in his old age, enjoys the earnings or economy of his youth,) yet sordid and illiberal habits are generally found to accompany avarice and parsimony, and, consequently, render the possessor of them contemptible; on the contrary, generosity, if it does not launch into prodigality, but is guided by the hand of prudence, will render a man respected and esteemed.

The Strange Notion of Progress

Abū Tāleb's evident surprise at the modern Western belief in progress and the infinite perfectibility of human knowledge reflects the fact that before the advent of the British this idea had not occurred to Indian thinkers.

[From *The Travels of Mirza Abū Tāleb Khān*, II, 165–66]

The English have very peculiar opinions on the subject of *perfection*. They insist that it is merely an ideal quality, and depends entirely upon comparison; that mankind have risen, by degrees, from the state of savages to the exalted dignity of the great philosopher Newton; but that, so far from having yet attained *perfection,* it is possible that, in future ages, philosophers will look with as much contempt on the acquirements of Newton as we now do on the rude state of the arts among savages. If this axiom of theirs be correct, man has yet much to learn, and all his boasted knowledge is but vanity.

HENRY DEROZIO: POET AND EDUCATOR

One of the most brilliant figures in the intellectual world of Calcutta in the early nineteenth century was the Christian poet Henry Louis Vivian Derozio (1809–1831). His father, a successful merchant, was probably of mixed Portuguese and Indian descent, while both his mother and the stepmother who brought him up were English. He thus belonged to that tiny racial group accepted neither by the British ruling class, nor by Hindu and Muslim society—the so-called Anglo-Indians.

Derozio was raised in the Protestant faith and received the best English education available in Calcutta. Nevertheless, his part-Indian ancestry disqualified him from a responsible government post. Finding office work for his father distasteful, he turned for a living to his uncle's indigo factory in the country. There, on the banks of the Ganges, he composed romantic poems whose publication made him the talk of Calcutta at seventeen. Two years later he was appointed assistant headmaster at the famous Hindu College, where the brightest young Bengalis were flocking to learn the new knowledge from the West. Here he found his true calling, and in two years achieved an ascendancy over the minds and hearts of his students that lasted long after his premature death.

Derozio's influence was as great outside the classroom as in. The discussion group he founded, the Academic Association, drew not only his pupils but some of the best minds in the city, both Indian and British. With keen intellect and unbounded fancy he expanded on such subjects as "free will . . . fate, faith, the sacredness of truth, the high duty of cultivating virtue and the meanness of vice, the nobility of patriotism, the attributes of God, and the arguments for and against the existence of the Deity . . . the hollowness of idolatry and the shams of the priesthood. . . ." According to his biographer, these themes ". . . stirred to their very depths the young, fearless, hopeful hearts of the leading Hindoo youths of Calcutta." [1]

Like Socrates in ancient Athens, Derozio soon found his influence on the young denounced by the orthodox as pernicious. Parents kept their sons from attending the Hindu College, and finally the board of managers demanded his resignation. His rejoinder, reproduced below, shows that deep love of intellectual freedom which is one of the best traditions of the modern West.

In another respect Derozio represents the first echo in India of Western ideas and attitudes. His verse carries the flavor of his contemporaries, the English romantic poets, and the sentiments he expresses remind us of theirs. His patriotism is an especially significant example. His poems to India are virtually the first expressions of Indian nationalist thought, and their appearance among other poetry whose inspiration is clearly derivative dramatizes the fact that modern nationalism is essentially an alien importation into the Indian world of ideas.

While battling the bonds of religious conservatism, he died of cholera at the age of twenty-two, leaving a generation of followers to carry on his work. One of his pupils, for example, was the Christian poet Michael Dutt, a pioneer in the creation of modern Bengali literature. His tremendous personal popularity with the youth of his time—despite his linguistic, racial, and religious affinity with the foreign rulers of the land—reflects the growing influence of Western thought among his countrymen. Symbol of the new India that was coming into being, Derozio was the first

[1] Thomas Edwards, *Biography of Henry Derozio,* in Bimanbehari Majumdar, *History of Political Thought from Rammohun to Dayananda,* I, 86–87.

and one of the finest flowers to spring from the implantation of European ideas in Indian soil.

HENRY DEROZIO
Letter Protesting His Dismissal

In 1831 the resistance of orthodox Hindus to Derozio's criticisms of their customs and beliefs culminated in his ouster from the Hindu College. One of the charges against Derozio was that he did not believe in the existence of God. To this he replied:

[From Bradley-Birt, *Poems of Henry Derozio,* pp. xlv–xlvii, li–lii]

I have never denied the existence of a God in the hearing of any human being. If it be wrong to speak at all upon such a subject, I am guilty, but I am neither afraid, nor ashamed to confess having stated the doubts of philosophers upon this head, because I have also stated the solution of these doubts. Is it forbidden anywhere to argue upon such a question? If so, it must be equally wrong to adduce an argument upon either side. Or is it consistent with an enlightened notion of truth to wed ourselves to only one view of so important a subject, resolving to close our eyes and ears against all impressions that oppose themselves to it?

How is any opinion to be strengthened but by completely comprehending the objections that are offered to it, and exposing their futility? And what have I done more than this? Entrusted as I was for some time with the education of youth peculiarly circumstanced, was it for me to have made them pert and ignorant dogmatists, by permitting them to know what could be said upon only one side of grave questions? Setting aside the narrowness of mind which such a course might have evinced, it would have been injurious to the mental energies and acquirements of the young men themselves. And (whatever may be said to the contrary), I can vindicate my procedure by quoting no less orthodox authority than Lord Bacon: "If a man," says this philosopher (and no one ever had a better right to pronounce an opinion upon such matters than Lord Bacon), "will begin with certainties he shall end in doubt." This, I need scarcely observe, is always the case with contented ignorance when it is roused too late to thought. One doubt suggests another, and universal scepticism is the consequence. I therefore thought it my duty to acquaint several of the College students with the substance of Hume's celebrated dialogue between Cleanthes and Philo, in which the most subtle and refined arguments against theism are adduced. But I have also furnished them with Dr. Reid's and Dugald Stewart's more acute replies to Hume —replies which to this day continue unrefuted. This is the head and front of my offending. If the religious opinions of the students have become unhinged in consequence of the course I have pursued, the fault is not mine. To produce convictions was not within my power; and if I am to be condemned for the atheism of some, let me receive credit for the theism of others. Believe me, my dear Sir, I am too thoroughly imbued with a deep sense of human ignorance, and of the perpetual vicissitudes of opinion, to speak with confidence even of the most unimportant matters. Doubt and uncertainty besiege us too closely to admit the boldness of dogmatism to enter an enquiring mind; and far be it from me to say "this is" and "that is not," when after the most extensive acquaintance with the researches of science, and after the most daring flights of genius, we must confess with sorrow and disappointment that humility becomes the highest wisdom, for the highest wisdom assures man of his ignorance.

In explaining the decision of the managers to dismiss him, one of them wrote that it ". . . was founded upon the expediency of yielding to popular clamor, the justice of which it was not incumbent on them to investigate." At this, Derozio hotly defended the principle of academic freedom, then virtually unknown in India.

Now that I have replied to your question, allow me to ask you, my dear Sir, whether the expediency of yielding to popular clamor can be offered in justification of the measures adopted by the Native [Indian] Managers of the College towards me? Their proceedings certainly do not record any condemnation of me, but does it not look very like condemnation of a man's conduct and character to dismiss him from office when popular clamor is against him? Vague reports and unfounded rumors went abroad concerning me; the Native Managers confirm them by acting towards me as they have done. Excuse my saying it, but I believe there was a determination on their part to get rid of me, not to satisfy popular clamor, but their own bigotry. Had my religion and morals been investigated by them, they could have had no grounds to proceed against me. They therefore thought it most expedient to make no enquiry, but with anger and precipitation to remove me from the institution. The slovenly manner in which they have done so is a sufficient indication of the spirit by which they were moved; for in their rage they have forgotten what was due even to common decency. Every person who has heard of the way in which they have acted is indignant; but to complain of their injustice would be paying them a greater compliment than they deserve.

In concluding this letter allow me to apologize for its inordinate length, and to repeat my thanks for all that you have done for me in the unpleasant affair by which it has been occasioned.

I remain, etc.,

H. L. V. Derozio

India's Youth—The Hope of Her Future

That Derozio greatly enjoyed his work as an educator is clear from the following two sonnets. He placed his hopes on the young men then growing to maturity; where he failed to overcome the forces of orthodoxy, they would succeed. It is interesting to note the contradiction between his gloomy picture of India's past as a "tyrant's den" and his romantic picture of her former glories. In this respect Derozio foreshadows the mental conflict of later Indian nationalists as they sought to rid their country of the evils of the past, and at the same time to bolster their claim to self-rule by glorifying an ancient and honorable national heritage.

[From Bradley-Birt, *Poems of Henry Derozio,* pp. 43, 120]

SONNET TO THE PUPILS OF THE HINDU COLLEGE

Expanding like the petals of young flowers
I watch the gentle opening of your minds,
And the sweet loosening of the spell that binds
Your intellectual energies and powers,
That stretch (like young birds in soft summer hours)
Their wings, to try their strength. O, how the winds
Of circumstances, and freshening April showers
Of early knowledge, and unnumbered kinds
Of new perceptions shed their influence;
And how you worship truth's omnipotence.
What joyance rains upon me, when I see
Fame in the mirror of futurity,
Weaving the chaplets you have yet to gain,
Ah! then I feel I have not lived in vain.

SONNET

Your hand is on the helm—guide on young men
The bark that's freighted with your country's doom.
Your glories are but budding; they shall bloom
Like fabled amaranths Elysian, when
The shore is won, even now within your ken,
And when your torch shall dissipate the gloom
That long has made your country but a tomb,
Or worse than tomb, the priest's, the tyrant's den.
Guide on, young men; your course is well begun;
Hearts that are tuned to holiest harmony
With all that e'en in thought is good, must be
Best formed for deeds like those which shall be done
But you hereafter till your guerdon's won
And that which now is hope becomes reality.

Poems to India

Taking his cue from the patriotism of the Irish and English romantic poets,
Derozio dedicated two sonnets to India. These poems are virtually the first
expression of the sentiment of Indian nationalism which in the twentieth century
was to force the British to grant independence to India and Pakistan.
[From Bradley-Birt, *Poems of Henry Derozio,* pp. 1, 2]

THE HARP OF INDIA

Why hang'st thou lonely on yon withered bough?
    Unstrung, forever, must thou there remain?
Thy music once was sweet—who hears it now?
    Why doth the breeze sigh over thee in vain?—
    Silence hath bound thee with her fatal chain;
Neglected, mute and desolate art thou
    Like ruined monument on desert plain—
O! many a hand more worthy far than mine
    Once thy harmonious chords to sweetness gave,
And many a wreath for them did Fame entwine
    Of flowers still blooming on the minstrel's grave;
Those hands are cold—but if thy notes divine

> May be by mortal wakened once again,
> Harp of my country, let me strike the strain!

TO INDIA—MY NATIVE LAND

> My country! in thy day of glory past
> A beauteous halo circled round thy brow,
> And worshiped as a deity thou wast.
> Where is that glory, where that reverence now?
> Thy eagle pinion is chained down at last,
> And groveling in the lowly dust art thou:
> Thy minstrel hath no wreath to weave for thee
> Save the sad story of thy misery!
> Well—let me dive into the depths of time,
> And bring from out the ages that have rolled
> A few small fragments of those wrecks sublime,
> Which human eye may never more behold;
> And let the guerdon of my labor be
> My fallen country! one kind wish from thee!

RĀMMOHUN ROY: THE FATHER OF MODERN INDIA

Born of devout brāhman parents in 1772, Rāmmohun Roy showed an early interest in religious questions. An insatiable student, he mastered Persian, as had his forefathers, in order to qualify for government service, and read Euclid, Aristotle, and the Qur'ān in Arabic. At his mother's wish he next steeped himself in Sanskrit learning at Banaras, Hinduism's major intellectual center. Between the ages of fifteen and twenty he wandered through India in search of knowledge, going apparently as far as Tibet, where he seems to have spent several years studying Buddhism.

Eventually Rāmmohun entered the employ of the British, acquired a remarkable fluency in the English language, and rose as high as a non-Britisher could in the Bengal Civil Service. His success as an administrator and an assured income from landed estates enabled him to retire at forty-two and to settle permanently in Calcutta, then the political and intellectual capital of India.

For the next sixteen years of his life, Rāmmohun threw himself with characteristic vigor into an extraordinary number of projects for the reform and enlightenment of his fellow-men. He was one of the first Indians to found and edit newspapers, publishing them in English, Bengali, and Persian. He started several secondary schools, led a successful campaign against widow-burning, and organized a religious society (the Brāhmo Samāj, or Society of God), which was to exercise a deep influence on the intellectual, social, and religious life of modern India.

Rāmmohun carried on theological controversies with missionaries and orthodox brāhmans alike, and whether he was defending the precepts of Jesus or the teachings of the Vedas, his reasoning was always cogent and clear. So forceful were his arguments against the doctrine of the Trinity that he converted to Unitarianism the Scottish missionary with whom he was translating the New Testament into Bengali.

In the last years of his life he set a new precedent for Hindus by "crossing the black waters" to England, where he represented the powerless emperor of Delhi. While in London, he presented to a committee of Parliament recommendations on ways to improve the government of India, was given a dinner by the directors of the East India Company, and was everywhere honored as the unofficial ambassador of India to Britain. He died in Bristol in 1833, in the arms of his English Unitarian friends.

The first Indian whose ideas were profoundly affected by contact with modern Western culture, Rāmmohun Roy was also the first to give serious attention to the fundamental beliefs of the Christian religion. Although he rejected Christianity's doctrinal shell, he warmly welcomed its humanitarian message. At the same time, he singled out for attention those classical Hindu scriptures which came closest in content to an ethical monotheism, thereby offering to his fellow Hindus a means of reforming certain corrupt beliefs and practices without losing their self-respect. This strategic reinterpretation of Hinduism forestalled the impending conversion of numbers of educated Hindus who recognized as Rāmmohun did the merits of Christian ethics, for they could now claim that these merits were equally the property of their ancestral faith. For this and his other contributions to the regeneration of Hindu society and religion, Rāmmohun Roy well deserves the title given him by later generations—"The Father of Modern India."

RĀMMOHUN ROY

To the Believers of the Only True God

Rāmmohun Roy's great service to modern Hinduism has been to recover from obscurity the exalted religious ideas which centuries of neglect had overlaid with a hard caking of thoughtless custom and belief. In publicizing those portions of the Hindu scriptures which stress faith in one supreme Being, Rāmmohun attempted to demonstrate that idol-worship was an excrescence, not an essential part of his ancestral religion.

[From *Translation of an Abridgment of the Vedant,* pp. i–v, in *English Works,* pp. 3–5]

The greater part of Brahmuns, as well as of other sects of Hindoos, are quite incapable of justifying that idolatry which they continue to practice. When questioned on the subject, in place of adducing reasonable arguments in support of their conduct, they conceive it fully sufficient to quote their ancestors as positive authorities! And some of them are become very ill disposed towards me, because I have forsaken idolatry for the worship of the true and eternal God! In order, therefore, to vindicate my own faith, and that of our early forefathers, I have been endeavoring, for some time past, to convince my countrymen of the true meaning of our sacred books, and to prove that my aberration deserves not the opprobrium which some unreflecting persons have been so ready to throw upon me.

The whole body of the Hindoo theology, law, and literature is contained in the Veds [Vedas], which are affirmed to be coeval with the creation! These works are extremely voluminous; and being written in the most elevated and metaphorical style, are, as may be well supposed, in many passages seemingly confused and contradictory. Upwards of two thousand years ago, the great Byas [Vyāsa Bādarāyaṇa], reflecting on the perpetual difficulty arising from these sources, composed with great discrimination a complete and compendious abstract of the whole, and also reconciled those texts, which appeared to stand at variance. This work he termed *The Vedant* [Vedanta], which, compounded of two Sungscrit [Sanskrit] words, signifies *The resolutions of all the Veds.* It has continued to be most highly revered by all the Hindoos, and, in place of the more diffuse arguments of the Veds, is always referred to as equal authority. But, from its being concealed within the dark curtain of the Sungscrit language, and the Brahmuns permitting themselves alone to interpret, or even to touch any book of the kind, the Vedant, although perpetually quoted, is little known to the Public; and the practice of few Hindoos indeed bears the least accordance with its precepts!

In pursuance of my vindication, I have, to the best of my abilities, translated this hitherto unknown work, as well as an abridgement thereof, into the Hindoostanee and Bengalee languages, and distributed them, free of cost, among my own countrymen as widely as circumstances have possibly allowed. The present is an endeavor to render an abridgment of the same into English, by which I expect to prove to my European friends that the superstitious practices which deform the Hindoo religion have nothing to do with the pure spirit of its dictates!

I have observed, that, both in their writings and conversation, many Europeans feel a wish to palliate and soften the features of Hindoo idolatry, and are inclined to inculcate that all objects of worship are considered by their votaries as emblematical representations of the Supreme Divinity! If this were indeed the case, I might perhaps be led into some examination of the subject, but the truth is, the Hindoos of the present day have no such views of the subject, but firmly believe in the real existence of innumerable gods and goddesses, who possess, in their own departments, full and independent power; and to propitiate them, and not the true *God,* are Temples erected, and ceremonies performed. There can be no doubt, however, and it is my whole design to prove, that every rite has its derivation from the allegorical adoration of the true Deity; but, at the present day, all this is forgotten; and among many it is even heresy to mention it!

I hope it will not be presumed, that I intend to establish the preference of my faith over that of other men. The result of controversy on such a subject, however multiplied, must be ever unsatisfactory. For the reasoning faculty which leads men to certainty in things within its reach produces no effect on questions beyond its comprehension. I do no more than assert that if correct reasoning and the dictates of common sense induce the belief of a wise, uncreated Being who is the supporter and ruler of the boundless universe, we should also consider him, the most powerful and supreme existence,—far surpassing our powers of comprehension or description. And although men of uncultivated minds and even some learned individuals (but in this one point blinded by prejudice) readily choose as the object of their adoration any thing which they can always see and which they pretend to feed, the absurdity of such conduct is not, thereby, in the least degree diminished.

My constant reflections on the inconvenient or, rather, injurious rites introduced by the peculiar practice of Hindoo idolatry, which, more than any other pagan worship destroys the texture of society, together with compassion for my countrymen, have compelled me to use every possible effort to awaken them from their dream of error; and by making them acquainted with their scriptures, enable them to contemplate, with true devotion, the unity and omnipresence of nature's God.

By taking the path which conscience and sincerity direct, I, born a Brahmun, have exposed myself to the complainings and reproaches, even of some of my relations, whose prejudices are strong, and whose temporal advantage depends upon the present system. But, these, however accumulated, I can tranquilly bear, trusting that a day will arrive when my humble endeavors will be viewed with justice—perhaps acknowledged with gratitude. At any rate, whatever men may say, I cannot be deprived of this consolation: my motives are acceptable to that Being, who beholds in secret, and compensates openly!

The Superiority of the Christian Ethic

As the most learned and progressive Hindu of his time, Rāmmohun Roy was deeply interested in the new religious teachings being disseminated by the Christian missionaries. On reading the New Testament he formed the idea of bringing together only the ethical teachings it contains, leaving out the doctrinal passages—an idea which Jefferson had already put into practice in the West. He opened the volume with the following introduction.

[From *The Precepts of Jesus, the Guide to Peace and Happiness*, pp. xxi–xxiv; *English Works*, pp. 483–85]

A conviction in the mind of its total ignorance of the nature and of the specific attributes of the Godhead, and a sense of doubt respecting the real essence of the soul, give rise to feelings of great dissatisfaction with our limited powers, as well as with all human acquirements which fail to inform us on these interesting points. On the other hand, a notion of the existence of a supreme superintending power, the author and preserver of this harmonious system, who has organized and who regulates such an infinity of celestial and terrestrial objects, and a due estimation of that law which teaches that man should do unto others as he would wish to be done by, reconcile us to human nature, and tend to render our existence agreeable to ourselves and profitable to the rest of mankind. The former of these sources of satisfaction, namely, a belief in God, prevails generally, being derived either from tradition and instruction, or from an attentive survey of the wonderful skill and contrivance displayed in the works of nature. The latter, although it is partially taught also in every system of religion with which I am acquainted, is principally inculcated by Christianity. This essential characteristic of the Christian religion I was for a long time unable to distinguish as such, amidst the various doctrines I found insisted upon in the writings of Christian authors, and in the conversation of those teachers of Christianity with whom I have had the honor of holding communication. Amongst those opinions, the most prevalent seems to be that no one is justly entitled to the appellation of Christian who does not believe in the divinity of Christ, and of the Holy Ghost, as well as in the divine nature of God, the Father of all created beings. Many allow a much greater latitude to the term Christian, and consider it as comprehending all who acknowledge the Bible to contain the revealed will of God, however they may differ from others in their interpretations of particular passages of scripture; whilst some require from him who claims the title of Christian only an adherence to the doctrines of Christ, as taught by himself, without insisting on implicit confidence in those of the Apostles, as being, except when speaking from inspiration, like other men, liable to mistake and error. That they were so is obvious from the several instances of differences of opinion amongst the Apostles recorded in the Acts and Epistles.[1]

Voluminous works, written by learned men of particular sects for the purpose of establishing the truth, consistency, rationality, and priority of their own peculiar doctrines, contain such a variety of arguments, that I cannot hope to be able to adduce here any new reasonings of sufficient novelty and force to attract the notice of my readers. Besides, in matters of religion particularly, men in general, through prejudice and partiality to the opinions which they once form, pay little or no attention to opposite sentiments (however reasonable they may be) and often turn a

[1] See Acts 11.2, 3; 15.2, 7; 1 Corinthians 1.12; Galatians 2.11–13. [Roy's footnote]

deaf ear to what is most consistent with the laws of nature, and conformable to the dictates of human reason and divine revelation. At the same time, to those who are not biased by prejudice, and who are, by the grace of God, open to conviction, a simple enumeration and statement of the respective tenets of different sects may be a sufficient guide to direct their inquiries in ascertaining which of them is the most consistent with the sacred traditions, and most acceptable to common sense. For these reasons, I decline entering into any discussion on these points, and confine my attention at present to the task of laying before my fellow-creatures the words of Christ, with a translation from the English into Sungskrit, and the language of Bengal. I feel persuaded that by separating from the other matters contained in the New Testament, the moral precepts found in that book, these will be more likely to produce the desirable effect of improving the hearts and minds of men of different persuasions and degrees of understanding. For historical and some other passages are liable to the doubts and disputes of free-thinkers and anti-Christians, especially miraculous relations, which are much less wonderful than the fabricated tales handed down to the natives of Asia, and consequently would be apt at best to carry little weight with them. On the contrary, moral doctrines, tending evidently to the maintenance of the peace and harmony of mankind at large, are beyond the reach of metaphysical perversion, and intelligible alike to the learned and to the unlearned. This simple code of religion and morality is so admirably calculated to elevate men's ideas to high and liberal notions of one God, who has equally subjected all living creatures, without distinction of cast, rank, or wealth, to change, disappointment, pain, and death, and has equally admitted all to be partakers of the bountiful mercies which he has lavished over nature, and is also so well fitted to regulate the conduct of the human race in the discharge of their various duties to God, to themselves, and to society, that I cannot but hope the best effects from its promulgation in the present form.

A Counterattack Against the Missionaries

The Precepts of Jesus caused an uproar among the Protestant missionaries in Calcutta, and, because he rejected the divinity of Christ, Rāmmohun Roy found himself entangled in a theological controversy with Joshua Marshman, one of their leaders, for over three years. In defense of his position, Roy published three *Appeals to the Christian Public,* the last of which ran to 303 pages and was replete with citations in Greek and Hebrew. But this long controversy seems to have embittered Rāmmohun Roy, for in 1823 he started, under a pseudonym, *The Brahmunical Magazine; or, the Missionary and the Brahmun,* with the subtitle, "Being a Vindication of the Hindoo Religion Against the Attacks of Christian Missionaries."

[From *The Brahmunical Magazine* (1823), pp. 1–4; *English Works,* pp. 145–47]

For a period of upwards of fifty years, this country [Bengal] has been in exclusive possession of the English nation, during the first thirty years of which from their word and deed it was universally believed that they would not interfere with the religion of their subjects, and that they truly wished every man to act in such matters according to the dictates of his own conscience. Their possessions in Hindoostan and their political strength have, through the grace of God, gradually increased. But during the last twenty years, a body of English Gentlemen who are called missionaries have been publicly endeavoring, in several ways, to convert Hindoos and Mussulmans of this country into Christianity. The first way is that of publishing and distributing among the natives various books, large and small, reviling both religions, and abusing and ridiculing the gods and saints of the former; the second way is that of standing in front of the doors of the natives or in the public roads to preach the excellency of that of others; the third way is that if any natives of low origin become Christians from the desire of gain or from any other motives, these Gentlemen employ and maintain them as a necessary encouragement to others to follow their example.

It is true that the apostles of Jesus Christ used to preach the superiority of the Christian religion to the natives of different countries. But we must recollect that they were not the rulers of those countries where they preached. Were the missionaries likewise to preach the Gospel and distribute books in countries not conquered by the English, such as Turkey, Persia, &c. which are much nearer England, they would be esteemed a body of men truly zealous in propagating religion and in following the example of the founders of Christianity. In Bengal, where the English are the sole rulers, and where the mere name of Englishman is sufficient to frighten people, an encroachment upon the rights of her poor timid and humble inhabitants and upon their religion cannot be viewed in the eyes of God or the public as a justifiable act. For wise and good men always feel disinclined to hurt those that are of much less strength than themselves, and if such weak creatures be dependent on them and subject to their authority, they can never attempt, even in thought, to mortify their feelings.

We have been subjected to such insults for about nine centuries, and the cause of such degradation has been our excess in civilization and abstinence from the slaughter even of animals, as well as our division into castes which has been the source of want of unity among us.

It seems almost natural that when one nation succeeds in conquering another, the former, tho' their religion may be quite ridiculous, laugh at and despise the religion and manners of those that are fallen into their power. For example, Mussulmans, upon their conquest of India, proved highly inimical to the religious exercises of Hindoos. When the generals of Chungezkhan [Chingis Khan], who denied God and were like wild beasts in their manners, invaded the western part of Hindoostan, they universally mocked at the profession of God and of futurity expressed to them by the natives of India. The savages of Arracan on their invasion of the eastern part of Bengal always attempted to degrade the religion of Hindoos. In ancient days, the Greeks and the Romans, who were gross idolators and immoral in their lives, used to laugh at the religion and conduct of their Jewish subjects—a sect who were devoted to the belief of one God. It is therefore not uncommon if the English missionaries, who are of the conquerors of this country, revile and mock at the religion of its natives. But as the English are celebrated for the manifestation of humanity and for administering justice, and as a great many Gentlemen among them are noticed to have had an aversion to violate equity, it would tend to destroy their acknowledged character if they follow the example of the former savage conquerors in disturbing the established religion of the country; because to introduce religion by means of abuse and insult, or by affording the hope of worldly gain, is inconsistent with reason and justice. If by the force of argument they can prove the truth of their own religion and the falsity of that of Hindoos, many would of course embrace their doctrines, and in case they fail to prove this, they should not undergo such useless trouble, nor tease Hindoos any longer by their attempts at conversion. In consideration of the small huts in which Brahmuns of learning generally reside, and the simple food, such as vegetables &c. which they are accustomed to eat, and the poverty which obliges them to live upon charity, the missionary Gentlemen may not, I hope, abstain from controversy from contempt of them; for truth & true religion do not always belong to wealth and power, high names, or lofty palaces.

Hinduism Is Not Inferior to Christianity

Although he urged his countrymen to feel no resentment toward the missionaries, but only "compassion, on account of their blindness to the errors into which they themselves have fallen," Rāmmohun Roy was less than compassionate in his reply to a public letter charging him with having insulted the Christian religion. In this, his most extreme statement in defense of Hindu culture and religion, he advanced arguments which are still widely used in India today.

[From a letter to the editor of the *Bengal Hurkaru* (May 23, 1823); *English Works*, pp. 906, 908]

If by the "ray of intelligence" for which the Christian says we are indebted to the English, he means the introduction of useful mechanical arts, I am ready to express my assent and also my gratitude; but with respect to *science, literature,* or *religion,* I do not acknowledge that we are placed under any obligation. For by a reference to History it may be proved that the world was indebted to *our ancestors* for the first dawn of knowledge, which sprang up in the East, and thanks to the Goddess of Wisdom, we have still a philosophical and copious language of our own which distinguishes us from other nations who cannot express scientific or abstract ideas without borrowing the language of foreigners. . . .

Before "A Christian" indulged in a tirade about persons being "degraded by *Asiatic* effeminacy" he should have recollected that almost all the ancient prophets and patriarchs venerated by Christians, nay even Jesus Christ himself, a Divine Incarnation and the *founder* of the Christian Faith, were Asiatics. So that if a Christian thinks it degrading to be born or to reside in Asia, he directly reflects upon them. . . .

It is unjust in the Christian to quarrel with Hindoos because (he says) they cannot comprehend the sublime mystery of his religion [the Doctrine of the Trinity]; since he is equally unable to comprehend the sublime mysteries of ours, and since both these mysteries equally transcend the human understanding, one cannot be preferred to the other.

In Defense of Hindu Women

In a letter to an American friend, Rāmmohun Roy stated his willingness to support the moral principles preached by Jesus "even at the risk of my own life." Roy actually did risk his life while conducting his arduous campaign against the Hindu practice of suttee (satī) by which widows were encouraged to burn themselves to death on their husbands' funeral pyres. The threats of ultraconservative Hindus notwithstanding, Rāmmohun carried his campaign to a successful conclusion by helping the British to overcome their doubts about proscribing the custom. Having devastated his imaginary opponent by references to the highest Sanskrit authorities, he concluded his *Second Conference Between an Advocate and an Opponent of the Practice of Burning Widows Alive* with an appeal to humanitarian standards of justice and mercy, and a passionate defense of the rights of women.

[From *English Works*, pp. 359–63]

Advocate. I alluded in page 18, line 18, to the real reason for our anxiety to persuade widows to follow their husbands, and for our endeavors to burn them pressed down with ropes: namely, that women are by nature of inferior understanding, without resolution, unworthy of trust, subject to passions, and void of virtuous knowledge; they according to the precepts of the Shastru [shāstra] are not allowed to marry again after the demise of their husbands, and consequently despair at once of all worldly pleasure; hence it is evident that death to these unfortunate widows is preferable to existence, for the great difficulty which a widow may experience by living a purely ascetic life as prescribed by the Shastrus is obvious; therefore if she do not perform concremation, it is probable that she may be guilty of such acts as may bring disgrace upon her paternal and maternal relations, and those that may be connected with her husband. Under these circumstances we instruct them from their early life in the idea of concremation, holding out to them heavenly enjoyments in company with their husbands, as well as the beatitude of their relations, both by birth and marriage, and their reputation in this world. From this many of them, on the death of their husbands, become desirous of accompanying them; but to remove every chance of their trying to escape from the blazing fire, in burning them we first tie them down to the pile.

Opponent. The reason you have now assigned for burning widows alive is indeed your true motive, as we are well aware; but the faults which you have imputed to women are not planted in their constitution by nature. It would be therefore grossly criminal to condemn that sex to death merely from precaution. By ascribing to them all sorts of improper conduct, you have indeed successfully persuaded the Hindoo community to look down upon them as contemptible and mischievous creatures, whence they have been subjected to constant miseries. I have therefore to offer a few remarks on this head. Women are in general inferior to men in bodily strength and energy; consequently the male part of the community, taking advantage of their corporeal weakness, have denied to them those excellent merits that they are entitled to by nature, and afterwards they are apt to say that women are naturally incapable of acquiring those merits. But if we give the subject consideration, we may easily ascertain whether or not your accusation against them is consistent with justice. As to their inferiority in point of understanding, when did you ever afford them a fair opportunity of exhibiting their natural capacity? How then can you accuse them of want of understanding? If after instruction in knowledge and wisdom a person cannot comprehend or retain what has been taught him, we may consider him as deficient; but as you keep women generally void of education and acquirements, you cannot therefore in justice pronounce on their inferiority. On the contrary, Leelavutee, Bhanoomutee (the wife of the Prince of Kurnat) and that of Kalidas, are celebrated for their thorough knowledge of the Shastrus: moreover in the Vrihudarunyuk Oopunishad [*Brihad Āraṇyaka Upaniṣad*] of the Ujoor Ved [Yajur Veda] it is clearly stated, that Yagnuvulkyu [Yājnavalkya] imparted divine knowledge of the most difficult nature to his wife Muitreyee, who was able to follow and completely attain it!

Secondly. You charge them with want of resolution, at which I feel exceedingly surprised. For we constantly perceive in a country where the name of death makes the male shudder, that the female from her firmness of mind offers to burn with the corpse of her deceased husband; and yet you accuse those women of deficiency in point of resolution.

Thirdly. With regard to their trustworthiness, let us look minutely into the conduct of both sexes, and we may be enabled to ascertain which of them is the most frequently guilty of betraying friends. If we enumerate such women in each village or town as have been deceived by men, and such men as have been betrayed by women, I presume that the number of deceived women would be found ten times greater than that of the betrayed men. Men are in general able to read and write and manage public affairs, by which means they easily promulgate such faults as women occasionally commit, but never consider as criminal the misconduct of men towards women. One fault they have, it must be acknowledged; which is, by considering others equally void of duplicity as themselves to give their confidence too readily, from which they suffer much misery, even so far that some of them are misled to suffer themselves to be burnt to death.

In the fourth place, with respect to their subjection to the passions, this may be judged of by the custom of marriage as to the respective sexes; for one man may marry two or three, sometimes even ten wives and upwards; while a woman, who marries but one husband, desires at his death to follow him, forsaking all worldly enjoyments, or to remain leading the austere life of an ascetic.

Fifthly. The accusation of their want of virtuous knowledge is an injustice. Observe what pain, what slighting, what contempt, and what afflictions their virtue enables them to support! How many Kooleen [1] Brahmuns are there who marry ten or fifteen wives for the sake of money, that never see the greater number of them after the day of marriage, and visit others only three or four times in the course of their life. Still amongst those women, most, even without seeing or receiving any support from their husbands, living dependent on their fathers or brothers, and suffering much distress, continue to preserve their virtue. And when Brahmuns or those of other tribes bring their wives to live with them, what misery do the women not suffer? At marriage the wife is recognized as half of her husband, but in after conduct they are treated worse than inferior animals. For the woman is employed to do the work of a slave in the house, such as in her turn to clean the place very early in the morning, whether cold or wet, to scour the dishes, to wash the floor, to cook night and day, to prepare and serve food for her husband, father, and mother-in-law, sisters-in-law, brothers-in-law, and friends and connections! (For amongst Hindoos more than in other tribes relations long reside together, and on this account quarrels are more common amongst brothers respecting their worldly affairs.) If in the preparation

[1] Or Kûlin. An elite group found among certain Bengal brāhman subcastes. Their men were much sought after as husbands.

or serving up of the victuals they commit the smallest fault, what insult do they not receive from their husband, their mother-in-law, and the younger brothers of their husband? After all the male part of the family have satisfied themselves, the women content themselves with what may be left, whether sufficient in quantity or not. Where Brahmuns or Kayustus [2] are not wealthy, their women are obliged to attend to their cows, and to prepare the cow-dung for firing. In the afternoon they fetch water from the river or tank, and at night perform the office of menial servants in making the beds. In case of any fault or omission in the performance of those labors, they receive injurious treatment. Should the husband acquire wealth, he indulges in criminal amours to her perfect knowledge and almost under her eyes, and does not see her perhaps once a month. As long as the husband is poor she suffers every kind of trouble, and when he becomes rich she is altogether heartbroken. All this pain and affliction their virtue alone enables them to support. Where a husband takes two or three wives to live with him, they are subjected to mental miseries and constant quarrels. Even this distressed situation they virtuously endure. Sometimes it happens that the husband, from a preference for one of his wives, behaves cruelly to another. Amongst the lower classes, and those even of the better class who have not associated with good company, the wife on the slightest fault, or even on bare suspicion of her misconduct, is chastised as a thief. Respect to virtue and their reputation generally makes them forgive even this treatment. If, unable to bear such cruel usage, a wife leaves her husband's house to live separately from him, then the influence of the husband with the magisterial authority is generally sufficient to place her again in his hands; when, in revenge for her quitting him, he seizes every pretext to torment her in various ways, and sometimes even puts her privately to death. These are facts occurring every day, and not to be denied. What I lament is, that seeing the women thus dependent and exposed to every misery, you feel for them no compassion, that might exempt them from being tied down and burnt to death.

For Freedom of the Press

In 1823 the East India Company promulgated an ordinance restricting the freedom of the press by requiring all newspapers to be licensed under terms

[2] Kāyasthas, the caste of scribes, second to brāhmans in importance in Bengal.

laid down by the government. Rāmmohun Roy responded by drawing up a memorial to the governor-general on behalf of the Indian community, in which he contended that their loyalty depended on the continuing enjoyment of those civil liberties which had reconciled them to British rule—an argument echoed later by many an Indian nationalist.

[From *English Works,* pp. 441–43]

After this Rule and Ordinance shall have been carried into execution, your Memorialists are therefore extremely sorry to observe that a complete stop will be put to the diffusion of knowledge and the consequent mental improvement now going on, either by translations into the popular dialect of this country from the learned languages of the East, or by the circulation of literary intelligence drawn from foreign publications. And the same cause will also prevent those natives who are better versed in the laws and customs of the British nation from communicating to their fellow-subjects a knowledge of the admirable system of government established by the British, and the peculiar excellencies of the means they have adopted for the strict and impartial administration of justice. Another evil of equal importance in the eyes of a just ruler is that it will also preclude the natives from making the government readily acquainted with the errors and injustice that may be committed by its executive officers in the various parts of this extensive country; and it will also preclude the natives from communicating frankly and honestly to their Gracious Sovereign in England and his Council the real condition of His Majesty's faithful subjects in this distant part of his dominions and the treatment they experience from the local government; since such information cannot in future be conveyed to England, as it has heretofore been, either by the translations from the native publications inserted in the English newspapers printed here and sent to Europe, or by the English publications which the natives themselves had in contemplation to establish before this Rule and Ordinance was proposed.

After this sudden deprivation of one of the most precious of their rights, which has been freely allowed them since the establishment of the British power, a right which they are not, and cannot, be charged with having ever abused, the inhabitants of Calcutta would be no longer justified in boasting that they are fortunately placed by Providence under the protection of the whole British nation, or that the king of England

and his Lords and Commons are their legislators, and that they are secured in the enjoyment of the same civil and religious privileges that every Briton is entitled to in England.

Your Memorialists are persuaded that the British government is not disposed to adopt the political maxim so often acted upon by Asiatic princes that the more a people are kept in darkness, their rulers will derive the greater advantages from them; since, by reference to history, it is found that this was but a short-sighted policy which did not ultimately answer the purpose of its authors. On the contrary, it rather proved disadvantageous to them; for we find that as often as an ignorant people, when an opportunity offered, have revolted against their rulers, all sorts of barbarous excesses and cruelties have been the consequence; whereas a people naturally disposed to peace and ease, when placed under a good government from which they experience just and liberal treatment, must become the more attached to it, in proportion as they become enlightened and the great body of the people are taught to appreciate the value of the blessings they enjoy under its rule.

Every good ruler, who is convinced of the imperfection of human nature, and reverences the Eternal Governor of the world, must be conscious of the great liability to error in managing the affairs of a vast empire; and therefore he will be anxious to afford every individual the readiest means of bringing to his notice whatever may require his interference. To secure this important object, the unrestrained liberty of publication is the only effectual means that can be employed. And should it ever be abused, the established Law of the Land is very properly armed with sufficient powers to punish those who may be found guilty of misrepresenting the conduct or character of government, which are effectually guarded by the same laws to which individuals must look for protection of their reputation and good name.

Your Memorialists conclude by humbly entreating your Lordship to take this Memorial into your gracious consideration; and that you will be pleased by not registering the above Rule and Ordinance, to permit the natives of this country to continue in possession of the civil rights and privileges which they and their fathers have so long enjoyed under the auspices of the British nation, whose kindness and confidence they are not aware of having done anything to forfeit.

The Future of India

With remarkable accuracy, Rāmmohun Roy predicted the rise of Indian nationalism in a letter of 1828 to an English friend. At the same time he indicated that by enlightened and democratic government the connection between India and Britain might be prolonged to their mutual advantage.
[From *English Works*, p. xxiii]

Supposing that one hundred years hence the native character becomes elevated from constant intercourse with Europeans and the acquirement of general and political knowledge as well as of modern arts and sciences, is it possible that they will not have the spirit as well as the inclination to resist effectually any unjust and oppressive measures serving to degrade them in the scale of society? It should not be lost sight of that the position of India is very different from that of Ireland, to any quarter of which an English fleet may suddenly convey a body of troops that may force its way in the requisite direction and succeed in suppressing every effort of a refractory spirit. Were India to share one-fourth of the knowledge and energy of that country, she would prove from her remote situation, her riches and her vast population, either useful and profitable as a willing province, an ally of the British empire, or troublesome and annoying as a determined enemy.

In common with those who seem partial to the British rule from the expectation of future benefits arising out of the connection, I necessarily feel extremely grieved in often witnessing acts and regulations passed by government without consulting or seeming to understand the feelings of its Indian subjects and without considering that this people have had for more than half a century the advantage of being ruled by and associated with an enlightened nation, advocates of liberty and promoters of knowledge.

THE DECISION TO INTRODUCE
ENGLISH EDUCATION

No single act of British policy has had a more lasting influence on the evolution of modern Indian thought than the decision in 1835 to use governmental funds to support education in the English language and to adopt the curriculum prevalent in English schools. The introduction of this system of education had two main results. On the one hand it greatly accelerated the diffusion of Western ideas and the Western outlook on life among Indian intellectuals. On the other hand, both the rapid penetration of foreign ways and attitudes, and the publication of the Hindu classics in English translation stimulated movements defending Hinduism or demanding greater political opportunities for Indians— movements whose leaders often wrote, spoke, and thought in English.

The East India Company, in its initial caution to leave undamaged the traditional bases of Indian society and culture, had decided to sponsor Persian, Arabic, and Sanskrit studies as early as the 1770s. Later when the Company became the paramount power in India, many Indians realized that to get jobs with the new government they would have to learn English, even though Persian continued to be used for official purposes well into the nineteenth century. The more enlightened among them, men like Rāmmohun Roy, saw that tremendous advantages could be gained by direct contact with the whole corpus of Western learning which English education would make possible, and they therefore raised their voices against the antiquarian policy.

The Committee on Public Instruction was slow to react to the growing demand for a new educational system. When Thomas Babington Macaulay (fresh from England and thirty-four years old) was made its president in 1834, the Committee was hopelessly divided between the "Anglicists" and the "Orientalists." The former saw the need to train a host of loyal government servants able to conduct the routine clerical work of the Company. The latter feared that a Westernizing policy would offend the sensibilities of the Indian upper classes and possibly lead to their general rebellion. Seeing that a decision was needed, Macaulay ended the stalemate by supporting the Anglicists with all the weight of his influence and all the power of his pen. As soon as his recommendations were accepted he threw himself into the work of setting up the new system.

The introduction of English education in India has had profound social and political effects. The older elite were gradually replaced by a new class of Indians trained in a foreign language and a foreign culture, able to act as intermediaries between the British and the bulk of the people. Influenced by the secular spirit of English education, the members of this class gradually dropped their exclusive attachment to the religious traditions in which their ancestors had been raised. Breaking out of the mold of caste and custom they embraced Western ideas and standards of behavior. As Macaulay predicted, these men, "Indian in blood and color, but English in taste, in opinions, in morals, and in intellect," led their countrymen in reinvigorating India's regional languages and literatures. At the same time, wherever they went they helped to spread Western ways and ideas in the highways and byways of the land.

English education produced another drastic change in the Indian environment. By providing a common language and a common cultural background for men in all parts of India previously separated by linguistic, regional, and cultural differences, it offered Indians the opportunity of creating a common, modern culture of their own. It was only a question of time until these new conditions of all-Indian unity gave birth to political self-consciousness and to Indian nationalism itself.

A more ominous result was the effect of the new system on the relations between Hindus and Muslims. The substitution of English for Persian as the paramount language of government, diplomacy, and culture throughout the Indian subcontinent was naturally a bitter pill for Muslims to swallow. Resentful of the new order, Muslims tended to ignore it, "sulking in their tents," while Hindus flocked to the government and missionary schools in greater numbers than could be admitted. As time passed, the cultural gap between the two communities widened, until intelligent Muslims realized that English-educated Hindus were dominating the scene, both politically and economically. Long before the Muslims bestirred themselves to catch up, however, their Hindu rivals had begun the task of adjusting age-old beliefs and customs to the impact of European learning, and had moreover acquired a new pride in their own culture which made reconciliation with the Muslims increasingly difficult.

For thinking men in both communities, the introduction of English education ultimately revolutionized their traditional modes of thought and opened up to them a brave new world of almost limitless dimensions. Henceforth they might reject Western culture, they might recklessly embrace it, or they might respond to its challenge by revivifying and rein-terpreting the legacy of the past—but, however they reacted, they could not escape from its compelling presence.

SIR WILLIAM JONES
The Orientalist Viewpoint

The suspension of government support for the study of Persian, Arabic, and Sanskrit was stubbornly resisted by members of the Committee on Public In-struction who had studied these languages and discovered the riches contained in their literatures. These Orientalists owed much to the example of Sir Wil-liam Jones (1746–1794), a brilliant pioneer of Asian studies whose arrival in Calcutta in 1784 gave the decisive impulse to the founding of the Asiatick Society (now the Asiatic Society of Bengal).

The preface to Jones' *Grammar of the Persian Language* of 1771 eloquently stated the cultural and practical reasons why Englishmen should apply them-selves to mastering this tongue. He later had occasion also to praise Sanskrit for its ". . . wonderful structure; more perfect than the *Greek*, more copious than the *Latin*, and more exquisitely refined than either." [1]

Although the Orientalists were defeated on the question of educational policy, their high evaluation of India's classical heritage helped eventually to foster in English-educated Indians a pride in their own past which was of cardinal importance in the nineteenth-century renaissance of Hinduism and the rise of Hindu nationalism.

[From *The Works of Sir William Jones*, V, 165–66, 172–74]

The Persian language is rich, melodious, and elegant; it has been spoken for many ages by the greatest princes in the politest courts of Asia; and a number of admirable works have been written in it by historians, philoso-phers, and poets, who found it capable of expressing with equal advan-tage the most beautiful and the most elevated sentiments.

It must seem strange, therefore, that the study of this language should be so little cultivated at a time when a taste for general and diffusive learning seems universally to prevail; and that the fine productions of a celebrated nation should remain in manuscript upon the shelves of our public libraries, without a single admirer who might open their treasures to his countrymen, and display their beauties to the light; but if we con-sider the subject with a proper attention, we shall discover a variety of causes which have concurred to obstruct the progress of Eastern literature.

[1] *The Works of Sir William Jones*, III, 34.

Some men never heard of the Asiatick writings, and others will not be convinced that there is any thing valuable in them; some pretend to be busy, and others are really idle; some detest the Persians, because they believe in Mahomed, and others despise their language, because they do not understand it: we all love to excuse, or to conceal, our ignorance, and are seldom willing to allow any excellence beyond the limits of our own attainments: like the savages, who thought that the sun rose and set for them alone, and could not imagine that the waves, which surrounded their island, left coral and pearls upon any other shore.

Another obvious reason for the neglect of the Persian language is the great scarcity of books, which are necessary to be read before it can be perfectly learned: the greater part of them are preserved in the different museums and libraries of Europe, where they are shown more as objects of curiosity than as sources of information; and are admired, like the characters on a Chinese screen more for their gay colors than for their meaning. . . .

Since the literature of Asia was so much neglected, and the causes of that neglect were so various, we could not have expected that any slight power would rouse the nations of Europe from their inattention to it; and they would, perhaps, have persisted in despising it, if they had not been animated by the most powerful incentive that can influence the mind of man: interest was the magick wand which brought them all within one circle; interest was the charm which gave the languages of the East a real and solid importance. By one of those revolutions, which no human prudence could have foreseen, the Persian language found its way into India; that rich and celebrated empire, which, by the flourishing state of our commerce, has been the source of incredible wealth to the merchants of Europe. A variety of causes, which need not be mentioned here, gave the English nation a most extensive power in that kingdom: our India Company began to take under their protection the princes of the country, by whose protection they gained their first settlement; a number of important affairs were to be transacted in peace and war between nations equally jealous of one another, who had not the common instruments of conveying their sentiments; the servants of the company received letters which they could not read, and were ambitious of gaining titles of which they could not comprehend the meaning; it was found highly dangerous to employ the natives as interpreters, upon whose fidelity they could not depend; and it was at last discovered, that they must apply themselves to the study of the Persian language, in which all the letters from the Indian princes were written. A few men of parts and taste, who resided in Bengal, have since amused themselves with the literature of the East, and have spent their leisure in reading the poems and histories of Persia; but they found a reason in every page to regret their ignorance of the Arabick language, without which their knowledge must be very circumscribed and imperfect. The languages of Asia will now, perhaps, be studied with uncommon ardor; they are known to be useful, and will soon be found instructive and entertaining; the valuable manuscripts that enrich our publick libraries will be in a few years elegantly printed; the manners and sentiments of the Eastern nations will be perfectly known; and the limits of our knowledge will be no less extended than the bounds of our empire.

RĀMMOHUN ROY

Letter on Education

Having established several schools at his own expense, at which the young men of Bengal could acquire through the medium of English the best and most modern European education, Rāmmohun Roy was sincerely shocked when the government decided in 1823 to found and support a new college for Sanskrit studies. His letter protesting against the plan shows how warmly he welcomed the introduction of Western learning among his countrymen. The superb English in which he couched his appeal, and the fact that Roy represented the most advanced section of the Hindu community, provided the Anglicists on the Committee on Public Instruction with powerful ammunition in their struggle against the Orientalists.

[From *English Works*, pp. 471–74]

To His Excellency the Right Honorable Lord Amherst,
    Governor-General in Council
My Lord,

Humbly reluctant as the natives of India are to obtrude upon the notice of government the sentiments they entertain on any public measure, there are circumstances when silence would be carrying this respectful feeling to culpable excess. The present rulers of India, coming from a distance of many thousand miles to govern a people whose language, literature, manners, customs, and ideas, are almost entirely new and strange to them, cannot easily become so intimately acquainted with their real circumstances as the natives of the country are themselves. We should therefore be guilty of a gross dereliction of duty to ourselves and afford our rulers just grounds of complaint at our apathy did we omit, on occasions of importance like the present, to supply them with such accurate information as might enable them to devise and adopt measures calculated to be beneficial to the country, and thus second by our local knowledge and experience their declared benevolent intentions for its improvement.

The establishment of a new Sanscrit School in Calcutta evinces the laudable desire of government to improve the natives of India by education—a blessing for which they must ever be grateful, and every well-wisher of the human race must be desirous that the efforts made to promote it should be guided by the most enlightened principles, so that the stream of intelligence may flow in the most useful channels.

When this seminary of learning was proposed, we understood that the government in England had ordered a considerable sum of money to be annually devoted to the instruction of its Indian subjects. We were filled with sanguine hopes that this sum would be laid out in employing European gentlemen of talent and education to instruct the natives of India in mathematics, natural philosophy, chemistry, anatomy, and other useful sciences, which the natives of Europe have carried to a degree of perfection that has raised them above the inhabitants of other parts of the world.

While we looked forward with pleasing hope to the dawn of knowledge thus promised to the rising generation, our hearts were filled with mingled feelings of delight and gratitude, we already offered up thanks to Providence for inspiring the most generous and enlightened nations of the West with the glorious ambition of planting in Asia the arts and sciences of modern Europe.

We find that the government are establishing a Sanscrit school under Hindu pandits to impart such knowledge as is already current in India. This seminary (similar in character to those which existed in Europe before the time of Lord Bacon) can only be expected to load the minds of youth with grammatical niceties and metaphysical distinctions of little or no practical use to the possessors or to society. The pupils will there acquire what was known two thousand years ago with the addition of vain and empty subtleties since then produced by speculative men such as is already commonly taught in all parts of India.

The Sanscrit language, so difficult that almost a lifetime is necessary for its acquisition, is well known to have been for ages a lamentable check to the diffusion of knowledge, and the learning concealed under this almost impervious veil is far from sufficient to reward the labor of acquiring it. But if it were thought necessary to perpetuate this language for the sake of the portion of valuable information it contains, this might be much more easily accomplished by other means than the establishment of a new Sanscrit College; for there have been always and are now numerous professors of Sanscrit in the different parts of the country engaged in teaching this language, as well as the other branches of literature which are to be the object of the new seminary. Therefore their more diligent cultivation, if desirable, would be effectually promoted, by holding out premiums and granting certain allowances to their most eminent professors, who have already undertaken on their own account to teach them, and would by such rewards be stimulated to still greater exertion.

From these considerations, as the sum set apart for the instruction of the natives of India was intended by the government in England for the improvement of its Indian subjects, I beg leave to state, with due deference to your Lordship's exalted situation, that if the plan now adopted be followed, it will completely defeat the object proposed, since no improvement can be expected from inducing young men to consume a dozen years of the most valuable period of their lives in acquiring the niceties of Vyakaran or Sanscrit Grammar, for instance, in learning to discuss such points as the following: *khada,* signifying to eat, *khadati* he or she eats, query, whether does *khadati* taken as a whole convey the meaning he, she, or it eats, or are separate parts of this meaning conveyed by distinctions of the words, as if in the English language it were asked how much meaning is there in the *eat* and how much in the *s,* and is the whole meaning of the word conveyed by these two portions of it distinctly or by them taken jointly?

Neither can much improvement arise from such speculations as the following which are the themes suggested by the Vedanta: In what manner is the soul absorbed in the Deity? What relation does it bear to the Divine Essence? Nor will youths be fitted to be better members of society by the Vedantic doctrines which teach them to believe that all visible things have no real existence, that as father, brother, etc. have no real entity, they consequently deserve no real affection, and therefore the sooner we escape from them and leave the world the better.

Again, no essential benefit can be derived by the student of the *Mimamsa* from knowing what it is that makes the killer of a goat sinless by pronouncing certain passages of the Vedanta and what is the real nature and operative influence of passages of the Vedas, &c.

The student of the Nyaya Shastra cannot be said to have improved his mind after he has learned from it into how many ideal classes the objects in the universe are divided, and what speculative relation the soul bears to the body, the body to the soul, the eye to the ear, &c.

In order to enable your Lordship to appreciate the utility of encouraging such imaginary learning as above characterized, I beg your Lordship will be pleased to compare the state of science and literature in Europe before the time of Lord Bacon with the progress of knowledge made since he wrote.

If it had been intended to keep the British nation in ignorance of real knowledge, the Baconian philosophy would not have been allowed to displace the system of the schoolmen which was the best calculated to perpetuate ignorance. In the same manner the Sanscrit system of education would be the best calculated to keep this country in darkness, if such had been the policy of the British legislature. But as the improvement of the native population is the object of the government, it will consequently promote a more liberal and enlightened system of instruction, embracing mathematics, natural philosophy, chemistry, anatomy, with other useful sciences, which may be accomplished with the sums proposed by employing a few gentlemen of talent and learning educated in Europe and providing a college furnished with necessary books, instruments, and other apparatus.

In presenting this subject to your Lordship, I conceive myself discharging a solemn duty which I owe to my countrymen, and also to that enlightened sovereign and legislature which have extended their benevolent care to this distant land, actuated by a desire to improve the inhabitants, and therefore humbly trust you will excuse the liberty I have taken in thus expressing my sentiments to your Lordship.

I have the honor, etc.,

Rammohun Roy

THOMAS BABINGTON MACAULAY
Minute on Education

Following Rāmmohun Roy's letter on education by twelve years, Macaulay, in his famous "Minute on Education," used many of the arguments and even some of the phraseology of his predecessor. His exaggeratedly low opinion of classical Sanskrit and Arabic literature was born of his almost total ignorance in this realm of knowledge. His judgment was nevertheless basically well-intended, for his purpose was not the eradication of non-Western learning in India, but its regeneration through contact with the best learning produced by the modern West.

After citing and giving his interpretation of the Act of Parliament providing for ". . . the revival and promotion of literature . . . and for the introduction and promotion of a knowledge of the sciences" in India, Macaulay continued his argument.

[Macaulay, *Prose and Poetry,* pp. 721–24, 725, 728–29]

We now come to the gist of the matter. We have a fund to be employed as government shall direct for the intellectual improvement of the people of this country. The simple question is, what is the most useful way of employing it?

All parties seem to be agreed on one point, that the dialects commonly spoken among the natives of this part of India contain neither literary nor scientific information, and are, moreover, so poor and rude that, until they are enriched from some other quarter, it will not be easy to translate any valuable work into them. It seems to be admitted on all sides that the intellectual improvement of those classes of the people who have the means of pursuing higher studies can at present be effected only by means of some language not vernacular amongst them.

What then shall that language be? One-half of the committee maintain that it should be the English. The other half strongly recommend the Arabic and Sanscrit. The whole question seems to me to be, which language is the best worth knowing?

I have no knowledge of either Sanscrit or Arabic. But I have done what I could to form a correct estimate of their value. I have read translations of the most celebrated Arabic and Sanscrit works. I have conversed both here and at home with men distinguished by their proficiency in the Eastern tongues. I am quite ready to take the Oriental learning at the valuation of the Orientalists themselves. I have never found one among them who could deny that a single shelf of a good European library was worth the whole native literature of India and Arabia. The intrinsic superiority of the Western literature is, indeed, fully admitted by those members of the committee who support the Oriental plan of education.

It will hardly be disputed, I suppose, that the department of literature in which the Eastern writers stand highest is poetry. And I certainly never met with any Orientalist who ventured to maintain that the Arabic and Sanscrit poetry could be compared to that of the great European nations. But when we pass from works of imagination to works in which facts are recorded, and general principles investigated, the superiority of the Europeans becomes absolutely immeasurable. It is, I believe, no exaggeration to say, that all the historical information which has been collected from all the books written in the Sanscrit language is less valuable than what may be found in the most paltry abridgments used at preparatory schools in England. In every branch of physical or moral philosophy, the relative position of the two nations is nearly the same.

How, then, stands the case? We have to educate a people who cannot at present be educated by means of their mother-tongue. We must teach them some foreign language. The claims of our own language it is hardly necessary to recapitulate. It stands preeminent even among the languages of the West. It abounds with works of imagination not inferior to the noblest which Greece has bequeathed to us; with models of every species of eloquence; with historical compositions, which, considered merely as narratives, have seldom been surpassed, and which, considered as vehicles of ethical and political instruction, have never been equaled; with just and lively representations of human life and human nature; with the most profound speculations on metaphysics, morals, government, jurisprudence, and trade; with full and correct information respecting every experimental science which tends to preserve the health, to increase the comfort, or to expand the intellect of man. Whoever knows that language has ready access to all the vast intellectual wealth, which all the wisest nations of the earth have created and hoarded in the course of ninety generations. It may safely be said that the literature now extant in that language is of far greater value than all the literature which three hundred years ago was extant in all the languages of the world together. Nor is this all. In India, English is the language spoken by the ruling class. It is spoken by the higher class of natives at the seats of government. It is likely to become the language of commerce throughout the seas of the East. It is the language of two great European communities which are rising, the one in the south of Africa, the other in Australasia, communities which are every year becoming more important and more closely connected with our Indian empire. Whether we look at the intrinsic value of our literature, or at the particular situation of this country, we shall see the strongest reason to think that, of all foreign tongues, the English tongue is that which would be the most useful to our native subjects.

The question now before us is simply whether, when it is in our power to teach this language, we shall teach languages in which, by universal confession, there are no books on any subject which deserve to be compared to our own; whether, when we can teach European science, we shall teach systems which, by universal confession, whenever they differ from those of Europe, differ for the worse; and whether, when we can patronize sound philosophy and true history, we shall countenance, at the public expense, medical doctrines which would disgrace an English farrier, astronomy which would move laughter in girls at an English boarding school, history abounding with kings thirty feet high and reigns thirty thousand years long, and geography, made up of seas of treacle and seas of butter.

We are not without experience to guide us. History furnishes several analogous cases, and they all teach the same lesson. There are in modern times, to go no further, two memorable instances of a great impulse given to the mind of a whole society—of prejudices overthrown, of knowledge diffused, of taste purified, of arts and sciences planted in countries which had recently been ignorant and barbarous.

The first instance to which I refer is the great revival of letters among the Western nations at the close of the fifteenth and beginning of the sixteenth century. At that time almost every thing that was worth reading was contained in the writings of the ancient Greeks and Romans. Had our ancestors acted as the Committee of Public Instruction has hitherto acted; had they neglected the language of Cicero and Tacitus; had they confined their attention to the old dialects of our own island; had they printed nothing and taught nothing at the universities but chronicles in Anglo-Saxon, and romances in Norman-French, would England have been what she now is? What the Greek and Latin were to the contemporaries of More and Ascham, our tongue is to the people of India. The literature of England is now more valuable than that of classical antiquity. I doubt whether the Sanscrit literature be as valuable as that of our Saxon and Norman progenitors. In some departments, in history, for example, I am certain that it is much less so.

Another instance may be said to be still before our eyes. Within the last hundred and twenty years, a nation which has previously been in a state as barbarous as that in which our ancestors were before the Crusades, has gradually emerged from the ignorance in which it was sunk, and has taken its place among civilized communities. I speak of Russia. There is now in that country a large educated class, abounding with persons fit to serve the state in the highest functions, and in no wise inferior to the most accomplished men who adorn the best circles of Paris and London. There is reason to hope that this vast empire, which in the time of our grandfathers was probably behind the Punjab, may, in the time of our grandchildren, be pressing close on France and Britain in the career of improvement. And how was this change effected? Not by flattering national prejudices, not by feeding the mind of the young Muscovite with old women's stories which his rude fathers had believed, not by filling his head with lying legends about St. Nicholas, not by encouraging him to study the great question—whether the world was or was not created on the 13th of September, not by calling him "a learned native" when he has mastered all these points of knowledge, but by teaching him those foreign languages in which the greatest mass of information had been laid up, and thus putting all that information within his reach. The languages of Western Europe civilized Russia. I cannot doubt that they will do for the Hindoo what they have done for the Tartar.

Macaulay next showed that the demand for English education was far greater than that for Sanskrit and Arabic.

All the declamations in the world about the love and reverence of the natives for their sacred dialects will never, in the mind of any impartial person, outweigh the undisputed fact that we cannot find, in all our vast empire, a single student who will let us teach him those dialects unless we will pay him. . . . Why then is it necessary to pay people to learn Sanscrit and Arabic? Evidently because it is universally felt that the Sanscrit and Arabic are languages, the knowledge of which does not compensate for the trouble of acquiring them. On all such subjects the state of the market is the decisive test.

[Answering the claims of the Orientalists, he asserted:] But there is yet another argument which seems even more untenable. It is said that the Sanscrit and Arabic are the languages in which the sacred books of a hundred millions of people are written, and that they are, on that account, entitled to peculiar encouragement. Assuredly it is the duty of the British government in India to be not only tolerant, but neutral on all religious questions. But to encourage the study of a literature admitted to be of small intrinsic value, only because that literature inculcates the most serious errors on the most important subjects, is a course hardly reconcilable with reason, with morality, or even with that very neutrality which ought, as we all agree, to be sacredly preserved. It is confessed that a language is barren of useful knowledge. We are to teach it because it is fruitful of monstrous superstitions. We are to teach false history, false astronomy, false medicine, because we find them in company with a false religion. We abstain, and I trust shall always abstain, from giving any public encouragement to those who are engaged in the work of converting natives to Christianity. And while we act thus, can we reasonably and decently bribe men out of the revenues of the state to waste their youth in learning how they are to purify themselves after touching an ass, or what text of the Vedas they are to repeat to expiate the crime of killing a goat?

It is taken for granted by the advocates of Oriental learning that no native of this country can possibly attain more than a mere smattering of English. They do not attempt to prove this; but they perpetually insinuate it. They designate the education which their opponents recommend as a mere spelling book education. They assume it as undeniable, that the question is between a profound knowledge of Hindoo and Arabian literature and science on the one side, and a superficial knowledge of the rudiments of English on the other. This is not merely an assumption, but an assumption contrary to all reason and experience. We know that foreigners of all nations do learn our language sufficiently to have access to all the most abstruse knowledge which it contains, sufficiently to relish even the more delicate graces of our most idiomatic writers. There are in this very town natives who are quite competent to discuss political or scientific questions with fluency and precision in the English language. I have heard the very question on which I am now writing discussed by native gentlemen with a liberality and an intelligence which would do credit to any member of the Committee of Public Instruction. Indeed it is unusual to find, even in the literary circles of the continent, any foreigner who can express himself in English with so much facility and correctness as we find in many Hindoos. Nobody, I suppose, will contend that English is so difficult to a Hindoo as Greek to an Englishman. Yet an intelligent English youth, in a much smaller number of years than our unfortunate pupils pass at the Sanscrit College, becomes able to read, to enjoy, and even to imitate, not unhappily, the compositions of the best Greek authors. Less than half the time which enables an English youth to read Herodotus and Sophocles ought to enable a Hindoo to read Hume and Milton.

To sum up what I have said, I think it clear that we are not fettered by the Act of Parliament of 1813; that we are not fettered by any pledge expressed or implied; that we are free to employ our funds as we choose; that we ought to employ them in teaching what is best worth knowing; that English is better worth knowing than Sanscrit or Arabic; that the natives are desirous to be taught English, and are not desirous to be taught Sanscrit or Arabic; that neither as the languages of law, nor as the languages of religion, have the Sanscrit and Arabic any peculiar claim to our engagement; that it is possible to make natives of this country thoroughly good English scholars; and that to this end our efforts ought to be directed.

In one point I fully agree with the gentlemen to whose general views I am opposed. I feel with them, that it is impossible for us, with our limited means, to attempt to educate the body of the people. We must at present do our best to form a class who may be interpreters between us and the millions whom we govern; a class of persons, Indian in blood and color, but English in taste, in opinions, in morals, and in intellect. To that class we may leave it to refine the vernacular dialects of the country, to enrich those dialects with terms of science borrowed from the Western nomenclature, and to render them by degrees fit vehicles for conveying knowledge to the great mass of the population.

CHAPTER XXII

THE RENASCENCE OF HINDUISM

Just as the Muslim conquest had injected a fresh stream of religious thought into the veins of Hindu society, so the British conquest brought with it new views of the world, man, and God. Confronted with the message of Islam that all believers are equal in the sight of their Maker, religious leaders like Kabīr and Nānak had come forth in the fifteenth and sixteenth centuries to translate this teaching into traditional Hindu terms. Similarly in the nineteenth century a series of creative individuals emerged from the ranks of Hindu society to respond to the combined challenge of Christian religious ideas and of modern Western rationalist and utilitarian thought.

The renascence of Hinduism grew out of the favorable conditions created by the new rulers of India. The establishment of law and order under British administration provided Hindus with an unprecedented opportunity to improve their position vis-à-vis their former rulers, the Muslims. While the latter remained resentful of (and to a certain extent distrusted by) the new conquerors, educated Hindus entered the service of the Christian power in growing numbers. They studied English, read enthusiastically the classics of English literature, and became virtually the Anglicized Indians Macaulay had intended them to become.

Some Hindus became Christians, others clung stubbornly to orthodoxy, while a third group tried to combine the best features of both religions. Rāmmohun Roy carefully distinguished between English virtues and English errors, and defended Hinduism against the criticisms of the missionaries as vigorously as he challenged the orthodox to abandon its excrescences. Rāmmohun's policy of war on two fronts set the keynote for later champions of Hinduism against Christianity. The more deeply they were imbued by English education with a humanitarian outlook, the more keenly sensitive they became when faced with the missionaries' charge that Hinduism was a pagan and idolatrous religion, laden with barbarous customs. In order to defend Hinduism, therefore, they first had to reform it.

The Brāhmo Samāj remained for two generations after Rāmmohun Roy's death the focus of efforts to purify Hinduism and to immunize it against the Christian virus by a partial incorporation of Christian ideas and practices. Debendranāth Tagore first strengthened the Samāj's corporate worship and noble monotheism. Next Keshub Chunder Sen used revivalist sermons and Brāhmo missionaries to spread a gospel which became so close to Christian in its content that his conversion was thought imminent. The initiative then passed to Swāmī Dayānanda, who based his radical social reforms entirely on the authority of the Vedas.

Amid the hubbub of these self-conscious efforts to check the advance of Christian influence, Hindu society suddenly discovered in its midst a genuine saint and mystic. In the end, Sri Rāmakrishna's simple devotion to the traditional concepts and deities of his faith proved a more effective force than all the oratory of his predecessors. As Jesus was followed by Saint Paul, Rāmakrishna had dynamic Swāmī Vivekānanda to preach his "Gospel" to India and to the world.

The Hindu response to the Christian challenge had now come full circle from resistance, through defense by imitation, to proud self-confidence. In large part, the mounting pressure of Western secular institutions and missionary activity on Hindu society was responsible for solidifying the Hindu stand as the nineteenth century progressed. At the same time, the attention and praise which classical Indian thought was receiving from a host of European scholars added considerably to the momentum of the Hindu revival. Many Westernized Indians first took interest in the *Bhagavad Gītā* and the story of the Buddha on making their acquaintance in Sir Edwin Arnold's poetic English translations. Their self-confidence turned to pride when they read the dictum of Professor Max Müller, England's foremost Sanskritist, that in India ". . . the human mind has most fully developed some of its choicest gifts, has most deeply pondered on the greatest problems of life." [1]

Even more encouraging were the growing numbers of Europeans who rejected Western civilization and became rabid partisans of Indian culture. In 1875 the Russian Madame Blavatsky and the American Colonel

[1] F. Max Müller: *India, What Can It Teach Us?*, p. 6.

Olcott founded the Theosophical Society, which held reincarnation, karma, and other Hindu or Buddhist conceptions as central doctrines. In 1882 they moved the headquarters of the Society to Adyar, Madras. Mrs. Annie Besant, the Society's next leader, made India her permanent home from 1893 onward, and took such a prominent part in Indian politics that in 1917 she became President of the Indian National Congress—the fifth and last Britisher to receive this honor. Then came Irish-born Margaret Noble, Vivekānanda's most fervent disciple, who settled in Calcutta, took the name of Sister Niveditā (i.e., the dedicated one), and made a deep impression on Bengali thought and culture in the first decade of this century.

In the last analysis, however, European influences—whether friendly or hostile—of necessity played but a secondary role in the renascence of Hinduism. It was primarily through the efforts of a series of devout and devoted men that this ancient religion was able to recover in such a remarkable manner the deepest sources of its original inspiration. Even though their efforts primarily affected only the Western-educated (a tiny fraction of the total mass of Hindu society), this minority nevertheless possessed an influence far greater than its numbers would indicate. For they provided the leaders of the future—the Tagores and the Gāndhis— whose understanding of their Hindu heritage was decisively shaped by that galaxy of religious thinkers who had preceded them in the nineteenth century.

DEBENDRANĀTH TAGORE: RE-CREATOR OF THE BRĀHMO SAMĀJ

The influence of Rāmmohun Roy on succeeding generations was kept alive by the Brāhmo Samāj (the Society of God), the religious society he had founded in 1828. After Roy's death in England, his close friend Dwārkanāth Tagore, one of India's first entrepreneurial capitalists, gave the little group his financial support, but its numbers dwindled steadily. Meanwhile, Dwārkanāth's eldest son Debendranāth (1817–1905), who used to play in Rāmmohun's yard as a boy in Calcutta, had started a small association of his own which met monthly to discuss religious questions.

In 1843 Debendranāth merged his group with the remnant of Rāmmohun Roy's, preserving the original name but injecting a new spirit into the older organization.

Under Debendranāth's devoted leadership, the Brāhmo Samāj attracted numbers of Bengal's ablest young men, many of them belonging like himself to the brāhman caste. Their spiritual center was the common worship of the one true God. Like Rāmmohun Roy, the Brāhmos (as they came to be called) opposed both the idolatry of popular Hinduism and the tactics of the Christian missionaries. Debendranāth recounts in his *Autobiography* an incident which illustrates his zeal in defense of purified Hinduism. Hearing that graduates of mission schools were becoming converts to Christianity, he called a mass meeting of the leading Hindu citizens of Calcutta and raised sufficient funds to start a free school for their children. "Thenceforward the tide of Christian conversion was stemmed," he wrote, "and the designs of the missionaries were knocked on the head." [1]

At heart, Debendranāth's nature was more devotional than combative. When his fiery young disciple, Keshub Chunder Sen, split the Samāj by insisting that Brāhmos discontinue wearing the sacred thread used by high-caste Hindus, Debendranāth withdrew from active leadership of his remaining followers and spent many months traveling to places of pilgrimage or meditating in the Himalayas. His piety throughout his long life earned him the honorific title of *Maharshi*, "the great sage."

In addition to his work in strengthening the Brāhmo Samāj Debendranāth continued the work, started by Rāmmohun Roy, of rediscovering and reviving Hindu monotheism. To find an authoritative scriptural canon for the Samāj he sent four students to Banaras, each assigned to learn one of the four Vedas. The results of their researches being inconclusive, Debendranāth came increasingly to rely on personal intuition as his authority and even composed a creed and a sacred book for the use of Brāhmos. The lofty theism and deeply devotional spirit of these documents seem to spring from the same blend of Upanishadic and Christian inspirations we find in the writings of Rāmmohun Roy. Debendranāth Tagore's contribution to the revitalization of Hinduism was therefore a happy combination of preserving and of adding creatively to its best traditions.

[1] Debendranāth Tagore, *Autobiography*, p. 39.

DEBENDRANĀTH TAGORE

The Conflict Between Sanskritic and Western Education

Debendranāth tells in his *Autobiography* the story of his search for religious certainty. The following passage relates the way in which he resolved the apparent conflict between the two intellectual traditions in which he was educated.

[From Debendranāth Tagore, *Autobiography*, pp. 9–10]

As on the one hand there were my Sanskrit studies in the search after truth, so on the other hand there was English. I had read numerous English works on philosophy. But with all this, the sense of emptiness of mind remained just the same, nothing could heal it, my heart was being oppressed by that gloom of sadness and feeling of unrest. Did subjection to nature comprise the whole of man's existence? I asked. Then indeed are we undone. The might of this monster is indomitable. Fire, at a touch, reduces everything to ashes. Put out to sea in a vessel, whirlpools will drag you down to the bottom, gales will throw you into dire distress. There is no escape from the clutches of this Nature-fiend. If bowing down to her decree be our end and aim, then indeed are we undone. What can we hope for, whom can we trust? Again I thought, as things are reflected on a photographic plate by the rays of the sun, so are material objects manifested to the mind by the senses, this is what is called knowledge. Is there any other way but this of obtaining knowledge? These were the suggestions that Western philosophy had brought to my mind. To an atheist this is enough, he does not want anything beyond nature. But how could I rest fully satisfied with this? My endeavor was to obtain God, not through blind faith but by the light of knowledge. And being unsuccessful in this, my mental struggles increased from day to day. Sometimes I thought I could live no longer.

Suddenly, as I thought and thought, a flash as of lightning broke through this darkness of despondency. I saw that knowledge of the material world is born of the senses and the objects of sight, sound, smell, touch, and taste. But together with this knowledge, I am also enabled to know that I am the knower. Simultaneously with the facts of seeing, touching, smelling, and thinking, I also come to know that it is I who see, touch, smell, and think. With the knowledge of objects comes the knowledge of the subject, with the knowledge of the body comes the knowledge of the spirit within. It was after a prolonged search for truth that I found this bit of light, as if a ray of sunshine had fallen on a place full of extreme darkness. I now realized that with the knowledge of the outer world we come to know our inner self. After this, the more I thought over it, the more did I recognize the sway of wisdom operating throughout the whole world. For us the sun and moon rise and set at regular intervals, for us the wind and rain are set in motion in the proper seasons. All these combine to fulfil the one design of preserving our life. Whose design is this? It cannot be the design of matter, it must be the design of mind. Therefore this universe is propelled by the power of an intelligent being.

I saw that the child, as soon as born, drinks at its mother's breast. Who taught it to do this? He alone, who gave it life. Again who put love into the mother's heart? Who but He that put milk into her breast. He is that God who knows all our wants, whose rule the universe obeys. When my mind's eye had opened thus far, the clouds of grief were in a great measure dispelled. I felt somewhat consoled.

One day, while thinking of these things I suddenly recalled how, long ago, in my early youth, I had once realized the Infinite as manifested in the infinite heavens. Again I turned my gaze towards this infinite sky, studded with innumerable stars and planets, and saw the eternal God, and felt that this glory was His. He is infinite wisdom. He from whom we have derived this limited knowledge of ours, and this body, its receptacle, is Himself without form. He is without body or senses. He did not shape this universe with his hands. By His will alone did He bring it into existence. He is neither the Kali [1] or Kalighat,[2] nor the family Shalgram.[3] Thus was laid the axe at the root of idolatry.

The Call to Renunciation

Had he followed in his father's footsteps, Debendranāth could have become one of India's wealthiest men. But his innermost desire was to seek salvation through the traditional path of renunciation.

[From Debendranāth Tagore, *Autobiography*, p. 41]

My father was in England. The task of managing his various affairs devolved upon me. But I was not able to attend to any business matters

---

[1] Kālī—the Great Goddess.   [2] The temple of Kālī in Calcutta.   [3] The family idol.

properly. My subordinates used to do all the work, I was only concerned with the Vedas, the Vedanta, religion, God, and the ultimate goal of life. I was not even able to stay quietly in the house. My spirit of renunciation became deeper under all this stress of work. I felt no inclination to become the owner of all this wealth. To renounce everything and wander about alone, this was the desire that reigned in my heart. Imbued with His love I would roam in such lonely places that none would know; I would see His glory on land and water, would witness His mercy in different climes, would feel His protective power in foreign countries, in danger and peril; in this enthusiastic frame of mind I could no longer stay at home.

A Decisive Dream

When his father died, Debendranāth was faced with the choice of performing the customary Hindu funeral rites, in which offerings are made to various gods, or of remaining true to his vow to renounce idolatry. The decision came to him in this dream, whose conclusion gives us a good insight into the Hindu conceptions of religion and filial piety.

[From Debendranāth Tagore, *Autobiography*, pp. 48–49]

Which would triumph, the world or religion?—one could not tell—this was what worried me. My constant prayer to God was "Vouchsafe strength unto my weak heart, be Thou my refuge." All these anxieties and troubles would not let me sleep at night, my head felt dazed on the pillow. I would now doze off and again wake up. It was as if I was sleeping on the borderland between waking and sleeping. At such a time some one came to me in the dark and said "Get up," and I at once sat up. He said "Get out of bed" and I got up; he said "follow me" and I followed. He went down the steps leading out of the inner apartments, I did the same and came out into the courtyard with him. We stood before the front door. The durwans[4] were sleeping. My guide touched the door, and the two wings flew open at once. I went out with him into the street in front of the house. He seemed to be a shadowlike form. I could not see him clearly, but felt myself constrained to do immediately whatever he bade me. From thence he mounted up upwards to the sky, I also followed him. Clusters of stars and planets were shedding a bright

[4] Doorkeepers.

lustre, right and left and in front of me, and I was passing through them. On the way I entered a sea of mist, where the stars and planets were no longer visible. After traversing the mist for some distance I came upon a still full moon, like a small island in that vaporous ocean. The nearer I came the larger grew that moon. It no longer appeared round, but flat like our earth. The apparition went and stood on that earth, and I did likewise. The ground was all of white marble. Not a single blade of grass was there—no flowers, no fruit. Only that bare white plain stretched all around. The moonlight there was not derived from the sun. It shone by virtue of its own light. The rays of the sun could not penetrate the surrounding mist. Its own light was very soft, like the shade we have in the daytime. The air was pleasing to the senses. In the course of my journey across this plain I entered one of its cities. All the houses and all the streets were of white marble, not a single soul was to be seen in the clean and bright and polished streets. No noise was to be heard, everything was calm and peaceful. My guide entered a house by the road and went up to the second floor, I also went with him. I found myself in a spacious room, in which there were a table and some chairs of white marble. He told me to sit down, and I sat down in one of the chairs. The phantom then vanished. Nobody else was there. I sat silent in that silent room; shortly afterwards the curtain of one of the doors in front of the room was drawn aside and my mother appeared. Her hair was down, just as I had seen it on the day of her death. When she died, I never thought that she was dead. Even when I came back from the burning ground after performing her funeral ceremonies, I could not believe that she was dead. I felt sure that she was still alive. Now I saw that living mother of mine before me. She said "I wanted to see thee, so I sent for thee. Hast thou really become one who has known Brahma? Sanctified is the family, fulfilled is the mother's desire." On seeing her, and hearing these sweet words of hers my slumber gave way before a flood of joy. I found myself still tossing on my bed.

The Brāhmo Samāj and Its Relation to Orthodox Hinduism

After Keshub Chunder Sen had seceded from the Samāj, taking the majority of Brāhmos with him, Debendranāth pronounced in 1867 the following message on "gradualism" in matters of social reform.

[From Debendranāth Tagore, *Autobiography*, pp. 152–53]

We are worshipers of Brahma, the Supreme Being. In this we are at one with Orthodox Hinduism, for all our shastras declare with one voice the supremacy of the worship of Brahma, enjoining image worship for the help of those who are incapable of grasping the highest Truth.

Our first point of distinction is in the positive aspect of our creed wherein worship is defined as consisting in "Loving Him and doing the works He loveth"—this at once differentiates us from all religions and creeds which postulate a special or verbal revelation or wherein definite forms, rites, or ceremonials are deemed essential one way or the other.

The negative aspect of our creed which prohibits the worship of any created being or thing as the Creator further distinguishes us from all who are addicted to the worship of avatars or incarnations or who believe in the necessity of mediators, symbols, or idols of any description.

We base our faith on the fundamental truths of religion, attested by reason and conscience and refuse to permit man, book, or image to stand in the way of the direct communion of our soul with the Supreme Spirit.

This message of the Brāhmo Samāj in the abstract does not materially differ from the doctrines of the pure theistic bodies all the world over. Viewed historically and socially, however, the Brāhmo Samāj has the further distinction of being the bearer of this message to the Hindu people. This was the idea of its founder Ram Mohun Roy, this points to the duty incumbent upon all Brahmos of today, and will serve as the guiding principle in the selection of texts, forms, and ceremonials as aids to the religious life.

We are in and of the great Hindu community and it devolves upon us by example and precept to hold up as a beacon the highest truths of the Hindu shastras. In their light must we purify our heritage of customs, usages, rites, and ceremonies and adapt them to the needs of our conscience and our community. But we must beware of proceeding too fast in matters of social change, lest we be separated from the greater body whom we would guide and uplift.

While we should on no account allow any consideration of country, caste, or kinship to prevent our actions being consistent with our faith, we must make every allowance for, and abstain from, persecuting or alienating those who think differently from us. Why should we needlessly wound the feelings of our parents and elders by desecrating an image which they regard with the highest reverence, when all that our conscience can demand of us is to refrain from its adoration?

The steering of this middle course is by no means an easy task, but during my long experience I have been led greatly to hope for a brighter future by the sympathetic response of our orthodox brethren to the ideal held up before them. The amount of conformity nowadays expected by even the most orthodox, demands so little of us that a little tact and common sense will in most cases be sufficient to obviate all friction.

Nevertheless, great as are the claims of our land and our people, we must never forget that we are Brahmos first, and Indians or Hindus afterwards. We must on no account depart from our vow of renouncing the worship of images and incarnations, which is of the essence of our religion. It is a sound policy on our part to sink our minor differences, but on matters of principle no compromise is possible. Our Motherland is dear to us, but Religion is dearer, Brahma is dearest of all, dearer than son, dearer than riches, supreme over everything else.

A Farewell Message to His Followers

In 1889, thinking that he was about to die, Debendranāth set down eighteen principles for his followers. Combined in this document we find both the Christian emphasis on brotherly love and the Hindu conception of the relationship between *Ātman* and *Brāhman*. The Sanskrit texts of passages in quotation marks have been omitted.

[From Debendranāth Tagore, *Autobiography*, pp. 191–95.]

Dearly Beloved Brethren,

"Be ye united together; speak ye in unity; united know ye each the heart of the other. As the gods of old with one mind received each his offering due, even so be ye of one mind!"

"Harmonious may your efforts be, and harmonious your thoughts and heart, so that beauteous Peace may dwell in your midst!" "Live ye all one in heart and speech." This loving blessing and benediction which I have just expressed in Vedic words, it is meet ye should keep well in view, in the midst of the world's wranglings and jars. If to this end ye follow the way, then shall ye become gainers of your end. This way is the way of unity. If ye follow this way, all contentions shall depart from amongst you. Peace shall reign, and the Brāhmo religion shall have triumph.

1. The Brāhmo religion is a spiritual religion. Its seed-truth is this: By the soul shalt thou know the Supreme Soul. When God is seen in the soul, then, indeed, is He seen everywhere. The dearest dwelling-place

of Him who is the root of all this complexity, the One Sovereign of all this universe, is the soul of man. If ye know not the soul, then all is empty. The soul is of the knowledge of God.

2. In this body dwells the soul, and within it, in the pure refulgence of spiritual consciousness, the pure, bodiless Supreme Soul is to be seen. With mind and body subdued, unattached to all outward things, even-minded in sorrow and joy, self-contained, the Supreme Soul is to be viewed. This is spiritual union. When with love ye are united in this spiritual union, ye shall be delivered from all sin and shall attain the steps of salvation. After death, the body will be left here, but, united in this spiritual union, the soul shall dwell with the Soul Supreme for ever.

3. As for the health of the body ye partake of your regular daily meals, so for the soul's health the worship of God must be performed every day. The worship of God is the soul's sustenance.

4. "Loving Him and the doing of deeds pleasant in His sight, this, indeed, is His worship." That Brahma, who is beyond Time and Space, and who yet pervades Time and Space, the Witness of all, Truth, Wisdom, and Infinity—knowing Him to be the Soul's Ruler, and the Heart's Lord—adore Him every day with love, and, for the good of the world, be engaged in the performance of works of righteousness which are pleasing in His sight. Never dissever these two ever-united limbs of God's worship.

5. Let only that be done which promoteth well-being. Do no evil to an evil-doer. If any should work unrighteousness, it should not be requited by unrighteousness. Always be righteous. Evil should be overcome by good, and unrighteousness by righteousness.

6. Contend with no one. Restrain anger; and, imbued with love and charity, behave justly to all. Let love be thy rule of conduct with regard to others.

7. By day and night instruct yourselves—govern yourselves—and accept righteousness as the end of existence. For him who can subdue his heart and senses, there remains no cause for sorrow and suffering. For him who cannot restrain himself there is suffering on every side.

8. He who desireth the good of mankind must look on others as he looks on himself. It behoves thee to love thy neighbor, since it pleases thee to be loved by him, and to avoid giving pain by hatred, since it causes thee pain to be hated by another. Thus in all things shalt thou deal with others by comparing them with thyself; for as pleasure and pain affect

thee, so do they affect all creatures. Such conduct alone is the means of attaining well-being.

9. He who adores God and loves man is a saint. Such a man never rejoices in finding fault with men, for man is beloved of him. He is pained by the sight of a fault in others, and lovingly does he labor for its correction. He loves man as man; and owing to that love, is pleased by the sight of good, and grieved by the sight of evil in man. Therefore he is unable to proclaim the faults of others with rejoicing.

10. The satisfaction of the inner spirit, or, in other words, a good conscience, is the unfailing fruit of the practice of righteousness. In this favor of conscience is felt the favor of God. If the inner spirit is satisfied, all sufferings cease. Without the practice of righteousness, the inner spirit is never satisfied. The mind may find enjoyment in the pleasures of the world, but if the conscience is diseased, then even the height of worldly bliss becomes valueless. Therefore, by the practice of righteousness, ye shall preserve a clear conscience, and ye shall abandon all things whereby the satisfaction of the spirit may be marred.

11. Ye shall seek the practice of righteousness to the utmost of your power. If, after the exercise of all your power, ye fail to attain the end, yet ye shall acquire merit thereby. God does not reckon what portion of His infinite work is performed by individuals. Let every one use the powers given him, without reservation; this is God's ordinance.

12. Ye shall abjure sinful thoughts, sinful speech, and sinful acts. Those who do not sin in thought, word, deed, or judgment—such saints truly practice austerity; not those who mortify the flesh. Therefore, abstaining from sin, engage in good works. Persevering on the road of righteousness, ye shall earn your livelihood.

13. If, by perseverence on the road of righteousness, ye are completely cast down, even then ye shall not turn your thoughts to unrighteous means. Protect dharma with your lives, and dharma will protect you.

14. Not father or mother, nor wife or child, nor friend or relation, remains as our stay in the next world. Righteousness alone remains. Alone a man is born, alone he dies, alone he enjoys the good fruits of his righteous acts, and alone he suffers the evil consequences of his bad deeds. Friends, leaving on the earth his body like a stock or stone, turn away from him; but righteousness follows him whither he goeth. Therefore, ye shall, step by step, acquire righteousness, which shall be your stay.

Dharma is our friend in this world, and dharma is the guide to the next. "Dharma is as honey unto all creatures."

15. "Not by wealth, nor by children, nor by works, but by renunciation alone, is immortality attained." Renunciation is not the renunciation of the world by becoming an anchorite, dwelling in the wilderness, but dwelling at home, and living in the world, all lusts of the heart should be cast out.

"When all lusts that dwell in the heart of man are cast out, then the mortal becomes immortal, and even on earth attains God."

16. With all diligence shall ye cherish your wives and children and relations; but, being yourselves free from desire, remain unattached to the fruit of your acts, and then ye shall be able to mount the steps of salvation. God's own love furnishes the most perfect example. See how mindful He is of the interests of the world. He never forgets to give food even to a single worm or insect. Even in the bowels of arid mountains, He supplies nourishment to living creatures. Yet He keeps nothing for Himself. He is always giving to all, and never receives. By the light of this example, ye, too, forgetting yourselves, shall be vowed to work for the good of the world. Being united to Him, ye shall perform the duties of life. That which ye shall know to be His command, ye must obey with your lives. That which ye shall know to be against His will, ye shall shun like poison. If thus, forgetful of self, ye perform His work, then be sure He will not forget you, with gratitude receive it as plenty. In whatever condition He may place you, with that be contented. In seasons of prosperity, live in obedience to Him; and, in seasons of adversity, take refuge in Him; and ye shall not be perplexed. At the time of action, act resting in Him; at the time of rest, rest even in Him. This body will move about on earth, but your souls will be united with Him. Even in death there is no dissolution of this union.

17. Blessed is that soul which, self-subdued, freed from sin and impurity like the moon from the shadow of eclipse, and casting off the pride of flesh, can rest in the Supreme Soul. That soul is not cast down by disease, is not frightened by death; it sees from here the abode of God; to it the door of the infinitude of progress is opened, and before it millions on millions of heavens shine forth. On this side is the billowy world of change, on the other side the Peaceful Abode of God; in the middle God

Himself, like a bridge, preserves the position of both. Neither day nor night, nor death, disease, or sorrow, nor good or evil deed, is able to cross this bridge. All kinds of sin fall back from there. Sin has no power in the Sinless Abode of Brahma. The liberated soul, leaving behind him the sin and sorrow of this world, attains the Abode of Brahma, beyond this world. There the blind cease to be blind; the sin-stricken become free from sin; for the Abode of Brahma is for ever resplendent; to that splendor there is no end.

18. Following the previous teachings of Brahma-dharma, I make you this offering of my last words. May ye realize it in your lives and attain to everlasting salvation—this is my prayer!

Om—Peace, Peace, Peace.

KESHUB CHUNDER SEN AND THE INDIANIZATION OF CHRISTIANITY

The stormy career of Keshub Chunder Sen [1] encompassed both the peak and the later decline of the influence of the Brāhmo Samāj on Indian intellectual life. With his great energy and oratorical skill he brought to fulfillment the openness to Christian inspiration of Rāmmohun Roy and the intuitionist doctrine of Debendranāth Tagore. Yet his very enthusiasm was his undoing, for by the time of his death he had shattered the Samāj into three separate organizations, and damaged its prestige irrevocably.

Keshub's grandfather was a contemporary and friend of Rāmmohun Roy, but did not share the great reformer's ideas on religion. The Sen family was one of the most Westernized in Bengal, and young Keshub grew up speaking English more fluently than Bengali. His career as a student at the Hindu College was marred by his failure in mathematics, but he took great interest in philosophy and ethics. At nineteen his religious spirit found its natural orbit in the Brāhmo Samāj. Within a short time Keshub had become Debendranāth's most beloved disciple. When he was excommunicated by his own family for having taken his wife to

[1] Or Keshab Chandra Sen.

a Brāhmo ceremony, Keshub found shelter in the home of his religious teacher.

With unquenchable energy, Keshub threw himself into the activities of the Brāhmo Samāj, founding discussion groups and schools, organizing famine relief, advocating remarriage for widows and education for young women, writing religious tracts, and giving sermons. His fiery oratory in fluent English stirred educated audiences in many parts of India, especially in Bombay, and branches of the Samāj sprang up in cities beyond the borders of Bengal.

Keshub's zeal for social reform carried him far beyond the moderate position taken by Debendranāth. The two finally parted in 1865 over the wearing of the sacred thread and Keshub set up an independent organization which he named the Brāhmo Samāj of India. From this point on, his faith in inspiration as the guide to action grew more pronounced. In 1878 another and more fatal fission took place within his own movement. Despite his prolonged advocacy of a minimum age for Brāhmo marriages, and his opposition to idolatry, he was persuaded to marry his thirteen-year-old daughter to a Hindu prince, feeling that such was the will of God. Scandalized by this betrayal of his previous principles, most of his followers abandoned him and set up a third group, the Sādhāran (General) Brāhmo Samāj.

In the last years of his life Keshub experimented in synthesizing elements from the world's major religions. Although he borrowed devotional and yogic practices from Hinduism, he drew even more heavily on Christian teachings and practices. The New Dispensation which he proclaimed in 1879 appropriated much from the Christian church which it claimed to supplant, including among other things a direct revelation from God, apostles, missionaries, monastic orders, and the doctrines of sin, salvation, and the divinity of Christ.

Of Keshub's work little remained after his death in 1884 at the age of forty-one. The flaming enthusiasm which had launched him on so many enterprises, and the eloquent oratory which electrified so many audiences, left surprisingly few monuments. But the force of his example was felt in Bengal for decades, and his methods—particularly his oratorical conquests and his synthesizing of Indian and Western ideas—have been imitated by later religious leaders and nationalist politicians alike.

KESHUB CHUNDER SEN

Enthusiasm

Two years before his death Keshub penetratingly summed up his nature and the activities into which it had plunged him.

[From Mozoomdar, *Life and Teachings of Keshub Chunder Sen*, pp. 15–16]

If I ask thee, O Self, in what creed wast thou baptized in early life? The self answers in the baptism of fire. I am a worshiper of the religion of fire, I am partial to the doctrine of enthusiasm. To me a state of being on fire is the state of salvation. My heart palpitates as soon as I perceive any coldness in my life. When the body becomes cold, it is death, when religion becomes cold, it is death also. It may take time to know whether I am a sinner or not, but it is easy to know whether I am alive or dead; I at once decide this by finding whether I am warm or cold. I live in the midst of fire, I love, embrace, and exalt fire. Every sign of heat fills me with joy, hope, zeal. As soon as I feel the fire is losing its heat, I feel as if I would jump into the sea and drown myself. When I find that a man after five years of enthusiasm is getting to be lukewarm, I at once conclude he is on the highway of a sinful life, that before long death will tread on his neck. I have always felt a cold condition to be a state of impurity. Coldness and hell have always been the same to my mind. Around my own life, around the society in which I lived, I always kept burning the flame of enthusiasm. When I succeeded in serving one body of men, I always sought another body whom I might serve. When I successfully worked in one department of life, I always sighed to work in other departments also. When I gathered truths from one set of scriptures, I have longed for others, and before finishing these I have looked out for others again, lest anything should become old or cold to me. This is my life that I am continually after new ideas, new acquirements, new enjoyments.

Loyalty to the British Nation

Keshub was only voicing the sentiments of his time when he declared British rule providential for India. His conviction that India had a reciprocal contribution to make to England was a relatively new idea, and one which was to take on increasing importance in the nationalist era. This speech was delivered in Calcutta in 1877, shortly after Queen Victoria had assumed the title of Empress of India.

[From "Philosophy and Madness in Religion," in *Keshub Chunder Sen's Lectures in India,* pp. 322–26]

Loyalty shuns an impersonal abstraction. It demands a person, and that person is the sovereign, or the head of the state, in whom law and constitutionalism are visibly typified and represented. We are right then if our loyalty means not only respect for law and the Parliament, but personal attachment to Victoria, Queen of England and Empress of India. [Applause.] What makes loyalty so enthusiastic is not, however, the presence of purely secular feelings, but of a strong religious sentiment. By loyalty I mean faith in Providence. It is this faith which gives loyalty all its sanctity and solidity, and establishes it in the individual heart and in society as a holy passion. Do you not believe that there is God in history? Do you not recognize the finger of special providence in the progress of nations? Assuredly the record of British rule in India is not a chapter of profane history, but of ecclesiastical history. [Cheers.] The book which treats of the moral, social, and religious advancement of our great country with the help of Western science, under the paternal rule of the British nation, is indeed a sacred book. There we see clearly that it is Providence that rules India through England. [Applause.] Were you present at the magnificent spectacle at Delhi, on the day of the assumption of the imperial title by our sovereign? Some men have complained that no religious ceremony was observed on the occasion, and indeed opinion is divided on this point. None, however, can gainsay the fact that the whole affair, from beginning to end was a most solemn religious ceremony, and I rejoice I am privileged to say this in the presence of our noble-hearted Viceroy. Was any devout believer in Providence there? To him I appeal. Let him say whether the imperial assemblage was not a spectacle of deep moral and religious significance. Did not the eye of the faithful believer see that God Himself stretched His right hand and placed the Empress' crown upon Victoria's head? [Loud cheers.] And did he not hear the Lord God say unto her: "Rule thy subjects with justice and truth and mercy, according to the light given unto thee and thy advisers, and let righteousness and peace and prosperity dwell in the Empire"? [Applause.]

Would you characterize this sight and this sound as a visionary dream?

Is there no truth in the picture? Who can deny that Victoria is an instrument in the hands of Providence to elevate this degraded country in the scale of nations, and that in her hands the solemn trust has lately been most solemnly reposed? Glory then to Empress Victoria! [Applause.] Educated countrymen, you are bound to be loyal to your Divinely-appointed sovereign. Not to be loyal argues base ingratitude and absence of faith in Providence. You are bound to be loyal to the British government, that came to your rescue, as God's ambassador, when your country was sunk in ignorance and superstition and hopeless jejuneness, and has since lifted you to your present high position. This work is not of man, but of God, and He has done it, and is doing it, through the British nation. As His chosen instruments, then, honor your sovereign and the entire ruling body with fervent loyalty. The more loyal we are, the more we shall advance with the aid of our rulers in the path of moral, social, and political reformation. India in her present fallen condition seems destined to sit at the feet of England for many long years, to learn Western art and science. And, on the other hand, behold England sits at the feet of hoary-headed India to study the ancient literature of this country. [Applause.] All Europe seems to be turning her attention in these days towards Indian antiquities, to gather the priceless treasures which lie buried in the literature of Vedism and Buddhism. Thus while we learn modern science from England, England learns ancient wisdom from India. Gentlemen, in the advent of the English nation in India we see a reunion of parted cousins, the descendants of two different families of the ancient Aryan race. Here they have met together, under an overruling Providence, to serve most important purposes in the Divine economy. The mutual intercourse between England and India, political as well as social, is destined to promote the true interests and lasting glory of both nations. We were rejoiced to see the rajahs and maharajahs of India offering their united homage to Empress Victoria and her representative at the imperial assemblage. Far greater will be our rejoicing when all the chiefs and people of India shall be united with the English nation, in a vast international assemblage, before the throne of the King of Kings and the Lord of Lords! [Loud cheers.] May England help us to draw near to that consummation, by giving us as much of the light of the West as lies in her power! That is her mission in India. May she fulfill it nobly and honorably. Let England give us her industry and arts, her exact sciences and her practical philosophy, so much needed in a land where superstition and prejudices prevail to an alarming extent. But we shall not forget our ancient sages and Rishis. Ye venerable devotees of ancient India! teach us meditation and asceticism and loving communion. Let England baptize us with the spirit of true philosophy. Let the sages of Aryan India baptize us with the spirit of heavenly madness. Let modern England teach hard science and fact; let ancient India teach sweet poetry and sentiment. Let modern England give us her fabrics; but let the gorgeous East lend her charming colors. Come then, fellow countrymen and friends, and accept this divine creed, in which you will find all that is goodliest, fairest, and sweetest, based upon a foundation scientific, strong and sound—a creed in which truth and love are harmonized. Let us have only fifty young men from our universities, trained in science and philosophy, and baptized with the spirit of madness, and let these men go forth as missionary-soldiers of God, conquering and to conquer, and in the fullness of time the banners of truth shall be planted throughout the length and breadth of the country. [Loud cheers.]

The Asiatic Christ

Whereas Rāmmohun Roy welcomed only the moral influence of Jesus, Keshub embraced Christ as the fulfillment of India's devotional striving. He also took Roy's assertion that Jesus was an Asian by birth and used it as an argument for better understanding between the rulers and the ruled in India.

[From "Jesus Christ: Europe and Asia," in *Keshub Chunder Sen's Lectures in India*, pp. 33-34]

Europeans and natives are both the children of God, and the ties of brotherhood should bind them together. Extend, then, to us, O ye Europeans in India! the right hand of fellowship, to which we are fairly entitled. If, however, our Christian friends persist in traducing our nationality and national character, and in distrusting and hating Orientalism, let me assure them that I do not in the least feel dishonored by such imputations. On the contrary, I rejoice, yea, I am proud, that I am an Asiatic. And was not Jesus Christ an Asiatic? [Deafening applause.] Yes, and his disciples were Asiatics, and all the agencies primarily employed for the propagation of the Gospel were Asiatic. In fact, Christianity was founded and developed by Asiatics, and in Asia.

When I reflect on this, my love for Jesus becomes a hundredfold intensified; I feel him nearer my heart, and deeper in my national sympathies. Why should I then feel ashamed to acknowledge that nationality which he acknowledged? Shall I not rather say he is more congenial and akin to my Oriental nature, more agreeable to my Oriental habits of thought and feeling? And is it not true that an Asiatic can read the imageries and allegories of the Gospel, and its descriptions of natural sceneries, of customs, and manners, with greater interest, and a fuller perception of their force and beauty, than Europeans? [Cheers.] In Christ we see not only the exaltedness of humanity, but also the grandeur of which Asiatic nature is susceptible. To us Asiatics, therefore, Christ is doubly interesting, and his religion is entitled to our peculiar regard as an altogether Oriental affair. The more this great fact is pondered, the less I hope will be the antipathy and hatred of European Christians against Oriental nationalities, and the greater the interest of the Asiatics in the teachings of Christ. And thus in Christ, Europe and Asia, the East and the West, may learn to find harmony and unity. [Deafening applause.]

An Indian National Church

With characteristic enthusiasm, Keshub saw in the simple theism of the Brāhmo Samāj a platform on which the major religious traditions of India—Hindu, Muslim, Christian—could unite. The resulting faith, he thought, would sustain not only the future church of India, but would qualify India to take part in a world-wide religious brotherhood. Keshub's expectation that Hindus and Muslims would willingly merge into this national church is but one more example of his supreme optimism.

[From "The Future Church," in *Keshub Chunder Sen's Lectures in India,* pp. 155–60]

I have briefly described the general features of the church of the future—its worship, creed, and gospel. Before I conclude I must say a few words with special reference to this country. There are some among us who denounce Mahomedanism as wholly false, while others contend that Hinduism is altogether false. Such opinions are far from being correct; they only indicate the spirit of sectarian antipathy. Do you think that millions of men would to this day attach themselves so devotedly to these systems of faith unless there was something really valuable and true in them? This cannot be. There is, no doubt, in each of these creeds, much to excite to ridicule, and perhaps indignation—a large amount of superstition, prejudice, and even corruption. But I must emphatically say it is wrong to set down Hinduism or Mahomedanism as nothing but a mass of lies and abominations, and worthy of being trampled under foot. Proscribe and eliminate all that is false therein: there remains a residue of truth and purity which you are bound to honor. You will find certain central truths in these systems, though surrounded by errors, which constitute their vitality, and which have preserved them for centuries in spite of opposition, and in which hundreds of good men have always found the bread of life. It is these which form even now the mighty pillars of Hinduism and Mahomedanism, and challenge universal admiration and respect. It is idle to suppose that such gigantic systems of faith will be swept away by the fervor of youthful excitement, or the violent fulminations of sectarian bigotry, so long as there is real power in them. All the onslaughts which are being leveled against them in this age of free inquiry and bold criticism will tend, not to destroy them, but to purify them and develop their true principles. The signs of the times already indicate this process of purification and development; and I believe this process will gradually bring Hinduism and Mahomedanism, hitherto so hostile to each other, into closer union, till the two ultimately harmonize to form the future church of India.

The Hindu's notion of God is sublime. In the earliest Hindu scriptures God is represented as the Infinite Spirit dwelling in His own glory, and pervading all space, full of peace and joy. On the other hand, the Mahomedans describe their God as infinite in power, governing the universe with supreme authority as the Lord of all. Hence the principal feature of the religion of the Hindu is quiet contemplation, while that of the religion of the Mahomedan is constant excitement and active service. The one lives in a state of quiet communion with his God of peace; the other lives as a soldier, ever serving the Almighty Ruler, and crusading against evil. These are the primary and essential elements of the two creeds, and, if blended together, would form a beautiful picture of true theology, which will be realized in the future church of this country. As the two creeds undergo development, their errors and differences will disappear, and they will harmoniously coalesce in their fundamental and vital principles. The future creed of India will be a composite faith, resulting from the union of the true and divine elements of

Hinduism and Mahomedanism, and showing the profound devotion of the one and the heroic enthusiasm of the other. The future sons and daughters of this vast country will thus inherit precious legacies from Hinduism and Mahomedanism, and, while enjoying the blessings of the highest and sweetest communion with the God of love, will serve Him in the battlefield of life with fidelity to truth and unyielding opposition to untruth and sin. As regards Christianity and its relation to the future church of India, I have no doubt in my mind that it will exercise great influence on the growth and formation of that church. The spirit of Christianity has already pervaded the whole atmosphere of Indian society, and we breathe, think, feel, and move in a Christian atmosphere. Native society is being roused, enlightened, and reformed under the influence of Christian education. If it is true that the future of a nation is determined by all the circumstances and agencies which today influence its nascent growth, surely the future church of this country will be the result of the purer elements of the leading creeds of the day, harmonized, developed, and shaped under the influence of Christianity.

But the future church of India must be thoroughly national; it must be an essentially Indian church. The future religion of the world I have described will be the common religion of all nations, but in each nation it will have an indigenous growth, and assume a distinctive and peculiar character. All mankind will unite in a universal church; at the same time, it will be adapted to the peculiar circumstances of each nation, and assume a national form. No country will borrow or mechanically imitate the religion of another country; but from the depths of the life of each nation its future church will naturally grow up. And shall not India have its own national church? Dr. Norman McLeod, in expounding last year, in this very hall, his ideas of the future church of this country, said emphatically that it would be a purely Indian church, and not a reproduction of any of the established churches of the West. Though I differ from that learned and liberal-minded gentleman in regard to the doctrines and tenets of that church as set forth by him, I fully agree with him that that church must have a strictly national growth and a national organization. Neither will Germany adopt the religious life of China, nor will India accept blindly that of England or of any other European country. India has religious traditions and associations, tastes and customs, peculiarly sacred and dear to her, just as every other country has, and it is idle to expect that she will forego these; nay, she cannot do so,

MODERN INDIA AND PAKISTAN

as they are interwoven with her very life. In common with all other nations and communities, we shall embrace the theistic worship, creed, and gospel of the future church—we shall acknowledge and adore the Holy One, accept the love and service of God and man as our creed, and put our firm faith in God's almighty grace as the only means of our redemption. But we shall do all this in a strictly national and Indian style. We shall see that the future church is not thrust upon us, but that we independently and naturally grow into it; that it does not come to us as a foreign plant, but that it strikes its roots deep in the national heart of India, draws its sap from our national resources, and develops itself with all the freshness and vigor of indigenous growth. One religion shall be acknowledged by all men, One God shall be worshiped throughout the length and breadth of the world; the same spirit of faith and love shall pervade all hearts; all nations shall dwell together in the Father's house—yet each shall have its own peculiar and free mode of action. There shall, in short, be unity of spirit, but diversity of forms; one body, but different limbs; one vast community, with members laboring, in different ways and according to their respective resources and peculiar tastes, to advance their common cause. Thus India shall sing the glory of the Supreme Lord with Indian voice and with Indian accompaniments, and so shall England and America, and the various races and tribes and nations of the world, with their own peculiar voice and music, sing His glory; but all their different voices and peculiar modes of chanting shall commingle in one sweet and swelling chorus—one universal anthem proclaiming in solemn and stirring notes, in the world below and the heavens above, "the Fatherhood of God and the brotherhood of man." May the Merciful Lord hasten the advent of the true church, and establish peace and harmony among His children! And as His name has been solemnly chanted tonight in this splendid hall by an immense concourse of worshipers of various races and tribes, so may all His children assemble in His holy mansions, and blending their million voices in one grand chorus, glorify Him time without end.

The New Dispensation

The central idea of Keshub's New Dispensation was that the new faith constituted a direct continuation of the Old and New Testament revelations. Implicit in his bold claims lay the assumption that the Hindu religious genius was able to reconcile and harmonize all conflicting creeds. This daring concept of India's spiritual mission to the world has been voiced by many of her thinkers since Keshub's time.

[From "We Apostles of the New Dispensation," in *Keshub Chunder Sen's Lectures in India*, pp. 464–68, 484–85]

Admit, then, that Paul was a necessary logical adjunct and consequent of Christ, as Moses was, indeed, his antecedent. Does the continuity stop here? No. If the New Testament follows the Old in the line of logical sequence, the new dispensation follows as necessarily all the old dispensations which have gone before it. If you cannot separate Paul from Christ, surely you cannot separate us from Paul. Are we not servants of Paul and apostles of Jesus? Yes. You cannot regard us otherwise. When I say the New Dispensation is a sequence of the Christian dispensation you will no doubt admit a chronological succession. You will perhaps go further, and trace a theological connection. But you have yet to discover a logical succession. Students of logic will yet recognize in the present movement a deduction and a sequence resulting from the Christian dispensation. You cannot deny us. We are the fulfillment of Moses. He was simply the incarnation of Divine conscience. But there was no science in his teachings, that science which in modern times is so greatly honored. Let Moses grow into modern science, and you have the new dispensation, which may be characterized as the union of the conscience and science. As for Christ, we are surely among his honored ambassadors. We are a deduction and corollary from his teachings. The new dispensation is Christ's prophecy fulfilled. Did not Jesus predict and foreshadow a fuller dispensation of light and grace? Did he not say the Comforter would come after him, and guide the world "into all truth"? Do you not remember those prophetic words?: "I have yet many things to say unto you, but ye cannot bear them now. Howbeit when he, the spirit of truth, is come, he will guide you into all truth." And touching the subject of synthetic unity, one can hardly conceive a clearer foreboding than is to be found in those words of Paul: "That in the dispensation of the fullness of time he might gather together in one all things in Christ, both which are in heaven and which are in earth, even in him." Inasmuch as the present dispensation sums up all things in a divine synthesis unifying all in God, and seeks new light in the direct inspiration of the Comforter or Holy Spirit, one cannot fail to recognize in it the fulfillment of an ancient prophecy, the realization of Christian and Pauline anticipations. What do we see before us in India today but the fruit of that tree, whose seed Jesus planted, and Paul watered, centuries ago? The unbeliever may hold that Christ wholly denies us, and is far away from us. But faith points to his spirit in us, and maintains an unbroken continuity of dispensation. Wherever a dozen disciples are gathered in his name, he is there. We in India are imbued with his spirit. If it be true that the faith of our ancient Aryan ancestors has permeated us, it is equally true that Christ has leavened us and Christianized us. The Acts of his Hindu Apostles will form a fresh chapter in his universal gospel. Can he deny us, his logical succession? Surely he cannot. And so Paul too. Wilt thou reject us, Saint Paul? Revered Brother, wilt thou cast us away as thine enemies? Is not thy spirit in us? Let our lives testify. Gentlemen, what was Paul's great mission? To obliterate the distinction between Jew and Gentile. "I speak to you Gentiles," said he; "inasmuch as I am the apostle of Gentiles, I magnify mine office." "There is no difference between the Jew and the Greek: for the same Lord over all is rich unto all that call upon him." Again, in his Epistle to the Corinthians, "By one Spirit are we all baptized into one body, whether we be Jews or Gentiles." Paul was raised by God to break caste, and level the distinctions of race and nationality; and nobly did he fulfill his mission. The Jew and the Gentile he made into one body. The modern Pauls of the new dispensation are carrying on a similar crusade against caste in India. The obnoxious distinctions between Brahmin and Sudra, between Hindu and Yavana, between Asiatic and European, the new gospel of love thoroughly proscribes.

In the kingdom of God there is no invidious distinction, and therefore this dispensation gathers all men and nations, all races and tribes, the high and the low, and seeks to establish one vast brotherhood among the children of the great God, who hath made of one blood all nations of men. Let them that have eyes see that in the midst of the great spiritual revolution and revival going on in this land, Moses and Christ and Paul are gathering through us the many tribes of Israel, and uniting all in the name of the kingdom of heaven. . . .

In all ages devout and godly men have eaten the flesh of saints and been in turn eaten by others. Divinity went into the flesh of Christ.

Then Christ was eaten by Paul and Peter. They were eaten by the fathers and the martyrs and all the saints in Christendom, and all these have we of modern times eaten, assimilated, and absorbed, making their ideas and character our own. Thus one nation may swallow another, and be identified with it. Thus one generation may draw into itself the character and faith of another generation. And we too may enter into each other and dwell in each other. We Hindus are specially endowed with, and distinguished for, the yoga faculty, which is nothing but this power of spiritual communion and absorption. This faculty, which we have inherited from our forefathers, enables us to annihilate space and time, and bring home to our minds an external Deity and an external humanity. Waving the magic wand of yoga, we say to the Ural mountains and the river Ural, Vanish, and lo! they disappear. And we command Europe to enter into the heart of Asia, and Asia to enter into the mind of Europe, and they obey us, and we instantly realize within ourselves an European Asia and an Asiatic Europe, a commingling of oriental and occidental ideas and principles. We say to the Pacific, Pour thy waters into the Atlantic; and we say to the West, Roll back to the East. We summon ancient India to come into modern India with all her rishis and saints, her asceticism and communion and simplicity of character, and behold a transfiguration! The educated modern Hindu cast in Vedic mold! How by yoga one nation becomes another! How Asia eats the flesh and drinks the blood of Europe! How the Hindu absorbs the Christian; how the Christian assimilates the Hindu! Cultivate this communion, my brethren, and continually absorb all that is good and noble in each other. Do not hate, do not exclude others, as the sectarians do, but include and absorb all humanity and all truth. Let there be no antagonism, no exclusion. Let the embankment which each sect, each nation, has raised, be swept away by the flood of cosmopolitan truth, and let all the barriers and partitions which separate man from man be pulled down, so that truth and love and purity may flow freely through millions of hearts and through hundreds of successive generations, from country to country, from age to age. Thus shall the deficiencies of individual and national character be complemented, and humanity shall attain a fuller and more perfect standard of religious and moral life.

DAYĀNANDA SARASWATĪ: VEDIC REFORMER

While Keshub Chunder Sen was preaching an Indianized version of Christianity in Bengal, a stern ascetic arose in northern India who vigorously rejected Western ideas and undertook instead to revive the ancient religion of the Aryans. Swāmī Dayānanda Saraswatī (1824–1883) was even more ardent a reformer than Keshub, yet he drew his strength from purely indigenous sources. Standing foursquare on the authority of the Vedas, he fearlessly denounced the evils of post-Vedic Hinduism.

Dayānanda was born into a brāhman family in a princely state of Gujarat, a section of western India relatively untouched by British cultural influence. His well-to-do father instructed him in Sanskrit and Shaivism from the age of five, but Dayānanda revolted against idol-worship at fourteen, and to avoid being married ran away from home at nineteen to become a sannyāsī (religious mendicant) of the *Sarasvatī* order. He spent the next fifteen years as a wandering ascetic, living in jungles, in Himalayan retreats, and at places of pilgrimage throughout northern India. A tough, blind old teacher completed his education by literally beating into him a reverence for the four Vedas and a disdain for all later scriptures.

For the rest of his life Dayānanda lectured in all parts of India on the exclusive authority of the Vedas. Time after time he challenged all comers to religious debates, but few could withstand his forceful forensic attack. Idol-worship is not sanctioned by the Vedas, he pointed out, nor is untouchability, nor child marriage, nor the subjection of women to unequal status with men. The study of the Vedas should be open to all, not just to brāhmans, and a man's caste should be in accordance with his merits. Such revolutionary teachings evoked the wrath of the orthodox and numerous attempts were made on Dayānanda's life. His great physical strength saved him from swordsmen, thugs, and cobras, but the last of many attempts to poison him succeeded. Like John the Baptist, he accused a princely ruler of loose living, and the woman in question instigated his death by having ground glass put in his milk.

Dayānanda's energetic and sometimes acrimonious method of preaching epitomized the change among Hindu religious leaders from a passive or defensive attitude to an active and aggressive one. His claims were sometimes extravagant, however, as with his assertion that firearms and electricity were described in the Vedas. His followers dubbed him "the Luther of India," and considering the fervor of his reforms and the great importance which he attached to the Vedas as a holy "book," the analogy is quite apt. The Ārya Samāj (the Society of the Āryas, or "noble men") which he established at Bombay in 1875 has since reflected the militant character of its founder, and from its stronghold in the Punjab has contributed to the rise of Hindu nationalism.

DAYĀNANDA SARASWATĪ
Of Mice and Idols

A major turning point in Dayānanda's life came at fourteen, when he observed for the first time a special all-night fast and vigil in honor of the god Shiva. What other Hindu boys accepted unthinkingly caused in him such revulsion that he waged war on idolatry for the rest of his days.

[From Har Bilas Sarda, *Life of Dayanand Saraswati*, pp. 5–6]

Wherever the *Siva Purāna*[1] was to be read and explained, there my father was sure to take me along with him. Finally unmindful of my mother's remonstrances, he imperatively demanded that I should begin practicing Parthiva Puja.[2] When the great day of gloom and fasting—called Shivaratri—arrived, this day falling on the 13th of Vadya of Magh,[3] my father regardless of the protest of my mother that my strength might fail, commanded me to keep a fast adding that I had to be initiated on that night into the sacred legend and participate in that night's long vigil in the temple of Shiva. Accordingly, I followed him along with other young men, who accompanied their parents. This vigil is divided into four parts called *paharas,* consisting of three hours each. Having completed my task, namely, having sat up for the first two paharas till the hour of midnight, I remarked that the pujaris, or temple servants and some of the lay devotees, after having left the inner temple, had fallen asleep outside. Having been taught for years that by sleeping on that particular night, the worshiper loses all the good effect of his devotion, I tried to refrain from drowsiness by bathing my eyes now

[1] Didactic tale of Shiva. [2] The worship of the clay emblem of Shiva.
[3] Vadya, the dark, or second fortnight of the lunar month. Māgha, the eleventh month of the Hindu calendar.

and then with cold water. But my father was less fortunate. Unable to resist fatigue, he was the first to fall asleep, leaving me to watch alone.

Thoughts upon thoughts crowded upon me, and one question arose after another in my disturbed mind. Is it possible, I asked myself, that this semblance of man, the idol of a Personal God that I see bestriding his bull before me, and who, according to all religious accounts, walks about, eats, sleeps, and drinks; who can hold a trident in his hand, beat upon his dumroo [drum], and pronounce curses upon men—is it possible that he can be the Mahadeva, the great Deity, the same that is invoked as the Lord of Kailas,[4] the supreme being and the Divine hero of all the stories we read of in the Puranas? Unable to resist such thoughts any longer, I awoke my father abruptly asking him to enlighten me and tell me whether this hideous emblem of Shiva in the temple was identical with the Mahadeva (Great God) of the scriptures, or something else. "Why do you ask it?" said my father. Because, I answered, I feel it impossible to reconcile the idea of an omnipotent, living God, with this idol, which allows the mice to run upon its body, and thus suffers its image to be polluted without the slightest protest. Then my father tried to explain to me that this stone representation of the Mahadeva of Kailasa, having been consecrated with the Veda mantras in the most solemn way by the holy Brahmins, became in consequence the God himself, and is worshiped as such, adding that as Shiva cannot be perceived personally in this Kali Yug—the age of mental darkness—we have the idol in which the Mahadeva of Kailasa is worshiped by his votaries; this kind of worship is pleasing to the great Deity as much as if, instead of the emblem, he were there himself. But the explanation fell short of satisfying me. I could not, young as I was, help suspecting misinterpretation and sophistry in all this. Feeling faint with hunger and fatigue, I begged to be allowed to go home. My father consented to it, and sent me away with a sepoy, only reiterating once more his command that I should not eat. But when once home, I told my mother of my hunger and she fed me with sweetmeats, and I fell into profound sleep.

In the morning, when my father returned and learnt that I had broken my fast, he felt very angry. He tried to impress me with the enormity of sin; but do what he could I could not bring myself to believe that that idol and Mahadeva were one and the same God, and therefore, could

[4] A mountain peak of the Himalayas where Shiva's Heaven is believed to be situated.

not comprehend why I should be made to fast for the worship of the former. I had, however, to conceal my lack of faith, and bring forward as an excuse for abstaining from regular worship my ordinary studies, which really left me little or rather no time for anything else. In this I was strongly supported by my mother and even my uncle who pleaded my cause so well that my father had to yield at last and allowed me to devote my whole attention to my studies.

A Debate with a Christian and a Muslim

Dayānanda loved to engage in religious debates, usually with orthodox Hindus, but occasionally with representatives of other faiths. The following summary of his debate with a Christian minister and a Muslim *maulvi* [5] gives a good picture of his harshly critical attitude toward their respective religions—an attitude which led his later followers into intermittent friction with India's Muslims.

[From Har Bilas Sarda, *Life of Dayanand Saraswati*, pp. 170–72]

As time was short, after some talk it was decided that the question "What is salvation and how to attain it," should be discussed. As both the Christians and the Muslims declined to open the debate, Swamiji opened it. He said:

"Mukti or salvation means deliverance, in other words, to get rid of all suffering, and to realize God, to remain happy and free from rebirth. Of the means to attain it, the first is to practice truth, that is truth which is approved both by one's conscience and God. That is truth, in uttering which, one gets encouragement, happiness, and fearlessness. In uttering untruth, fear, doubt, and shame are experienced. As the third mantra of the fortieth chapter of Yajurveda says, those who violate God's teachings, that is, those who speak, act, or believe against one's conscience are called Asur, Rakkhshas, wicked and sinful. The second means to attain salvation is to acquire knowledge of the Vedas and follow truth. The third means is to associate with men of truth and knowledge. The fourth is by practicing Yoga, to eliminate untruth from the mind and the soul, and to fix it in truth. The fifth is to recite the qualities of God and meditate on them. The sixth is to pray to God to keep one steadfast in truth (gyana), realization of the reality and dharma, to keep one away from

[5] A term denoting a Muslim learned in Islamic law and theology.

untruth, ignorance and adharma, and to free one from the woes of birth and death and obtain mukti. When a man worships God wholeheartedly and sincerely, the merciful God gives him happiness. Salvation, dharma, material gain and fulfillment of desires, and attainment of truth are the results of one's efforts, and not otherwise. To act according to the teaching of God is dharma and violation of it is adharma. Only rightful means should be adopted to attain success and prosperity. Injustice, untruth and unrighteous means should not be made use of to gain happiness.

Rev. Scott said:

"Salvation does not mean deliverance from woes. Salvation only means to be saved from sins and to obtain Heaven. God had created Adam pure, but he was misled by Satan and committed sin which made all his descendants sinful. Man commits sin of his own accord as the clock works by itself, that is to say, one cannot avoid committing sin by one's own effort and so cannot get salvation. One can obtain salvation only by believing in Christ. Wherever Christianity spreads, people are saved from sin. I have attained salvation by believing in Christ."

Maulvi Muhammad Hasim said:

"God does what he wishes to do; whom He wishes He gives salvation, just as a judge acquits those with whom he is pleased and punishes those with whom he is displeased. God does what He likes. He is beyond our control. We must trust whoever is the ruler for the time being. Our Prophet is the ruler of the present time. We can get salvation by putting our trust in Him. With knowledge we can do good work, but moksha or salvation lies in His hands."

Swamiji replied that:

"Suffering is the necessary result of sin; whoever avoids sin will be saved from suffering. The Christians believe God to be powerful; but to believe that Satan misled Adam to commit sin is to believe that God is not All powerful; for, if God had been All powerful, Satan could not have misled Adam, who had been created pure by God. No sensible man can believe that Adam committed sin and all his descendants became sinful. *He alone undergoes suffering who commits sin; no one else.* You say that Satan misleads everyone, I therefore ask you who misled Satan. If you say no one misled him, then as Satan misled himself, so must Adam have done it. Why believe in Satan then? If you say, somebody else must have misled Satan, then the only one who could have done it was God. In that case when God himself misleads and gets others to commit sin, then how can He save people from sin. Satan disturbs and spoils God's creation, but God neither punishes him nor imprisons him, nor puts him to death. This proves that God is powerless to do so. Those who believe in Satan cannot avoid committing sins, for they believe that Satan gets them to commit sin and they themselves are not sinful. Again, when God's only son suffered crucifixion for the sins of all people, then the people need not be afraid of being punished for their sins and they can go on committing sins with impunity. The illustration of the clock given by the Padree sahib is also inappropriate. "The clock works only as its *maker has given it the power* to do. The clock cannot alter it. Then again how can you continue to live in Paradise. Adam was misled there by Satan into eating wheat. Will you not eat wheat and be expelled from Paradise? You gentlemen believe God to be like a man. Man has limited knowledge and does not know everything, he therefore stands in need of recommendation of someone who possesses knowledge. But God is All-knowing and All-powerful. He does not stand in need of any recommendation or help from any prophet or anyone else; otherwise, where would be the difference between God and man? Nor does He according to you remain just, for He does not do justice, if he pardons the culprit on the recommendations of anybody. If God is present everywhere, He cannot have a body; for if he has a body, He will be subject to limitation and will not be infinite, and then he must be subject to birth and death. Is God incapable of saving his worshipers without Christ's intervention? Nor has God any need of a prophet. It is true that where there are good people in a country, people improve because of good men's teachings. As regards the Maulvi sahib, he is wrong in saying that God does what He likes, because then He does not remain just. As a fact, he gives salvation only to those whose works deserve it. Without sin and righteousness there can be no suffering and no happiness. God is the ruler for all time. If God gives salvation on the recommendation of others, he becomes dependent. God is All-powerful. It is a matter of surprise that though the Mussalmans believe God to be one and without a second, yet they made the prophet take part with God in bestowing salvation."

The Virtues of Europeans

For all his disdain for the Christian religion, Swāmī Dayānanda was not oblivious to the good qualities of India's British rulers, particularly those virtues (such as marrying the person of one's choice) for which he found support in the Vedas.

[From *The Light of Truth*, pp. 443–44]

Q. Look at the Europeans! They wear boots, jackets, and trousers, live in hotels, and eat of the hands of all. These are the causes of their advancement.

A. This is your mistake, since the Muhammadans and low-caste people eat of the hands of every one and yet they are so backward. The causes of their advancement are:

1. The custom of child-marriage does not prevail among them.

2. They give their boys and girls sound training and education.

3. They *choose* their own life-partners. Such marriages are called *Swyamvara*,[1] because a maid chooses her own consort.

4. They do not allow their children to associate with bad people. Being well educated, they do not fall into the snares of any unprincipled person.

5. Whatever they do, they do after discussing it thoroughly among themselves and referring it to their representative assembly.

6. They sacrifice everything, their wealth, their hearts, aye, their very lives, for the good of their nation.

7. They are not indolent, on the contrary, live active lives.

8. They allow boots and shoes made in their country (or those made after their pattern in this country) to be taken into courts, and offices, but never Indian shoes. This must suffice to convince you that they value their boots much more than the natives of this country.

9. They have been in this country for more than one hundred years, and yet they wear thick clothing, as they used to do at home, up to this day. They have not changed the fashion of their country, but many among you have copied their dress. This shows that you are foolish, while they are wise. No wise man will ever imitate others.

10. Every one among them does his duty most faithfully.

11. They always obey orders (of their superiors).

[1] One's own choosing.

12. They help their countrymen in trade, etc.

It is the possession of such sterling qualities and the doing of such noble deeds that have contributed to the advancement of the Europeans. They have not become great by wearing boots, shoes, and eating in hotels and doing such other ordinary things or by doing evil things.

A Statement of My Beliefs

In an appendix to *The Light of Truth,* Swāmī Dayānanda summed up his credo, of which the essence is that God is one, and the Vedas are His word.
    [From *The Light of Truth,* pp. 677–78]

I believe in a religion based on universal and all-embracing principles which have always been accepted as true by mankind, and will continue to command the allegiance of mankind in the ages to come. Hence it is that the religion in question is called the *primeval eternal religion,* which means that it is above the hostility of all human creeds whatsoever. Whatever is believed in by those who are steeped in ignorance or have been led astray by sectaries is not worthy of being accepted by the wise. That faith alone is really true and worthy of acceptance which is followed by *Aptas,* i.e., those who are true in word, deed and thought, promote public good and are impartial and learned; but all that is discarded by such men must be considered as unworthy of belief and false.

My conception of God and all other objects in the universe is founded on the teachings of the Veda and other true Shastras, and is in conformity with the beliefs of all the sages, from Brahma [2] down to Jaimini.[3] I offer a statement of these beliefs for the acceptance of all good men. That alone I hold to be acceptable which is worthy of being believed by all men in all ages. I do not entertain the least idea of founding a new religion or sect. My sole aim is to believe in truth and help others to believe in it, to reject falsehood and help others to do the same. Had I been biased, I would have championed any one of the religions prevailing in India. But I have not done so. On the contrary, I do not approve of what is objectionable and false in the institutions of this or any other country, nor do I reject what is good and in harmony with the dictates of true religion, nor have I any desire to do so, since a contrary conduct is wholly unworthy of man. He alone is entitled to be called a man who

[2] The first promulgator of the Vedas.   [3] The author of the Pūrva Mīmāṃsā Sūtras.

possesses a thoughtful nature and feels for others in the same way as he does for his own self, does not fear the unjust, however powerful, but fears the truly virtuous, however weak. Moreover, he should always exert himself to his utmost to protect the righteous, and advance their good, and conduct himself worthily towards them even though they be extremely poor and weak and destitute of material resources. On the other hand, he should constantly strive to destroy, humble, and oppose the wicked, sovereign rulers of the whole earth and men of great influence and power though they be. In other words, a man should, as far as it lies in his power, constantly endeavor to undermine the power of the unjust and to strengthen that of the just, he may have to bear any amount of terrible suffering, he may have even to quaff the bitter cup of death in the performance of this duty, which devolves on him on account of being a man, but he should not shirk it.

Now I give below a brief summary of my beliefs. Their detailed exposition has been given in this book in its proper place.

1. He, Who is called *Brahma* or the Most High; who is *Paramātmā,* or the Supreme Spirit Who permeates the whole universe; Who is a true personification of Existence, Consciousness, and Bliss; Whose nature, attributes, and characteristics are Holy; Who is Omniscient, Formless, All-pervading, Unborn, Infinite, Almighty, Just, and Merciful; Who is the author of the universe, sustains and dissolves it; Who awards all souls the fruits of their deeds in strict accordance with the requirements of absolute justice and is possessed of the like attributes—even *Him* I believe to be the Great God.

2. I hold that the four Vedas—the repository of Knowledge and Religious Truths—are the Word of God. They comprise what is known as the *Sanhita—Mantra* [4] portion only. They are absolutely free from error, and are an authority unto themselves. In other words, they do not stand in need of any other book to uphold their authority. Just as the sun (or a lamp) by his light, reveals his own nature as well as that of other objects of the universe, such as the earth—even so are the *Vedas.*

---

[4] The collections of hymns which make up the first part of each of the four Vedas. See Chapter I.

SRI RĀMAKRISHNA: MYSTIC AND
SPIRITUAL TEACHER

Sri Rāmakrishna (1836–1886) was among the most saintly of the many religious leaders to whom modern India has given birth. A son of Bengal, like Debendranāth and Keshub, he was, unlike them, a child of the soil and never lost his rustic simplicity. Like Dayānanda, he personified the rebirth of an ancient tradition in the midst of an era of increasing Westernization and modernization. But unlike that militant Gujarātī, he practiced and preached a gentle faith of selfless devotion to God and of ultimate absorption in Him.

Rāmakrishna imbibed from his boyhood days as the son of a village priest the spirit of devotion to Kālī, the Divine Mother, which the songs of Rāmprasād had made popular in rural Bengal in the eighteenth century. Ecstatic communion with the Divine, an aspect of this tradition, came naturally to the attractive young brāhman, and at the age of seven he experienced his first mystical trance. He received no formal education in Sanskrit or English, and could read and write Bengali only moderately well. Yet this "God-intoxicated" man attained to a wisdom that was the envy of many of his enlightened, English-educated contemporaries.

His elder brother took him at sixteen to Calcutta, where they were eventually installed as priests of a new temple on the Hooghly River, a branch of the Ganges. For the next twelve years Rāmakrishna put himself through every known type of spiritual discipline in an agonized search for God. Finally his efforts were rewarded with a series of mystical experiences during which he saw God in a variety of manifestations—as a Divine Mother, as Sītā, as Rāma, as Krishna, as Muhammad, as Jesus Christ, and worshiped Him in the manner of Muslims, Jains, and Buddhists—in each case suiting his dress, food and meditation to the particular religious tradition concerned.

Through the aid of Keshub Chunder Sen, who greatly admired him, Rāmakrishna began to attract disciples from among the Westernized middle class of Calcutta. His keen insight into the hearts of men made him an excellent teacher, and his natural simplicity and purity made a profound impression on these young men. From him they learned to draw strength from the living traditions of popular Hinduism; through them his teachings became known to all India and the world at large.

RĀMAKRISHNA
The World As Seen by a Mystic

Rāmakrishna lived in a state of consciousness so close to continual meditation that he was able to see great meaning in the smallest incidents. One of his disciples collected his sayings and anecdotes as he related them. They show us the world as he saw it—a world permeated by the presence of the Divine.
[From *The Gospel of Rāmakrishna*, pp. 207–14]

I practiced austerities for a long time. I cared very little for the body. My longing for the Divine Mother was so great that I would not eat or sleep. I would lie on the bare ground, placing my head on a lump of earth, and cry out loudly: "Mother, Mother, why dost Thou not come to me?" I did not know how the days and nights passed away. I used to have ecstasy all the time. I saw my disciples as my own people, like children and relations, long before they came to me. I used to cry before my Mother, saying: "O Mother! I am dying for my beloved ones (Bhaktas); do Thou bring them to me as quickly as possible."

At that time whatever I desired came to pass. Once I desired to build a small hut in the Panchavati [1] for meditation and to put a fence around it. Immediately after I saw a huge bundle of bamboo sticks, rope, strings, and even a knife, all brought by the tide in front of the Panchavati. A servant of the Temple, seeing these things, ran to me with great delight and told me of them. There was the exact quantity of material necessary for the hut and the fence. When they were built, nothing remained over. Everyone was amazed to see this wonderful sight.

When I reached the state of continuous ecstasy, I gave up all external forms of worship; I could no longer perform them. Then I prayed to my Divine Mother: "Mother, who will now take care of me? I have no power to take care of myself. I like to hear Thy name and feed Thy Bhaktas and help the poor. Who will make it possible for me to do these things? Send me someone who will be able to do these for me." As the answer to this prayer came Mathura Bābu,[2] who served me so long

[1] Five sacred trees planted together to form a grove used for contemplation.
[2] A wealthy disciple. Bābu is a respectful Bengali form of address.

and with such intense devotion and faith! Again at another time I said to the Mother: "I shall have no child of my own, but I wish to have as my child a pure Bhakta, who will stay with me all the time. Send me such an one." Then came Rākhāl (Brahmānanda).

Those who are my own are parts of my very Self.

ii

In referring to the time of joyous illumination which immediately followed His enlightenment, He exclaimed:

What a state it was! The slightest cause aroused in me the thought of the Divine Ideal. One day I went to the Zoological Garden in Calcutta. I desired especially to see the lion, but when I beheld him, I lost all sense-consciousness and went into samādhi. Those who were with me wished to show me the other animals, but I replied: "I saw everything when I saw the king of beasts. Take me home." The strength of the lion had aroused in me the consciousness of the omnipotence of God and had lifted me above the world of phenomena.

Another day I went to the parade ground to see the ascension of a balloon. Suddenly my eyes fell upon a young English boy leaning against a tree. The very posture of his body brought before me the vision of the form of Krishna and I went into samādhi.

Again I saw a woman wearing a blue garment under a tree. She was a harlot. As I looked at her, instantly the ideal of Sītā [3] appeared before me! I forgot the existence of the harlot, but saw before me pure and spotless Sītā, approached Rāma, the Incarnation of Divinity, and for a long time I remained motionless. I worshiped all women as representatives of the Divine Mother. I realized the Mother of the universe in every woman's form.

Mathura Bābu, the son-in-law of Rāshmoni, invited me to stay in his house for a few days. At that time I felt so strongly that I was the maid-servant of my Divine Mother that I thought of myself as a woman. The ladies of the house had the same feeling; they did not look upon me as a man. As women are free before a young girl, so were they before me. My mind was above the consciousness of sex.

What a Divine state it was! I could not eat here in the Temple. I would

[3] The consort of Rāma, hero of the *Rāmāyaṇa*. She exemplifies the Hindu ideal of womanhood.

walk from place to place and enter into the house of strangers after their meal hour. I would sit there quietly, without uttering a word. When questioned, I would say: "I wish to eat here." Immediately they would feed me with the best things they had.

iii

Once I heard of a poor Brāhmin who was a true devotee and who lived in a small hut in Bāghbāzār. I desired to see him, so I asked Mathura Bābu to take me to him. He consented, immediately ordered a large carriage, and drove me there. The Brāhmin's house was so small that he scarcely had room to receive us, and he was much surprised to see me coming with such a rich man in such a carriage!

At another time I wished to meet [Debendranāth] Tagore. He is a very rich man, but in spite of his enormous wealth he is devoted to God and repeats His Holy Name. For this reason I desired to know him. I spoke about him to Mathura Bābu. He replied: "Very well, Bābā,[4] I will take Thee to him; he was my classmate." So he took me and introduced me to him, saying: "This holy man has come to see you. He is mad after God." I saw in him a little pride and egotism. It is natural for a man who has so much wealth, culture, fame, and social position. I said to Mathura Bābu: "Tell me, does pride spring from true wisdom or from ignorance? He who has attained to the highest knowledge of Brāhman cannot possess pride or egotism, such as 'I am learned,' 'I am wise,' 'I am rich,' and so on." While I was speaking with [Debendranāth] Tagore, I went into a state from where I could see the true character of every individual. In this state the most learned pandits and scholars appear to me like blades of grass. When I see that scholars have neither true discrimination nor dispassion, then I feel that they are like straws; or they seem like vultures who soar high in the heavens, but keep their minds on the charnel-pits below on the earth. In [Debendranāth] I found both spiritual knowledge and worldly desire. He has a number of children, some of whom are quite young. A doctor was present. I said: "When you have so much spiritual knowledge, how can you live constantly in the midst of so much worldliness? You are like Rājā Janaka;[5] you can keep your mind on God, remaining amid worldly pleasures and luxury. Therefore I have come to see you. Tell me something of the Divine Be-

---

[4] An affectionate form of address.   [5] King Janaka, the father of Sītā.

ing." [Debendranāth] then read some passages from the Vedas and said: "This world is like a chandelier, and each Jiva (individual soul) is like a light in it." Long ago, when I spent nearly all my time meditating at the Panchavati, I saw the same thing. When [Debendranāth's] words harmonized with my experience, I knew that he must have attained to some true knowledge. I asked him to explain. He said: "Who would have known this world? God has created man to manifest His glory. If there were no light in the chandelier, it would be all dark. The chandelier itself would not be visible." After a long conversation [Debendranāth] Tagore begged me to come to the anniversary of the Brāhmo-Samāj. I answered: "If it be the will of the Lord. I go wherever He takes me."

Fix Your Mind on God

During one of his visits with Keshub Chunder Sen and his disciples, Rāmakrishna advised the Brāhmos to cultivate the liberating powers of the mind.
[From *The Gospel of Rāmakrishna*, pp. 158–60]

A Brāhmo: Revered Sir, is it true that God cannot be realized without giving up the world?

The Bhagavān,[6] smiling: Oh no! You do not have to give up everything. You are better off where you are. By living in the world you are enjoying the taste of both the pure crystallized sugar and of the molasses with all its impurities. You are indeed better off. Verily I say unto you, you are living in the world, there is no harm in that; but you will have to fix your mind on God, otherwise you cannot realize Him. Work with one hand and hold the Feet of the Lord with the other. When you have finished your work, fold His feet to your heart with both your hands.

Everything is in the mind. Bondage and freedom are in the mind. You can dye the mind with any color you wish. It is like a piece of clean white linen: dip it in red and it will be red, in blue it will be blue, in green it will be green, or any other color. Do you not see that if you study English, English words will come readily to you? Again, if a pandit studies Sanskrit, he will readily quote verse from Sacred Books. If you keep your mind in evil company, your thoughts, ideas, and words will be colored with evil; but keep in the company of Bhaktas, then your thoughts, ideas and words will be of God. The mind is everything. On

[6] Blessed One.

one side is the wife, on the other side is the child; it loves the wife in one way and the child in another way, yet the mind is the same.

By the mind one is bound; by the mind one is freed. If I think I am absolutely free, whether I live in the world or in the forest, where is my bondage? I am the child of God, the son of the King of kings; who can bind me? When bitten by a snake, if you assert with firmness: "There is no venom in me," you will be cured. In the same way, he who asserts with strong conviction: "I am not bound, I am free," becomes free.

Some one gave me a book of the Christians. I asked him to read it to me. In it there was only one theme—sin and sin, from the beginning to the end. (To Keshub) In your Brāhmo-Samāj the main topic is also sin. The fool who repeats again and again: "I am bound. I am bound," remains in bondage. He who repeats day and night: "I am a sinner, I am a sinner," becomes a sinner indeed.

Beware of the Wicked

Rāmakrishna's advice to his disciples was often of a very practical nature, as this example shows.
[From *The Gospel of Rāmakrishna,* pp. 42–44]

One of the devotees present said: But when a person is annoyed with me, Bhagavān, I feel unhappy. I feel that I have not been able to love everyone equally.

Rāmakrishna: When you feel that way, you should have a talk with that person and try to make peace with him. If you fail after such attempts, then you need not give it further thought. Take refuge with the Lord. Think upon Him. Do not let your mind be disturbed by any other thing.

Devotee: Christ and Chaitanya have both taught us to love all mankind.

Rāmakrishna: You should love everyone because God dwells in all beings. But to wicked people you should bow down at a distance. (To Bijoy, smiling): Is it true that people blame you because you mix with those who believe in a Personal God with form? A true devotee of God should possess absolute calmness and never be disturbed by the opinions of others. Like a blacksmith's anvil, he will endure all blows and persecutions and yet remain firm in his faith and always the same. Wicked people may say many things about you and blame you; but if you long for God, you should endure with patience. One can think on God even dwelling in the midst of wicked people. The sages of ancient times, who lived in forests, could meditate on God although surrounded by tigers, bears, and other wild beasts. The nature of the wicked is like that of a tiger or bear. They attack the innocent and injure them. You should be especially cautious in coming in contact with the following: First, the wealthy. A person who possesses wealth and many attendants can easily do harm to another if he so desires. You should be very guarded in speaking with him; sometimes it may even be necessary to agree with him in his opinion. Second, a dog. When a dog barks at you, you must not run, but talk to him and quiet him. Third, a bull. When a bull chases you, you should always pacify him by talking to him. Fourth, a drunkard. If you make him angry, he will call you names and swear at you. You should address him as a dear relative, then he will be happy and obliging.

When wicked people come to see me, I am very careful. The character of some of them is like that of a snake. They may bite you unawares. It may take a long time and much discrimination to recover from the effects of that bite. Or you may get so angry at them that you will wish to take revenge. It is necessary, however, to keep occasionally the company of holy men. Through such association right discrimination will come.

Parables and Sayings

There is much in Rāmakrishna's homely yet charming wisdom that reminds the reader of the teachings of Jesus. Both men took experiences from everyday life and used them to illustrate profound moral and religious truths. But despite the many similarities in the sayings and parables of the two teachers, it is clear that there remains a basic difference between the Hindu and the Judeo-Christian conception of the nature and means of salvation.

[From *Teachings of Sri Rāmakrishna*, pp. 31-94, 351]

The vegetables in the cooking pot move and leap till the children think they are living beings. But the grown-ups explain that they are not moving of themselves; if the fire be taken away they will soon cease to stir. So it is ignorance that thinks "I am the doer." All our strength is the strength of God. All is silent if the fire be removed. A marionette dances well, while the wires are pulled; but when the master's hand is gone, it falls inert. [p. 31]

The guru said: "Everything that exists is God," and the disciple understood this literally. Passing along the road, he met an elephant. The driver shouted from his high place: "Move away, move away!" But the disciple thought: "Why should I move away? I am God and so is the elephant. What fear can God have of himself?" Thinking thus he did not move. At last the elephant took him by his trunk and dashed him aside. He was severely hurt, and going back to his guru, he told his story. The guru said: "It is quite true that you are God. It is true that the elephant is God too, but God was also in the form of the elephant-driver. Why did you not listen to the God on top?" [p. 46]

. . . .

At a game of chess the onlookers can tell what is the correct move better than the players themselves. Men of the world think they are very clever; but they are attached to things of this world—money, honors, pleasure, etc. Being actually engaged in the play it is hard for them to hit upon the right move. Holy men who have given up the world are not attached to it. They are like the onlookers at a game of chess. They see things in their true light and can judge better than the men of the world. [p. 68]

. . . .

As a nail cannot be driven into a stone, yet it enters easily into the earth, so the advice of the pious does not affect the soul of a worldly man, while it pierces deep into the heart of a believer. [p. 94]

A man woke up at midnight and desired to smoke. He wanted a light, so he went to a neighbor's house and knocked at the door. Someone opened the door and asked him what he wanted. The man said: "I wish to smoke. Can you give me a light?" The neighbor replied: "Bah! What is the matter with you? You have taken so much trouble to come and [awaken] us at this hour, when in your hand you have a lighted lantern!" What a man wants is already within him; but he still wanders here and there in search of it. [p. 351]

[From Müller, *Rāmakrishna, His Life and Sayings,* pp. 134–80]
A disciple, having firm faith in the infinite power of his guru, walked over a river even by pronouncing his name. The guru, seeing this, thought

within himself: "Well, is there such a power even in my name? Then I must be very great and powerful, no doubt!" The next day he also tried to walk over the river pronouncing "I, I, I," but no sooner had he stepped into the waters than he sank and was drowned. Faith can achieve miracles, while vanity or egoism is the death of man. [p. 134]

. . . . .

A man after fourteen years of hard asceticism in a lonely forest obtained at last the power of walking over the waters. Overjoyed at this acquisition, he went to his guru, and told him of his grand feat. At this the master replied: "My poor boy, what thou hast accomplished after fourteen years' arduous labor, ordinary men do the same by paying a penny to the boatman." [p. 154]

. . . . .

When a wound is perfectly healed, the slough falls off it itself; but if the slough be taken off earlier, it bleeds. Similarly, when the perfection of knowledge is reached by a man, the distinctions of caste fall off from him, but it is wrong for the ignorant to break such distinctions. [p. 147]

. . . . .

The light of the gas illumines various localities with various intensities. But the life of the light, namely, the gas, comes from one common reservoir. So the religious teachers of all climes and ages are but as many lampposts through which is emitted the light of the spirit flowing constantly from one source, the Lord Almighty. [p. 148]

. . . .

The difference between the modern Brāhmaism [of the Brāhmo Samāj] and Hinduism is like the difference between the single note of music and the whole music. The modern Brahmas are content with the single note of Brahman, while the Hindu religion is made up of several notes producing a sweet and melodious harmony. [p. 153]

. . . .

As it is very difficult to gather together the mustard-seeds that escape out of a torn package, and are scattered in all directions; so, when the human mind runs in diverse directions and is occupied with many things in the world, it is not a very easy affair to collect and concentrate it. [p. 167]

. . . .

He who would learn to swim must attempt swimming for some days. No one can venture to swim in the sea after a single day's practice. So if you want to swim in the sea of Brahman, you must make many ineffectual attempts at first, before you can successfully swim therein. [p. 175]

As the village maidens carry four or five pots of water placed one over the other upon their heads, talking all the way with one another about their own joys and sorrows, and yet do not allow one drop of water to be spilt, so must the traveler in the path of virtue walk along. In whatever circumstances he may be placed, let him always take heed that his heart does not swerve from the true path. [p. 177]

. . . .

When an elephant is let loose, it goes about uprooting trees and shrubs, but as soon as the driver pricks him on the head with the goad he becomes quiet; so the mind when unrestrained wantons in the luxuriance of idle thoughts, but becomes calm at once when struck with the goad of discrimination. [p. 180]

. . . .

Know thyself, and thou shalt then know the non-self and the Lord of all. What is my ego? Is it my hand, or foot, or flesh, or blood, or muscle, or tendon? Ponder deep, and thou shalt know that there is no such thing as I. As by continually peeling off the skin of the onion, so by analyzing the ego it will be found that there is not any real entity corresponding to the ego. The ultimate result of all such analysis is God. When egoism drops away, Divinity manifests itself. [p. 180]

SWĀMĪ VIVEKĀNANDA: HINDU MISSIONARY TO THE WEST

Among Sri Rāmakrishna's disciples was a young Calcutta-born student on whom he showered special attention and praise. This boy Narendranāth Datta (1863–1902) came from a Kāyastha family of lawyers and received a good Western-style education. When he first visited Rāmakrishna he was planning to study law in England and then follow the profession which was the high road to success in British India. Within a year's time his interviews with the master mystic had changed the course of his life. He resolved to give up worldly pursuits and adopt the life of a sannyāsī. After twelve years of ascetic discipline he became famous as Swāmī Vivekānanda, the apostle to the world of his master's philosophy of God-realization.

Vivekānanda's meteoric career as missionary of Vedantic Hinduism to the West began in 1893 when he addressed the First World Parliament of Religions at Chicago. After four years of lecturing in America and England he returned to India a national hero and took up the task of regenerating his fellow-countrymen. He literally burned himself out in their service, dedicating the Rāmakrishna Mission to both social work and religious education, and rousing young men with his fiery speeches to devote themselves to uplifting the poor and starving millions of India.

Although he died at thirty-nine, Vivekānanda's example had a powerful impact on the thinking of his own and later generations. Despite his scorn for politics, his success in preaching to the world the greatness of Hinduism gave his countrymen an added sense of dignity and pride in their own culture. His zeal to serve the downtrodden masses opened a new dimension of activity to Indian nationalist leaders, whose Western outlook had heretofore isolated them from the vast majority of their countrymen. Gāndhi, the greatest to work in this new field, acknowledged his debt to the Swāmī in this respect.

Vivekānanda called India to become great by realizing her own possibilities and by living up to her own highest ideals. The heart and soul of his teaching was the message of his beloved master, Rāmakrishna: That each man was potentially divine, and so should both work to unleash the infinite power within himself, and should help other men to do the same.

VIVEKĀNANDA
Man Is God

In his series of lectures entitled "Practical Vedanta," delivered in London in 1896, Vivekānanda set forth the teachings of his master, Rāmakrishna. The central point of his message was that God is within man, that in his inmost being, man is God.

[From *The Complete Works of the Swami Vivekananda*, II, 324–25]

Do you not remember what the Bible says: "If you cannot love your brother whom you have seen, how can you love God whom you have not seen?" If you cannot see God in the human face, how can you see Him in the clouds, or in images made of dull, dead matter, or in mere fictitious stores of your brain? I shall call you religious from the day you begin to see God in men and women and then you will understand what is meant by turning the left cheek to the man who strikes you on the right. When you see man as God, everything, even the tiger, will be welcome. Whatever comes to you is but the Lord, the Eternal, the Blessed One, appearing to us in various forms, as our father, and mother, and friend, and child; they are our own soul playing with us.

As our human relationships can thus be made divine so our relationship with God may take any of these forms and we can look upon Him as our father or mother or friend or beloved. Calling God Mother is a higher idea than calling Him Father, and to call Him Friend is still higher, but the highest is to regard Him as the Beloved. The highest point of all is to see no difference between lover and beloved. You may remember, perhaps, the old Persian story, of how a lover came and knocked at the door of the beloved and was asked: "Who are you?" He answered: "It is I," and there was no response. A second time he came, and exclaimed: "I am here," but the door was not opened. The third time he came, and the voice asked from inside: "Who is there?" He replied: "I am thyself, my beloved," and the door opened. So is the relation between God and ourselves. He is in everything, He is everything. Every man and woman is the palpable, blissful, living God. Who says God is unknown? Who says He is to be searched after? We have found God eternally. We have been living in Him eternally. He is eternally known, eternally worshiped.

The Rationale of Caste and Idol-Worship

In contrast with the Brāhmo reformers and Dayānanda, Vivekānanda justified the caste system as good, and the worship of idols as useful for those who need them. Yet he interpreted these ancient practices in a way that brought them into harmony with the western ideals of social and religious equality.

[From *The Complete Works of the Swami Vivekananda*, III, 245–46, 460]

Caste is a natural order. I can perform one duty in social life, and you another; you can govern a country, and I can mend a pair of old shoes, but there is no reason why you are greater than I, for can you mend my shoes? Can I govern the country? I am clever in mending shoes, you are clever in reading Vedas, but there is no reason why you should trample on my head; why if one commits murder should he be praised, and if another steals an apple why should he be hanged! This will have to go. Caste is good. That is the only natural way of solving life. Men must form themselves into groups, and you cannot get rid of that. Wherever you go there will be caste. But that does not mean that there should be these privileges. They should be knocked on the head. If you teach Vedanta to the fisherman, he will say, I am as good a man as you, I am a fisherman, you are a philosopher, but I have the same God in me as you have in you. And that is what we want, no privileges for any one, equal chances for all; let every one be taught that the Divine is within, and every one will work out his own salvation. [pp. 245-46]

. . . .

This external worship of images has, however, been described in all our Shastras as the lowest of all the low forms of worship. But that does not mean that it is a wrong thing to do. Despite the many iniquities that have found entrance into the practices of image-worship as it is in vogue now, I do not condemn it. Aye, where would I have been, if I had not been blessed with the dust of the holy feet of that orthodox, image-worshiping Brahmana [Rāmakrishna]!

Those reformers who preach against image-worship, or what they denounce as idolatry—to them I say: "Brothers! If you are fit to worship God-without-Form discarding any external help, do so, but why do you condemn others who cannot do the same? A beautiful large edifice, the glorious relic of a hoary antiquity has, out of neglect or disuse, fallen into a dilapidated condition; accumulations of dirt and dust may be lying everywhere within it; may be, some portions are tumbling down to the ground. What will you do to it? Will you take in hand the necessary cleansing and repairs and thus restore the old, or will you pull the whole edifice down to the ground and seek to build another in its place, after a sordid modern plan whose permanence has yet to be established? We have to reform it, which truly means to make ready or perfect by necessary cleansing and repairs, not by demolishing the whole thing. There the function of reform ends." [p. 460]

India and the West

Vivekānanda developed the idea, put forth by Keshub, that India should take practical knowledge from Europe, and in exchange should teach religious wisdom to the world. In a speech about Rāmakrishna delivered in New York he stated most emphatically his claim that the Orient (by which he primarily meant India) was superior to the West in spiritual matters.

[From *The Complete Works of the Swami Vivekananda*, IV, 150–52]

"Whenever virtue subsides and vice prevails, I come down to help mankind," declares Krishna, in the *Bhagavad-Gītā*. Whenever this world of ours, on account of growth, on account of added circumstances, requires a new adjustment, a wave of power comes, and as man is acting on two planes, the spiritual and the material, waves of adjustment come on both planes. On the one side, of the adjustment on the material plane, Europe has mainly been the basis during modern times, and of the adjustment on the other, the spiritual plane, Asia has been the basis throughout the history of the world. Today, man requires one more adjustment on the spiritual plane; today when material ideas are at the height of their glory and power, today when man is likely to forget his divine nature, through his growing dependence on matter, and is likely to be reduced to a mere money-making machine, an adjustment is necessary; the voice has spoken, and the power is coming to drive away the clouds of gathering materialism. The power has been set in motion which, at no distant date, will bring unto mankind once more the memory of its real nature, and again the place from which this power will start will be Asia. This world of ours is on the plan of the division of labor. It is vain to say that one man shall possess everything. Yet how childish we are! The baby in its ignorance thinks that its doll is the only possession that is to be coveted in this whole universe. So a nation which is great in the possession of material power thinks that that is all that is to be coveted, that that is all that is meant by progress, that that is all that is meant by civilization, and if there are other nations which do not care for possession, and do not possess that power, they are not fit to live, their whole existence is useless! On the other hand, another nation may think that mere material civilization is utterly useless. From the Orient came the voice which once told the world, that if a man possesses everything that is under the sun and does not possess spirituality, what avails it? This is the Oriental type; the other is the Occidental type.

Each of these types has its grandeur, each has its glory. The present adjustment will be the harmonizing, the mingling of these two ideals. To the Oriental, the world of spirit is as real as to the Occidental is the world of senses. In the spiritual, the Oriental finds everything he wants or hopes for; in it he finds all that makes life real to him. To the Occidental he is a dreamer; to the Oriental, the Occidental is a dreamer, playing with ephemeral toys, and he laughs to think that grown-up men and women should make so much of a handful of matter which they will have to leave sooner or later. Each calls the other a dreamer. But the Oriental ideal is as necessary for the progress of the human race as is the Occidental, and I think it is more necessary. Machines never made mankind happy, and never will make. He who is trying to make us believe this, will claim that happiness is in the machine, but it is always in the mind. The man alone who is the lord of his mind can become happy, and none else. And what, after all, is power of machinery? Why should a man who can send a current of electricity through a wire be called a very great man, and very intelligent man? Does not Nature do a million times more than that every moment? Why not then fall down and worship Nature? What avails it if you have power over the whole of the world, if you have mastered every atom in the universe? That will not make you happy unless you have the power of happiness in yourself, until you have conquered yourself. Man is born to conquer Nature, it is true, but the Occidental means by "Nature" only the physical or external Nature. It is true that external Nature is majestic, with its mountains, and oceans, and rivers, and with the infinite powers and varieties. Yet there is a more majestic internal Nature of man, higher than the sun, moon, and the stars, higher than this earth of ours, higher than the physical universe, transcending these little lives of ours; and it affords another field of study. There the Orientals excel, just as the Occidentals excel in the other. Therefore it is fitting that, whenever there is a spiritual adjustment, it should come from the Orient. It is also fitting that when the Oriental wants to learn about machine-making, he should sit at the feet of the Occidental and learn from him. When the Occident wants to learn about the spirit, about God, about the soul, about the meaning and the mystery of this universe, he must sit at the feet of the Orient to learn.

Indian Thought to Conquer the World

In a lecture in Madras Swāmī Vivekānanda challenged his audience to conquer the West with India's spirituality. Through such speeches as this he instilled a feeling of self-confidence in the youth of the country, thus contributing to the later movement for national independence.

[From *The Complete Works of the Swami Vivekananda*, III, 276–77]

This is the great ideal before us, and every one must be ready for it—the conquest of the whole world by India—nothing less than that, and we must all get ready for it, strain every nerve for it. Let foreigners come and flood the land with their armies, never mind. Up, India, and conquer the world with your spirituality! Aye, as has been declared on this soil first, love must conquer hatred, hatred cannot conquer itself. Materialism and all its miseries can never be conquered by materialism. Armies when they attempt to conquer armies only multiply and make brutes of humanity. Spirituality must conquer the West. Slowly they are finding out that what they want is spirituality to preserve them as nations. They are waiting for it, they are eager for it. Where is the supply to come from? Where are the men ready to go out to every country in the world with the messages of the great sages of India? Where are the men who are ready to sacrifice everything, so that this message shall reach every corner of the world? Such heroic souls are wanted to help the spread of truth. Such heroic workers are wanted to go abroad and help to disseminate the great truths of the Vedanta. The world wants it; without it the world will be destroyed. The whole of the Western world is on a volcano which may burst tomorrow, go to pieces tomorrow. They have searched every corner of the world and have found no respite. They have drunk deep of the cup of pleasure and found it vanity. Now is the time to work so that India's spiritual ideas may penetrate deep into the West. Therefore, young men of Madras, I specially ask you to remember this. We must go out, we must conquer the world through our spirituality and philosophy. There is no other alternative, we must do it or die. The only condition of national life, of awakened and vigorous national life, is the conquest of the world by Indian thought.

America and India's Poor

While he was preaching the philosophy of the Vedanta to the people of the West, Vivekānanda was worrying about the poverty of his own countrymen. In 1894 he wrote from Chicago to the Mahārāja of Mysore, one of India's most enlightened princes, giving his opinion of American materialism, and asking for help in his new-found ambition to educate their nation's poor.

[From *The Complete Works of the Swami Vivekananda,* IV, 307–9]

Sri Narayana bless you and yours. Through your Highness' kind help it has been possible for me to come to this country. Since then I have become well-known here, and the hospitable people of this country have supplied all my wants. It is a wonderful country and this is a wonderful nation in many respects. No other nation applies so much machinery in their everyday work as do the people of this country. Everything is machine. Then again, they are only one-twentieth of the whole population of the world. Yet they have fully one-sixth of all the wealth of the world. There is no limit to their wealth and luxuries. Yet everything here is so dear. The wages of labor are the highest in the world; yet the fight between labor and capital is constant.

Nowhere on earth have women so many privileges as in America. They are slowly taking everything into their hands and, strange to say, the number of cultured women is much greater than that of cultured men. Of course, the higher geniuses are mostly from the rank of males. With all the criticism of the Westerners against our caste, they have a worse one —that of money. The almighty dollar, as the Americans say, can do anything here.

No country on earth has so many laws, and in no country are they so little regarded. On the whole our poor Hindu people are infinitely more moral than any of the Westerners. In religion they practice here either hypocrisy or fanaticism. Sober-minded men have become disgusted with their superstitious religions and are looking forward to India for new light. Your Highness cannot realize without seeing, how eagerly they take in any little bit of the grand thoughts of the holy Vedas, which resist and are unharmed by the terrible onslaughts of modern science. The theories of creation out of nothing, of a created soul, and of the big tyrant of a God sitting on a throne in a place called heaven, and of the eternal hell-fires, have disgusted all the educated; and the noble thoughts of the Vedas about the eternity of creation and of the soul, and about the God in our own soul, they are imbibing fast in one shape or other. Within fifty years the educated of the world will come to believe in the eternity of both soul and creation, and in God as our highest and perfect nature, as taught in our holy Vedas. Even now their learned priests are interpreting the Bible in that way. My conclusion is that they require more spiritual civilization, and we, more material.

The one thing that is at the root of all evils in India is the condition of the poor. The poor in the West are devils; compared to them ours are angels, and it is therefore so much the easier to raise our poor. The only service to be done for our lower classes is, to give them education, *to develop their lost individuality*. That is the great task between our people and princes. Up to now nothing has been done in that direction. Priest-power and foreign conquest have trodden them down for centuries, and at last the poor of India have forgotten that they are human beings. They are to be given ideas; their eyes are to be opened to what is going on in the world around them, and then they will work out their own salvation. Every nation, every man, and every woman must work out their own salvation. Give them ideas—that is the only help they require, and then the rest must follow as the effect. Ours is to put the chemicals together, the crystallization comes in the law of nature. Our duty is to put ideas into their heads, they will do the rest. This is what is to be done in India. It is this idea that has been in my mind for a long time. I could not accomplish it in India, and that was the reason of my coming to this country. The great difficulty in the way of educating the poor is this. Supposing even your Highness opens a free school in every village, still it would do no good, for the poverty in India is such, that poor boys would rather go to help their fathers in the fields, or otherwise try to make a living, than come to the school. Now if the mountain does not come to Mahomet, Mahomet must go to the mountain. If the poor boy cannot come to education, education must go to him. There are thousands of single-minded, self-sacrificing Sannyasins in our own country, going from village to village, teaching religion. If some of them can be organized as teachers of secular things also, they will go from place to place, from door to door, not only preaching but teaching also. Suppose two of these men go to a village in the evening with a camera, a globe, some maps, etc. They can teach a great deal of astronomy and geography to the ignorant. By telling stories about different nations, they can give the poor a hundred times more information through the ear than they can get in a lifetime through books. This requires an organization, which again means money. Men enough there are in India to work out this plan, but alas! they have no money. It is very difficult to set a wheel in motion, but when once set, it goes on with increasing velocity. After seeking help in my own country and failing to get any sympathy from the rich, I came over to this country through your Highness' aid. The Americans do not care a bit whether the poor of India die or live. And why should they, when our own people never think of anything but their own selfish ends?

My noble prince, this life is short, the vanities of the world are transient, but they alone live who live for others, the rest are more dead than alive. One such high, noble-minded, and royal son of India as your Highness can do much towards raising India on her feet again, and thus leave a name to posterity which shall be worshiped.

That the Lord may make your noble heart feel intensely for the suffering millions of India sunk in ignorance, is the prayer of—

Vivekananda

Modern India

In one of his last essays, written in Bengali in 1899, Vivekānanda declared India's independence of Western standards. Scouting blind imitation of foreign models as unmanly, he called on his compatriots to take pride in their past and to unite rich and poor, high and low castes, in order to make their nation strong.

[From *The Complete Works of the Swami Vivekananda,* IV, 408-13]

It has been said before that India is slowly awakening through her friction with the outside nations, and, as the result of this little awakening is the appearance, to a certain extent, of free and independent thought in modern India. On one side is modern Western science, dazzling the eyes with the brilliance of myriad suns, and driving in the chariot of hard and fast facts collected by the application of tangible powers direct in their incision; on the other are the hopeful and strengthening traditions of her ancient forefathers, in the days when she was at the zenith of her glory—traditions that have been brought out of the pages of her history by the great sages of her own land and outside, that run for numberless years and centuries through her every vein with the quickening of life drawn from universal love, traditions that reveal unsurpassed valor, superhuman genius, and supreme spirituality, which are the envy of the gods—these inspire her with future hopes. On one side, rank materialism, plenitude of fortune, accumulation of gigantic power, and intense sense-pursuits, have through foreign literature caused a tremendous stir; on the other, through the confounding din of all these discordant sounds, she hears, in low yet unmistakable accents, the heart-rending cries of her ancient gods, cutting her to the quick. There lie before her various strange luxuries introduced from the West—celestial drinks, costly well-served food, splendid apparel, magnificent palaces, new modes of conveyance—new manners, new fashions, dressed in which moves about the well-educated girl in shameless freedom; all these are arousing unfelt desires in her; again, the scene changes and in its place appear, with stern presence, Sītā, Sāvitrī,[1] austere religious vows, fastings, the forest retreat, the matted locks and orange garb of the semi-naked Sannyasin, Samadhi, and the search after the Self. On one side, is the independence of Western societies based on self-interest; on the other, is the extreme self-sacrifice of the Aryan society. In this violent conflict, is it strange that Indian society should be tossed up and down? Of the West, the goal is—individual independence, the language—money-making education, the means—politics; of India, the goal is—Mukti, the language—the Veda, the means—renunciation. For a time, modern India thinks, as it were: I am running this worldly life of mine in vain expectation of uncertain spiritual welfare hereafter, which has spread its fascination over me; and again, lo! spellbound she listens: "Here, in this world of death and change, O man, where is thy happiness?"

On one side, New India is saying: "We should have full freedom in the selection of husband and wife; because, the marriage in which are involved the happiness and misery of all our future life, we must have the right to determine, according to our own free will." On the other, Old India is dictating: "Marriage is not for sense enjoyment, but to perpetuate the race. This is the Indian conception of marriage. By the producing of children, you are contributing to, and are responsible for, the future good or evil of the society. Hence, society has the right to dictate whom

---

[1] Sāvitrī, famed in Indian legend for having saved her doomed husband from the God of Death.

you shall marry and whom you shall not. That form of marriage obtains in society, which is conducive most to its well-being; do you give up your desire of individual pleasure for the good of the many."

On one side New India is saying: "If we only adopt Western ideas, Western language, Western food, Western dress and Western manners, we shall be as strong and powerful as the Western nations"; on the other, Old India is saying: "Fools! By imitation, other's ideas never become one's own—nothing, unless earned, is your own. Does the ass in the lion's skin become the lion?"

On one side, New India is saying: "What the Western nations do are surely good, otherwise how did they become so great?" On the other side, Old India is saying: "The flash of lightning is intensely bright, but only for a moment; look out, boys, it is dazzling your eyes. Beware!"

Have we not then to learn anything from the West? Must we not needs try and exert ourselves for better things? Are we perfect? Is our society entirely spotless, without any flaw? There are many things to learn, we must struggle for new and higher things till we die—struggle is the end of human life. Sri Rāmakrishna used to say: "As long as I live, so long I learn." That man or that society which has nothing to learn is already in the jaws of death. Yes, learn we must many things from the West, but there are fears as well.

A certain young man of little understanding used always to blame Hindu Shastras before Sri Rāmakrishna. One day he praised the *Bhagavad-Gītā,* on which Sri Rāmakrishna said: "Methinks some European pandit has praised the *Gītā,* and so he has also followed suit."

O India, this is your terrible danger. The spell of imitating the West is getting such a strong hold upon you, that what is good or what is bad is no longer decided by reason, judgment, discrimination, or reference to the Shastras. Whatever ideas, whatever manners the white men praise or like, are good; whatever things they dislike or censure are bad! Alas! What can be a more tangible proof of foolishness than this?

The Western ladies move freely everywhere—therefore, that is good; they choose for themselves their husbands—therefore, that is the highest step of advancement; the Westerners disapprove of our dress, decorations, food, and ways of living—therefore, they must be very bad; the Westerners condemn image-worship as sinful—surely then, image-worship is the greatest sin, there is no doubt of it!

The Westerners say that worshiping a single Deity is fruitful of the highest spiritual good—therefore, let us throw our Gods and Goddesses into the river Ganges! The Westerners hold caste distinctions to be obnoxious—therefore, let all the different castes be jumbled into one! The Westerners say that child-marriage is the root of all evils—therefore, that is also very bad, of a certainty it is!

We are not discussing here whether these customs deserve countenance or rejection; but if the mere disapproval of the Westerners be the measure of the abominableness of our manners and customs, then it is our duty to raise our emphatic protest against it.

The present writer has, to some extent, personal experience of Western society. His conviction resulting from such experience has been that there is such a wide divergence between the Western society and the Indian as regards the primal course and goal of each, that any sect in India, framed after the Western model, will miss the aim. We have not the least sympathy with those who, never having lived in Western society and, therefore, utterly ignorant of the rules and prohibitions regarding the association of men and women that obtain there, and which act as safeguards to preserve the purity of the Western women, allow a free rein to the unrestricted intermingling of men and women in our society.

I observed in the West also, that the children of weaker nations, if born in England, give themselves out as Englishmen, instead of Greek, Portuguese, Spaniard, etc., as the case may be. All drift towards the strong, that the light of glory which shines in the glorious may anyhow fall and reflect on one's own body; i.e., to shine in the borrowed light of the great is the one desire of the weak. When I see Indians dressed in European apparel and costumes, the thought comes to my mind—perhaps they feel ashamed to own their nationality and kinship with the ignorant, poor, illiterate, downtrodden people of India! Nourished by the blood of the Hindu for the last fourteen centuries, the Parsee is no longer a "Native"! Before the arrogance of the casteless, who pretend to be and glorify themselves in being Brāhmans, the true nobility of the old, heroic, high-class Brāhman melts into nothingness! Again, the Westerners have now taught us that those stupid, ignorant, low-caste millions of India clad only in loin cloths are non-Aryans! They are therefore no more our kith and kin!

Oh India! With this mere echoing of others, with this base imitation of others, with this dependence on others, this slavish weakness, this vile detestable cruelty, wouldst thou, with these provisions only, scale the highest pinnacle of civilization and greatness? Wouldst thou attain, by means of thy disgraceful cowardice, that freedom deserved only by the brave and the heroic? Oh India! Forget not that the ideal of thy woman-hood is Sītā, Sāvitrī, Damayanti; [2] forget not that the God thou worship-est is the great Ascetic of ascetics, the all-renouncing Shankara, the Lord of Uma; [3] forget not that thy marriage, thy wealth, thy life are not for sense-pleasure, are not for thy individual personal happiness; forget not that thou art born as a sacrifice to the *Mother's* altar; forget not that thy social order is but the reflex of the Infinite Universal Motherhood; forget not that the lower classes, the ignorant, the poor, the illiterate, the cob-bler, the sweeper, are thy flesh and blood, thy brothers. Thou brave one, be bold, take courage, be proud that thou art an Indian, and proudly proclaim: "I am an Indian, every Indian is my brother." Say: "The ig-norant Indian, the poor and destitute Indian, the Brāhman Indian, the Pariah Indian, is my brother." Thou too clad with but a rag round thy loins proudly proclaim at the top of thy voice: "The Indian is my brother, the Indian is my life, India's gods and goddesses are my God, India's society is the cradle of my infancy, the pleasure-garden of my youth, the sacred heaven, the *Vārānasi,* [4] of my old age." Say, brother: "The soil of India is my highest heaven, the good of India is my good," and repeat and pray day and night: "O Thou Lord of Gauri, [5] O Thou Mother of the Universe, vouchsafe manliness unto me! O Thou Mother of Strength, take away my weakness, take away my unmanliness, and—*Make me a Man!"*

[2] Damayanti, celebrated in Indian legend for her devotion to her husband Nala.
[3] Umā, a name of the wife of Shiva or Shankara (the Gracious One).
[4] Banaras.   [5] A name for the wife of Shiva.

CHAPTER XXIII

NATIONALISM TAKES ROOT:
THE MODERATES

Before the British conquest, the concept of membership in a permanent political order embracing and involving them all seems to have been unknown to the inhabitants of India. Dynasties rather than nations were the centers of political power and the foci of personal loyalties. Powerful rulers like Ashoka, Samudragupta, and Harsha had indeed succeeded in bringing large parts of the subcontinent under their sway, but their empires dissolved with the death of the last strong ruler in each reigning line. Thanks largely to the genius of Akbar (1542–1605), the Mughal empire created a somewhat more durable administrative order, but internal dissensions and Persian-Afghan invasions led to the empire's dismemberment after the passing of the militant Aurangzeb (1619–1707). For a time the Mārāthas gave promise of re-establishing Hindu dominion, but again their rule could not even unite all of Hindudom around their standard, let alone bridge the gap between India's two major religious traditions.

A new chapter opened when British arms and diplomacy placed the whole of the subcontinent under one paramount power for the first time in history. They imposed not only peace and unity on India, but a relatively efficient administrative machinery as well. Gradually the sinews of a new nation were strengthened by the introduction of printing and journalism, railroads, a postal and telegraph system, and by the growth of an all-India economy centering in large modern cities accessible to ocean-going ships.

The new political and economic order attracted able Indians anxious to improve their status and increase their wealth by entering its service. A new class emerged to mediate between the foreign rulers or traders and the mass of the people. Using their knowledge of English as the key to advancement, Indian clerks and functionaries found employment in government posts; Indian lawyers pleaded in British-style courts; Indian businessmen dealt with foreign firms; and Indian teachers imparted to their countrymen the language and culture of the conquerors. This rising middle class demonstrated a loyalty to the British which outweighed the angry discontent of the old elite—both Muslim and Hindu. The supression of the latter in the Mutiny and Rebellion of 1857–58 only confirmed the entrenched position of their parvenu successors.

But the English education which provided so many willing collaborators for the British in India eventually proved the undoing of their empire. For one thing, the members of the new middle class—whether from the South or the North, from Bengal or from Mahārāshtra—could all communicate with each other through the medium of a common language. Equally important, their reading of the English classics instilled in them the Western ideals of justice, freedom, and love of country. As their numbers grew they found the good government jobs too few, with the best ones reserved for Europeans. To economic frustration was added the bitter sting of racial discrimination, for "the Mutiny" of 1857 had sharpened British suspicions of Indian loyalty, while the late nineteenth-century doctrines of social Darwinism and aggressive imperialism compounded to increase the white man's feeling of inherent superiority over his darker-skinned subjects. Ignoring the sympathetic statements made in Parliament and the conciliatory proclamation of Queen Victoria in 1858, Britishers in India saw little reason to grant Indians a greater measure of control over their own affairs.

Under these circumstances, it was not long before the seed-idea of nationalism implanted by their reading of Western books began to take root in the minds of intelligent and energetic Indians. A. O. Hume, a Scotsman sympathetic to their aspirations, made possible the first meeting (in 1885) of the Indian National Congress, which was intended to serve as a forum for the discussion of political reforms and patriotic projects. From this beginning as a safety-valve through which the upper classes could air their grievances, the Congress quickly transformed itself into an all-India nationalist organization.

The Moderates, the first men to come forward as leaders of the nationalist movement, shared a great many assumptions with those liberal Englishmen who advised and encouraged them. They believed in the providential character of British rule and in the gradual evolution of

India toward enlightenment and self-government under that rule. They regretted the backwardness of Hindu society and worked to bring about the reform of its grosser evils. The poverty of the people depressed them, and they therefore concerned themselves with plans for India's economic improvement. Although they were not men devoid of religious faith, they accepted the divorce of religion from government and maintained a secular view of politics which contrasted markedly with the religious outlook of the Extremists, who later posed a serious challenge to their leadership.

Having become, as Macaulay proposed, "English in taste, in opinions, in morals, and in intellect," the Indian Moderates gained certain advantages but at the same time ran certain risks in guiding the nationalist movement. Their familiarity with British culture enabled them to appeal to the best instincts of their rulers, from whom they demanded the same rights and liberties which all Britons took for granted. Their knowledge of the gradual rise of democratic government in English history furnished them with useful ammunition, and they repeatedly harked back to the assurances given by Parliament and Queen Victoria that Indians would be allowed to compete freely with Europeans for positions in the Indian Civil Service.

In relation to their rivals the Extremists, however, the position of the Moderates was bound to be a somewhat shaky one for several reasons. Their heavy reliance on British good faith embarrassed them whenever the concessions they asked for were refused or postponed. Moreover, the more anglicized they became in their thinking, the further they removed themselves from emotional rapport with the bulk of the population—the illiterate, poverty-stricken, and devoutly Hindu peasantry.

In one respect the Moderates did yeoman's service in tending to the needs of the peasantry. Unwilling to attack British rule for the political and social reforms it had introduced, they focused their attention on the obvious disparity between Britain's prosperity and India's poverty. Dādā-bhāi Naoroji, an Indian businessman resident in London, placed the blame for his country's plight on foreign rule, and in doing so was seconded by English socialist theoreticians. The Bengali leader Surendranāth Banerjea accepted Dādābhāi's thesis, while M. G. Rānade (pronounced Rānadé) sought a constructive solution in rapid industrialization under government auspices. Rānade's disciple G. K. Gokhale (pronounced Gokhalé) left the theorizing to others, and bent his efforts to reducing the load of taxation burdening the Indian people.

These four men were probably the most outstanding moderate leaders in the opening decades of the nationalist movement. It is significant that all were scholarly in temperament, and spent part of their early careers as teachers in colleges imparting English education to Indian students. Each possessed a flawless command of the English language and was able to hold his own in debates with Englishmen. Three of them—Naoroji, Banerjea, and Gokhale—made speaking tours in Great Britain to impress the British electorate with the importance of greater self-government for India. The same three were also elected presidents of the Congress, and all four were deeply involved in its work.

Although the Extremist leaders could muster far greater support through their appeal to Hindu symbols and traditions, it is doubtful that they could have succeeded in freeing India without the patient, more diplomatic efforts of the Moderates. Their greater willingness to cooperate with the British in instituting administrative reforms kept the nationalist movement from "going off the rails" into senseless violence, which could only lead to severe reprisals and political deadlock. Their contribution to the achievement of self-government has largely been forgotten by subsequent generations, but independent India's dedication to parliamentary democracy, economic development, and social progress stands as mute testimony to their farsighted wisdom.

DĀDĀBHĀI NAOROJI: ARCHITECT OF INDIAN NATIONALISM

Inevitable as the rise of Indian nationalism may seem to have been under the conditions created by British rule, its emergence would have been impossible without the strenuous efforts of devoted national leaders. The first of a long series of such men, Dādābhāi Naoroji drew the plans and laid the foundations for India's self-government.

This architect of Indian nationalism was neither Hindu nor Muslim, but a descendant of the followers of Zoroaster who had fled Persia after the Muslim conquest of that country. Settling as refugees along the western coast of India the Zoroastrians became known as Parsīs (Persians). When the British came to trade they emerged as the group most willing to do business, for they were bound neither by caste rules nor by prejudice against taking interest on loans, and as a minority group they had little to lose and much to gain by dealing with the Europeans. As a result of their trading contacts, the Parsīs became the most Westernized and the wealthiest single community in India.

Dādābhāi Naoroji was born in Bombay in 1825, the son of a Zoroastrian priest. His family name, Dordi, was little used; but the original meaning of the word (twisted rope made of coconut husk) had a symbolic significance for Dādābhāi, who was absolutely inflexible once he had made up his mind. "You may burn a *dordi*," he once said, "but you can never take the twist out of it. So it is with me. When once I form a decision, nothing will dislodge me from it."[1]

Tenacity of purpose was indeed his chief characteristic. He so distinguished himself in his studies at the Elphinstone Institution (Bombay's leading college) that he became at twenty-seven its Professor of Mathematics—the first Indian to attain such an academic rank. At thirty he left India to become a partner in the first Indian firm to do business in England. His aim in moving permanently to London, the heart of the empire, was not to gain wealth, but to enable himself to appeal directly to the British public for a better understanding of India's problems. For fifty years Dādābhāi delivered papers on Indian subjects to numerous learned societies, submitted memoranda and petitions to British officials concerned with India, and agitated both privately and publicly—all in the service of one cause: that Indians should be granted the same rights and privileges as other British subjects.

With his famous theory of "the drain" of India's wealth to Britain, Dādābhāi Naoroji sounded the keynote of Indian economic nationalism. But for all his bitter condemnation of the costliness of foreign government to his country, he never advocated violent action as a solution. His loyalty to the parliamentary system of government was rewarded in 1892 with his election to the British House of Commons on the Liberal ticket. The first Indian member of Parliament, he served both his London constituency and the interests of India for three years, succeeding in his attempt

[1] R. P. Masani, *Dadabhai Naoroji: The Grand Old Man of India*, p. 25.

to have a parliamentary commission investigate the financial administration of British India.

Dādābhāi punctuated his long residence in England with frequent visits to India. In 1873–74 he served as chief minister to the Indian state of Baroda to prevent it from being annexed by the British crown (the usual penalty for misgovernment in the princely states). He took a prominent part in the first session of the Indian National Congress in 1885, and was thrice elected its president—in 1886, 1893, and 1906. The younger generation of nationalist leaders all looked up to the patriarchal patriot for advice, and Gāndhi especially revered him. He died in Bombay in 1917, but to this day the affectionate title "the Grand Old Man of India" is associated with his name.

DĀDĀBHĀI NAOROJI
The Pros and Cons of British Rule

In the discussion following the presentation of a paper on India to a learned society in London in 1871, Dādābhāi drew up an impromptu account of the advantages and disadvantages of British rule to India. It shows both his fairness in recognizing the good the British had done, and his persistent criticism of the crushing cost to India of their rule.

> [From *Essays, Speeches, Addresses, and Writings . . . of the Hon'ble Dadabhai Naoroji*, pp. 131–36]

Credit—*In the Cause of Humanity:* Abolition of suttee and infanticide.

Destruction of Dacoits, Thugs, Pindarees,[1] and other such pests of Indian society.

Remarriage of Hindoo widows, and charitable aid in time of famine.

Glorious work all this, of which any nation may well be proud, and such as has not fallen to the lot of any people in the history of mankind.

In the Cause of Civilization: Education, both male and female. Though yet only partial, an inestimable blessing as far as it has gone, and leading gradually to the destruction of superstition, and many moral and social evils. Resuscitation of India's own noble literature, modified and refined by the enlightment of the West.

The only pity is that as much has not been done as might have been in this noble work; but still India must be, and is, deeply grateful.

[1] Armed thieves, highway murderers, robber bands.

Politically: Peace and order. Freedom of speech and liberty of the press. Higher political knowledge and aspirations. Improvement of government in the native States. Security of life and property. Freedom from oppression caused by the caprice or avarice of despotic rulers, and from devastation by war. Equal justice between man and man (sometimes vitiated by partiality to Europeans). Services of highly educated administrators, who have achieved the above-mentioned good results.

Materially: Loans for railways and irrigation. (I have been particularly charged with ignoring this, but I consider it one of the greatest benefits you have conferred upon India, inasmuch as it has enabled us to produce more than we could before, though there is not yet enough for all India's ordinary wants, and I have said this in my paper.) I cannot ascertain the exact amount of investments in irrigation works, but I take them to be about £10,000,000, making the total £110,000,000. The development of a few valuable products, such as indigo, tea, coffee, silk, &c. Increase of exports. Telegraphs.

Generally: A slowly growing desire of late to treat India equitably, and as a country held in trust. Good intentions.

No nation on the face of the earth has ever had the opportunity of achieving such a glorious work as this. I hope in this credit side of the account I have done no injustice, and if I have omitted any item which anyone may think of importance, I shall have the greatest pleasure in inserting it. I appreciate, and so do my countrymen, what England has done for India, and I know that it is only in British hands that her regeneration can be accomplished. Now for the debit side.

Debit—*In the Cause of Humanity:* Nothing. Everything, therefore, is in your favor under this head.

In the Cause of Civilization: As I have said already, there has been a failure to do as much as might have been done, but I put nothing to the debit. Much has been done, or I should not be standing here this evening.

Politically: Repeated breach of pledges to give the natives a fair and reasonable share in the higher administration of their own country, which has much shaken confidence in the good faith of the British word. Political aspirations and the legitimate claim to have a reasonable voice in the legislation and the imposition and disbursement of taxes, met to a very slight degree, thus treating the natives of India not as British subjects, to whom representation is a birthright.

(I stop here a moment to say a word as to a mistake into which my friend, Mr. Hyde Clarke, fell, in supposing that I desired the government of India to be at once transferred to the natives. In my belief a greater calamity could not befall India than for England to go away and leave her to herself.)

Consequent on the above, an utter disregard of the feelings and views of the natives. The great moral evil of the drain of the wisdom and practical administration and statesmanship, leaving none to guide the rising generation. (Here, again, have I been misunderstood. I complain not of Englishmen returning to their own country, but of the whole administration being kept entirely in English hands, so that none of the natives are brought up to and taught the responsibilities and duties of office, so that we have none amongst ourselves to guide us as our elders and to teach us our duties as citizens and as moral beings. A foster mother or nurse will never supply the place of the real mother, and the natives will therefore naturally follow their own leaders, unless you prove more kind, humane, and considerate. Draw these leaders on your side.) The indifference to India, even of a large portion of those who have had an Indian career, and who are living on Indian pensions. The culpable indifference of a large portion of the people, the public press, and Parliament of this country to the interests of India; therefore, periodical committees of inquiry are absolutely necessary, for the knowledge that such will take place would be a check on careless administration. With regard to the native states, though their system is improving, it is most unjust that their cases should be decided in secret. The frequent change of officials is a constant source of disturbance in policy, and though it may be unavoidable, it is none the less hard upon India.

Financially: All attention is engrossed in devising new modes of taxation, without any adequate effort to increase the means of the people to pay; and the consequent vexation and oppressiveness of the taxes imposed, imperial and local. Inequitable financial relations between England and India, i.e. the political debt of £100,000,000 clapped on India's shoulders, and all home charges also, though the British exchequer contributes nearly £3,000,000 to the expenses of the colonies. The crushing and economically rude and unintelligent policy of making the present generation pay the whole cost of public works for the benefit of the future, instead of making the political like all other machinery, and distributing the weight so as to make a small power lift a large weight by the aid of time. The results of trying to produce something out of nothing, of the want of intelligent adaptation of financial machinery, and of much reckless expenditure; in financial embarrassments, and deep discontent of the people.

Materially: The political drain,[2] up to this time, from India to England, of above £500,000,000, at the lowest computation, in principal alone, which with interest would be some thousands of millions. The further continuation of this drain at the rate, at present, of above £12,000,000, with a tendency to increase. (I do not mean this as a complaint; you must have a return for the services rendered to India, but let us have the means of paying. If I have a manager to whom I pay £1,000 a year, and he only makes the business produce £400, so that £600 a year must be paid him out of capital, any man of business can see what will be the result. Peace and order will soon be completely established by the closing of the concern.)

The consequent continuous impoverishment and exhaustion of the country, except so far as it has been very partially relieved and replenished by the railway and irrigation loans, and the windfall of the consequences of the American war, since 1850. Even with this relief, the material condition of India is such that the great mass of the poor people have hardly 2d a day and a few rags, or a scanty subsistence.

The famines that were in their power to prevent, if they had done their duty, as a good and intelligent government. The policy adopted during the last fifteen years of building railways, irrigation works, etc., is hopeful, has already resulted in much good to your credit, and if persevered in, gratitude and contentment will follow.

[An] increase of exports [without adequate compensation]; [a] loss of manufacturing industry and skill. Here I end the debit side. . . .

To sum up the whole, the British rule has been—morally, a great blessing; politically peace and order on one hand, blunders on the other, materially, impoverishment (relieved as far as the railway and other loans go). The natives call the British system "Sakar ki Churi," the knife of sugar. That is to say there is no oppression, it is all smooth and sweet, but it is the knife, notwithstanding. I mention this that you should

---

[2] Dādābhāi refers to the export from India of the savings and pensions of British officials, and to other costs of British rule such as supplies and military expenditures.

know these feelings. Our great misfortune is that you do not know our wants. When you will know our real wishes, I have not the least doubt that you would do justice. The genius and spirit of the British people is fair play and justice. The great problems before the English statesmen are two: 1) To make the foreign rule self-supporting, either by returning to India, in some shape or other, the wealth that has been, and is being, drawn from it, or by stopping that drain in some way till India is so far improved in its material condition as to be able to produce enough for its own ordinary wants and the extraordinary ones of a costly distant rule. If you cannot feel yourself actuated by the high and noble ambition of the amelioration of 200,000,000 of human beings, let your self-interest suggest to you to take care of the bird that gives the golden egg of £12,000,000 a year to your nation, and provisions to thousands of your people of all classes. In the name of humanity, I implore our rulers to make up their minds not to prevent the restoration of the equilibrium, after the continuous exhaustion by drain and by horrible famines. I do not in the least grudge any legitimate benefit England may derive for its rule in India. On the contrary, I am thankful for its invaluable moral benefits; but it is the further duty of England to give us such a government, and all the benefit of its power and credit, as to enable us to pay, without starving or dying by famine, the tribute or price for the rule; 2) How to satisfy reasonably the growing political aspirations and just rights of a people called British subjects to have a fair share in the administration and legislation of their own country. If the Select Committee solve these two problems, before which all other difficulties, financial or others, are as nothing, they will deserve the blessings of 200,000,000 of the human race.

The Blessings of British Rule

Dādābhāī's presidential address at the second session of the Congress in 1886 rings with protestations of loyalty and gratitude to British rule for the unity, peace, civil liberties and education it brought to the Indian people.

[From *Essays, Speeches, Addresses, and Writings . . . of the Hon'ble Dadabhai Naoroji*, pp. 332–33]

The assemblage of such a Congress is an event of the utmost importance in Indian history. I ask whether in the most glorious days of Hindu rule, in the days of Rajahs like the great Vikram,[3] you could imagine the possibility of a meeting of this kind, where even Hindus of all different provinces of the kingdom could have collected and spoken as one nation. Coming down to the later empire of our friends, the Mahomedans, who probably ruled over a larger territory at one time than any Hindu monarch, would it have been, even in the days of the great Akbar himself, possible for a meeting like this to assemble composed of all classes and communities, all speaking one language, and all having uniform and high aspirations of their own?

Well, then, what is it for which we are now met on this occasion? We have assembled to consider questions upon which depend our future, whether glorious or inglorious. It is our good fortune that we are under a rule which makes it possible for us to meet in this manner. [Cheers.] It is under the civilizing rule of the Queen and people of England that we meet here together, hindered by none, and are freely allowed to speak our minds without the least fear and without the least hesitation. Such a thing is possible under British rule and British rule only. [Loud cheers.] Then I put the *question* plainly: Is this Congress a nursery for sedition and rebellion against the British Government [cries of "no, no"]; or is it another stone in the foundation of the stability of that Government [cries of "yes, yes"]? There could be but one answer, and that you have already given, because we are thoroughly sensible of the numberless blessings conferred upon us, of which the very existence of this Congress is a proof in a nutshell. [Cheers.] Were it not for these blessings of British rule I could not have come here, as I have done, without the least hesitation and without the least fear that my children might be robbed and killed in my absence; nor could you have come from every corner of the land, having performed, within a few days, journeys which in former days would have occupied as many months. [Cheers.] These simple facts bring home to all of us at once some of those great and numberless blessings which British rule has conferred upon us. But there remain even greater blessings for which we have to be grateful. It is to British rule that we owe the education we possess; the people of England were sincere in the declarations made more than half a century ago that India was a sacred charge entrusted to their care by Providence, and that they were bound to administer it for the good of India, to the

[3] Vikramāditya, a great and good king in Indian legend.

glory of their own name, and the satisfaction of God. [Prolonged cheer-
ing.] When we have to acknowledge so many blessings as flowing from
British rule—and I could descant on them for hours, because it would
simply be recounting to you the history of the British empire in India—
is it possible that an assembly like this, every one of whose members is
fully impressed with the knowledge of these blessings, could meet for
any purpose inimical to that rule to which we owe so much? [Cheers.]

The thing is absurd. Let us speak out like men and proclaim that we
are loyal to the backbone [cheers]; that we understand the benefits
English rule has conferred upon us; that we thoroughly appreciate the
education that has been given to us, the new light which has been
poured upon us, turning us from darkness into light and teaching us
the new lesson that kings are made for the people, not people for their
kings; and this new lesson we have learned amidst the darkness of Asiatic
despotism only by the light of free English civilization. [Loud cheers.]

The Moral Impoverishment of India

The frustration felt by the swelling ranks of educated Indians who were excluded from government positions is well expressed in Dādābhāi's memorandum of 1880. Note the veiled threat with which this selection concludes.

[From *Essays, Speeches, Addresses, and Writings . . . of the Hon'ble
Dadabhai Naoroji*, pp. 465–67]

In this Memorandum I desire to submit for the kind and generous consideration of His Lordship the Secretary of State for India, that from the
same cause of the deplorable drain, besides the material exhaustion of
India, the moral loss to her is no less sad and lamentable.

With the material wealth go also the wisdom and experience of the
country. Europeans occupy almost all the higher places in every department of government, directly or indirectly under its control. While
in India they acquire India's money, experience, and wisdom, and
when they go, they carry both away with them, leaving India so much
poorer in material and moral wealth. Thus India is left without, and
cannot have, those elders in wisdom and experience, who in every country are the natural guides of the rising generations in their national
and social conduct, and of the destinies of their country—and a sad, sad
loss this is!

Every European is isolated from the people around him. He is not their mental, moral or social leader, or companion. For any mental or moral influence or guidance or sympathy with the people, he might just as well be living in the moon. The people know not him, and he knows not, nor cares for the people. Some honorable exceptions do, now and then, make an effort to do some good they can, but in the very nature of things, these efforts are always feeble, exotic, and of little permanent effect. These men are not always in the place, and their works die away when they go.

The Europeans are not the natural leaders of the people. They do not belong to the people. They cannot enter into their thoughts and feelings; they cannot join or sympathize with their joys or griefs. On the contrary, every day the estrangement is increasing. Europeans deliberately and openly widen it more and more. There may be very few social institutions started by Europeans in which natives, however fit and desirous to join, are not deliberately and insultingly excluded. The Europeans are and make themselves strangers in every way. All they effectually do is to eat the substance of India, material and moral, while living there, and when they go, they carry away all they have acquired, and their pensions and future usefulness besides.

This most deplorable moral loss to India needs most serious consideration, as much in its political as in its national aspect. Nationally disastrous as it is, it carries politically with it its own nemesis. Without the guidance of elderly wisdom and experience of their own natural leaders, the education which the rising generations are now receiving is naturally leading them (or call it misleading them, if you will) into directions which bode no good to the rulers, and which, instead of being the strength of the rulers as it ought to and can be, will turn out to be their great weakness. The fault will be of the rulers themselves for such a result. The power that is now being raised by the spread of education, though yet slow and small, is one that in time must, for weal or woe, exercise great influence. In fact it has already begun to do so. However strangely the English rulers, forgetting their English manliness and moral courage, may, like the ostrich, shut their eyes by gagging acts or otherwise, to the good or bad influences they are raising around them, this good or evil is rising nevertheless. The thousands that are being sent out by the universities every year find themselves in a most anomalous position. There is no place for them in their motherland. They may beg in the streets or break stones on the roads, for aught the rulers seem to care for their natural rights, position, and duties in their own country. They may perish or do what they like or can, but scores of Europeans must go from this country to take up what belongs to them, and that, in spite of every profession for years and years past and up to the present day, of English statesmen, that they must govern India for India's good, by solemn acts and declarations of Parliament, and above all, by the words of the August Sovereign Herself. For all practical purposes all these high promises have been hitherto, almost wholly, the purest romance, the reality being quite different.

The educated find themselves simply so many dummies, ornamented with the tinsel of school education, and then their whole end and aim of life is ended. What must be the inevitable consequence? A wild, spirited horse, without curb or reins, will run away wild, and kill and trample upon every one that came in his way. A misdirected force will hit anywhere and destroy anything. The power that the rulers are, so far to their credit, raising, will, as a nemesis recoil against themselves, if with this blessing of education they do not do their whole duty to the country which trusts to their righteousness, and thus turn this good power to their own side. The nemesis is as clear from the present violence to nature, as disease and death arise from uncleanliness and rottenness. The voice of the power of the rising education is, no doubt, feeble at present. Like the infant, the present dissatisfaction is only crying at the pains it is suffering. Its notions have not taken any form or shape or course yet, but it is growing. Heaven only knows what it will grow to! He who runs may see, that if the present material and moral destruction of India continued, a great convulsion must inevitably arise, by which either India will be more and more crushed under the iron heel of despotism and destruction, or may succeed in shattering the destroying hand and power. Far, far is it from my earnest prayer and hope that such should be the result of the British rule.

"SURRENDER-NOT" BANERJEA: BENGALI MODERATE

The Hindu renascence in nineteenth-century Bengal was accompanied by a gradual political awakening in that province. Politics, however, unlike religion, came as a comparatively new category of thought to Bengali Hindus after centuries of domination by Muslim rulers. The example set by Rāmmohun Roy thus lay neglected until the new English-educated middle-class gave birth several generations later to a group of men infused with new ideals of patriotism and self-government.

To this group Allan Octavian Hume, the retired civil servant who fathered the organization of the Indian National Congress, appealed with his letter of 1883, addressing the graduates of Calcutta University. "You are the salt of the land," he wrote. "And if amongst even you, the elite, fifty men cannot be found with sufficient power of self-sacrifice, sufficient love for and pride in their country, sufficient genuine and unselfish heart-felt patriotism to take the initiative, and if needs be, devote the rest of their lives to the Cause—then there is no hope for India." [1]

To one Calcutta University graduate Hume's appeal was entirely superfluous, for Surendranāth Banerjea (1848–1926) had already cast himself into the stormy sea of national service. A brāhman and the son of a doctor, Surendranāth had been one of the first Indians to be admitted to the select Indian Civil Service, the so-called "steel frame" of British administration; but his failure to correct a false report prepared in his name by a subordinate had caused him to be dismissed—a punishment far more severe than English members of the I.C.S. received for similar oversights. Undismayed, Surendranāth journeyed to London to appeal his case. When the appeal was denied, he appeared for bar examinations, only to be refused again. With the two swiftest roads to success—the civil service and the law—closed to him, Surendranāth returned to Calcutta, convinced that "the personal wrong done to me was an illustration of the impotency of our people," and determined to spend his life "redressing our wrongs and protecting our rights, personal and collective." [2]

The rest of his long life was only the acting out of this resolve. Starting as a teacher, he soon founded a patriotic association, then a newspaper, then a college. As Keshub Chunder Sen had captivated audiences in many parts of the land with his revivalist sermons, so Surendranāth used his oratorical gifts to rouse Indians from Bengal to the Punjab to a greater sense of loyalty to their country. When he was jailed for

[1] William Wedderburn, *Allan Octavian Hume, C.B.*, pp. 51–52.
[2] Surendranāth Banerjea, *A Nation in Making, Being the Reminiscences of Fifty Years in Public Life*, p. 33.

criticizing a British judge, he started the tradition (still popular in India) of welcoming imprisonment in order to demonstrate the injustice of a governmental law or policy.

Surendranāth's career dramatizes the change of heart in countless educated Indians from blind loyalty to British rule to stubborn resistance against its evils. Despite his sufferings at the hands of the authorities, Surendranāth insisted that only constitutional means be used in the struggle for self-government. When the Extremists cried for more drastic measures against the foreigner, he opposed them as firmly as he opposed the British. Twice president of the Congress, he left it in 1918 to head the All-India Liberal Federation when the younger Congress leaders threatened to obstruct the introduction of the important Montagu-Chelmsford Reforms. His persistence in his chosen course earned him the respect of Indians and British alike and won him the aptly coined nickname of "Surrender-not" Banerjea.

SURENDRANĀTH BANERJEA

The Need for Indian Unity

Understanding between Hindus and Muslims formed a major plank in the Moderates' platform. In one of Surendranāth's earliest speeches (in 1878) he exhorted the young men of the country to strive for unity as a patriotic duty.
[From *Speeches and Writings of Hon. Surendranath Banerjea*, pp. 227–31]

Young men, whom I see around me in such large numbers, you are the hopes of your families. May I not also say, you are the hopes of your country? Your country expects great things from you. Now I ask, how many of you are prepared, when you have finished your studies at the college, to devote your lives, to consecrate your energies to the good of your country? I repeat the question and I pause for a reply. [Here the speaker paused for a few seconds. Cries of "all, all" from all sides of the gallery]. The response is in every way worthy of yourselves and of the education which you are receiving. May you prove true to your resolve, and carry out in life the high purposes which animate your bosoms.

Gentlemen, I have a strong conviction and an assured belief that there comes a time in the history of a nation's progress, when every man may verily be said to have a mission of his own to accomplish. Such a time has now arrived for India. The fiat has gone forth. The celestial mandate has been issued that every Indian must now do his duty, or stand condemned before God and man. There was such a time of stirring activity in the glorious annals of England, when Hampden offered up his life for the deliverance of his own country, when Algernon Sydney laid down his head on the block to rid his country of a hated tyrant, when English bishops did not hesitate in the discharge of their duty to their Fatherland to descend from the performance of their ecclesiastical functions and appear as traitors before the bar of a Criminal Court. These are glorious reminiscences in England's immortal history, which Englishmen to this day look back upon with pride and satisfaction. It is not indeed necessary for us to have recourse to violence in order to obtain the redress of our grievances. Constitutional agitation will secure for us those rights, the privileges which in less favoured countries are obtained by sterner means. But peaceful as are the means to be enforced, there is a stern duty to be performed by every Indian. And he who fails in that duty is a traitor before God and man.

In holding up for your acceptance the great principle of Indian unity, I do not lay claims to originality. Three hundred years ago, in the Punjab, the immortal founder of Sikhism, the meek, the gentle, the blessed Nānak preached the great doctrine of Indian unity and endeavored to knit together Hindus and Musulmans under the banner of a common faith. That attempt was eminently successful. Nānak became the spiritual founder of the Sikh empire. He preached the great doctrine of peace and good will between Hindus and Musulmans. And standing in the presence of his great example, we too must preach the great doctrine of peace and good will between Hindus and Musulmans, Christians and Parsees, aye between all sections of the great Indian community. Let us raise aloft the banner of our country's progress. Let the word "Unity" be inscribed there in characters of glittering gold. We have had enough of past jealousies, past dissensions, past animosities. The spirits of the dead at Paniput [1] will testify to our bloody strifes. The spirits of the dead in other battlefields will testify to the same fact. There may be religious differences between us. There may be social differences

---

[1] Pānīpat, the site of numerous pitched battles in Indian history. It lies about fifty miles north of Delhi.

between us. But there is a common platform where we may all meet, the platform of our country's welfare. There is a common cause which may blind [bind] us together, the cause of Indian progress. There is a common Divinity, to whom we may uplift our voices in adoration, the Divinity who presides over the destinies of our country. In the name then of a common country, let us all, Hindus, Musulmans, Christians, Parsees, members of the great Indian community, throw the pall of oblivion over jealousies and dissensions of bygone times and embracing one another in fraternal love and affection, live and work for the benefit of a beloved Fatherland. Under English auspices there is indeed a great future for India. I am confident of the great destinies that are in store for us. You and I may not live to see that day. These eyes of ours may not witness that spectacle of ineffable beauty. It may not be permitted to us to exclaim Simeonlike, "Now Lord, lettest thou thy servant depart in peace." It may not be permitted to us to exclaim like the Welsh Bard on the heights of Snowdon, "Visions of glory, spare my aching sight." But is it nothing to know when you are dying, when you are about to take leave of this world, of its joys and sorrows, when the past of your life is unfurled before you, when eternity opens wide its portals, is it nothing to know at that last awful, supreme moment of your lives, that you have not lived in vain, that you have lived for the benefit of others, that you have lived to help in the cause of your country's regeneration? Let us all lead worthy, honorable, and patriotic lives, that we may all live and die happily and that India may be great. This is my earnest and prayerful request. May it find a response in your sympathetic hearts.

Faith in England

The backbone of the Moderates' creed was faith that the British would grant self-government to India when she was prepared for it. Surendranāth enunciated this creed in the peroration of his presidential address to the Congress in 1895.

[From *Speeches and Writings of the Hon. Surendranath Banerjea*, pp. 93–96]

We feel that in this great struggle in which we are engaged, the moral sympathies of civilized humanity are with us. The prayers of the good and the true in all parts of the world follow us. They will welcome as glad tidings of great joy the birth of an emancipated people on the banks of the Ganges. For, have they not all read about our ancient civilization; how, in the morning of the world, before the Eternal City had been built upon the Seven Hills, before Alexander had marched his army to the banks of the Tigris, before Babylonian astronomers had learnt to gaze upon the starry world, our ancestors had developed a great civilization, and how that civilization has profoundly influenced the course of modern thought in the highest concerns of man? Above all, we rely with unbounded confidence on the justice and generosity of the British people and of their representatives in Parliament.

It is not that we mistrust the authorities here. But the higher we mount, the purer is the atmosphere. The impurities generated by local causes cannot touch those who, removed from local influences, represent in a loftier sphere of responsibility the majesty and the greatness of the English nation. Let us freely acknowledge the tribute we owe to the British government in India. What government could have accorded a speedier recognition to Congress claims than the government of India has done? Within the lifetime of a generation we have achieved changes —beneficent changes of far-reaching moment—which it would have taken many generations to accomplish elsewhere, which in less fortunately situated countries could not have been accomplished except, perhaps, after bloodshed and tumult. All this we freely acknowledge. For all this we are truly grateful. All this fills [us] with hope for the future.

Nevertheless we feel that much yet remains to be done, and the impetus must come from England. To England we look for inspiration and guidance. To England we look for sympathy in the struggle. From England must come the crowning mandate which will enfranchise our peoples. England is our political guide and our moral preceptor in the exalted sphere of political duty. English history has taught us those principles of freedom which we cherish with our lifeblood. We have been fed upon the strong food of English constitutional freedom. We have been taught to admire the eloquence and genius of the great masters of English political philosophy. We have been brought face to face with the struggles and the triumphs of the English people in their stately march towards constitutional freedom. Where will you find better models of courage, devotion, and sacrifice; not in Rome, not in Greece, not even in France in the stormy days of the Revolution—courage tempered by caution, enthusiasm leavened by sobriety, partisanship softened by a large-hearted charity—all subordinated to the one predominating sense of love of country and love of God.

We should be unworthy of ourselves and of our preceptors—we should, indeed, be something less than human—if, with our souls stirred to their inmost depths, our warm Oriental sensibilities roused to an unwanted pitch of enthusiasm by the contemplation of these great ideals of public duty, we did not seek to transplant into our own country the spirit of those free institutions which have made England what she is. In the words of Lord Lansdowne, a wave of unrest is passing through this country. But it is not the unrest of discontent or disloyalty to the British government—it is the unrest which is the first visible sign of the awakening of a new national life. It is the work of Englishmen—it is the noblest monument of their rule—it is the visible embodiment of the vast moral influence which they are exercising over the minds of the people of India. Never in the history of the world have the inheritors of an ancient civilization been so profoundly influenced by the influx of modern ideas. In this Congress from year to year we ask England to accomplish her glorious work. The course of civilization following the path of the sun has traveled from East to West. The West owes a heavy debt to the East. We look forward to the day when that debt will be repaid, not only by the moral regeneration, but by the political enfranchisement of our people.

Faith in Social Progress

In concluding his memoirs in his old age, Surendranāth looked back at the changes that had taken place in Hindu society during his lifetime, and summed up that faith in gradual reform which is one of the hallmarks of a Moderate.

[From *A Nation in Making,* pp. 397–98]

I feel that if we have to advance in social matters, we must, so far as practicable, take the community with us by a process of steady and gradual uplift, so that there may be no sudden disturbance or dislocation, the new being adapted to the old, and the old assimilated to the new. That has been the normal path of progress in Hindu society through the long centuries. It would be idle to contend that Hindu society is today where it was two hundred years ago. It moves slowly, perhaps more slowly than many would wish, but in the words of Galileo "it does move," more or less according to the lines of adaptation that I have indicated. The question of sea-voyage, or child-marriage, or even enforced widowhood, is not today where it was in the latter part of the last century. Fifty years ago I was an outcaste (being an England-returned Brahmin) in the village where I live. Today I am an honored member of the community. My public services have, perhaps, partly contributed to the result. But they would have been impotent, as in the case Ram Mohun Roy for many long years after his death, if they were not backed by the slow, the silent, the majestic forces of progress, working noiselessly but irresistibly in the bosom of society, helping on the fruition of those ideas which have been sown in the public mind. Remarkable indeed have been, in many respects, the relaxations and the removal of restrictions of caste. Dining with non-Hindus, which was an abomination not many years ago, is now connived at, if not openly countenanced. A still more forward step towards loosening the bonds of caste has been taken within the last few years. The barriers of marriage between some sub-castes have been relaxed, and marriages between hitherto prohibited sub-castes of Brahmins and Kayasthas [scribes] are not infrequent, and I have had some personal share in this reform. Beneficent are the activities of the Brāhmo Samāj, but behind them is the slower but larger movement of the general community, all making towards progress.

M. G. RĀNADE: PIONEER MAHĀRĀSHTRIAN REFORMER

Western cultural influence, like British rule itself, came to different parts of India at different times. The coastal ports founded in the sixteenth and seventeenth centuries—Madras, Bombay, Calcutta—became and remain today the centers of the new order of life and thought. The spread of this order into the hinterland, however, was a slow and irregular process. Bengal, the home of a number of thinkers considered thus far, was the first province to fall entirely under British sway and therefore the first to react to the impact of Western ways and ideas.

On the opposite side of the Indian subcontinent, protected by their mountain fortresses in the Western Ghats, the proud kingdoms of

Mahārāshtra were among the last to surrender to foreign rule. The leadership which made this prolonged resistance possible came notably from two caste groups. The fighting Marāthā-Kunbi castes under Shivaji (1630?–1680) and his descendants, provided most of the military force, while the small but influential Chitpavan brāhman caste provided the peshwas (prime ministers) and intellectual leaders of later times. Even after the final defeat of the Peshwa's government in 1818 the city of Poona remained the center of Mahārāshtrian intellectual life. In the closing decades of the nineteenth century the Chitpavan brāhman caste produced three leaders whose names were to be inscribed in Indian nationalism's hall of fame—Rānade, Gokhale, and Tilak.

Mahādev Govind Rānade, the eldest of three children, was born in 1842 in a strictly orthodox household. An extremely serious student, he begged his father to send him to school in Bombay to complete his English education. At fourteen he entered the Elphinstone Institution, and at seventeen took his place in the first class to enroll in the new Bombay University. He distinguished himself by his diligence and originality of thought, and became a teacher of economics and later of history and literature at his first alma mater, now called the Elphinstone College. But he chose to make his career in the law, and before he was thirty received his first appointment as a subordinate judge in the government courts at Poona.

During his thirty years as a judge, Rānade gently but firmly worked for the reform of such social evils as child marriage, the non-remarriage of widows, and the seclusion of women. In many ways his efforts resembled those of Rāmmohun Roy, whom he admired as a patriot and as a godly man. Rānade was one of the early members of the Prārthanā Samāj (Prayer Society, modeled after the Brāhmo Samāj), whose founding in 1867 was sparked by Keshub Chunder Sen's earlier visits to Bombay. Under Rānade's judicious guidance, the Prārthanā Samāj did not cut itself off from the rest of Hindu society, but strove gradually to bring the orthodox around to its position. Despite the vociferous and sometimes violent opposition of Tilak and his school, Rānade's policy of moderation in social reform met with increasing success.

Disqualified from entering active politics by his judgeship, Rānade's contribution to the nationalist movement was largely in the realm of social and economic reform. In 1887, he founded the Indian National

Social Conference as a separate organization which met concurrently with the annual Congress sessions, and in 1890 inaugurated the Industrial Association of Western India. Rānade's views on economics grew out of his long and patient study of Indian problems. He concluded that their constructive solution lay in a vigorous policy of industrial and commercial development under British government auspices.

Rānade's infinite capacity for taking pains, his saintly disposition, and his devotion to the welfare of India inspired to greater patriotic endeavor the hundreds of younger men with whom he maintained contact in person or through correspondence. He was a Moderate in the best sense of the term—scholarly, patient, practical, constructive, never wasting his time in denouncing those who held other views. After his death in 1901 his memory continued to inspire the leaders of Western India— Gokhale, and after him Gāndhi, carrying on the tradition he initiated of social and economic reform as an integral part of selfless public service.

MAHĀDEV GOVIND RĀNADE
Revivalism versus Reform

The ludicrous impracticability of reviving ancient traditions merely because they were ancient was tellingly demonstrated by Rānade in one of his Social Conference addresses. Having explained why he rejected the suggestion of the Brāhmo and Ārya Samājists that all social reformers should convert to those faiths, he went on to analyze the four basic causes of the degeneration of Indian society.

[From Chintamini, *Indian Social Reform*, Part II, pp. 89–95]

While the new religious sects condemn us for being too orthodox, the extreme orthodox section denounce us for being too revolutionary in our methods. According to these last, our efforts should be directed to revive, and not to reform. I have many friends in this camp of extreme orthodoxy, and their watchword is that revival, and not reform, should be our motto. They advocate a return to the old ways, and appeal to the old authorities and the old sanction. Here also, as in the instance quoted above, people speak without realizing the full significance of their own words. When we are asked to revive our institutions and customs, people seem to be very much at sea as to what it is they seem to revive. What particular period of our history is to be taken as the old? Whether the period of the Vedas, of the Smritis, of the Puranas or of the Mahomedan or modern Hindu times? Our usages have been changed from time to time by a slow process of growth, and in some cases of decay and corruption, and we cannot stop at a particular period without breaking the continuity of the whole. When my revivalist friend presses his argument upon me, he has to seek recourse in some subterfuge which really furnishes no reply to the question—what shall we revive? Shall we revive the old habits of our people when the most sacred of our caste indulged in all the abominations as we now understand them of animal food and drink which exhausted every section of our country's zoology and botany? The men and the gods of those old days ate and drank forbidden things to excess in a way no revivalist will now venture to recommend. Shall we revive the twelve forms of sons, or eight forms of marriage, which included capture, and recognized mixed and illegitimate intercourse? Shall we revive the Niyoga system of procreating sons on our brother's wives when widowed? Shall we revive the old liberties taken by the Rishis and by the wives of the Rishis with the marital tie? Shall we revive the hecatombs of animals sacrificed from year's end to year's end, and in which human beings were not spared as propitiatory offerings? Shall we revive the Shakti worship of the left hand with its indecencies and practical debaucheries? Shall we revive the sati and infanticide customs, or the flinging of living men into the rivers, or over rocks, or hookswinging, or the crushing beneath Jagannath car? [1] Shall we revive the internecine wars of the Brahmins and Kshatriyas, or the cruel persecution and degradation of the aboriginal population? Shall we revive the custom of many husbands to one wife or of many wives to one husband? Shall we require our Brahmins to cease to be landlords and gentlemen, and turn into beggars and dependants upon the king as in olden times? These instances will suffice to show that the plan of reviving the ancient usages and customs will not work our salvation, and is not practicable. If these usages were good and beneficial, why were they altered by our wise ancestors? If they were bad and injurious, how can any claim be put forward for their restoration after so many ages? Besides, it seems to be forgotten that in a living organism,

---

[1] A huge wagon used to carry the idol of Jagannāth, "the Lord of the Universe," in the city of Puri. In fits of frenzy devotees would hurl themselves in front of its wheels. The word "juggernaut" derives from this source.

as society is, no revival is possible. The dead and the buried or burnt are dead, buried, and burnt once for all, and the dead past cannot therefore be revived except by a reformation of the old materials into new organized beings. If revival is impossible, reformation is the only alternative open to sensible people, and now it may be asked what is the principle on which this reformation must be based? People have very hazy ideas on this subject. It seems to many that it is the outward form which has to be changed, and if this change can be made, they think that all the difficulties in our way will vanish. If we change our outward manners and customs, sit in a particular way, or walk in a particular fashion, our work according to them is accomplished. I cannot but think that much of the prejudice against the reformers is due to this misunderstanding. It is not the outward form, but the inward form, the thought and the idea which determines the outward form, that has to be changed if real reformation is desired.

Now what have been the inward forms or ideas which have been hastening our decline during the past three thousand years? These ideas may be briefly set forth as isolation, submission to outward force or power more than to the voice of the inward conscience, perception of fictitious differences between men and men due to heredity and birth, passive acquiescence in evil or wrong doing, and a general indifference to secular well-being, almost bordering upon fatalism. These have been the root ideas of our ancient social system. They have as their natural result led to the existing family arrangements where the woman is entirely subordinated to the man and the lower castes to the higher castes, to the length of depriving men of their natural respect for humanity. All the evils we seek to combat result from the prevalence of these ideas. They are mere corollaries to these axiomatic assumptions. They prevent some of our people from realizing what they really are in all conscience, neither better nor worse than their fellows, and that whatever garb men may put on, they are the worse for assuming dignities and powers which do not in fact belong to them. As long as these ideas remain operative on our minds, we may change our outward forms and institutions, and be none the better for the change. These ideas have produced in the long course of ages their results on our character, and we must judge their good or bad quality, as Saint Paul says, by the fruits they have borne. Now that these results have been disastrous, nobody disputes or doubts, and the lesson to be drawn for our guidance in the future from this fact is that the current of these ideas must be changed, and in the place of the old worship we paid to them, we must accustom ourselves and others to worship and reverence new ideals. In place of isolation, we must cultivate the spirit of fraternity or elastic expansiveness. At present it is everybody's ambition to pride himself upon being a member of the smallest community that can be conceived, and the smaller the number of those with whom you can dine, or marry, or associate, the higher is your perfection and purity, the purest person is he who cooks his own food, and does not allow the shadow of even his nearest friend to fall upon his cooked food. Every caste and every sect has thus a tendency to split itself into smaller castes and smaller sects in practical life. Even in philosophy and religion, it is a received maxim that knowledge is for the few, and that salvation is only possible for the esoteric elect with whom only are the virtues of sanctity and wisdom, and that for the rest of mankind, they must be left to wander in the wilderness, and grovel in superstition and even vice, with only a coloring of so-called religion to make them respectable. Now all this must be changed. The new mold of thought on this head must be, as stated above, cast on the lines of fraternity, a capacity to expand outwards, and to make more cohesive inwards the bonds of fellowship. Increase the circle of your friends and associates, slowly and cautiously if you will, but the tendency must be towards a general recognition of the essential equality between man and man. It will beget sympathy and power. It will strengthen your own hands, by the sense that you have numbers with you, and not against you, or as you foolishly imagine, below you.

The next idea which lies at the root of our helplessness is the sense that we are always intended to remain children, to be subject to outside control and never to rise to the dignity of self-control by making our conscience and our reason the supreme, if not the sole, guide to our conduct. All past history has been a terrible witness to the havoc committed by this misconception. We are children, no doubt but the children of God, and not of man, and the voice of God is the only voice [to] which we are bound to listen. Of course, all of us cannot listen to this voice when we desire it, because from long neglect and dependence upon outside help, we have benumbed this faculty of conscience in us. With too many of us, a thing is true or false, righteous or sinful, simply because somebody in the past has said that it is so. Duties and obligations are duties and obligations, not because we feel them to be so, but because somebody reputed to be wise has laid it down that they are so. In small matters of manners and courtesies, this outside dictation is not without its use. But when we abandon ourselves entirely to this helpless dependence on other wills, it is no wonder that we become helpless as children in all departments of life. Now the new idea which should take up the place of this helplessness and dependence is not the idea of a rebellious overthrow of all authority, but that of freedom responsible to the voice of God in us. Great and wise men in the past, as in the present, have a claim upon our regards, but they must not come between us and our God—the Divine principle enthroned in the heart of every one of us high or low. It is this sense of self-respect, or rather respect for the God in us, which has to be cultivated. It is a very tender plant which takes years and years to make it grow. But there is the capacity and the power, and we owe it as a duty to ourselves to undertake the task. Revere all human authority, pay your respects to all prophets and all revelations, but never let this reverence and respect come in the way of the dictates of conscience, the Divine command in us.

Similarly there is no doubt that men differ from men in natural capacities, and aptitudes, and that heredity and birth are factors of considerable importance in our development. But it is at the same time true they are not the only factors that determine the whole course of our life for good or for evil, under a law of necessity. Heredity and birth explain many things, but this Law of Karma does not explain all things! What is worse, it does not explain the mystery that makes man and woman what they really are, the reflection and the image of God. Our passions and our feelings, our pride and our ambition, lend strength to these agencies, and with their help the Law of Karma completes our conquest, and in too many cases enforces our surrender. The new idea that should come in here is that this Law of Karma can be controlled and set back by a properly trained will, when it is made subservient to a higher will than ours. This we see in our everyday life, and Necessity, or the Fates are, as our own texts tell us, faint obstacles in the way of our advancement if we devote ourselves to the Law of Duty. I admit that this misconception is very hard to remove, perhaps the hardest of the old ideas. But removed it must be, if not in this life or generation, in many lives and generations, if we are ever to rise to our full stature.

The fourth old form or idea to which I will allude here is our acquiescence in wrong or evil doing as an inevitable condition of human life, about which we need not be very particular. All human life is a vanity and a dream, and we are not much concerned with it. This view of life is in fact atheism in its worst form. No man or woman really ceases to be animal who does not perceive or realize that wrong or evil-doing, impurity and vice, crime and misery, and sin of all kinds, is really our animal existence prolonged. It is the beast in us which blinds us to impurity and vice, and makes them even attractive. There must be nautches [2] in our temples, say our priests, because even the Gods cannot do without these impure fairies. This is only a typical instance of our acquiescence in impurity. There must be drunkenness in the world, there must be poverty and wretchedness and tyranny, there must be fraud and force, there must be thieves and the law to punish them. No doubt these are facts, and there is no use denying their existence, but in the name of all that is sacred and true, do not acquiesce in them, do not hug these evils to your bosom, and cherish them. Their contact is poisonous, not the less deadly because it does not kill, but it corrupts men. A healthy sense of the true dignity of our nature, and of man's high destiny, is the best corrective and antidote to this poison. I think I have said more than enough to suggest to your reflecting minds what it is that we have to reform. All admit that we have been deformed. We have lost our stature, we are bent in a hundred places, our eyes lust after forbidden things, our ears desire to hear scandals about our neighbors, our tongues lust to taste forbidden fruit, our hands itch for another man's property, our bowels are deranged with indigestible food. We cannot walk on our feet, but require stilts or crutches. This is our present social polity, and now we want this deformity to be removed; and the only way to remove it is to place ourselves under the discipline of better ideas and forms such as those I have briefly touched above. Now this is the work of the Reformer. Reforms in the matter of infant marriage and enforced widowhood, in the matter of temperance and purity, intermarriage between castes, the elevation of the low castes, and the re-admission of converts, and the regulation of our endowments and charities, are reforms only so far and no further as they check the influence of the old ideas and promote the growth of the new tendencies. The Reformer has to infuse in himself the light and warmth of nature,

[2] Women attached to temples as dancers (and sometimes as prostitutes).

and he can only do it by purifying and improving himself and his surroundings. He must have his family, village, tribe, and nation recast
in other and new molds, and that is the reason why Social Reform becomes our obligatory duty, and not a mere pastime which might be
given up at pleasure. Revival is, as I have said, impossible; as impossible
as mass-conversion into other faiths. But even if it were possible, its only
use to us would be if the reforms elevated us and our surroundings, if
they made us stronger, braver, truer men with all our faculties of endurance and work developed, with all our sympathies fully awakened
and refined, and if with our heads and hearts acting in union with a
purified and holy will, they made us feel the dignity of our being and
the high destiny of our existence, taught us to love all, work with all, and
feel for all.

Hindu-Muslim Cooperation

In his speech to the Indian Social Conference of 1899, Rānade stressed the
importance of religious toleration, suggesting that the members of each community avoid mutual recriminations, and cooperate instead in the work of social
reform.

[From Chintamini, *Indian Social Reform,* Part II, pp. 122–25]

If the lessons of the past have any value, one thing is quite clear, namely,
that in this vast country no progress is possible unless both Hindus and
Mahomedans join hands together, and are determined to follow the lead
of the men who flourished in Akbar's time and were his chief advisers
and councillors, and sedulously avoid the mistakes which were committed by his greatgrandson Aurangzib. Joint action from a sense of common interest, and a common desire to bring about the fusion of the
thoughts and feelings of men so as to tolerate small differences and
bring about concord—these were the chief aims kept in view by Akbar
and formed the principle of the new divine faith formulated in the
Din-i-ilahi.[3] Every effort on the part of either Hindus or Mahomedans
to regard their interests as separated and distinct, and every attempt made
by the two communities to create separate schools and interests among
themselves, and not to heal up the wounds inflicted by mutual hatred

[3] "Divine Faith," the synthesis of Hindu and Muslim religious ideas proclaimed by the
Mughal Emperor Akbar.

of caste and creed, must be deprecated on all hands. It is to be feared that this lesson has not been sufficiently kept in mind by the leaders of both communities in their struggle for existence and in the acquisition of power and predominance during recent years. There is at times a great danger of the work of Akbar being undone by losing sight of this great lesson which the history of his reign and that of his two successors is so well calculated to teach. The Conference which brings us together is especially intended for the propagation of this "din" [4] or "dharma," and it is in connection with that message chiefly that I have ventured to speak to you today on this important subject. The ills that we are suffering from are most of them, self-inflicted evils, the cure of which is to a large extent in our own hands. Looking at the series of measures which Akbar adopted in his time to cure these evils, one feels how correct was his vision when he and his advisers put their hand on those very defects in our national character which need to be remedied first before we venture on higher enterprises. Pursuit of high ideas, mutual sympathy and cooperation, perfect tolerance, a correct understanding of the diseases from which the body politic is suffering, and an earnest desire to apply suitable remedies—this is the work cut out for the present generation. The awakening has commenced, as is witnessed by the fact that we are met in this place from such distances for joint consultation and action. All that is needed is that we must put our hands to the plow, and face the strife and the struggle. The success already achieved warrants the expectation that if we persevere on right lines, the goal we have in view may be attained. That goal is not any particular advantage to be gained in power and wealth. It is represented by the efforts to attain it, the expansion and the evolution of the heart and the mind, which will make us stronger and braver, purer and truer men. This is at least the lesson I draw from our more recent history of the past thousand years, and if those centuries have rolled away to no purpose over our heads, our cause is no doubt hopeless beyond cure. That is however not the faith in me; and I feel sure it is not the faith that moves you in this great struggle against our own weak selves, than which nothing is more fatal to our individual and collective growth. Both Hindus and Mahomedans have their work cut out in this struggle. In the backwardness of female education, in the disposition to overleap the bounds of their own religion, in

[4] Arabic term for which the English word "religion" is only an approximate translation.

matters of temperance, in their internal dissensions between castes and creeds, in the indulgence of impure speech, thought, and action on occasions when they are disposed to enjoy themselves, in the abuses of many customs in regard to unequal and polygamous marriages, in the desire to be extravagant in their expenditure on such occasions, in the neglect of regulated charity, in the decay of public spirit in insisting on the proper management of endowments—in these and other matters both communities are equal sinners, and there is thus much ground for improvement on common lines. Of course the Hindus, being by far the majority of the population, have other difficulties of their own to combat with; and they are trying in their gatherings of separate castes and communities to remedy them each in their own way. But without co-operation and conjoint action of all communities, success is not possible, and it is on that account that the general Conference is held in different places each year to rouse local interest, and help people in their separate efforts by a knowledge of what their friends similarly situated are doing in other parts. This is the reason of our meeting here, and I trust that this message I have attempted to deliver to you on this occasion will satisfy you that we cannot conceive a nobler work than the one for which we have met here today.

India's Need: State Guidance of Economic Development

Rānade's essay of 1892 on "Indian Political Economy" may be regarded as the cornerstone of the economic theory which underlies the present Five Year Plans. He first showed that English *laissez faire* doctrines were being challenged by more recent theories of the science of economics and were not necessarily relevant to India's problems; then continued with a diagnosis of the Indian economy.

[From Rānade, *Essays on Indian Economics*, pp. 22–25, 33–36]

This resumé of the past and contemporary history of the growth of economic Sciences in England, France, Germany, Italy, and America will satisfy the student that modern European thought does not at all countenance the view of the English writers of the Ricardian School, that the principles of the science, as they have enunciated them in their textbooks, are universally and necessarily true for all times and places, and for all stages of advancement. Modern thought is veering to the conclusion that the individual and his interests are not the center round which the theory should revolve, that the true center is the body politic of which that individual is a member, and that collective defense and well-being, social education and discipline, and the duties, and not merely the interests, of men, must be taken into account, if the theory is not to be merely utopian. The method to be followed is not the deductive but the historical method, which takes account of the past in its forecast of the future; and relativity, and not absoluteness, characterizes the conclusions of economical science. There are those who seek to get over this difficulty by differentiating the science from what they are disposed to call the art of economy. This divorce of theory and practice is, however, a mischievous error, which relegates the science to the sterility of an ideal dream or a puzzle, and condemns the art to the position of a rule of the thumb. Theory is only enlarged practice, practice is theory studied in its relation to proximate causes. The practice is predetermined by the theory which tests its truth, and adapts it to different conditions by reason of its grasp of the deep-seated, permanent, and varied basal truths. I hope thus to have shown that the nature of the subject itself as a branch of social science, which is best studied historically and not deductively, the actual practice of the most civilized nations and the history of the growth of its theory given above alike establish the doctrine of relativity, and the predominant claim of collective welfare over individual interests, as the principal features in which the highest minds of the present day chiefly differ from the economical writers of the old school, with their *a priori* conclusions based on individual self-interest and unrestricted competition.

We have next to consider the bearings of this enlarged view of the science in its Indian aspects. The characteristics of our social life are the prevalence of status over contract, of combination over competition. Our habits of mind are conservative to a fault. The aptitudes of climate and soil facilitate the production of raw materials. Labor is cheap and plentiful, but unsteady, unthrifty, and unskilled. Capital is scarce, immobile, and unenterprising. Cooperation on a large scale of either capital or labor is unknown. Agriculture is the chief support of nearly the whole population, and this agriculture is carried on under conditions of uncertain rainfall. Commerce and manufactures on a large scale are but recent importations, and all industry is carried on, on the system of petty farming, retail dealing, and job working by poor people on borrowed capital. There is an almost complete absence of a landed gentry or wealthy middle class. The land is a monopoly of the State. The desire for accumulation is very weak, peace and security having been almost unknown over large areas for any length of time till within the last century. Our laws and institutions favour a low standard of life, and encourage subdivision and not concentration of wealth. The religious ideals of life condemn the ardent pursuit of wealth as a mistake to be avoided as far as possible. These are old legacies and inherited weaknesses. Stagnation and dependence, depression and poverty—these are written in broad characters on the face of the land and its people. To these must be added the economical drain of wealth and talents, which foreign subjection has entailed on the country. As a compensation against all these depressing influences, we have to set off the advantage of a free contact with a race which has opened the country to the commerce of the world, and by its superior skill and resources has developed communications in a way previously unknown. If we wish to realize our situation fully, we may not overlook this factor, because, it represents the beam of light which alone illumines the prevailing darkness. It cannot well be a mere accident that the destinies of this country have been entrusted to the guidance of a nation whose characteristic strength is opposed to all our weaknesses, whose enterprise, chiefly in commerce and manufactures, knows no bounds, whose capital overflows the world, among whom contract has largely superseded status, and competition and cooperation play a predominant part, whose view of life is full of hope, and whose powers of organization have never been surpassed.

Rānade next advanced several reasons why industrial enterprise should be encouraged, and urged government action to populate untilled lands, protect peasants against excessive taxation, and prevent exploitation by landlords or money-lenders. In his conclusion he argued that the state should play a more active role in the economic development of the country.

Lastly comes the great department of governmental interference. The meddlesomeness of the mercantile system provoked a reaction against state control and guidance towards the end of the last century in favor of natural liberty. The doctrines of this negative school have now in their turn been abused by a too logical extension of its principles. There is a decided reaction in Europe against the *laissez faire* system. Even in England, the recent factory legislation, the qualified recognition by law of Trades-Unionism, the poor law system, and the Irish Land Settlement, are all instances which indicate the same change of view. Speaking roughly, the province of state interference and control is practically being extended so as to restore the good points of the mercantile system without its absurdities. The State is now more and more recognized as the national organ for taking care of national needs in all matters in which individual and cooperative efforts are not likely to be so effective and economic as national effort. This is the correct view to take of the true functions of a state. To relegate them to the simple duty of maintaining peace and order is really to deprive the community of many of the advantages of the social union. Education, both liberal and technical, post and telegraphs, railway and canal communications, the pioneering of new enterprise, the insurance of risky undertakings—all these functions are usefully discharged by the State. The question is one of time, fitness, and expediency, not one of liberty and rights. In our own country the State has similarly enlarged its functions with advantage. The very fact that the rulers belong to a race with superior advantages imposes this duty on them of attempting things which no native rulers, past or present, could as well achieve, or possibly even think of. This obligation is made more peremptory by the fact that the State claims to be the sole landlord, and is certainly the largest capitalist in the country. While the State in India has done much in this way in the working of iron and coal fields, and in the experiments made about cotton and tobacco, and in tea and coffee and cinchona Plantations, it must be admitted that, as compared with its resources and the needs of the country, these attempts are as nothing by the side of what has been attempted with success in France, Germany, and other countries, but which, unhappily, has not been attempted in this country. Even if political considerations forbid independent action in the matter of differential duties, the pioneering of new enterprises is a duty which the government might more systematically undertake with advantage. In truth, there is no difference of principle between lending such support and guidance, by the free use of its credit and superior organization, in pioneering industrial undertaking or subsidizing private cooperative effort, and its guaranteeing minimum interest to railway companies. The building up of national, not merely state, credit on broad foundations by helping people to acquire confidence in a free and largely ramified banking system, so advantageously worked in Europe under different forms, has also not been attempted here. There is, lastly, the duty cast on it of utilizing indigenous resources, and organizing them in a way to produce in India in state factories all products of skill which the state departments require in the way of stores. These are only a few of the many directions in which, far more than exchange and frontier difficulties, the highest statesmanship will have a field all its own for consideration and action. They will, no doubt, receive such consideration if only the minds of the rulers were once thoroughly freed from the fear of offending the so-called maxims of rigid economical science. It is time that a new departure should take place in this connection, and it is with a view to drawing public attention to this necessity that I have ventured to place before you the results of modern economic thought. In this, as in other matters, the conditions of Indian life are more faithfully reproduced in some of the continental countries and in America than in happy England, proud of its position, strong in its insularity, and the home of the richest and busiest community in the modern industrial world. If the attempt I have made leads to a healthy and full discussion of the change of policy I advocate, I shall regard myself amply repaid for my trouble.

G. K. GOKHALE: SERVANT OF INDIA

The work of reform begun by Rānade was ably shouldered by his younger friend and colleague G. K. Gokhale. So close was the personal relationship between the two men during Rānade's lifetime—for years they met weekly to discuss their ideas and projects—that Gokhale's excursions into active politics can be regarded as the logical extension of his teacher's endeavors. Sprung from the same proud Mahārāshtrian stock, both leaders nevertheless clung to the policy of cooperation with the government and of moderate opposition to its evils. Gokhale, however, had to endure the merciless attacks of the Extremists during the stormiest decade in Indian politics up to that time.

Gopāl Krishna Gokhale (1866–1915) dedicated his life to public service at the age of nineteen, on his graduation from Elphinstone College, by joining the Deccan Education Society in Poona. Members of the Society took a vow of poverty for twenty years in order to devote their time exclusively to educating their fellow-countrymen. For his part, Gokhale became a teacher of English and mathematics in the Fergusson College which the Society founded in 1885. He soon met Justice Rānade and began his long and fruitful apprenticeship under him—examining documents, weighing evidence, analyzing fiscal data, and preparing comprehensive memoranda on public questions.

Gokhale attracted public attention with the sagacity of his carefully prepared speeches, and in 1899 was elected a member of the recently formed Legislative Council for the state of Bombay. When only thirty-six, he became the Indian representative of this state on the Imperial Legislative Council, despite its limited powers the highest law-making body in India. For the last thirteen years of his life he wore himself out with his efforts to secure government cooperation in granting much needed financial and administrative reforms for India. "No taxation without representation," was the essence of his demand, and his annual speeches on the imperial budget effected many concessions from harassed ministers of finance.

In 1905 Gokhale founded the Servants of India Society in Poona, modeling it after the lay and monastic orders of the Catholic Church. Famine relief, education, Hindu-Muslim unity, and the elevation of the lowest castes were among the fields in which it carried on the work begun by its founder. Gokhale also took great interest in the problems of Indian emigrants to South Africa, giving freely of his advice and encouragement to their leader, M. K. Gāndhi. Although bitterly reviled by Tilak and other advocates of violent action to end foreign rule, Gokhale's readiness to cooperate with the British in introducing gradual reforms helped to pave the way for the eventual peaceful transfer of power to an independent India.

GOPĀL KRISHNA GOKHALE
Taxation Without Representation

Soon after taking his place in the Imperial Legislative Council, Gokhale made the first of his annual budget speeches. His attacks on the government's taxation policy are representative of the Moderates' preoccupation with the economic shortcomings of British rule.

[From *Speeches of the Honourable Mr. G. K. Gokhale,* pp. 1-2, 8-11]

Your Excellency, I fear I cannot conscientiously join in the congratulations which have been offered to the Hon'ble Finance Member on the huge surplus which the revised estimates show for the last year. A surplus of seven crores [1] of rupees is perfectly unprecedented in the history of Indian finance, and coming as it does on the top of a series of similar surpluses realized when the country has been admittedly passing through very trying times, it illustrates to my mind in a painfully clear manner the utter absence of a due correspondence between the condition of the people and the condition of the finances of the country. Indeed, my Lord, the more I think about this matter the more I feel—and I trust Your Lordship will pardon me for speaking somewhat bluntly—that these surpluses constitute a double wrong to the community. They are a wrong in the first instance in that they exist at all—that government should take so much more from the people than is needed in times of serious depression and suffering; and they are also a wrong, because they lend themselves to easy misinterpretation and, among other things, render possible the phenomenal optimism of the Secretary of State for India, who seems to imagine that all is for the best in this best of lands. A slight examination of these surpluses suffices to show that they are mainly, almost entirely, currency surpluses, resulting from the fact that government still maintain the same high level of taxation which they considered to be necessary to secure financial equilibrium when the rupee stood at its lowest. . . .

A taxation so forced as not only to maintain a budgetary equilibrium but to yield as well "large, continuous, progressive surpluses"—even in years of trial and suffering—is, I submit, against all accepted canons of finance. In European countries, extraordinary charges are usually met out of borrowings, the object being to avoid, even in times of pressure, impeding the even, normal development of trade and industry by any sudden or large additions to the weight of public burdens. In India, where the economic side of such questions finds such scant recognition, and the principle of meeting the charges of the year with the resources of the year is carried to a logical extreme, the anxiety of the Financial Administration is not only to make both ends meet in good and bad years alike, but to present large surpluses year after year. The Hon'ble Finance Member remarks in his Budget Statement under "Army Services": "It must be remembered that India is defraying from revenues the cost of undertaking both rearmament and the reform of military reorganization in important departments. I believe that this is an undertaking which has not been

[1] One crore equals ten millions.

attempted by other countries without the assistance of loans in some form or other. Even in England, extraordinary military requirements for fortifications and barracks have been met by loans for short terms of years repayable by installments out of revenues. If profiting by a period of political tranquillity we can accomplish this task without the raising of a loan and the imposition of a permanent burden on future generations, I think that we shall be able to congratulate ourselves on having done that which even the richest nations of Europe have not considered it advisable to attempt."

Every word of this citation invites comment. How comes it that India is doing in regard to these extraordinary charges that which even the richest nations of Europe have not considered it advisable to attempt? The obvious answer is that in those countries it is the popular assemblies that control taxation and expenditure; in India the tax-payer has no constitutional voice in the shaping of these things. If we had any votes to give, and the government of the country had been carried on by an alternation of power between two parties, both alike anxious to conciliate us and bid for our support, the Hon'ble Member would assuredly have told a different tale. But I venture to submit, my Lord, that the consideration which the people of Western countries receive in consequence of their voting power should be available to us, in matters of finance at any rate, through an "intelligent anticipation"—to use a phrase of Your Lordship's —of our reasonable wishes on the part of government.

But even thus—after doing what the richest nations of Europe shrink from attempting—meeting all sorts of extraordinary charges, amounting to about 70 crores in sixteen years, out of current revenues—we have "large, continuous, progressive surpluses," and this only shows, as Colonel Chesney points out in the March number of the *Nineteenth Century and After,* that more money is being taken from the people than is right, necessary, or advisable, or, in other words, the weight of public taxation has been fixed and maintained at an unjustifiably high level. Taxation for financial equilibrium is what we all can understand, but taxation kept up in the face of the difficulties and misfortunes of a period of excessive depression and for "large, continuous and progressive surpluses" is evidently a matter which requires justification. At all events, those who have followed the course of the financial history of the period will admit that the fact viewed *per se* that "such large, continuous, and progressive surpluses" have occurred during the period—as a result not of a normal expansion of fiscal resources but of a forced up and heavy taxation—does not connote, as Lord George Hamilton contends, an advancing material prosperity of the country or argue any marvelous recuperative power on the part of the masses—as the Hon'ble Sir Edward Law urged last year. To them, at any rate, the apparent paradox of a suffering country and an overflowing treasury stands easily explained and is a clear proof of the fact that the level of national taxation is kept unjustifiably high, even when government are in a position to lower that level.

Improving the Lot of Low-Caste Hindus

One of Gokhale's chief concerns in the realm of social reform was the lot of the so-called "untouchables." The appeal launched in this speech to a social conference in 1903 was answered after his death by Gāndhi's devotion to their cause.

[From *Speeches of the Honourable Mr. G. K. Gokhale,* pp. 740–47]

Mr. President and Gentlemen: The proposition which has been entrusted to me runs thus—"That this Conference holds that the present degraded condition of the low castes is, in itself and from the national point of view, unsatisfactory, and is of opinion that every well-wisher of the country should consider it his duty to do all he can to raise their moral and social condition by trying to rouse self-respect in these classes and placing facilities for education and employment within their reach."

Gentlemen, I hope I am not given to the use of unnecessarily strong language and yet I must say that this resolution is not as strongly worded as it should have been. The condition of the low castes—it is painful to call them low castes—is not only unsatisfactory as this resolution says, it is so deeply deplorable that it constitutes a grave blot on our social arrangements; and, further, the attitude of our educated men towards this class is profoundly painful and humiliating. I do not propose to deal with this subject as an antiquarian; I only want to make a few general observations from the standpoint of justice, humanity, and national self-interest. I think all fair-minded persons will have to admit that it is absolutely monstrous that a class of human beings, with bodies similar to our own, with brains that can think and with hearts that can feel, should be perpetually condemned to a low life of utter wretchedness,

servitude, and mental and moral degradation, and that permanent barriers should be placed in their way so that it should be impossible for
them ever to overcome them and improve their lot. This is deeply revolt-
ing to our sense of justice. I believe one has only to put oneself mentally
into their place to realize how grievous this injustice is. We may touch a
cat, we may touch a dog, we may touch any other animal, but the touch
of these human beings is pollution! And so complete is now the mental
degradation of these people that they themselves see nothing in such
treatment to resent, that they acquiesce in it as though nothing better
than that was their due.

I remember a speech delivered seven or eight years ago by the late Mr.
Rānade in Bombay, under the auspices of the Hindu Union Club. That
was a time when public feeling ran high in India on the subject of the
treatment which our people were receiving in South Africa. Our friend,
Mr. Gāndhi, had come here on a brief visit from South Africa and he
was telling us how our people were treated in Natal and Cape Colony
and the Transvaal—how they were not allowed to walk on footpaths or
travel in first-class carriages on the railway, how they were not admitted
into hotels, and so forth. Public feeling, in consequence, was deeply
stirred, and we all felt that it was a mockery that we should be called
British subjects, when we were treated like this in Great Britain's colonies. Mr. Rānade felt this just as keenly as any one else. He had been a
never-failing adviser of Mr. Gāndhi, and had carried on a regular correspondence with him. But it was Mr. Rānade's peculiar greatness that he
always utilized occasions of excitement to give a proper turn to the
national mind and cultivate its sense of proportion. And so, when every
one was expressing himself in indignant terms about the treatment which
our countrymen were receiving in South Africa, Mr. Rānade came forward to ask if we had no sins of our own to answer for in that direction.
I do not exactly remember the title of his address. I think it was "Turn
the searchlight inwards," or some such thing. But I remember that it was
a great speech—one of the greatest that I have ever been privileged to hear.
He began in characteristic fashion, expressing deep sympathy with the
Indians in South Africa in the struggle they were manfully carrying on.
He rejoiced that the people of India had awakened to a sense of the
position of their countrymen abroad, and he felt convinced that this
awakening was a sign of the fact that the dead bones in the valley were

once again becoming instinct with life. But he proceeded to ask: "Was this sympathy with the oppressed and downtrodden Indians to be confined to those of our countrymen only who had gone out of India? Or was it to be general and to be extended to all cases where there was oppression and injustice?" It was easy, he said, to denounce foreigners, but those who did so were bound in common fairness to look into themselves and see if they were absolutely blameless in the matter. He then described the manner in which members of low caste were treated by our own community in different parts of India. It was a description which filled the audience with feelings of deep shame and pain and indignation. And Mr. Rānade very justly asked whether it was for those who tolerated such disgraceful oppression and injustice in their own country to indulge in all that denunciation of the people of South Africa. This question, therefore, is, in the first place, a question of sheer justice.

Next, as I have already said, it is a question of humanity. It is sometimes urged that if we have our castes, the people in the West have their classes, and after all, there is not much difference between the two. A little reflection will, however, show that the analogy is quite fallacious. The classes of the West are a perfectly elastic institution, and not rigid or cast-iron like our castes. Mr. Chamberlain, who is the most masterful personage in the British empire today, was at one time a shoemaker and then a screwmaker. Of course, he did not make shoes himself, but that was the trade by which he made money. Mr. Chamberlain today dines with royalty, and mixes with the highest in the land on terms of absolute equality. Will a shoemaker ever be able to rise in India in the social scale in a similar fashion, no matter how gifted by nature he might be? A great writer has said that castes are eminently useful for the preservation of society, but that they are utterly unsuited for purposes of progress. And this I think is perfectly true. If you want to stand where you were a thousand years ago, the system of castes need not be modified in any material degree. If, however, you want to emerge out of the slough in which you have long remained sunk, it will not do for you to insist on a rigid adherence to caste. Modern civilization has accepted greater equality for all as its watchword, as against privilege and exclusiveness, which were the root-ideas of the old world. And the larger humanity of these days requires that we should acknowledge its claims by seeking the amelioration of the helpless condition of our downtrodden countrymen.

Finally, gentlemen, this is a question of national self-interest. How can we possibly realize our national aspirations, how can our country ever hope to take her place among the nations of the world, if we allow large numbers of our countrymen to remain sunk in ignorance, barbarism, and degradation? Unless these men are gradually raised to a higher level, morally and intellectually, how can they possibly understand our thoughts or share our hopes or cooperate with us in our efforts? Can you not realize that so far as the work of national elevation is concerned, the energy, which these classes might be expected to represent, is simply unavailable to us? I understand that that great thinker and observer—Swāmī Vivekānanda—held this view very strongly. I think that there is not much hope for us as a nation unless the help of all classes, including those that are known as low castes, is forthcoming for the work that lies before us. Moreover, is it, I may ask, consistent with our own self-respect that these men should be kept out of our houses and shut out from all social intercourse as long as they remain within the pale of Hinduism, whereas the moment they put on a coat and a hat and a pair of trousers and call themselves Christians, we are prepared to shake hands with them and look upon them as quite respectable? No sensible man will say that this is a satisfactory state of things. Of course, no one expects that these classes will be lifted up at once morally and intellectually to a position of equality with their more-favored countrymen.

This work is bound to be slow and can only be achieved by strenuous exertions for giving them education and finding for them honourable employment in life. And, gentlemen, it seems to me that, in the present state of India, no work can be higher or holier than this. I think if there is one question of social reform more than another that should stir the enthusiasm of our educated young men and inspire them with an unselfish purpose, it is this question of the degraded condition of our low castes. Cannot a few men—five percent, four percent, three, two, even one percent—of the hundreds and hundreds of graduates that the university turns out every year, take it upon themselves to dedicate their lives to this sacred work of the elevation of low castes? My appeal is not to the old or the middle-aged—the grooves of their lives are fixed—but I think I may well address such an appeal to the young members of our community—to those who have not yet decided upon their future course and who entertain the noble aspiration of devoting to a worthy cause

702 MODERN INDIA AND PAKISTAN

the education which they have received. What the country needs most at the present moment is a spirit of self-sacrifice on the part of our educated young men, and they may take it from me that they cannot spend their lives in a better cause than raising the moral and intellectual level of these unhappy low castes and promoting their general well-being.

The Servants of India Society

The charter of the Servants of India Society embodies Gokhale's most cherished aims for the uplift of his country.

[From *Speeches of the Honourable Mr. G. K. Gokhale,* Appendix, pp. 182–83, 184]

For some time past, the conviction has been forcing itself on many earnest and thoughtful minds that a stage has been reached in the political education and national advancement of the Indian people, when, for further progress, the devoted labors of a specially trained agency, applying itself to the task in a true missionary spirit, are required. The work that has so far been done has indeed been of the highest value. The growth, during the last fifty years, of a feeling of common nationality, based upon common tradition, common disabilities, and common hopes and aspirations, has been most striking. The fact that we are Indians first, and Hindoos, Mahomedans, Parsees, or Christians afterwards, is being realized in a steadily increasing measure, and the idea of a united and renovated India, marching onwards to a place among the nations of the world worthy of her great past, is no longer a mere idle dream of a few imaginative minds, but is the definitely accepted creed of those who form the brain of the community—the educated classes of the country. A creditable beginning has already been made in matters of education and of local self-government; and all classes of the people are slowly but steadily coming under the influence of liberal ideas. The claims of public life are every day receiving wider recognition, and attachment to the land of our birth is growing into a strong and deeply cherished passion of the heart. The annual meetings of the National Congress and of provincial and other conferences, the work of political associations, the writings in the columns of the Indian press—all bear witness to the new life that is coursing in the veins of the people. The results achieved so far are undoubtedly most gratifying, but they only mean that the jungle has been cleared and the foundations laid. The great work of rearing the super-structure has yet to be taken in hand, and the situation demands, on the part of workers, devotion and sacrifices proportionate to the magnitude of the task.

The Servants of India Society has been established to meet in some measure these requirements of the situation. Its members frankly accept the British connection, as ordained, in the inscrutable dispensation of Providence, for India's good. Self-government on the lines of English colonies is their goal. This goal, they recognize, cannot be attained without years of earnest and patient work and sacrifices worthy of the cause. Moreover, the path is beset with great difficulties—there are constant temptations to turn back—bitter disappointments will repeatedly try the faith of those who have put their hand to the work. But the weary toil can have but one end, if only the workers grow not faintheartcd on the way. One essential condition of success is that a sufficient number of our countrymen must now come forward to devote themselves to the cause in the spirit in which religious work is undertaken. Public life must be spiritualized. Love of country must so fill the heart that all else shall appear as of little moment by its side. A fervent patriotism which rejoices at every opportunity of sacrifice for the motherland, a dauntless heart which refuses to be turned back from its object by difficulty or danger, a deep faith in the purpose of Providence that nothing can shake —equipped with these, the worker must start on his mission and reverently seek the joy which comes of spending oneself in the service of one's country.

The Servants of India Society will train men, prepared to devote their lives to the cause of the country in a religious spirit, and will seek to promote, by all constitutional means, the national interests of the Indian people. Its members will direct their efforts principally towards: 1) creating among the people, by example and by precept, a deep and passionate love of the motherland, seeking its highest fulfillment in service and sacrifice; 2) organizing the work of political education and agitation and strengthening the public life of the country; 3) promoting relations of cordial goodwill and cooperation among the different communities; 4) assisting educational movements, especially those for the education of women, the education of backward classes and industrial and scientific education; and 5) the elevation of the depressed classes. The headquarters of the Society will be at Poona, where it will maintain a Home for its members, and attached to it, a library for the study of political questions. The following constitution has been adopted for the Society.

1. The Society shall be called "The Servants of India Society."

2. The objects of the Society are to train men to devote themselves to the service of India as national missionaries and to promote by all constitutional means the national interests of the Indian people. . . .

[Items 3 to 8 and 10 onward deal with organizational questions.]

9. Every member, at the time of admission, shall take the following seven vows:

(*a*) That the country will always be the first in his thoughts and he will give to her service the best that is in him.

(*b*) That in serving the country he will seek no personal advantage for himself.

(*c*) That he will regard all Indians as brothers, and will work for the advancement of all, without distinction of caste or creed.

(*d*) That he will be content with such provision for himself and his family, if he has any, as the Society may be able to make. He will devote no part of his energies to earning money for himself.

(*e*) That he will lead a pure personal life.

(*f*) That he will engage in no personal quarrel with any one.

(*g*) That he will always keep in view the aims of the Society and watch over its interests with the utmost zeal, doing all he can to advance its work. He will never do anything which is inconsistent with the objects of the Society.

CHAPTER XXIV

THE MARRIAGE OF POLITICS AND RELIGION: THE EXTREMISTS

In much the same way as the opening of India to Western cultural influence stimulated the renascence of Hinduism, so the imposition of foreign rule inevitably evoked powerful indigenous reactions in the political sphere. The militant xenophobia which had found expression in scattered attempts at die-hard resistance to British conquest, and in the unorganized uprising of 1857–58, finally crystallized in the late nineteenth century in the group of zealous nationalists known as the Extremists. This group possessed two weapons which were unavailable to previous opponents of British rule. Firstly, they shared with their Moderate rivals the use of a common "national" language, English, and through it enjoyed the opportunities for political agitation provided by the press, the schools, and the Indian National Congress. Secondly, they were able to draw on the newly formulated ideals of renascent Hinduism and to create a potent ideology out of the marriage between these ideals and the imported concepts of patriotism and national unity.

Being impatient to throw off the foreign yoke, the Extremists concentrated on building up mass support for the nationalist movement. To create this support and to unify the Westernized elite with the illiterate peasantry they appealed to three principal ties common to both the educated and the uneducated—language, history, and religion. Casting off the use of English wherever possible, they wrote and spoke in the regional languages understood by the common people. As a means of heightening patriotic fervor they fostered pride in a glorious past, when Hindu kings and warriors ruled the land. Most effective of all because it had the broadest appeal was the use of religious symbolism and terminology to instill in all Hindus a fervent devotion to the Motherland.

In contrast to the Moderates, the Extremists regarded such tasks as social reform and Hindu-Muslim cooperation as merely side issues draining energies from the political struggle and weakening Hindu solidarity. At times their anger at Muslim collaboration with the British spurred them to engage openly in anti-Muslim activity, heedless of the fact that in so doing they were ruining the chances of creating an independent but undivided India. The 1905 Partition of Bengal into Hindu and Muslim majority areas drove a further wedge between the two religious communities, for it encouraged prominent Muslims to enter into a tacit alliance with the British against Hindu ambitions (the Muslim League was founded in 1906, and its demand for separate electorates was granted in 1909). The danger that the more numerous and better-educated Hindu community would preempt the positions of power and influence in self-governing India gave many Muslims a pressing reason to convert to friendship their traditional hostility to the British.

Both Moderates and Extremists insisted that divided Bengal be reunited, but the latter urged that radical measures be taken to coerce the ruling power. In essence, their program was much like the one Gāndhi introduced fifteen years later, being based on the principle of reducing Indian dependence on the British in every possible way. Its principal aims were the boycott of foreign goods, the use of Indian-made articles (or Swadeshi—"one's own country"), the strengthening of an indigenous system of education, and in time the creation of a parallel government of, by, and for the Indian people.

Such a bold stand, coupled with the religious ideology that motivated it, captured the imagination of younger men more readily than did the cautious policies of the Moderates, and the following of the Extremists increased rapidly in numbers after 1905. Their abortive attempt to gain control of the Congress led to a schism in that body at the 1907 session. For the next decade most of the Extremist leaders were either in jail, in exile, or in retirement, but the continuance of terrorist activity—climaxing in an attempt on the Viceroy's life in 1912—showed that their memory was still honored in their absence. The rescinding of the Partition of Bengal in 1911 and the altered situation produced by the First World War made it possible for the Moderates and the Extremists to patch up their quarrel in 1916. The death of the Extremists' greatest leader, Tilak, in 1920 marked the end of an era, for in that same year the Congress came under Gāndhi's uniquely effective control.

Although the heyday of the Extremists was short-lived, their chief contribution to modern Indian thought—the creation of Hindu nationalism through the union of religious and political ideals—is likely to endure for some time to come. It is entirely possible that as the influence of English culture (by which all of them were deeply affected, but against which all reacted in one way or another) diminishes in independent India, a more virulent and violent form of this nationalism may yet emerge.

BANKIM CHANDRA CHATTERJEE: NATIONALIST AUTHOR

Gokhale's saying, "What Bengal thinks today, all India thinks tomorrow," is nowhere more applicable than in the case of the Bengali writer Bankim Chandra Chatterjee. Bankim, although he took no part in politics, first employed the triple appeal of language, history, and religion which enabled Hindu nationalism to win such widespread support in the opening decade of the twentieth century. His historical novels in Bengali reminded his readers that their glorious past should inspire them to achieve an equally glorious future, and demonstrated the power of the pen as an instrument for stirring up patriotic emotions in times when overt political action was impossible.

Bankim was born near Calcutta in 1838, the son of a brāhman landlord and local deputy collector of revenue. A brilliant student, he passed through the anglicized educational system with distinction and was in 1858 one of two in Calcutta University's first graduating class. He was immediately offered a position as deputy magistrate in the Bengal civil service, and for all but one year held this same rank until his retirement in 1891—a mute comment on the opportunities for advancement given to Indians in government service. Fortunately he found an outlet for his natural talent in another direction, and throughout his career as an official used his spare time to write stories and novels which captured the imagination of literate Bengal. Bankim employed a new prose style which combined the virtues of Sanskritized Bengali and the vigor of the common speech, and for the first time since the introduction of English education made it respectable for Bengalis to write in their own mother tongue.

Nationalism in all parts of the world has often been associated with attachment to a common language and its accompanying literary heritage. Bankim could thus be credited with quickening Bengali, as distinct from an all-Indian, nationalism. But this distinction was rendered largely superfluous after 1905, when the agitation against the Partition of Bengal took on a nation-wide character. By the same token, the poem *Bande Mātaram* (*Hail to the Mother*) which first appeared in one of his novels soon became the *Marseillaise* of the nationalist movement throughout the country.

Bankim's original concept, "the Mother" of *Bande Mātaram*, referred at the same time to the land of Bengal and to the female aspect of the Hindu deity. From this fusion of the hitherto separate objects of patriotic and religious devotion sprang the central concept of modern Hindu nationalism. The concept of the divine Motherland, equating as it did love of country with love of God, made an instinctive appeal to the devout Hindu peasantry, for whom the secular reformism and Westernized nationalism of the Moderate leaders remained beyond comprehension.

For all the strength of dedication and mass appeal it generated, Hindu nationalism acted as a regressive force both in hindering social reform and in exacerbating the latent hostility between Hindus and Muslims. Bankim's novels faithfully reflect these two shortcomings, for with rare exceptions they picture well-meaning reformers as fools and Muslims as knaves. Nevertheless, his magic blend of religious sentiment, glorification of the Hindu past, and a beautiful style assured Bankim of lasting popularity among Bengalis, and exerted a far-reaching influence on the rise of extremist Hindu nationalism throughout India.

BANKIM CHANDRA CHATTERJEE
The Language of the Masses

In a letter to the editor of a new English-language periodical, Bankim explained why he, too, was founding a review—in Bengali. His concluding remarks illustrate the linguistic complexity of India as a whole, and remain almost as true today as when they were written.

[From "Letter from Bankim Chandra Chatterjee," in *Bengal: Past and Present*, Vol. VIII, Part 2 (April–June, 1914), pp. 273–74]

I wish you every success in your project. I have myself projected a Bengali magazine with the object of making it the medium of communication and sympathy between the educated and the uneducated classes. You rightly say that the English for good or evil has become our vernacular; and this tends daily to widen the gulf between the higher and the lower ranks of Bengali society. This I think is not exactly what it ought to be; I think that we ought to *disanglicize* ourselves, so to speak, to a certain extent, and to speak to the masses in the language which they understand. I therefore project a Bengali magazine. But this is only half the work we have to do. No purely vernacular organ can completely represent the Bengali culture of the day. Just as we ought to address ourselves to the masses of our own race and country, we have also to make ourselves intelligible to the other Indian races, and to the governing race. There is no hope for India until the Bengali and the Panjabi understand and influence each other, and can bring their joint influence to bear upon the Englishman. This can be done only through the medium of the English, and I gladly welcome your projected periodical.

Hail to the Mother

In *Ānandamath* (*The Abbey of Bliss*), his most famous novel, Bankim took as his theme the Sannyāsī Rebellion in Bengal of the 1770s, attributing to these raiding ascetics a sort of religious nationalism whose focus was God in the form of the Mother. He neatly avoided the charge of disloyalty to British rule by making the Muslims (still the titular rulers of Bengal) the villains of the piece. In this excerpt, Bhavānanda, one of the sannyāsīs, reveals to a new disciple the group's mission and the *mystique* which sustains it.

[From *Abbey of Bliss*, pp. 31–37; *Bande Mātaram* translation in Ghose, *Collected Poems and Plays*, II, 227–28]

In that smiling moonlit night, the two silently walked across the plain. Mahendra [the disciple] was silent, sad, careless, and a little curious.

Bhavananda suddenly changed his looks. He was no more the steady and mild anchorite, nor wore any more the warlike hero's face—the face of the slayer of a captain of forces. Not even was there in his mien the proud disdain with which he had scolded Mahendra even now. It seemed as if his heart was filled with joy at the beauteous sight of the earth, lulled in peace and beaming under the silvery moon, and of the glory in her wilds and woods and hills and streams, and grew cheery like the ocean smiling with the rise of the moon. Bhavananda grew chatty, cheerful, cordial, and very eager to talk. He made many an attempt to open a conversation with his companion but Mahendra would not speak. Having no option left, he then began to sing to himself:

> Mother, I bow to thee!
> Rich with thy hurrying streams,
> Bright with thy orchard gleams,
> Cool with thy winds of delight,
> Dark fields waving, Mother of might,
> Mother free.

Mahendra was a little puzzled to hear the song; he could not grasp anything. Who could be the mother, he thought.

> Rich with thy hurrying streams,
> Bright with orchard gleams.
> Cool with thy winds of delight,
> Dark fields waving, Mother of might,
> Mother free.

He asked, "Who is the mother?" Bhavananda did not answer but sang on:

> Glory of moonlight dreams
> Over the branches and lordly streams,
> Clad in thy blossoming trees,
> Mother, giver of ease,
> Laughing low and sweet!
> Mother, I kiss thy feet,
> Speaker sweet and low!
> Mother, to thee I bow.

"It is the country and no mortal mother," cried Mahendra. "We own no other mother," retorted Bhavananda; "they say, 'the mother and the land of birth are higher than heaven.' We think the land of birth to be no other than our mother herself. We have no mother, no father, no brother, no wife, no child, no hearth or home, we have only got the mother—

> Rich with hurrying streams,
> Bright with orchard gleams.

Mahendra now understood the song and asked Bhavananda to sing again.

He sang:

> Mother, I bow to thee!
> Rich with thy hurrying streams,
> Bright with thy orchard gleams,
> Cool with thy winds of delight,
> Dark fields waving, Mother of might,
> Mother free.
> Glory of moonlight dreams
> Over thy branches and lordly streams,
> Clad in thy blossoming trees,
> Mother, giver of ease,
> Laughing low and sweet!
> Mother, I kiss thy feet,
> Speaker sweet and low!
> Mother, to thee I bow.
> Who hath said thou art weak in thy lands,
> When the swords flash out in twice seventy million hands
> And seventy million voices roar [1]
> Thy dreadful name from shore to shore?
> With many strengths who are mighty and stored,
> To thee I call, Mother and Lord!
> Thou who savest, arise and save!
> To her I cry who ever her foemen drave
> Back from plain and sea
> And shook herself free.
> Thou art wisdom, thou art law,
> Thou our heart, our soul, our breath,
> Thou the love divine, the awe
> In our hearts that conquers death.
> Thine the strength that nerves the arm,
> Thine the beauty, thine the charm.
> Every image made divine
> In our temples is but thine.
> Thou art Durga,[2] Lady and Queen,
> With her hands that strike and her swords of sheen,
> Thou art Lakshmi [3] lotus-throned,

---

[1] When used as a national anthem, this figure was changed to 300 million.
[2] The Goddess Mother, much-worshiped in Bengal.   [3] The Goddess of Wealth.

And the Muse a hundred-toned.
Pure and Perfect without peer,
Mother, lend thine ear.
Rich with thy hurrying streams,
Bright with thy orchard gleams,
Dark of hue, O candid-fair
In thy soul, with jewelled hair
And thy glorious smile divine,
Loveliest of all earthly lands,
Showering wealth from well-stored hands!
Mother, mother mine!
Mother sweet, I bow to thee
Mother great and free!

Mahendra saw that the outlaw was weeping as he sang. He then asked in wonder, "Who may you be, please?"

Bhavananda answered, "We are the Children."

"Children! Whose children are you?"

"Our mother's."

"Well, but does a child worship its mother with the proceeds of robbery?"

"We do nothing of the sort."

"Presently you looted a cart."

"Was that robbery? Whom did we rob?"

"Why, of course the king!"

"The king! What right has he to take this money?"

"It is the royal portion which goes to the king."

"How do you call him a king who does not rule his kingdom?"

"I fear you will be blown up before the sepoy's cannons one of these days."

"We have seen plenty of sepoys; even today we have had some."

"You haven't yet known them aright, you will know them one day however."

"What then? One never dies more than once."

"But why should you willingly invite death?"

"Mahendra Sinha, I thought you to be a man amongst men, but I now see there is little to choose between you and the rest of your lot—you are only the sworn consumer of milk and butter. Just think of the snake. It creeps on the ground; I cannot think of any creature lower and meaner than it; but put your foot on its neck and it will spread its fangs to bite you. But can nothing disturb *your* equanimity? Look round and see, look at Magadha, Mithila, Kasi, Kanchi,[4] Delhi, Kashmir—where do you find such misery as here? Where else do the people eat grass for want of better food? Where do they eat thorns and white-ants' earth and wild creepers? Where do men think of eating dogs and jackals and even carcasses? Where else can you find men getting so anxious about the money in their coffers, the *salgram* [5] in their temples, the females in the Zenana,[6] and the child in the mother's womb? Yes, here they even rip open the womb! In every country the bond that binds a sovereign to his subjects is the protection that he gives; but our Mussulman king—how does he protect us? Our religion is gone; so is our caste, our honor and the sacredness of our family even! Our lives even are now to be sacrificed. Unless we drive these tipsy longbeards away, a Hindu can no longer hope to save his religion."

"Well, but how can you drive them away?"

"We will beat them."

"Alone, will you? With a slap, I presume."

The outlaw sang:

> Who hath said thou art weak in thy lands,
> When the swords flash out in twice seventy million hands
> And seventy million voices roar
> Thy dreadful name from shore to shore?

M: "But I see you are alone."

Bh: "Why, only now you saw two hundred of us."

M: "Are they all children?"

Bh: "They are, all of them."

"How many more are there?"

"Thousands of them; we will have more by and by."

"Suppose you get ten or twenty thousands. Could you hope to depose the Mussulman king with them?"

"How many soldiers had the English at Plassey?"

"Tut! to compare the English with the Bengali!"

"Why not? Physical strength does not count for much; the bullet won't be running faster, I ween, if I am stronger."

[4] Names of ancient Indian cities and kingdoms, used here in lieu of modern place-names.
[5] Family idol.   [6] The rooms of a house in which women are secluded.

"Then why this great difference between the English and the Mussulman?"

"Because an Englishman would die sooner than fly; the Mussulman will fly with the first breath of fire and look about for *sherbet*.[7] Secondly, the English have determination: what they want to do they will see done. The Mussulman soldiers come to die for pay, and even that they don't always get. Lastly there is courage. A cannon ball falls only on one spot and cannot kill two hundred men together. Yet, when such a ball falls before the Mussulmans, they fly away in a body, while no Englishman would even fly before a shower of balls."

"Have you these qualities?"

"No, but you don't pluck them like ripe fruits from trees; they come by practice."

"What is your practice?"

"Don't you see we are all anchorites? Our renunciation is for the sake of this practice alone. When our mission is done or the practice is completed, we shall go back to our homes. We too have wives and children."

"You have left them all? How could you break the ties of family life?"

"A Child must not lie! I will not brag in vain to you. No body can ever cut the bond. He who says that he never cares for the family bonds either did never love or merely brags. We don't get rid of the bonds but simply keep our pledge. Will you enter our order?"

"Till I hear of my wife and child, I can say nothing."

"Come and you will see them."

So saying they began to walk along. Bhavananda sang the song "Hail Mother" again. Mahendra had a good voice and had some proficiency in music which he loved; so he joined Bhavananda in his song. He found that it really brought tears to the eye. "If I have not got to renounce my wife and daughter," said he, "you may initiate me into your order."

"He who takes this vow," said Bhavananda, "has to give up his wife and children. If you take it, you need not see your wife and daughter. They will be well kept, but till the mission is fulfilled, you are not to see their face[s]."

"I don't care to take your vow," blurted out Mahendra.

Mahendra does take the vow, but is later reunited with his wife and daughter.

[7] A chilled sweet drink.

Why the British Came to Rule India

In the final chapter of *The Abbey of Bliss,* after the sannyāsīs have routed both
the Muslims and the British, Bankim has a supernatural figure explain to
their leader Satyānanda, that the British have been forced to rule in India in
order that Hinduism might regain its pristine power.

[From *Ānandamath,* Part IV, Chapter 8. Tr. by T. W. Clark]

S: Come, I'm ready. But, my lord, clear up this doubt in my mind. Why
at the very moment in which I have removed all barriers from before our
eternal Faith, do you order me to cease?

He: Your task is accomplished. The Muslim power is destroyed. There
is nothing else for you to do. No good can come of needless slaughter.

S: The Muslim power has indeed been destroyed, but the dominion of
the Hindus has not yet been established. The British still hold Calcutta.

He: Hindu dominion will not be established now. If you remain at your
work, men will be killed to no purpose. Therefore come.

S: (greatly pained) My lord, if Hindu dominion is not going to be
established, who will rule? Will the Muslim kings return?

He: No. The English will rule.

S: (turning tearfully to the image of her who symbolized the land of
his birth) Alas, my Mother! I have failed to set you free. Once again you
will fall into the hands of infidels. Forgive your son. Alas, my Mother!
Why did I not die on the battlefield?

He: Grieve not. You have won wealth; but it was by violence and robbery, for your mind was deluded. No pure fruit can grow on a sinful
tree. You will never set your country free in that way. What is going to
happen now is for the best. If the English do not rule, there is no hope
of a revival of our eternal Faith. I tell you what the wise know. True
religion is not to be found in the worship of 33 crores of gods; that is a
vulgar, debased religion, which has obscured that which is true. True
Hinduism consists in knowledge not in action. Knowledge is of two
kinds, physical and spiritual. Spiritual knowledge is the essential part of
Hinduism. If however physical knowledge does not come first, spiritual
knowledge will never comprehend the subtle spirit within. Now physical
knowledge has long since disappeared from our land, and so true religion
has gone too. If you wish to restore true religion, you must first teach
this physical knowledge. Such knowledge is unknown in this country

because there is no one to teach it. So we must learn it from foreigners. The English are wise in this knowledge, and they are good teachers. Therefore we must make the English rule. Once the people of India have acquired knowledge of the physical world from the English, they will be able to comprehend the nature of the spiritual. There will then be no obstacle to the true Faith. True religion will then shine forth again of itself. Until that happens, and until Hindus are wise and virtuous and strong, the English power will remain unbroken. Under the English our people will be happy; and there will be no impediment to our teaching our faith. So, wise one, stop fighting against the English and follow me.

S: My lord, if it was your intention to set up a British government, and if at this time a British government is good for the country, then why did you make use of me to fight this cruel war?

He: At the present moment the English are traders. Their minds are set on amassing wealth. They have no desire to take up the responsibilities of government. But as a result of the rebellion of the Children, they will have to; because they will get no money if they do not. The rebellion took place to make the English ascend the throne. Come with me now. Know and you will understand.

S: My lord. I do not desire knowledge. It cannot help me. I have vowed a vow and I must keep it. Bless me, and let me not be shaken in my devotion to my Mother.

He: Your vow is fulfilled. You have brought fortune to your Mother. You have set up a British government. Give up your fighting. Let the people take to their plows. Let the earth be rich with harvest and the people rich with wealth.

S: (weeping hot tears) I will make my Mother rich with harvest in the blood of her foes.

He: Who is the foe? There are no foes now. The English are friends as well as rulers. And no one can defeat them in battle.

S: If that is so, I will kill myself before the image of my Mother.

He: In ignorance? Come and know. There is a temple of the Mother in the Himalayas. I will show you her image there.

So saying, He took Satyānanda by the hand. What incomparable beauty! In the dim light, in the deep recesses of Vishnu's temple, two human forms radiant with light stood before a mighty four-armed figure.

One held the other by the hand. Who held the hand; and whose was the hand he held? Knowledge was holding Devotion by the hand; Faith that of Action; Self-sacrifice that of Glory; Heavenly Joy that of Earthly Peace. Satyānanda was the Earthly Peace; He was Heavenly Joy. Satyānanda was Glory; He was Self-sacrifice.

And Self-sacrifice led away Glory.

BĀL GANGĀDHAR TILAK: "FATHER OF INDIAN UNREST"

Impressed by his grandfather's recollections of the days before British rule reached Mahārāshtra, and of the Mutiny and Rebellion of 1857–58, it is not surprising that Bāl Gangādhar Tilak (1856–1920) should have grown up questioning the right of the British to govern his land. Like Rānade and Gokhale (with whom he fought a running political duel for many years) Tilak was descended from the Chitpavan brāhman caste, but unlike them he maintained an uncompromising hostility to foreign domination.

In addition to the Marāthā history he imbibed at his grandfather's knee, Tilak learned Sanskrit and English from his father, a schoolteacher and deputy inspector of education in a small town on India's western seacoast. When he was ten, the family moved to Poona, but at sixteen Tilak was an orphan. A self-reliant but weak-bodied youth, he devoted a year to building up his physique with exercises. After receiving his B.A., he took a Bachelor of Laws degree, but refused to enter government service, the usual haven of educated Indians in those days. Instead, with a few like-minded friends he started a school and two newspapers in order to spread Western knowledge among the people of their native region of Mahārāshtra. After helping to found the Deccan Education Society and Fergusson College, Tilak opposed the reform program of Agarkar and Gokhale and resigned from the group in 1890.

Tilak now purchased from the group the Marāthī weekly *Kesari* (The Lion), which he had named and helped to edit, and its English counterpart, the *Mahratta*.[1] Henceforth he poured his energies into educating the people of his province through the columns of these newspapers.

[1] The old spelling for Marāthā.

His Marāthī style was particularly effective and made a direct appeal to the villagers who would gather to have it read to them. Tilak also promoted in his papers the celebration of two new annual festivals—one dedicated to the Hindu god Ganesh, the other honoring the Marāthā hero Shivaji. His purpose in organizing these festivals was to develop in the Marāthā people a sense of pride in their common history and religion; however, the Muslim community could not ignore the fact that one of them was made to coincide with their own festival of Muharram, and the other extolled the Mughal empire's fiercest enemy. As eaters of beef, Muslims were further alarmed at the anti-cowkilling agitation which had been started by Dayānanda, and which Tilak continued to sponsor.

Tilak's success in arousing popular enthusiasm through these activities began to worry the government after the assassination of two British officials in Poona in 1897. Tilak was accused of fanning hatred for the officials with his *Kesari* articles, and was sentenced to jail for eighteen months. Imprisonment only whetted his fighting spirit, and the Bengal agitation of 1905 found him in the front lines of the fray. "Militancy—not mendicancy" was the slogan the Extremist faction used to disparage the Moderates, and his cry "Freedom is my birthright and I will have it" swept the country. When the Extremists failed to wrest control of the Congress from the Moderates at the 1907 session, Tilak defied the chairman (who refused to recognize him); whereupon the meeting degenerated into a riot in which shoes and chairs flew through the air.

Shortly afterward Tilak was again arrested and tried for countenancing political assassination in his speeches and writings. He was sentenced to six years' rigorous confinement in Mandalay, Upper Burma. Books helped him to pass the time, and he returned to his Sanskrit studies. Earlier he had written two books arguing that the Vedas were over six thousand years old. His *magnum opus,* written in prison, was his lengthy commentary on the *Bhagavad Gītā.*

Tilak's interpretation of the *Gītā,* emphasizing as it does the importance of action in this world, gives us the key to his own character and to the influence he has had on political thought in twentieth-century India. He stressed that Hinduism's most popular sacred poem preached political as well as religious activity, and hinted that violence in a righteous cause was morally justifiable. His followers, however, cut themselves loose from the known but foreign standards to which the

Moderates remained attached and drifted into the uncharted depths of revolutionary violence and terrorism. Tilak himself never used such methods, but when others used them he maintained a silence which implied assent. The "father of Indian unrest," as the British journalist Valentine Chirol called him, was not the man to reprimand his own offspring.

By the time of his death in 1920 Tilak had tempered his opposition to British rule sufficiently to favor contesting the elections provided for under the Montagu-Chelmsford Reforms of 1919, in contrast to the younger Gāndhi, who wished to boycott them. But Tilak's example of fearless defiance was remembered by those who came after him, and the title of Lokamānya—"Honored by the People"—is still used as a reminder of his efforts to transform the nationalist cause from an upper-class into a truly popular movement.

BĀL GANGĀDHAR TILAK
The Tenets of the New Party

At the end of the Congress session of 1906, it was clear that the gap between the Moderates and the Extremists had been bridged only temporarily by the mediation of Dādābhāi Naoroji. At this juncture Tilak delivered an address summarizing the aims and methods of the new party of which he was the leader.

[From *Bal Gangadhar Tilak: His Writings and Speeches*, pp. 55–57, 61, 63–67]

Calcutta, 2d January, 1907

Two new words have recently come into existence with regard to our politics, and they are *Moderates* and *Extremists*. These words have a specific relation to time, and they, therefore, will change with time. The Extremists of today will be Moderates tomorrow, just as the Moderates of today were Extremists yesterday. When the National Congress was first started and Mr. Dādābhāi's views, which now go for Moderates, were given to the public, he was styled an Extremist, so that you will see that the term Extremist is an expression of progress. We are Extremists today and our sons will call themselves Extremists and us Moderates. Every new party begins as Extremists and ends as Moderates. The sphere of practical politics is not unlimited. We cannot say what will or will not happen 1,000 years hence—perhaps during that long period, the whole of the white race will be swept away in another glacial period. We must, therefore, study the present and work out a program to meet the present condition.

It is impossible to go into details within the time at my disposal. One thing is granted, namely, that this government does not suit us. As has been said by an eminent statesman—the government of one country by another can never be a successful, and therefore, a permanent government. There is no difference of opinion about this fundamental proposition between the old and new schools. One fact is that this alien government has ruined the country. In the beginning, all of us were taken by surprise. We were almost dazed. We thought that everything that the rulers did was for our good and that this English government has descended from the clouds to save us from the invasions of Tamerlane and Chingis Khan, and, as they say, not only from foreign invasions but from internecine warfare, or the internal or external invasions, as they call it. We felt happy for a time, but it soon came to light that the peace which was established in this country did this, as Mr. Dādābhāi has said in one place—that we were prevented from going at each other's throats, so that a foreigner might go at the throat of us all. *Pax Britannica* has been established in this country in order that a foreign government may exploit the country. That this is the effect of this *Pax Britannica* is being gradually realized in these days. It was an unhappy circumstance that it was not realised sooner. We believed in the benevolent intentions of the government, but in politics there is no benevolence. Benevolence is used to sugar-coat the declarations of self-interest and we were in those days deceived by the apparent benevolent intentions under which rampant self-interest was concealed. That was our state then. But soon a change came over us. English education, growing poverty, and better familiarity with our rulers, opened our eyes and our leaders; especially, the venerable leader who presided over the recent Congress was the first to tell us that the drain from the country was ruining it, and if the drain was to continue, there was some great disaster awaiting us. So terribly convinced was he of this that he went over from here to England and spent twenty-five years of his life in trying to convince the English people of the injustice that is being done to us. He worked very hard. He had conversations and interviews with secretaries of state, with members of Parliament—and with what result?

He has come here at the age of eighty-two to tell us that he is bitterly disappointed. Mr. Gokhale, I know, is not disappointed. He is a friend of mine and I believe that this is his honest conviction. Mr. Gokhale is not disappointed but is ready to wait another eighty years till he is disappointed like Mr. Dādābhāi. . . .

You can now understand the difference between the old and the new parties. Appeals to the bureaucracy are hopeless. On this point both the new and old parties are agreed. The old party believes in appealing to the British nation and we do not. That being our position, it logically follows we must have some other method. There is another alternative. We are not going to sit down quiet. We shall have some other method by which to achieve what we want. We are not disappointed, we are not pessimists. It is the hope of achieving the goal by our own efforts that has brought into existence this new party.

There is no empire lost by a free grant of concession by the rulers to the ruled. History does not record any such event. Empires are lost by luxury, by being too much bureaucratic or overconfident or from other reasons. But an empire has never come to an end by the rulers conceding power to the ruled. . . .

We have come forward with a scheme which if you accept [it], shall better enable you to remedy this state of things than the scheme of the old school. Your industries are ruined utterly, ruined by foreign rule; your wealth is going out of the country and you are reduced to the lowest level which no human being can occupy. In this state of things, is there any other remedy by which you can help yourself? The remedy is not petitioning but boycott. We say prepare your forces, organize your power, and then go to work so that they cannot refuse you what you demand. A story in *Mahabharata* tells that Sri Krishna was sent to effect a compromise, but the Pandavas and Kauravas were both organizing their forces to meet the contingency of failure of the compromise. This is politics. Are you prepared in this way to fight if your demand is refused? If you are, be sure you will not be refused; but if you are not, nothing can be more certain than that your demand will be refused, and perhaps, forever. We are not armed, and there is no necessity for arms either. We have a stronger weapon, a political weapon, in boycott. We have perceived one fact, that the whole of this administration, which is carried on by a handful of Englishmen, is carried on with our assistance. We are all in subordinate service. This whole government is carried on with our assistance and they try to keep us in ignorance of our power of cooperation between ourselves by which that which is in our own hands at present can be claimed by us and administered by us. The point is to have the entire control in our hands. I want to have the key of my house, and not merely one stranger turned out of it. Self-government is our goal; we want a control over our administrative machinery. We don't want to become clerks and remain [clerks]. At present, we are clerks and willing instruments of our own oppression in the hands of an alien government, and that government is ruling over us not by its innate strength but by keeping us in ignorance and blindness to the perception of this fact. Professor Seely [1] shares this view. Every Englishman knows that they are a mere handful in this country and it is the business of every one of them to befool you in believing that you are weak and they are strong. This is politics. We have been deceived by such policy so long. What the new party wants you to do is to realize the fact that your future rests entirely in your own hands. If you mean to be free, you can be free; if you do not mean to be free, you will fall and be for ever fallen. So many of you need not like arms; but if you have not the power of active resistance, have you not the power of self-denial and self-abstinence in such a way as not to assist this foreign government to rule over you? This is boycott and this is what is meant when we say, boycott is a political weapon. We shall not give them assistance to collect revenue and keep peace. We shall not assist them in fighting beyond the frontiers or outside India with Indian blood and money. We shall not assist them in carrying on the administration of justice. We shall have our own courts, and when time comes we shall not pay taxes. Can you do that by your united efforts? If you can, you are free from tomorrow. Some gentlemen who spoke this evening referred to half bread as against the whole bread. I say I want the whole bread and that immediately. But if I can not get the whole, don't think that I have no patience.

I will take the half they give me and then try for the remainder. This is the line of thought and action in which you must train yourself. We have not raised this cry from a mere impulse. It is a reasoned impulse. Try to understand that reason and try to strengthen that impulse by your logical convictions. I do not ask you to blindly follow us. Think

[1] Refers to Sir John Robert Seeley, author of *The Expansion of England* (London, 1895).

over the whole problem for yourselves. If you accept our advice, we feel sure we can achieve our salvation thereby. This is the advice of the new party. Perhaps we have not obtained a full recognition of our principles. Old prejudices die very hard. Neither of us wanted to wreck the Congress, so we compromised, and were satisfied that our principles were recognized, and only to a certain extent. That does not mean that we have accepted the whole situation. We may have a step in advance next year, so that within a few years our principles will be recognized, and recognized to such an extent that the generations who come after us may consider us Moderates. This is the way in which a nation progresses, and this is the lesson you have to learn from the struggle now going on. This is a lesson of progress, a lesson of helping yourself as much as possible, and if you really perceive the force of it, if you are convinced by these arguments, then and then only is it possible for you to effect your salvation from the alien rule under which you labor at this moment.

There are many other points but it is impossible to exhaust them all in an hour's speech. If you carry any wrong impression come and get your doubts solved. We are prepared to answer every objection, solve every doubt, and prove every statement. We want your cooperation; without your help we cannot do anything singlehanded. We beg of you, we appeal to you, to think over the question, to see the situation, and realize it, and after realizing it to come to our assistance, and by our joint assistance to help in the salvation of the country.

The Message of the Bhagavad Gītā

Differing from the nondualistic interpretation of the *Gītā* as pointing the path to renunciation of the world, Tilak held that it preached a life of desireless action *in* the world. In the conclusion to his *Mystic Import of the Bhagavad Gītā* he links this message with the revival of India's political fortunes.

[From Tilak, *Srimad Bhagavadgītā Rahasya*, II, 712–13]

The religion of the *Gītā*, which is a combination of spiritual knowledge, devotion, and action, which is in all respects undauntable and comprehensive, and is further perfectly equable, that is, which does not maintain any distinction, but gives release to everyone in the same measure, and at the same time shows proper forbearance towards other religions, is thus seen to be the sweetest and immortal fruit of the tree of the Vedic religion. In the Vedic religion, higher importance was given in the beginning principally to the sacrifice of wealth or of animals, that is to say, principally to action in the shape of ritual; but, when the knowledge expounded in the Upanishads taught later on that this ritualistic religion of the Shrutis was inferior, Sānkhya philosophy came into existence out of it. But as this knowledge was unintelligible towards abandonment of action, it was not possible for ordinary people to be satisfied merely by the religion of the Upanishads, or by the unification of the Upanishads and the Sānkhya philosophy in the Smritis. Therefore, the *Gītā* religion fuses the knowledge of the Brahman contained in the Upanishads, which is cognoscible only to the intelligence, with the "king of mysticisms" (*rāja-guhya*) of the worship of the perceptible which is accessible to love, and consistently with the ancient tradition of ritualistic religion, it proclaims to everybody, though nominally to Arjuna, that, "[to] perform lifelong your several worldly duties according to your respective positions in life, desirelessly, for the universal good, with a self-identifying vision, and enthusiastically, and thereby perpetually worship the deity in the shape of the Paramātman (the Highest Ātman), which is eternal, and which uniformly pervades the body of all created things as also the cosmos; because, therein lies your happiness in this world and in the next"; and on that account, the mutual conflict between action, spiritual knowledge (jnāna), and love (devotion) is done away with, and the single *Gītā* religion, which preaches that the whole of one's life should be turned into a sacrifice (yajna), contains the essence of the entire Vedic religion. When hundreds of energetic noble souls and active persons were busy with the benefit of all created things, because they looked upon that as their duty, as a result of their having realized this eternal religion, this country was blessed with the favor of the Parameshvara,[1] and reached the height not only of knowledge but also of prosperity; and it need not be said in so many words, that when this ancient religion, which is beneficial in this life and in the next, lost following in our country, it (our country) reached its present fallen state. I, therefore, now pray to the Parameshvara, at the end of this book, that there should come to birth again in this our country such noble and pure men as will worship the Parameshvara according to this equable and brilliant religion of the *Gītā,* which harmonizes devotion, spiritual knowledge, and energism. . . .

[1] The Highest God.

AUROBINDO GHOSE: MYSTIC PATRIOT

The agitation against the Partition of Bengal drew into public life one of the most fascinating figures modern India has produced—a completely Westernized intellectual who became a fanatic nationalist and ended his days an accomplished yogi. Aurobindo Ghose (1872–1950)—or Sri Aurobindo, as he is known to his followers—spent only four years in active politics, but in that brief span his passionate devotion to the national cause won him reknown as an Extremist leader second only to Tilak in nation-wide popularity.

Aurobindo's father, an English-educated Bengali doctor, was so determined to give his son a completely European education that he sent him to a convent school at five and to England at seven. Isolated from all Indian influences, Aurobindo studied in England until he was twenty. Leaving Cambridge University, he returned to India in 1893 to enter the civil service of the progressive princely state of Baroda. Sensing himself "denationalized" by his foreign education, he turned his attention to Indian culture and politics. He was inspired by the writings of Rāmakrishna, Vivekānanda, and the novels of Bankim Chandra Chatterjee, and after studying Sanskrit was able to appreciate in the original the Upanishads and the Gītā.

His fascination with Hindu culture, when combined with the sense of patriotism he had imbibed along with the rest of his English education, naturally led Aurobindo to sympathize with the Extremist politicians. Despite the fact that he was unusually shy, during the agitation against the Partition of Bengal he gave up his post as vice-principal of Baroda College and threw himself into the maelstrom of Bengal politics. His articles in the English-language weekly Bande Mataram made him famous, especially after the government tried and failed to prove seditious their deftly phrased innuendos. In 1907 Aurobindo led a large Bengali delegation to the crucial Congress session at Tilak's request, and served as Lokamanya's right-hand man during the stormy days of the split between the Moderates and the Extremists.

Shortly afterward Aurobindo consulted a Hindu holy man who advised him to void his mind of all thought so as to be able to receive supermental inspiration. He followed this advice faithfully, and when he found himself jailed as a suspected member of a bombing plot, he heard the voice of Vivekānanda guiding him in his practice of yoga, and saw all men as incarnations of God. After his release Aurobindo gradually withdrew from political life, and in 1910 abandoned Bengal—and his wife—for the French settlement of Pondichéry, where he spent his remaining forty years doing spiritual exercises and writing. All efforts to bring him back into the political arena proved ineffectual.

Brief as his political career was, Aurobindo defined the essence of religious nationalism in a manner which for sheer passion has never been surpassed. Because of his prolonged absence from India, Aurobindo came to idealize both his native land and its ancestral faith and to identify one with the other in a way no previous thinker had dared to do. The very fervor of his faith in "India" helped his Hindu countrymen to transcend the many differences of caste, language, and custom which had hindered the development among them of allegiance to one nation.

Aurobindo was free of the region-centered nationalism which limited the effectiveness of a Bengali like Bankim or a Mahārāshtrian like Tilak. Along with Bankim and Tilak, however, he failed to perceive that the greater the zeal of the Hindu nationalists became, the more difficult grew the task of uniting both Hindus and Muslims in loyalty to a single non-British government.

AUROBINDO GHOSE
The Doctrine of Passive Resistance

In a series of articles under this heading penned in April, 1907, Aurobindo outlined the Extremists' program of national self-reliance. Both the negative and the positive aspects of this program were later utilized by Gāndhi.

[From Ghose, *The Doctrine of Passive Resistance*, pp. 73–74, 77–79]

We desire to put an end to petitioning until such a strength is created in the country that a petition will only be a courteous form of demand. We wish to kill utterly the pernicious delusion that a foreign and adverse interest can be trusted to develop us to its own detriment, and entirely to do away with the foolish and ignoble hankering after help from our natural adversaries. Our attitude to bureaucratic concession is that of Laocoon: "We fear the Greeks even when they bring us gifts." Our policy is self-development and defensive resistance. But we would extend the policy of self-development to every department of national life; not only

Swadeshi and National Education, but national defense, national arbitration courts, sanitation, insurance against famine or relief of famine—whatever our hands find to do or urgently needs doing, we must attempt ourselves and no longer look to the alien to do it for us. And we would universalize and extend the policy of defensive resistance until it ran parallel on every line with our self-development. We would not only buy our own goods, but boycott British goods; not only have our own schools, but boycott government institutions; not only organize our league of defense, but have nothing to do with the bureaucratic executive except when we cannot avoid it. At present even in Bengal where boycott is universally accepted, it is confined to the boycott of British goods and is aimed at the British merchant and only indirectly at the British bureaucrat. We would aim it directly both at the British merchant and at the British bureaucrat who stands behind and makes possible exploitation by the merchant. . . .

The double policy of self-development and defensive resistance is the common standing-ground of the new spirit all over India. Some may not wish to go beyond its limits, others may look outside it; but so far all are agreed. For ourselves we avow that we advocate passive resistance without wishing to make a dogma of it. In a subject nationality, to win liberty for one's country is the first duty of all, by whatever means, at whatever sacrifice; and this duty must override all other considerations. The work of national emancipation is a great and holy yajna [1] of which boycott, Swadeshi, national education, and every other activity, great and small, are only major or minor parts. Liberty is the fruit we seek from the sacrifice and the Motherland the goddess to whom we offer it; into the seven leaping tongues of the fire of the yajna we must offer all that we are and all that we have, feeding the fire even with our blood and lives and happiness of our nearest and dearest; for the Motherland is a goddess who loves not a maimed and imperfect sacrifice, and freedom was never won from the gods by a grudging giver. But every great yajna has its Rakshasas [2] who strive to baffle the sacrifice, to bespatter it with their own dirt, or by guile or violence put out the flame. Passive resistance is an attempt to meet such disturbers by peaceful and self-contained *Brahmatej;* [3] but even the greatest Rishis of old could not, when the Rakshasas were fierce and determined, keep up the sacrifice

[1] Ritual sacrifice. [2] Demons. [3] Divine power.

without calling in the bow of the Kshatriya. We should have the bow of the Kshatriya ready for use, though in the background. Politics is especially the business of the Kshatriya, and without Kshatriya strength at its back, all political struggle is unavailing.

Vedantism accepts no distinction of true or false religions, but considers only what will lead more or less surely, more or less quickly to moksha, spiritual emancipation and the realization of the Divinity within. Our attitude is a political Vedantism. India, free, one and indivisible, is the divine realization to which we move, emancipation our aim; to that end each nation must practice the political creed which is the most suited to its temperament and circumstances; for that is the best for it which leads most surely and completely to national liberty and national self-realization. But whatever leads only to continued subjection must be spewed out as mere vileness and impurity. Passive resistance may be the final method of salvation in our case or it may be only the preparation for the final sadhana.[4] In either case, the sooner we put it into full and perfect practice, the nearer we shall be to national liberty.

Nationalism Is the Work of God

Addressing a Bombay audience soon after the Moderate-Extremist split, Aurobindo made his mind a blank and spoke as the spirit moved him. The result was a startling declaration of the religious significance of Indian nationalism.

[From Ghose, *Speeches,* pp. 7–9]

There is a creed in India today which calls itself Nationalism, a creed which has come to you from Bengal. This is a creed which many of you have accepted when you called yourselves Nationalists. Have you realized, have you yet realized what that means? Have you realized what it is that you have taken in hand? Or is it that you have merely accepted it in the pride of a superior intellectual conviction? You call yourselves Nationalists. What is Nationalism? Nationalism is not a mere political program; Nationalism is a religion that has come from God; Nationalism is a creed which you shall have to live. Let no man dare to call himself a Nationalist if he does so merely with a sort of intellectual pride, thinking that he is more patriotic, thinking that he is something higher

---

[4] Spiritual discipline leading to attainment of the highest good.

than those who do not call themselves by that name. If you are going to be a nationalist, if you are going to assent to this religion of Nationalism, you must do it in the religious spirit. You must remember that you are the instruments of God. What is this that has happened in Bengal? You call yourselves Nationalists, but when this happens to you, what will you do? This thing is happening daily in Bengal, because, in Bengal, Nationalism has come to the people as a religion, and it has been accepted as a religion. But certain forces which are against that religion are trying to crush its rising strength. It always happens when a new religion is preached, when God is going to be born in the people, that such forces rise with all their weapons in their hands to crush the religion. In Bengal too a new religion, a religion divine and sattwic[1] has been preached, and this religion they are trying with all the weapons at their command to crush. By what strength are we in Bengal able to survive? Nationalism is not going to be crushed. Nationalism survives in the strength of God and it is not possible to crush it, whatever weapons are brought against it. Nationalism is immortal; Nationalism cannot die; because it is no human thing, it is God who is working in Bengal. God cannot be killed, God cannot be sent to jail. When these things happen among you, I say to you solemnly, what will you do? Will you do as they do in Bengal? [Cries of "Yes."] Don't lightly say "yes." It is a solemn thing; and suppose that God puts you this question, how will you answer it? Have you got a real faith? Or is it merely a political aspiration? Is it merely a larger kind of selfishness? Or is it merely that you wish to be free to oppress others, as you are being oppressed? Do you hold your political creed from a higher source? Is it God that is born in you? Have you realized that you are merely the instruments of God, that your bodies are not your own? You are merely instruments of God for the work of the Almighty. Have you realized that? If you have realized that, then you are truly Nationalists; then alone will you be able to restore this great nation. In Bengal it has been realized clearly by some, more clearly by others, but it has been realized and you on this side of the country must also realize it. Then there will be a blessing on our work, and this great nation will rise again and become once more what it was in the days of its spiritual greatness.

[1] Pure, holy.

India's Mission: The Resurrection of Hinduism

In a memorable speech to the Society for the Protection of Religion after his release from prison in 1908, Aurobindo relayed to his countrymen the messages which had mystically come to him during his confinement. He was first of all to dedicate himself to God's work. Secondly, through her national revival, India was to spread the universal truth of Hinduism throughout the world.

[From Ghose, *Speeches,* pp. 76–80]

The second message came and it said: "Something has been shown to you in this year of seclusion, something about which you had your doubts and it is the truth of the Hindu religion. It is this religion that I am raising up before the world, it is this that I have perfected and developed through the rishis, saints, and avatars, and now it is going forth to do my work among the nations. I am raising up this nation to send forth my word. This is the Sanatan Dharma, this is the eternal religion which you did not really know before, but which I have now revealed to you. The agnostic and the sceptic in you have been answered, for I have given you proofs within and without you, physical and subjective, which have satisfied you. When you go forth, speak to your nation always this word, that it is for the Sanatan Dharma that they arise, it is for the world and not for themselves that they arise. I am giving them freedom for the service of the world. When therefore it is said that India shall rise, it is the Sanatan Dharma that shall rise. When it is said that India shall be great, it is the Sanatan Dharma that shall be great. When it is said that India shall expand and extend itself, it is the Sanatan Dharma that shall expand and extend itself over the world. It is for the dharma and by the dharma that India exists. To magnify the religious means to magnify the country. I have shown you that I am everywhere and in all men and in all things, that I am in this movement and I am not only working in those who are striving for the country but I am working also in those who oppose them and stand in their paths. I am working in everybody and whatever men may think or do they can do nothing but help on my purpose. They also are doing my work, they are not my enemies but my instruments. In all your actions you are moving forward without knowing which way you move. You mean to do one thing and you do another. You aim at a result and your efforts subserve one that is different or contrary. It is Shakti [2] that has gone forth and entered into the people. Since long ago I have been preparing this uprising and now the time has come and it is I who will lead it to its fulfillment."

This then is what I have to say to you. The name of your society is "Society for the Protection of Religion." Well, the protection of the religion, the protection and upraising before the world of the Hindu religion, that is the work before us. But what is the Hindu religion? What is this religion which we call Sanatan, eternal? It is the Hindu religion only because the Hindu nation has kept it, because in this Peninsula it grew up in the seclusion of the sea and the Himalayas, because in this sacred and ancient land it was given as a charge to the Aryan race to preserve through the ages. But it is not circumscribed by the confines of a single country, it does not belong peculiarly and forever to a bounded part of the world. That which we call the Hindu religion is really the eternal religion, because it is the universal religion which embraces all others. If a religion is not universal, it cannot be eternal. A narrow religion, a sectarian religion, an exclusive religion can live only for a limited time and a limited purpose. This is the one religion that can triumph over materialism by including and anticipating the discoveries of science and the speculations of philosophy. It is the one religion which impresses on mankind the closeness of God to us and embraces in its compass all the possible means by which man can approach God. It is the one religion which insists every moment on the truth which all religions acknowledge that He is in all men and all things and that in Him we move and have our being. It is the one religion which enables us not only to understand and believe this truth but to realize it with every part of our being. It is the one religion which shows the world what the world is, that it is the Lila of Vasudeva.[3] It is the one religion which shows us how we can best play our part in that Lila, its subtlest laws and its noblest rules. It is the one religion which does not separate life in any smallest detail from religion, which knows what immortality is and has utterly removed from us the reality of death.

This is the word that has been put into my mouth to speak to you today. What I intended to speak has been put away from me, and

[2] Divine creative power.   [3] The play or sport of God.

beyond what is given to me I have nothing to say. It is only the word that is put into me that I can speak to you. That word is now finished. I spoke once before with this force in me and I said then that this movement is not a political movement and that nationalism is not politics but a religion, a creed, a faith. I say it again today, but I put it in another way. I say no longer that nationalism is a creed, a religion, a faith; I say that it is the Sanatan Dharma which for us is nationalism. This Hindu nation was born with the Sanatan Dharma, with it it moves and with it it grows. When the Sanatan Dharma declines, then the nation declines, and if the Sanatan Dharma were capable of perishing, with the Sanatan Dharma it would perish. The Sanatan Dharma, that is nationalism. This is the message that I have to speak to you.

BRAHMABĀNDHAB UPĀDHYĀY: HINDU CATHOLIC NATIONALIST

A Hindu sannyāsī, a Roman Catholic, a fiery nationalist—all three descriptions apply equally well to the Bengali brāhman Brahmabāndhab Upādhyāy (1861–1907).

Brahmabāndhab grew up in a village near Calcutta, the third and youngest son of an inspector of police. His mother had died before he was a year old; one of his uncles, Kāli Charan Banerjee, later a prominent Protestant minister, used to visit the family frequently and teach the boy reading and writing.

Brahmabāndhab was an avid student of Sanskrit literature, and had read the *Mahābhārata* and *Rāmāyaṇa* many times before entering his 'teens. The novels of Bankim Chandra Chatterjee excited his fertile imagination, and Surendranāth Banerjea's speeches inspired him to dedicate himself to patriotic service. At seventeen he ran away from college to "learn the art of fighting and drive out the English."[1] Unable to enlist in the Mahārāja of Gwalior's army, after a period of wandering he returned disillusioned to Calcutta and became a teacher in a boys' school.

Calcutta in the early 1880s was the scene of an unusual religious fer-

[1] Quoted in B. Animananda, *The Blade*, p. 14.

ment. Brahmabāndhab fell under the influence of Keshub Chunder Sen, and through him met Rāmakrishna, with whom he was less deeply impressed. He also became a good friend of Narendranāth Datta, the future Vivekānanda. In 1887 he joined the Brāhmo Samāj and soon emigrated with a few friends to found a school for the teaching of Sanskrit and moral character in the province of Sind, in western India.

Four years later, after much reading and prayer, his restless spirit embraced Christianity, first as a Protestant, and then as a Roman Catholic. He nevertheless continued to consider himself as every inch a Hindu, and from 1894 until his death followed strictly the celibate and dietary regimen of a Hindu sannyāsī. Throughout this period he tried to reconcile Hindu philosophy with Christian theology, but his efforts to this end were regarded with some anxiety by the Catholic hierarchy, which twice forbade him to write on the subject.

In 1901 Brahmabāndhab joined Rabindranāth Tagore in setting up a rural school on classical lines at Shāntiniketan. In 1902 he made a trip to Rome and England, feeling that by lecturing on Indian thought at Oxford and Cambridge he was carrying on the work begun by Vivekānanda.

A new phase in his life began in 1905, when his weekly Calcutta newspaper *Sandhyā* (*Twilight*) became a sort of headquarters for the great anti-Partition agitation. Although less important as a political figure than they, he worked with Aurobindo, Tilak, Bepin Chandra Pāl and other Extremist leaders. In 1907 the government arrested and tried him for seditious journalism, for he had written some passionately anti-British editorials in his paper. During the trial he underwent a minor operation and died of lockjaw from a resulting infection.

The life of Brahmabāndhab Upādhyāy illustrates once more the fact that for Hindu nationalists the religious and political spheres of action were virtually inseparable. Moreover, his success in adopting the Christian faith while retaining his status as a brāhman testifies to the great freedom of thought which Hindu society permits to its members. It is also possible to conclude from his experience that if Christianity is to win future converts in Asia it will depend increasingly on the sort of religious synthesis Brahmabāndhab tried to create.

BRAHMABĀNDHAB UPĀDHYĀY
Hinduism's Contribution to Christianity

In an article of 1897 Brahmabāndhab stated his aim of explaining Christian doctrine in terms of Hindu concepts. The influence of Keshab Chunder Sen is perceptible in this passage.

[From Animananda, *The Blade,* pp. 67–68]

Christianity has again after a long period come in contact with a philosophy which, though it may contain more errors—because the Hindu mind is synthetic and speculative—still unquestionably soars higher than her Western sister. Shall we, Catholics of India, now . . . [let Hindus make] it their weapon against Christianity or shall we look upon it in the same way as St. Thomas looked upon the Aristotelian system? We are of [the] opinion that attempts should be made to win over Hindu philosophy to the service of Christianity as Greek philosophy was won over in the Middle Ages.

We have no definite idea as regards the *modus operandi* of making Hindu philosophy the handmaid of Christianity. The task is difficult and beset with many dangers. But we have a conviction and it is growing day by day that the Catholic Church will find it hard to conquer India unless she makes Hindu philosophy hew wood and draw water for her. The more we meditate on the cogitations of Hindu philosophy concerning the Supreme Being, on its marvelous but fruitless effort to penetrate into His inner nature . . . the more light is thrown upon the ever-mysterious Christian doctrine of the One God, one yet multiple, absolute yet related within Himself, discovering in it a new fitness to appease the noblest cravings of man and satisfy the demands of the loftiest intellect. . . .

The development of the Christian religion has not come to an end. It will grow, blossom, and fructify till the end of time. Indian soil is humid and its humidity will make the ever-new Christian revelation put forth newer harmonies and newer beauties revealing more clearly the invincible integrity of the Universal Faith deposited in the Church by the Apostles of Jesus Christ. The Hindu mind and heart, coming under the dominion of the One, Holy, Apostolic and Catholic Church, will sing a *new* canticle which will fill the earth with sweetness from end to end.

Hindu Catholicism

Pride in Hindu upbringing, Brahmabāndhab asserted, is totally compatible with Catholic faith, which is universal.

[From Animananda, *The Blade*, pp. 71–73]

By birth we are Hindus and shall remain *Hindu* till death. But as *dvija* (twice-born) by virtue of our sacramental rebirth, we are *Catholic*, we are members of an indefectible communion embracing all ages and climes.

In customs and manners, in observing caste and social distinctions, in eating and drinking, in our life and living, we are genuine Hindus; but in our faith we are neither Hindus nor European, nor American, nor Chinese, but all inclusive. Our faith fills the whole world and is not confined to any country or race; our faith is universal and consequently includes all truths.

Our thought and thinking is emphatically Hindu. We are more speculative than practical, more given to synthesis than analysis, more contemplative than active. It is extremely difficult for us to learn how to think like the Greeks of old or the scholastics of the Middle Ages. Our brains are molded in the philosophic cast of our ancient country.

We are proud of the stability of the Hindu race. Many a mighty race did rise and fall, but we continue to exist, though we had to buffet many a religious deluge and weather many a political storm. We believe in the future greatness of our race and in this belief we shall live and die.

The more strictly we practice our universal faith, the better do we grow as Hindus. All that is noblest and best in the Hindu character, is developed in us by the genial inspiration of the perfect Narahari (God-man) [Jesus Christ], our pattern and guide. The more we love Him, the more we love our country, the prouder we become of our past glory.

Do we really believe in Hinduism? The question must be understood before it can be answered. Hinduism has no definite creed. Kapila and Vyasa [1] were opposed to each other and yet both of them are con-

---

[1] The founders of the Sānkhya and Vedanta systems respectively.

sidered to be rishis. The Hindu Vedantists of the school of *Ramanuja* look down upon the Hindu Vedantists of the school of *Sankara* as blasphemers; the *Vaishnava* doctrines differ as widely as the poles from the Shaiva doctrine; even the gods have been made to fight one another in the Puranas. The test of being a Hindu cannot therefore lie in religious opinions.

However we are fully imbued with the *spirit* of Hinduism. We hold with the Vedantists that there is one eternal Essence from which proceed all things. We believe with the *Vaishnavas* in the necessity of incarnation and in the doctrine that man cannot be saved without grace. We agree in spirit with Hindu lawgivers in regard to their teaching that sacramental rites (Sankaras) are vehicles of sanctification. With wondering reverence do we look upon their idea of establishing a sacerdotal hierarchy vested with the highest authority in religious and social matters.

In short, we are Hindus so far as our physical and mental constitution is concerned, but in regard to our immortal souls we are Catholic. We are Hindu Catholics.

Independence for India

Love of India and scorn of the foreigner are expressed in these excerpts from the *Sandhyā* of the anti-Partition days.

[From Animananda, *The Blade,* pp. 136, 137]

I swear by the moon and the sun that I have heard in my heart of hearts this message of freedom. As the tree in winter gets a new life with the touch of the breeze of spring, as you feel joy at the return of love, as the heart of a hero dances to the call of the trumpet of war, so a feeling has throbbed in my heart.

But independence will mean both freedom from our slave complex and freedom from gerrymandering politics.

With the spread of English rule and culture, India lost her own ideal of civilization. Our educated classes think as they have been taught by their Firinghi [2] masters. Our minds have been conquered. We have become slaves. The faith in our own culture and the love for things Indian are gone. India will reach Swaraj the day she will again have a faith in herself. Rāmakrishna had gone in that line. So did Bamkim. So did

[2] Foreigner.

Vivekānanda. The whole mass of our people must now be made to appreciate things Indian and to return to our ancient way. That is Swadesh as opposed to Bidesh.[3] [p. 136]

I see the fort of *Swaraj* built in various places. There shall be no connection with the foreigner. These forts will be purified by the incense of sacrifice, resounding with the cry of victory, filled to overflowing with corn and grain.

Foreigners will not enter there. There we shall be our own masters, from the Thakurghar [4] to the cowshed. All our laws will be observed there, our own Varna-Asram. Let the Englishman be like the *Chaukidar* or *Jamadar*,[5] like the watching dog at the door: "If the dog enters your kitchen you break the cooking pot and chase him out." Outside this, our own jurisdiction, we shall observe the laws of the Firinghi for fear of assault and we shall pay the taxes. But if he were to trespass on our God-given rights, woe betide him? We shall give thrashing for thrashing. [p. 137]

"First Let the Mother Be Free . . ."

The sedition charge for which Brahmabāndhab was tried in 1907 rested primarily on this editorial, which extols India as the Mother in the same way as did the sannyāsīs of Bankim's *Abbey of Bliss.*
[From Animananda, *The Blade,* pp. 170–71]

We have said over and over again that we are not Swadeshi only so far as salt and sugar are concerned. Our aspirations are higher than the Himalayas. Our pain is as intense as if we had a volcano in us. What we want is the emancipation of India. Our aim is that India may be free, that the stranger may be driven from our homes, that the continuity of the learning, the civilization and the system of the rishis may be preserved. We have often heard the voice from heaven: Selfish men! We have not entered the lists to play the mudi [grocer].

First free the Mother from her bondage, then seek your own deliverance. The fire of desire has been kindled within our bosom. We do not know whence. Heaven we do not want. Deliverance we seek not. O Mother! let us be born again and again in India till your chains fall

---

[3] "One's own country" as opposed to "a foreign country."   [4] Lord's house.
[5] Doorkeeper or guard.

off. First let the Mother be free, and then shall come our own release
from the worldly bonds. This is no mere child's play. O Feringhi [*sic*],
here I am with my neck outstretched—offer it up as a sacrifice. You will
see, I shall again be born in the land of Bengal and shall cause much
more serious confusion. Can you intimidate us? Our power is more
than human. It is divine. We have heard the voice telling us that the
period of India's suffering is about to close, that the day of her deliverance is near at hand. It is because we have heard the voice that we have
left our forest-home and came to town. Your overweening pride is due
to your possessing a few cannon and guns. Just see to what plight you
are reduced. You imagine that by causing a *Kabulyat*[6] of loyalty to be
written, you will drive us to a corner. But the signatories of that document are nonentities. We have all the advantages of the ancient greatness of India on our side. We are immortal. If you are wise, you should
help towards the attainment of deliverance by India. Otherwise, come,
let us descend into the arena of war. We hereby summon you to battle.
See what a mighty contest presently begins all over the country. The
sons of the Mother are preparing themselves. All the arms—fiery
(Agneya), watery (Varuna), airy (Vayabya)—in her vaults, are being
polished. Hark, the flapping of the fourfold arms of the Mother? Are we
afraid of your cannon and guns? Arm brothers, arm! The day of deliverance is near. We have heard the voice and we cannot fail to see the chains
of India removed before we die. It is now too late to recede.

[6] Certificate.

CHAPTER XXV

THE MUSLIM REVIVAL

The coming of the British and of Western civilization had, initially at least, a very different impact on the Hindus and Muslims of India. The former, as we have seen, responded to the new situation with both an eagerness to learn from the British whatever would contribute to their own advancement, and a desire to preserve their own sense of national identity by returning to Hindu traditions long neglected. Thus, during the period of British ascendancy, Hindus who had, under Mughal dominance, tended to accept as their own much that was most glorious in Indo-Muslim civilization, found their loyalty to it seriously undermined by these new interests or allegiances. Indian Muslims, on the other hand, clung tenaciously to cultural traditions bound up with the practice of their religion and to the memory of a brilliant civilization which, in their eyes, was irreplaceable by anything the West had to offer.

As time passed the divergent loyalties of Hindus and Muslims were manifested particularly in their differing views of history. The Hindu revival and a new sense of nationalism led to reexamination and, to some extent, recreation of the past. It was, however, a past which Muslims felt they could not share, a "heathen past" in which they could take no pride. For them it was the days of Muslim domination and the exploits of Muslim conquerors to which they turned for inspiration. For Hindus, on the other hand, the period before the Muslim conquest was the age of freedom and national glory, while the long centuries of Muslim domination came to be looked upon as a humiliation, openly referred to as "the days of subjugation and slavery." Hindu rebels against Muslim authority were hailed as patriots who bravely resisted the alien invader and ruler. To Muslims these same men were the villains of history, who had weakened

---

The present chapter, as well as Chapter XXVII, "Pakistan: Its Founding and Future," have been prepared by Dr. I. H. Qureshī of the Center of Pakistan Studies, Columbia University, particularly with a view to highlighting those developments in the recent past which have contributed to the consciousness among Indian Muslims of separate nationhood.

India from within and prepared the way for the Western aggressor. Thus, the sense of a common attitude toward a common history, which contributes so much to the feeling of unity among a people, was, if it had ever existed in India, almost wholly dissipated.

In the eighteenth century we have already seen, in the views of Abū Tāleb, the near-contempt in which even this remarkably curious and sophisticated Muslim held the Western civilization he observed in Britain. We have noted, too, his prediction that Indian Muslims would continue to ignore Western learning out of "zeal for their own religion." This attitude, indeed, largely prevailed in the Muslim community until, in the mid-nineteenth century, Syed Ahmad Khān appeared to rouse it to a more forward-looking and realistic view of its mission in the modern world.

SYED AHMAD KHĀN AND THE ALĪGARH MOVEMENT

Muslim nationalism had tried to assert itself in many ways before the Sepoy Mutiny, and yet had failed to retrieve its lost position. Almost everywhere it had met with reverses; and the successes it did achieve, such as the victory over the Mārāthas at Panipat (1761), were short-lived. Muslim participation in the Mutiny itself was a last desperate effort, which succeeded only in convincing the British of the Muslims' responsibility for the outbreak. As a result the Muslims were heavily punished, and would have been completely and irretrievably ruined but for the efforts of Sir Syed Ahmad Khān (1817–1898).

Syed Ahmad was born at Delhi to a noble family respected for its learning and piety. He was given an excellent education in the traditional Muslim style. At the time of the Mutiny he was serving the Company's government in a subordinate judicial post, the higher grades being, at that time, not open to Indians. Farsighted enough to see that the Mutiny was unlikely to succeed, he remained faithful to the British and helped them by saving the lives of those in danger.

Syed Ahmad could see that the Muslims would make no progress if they did not accept the fact that British rule had come to stay indefinitely.

The Muslims were weak and disorganized as a result of the failure of the Mutiny. They were backward because of their hostility to the new educational system established by the British. Only a constructive program could save them, and such a program, for its success, needed the enthusiasm of the community as well as the cooperation of the British. There was still, however, considerable reluctance on the part of the British to believe that Muslims could be loyal to British rule. The Muslims, for their part, found it hard to swallow their pride and loyally serve a regime which they had come to hate as the source of all their troubles. There were, however, hopeful factors in the situation as well. The British had come to realize that it was not in the interests of the empire for a large and brave community to remain sullen and unreconciled; an effort to win its confidence was worthwhile. Among the Muslims, too, there was an increasing number who saw the need for allaying the suspicions of the British, without whose help the Muslim community could not be rescued from its low condition.

Syed Ahmad started work on all fronts. He wrote voluminously to allay British misgivings about the Muslims and Islam itself. He carried on incessant propaganda among his own people to convince them of the futility of any attempt to overthrow British rule, and the desirability of taking full advantage of the possibilities for self-improvement which the stability of the British empire offered. Syed Ahmad laid the greatest emphasis upon education and scientific knowledge and established a society for popularizing science among the Muslims. His greatest achievement was the founding of the Muhammadan Anglo-Oriental College, which was to educate Muslim youth in Western knowledge without neglecting their religious training. Sir Syed's aim was to produce a progressive, educated, well-informed Muslim, capable of success in the modern world without in any way forswearing his loyalty to the tenets of Islam. This college, founded in 1875, was raised to the status of a university in 1921, as the Muslim University of Aligarh.

Sir Syed published a magazine in Urdu called the *Improvement of Manners and Morals* (*Tahdhīb-ul-Akhlāq*), devoted mainly to social and religious problems. His immediate aim was to assimilate the best in Western life and thought into Indo-Muslim culture without in any way compromising the fundamentals of his faith. Through this, however, he was led further to give a new interpretation to Islam. First of all he criticized those beliefs and opinions which had no basis in scripture and yet had become part and parcel of Muslim belief or practice. Then he took up the Qur'ān and the traditions of the Prophet, attempting to explain them in the light of contemporary scientific knowledge. On account of his strong distaste for the supernatural and the irrational he and his followers were called *necharis*—believers in Nature. Though he was vehemently criticized in his lifetime by the conservative sections of his community, he had a profound influence upon the religious opinions of the Muslims of the subcontinent and today his basic ideas are accepted by all but a handful of ultraconservative theologians.

In politics, Sir Syed was a fearless critic of the government. His treatise on the causes of the Mutiny was not pleasing to the reactionary sections of British officialdom in India, and it was only his record of service as a moderating influence against more violent forms of anti-British feelings that helped him to escape the consequences of such boldness. He was, however, a firm believer in the need for cooperation between his community and the British government. He therefore advised the Muslims to stand aloof from the Indian National Congress when it was organized, and remained throughout a critic of its policies. His opposition to the Congress was based upon the belief that a system of representative government, if introduced in the subcontinent, would ultimately lead to rule by the Hindu majority. He believed that the people of India were not sufficiently integrated to be able to run a democratic government without its becoming a disguised rule of the Hindus over the Muslims. So fearful was he of such an eventuality that despite his bitter memories of the Muslim's treatment at the hands of he British, he accepted British rule in preference to Hindu hegemony. Though the Muslim attitude towards British rule changed again after Sir Syed's death, their misgivings about a government run by Hindus remained. In this respect Sir Syed may be considered one of the founders of the Pakistan Movement, though of course, there is no reference to Pakistan or to a separate Muslim state in his writings, since he foresaw no early end to the British empire in India. As one of the first modernists in the world of Islam, moreover, he laid the groundwork for the synthesis of Indian Islam and Western knowledge which has helped make the Pakistanis one of the most advanced Muslim nations in the world. Above all he manifested in his own person those qualities which he put forward as ideals for his people: devotion to Islam, intolerance of superstition and obscurantism, a willingness to accept all that the progress of human knowledge had to offer, and a readiness to make whatever sacrifice was required in the service of his people.

SYED AHMAD KHĀN

Religion and the Supernatural
[From Syed Ahmad Khān, Akhari Madamin, pp. 74–77]

There are so many natural mysteries in the universe which are beyond the understanding of men that they can not be counted. . . . These mysteries which we watch every day no longer strike us as miraculous and we become indifferent to them, but when man begins to believe in some religion or considers a person holy, he always attributes miracles to them. He accepts any miracles which are attributed to them; indeed he does not accept the truth of a religion or the holiness of a person without those miracles. . . .

The Prophet of God (Muhammad), on whom be peace and blessings, reiterated again and again: "I am a man like you; it has been revealed to me that your Lord is the one God;" but people were not content with this, and ascribed miracles to him. They base their faith in the Prophet upon these miracles.

The same attitude is adopted toward the saints; until it is accepted that they performed miracles . . . people do not find it possible to believe that they were saints.

In short it has become a habit with men that they ascribe miracles and supernatural attributes to an object or a person whom they consider to be holy or sacred. This is why men have interpolated supernatural factors into Islam, which are not worthy of belief, but such credulous persons believe in them.

However, this is a grievous mistake. Any religion which is true or claims to be true can not contain such elements in it as are contrary to nature and offend human reason, so that a sensible person would find it impossible to believe in them. A true faith in its pristine purity is absolutely free from such supernatural and irrational elements. It is always at a later time that those who hanker for the supernatural interpolate into it supernatural and miraculous elements. I am sincerely convinced about Islam that it is absolutely free from such strange stories and unnatural and irrational mysteries. May God save us from such mystery worshipers!

The Qur'ān and Science
[From Syed Ahmad Khān, *Akhari Madamin*, p. 84]

The Qur'ān does not prove that the earth is stationary, nor does it prove that the earth is in motion. Similarly it can not be proved from the Qur'ān that the sun is in motion, nor can it be proved from it that the sun is stationary. The Holy Qur'ān was not concerned with these problems of astronomy; because the progress in human knowledge was to decide such matters itself. The Qur'ān had a much higher and a far nobler purpose in view. It would have been tantamount to confusing the simple Bedouins by speaking to them about such matters and to throwing into perplexity even the learned, whose knowledge and experience had not yet made the necessary progress, by discussing such problems. The real purpose of a religion is to improve morality; by raising such questions that purpose would have been jeopardized. In spite of all this I am fully convinced that the Work of God and the Word of God can never be antagonistic to each other; we may, through the fault of our knowledge, sometimes make mistakes in understanding the meaning of the Word.

Western Education
[From a letter to Mawlawi Tasadduq, in *Sir Syed ke chand nadir khutut*]

I have been accused by people, who do not understand, of being disloyal to the culture of Islam, even to Islam itself. There are men who say that I have become a Christian. All this I have drawn upon myself because I advocate the introduction of a new system of education which will not neglect the Islamic basis of our culture, nor, for that matter, the teaching of Islamic theology itself, but which will surely take account of the changed conditions in this land. Today there are no Muslim rulers to patronize those who are well versed in the old Arabic and Persian learning. The new rulers insist upon a knowledge of their language for all advancement in their services and in some of the independent professions like practising law as well. If the Muslims do not take to the system of education introduced by the British, they will not only remain a backward community but will sink lower and lower until there will be no hope of recovery left to them. Is this at all a pleasing prospect? Can we serve the cause of Islam in this way? Shall we then be able to ward off the obliteration of all that we hold dear for any length of time?

If the choice were to lie between giving up Islam itself and saving ourselves from apostasy, I should have unhesitatingly chosen the latter even if it had meant utter destruction for myself and my people. That, however, is not the choice. The adoption of the new system of education does not mean the renunciation of Islam. It means its protection. We are justly proud of the achievements of our forefathers in the fields of learning and culture. We should, however, remember that these achievements were possible only because they were willing to act upon the teachings of the Prophet upon whom be peace and blessings of God. He said that knowledge is the heritage of the believer, and that he should acquire it wherever he can find it. He also said that the Muslims should seek knowledge even if they have to go to China to find it. It is obvious that the Prophet was not referring to theological knowledge in these sayings; China at that time was one of the most civilized countries of the world, but it was a non-Muslim country and could not teach the Muslims anything about their own religion. Islam, Islamic culture, and the Muslims themselves prospered as long as the Prophet was followed in respect of these teachings; when we ceased to take interest in the knowledge of others, we began to decline in every respect. Did the early Muslims not take to Greek learning avidly? Did this in any respect undermine their loyalty to Islam?

It is not only because the British are today our rulers, and we have to recognize this fact if we are to survive, that I am advocating the adoption of their system of education, but also because Europe has made such remarkable progress in science that it would be suicidal not to make an effort to acquire it. Already the leeway between our knowledge and that of Europe is too great. If we go on with our present obstinacy in neglecting it, we shall be left far behind. How can we remain true Muslims or serve Islam, if we sink into ignorance? The knowledge of yesterday is often the ignorance of tomorrow, because knowledge and ignorance are, in this context, comparative terms. The truth of Islam will shine the more brightly if its followers are well educated, familiar with the highest in the knowledge of the world; it will come under an eclipse if its followers are ignorant and backward.

The Muslims have nothing to fear from the adoption of the new education if they simultaneously hold steadfast to their faith, because Islam is not irrational superstition; it is a rational religion which can march hand in hand with the growth of human knowledge. Any fear to the contrary betrays lack of faith in the truth of Islam.

The Indian National Congress
[From Syed Ahmad Khān, *Akhari Madamin*, pp. 46–50]

Long before the idea of founding the Indian National Congress was mooted, I had given thought to the matter whether representative government is suited to the conditions of India. I studied John Stuart Mill's views in support of representative government. He has dealt with this matter exceedingly well in great detail. I reached the conclusion that the first requisite of a representative government is that the voters should possess the highest degree of homogeneity. In a form of government which depends for its functioning upon majorities, it is necessary that the people should have no differences in the matter of nationality, religion, ways of living, customs, mores, culture, and historical traditions. These things should be common among a people to enable them to run a representative government properly. Only when such homogeneity is present can representative government work or prove beneficial. It should not even be thought of when these conditions do not exist.

In a country like India where homogeneity does not exist in any one of these fields, the introduction of representative government can not produce any beneficial results; it can only result in interfering with the peace and prosperity of the land. I sincerely hope that whichever party comes into power in Great Britain—be they the Conservatives, the Liberals, the Unionists, or the Radicals—they will remember that India is a continent; it is not a small and homogeneous country like England, Scotland, Wales, or Ireland. India is inhabited by different peoples, each one of whom is numerically large and different from the others in its culture, its moral code, its social organization, its political outlook, its religion, its physique, and its historical associations. These peoples have never been united since the downfall of the Muslim empire. Instead of being able to organize some other form of government they have just indulged in mutual fighting and internecine wars. . . . All the difficulties with which Ireland has been faced are due to the fact that the British are the rulers and the Irish are the ruled, and the two peoples are different from each other . . . and yet there is great resemblance between the two; they have the same complexion, their religions are not so different; they can intermarry; their cultures are similar; so are their mores. . . .

The aims and objects of the Indian National Congress are based upon an ignorance of history and present-day realities; they do not take into consideration that India is inhabited by different nationalities; they presuppose that the Muslims, the Marathas, the Brahmins, the Kshatriyas, the Banias, the Sudras, the Sikhs, the Bengalis, the Madrasis, and the Peshawaris can all be treated alike and all of them belong to the same nation. The Congress thinks that they profess the same religion, that they speak the same language, that their way of life and customs are the same, that their attitude to History is similar and is based upon the same historical traditions. . . . For the successful running of a democratic government it is essential that the majority should have the ability to govern not only themselves but also unwilling minorities. . . . I consider the experiment which the Indian National Congress wants to make fraught with dangers and suffering for all the nationalities of India, specially for the Muslims. The Muslims are in a minority, but they are a highly united minority. At least traditionally they are prone to take the sword in hand when the majority oppresses them. If this happens, it will bring about disasters greater than the ones which came in the wake of the happenings of 1857. . . . The Congress cannot rationally prove its claim to represent the opinions, ideals, and aspirations of the Muslims.

THE MUSLIM SEARCH FOR FREEDOM

After the death of Sir Syed Ahmad Khān, Muslim leaders from the Alīgarh school maintained the policy of cooperation with the British; but by its very nature such a policy could not endure for long. Though years of constructive effort had improved the position of the Muslims, there was still a good deal of ground to cover before they could reach the level of educational and economic progress already achieved by the Hindus. The Muslims became increasingly conscious of the fact that mere loyalty to the British could not meet their needs. They had to organize if they were to make their voice heard by the government and the other communities of India.

Muslim suspicions of the Indian National Congress were not allayed by the fact that its control had passed from the hands of the liberals and moderate elements into those of the Maratha leader Tilak, whose anti-Muslim opinions and activities were well-known. The partition of Bengal (1905) gave the Muslims of East Bengal a majority in the newly constituted province of East Bengal and Assam, where they could develop the resources of a Muslim majority area to their advantage. Vehement Hindu opposition to the partition seemed to Muslims additional evidence that the Hindus were reluctant to part with their own power and influence. The Muslims had also been alarmed by the growing hostility shown by Hindu revivalist movements like the Ārya Samāj and the Mārātha glorification of Shivaji's rebellion against the Mughal empire. All these factors led them to establish the All-India Muslim League in 1906. Despite Muslim opposition to the introduction of representative institutions, it was already clear that the British could not resist Hindu pressure in this direction indefinitely. Besides, British elections had brought into office a liberal government in 1905, and some change in the Indian system of government was expected. The Muslims, therefore, sent a deputation to the Governor-General, Lord Minto, stressing their fears lest representative institutions be extended without any safeguards to protect Muslim interests. The deputation succeeded in getting from the Governor-General a promise of separate electorates for the Muslims. This was to remain the cornerstone of Muslim policy as long as British rule lasted on the subcontinent. Acceptance of the principle of separate electorates was the first official recognition on the part of the British that the Muslims and the Hindus were not a single people.

At this point Muslim policy entered a new phase. The Muslims began to be stirred again by dreams of freedom but were still apprehensive lest one form of domination be exchanged for another. They therefore continued to look for legal and constitutional safeguards, until the goal of a separate state for Muslims became clearer and better defined. In the meantime Muslims felt their way along amidst much confusion of thought and difference of opinion. The most important figures of this period are Iqbāl and Muhammad Alī. In the religious field the tendency to bring the interpretation of Islam into line with contemporary knowledge gained momentum and produced, among a host of less-known authors, Amīr Alī, who became famous for his *The Spirit of Islam*.

MUHAMMAD IQBĀL: POET AND PHILOSOPHER OF THE ISLAMIC REVIVAL

Sir Syed had brought rationalism and the desire for knowledge and progress to the Indian Muslims; Iqbāl brought them inspiration and a philosophy. Next to the Qur'ān, there is no single influence upon the consciousness of the Pakistani intelligentsia so powerful as Iqbāl's poetry. In his own time it kindled the enthusiasm of Muslim intellectuals for the values of Islam, and rallied the whole Muslim community once again to the banner of their faith. For this reason Iqbāl is looked upon today as the spiritual founder of Pakistan.

Muhammad Iqbāl (1873–1938) was born at Sialkot in the Punjab in the year 1873. His parents, devout and pious Muslims, inculcated in him the teachings of Islam. Eventually Iqbāl was sent to the Government College at Lahore where he graduated in 1899 and was appointed a lecturer in philosophy. After studying philosophy at Cambridge and in Germany, and having also qualified as a barrister-at-law, he came back to his teaching at Lahore in 1908. Two years later, in order to free himself from this type of service to a foreign government, he gave up teaching and started the private practice of law. Still, his heart was not in the legal profession, and he undertook only enough work to keep himself in modest comfort. For the most part, his time was spent in study and writing. It was not long before he came to be recognized as a thinker of importance and the greatest Urdu poet of his time.

While in Europe, Iqbāl had come into contact with the leading schools of Western philosophy, and was particularly influenced by Nietzsche and Bergson. These influences are evident in his own thought, and yet the main source of Iqbāl's ideas is the Islamic tradition itself. His knowledge of Islamic thought and literature, especially of the Persian classics, was profound. Above all he was indebted to the great mystic thinker of Turkey, Jalāl-u'd-dīn Rūmī, whom he quotes again and again with deep appreciation. Iqbāl had an aversion, however, for those Sufis who tended toward a mystical quietism. Their philosophy of inaction he held responsible for the decadence of Islam. Action is life and inaction is death, he taught. In strife with evil, not in the peace of the grave, lies the true meaning of human life. Iqbāl had a burning conviction that Islam provided the remedy for many of the world's ills. The division of humanity into national and racial groups, according to him, was the greatest curse of the day. Injustice in any form was abhorrent and had to be fought. The evils of colonialism, the tyranny of the landlord over the unprotected tenant, the cupidity of capitalism, and the exploitation of the resources of a weaker people by a stronger nation, were all hateful in his eyes. The real remedy lay, according to him, in the cultivation of the innate greatness of the human self, so that realizing its real qualities, it would become incapable of meaner tendencies like greed, injustice, and fear. Such development of the Self, he insisted, is possible only through a true understanding of the relationship between God and man. Even God does not demand the destruction of the Self; He is desirous that the Self should be developed to its fullest capacity. The Self, however, finds its fullest meaning only through identification with the life of the community, and for that purpose the community should be organized on a righteous basis. Such a community is the community of Islam, because its sole foundation is the acceptance of God and the Law, which is the criterion of righteousness. As Islam recognizes no superiority of birth or rank or wealth within its bosom and judges excellence by righteousness alone, the fullest cultivation of the Self is possible within its fold. This community, moreover, is not limited by time or space, according to the Islamic doctrine that all truth from God revealed anywhere at any time is Islam, Muhammad being the final recipient of this truth in its most perfect form. Such a community was not meant to be fragmented into nations. The means by which the Self can develop to its full height is Love, which is the Sufic word for the ecstatic devotion to God. Whereas human reason is limited by time and space, Love is not; it is therefore capable of creating immutable qualities in the Self. Iqbāl thinks that real Time is not the linear time of which we have a feeling, nor the limited time of the scientist, because he must think in terms of transient and limited space, but that it is higher and everlasting. It is infinite and eternal, indeed an attribute of God himself. It is in this Time that the Self finds its ultimate fulfillment.

Realizing the importance of his message to the whole Islamic world Iqbāl began to write in Persian, which is more widely understood and read in the Muslim world than Urdu. Urdu itself was not his mother tongue but had been the literary language of the Punjab for more than a century. In Urdu, he ranks high as a philosophic poet and is considered next only to Ghalib (1796–1869) in charm, depth, and richness of ideas.

Unfortunately Iqbāl's poetry is difficult to translate; even in the excellent translations reproduced below, they lose a good deal of the charm and force of the original.

In 1922, Iqbāl accepted a knighthood conferred upon him in recognition of his greatness as a poet, but only on the understanding that it was not a reward for any service he had rendered the government. He also somewhat halfheartedly participated in the political activities of his province and local community. Elected to the provincial legislature, he participated in its debates, but made no great mark as a legislator. In addition he served as a delegate to the Round Table Conference in London in 1931. Temperamentally, he was not suited to politics, and his only real contribution in this field was made as president of the All-India Muslim League session of 1930, when he declared that he would like to see the Northwestern areas, where Muslims were in a majority, constituted a separate state. Though his ideas on the subject were still vague and aroused no immediate response, this was the first time that the idea of a separate state for the Muslims had been put forward from the platform of a political party.

Toward the end of his life Iqbāl became convinced that the Muslims in India were threatened with extermination. He called the endless succession of Hindu-Muslim riots a virtual civil war, which he foresaw would develop in magnitude as time passed. Feeling that the Muslims were unprepared for a final showdown, ill-organized and without a leader, he singled out Jinnāh as the one person capable of serving the Muslims and in whose capacity and leadership he had the fullest confidence and faith.

Iqbāl died in 1938, deeply mourned by the Muslims in India and by Muslims in other lands as well. Today admirers come from afar to visit his tomb, and Pakistan recognizes him as its national poet. One of the earliest actions of the government of Pakistan was to found an academy for the study of his teachings.

MUHAMMAD IQBĀL

Fate

[From Kiernan, *Poems from Iqbal,* p. 64]

Satan

Oh God, Creator! I did not hate your Adam,
That captive of Far-and-Near and Swift-and-Slow;

And what presumption could refuse to *You*
Obedience? If I would not kneel to him,
The cause was Your own foreordaining will.

God

When did that mystery dawn on you? before,
Or after your sedition?

Satan

After, oh brightness
Whence all the glory of all being flows.

God (to His angels)

See what a groveling nature taught him this
Fine theorem! His not kneeling, he pretends,
Belonged to My foreordinance; gives his freedom
Necessity's base title;—wretch! his own
Consuming fire he calls a wreath of smoke.

Freedom

[From Kiernan, *Poems from Iqbal,* p. 90]

The freeman's veins are firm as veins of granite;
The bondman's weak as tendrils of the vine,
And his heart too despairing and repining—
The free heart has life's tingling breath to fan it.
Quick pulse, clear vision, are the freeman's treasure;
The unfree, to kindness and affection dead,
Has no more wealth than tears of his own shedding
And those glib words he has in such good measure.

Bondman and free can never come to accord:
One is the heavens' lackey, one their lord.

The Self

In order to stir the Muslims from their lethargy and despair, in the following poems from *The Secrets of the Self* Iqbāl extols a positive, active attitude to the world, rather than the world-negating quietism preached by certain Sufis. He also emphasizes the importance of the individual in the world ("The Self").

By "desire" Iqbāl meant primarily the striving after ideals as the source of man's activity and progress.
[From Iqbāl, *The Secrets of the Self*, pp. 16, 18–19]

The form of existence is an effect of the Self,
Whatsoever thou seest is a secret of the Self,
When the Self awoke to consciousness,
It revealed the universe of Thought.
A hundred worlds are hidden in its essence:
Self-affirmation brings Not-self to light.

. . . .

Subject, object, means, and causes—
All these are forms which it assumes for the purpose of action.
The Self rises, kindles, falls, glows, breathes,
Burns, shines, walks, and flies.
The spaciousness of time is its arena,
Heaven is a billow of the dust on its road.
From its rose-planting the world abounds in roses;
Night is born of its sleep, day springs from its waking.

Desire
[From Iqbāl, *The Secrets of the Self*, pp. 23, 25–27]

Life is preserved by purpose:
Because of the goal its caravan-bell tinkles.
Life is latent in seeking,
Its origin is hidden in desire.
Keep desire alive in thy heart,
Lest thy little dust become a tomb.

. . . .

'Tis desire that enriches life,
And the mind is a child of its womb.
What are social organization, customs, and laws?
What is the secret of the novelties of science?
A desire which realized itself by its own strength
And burst forth from the heart and took shape.

. . . .

Rise intoxicated with the wine of an ideal,
An ideal shining as the dawn
A blazing fire to all that is other than God,
An ideal higher than Heaven—
Winning, captivating, enchanting men's hearts;
A destroyer of ancient falsehood,
Fraught with turmoil, an embodiment of the Last Day.
We live by forming ideals,
We glow with the sunbeams of desire!

Love

Iqbāl uses Love for the ecstatic love of God, not in any quietist, passive sense,
but as the source of the highest inspiration for true knowledge and effective,
righteous action.

[From Iqbāl, *The Secrets of the Self*, pp. 28–29]

The luminous point whose name is the Self
Is the life-spark beneath our dust.
By love it is made more lasting,
More living, more burning, more glowing.
From love proceeds the radiance of its being
And the development of its unknown possibilities.
Its nature gathers fire from love,
Love instructs it to illumine the world.
Love fears neither sword nor dagger,
Love is not born of water and air and earth.
Love makes peace and war in the world,
Love is the fountain of life, love is the flashing sword of death.
The hardest rocks are shivered by love's glance:
Love of God at last becomes wholly God.

Time

Iqbāl believed that the conception of time as finite and limited induced a passive attitude toward life; if time itself is limited, nothing that exists in time
can be of everlasting value and all that is achieved by human action must
perish. To combat this tendency Iqbāl held that time is eternal and, therefore,

human action has a lasting importance. This idea militated against both inaction and mere expediency.

[From Iqbāl, *The Secrets of the Self*, pp. 137–38]

> The cause of time is not the revolution of the sun:
> Time is everlasting, but the sun does not last forever.
> Time is joy and sorrow, festival and fast;
> Time is the secret of moonlight and sunlight.
> Thou hast extended time, like space,
> And distinguished yesterday from tomorrow.
> Thou hast fled, like a scent, from thine own garden;
> Thou hast made thy prison with thine own hand.
> Our time which has neither beginning nor end,
> Blossoms from the flower bed of our mind.
> To know its root quickens the living with new life:
> Its being is more splendid than the dawn.
> Life is of time, and time is of life.

Muslims Are One in Soul

In the following passages from his *Mysteries of Selflessness* Iqbāl attempts to correct the overindividualistic effect of his previous work, *The Secrets of the Self*, by emphasizing the Muslim community. Reflecting the concern of Muslims at that time over the fate of the Ottoman empire and other Muslim lands conquered or threatened by European powers, Iqbāl propagates pan-Islamism based on the doctrine of an indivisible Muslim community. The Muslims are united throughout space and time by a common faith and a common history.

[From Iqbāl, *The Mysteries of Selflessness*, p. 20]

> A common aim shared by the multitude
> Is unity which, when it is mature,
> Forms the Community; the many live
> Only by virtue of the single bond.
> The Muslim's unity from natural faith
> Derives, and this the Prophet taught us,
> So that we lit a lantern on truth's way.
> This pearl was fished from his unfathomed sea,
> And of his bounty we are one in soul.

Let not this unity go from our hands,
And we endure to all eternity.

Muslims Profess No Fatherland
[From Iqbāl, *The Mysteries of Selflessness*, p. 29]

Our Essence is not bound to any place;
The vigor of our wine is not contained
In any bowl; Chinese and Indian
Alike the shard that constitutes our jar,
Turkish and Syrian alike the clay
Forming our body; neither is our heart
Of India, or Syria, or Rum,
Nor any fatherland do we profess
Except Islam.

The Concept of Country Divides Humanity
[From Iqbāl, *The Mysteries of Selflessness*, p. 32]

Now brotherhood has been so cut to shreds
That in the stead of community
The country has been given pride of place
In men's allegiance and constructive work;
The country is the darling of their hearts,
And wide humanity is whittled down
Into dismembered tribes. . . .
Vanished is humankind; there but abide
The disunited nations. Politics
Dethroned religion. . . .

The Muslim Community Is Unbounded in Time
[From Iqbāl, *The Mysteries of Selflessness*, pp. 36–37]

. . . When the burning brands
Of time's great revolution ring our mead,
Then Spring returns. The mighty power of Rome,
Conqueror and ruler of the world entire,
Sank into small account; the golden glass
Of the Sassanians was drowned in blood;

Broken the brilliant genius of Greece;
Egypt too failed in the great test of time,
Her bones lie buried neath the pyramids.
Yet still the voice of the muezzin rings
Throughout the earth, still the Community
Of World-Islam maintains its ancient forms.
Love is the universal law of life,
Mingling the fragmentary elements
Of a disordered world. Through our hearts' glow
Love lives, irradiated by the spark
There is no god but God.

The Importance of History
[From Iqbāl, *The Mysteries of Selflessness,* pp. 60–62]

Like to a child is a community
Newborn, an infant in its mother's arms;
All unaware of Self. . . .
But when with energy it falls upon
The world's great labors, stable then becomes
This new-won consciousness; it raises up
A thousand images, and casts them down;
So it createth its own history. . . .
The record of the past illuminates
The conscience of a people; memory
Of past achievements makes it Self-aware;
But if that memory fades, and is forgot,
The folk again is lost in nothingness. . . .
What thing is history, O Self-unaware?
A fable? Or a legendary tale?
Nay, 'tis the thing that maketh thee aware
Of thy true Self, alert unto the task,
A seasoned traveler; this is the source
Of the soul's ardor, this the nerves that knit
The body of the whole community.
This whets thee like a dagger on its sheath,
To dash thee in the face of all the world. . . .
If thou desirest everlasting life,

Break not the thread between the past and now
And the far future. What is Life? A wave
Of consciousness of continuity,
A gurgling wine that flames the revelers.

Muslims Are Bound Together by Faith Alone
[From Iqbāl, *The Mysteries of Selflessness,* pp. 75–76]

The bond of Turk and Arab is not ours,
The link that binds us is no fetter's chain
Of ancient lineage; our hearts are bound
To the beloved Prophet of Hejaz,
And to each other are we joined through him.
Our common thread is simple loyalty
To him alone; the rapture of his wine
Alone our eyes entrances; from what time
This glad intoxication with his love
Raced in our blood, the old is set ablaze
In new creation. As the blood that flows
Within a people's veins, so is his love
Sole substance of our solidarity.
Love dwells within the spirit, lineage
The flesh inhabits; stronger far than race
And common ancestry is love's firm cord.
True loverhood must overleap the bounds
Of lineage, transcend Arabia
And Persia. Love's community is like
The light of God; whatever being we
Possess, from its existence is derived.
"None seeketh when or where God's light was born;
What need of warp and woof, God's robe to spin?" [1]
Who suffereth his foot to wear the chains
Of clime and ancestry is unaware
How *He begat not, neither was begot.*[2]

---

[1] A quotation from Jalāl-u'd-dīn Rūmī.
[2] One of the most repeated verses of the Qur'ān.

The Need for Understanding Islam in the Light of
Modern Knowledge
[From Iqbāl, *Reconstruction of Religious Thought in Islam*, pp. 7–8]

During the last five hundred years religious thought in Islam has been practically stationary. There was a time when European thought received inspiration from the world of Islam. The most remarkable phenomenon of modern history, however, is the enormous rapidity with which the world of Islam is spiritually moving towards the West. There is nothing wrong in this movement, for European culture, on its intellectual side, is only a further development of some of the most important phases of the culture of Islam. Our only fear is that the dazzling exterior of European culture may arrest our movement and we may fail to reach the true inwardness of that culture. During all the centuries of our intellectual stupor Europe has been seriously thinking on the great problems in which the philosophers and scientists of Islam were so keenly interested. Since the Middle Ages, when the schools of Muslim theology were completed, infinite advance has taken place in the domain of human thought and experience. The extension of man's power over nature has given him a new faith and a fresh sense of superiority over the forces that constitute his environment. New points of view have been suggested, old problems have been restated in the light of fresh experience, and new problems have arisen. It seems as if the intellect of man is outgrowing its own most fundamental categories—time, space, and causality. With the advance of scientific thought even our concept of intelligibility is undergoing a change. The theory of Einstein has brought a new vision of the universe and suggests new ways of looking at the problems common to both religion and philosophy. No wonder then that the younger generation of Islam in Asia and Africa demand a fresh orientation of their faith. With the reawakening of Islam, therefore, it is necessary to examine, in an independent spirit, what Europe has thought and how far the conclusions reached by her can help us in the revision and, if necessary, reconstruction, of theological thought in Islam. Besides this it is not possible to ignore the generally antireligious and especially anti-Islamic propaganda in Central Asia which has already crossed the Indian frontier.

The Role of Religion in the World of Today
[From Iqbāl, *Reconstruction of Religious Thought in Islam,* pp. 186–88]

Thus, wholly overshadowed by the results of his intellectual activity, the modern man has ceased to live soulfully, i.e., from within. In the domain of thought he is living in open conflict with himself; and in the domain of economic and political life he is living in open conflict with others. He finds himself unable to control his ruthless egoism and his infinite gold-hunger which is gradually killing all higher striving in him and bringing him nothing but life-weariness. Absorbed in the "fact," that is to say, the optically present source of sensation, he is entirely cut off from the unplumbed depths of his own being. In the wake of his systematic materialism has at last come that paralysis of energy which Huxley apprehended and deplored. The condition of things in the East is no better. The technique of medieval mysticism by which religious life, in its higher manifestations, developed itself both in the East and in the West has now practically failed. And in the Muslim East it has, perhaps, done far greater havoc than anywhere else. Far from reintegrating the forces of the average man's inner life, and thus preparing him for participation in the march of history, it has taught him a false renunciation and made him perfectly contented with his ignorance and spiritual thralldom. No wonder then that the modern Muslim in Turkey, Egypt, and Persia is led to seek fresh sources of energy in the creation of new loyalties, such as patriotism and nationalism which Nietzsche described as "sickness and unreason," and "the strongest force against culture." Disappointed of a purely religious method of spiritual renewal which alone brings us into touch with the everlasting fountain of life and power by expanding our thought and emotion, the modern Muslim fondly hopes to unlock fresh sources of energy by narrowing down his thought and emotion. Modern atheistic socialism, which possesses all the fervor of a new religion, has a broader outlook; but having received its philosophical basis from the Hegelians of the left wing, it rises in revolt against the very source which could have given it strength and purpose. Both nationalism and atheistic socialism, at least in the present state of human adjustments, must draw upon the psychological forces of hate, suspicion, and resentment which tend to impoverish the soul of man and close up his hidden sources of spiritual energy. Neither the technique of medieval mysticism nor nationalism nor atheistic socialism can cure the ills of a despairing humanity. Surely the present moment is one of great crisis in the history of modern culture. The modern world stands in need of biological renewal. And religion, which in its higher manifestations is neither dogma, nor priesthood, nor ritual, can alone ethically prepare the modern man for the burden of the great responsibility which the advancement of modern science necessarily involves, and restore to him that attitude of faith which makes him capable of winning a personality here and retaining it hereafter. It is only by rising to a fresh vision of his origin and future, his whence and whither, that man will eventually triumph over a society motivated by an inhuman competition, and a civilization which has lost its spiritual unity by its inner conflict of religious and political values.

Islam and Human Dignity

Iqbāl opposed the way of life of the West which according to him looked upon man as "a *thing* to be exploited and not as a *personality* to be developed." He thought that Islam, freed from the shackles of theological thought of the previous ages, was capable of giving a better deal to man by emphasizing its doctrines of equality and regard for human dignity.

[From Iqbāl, *Speeches and Statements.* . . . , pp. 52–56]

The present struggle in India is sometimes described as India's revolt against the West. I do not think it is a revolt against the West; for the people of India are demanding the very institutions which the West stands for. . . . Educated urban India demands democracy. The minorities, feeling themselves as distinct cultural units and fearing that their very existence is at stake, demand safeguards, which the majority community, for obvious reasons, refuses to concede. The majority community pretends to believe in a nationalism theoretically correct, if we start from Western premises, belied by facts, if we look to India. Thus the real parties to the present struggle in India are not England and India, but the majority community and the minorities of India which can ill afford to accept the principle of Western democracy until it is properly modified to suit the actual conditions of life in India.

Nor do Mahātmā Gāndhi's political methods signify a revolt in the psychological sense. These methods arise out of a contact of two opposing types of world-consciousness, Western and Eastern. The Western man's mental texture is chronological in character. He lives and moves and has his being in time. The Eastern man's world-consciousness is nonhistorical. To the Western man things gradually become; they have a past, present, and future. To the Eastern man they are immediately rounded off, timeless, purely present. That is why Islam which sees in the time-movement a symbol of reality appeared as an intruder in the static world-pictures of Asia. The British as a Western people cannot but conceive political reform in India as a systematic process of gradual evolution. Mahātmā Gāndhi as an Eastern man sees in this attitude nothing more than an ill-conceived unwillingness to part with power and tries all sorts of destructive negations to achieve immediate attainment. Both are elementally incapable of understanding each other. The result is the appearance of a revolt.

These phenomena, however, are merely premonitions of a coming storm, which is likely to sweep over the whole of India and the rest of Asia. This is the inevitable outcome of a wholly political civilization which has looked upon man as a *thing* to be exploited and not as a *personality* to be developed and enlarged by purely cultural forces. The peoples of Asia are bound to rise against the acquisitive economy which the West has developed and imposed on the nations of the East. Asia cannot comprehend modern Western capitalism with its undisciplined individualism. The faith which you represent recognizes the worth of the individual, and disciplines him to give away his all to the service of God and man. Its possibilities are not yet exhausted. It can still create a new world where the social rank of man is not determined by his caste or color, or the amount of dividend he earns, but by the kind of life he lives; where the poor tax the rich, where human society is founded not on the equality of stomachs but on the equality of spirits, where an untouchable can marry the daughter of a king, where private ownership is a trust, and where capital cannot be allowed to accumulate so as to dominate the real producer of wealth. This superb idealism of your faith, however, needs emancipation from the medieval fancies of theologians and legists. Spiritually we are living in a prison-house of thoughts and emotions which during the course of centuries we have woven round ourselves. And be it further said to the shame of us—men of [the] older generation —that we have failed to equip the younger generation for the economic, political, and even religious crises that the present age is likely to bring. The whole community needs a complete overhauling of its present mentality in order that it may again become capable of feeling the urge of fresh desires and ideals. The Indian Muslim has long ceased to explore the depths of his own inner life. The result is that he has ceased to live in the full glow and color of life, and is consequently in danger of an unmanly compromise with forces which, he is made to think, he cannot vanquish in open conflict. He who desires to change an unfavorable environment must undergo a complete transformation of his inner being. God changeth not the condition of a people until they themselves take the initiative to change their condition by constantly illuminating the zone of their daily activity in the light of a definite ideal. Nothing can be achieved without a firm faith in the independence of one's own inner life. This faith alone keeps a people's eye fixed on their goal and saves them from perpetual vacillation. . . . The flame of life cannot be borrowed from others; it must be kindled in the temple of one's own soul.

A Separate State for the Muslims

Iqbāl's presidential address before the All-India Muslim League, Allahabad, December 29, 1930, from which this reading is taken, is his most important political statement in relation to the later establishment of a separate state for the Muslims in India. His argument is that a polity making religion a purely private matter, as in European states, dooms religion. Islam, on the other hand, is organically connected with the social order and in India needs an autonomous area for its full expression and development.

[From Iqbāl, *Speeches and Statements* . . . , pp. 3–12, 34–36]

It cannot be denied that Islam, regarded as an ethical ideal plus a certain kind of polity—by which expression I mean a social structure regulated by a legal system and animated by a specific ethical ideal—has been the chief formative factor in the life-history of the Muslims of India. It has furnished those basic emotions and loyalties which gradually unify scattered individuals and groups and finally transform them into a well-defined people. Indeed it is no exaggeration to say that India is perhaps the only country in the world where Islam, as a people-building force, has worked at its best. . . . The ideas set free by European political thinking, however, are now rapidly changing the outlook of the present generation of Muslims both in India and outside India. Our younger men, inspired by these ideas, are anxious to see them as living forces in their own countries, without any critical appreciation of the facts which have determined their evolution in Europe. . . . Islam does not bifurcate the unity of man into an irreconcilable duality of spirit and matter. In Islam God and the universe, spirit and matter, Church and State, are organic to each other. Man is not the citizen of a profane world to be renounced in the interest of a world of spirit situated elsewhere. To Islam matter is spirit realizing itself in space and time. Europe uncritically accepted the duality of spirit and matter probably from Manichaean thought. Her best thinkers are realizing this initial mistake today, but her statesmen are indirectly forcing the world to accept it as an unquestionable dogma. It is, then, this mistaken separation of spiritual and temporal which has largely influenced European religious and political thought and has resulted practically in the total exclusion of Christianity from the life of European states. The result is a set of mutually ill-adjusted states dominated by interests not human but national. . . . In the world of Islam we have a universal polity whose fundamentals are believed to have been revealed, but whose structure, owing to our legists' want of contact with [the] modern world, stands today in need of renewed power by fresh adjustments. I do not know what will be the final fate of the national idea in the world of Islam. Whether Islam will assimilate and transform it, as it has assimilated and transformed before many ideas expressive of a different spirit, or allow a radical transformation of its own structure by the force of this idea, is hard to predict. Professor Wensinck of Leiden (Holland) wrote to me the other day: "It seems to me that Islam is entering upon a crisis through which Christianity has been passing for more than a century. The great difficulty is how to save the foundations of religion when many antiquated notions have to be given up. It seems to me scarcely possible to state what the outcome will be for Christianity, still less what it will be for Islam." At the present moment the national idea is racializing the outlook of Muslims, and thus materially counteracting the humanizing work of Islam. And the growth of racial consciousness may mean the growth of standards different and even opposed to the standards of Islam. . . .

What, then, is the problem and its implications? Is religion a private affair? Would you like to see Islam, as a moral and political ideal, meeting the same fate in the world of Islam as Christianity has already met in Europe? Is it possible to retain Islam as an ethical ideal and to reject it as a polity in favor of national polities, in which a religious attitude is not permitted to play any part? This question becomes of special importance in India where the Muslims happen to be in a minority. The proposition that religion is a private individual experience is not surprising on the lips of a European. In Europe the conception of Christianity as a monastic order, renouncing the world of matter and fixing its gaze entirely on the world of spirit led, by a logical process of thought, to the view embodied in this proposition. The nature of the Prophet's religious experience, as disclosed in the Qur'ān, however, is wholly different. It is not mere experience in the sense of a purely biological event, happening inside the experient and necessitating no reactions on his social environment. It is individual experience creative of a social order. Its immediate outcome is the fundamentals of a polity with implicit legal concepts whose civic significance cannot be belittled merely because their origin is revelational. The religious ideal of Islam, therefore, is organically related to the social order which it has created. The rejection of the one will eventually involve the rejection of the other. Therefore the construction of a polity on national lines, if it means a displacement of the Islamic principle of solidarity, is simply unthinkable to a Muslim. This is a matter which at the present moment directly concerns the Muslims of India. "Man," says Renan, "is enslaved neither by his race, nor by his religion, nor by the course of rivers, nor by the direction of mountain ranges. A great aggregation of men, sane of mind and warm of heart, creates a moral consciousness which is called a nation." Such a formation is quite possible, though it involves the long and arduous process of practically remaking men and furnishing them with a fresh emotional equipment. It might have been a fact in India if the teaching of Kabīr and the Divine Faith of Akbar had seized the imagination of the masses of this country. Experience, however, shows that the various caste-units and religious units in India have shown no inclination to sink their respective individualties in a larger whole. Each group is intensely jealous of its collective existence. The formation of the kind of moral consciousness which constitutes the essence of a nation in Renan's sense demands a price which the peoples of India are not prepared to pay. The unity of an Indian nation, therefore, must be sought, not in the negation but in the mutual harmony and cooperation of the many. True statesmanship cannot ignore facts, however unpleasant they may be. The only practical course is not to assume the existence of a state of things which does not exist, but to recognize facts as they are, and to exploit them to our greatest advantage. . . . And it is on the discovery of Indian unity in this direction that the fate of India as well as Asia really depends. India is Asia in miniature. Part of her people have cultural affinities with nations in the east and part with nations in the middle and west of Asia. If an effective principle of co-operation is discovered in India, it will bring peace and mutual good-will to this ancient land which has suffered so long, more because of her situation in historic space than because of any inherent incapacity of her people. And it will at the same time solve the entire political problem of Asia.

It is, however, painful to observe that our attempts to discover such a principle of internal harmony have so far failed. Why have they failed? Perhaps we suspect each other's intentions and inwardly aim at dominating each other. Perhaps in the higher interests of mutual cooperation, we cannot afford to part with the monopolies which circumstances have placed in our hands and conceal our egoism under the cloak of a nationalism, outwardly stimulating a large-hearted patriotism, but inwardly as narrow-minded as a caste or a tribe. Perhaps, we are unwilling to recognize that each group has a right to free development according to its own cultural traditions. But whatever may be the causes of our failure, I still feel hopeful. Events seem to be tending in the direction of some sort of internal harmony. And as far as I have been able to read the Muslim mind, I have no hesitation in declaring that if the principle that the Indian Muslim is entitled to full and free development on the lines of his own culture and tradition in his own Indian home-lands is recognized as the basis of a permanent communal settlement, he will be ready to stake his all for the freedom of India. The principle that each group is entitled to free development on its own lines is not inspired by any feeling of narrow communalism. There are communalisms and communalisms. A community which is inspired by feelings of ill-will toward other communities is low and ignoble. I entertain the highest respect for the customs, laws, religious, and social institutions of other communities. Nay, it is my duty according to the teaching of the Qur'ān, even to defend their places of worship, if need be. Yet I love the communal group which is the source of my life and behavior and which has formed me what I am by giving me its religion, its literature, its thought, its culture and thereby recreating its whole past as a living factor in my present consciousness. . . .

Communalism in its higher aspect, then, is indispensable to the formation of a harmonious whole in a country like India. The units of Indian society are not territorial as in European countries. India is a continent of human groups belonging to different races, speaking different languages and professing different religions. Their behavior is not at all determined by a common race-consciousness. Even the Hindus do not form a homogeneous group. The principle of European democracy cannot be applied to India without recognizing the fact of communal groups. The Muslim demand for the creation of a Muslim India within India is, therefore, perfectly justified. The resolution of the All-Parties Muslim Conference at Delhi, is, to my mind, wholly inspired by this noble ideal of a harmonious whole which, instead of stifling the respective individualities of its component wholes, affords them chances of fully working out the possibilities that may be latent in them. And I have no doubt that this House will emphatically endorse the Muslim demands embodied in this resolution. Personally, I would go further than the demands embodied in it. *I would like to see the Punjab, North-West Frontier Province, Sind and Baluchistan amalgamated into a single State. Self-government within the British empire or without the British empire, the formation of a consolidated North-West Indian Muslim State appears to me to be the final destiny of the Muslims, at least of North-West India.*[1]

MUSLIM UNITY OF WILL TO BE PROVIDED BY ISLAM

In conclusion I cannot but impress upon you that the present crisis in the history of India demands complete organization and unity of will and purpose in the Muslim community, both in your own interest as a community, and in the interest of India as a whole. The political bondage of India has been and is a source of infinite misery to the whole of Asia. It has suppressed the spirit of the East and wholly deprived her of that joy of self-expression which once made her the creator of a great and glorious culture. We have a duty towards India where we are destined to live and die. We have a duty towards Asia, especially Muslim Asia. And since 70 millions of Muslims in a single country constitute a far more valuable

[1] The italics are Dr. Qureshi's.

asset to Islam than all the countries of Muslim Asia put together, we must look at the Indian problem not only from the Muslim point of view but also from the standpoint of the Indian Muslim as such. Our duty towards Asia and India cannot be loyally performed without an organized will fixed on a definite purpose. In your own interest, as a political entity among other political entities of India, such an equipment is an absolute necessity. Our disorganized condition has already confused political issues vital to the life of the community. I am not hopeless of an intercommunal understanding, but I cannot conceal from you the feeling that in the near future our community may be called upon to adopt an independent line of action to cope with the present crisis. And an independent line of political action, in such a crisis, is possible only to a determined people, possessing a will focalized by a single purpose. Is it possible for you to achieve the organic wholeness of a unified will? Yes, it is. Rise above sectional interests and private ambitions, and learn to determine the value of your individual and collective action, however directed on material ends, in the light of the ideal which you are supposed to represent. Pass from matter to spirit. Matter is diversity; spirit is light, life and unity. One lesson I have learnt from the history of Muslims. At critical moments in their history it is Islam that has saved Muslims and not vice versa. If today you focus your vision on Islam and see inspiration from the ever-vitalizing idea embodied in it, you will be only reassembling your scattered forces, regaining your lost integrity, and thereby saving yourself from total destruction. One of the profoundest verses in the Holy Qur'ān teaches us that the birth and rebirth of the whole of humanity is like the birth of a single individual. Why cannot you who, as a people, can well claim to be the first practical exponents of this superb conception of humanity, live and move and have your being as a single individual? . . . In the words of the Qur'ān: "Hold fast to yourself; no one who erreth can hurt you, provided you are well guided."

MUHAMMAD ALĪ AND THE KHILĀFAT MOVEMENT

If Iqbāl was the philosopher of the new awakening of the Indian Muslims, Muhammad Alī (1879–1930) was its man of action. To Muslim political life he contributed a most vital asset—mass support. Hitherto politics had been the preserve of a few intellectuals; now popular opinion began to play a part in the determination of policy. Thus when Jinnāh later launched his campaign for Pakistan, it was the support given him by the Muslim masses which brought success, as well as the help of trained workers who had received their political baptism under Muhammad Alī in the Khilāfat Movement.

Muhammad Alī was born at Rampur, a small Muslim princely state in northern India. Following his education at Aligarh and Oxford, he entered the civil service of Baroda, which, at that time, was one of the most progressive Indian states. Gradually, however, his interest in public affairs and particularly in the welfare of his community drew him away from civil service. After starting an independent weekly review, the *Comrade,* which attracted the attention of educated Muslims, Muhammad Alī found himself engaged in politics. He was one of the original members of the Muslim League, and it was through his efforts that the founder of Pakistan, Muhammad Alī Jinnāh, was persuaded to join the League in 1913.

An ardent Muslim, Muhammad Alī's loyalty was not limited to Islam in India; the difficulties of Muslims anywhere in the world elicited his sympathy and active concern. In this he was a true representative of the ideals of Islam and the feelings of Indian Muslims. The European onslaught upon the Ottoman empire, beginning with the Italian occupation of Tripoli, the Balkan Wars, and the events leading up to the First World War created grave misgivings in the minds of the Indian Muslims regarding the future of the secular power of Islam in the world and the freedom of the Muslim peoples. They had themselves tasted the humiliation of subjugation and there was a great upsurge of sympathy among them for suffering Muslims elsewhere, as well as of antagonism toward the West and in particular Great Britain. These feelings were powerfully expressed and represented by Muhammad Alī.

When the First World War came, he saw that the Turks might be tempted to join the Germans in the hope of recovering the territories they had lost to Great Britain, especially Egypt. A long article of his in the *Comrade* entitled "The Choice of the Turks," begged the Allies to win over the Turks by making good the losses which had been inflicted upon the Ottoman empire despite its traditional friendship with Great Britain.

This article, though well intentioned, was so outspoken about the record of British relations with Turkey that it was proscribed by the government, and in spite of Muhammad Alī's earlier support of the Allied cause, his press, review, and Urdu daily, the *Hamdard,* were suppressed. Muhammad Alī himself was jailed.

The British, nevertheless, realized that the war between Britain and Turkey placed a great strain upon the loyalty of Indian Muslims to the British Empire. To allay Muslim fears Lloyd George stated in Parliament that it was not the intention of the British government to deprive the Turks of their homelands. When, despite these assurances, territories inhabited by the Turks, such as parts of Anatolia, were wrested from Turkey after the war (1920), Muslim opinion on the subcontinent was shocked. Even the release of Muhammad Alī did not allay mounting feeling over this betrayal, and he soon found himself in the forefront of popular agitation.

It was on the issue of the Caliphate (*Khilāfat*) that Muslim leaders felt they could most effectively appeal to the non-Muslim world including Great Britain. The Ottoman sultans had long claimed to be the caliphs, or supreme religious authority of the Muslim world, a claim never seriously challenged because, within the Ottoman empire, it was identified with the political sovereignty of the sultanate, and, outside the Ottoman empire, had no practical significance. But now that the Indian Muslims had lost their own liberty, they had reason to feel a strong emotional attachment to a caliph whom they could claim as their own sovereign, even though only in a nominal and religious sense. Indeed, before the First World War, prayers for the Turkish sultan had already come to be included in the Friday *Khutbah* (sermon) in the mosques of India.

The Indian Muslims, therefore, based their case for Turkey upon loyalty to the caliphate, arguing that in so far as it was necessary that the caliph should possess sufficient power to defend the vital interests of Islam, any further diminution in his territories would reduce the institution to a farce. Moreover it was necessary that the sacred places of Islam, Mecca and Medina, should be free from non-Muslim influence, and since the Sharif of Mecca, Husain, was merely a British puppet, he could not serve as true guardian of the sanctuaries. To Indian Muslims these arguments had a strong religious appeal, and the Khilāfat Movement quickly gathered momentum.

The time was ripe for a genuine mass movement in India. Gāndhi was now home from South Africa, having perfected his methods of passive resistance and nonviolent noncooperation. Believing that if the Hindus and Muslims joined forces they could seriously embarrass the government, he supported the Khilāfat Movement; and the Muslims, in turn, guided by Muhammad Alī, accepted Gāndhi's leadership. As the movement gathered strength, Hindus and Muslims fraternized and it seemed that communal unity had been achieved. However, scattered outbreaks of violence convinced Gāndhi that the movement was getting out of hand and might give the British an opportunity to retaliate with superior force. He therefore called off the militant part of the movement. In the meantime, Muhammad Alī and others had been put on trial and sentenced to two years' imprisonment for a resolution they had passed at a meeting asking Indian troops not to serve the British. On the other hand, Gāndhi's calling off of the campaign was interpreted by the British as a confession of weakness on his part. As a result Gāndhi and many other leaders were imprisoned, and the noncooperation movement came to an end. The Khilāfat Movement itself hung on a while longer until the Turks unexpectedly delivered the coup de grace by abolishing the caliphate in 1924.

Muslims felt that they could have gone no further than they did in the Khilāfat Movement to cultivate good relations with the Hindus, without yielding on matters of fundamental principle. Nevertheless, violent agitation was stirred up by the Hindu Ārya Samāj in protest against injuries done Hindus by Muslims during one of the outbreaks. After the imprisonment of the Congress and Khilāfat leaders, the Ārya Samājists launched two movements aimed at Muslims. One of these, called *Sangathan* (lit. holding-together), sought to organize the Hindus into a militant group "capable of defending themselves" against the Muslims, who were called bullies in this connection even by Gandhi. A secret militant branch of this movement was the Rāshtrīya Svayam Sevak Sangh (National Self-Help Society), established in 1926, which finally came out into the open in the pre-Partition days. The other movement was called *Suddhi* (purification), which aimed at the mass conversion of the Muslims to Hinduism. Muhammad Alī took the attitude that if the Hindus wanted to organize themselves, no one could object; likewise he held that the Muslims, who themselves belonged to a missionary religion, could not well object to the Hindus organizing missionary activities even on a mass scale. However, his view was not shared by Muslims, and good will yielded to animosity on both sides until a wave of communal riots had begun. The causes of these riots were often trivial, but they were symptoms of a deeper malady.

Soon differences of opinion sprang up between the Hindu and Muslim Congress leaders. Muslim leaders, including Muhammad Alī, complained that the Hindu leaders did not try to curb the growing anti-Muslim feeling among the Hindus; nor did they exercise their influence with their own community to remove the causes of discord. About Gāndhi, Muhammad Alī said: "The Mussalmans have been oppressed and persecuted by the excesses of the Hindu majority in the last ten years, but Mr. Gāndhi never tried to improve matters or condemn Hindu terrorism against the Muslims. He never denounced the movements of Shuddhi and Sangathan . . . which openly and clearly aimed at the annihilation of the Muslims in India."

Muhammad Alī now moved further and further away from the Congress of which he had once been president. He was dissatisfied with the provisions of the Nehru Report,[1] which, he argued, would result in Hindu domination. The final break came in 1930, when Gāndhi started the second civil disobedience movement; Muhammad Alī advised the Muslims to stand aloof from it, and they did. That same year Muhammad Alī died in London, where he had gone against the advice of his doctors to participate in the first Round Table Conference. He had sworn that he would not return again to a "slave country" and at the request of Muslims in Palestine, who respected him as a great Muslim leader, he was buried in Jerusalem.

MUHAMMAD ALĪ
The Communal Patriot

In this famous article written for the *Comrade* in 1912 Muhammad Alī pleaded for mutual understanding of the very real factors creating communal feeling, and argued that genuine Indian nationalism, which he then still supported,

[1] As a challenge to the British Simon Commission, an Indian All-Parties Convention met in 1928. The Convention, with a large Hindu majority, appointed a commission under Motīlāl Nehru (Jawāharlāl Nehru's father) to draw a draft constitution. The Convention accepted the principle of reservation of seats for the minorities, but not separate electorates, which the Muslims demanded. Jinnāh split with the Congress on this occasion and held an All-India Muslim Conference on January 1, 1929. The Nehru Report came out later in 1929.

could only be achieved by allowing for basic differences of interest rather than suppressing them.

[From Muhammad Alī, *Select Writings* . . . , pp. 65–70]

How does India justify her "communal patriots"? The "Nationalist" of the Congress school would swear by "nationality" and patriotism and vehemently deny that any such monster could exist in his ranks, and point, with a mild, deprecating gesture, to "Muslim Leaguers" and their cries for "separate electorates." The Muslims would hold forth on the woes of "minorities," the imperative duty of self-preservation, and the aggressive spirit and character of Hindu "nationalism." These self-righteous attitudes prove not only that the problem is not even half-understood, but also that the "patriotism" in vogue in this country is exclusively Hindu or Muslim. Discussions on this subject have seldom been inspired by intellectual honesty and courage. Much of the "patriotic" literature is fumbling, shallow, and jejune. Not only it lacks sincerity and breadth of outlook, but it also betrays inordinate fondness for crude subterfuges and cheap claptrap with a view to secure some paltry advantage in the struggle for race ascendancy. The "communal patriot" only reflects in his inadequacy, narrowness, and fanaticism, the temper of his people. Without attempting a detailed analysis of the factors that hamper the growth of a truly Indian patriotism, it may be worth while studying how the communal fanatic has been evolved. Many centuries of Muslim rule in India had given the Hindus an immense power of adaptability to varying political conditions. They readily availed themselves of the facilities for education and material progress which British rule brought within their reach, because they were not burdened like the Muslims with a pride of race and powerful traditions of empire. Western literature gave them a free access to ideas of political freedom and democracy and they naturally and justly began to dream of self-government and organized national existence. They looked back and searched for fresh inspiration, but the oracles of the past were dumb. Before them lay a boundless sea of hope, aspiration, and experiment. If the past could not offer a chart and compass for the new voyage, clearly the fault lay with the Muslims who had viciously strayed into Bharat and demolished its political features and landmarks. Instead of accepting philosophically what could not be undone, they began to quarrel with history. This attitude speedily produced amongst the majority of the educated Hindus the unfortunate habit of ignoring the one great reality of the Indian situation—the existence of about 70 million Muslims who had made a permanent home in this country. Whatever may be the inspiration of Hinduism as a religious creed, the educated Hindus made it a rallying symbol for political unity. The aspiration for self-government arrested all movements for social reform which the early impulse towards liberalism had called forth amongst the educated Hindus. Past history was ransacked for new political formulas; and by a natural and inevitable process "nationality" and "Patriotism" began to be associated with Hinduism. The Hindu "communal patriot" sprang into existence with "Swaraj" as his war-cry. He refuses to give quarter to the Muslims unless the latter quietly shuffles off his individuality and becomes completely Hinduized. He knows, of course, the use of the words like "India" and "territorial nationality," and they form an important part of his vocabulary. But the Muslims weigh on his consciousness all the same, as a troublesome irrelevance; and he would thank his stars if some great exodus or even a geological cataclysm could give him riddance.

The Muslim "communal patriot" owes his origin to a very different set of circumstances. His community lagged behind in the race by moodily sulking in its tents and declining, for a considerable time, to avail itself of the facilities for intellectual and material progress. When it made up its mind to accept the inevitable and move with the times, it suddenly found itself face to face with a community vastly superior to it in number, in wealth, in education, in political organization and power, in a word a united community uttering new accents and pulsating with a new hope. The spectacle of a go-ahead Hinduism, dreaming of self-government and playing with its ancient gods, clad in the vesture of democracy, dazed the conservative Muslim, who was just shaking himself free from the paralyzing grip of the past. He realized that the spirit of the fight had changed. The weapons were new and so were the ways to use those weapons. He felt as if he was being treated as an alien, as a meddlesome freak, who had wantonly interfered with the course of Indian history. Strange incidents were raked up from his long and eventful career, which he was called upon to justify. He had come as a conqueror and had freely given to India the best that was in him. With the loss of empire he felt as if he were to lose his self-respect as well. The "communal patriots" amongst the Hindus treated him as a prisoner in the dock, and loudly complained of him as an impossible factor in the scheme of India's future. Then, again, the new conditions of political success alarmed him. It was to him a painful education to learn that wisdom consisted in lung-power multiplied by the millions and political strength lay in the counting of heads. His community was small in numbers, ignorant, and poor. He was a negligible quantity in the visions of the Hindu "patriot." His religion and history had given him an individuality which he was very loth to lose. As a consequence he drew within his shell and nursed ideals of communal patriotism. He has been scared into this attitude in self-defense. The Hindu "communal patriot" has an advantage over him in the choice of his formulas. While the former boldly walks a road in the garb of India's champion, the latter, less mobile and more unfortunate, formulates even his unimpeachable right to live in terms of apology.

This is, in broad outline, the atmosphere in which the Hindu-Muslim problem has taken its rise. The race antagonism owes its virulence mainly to a false reading of history. The past has flung out its dead hand to paralyze the present. Practical issues of politics are swayed by the foolish but eminently real resentment of the Hindu "patriot" at the political domination of the Muslim in a bygone period of Indian history and by the equally foolish yet powerful sentiment of the Muslim about his vanished power and prestige and empire. The temper of the "communal patriots" has grown aggressive and bellicose on the one hand, and suspicious, sensitive, and irritable on the other. The Hindu tries to ignore the Muslim, the latter retaliates by assuming that all "nationalist" desires are a snare, if not a delusion. Yet the fiction is industriously kept up about the identity of interests, and the organs of Hindu "nationalism" use facile phrases about Indian unity, as if there existed no vital differences of feeling, temper, ideals, and standpoints. The first step towards the solution of the problem is to recognize honestly and courageously that the problem in all its magnitude and many-sided aspects exists. We must clearly recognize that the Hindus and the Muslims dwell apart in thought and sentiment, that the Hindu "patriot" is at times intolerant and grasping, that he dreams of the India that is to be as a modern shrine he is going to build for his gods, that the Muslim is getting a little too clannish, that he is only dimly aware of what it means to feel a generous enthusiasm for such great secular causes as self-government and nationality, and that he broods over his loss and moves about in a world of unsubstantial shadows. It is when we have recognized all this that any progress in the direction of Hindu-Muslim *rapprochement* will become possible. The Muslim who imagines his community to be entirely free of blame is either a man of simple texture or a politician of a very complex type. The Hindu who talks of his community as wholly innocent must be talking with his tongue in his cheek.

Let us look at the facts. To take an important instance, separate representation of the Muslims in the legislative chambers of the country has been denounced with a vehemence that must have struck even the Hindu "communal patriots" themselves as a little tactless and crude. With the existing state of racial feeling, the cry for mixed electorates cannot but alarm the Muslims and create in their minds a strong suspicion of Hindu motives. . . . It is because the immediate, the practical issues of the day divide the Hindus and the Muslims that communal representation has become a cardinal feature in the political evolution of the country. If the Hindu "patriot" is not thinking of an exclusively Hindu India, if he wants the Muslims to exercise their due influence on Indian affairs his demand for the mixed electorates is an insoluble riddle. . . . Let us take another question which is said to have been a powerful factor in the growth of racial bitterness. Cows have been responsible for many riots in the country and many riotous campaigns in the Press. If only the Muslims gave up eating beef, we are told by many well-meaning persons, the Hindu-Muslim relations would grow in good will and cordiality at a bound. . . . It is sometimes forgotten that to a non-Hindu a cow is an ordinary quadruped and no more. A Muslim who eats beef does so on the score of its comparative cheapness. It is not possible that the Hindu, while retaining all his reverence for the animal, should leave others to their own notions of its utility, as long as they are not wantonly offensive? The educated Hindu who assures us that cow-killing lies at the root of racial bitterness makes rather a large demand on our credulity. India may be in varying stages of development from the twelfth century onward, but the sense of proportion of her educated sons is surely quite abreast of the twentieth's.

We need not multiply instances to show how the attitude of the Hindu "communal patriots" has alarmed the Muslims and driven them into a comparative isolation. The walls of separation can be broken down only if a radical change takes place in the conceptions of communal duty and patriotism. The responsibility of the Hindus is much greater in the matter, because they are more powerful and have sometimes used their strength with strange disregard to consequences. The Muslims stand aloof because they are afraid of being completely swallowed up. Any true patriot of India working for the evolution of Indian nationality will have to accept the communal individuality of the Muslims as the basis of his constructive effort. This is the irreducible factor of the situation, and the politician who ignores it has no conception of the task that awaits India's statesmen. People talk sometimes of the need of the Muslims joining hands with the Hindus, because some incidents in contemporary history have not been exactly to their liking. They conceive of Muslim "policy" as something wholly apart from Muslim interests, entirely unrelated to contemporary facts and past history, something necessary for a bargain, a toy that one might have for the mere fun of politics. Soft-headed and some self-advertising folk have gone about proclaiming that the Muslims should join the Congress because the government had revoked the Partition of Bengal or because Persia and Turkey are in trouble. We were simply amused at this irresponsible fatuity. But when a responsible body like the London Branch of the All-India Muslim League talks of closer cooperation between the Hindus and Muslims because the Muslims of Tripoli and Persia have been the victims of European aggressions, we realize for the first time that even sane and level-headed men can run off at a tangent and confuse the issues. What has the Muslim situation abroad to do with the conditions of the Indian Muslims? Either their interests come actually into conflict with those of the Hindus, or they have been all along guilty of a great political meanness and hypocrisy. Has the Indian situation undergone a change? Are the Hindu "communal patriots" less militant today and have they grown more considerate and careful about Muslim sentiments? Have the questions that really divide the two communities lost their force and meaning? If not, then the problem remains exactly where it was at any time in recent Indian history. Boards of arbitration, peace syndicates and solemn pacts about cows cannot solve it any more than we can by a spell of occult words control the winds and the tides. The communal sentiment and temper must change, and interests must grow identical before the Hindus and the Muslims can be welded into a united nationality. The problem is great, in fact, one of the greatest known to history. None, however, need despair, as the influences of education, and the leveling, liberalizing tendencies of the times are bound to succeed in creating political individuality out of the diversity of creed and race. Any attempt to impose artificial unity is sure to end in failure, if not in disaster.

The Muslim and Urdu

One of the most sensitive issues which developed with the rise of Indian nationalism arose over the drive for unification of language and script, which some considered a prerequisite to greater unity of thought and action. As a Muslim, Muhammad Alī was deeply concerned over the fate of Islamic culture and religion if the common language of the Muslim minority should be set aside. In this article he deals with the question of linguistic nationalism which even today is one of the most serious unresolved problems of independent India and Pakistan.

[From Muhammad Alī, *Select Writings* . . . , p. 40–43]

The question then arises, what shall be the fate of Urdu? It is our hope that there will always be a body of Hindu lovers of literature who will not willingly let it die. But our fear is that the tidal wave of a narrow and aggressive politics may sweep them away also, and party passions may prove too much for poetic sensibility. Prudence does not sanction an indolent optimism. But another question arises. Why not let Urdu be swept away altogether? Why not let that share the hecatomb of many good things which the "nationalism" of today has ordered? Let it also be the peace offering of Muslim India to the insatiable goddess of numbers!

The answer to this question, suggested as it is by the policy of working on the lines of least resistance, cannot be given till we have examined fully what Urdu now means to [the] Muslims of India. It will not perhaps be contradicted that Urdu is the vernacular of the Muslims of Northern India, if we exclude the portions of the North-West Frontier Province where Pushtu is mostly spoken. In the United Provinces, whatever language may be the vernacular of the Hindus, Urdu is undoubtedly the vernacular of the Muslims. In the Punjab, too, although Punjabi is often spoken at home, Urdu is the written language and the language of refined intercourse, while in Eastern Punjab, in which Delhi and its neighboring districts are included, Urdu is, of course, the only vernacular. In Behar, Rajputana, Central India, and the Central Provinces, Urdu is the mother tongue of the Muslims. Even in the South, in the Dominions of His Highness the Nizam, Urdu is the vernacular of the Muslims. There now remain for consideration the extreme South and Eastern and Western India. In these parts Muslims are somewhat sharply divided into two classes, the descendants of Muslim officials who were sent from Delhi to the outlying provinces, and were originally, at least, of non-Indian extraction; and the Neo-Muslims, the converts whose Indian origin is beyond doubt and the period of whose ancestors is often not very remote.

Those who belong to the former class still retain Urdu, which they brought from Delhi as their mother tongue, although they have learnt the commoner languages of their respective provinces. In Gujarat, for instance, they speak and write in Gujarati like the best of Hindus, but one would never hear them converse amongst themselves and at home in anything but what is known there as Mussalmani and is, of course, no other than Urdu as spoken in Gujarat. Urdu, then is the language in which they think although they may carry on business in the languages used generally by the Hindus of their province, such as Gujarati, Marathi, Sindhi, Kachhi, or Bengali.

Those who come under the latter category have retained the use of the vernacular which their Hindi ancestors used before and which their neighbors use now, for instance, the Khojas of Bombay speak Kachhi and write in Gujarati. Exceptions, of course, exist, such as the well-known and highly cultured Tayebji family of Bombay in which Urdu has been deliberately adopted as the language of daily intercourse, although Gujarati has not been given up for business purposes. But it may safely be asserted that, as a general rule, the literates among these Neo-Muslims have learnt some Urdu partly for purposes of intercourse with other Muslims and partly for religious purposes. For, incredible as it may seem, in spite of the fact that until recently and for long centuries Persian was the court language and the language of literary composition and Arabic was the classical language which the Muslims studied both for general culture and religious purposes, Urdu has been enriched during the last two generations by translations of almost every important work on Muslim theology. The Qur'ān and the Traditions and Commentaries have all been translated by more than one writer into Urdu.

If Urdu is to be sacrificed, we deprive millions of Muslims—and these the best of Muslims, if heredity counts for anything—of their tongue in

which they lisped as children and in which they think today. In addition
to this we deprive them and the remaining millions of Muslims of the
consolation which their religion has to offer to them. For our part we
think it is the loss to the latter whose mother tongue is not Urdu that is ir-
reparable. It is possible for Muslims, as it is being made possible for
Hindus in Northern India, to give up the use of a familiar Persian word
or Arabic expression and substitute for it a strange word or expression
from Sanskrit for ordinary purposes of life. Time and use would make
strange phrases familiar and time and disuse would make familiar
phrases strange. But what of the familiar word and phrase of religious
literature? Language is the expression of thought, and where thought
differs so radically as in Islam and Hinduism can the same language
express it adequately in each case? Consider it whichever way we like,
it has to be confessed in the end that Urdu is [the] irreducible minimum
to which the most compromising Muslims would consent. Not that there
is no room in Urdu for a longer admixture of Sanskrit words, but they
can glide in naturally and smoothly; they cannot be pushed by force. If
Muslims study Sanskrit in larger numbers than they do today, they are
bound to use a larger number of such words. . . . Nor would there be
a keen desire on the part of the Muslims to enrich Urdu with such words
if the Hindus follow the opposite policy of excluding words of Arabic
and Persian origin. . . .

This brings us to the question of a script, though we are concerned here
mainly with that of language. Islam was neither insular nor peninsular,
and if Muslims lacked something in their love for the land they lived in,
they have been charged with a little too much of it for the lands of others.
Their conquest brought them worldly gain and afforded them facilities
for conversion. Just as in the case of European nations today, commerce
follows conquest, in the history of Islam the faith followed the flag. For
a world-wide empire, a common language was an impossibility, and, as
we have shown, Arabic was not imposed on the conquered lands. But a
common script facilitated a common understanding, and today, while
Arabic, Persian, Turki, Pushtu, Urdu, and many other languages are used
by Muslims, the Arabic script is common to all. Herein, again, the irreducible minimum was found by people ready to compromise. Efforts
are now being made in India to have a common script. So long as Islam
remains a world-wide religion and Muslims retain their present sympa-

thies with other Muslims no matter where they be, Indian Muslims cannot give up their present script for Devanāgrī. We have heard a great deal of the scientific character of the latter, but few of its advocates have examined its suitability for transcription of Arabic words, and all seem to ignore the fact that the Arabic script is perhaps the only form of shorthand which is a common blessing for many millions. Granting, for argument's sake, that Devanāgrī is more scientific, does it entitle it to any greater consideration than that which such a shrewd and businesslike nation as the Americans paid to Mr. Roosevelt's short list of phonetically spelt words? And, finally, in the matter of script, even more than in the case of language, the general adoption of Devanāgrī to the exclusion of Arabic character would be to curtail the facilities of intercourse between India and other Asiatic countries.

The only conclusion at which we can arrive is that neither in the matter of language nor in that of script can the Muslims afford to concede more than what they have already done in adopting Urdu as their only vernacular or their second vernacular, and retaining the script that is practically common to the Islamic world. But unless we take practical steps to safeguard the language and the script, both are endangered by the narrow and exclusive "nationalism" which is growing more and more militant every day.

CHAPTER XXVI

TAGORE AND GĀNDHI

Two towering figures dominated the Indian scene in the first half of the twentieth century, overshadowing all rivals in their respective fields of endeavor. Each achieved such international renown that he thereby automatically increased India's prestige abroad. Each in his own way spent many years in the service of his countrymen. And yet there could scarcely be two men more different from one another in temperament and interests. Tagore's nature was that of a poet; Gāndhi's that of a states-man. Tagore's realm was artistic expression; Gāndhi's ethical action. Even the clothes they chose reflected the contrast between them, for Tagore was fond of dressing in flowing silken robes, while Gāndhi wore nothing but the simplest hand-spun garments.

In a sense these two remarkable men brought to their finest fruition the potentialities created in modern India by the engrafting of new pat-terns of thought and action onto various "stems" of traditional culture. Both Tagore and Gāndhi made themselves masters of the English language and were considerably affected by their contact with Western culture. How then can one explain the contrary directions in which their minds developed? Perhaps the distinctive regional cultures in which they grew to manhood affected them most decisively. Cosmopolitan Bengal, where English thought left its deepest imprint, produced the Brāhmo Samāj in whose bosom Tagore was born. Isolated Gujarat, on the opposite side of the subcontinent, and the home of the Vedist Dayānanda, clung longer to the older Vaishnava and Jaina traditions which influenced Gāndhi so deeply.

For whatever reasons, Tagore and Gāndhi certainly disagreed funda-mentally in their diagnoses of India's ills and their prescriptions for her cure. For a time this disagreement clouded their personal friendship, which had dated from 1915 when Tagore had invited Gāndhi, fresh from South Africa, to bring his followers to Shāntiniketan for want of a more congenial temporary haven. Addressing Gāndhi on this occasion as Mahātmā (great soul), Tagore seems to have been the first to use the famous title. Their public controversy over the methods of Gāndhi's noncooperation movement flared up in 1921, and passages from their eloquent debate are reproduced in this chapter. Gāndhi's 1933 fast against untouchability brought about a dramatic reconciliation between the two men, and Gāndhi ended his fast with a sip of fruit juice while Tagore sat nearby. Visiting Shāntiniketan after the poet's death, Gāndhi is said to have remarked that he had begun by thinking that he and Tagore were poles apart, but now believed that in fundamentals they were one.

Jawaharlāl Nehru, who admired both men greatly (perhaps because they served as models for the two sides of his own personality) has written: "Tagore was primarily the man of thought, Gandhi of concentrated and ceaseless activity. Both, in their different ways, had a world outlook, and both were at the same time wholly India. They seemed to represent different but harmonious aspects of India and to complement one another." [1]

RABĪNDRANĀTH TAGORE: POET, EDUCATOR, AND AMBASSADOR TO THE WORLD

The fourteenth of Maharshi Debendranāth Tagore's fifteen children, Rabīndranāth Tagore (1861–1941) grew to manhood in a highly cultured family environment. A number of his brothers and sisters were artistically inclined—one composed music, another staged amateur theatricals, and several contributed to the literary magazine edited by their eldest brother, who was also a philosopher. The venerable Debendranāth gave special attention to his youngest son's education, and after investing him with the brāhmanical sacred thread, took him on an extended pilgrimage to Amritsar and the Himalayas. Rabīndranāth's religious views were decisively shaped by his father's influence.

A steady income from the family's landed estates deprived Rabīndranāth of the necessity of earning his own livelihood, and he was allowed to give up formal studies at the age of thirteen. Living at home, he began to experiment with writing verse. Encouraged by his older

[1] Jawaharlāl Nehru, The Discovery of India, 342–43.

siblings, he went on to win renown at twenty with his first volume of Bengali poems, Bankim Chandra Chatterjee himself hailing their appearance. Year after year his writing matured in style and grew richer in content. Translating into English from the devotional poems written after the death of his wife and three of his five children, he published in 1912 the collection entitled *Gītāñjali* (*Song Offerings*). A year later the world was startled to hear that he had been awarded the Nobel Prize for Literature. Educated India went wild with excitement, sensing that Rabīndranāth had vindicated Indian culture in the eyes of the West. As for the poet, he is said to have cried, "I shall never have any peace again." [1]

Although his prediction proved correct, the ceaseless activity in which he spent the rest of his life was mostly of his own making. He had already founded a school at Shāntiniketan, the rural retreat where his father used to pass days in meditation. He now began to develop there a center of Indian culture, where all the creative and performing arts could thrive in a new birth. In 1921, as a crowning step in his educational work, Tagore opened his Vishva-Bhāratī [2] University at Shāntiniketan, dedicating it to his ideal of world brotherhood and cultural interchange.

Like his father, Rabīndranāth loved to travel, and he seldom refused the many invitations which came to him from all parts of the world. In addition to many tours within India, he lectured on five occasions in the United States, five times in Europe, three times in Japan, and once each in China, South America, Soviet Russia, and Southeast Asia. He made good use of his opportunities to address important audiences by denouncing—especially after the First World War—the evils of nationalism and materialism. Mankind could only save itself from destruction, he declared, by a return to the spiritual values which permeate all religions. Asia, the home of the world's great faiths, lay under a special obligation to lead this religious revival, and to India, the home of both Hinduism and Buddhism, belonged the mission of reawakening herself, Asia, and the world. Although this message, like that of Vivekānanda, stressed India's role as spiritual teacher to mankind, Tagore

[1] E. J. Thompson, *Rabindranath Tagore, His Life and Work*, p. 44.
[2] Translatable as either "universal learning" or "all-India."

never tired of reminding his countrymen that they also needed to learn from the West's vitality and dedicated search for truth.

Through an irony of fate, this preacher of the complementary relationship between Asian and Western cultures returned from a triumphant European tour in 1921 to find Gāndhi leading a mass movement of noncooperation with every aspect of British influence in India, including the prevailing form of English education. Rabīndranāth publicly opposed the Mahātmā and was accordingly accused of taking an "unpatriotic" position. He had already been virtually ostracized for his withdrawal in 1908 from Bengal politics in disgust at the extremist excesses of the anti-Partition agitation. On both occasions he bore his isolation stoically and without yielding his ground, much like the great Bengali whom he considered his spiritual kinsman—Rāmmohun Roy.

Shy and aloof, Tagore was able to look more dispassionately on the events of his time than those who hurled themselves into the struggle against British rule. Reversing Tilak's dictum that social reform diverted and divided the movement for independence, Tagore held that the clamor for political rights distracted men from more fundamental tasks such as erasing caste barriers, reconciling Hindus and Muslims, uplifting the poor and helpless villagers, and liberating men's minds and bodies from a host of self-made but unnecessary burdens.

Right down to his eightieth year, Tagore never lost his childlike wonderment at the variety and beauty of the creation and he expressed his delight with life in a ceaseless outpouring of poetry, prose, drama, and song. By making the speech of the common people the medium for his masterly style he revolutionized and revitalized Bengali literature. His interests, although basically esthetic, were truly universal; in his seventies he wrote a textbook on elementary science which explained the theory of relativity and the working of the solar system. In an age of growing xenophobia he sought to keep India's windows open on the world. For his creativity, his breadth of vision, and his zeal in championing man's freedom from arbitrary restraints—whether social, political or religious—Tagore deserves comparison with the great artist-philosophers of Renaissance humanism in the West.

RABĪNDRANĀTH TAGORE
The Sunset of the Century

Written originally in Bengali on the last day of the nineteenth century, this poem embodied Tagore's protest against the aggressive nationalism which brought on the Boer War then raging in South Africa. He implied that by patient cultivation of spiritual virtues India and "the East" would take their proper place in world civilization after the militant power of Western nationalism had ceased to control mankind.

[From Tagore, *Nationalism*, 133–35]

I

The last sun of the century sets amidst the blood-red clouds of the West and the whirlwind of hatred.

The naked passion of self-love of Nations, in its drunken delirium of greed, is dancing to the clash of steel and the howling verses of vengeance.

2

The hungry self of the Nation shall burst in a violence of fury from its own shameless feeding.

For it has made the world its food.

And licking it, crunching it, and swallowing it in big morsels,

It swells and swells,

Till in the midst of its unholy feast descends the sudden shaft of heaven piercing its heart of grossness.

3

The crimson glow of light on the horizon is not the light of thy dawn of peace, my Motherland.

It is the glimmer of the funeral pyre burning to ashes the vast flesh—the self-love of the Nation—dead under its own excess.

Thy morning waits behind the patient dark of the East,

Meek and silent.

4

Keep watch, India.

Bring your offerings of worship for that sacred sunrise.

Let the first hymn of its welcome sound in your voice and sing

"Come, Peace, thou daughter of God's own great suffering.

Come with thy treasure of contentment, the sword of fortitude,
And meekness crowning thy forehead."

5

Be not ashamed, my brothers, to stand before the proud and the powerful
With your white robe of simpleness.
Let your crown be of humility, your freedom the freedom of the soul.
Build God's throne daily upon the ample bareness of your poverty
And know that what is huge is not great and pride is not everlasting.

"Where the Mind Is Without Fear"

One of the hundred-odd poems which comprise the prize-winning volume
Gītāñjali listed in a rising crescendo Tagore's ambitions for his native India.
    [From *Collected Poems and Plays of Rabindranath Tagore*, p. 16]

Where the mind is without fear and the head is held high;
Where knowledge is free;
Where the world has not been broken up into fragments by narrow
    domestic walls;
Where words come out from the depth of truth;
Where tireless striving stretches its arms towards perfection;
Where the clear stream of reason has not lost its way into the dreary
    desert sand of dead habit;
Where the mind is led forward by thee into everwidening thought and
    action—
Into that heaven of freedom, my Father, let my country awake.

Jana Gana Mana

In addition to composing the melody for the famous *Bande Mātaram* song
in 1912, Tagore wrote both words and music for the hymn *Jana Gana Mana*
(The Mind of the Multitude of the People), which after independence became the national anthem of India.
    [From Sykes, *Rabindranath Tagore*, p. 69]

Thou art the ruler of the minds of all people,
    Thou Dispenser of India's destiny.
Thy name rouses the hearts
    Of the Punjab, Sind, Gujrat, and Maratha,

Of Dravid, Orissa, and Bengal.
It echoes in the hills of the Vindhyas and Himālayas,
    Mingles in the music of Jumna and Ganges,
    And is chanted by the waves of the Indian sea.
They pray for Thy blessing and sing Thy praise,
    Thou Dispenser of India's destiny,
    Victory, Victory, Victory to Thee.

The Evils of Nationalism

Lecturing to American audiences in 1917, Tagore denounced the nationalistic
trend of the times. Crucial to his argument was the distinction he drew between the Western nation and the spirit of the West.
    [From Tagore, *Nationalism*, pp. 18–22]

Before the Nation came to rule over us we had other governments
which were foreign, and these, like all governments, had some element
of the machine in them. But the difference between them and the government by the Nation is like the difference between the hand-loom and
the power-loom. In the products of the hand-loom the magic of man's
living fingers finds its expression, and its hum harmonizes with the
music of life. But the power-loom is relentlessly lifeless and accurate
and monotonous in its production.

We must admit that during the personal government of the former
days there have been instances of tyranny, injustice, and extortion. They
caused sufferings and unrest from which we are glad to be rescued. The
protection of law is not only a boon, but it is a valuable lesson to us. It
is teaching us the discipline which is necessary for the stability of civilization and for continuity of progress. We are realizing through it that
there is a universal standard of justice to which all men, irrespective of
their caste and color, have their equal claim.

This reign of law in our present government in India has established
order in this vast land inhabited by peoples different in their races and
customs. It has made it possible for these peoples to come in closer
touch with one another and cultivate a communion of aspiration.

But this desire for a common bond of comradeship among the different races of India has been the work of the spirit of the West, not
that of the Nation of the West. Wherever in Asia the people have re-

ceived the true lesson of the West it is in spite of the Western Nation. Only because Japan had been able to resist the dominance of this Western Nation could she acquire the benefit of the Western civilization in fullest measure. Though China has been poisoned at the very spring of her moral and physical life by this Nation, her struggle to receive the best lessons of the West may yet be successful if not hindered by the Nation. It was only the other day that Persia woke up from her age-long sleep at the call of the West to be instantly trampled into stillness by the Nation. The same phenomenon prevails in this country also, where the people are hospitable, but the Nation has proved itself to be otherwise, making an Eastern guest feel humiliated to stand before you as a member of the humanity of his own motherland.

In India we are suffering from this conflict between the spirit of the West and the Nation of the West. The benefit of the Western civilization is doled out to us in a miserly measure by the Nation, which tries to regulate the degree of nutrition as near the zero-point of vitality as possible. The portion of education allotted to us is so raggedly insufficient that it ought to outrage the sense of decency of a Western humanity. We have seen in these countries how the people are encouraged and trained and given every facility to fit themselves for the great movements of commerce and industry spreading over the world, while in India the only assistance we get is merely to be jeered at by the Nation for lagging behind. While depriving us of our opportunities and reducing our education to the minimum required for conducting a foreign government, this Nation pacifies its conscience by calling us names, by sedulously giving currency to the arrogant cynicism that the East is East and the West is West and never the twain shall meet. If we must believe our schoolmaster in his taunt that, after nearly two centuries of his tutelage, India not only remains unfit for self-government but unable to display originality in her intellectual attainments, must we ascribe it to something in the nature of Western culture and our inherent incapacity to receive it or to the judicious niggardliness of the Nation that has taken upon itself the white man's burden of civilizing the East? That Japanese people have some qualities which we lack we may admit, but that our intellect is naturally unproductive compared to theirs we cannot accept even from them whom it is dangerous for us to contradict.

The truth is that the spirit of conflict and conquest is at the origin and in the center of Western nationalism; its basis is not social cooperation. It has evolved a perfect organization of power, but not spiritual idealism. It is like the pack of predatory creatures that must have its victims. With all its heart it cannot bear to see its hunting-grounds converted into cultivated fields. In fact, these nations are fighting among themselves for the extension of their victims and their reserve forests. Therefore the Western Nation acts like a dam to check the free flow of Western civilization into the country of the No-Nation. Because this civilization is the civilization of power, therefore it is exclusive, it is naturally unwilling to open its sources of power to those whom it has selected for its purposes of exploitation.

But all the same moral law is the law of humanity, and the exclusive civilization which thrives upon others who are barred from its benefit carries its own death-sentence in its moral limitations. The slavery that it gives rise to unconsciously drains its own love of freedom dry. The helplessness with which it weighs down its world of victims exerts its force of gravitation every moment upon the power that creates it. And the greater part of the world which is being denuded of its self-sustaining life by the Nation will one day become the most terrible of all its burdens, ready to drag it down into the bottom of destruction. Whenever Power removes all checks from its path to make its career easy, it triumphantly rides into its ultimate crash of death. Its moral brake becomes slacker every day without its knowing it, and its slippery path of ease becomes its path of doom.

Gāndhi—The Frail Man of Spirit

Tagore was lecturing in Europe and America when Gāndhi started his first great noncooperation campaign. From this distance the poet began to see the significance of Gāndhi's methods, and his admiration is shown in the following letter to his friend C. F. Andrews.

[From Andrews, *Letters to a Friend*, pp. 127–28]

Chicago, March 2d, 1921

Your last letter gives wonderful news about our students in Calcutta.[1] I hope that this spirit of sacrifice and willingness to suffer will grow in

[1] Referring to the boycott of schools and colleges by thousands of students.

strength; for to achieve this is an end in itself. This is the true freedom! Nothing is of higher value—be it national wealth or independence— than disinterested faith in ideals, in the moral greatness of man.

The West has its unshakable faith in material strength and prosperity; and therefore, however loud grows the cry for peace and disarmament, its ferocity growls louder, gnashing its teeth and lashing its tail in impatience. It is like a fish, hurt by the pressure of the flood, planning to fly in the air. Certainly the idea is brilliant, but it is not possible for a fish to realize. We, in India, have to show the world what is that truth which not only makes disarmament possible but turns it into strength.

The truth that moral force is a higher power than brute force will be proved by the people who are unarmed. Life, in its higher development, has thrown off its tremendous burden of armor and a prodigious quantity of flesh, till man has become the conqueror of the brute world. The day is sure to come when the frail man of spirit, completely unhampered by airfleets and dreadnoughts, will prove that the meek are to inherit the earth.

It is in the fitness of things that Mahātmā Gāndhi, frail in body and devoid of all material resources, should call up the immense power of the meek that has been waiting in the heart of the destitute and insulted humanity of India. The destiny of India has chosen for its ally the power of soul, and not that of muscle. And she is to raise the history of man from the muddy level of physical conflict to the higher moral altitude.

What is *Swarāj!* [2] It is māyā; [3] it is like a mist that will vanish, leaving no stain on the radiance of the Eternal. However we may delude ourselves with the phrases learnt from the West, *Swarāj* is not our objective. Our fight is a spiritual fight—it is for Man. We are to emancipate Man from the meshes that he himself has woven round him—these organizations of national egoism. The butterfly will have to be persuaded that the freedom of the sky is of higher value than the shelter of the cocoon. If we can defy the strong, the armed, the wealthy—revealing to the world the power of the immortal spirit—the whole castle of the Giant Flesh will vanish in the void. And then Man will find his *Swarāj*.

We, the famished ragged ragamuffins of the East, are to win freedom for all humanity. We have no word for "Nation" in our language. When

[2] Self-rule. [3] Illusion.

we borrow this word from other people, it never fits us. For we are to make our league with *Nārāyan*,[4] and our triumph will not give us anything but victory itself: victory for God's world. I have seen the West; I covet not the unholy feast in which she revels every moment, growing more and more bloated and red and dangerously delirious. Not for us is this mad orgy of midnight, with lighted torches, but awakenment in the serene light of the morning.

Gāndhi versus Truth

Even before Tagore returned to India in 1921, he saw that Gāndhi's nationalism clashed with his own internationalism. A meeting between the two at Tagore's Calcutta house failed to resolve their differences. Finally, Tagore published an article entitled "The Call of Truth," expressing his criticisms of Gāndhi's narrow conception of *Swarāj* and the way to achieve it.

[From Tagore, "The Call of Truth," in *Modern Review*, XXX, 4, 429–33]

The Mahātmā has won the heart of India with his love; for that we have all acknowledged his sovereignty. He has given us a vision of the shakti [1] of truth; for that our gratitude to him is unbounded. We read about truth in books: we talk about it: but it is indeed a red-letter day, when we see it face to face. Rare is the moment, in many a long year, when such good fortune happens. We can make and break Congresses every other day. It is at any time possible for us to stump the country preaching politics in English. But the golden rod which can awaken our country in Truth and Love is not a thing which can be manufactured by the nearest goldsmith. To the wielder of that rod our profound salutation! But if, having seen truth, our belief in it is not confirmed, what is the good of it all? Our mind must acknowledge the truth of the intellect, just as our heart does the truth of love. No Congress or other outside institution succeeded in touching the heart of India. It was roused only by the touch of love. Having had such a clear vision of this wonderful power of Truth, are we to cease to believe in it, just where the attainment of *Swarāj* is concerned? Has the truth, which was needed in the process of awakenment, to be got rid of in the process of achievement? . . .

From our master, the Mahātmā—may our devotion to him never grow

---

[4] The godlike element in man.   [1] Divine creative power.

less!—we must learn the truth of love in all its purity, but the science and art of building up *Swarāj* is a vast subject. Its pathways are difficult to traverse and take time. For this task, aspiration and emotion must be there, but no less must study and thought be there likewise. For it, the economist must think, the mechanic must labor, the educationist and statesman must teach and contrive. In a word, the mind of the country must exert itself in all directions. Above all, the spirit of inquiry throughout the whole country must be kept intact and untrammelled, its mind not made timid or inactive by compulsion, open or secret.

We know from past experience that it is not any and every call to which the country responds. It is because no one has yet been able to unite in Yoga [2] all the forces of the country in the work of its creation, that so much time has been lost over and over again. And we have been kept waiting and waiting for him who has the right and the power to make the call upon us. In the old forests of India, our gurus, in the fullness of their vision of the Truth had sent forth such a call saying: "As the rivers flow on their downward course, as the months flow on to the year, so let all seekers after truth come from all sides." The initiation into Truth of that day has borne fruit, undying to this day, and the voice of its message still rings in the ears of the world.

Why should not our Guru of today, who would lead us on the paths of Karma, send forth such a call? Why should he not say: "Come ye from all sides and be welcome. Let all the forces of the land be brought into action, for then alone shall the country awake. Freedom is in complete awakening, in full self-expression." God has given the Mahātmā the voice that can call, for in him there is the Truth. Why should this not be our long-awaited opportunity?

But his call came to one narrow field alone. To one and all he simply says: Spin and weave, spin and weave. Is this the call: "Let all seekers after truth come from all sides"? Is this the call of the New Age to new creation? When nature called to the bee to take refuge in the narrow life of the hive, millions of bees responded to it for the sake of efficiency, and accepted the loss of sex in consequence. But this sacrifice by way of self-atrophy led to the opposite of freedom. Any country, the people of which can agree to become neuters for the sake of some temptation, or command, carries within itself its own prison-house. To spin

---

[2] Here used in the sense of "a harmonious union."

is easy, therefore for all men it is an imposition hard to bear. The call to the ease of mere efficiency is well enough for the Bee. The wealth of power that is Man's can only become manifest when his utmost is claimed.

Sparta tried to gain strength by narrowing herself down to a particular purpose, but she did not win. Athens sought to attain perfection by opening herself out in all her fullness—and she did win. Her flag of victory still flies at the masthead of man's civilization. It is admitted that European military camps and factories are stunting man, that their greed is cutting man down to the measure of their own narrow purpose, that for these reasons joylessness darkly lowers over the West. But if man be stunted by big machines, the danger of his being stunted by small machines must not be lost sight of. The charkha[3] in its proper place can do no harm, but will rather do much good. But where, by reason of failure to acknowledge the differences in man's temperament, it is in the wrong place, there thread can only be spun at the cost of a great deal of the mind itself. Mind is no less valuable than cotton thread.

Some are objecting: "We do not propose to curb our minds forever, but only for a time." But why should it be even for a time? Is it because within a short time spinning will give us *Swarāj?* But where is the argument for this? *Swarāj* is not concerned with our apparel only —it cannot be established on cheap clothing; its foundation is in the mind, which, with its diverse powers and its confidence in those powers, goes on all the time creating *Swarāj* for itself. In no country in the world is the building up of *Swarāj* completed. In some part or other of every nation, some lurking greed or illusion still perpetuates bondage. And the root of such bondage is always within the mind. Where then, I ask again, is the argument, that in our country *Swarāj* can be brought about by everyone engaging for a time in spinning? A mere statement, in lieu of argument, will surely never do. If once we consent to receive fate's oracle from human lips, that will add once more to the torments of our slavery, and not the least one either. If nothing but oracles will serve to move us, oracles will have to be manufactured, morning, noon and night, for the sake of urgent needs, and all other voices would be defeated. Those for whom authority is needed in place of reason will invariably accept despotism in place of freedom. It is like cutting at the

[3] Spinning wheel.

root of a tree while pouring water on the top. This is not a new thing, I know. We have enough magic in the country—magical revelation, magical healing, and all kinds of divine intervention in mundane affairs. That is exactly why I am so anxious to reinstate reason on its throne. As I have said before, God himself has given the mind sovereignty in the material world. And I say today, that only those will be able to get and keep *Swarāj* in the material world who have realized the dignity of self-reliance and self-mastery in the spiritual world, those whom no temptation, no delusion, can induce to surrender the dignity of intellect into the keeping of others.

Consider the burning of cloth, heaped up before the very eyes of our motherland shivering and ashamed in her nakedness. What is the nature of the call to do this? Is it not another instance of a magical formula? The question of using or refusing cloth of a particular manufacture belongs mainly to economic science. The discussion of the matter by our countrymen should have been in the language of economics. If the country has really come to such a habit of mind that precise thinking has become impossible for it, then our very first fight should be against such a fatal habit, to the temporary exclusion of all else if need be. Such a habit would clearly be the original sin from which all our ills are flowing. But far from this, we take the course of confirming ourselves in it by relying on the magical formula that foreign cloth is "impure." Thus economics is bundled out and a fictitious moral dictum dragged into its place. . . .

The command to burn our foreign clothes has been laid on us. I, for one, am unable to obey it. Firstly, because I conceive it to be my very first duty to put up a valiant fight against this terrible habit of blindly obeying orders, and this fight can never be carried on by our people being driven from one injunction to another. Secondly, I feel that the clothes to be burnt are not mine, but belong to those who most sorely need them. If those who are going naked should have given us the mandate to burn, it would, at least, have been a case of self-immolation and the crime of incendiarism would not lie at our door. But how can we expiate the sin of the forcible destruction of clothes which might have gone to women whose nakedness is actually keeping them prisoners, unable to stir out of the privacy of their homes?

I have said repeatedly and must repeat once more that we cannot afford to lose our mind for the sake of any external gain. Where Mahātmā Gāndhi has declared war against the tyranny of the machine which is oppressing the whole world, we are all enrolled under his banner. But we must refuse to accept as our ally the illusion-haunted, magic-ridden, slave-mentality that is at the root of all the poverty and insult under which our country groans. Here is the enemy itself, on whose defeat alone *Swarāj* within and without can come to us.

The time, moreover, has arrived when we must think of one thing more, and that is this. The awakening of India is a part of the awakening of the world. The door of the New Age has been flung open at the trumpet blast of a great war. We have read in the *Mahābhārata* how the day of self-revelation had to be preceded by a year of retirement. The same has happened in the world today. Nations had attained nearness to each other without being aware of it, that is to say, the outside fact was there, but it had not penetrated into the mind. At the shock of the war, the truth of it stood revealed to mankind. The foundation of modern, that is Western, civilization was shaken; and it has become evident that the convulsion is neither local nor temporary, but has traversed the whole earth and will last until the shocks between man and man, which have extended from continent to continent, can be brought to rest, and a harmony be established.

From now onward, any nation which takes an isolated view of its own country will run counter to the spirit of the New Age, and know no peace. From now onward, the anxiety that each country has for its own safety must embrace the welfare of the world. . . .

I have condemned, in unsparing terms, the present form and scope of the League of Nations and the Indian Reform Councils. I therefore feel certain that there will be no misunderstanding when I state that, even in these, I find signs of the Time Spirit, which is moving the heart of the West. Although the present form is unacceptable, yet there is revealed an aspiration, which is towards the truth, and this aspiration must not be condemned. In this morning of the world's awakening, if in only our own national striving, there is no response to its universal aspiration, that will betoken the poverty of our spirit. I do not say for a moment that we should belittle the work immediately to hand. But when 'the bird is roused by the dawn, all its awakening is not absorbed in its search for food. Its wings respond unweariedly to the call of the sky, its throat pours forth songs for joy of the new light. Universal humanity has sent us its call today. Let our mind respond in its own language; for response is the only true sign of life. When of old we were immersed in the politics of dependence on others, our chief business was the compilation of others' shortcomings. Now that we have decided to dissociate our politics from dependence, are we still to establish and maintain it on the same recital of others' sins? The state of mind so engendered will only raise the dust of angry passion, obscuring the greater world from our vision, and urge us more and more to take futile short cuts for the satisfaction of our passions. It is a sorry picture of India, which we shall display if we fail to realize for ourselves the greater India. This picture will have no light. It will have in the foreground only the business side of our aspiration. Mere business talent, however, has never created anything.

In the West, a real anxiety and effort of their higher mind to rise superior to business considerations is beginning to be seen. I have come across many there whom this desire has imbued with the true spirit of the sannyasin,[4] making them renounce their home-world in order to achieve the unity of man, by destroying the bondage of nationalism; men who have within their own soul realized the advaita [5] of humanity. Many such have I seen in England who have accepted persecution and contumely from their fellow-countrymen in their struggles to free other peoples from the oppression of their own country's pride of power. Some of them are amongst us here in India. I have seen sannyāsins too in France—Romain Rolland for one, who is an outcast from his own people. I have also seen them in the minor countries of Europe. I have watched the faces of European students all aglow with the hope of a united mankind, prepared manfully to bear all the blows, cheerfully to submit to all the insults, of the present age for the glory of the age to come. And are we alone to be content with telling the beads of negation, harping on others' faults and proceeding with the erection of *Swarāj* on a foundation of quarrelsomeness? Shall it not be our first duty in the dawn to remember Him, who is One, who is without distinction of class or color, and who with his varied shakti makes true provision for the inherent need of each and every class; and to pray to the Giver of Wisdom to unite us all in right understanding.

[4] Religious mendicant.   [5] Non-duality.

The Spirit of Asia

Like Keshub Chunder Sen and Swāmī Vivekānanda, Tagore believed that all
Asia was united by a profound spirituality from which the more materialistic
nations of the West could benefit. In his lectures of 1924 to audiences in China
he stressed Asia's need to find her own soul, in order that her message to mankind might not perish.

[From Tagore, *Talks in China*, pp. 64, 66–67, 156–57]

My friends, I have come to ask you to reopen the channel of communion
which I hope is still there; for though overgrown with weeds of oblivion
its lines can still be traced. I shall consider myself fortunate if, through
this visit, China comes nearer to India and India to China—for no political or commercial purpose, but for disinterested human love and for
nothing else. . . .

In Asia we must seek our strength in union, in an unwavering faith in
righteousness, and never in the egotistic spirit of separateness and self-
assertion. It is from the heart of the East that the utterance has sprung
forth: "The meek shall inherit the earth." For the meek never waste
energy in the display of insolence, but are firmly established in true prosperity through harmony with the All.

In Asia we must unite, not through some mechanical method of organization, but through a spirit of true sympathy. The organized power
of the machine is ready to smite and devour us, from which we must
be rescued by that living power of spirit which grows into strength, not
through mere addition, but through organic assimilation. . . .

It will never do for the Orient to trail behind the West like an overgrown appendix, vainly trying to lash the sky in defiance of the divine.
For humanity this will not only be a useless excess, but a disappointment
and a deception. For if the East ever tries to duplicate Western life, the
duplicate is bound to be a forgery.

The West has no doubt overwhelmed us with its flood of commodities,
tourists, machine guns, school masters, and a religion which is great, but
whose followers are intent upon lengthening the list of its recruits, and
not upon following it in details that bring no profit, or in practices that
are inconvenient. But one great service the West has done us by bringing
the force of its living mind to bear upon our life; it has stirred our

thoughts into activity. For its mind is great; its intellectual life has in its center intellectual probity, the standard of truth.

The first effect of our mind being startled from its sleep was to make it intensely conscious of what was before it; but now that the surprise of awakening has subsided, the time has come to know what is within. We are beginning to know ourselves. We are finding our own mind, because the mind of the West claims our attention.

I have no doubt in my own mind that in the East our principal characteristic is not to set too high a price upon success through gaining advantage, but upon self-realization through fulfilling our dharma, our ideals. Let the awakening of the East impel us consciously to discover the essential and the universal meaning of our own civilization, to remove the debris from its path, to rescue it from the bondage of stagnation that produces impurities, to make it a great channel of communication between all human races.

M. K. GĀNDHI: INDIA'S "GREAT SOUL"

Known to the world as the greatest Indian of modern times, Mohandās Karamchand Gāndhi (1869–1948) was more a man of action, a karmayogin, than a thinker. He himself declared, when asked for his message to mankind, "My life is my message." Nevertheless, in working out the philosophy which sustained him through a lifetime of striving, Gāndhi wove together and gave new strength to many strands of both Indian and Western thought.

From his pious mother, young Mohandās imbibed the devotional spirit of Vaishnavite Hinduism. Western secular influences were weak and Jain influences strong in his native Gujarat, and the importance of ahimsā (noninjury or nonviolence to all creatures) and ascetic self-discipline was impressed on him by the examples of his mother, who fasted frequently, and of Jain friends of the family. Although the Gāndhis belonged to the vaishya caste and were originally merchants, Mohandās' father, uncle, and grandfather had served as prime ministers to several small princely states.

A youngest son, and an unusually bright and ambitious youth, Mohandās resolved to study law in order to follow in his father's footsteps.

By the time he sailed for England at eighteen, leaving behind his wife and infant son, his mind had been deeply and permanently molded by traditional Indian influences.

His three years as a student in London turned Gāndhi into a Westernized and nattily dressed young barrister. His associations with Englishmen were pleasant: he became an active member of the London Vegetarian Society and was introduced by English theosophists to the *Bhagavad Gītā* in Sir Edwin Arnold's translation. He studied the New Testament and often attended church in order to hear sermons by the best preachers of the day. He returned to Gujarāt at twenty-one, convinced that "next to India, I would rather live in London than in any other place in the world." [1]

After two years of unsuccessful law practice, Gāndhi was called to South Africa to help a Gujarātī Muslim merchant with a court case. Insisting on traveling first class, he was shoved out of carriages and beaten by white South Africans. These brutal encounters with racial intolerance came as a great shock to him after his close relations with English friends in London. He decided to stay on in South Africa to help the Indians there fight for their rights. To unite the disorganized Indian community he founded the Natal Indian Congress. At twenty-seven he toured India to enlist support for the cause he had made his own. On this mission he met Banerjea, Rānade, Gokhale, and Tilak, and felt so drawn to Gokhale that he came to consider himself as the latter's disciple.

Twenty years in the invigorating climate of the South African frontier, far from the restrictions of caste- and custom-conscious India, gave Gāndhi a unique opportunity to evolve religious and ethical beliefs of his own. The seed of pacifist anarchism had already been sown in his mind by his reading of Kropotkin's essays, which were being published in London during his student days there. Tolstoy's *The Kingdom of God Is Within You* now "overwhelmed" him with its message of Christian pacifism. Ruskin's *Unto This Last* made real to him the significance of manual labor as an expression of solidarity between the educated and the uneducated, and he acted immediately on this insight by starting a rural settlement for his growing band of followers. His studies of the Sermon on the Mount and the *Gītā* led him to the conclusion that the ideal life was one of selfless action in the service of one's fellow men, and the best

[1] D. G. Tendulkar, *Mahātmā. Life of Mohandas Karamchand Gandhi*, I, 39.

method of righting wrongs was to protest nonviolently and to suffer lovingly rather than submit to injustice. Last but not least, as he testified in his autobiography, *The Story of My Experiments with Truth,* the example of his wife, Kasturbā, proved to him how passive resistance to a wrong-doer could shame him into repentance.

Applying these principles to the struggle for fair treatment to the Indian community in South Africa, Gāndhi coined the term *satyāgraha* (literally, truth-insistence), defining it as "soul-force" or "the force which is born of truth and love or nonviolence." Time and again he and his followers deliberately and gladly went to jail rather than obey anti-Indian legislation. Thoreau's essay on "Civil Disobedience," read during one of his imprisonments, confirmed his view that an honest man is duty-bound to violate unjust laws. To fit himself for a life of voluntary hardship, Gāndhi continued to simplify his diet and dress, took a vow of celibacy, and disciplined his mind and body with prayer and fasting. His great *satyāgraha* campaign of 1913–14 ending successfully, he returned to India in 1915.

Gāndhi's use of peasant dress, his tireless advocacy of hand spinning and weaving, and his devotion to the cause of India's untouchables startled the older school of nationalist leaders and won the admiration of younger middle-class patriots. Because he had given up all worldly attachments, illiterate villagers trusted him unquestioningly. With the death of Tilak in 1920, he became the unchallenged master of the Congress. He brought to the task a Moderate's abhorrence of violence and willingness to arrive at compromises, together with an Extremist's passion for action and quasi-religious appeal to the masses. Under his leadership the Congress was transformed into a fighting political army with hundreds of thousands of active members and sympathizers. In three major campaigns, spaced roughly ten years apart, he and his nonviolent army demonstrated their dissatisfaction with British reforms by inviting imprisonment and filling the jails to overcrowding.

Gāndhi's method of nonviolent noncooperation with British rule proved uniquely effective in the Indian situation where a resort to violence would have provoked severe repression and also embarrassed those English liberals and Laborites who were instrumental in finally freeing India. Whether *satyāgraha* would, as Gāndhi claimed, have worked equally well against a government of men fettered neither by Christian consciences nor by the sovereign rule of law has yet to be proved. The eventual achievement of Indian independence in 1947 was the outcome of a combination of circumstances—probably the most important being the weakening effect of two world wars on Britain's power and prestige in Asia—but the presence of a disciplined political organization under a revered leader greatly facilitated the transfer of power. Gāndhi, however, was deeply grieved at the partition of British India into the two states of India and Pakistan, and heartbroken at the ensuing communal warfare between Hindus and Sikhs on the one hand and Muslims on the other. His last of many political fasts were undertaken to persuade the rioters to come to their senses and to promote amity between the rival governments. On January 30, 1948, a Mahārāshtrian Hindu nationalist, feeling that Gāndhi had been too conciliatory to the Muslims, fatally shot him at his daily prayer meeting.

Gāndhi's remarkably protean thought mirrored the many influences, both Indian and Western, to which he subjected himself. The most ardent of Indian nationalists, he can also be considered the greatest representative of the renascence of Hinduism. At the same time, his long residence in Christian communities sharpened his unusual sense of sinfulness and his desire to serve the humblest of his fellow men. Gāndhi took seriously the New Testament injunction to return good for evil, and often referred to Jesus as "the Prince of Civil Resisters." A child of the Victorian era, he developed a puritanical zeal which spurred him on to act in strict accordance with his conscience, whatever the consequences. Significantly, Newman's "Lead, kindly light . . . one step enough for me," was his favorite hymn.

Harmony between thought and deed thus meant far more to Gāndhi than consistency between one thought and another. Because his mind operated in two different dimensions—the religious, with its insistence on absolute perfection and purity, and the political, with its emphasis on practicality and expediency—he often seemed to contradict himself. Summing up the conflict between these two sides of his nature, he once remarked, "Men say I am a saint losing myself in politics. The fact is I am a politician trying my hardest to be a saint." [2] Gandhi's great strength as a political leader, however, and the key to his compelling personality,

[2] L. Fischer, *Gandhi, His Life and Message for the World*, p. 35, citing Henry Polak as his source.

lay precisely in his saintliness, his transparent honesty, and his constant willingness to see new points of view, to admit mistakes, but above all to be faithful to the truth as he saw it at the moment.

MOHANDĀS K. GĀNDHI
Hind Swarāj

Hind Swarāj (*Indian Home Rule*) was Gāndhi's first full-dress statement of his social and political ideals. Written in 1909 during a sea-voyage from London to South Africa, it took the form of a dialogue between the author and a skeptical friend. In a preface to a later edition Gāndhi explained that he wrote it to stop the "rot" of extremism and anarchism that was setting in among Indians in South Africa and elsewhere. To accomplish this end, Gāndhi seems to go the anarchists one better by advocating the complete rejection of modern Western civilization. In his conclusion he set forth clearly the doctrine of passive resistance, which follows as a logical corollary of his antagonism to "modern" civilization and all its ways.

Although Gāndhi was later forced to modify some of the extreme positions taken in *Hind Swarāj,* he never recanted the basic principles outlined in this manifesto. In his preface to the edition of 1938, he wrote that ". . . after the stormy thirty years through which I have . . . passed [since writing it], I have seen nothing to make me alter the views expounded in it."

Starting with a discussion of the political situation in India, Gāndhi criticized the British system of parliamentary government, and concluded:

[From Gāndhi, *Hind Swarāj,* pp. 24–76]

If India copies England, it is my firm conviction that she will be ruined.

Reader: To what do you ascribe this state of England?

Editor: It is not due to any peculiar fault of the English people, but the condition is due to modern civilization. It is a civilization only in name. Under it the nations of Europe are becoming degraded and ruined day by day.

Reader: Now you will have to explain what you mean by civilization.

Editor: It is not a question of what I mean. Several English writers refuse to call that civilization which passes under that name. Many books have been written upon that subject. Societies have been formed to cure the nation of the evils of civilization. A great English writer has written a work called "Civilization: Its Cause and Cure." Therein he has called it a disease.

Reader: Why do we not know this generally?

Editor: The answer is very simple. We rarely find people arguing against themselves. Those who are intoxicated by modern civilization are not likely to write against it. Their care will be to find out facts and arguments in support of it, and this they do unconsciously, believing it to be true. A man whilst he is dreaming, believes in his dream; he is undeceived only when he is awakened from his sleep. A man laboring under the bane of civilization is like a dreaming man. What we usually read are the works of defenders of modern civilization, which undoubtedly claims among its votaries very brilliant and even some very good men. Their writings hypnotize us. And so, one by one, we are drawn into the vortex.

Reader: This seems to be very plausible. Now will you tell me something of what you have read and thought of this civilization?

Editor: Let us first consider what state of things is described by the word "civilization." Its true test lies in the fact that people living in it make bodily welfare the object of life. We will take some examples. The people of Europe today live in better-built houses than they did a hundred years ago. This is considered an emblem of civilization, and this is also a matter to promote bodily happiness. Formerly, they wore skins, and used spears as their weapons. Now, they wear long trousers, and, for embellishing their bodies, they wear a variety of clothing, and, instead of spears, they carry with them revolvers containing five or more chambers. If people of a certain country, who have hitherto not been in the habit of wearing much clothing, boots, etc., adopt European clothing, they are supposed to have become civilized out of savagery. Formerly, in Europe, people plowed their lands mainly by manual labor. Now, one man can plow a vast tract by means of steam engines and can thus amass great wealth. This is called a sign of civilization. Formerly, only a few men wrote valuable books. Now, anybody writes and prints anything he likes and poisons people's minds. Formerly, men traveled in wagons. Now, they fly through the air in trains at the rate of four hundred and more miles per day. This is considered the height of civilization. It has been stated that, as men progress, they shall be able to travel in airships and reach any part of the world in a few hours. Men will not need the use of their hands and feet. They will press a button, and they will have their clothing by their side. They will press another button, and they will have their newspaper. A third, and a motor-car will be in waiting for them. They will have a variety of delicately dished up food. Everything will be done by machinery. Formerly, when people wanted to fight with one another, they measured between them their bodily strength; now it is possible to take away thousands of lives by one man working behind a gun from a hill. This is civilization. Formerly, men worked in the open air only as much as they liked. Now thousands of workmen meet together and for the sake of maintenance work in factories or mines. Their condition is worse than that of beasts. They are obliged to work, at the risk of their lives, at most dangerous occupations, for the sake of millionaires. Formerly, men were made slaves under physical compulsion. Now they are enslaved by temptation of money and of the luxuries that money can buy. There are now diseases of which people never dreamt before, and an army of doctors is engaged in finding out their cures, and so hospitals have increased. This is a test of civilization. Formerly, special messengers were required and much expense was incurred in order to send letters; today, anyone can abuse his fellow by means of a letter for one penny. True, at the same cost, one can send one's thanks also. Formerly, people had two or three meals consisting of home-made bread and vegetables; now, they require something to eat every two hours so that they have hardly leisure for anything else. What more need I say? All this you can ascertain from several authoritative books. These are all true tests of civilization. And if anyone speaks to the contrary, know that he is ignorant. This civilization takes note neither of morality nor of religion. Its votaries calmly state that their business is not to teach religion. Some even consider it to be a superstitious growth. Others put on the cloak of religion, and prate about morality. But, after twenty years' experience, I have come to the conclusion that immorality is often taught in the name of morality. Even a child can understand that in all I have described above there can be no inducement to morality. Civilization seeks to increase bodily comforts, and it fails miserably even in doing so.

This civilization is irreligion, and it has taken such a hold on the people in Europe that those who are in it appear to be half-mad. They lack real physical strength or courage. They keep up their energy by intoxication. They can hardly be happy in solitude. Women, who should be the queens of households, wander in the streets or they slave away in factories. For the sake of a pittance, half a million women in England alone are laboring under trying circumstances in factories or similar institutions. This awful fact is one of the causes of the daily growing suffragette movement.

This civilization is such that one has only to be patient and it will be self-destroyed. According to the teaching of Mahomed this would be considered a Satanic Civilization. Hinduism calls it the Black Age. I cannot give you an adequate conception of it. It is eating into the vitals of the English nation. It must be shunned. Parliaments are really emblems of slavery. If you will sufficiently think over this, you will entertain the same opinion and cease to blame the English. They rather deserve our sympathy. They are a shrewd nation and I therefore believe that they will cast off the evil. They are enterprising and industrious, and their mode of thought is not inherently immoral. Neither are they bad at heart. I therefore respect them. Civilization is not an incurable disease, but it should never be forgotten that the English people are at present afflicted by it. [pp. 24-27]

Gāndhi next explained that the English gained India because Indians yielded to the blandishments of their silver bullion; he condemned the railway as a "distributing agency for the evil one," and "a most dangerous institution"; charged lawyers with enslaving India by their cooperation with the British legal system; and ridiculed doctors for encouraging vice by curing the diseases acquired through overindulgence. He went on to draw an idyllic picture of pre-British India, whose civilization he characterized as "unquestionably" the world's best.

Reader: You have denounced railways, lawyers and doctors. I can see that you will discard all machinery. What then, is civilization?

Editor: The answer to that question is not difficult. I believe that the civilization India has evolved is not to be beaten in the world. Nothing can equal the seeds sown by our ancestors. Rome went, Greece shared the same fate; the might of the Pharaohs was broken; Japan has become Westernized; of China nothing can be said; but India is still, somehow or other, sound at the foundation. The people of Europe learn their lessons from the writings of the men of Greece or Rome, which exist no longer in their former glory. In trying to learn from them, the Europeans imagine that they will avoid the mistakes of Greece and Rome. Such is their pitiable condition. In the midst of all this India remains immovable and that is her glory. It is a charge against India that her people are so uncivilized, ignorant, and stolid, that it is not possible to induce them to adopt any changes. It is a charge really against our merit. What we have tested and found true on the anvil of experience, we dare not change. Many thrust their advice upon India, and she remains steady. This is her beauty: it is the sheet-anchor of our hope.

Civilization is that mode of conduct which points out to man the path of duty. Performance of duty and observance of morality are convertible terms. To observe morality is to attain mastery over our mind and our passions. So doing, we know ourselves. The Gujarātī equivalent for civilization means "good conduct."

If this definition be correct, then India, as so many writers have shown, has nothing to learn from anybody else, and this is as it should be. We notice that the mind is a restless bird; the more it gets the more it wants, and still remains unsatisfied. The more we indulge our passions the more unbridled they become. Our ancestors, therefore, set a limit to our indulgences. They saw that happiness was largely a mental condition. A man is not necessarily happy because he is rich, or unhappy because he is poor. The rich are often seen to be unhappy, the poor to be happy. Millions will always remain poor. Observing all this, our ancestors dissuaded us from luxuries and pleasures. We have managed with the same kind of plow as existed thousands of years ago. We have retained the same kind of cottages that we had in former times and our indigenous education remains the same as before. We have had no system of life-corroding competition. Each followed his own occupation or trade and charged a regulation wage. It was not that we did not know how to invent machinery, but our forefathers knew that, if we set our hearts after such things, we would become slaves and lose our moral fibre. They, therefore, after due deliberation decided that we should only do what we could with our hands and feet. They saw that our real happiness and health consisted in a proper use of our hands and feet. They further reasoned that large cities were a snare and a useless encumbrance and that people would not be happy in them, that there would be gangs of thieves and robbers, prostitution, and vice flourishing in them and that poor men would be robbed by rich men. They were, therefore, satisfied with small villages. They saw that kings and their swords were inferior to the sword of ethics, and they, therefore, held the sovereigns of the earth to be inferior to the Rishis and the Fakirs. A nation with a constitution like this is fitter to teach others than to learn from others. This nation had courts, lawyers, and doctors, but they were all within bounds. Everybody knew that these professions were not particularly superior; moreover, these *vakils* and *vaids* [1] did not rob people; they were considered people's dependants, not their masters. Justice was tolerably fair. The ordinary rule was to avoid courts. There were no touts to lure people into them. This evil, too, was noticeable only in and around capitals. The common people lived independently and followed their agricultural occupation. They enjoyed true Home Rule.

And where this cursed modern civilization has not reached, India remains as it was before. The inhabitants of that part of India will very properly laugh at your new-fangled notions. The English do not rule over them, nor will you ever rule over them. Those in whose name we speak we do not know, nor do they know us. I would certainly advise you and those like you who love the motherland to go into the interior that has not yet been polluted by the railways and to live there for six months; you might then be patriotic and speak of Home Rule.

Now you see what I consider to be real civilization. Those who want to change conditions such as I have described are enemies of the country and are sinners.

Reader: It would be all right if India were exactly as you have described it, but it is also India where there are hundreds of child widows, where two-year-old babies are married, where twelve-year-old girls are mothers and housewives, where women practice polyandry, where the practice of *niyoga* [2] obtains, where, in the name of religion, girls dedicate themselves to prostitution, and in the name of religion sheep and goats are killed. Do you consider these also symbols of the civilization that you have described?

Editor: You make a mistake. The defects that you have shown are defects. Nobody mistakes them for ancient civilization. They remain in spite of it. Attempts have always been made and will be made to remove them. We may utilize the new spirit that is born in us for purging ourselves of these evils. But what I have described to you as emblems of modern civilization are accepted as such by its votaries. The Indian civilization, as described by me, has been so described by its votaries. In no part of the world, and under no civilization, have all men attained

---

[1] Lawyers and doctors.

[2] Temporary cohabitation, enjoined for the sake of giving a childless widow a son.

perfection. The tendency of the Indian civilization is to elevate the moral being, that of the Western civilization is to propagate immorality. The latter is godless, the former is based on a belief in God. So understanding and so believing, it behoves every lover of India to cling to the old Indian civilization even as a child clings to the mother's breast.

Reader: I appreciate your views about civilization. I will have to think over them. I cannot take them in all at once. What, then, holding the views you do, would you suggest for freeing India?

Editor: I do not expect my views to be accepted all of a sudden. My duty is to place them before readers like yourself. Time can be trusted to do the rest. We have already examined the conditions for freeing India, but we have done so indirectly; we will now do so directly. It is a world-known maxim that the removal of the cause of a disease results in the removal of the disease itself. Similarly if the cause of India's slavery be removed, India can become free.

Reader: If Indian civilization is, as you say, the best of all, how do you account for India's slavery?

Editor: This civilization is unquestionably the best, but it is to be observed that all civilizations have been on their trial. That civilization which is permanent outlives it. Because the sons of India were found wanting, its civilization has been placed in jeopardy. But its strength is to be seen in its ability to survive the shock. Moreover, the whole of India is not touched. Those alone who have been affected by Western civilization have become enslaved. We measure the universe by our own miserable foot-rule. When we are slaves, we think that the whole universe is enslaved. Because we are in an abject condition, we think that the whole of India is in that condition. As a matter of fact, it is not so, yet it is as well to impute our slavery to the whole of India. But if we bear in mind the above fact, we can see that if we become free, India is free. And in this thought you have a definition of *Swarāj*. It is *Swarāj* when we learn to rule ourselves. It is, therefore, in the palm of our hands. Do not consider this *Swarāj* to be like a dream. There is no idea of sitting still. The *Swarāj* that I wish to picture is such that, after we have once realized it, we shall endeavor to the end of our lifetime to persuade others to do likewise. But such *Swarāj* has to be experienced, by each one for himself. One drowning man will never save another. Slaves ourselves, it would be a mere pretension to think of freeing others. Now you will have seen that it is not necessary for us to have as our goal the expulsion of the English. If the English become Indianized, we can accommodate them. If they wish to remain in India along with their civilization, there is no room for them. It lies with us to bring about such a state of things.

Reader: It is impossible that Englishmen should ever become Indianized.

Editor: To say that is equivalent to saying that the English have no humanity in them. And it is really beside the point whether they become so or not. If we keep our own house in order, only those who are fit to live in it will remain. Others will leave of their own accord. Such things occur within the experience of all of us.

Reader: But it has not occurred in history.

Editor: To believe that what has not occurred in history will not occur at all is to argue disbelief in the dignity of man. At any rate, it behoves us to try what appeals to our reason. All countries are not similarly conditioned. The condition of India is unique. Its strength is immeasurable. We need not, therefore, refer to the history of other countries. I have drawn attention to the fact that, when other civilizations have succumbed, the Indian has survived many a shock. [pp. 43-47]

. . . .

Reader: I cannot follow this. There seems little doubt that we shall have to expel the English by force of arms. So long as they are in the country we cannot rest. . . .

Editor: . . . I believe that you want the millions of India to be happy, not that you [merely] want the reins of government in your hands. If that be so, we have to consider only one thing: how can the millions obtain self-rule? You will admit that people under several Indian princes are being ground down. The latter mercilessly crush them. Their tyranny is greater than that of the English, and if you want such tyranny in India, then we shall never agree. My patriotism does not teach me that I am to allow people to be crushed under the heel of Indian princes if only the English retire. If I have power, I should resist the tyranny of Indian princes just as much as that of the English. By patriotism I mean the welfare of the whole people, and if I could secure it at the hands of the English, I should bow down my head to them. If any Englishman dedicated his life to securing the freedom of India, resisting tyranny, and serving the land, I should welcome that Englishman as an Indian.

Again [you say that] India can fight . . . only when she has arms. You have not considered this problem at all. The English are splendidly armed; that does not frighten me, but it is clear that, to pit ourselves against them in arms, thousands of Indians must be armed. If such a thing be possible, how many years will it take? Moreover, to arm India on a large scale is to Europeanize it. Then her condition will be just as pitiable as that of Europe. This means, in short that India must accept European civilization, and if that is what we want, the best thing is that we have among us those who are so well trained in that civilization. We will then fight for a few rights, will get what we can and so pass our days. But the fact is that the Indian nation will not adopt arms, and it is well that it does not. [p. 49]

Introducing the concept of "soul-force" or "passive resistance," Gāndhi argued that it is the only method by which home rule can be regained.

Thousands, indeed tens of thousands, depend for their existence on a very active working of this force. Little quarrels of millions of families in their daily lives disappear before the exercise of this force. Hundreds of nations live in peace. History does not and cannot take note of this fact. History is really a record of every interruption of the even working of the force of love or of the soul. Two brothers quarrel; one of them repents and reawakens the love that was lying dormant in him; the two again begin to live in peace; nobody takes note of this. But if the two brothers, through the intervention of solicitors or some other reason, take up arms or go to law—which is another form of the exhibition of brute force—their doings would be immediately noticed in the press, they would be the talk of their neighbors and would probably go down to history. And what is true of families and communities is true of nations. There is no reason to believe that there is one law for families and an-other for nations. History, then, is a record of an interruption of the course of nature. Soul-force, being natural, is not noted in history.

Reader: According to what you say, it is plain that instances of this kind of passive resistance are not to be found in history. It is necessary to understand this passive resistance more fully. It will be better, there-fore, if you enlarge upon it.

Editor: Passive resistance is a method of securing rights by personal suffering; it is the reverse of resistance by arms. When I refuse to do a thing that is repugnant to my conscience, I use soul-force. For instance, the government of the day has passed a law which is applicable to me. I do not like it. If by using violence I force the government to repeal the law, I am employing what may be termed body-force. If I do not obey the law and accept the penalty for its breach, I use soul-force. It involves sacrifice of self.

Everybody admits that sacrifice of self is infinitely superior to sacrifice of others. Moreover, if this kind of force is used in a cause that is unjust, only the person using it suffers. He does not make others suffer for his mistakes. Men have before now done many things which were subsequently found to have been wrong. No man can claim that he is absolutely in the right or that a particular thing is wrong because he thinks so, but it is wrong for him so long as that is his deliberate judgment. It is therefore meet that he should not do that which he knows to be wrong, and suffer the consequence whatever it may be. This is the key to the use of soul-force.

Reader: You would then disregard laws—this is rank disloyalty. We have always been considered a law-abiding nation. You seem to be going even beyond the extremists. They say that we must obey the laws that have been passed, but that if the laws be bad, we must drive out the law-givers even by force.

Editor: Whether I go beyond them or whether I do not is a matter of no consequence to either of us. We simply want to find out what is right and to act accordingly. The real meaning of the statement that we are a law-abiding nation is that we are passive resisters. When we do not like certain laws, we do not break the heads of law-givers but we suffer and do not submit to the laws. That we should obey laws whether good or bad is a new-fangled notion. There was no such thing in former days. The people disregarded those laws they did not like and suffered the penalties for their breach. It is contrary to our manhood if we obey laws repugnant to our conscience. Such teaching is opposed to religion and means slavery. If the government were to ask us to go about without any clothing, should we do so? If I were a passive resister, I would say to them that I would have nothing to do with their law. But we have so forgotten ourselves and become so compliant that we do not mind any degrading law.

A man who has realized his manhood, who fears only God, will fear no one else. Man-made laws are not necessarily binding on him. Even the government does not expect any such thing from us. They do not say:

"You must do such and such a thing," but they say: "If you do not do it, we will punish you." We are sunk so low that we fancy that it is our duty and our religion to do what the law lays down. If man will only realize that it is unmanly to obey laws that are unjust, no man's tyranny will enslave him. This is the key to self-rule or home-rule.

It is a superstition and ungodly thing to believe that an act of a majority binds a minority. Many examples can be given in which acts of majorities will be found to have been wrong and those of minorities to have been right. All reforms owe their origin to the initiation of minorities in opposition to majorities. If among a band of robbers a knowledge of robbing is obligatory, is a pious man to accept the obligation? So long as the superstition that men should obey unjust laws exists, so long will their slavery exist. And a passive resister alone can remove such a superstition.

To use brute-force, to use gunpowder, is contrary to passive resistance, for it means that we want our opponent to do by force that which we desire but he does not. And if such a use of force is justifiable, surely he is entitled to do likewise by us. And so we should never come to an agreement. We may simply fancy, like the blind horse moving in a circle round a mill, that we are making progress. Those who believe that they are not bound to obey laws which are repugnant to their conscience have only the remedy of passive resistance open to them. Any other must lead to disaster.

Reader: From what you say I deduce that passive resistance is a splendid weapon of the weak, but that when they are strong they may take up arms.

Editor: This is gross ignorance. Passive resistance, that is, soul-force, is matchless. It is superior to the force of arms. How, then, can it be considered only a weapon of the weak? Physical-force men are strangers to the courage that is requisite in a passive resister. Do you believe that a coward can ever disobey a law that he dislikes? Extremists are considered to be advocates of brute force. Why do they, then, talk about obeying laws? I do not blame them. They can say nothing else. When they succeed in driving out the English and they themselves become governors, they will want you and me to obey their laws. And that is a fitting thing for their constitution. But a passive resister will say he will not obey a law that is against his conscience, even though he may be blown to pieces at the mouth of a cannon.

What do you think? Wherein is courage required—in blowing others to pieces from behind a cannon, or with a smiling face to approach a cannon and be blown to pieces? Who is the true warrior—he who keeps death always as a bosom-friend, or he who controls the death of others? Believe me that a man devoid of courage and manhood can never be a passive resister.

This however, I will admit: that even a man weak in body is capable of offering this resistance. One man can offer it just as well as millions. Both men and women can indulge in it. It does not require the training of an army; it needs no jiu-jitsu. Control over the mind is alone necessary, and when that is attained, man is free like the king of the forest and his very glance withers the enemy.

Passive resistance is an all-sided sword, it can be used anyhow; it blesses him who uses it and him against whom it is used. Without drawing a drop of blood it produces far-reaching results. It never rusts and cannot be stolen. Competition between passive resisters does not exhaust. The sword of passive resistance does not require a scabbard. It is strange indeed that you should consider such a weapon to be a weapon merely of the weak.

Reader: You have said that passive resistance is a specialty of India. Have cannons never been used in India?

Editor: Evidently, in your opinion, India means its few princes. To me it means its teeming millions on whom depends the existence of its princes and our own.

Kings will always use their kingly weapons. To use force is bred in them. They want to command, but those who have to obey commands do not want guns: and these are in a majority throughout the world. They have to learn either body-force or soul-force. Where they learn the former, both the rulers and the ruled become like so many madmen; but where they learn soul-force, the commands of the rulers do not go beyond the point of their swords, for true men disregard unjust commands. Peasants have never been subdued by the sword, and never will be. They do not know the use of the sword, and they are not frightened by the use of it by others. That nation is great which rests its head upon death as its pillow. Those who defy death are free from all fear. For those who are laboring under the delusive charms of brute-force, this picture is not overdrawn. The fact is that, in India, the nation at large has generally used passive resistance in all departments of life. We cease to cooperate with our rulers when they displease us. This is passive resistance.

I remember an instance when, in a small principality, the villagers were offended by some command issued by the prince. The former immediately began vacating the village. The prince became nervous, apologized to his subjects, and withdrew his command. Many such instances can be found in India. Real Home Rule is possible only where passive resistance is the guiding force of the people. Any other rule is foreign rule.

Reader: Then you will say that it is not at all necessary for us to train the body?

Editor: I will certainly not say any such thing. It is difficult to become a passive resister unless the body is trained. As a rule, the mind, residing in a body that has become weakened by pampering, is also weak, and where there is no strength of mind there can be no strength of soul. We shall have to improve our physique by getting rid of infant marriages and luxurious living. If I were to ask a man with a shattered body to face a cannon's mouth I should make a laughing-stock of myself.

Reader: From what you say, then, it would appear that it is not a small thing to become a passive resister, and, if that is so, I should like you to explain how a man may become one.

Editor: To become a passive resister is easy enough but it is also equally difficult. I have known a lad of fourteen years become a passive resister; I have known also sick people do likewise; and I have also known physically strong and otherwise happy people unable to take up passive resistance. After a great deal of experience it seems to me that those who want to become passive resisters for the service of the country have to observe perfect chastity, adopt poverty, follow truth, and cultivate fearlessness.

Chastity is one of the greatest disciplines without which the mind cannot attain requisite firmness. A man who is unchaste loses stamina, becomes emasculated and cowardly. He whose mind is given over to animal passions is not capable of any great effort. This can be proved by innumerable instances. What, then, is a married person to do is the question that arises naturally; and yet it need not. When a husband and wife gratify the passions, it is no less an animal indulgence on that account. Such an indulgence, except for perpetuating the race, is strictly prohibited. But a passive resister has to avoid even that very limited indulgence because he can have no desire for progeny. A married man, therefore, can observe perfect chastity. This subject is not capable of being treated at greater length. Several questions arise: How is one to carry one's wife with one? what are her rights? and other similar questions. Yet those who wish to take part in a great work are bound to solve these puzzles.

Just as there is necessity for chastity, so is there for poverty. Pecuniary ambition and passive resistance cannot well go together. Those who have money are not expected to throw it away, but they *are* expected to be indifferent about it. They must be prepared to lose every penny rather than give up passive resistance.

Passive resistance has been described in the course of our discussion as truth-force. Truth, therefore, has necessarily to be followed and that at any cost. In this connection, academic questions such as whether a man may not lie in order to save a life, etc., arise, but these questions occur only to those who wish to justify lying. Those who want to follow truth every time are not placed in such a quandry; and if they are, they are still saved from a false position.

Passive resistance cannot proceed a step without fearlessness. Those alone can follow the path of passive resistance who are free from fear, whether as to their possessions, false honor, their relatives, the government, bodily injuries or death.

These observances are not to be abandoned in the belief that they are difficult. Nature has implanted in the human breast ability to cope with any difficulty or suffering that may come to man unprovoked. These qualities are worth having, even for those who do not wish to serve the country. Let there be no mistake, as those who want to train themselves in the use of arms are also obliged to have these qualities more or less. Everybody does not become a warrior for the wish. A would-be warrior will have to observe chastity and to be satisfied with poverty as his lot. A warrior without fearlessness cannot be conceived of. It may be thought that he would not need to be exactly truthful, but that quality follows real fearlessness. When a man abandons truth, he does so owing to fear in some shape or form. The above four attributes, then, need not frighten anyone. It may be as well here to note that a physical-force man has to have many other useless qualities which a passive resister never needs. And you will find that whatever extra effort a swordsman needs is due to lack of fearlessness. If he is an embodiment of the latter, the sword will drop from his hand that very moment. He does not need its support. One who is free from hatred requires no sword. A man with a stick suddenly came face to face with a lion and instinctively raised his weapon in self-defense. The man saw that he had only prated about fearlessness when there was none in him. That moment he dropped the stick and found himself free from all fear. [pp. 57–63]

In the manner of a lawyer summing up his brief, Gāndhi reduced his argument to its essentials in this final portion of *Hind Swarāj*. After his prophetic last sentence, he appended a list of twenty authoritative books, eighteen of them by Europeans, and eight testimonies to the superiority of Indian civilization, all of them by Englishmen.

Reader: What then, would you say to the English?

Editor: To them I would respectfully say: "I admit you are my rulers. It is not necessary to debate the question whether you hold India by the sword or by my consent. I have no objection to your remaining in my country, but although you are the rulers, you will have to remain as servants of the people. It is not we who have to do as you wish, but it is you who have to do as we wish. You may keep the riches that you have drained away from this land, but you may not drain riches henceforth. Your function will be, if you so wish, to police India; you must abandon the idea of deriving any commercial benefit from us. We hold the civilization that you support to be the reverse of civilization. We consider our civilization to be far superior to yours. If you realize this truth, it will be to your advantage and, if you do not, according to your own proverb, you should only live in our country in the same manner as we do. You must not do anything that is contrary to our religions. It is your duty as rulers that for the sake of the Hindus you should eschew beef, and for the sake of Mahomedans you should avoid bacon and ham. We have hitherto said nothing because we have been cowed down, but you need not consider that you have not hurt our feelings by your conduct. We are not expressing our sentiments either through base selfishness or fear, but because it is our duty now to speak out boldly. We consider your schools and law courts to be useless. We want our own ancient schools and courts to be restored. The common language of India is not

English but Hindi. You should, therefore, learn it. We can hold communication with you only in our national language.

"We cannot tolerate the idea of your spending money on railways and the military. We see no occasion for either. You may fear Russia;[3] we do not. When she comes we shall look after her. If you are with us, we may then receive her jointly. We do not need any European cloth. We shall manage with articles produced and manufactured at home. You may not keep one eye on Manchester and the other on India. We can work together only if our interests are identical.

"This has not been said to you in arrogance. You have great military resources. Your naval power is matchless. If we wanted to fight with you on your own ground, we should be unable to do so, but if the above submissions be not acceptable to you, we cease to play the part of the ruled. You may, if you like cut us to pieces. You may shatter us at the cannon's mouth. If you act contrary to our will, we shall not help you; and without our help, we know that you cannot move one step forward.

"It is likely that you will laugh at all this in the intoxication of your power. We may not be able to disillusion you at once; but if there be any manliness in us, you will see shortly that your intoxication is suicidal and that your laugh at our expense is an aberration of intellect. We believe that at heart you belong to a religious nation. We are living in a land which is the source of religions. How we came together need not be considered, but we can make mutual good use of our relations.

"You, English, who have come to India are not good specimens of the English nation, nor can we, almost half-Anglicized Indians, be considered good specimens of the real Indian nation. If the English nation were to know all you have done, it would oppose many of your actions. The mass of the Indians have had few dealings with you. If you will abandon your so-called civilization and search into your own scriptures, you will find that our demands are just. Only on condition of our demands being fully satisfied may you remain in India; and if you remain under those conditions, we shall learn several things from you and you will learn many from us. So doing we shall benefit each other and the world. But that will happen only when the root of our relationship is sunk in a religious soil."

[3] Russia's conquest of Central Asia in the latter half of the nineteenth century had alarmed the British, who feared a possible invasion of India through the Khyber Pass.

Reader: What will you say to the nation?

Editor: Who is the nation?

Reader: For our purposes it is the nation that you and I have been thinking of, that is those of us who are affected by European civilization, and who are eager to have Home Rule.

Editor: To these I would say: "It is only those Indians who are imbued with real love who will be able to speak to the English in the above strain without being frightened, and only those can be said to be so imbued who conscientiously believe that Indian civilization is the best and that the European is a nine-days' wonder. Such ephemeral civilizations have often come and gone and will continue to do so. Those only can be considered to be so imbued who, having experienced the force of the soul within themselves, will not cower before brute-force, and will not, on any account, desire to use brute-force. Those only can be considered to have been so imbued who are intensely dissatisfied with the present pitiable condition, having already drunk the cup of poison.

"If there be only one such Indian, he will speak as above to the English and the English will have to listen to him." [pp. 72–74]

Reader: This is a large order. When will all carry it out?

Editor: You make a mistake. You and I have nothing to do with the others. Let each do his duty. If I do my duty, that is, serve myself, I shall be able to serve others. Before I leave you, I will take the liberty of repeating;

1. Real home-rule is self-rule or self-control.

2. The way to it is passive resistance: that is soul-force or love-force.

3. In order to exert this force, Swadeshī in every sense is necessary.

4. What we want to do should be done, not because we object to the English or because we want to retaliate, but because it is our duty to do so. Thus, supposing that the English remove the salt-tax, restore our money, give the highest posts to Indians, withdraw the English troops, we shall certainly not use their machine-made goods, nor use the English language, nor many of their industries. It is worth noting that these things are, in their nature, harmful; hence we do not want them. I bear no enmity towards the English but I do towards their civilization.

In my opinion, we have used the term *Swarāj* without understanding its real significance. I have endeavored to explain it as I understand it, and my conscience testifies that my life henceforth is dedicated to its attainment. [p. 76]

Reply to Tagore

Referring to the poet as "the great sentinel" who was exquisitely jealous of India's honor, Gāndhi answered Tagore's criticisms in his weekly magazine, *Young India*. He justified his program of spinning, burning foreign cloth, and boycotting English education by an eloquent appeal on behalf of the starving millions with whom he had identified himself.

[From Gāndhi, *Young India, 1919–1922*, pp. 670–74]

To a people famishing and idle, the only acceptable form in which God can dare appear is work and promise of food as wages. God created man to work for his food, and said that those who ate without work were thieves. Eighty percent of India are compulsory thieves half the year. Is it any wonder if India has become one vast prison? Hunger is the argument that is driving India to the spinning wheel. The call of the spinning wheel is the noblest of all. Because it is the call of love. And love is *Swarāj*. The spinning wheel will "curb the mind" when the time is spent on necessary physical labor can be said to do so. We must think of millions who are today less than animals, who are almost in a dying state. The spinning wheel is the reviving draught for the millions of our dying countrymen and countrywomen. "Why should I who have no need to work for food, spin?" may be the question asked. Because I am eating what does not belong to me. I am living on the spoliation of my countrymen. Trace the course of every pice [1] that finds its way into your pocket, and you will realize the truth of what I write. *Swarāj* has no meaning for the millions if they do not know how to employ their enforced idleness. The attainment of this *Swarāj* is possible within a short time and it is so possible only by the revival of the spinning wheel.

I do want growth, I do want self-determination, I do want freedom, but I want all these for the soul. I doubt if the steel age is an advance upon the flint age. I am indifferent. It is the evolution of the soul to which the intellect and all our faculties have to be devoted. I have no difficulty in imagining the possibility of a man armored after the modern style making some lasting and new discovery for mankind, but I have less difficulty in imagining the possibility of a man having nothing but a bit of flint and a dail for lighting his path or his matchlock ever singing new hymns of praise and delivering to an aching world a message

[1] One-fourth anna, or one forty-eighth of a rupee.

of peace and good will upon earth. A plea for the spinning wheel is a plea for recognizing the dignity of labor.

I claim that in losing the spinning wheel we lost our left lung. We are therefore suffering from galloping consumption. The restoration of the wheel arrests the progress of the fell disease. There are certain things which all must do in all climes. There are certain things which all must do in certain climes. The spinning wheel is the thing which all must turn in the Indian clime for the transition stage at any rate and the vast majority must for all time.

It was our love of foreign cloth that ousted the wheel from its position of dignity. Therefore I consider it a sin to wear foreign cloth. I must confess that I do not draw a sharp or any distinction between economics and ethics. Economics that hurt the moral well-being of an individual or a nation are immoral and therefore sinful. Thus the economics that permit one country to prey upon another are immoral. It is sinful to buy and use articles made by sweated labor. It is sinful to eat American wheat and let my neighbor the grain dealer starve for want of custom. Similarly it is sinful for me to wear the latest finery of Regent Street, when I know that if I had but worn the things woven by the neighboring spinners and weavers, that would have clothed me, and fed and clothed them. On the knowledge of my sin bursting upon me, I must consign the foreign garments to the flames and thus purify myself, and henceforth rest content with the rough khādī [2] made by my neighbors. On knowing that my neighbors may not, having given up the occupation, take kindly to the spinning wheel, I must take it up myself and thus make it popular.

I venture to suggest to the Poet that the clothes I ask him to burn must be and are his. If they had to his knowledge belonged to the poor or the ill-clad, he would long ago have restored to the poor what was theirs. In burning *my* foreign clothes I burn my shame. I must refuse to insult the naked by giving them clothes they do not need, instead of giving them work which they sorely need. I will not commit the sin of becoming their patron, but on learning that I had assisted in impoverishing them, I would give them a privileged position and give them neither crumbs nor cast off clothing, but the best of my food and clothes and associate myself with them in work.

[2] Homespun cloth.

Nor is the scheme of noncooperation or Swadeshī an exclusive doctrine. My modesty has prevented me from declaring from the house top that the message of noncooperation, nonviolence, and Swadeshī, is a message to the world. It must fall flat, if it does not bear fruit in the soil where it has been delivered. At the present moment India has nothing to share with the world save her degradation, pauperism and plagues. Is it her ancient Shāstras that we should send to the world? Well they are printed in many editions, and an incredulous and idolatrous world refuses to look at them, because we, the heirs and custodians, do not live them. Before, therefore, I can think of sharing with the world, I must possess. Our noncooperation is neither with the English nor with the West. Our noncooperation is with the system the English have established, with the material civilization and its attendant greed and exploitation of the weak. Our noncooperation is a retirement within ourselves. Our non-cooperation is a refusal to cooperate with the English administrators on their own terms. We say to them, "Come and cooperate with us on our terms, and it will be well for us, for you and the world." We must refuse to be lifted off our feet. A drowning man cannot save others. In order to be fit to save others, we must try to save ourselves. Indian nationalism is not exclusive, nor aggressive, nor destructive. It is health-giving, re-ligious, and therefore humanitarian. India must learn to live before she can aspire to die for humanity. The mice which helplessly find them-selves between the cat's teeth acquire no merit from their enforced sacrifice.

True to his poetical instinct the Poet lives for the morrow and would have us do likewise. He presents to our admiring gaze the beautiful picture of the birds early in the morning singing hymns of praise as they soar into the sky. These birds had their day's food and soared with rested wings in whose veins new blood had flown during the previous night. But I have had the pain of watching birds who for want of strength could not be coaxed even into a flutter of their wings. The hu-man bird under the Indian sky gets up weaker than when he pretended to retire. For millions it is an eternal vigil or an eternal trance. It is an indescribably painful state which has to be experienced to be realized. I have found it impossible to soothe suffering patients with a song from Kabīr. The hungry millions ask for one poem—invigorating food. They cannot be given it. They must earn it. And they can earn only by the sweat of their brow.

Through Love to God

In bringing to a close his exceedingly frank autobiography (which is a classic of its kind), Gāndhi gave a succinct statement of his ethico-religious beliefs. For him, Truth is God, and ahimsā (which in Gāndhi's usage of the term corresponds closely to the Christian concept of love) is the way to achieve the traditional Hindu ideal of "God-realization."
    [From Gāndhi, *Autobiography*, pp. 615–16]

My uniform experience has convinced me that there is no other God than Truth. And if every page of these chapters does not proclaim to the reader that the only means for the realization of Truth is ahimsā, I shall deem all my labor in writing these chapters to have been in vain. And, even though my efforts in this behalf may prove fruitless, let the readers know that the vehicle, not the great principle, is at fault. After all, however sincere my strivings after ahimsā may have been, they have still been imperfect and inadequate. The little fleeting glimpses, therefore, that I have been able to have of Truth can hardly convey an idea of the indescribable luster of Truth, a million times more intense than that of the sun we daily see with our eyes. In fact what I have caught is only the faintest glimmer of that mighty effulgence. But this much I can say with assurance, as a result of all my experiments, that a perfect vision of Truth can only follow a complete realization of ahimsā.

To see the universal and all-pervading Spirit of Truth face to face one must be able to love the meanest of creation as oneself. And a man who aspires after that cannot afford to keep out of any field of life. That is why my devotion to Truth has drawn me into the field of politics; and I can say without the slightest hesitation, and yet in all humility, that those who say that religion has nothing to do with politics do not know what religion means.

Identification with everything that lives is impossible without self-purification; without self-purification the observance of the law of ahimsā must remain an empty dream; God can never be realized by one who is not pure of heart. Self-purification therefore must mean purification in all the walks of life. And purification being highly infectious, purification of oneself necessarily leads to the purification of one's surroundings.

But the path of self-purification is hard and steep. To attain to perfect purity one has to become absolutely passion-free in thought, speech, and action; to rise above the opposing currents of love and hatred, attachment and repulsion. I know that I have not in me as yet that triple purity, in spite of constant ceaseless striving for it. That is why the world's praise fails to move me, indeed it very often stings me. To conquer the subtle passions seems to me to be harder far than the physical conquest of the world by the force of arms. Ever since my return to India I have had experiences of the dormant passions lying hidden within me. The knowledge of them has made me feel humiliated though not defeated. The experiences and experiments have sustained me and given me a great joy. But I know that I have still before me a difficult path to traverse. I must reduce myself to zero. So long as a man does not of his own free will put himself last among his fellow creatures, there is no salvation for him. Ahimsā is the farthest limit of humility.

In bidding farewell to the reader, for the time being at any rate, I ask him to join with me in prayer to the God of Truth that He may grant me the boon of ahimsā in mind, word, and deed.

Hindu-Muslim Unity

The following passages from a statement issued shortly before a meeting in 1938 with Muslim League leader Jinnāh show Gāndhi's deep longing to establish concord between Hindus and Muslims. By the very nature of Islam, however, Indian Muslims were unable to reciprocate his readiness to include the best of their religion in his.
[From Gāndhi, *Communal Unity*, pp. 217–18]

My Hinduism is not sectarian. It includes all that I know to be best in Islam, Christianity, Buddhism, and Zoroastrianism. I approach politics as everything else in a religious spirit. Truth is my religion and ahimsā is the only way of its realization. I have rejected once and for all the doctrine of the sword. The secret stabbings of innocent persons, and the speeches I read in the papers, are hardly the thing leading to peace or an honorable settlement.

Again I am not approaching the forthcoming interview in any representative capacity. I have purposely divested myself of any such. If there are to be any formal negotiations, they will be between the President of the Congress and the President of the Muslim League. I go as a lifelong worker in the cause of Hindu-Muslim unity. It has been my passion from early youth. I count some of the noblest of Muslims as my friends. . . .

I may not leave a single stone unturned to achieve Hindu-Muslim unity. God fulfills Himself in strange ways. He may, in a manner least known to us, both fulfill Himself through the interview and open a way to an honorable understanding between the two communities. It is in that hope that I am looking forward to the forthcoming talk. We are friends, not strangers. It does not matter to me that we see things from different angles of vision. I ask the public not to attach any exaggerated importance to the interview. But I ask all lovers of communal peace to pray that the God of truth and love may give us both the right spirit and the right word and use us for the good of the dumb millions of India.

The Message of Asia

Addressing the Inter-Asian Relations Conference convened at Delhi in April, 1947, Gāndhi reiterated the belief of many Indian intellectuals that all Asia shared their traditional concern for religious and spiritual values.
[From Gāndhi, *Communal Unity,* pp. 579–80]

What I want you to understand is the message of Asia. It is not to be learnt through Western spectacles or by imitating the atom bomb. If you want to give a message to the West, it must be the message of love and the message of truth. I do not want merely to appeal to your head. I want to capture your heart.

In this age of democracy, in this age of awakening of the poorest of the poor, you can redeliver this message with the greatest emphasis. You will complete the conquest of the West not through vengeance because you have been exploited, but with real understanding. I am sanguine if all of you put your hearts together—not merely heads—to understand the secret of the message these wise men [1] of the East have left to us, and if we really become worthy of that great message, the conquest of the West will be completed. This conquest will be loved by the West itself.

[1] He had previously mentioned Zoroaster, Buddha, Moses, Jesus, Muhammad, Krishna, and Rāma.

The West is today pining for wisdom. It is despairing of a multiplication of atom bombs, because atom bombs mean utter destruction not merely of the West but of the whole world, as if the prophecy of the Bible is going to be fulfilled and there is to be a perfect deluge. It is up to you to tell the world of its wickedness and sin—that is the heritage your teachers and my teachers have taught Asia.

CHAPTER XXVII

PAKISTAN: ITS FOUNDING AND FUTURE

When Iqbāl told the All-India Muslim League in December, 1930, that he hoped to see the Muslim areas of the subcontinent become a separate state, it was not the first time this idea had been put forward. Earlier the famous pan-Islamist thinker, Saiyid Jamāl-u'd-dīn al-Afghānī (1838/39–1897) had written that the destiny of the Muslims of Central Asia was to form a state with Afghanistan and the Muslim majority area in northwestern India. Some kind of separation from the other areas of India and autonomous integration into a single entity was also advocated by several other contemporary thinkers. An Indian Muslim student at Cambridge, Chaudhari Rahmat Alī, coined the word Pakistan, by taking the *P* from Punjab, *A* from Afghania (by which name he preferred to call the North-Western Frontier Province), *K* from Kashmir, *S* from Sind, and *Tan* from Baluchistan. The *I* between *K* and *S* does not occur if the name Pakistan is written in Urdu. The synthetic name also has a meaning—the Land of the Pure.

Rahmat Alī had had no political experience. He expressed his ideas with greater fervor and enthusiasm than practical reasoning. In the propagation of the idea of Pakistan, however, the part played by him should not be underestimated. Gradually the majority of Indian Muslim students studying in Great Britain came to subscribe to his ideal. This was no mean achievement, as they represented the future leadership of the Indo-Muslim intelligentsia. Moreover, he had to wean them away from Communism, which was then quite fashionable among the students. His deep influence upon them was soon shown in their personal lives, when they withdrew from the frivolities of undergraduate life and became sincere and practicing Muslims. So great was their enthusiasm that sometimes to get a manifesto printed or a note inserted in a newspaper they would go without lunch for weeks to save the necessary money.

Rahmat Alī issued his first manifesto in 1933. At that time his ideas were dismissed with contempt by practical politicians as the wild musings of an irresponsible student. But by the end of 1937, the idea of a separate Muslim state had begun to spread with such rapidity that the politicians themselves were astonished. In 1940, the All-India Muslim League in its Lahore session demanded that Muslim majority areas lying in contiguity should become sovereign states. This idea won at least partial acceptance in the Cripps proposals of 1942. By 1947 Pakistan itself had been achieved. Rahmat Alī died in 1948, disappointed because the Muslim League had accepted a much smaller Pakistan than he had envisaged. Nevertheless, few other university students have lived to see a dream of such magnitude so substantially realized in so short a time.

RAHMAT ALĪ

Sovereign Nations in Homeland or Sub-Nations in Hindoolands?

[From Rahmat Alī, *India* . . . , pp. 3–5]

Nations of Dinia: [1]

It is time to realize that we, the non-Indian nations, who comprise the Muslims, Dravidians, Akhoots [the untouchables],[2] Christians, Sikhs, Buddhs,[3] and Parsis, are, and ever have been, the victims of "the Myth of Indianism." That is the myth which teaches that India is, "the country of India," i.e., the exclusive domain of Caste Hindooism and Caste Hindoos; and which has been built up by the Caste Hindoos, buttressed by the British, and, thanks to our own folly, believed by the world.

PAST RECORD OF THE MYTH

False in its origin and foul in its teachings, this myth, from its very beginning, has wrought havoc and ruin to the cause of human freedom in the world. Throughout the ages it has compromised the status of Asia,

---

[1] India. Dinia is an anagram of India coined by Rahmat Alī on the basis of Arabic *din* "faith, religion." Thus Dinia is the land of religions, while India is the land of the Hindus.

[2] The real word is *acchūt*, meaning "untouchable." Rahmat Alī changed the word into Akhoots—by stretching Arabic grammar, it comes nearer *akhuwwat*, Arabic for "brotherhood."

[3] The Urdu word for Buddhists.

distorted the history of Dinia, and degraded our peoples who have had the misfortune to live and to die in its sphere of domination.

Indeed, such is its evil spirit that, though left stripped of every excuse for its mischievous activity since 711, yet, throughout the last thirteen centuries of its vogue, it has mentally enslaved and socially enchained, nationally "minoritized" and territorially disinherited, us all. Not only that. It has frustrated our spiritual missions and perverted our civilizations, caged us in India, and made India herself a country of doom for all—the Indian as well as the non-Indian nations.

PRESENT ROLE OF THE MYTH

Nor has it stopped there. On the contrary, thanks to its priests and parasites, it has remained as active as ever and is now busily engaged in sabotaging the revival and recognition of us all as nations.

That is the cynical role which it is playing at present through its first believers, the Caste Hindoos, and its latest beneficiaries, the British imperialists, who, in spite of their other differences, are cooperating with one another to canonize it anew and to preach its fatal cult with a view to perpetuating its strangle-hold on us all in the continent of Dinia.

Why are they doing that?

The Caste Hindoos, who are more numerous than all our nations combined, are doing it because to them the existence of the myth gives an opportunity first of keeping us mixed with themselves, then of disintegrating us as nations, and finally of absorbing us into their Indian nation. The British are doing it because to them, as an imperial power, the existence of the myth gives an opportunity first of keeping us and the Caste Hindoos intermingled, then of exploiting our conflict, resulting from that intermingling, to strengthen their hold on India, and finally of justifying before the world, by citing the record of that conflict, their imperial rule over all the nations in India.

So it is to maintain their respective positions of sublordship and overlordship that both the Caste Hindoos and the British imperialists are hymning the myth and hypnotizing us—the non-Indian nations—into accepting its teachings and, thereby, committing national self-immolation and submitting to the Indo-British Condominium.

To rationalize—and to realize—their aims, they are using two main arguments. First, that the unity of "the country of India" is too natural to permit of its partition into separate homelands for all the Indian and the non-Indian nations. Secondly, that the constitutional principle of "one country, one nation" is so decisive as to reduce even one hundred and ten million Muslims, sixty million Akhoots, forty million Dravidians, seven million Christians, and six million Sikhs, to the position of mere sub-nations and satellites of the Indian nation, and thereby to disqualify each one of us from claiming the status of distinct sovereign nations in our own homelands, i.e., the areas to which we are individually entitled in proportion to our populations in the "country of India."

It is obvious that both these arguments are pure cant and casuistry. For the assumption of the unity of the so-called "country of India" is contradicted by the facts of its geography and history; and the application to its case of the constitutional principle of "one country, one nation" is disputed by all the canons of international law.

MIGHT WITH METHOD

The truth is that, in their heart of hearts, both the British imperialists and the Caste Hindoos know this. Yet, in utter disregard of that knowledge, they assume the unity of India, invoke the principle of "one country, one nation," and enforce both—the mythical unity and the constitutional principle.

What does all this mean?

It means might with method; in other words, a firm stand by the Anglo-Hindoo Entente for their own present and future purposes; and a final warning to us, the non-Indian nations, that, in the name of the myth, they won't let us be sovereign nations in separate homelands in the continent of Dinia, but will hold us down as the sub-nations and satellites of the India nation in "the country of India."

OUR CHOICE: MYTH-DESTRUCTION OR SELF-DESTRUCTION

False but final, that is their position. What is ours? It can only be summed up as a choice between life and death; that is to say, between myth-destruction and self-destruction. For it is sun-clear that if we do not destroy the myth, the myth will certainly destroy us.

It is, therefore, time for us all to realize the fatefulness of our position, and, in that realization, make our choice.

As we do that, we must remember that, for each one of us, everything is at stake; and that, to save everything, this is our last and our best opportunity. For now, as never before, the myth is not only discredited but also damned; and its supporters, though materially powerful, are morally powerless. They are aware both of the weakness of their case and of the strength of ours. So, if now we all challenge the myth and give it a smashing blow, it will die a deserved death, and we shall all be free. But if we dilly-dally and miss this opportunity, the Indo-British Entente will reimpose it upon us in all its tyranny. In that case, everything will be lost, and we shall all be the slaves of the Indian nation, perhaps for centuries, perhaps forever. . . .

THE WRITING ON THE WALL

Let them [the other minority communities] make no mistake about it. In the country of India—as for the Muslims, so for them—the fate of national subordination is inescapable. They cannot dodge it; they cannot defy it; they cannot defeat it. The reason is that, even if they achieve the recognition of their distinct nationhoods in the country of India, they can never be sovereign nations in separate homelands. On the contrary, they will ever be the sub-nations and satellites of the Indian nation in, at best, the renamed regions of India—which is, and ever will be, another name for the Hindoo lands.

MUHAMMAD ALĪ JINNĀH AND THE FOUNDING OF PAKISTAN

The founder of Pakistan, Muhammad Alī Jinnāh, was born at Karachi in the year 1876. His father was a merchant of modest means, yet affluent enough to send his son to England for training as a barrister. The house where Muhammad Alī Jinnāh was born, and which is now maintained as a museum by the government of Pakistan, evinces middle-class respectability without much comfort or any trace of luxury. In England Jinnāh was attracted by the political views of the British liberals and he saw an Indian Parsi, Dādābhāi Naoroji, elected to the British Parliament from Central Finsbury, reflecting the growing strength of British liberalism.

Shortly after returning to India in 1896, Jinnāh moved to Bombay, which, being a much larger city, promised greater opportunities to the young barrister. The first three years were years of grim struggle, after which the tide began to turn. Through his ability, integrity, and hard work, Jinnāh ultimately found himself one of the best-known lawyers in the subcontinent. He had devoted himself to his profession to the exclusion of other interests; but having made his mark and ensured his financial independence, Jinnāh's thoughts turned in the direction of politics. His earlier contacts with British liberalism had created an interest in public affairs which now asserted itself. He joined the Indian National Congress and simultaneously took up a secretaryship to Dādābhāi Naoroji, through which he served his apprenticeship in Indian politics. In 1909 the Bombay Muslim constituency elected him to the imperial Legislative Council of the government of India, where his ability and independence soon won him recognition. He came into contact with the able Marātha leader, Gokhale, and a warm friendship grew up between the two men. In Gokhale he found the kind of Hindu patriot who, he thought, had the same approach to Indian politics as himself; Gokhale, for his part, considered Jinnāh to be a potential ambassador of Hindu-Muslim unity.

In 1913, while the two friends were in England for a holiday, Jinnāh was persuaded by Muhammad Alī, editor of the *Comrade,* to join the Muslim League. He did this on the assurance that the aims of the League were now similar to those of the Congress, and that his membership in the League would not imply disloyalty to "the larger national cause to which his life was dedicated." A few months later he led a delegation to England to put the views of the Indian National Congress regarding the Council of India Bill before the Secretary of State for India. Consideration of the bill was postponed, however, because the First World War broke out in August, 1914. Still Jinnāh continued to work for a Hindu-Muslim understanding and brought about the Lucknow Pact between the Congress and the League in 1916, by which the Congress accepted the principle of separate electorates for the Muslims. In 1917 Montagu, the Secretary of State for India, went to the subcontinent to assess the situation regarding a further installment of self-rule. His description of Jinnāh is interesting:

They were followed by Jinnāh, young, perfectly mannered, impressive looking, armed to the teeth with dialectics. . . . I was rather tired and I funked him.

Chelmsford tried to argue with him, and was tied up into knots. Jinnāh is a very clever man, and it is, of course, an outrage that such a man should have no chance of running the affairs of his own country.[1]

The end of the First World War saw the rise of Gāndhi as the leader of the national movement. Jinnāh, however, had no use for the new techniques of civil disobedience and noncooperation; nor had he much liking for the Khilāfat Movement. This movement reflected, indeed, a romanticism in politics upon which the Muslims had fed so long that they had lost a sense of realities. Their attitude towards political problems was seldom based upon a clear appreciation of all the factors involved. The unrealistic aims of this movement, the unqualified acceptance of Gāndhi's leadership, the confidence that withdrawal of the British would automatically solve the Hindu-Muslim problem, and unbounded faith in the willingness and power of the Congress Hindu leaders to settle Hindu-Muslim differences were all manifestations of this romanticism. When the spell was broken by the inauguration of the Shuddhi and Sangathan Movements and the unwillingness or inability of the Congress Hindu leaders to curb such extremism, the Muslims' disappointment was extreme. Especially after the death of Muhammad Alī in 1930 it was felt that new policies and new leadership were needed.

Nevertheless, Jinnāh's emergence as the leader could not have been foretold at that time, since he had none of the qualities the Muslims had been accustomed to look for in a leader. Jinnāh was a realist who never permitted his vision to be obscured by emotionalism. Though an ardent Muslim, he did not wear his religion in his buttonhole, whereas the Muslim masses were steeped in sentimentalism and religiosity. Jinnāh was aristocratic by temperament and Western in outlook; the masses distrusted Westernized leaders who lived in a style so different from their own. He was a statesman and a true leader who spoke simply and to the point; the masses wanted a demagogue. Jinnāh did not offer a ready-made solution to the problems confronting his people. He was a cautious man and given to feeling his ground before saying a word, to weighing the pros and cons of a policy before recommending it to anyone. The only qualities in him which could be appreciated at first sight were his independence, courage, integrity, ability, and perseverance. Moreover, his strict sense of discipline, which reconciled him to the loss

[1] Edwin S. Montagu. *An Indian Diary*, p. 57 f.

of politically important allies rather than tolerate indiscipline, did nothing to enhance his popularity.

Still Jinnāh could see that the Muslims needed policies which would safeguard their position. His faith in the old liberal leaders of Indian nationalism was yielding to doubt over the newer forces which had made their appearance. The older liberal leaders had been able to keep the ideals of nationalism clearly defined; now mass feelings were so aroused that agreement on well-defined aims would be impossible. In the beginning Jinnāh worked tirelessly to forge some agreement with the Congress. There still seemed some hope of re-establishing a *modus vivendi,* if the Muslim position were sufficiently understood by the Congress. This hope declined, however, when the Congress in the 1937 elections was able to win so overwhelmingly in provinces possessing Hindu majorities that it did not need the support of any other community to form a government. The Congress decided to form exclusively Congress ministries. Legally the position taken by the Congress was unassailable; but to the Muslims it indicated that the Congress would care little for their cooperation in the hour of its final triumph. Inevitably the two communities began to act upon their deep-rooted instincts and move away from each other. The search for safeguards and formulas proved vain and the emotions of the two peoples asserted themselves with such force that all were helpless in their grip.

Jinnāh had wanted to be the architect of Hindu-Muslim unity. With his usual perseverance, he continued his pursuit of this aim until it became clear that such efforts were doomed to fail. In the fall of 1939 he told a small delegation of Muslim students from Cambridge, who were advocates of Pakistan, "I am getting more and more convinced that you are right in spite of myself." Yet once he became convinced, no obstacle could stand in his way. The Muslim masses of India gave him such support and loyalty as they had given no one before in their history, acclaiming him as their Qaid-i-azam—"the supreme leader." Under his command they marched forward to establish Pakistan as a fact—a country with a population of more than seventy-six million people, which had been dismissed less than two decades before as a fantasy unworthy of consideration.

In 1949, when the cortege of his funeral emerged from the gates of his palace, hundreds of thousands of people who had been waiting, grief-

stricken, shouted spontaneously in unison: *"Qaid-i-azam zindah bād!"*—
"Long live our supreme leader!" Today, too, a grateful people still honors
him as the father of their nation.

MUHAMMAD ALĪ JINNĀH
An International Problem

The selection is taken from Jinnāh's presidential address to the Muslim League
session at Lahore in March, 1940, which marked the adoption by the League
of the principle of a separate Muslim state.

[From Jinnāh, *Some Recent Speeches and Writings,* I, 174–80]

The British government and Parliament, and more so the British nation, have been for many decades past brought up and nurtured with
settled notions about India's future, based on developments in their own
country which has built up the British constitution, functioning now
through the Houses of Parliament and the system of cabinet. Their concept of party government functioning on political planes has become the
ideal with them as the best form of government for every country, and
the one sided and powerful propaganda, which naturally appeals to the
British, has led them into a serious blunder, in producing the constitution envisaged in the Government of India Act of 1935. We find that
the most leading statesmen of Great Britain, saturated with these notions,
have in their pronouncements seriously asserted and expressed a hope that
the passage of time will harmonize the inconsistent elements of India.

A leading journal like the London *Times,* commenting on the Government of India Act of 1935, wrote: "Undoubtedly the differences between the Hindus and Muslims are not of religion in the strict sense
of the word but also of law and culture, that they may be said, indeed,
to represent two entirely distinct and separate civilizations. However, in
the course of time, the superstition will die out and India will be molded
into a single nation." So, according to the London *Times,* the only difficulties are superstitions. These fundamental and deep-rooted differences,
spiritual, economic, cultural, social, and political, have been euphemized
as mere "superstitions." But surely it is a flagrant disregard of the past
history of the subcontinent of India as well as the fundamental Islamic
conception of society vis-à-vis that of Hinduism to characterize them as

mere "superstitions." Notwithstanding a thousand years of close contact, nationalities, which are as divergent today as ever, cannot at any time be expected to transform themselves into one nation merely by means of subjecting them to a democratic constitution and holding them forcibly together by unnatural and artificial methods of British parliamentary statute. What the unitary government of India for one hundred fifty years had failed to achieve cannot be realized by the imposition of a central federal government. It is inconceivable that the fiat or the writ of a government so constituted can ever command a willing and loyal obedience throughout the subcontinent by various nationalities except by means of armed force behind it.

The problem in India is not of an intercommunal character but manifestly of an international one, and it must be treated as such. So long as this basic and fundamental truth is not realized, any constitution that may be built will result in disaster and will prove destructive and harmful not only to the Mussalmans but to the British and Hindus also. If the British government are really in earnest and sincere to secure [the] peace and happiness of the people of this subcontinent, the only course open to us all is to allow the major nations separate homelands by dividing India into "autonomous national states." There is no reason why these states should be antagonistic to each other. On the other hand, the rivalry and the natural desire and efforts on the part of one to dominate the social order and establish political supremacy over the other in the government of the country will disappear. It will lead more towards natural good will by international pacts between them, and they can live in complete harmony with their neighbors. This will lead further to a friendly settlement all the more easily with regard to minorities by reciprocal arrangements and adjustments between Muslim India and Hindu India, which will far more adequately and effectively safeguard the rights and interests of Muslims and various other minorities.

It is extremely difficult to appreciate why our Hindu friends fail to understand the real nature of Islam and Hinduism. They are not religions in the strict sense of the word, but are, in fact, different and distinct social orders, and it is a dream that the Hindus and Muslims can ever evolve a common nationality, and this misconception of one Indian nation has gone far beyond the limits and is the cause of most of your troubles and will lead India to destruction if we fail to revise our

notions in time. The Hindus and Muslims belong to two different religious philosophies, social customs, literatures. They neither intermarry
nor interdine together and, indeed, they belong to two different civilizations which are based mainly on conflicting ideas and conceptions. Their
aspects on life and of life are different. It is quite clear that Hindus and
Mussalmans derive their inspiration from different sources of history. They
have different epics, different heroes, and different episodes. Very often
the hero of one is a foe of the other and, likewise, their victories and defeats overlap. To yoke together two such nations under a single state,
one as a numerical minority and the other as a majority, must lead to
growing discontent and final destruction of any fabric that may be so
built up for the government of such a state.

History has presented to us many examples, such as the union of
Great Britain and Ireland, Czechoslovakia, and Poland. History has also
shown us many geographical tracts, much smaller than the subcontinent
of India, which otherwise might have been called one country, but which
have been divided into as many states as there are nations inhabiting
them. [The] Balkan Peninsula comprises as many as seven or eight sovereign states. Likewise, the Portuguese and the Spanish stand divided in
the Iberian Peninsula. Whereas under the plea of the unity of India and
one nation, which does not exist, it is sought to pursue here the line of
one central government, we know that the history of the last twelve
hundred years has failed to achieve unity and has witnessed, during the
ages, India always divided into Hindu India and Muslim India. The
present artificial unity of India dates back only to the British conquest and
is maintained by the British bayonet, but termination of the British
regime, which is implicit in the recent declaration of His Majesty's government, will be the herald of the entire break-up with worse disaster
than has ever taken place during the last one thousand years under
Muslims. Surely that is not the legacy which Britain would bequeath
to India after one hundred fifty years of her rule, nor would Hindu
and Muslim India risk such a sure catastrophe.

Muslim India cannot accept any constitution which must necessarily
result in a Hindu majority government. Hindus and Muslims brought
together under a democratic system forced upon the minorities can only
mean Hindu rāj [rule]. Democracy of the kind with which the Congress
High Command is enamored would mean the complete destruction of

what is most precious in Islam. We have had ample experience of the working of the provincial constitutions during the last two and a half years and any repetition of such a government must lead to civil war and raising of private armies as recommended by Mr. Gāndhi to [the] Hindus of Sukkur when he said that they must defend themselves violently or nonviolently, blow for blow, and if they could not, they must emigrate.

Mussalmans are not a minority as it is commonly known and understood. One has only got to look round. Even today, according to the British map of India, four out of eleven provinces, where the Muslims dominate more or less, are functioning notwithstanding the decision of the Hindu Congress High Command to noncooperate and prepare for civil disobedience. Mussalmans are a nation according to any definition of a nation, and they must have their homelands, their territory, and their state. We wish to live in peace and harmony with our neighbors as a free and independent people. We wish our people to develop to the fullest our spiritual, cultural, economic, social, and political life in a way that we think best and in consonance with our own ideals and according to the genius of our people. Honesty demands and the vital interests of millions of our people impose a sacred duty upon us to find an honorable and peaceful solution, which would be just and fair to all. But at the same time we cannot be moved or diverted from our purpose and objective by threats or intimidations. We must be prepared to face all difficulties and consequences, make all the sacrifices that may be required of us to achieve the goal we have set in front of us.

The Aims of Pakistan

These excerpts from Jinnāh's speeches, made after the adoption by the Muslim League of the principle of a separate state, suggest the type of political program he hoped the Muslims would pursue. Despite his opposition to majority rule by the Hindus over Muslims, he hoped the latter would adopt for themselves the ideals of liberal and social democracy.

[From Jinnāh, *Some Recent Speeches and Writings,* I, 519–21, 560–62]

The progress that Mussalmans, as a nation, have made, during these three years, is a remarkable fact. Never before in the history of the world has a nation rallied around a common platform and a common ideal in such a short time as the Muslims have done in this vast subcontinent. Never before has a nation, miscalled a minority, asserted itself so quickly, and so effectively. Never before has the mental outlook of a nation been unified so suddenly. Never before has the solidarity of millions of population been established and demonstrated in so limited a time and under such peculiar circumstances as are prevalent in India. Three years ago Pakistan was a resolution. Today it is an article of faith, a matter of life and death with Muslim India. . . .

We have created a solidarity of opinion, a union of mind and thought. Let us concentrate on the uplift of our people for their educational, political, economic, social and moral well-being. Let us cooperate with and give all help to our leaders to work for our collective good. Let us make our organization stronger and put it on a thorough[ly] efficient footing. In all this, the final sanction and censure rests with and upon the verdict of our people. We, the Muslims, must rely mainly upon our own inherent qualities, our own natural potentialities, our own internal solidarity and our own united will to face the future.

I particularly appeal to our intelligentsia and Muslim students to come forward and rise to the occasion. Train yourselves, equip yourselves for the task that lies before us. The final victory depends upon you and is within our grasp. You have performed wonders in the past. You are still capable of repeating the history. You are not lacking in the great qualities and virtues in comparison with the other nations. Only you have to be fully conscious of that fact and act with courage, faith and unity, [pp. 519–21]

. . . . .

You will elect your representatives to the constitution-making body. You may not know your power, you may not know how to use it. This would be your fault. But I am sure that democracy is in our blood. It is in our marrows. Only centuries of adverse circumstances have made the circulation of that blood cold. It has got frozen and your arteries have not been functioning. But, thank God, the blood is circulating again, thanks to the Muslim League efforts. It will be a people's government. Here I should like to give a warning to the landlords and capitalists who have flourished at our expense by a system which is so vicious, which is so wicked and which makes them so selfish that it is difficult to reason with

them. [Tremendous applause.] The exploitation of the masses has gone
into their blood. They have forgotten the lessons of Islam. Greed and
selfishness have made these people subordinate others to their interests
in order to fatten themselves. It is true we are not in power today. You
go anywhere to the countryside. I have visited villages. There are millions and millions of our people who hardly get one meal a day. Is this
civilization? Is this the aim of Pakistan? [Cries of no, no.] Do you
visualize that millions have been exploited and cannot get one meal a
day? If that is the idea of Pakistan I would not have it. [Cheers.] If they
are wise they will have to adjust themselves to the new modern conditions
of life. If they don't, God help them. [Hear, hear, renewed cheers and
applause.] Therefore let us have faith in ourselves. Let us not falter or
hesitate. That is our goal. We are going to achieve it. [Cheers.] The constitution of Pakistan can only be framed by the Millat [the Muslim community or nation] and the people. Prepare yourselves and see that you
frame a constitution which is to your heart's desire. There is a lot of
misunderstanding. A lot of mischief is created. Is it going to be an
Islamic government? Is it not begging the question? Is it not a question of passing a vote of censure on yourself? The constitution and the
government will be what the people will decide. The only question is
that of minorities.

The minorities are entitled to get a definite assurance and ask: "Where
do we stand in the Pakistan that you visualize?" That is an issue of
giving a definite and clear assurance to the minorities. We have done
it. We have passed a resolution that the minorities must be protected and
safeguarded to the fullest extent and as I said before any civilized
government will do it and ought to do it. So far as we are concerned our
own history, our Prophet have given the clearest proof that non-Muslims
have been treated not only justly and fairly but generously. [pp. 560–62]

PAKISTAN'S COURSE IN THE MODERN WORLD

Pakistan, emerging so suddenly as a nation, was immediately faced with
grave problems affecting not only its future but also the fundamental
basis of the state. What would be its relationship to the rest of the world,
and especially to its neighbors? How far should the government go to-

ward assuming the responsibilities of a welfare state, or toward adopting the political institutions of the democratic West? Above all, what would be the status of the Islamic religion, which had been such a crucial factor in the determination of Indian Muslims to found a separate state?

This last question, of course, was the subject of the most intense controversy. There were few Muslims, it is true, who advocated a completely secular state. Most people agreed that Islam should hold a place of special importance in the life of the nation. Nevertheless, there was much difference of opinion as to what its precise role should be. Some held that the principles of Islam should be applied in strict accordance with the precedents established in earlier tradition; others that there should be enough flexibility in their application to allow for the needs of contemporary society. Naturally enough this controversy soon focused on the problem of adopting a constitution. The main exponents of the conservative point of view were the ulama, or recognized theologians of Islam; representatives of the more liberal and progressive approach included a majority of the political leaders of Pakistan, including its first prime minister, Liāquat Alī Khān.

LIĀQUAT ALĪ KHĀN: ARCHITECT OF PAKISTAN

The credit for creating a government in Pakistan out of the chaos which followed Partition goes mainly to Liāquat Alī Khān (1895–1951). Jinnāh was the founder of Pakistan, Liāquat its chief architect.

Born to a rich and noble family which had extensive landed property in the Punjab and the United Provinces, Liāquat was educated at Alīgarh and Oxford and, having been called to the bar from the Inner Temple, he entered politics as a Muslim Leaguer. He was a member of the United Provinces Legislative Council from 1926 to 1940, when he was elected to the central legislature. From 1936 to 1947 he was the general secretary of the Muslim League and Jinnāh's right-hand man. On the establishment of Pakistan in August, 1947, he became its first prime minister until his death in 1951. Despite his wealthy origins and success in public life, Liāquat died a poor man.

During Liāquat's tenure, the reputation of Pakistan as a progressive and stable state increased steadily. A powerful speaker, whose addresses thrilled and inspired the masses, Liāquat still was no demagogue but a coolheaded statesman dedicated to the service of his country. Though he fully shared his people's love for Islam, there was no narrowness or bigotry in his soul; he judged issues on their merits and combined breadth of outlook with regard for detail. When finally struck down by the bullets of an assassin, the only words he muttered were the Muslim formula of faith and the prayer, "May God protect Pakistan."

LIĀQUAT ALĪ KHĀN
Pakistan As an Islamic State

The Objectives Resolution was adopted by the Constituent Assembly of Pakistan on March 7, 1949, after a debate lasting for six days. It has since been incorporated into the constitution of Pakistan. Liāquat Alī Khān's speech moving the Objectives Resolution represents the ideas of the liberal wing of Muslim opinion which has since been dominant in the government of Pakistan notwithstanding several changes in its composition.

[From *The Constituent Assembly of Pakistan Debates*, Vol. V, No. 1, pp. 1–7]

Sir, I beg to move the following Objectives Resolution embodying the main principles on which the constitution of Pakistan is to be based:

"In the name of Allāh, the Beneficent, the Merciful;

WHEREAS sovereignty over the entire universe belongs to God Almighty alone and the authority which He has delegated to the State of Pakistan through its people for being exercised within the limits prescribed by Him is a sacred trust;

This Constituent Assembly representing the people of Pakistan resolves to frame a constitution for the sovereign independent State of Pakistan;

WHEREIN the State shall exercise its powers and authority through the chosen representatives of the people;

WHEREIN the principles of democracy, freedom, equality, tolerance, and social justice, as enunciated by Islam, shall be fully observed;

WHEREIN the Muslims shall be enabled to order their lives in the individual and collective spheres in accord with the teachings and requirements of Islam as set out in the Holy Qur'ān and the Sunna; [1]

WHEREIN adequate provision shall be made for the minorities freely to profess and practice their religions and develop their cultures;

[1] The customs and sayings of the Holy Prophet.

WHEREBY the territories now included in or in accession with Pakistan and such other territories as may hereafter be included in or accede to Pakistan shall form a Federation wherein the units will be autonomous with such boundaries and limitations on their powers and authority as may be prescribed;

WHEREIN shall be guaranteed fundamental rights including equality of status, of opportunity, and before law, social, economic, and political justice and freedom of thought, expression, belief, faith, worship and association, subject to law and public morality.

WHEREIN adequate provision shall be made to safeguard the legitimate interests of minorities and backward and depressed classes;

WHEREIN the independence of the judiciary shall be fully secured;

WHEREIN the integrity of the territories of the Federation, its independence and all its rights including its sovereign rights on land, sea and air shall be safeguarded;

So that the people of Pakistan may prosper and attain their rightful and honored place amongst the nations of the world and make their full contribution towards international peace and progress and happiness of humanity."

Sir, I consider this to be a most important occasion in the life of this country, next in importance only to the achievement of independence, because by achieving independence we only won an opportunity of building up a country and its polity in accordance with our ideals. I would like to remind the House that the Father of the Nation, Qaid-i-azam, gave expression to his feelings on this matter on many an occasion, and his views were endorsed by the nation in unmistakable terms. Pakistan was founded because the Muslims of this subcontinent wanted to build up their lives in accordance with the teachings and traditions of Islam, because they wanted to demonstrate to the world that Islam provides a panacea to the many diseases which have crept into the life of humanity today. It is universally recognized that the source of these evils is that humanity has not been able to keep pace with its material development, that the Frankenstein monster which human genius has produced in the form of scientific inventions, now threatens to destroy not only the fabric of human society but its material environment as well, the very habitat in which it dwells. It is universally recognized that if man had not chosen to ignore the spiritual values of life and if his faith in God had not been weakened, this scientific development would not have endangered his very existence. It is God-consciousness alone which can save humanity, which means that all power that humanity possesses must be used in accordance with ethical standards which have been laid down by inspired teachers known to us as the great Prophets of different religions. We, as Pakistanis, are not ashamed of the fact that we are overwhelmingly Muslims and we believe that it is by adhering to our faith and ideals that we can make a genuine contribution to the welfare of the world. Therefore, Sir, you would notice that the Preamble of the Resolution deals with a frank and unequivocal recognition of the fact that all authority must be subservient to God. It is quite true that this is in direct contradiction to the Machiavellian ideas regarding a polity where spiritual and ethical values should play no part in the governance of the people and, therefore, it is also perhaps a little out of fashion to remind ourselves of the fact that the State should be an instrument of beneficence and not of evil. But we, the people of Pakistan, have the courage to believe firmly that all authority should be exercised in accordance with the standards laid down by Islam so that it may not be misused. All authority is a sacred trust, entrusted to us by God for the purpose of being exercised in the service of man, so that it does not become an agency for tyranny or selfishness. I would, however, point out that this is not a resuscitation of the dead theory of divine right of kings or rulers, because, in accordance with the spirit of Islam, the Preamble fully recognizes the truth that authority has been delegated to the people, and to none else, and that it is for the people to decide who will exercise that authority.

For this reason it has been made clear in the Resolution that the State shall exercise all its powers and authority through the chosen representatives of the people. This is the very essence of democracy, because the people have been recognized as the recipients of all authority and it is in them that the power to wield it has been vested.

Sir, I just now said that the people are the real recipients of power. This naturally eliminates any danger of the establishment of a theocracy. It is true that in its literal sense, theocracy means the Government of God; in this sense, however, it is patent that the entire universe is a theocracy, for is there any corner in the entire creation where His authority does not exist? But in the technical sense, theocracy has come to mean a government by ordained priests, who wield authority as being specially appointed by those who claim to derive their rights from their sacerdotal position. I cannot overemphasize the fact that such an idea is absolutely foreign to Islam. Islam does not recognize either priesthood or any sacerdotal authority; and, therefore, the question of a theocracy simply does not arise in Islam. If there are any who still use the word theocracy in the same breath as the polity of Pakistan, they are either laboring under a grave misapprehension, or indulging in mischievous propaganda.

You would notice, Sir, that the Objectives Resolution lays emphasis on the principles of democracy, freedom, equality, tolerance, and social justice, and further defines them by saying that these principles should be observed in the constitution as they have been enunciated by Islam. It has been necessary to qualify these terms because they are generally used in a loose sense. For instance, the Western Powers and Soviet Russia alike claim that their systems are based upon democracy, and, yet, it is common knowledge that their polities are inherently different. . . . When we use the word democracy in the Islamic sense, it pervades all aspects of our life; it relates to our system of government and to our society with equal validity, because one of the greatest contributions of Islam has been the idea of the equality of all men. Islam recognizes no distinctions based upon race, color, or birth. Even in the days of its decadence, Islamic society has been remarkably free from the prejudices which vitiated human relations in many other parts of the world. Similarly, we have a great record in tolerance, for under no system of government, even in the Middle Ages, have the minorities received the same consideration and freedom as they did in Muslim countries. When Christian dissentients and Muslims were being tortured and driven out of their homes, when they were being hunted as animals and burnt as criminals—even criminals have never been burnt in Islamic society—Islam provided a haven for all who were persecuted and who fled from tyranny. It is a well-known fact of history that, when anti-Semitism turned the Jews out of many a European country, it was the Ottoman empire which gave them shelter. The greatest proof of the tolerance of Muslim peoples lies in the fact that there is no Muslim country where strong minorities do not exist, and where they have not been able to preserve their religion and culture. Most of all, in this subcontinent of India, where the Muslims wielded unlimited authority, the rights of non-Muslims were cherished and protected. I may point out, Sir, that it was under Muslim patronage that many an indigenous language developed in India. My friends from Bengal would remember that it was under the encouragement of Muslim rulers that the first translations of the Hindu scriptures were made from Sanskrit into Bengali. It is this tolerance which is envisaged by Islam, wherein a minority does not live on sufferance, but is respected and given every opportunity to develop its own thought and culture, so that it may contribute to the greater glory of the entire nation. In the matter of social justice as well, Sir, I would point out that Islam has a distinct contribution to make. Islam envisages a society in which social justice means neither charity nor regimentation. Islamic social justice is based upon fundamental laws and concepts which guarantee to man a life free from want and rich in freedom. It is for this reason that the principles of democracy, freedom, equality, tolerance, and social justice have been further defined by giving to them a meaning which, in our view, is deeper and wider than the usual connotation of these words.

The next clause of the Resolution lays down that Muslims shall be enabled to order their lives in the individual and collective spheres in accord with the teachings and requirements of Islam as set out in the Holy Qur'ān and the Sunna. It is quite obvious that no non-Muslim should have any objection if the Muslims are enabled to order their lives in accordance with the dictates of their religion. You would also notice, Sir, that the State is not to play the part of a neutral observer, wherein the Muslims may be merely free to profess and practice their religion, because such an attitude on the part of the State would be the very negation of the ideals which prompted the demand of Pakistan, and it is these ideals which should be the cornerstone of the State which we want to build. The State will create such conditions as are conducive to the building up of a truly Islamic society, which means that the State will have to play a positive part in this effort. You would remember, Sir, that the Qaid-i-azam and other leaders of the Muslim league always made unequivocal declarations that the Muslim demand for Pakistan was based upon the fact that the Muslims had a way of life and a code of conduct. They also reiterated the fact that Islam is not merely a rela-

THE FOUNDING OF PAKISTAN

tionship between the individual and his God, which should not, in any
way, affect the working of the State. Indeed, Islam lays down specific
directions for social behavior, and seeks to guide society in its attitude
towards the problems which confront it from day to day. Islam is not
just a matter of private beliefs and conduct. It expects its followers to
build up a society for the purpose of good life—as the Greeks would have
called it, with this difference, that Islamic "good life" is essentially based
upon spiritual values. For the purpose of emphasizing these values and
to give them validity, it will be necessary for the State to direct and
guide the activities of the Muslims in such a manner as to bring about a
new social order based upon the essential principles of Islam, including
the principles of democracy, freedom, tolerance, and social justice. These
I mention merely by way of illustration; because they do not exhaust the
teachings of Islam as embodied in the Qu'rān and the Sunna. There can
be no Muslim who does not believe that the word of God and the life
of the Prophet are the basic sources of his inspiration. In these there is
no difference of opinion amongst the Muslims and there is no sect in
Islam which does not believe in their validity. Therefore, there should
be no misconception in the mind of any sect which may be in a minority
in Pakistan about the intentions of the State. The State will seek to create an Islamic society free from dissensions, but this does not mean that
it would curb the freedom of any section of the Muslims in the matter
of their beliefs. No sect, whether the majority or a minority, will be permitted to dictate to the others and, in their own internal matters and
sectional beliefs, all sects shall be given the fullest possible latitude and freedom. Actually we hope that the various sects will act in accordance with
the desire of the Prophet who said that the differences of opinion amongst
his followers are a blessing. It is for us to make our differences a source
of strength to Islam and Pakistan, not to exploit them for narrow interests which will weaken both Pakistan and Islam. Differences of opinion very often lead to cogent thinking and progress, but this happens
only when they are not permitted to obscure our vision of the real goal,
which is the service of Islam and the furtherance of its objects. It is,
therefore, clear that this clause seeks to give the Muslims the opportunity
that they have been seeking, throughout these long decades of decadence
and subjection, of finding freedom to set up a polity, which may prove

848 MODERN INDIA AND PAKISTAN

to be a laboratory for the purpose of demonstrating to the world that Islam is not only a progressive force in the world, but it also provides remedies for many of the ills from which humanity has been suffering.

Pakistan's Mission in Asia

In 1950, when an honorary degree was conferred on Liāquat Alī Khān by the University of Kansas City (Mo.), he delivered an address, "Pakistan, the Heart of Asia," from which are taken these excerpts, expressing his conviction that Pakistan stands as a bastion of religious and democratic ideals amidst the political and social upheavals shaking all of Asia.

[From Liāquat Alī Khān, *Pakistan, the Heart of Asia*, pp. 55–61]

Pakistan is a new state; or to be more exact, a new democracy. As a democracy it is not yet three years old. There was a time when your country, where the traditions of civil liberty, freedom, and democracy have now taken such firm root, was a new and young democracy and the memory of your struggle for independence was yet fresh in the minds of men. If you can, in your imagination, reconstruct those times for a little while, you will in many ways be reading the history of Pakistan and of the first three years of its new life.

Till three years ago, Pakistan was only an ideal and a longing. In the vast subcontinent where present-day Bhārat [India] and Pakistan were situated and where the British held sway, there lived a hundred million Muslims who for centuries had made this part of the world their homeland. They lived, side by side, with three hundred million others—mostly Hindus who had come to this continent in an earlier era. As the day of freedom for these four hundred million people drew near, it became increasingly obvious that at the end of the British rule the one hundred million Muslims would have to live their new life as a perpetual political minority. Long experience and the history of several centuries had taught them that under a dominating majority of three to one, freedom from British rule would mean to the Muslims not freedom but merely a change of masters. . . .

We believed then [before Partition] and we believe now that the demand of the Muslims in British India to have a separate state of their own was, both on human and geopolitical grounds, a very reasonable demand. To millions of Muslims it meant the only opportunity for genuine freedom and genuine self-government. To millions of Hindus it gave the same opportunity for developing their own culture, untrammeled by the constant discontent of a large and unmanageable minority. From the point of view of world peace the creation of two independent and comparatively homogeneous states instead of a single uneasy and unwieldy state with great strains and stresses within the body politic was the greatest contribution that could be made towards the creation of a stable new Asia. Peace-loving men and women who today lament the strained relations between Pakistan and Bhārat—and none laments them more than we do—should at least have this consolation that had Pakistan not been separated from the rest of British India, far more serious and dangerous cracks would have appeared in that subcontinent resulting in untold upheavals. Potentially, therefore, the creation of Pakistan has by itself dissolved what would have been a perpetual danger zone in Asia.

But it has done more than that. Cast your mind on all the countries of Asia one after another. Almost everywhere you will see intense nationalism, great backwardness, impatience with colonial rule, and, in some, a greater or lesser degree of democratic rule. But in many of them you will also see internal strains, moral doubts, ideological conflicts, waverings, hesitations, and confusions. Halting democracies and ideological confusions create great anxieties for the governments in Asia, for the peoples of Asia and for peace-loving and world-minded people anywhere. In the midst of these Pakistan stands unified. It stands unified because its people are free from mental confusions which elsewhere create disruption and cast menacing shadows on the future. They have chosen for themselves the part chalked out for them by their simple, practical, clear-cut beliefs and decisions. Foremost amongst those beliefs are the belief in the supreme sovereignty of God, belief in the equality of men, belief in democracy and the right of the people to be governed by their own freely chosen representatives, belief in individual destiny, in the fundamental freedoms of every single man and woman, in the right of every individual to the fruits of his own honest effort, belief in the sanctity of human life and human liberty, belief in the sanctity of the home, belief in universal peace but an equally strong belief in resisting aggression, tyranny, and exploitation. We did not have to acquire or inculcate these beliefs after the foundation of our new state. On the contrary, we founded a new state because we wanted to practice these beliefs without being inhibited by the contiguity, and without being thwarted by the domination, of other conflicting ways of life. For us to be undemocratic, or to ignore individual rights whether of property, belief or expression, or to bend our knee to aggression, is to destroy completely the very ideals which inspired us in our demand for Pakistan.

This intensity of purpose and this firm faith have, during the last three years, been demonstrated in ways which surprised our critics and our friends, and in some ways went beyond our own expectations. When British India was partitioned we, the Pakistanis, were asked to set up a new state of eighty million people within a period of two months. We had no capital and no flag. Our administrative machinery had to be built up from scratch. We were allotted an army, but its personnel was dispersed far and wide and could not come together for months. We had no military equipment. Our share of the military equipment of British India which was allotted to us on paper remains largely undelivered even today when three years have elapsed. Being a backward people we had no industry, no engineers, and practically no traders. Within a few months of independence seven million homeless refugees driven out of India came over to us in a miserable plight to seek shelter. Had it not been for the unity of our people we might have floundered. But today after three years we are stronger than before. And in spite of some very anxious moments when our international rights and our freedom seemed to be in jeopardy, we are still free.

What are the demands that our freedom makes on us? Our first duty is to ourselves. I do not say this in any spirit of selfishness or chauvinism. A free people must maintain their own freedom first. Otherwise they disgrace the fair name of free men and women all over the world. But the maintenance of freedom requires constant vigilance. "Liberty does not descend upon a people; a people must raise themselves to it. It is a fruit that must be earned before it can be enjoyed." That freedom means freedom only from foreign domination is an outworn idea. It is not merely governments that should be free but the people themselves who should be free; and no freedom has any real value for the common man or woman unless it also means freedom from want, freedom from disease, freedom from ignorance. This is the main task which confronts us if we are to take our rightful place in the modern world. We cannot hold the clock back and therefore it is *we* who must go forward at a double pace, bending all our resources and all our energies to this great purpose. Students of history are aware that during the last two or three centuries of foreign domination our people have not kept pace with the march of civilization. It was during these centuries that Western civilization, of which you are the proud torch-bearers, discovered a use for science, which, though not new, was so fast in tempo and so vast in its magnitude that it gave civilization a new orientation altogether. This was the phase that for various reasons our people missed. The result is that today we find multitudes emerging as large, free nations in Asia with their material and mental resources utterly undeveloped and with their standards of living so low that the world conscience should not be content to leave them stagnant. Our ancient steadfast faith which is such a source of strength to us on the ideological front in these modern uneasy times must be wedded to the pioneering virility of modern technology. This is the synthesis we must achieve and achieve quickly, not merely for the sake of progress but for the sake of world peace itself.

For I sincerely believe that war and peace and progress and prosperity are all indivisible today. The innumerable millions of Asia, heirs to ancient cultures and ancient civilizations, have, after centuries of suppression, entered upon a new and dynamic phase of nationalism. Most of them were accustomed to looking at the West from the position of subject peoples and could see little beyond the less attractive side of what to them was Western civilization. Their newly won freedom has, however, corrected their vision and they are better able to see both the Western world and their own surroundings in their true perspective. While on the one hand they are filled with admiration at the sight of the progress and the advancement of civilization in such great countries as the United States of America, they are more impatient than ever before with their own misery and backwardness and are keenly searching the horizons for the signs of a bright day. They are acutely aware of the great contrast between their own standard of living and the standards of living in the Western world. This disequilibrium is in many ways most disquieting and has in it the seeds of unpredictable upheavals. For the sake of world peace, for the sake of world civilization, Asia must be made stable but it cannot be made stable unless discontent is removed and the germs of disruption are killed by better and cleaner living which means no more and no less than enabling the peoples of Asia to enjoy the fullest advantages of freedom and democracy. In this situation, we consider the role of Pakistan to be that of a stabilizing factor in a backward and discontented part of the world. We hope to be able to play this role successfully by our strong faith in God, in democracy and in our own unity, by the resources of our lands and waters and by our will to work. On these points Pakistan stands firm.

What, however, is the role of the Western world in this situation? It is to demonstrate that true democracy is international in its very conception and does not shirk its responsibility for the maintenance of world peace; that it discharges this responsibility by defying not only this or that particular aggressor, but aggression everywhere; and that it has a constructive and not merely a defiant outlook. We conceive the role of the Western world to be the enlightened one of sharing its great fund of knowledge, skill, and experience with those who were denied their opportunities but who constitute a major part of the world's population and without whose progress, the world will limp along only on one leg, if at all. I have met many liberal-minded and thoughtful men in your country to whom these are the only aims worth pursuing in the domain of international affairs today. I am certain therefore that the vast majority of your people regard the emergence of the democracy of Pakistan, its progress, and future development, as of great importance in Asia for they are convinced that Pakistan's strength will be a happy augury for peace.

THE CONSERVATIVE STAND

The most powerful conservative force in Pakistan today is represented by the ulamā, or theologians of Islam, who have fought for an Islamic constitution and for a legal system adhering strictly to traditional Islamic law. One of the chief spokesmen for this point of view has been Syed Abū'l-A'lā Maudoodī (1903–), himself a journalist rather than a theologian. Known for the clarity and elegance of his style in Urdu, Maudoodī devoted himself to the study of Islamics and won respect for his opinions even in the most learned circles. In 1929 he published *Holy War in Islam* (*al-jihād fī-'l-Islām*), and in 1932 started *Exegesis of the Qur'ān* (*Tarjumān-u'l-Qur'ān*), a monthly devoted to the discussion of Islamic subjects. This journal had a deep influence upon contemporary Muslim thought. Maudoodī's main thesis was that the Muslims, to be effective in the pursuit of their ideals, must have only one loyalty—their Faith. He criticized those theologians who had thrown in their lot with the Indian National Congress; but such popularity as this brought him waned considerably when he took an unsympathetic attitude toward the movement for Pakistan. Maudoodī transferred his headquarters to Pathankot in East Punjab and established a center there which prospered until Partition. Then, as the result of disturbances, he and his colleagues had to flee for their lives to Pakistan, where he became a staunch supporter of the new state.

Maudoodī had organized a movement called the Islamic Association (Jamāat-i-Islāmi) to spread among Muslims his ideas regarding the renaissance of true Islam. In Pakistan this body has since come into frequent conflict with the government because of its politics. It has consistently agitated for the enactment of an Islamic constitution. Maudoodī's ideas are more fundamentalist than those of the Muslim League and other Muslim political parties. His party has occasionally won isolated seats in provincial elections, but this does not represent its real strength, as it has many cells of workers in all schools and colleges, factories, government offices, and many townships and villages. The party undertakes relief and medical work in poorer or calamity-stricken areas. Most of this work is financed through the sale of party literature, especially the writings of Maudoodī himself, which reach a wide audience.

SYED ABŪ'L-AʿLĀ MAUDOODĪ

Islamic Law and Constitution

[From Maudoodī, *Islamic Law and Constitution*, p. 14 ff.]

Commencing with stagnation in the domains of knowledge and learning, research and discovery, and thought and culture, it [the degeneration of the Muslims] finally culminated in our political breakdown, making many a Muslim country the slave of non-Muslim imperialist powers. Political slavery gave birth to an inferiority complex and the resultant intellectual serfdom, which eventually swept the entire Muslim world off its feet, so much so that even those Muslim countries which were able to retain their political freedom could not escape its evil influences. The ultimate consequence of this evil situation was that when Muslims woke up again to the call of progress, they were incapable of looking at things except through the colored glasses of Western thought. Nothing which was not Western could inspire confidence in them. Indeed, the adoption of Western culture and civilization and aping the West even in the most personal things became their craze. Eventually, they succumbed totally to the slavery of the West.

This trend towards Westernism was also the result of the disappointment which came from the side of the Muslim religious leaders. Being themselves the victims of the widespread degeneration that had engulfed the entire Muslim world, they were incapable of initiating any constructive movement or taking any revolutionary step which could combat the evils afflicting Muslim society. Quite naturally, this disappointment turned the discontented Muslims towards that system of life which had the glamour of being successful in the modern world. Thus they adopted modern thought and the new culture of the West and blindly aped Western morals and manners. Slowly but surely the religious leaders were pushed into the background and were replaced, as regards power and control over the people, by men bereft of all knowledge of their religion and imbued only with the spirit of modern thought and Western ideals. That is why we find that many a Muslim country has, in the recent past, either completely abrogated the Islamic law or confined its operation to the domain of purely personal matters—a position conferred on the non-Muslims in a truly Islamic state.

In all Muslim countries suffering from foreign domination, the leadership of political and cultural movements fell into the hands of those who were shorn of all Islamic background. They adopted the creed of "Nationalism," directed their efforts towards the cause of *national* independence and prosperity along secular lines, and tried to copy step by step the advanced nations of our age. So, if these gentlemen are vexed with the demand for Islamic constitution and Islamic laws, it is just natural for them. It is also natural for them to sidetrack or suppress the issue, as they are ignorant even of the A B C of the Islamic Sharī'a. Their education and intellectual development has alienated them so completely from the spirit and the structure of Islamic ideology that it is at least for the moment impossible for them to understand such demands.

As regards the Muslim religious leadership, it fares in no way better, because our religious institutions are tied up to the intellectual atmosphere of eight centuries ago, as a consequence of which they have not been able to produce such leaders of Islamic thought and action as could be capable of administering the affairs of a modern state in the light of Islamic principles. This is, indeed, a very real obstacle facing the Islamic countries in their march towards the goal of Islamic revolution.

This is the situation obtaining throughout the Muslim world and impeding the path of the establishment of Islamic constitution. The case of Pakistan is not, however, the same as that of other Muslim countries, certain similarities of situation notwithstanding. This is so because it has been achieved exclusively with the object of becoming the home land of Islam. For the last ten years, we have been ceaselessly fighting for the recognition of the fact that we are a separate nation by virtue of our adherence to Islam. We have been proclaiming from house-tops that we have a distinct culture of our own, and that we possess a world view, an outlook on life, and a code of living fundamentally different from those of non-Muslims. We have all along been demanding a separate homeland for the purpose of translating into practice the ideals envisaged by Islam, and, at last, after a long and arduous struggle, in which we sustained a heavy loss of life and property and suffered deep humiliation in respect of the honor and chastity of a large number of our womenfolk, we have succeeded in attaining our cherished goal—this country of Pakistan. If, now, after all these precious sacrifices, we fail to achieve the real and ultimate objective of making Islam a practical, constitutional reality which inspired us to fight for Pakistan, our entire struggle becomes futile and all our sacrifices meaningless.

Indeed, if a secular and Godless, instead of Islamic, constitution was to be introduced and if the British Criminal Procedure Code had to be enforced instead of the Islamic Shari'a what was the sense in all this struggle for a separate Muslim homeland? We could have had it without that. Similarly, if we simply intended to implement any socialist program, we could have achieved it in collaboration with the Communist and Socialist parties of India without plunging the nation into this great blood-bath and mighty ordeal.

The fact is that we are already committed before God and man and at the altar of History about the promulgation of Islamic constitution and no going back on our words is possible. Whatever the hurdles and however great they are, we have to continue our march towards our goal of a full-fledged Islamic state in Pakistan.

The Islamic Law and Modern Needs
[From Maudoodī, *Islamic Law and Constitution*, p. 38 ff.]

The first objection that is raised is that because the Islamic laws were framed thirteen centuries ago in the light of the requirements of a primitive society, they cannot be of any use for a modern state of our days.

I doubt very much whether people who take this stand are conversant even with the elementary knowledge of the Islamic law. In all probability, they have heard from somewhere that the fundamentals of the Islamic law were enunciated more than thirteen hundred years ago, and they have assumed that this law has remained static since then and has failed to respond to the requirements of changing conditions of human life. On this misconception they have further assumed that the Islamic law will be unsuited to the needs of the present-day society and will clog the wheels of progress. These critics fail to realize, however, that the laws propounded thirteen and a half centuries ago, did not remain in a vacuum; they formed part and parcel of the life of Muslim society and brought into being a *state* which was run in the light of these laws. This naturally provided an opportunity of evolution to Islamic law from the earliest days, as it had to be applied to day-to-day matters through the process of *Ta'wīl, Qiyās, Ijtihād,* and *Istihsān.*[1]

Very soon after its inception, Islam began to hold sway over nearly half the civilized world stretching from the Pacific to the Atlantic and, during the following twelve hundred years, the Islamic Law continued to administer the affairs of all Muslim states. This process of the evolution of Islamic law, therefore, did not stop for a moment up to the beginning of the nineteenth century, because it had to meet the challenge of the ever-changing circumstances and face countless problems confronting different countries in different stages of history. Even in our Indo-Pakistan subcontinent, the Islamic civil and penal codes were in vogue up to the beginning of the nineteenth century.

Thus, it is only for the last one hundred years that the Islamic law remained inoperative and suffered stagnation. But, firstly, this period

[1] *Ta'wīl* is the process of enlarging the applicability of a text by finding analogous situations; *qiyās* is to determine how one should act in the spirit of Islam, if there is no clear injunction available; *ijtihād* is the application of human reason in the interpretation of the meaning of a text; *istihsān* is to find the best procedure in the light of the teachings of Islam.

does not form a big gap and we can easily make up for the loss with some amount of strenuous effort; secondly, we possess full records of the development of our jurisprudence, century by century, and there can be absolutely no ground for frustration or despondency, and our path of legal progress is thus already illumined.

Once we have grasped the fundamental principles and the basic facts concerning the evolution of the Islamic system of law, we cannot remain in doubt that this law shall be as responsive to the urges of a progressive society in the present and the future as it has been in the past. Only those who suffer from ignorance can fall a prey to such nonsense, while those who have a grasp of Islam and the Islamic law are aware of its potentialities of progress, and those who possess even a cursory knowledge of the history of its development can never suspect it of being an antiquated or stagnant system of life which cannot keep pace with the march of history.

Gradual Reform
[From Maudoodī, *Islamic Law and Constitution*, p. 47 ff.]

If we really wish to see our Islamic ideals translated into reality, we should not overlook the natural law that all stable changes in the collective life of a people come about gradually. The more sudden a change, the more shortlived it is. For a permanent change it is necessary that it should be free from extremist bias and unbalanced approach.

The best example of this gradual change is the revolution brought about by the Holy Prophet (peace be on him) in Arabia. One who is acquainted even superficially with the history of the Prophet's achievements knows that he did not enforce the entire body of Islamic laws with one stroke. Instead, the society was prepared gradually for their enforcement. The Prophet (peace be on him) uprooted the practices of the "Age of Ignorance" one by one and substituted for them new, moderate principles of human conduct. He started his efforts for reformation by inculcating belief in the fundamentals of Islam, namely, the unity of God, the Life Hereafter and the Institution of Prophethood and by inducing the people to live a life of righteousness and piety. Those who accepted this message were trained by him to believe in and practice the Islamic Way of Life. When this was achieved to a considerable degree, the Prophet went a step further and established an Islamic State in Medina with the sole object of making the social life of the country conform to the Islamic pattern. . . .

Coming to our own times and our own country, Pakistan, if we wish to promulgate Islamic Law here, it would mean nothing less than the demolition of the entire structure built by your British masters and the erection of a new one in its place. It is obvious that this cannot be achieved by just an official proclamation or a parliamentary bill, because it is a stupendous task and demands a good deal of hard and systematic work on the basis of an all-embracing program. For instance, we need a thorough reorientation of our educational system. At present, we find two kinds of educational institutions running simultaneously in our country, namely, the old, religious "madrasahs" and the modern, secular universities and colleges. None of them can produce people needed to run a modern Islamic State. The old-fashioned schools are steeped in conservatism to such an extent that they have lost all touch with the modern world. Their education has been disconnected from the practical problems of life and has thus become barren and lifeless. It cannot, therefore, produce people who might be able to serve, for instance, as judges and magistrates of a progressive modern state. As for our modern, secular institutions, they produce people who are ignorant of even a rudimentary knowledge of Islam and its laws. Moreover, we can hardly find such persons among those whose mentality has not been affected by the poisonous content and the thoroughly materialistic bias of modern, secular education.

There is yet another difficulty. The Islamic law has not been in force for the last century or so. Consequently our legal code has become stagnant and has lagged behind the march of time, while our urgent need is to bring it abreast of the latest developments of the modern age. Obviously, this would require a considerable amount of hard work.

There is, however, an even bigger hurdle. Living as slaves of an alien power and deprived of the Islamic influence for a long time, the pattern of our moral, cultural, social, economic and political life has undergone a radical change, and is today far removed from Islamic ideals. Under such circumstances it cannot be fruitful, even if it were possible, to change the legal structure of the country all at once, because then the general pattern of life and the legal structure will be poles apart, and the legal change will have to suffer the fate of a sapling planted in an uncongenial soil and facing hostile weather. It is, therefore, inevitable that the required reform should be gradual and the changes in the laws should be effected in such a manner as to balance favorably the change in the moral, educational, social, cultural and political life of the nation.

The Sources of Islamic Law

Maudoodī holds that the Islamic law is not static, but he concedes that it will have to be redefined if it has to become the fundamental law of Pakistan.

[From Maudoodī, *Islamic Law and Constitution*, p. 99 f.]

We should first clearly understand the nature of the problem that confronts us. When we say that this country should have an Islamic constitution, we do not mean that we possess a constitution of the Islamic state in a written form and that the only thing that is required to be done is to enforce it. The core of the problem is that we want an unwritten constitution to be transformed into a written one. What we term as Islamic constitution is really an unwritten constitution drawn from certain specific sources, and it is from this that we have to evolve a written constitution in keeping with the present-day requirements of our country.

An unwritten constitution is nothing unique or strange for the world. Indeed, up to the end of the eighteenth century, the structure of government throughout the world rested on unwritten constitutions; and even today the British government is functioning without a written constitution. As for a written constitution, even this great government, if it desires to have one, will inescapably have to take recourse to the various sources of its unwritten constitution to collect its material therefrom and then codify it article-wise. Our own need at the present moment is almost of the same kind.

There are four sources of the unwritten Islamic constitution:

1. *The Qur'ān* is the first and primary source, containing as it does all the fundamental directives and instructions from God. These directives and injunctions cover the entire gamut of man's existence. Herein are to be found not only directives relating to individual conduct but also principles regulating all the aspects of the social and cultural life of man.

It has also been clearly shown therein as to whether and why Muslims should endeavor to create and establish a state of their own.

2. *The Sunna* is the second source. It shows the way how, in accordance with the Qur'anic directives, the Prophet (peace be on him) translated into practical life the ideological spirit of Islam and developed it into a positive social order, finally elevating it to a full-fledged state. These things we can know from the Sunna and Sunna alone, thereby also learning how to ascertain the precise sense, purport and meaning of the Qur'anic directives. In other words the Sunna is the practical application of Qur'anic principles to mankind's social existence and we can, therefore, obtain the greatest possible number of invaluable precedents relating to Islamic constitution from this very important source.

3. *The Conventions of Khilāfat-i-Rāshidah* [1] form the third source. After the passing away of the Holy Prophet, the Righteous Caliphs managed the Islamic state in the best Islamic traditions, and books of Hadīth, History, and Biography are replete with glittering precedents of that golden era. It has been accepted in Islam from the very beginning that interpretations of the Qur'ān and the Sunna having the unanimous approval of all the Companions (technically known as ijmā') and the decisions of the Caliphs relating to constitutional and judicial problems accepted by the Companions should be binding on all and for all time. In other words, such interpretations and such decisions have to be accepted *in toto,* as the consensus of the Companions on any matter is tantamount to an authoritative exposition of the law. Wherever they have differed, it is but too evident there that two or even more interpretations were actually probable and one may be preferred to the other on the basis of sound reasoning. In cases of general consensus, however, the decision is inescapably the only logical one and has to be accepted as the only authoritative rule. As all the Companions were direct disciples of the Holy Prophet, trained by him personally, their general consensus in matters of interpretations and decisions was bound to be free from even the most trifling chance of error.

4. *The Rulings of Great Jurists* comprise the fourth source. These are the decisions of top-ranking jurists in regard to various constitutional problems of their times. They may not be of eternal validity, yet it cannot

[1] *Khilāfat-i-Rāshidah,* the period of the rule of the first four caliphs after the death of the Prophet, also known as the Republic, which lasted for thirty years.

be gainsaid that they contain fundamentals of the best guidance for a proper understanding of the Islamic constitution.

For writing down the constitution of an Islamic state, we will have to collect relevant material from all these sources, in the same way as the people of England, were they inclined to reduce their constitution to writing, would have to refer to their Common Law decisions and conventions and note down all the inferences therefrom and from judgments of their courts relating to constitutional problems.

THE ULAMĀ

A convention of learned theologians, representing all schools of Islamic thought, was held January 21–24, 1951. It unanimously recommended that the following principles be incorporated in the constitution of an Islamic state. Though their point of view has not met with general acceptance, it is significant as the expression of the most conservative force in present-day Pakistan.

Basic Principles of an Islamic State

The Constitution of an Islamic state should comprehend the following basic principles:

1. Ultimate Sovereignty over all Nature and all Law shall be affirmed in *Allāh,* the Lord of the universe, alone.

2. The law of the land shall be based on the Qur'ān and the Sunna, and no law shall be passed nor any administrative order issued, in contravention of the Qur'ān and the Sunna. *Explanatory Note:* If there be any laws in force in the country which are in conflict with the Qur'ān or the Sunna, it would be necessary to lay down (in the Constitution) that such laws shall be gradually, within a specified period, amended in conformity with the Islamic Law or repealed.

3. The State shall be based not on geographical, racial, linguistic or any other materialistic concepts, but on those principles and ideals which form the life-blood of Islamic ideology.

4. It shall be incumbent upon the State to uphold the Right (*Marūf*) and to suppress the Wrong (*Munkar*) as presented in the Qur'ān and

the Sunna, to take all measures necessary for the revival and advancement of the cultural pattern of Islam, and to make provision for Islamic education in accordance with the requirements of the various recognized schools of thought.

5. It shall be incumbent upon the State to strengthen the bonds of unity and brotherhood among all the Muslims of the world and to inhibit among the Muslim citizens of the State the growth of all prejudicial tendencies based on distinctions of race or language or territory or any other materialistic consideration so as to preserve and strengthen the unity of the *Millat-al-Islamiah*.[1]

6. It shall be the responsibility of the government to guarantee the provision of basic human necessities, i.e., food, clothing, housing, medical relief, and education to all citizens who might temporarily or permanently be incapable of earning their livelihood due to unemployment, sickness, or other reason, and to make no distinction of religion or race in that regard.

CITIZEN'S RIGHTS

7. The citizens shall be entitled to all the rights conferred upon them by the Islamic law, i.e., they shall be assured, within the limits of the law, of full security of life, property and honor, freedom of religion and belief, freedom of worship, freedom of person, freedom of expression, freedom of movement, freedom of association, freedom of occupation, equality of opportunity, and the right to benefit from public services.

8. No citizen shall, at any time, be deprived of these rights, except under the law, and none shall be awarded any punishment on any charge without being given full opportunity of defense and without the decision of a court of law.

9. The recognized Muslim schools of thought shall have, within the limits of the law, complete religious freedom. They shall have the right to impart religious instruction to their adherents and the freedom to propagate their views. Matters coming under the purview of Personal Law shall be administered in accordance with their respective codes of jurisprudence (*fiqh*), and it will be desirable to make provision for the administration of such matters by their respective judges (*qādīs*).

10. The non-Muslim citizens of the State shall have, within the limits

[1] The Muslim community.

of the law, complete freedom of religion and worship, mode of life, culture and religious education. They shall be entitled to have all their matters concerning Personal Law administered in accordance with their own religious code, usages, and customs.

11. All obligations assumed by the State, within the limits of the Shari'a, towards the non-Muslim citizens shall be fully honored. They shall be entitled equally with the Muslim citizens to the rights of citizenship as enunciated in paragraph 7 above.

GOVERNANCE OF THE STATE

12. The Head of the State shall always be a male Muslim in whose piety, learning, and soundness of judgment the people or their elected representatives have full confidence.

13. The responsibility for the administration of the State shall primarily vest in the Head of the State, although he may delegate any part of his powers to any individual or body.

14. The function of the Head of the State shall not be autocratic but consultative (Shura'i), i.e., he will discharge his duties in consultation with persons holding responsible positions in the Government and with the elected representatives of the people.

15. The Head of the State shall have no right to suspend the Constitution wholly or partly or to run the administration in any other way but on a consultative basis.

16. The body empowered to elect the Head of the State shall also have the power to remove him by a majority of vote.

17. In respect of civic rights, the Head of the State shall be on the level of equality with other Muslims and shall not be above the law.

18. All citizens, whether members of the Government and officials or private persons, shall be subject to the same laws and the jurisdiction of the same courts.

19. The judiciary shall be separate from and independent of the executive, so that it may not be influenced by the executive in the discharge of its duties.

20. The propagation and publicity of such views and ideologies as are calculated to undermine the basic principles and ideals on which the Islamic State rests, shall be prohibited.

21. The various zones or regions of the country shall be considered

864 MODERN INDIA AND PAKISTAN

administrative units of a single state. They shall not be racial, linguistic, or tribal units but only administrative areas which may be given such powers under the supremacy of the Center as may be necessary for administrative convenience. They shall not have the right to secede.

22. No interpretation of the Constitution which is in conflict with the provisions of the Qur'ān or the Sunna shall be valid.

THE LIBERAL APPROACH

An influential school of thought in Pakistan which differs from the orthodox ulamā believes in a more radical interpretation of the principles contained in the Qur'ān and the traditions of the Prophet. That is, it does not contest the orthodox belief in the validity of the basic principles of Islam, nor does it reject all earlier thinking concerning them, but it insists that the interpretation of these principles should be freed from the shackles of inherited opinion and should make allowance for the changed needs of the times. The difference between the conservative and liberal approaches is thus not one of principle but of degree.

The selections included here are from the speeches and writings of Ishtiāq Husain Qureshī, who has compiled this section of our readings on the rise and growth of Pakistani nationalism. Qureshī was born in India in 1903 and completed his education at the University of Delhi and at Cambridge, where he was a member of Rahmat Alī's group. Even as a student he took part in the noncooperation and Khilāfat movements, and subsequently became a member of the District Congress Committee of Etah and of the Provincial Khilāfat Committee of the United Provinces. As a result of his efforts in behalf of the Muslim League on the eve of Partition, he was elected to the Constituent Assembly of India on the Muslim League ticket and later to the Constituent Assembly for Pakistan, of which he remained a member until its dissolution in 1954. Appointed to the government of Pakistan in early 1949, Qureshī rose from deputy minister to minister with full cabinet rank (1951–1954). The author of numerous works on Indo-Muslim institutions and culture, he has held the chairs of History and Political Science in the Universities of Delhi and Lahore, and more recently has come to the United States as visiting professor at Columbia University.

ISHTIĀQ HUSAIN QURESHĪ
The Basic Principles of an Islamic Polity

[From All-Pakistan Political Science Conference, *Proceedings*, 1950, Presidential address of Session III, pp. 1–5]

The constitution of a country must reflect the ideals on which its people want to base their political life. In Pakistan these ideals have never been debatable or ambiguous and have now been clearly set forth in the Objectives Resolution passed by the Assembly, with which all of you are familiar. The most outstanding feature of the Objectives Resolution is that the constitution of Pakistan shall be based on the ideals of Islam. The implementation of this decision, I would point out, requires the utmost circumspection and is beset with formidable difficulties. Broadly speaking, we are fully familiar with the ideology of Islam, but we have failed to keep abreast of the progress made by the world in the development of political institutions and the social fabric alike. We have now been suddenly faced with the great task of applying our ideology to modern needs. . . . If Islam were simply a code of certain rigid laws or even legal concepts, it would, perhaps, have been easy enough to apply them to such spheres of political life as were covered by it. But Islam is a dynamic force, a concept of life not of law, a guidance for the springs of thought and action and not a static code of action. In other words, Islam is a live and dynamic ideology and not a dead unprogressive and static collection of injunctions and prohibitions. It requires a new interpretation at every stage of our development and cannot be content merely with precedents and past usage. Islam does not discard precedents and traditions, but it lays emphasis upon the progressive unfolding of the creative instincts of mankind in accordance with the eternal principles defined by revelation. Islam limits the field of human deliberation within the precincts of moral and spiritual righteousness, but within these limitations it gives the human spirit the fullest freedom to find new methods of fulfillment in creative effort. If this analysis of the spirit of Islam is correct, you would understand what a difficult task we have set ourselves in this twentieth century by proclaiming to the world that our constitution will be based upon Islamic principles, because these principles have to be interpreted in accordance with all that is best and profound in human thought today.

At every step, however, we may be pulled by conflicting forces. On the one hand, we have a group of persons who seem to think that it is no longer possible to go beyond the institutions or even the procedure adopted in the early days of Islam when conditions were entirely different. These persons would want us to reproduce a society which no longer exists and a polity which was suited to that society. They would make us believe that all that was done at that time was the final interpretation of Islam and [that] it is not possible for the human intellect to deviate from it in any detail. This position is fallacious as I will try to show very shortly. If we were told to follow the principles which guided the creators of the Republic after the death of the Prophet, there could have been no difference of opinion with them. But when for every action or institution we are expected to find a precedent, we are being asked to act in a most un-Islamic manner. We must distinguish from the principle and the methods of its expression, from the spirit and the form which the action to fulfill it had to take in those circumstances. To give you a parallel, whereas a person who says that the Hāj [pilgrimage to Mecca] is a religious obligation is speaking the truth, he would not be in his senses if he insisted that the journey must be made on camels and not by any modern vehicle of transport. A constitution, I must emphasize, is only an instrument, a vehicle for achieving certain ends. It should be such as can serve those ends, it is true, but it should not be considered to be the end in itself. . . .

The moral concepts of our people are based upon the teachings of our religion. If, therefore, the polity of Pakistan is to be based upon a firm foundation of a righteous ideology, there is no motive force, but that of Islam which can act as the basis. To ask an overwhelmingly Muslim people to discard its innermost convictions in framing its constitution is to ask it to commit suicide. Therefore, there should be no doubt in the mind of any Pakistani, whether a Muslim or a non-Muslim, that the only enduring polity which can ensure justice and fairplay to all and which can make a contribution to the welfare of . . . humanity can be one which is based upon the principles of Islam. For the sake of a handful of persons who may have come to disbelieve either in Islam itself or in its dynamic possibilities this essential need cannot be overlooked.

Thus the only rational conclusion which emerges is that the Constituent Assembly was right in setting for itself the ideal of Islam as the main objective to be achieved in its constitution; but this ideal should be given a rational, dynamic interpretation. It is in this matter of interpretation, as I said before, that our main difficulties lie. For one thing, the critics of my views may ask me how we can distinguish the essence from the form. In other words, how far is it possible to define the principles which should actuate an Islamic polity, and how far can we go in discarding precedents without injuring the principles? Fortunately, so far as I can see, this question was answered for us in a most miraculous manner by the Prophet himself. Some time before his death, in his last Hāj, the fulfillment of his mission was proclaimed by revelation in the verse which heralded the completion of the faith for the Muslims. At that time it was realized by the Prophet as well as his companions that his mission having been fulfilled, his life in this world was also to come to an end; and yet he did not define any political institutions or lay down any definitive forms of government for his people. This I take to mean that having, by his teachings and through revelation, given to his people an ideology, he abstained from laying down any hard and fast rules for organizing the governmental or administrative machinery of his people. A complete code of principles was now in the hands of the community, but it was not fettered by any rigid rules in the matter of applying those principles to the needs of government. The foundations of the polity were laid in the Qur'ān and the teachings of the Prophet, the edifice was to be built in accordance with the needs of the successive generations by the creative spirit of the Muslim peoples guided by the teachings of Islam. Is this action of the great Exemplar not a clear guidance for us? Does it not show us that for guidance in the matter of framing a constitution for Pakistan we should turn to the principles contained in the teachings of the Qur'ān and the Prophet and should look upon precedents only as an ephemeral interpretation of those principles?

So far as constitutional matters, as apart from moral behavior and rules of conduct in certain circumstances, are concerned, we find two principles clearly narrated in the Qur'ān. The first principle is that the Muslims should obey God, His Prophet, and those who from amongst themselves are put in authority over them; the other principle, repeated at various places, is that Muslims should cooperate in righteousness and justice, but never in unrighteousness and injustice. These are important constitutional principles which form the basic principle of good government. The first verse properly interpreted means that a Muslim's first duty is to God and he should do nothing which comes into conflict with that duty. He should not, whatever be the cost, compromise his allegiance to the clear injunctions of the Qur'ān and the teachings of the Prophet by obeying any un-Islamic orders of the State. In other words, a really Islamic government can never ask its people to carry out an un-Islamic policy or to follow an order which is in clear contravention of Islam. And this is further strengthened by the second verse which I have quoted. The basis of human action should be moral and not merely political. There should be no divorce between fundamental morality and political activity. This refers to states and individuals alike. A Muslim state should so frame its policies that it does not become an engine of oppression at home or a supporter of injustice abroad. The individual should refrain from any activity which is unrighteous, unjust, or immoral. He must refuse to subordinate his moral principles to other considerations. This view carried to its logical interpretation confers the right of disobedience on the individual; but then he should be quite clear in his mind that he is in the right. If he is in doubt, he must obey the government so that the bonds of discipline and unity are not broken asunder. Thus by a two-fold emphasis upon righteousness, Islam attempts to build up a righteous polity, but, having provided that, it expects complete discipline. Where it is absolutely clear that on obeying an order a man is likely to contravene an injunction of God, he must disobey, but in all other circumstances, he must abide by the dictates of the government.

It should, however, be emphasized that the right of disobedience is to be used only in extreme circumstances. It is even possible to hold that this right does not exist. Having laid down a severe moral code for the State, it may be argued, Islam does not envisage any circumstances in which it can palpably deviate from the right path. The order to obedience is positive, the right of disobedience can only be inferred. Actually if the state is effectively prevented from disobeying the injunctions of Islam, the right of disobedience would automatically disappear. But has Islam provided effective safeguards against the deviation of the state from the right path? Legally it could have been laid down that a body of jurists would have the authority to declare any action of the government illegal, which ruling would be binding. But no such authority was ever set up nor envisaged, for the simple reason that Islam does not invest any body of jurists or lawyers with political power. This is in keeping with its refusal to set up a priestly class. Islam is a religion without any priests; it is a Faith, not a church, it trusts its followers and does not seek to set up human guardians over their conscience.

This is in accordance with the great political sagacity which the liberal creed of Islam has displayed in other fields. A state will remain Muslim to the extent and for the time that its people are Muslim. An Islamic state cannot be forced upon an un-Islamic people. Islam, therefore, concentrates on the necessity of making the people true Muslims and for this purpose has laid it down that there should always be a group of persons among the believers, who by their precept and example, hold aloft the torch of true Islam and preach righteousness and true belief, but these persons have not been given any political power, because Islam does not believe in compulsion which defeats its own purpose. The true safeguard against the state deviating from the path of truth is, therefore, an effective machinery for the dissemination of true knowledge so that the mass of the people may abide by the ideals of Islam. Having provided that, Islam trusts the people to run the government in accordance with the tenets of the Faith.

The government has, therefore, to be organized on a basis which makes it possible that all decisions should be the results of mutual consultation. This brings me to the third fundamental principle which has been clearly defined in the Qur'ān. Muslims are expected to order their affairs by mutual consultation, which is the basis of democracy. It is inherent in the idea of consultation that the majority view shall prevail and personal opinions shall be subordinated to discipline and requirements of unity.

Sovereignty in a Truly Islamic State

This excerpt from Qureshī's presidential address before the second all-Pakistan Political Science Conference, 1951, is directed against the claims of the ulamā to be the sole authoritative interpreters of Islamic law, *Shar'* (Sharī'a). The author's faith in democracy has been shared by most leading politicians in Pakistan.

[From the second All-Pakistan Political Science Conference, *Proceedings*, 1951, Presidential address of Session I, pp. 2–8]

The political sovereign in Pakistan, like any other country, are the people. This does not come into conflict with the idea of the sovereignty of God. God is sovereign in the universe and His will cannot be challenged by anyone. In that sense God is sovereign in every country, Muslim or non-Muslim. He is equally sovereign in those socialist countries where His authority is challenged and His existence denied as He is in countries where people prostrate themselves before Him five times a day in recognition of the fact that He is the sole arbiter of their fates, their Creator and Master. But when we are talking of the real sovereign this idea does not remain relevant. In spite of the sovereignty of God there have been states, nations, and communities which have denied His existence. It is not inconceivable, howsoever improbable it may be, that the people of Pakistan may cease to believe in God. It is in the very nature of the freedom given by his Creator to man that he should be free to act in accordance with his beliefs and convictions. If the people of Pakistan— God forbid—stray from the path of the Truth, the sovereignty of God will not cease, but the authority of the people will direct the life in the country in entirely different channels. In a worldly sense, therefore, the people of Pakistan possess at present the final authority even to decide whether they shall be Muslims or not. It is, therefore, obvious that the people of Pakistan are as sovereign as the people of any other country because they can, if they so desire, make any decisions, for better, for worse.

The concept of legal sovereignty has been strong in the annals of Islam. Looking at the past, the Muslims have recognized the sovereignty of the law. No authority has been permitted to stand between the law and its majesty. The law of Islam—the *Shar'*—has been considered to be the final legal authority in all Muslim countries. The highest executive in the land—the caliph, for that matter, the Prophet himself—was not considered higher than the law. The law equally applied to everyone because the Islamic conception of law is different from the Western conception. In the West, the law is the will of the sovereign. In Islamic countries the law is the will of God. In this sense we might say that Islam recognizes the sovereignty of God and, therefore, in a limited sense a Muslim state is a theocratic state. But the terms "theocracy" as well as the sovereignty of God have been misapplied in many communities and, therefore, they are not applicable to an Islamic state. Theocracy in the West is a kingdom of God where authority vests in specially ordained priests who exercise it on behalf of God. This is not the conception of Islam. Islam has no priesthood and, therefore, no special agents of God to administer the law which expresses His will.

It would be of some interest to us to analyze the position as envisaged by Islam and to remove the pitfalls which exist for the unwary in this quest. Islam envisages a Muslim people guided by the teachings of Islam in ordering its affairs. This community, for the purposes of convenience, elected, in the earlier days, a high executive, called the caliph, to carry on the business of the State on its behalf. This executive of the State, the caliph and later the sultan, was only an agent to carry out the will of the people and the people being Muslims naturally demanded that their affairs should be conducted in accordance with their beliefs and convictions. The *Shar'* included within its fold three main principles, two immutable and one mutable. The immutable principles are the Qur'ān and the authentic Hadīth of the Prophet; the latter, according to the Muslims is not so much an enlargement as an interpretation of the principles enunciated in the revelation. The mutable factor is the interpretation of these principles which has been arrived at by the application of human reason to apply them to the changing needs of humanity in different conditions. It is wrong, therefore, to say that the *Shar'* is entirely immutable. The first two principles of it certainly are immutable, but, as I have pointed out, the third principle which is so necessary for the application of Islamic principles to our own lives must necessarily be progressive. In the body of Islamic law known to us today there is considerable contribution of this third principle and it needs reconsideration for being applied in circumstances which have so considerably altered.

The recognition of the legal sovereignty of a code of law has certain implications: one of these is that the courts would directly administer it without the interference of the legislature or the executive authority. This method was followed during the Middle Ages in all Islamic countries. But today there are very few countries where this conception prevails. Those Muslim countries which had to give up this practice had certain valid reasons to do so. As I have pointed out earlier, the *Shar'*, as it exists today, has a considerable corpus of judge-made law. Unfortunately, the tendency amongst Muslim jurists has been, like other judges, of basing their interpretation on the past body of previous interpretations. This was healthy, because otherwise it would have been impossible to maintain a continuity of tradition in the Muslim legal system. However, after a lapse of many centuries, with changing conditions, whereas the immutable principles upon which the *Shar'* is based continued to be valid, the line of reasoning which led to the interpretation of these eternal principles was not always in keeping with the progress that human knowledge had made. To leave the courts to decide what is in accordance with Islamic law, it is necessary to define Islamic law properly and to separate the grain from the husk. From such a complex mass it is not within the capacity of every lawyer or judge to extricate the basic principles, because this will in itself involve fresh interpretation. For the purposes of uniformity it is also necessary that a sound tradition should grow up and, if the judge-made law makes deviations either from the principles or the needs of the people, it should be possible to correct the mistakes through a different human agency.

This analysis brings us to the fundamental considerations which hold today in determining the legal sovereign in our new constitution. Should we accept the *Shar'* as it stands today without any reinterpretation or reorientation? Should we have a legislature and what part has the legislature to play if the sovereignty of the *Shar'* is accepted? Would it be wise to put any limitations on the power of the legislature which may be enforced constitutionally? And, lastly, what would be the relationship between the legal sovereign that we may choose to accept and the political sovereign, on one hand, and the real sovereign, on the other? . . .

It has been recognized in all Muslim countries that in many respects the mutable part of the *Shar'* requires considerable overhauling and the immutable bases need a new interpretation. This feeling has been shared by some of the leading theologians of the Muslim world. Therefore, it would not be in keeping with the progressive tendencies of Islam to recognize the *Shar'* in its present form as the legal sovereign. It may be argued that there is no difficulty in accepting the Qur'ān and the Sunna as the legal sovereign; but until a new interpretation is accepted by the people, the difference in interpretation will create not only difficulties but discord as well. How the interpretation should be revised and made acceptable to the people is quite a different problem. It will require considerable research, careful thinking and propagation amongst the people. If the work is left entirely to the courts, it is obvious that the interpretation will be only legalistic and not necessarily wise or sound; besides, to make it universally acceptable it is necessary in this twentieth century that every interpretation should be put in the public forum so that the combined judgment of the people may accept the one which it finds the most rational. It is a well-known principle of legislation that a law should conform to the moral conscience of the people, otherwise it will fail in its application. The moral conscience of the people can be swayed in favor or against an interpretation only with the help of public discussion. Treated as the close preserve of a few lawyers, theologians, jurists, or judges, the law would gradually find itself in disharmony with public sentiment. Our present attitude towards the dictates of the *Shar'* will completely illustrate my point. Our theologians, learned in the traditions of the Islamic legal system, have kept the torch burning, but have failed to spread its light among the people, because they have not trusted the people. They have considered the interpretation of the principles of Islam as their close preserve and by not taking the people into their confidence have created a wide gulf between their own views and the outlook of the intelligent sections of the nation. In every Muslim country, therefore, there has come into existence a wide gulf between the ulamā of the orthodox schools and the intelligentsia. This has done a great harm to Islam, because, as the result of this division, Islam has ceased to play that vital role in the life of the people which was its due. The intensity of these antagonisms varies from country to country and even in the same country from class to class but it does exist everywhere, yielding a most pernicious crop of laxity and indifference. But it is a disease which must be rooted out from the body politic of Islam.

It is obvious that the only place where discussions can take place in connection with the reinterpretation and reorientation of the *Shar'* is the legislature, because as the supreme representative of the people, the legislature alone can speak for them and accept on their behalf what seems rational and proper out of the mass of argument and commentary putting forward different points of view. Another happy result of these discussions will be that every problem shall come into the public forum and will be discussed from a million platforms; and, as problems are discussed they will sink into the subconscious mind of the people and ultimately become a part of their convictions. Thus interpretation and conviction will go hand in hand. It has been suggested by some that the constitution should provide for a body of learned theologians and jurists to veto any legislation that they consider to be against the *Shar'*. This would be a most retrograde step, because then the responsibility of understanding and interpreting Islam will be limited to a few persons rather than the entire nation. All the difficulties which would arise if the courts are left with the interpretation of the Qur'ān and the Sunna will be accentuated if a body like this is set up to control the activities of the legislature. Instead of harmony it would create resentment and even rebellion.

It has been argued that none except those who are deeply steeped in legal knowledge and theology have the capacity to interpret the Qur'ān. This is true in a limited sense; when it comes to the application of a law to a case with legal nicety, the layman is at a grave disadvantage. The comprehensive principles and their broad application to the life of the community is not so technically legal. Only a lawyer can be a judge; but a legislator need not be a trained lawyer. The legislator accepts principles which are given a legal garb by experts and a judge-made law grows up around that legislation. It is, therefore, a mistake to think that only the ulamā are capable of legislating in accordance with the principles enunciated in the Qur'ān and the Sunna. The last of the Prophets was born amongst a backward and uneducated people; he did not limit his mission to trained jurists and lawyers. It is quite likely that the legislature may make mistakes, but these mistakes will be rectified in course of time. On the other hand if the interpretation of Islamic principles is to be based entirely upon authoritative rulings of judges and jurists, their mistakes would take long to rectify, for then the entire approach would be authoritative and not persuasive. For achieving a quick rectification of mistakes, the legislature will have to be left unhampered and it would be unwise to put any limitations on its authority.

This does not mean that our experts in Islamic learning and law will have no influence. Their learning and piety will add authority to their opinion. There is, however, much difference between the authority which the opinion of an expert possesses and the legal sanction behind it. Once the opinions of a small body of experts begin to be vested with the authority of the law, the freedom of the mass of the people to choose from amongst the interpretations vanishes. Besides, persuasion and discussion are at a discount; they gradually disappear. There is a danger of the emergence of a class or a set of persons vested with sacerdotal authority. Islam does not tolerate the growth of a priesthood, nor does it encourage the division of the people into a clergy and the laity. Indeed no particular class has been given any authority to interpret the principles of Islam. The reason for this attitude is that the growth of a class vested with any sacerdotal authority or religious sanctity discourages the mass of the people from acquiring the true knowledge of the Faith. Real knowledge becomes the monopoly of the few and creates indifference among the rest. Sometimes it even engenders hostility. Although the history of the ulamā of Islam has been remarkably free from a class consciousness based upon selfish motives, yet there are many instances in which certain sections of the ulamā have exploited their position to the detriment of the *millat* [the Muslim community or nation]. Islam envisages the Muslims as a secular society believing in the principles of Islam and, therefore, acting upon its precepts. It trusts the mass of the Muslims to do their duty. It does provide for discipline and goes even to the extent of punishing the black sheep, but so far as the Muslims as a community are concerned, they have been entrusted, and no one else, to organize themselves into an instrument for practicing and propagating, by precept and example, the message that was delivered to our Prophet in its final form. There is a tradition of the Prophet which says that there shall be no consensus on an error amongst his people. This is not only a prophecy but is also the embodiment of the trust that Islam places in its followers. If the mass of the people are Muslims and their faith is sound, they will instinctively accept the correct interpretation. If they do not accept the correct interpretation and wilfully persist in error, it is obvious that no authority can put them right. The Muslim people, therefore, are the sole authority, guided, of course, by the advice of the experts to decide which interpretation they would follow. The advice, however, has no binding authority. To leave the legislature unhampered, therefore, will be in keeping with the spirit of Islam.

By adopting this attitude Islam has acted in accordance with human nature. All philosophies and religions can thrive only on conviction and a voluntary surrender of the human will to their precepts. No conviction or religion can be forced upon a people. Attempts to do so result either in failure or in disasters. From the point of view of political philosophy, this attitude of Islam is not only correct but the very essence of wisdom. From the analysis of the theory of sovereignty which I have given in the beginning it would be obvious that Islam seeks to establish a complete harmony among the real sovereign, the political sovereign, and the legal sovereign. The legal sovereign shall be the Muslim law; but its definition shall be in the hands of a legislature representing the people which will, by deliberation and discussion, decide how to apply the principles of Islam to the needs of the community in varying circumstances. If the people of Pakistan are overwhelmingly Muslims and their representatives in the legislature represent their opinions and views, it is obvious that they will be honest guardians of the teachings of Islam. The political sovereign shall be the people who will elect and dismiss their legislatures and their governments. We have accepted this principle in our Objectives Resolution wherein we have recognized that the people are the vehicle of the authority delegated by God to the state of Pakistan. The real sovereign will be basically the principles of Islam, which influence the public mind only if the problems are brought into the public forum and discussed at full length. If we want that Islam should be the real sovereign in Pakistan we will have to strengthen the Islamic elements in the education of our children and our people. And one of the methods of education is that the problems facing the community shall be discussed openly, permitting all those who have something to say to participate in the discussion.

CHAPTER XXVIII

SIX PATHS TO
INDIA'S FUTURE

The intellectual climate of India has always allowed a great variety of ideas to flourish and coexist with one another. The modern period of Indian thought reveals this luxuriant tendency as much as do the classical and medieval periods, with one significant difference. Whereas the speculations of the literate class (both Hindu and Muslim) had traditionally centered in religion, by the time the British withdrew from the subcontinent educated Indians and Pakistanis were primarily concerned with urgent economic and political problems.

This remarkable transformation of values had of course by no means permeated the entire society in the space of a century and a half. Hundreds of millions of peasant- and artisan-villagers in South Asia continue to abide by the rules and precepts laid down centuries ago in their sacred books, and the thought of changing their traditional way of life would seem to them as fantastic and dangerous as travel to other solar systems may seem to the average Westerner today. Genuine Hindu saints, such as Rāmana Maharshi in South India, continue to appear, and pilgrimages to holy places have actually increased with the advent of modern transportation. Even among the educated and Westernized fraction of the population there is no lack of interest in religious speculation and no dearth of writing on religious subjects.

Nevertheless, now that independent India has become a part of the modern world, the pull of the tide is today strongly secular, drawing men's minds toward the practical tasks involved in creating a better social order. Many prescriptions are being offered as to the best means of achieving this goal, some old and some new. The moderate program of social reform and gradual political change initiated by Rāmmohun Roy could be said to be the dominant philosophy of the Congress Party which governs India today. Meanwhile, Gāndhi's more radical social gospel is still being preached by his disciple Vinobā Bhāve, under whom the *bhūdān* (land-gift) movement has reached astounding proportions.

As these older traditions, including the Hindu nationalism of the Extremists, have continued into independent India, so younger ones have emerged in recent decades, each proclaiming a different path to a better future. The seed-time of these philosophies, interestingly enough, was the Gāndhian era, when many of the younger leaders brought to the fore by the intensification of the nationalist movement found the Mahātmā's ideas medieval, much as they admired him personally. Inevitably their minds reached out for more modern ideas to Europe, where many had lived as students. Ideologies such as Fascism, Socialism, and Communism seemed to answer India's needs in two ways. Not only did the collectivist spirit common to them all promise to heal the psychological and economic gap between the tiny educated elite and the impoverished mass of the population, but British Socialists, German and Italian Fascists, and Russian Communists also offered to provide moral and often material assistance to the independence movement.

In this concluding chapter of our survey of more than three thousand years of Indian thought, the doctrines of six contrasting schools—not of metaphysics but of political philosophy—are presented by authoritative spokesmen. Hindu nationalism in its most virulent form, dictatorial National Socialism, liberal Democratic Socialism, revolutionary International Communism, evolutionary National Communism, and Gāndhian decentralism—all vie with one another for control of men's minds in independent India. Which school, if any, will win out is perhaps in the long run less important than the fact that all together have been slowly but surely acting to leaven the dough of age-old custom and belief with the bitter yeast of politics.

V. D. SĀVARKAR: HINDU NATIONALIST

Unaffected by the new political ideas that came into India after the First World War, but exacerbated by the rise of Muslim nationalism, the tradition of extremist Hindu nationalism has been carried forward into the post-independence period by a group of zealots deeply imbued with its ideology. Its most outstanding proponent and theoretician in recent decades has been Vinayak Damodar Sāvarkar. Born in 1883, and a Chitpāvan brāhman like his fellow-Mahārāshtrians Rānade, Gokhale and Tilak, Sāvarkar was the second son of a landowner known for both his Sanskrit scholarship and his Western-style education. Two incidents from his youth presaged his lifelong antipathy to those he considered Hindu-ism's foes. At the age of ten, hearing of bloody Hindu-Muslim riots in the United Provinces, he led a gang of his schoolmates in a stone-throwing attack on the village mosque. At sixteen, his anger at the hanging of two Mahārāshtrian terrorists made him vow to devote his life to driving the British out of India.

On entering Fergusson College at Poona, Sāvarkar quickly organized a patriotic society among his fellow-students. Through poems, articles, and speeches he reminded them of India's glorious past and the need to regain her freedom. In 1905 he arranged for a huge bonfire of foreign cloth and persuaded Tilak to speak to the crowd gathered around it. For this he was rusticated from his college, but with Tilak's help secured a scholarship to study in London from an Indian patriot there, on the understanding that he would never enter government service.

From 1906 to 1910, in the guise of a student of law, the young Sāvarkar bearded the British lion in its den. His "New India" group learned the art of bomb-making from a Russian revolutionary in Paris, and planned the assassination of the hated Lord Curzon. One member of the group electrified London when he shot and killed an important official of the India Office and then went proudly to the gallows. Sāvarkar himself was arrested a few months later, but by this time he had already published his nationalistic interpretation of the 1857–58 Mutiny and Rebellion, entitling it *The First Indian War of Independence of 1857*.

When the ship carrying him back to India for trial stopped at Mar-seilles, Sāvarkar created an international incident by swimming ashore and claiming asylum on French soil. The Hague International Tribunal ultimately judged his recapture by the British authorities irregular but justifiable, but by this time he had already been twice sentenced to life-imprisonment. In 1911 Sāvarkar was transported to the Andaman Islands (India's "Devil's Island" in the tropical Bay of Bengal) where he found his elder brother, a renowned terrorist, already there before him.

Agitation in India secured his release from confinement in 1924, but until 1937 his movements were restricted and he was forbidden to take part in politics. Nehru, Bose, and Roy all sent him congratulatory messages on his final return to the political arena, and the Hindu Mahāsabhā (Great Assembly of Hindus), founded in 1919 and the largest Hindu communal party, elected him as their president for seven consecutive years, until failing health forced him to resign.

Intending to unite and strengthen all Hindudom, Sāvarkar advocated the removal of inter-caste barriers, the entry of untouchables into orthodox temples, and the reconversion of Hindus who had become Muslims or Christians. During the Second World War he propagated the slogan: "Hinduize all politics and militarize Hindudom," and urged Hindus to enlist in the armed forces in order to learn the arts of war.

Sāvarkar and Gāndhi had disagreed from the time of their discussions in London in 1909 (which may have been what provoked the latter to write his famous *Hind Swarāj*). Sāvarkar now made no bones about his conviction that Gāndhi's doctrine of absolute nonviolence was "absolutely sinful." [1] As the fateful hour of independence from British rule drew near, Sāvarkar and the Mahāsabhā strenuously opposed the Muslim League's demand for Pakistan. Gāndhi's apparent vacillation on this issue and his post-Partition fasts for the protection of India's Muslims and for good-will toward Pakistan infuriated many Hindu nationalists. Early in 1948 one of them, to avenge what he felt was Gāndhi's betrayal of the Hindu cause, felled him with three pistol shots.

The assassin, N. V. Godse, although no longer a member of the Mahāsabhā, was still known as a devoted lieutenant of Sāvarkar, who consequently had to stand trial with him. Acquitted because of lack of evidence linking him to the crime itself, but too ill to lead an active life, Sāvarkar retired to his home in Bombay. The ideology he helped to shape continues to animate the Hindu nationalist organizations, which in addition to the Hindu Mahāsabhā now include the Rāshtriya Swayamsevak Sangh (National Self-Service Organization), the Jan Sangh (People's Party), and Rām Rājya Parishad (Followers of the Divine Kingdom). Although greatly overshadowed by the Congress Party, their appeal to both patriotic and religious sentiment gives them a potentially strong position in India politics.

[1] Dhananjay Keer, *Savarkar and His Times*, p. 219.

VINAYAK SĀVARKAR
The Glories of the Hindu Nation

Deprived of writing materials during his days of imprisonment, Sāvarkar scratched on the whitewashed walls of his cell and then committed to memory the notes for his treatise on *Hindutva* ("Hindu-ness"). In the final portion of this work, published in 1924, he exultantly cited the geographical, racial, cultural, numerical, and religious ways in which the Hindu nation is superior to all other polities.

[From Sāvarkar, *Hindutva*, pp. 108–16]

So far we have not allowed any considerations of utility to prejudice our inquiry. But having come to its end it will not be out of place to see how far the attributes, which we found to be the essentials of *Hindutva,* contribute towards [the] strength, cohesion, and progress of our people. Do these essentials constitute a foundation so broad, so deep, so strong, that basing upon it the Hindu people can build a future which can face and repel the attacks of all the adverse winds that blow; or does the Hindu race stand on feet of clay?

Some of the ancient nations raised huge walls so as to convert a whole country into a fortified castle. Today their walls are trodden to dust or are but scarcely discernible by a few scattered mounds here and there; while the people they were meant to protect are not discernible at all! Our ancient neighbors, the Chinese, labored from generation to generation and raised a rampart, embracing the limits of an empire—so wide, so high, so strong—a wonder of human world. That too, as all human wonders must, sank under its own weight. But behold the ramparts of Nature! Have they not, these Himalayas, been standing there as one whose desires are satisfied—so they seemed to the Vedic bard—so they seem to us today. These are *our* ramparts that have converted this vast continent into a cosy castle.

You take up buckets and fill your trenches with water and call it [a] moat. Behold, Varuna[1] himself, with his one hand pushing continents aside, fills the gap by pouring seas on seas with the other! This Indian ocean, with its bays and gulfs, is *our* moat.

These are our frontier lines bringing within our reach the advantages of an inland as well as an insular country.

[1] God of the Waters.

She is the richly endowed daughter of God—this our Motherland. Her rivers are deep and perennial. Her land is yielding to the plow and her fields are loaded with golden harvests. Her necessaries of life are few and a genial nature yields them all almost for the asking. Rich in her fauna, rich in her flora, she knows she owes it all to the immediate source of light and heat—the sun. She covets not the icy lands; blessed be they and their frozen latitudes. If heat is at times "enervating" here, cold is at times benumbing there. If cold induces manual labor, heat removes much of its very necessity. She takes more delight in quenched thirst than in the parched throat. Those who have not, let them delight in exerting to have. But those who have—may be allowed to derive pleasure from the very fact of having. Father Thames is free to work at feverish speed, wrapped in his icy sheets. She loves to visit her ghats and watch her boats gliding down the Ganges, on her moonlit waters. With the plow, the peacocks, the lotus, the elephant, and the *Gītā,* she is willing to forego, if that must be, whatever advantage the colder latitudes enjoy. She knows she cannot have all her own way. Her gardens are green and shady, her granaries well stocked, her waters crystal, her flowers scented, her fruits juicy, and her herbs healing. Her brush is dipped in the colors of dawn and her flute resonant with the music of Gokul.[2] Verily Hind is the richly endowed daughter of God.

Neither the English nor the French—with the exception of [the] Chinese and perhaps the Americans, no people are gifted with a land that can equal in natural strength and richness the land of *Sindhustān.*[3] A country, a common home, is the first important essential of stable strong nationality; and as of all countries in the world our country can hardly be surpassed by any in its capacity to afford a soil so specially fitted for the growth of a great nation; we Hindus, whose very first article of faith is the love we bear to the common Fatherland, have in that love the strongest talismanic tie that can bind close and keep a nation firm and enthuse and enable it to accomplish things greater than ever.

The second essential of *Hindutva* puts the estimate of our latent powers of national cohesion and greatness yet higher. No country in the world, with the exception of China again, is peopled by a race so homogeneous,

[2] The village near Mathura where Krishna is said to have spent his boyhood.
[3] "Land of the Rivers." *Sindhu* (river) is presumably the earlier form from which *Hindu* derives.

yet so ancient and yet so strong both numerically and vitally. The Americans too, whom we found equally fortunate with us so far as the gift of an excellent geographical basis of nationality is concerned, are decidedly left behind. Mohamedans are no race nor are the Christians. They are a religious unit, yet neither a racial nor a national one. But we Hindus, if possible, are all the three put together and live under our ancient and common roof. The numerical strength of our race is an asset that cannot be too highly prized.

And culture? The English and the Americans feel they are kith and kin because they possess a Shakespeare in common. But not only a Kalidas or a Bhas, but Oh Hindus! ye possess a Ramayan and a Mahabharat in common—and the Vedas! One of the national songs the American children are taught to sing attempts to rouse their sense of eternal self-importance by pointing out to the hundred years twice told that stand behind their history. The Hindu counts his years not by centuries but by cycles—the *Yug* and the *Kalpa* [4]—and amazed asks: "O Lord of the line of Raghu [Rama], where has the kingdom of Ayodhya gone? O Lord of the line of Yadu [Krishna], where has Mathura gone!!" He does not attempt to rouse the sense of self-importance so much as the sense of proportion, which is Truth. And that has perhaps made him last longer than Ramses and Nebuchadnezzar. If a people that had no past have no future, then a people that had produced an unending galaxy of heroes and heroworshipers and who are conscious of having faught [fought] with and vanquished the forces whose might struck Greece and Rome, the Pharaohs and the Incas, dead, have in their history a guarantee of their future greatness more assuring than any other people on earth yet possess.

But besides culture the tie of common holyland has at times proved stronger than the chains of a Motherland. Look at the Mohamedans. Mecca to them is a sterner reality than Delhi or Agra. Some of them do not make any secret of being bound to sacrifice all India if that be to the glory of Islam or [if it] could save the city of their prophet. Look at the Jews. Neither centuries of prosperity nor sense of gratitude for the shelter they found can make them more attached or even equally attached to the several countries they inhabit. Their love is, and must necessarily be, divided between the land of their birth and the land of their prophets.

[4] The age and the eon.

If the Zionists' dreams are ever realized—if Palestine becomes a Jewish state and it will gladden us almost as much as our Jewish friends—they, like the Mohamedans, would naturally set the interests of their holyland above those of their Motherlands in America and Europe, and, in case of war between their adopted country and the Jewish state, would naturally sympathize with the latter, if indeed they do not bodily go over to it. History is too full of examples of such desertions to cite particulars. The Crusades again, attest to the wonderful influence that a common holyland exercises over peoples widely separated in race, nationality, and language, to bind and hold them together.

The ideal conditions, therefore, under which a nation can attain perfect solidarity and cohesion would, other things being equal, be found in the case of those people who inhabit the land they adore, the land of whose forefathers is also the land of their Gods and Angels, of Seers and Prophets; the scenes of whose history are also the scenes of their mythology.

The Hindus are about the only people who are blessed with these ideal conditions that are at the same time incentive to national solidarity, cohesion, and greatness. Not even the Chinese are blessed thus. Only Arabia and Palestine—if ever the Jews can succeed in founding their state there —can be said to possess this unique advantage. But Arabia is incomparably poorer in the natural, cultural, historical, and numerical essentials of a great people; and even if the dreams of the Zionists are ever realized into a Palestine state still they too must be equally lacking in these.

England, France, Germany, Italy, Turkey proper, Persia, Japan, Afganistan, [the] Egypt of today (for the old descendants of "Punto" and their Egypt is dead long since)—and other African states, Mexico, Peru, Chilly [Chile] (not to mention states and nations lesser than all these)— though racially more or less homogeneous, are yet less advantageously situated than we are in geographical, cultural, historical, and numerical essentials, besides lacking the unique gift of a sanctified Motherland. Of the remaining nations Russia in Europe, and the United States in America, though geographically equally well-gifted with us, are yet poorer, in almost every other requisite of nationality. China alone of the present comity of nations is almost as richly gifted with the geographical, racial, cultural, and numerical essentials as the Hindus are. Only in the possession of a common, a sacred, and a perfect language, the Sanskrit, and a sanctified Motherland, we are so far [as] the essentials that contribute to national solidarity are concerned more fortunate.

Thus the actual essentials of *Hindutva* are, as this running sketch reveals, also the ideal essentials of nationality. If we would we can build on this foundation of *Hindutva,* a future greater than what any other people on earth can dream of—greater even than our own past; provided we are able to utilize our opportunities! For let our people remember that great combinations are the order of the day. The leagues of nations, the alliances of powers, Pan-Islamism, Pan-Slavism, Pan-Ethiopism—all little beings are seeking to get themselves incorporated into greater wholes, so as to be better fitted for the struggle for existence and power. Those who are not naturally and historically blessed with numerical or geographical or racial advantages are seeking to share them with others. Woe to those who have them already as their birthright and know them not; or worse, despise them! The nations of the world are desperately trying to find a place in this or that combination for aggression:—can any one of you, Oh Hindus! whether Jain or Samāji [5] or Sanātani [6] or Sīkh or any other subsection, afford to cut yourselves off or fall out and destroy the ancient, the natural, and the organic combination that already exists? —a combination that is bound not by any scraps of paper nor by the ties of exigencies alone, but by the ties of blood and birth and culture? Strengthen them if you can; pull down the barriers that have survived their utility, of castes and customs, of sects and sections. What of interdining? But intermarriages between provinces and provinces, castes and castes, be encouraged where they do not exist. But where they already exist as between the Sīkhs and Sanātanies, Jains and Vaishnavas, Lingayats [7] and Non-Lingayats—suicidal be the hand that tries to cut the nuptial tie. Let the minorities remember they would be cutting the very branch on which they stand. Strengthen every tie that binds you to the main organism, whether of blood or language or common festivals and feasts or culture love you bear to the common Motherland. Let this ancient and noble stream of Hindu blood flow from vein to vein . . . till at last the Hindu people get fused and welded into an indivisible whole, till our race gets consolidated and strong and sharp as steel.

Just cast a glance at the past, then at the present: Pan-Islamism in Asia,

[5] A member of the Brāhmo or Ārya Samāj.   [6] Orthodox Hindu.
[7] A Hindu sect devoted exclusively to the worship of Shiva.

the political leagues in Europe, the Pan-Ethiopic movement in Africa and America—and then see, Oh Hindus, if your future is not entirely bound up with the future of India and the future of India is bound up, in the last resort, with Hindu strength. We are trying our best, as we ought to do, to develop the consciousness of and a sense of attachment to the greater whole, whereby Hindus, Mohamedans, Parsis, Christians, and Jews, would feel as Indians first and every other thing afterwards. But whatever progress India may have made to that goal one thing remains almost axiomatically true—not only in India but everywhere in the world —that a nation requires a foundation to stand upon and the essence of the life of a nation is the life of that portion of its citizens whose interests and history and aspirations are most closely bound up with the land and who thus provide the real foundation to the structure of their national state. Take the case of Turkey. The young Turks after the revolution had to open their parliament and military institutions to Armenians and Christians on a nonreligious and secular basis. But when the war with Servia came the Christians and Armenians first wavered and then many a regiment consisting of them went bodily over to the Servians, who politically and racially and religiously were more closely bound up with them. Take the case of America. When the German war broke out she suddenly had to face the danger of desertions of her German citizens; while the Negro citizens there sympathize more with their brethren in Africa than with their white countrymen. The American state, in the last resort, must stand or fall with the fortunes of its Anglo-Saxon constituents. So with the Hindus, they being the people, whose past, present, and future are most closely bound with the soil of Hindusthan as *Pitṛbhū*,[8] as *Puṇyabhū*,[9] they constitute the foundation, the bedrock, the reserved forces of the Indian state. Therefore even from the point of Indian nationality, must ye, Oh Hindus, consolidate and strengthen Hindu nationality: not to give wanton offense to any of our non-Hindu compatriots, in fact to any one in the world but in just and urgent self-defense of our race and land; to render it impossible for others to betray her or to subject her to unprovoked attacks by any of those "Pan-isms" that are struggling forth from continent to continent. As long as other communities in India or in the world are not respectively planning India first or Mankind first, but all are busy in organizing offensive and defensive alliances and com-

---

[8] Ancestral land.   [9] Holy land.

binations on entirely narrow racial or religious or national basis, so long, at least so long, Oh Hindus, strengthen if you can those subtle bonds that like nerve-threads bind you in One Organic Social Being. Those of you who in a suicidal fit try to cut off the most vital of those ties and dare to disown the name Hindu will find to their cost that in doing so they have cut themselves off from the very source of our racial life and strength.

The presence of only a few of these essentials of nationality which we have found to constitute *Hindutva* enabled little nations like Spain or Portugal to get themselves lionized in the world. But when all of those ideal conditions obtain here what is there in the human world that the Hindus cannot accomplish?

Thirty crores of people, with India for their basis of operation, for their Fatherland and for their Holyland, with such a history behind them, bound together by ties of a common blood and common culture can dictate their terms to the whole world. A day will come when mankind will have to face the force.

Equally certain it is that whenever the Hindus come to hold such a position whence they could dictate terms to the whole world—those terms cannot be very different from the terms which [the] *Gītā* dictates or the Buddha lays down. A Hindu is most intensely so, when he ceases to be a Hindu; and with a Kabir claims the whole earth for a Benares . . . or with a Tukaram exclaims: "My country? Oh brothers, the limits of the Universe—there the frontiers of my country lie."

SUBHĀS CHANDRA BOSE: NATIONAL SOCIALIST LEADER

"The earliest recollection I have of myself is that I used to feel like a thoroughly insignificant being." [1] So wrote the man who rose to become one of the most controversial figures in modern Indian politics. The sixth son and ninth child of a successful Bengali lawyer in Orissa, Subhās Chandra Bose (1897-1945) showed from his youth a burning desire to excel. Throughout his scholastic career he generally stood at the top of his class. His primary education was gained at a Baptist mission school,

[1] *Netaji's Life and Writings, Part One, An Indian Pilgrim; Or, Autobiography of Subhas Chandra Bose, 1897-1920*, p. 3.

but his parents insisted on his studying Sanskrit at the same time. At the age of fifteen Subhās discovered in the writings of Swāmī Vivekānanda the ideals of self-purification and social service. Soon afterward, as a student at Presidency College of the University of Calcutta, he became a great admirer of Aurobindo Ghose's mystic nationalism.

Subhās grew to manhood during the First World War, and found military life so appealing that he joined the Calcutta University unit of the India Defense Force. After finishing his B.A. in 1919, he was sent by his father to Cambridge to prepare for the Indian Civil Service. He succeeded in passing the rigorous I.C.S. examination, but a few months later resigned from the Service and returned to India to join the noncooperation movement, which was then at its height.

Subhās Chandra Bose's career both paralleled and rivaled that of his contemporary, Jawaharlāl Nehru. Each got his start under the wing of an outstanding Congress statesman—Bose under the Bengali lawyer Chittaranjan Dās, and Nehru under his father, Motilāl Nehru, who was a very close friend of Dās. Both Subhās and Jawaharlāl agitated for Congress to adopt the goal of complete independence (as opposed to dominion status) in the late 1920s; both were interested in spreading socialist ideas and in bringing the youth of the country into the nationalist movement. With his emergence as the spokesman for Bengal in the 1930s, however, Bose grew increasingly impatient with Gāndhi's leadership and his favoritism toward Nehru. Finally, in 1939, he openly disobeyed Gāndhi by running for a second term as Congress president and proposing a renewal of civil disobedience under his own direction. Although re-elected, Bose was so hampered by Gāndhi's noncooperation with his program that he resigned within a few months and founded his own leftist party, the Forward Bloc.

In 1941, making a dramatic escape from police surveillance after his release from jail for the eleventh time, Bose traveled via Afghanistan and Russia to Germany. Fascism had long attracted him and during his visits to Europe in the 1930s he had met Mussolini several times. He now called on Hitler and secured his backing in forming an Indian National Army, to be made up of captured Indian soldiers and officers. In 1943 a German submarine took him to Indonesia, whence he flew to Japan. General Tojo welcomed his collaboration and soon he was back in Southeast Asia organizing his Indian National Army there. As a military venture the I.N.A. had no effect, but it did create in the British grave doubts about the loyalty of their Indian troops, upon whom their rule in India ultimately depended.

Bose seems to have pictured himself as a sort of Indian Führer, and his troops and admirers addressed him as Netājī—"the leader." Rumors that he is still alive persist in India despite the attested fact that he died after a plane crash on Taiwan in 1945. Had he lived, there is little doubt that he would have greatly complicated the political negotiations of the post-war period. Bose owed his personal popularity in large part to the continuing appeal of quasi-religious nationalism, but he added to the Extremist tradition the glamor of military discipline under a colorful leader. His death and the failure of Fascism abroad brought to a sudden close this brief period of Indian interest in National Socialist ideology.

SUBHĀS CHANDRA BOSE
A Philosophy of Activism

Speaking to a conference of students in the 1920s, Bose attacked the theories of both Gāndhi and Aurobindo for their passive and antimodern tendencies. Stressing the importance of sound leadership, he called for an optimistic and combative outlook on life.
[From *Netaji Speaks to the Nation*, pp. 44–47]

As I look around me today, I am struck by two movements or two schools of thought about which, however small and insignificant I may be, it is my duty to speak out openly and fearlessly. I am referring to the two schools of thought, which have their centers at Sabarmati and Pondichéry. I am not considering the fundamental philosophy underlying those two schools of thought. This is not the time for metaphysical speculation. I shall talk to you today as [a] pragmatist, as one who will judge the intrinsic value of a school of thought [not] from a metaphysical point of view, but from experience of its actual effects and consequences.

The actual effect of the propaganda carried on by the Pondichéry school or thought is to create a feeling and an impression that there is nothing higher or nobler than peaceful contemplation, that Yoga means Pranayama and Dhyana, that while action may be tolerated as good, this propaganda has led many a man to forget that spiritual progress under the present-day conditions is possible only by ceaseless and unselfish action, that the best way to conquer nature is to fight her, and that it is weakness to seek refuge in contemplation when we are hemmed in on all sides by dangers and difficulties.

It is the passivism, not philosophic but actual, inculcated by these schools of thought against which I protest. In this holy land of ours, Ashramas [1] are not new institutions and ascetics and Yogis are not novel phenomena. They have held and they will continue to hold an honored place in society. But it is not their lead we shall have to follow if we are to create a new India at once free, happy, and great.

Friends, you will pardon me if in a fit of outspokenness I have trod on your sentiments. As I have just said I do not for one moment consider the fundamental philosophy underlying the two schools of thought but the actual consequences from a pragmatic point of view. In India we want today a philosophy of activism. We must be inspired by robust optimism. We have to live in the present and to adapt ourselves to modern conditions. We can no longer live in an isolated corner of the world. When India is free, she will have to fight her modern enemies with modern methods, both in the economic and in the political spheres. The days of the bullock-cart are gone and are gone for ever. Free India must prepare herself for any eventuality as long as the whole world does not accept wholeheartedly the policy of disarmament.

I am not one of those who in their zeal for modernism forget the glories of the past. We must take our stand on our past. India has a culture of her own which she must continue to develop along her own distinctive channels. In philosophy, literature, art, science, we have something new to give to the world which the world eagerly awaits. In a word, we must arrive at a synthesis. Some of our best thinkers and workers are already . . . engaged in the important task. We must resist the cry of "Back to the Vedas" on the one side, and on the other the meaningless craze for fashion and change of modern Europe. It is difficult to restrict a living movement within proper bound[s], but I believe that if the pioneers and leaders of the movement are on the right track, things will take their proper shape in due time.

A Synthesis Between Communism and Fascism

Writing in 1934, Bose stated his ambition of creating in India a synthesis of the new totalitarian ideologies of Europe. In passing he repudiated the hope of

[1] Religious communities or hermitages.

preserving parliamentary democracy to which Nehru, despite his sympathies for the Communist ideal, has continued to cling.

[From Bose, *The Indian Struggle, 1920–1934,* pp. 345–47]

A question which is on everybody's lips in Europe is: "What is the future of Communism in India?" In this connection it is worth while quoting the expressed opinion of Pandit Jawaharlāl Nehru, whose popularity in India today is, according to the [present] writer, second only to that of Mahātmā Gāndhi. In a press statement issued on December 18, 1933, he said: "I do believe that fundamentally the choice before the world today is one between some form of Communism and some form of Fascism, and I am all for the former, that is Communism. I dislike Fascism intensely and indeed I do not think it is anything more than a crude and brutal effort of the present capitalist order to preserve itself at any cost. There is no middle road between Fascism and Communism. One has to choose between the two and I choose the Communist ideal. In regard to the methods and approach to this ideal, I may not agree with everything that the orthodox Communists have done. I think that these methods will have to adapt themselves to changing conditions and may vary in different countries. But I do think that the basic ideology of Communism and its scientific interpretation of history is sound."

The view expressed here is, according to the [present] writer, fundamentally wrong. Unless we are at the end of the process of evolution or unless we deny evolution altogether, there is no reason to hold that our choice is restricted to two alternatives. Whether one believes in the Hegelian or in the Bergsonian or any other theory of evolution—in no case need we think that creation is at an end. Considering everything, one is inclined to hold that the next phase in world-history will produce a synthesis between Communism and Fascism. And will it be a surprise if that synthesis is produced in India? The view has been expressed in the Introduction that in spite of India's geographical isolation, the Indian awakening is organically connected with the march of progress in other parts of the world and facts and figures have been mentioned to substantiate that view. Consequently, there need be no surprise if an experiment, of importance to the whole world, is made in India—especially when we have seen with our own eyes that another experiment (that of Mahātmā Gāndhi) made in India has roused profound interest all over the world.

In spite of the antithesis between Communism and Fascism, there are

certain traits common to both. Both Communism and Fascism believe
in the supremacy of the State over the individual. Both denounce par-
liamentarian democracy. Both believe in party rule. Both believe in the
dictatorship of the party and in the ruthless suppression of all dissenting
minorities. Both believe in a planned industrial reorganization of the
country. These common traits will form the basis of the new synthesis.
That synthesis is called by the writer "Samyavada"—an Indian word,
which means literally "the doctrine of synthesis or equality." It will be
India's task to work out this synthesis.

Proclamation of the Provisional Government of Azād Hind [1]

Bose's career came to a climax on October 21, 1943, when he proclaimed
from Singapore the establishment of a provisional government of Free India,
with himself as "Head of State, Prime Minister and Minister for War, Minister
for Foreign Affairs and Supreme Commander of the Indian National Army." [2]
His proclamation on that occasion set forth the program and claims of the I.N.A.

[From *Netaji Speaks to the Nation*, pp. 315–18]

Having goaded Indians to desperation by its hypocrisy, and having
driven them to starvation and death by plunder and loot, British rule in
India has forfeited the good will of the Indian people altogether, and is
now living a precarious existence. It needs but a flame to destroy the
last vestige of that unhappy rule. To light that flame is the task of India's
Army of Liberation. Assured of the enthusiastic support of the civil
population at home and also of a large section of Britain's Indian Army,
and backed by gallant and invincible allies abroad, relying in the first instance on its own strength, India's Army of Liberation is confident of
fulfilling its historic role.

Now that the dawn of freedom is at hand, it is the duty of the people
to set up [a] provisional government of their own, and launch the last
struggle under the banner of that government. But with all the Indian
leaders in prison and the people at home totally disarmed—it is not possible to set up a provisional government within India or to launch an
armed struggle under the aegis of that government. It is, therefore, the
duty of the Indian Independence League in East Asia, supported by all
patriotic Indians at home and abroad, to undertake this task—the task

[1] Free India.   [2] *Netaji Speaks to the Nation*, p. 318.

of setting up a provisional government of Azad Hind (Free India), and of conducting the last fight for freedom, with the help of the Army of Liberation (that is, the Azad Hind Fauj or the Indian National Army) organized by the League.

Having been constituted as the Provisional Government of Azad Hind by the Indian Independence League in East Asia, we enter upon our duties with a full sense of the responsibility that has devolved on us. We pray that Providence may bless our work and our struggle for emancipation of our Motherland, and our comrades in arms for the cause of her freedom, for her welfare and her exaltation among the nations of the world.

The provisional government is entitled to and hereby claims the allegiance of every Indian. It guarantees religious liberty, as well as equal rights and equal opportunities to all its citizens. It declares its firm resolve to pursue the happiness and prosperity of the whole nation and of all its parts, cherishing all the children of the nation equally and transcending all the differences cunningly fostered by an alien government in the past.

In the name of God, in the name of by-gone generations, who have welded the Indian people into one nation, and in the name of the dead heroes who have bequeathed to us a tradition of heroism and self-sacrifice, we call upon the Indian people to rally round our banner, and to strike for India's freedom. We call upon them to launch the final struggle against the British and all their allies in India, and to prosecute the struggle with valor and perseverance and with full faith in final victory —until the enemy is expelled from Indian soil, and the Indian people are once again a free nation.

JAWAHARLĀL NEHRU: DEMOCRATIC SOCIALIST

Descended from a proud line of Kashmiri brāhmans, Jawaharlāl Nehru was born in 1889 in Allahabad, where the Ganges and Jumna rivers converge. His ancestors had settled in Delhi and served at the court of the Mughal emperors, but his father, Motilāl Nehru, had moved on to Allahabad to become a successful and wealthy lawyer at the high court there. As Jawaharlāl wrote of his childhood, "An only son of prosperous parents is apt to be spoilt, especially so in India."[1] The apple of his father's eye, he studied at home under a series of English governesses and tutors. When he was fifteen, his father sent him to Harrow; at seventeen he entered Cambridge University; and at twenty he went down to London to take his law degree at the Inns of Court, where Gāndhi had studied some two decades earlier. After seven formative years in England, Jawaharlāl returned to India in 1912 to practice law with his father.

Motilāl Nehru possessed a powerful personality and a patrician bearing, and his son admired him tremendously. Jawaharlāl would no doubt have been drawn to politics of his own accord, but his father's position as leading Moderate in the Indian National Congress made the attraction an irresistible one. He joined the Congress and began to speak at its sessions, but it was not until 1920, when Gāndhi launched his great noncooperation movement against British rule, that Jawaharlāl found full expression for his energies. He made tours in remote village areas discovering the hard lot of the peasantry, organized volunteer workers, and delivered speeches to large patriotic gatherings. "I experienced [then] the thrill of mass-feeling, the power of influencing the mass,"[2] he tells us, and this power has been one of the keys to his success as a national leader. The climax of his activities came when, for the first of many times in his career, he went gladly to jail as a political prisoner.

Jawaharlāl was disappointed by Gāndhi's sudden suspension of the movement in 1922 after an outbreak of violence, and in the following years he felt himself groping for a clearer analysis of and a more predictable solution to India's problems than those provided by the Mahātmā's intuitive and moralistic mind. A trip to Europe for his wife's health in 1926–27 gave him a new perspective on the conflict between Indian nationalism and British rule. Conversations with Socialists and Communists in Europe—especially at the Congress of the League of Oppressed Peoples at Brussels—convinced him that the principal international conflict was between capitalist imperialism and anticapitalist socialism. A week's visit to Russia impressed him with the achievements of the Soviet system, and with the common interest of Russia and India in opposing British imperialism.[3]

---

[1] Jawaharlāl Nehru: *An Autobiography*, p. 1.   [2] *Ibid.*, p. 77.
[3] Jawaharlāl Nehru: *Soviet Russia, Some Random Sketches and Impressions*.

Back in India once more, Jawaharlāl threw himself with renewed vigor into the national struggle, for he now saw it as part of a world-wide movement to liberate mankind from every kind of oppression and exploitation. He demanded that the Congress declare its ultimate goal to be, not dominion status (as his father wished), but complete independence. Jawaharlāl was supported by Subhās Chandra Bose and others, and Gāndhi wisely yielded to their demand in order to keep the nationalist movement from splitting into Moderate and Extremist wings, as it had in 1907. Gāndhi went on to persuade the Congress to accept Jawaharlāl as its president on the eve of the second nation-wide campaign of civil disobedience, which lasted from 1930 to 1934.

From this time onward Jawaharlāl came increasingly to be regarded as Gāndhi's heir-apparent. Devotion to the cause of Indian freedom, and compassion for the lot of their nation's poor, created between the two men an indissoluble bond. In their attitudes toward other questions, however, Nehru and Gāndhi were poles apart. Religion held no meaning for Nehru, while for his guru it was all-important. Gāndhi held non-violence and simple living to be ends in themselves, but Nehru considered them merely as practical expedients in the political struggle. Gāndhi's ideal India was a decentralized family of self-sufficient villages; Nehru's ideal India was a centralized modern state with a planned industrial economy. Despite their intellectual differences, however, Nehru found in Gāndhi a faithful friend and a wise counsellor. At one time he telegraphed him, "I feel lost in a strange country where you are the only familiar landmark . . . ,"[4] and after Gāndhi's assassination he mourned, "the light has gone out of our lives and there is darkness everywhere."[5]

India has been fortunate in having Jawaharlāl Nehru as her Prime Minister since receiving independence in 1947, for he has provided the dynamic leadership necessary to preserve national unity and accelerate economic progress. His sponsorship of a "third force" of neutralist nations and his role as mediator between the Western democracies and the Communist powers have enhanced India's position in world affairs. If he has tended, in his public statements, to be more critical of the West than of the Communist powers, it should be remembered that he is

[4] Anup Singh, *Nehru, the Rising Star of India*, p. 143.
[5] *Independence and After. A Collection of the More Important Speeches of Jawaharlal Nehru from September 1946 to May 1949*, p. 17.

still a convinced Socialist. At the same time, his commitment to uphold parliamentary government and to defend civil liberties constitutes, during his lifetime, one of the strongest bulwarks of democracy in India.

JAWAHARLĀL NEHRU
Communalism—A Reactionary Creed

Nehru abhorred the political groups who based their power on the membership of a particular religious community—whether Hindu, Muslim, or Sikh. His determination to make independent India a secular state shows clearly in this attack on communalism in an article written in the 1930s. He later used these same arguments in opposing Jinnah's demand for a separate Muslim state.

[From Nehru, *Recent Essays and Writings,* pp. 76–77]

Communalism is essentially a hunt for favors from a third party—the ruling power. The communalist can only think in terms of a continuation of foreign domination and he tries to make the best of it for his own particular group. Delete the foreign power and communal arguments and demands fall to the ground. Both the foreign power and the communalists, as representing some upper class groups, want no essential change of the political and economic structure; both are interested in the preservation and augmentation of their vested interests. Because of this, both cannot tackle the real economic problems which confront the country, for a solution of these would upset the present social structure and divest the vested interests. For both, this ostrich-like policy of ignoring real issues is bound to end in disaster. Facts and economic forces are more powerful than governments and empires and can only be ignored at peril.

Communalism thus becomes another name for political and social reaction and the British government, being the citadel of this reaction in India, naturally throws its sheltering wings over a useful ally. Many a false trail is drawn to confuse the issue; we are told of Islamic culture and Hindu culture, of religion and old custom, of ancient glories and the like. But behind all this lies political and social reaction, the communalism must therefore be fought on all fronts and given no quarter. Because the inward nature of communalism has not been sufficiently realized, it has often sailed under false colors and taken in many an unwary person. It is an undoubted fact that many a Congressman has almost unconsciously partly succumbed to it and tried to reconcile his nationalism with this narrow and reactionary creed. A real appreciation of its true nature would demonstrate that there can be no common ground between the two. They belong to different species. It is time that Congressmen and others who have flirted with Hindu or Muslim or Sikh or any other communalism should understand this position and make their choice. No one can have it both ways, and the choice lies between political and social progress and stark reaction. An association with any form of communalism means the strengthening of the forces of reaction and of British imperialism in India; it means opposition to social and economic change and a toleration of the present terrible distress of our people; it means a blind ignoring of world forces and events.

The World-View of a Socialist

In his presidential address of 1936, Nehru frankly declared to the Congress his faith in Socialism. Both the international situation and the domestic problems of India seemed to him to prove the superiority of Socialism as a political creed. At the same time, Nehru emphasized the importance of civil liberties and of persuasion rather than coercion, but paid scant heed to the fact that these democratic values scarcely existed in the state he took as his model, Soviet Russia.

[From *Important Speeches of Jawaharlal Nehru,* pp. 4–6, 8, 12–14]

During the troubled aftermath of the Great War came revolutionary changes in Europe and Asia, and the intensification of the struggle for social freedom in Europe, and a new aggressive nationalism in the countries of Asia. There were ups and downs, and sometimes it appeared as if the revolutionary urge had exhausted itself and things were settling down. But economic and political conditions were such that there could be no settling down, the existing structure could no longer cope with these new conditions, and all its efforts to do so were vain and fruitless. Everywhere conflicts grew and a great depression overwhelmed the world and there was a progressive deterioration, everywhere except in the wide-flung Soviet territories of the U.S.S.R., where, in marked contrast with the rest of the world, astonishing progress was made in every direction. Two rival economic and political systems faced each other in the world and, though they tolerated each other for a while, there was an inherent antagonism between them, and they played for mastery on the stage of the world. One of them was the capitalist order which had inevitably developed into vast imperialisms, which, having swallowed the colonial world, were intent on eating each other up. Powerful still and fearful of war which might endanger their possessions, yet they came into inevitable conflict with each other and prepared feverishly for war. They were quite unable to solve the problems that threatened them and helplessly they submitted to slow decay. The other was the new socialist order of the U.S.S.R. which went from progress to progress, though often at terrible cost, and where the problems of the capitalist world had ceased to exist.

Capitalism, in its difficulties, took to Fascism with all its brutal suppression of what Western civilization had apparently stood for; it became, even in some of its homelands, what its imperialist counterpart had long been in the subject colonial countries. Fascism and imperialism thus stood out as the two faces of the [now] [1] decaying capitalism, and though they varied in different countries according to national characteristics and economic and political conditions, they represented the same forces of reaction and supported each other, and at the same time came into conflict with each other, for such conflict was inherent in their very nature. Socialism in the West and the rising nationalism of the eastern and other dependent countries opposed this combination of Fascism and imperialism. Nationalism in the East, it must be remembered, was essentially different from the new and terribly narrow nationalism of Fascist countries; the former was the historical urge to freedom, the latter the last refuge of reaction.

Thus we see the world divided up into two vast groups today—the imperialist and Fascist on one side, the Socialist and nationalist on the other. There is some overlapping of the two and the line between them is difficult to draw, for there is mutual conflict between the fascist and imperialist powers, and the nationalism of subject countries has sometimes a tendency to Fascism. But the main division holds and if we keep it in mind, it will be easier for us to understand world conditions and our own place in them.

Where do we stand then, we who labor for a free India? Inevitably we take our stand with progressive forces of the world which are ranged against Fascism and imperialism. We have to deal with one imperialism

[1] The original has "new." [Ed.]

in particular, the oldest and the most far-reaching of the modern world, but powerful as it is, it is but one aspect of world-imperialism, and that is the final argument for Indian independence and for the severance of our connection with the British empire. Between Indian nationalism, Indian freedom, and British imperialism there can be no common ground, and if we remain within the imperialist fold, whatever our name or status, whatever outward semblance of political power we might have, we remain cribbed and confined and allied to and dominated by the reactionary forces and the great financial vested interests of the capitalist world. The exploitation of our masses will still continue and all the vital social problems that face us will remain unsolved. Even real political freedom will be out of our reach, much more so than radical social changes. . . .

But of one thing I must say a few words for to me it is one of the most vital things that I value. That is the tremendous deprivation of civil liberties in India. A government that has to rely on the Criminal Law Amendment Act and similar laws, that suppresses the press and literature, that bans hundreds of organizations, that keeps people in prison without trial, and that does so many other things that are happening in India today, is a government that has ceased to have even a shadow of a justification for its existence. I can never adjust myself to those conditions, I find them intolerable. And yet I find many of my own countrymen complacent about them, some even supporting them, some, who have made the practice of sitting on a fence into a fine art, being neutral when such questions are discussed. And I have wondered what there was in common between them and me and those who think like I do. We in the Congress welcome all cooperation in the struggle for Indian freedom; our doors are ever open to all who stand for that freedom and are against imperialism. But they are not open to the allies [of] [2] imperialism and the supporters of repression and those who stand by the British government in its suppression of civil liberty. We belong to opposite camps. . . .

Perhaps you have wondered at the way I have dealt at some length with the background of international affairs and not touched so far the immediate problems that fill your minds. You may have grown impatient. But I am convinced that the only right way of looking at our own problem is to see them in their proper place in a world setting. I am

[2] The original has "to" here. [Ed.]

convinced that there is intimate connection between world events and our national problem is but a part of the world problem of capitalist-imperialism. To look at each event apart from the others and without understanding the connection between them must lead us to the formation of erratic and erroneous views. Look at the vast panorama of world change today, where mighty forces are at grips with each other and dreadful war darkens the horizon. Subject peoples struggling for freedom and imperialism crushing them down; exploited classes facing their exploiters and seeking freedom and equality. Italian imperialism bombing and killing the brave Ethiopians; Japanese imperialism continuing in aggression in North China and Mongolia; British imperialism piously objecting to other countries misbehaving, yet carrying on in much the same way in India and the Frontier; and behind it all a decaying economic order which intensifies all these conflicts. Can we not see an organic connection in all these various phenomena? Let us try to develop the historic sense so that we can view current events in proper perspective and understand their real significance. Only then can we appreciate the march of history and keep step with it.

I realize that in this address I am going a little beyond the usual beat of the Congress president. But I do not want you to have me under any false pretenses and we must have perfect frankness with each other. Most of you must know my views on social and economic matters, for I have often given expression to them. Yet you chose me as president. I do not take that choice to mean an endorsement by you all, or by a majority, of those views, but I take it that this does mean that those views are spreading in India and that most of you will be indulgent in considering them at least.

I am convinced that the only key to the solution of the world's problems and of India's problems lies in Socialism, and when I use this word I do so not in a vague humanitarian way but in the scientific economic sense. Socialism is, however, something even more than an economic doctrine; it is a philosophy of life and as such also it appeals to me. I see no way of ending the poverty, the vast unemployment, the degradation, and the subjection of the Indian people except through Socialism. That involves vast and revolutionary changes in our political and social structure, the ending of vested interests in land and industry, as well as the feudal and autocratic Indian states system. That means the ending of private property, except in a restricted sense, and the replacement of the present profit system by a higher ideal of cooperative service. It means ultimately a change in our instincts, habits and desires. In short, it means a new civilization, radically different from the present capitalist order. Some glimpse we can have of this new civilization in the territories of the U.S.S.R. Much has happened there which has pained me greatly and with which I disagree, but I look upon that great and fascinating unfolding of a new order and a new civilization as the most promising feature of our dismal age. If the future is full of hope it is largely because of Soviet Russia and what it has done, and I am convinced that, if some world catastrophe does not intervene, this new civilization will spread to other lands and put an end to the wars and conflicts which capitalism feeds.

I do not know how or when this new order will come to India. I imagine that every country will fashion it after its own way and fit it in with its national genius. But the essential basis of that order must remain and be a link in the world order that will emerge out of the present chaos.

Socialism is thus for me not merely an economic doctrine which I favor, it is a vital creed which I hold with all my head and heart. I work for Indian independence because the nationalist in me cannot tolerate an alien domination; I work for it even more because for me it is the inevitable step to social and economic change. I should like the Congress to become a socialist organization and to join hands with the other forces that in the world are working for the new civilization. But I realize that the majority in the Congress, as it is constituted today, may not be prepared to go thus far. We are a nationalist organization and we think and work on the nationalist plan. It is evident enough now that this is too narrow even for the limited objective of political independence and so we talk of the masses and their economic needs. But still most of us hesitate, because of our nationalist backgrounds, to take a step which might frighten away some vested interests. Most of those interests are already ranged against us and we can expect little from them except opposition even in the political struggle.

Much as I wish for the advancement of Socialism in this country, I have no desire to force the issue on the Congress and thereby create difficulties in the way of our struggle for independence. I shall cooperate gladly and with all the strength in me with all those who work for independence even though they do not agree with the socialist solution. But I shall do so stating my position frankly and hoping in course of time to convert the Congress and the country to it, for only thus can I see it achieving independence.

On the Threshold of a New Era

More than most modern Indians, Nehru possessed and cultivated a deep awareness of his country's past. This sense of history stands out in his speech to the Constituent Assembly in 1946 as it prepared to adopt its basic "Declaration of Objectives." It is important to note, however, that the three examples which he cited as models of constituent assemblies are all taken not from Indian but from Western history.

[From Nehru, *Independence and After*, pp. 346–48]

As I stand here, Sir, I feel the weight of all manner of things crowding upon me. We are at the end of an era and possibly very soon we shall embark upon a new age; and my mind goes back to the great past of India, to the 5,000 years of India's history, from the very dawn of that history which might be considered almost the dawn of human history, till today. All that past crowds upon me and exhilarates me and, at the same time, somewhat oppresses me. Am I worthy of that past? When I think also of the future, the greater future I hope, standing on this sword's edge of the present between the mighty past and the mightier future, I tremble a little and feel overwhelmed by this mighty task. We have come here at a strange moment in India's history. I do not know, but I do feel, that there is some magic in this moment of transition from the old to the new, something of that magic which one sees when the night turns into day and even though the day may be a cloudy one, it is day after all, for when the clouds move away, we can see the sun again. Because of all this I find a little difficulty in addressing this House and putting all my ideas before it and I feel also that in this long succession of thousands of years, I see the mighty figures that have come and gone and I see also the long succession of our comrades who have labored for the freedom of India. And now we stand on the verge of this passing age, trying, laboring, to usher in the new. I am sure the House will feel the solemnity of this moment and will endeavor to treat this Resolution which it is my proud privilege to place before it in a correspondingly solemn manner. I believe there are a large number of amendments coming before the House. I have not seen most of them. It is open to the House, to any member of this House, to move any amendment and it is for the House to accept it or reject it, but I would, with all respect, suggest that this is not the moment for us to be technical and legal about small matters when we have big things to face, big things to say and big things to do, and, therefore, I hope that the House will consider this Resolution in a broadminded manner and not lose itself in wordy quarrels and squabbles.

I think also of the various constituent assemblies that have gone before and of what took place at the making of the great American nation when the fathers of that nation met and fashioned a constitution which has stood the test for so many years, more than a century and a half, and of the great nation that has resulted, which has been built up on the basis of that constitution. My mind goes back to that mighty revolution which took place also over one hundred fifty years ago and the constituent assembly that met in that gracious and lovely city of Paris which has fought so many battles for freedom. My mind goes back to the difficulties that that constituent assembly had to face from the king and other authorities, and still it continued. The House will remember that when these difficulties came and even the room for a meeting was denied to that constituent assembly, they betook themselves to an open tennis court and met there and took the oath, which is called the Oath of the Tennis Court. They continued meeting in spite of kings, in spite of the others, and did not disperse till they had finished the task they had undertaken. Well, I trust that it is in that solemn spirit that we too are meeting here and that we too whether we meet in this chamber or in other chambers, or in the fields or in the market place, will go on meeting and continue our work till we have finished it.

Then my mind goes back to a more recent revolution which gave rise to a new type of state, the revolution that took place in Russia and out of which has arisen the Union of the Soviet Socialist Republics, another mighty country which is playing a tremendous part in the world, not only a mighty country, but for us in India, a neighboring country.

So our mind goes back to these great examples and we seek to learn from their success and to avoid their failures. Perhaps we may not be able to avoid failures, because some measure of failure is inherent in human effort. Nevertheless, we shall advance, I am certain, in spite of obstructions and difficulties, and achieve and realize the dream that we have dreamt so long.

India's Role in World Affairs

In contrast to the theory of Keshub, Vivekānanda, Tagore, and others to whom India was important in the world mainly for her "spirituality," Nehru saw India as the emerging "giant" of world affairs, able to stand on an equal footing with any other nation.

[From Nehru, *Independence and After*, pp. 231–33]

One of the major questions of the day is the readjustment of the relations between Asia and Europe. When we talk of Asia, remember that India, not because of any ambition of hers, but because of the force of circumstances, because of geography, because of history and because of so many other things, inevitably has to play a very important part in Asia. And not only that; India becomes a kind of meeting ground for various trends and forces and a meeting ground between what might roughly be called the East and the West.

Look at the map. If you have to consider any question affecting the Middle East, India inevitably comes into the picture. If you have to consider any question concerning Southeast Asia, you cannot do so without India. So also with the Far East. While the Middle East may not be directly connected with Southeast Asia, both are connected with India. Even if you think in terms of regional organizations in Asia, you have to keep in touch with the other regions. And whatever regions you may have in mind, the importance of India cannot be ignored.

One of the major questions of the day is the readjustment of the relations between Asia and Europe. In the past, especially by virtue of her economic and political domination, the West ignored Asia, or at any rate did not give her the weight that was due to her. Asia was really given a back seat and one unfortunate result of it was that even the statesmen did not recognize the changes that were taking place. There is, I believe, a considerable recognition of these changes now, but it is not enough yet. Even in the Councils of the United Nations, the problems of Asia, the outlook of Asia, the approach of Asia have failed to evoke the enthusiasm they should. There are many ways of distinguishing between what may be called the approach of Asia and the approach of Europe. Asia today is primarily concerned with what may be called the immediate human problems. In each country of Asia—under-developed countries more or less—the main problem is the problem of food, of clothing, of education, of health. We are concerned with these problems. We are not directly concerned with problems of power politics. Some of us, in our minds, may perhaps think of that.

Europe, on the other hand, is also concerned with these problems, no doubt, in the devastated regions. Europe has a legacy of conflicts of power, and of problems which come from the possession of power. They have the fear of losing that power and the fear of some one else getting greater power and attacking one country or the other. So that the European approach is a legacy of the past conflicts of Europe.

I do not mean to say that we in Asia are in any way superior, ethically or morally, to the people of Europe. In some ways I imagine that we are worse. There is, however, a legacy of conflict in Europe. In Asia, at the present moment at least, there is no such legacy. The countries of Asia may have their quarrels with their neighbors here and there, but there is no basic legacy of conflict such as the countries of Europe possess. That is a very great advantage of Asia and it would be folly in the extreme for the countries of Asia, for India, to be dragged in the wake of the conflicts in Europe. We might note that the world progressively tends to become one—one in peace, and it is likely to be one, in a sense of war. No man can say that any country can remain apart when there is a major conflagration. But still one can direct one's policy towards avoiding this conflict and being entangled in it.

So the point I wish the House to remember is this: first of all, the emergence of India in world affairs is something of major consequence in world history. We who happen to be in the government of India or in this House are men of relatively small stature. But it has been given to us to work at a time when India is growing into a great giant again. So, because of that, in spite of our own smallness, we have to work for great causes and perhaps elevate ourselves in the process.

M. N. ROY: FROM INTERNATIONAL
COMMUNIST TO RADICAL HUMANIST

Perhaps the most potent of the political ideologies which entered India in the twentieth century came not from Western Europe but via Russia —a country with which Indians had previously had very little direct contact. Vladimir I. Lenin had long seen the nationalist movements in Asia as useful adjuncts to the revolution he expected to sweep Europe. Immediately on seizing power in Russia in 1917, his Bolshevik Party championed the right of colonial peoples to complete independence of foreign rule. Although British vigilance prevented Communist literature from entering the Indian empire openly and in quantity, the news that Bolshevik Russia stood ready to help their cause gave new hope to the numerous Indians in exile all over the world.

One of these was Narendranāth Bhattāchārya (1887–1954), who had slipped out of India in 1915 to make contact in Java with German agents bringing arms for an Indian insurrection. This plot having failed, he continued eastward to the United States and settled in Mexico under the name of Mānabendra Nāth Roy. When news of the Bolshevik Revolution reached him, he first helped found the Mexican Communist Party and then hurried to Moscow. There he made such a favorable impression on Lenin that he was put on the Executive Committee of the newly founded Communist International. For a time Roy was busy in Tashkent, Central Asia, training for revolutionary work Indians who had come to Russia via Afghanistan. His career as an international Communist leader extended through the 1920s, but after his unsuccessful mission to China in 1927 and the victory of Stalin over Trotsky he fell from favor and left Russia for Germany.

Severing his connection with the Comintern in 1929, Roy returned incognito to India, but was arrested by the British authorities and imprisoned for six years. On his release he attempted to organize a non-Stalinist Marxist party within the Indian National Congress. During the Second World War he opposed Gāndhi and Nehru, whom he called the tools of Indian Fascism, and supported the Allied cause. After independence he abandoned Marxism and sought in the rational and secular humanism of Europe the basis for a new social order.

Notwithstanding his disillusionment with Communism, M. N. Roy remained an internationalist to the end of his life, and the Radical Humanist group which he founded has ties with similar groups in the Western world. Significantly, he also retained from his Communist period a belief in materialism and a deep suspicion of the religious outlook on life, which has played such a dominant role throughout the history of Indian culture. It was precisely what others considered "changeless" in India that he wanted most to change.

MĀNABENDRA NĀTH ROY
The Anti-Imperialist Struggle in India

Roy's article of this title, written in 1924, is a typical expression of his hopes for an Indian revolution, whose momentum was to come from the hitherto unorganized energies of the workers and peasants.
  [From M. N. Roy, "Anti-Imperialist Struggle in India," in *The Communist International*, No. 6 (1924), pp. 83, 92–93]

Slowly but surely British domination in India is being undermined. It is true that this historic process is not so speedy as many expected or even prophesied. Nevertheless, the process is going on unceasingly. The depression that followed the sudden collapse of the great noncooperation movement lasted rather long, only to be enlivened, not by an intensified revolutionary activity, but by a concerted effort on the part of the bourgeoisie to challenge the absolute position of imperialism on constitutional lines. The development of this new stage has been during the last twelve months. It has culminated in a political deadlock which has not only nonplussed the nationalist bourgeoisie, but has also placed the British government in a somewhat uncomfortable position. Some decisive action must be taken from one side or the other to break this deadlock. For the nationalists, it is necessary either to compromise with imperialism or to go a few steps further towards revolution. Imperialism, on the other hand, is faced with the alternatives: to placate the nationalist bourgeoisie with concessions or to adopt openly the policy of blood and iron.

It is obvious what should be the nature of our activities. While supporting the nationalist bourgeoisie in every act of resistance to imperialism, we should mobilize the revolutionary mass energy which the nationalist bourgeoisie is afraid of touching. The rapid crystallization of bourgeois nationalism around a reformist program has left the field clear. For the first time in the history of the Indian national movement, there will come into existence a political party demanding separation from the empire. Nationalist elements, which up till now followed the bourgeoisie, will enter this party; because the program of reformism advocated by the bourgeoisie neglects their interests altogether. To aid the organization of this party of revolutionary nationalism is our immediate task. The objective situation is quite ripe, although there are enormous subjective difficulties. The masses are very restive. The peasantry is a veritable inflammable material, while the city proletariat demonstrates its revolutionary zeal whenever there is an opportunity. The process of uniting all these revolutionary elements into an anti-imperialist army is going on steadily. The collapse of bourgeois nationalism, as expressed by the present Parliamentary deadlock, will only accentuate this process. The people will see that the reformist program of the bourgeoisie does not lead anywhere. The center of gravity of the nationalist movement will be shifted back to its proper place—namely, mass action. As soon as the rank and file of the nationalist forces are freed from the reformist leadership of the bourgeoisie, they will begin to follow the standard of revolution, because in that case, they will be convinced that the anti-imperialist struggle cannot be conducted successfully in a different way. There is every indication that things are moving in that direction, and that the next stage of the Indian movement will be a great advance towards revolution.

Revolution—Necessary and Inevitable

Belief in the inevitability of the proletarian revolution being a central tenet in the Communist faith, M. N. Roy declared himself simply a servant of this historical process. Not he, but the British were to blame for refusing to cooperate with the inevitable, he asserted in the statement he intended (but was not allowed) to make at his trial for conspiracy in 1931.

[From M. N. Roy, *I Accuse*, pp. 26–27, 28–29]

The evidence proves that I pointed out the inevitability of a revolutionary change in the social and political conditions of India and that the welfare of the toiling masses was dependent upon the revolution. I have been working for the welfare of the Indian masses and have urged the elimination of all obstacles in the way to that goal. I tried to organize a working class party because it is necessary for the liberation of the masses from political slavery, economic exploitation, and social degradation. The party is a historic necessity and has a historically revolutionary mission. It is neither a conspiracy nor a weapon in any conspiracy. The British king, as well as any other power that stands in the way of the progress and prosperity of the Indian masses, must go.

Of course, our attempt to organize a party of the workers and peasants would be a quixotic venture had the condition of the masses been really what the public prosecutor imagines it to be. In his opening address he told the assessors that the Indian peasants were happy in their misery and that I was trying to disturb their happiness for some sinister purpose of mine. I have already given a few facts and figures to show that "happy peasants" live only in the imagination of the public prosecutor, unless the gentleman would venture to advance a theory that the less one eats and the more one toils the happier he is.

In reality, the government is against the most harmless economic program, for its enforcement would mean loss to imperialism and its Indian allies, the princes, big landlords, and capitalists. Therefore, the realization of the program will necessarily mean violation of the laws of the imperialist government. The function of the laws is to hold the masses on the starvation level so that foreign imperialism and its native allies can grow rich, and to suppress the attempts of the masses to rise above the present conditions.

I have not preached violent revolution. I have maintained that revolution is a historic necessity. From time to time, surging forces of social progress reach the period of a violent outburst. This is caused by the resistance of the old to the new. An impending revolution produces its pioneers who force events and herald the maturing of the conflict. The task of the revolutionary vanguard is to expedite the historical process caused by objective necessity. They consciously organize the forces of the revolution and lead them to victory. I have acted as a pioneer of the Indian revolution; but the revolution itself is not my invention. It grows out of the historical conditions of the country. I have simply been one who perceived it earlier than others.

I do not make a secret of my determination of helping the organization of the great revolution which must take place in order to open up
before the Indian masses the road to liberty, progress, and prosperity.
The impending revolution is an historic necessity. Conditions for it are
maturing rapidly. Colonial exploitation of the country creates those
conditions. So, I am not responsible for the revolution, nor is the Communist International. Imperialism is responsible for it. My punishment,
therefore, will not stop the revolution. Imperialism has created its own
grave-digger, namely, the forces of national revolution. These will continue operating till their historic task is accomplished. No law, however
ruthless may be the sanction behind it, can suppress them.

India's Message to the World

In one of his most pungent essays, M. N. Roy sought to debunk the popular
notion that Indian spirituality in general, and Gāndhism in particular, held
an important message for the world. On the contrary, he argued, it was only
by following the philosophy of materialism (to which classical Indian thought
had also given expression) that modern civilization could go forward.

[From M. N. Roy, *India's Message* (*Fragments of a Prisoner's Diary,* II),
pp. 190–91, 209–11, 217–18]

The "decline of the West" being in reality only the decline of capitalism,
the crisis of Western civilization means only disintegration of the
bourgeois social order. In that context, India's "spiritual mission" appears to be a mission with a mundane purpose, namely, to salvage
a social system based upon the love of lucre and lust for power. It is not
suggested that the believers in India's spiritual mission are all conscious
of its reactionary implication. Probably very few of them are. Most of
them may be credited with a sincere antipathy for capitalism. But
antipathy does not necessarily give birth to a desire to go farther than
capitalism. It indicates an attachment to pre-capitalist social conditions,
which are idealized. Objectively, it is therefore the token of a reactionary
social outlook. Indian spiritualism is not different from the Western
kind. The merit of a philosophy is to be judged by its historical role and
social significance. The sincerity or otherwise of its protagonists is altogether beside the point.

The preachers of India's "world mission" nevertheless take their stand
on the dogmatic assertion that Indian philosophy is different from West-

ern idealism. The basic principles of idealist philosophy, together with the survey of its medieval and pre-Christian background, prove that this assertion is utterly groundless. While the emotional aspect of Indian speculation is well matched, if not surpassed, by Christian mysticism, intellectually it can hardly claim superiority to Western idealism, either modern or ancient. As regards transcendental fantasies, the Western mind has been no less fertile. The great Sage of Athens, the seers of Alexandria, the saints of early Christianity, the monks of the Middle Ages—that is a record which can proudly meet any competition. On the question of moral doctrines, Christianity stands unbeaten on the solid ground of the Jewish, Socratic, and Stoic traditions. Should the modern West be accused of not having lived up to those noble principles, could India conscientiously be absolved of a similar charge? The claim that the Indian people as a whole are morally less corrupt, emotionally purer, idealistically less worldly, in short, spiritually more elevated, than the bulk of the Western society, is based upon a wanton disregard for reality. . . .

The most commonly agreed form of India's world message is Gandhism. Not only does it dominate the nationalist ideology: it has found some echo outside of India. It is as the moralizing mysticism of Gāndhi that Indian thought makes any appeal to the Western mind. Therefore, an analysis of Gandhism will give a correct idea of the real nature of India's message to the world.

But Gandhism is not a coordinated system of thought. There is little of philosophy in it. In the midst of a mass of platitudes and hopeless self-contradictions, it harps on one constant note—a conception of morality based upon dogmatic faith. But what Gāndhi preaches is primarily a religion: the faith in God is the only reliable guide in life. The fact that even in the twentieth century India is swayed by the naive doctrines of Gāndhi speaks for the cultural backwardness of the masses of her people. The subtlety of the Hindu philosophy is not the measure of the intellectual level of the Indian people as a whole. It was the brain-child of a pampered intellectual elite sharing power and privileges with the temporal ruling class. It still remains confined to the comparatively small circle of intellectuals who try to put on a thin veneer of modernism, and represents nothing more than a nostalgia. The popularity of Gāndhi and the uncritical acceptance of his antics as the highest of human wisdom knock the bottom off the doctrine that the Indian people as a whole are morally and spiritually superior to the Western. The fact is that the great bulk of the Indian people are steeped in religious superstitions. Otherwise, Gandhism would have no social background and disappear before long. They have neither any understanding of philosophical problems nor are they concerned with metaphysical speculations in preference to material questions. As normal human beings, they are engrossed with the problems of worldly life, and being culturally backward, necessarily think in terms of religion, conceive their earthly ideals, their egoistic aspirations, in religious forms. Faith is the mainstay of their existence, prejudice the trusted guide of life, and superstition their only philosophy.

Gandhism is the ideological reflex of this social background. It sways the mass mind, not as a moral philosophy, but as a religion. It is neither a philosopher nor a moralist who has become the idol of the Indian people. The masses pay their homage to a Mahātmā—a source of revealed wisdom and agency of supernatural power. The social basis of Gandhism is cultural-backwardness; its intellectual mainstay, superstition. . . .

The Gandhist utopia thus is a static society—a state of absolute social stagnation. It is an utopia because it can never be realized. Absolute stagnation is identical with death. To begin with, all resistance to the established order must cease. That would offer absolute guarantee to the *status quo*. The ruling classes would refrain from using force simply because it would not be necessary. Their power and privilege, being completely undisputed, would require no active defense. But this idyllic picture can be drawn only by the cold hand of death. Life expresses itself as a movement—individually, in space, and collectively, in time. And movement implies overwhelming of obstacles on the way. Disappearance of all resistance to the established order would mean extinction of social life. Perfect peace reigns only in the grave.

Neither the preachers nor the proselytes of Gandhism, however, would have the consistency of carrying their cult to the nihilistic extreme. There would be a certain macabre majesty in such a boldness. But with all the absoluteness of its standards, Gandhism remains on the ground of the relative. After all, it prescribes a practical cure for the evils of the world. Philosophically, it is pragmatic. And the remedy suggested is the reactionary program of forcibly keeping society in a relatively static condition. Gandhism offers this program because it is the quintessence of an ideology which developed on the background of a static society.

But India's spiritual message, while still finding an echo in the ruins of the native society, can have no standing appeal to the world of modern civilization. There, the society is armed with potentialities which preclude its falling into a state of stagnation. Modern civilization is a dynamic process. It must go forward. Not only the masses, but even the capitalist rulers of the West must reject the ideology of social stagnation. And precisely in this dynamic nature of the civilization, developed under its aegis, does the nemesis of capitalism lie. It cannot carry civilization farther, nor can it hold it back in a static state permanently as a guarantee for its continued existence. The perspective, therefore, is an advance of modern civilization over the boundaries of capitalism. The materialist philosophy throws a flood of light on that perspective of the future of mankind. India's spiritual message, on the contrary, would teach the West to turn back upon the goal within reach, and relapse into medieval barbarism.

Radical Humanism

In August, 1947, M. N. Roy presented a summary of his new political ideals, which were founded, not on dogma or Machiavellianism, but on human reason and morality.

[From M. N. Roy, *New Humanism: A Manifesto*, pp. 34–47]

The question of all questions is: Can politics be rationalized? An affirmative answer to this controversial question would not take us very far unless rationalism was differentiated from the metaphysical concept of reason. To replace the teleology of Marxist materialism by an appeal to the mystical category of reason would not be an advance.

The cognate question is about the relation of politics and morality: Must revolutionary political practice be guided by the Jesuitic dictum —the end justifies the means? The final sanction of revolution being its moral appeal—the appeal for social justice—logically, the answer to the latter question must be in the negative. It is very doubtful if a moral object can ever be attained by immoral means. In critical moments, when larger issues are involved and greater things are at stake, some temporary compromise in behavior may be permissible. But when practices repugnant to ethical principles and traditional human values are stabilized as the permanent features of the revolutionary regime, the means defeat the end. Therefore Communist political practice has not taken the world, not even the working class, anywhere near a new order of freedom and social justice. On the contrary, it has plunged the army of revolution—proletarian as well as nonproletarian—in an intellectual confusion, spiritual chaos, emotional frustration, and a general demoralization.

To overcome this crisis, the fighters for a new world order must turn to the traditions of Humanism and moral Radicalism. The inspiration for a new philosophy of revolution must be drawn from those sources. The nineteenth-century Radicals, actuated by the humanist principle of individualism, realized the possibility of a secular rationalism and a rationalist ethics. They applied to the study of man and society the principles and methods of the physical sciences. Positive knowledge of nature—living as well as inanimate—being so much greater today than a hundred years ago, the Radical scientific approach to the problem of man's life and interrelations is bound to be more successful. Today we can begin with the conviction that it is long since man emerged from the jungle of "pre-history," that social relations can be rationally harmonized, and that therefore appreciation of moral values can be reconciled with efforts for replacing the corrupt and corrosive *status quo* by a new order of democratic freedom. A moral order will result from a rationally organized society, because, viewed in the context of his rise out of the background of a harmonious physical universe, man is essentially rational and therefore moral. Morality emanates from the rational desire for harmonious and mutually beneficial social relations.

Man did not appear on the earth out of nowhere. He rose out of the background of the physical universe, through the long process of biological evolution. The umbilical cord was never broken: man, with his mind, intelligence, will, remains an integral part of the physical universe. The latter is a cosmos—a law-governed system. Therefore, man's being and becoming, his emotions, will, ideas are also determined: man is essentially rational. The reason in man is an echo of the harmony of the universe. Morality must be referred back to man's innate rationality. Only then, man can be moral, spontaneously and voluntarily. Reason is only sanction for morality, which is an appeal to conscience, and conscience, in its turn, is the instinctive awareness of, and reaction to, environments. In the last analysis, conscience is nothing mystic or mysterious. It is a biological function, as such mechanistic, on the level of consciousness. The innate rationality of man is the only guarantee of a harmonious order, which will also be a moral order, because morality is a rational function. Therefore, the purpose of all social endeavor should be to make man increasingly conscious of his innate rationality.

Any effort for a reorganization of society must begin from the unit of society—from the root, so to say. Such an effort to develop a new philosophy of revolution, on the basis of the entire stock of human heritage, and then to elaborate the theory and formulate the principles of the practice of political action and economic reconstruction, therefore, can be called Radicalism.

Radicalism thinks in terms neither of nation nor of class; its concern is man; it conceives freedom as freedom of the individual. Therefore, it can also be called New Humanism, new, because it is Humanism enriched, reinforced and elaborated by scientific knowledge and social experience gained during the centuries of modern civilization.

Humanism is cosmopolitan. It does not run after the utopia of internationalism, which presupposes the existence of autonomous national states. The one makes of the other a pious desire or wishful thinking. A cosmopolitan commonwealth of free men and women is a possibility. It will be a spiritual community, not limited by the boundaries of national states— capitalist, fascist, communist or of any other kind—which will gradually disappear under the impact of cosmopolitan Humanism. That is the Radical perspective of the future of mankind.

THE APPEALS OF "NATIONAL" COMMUNISM

Imitation being the truest form of flattery, Western Europe and America should take pride in the fact that India's educated elite now desire ardently to rid their society of ancient inequalities, to build a modern, industrial economy, and to make India a strong national state. When a young nation comes to be dominated by such desires, but finds that it has been left far behind in the race for modernity, it commonly reacts by making desperate attempts to "catch up" with the rest of the world. The

success of similar endeavors by other late-comer nations is bound to make
a deep impression on the most recent entrant in the race. Some fifty years
ago, India was thrilled by Japan's victory over Tsarist Russia. Today, a
large percentage of the Indian intelligentsia look to Soviet Russia and
Communist China as models for their own country's future development.

This frame of mind, compounded as it is of nationalistic strivings and
of admiration for the achievements of Communist states, might aptly be
termed "National" Communism. While not committing itself to the international conspiracy in which M. N. Roy played so conspicuous a part,
National Communism promises to strengthen and modernize politically
independent but economically underdeveloped countries through the
Communist program of accelerated industrialization and social reorganization. National Communism diverges from Democratic Socialism, with
which it otherwise has much in common, at the point where this increasing acceleration involves the sacrifice of parliamentary democracy and
civil liberties.

The sheer magnitude of India's population, now over the 380,000,000
mark, seems to render irrelevant the experience of countries like the
United States, where an abundance of land and mineral resources have
been exploited by a fairly small population during several centuries of
undisturbed isolation. Indian free enterprise, faced with much more urgent problems and equipped with much scantier resources, lacks the
capacity to undertake the large-scale development projects required by
the situation, and is in any case less public-spirited and more monopolistic
than its American counterpart. Foreign aid is gratefully accepted, but a
deep-seated prejudice exists in India against capitalists in general and
Western capitalists in particular.

Prime Minister Nehru, in articulating these suspicions, once explained
them as a product of persisting attachment to the classical hierarchy of
occupations. Of the traditional culture of India he wrote: "it is fighting
silently and desperately against a new and all-powerful opponent—the
bania [1] civilization of the capitalist West. It will succumb to this newcomer, for the West brings science, and science brings food for the hungry
millions. But the West also brings an antidote to the evils of this cut-
throat civilization—the principles of socialism, of cooperation, and service
to the community for the common good. This is not so unlike the old

[1] Merchant.

Brahman ideal of service, but it means the brahmanization (not in the religious sense, of course) of all classes and groups and the abolition of class distinctions." [2] Thus capitalism has been associated with the tradition of the Vaishyas, the lowest of the three "twice-born" castes, and Socialism or Communism with the more prestigious brāhman tradition.

As with every nation, Indians tend to see the outside world as it is reflected in the mirror of their own preconceptions. Many find this stereotype of idealistic socialism opposing materialistic capitalism helpful in interpreting the "cold war" between Soviet Russia and the United States of America. China's entrance into the Communist camp has further enhanced the latter's prestige, and has also heightened pan-Asian sentiment in India. Another source of sympathy for Russia and China is the absence of marked racial discrimination in these countries. Finally, there is the simple fact that in modern times Indians have become much better acquainted through reading and travel with Western Europe and North America than with these giant neighboring countries. Just as familiarity may breed contempt, so distance (in this case not so much geographical as psychological) may lend enchantment.

Prime Minister Nehru's policy of friendship with Soviet Russia and the People's Republic of China has made it possible for the Communist Party of India to appeal to nationalist sentiment by loudly championing India's present role in world affairs. In domestic policies however, the Communists have emerged as the strongest opposition party to the Congress government. The effectiveness of their National Communist program was demonstrated in the 1957 general elections, when they unexpectedly won a sufficiently large plurality in the Kerala legislature to assume parliamentary control of that state.

On the purely personal level, the combination of nationalist and Communist ideals appeals to many Westernized intellectuals who would like to improve the hard lot of the common people. Accustomed to middle-class standards of morality and material well-being, they often feel keenly the gap between their lives and those of the un-Westernized, uneducated, and impoverished peasants and urban laborers. Doctrines which emphasize solidarity between the educated elite and "the masses" alleviate the feelings of guilt created by the alienation of the former from the latter. They also promise full employment and the hope of transforming village

[2] *Jawaharlal Nehru, An Autobiography,* p. 432.

India (where 85 percent of her population lives) in the image of the Westernized city-dwellers rather than, as Gāndhi proposed, remaking the Westernized minority in the image of the peasant majority.

To illustrate some of the appeals of National Communism two writers have been chosen, neither a Communist Party member, but each in substantial agreement with one or more aspects of the National Communist line. J. C. Kumarappa, an Indian Christian, took his M.A. in economics at Columbia University, and on his return to India became a leading exponent of Gāndhian economic theory, and head of Gāndhi's village hand-industry program. Although he does not subscribe to their emphasis on rapid industrialization, he does accept the National Communist diagnosis of the world situation and sees "American machinations" as a great danger to his country.

Romesh Thapar expresses a more comprehensive and optimistic outlook, for he expects the gradual emergence of a socialist order throughout the world. Thapar edited the Communist Party's weekly organ from 1949 to 1951 (a period when most of its leaders were in hiding or in prison), and was secretary to the Indian delegation at the Warsaw Peace Congress of 1950. His writings, although sometimes critical of the Party, seem to have a degree of influence on its policy. This fact in itself is symptomatic of the importance the Party attaches to winning the minds of the Indian intelligentsia as a whole—a task in which to date it has had surprising success.

J. C. KUMARAPPA
The American Plot Against India

In 1952 a book entitled *American Shadow Over India* appeared which construed as subversive to India American activities in India in such varied fields as trade, investments, economic aid, intelligence activities, propaganda, Christian missions, motion pictures, and books. The selection which follows is J. C. Kumarappa's foreword to this book.

[From L. Natarajan, *American Shadow Over India*, pp. xi–xiii]

In centuries past every nation was at liberty to express its way of life and thought and its national culture. From time to time this freedom was interfered with by neighboring chieftains who descended on prosperous people for the loot they could get. Their followers stayed behind, in some cases to found dynasties of their own.

Since the Industrial Revolution these personal ambitions have given way to organized exploitation of the weak. This is done by holding down the unwary in groups, in geographical units, or as whole nations. The methods adopted have been termed variously according to their nature, but in effect they were all the same. It was to secure raw materials or labor for large-scale mechanized industries. This was a development over individual slavery, serfdom or feudalism.

Britain came to India with a feudal background and hence her relations with her colonies were characterized by a socio-economic order which took the form of political imperialism. This carried with it certain duties towards the subject nations even though exploitation was the ultimate purpose. This method laid the responsibility for good government on the so-called "Metropolitan Country."

A little later in the field came the Americans. They appeared on the scene with a tradition of slavery. Hence their mode of control of "undeveloped" countries took on a different color from the British one. They are following a financial imperialism which is practically irresponsible for the welfare of those who come under its grip.

Further, at this time, there is an attempt to gather together the nations of the world under two prevailing ideologies of either private enterprise or for social justice. In this struggle for proselytes the world is being divided into two competing groups. The U.S.A. stands for private enterprise based on private property leading to private profit while the U.S.S.R. advocates social justice based on the fundamental equality of man and the need therefore for equality in opportunities of life.

These two camps are splitting the world into two blocs. Russia is going about her work in a missionary spirit by practicing what she preaches and demonstrating her theories by experiments and thus strives to gather adherents by convincing the neighbors.

The U.S.A. is proceeding on various plans to entrap the nations by guile, by compulsion, by coercion and financial entanglements. These methods are not calculated to liberate its victims but to carry on its nefarious purpose like the spider. The webs are woven so well and close that the victim hardly realizes what is happening and all its struggles only make the end come sooner.

Unfortunately, people are far too busy today to halt and take note of what is taking place round them. The hurry and flurry of life hardly leave them any leisure to stand up and look at their surroundings and appraise the situation. Advantage is taken of this pressure of life to hasten the end.

For over a century and a half, the U.S.A. has been spreading her financial nets the world over. India was somewhat in a protected position because of British vested interests and jealousies. Of late, this protective fencing has been disbanded and India presents an open field of ruthless exploitation. It is sad that this should happen under the leadership of a patriot of the order of Nehru. The wiles of the Americans, who go about their work with the aid of modern psychology, are a little too much for the straightforward, simple, trusting statesman.

It is, therefore, all the more necessary for the man in the street to be well-informed of what is going on to entrap him. Hence it is a boon to India that full information should be made available in a small compass, without much argumentation, with proper references and documentation. This little book is a mine of such information. The author has laid us under a deep debt for the pains he has taken to glean valuable material and place it at our disposal in so lucid a fashion. He traces the American machinations to get India within its financial web for over a century. It is a fascinating story and we may well be warned by the danger. If we do not avail ourselves of the timely warning we shall, before long, be overtaken by the tragedy that has befallen Korea.[1] May we awake and beware before it is too late.

ROMESH THAPAR
India's Socialist Future

In the concluding chapter of his *India in Transition*, Romesh Thapar pictures Socialism (using the word as Communists do to denote the intermediate stage between capitalism and pure Communism) established throughout the world. He implies by his criticism of "the evils of Stalinist practice" that he expects the new world order to be based on democratic values.

[From Romesh Thapar, *India in Transition*, pp. 259–64]

Each land and people has its prophets and visionaries. Learning from the past and the present, they project that experience into the future to understand the processes which will mold events yet unrecorded.

---

[1] Kumarappa accepts the Communist allegation that South Korea, encouraged by the U.S.A., was responsible for starting the Korean War.

India is a rewarding field for such study and speculation. Perhaps no other people in the world have found themselves in so interesting a situation; the more so when it is compared with the immediate perspectives before those powers who are today making world events.

In the U.S.A., the enlightened may feel the torture of the McCarthy witch-hunts, the democratic-minded mass may be tormented by the international dealings of the State Department, but they are now beginning to locate the cause of these aberrations. If prosperity dulls their senses, makes them impotent to counter policies which can only spell ruin in the final accounting, the wide-awake among them do know that, sooner or later, the truth will out. Each day the blinkers are being lifted. Cold war policies are boomeranging on those who initiated them. It is the climate in which the thought of a Franklin Delano Roosevelt, steeled and sharpened, will again rise triumphant.

Great Britain, corrupted and corroded by centuries of international swindling, bungles along at the bidding of her master across the Atlantic. Her empire dwindles, and sometimes a morsel, here and there, is digested by the senior partner in "Imperialism Limited." The theme of democracy at home and brutal autocracy abroad no longer inspires. The British people must return to their island home. Then they will learn to live on soil that is their own.

For France, the transformation has already begun. Today, in Africa, we are witnessing her last frenzied attempts to retain the trappings of a "big power." But the working people of that gifted land now realize that these trappings are but chains holding back the fulfillment of many dreams. The cobwebs are being removed. A new, strong voice is heard proclaiming the path to real and lasting greatness.

Germany and Japan, conserving the industrial strength of giants, have healed the wounds caused by their costly military ventures. Their domestic problems are many, but the solutions lie within their grasp. Significantly, these arsenals of the West and the East now depend for their progress on peace. Their future is not clouded by stratagems of empire, only by the logic of international tension and foreign intervention.

China, now risen again, is a great source of hope. These ancient people have battled against immense odds and now they work with a single resolve to turn a vast country into a modern, industrialized nation. By 1962, they will have outstripped the rest of Asia in economic development. They are able to do so, for they have found the weapons to triumph over man-made tragedy and disaster. No obstacles, no errors, can halt their advance.

Even more decisive will be the advance of the Soviet peoples—that is, when they have purged their society of the evils of Stalinist practice. This practice has distorted their life and the life of those allied to them in Eastern Europe. It will take time and courage to overcome the distortions. The task is immense; the trials, too.

Free India, born in this crucial period of transition and beginning a delayed journey into a future that is often the past of many advanced peoples, feels the impact of all this emotion and experience. There was a time when, on the banks of the Indus and its tributaries, she led the advance of civilization. Today, she learns, and while she emulates, creatively develops the experience of other peoples.

This process her prophets and visionaries interpret according to their respective attitudes. We must look for the most intelligent and consistent interpretation.

The transition which India is making is from the age of cow-dung to the age of the atom. Naturally, in the course of it, many values and traditions, concepts and practices, will experience a violent shaking. But, if experience is of any use, the transition will be made rapidly and without the degree of sacrifice which other nations had to undergo. True, this generation is condemned to hard labor, but at least it knows that the effort is linked to the creation of a society which will be very different from the familiar capitalist jungle. This is the dominant fact of our time, a fact that will condition attitudes and action.

Today, there may be serious linguistic tensions in the land. Tomorrow, there may be cleavages between the North and South. The day after, a series of international intrigues may be launched against the freedom and sovereignty of the land. Even more critical events are possible, but the confusion and uncertainty will pass as surely as the day follows night. We live in an age where science and scientific planning are steadily overcoming traditional anarchy in every field.

We have seen how the policies of India, both foreign and domestic, during the first decade of her independent nationhood have been molded by the facts of our era. The formative process will proceed with greater vigor and momentum as the field of economic and political controversy narrows. Such a narrowing is most visible in the former colonial world, where the philosophy of dog-eat-dog no longer makes sense and there is no large and established group to propagate it effectively. Moreover, should such an attempt be made, the technological advance of the socialist world and its ability to aid Asia and Africa will very soon destroy the possibility of such a philosophy becoming popular. India is striking out on a path which has been cleared by the processes of historical experience made available to her by her own past and the past of other lands.

India's progress to Socialism, the ordered and equitable way of life, can be peaceful and sustained. In many ways the foundations are being laid with each day that passes. On one side socialistic measures are being extended, and on the other a growing mass consolidation creates the sanction for their wider application and implementation. If a tiny minority attempts to place hindrances in the way, it can only succeed in causing a temporary dislocation. If this same minority seeks to make the dislocation permanent, it will realize to its cost that the determination of the people can not be tampered with for long.

In many respects India will also lead experiment into the mysteries of this new transition to socialism, for she is ahead of others who, like her, are also advancing in the same direction—Indonesia, Burma, Egypt, and such newly risen nations. It is certain that developments unique in political and economic science will take place. They will require profound and creative understanding, for they will be inexplicable in terms of the usual yardsticks. Those who doubt this should remember that the first years of freedom of countries like India, Indonesia, Burma, and Egypt have provided many such revealing examples.

India, in common with other lands, will feel the glow of new experience, the tensions of new problems, and the elation of finding new solutions. She does not have to go through the harrowing experiences of early industrial revolutions. She need not repeat the errors made by others. She can look forward to substantial, lightning advances, for she has begun her journey into the atomic age, made possible by the achievements of world science.

To realize what this means, one has only to consider how the discovery of fire, of the wheel, of a new metal, dramatically changed the story of mankind. How much more decisive will be the impact of atomic energy and its uses. For the first time, science offers us unlimited energy to transform the deserts, the mountains, and the oceans; it is energy which has lain hidden for centuries in tiny drops of water. The boundaries of endeavor are now vastly extended. Even the planets in space and beyond are within reach.

What all this means is too early to say. One conclusion is inescapable. It has become a crucial duty to guard and protect the possibilities of such development. Only scientific social organization can do this. How is it to be achieved without sacrificing the great achievements of mankind? This is the central task of political, economic, social, and cultural leadership.

History shows that as our forefathers gained control over mighty nature, they also, strangely enough, lost control over their own relations with one another. They became helpless victims of vast, overwhelming, and often intangible forces which dragged them into bloody conflicts, class struggles, racial and communal strife, and international war.

But history will also record the dominant fact of today—that the greatest effort of man, of all men, is the effort to save the world of the mid-twentieth century from atomic destruction.

Is it possible then that, learning from this living experience, he will succeed in mastering by reason, and hence peacefully, other forces in society which have hitherto kept him poor, hungry, and ignorant?

The answer lies with us. We can set our world on fire or build on it as we have never built before.

VINOBĀ BHĀVE: GANDHIAN DECENTRALIST

During his lifetime, Gāndhi emphasized that his twin principles of truth and nonviolence could solve a wide variety of human problems. Since the achievement of political independence, some of the social and economic implications of these principles are being worked out by a small group of devoted disciples. The leader of this growing band is the Mahārāshtrian brāhman Vinobā Bhāve—often referred to as Āchārya, "the teacher" or "preceptor."

Vinobā was born in 1895 and spent part of his youth in the pilgrimage town of Wai, at the headwaters of the Kistna River. His mother was a pious and generous woman; his father was a textile expert who wanted his sons to go to England for their higher education. Showing an early inclination toward an ascetic life in his late 'teens, Vinobā gave up his studies, burned his all-important school certificates, and set off for holy Banaras. Reading a newspaper version of a public lecture by Gāndhi (then fresh from South Africa) he felt so drawn by the latter's combined moral and political program that he joined his ashram at Sabarmati, near Ahmedabad.

Vinoba distinguished himself by his austerity and reliability, and Gāndhi sent him in 1921 to Wardha, in central India, to open a new ashram there. At the start of the 1940 civil disobedience movement, Gāndhi chose Vinobā to be the first satyāgrahi (practitioner of *satyā-graha* [1]) to court arrest. During the ensuing years of imprisonment, Vinobā, already a master of Sanskrit, set himself to learning Arabic and the four Dravidian languages of South India. After Gāndhi's assassination, Vinobā was generally looked to as the Mahātmā's heir and successor in the realm of nonviolent theory and practice.

It was in 1951, while walking through the disturbed areas of Hyderabad State, that Vinobā hit upon an alternative to the terrorizing and looting of wealthy landlords which Communist leaders were inciting in this part of India. Placing the emphasis on voluntary donations, he begged land from those who had more than they needed in order to give it to those who had none. His new method of distributing wealth had an immediate practical appeal to the embattled large landholders of Hyderabad. Those in the many other provinces which he has since toured on foot have also responded on ethical and religious grounds. By April 1957 over four million acres—including 2,500 villages—had been donated to the *bhūdān* (land-gift) movement, although only one-seventh of that amount had been redistributed by that date.

The philosophy behind the *bhūdān* mission is essentially that of Gāndhi, for Vinobā, like his guru before him, seeks a society ruled by love instead of coercion, and envisions an India composed of a network of self-sufficient village communities. Although agreeing with the Communists in desiring the ultimate "withering away" of the state, his program of radical decentralization contrasts sharply with their clear intention to centralize both economic and political power in the hands of a single, monolithic party.

[1] See p. 801.

VINOBĀ BHĀVE

Communism and Sarvodaya

The word *sarvodaya*—"the welfare of all"— was coined by Gāndhi to denote the full range of his attempts at social and rural uplift. In a speech to Gandhian workers in Kerala in 1957, Vinobā compared the aims and methods of *Sarvodaya* with those of Communism and found them in substantial agreement. These remarks, which show Vinobā's indifference to parliamentary government, as well as his waving aside of all differences with the Communists except their espousal of violent means, have since caused no little consternation among the advocates of parliamentary democracy in India.

[From Bhave, "Communism and Sarvodaya," reprinted from *Sarvodaya*, May, 1957, in *New Age, Political Monthly of the Communist Party*, Vol. VI, No. 10 (October, 1957), pp. 41–45]

Some think that the Communists are believers in violence and in [a] destructive program. There are differences between my view point and theirs. I have told them that their ideology is a good one. But I do not consider that Communism is itself attached to destructive work. The Communist ideology is worthy of consideration. It contains one great idea which is not found in any other earlier ideologies. But I do not want to discuss on this point. I had already written a small article discussing about Communism. I had referred to Marx in it as the *Maha Muni* or the great saint. By reading Marx there has been a great change in the minds of innumerable people. But I am surprised to hear that the Communists do not believe in the change of mind. This is an important point in which I differ from them. I ask them why they say that there is no room for change of heart in their philosophy while their own lives are examples for change of heart. And, therefore, I consider Communism by itself is a very good and great thing. But what is the means to realize it? . . .

Some believe that there was [a] satya-yuga [age of truth] in which there was no need for the state. Some others believe that there was never a satya-yuga but it is yet to come and it is bound to come. Those who say that satya-yuga is a matter of [the] past can be called traditionalists; those who believe that satya-yuga is yet to come are Communists. The traditionalists and the Communists are both believers in satya-yuga. One group describes the one that had passed away and the other that of the one yet to come. But what do I say? The past is not in my hands nor the future. The present only is in my hands, and, therefore, we want to make the satya-yuga a reality of the present. . . .

Some of the Jana Sangh Party [1] used to meet me. They used to tell me: "You talk about ahimsa, but it will never be practicable in this kali-yuga [2]; it was only possible in the satya-yuga of the past." These are traditionalists. They do not believe that nonviolence would go well with the present. They oppose us thus, while the Communists oppose us by saying that we are only wandering in an utopia. They say: "For the present we have to be prepared to make use of violence. But ultimately nonviolence will come to prevail, that is, for achieving nonviolence in the end we have to use a little violence today and we must be prepared for it. Therefore, you have to suspend your nonviolence for a little." But if we are to prepare ourselves mentally for some violence today hoping that nonviolence is bound to come at some distant stage, it is possible that nonviolence itself would never be realized. In this way we differ.

About the conception of satya-yuga there is no difference between us. There is no difference either in our conception of the ideal order of society and its nature. While saying this I pass over the minor differences. The Communists describe the new order of society which is to come or their conception of satya-yuga in the same way as the traditionalists describe their satya-yuga and the paradise. I ask the traditionalists to show me the steps to the paradise which attracts me. They say: "We can show you the steps but you can see them only after death." So if we are to reach their paradise we have first to die. What purpose will it serve me if I cannot reach it though their paradise attracts me?

I ask the Communists also to tell me how to reach their paradise. They answer that I should now be prepared for some violence and killing. One says that paradise can be reached after death and the other tells me that the paradise will come after I kill another. Therefore both ways do not appear to be helpful to us.

They also feel some difficulty in understanding us. They tell us: "What you preach is nice and good but you are not the first man to preach like this. Before you hundreds of prophets and seers had come and gone. You are only repeating what they had said. Will you succeed where Buddha and Christ could not succeed? Is the teaching of nonviolence in the Bible less than what you say? [The] Bible is already translated in over [a]

[1] See p. 880.   [2] Dark age.

thousand languages. Even the soldiers who work in the army have their Bible in their pockets with them when they fight and die. They always have the name of God on their lips and read the Bible on Sundays. They forget it during the rest of the week. The world goes on in this way. What effect will your preaching have? If what you speak is something that is going to really happen you may demonstrate it before us. But we do not have faith." Their difficulty is that they cannot accept what we say though our idea may be perfect and appealing. But what is the use of going on arguing like this?

If we have the conviction that we can create a new force through our idea we must make up our mind now. Though I did not expect [had no expectations of it], when the first offer of the land came at Pochampalli, I began to think deeply that night over the significance of this incident. I thought there must be some divine indication in this. With some faith in arithmetic as in God I began to calculate. I thought that 5 crores of acres got in this way would solve the land problem. Yet there was a doubt and fear in my mind as to how it would be possible to get 5 crores of acres even as the 100 acres which I got that day. When I began to think that it may not be possible, the picture of the Communists came to my mind immediately. I had already known about all their violent activities there which I do not want to describe here. If I cannot get land by persuasion and love, I thought that I should have faith in the Communists and should follow them. If this *Sarvodaya* method is not possible it will have to be accepted that Communism alone can achieve the objective. Thus we came close to each other. Two points at the end of a circle are close to each other. The point where the circle ends is also the beginning of the circle. That which is the farthest is also the nearest.

Though Communism permits violence we have to accept that it is the compassion that inspires it. This is a paradox. The compassion is the motive force but the faith is in violence. This paradox is not a thing of [the] recent past. This has persisted since time immemorial. In the *Geetha Pravachana* [3] I have mentioned that a great apostle of ahimsa had to bear arms and fight for twenty-one times. This contradiction was in Parasurama [4] who is an incarnation of compassion. He had an axe in his

---

[3] Vinobā's *Commentary on the Gita*.
[4] A brāhman hero, an incarnation of Vishnu, who slew thousands of kshatriyas.

hand. From that time always this contradiction has persisted in the world. We have to cut at this. We have to demonstrate the power of both love and peace.

What is happening today? Those who chant peace thrice are for [the] status quo that nothing should be changed. They are afraid of any change. On the other side those who want to create revolution do not want the discipline of nonviolence. They are not believers in violence nor believers in nonviolence. Only compassion moves them. But, that the compassionate follow violence is not a new contradiction of the present day. Nor should we be surprised at it. They say: "All lives are full of contradictions. There is not an individual in which there is no contradiction. Therefore come with us for a while with a contradiction suspending your nonviolence and accept some violence. Violence is the most ancient and has come from the beginning of the time. But what we want to bring about ultimately is nonviolence." They believe that violence has prevailed from the beginning and if peace could be stably established it would be permanent and eternal. But they feel that the eternal nonviolence can be brought about by the use of some violence in the intermediate stage in which we are. They say: "You can have belief in nonviolence [but] for the time being take your arms. Don't you feel for the poor and for their sake can't you do a little violence? If you don't do [so] you will be helpless for ever." This line of objection is worthy of consideration.

The seekers of peace maintain [the] status quo; and the revolutionaries become followers of violence. We are revolutionaries but we desire to act through peace. It behoves us to take the responsibility to demonstrate that every issue in this world can be solved through peace. I say to this large assembly of *sevaks* [constructive workers]. The achievements during the last six years have made them feel that revolution is possible through peace. Those who believed that revolution is not possible through peaceful means [the Communists] have come to doubt if revolution is not possible through peace. If this is the result of the last six years of our activity, I think that this is much more than what we expected.

Renunciation As a Force for Social Good

The ancient ideal of the renunciation of worldly goods and concerns has found a new purposefulness in Vinobā's program. In addition to the giving of land to the landless, he has requested the giving of one-sixth of one's property and wealth for use by the community (*sampattidān*) and finally the giving of one's entire life for the service of the poor (*jīvandān*).

[From Ramabhai, *Vinoba and His Mission*, pp. 181, 182, 184]

We consider stealing to be a crime, but connive at those who encourage this antisocial activity by amassing heaps of money. In a story in a[n] Upanishad a king says: "In my kingdom, there is neither a thief nor a miser." As we know it is the miser who gives rise to the thief. We condemn the thieves to rot in the prisonhouse, but let their creators roam about in complete freedom. They even occupy seats of honor and respectability in the society. Is this justice? . . .

The highly expensive administrative and other departments of the government are known as "services." And there are services galore: Civil Service, Medical Service, Educational Service. The officials of the Civil Service are paid four figure salaries [in rupees per month], while their masters, the poor of the country, whom they profess to serve have to live on a pittance of annas eight [one-half rupee] a day. It is a tragic paradox that those who earn laks [hundreds of thousands] are called servants, while those who produce food for the nation are regarded as self-seekers working merely to feather their own nest. . . .

It is in order to put an end to this hypocrisy that I have put forward the idea of land being the common property of all. All that we have, our land and property and intelligence—everything has to be an offering to the society. . . .

Today he who earns money does also earn worry. Though he may make money, he loses something more precious than money, namely, the love of his fellow-men, the love of friends and neighbors. That is why even the moneyed are unhappy in the existing society. Both the rich and the poor are unhappy. The remedy is to change the order and place it on the secure basis of nonpossession. . . .

There is one thing which we will demonstrate through *Sampattidan:* that nonpossession is a force for social good. We have long known that nonpossession brings about individual purification. We have to realize that it can also serve as a powerful means of social wellbeing. We have to prove that it is not only spiritually efficacious but it can help us in constructing [a] better and richer worldly life. The Gandhi Memorial Fund collected ten crore rupees. But not even [a] hundred crores will suffice for all we want to do. The need of the hour is to mobilize all our wealth in every form and press it into the service of the society. The *Sampattidan* way will turn every house into a bank on which the society can draw freely for all its wants. And because what is offered will be used locally, it will make a very easily workable plan. It will directly lead to the building up of the collective strength of the people. It will unite them with one another and release tremendous energy for constructive effort. We know that [the] practice[s] of equality and renunciation are good, but we have to look at them afresh and see them as forces for promoting social welfare.

INDIC WORD LIST

The following is a list of Sanskrit (S) and Pāli (P) terms and proper names printed in roman type in the text together with the corresponding transliteration in accordance with L. Renou's *Grammaire Sanscrite* (Paris, 1930). There is no listing for those terms whose orthodox spellings do not differ from popular ones, as used in the text. Some Hindī (H), Bengālī (B), and Dravidian (D), i.e., Tamil, Telegu, etc., words are also included in cases where a significant word is borrowed from the Sanskrit or where the orthography may be misleading.

āchārya	ācārya	Bhartrihari	Bhartṛhari
Agneya	Āgneya	bhāshya	bhāṣya
ahimsā	ahiṃsā	Bhatta Lollata	Bhaṭṭa Lollaṭa
Amar Dās (H)	Amar Dās	Bhatta Nāyaka	Bhaṭṭa Nāyaka
Ambashtha	Ambaṣṭha	Bhavananda	Bhavānanda
Amritachandra	Amṛtacandra	bhikshu	bhikṣu
Anathapindaka	Anāthapiṇḍaka	Bhīshma	Bhīṣma
Angiras	Aṅgiras	Bhoodan (H)	Bhūdāna (S)
Apabhramsha	Apabhraṃśa	Bhrigu	Bhṛgu
Āranyaka	Āraṇyaka	brahmachārī	brahmacārī
Ardha-magadhi	Ardha-māgadhī	brahmacharya	brahmacarya
Āruni	Āruṇi	brāhman	brāhmaṇa
Aryan	Āryan	Brāhmana	Brāhmaṇa
Asanga	Asaṅga	Brahmanaspati	Brahmaṇaspati
Āshmarathya	Āśmarathya	Brihaspati	Bṛhaspati
Ashoka	Aśoka (Pāli, Asoka)	Brindavan (H)	Vṛndāvana (S)
		Chaitanya	Caitanya
āshrama	āśrama	Chāndāla	Cāṇḍāla
Ashvaghosha	Aśvaghoṣa	Chandragupta	Candragupta
Āshvalāyana	Āśvalāyana	Charkha (H)	Carkha
ashvamedha	aśvamedha	Chaulukya	Caulukya
Ashvin	Aśvin	Chetaka	Cetaka
Asur (H)	Asura (S)	chit	cit
Audulomi	Auḍulomi	Chola (D)	Cōḷa
Avalokiteshvara	Avalokiteśvara	Dadu	Dādū
avatār (H)	avatāra (S)	Dadu-panthi	Dādū-panthī
Ayodhya	Ayodhyā	Daksha	Dakṣa
Bādarāyana	Bādarāyaṇa	Damayanti	Damayantī
bhajan (H)	bhajana	Dandin	Daṇḍin

darshana	darśana	Krita	Kṛta
Devanagri (H)	Devanāgarī	kshatra	kṣatra
Dhananjaya	Dhanañjaya	Kshatriya	Kṣatriya
Dhritarāshtra	Dhṛtarāṣṭra	Kshemendra	Kṣemendra
dhyana	dhyāna	Kurukshetra	Kurukṣetra
Dinnāga	Diṅnāga	Kushāna	Kuṣāṇa
Drona	Droṇa	Kusinara (P)	Kusināra
Duhshanta	Duḥṣanta (Duṣ-	Lakshmī	Lakṣmī
	yanta)	Lila	Līlā
Ganesha	Gaṇeśa	Lingayat	Liṅgāyat
Ganges	Gaṅgā (S)	Lokāchārya	Lokācārya
Garuda	Garuḍa	Mahadev (H)	Mahādeva (S)
Gaudapāda	Gauḍapāda	Maha Muni	Mahāmuni (S)
Gauri	Gaurī	maharaja(h)	mahārāja
Gaya	Gayā	Maharashtra	Mahārāṣṭra
ghee	ghī (H)	maharshi	maharṣi
Giridhar	Giridhara (S)	Mahāsānghika	Mahāsaṅghika
Gokul (H)	Gokula (S)	Mahendra Sinha	Mahendra Siṅha
Gopāl (H)	Gopāla (S)	Māhishya	Māhiṣya
Gudākesha	Guḍākeśa	Maladhārī He-	Maladhārī He-
guna	guṇa	machandra	macandra
gyana (B)	jñāna (S)	Mammata	Mammaṭa
Harsha	Harṣa	Marīchi	Marīci
Hemachandra	Hemacandra	Mathura	Mathurā
Himalaya	Himālaya	Mīmāmsā	Mīmāṃsā
Īshvara	Īśvara	Mīmāmsaka	Mīmāṃsaka
Īshvarakrishna	Īśvarakṛṣṇa	moksha	mokṣa
Jagannath	Jagannātha (S)	Mrigaputra	Mṛgaputra
Jain	Jaina	Narasimha	Narasiṃha
Jan(a) Sangh	Jana Saṅgha (S)	Nārāyana	Nārāyaṇa
(H)		Nigantha	Nirgrantha
Jayasimha	Jayasiṃha	Nātaputta	Jñātṛputra (S);
jnāna	jñāna		Nigaṇṭha
Jnānadeva	Jñānadeva		Nātaputta (P)
Jnāneshvara	Jñāneśvara	Nīlakantha Dīk-	Nīlakaṇṭha Dīk-
Jnātrika	Jñātṛka	shita	ṣita
Kailash(a)	Kailāsa	Nirvāna	Nirvāṇa
Kalinga	Kaliṅga	Nishāda	Niṣāda
Kanāda	Kaṇāda	Om	Oṃ
Kanchi	Kāñcī	Pakudha Kac-	Pakudha Kac-
Kānchīpuram	Kāñcīpura	chāyana (P)	cāyana
Karana	Karaṇa	Pali	Pāli
Karna	Karṇa	Pāndava	Pāṇḍava
Kāshakritsna	Kāśakṛtsna	pandit (H)	paṇḍita (S)
Kashi	Kāśī	Pāndu	Pāṇḍu
Kaundinya	Kauṇḍinya	Pāndya	Pāṇḍya
Kautilya	Kauṭilya	Pānini	Pāṇini
Kayastha	Kāyastha	Parameshvara	Parameśvara
Krishna	Kṛṣṇa	Parashurāma	Paraśurāma

Pārshva	Pārśva	samhitā	saṃhitā
Parthiva Puja	Pārthiva Pūjā	samsāra	saṃsāra
Pataliputra	Pāṭaliputra	samskāra	saṃskāra
Patanjali	Patañjali	Sanatan Dharma	Sanātana
Pava	Pāvā	(H)	Dharma (S)
Pindaree	Piṇḍarī	Sandhya	Sandhyā
prajna	prajñā	Sanjaya Belatthi-	Sañjaya Belaṭṭhi-
Prakrit (Prākrit)	Prākṛta (S)	putta (P)	putta
prakriti	prakṛti	Sānkhya	Sāṅkhya
prāna	prāṇa	Sanskrit	Saṃskṛta (S)
Pranayama	Prāṇāyāma	Saraswatī	Sarasvatī
Prithā	Pṛthā	sati, suttee	satī (S)
purāna	purāṇa	satyagrahi	satyāgrahī
Purāna Kassapa	Purāṇa Kassapa	Saurashtra	Saurāṣṭra
(P)		Savitar	Savitṛ
Purandaradāsa	Puraṅdaradāsa	Shaiva	Śaiva
purusha	puruṣa	Shakra	Śakra
purushārtha	puruṣārtha	shakti	śakti
Pūrva Mīmāmsā	Pūrva Mīmāṃsā	Shakuntalā	Śakuntalā
Pūrva Mīmām-	Pūrva Mīmāṃ-	Shākya	Śākya
saka	saka	Shālīki	Śālīki
Pūshan	Pūṣan	Shāndilya	Śāṇḍilya
Pushyamitra Shun-	Puṣyamitra Śuṅga	Shankara	Śaṅkara
ga		Shankaradeva	Śaṅkaradeva
raj (H)	rājya (S)	Shāntideva	Śāntideva
raja (H)	rājā	Shantiniketan	Śāntiniketana
rakshasa (Rakkh-	rākṣasa (Rakṣas)	Shāriputra	Śāriputra
shas)		Shārngadeva	Śārṅgadeva
Ramakrishna	Rāmakṛṣṇa	shāstra	śāstra
Rāmana Maharshi	Rāmaṇa Maharṣi	Shauraseni	Śauraseni
Ramananda	Rāmānanda	Shesha	Śeṣa
Rām Rājya Pāri-	Rām Rājya Pari-	Shitala	Śītalā
shad (H)	ṣad	Shiva	Śiva
Rashtriya Svayam	Rāṣṭriya Svayam	Shivajī	Śivaji
Sevak Sangh	Sevak Saṅgh	Shrāvastī	Śrāvastī
(H)		Shrī	Śrī
Rāvana	Rāvaṇa	Shrīdhara Ven-	Śrīdhara Veṅka-
Rig Veda	*Ṛg Veda*	katesha	teśa
Rishabhadeva	Ṛṣabhadeva	Shrīkantha	Śrīkaṇṭha
rishi	ṛṣi	Shrīvaishnava	Śrīvaiṣṇava
rita	ṛta	shruti	śruti
Sabha	Sabhā	Shuddhi	Śuddhi
Sādhāran	Sādhāraṇa	shūdra	śūdra
(Brahmo Sa-	Brahma Sa-	Shuka	Śuka
maj) (B)	māja (S)	Shukra	Śukra
Sakar ki Churi	Sakar kī chūrī	Shunga	Śuṅga
	(H)	Shvetaketu	Śvetaketu
Sāl (H)	Śāla	Shvetāmbara	Śvetāmbara
Samāj (H)	Samāja	Singāla (P)	Siṅgāla

smriti	smṛti	Vibhīshana	Vibhīṣaṇa
Sri	Śrī	Vijnānavāda	Vijñānavāda
Swadeshī (H)	Svadeśī (S)	Vijnānavādin	Vijñānavādin
Swami	Svāmi	Vīrashaiva	Vīraśaiva
Swamiji	Svāmiji	Virochana	Virocana
swaraj (H)	svarājya (S)	Virūdhaka	Virūḍhaka
Tīrthankara	Tīrthaṅkara	Virūpāksha	Virūpākṣa
Trishalā	Triśalā	Vishishtādvaita	Viśiṣṭādvaita
Tukārām	Tukārāma	Vishnu	Viṣṇu
Tvashtar	Tvaṣṭṛ	Vishnuchitta	Viṣṇucitta
Uddālaka Āruni	Uddālaka Āruṇi	(Periyālvār,	
Ujjain	Ujjayinī (S)	D)	
Upanishad	Upaniṣad	Vishva-Bhārati	Viśva-Bhārati
Uttara Mīmāmsā	Uttara Mīmāṃsā	Vrishni	Vṛṣṇi
Uttar Pradesh	Uttara Pradeśa	Vritra	Vṛtra
	(S)	Vyakaran (H)	Vyākāraṇa (S)
Vāch	Vāc	Yādavaprakāsha	Yādavaprakāśa
Vāgīsha (Tirunā-	Vāgīśa	Yajna	Yajña
vukkarashu,		yaksha	yakṣa
D)		Yamuna	Yamunā (Jum-
Vaishali	Vaiśālī		na)
Vaisheshika	Vaiśeṣika	Yāmuna Āchār-	Yāmunācārya (S)
Vaishnava	Vaiṣṇava	ya (Ālavan-	
Vaishravana	Vaiśravaṇa	dār, D)	
Vaishya	Vaiśya	Yogāchāra	Yogācāra
varna	varṇa	yogi	yogī
Varuna	Varuṇa	Yudhishthira	Yudhiṣṭhira
Vedānta Deshika	Vedānta Deśika		

BIBLIOGRAPHY

" 'Abd," Encyclopedia of Islam. New ed. Leiden, E. J. Brill, 1954–57.

Abū'l Fazl. Ā'īn-i-akbarī. Vol. 3 of Akbarnāma, q.v.

—— Akbarnāma [Akbar-Nama]. Translated by H. Blochmann, et al. 3 vols. Calcutta, Asiatic Society, 1873–1948. (Bibliotheca Indica)

Abū Tāleb. The Travels of Mirza Abu Taleb Khan. Translated by Charles Stewart. 2d ed., 3 vols. London, R. Watts, 1814.

Ācārāṅga Sūtra (Āyāraṅga Sutta). Edited by Hermann Jacobi. London, Oxford, 1882. (Pali Text Society)

" 'Āda," Encyclopedia of Islam. New ed. Leiden, E. J. Brill, 1954–57.

Alī, Chaudhari Rahmat. India, the Continent of Dinia, or the Country of Doom. Cambridge, Dinia Continental Movement, 1946.

Alī, Muhammad. Select Writings and Speeches of Maulana Mohamed Ali. Compiled and ed. by Afzad Iqbal. Lahore, M. Ashraf, 1944.

Ānanda Ranga Pillai. The Private Diary of Ananda Ranga Pillai. Ed. by J. Frederick Price. 12 vols. Madras, Government Press, 1904.

Animananda, B. The Blade. Calcutta, Roy and Son, n.d.

Āryadeva. Cittaviśuddhiprakaraṇa. Edited by P. B. Patel. Calcutta, Visva-Bharati, 1949.

Asanga. Mahāyānasūtrālaṅkāra. Edited by Sylvain Lévi. Paris, H. Champion, 1907–11.

Ashoka's Edicts. Translated by Jules Bloch as Les Inscriptions d'Asoka. Paris, Société d'édition "Les Belles Lettres," 1950.

Ashvaghosha. Buddhacarita. Edited by E. H. Johnston. Calcutta, Baptist Mission Press, 1936.

Āshvalāyana. Gṛhya Sūtra. Edited by T. Ganapati Sāstrī. Trivandrum, Government Press, 1923.

Aṣṭasāhasrikā Prajñāpāramitā. Edited by R. Mitra. Calcutta, Asiatic Society of Bengal, 1888. (Bibliotheca Indica)

Atharva Veda. Edited by R. Roth and W. D. Whitney. Berlin, Ferd. Dümmler's Verlagsbuchhandlung, 1855–56. 2d ed. rev. by M. Lindenau, 1924.

Badā'ūnī, Abd'ul Qādir. Muntakhab ut-Tawārīkh. Translated by G. S. A. Ranking and W. H. Lowe. 3 vols. Calcutta, The Asiatic Society, 1895–1925. (Bibliotheca Indica)

Banerjea, Surendranāth. A Nation in Making, Being the Reminiscences of Fifty Years in Public Life. London, Oxford, 1925.
—— The Speeches and Writings of Hon. Surendranāth Banerjea. Madras, Natesan, 1927?.

Bāqir Khān, Muhammad. Mau'iza-yi-Jahāngīrī. Persian Ms. No. 1666. London, India Office Library.

Barnī, Ziā ud-dīn. Fatāwa-yi-Jahāndārī. Persian Ms. No. 1149. London, India Office Library.
—— Tārīkh-i-Fīrūz Shāhī. Calcutta, 1860–62. (Bibliotheca Indica)

Baudhāyana Śrauta Sūtra. Edited by W. Caland. Calcutta, Asiatic Society of Bengal, 1904–24.

Bhagavad Gītā. Edited by Shripad Krishna Belvalkar. Poona, Bhandarkar Oriental Research Institute, 1945.

Bhāgavata Purāṇa. Edited by Vāsudeva Lakshmana Sharman Panshīkar. Bombay, Nirnayasāgara Press, 1929.

Bhāi Gurdās. War I 38. Lithographed ed. Lahore, 1879.

Bharata. Nāṭya Śāstra. Edited by Joanny Grosset. Paris, Ernest Leroux, 1898.

Bhāve, Vinoba. "Communism and Sarvodaya" in Sarvodaya, May, 1957. Reprinted in New Age, Political Monthly of the Communist Party, VI:10 (October 1957), 41–45.

Bose, Subhās Chandra. The Indian Struggle, 1920–1934. London, Wishart and Co., 1935.
—— Netaji's Life and Writings, Part One, An Indian Pilgrim; Or, Autobiography of Subhas Chandra Bose, 1897–1920. Calcutta, Thacker Spink and Co., 1948.
—— Netaji Speaks to the Nation. Edited by Durlab Singh. Lahore, Hero Publications, 1946.

Bradley-Birt, Francis Bradley. Poems of Henry Louis Vivian Derozio, A Forgotten Anglo-Indian Poet. London, Oxford, 1923.

Brahma Purāṇa. Edited by the pandits of the Ānandāśrama. Poona, Ānandāśrama Press, 1895.

Bṛhad Āraṇyaka Upaniṣad. Edited by E. Röer. 3 vols. Calcutta, Asiatic Society of Bengal, 1849–56.

Bright, J. S. (ed.). Important Speeches of Jawaharlal Nehru. 2d rev. ed. Lahore, Indian Printing Works, 1946.

Bukhārī, 'Abd ul-Haqq al-Dihlawī al. Takmīl-ul-Imām. Persian Ms. No. 2756. London, India Office Library.

Chaitanya. Śikṣāṣṭaka. In Raghavan, q.v.

Chāndogya Upaniṣad. Edited by T. R. Krishnāchārya. Bombay, Nirnayasāgara Press, 1904.

Chatterjee, Bankim Chandra. Anandamath. Translated by T. W. Clark. Manuscript.
—— The Abbey of Bliss, a Translation of Bankim Chandra Chatterjee's An-

andamath. Translated by Nares Chandra Sen-Gupta. Calcutta, P.M. Neogi, 1906.

—— Letter from Bankim Chandra Chatterjee to Dr. Sambhu Chandra Mooker-jee of March 14, 1872. "The Secretary's Notes," *Bengal: Past and Present,* VIII (1914), Calcutta.

Chintamini, C. Y. (ed.). Indian Social Reform. 4 parts. Madras, Thompson and Co., 1901.

Conze, Edward (ed.). Buddhist Texts, Through the Ages. Oxford, Bruno Cassirer, 1954.

Dārā Shikōh. Hasanat-ul-'Arifīn. Lithographed ed. Delhi, 1891.

—— "Iksir-i-Azam," *Journal of the Royal Asiatic Society of Bengal,* V:1 (1939),
—— Risāla'i Haqq Numā'. Lithographed ed. Allahabad, 1921.

Dayānanda Saraswatī, Swami. The Light of Truth; or the English translation of the Satyartha-Prakasha. Lahore, 1927?.

Dhammapada. Edited by Sūriyagoda Sumangala Thera. London, Oxford, 1914. (Pali Text Society)

Dīgha Nikāya. Edited by T. W. Rhys Davids and J. Estlin Carpenter. 3 vols. London, Oxford, 1890–1911. (Pali Text Society)

Edwards, Thomas. Biography of Henry Derozio. Cited in Majumdar, vol. I, q.v.

Fakhr-i-Mudir. Shajara-yi-Ansab. Introduction published as Ta'rīkh-i Fakhr ud-dīn Mubārakshāh. Edited by E. Denison Ross. London, 1927.

Fischer, Louis. Gandhi, His Life and Message for the World. New York, New American Library, 1954.

Gāndhi, Mohandās Karamchand. An Autobiography, or the Story of My Ex-periments with Truth. Translated by Mahadev Desai. Ahmedabad, Navajivan, 1927.

—— Communal Unity. Ahmedabad, Navajivan, 1949.

—— Hind Swarāj, or Indian Home Rule. Ahmedabad, Navajivan, 1946.

—— Young India, 1919–1922. New York, Huebsch, 1922.

Gautama. Dharma Sūtra [Gautama. Dharma Śāstra or Samhitā]. Edited by A. F. Stenzler. London, Trübner and Co., 1876.

Ghose, Aurobindo. Collected Poems and Plays. 2 vols. Pondicherry, Sri Auro-bindo Asram, 1942.

—— The Doctrine of Passive Resistance. Calcutta, Arya Publishing House, 1948.

—— Speeches. Calcutta, Arya Publishing House, 1948.

Ghulām Husayn Khān Tabātabā'i, Siyar-ul-Mutaakh-khirīn. Translated by M. Raymond [Hajee Mustapha]. 4 vols. Calcutta, T. D. Chatterjee [1902].

Gokhale, G. K. Speeches of the Honourable Mr. G. K. Gokhale. Madras, Natesan, 1908.

Hamadānī, Shaikh. Zakhīrat ul-Mulūk. Persian Ms. No. 1130. London, India Office Library.

Haribhadra. Samarāicca Kahā [Samarāditya Kathā]. Edited by Hermann Jacobi. Calcutta, Asiatic Society of Bengal, 1908–1926. (Bibliotheca Indica)

Hasrat, Bikrania Jit. Dara Shikuh [Shikoh]: Life and Works. Calcutta, Visva-
bharati, 1953.

Hemachandra. Mahāvīracarita. Translated by M. Patel. Quoted in The Life of
Hemachandrāchārya, by G. Bühler. Santiniketan, 1936.

Hujwīrī, Shaikh 'Alī. Kashf ul-Mahjūb. Translated by R. A. Nicholson, 2d ed.
London, Luzac, 1936.

Husainī, Abū Tālib al-. Tūzuk-i-Tīmūrī. Edited by J. White. Oxford, Clarendon Press, 1783.

Iqbāl, Muhammad. The Mysteries of Selflessness. Translated by Arthur J. Ar-
berry. London, John Murray, 1953. (The Wisdom of the East Series)

—— Poems from Iqbal. Translated by V. G. Kiernan. London, John Murray,
1955. (The Wisdom of the East Series)

—— The Reconstruction of Religious Thought in Islam. Published by Javid
Iqbal. Lahore, M. Ashraf, 1944.

—— The Secrets of the Self. Translated by R. A. Nicholson. Rev. ed. Lahore,
M. Ashraf, 1944.

—— Speeches and Statements of Iqbal. Compiled by "Shamloo." Lahore,
Hamidullah Khan for al-Manar Academy, 1944.

Īshvarakrishna. Sāṅkhya Kārikās. Edited by Pandit Sri Harirām Shukla. Banaras, Chowkhamba Sanskrit Series Office, 1932.

Jagannātha Pandita. Rasagaṅgādhara. Edited by Pandit Gangādhara Shāstrī.
Banaras, Braj B. Das and Co., 1885–1903.

Jain, Champat Rai. Essays and Addresses. Allahabad, The India Press, 1930.

Jinabhadra. Gaṇadharavāda (Gaṇaharavā). Edited by Muni Patnaprabha Vi-
jaya. Ahmedabad, 1950.

Jinasena. Mahāpurāṇa. Edited by P. Jain. 2 vols. Banaras, 1951.

Jinnāh, Mohamed [Muhammad] Alī. Some Recent Speeches and Writings of
Mr. Jinnah. Edited by Jamīl-ud-dīn Ahmad. 2 vols. Lahore, M. Ashraf,
1946–47.

Jitam te Sūtra. In V. Raghavan, q.v.

Jnānadeva (Jnāneshvara), Jñāneśvarī [Dnyāneshwarī]. Edited by Vināyaka
Bovā Sākhare. 3d ed. Poona, Indirā Press, 1922.

Jnānasambandha. Tirunāvukkarashu. In Kingsbury, q.v.

Jones, Sir William. The Works of Sir William Jones. 13 vols. London, 1807.

Kālidāsa. Raghuvaṃśa. Edited by Ramtaij Pandeya. Banaras, Chowkhamba
Sanskrit Series Office, 1926.

Kautilya. Artha Śāstra. Edited by J. Jolly and R. Schmidt. 2 vols. Lahore,
Punjab Sanskrit Book Depot, 1923–24.

Keer, Dhananjay. Savarkar and His Times. Bombay, A. V. Keer, 1950.

Khān, Liāquat Alī. Pakistan, the Heart of Asia. Cambridge, Massachusetts,
Harvard University Press, 1950.

—— The Constituent Assembly of Pakistan Debates. V:1 (1949), pp. 1–7.

Khān, Sir Syed Ahmad. Akhari Madamin. Compiled by Muhammad Imām ud-dīn Gujerat and Maulvi Ahmad Baba Makhdumi. 3d ed. Lahore, Malik Chunan ud-dīn, n.d.

—— "Letter to Mawlawi Tasadduq Husain," Sir Syed ke chand nadir khutut. Compiled by Ahmad Husain Yaqubi. Meerut, Nandar Press, 1900.

Khaqānī, Nūr ud-dīn Muhammad. Akhlāq-i-Jahāngīrī. Persian Ms. No. 1547. London, India Office Library.

Khuddaka Pāṭha. Edited by Helmer Smith. London, Oxford, 1915. (Pali Text Society)

Kingsbury, F., and G. E. Phillips. Hymns of the Tamil Śaivite Saints. Calcutta, Association Press, 1921. (Heritage of India Series)

Kulashekhara. Mukundamālā. Edited by K. R. Pisharoti. *Annamalai University Journal* (April and October 1932). (Annamalai University Sanskrit Series, 1)

Kumārapālapratibodha (Apabhraṃśa section). Edited by Ludwig Alsdorf. Hamburg, Friederichsen, De Gruyter and Co., 1928.

Kumarappa, J. C. "Foreword," in American Shadow over India, by L. Natarajan. Bombay, People's Publishing House, 1952.

Kundakunda. Pravacanasāra (Pavayaṇasāra). Edited by A. N. Upadhya. Bombay, Manikachandra Digambara Jaina Granthamālā Samiti, 1935.

Lalitavistara. Edited by S. Lefmann. Halle, Buchhandlung des Waisenhauses, 1902–08.

Lallā. Lallā-vākyāni or the Wise Sayings of Lal Ded. Edited and translated by Sir G. Grierson and L. D. Barnett. London, Royal Asiatic Society, 1920.

Laṅkāvatāra Sūtra. Edited by Bunyiu Nanjio. Kyoto, Otani University Press, 1923.

Lokāchārya. Tattvatraya. Edited by Swami Samshodhya. Banaras, 1900. (Chowkhamba Sanskrit Series, vol. 4)

Macaulay, Thomas Babington. Macaulay, Prose and Poetry. Selected by G. M. Young. Cambridge, Massachusetts, Harvard University Press, 1952.

Macauliffe, Max Arthur. The Sikh Religion. Its Gurus, Sacred Writings and Authors. 6 vols. Oxford, Clarendon Press, 1909.

Macdonell, A. A. (tr.). Hymns from the Rigveda. London, Oxford, 1923. (Heritage of India Series)

Mahābhārata. Edited by V. S. Sukthankar, S. K. Belvalkar, et al. Poona, Bhandarkar Oriental Research Institute, 1925–.

Mahāprajñāpāramitā. Translated by Arthur Waley. In Conze, q.v.

Majjhima Nikāya. Edited by V. Trenckner and R. Chalmers. 3 vols. London, Oxford, 1888–1899. (Pali Text Society)

Majumdar, Bimanbehari. History of Political Thought from Rammohun to Dayananda. 1 vol. to date. Calcutta, University of Calcutta, 1934.

Malcolm, Sir John. Sketch of the Sikhs. London, 1812.

Mammata. Kāvyaprakāśa. Edited by Shivaprasāda Bhattāchārya. Banaras, Government Sanskrit Library, Sarasvati Bhavana, 1933.

Māṇikkavāchakar. Tiruccatakam. In Kingsbury, q.v.

Maṇimēgalai. Edited by K. V. Settiyar. Tirunelvēli [Tinnevelly], 1946.

Manu. Dharma Śāstra [Mānavadharmaśāstra or Manusmṛti]. Edited by J. Jolly. London, Trübner and Co., 1887. (Trübner Oriental Series)

Marghīnānī, Maulana Burhān ud-dīn. Hidāya. Translated by C. Hamilton. London, W. H. Allen, 1791.

Masani, R. P. Dadabhai Naoroji: The Grand Old Man of India. London, Allen and Unwin, 1939.

Maudoodī, Syed Abū'l-A'lā. Islamic Law and Constitution. Published by Jamaʿat-i-Islami, Lahore. Karachi, Pakistan Herald Press, 1955.

Max Müller, F. India. What Can It Teach Us? New ed. London, Longmans, Green, 1892.

—— (ed.). Ramakrishna, His Life and Sayings. New York, Scribner's, 1899.

Mihrābī, Ibn 'Umar. Hujjat ul-Hind. Add. 5602. London, British Museum.

Milindapañha. Edited by V. Trenckner. London, Williams and Norgate, 1880.

Montagu, Edwin S. An Indian Diary. Edited by Venetia Montagu. London, William Heinemann Ltd., 1930.

Mozoomdar, P. C. The Life and Teachings of Keshub Chunder Sen. Calcutta, Thomas, 1887.

Muhammad Mujīr Wājib Adīb. Miftāh al Jinān. Persian Ms. No. 927. London, India Office Library.

Muhsin-i-Fānī. Dabistān-i-Mazāhib. Translated by David Shea and Anthony Troyer. 3 vols. Paris, 1843. 2d ed. Washington and London, M. W. Dunne, 1901.

Muṇḍaka Upaniṣad. Edited by T. R. Krishnāchārya. Bombay, Nirnayasāgara Press, 1903.

Nāladiyār. Edited and translated by G. U. Pope. Oxford, Clarendon Press, 1893.

Naoroji, Dādābhāi. Essays, Speeches, Addresses, and Writings (on Indian Politics) of the Hon'ble Dadabhai Naoroji. Edited by Chundal Lallubhai Parekh. Bombay, Caxton Printing Works, 1887.

Nārada. Bhakti Sūtras. Edited and translated by Nandlal Sinha. Allahabad, Panini Office, 1911–12. (Sacred Books of the Hindus)

Narasiṃha Purāṇa. Edited by Uddhavāchārya Aināpure. Bombay, Gopāla Nārāyana Co., 1911.

Nehru, Jawaharlāl. An Autobiography. London, John Lane, 1937.

—— The Discovery of India. New York, Day, 1946.

—— Independence and After. A Collection of the More Important Speeches of Jawaharlal Nehru from September 1946 to May 1949. New Delhi, Government of India, 1949.

—— Recent Essays and Writings. Allahabad, Kitabistan, 1934.

—— Soviet Russia, Some Random Sketches and Impressions. Allahabad, Law Journal Press, 1928.

Nīlakantha Dīkshita. Ānandasāgarastava. Edited by Pandita Durgāprasāda and

Kāshīnātha Pānduranga Paraba. Kāvyamālā Pt. 11. Bombay, Nirnayasāgara Press, 1895.

Nizām ud-dīn Ahmad. Tabaqāt-i-Akbarī. 3 vols. Translated by B. De. Calcutta, The Asiatic Society, 1913, 1927 and 1936. (Bibliotheca Indica)

Orr, W. G. A Sixteenth-century Indian Mystic. With a Foreword by Nicol Macnicol. London, Lutterworth Press, 1947.

Pañcaviṃśatisāhasrikā Prajñāpāramitā. Edited by N. Dutt. Calcutta, 1934.

Qureshī, Ishtiāq Husain. "Presidential Address of Session III," Proceedings, All-Pakistan Political Science Conference. Lahore, Panjab University Press, 1950.

—— "Presidential Address of Session I," Proceedings, 2d All-Pakistan Political Science Conference. Lahore, 1951.

Raghavan, V. Prayers, Praises, and Psalms. Madras, G. A. Natesan and Co., 1938.

Rāmabhāi, Suresh. Vinoba and His Mission. Sevagram, A. W. Sahasvabuddhe, 1954.

Rāmakrishna. The Gospel of Ramakrishna. New York, The Vedānta Society, 1907.

—— Teachings of Sri Ramakrishna. Almora, Advaita Āshrama, 1934.

Rāmānuja. Śaraṇāgatigadya [Gadyatraya]. In Raghavan, q.v.

Rānade, M. G. Essays on Indian Economics. Madras, Natesan, 1906.

Rāzī, Fakhr ud-dīn al-. Jāmi ul-'Ulūm. (An Encyclopedia of the Sciences.) Lithographed edition. Bombay, 1904.

R̥g Veda. Edited by Th. Aufrecht. 2 vols. Berlin, Ferd. Dümmler's Verlagsbuchhandlung, 1861, 1863.

Roy, M. N. I Accuse. New York, Roy Defense Committee of India, 1932.

—— India's Message (Fragments of a Prisoner's Diary, Volume Two). 2d rev. ed. Calcutta, Renaissance Publishers Ltd., 1950.

—— New Humanism, A Manifesto. Calcutta, Renaissance Publishers, Ltd., 1947.

—— "Anti-Imperialist Struggle in India," The Communist International, No. 6 (1924).

Roy, Rāmmohun. The English Works of Raja Rammohun Roy. Allahabad, The Pānini Office, 1906; Calcutta, Sādhāran Brāhmo Samāj, 1945–51.

Saddharmapuṇḍarīka. Edited by H. Kern and Bunyiu Nanjio. St. Petersburg, Académie impériale des sciences, 1912.

Saṃyutta Nikāya. Edited by Léon Feer and C. A. F. Rhys Davids. 6 vols. London, Oxford, 1884–1904. (Pali Text Society)

Saraha. Dohākośa. Translated by D. S. Snellgrove. In Conze, q.v.

Sarda, Har Bilas. Life of Dayanand Saraswati. Ajmer, Vedic Yantrālaya, 1946.

Śatapatha Brāhmaṇa. Vols. 1–3, 5–7, 9. Edited by Āchārya Satyavrata Sāmashramī and Hitavrata Samakantha. Calcutta, Asiatic Society of Bengal, 1900–1912. (Bibliotheca Indica)

Sāvarkar, Vinayak D. Hindutva [Who is a Hindu?]. 4th ed. Poona, S. P. Gokhale, 1949.

Sen, Keshub Chunder. Keshub Chunder Sen's Lectures in India. London, Cassell, 1901.

Shankara. Brahmasūtrabhāṣya. Edited by M. A. Shāstrī and Bhārgav Shāstrī, Shāstrāchārya. Bombay, Nirnayasāgara Press, 1938.

—— Kāśīpañcaka. In Raghavan, q.v.

—— Saundaryalaharī. In Raghavan, q.v.

—— Śivabhujaṅga Stotra. In Raghavan, q.v.

—— Subrahmaṇyabhujaṅga Stotra. In Raghavan, q.v.

Shāntideva. Śikṣasamuccaya. Edited by Cecil Bendall. St. Petersburg, Imperial Academy of Sciences, 1902. (Bibliotheca Buddhica)

Sharaf ud-dīn Yahyā, Shaikh. Maktūbāt-i-Sa'dī. Translated by Baijnath Singh as Letters from a Sufi Teacher. Banaras, Theosophical Publishing Society, 1909.

Sharngadeva. Saṅgītaratnākara. Edited by Mangesha Rāmakrishna Telanga. 2 vols. Poona, Ānandāshrama Press, 1896, 1897.

Sijzī, Amīr Hasan. Fawā'id ul-Fuwād. Lithographed ed. Delhi, 1865.

Singh, Anup. Nehru, the Rising Star of India. New York, John Day, 1939.

Singh, Kushwant. The Sikhs. London, G. Allen and Unwin, 1953.

Sirhindī, Shaikh Ahmad. Maktūbāt. Persian Ms. No. 1037. London, India Office Library.

Skanda Purāṇa. Sūta Saṃhitā. Edited by Vāsudeva Shāstrī Panashīkara. 3 vols. Poona, Ānandāshrama Press, 1924–25.

Somadeva. Nītivākyāmṛta. Edited by Pandit Pannālāla Sonī. Bombay, Māni-kachandra Digambara Jaina Granthamālā Samiti, 1922.

Srīdhara Venkatesha. Ākhyāśasṭi. In Raghavan, q.v.

Storey, C. A. "Persian Literature," Section II, 2. History of India, 1939.

Śukra Nīti. Edited by Pandit Mihirachandrajī. Bombay, Venkateshvara Press, 1907.

Sūtrakṛtāṅga Sūtra (Sūyagaḍaṃga Sutta). Edited by P. L. Vaidya. Poona, Motīlāla Lādhājī, 1928.

Sutta Nipāta. Edited by Dines Andersen and Helmer Smith. London, Oxford, 1913. (Pali Text Society)

Suvarṇaprabhāsa Sūtra [Suvarṇabhāsottamasūtra]. Das Goldglanz-sūtra; ein Sanskrittext des Mahāyāna-buddhismus. Edited by Johann Nobel. Leipzig, Otto Harrassowitz, 1937.

Sykes, Marjorie. Rabindranath Tagore. Calcutta, Longmans, Green, 1943.

Tagore, Debendranāth. The Autobiography of Maharshi Devendranath [sic] Tagore. Calcutta, S. K. Lahiri and Co., 1909.

Tagore, Rabīndranāth. Collected Poems and Plays of Rabindranath Tagore. London, Macmillan, 1936.

—— Letters to a Friend. Edited by C. F. Andrews. London, Allen and Unwin, 1928.

—— Nationalism. 2d ed. London, Macmillan, 1950.

—— Songs of Kabir. Assisted by Evelyn Underhill. New York, Macmillan, 1917.

—— Talks in China. Calcutta, Visva-Bharati, 1925.

—— "The Call of Truth," *Modern Review*, XXX (1921), Calcutta.

Taittirīya Āraṇyaka. Edited by Rājendralāla Mitra. Calcutta, Asiatic Society of Bengal, 1872. (Bibliotheca Indica)

Taittirīya Brāhmaṇa. Edited by Rājendralāla Mitra. 3 vols. Calcutta, Asiatic Society of Bengal, 1859, 1862, 1890. (Bibliotheca Indica)

Taittirīya Upaniṣad. Edited by E. Röer. Calcutta, Asiatic Society of Bengal, 1850. (Bibliotheca Indica)

Tendulkar, D. G. Mahātmā. Life of Mohandas Karamchand Gandhi. 8 vols. Bombay, V. K. Jhaveri and D. G. Tendulkar, 1951–54.

Thapar, Romesh. India in Transition. Bombay, Current Book House, 1956.

Thompson, Edward John. Rabindranath Tagore. His Life and Work. London, Oxford, 1921.

Thompson, F. W. The Practical Philosophy of the Muhammadan People. London, 1839.

Tilak. Bāl Gangādhar Tilak; His Writings and Speeches. 3d ed. Madras, Ganesh, 1922.

—— Śrīmad Bhagavadgītā Rahasya, or Karma-Yoga-Śāstra. 2 vols. Poona, R. B. Tilak, 1935–36.

Tukārām. A Complete Collection of the Poems of Tukārām. Edited by Vishnu Parashuram Shāstrī Pandit. 2 vols. Bombay, Induprakāsha Press, 1869, 1873.

Tulasīdās. Rāmacaritamānasa. Edited by Yādava Shamkara Jāmadāra. Poona, Vadyakapatrikā Press, 1913.

Utpaladeva. Śivastotrāvali. In Raghavan, q.v.

Uttarādhyayana Sūtra (Uttarajjhayaṇa). Edited by J. Charpentier. Upsala, Appelbergs Boktrycheri Aktiebolag, 1922.

Vādirāja. Haryaṣṭaka. In Raghavan, q.v.

—— Kṛṣṇastuti. In Raghavan, q.v.

Vaiśeṣika Sūtra. Edited and translated by Nandalal Sinha. Allahabad, Pānini Office, 1911. (Sacred Books of the Hindus)

Vālmiki. Rāmāyaṇa. Edited by T. R. Krishnāchārya and T. R. Vyāsāchārya. Bombay, Nirnayasāgara Press, 1911–13.

Vāmana Purāṇa. Ms. form, ff. 4, 162. Bombay, Venkateshvara Press, 1903.

Vātsyāyana. Kāma Sūtra. Edited by Pandit Durgāprasād. Bombay, Nirnayasāgara Press, 1891.

Vedānta Deshika. Aṣṭabhujāṣṭaka. In Raghavan, q.v.

Vijñānabhairava Tantra. Edited by Mukunda Rāma Shāstrī. Srinagar, 1918.

Vinaya Piṭaka (Mahāvagga). Edited by Hermann Oldenberg. 5 vols. London, Oxford, 1929.

Viṣṇu Purāṇa. Edited by Pandit Jibānanda Vidyāsāgara. Calcutta, Saraswati Press, 1882.

Vivekānanda. The Complete Works of Swami Vivekananda. 7 vols. Almora, Advaita Āshrama, 1924–32.

Walī-Ullāh, Shah. "al-Tafhīmāt ul-Ilāhīya." Translated by Fazl Mahmūd Asīrī from 1906 ed. of Ahmadi Press, Delhi. Visva-Bharati Annals, IV (1951).

—— " 'Iqd al-Jīd fī Ahkām al-Ijtihād Wa'l Taqlīd." Translated by Muhammad Dā'ūd Rahbar. The Muslim World, XLV:4 (1955).

Wedderburn, William. Allan Octavian Hume, C. B. London, T. F. Unwin, 1913.

Westcott, G. H. Kabir and the Kabir Panth. Cawnpore, Christ Church Mission Press, 1907; Calcutta, S. Gupta, 1953.

Yājñavalkya Smṛti. Ein Beitrag zur Quellenkunde des indischen Rechts. Edited by Hans Losch. Leipzig, Otto Harrassowitz, 1927.

Yāmuna. Stotraratna. In Raghavan, q.v.

INDEX

Without the assistance of many publishers, a book of source readings such as this is not possible, and we are grateful for the cooperation of the following: Advaita Ashrama, Almora, India; Allen & Unwin, Ltd., London; All-Pakistan Political Science Association, Lahore; Mohammad Ashraf, Lahore; Asiatic Society of Mangal, Calcutta; Sri Aurobindo Ashram, Pondichéry, India; The Bodley Head, Ltd., London; Clarendon Press, Oxford; Current Book House, Bombay; Ganesh and Co., Ltd., Madras, India; S. P. Gokhale, Poona, India; Harvard University Press, Cambridge, Mass.; Hero Publications, Lahore; Indian Printing Works, Lahore; The India Press, Allahabad, India; Kitabistan, Allahabad, India; S. K. Lahin and Co., Calcutta; Luzac and Co., London; Macmillan & Co., Ltd., London and New York; al-Manar Academy, Lahore; Modern Review, Calcutta; John Murray, London, and the "Wisdom of the East" series; The Muslim World; G. A. Natesan and Co., Madras, India; The Navajivan Trust, Ahmedabad, India; P. M. Neogi, Calcutta; Orient Longmans Ltd., Calcutta; Oxford University Press, London; Pakistan Herald Press, Karachi; Panjab University Press, Lahore; People's Publishing House, Ltd., Bombay; Renaissance Publishers, Ltd., Calcutta; Roy and Son, Calcutta; A. W. Sahasvabuddhe, Sevagram, India; Sadharan Brahmo Samaj, Calcutta; Sarvodaya, Bombay; Theosophical Publishing Society, Banaras, India; Thomas and Co., Calcutta; Thompson and Co. Ltd., Madras, India; R. B. Tilak, Poona, India; The Vedanta Society, New York; Vedic Yantralaya, Ajmer, India; The Viking Press, Inc., New York; Visvabharati, Calcutta.